WITHDRAWN

Dictionary of Literary Biography

1 *The American Renaissance in New England*, edited by Joel Myerson (1978)

2 *American Novelists Since World War II*, edited by Jeffrey Helterman and Richard Layman (1978)

3 *Antebellum Writers in New York and the South*, edited by Joel Myerson (1979)

4 *American Writers in Paris, 1920-1939*, edited by Karen Lane Rood (1980)

5 *American Poets Since World War II*, 2 parts, edited by Donald J. Greiner (1980)

6 *American Novelists Since World War II, Second Series*, edited by James E. Kibler Jr. (1980)

7 *Twentieth-Century American Dramatists*, 2 parts, edited by John MacNicholas (1981)

8 *Twentieth-Century American Science-Fiction Writers*, 2 parts, edited by David Cowart and Thomas L. Wymer (1981)

9 *American Novelists, 1910-1945*, 3 parts, edited by James J. Martine (1981)

10 *Modern British Dramatists, 1900-1945*, 2 parts, edited by Stanley Weintraub (1982)

11 *American Humorists, 1800-1950*, 2 parts, edited by Stanley Trachtenberg (1982)

12 *American Realists and Naturalists*, edited by Donald Pizer and Earl N. Harbert (1982)

13 *British Dramatists Since World War II*, 2 parts, edited by Stanley Weintraub (1982)

14 *British Novelists Since 1960*, 2 parts, edited by Jay L. Halio (1983)

15 *British Novelists, 1930-1959*, 2 parts, edited by Bernard Oldsey (1983)

16 *The Beats: Literary Bohemians in Postwar America*, 2 parts, edited by Ann Charters (1983)

17 *Twentieth-Century American Historians*, edited by Clyde N. Wilson (1983)

18 *Victorian Novelists After 1885*, edited by Ira B. Nadel and William E. Fredeman (1983)

19 *British Poets, 1880-1914*, edited by Donald E. Stanford (1983)

20 *British Poets, 1914-1945*, edited by Donald E. Stanford (1983)

21 *Victorian Novelists Before 1885*, edited by Ira B. Nadel and William E. Fredeman (1983)

22 *American Writers for Children, 1900-1960*, edited by John Cech (1983)

23 *American Newspaper Journalists, 1873-1900*, edited by Perry J. Ashley (1983)

24 *American Colonial Writers, 1606-1734*, edited by Emory Elliott (1984)

25 *American Newspaper Journalists, 1901-1925*, edited by Perry J. Ashley (1984)

26 *American Screenwriters*, edited by Robert E. Morsberger, Stephen O. Lesser, and Randall Clark (1984)

27 *Poets of Great Britain and Ireland, 1945-1960*, edited by Vincent B. Sherry Jr. (1984)

28 *Twentieth-Century American-Jewish Fiction Writers*, edited by Daniel Walden (1984)

29 *American Newspaper Journalists, 1926-1950*, edited by Perry J. Ashley (1984)

30 *American Historians, 1607-1865*, edited by Clyde N. Wilson (1984)

31 *American Colonial Writers, 1735-1781*, edited by Emory Elliott (1984)

32 *Victorian Poets Before 1850*, edited by William E. Fredeman and Ira B. Nadel (1984)

33 *Afro-American Fiction Writers After 1955*, edited by Thadious M. Davis and Trudier Harris (1984)

34 *British Novelists, 1890-1929: Traditionalists*, edited by Thomas F. Staley (1985)

35 *Victorian Poets After 1850*, edited by William E. Fredeman and Ira B. Nadel (1985)

36 *British Novelists, 1890-1929: Modernists*, edited by Thomas F. Staley (1985)

37 *American Writers of the Early Republic*, edited by Emory Elliott (1985)

38 *Afro-American Writers After 1955: Dramatists and Prose Writers*, edited by Thadious M. Davis and Trudier Harris (1985)

39 *British Novelists, 1660-1800*, 2 parts, edited by Martin C. Battestin (1985)

40 *Poets of Great Britain and Ireland Since 1960*, 2 parts, edited by Vincent B. Sherry Jr. (1985)

41 *Afro-American Poets Since 1955*, edited by Trudier Harris and Thadious M. Davis (1985)

42 *American Writers for Children Before 1900*, edited by Glenn E. Estes (1985)

43 *American Newspaper Journalists, 1690-1872*, edited by Perry J. Ashley (1986)

44 *American Screenwriters, Second Series*, edited by Randall Clark, Robert E. Morsberger, and Stephen O. Lesser (1986)

45 *American Poets, 1880-1945, First Series*, edited by Peter Quartermain (1986)

46 *American Literary Publishing Houses, 1900-1980: Trade and Paperback*, edited by Peter Dzwonkoski (1986)

47 *American Historians, 1866-1912*, edited by Clyde N. Wilson (1986)

48 *American Poets, 1880-1945, Second Series*, edited by Peter Quartermain (1986)

49 *American Literary Publishing Houses, 1638-1899*, 2 parts, edited by Peter Dzwonkoski (1986)

50 *Afro-American Writers Before the Harlem Renaissance*, edited by Trudier Harris (1986)

51 *Afro-American Writers from the Harlem Renaissance to 1940*, edited by Trudier Harris (1987)

52 *American Writers for Children Since 1960: Fiction*, edited by Glenn E. Estes (1986)

53 *Canadian Writers Since 1960, First Series*, edited by W. H. New (1986)

54 *American Poets, 1880-1945, Third Series*, 2 parts, edited by Peter Quartermain (1987)

55 *Victorian Prose Writers Before 1867*, edited by William B. Thesing (1987)

56 *German Fiction Writers, 1914-1945*, edited by James Hardin (1987)

57 *Victorian Prose Writers After 1867*, edited by William B. Thesing (1987)

58 *Jacobean and Caroline Dramatists*, edited by Fredson Bowers (1987)

59 *American Literary Critics and Scholars, 1800-1850*, edited by John W. Rathbun and Monica M. Grecu (1987)

60 *Canadian Writers Since 1960, Second Series*, edited by W. H. New (1987)

61 *American Writers for Children Since 1960: Poets, Illustrators, and Nonfiction Authors*, edited by Glenn E. Estes (1987)

62 *Elizabethan Dramatists*, edited by Fredson Bowers (1987)

63 *Modern American Critics, 1920-1955*, edited by Gregory S. Jay (1988)

64 *American Literary Critics and Scholars, 1850-1880*, edited by John W.

Rathbun and Monica M. Grecu (1988)

65 *French Novelists, 1900-1930,* edited by Catharine Savage Brosman (1988)

66 *German Fiction Writers, 1885-1913,* 2 parts, edited by James Hardin (1988)

67 *Modern American Critics Since 1955,* edited by Gregory S. Jay (1988)

68 *Canadian Writers, 1920-1959, First Series,* edited by W. H. New (1988)

69 *Contemporary German Fiction Writers, First Series,* edited by Wolfgang D. Elfe and James Hardin (1988)

70 *British Mystery Writers, 1860-1919,* edited by Bernard Benstock and Thomas F. Staley (1988)

71 *American Literary Critics and Scholars, 1880-1900,* edited by John W. Rathbun and Monica M. Grecu (1988)

72 *French Novelists, 1930-1960,* edited by Catharine Savage Brosman (1988)

73 *American Magazine Journalists, 1741-1850,* edited by Sam G. Riley (1988)

74 *American Short-Story Writers Before 1880,* edited by Bobby Ellen Kimbel, with the assistance of William E. Grant (1988)

75 *Contemporary German Fiction Writers, Second Series,* edited by Wolfgang D. Elfe and James Hardin (1988)

76 *Afro-American Writers, 1940-1955,* edited by Trudier Harris (1988)

77 *British Mystery Writers, 1920-1939,* edited by Bernard Benstock and Thomas F. Staley (1988)

78 *American Short-Story Writers, 1880-1910,* edited by Bobby Ellen Kimbel, with the assistance of William E. Grant (1988)

79 *American Magazine Journalists, 1850-1900,* edited by Sam G. Riley (1988)

80 *Restoration and Eighteenth-Century Dramatists, First Series,* edited by Paula R. Backscheider (1989)

81 *Austrian Fiction Writers, 1875-1913,* edited by James Hardin and Donald G. Daviau (1989)

82 *Chicano Writers, First Series,* edited by Francisco A. Lomelí and Carl R. Shirley (1989)

83 *French Novelists Since 1960,* edited by Catharine Savage Brosman (1989)

84 *Restoration and Eighteenth-Century Dramatists, Second Series,* edited by Paula R. Backscheider (1989)

85 *Austrian Fiction Writers After 1914,* edited by James Hardin and Donald G. Daviau (1989)

86 *American Short-Story Writers, 1910-1945, First Series,* edited by Bobby Ellen Kimbel (1989)

87 *British Mystery and Thriller Writers Since 1940, First Series,* edited by Bernard Benstock and Thomas F. Staley (1989)

88 *Canadian Writers, 1920-1959, Second Series,* edited by W. H. New (1989)

89 *Restoration and Eighteenth-Century Dramatists, Third Series,* edited by Paula R. Backscheider (1989)

90 *German Writers in the Age of Goethe, 1789-1832,* edited by James Hardin and Christoph E. Schweitzer (1989)

91 *American Magazine Journalists, 1900-1960, First Series,* edited by Sam G. Riley (1990)

92 *Canadian Writers, 1890-1920,* edited by W. H. New (1990)

93 *British Romantic Poets, 1789-1832, First Series,* edited by John R. Greenfield (1990)

94 *German Writers in the Age of Goethe: Sturm und Drang to Classicism,* edited by James Hardin and Christoph E. Schweitzer (1990)

95 *Eighteenth-Century British Poets, First Series,* edited by John Sitter (1990)

96 *British Romantic Poets, 1789-1832, Second Series,* edited by John R. Greenfield (1990)

97 *German Writers from the Enlightenment to Sturm und Drang, 1720-1764,* edited by James Hardin and Christoph E. Schweitzer (1990)

98 *Modern British Essayists, First Series,* edited by Robert Beum (1990)

99 *Canadian Writers Before 1890,* edited by W. H. New (1990)

100 *Modern British Essayists, Second Series,* edited by Robert Beum (1990)

101 *British Prose Writers, 1660-1800, First Series,* edited by Donald T. Siebert (1991)

102 *American Short-Story Writers, 1910-1945, Second Series,* edited by Bobby Ellen Kimbel (1991)

103 *American Literary Biographers, First Series,* edited by Steven Serafin (1991)

104 *British Prose Writers, 1660-1800, Second Series,* edited by Donald T. Siebert (1991)

105 *American Poets Since World War II, Second Series,* edited by R. S. Gwynn (1991)

106 *British Literary Publishing Houses, 1820-1880,* edited by Patricia J. Anderson and Jonathan Rose (1991)

107 *British Romantic Prose Writers, 1789-1832, First Series,* edited by John R. Greenfield (1991)

108 *Twentieth-Century Spanish Poets, First Series,* edited by Michael L. Perna (1991)

109 *Eighteenth-Century British Poets, Second Series,* edited by John Sitter (1991)

110 *British Romantic Prose Writers, 1789-1832, Second Series,* edited by John R. Greenfield (1991)

111 *American Literary Biographers, Second Series,* edited by Steven Serafin (1991)

112 *British Literary Publishing Houses, 1881-1965,* edited by Jonathan Rose and Patricia J. Anderson (1991)

113 *Modern Latin-American Fiction Writers, First Series,* edited by William Luis (1992)

114 *Twentieth-Century Italian Poets, First Series,* edited by Giovanna Wedel De Stasio, Glauco Cambon, and Antonio Illiano (1992)

115 *Medieval Philosophers,* edited by Jeremiah Hackett (1992)

116 *British Romantic Novelists, 1789-1832,* edited by Bradford K. Mudge (1992)

117 *Twentieth-Century Caribbean and Black African Writers, First Series,* edited by Bernth Lindfors and Reinhard Sander (1992)

118 *Twentieth-Century German Dramatists, 1889-1918,* edited by Wolfgang D. Elfe and James Hardin (1992)

119 *Nineteenth-Century French Fiction Writers: Romanticism and Realism, 1800-1860,* edited by Catharine Savage Brosman (1992)

120 *American Poets Since World War II, Third Series,* edited by R. S. Gwynn (1992)

121 *Seventeenth-Century British Nondramatic Poets, First Series,* edited by M. Thomas Hester (1992)

122 *Chicano Writers, Second Series,* edited by Francisco A. Lomelí and Carl R. Shirley (1992)

123 *Nineteenth-Century French Fiction Writers: Naturalism and Beyond, 1860-1900,* edited by Catharine Savage Brosman (1992)

124 *Twentieth-Century German Dramatists, 1919-1992,* edited by Wolfgang D. Elfe and James Hardin (1992)

125 *Twentieth-Century Caribbean and Black African Writers, Second Series,* edited by Bernth Lindfors and Reinhard Sander (1993)

126 *Seventeenth-Century British Nondramatic Poets, Second Series,* edited by M. Thomas Hester (1993)

127 *American Newspaper Publishers, 1950-1990,* edited by Perry J. Ashley (1993)

128 *Twentieth-Century Italian Poets, Second Series,* edited by Giovanna Wedel De Stasio, Glauco Cambon, and Antonio Illiano (1993)

129 *Nineteenth-Century German Writers, 1841-1900,* edited by James Hardin and Siegfried Mews (1993)

130 *American Short-Story Writers Since World War II,* edited by Patrick Meanor (1993)

131 *Seventeenth-Century British Nondramatic Poets, Third Series*, edited by M. Thomas Hester (1993)

132 *Sixteenth-Century British Nondramatic Writers, First Series*, edited by David A. Richardson (1993)

133 *Nineteenth-Century German Writers to 1840*, edited by James Hardin and Siegfried Mews (1993)

134 *Twentieth-Century Spanish Poets, Second Series*, edited by Jerry Phillips Winfield (1994)

135 *British Short-Fiction Writers, 1880–1914: The Realist Tradition*, edited by William B. Thesing (1994)

136 *Sixteenth-Century British Nondramatic Writers, Second Series*, edited by David A. Richardson (1994)

137 *American Magazine Journalists, 1900–1960, Second Series*, edited by Sam G. Riley (1994)

138 *German Writers and Works of the High Middle Ages: 1170–1280*, edited by James Hardin and Will Hasty (1994)

139 *British Short-Fiction Writers, 1945–1980*, edited by Dean Baldwin (1994)

140 *American Book-Collectors and Bibliographers, First Series*, edited by Joseph Rosenblum (1994)

141 *British Children's Writers, 1880–1914*, edited by Laura M. Zaidman (1994)

142 *Eighteenth-Century British Literary Biographers*, edited by Steven Serafin (1994)

143 *American Novelists Since World War II, Third Series*, edited by James R. Giles and Wanda H. Giles (1994)

144 *Nineteenth-Century British Literary Biographers*, edited by Steven Serafin (1994)

145 *Modern Latin-American Fiction Writers, Second Series*, edited by William Luis and Ann González (1994)

146 *Old and Middle English Literature*, edited by Jeffrey Helterman and Jerome Mitchell (1994)

147 *South Slavic Writers Before World War II*, edited by Vasa D. Mihailovich (1994)

148 *German Writers and Works of the Early Middle Ages: 800–1170*, edited by Will Hasty and James Hardin (1994)

149 *Late Nineteenth- and Early Twentieth-Century British Literary Biographers*, edited by Steven Serafin (1995)

150 *Early Modern Russian Writers, Late Seventeenth and Eighteenth Centuries*, edited by Marcus C. Levitt (1995)

151 *British Prose Writers of the Early Seventeenth Century*, edited by Clayton D. Lein (1995)

152 *American Novelists Since World War II, Fourth Series*, edited by James and Wanda Giles (1995)

153 *Late-Victorian and Edwardian British Novelists, First Series*, edited by George M. Johnson (1995)

154 *The British Literary Book Trade, 1700–1820*, edited by James K. Bracken and Joel Silver (1995)

155 *Twentieth-Century British Literary Biographers*, edited by Steven Serafin (1995)

156 *British Short-Fiction Writers, 1880–1914: The Romantic Tradition*, edited by William F. Naufftus (1995)

157 *Twentieth-Century Caribbean and Black African Writers, Third Series*, edited by Bernth Lindfors and Reinhard Sander (1995)

158 *British Reform Writers, 1789–1832*, edited by Gary Kelly and Edd Applegate (1995)

159 *British Short-Fiction Writers, 1800–1880*, edited by John R. Greenfield (1996)

160 *British Children's Writers, 1914–1960*, edited by Donald R. Hettinga and Gary D. Schmidt (1996)

161 *British Children's Writers Since 1960, First Series*, edited by Caroline Hunt (1996)

162 *British Short-Fiction Writers, 1915–1945*, edited by John H. Rogers (1996)

163 *British Children's Writers, 1800–1880*, edited by Meena Khorana (1996)

164 *German Baroque Writers, 1580–1660*, edited by James Hardin (1996)

165 *American Poets Since World War II, Fourth Series*, edited by Joseph Conte (1996)

166 *British Travel Writers, 1837–1875*, edited by Barbara Brothers and Julia Gergits (1996)

167 *Sixteenth-Century British Nondramatic Writers, Third Series*, edited by David A. Richardson (1996)

168 *German Baroque Writers, 1661–1730*, edited by James Hardin (1996)

169 *American Poets Since World War II, Fifth Series*, edited by Joseph Conte (1996)

170 *The British Literary Book Trade, 1475–1700*, edited by James K. Bracken and Joel Silver (1996)

171 *Twentieth-Century American Sportswriters*, edited by Richard Orodenker (1996)

172 *Sixteenth-Century British Nondramatic Writers, Fourth Series*, edited by David A. Richardson (1996)

173 *American Novelists Since World War II, Fifth Series*, edited by James R. Giles and Wanda H. Giles (1996)

174 *British Travel Writers, 1876–1909*, edited by Barbara Brothers and Julia Gergits (1997)

175 *Native American Writers of the United States*, edited by Kenneth M. Roemer (1997)

176 *Ancient Greek Authors*, edited by Ward W. Briggs (1997)

177 *Italian Novelists Since World War II, 1945–1965* edited by Augustus Pallotta (1997)

178 *British Fantasy and Science-Fiction Writers Before World War I*, edited by Darren Harris-Fain (1997)

179 *German Writers of the Renaissance and Reformation, 1280–1580*, edited by James Hardin and Max Reinhart (1997)

180 *Japanese Fiction Writers, 1868–1945*, edited by Van C. Gessel (1997)

181 *South Slavic Writers Since World War II*, edited by Vasa D. Mihailovich (1997)

182 *Japanese Fiction Writers Since World War II*, edited by Van C. Gessel (1997)

183 *American Travel Writers, 1776–1864*, edited by James J. Schramer and Donald Ross (1997)

Documentary Series

1 *Sherwood Anderson, Willa Cather, John Dos Passos, Theodore Dreiser, F. Scott Fitzgerald, Ernest Hemingway, Sinclair Lewis*, edited by Margaret A. Van Antwerp (1982)

2 *James Gould Cozzens, James T. Farrell, William Faulkner, John O'Hara, John Steinbeck, Thomas Wolfe, Richard Wright*, edited by Margaret A. Van Antwerp (1982)

3 *Saul Bellow, Jack Kerouac, Norman Mailer, Vladimir Nabokov, John Updike, Kurt Vonnegut*, edited by Mary Bruccoli (1983)

4 *Tennessee Williams*, edited by Margaret A. Van Antwerp and Sally Johns (1984)

5 *American Transcendentalists*, edited by Joel Myerson (1988)

6 *Hardboiled Mystery Writers: Raymond Chandler, Dashiell Hammett, Ross Macdonald*, edited by Matthew J. Bruccoli and Richard Layman (1989)

7 *Modern American Poets: James Dickey, Robert Frost, Marianne Moore*, edited by Karen L. Rood (1989)

8 *The Black Aesthetic Movement*, edited by Jeffrey Louis Decker (1991)

9 *American Writers of the Vietnam War: W. D. Ehrhart, Larry Heinemann, Tim O'Brien, Walter McDonald, John M. Del Vecchio,* edited by Ronald Baughman (1991)

10 *The Bloomsbury Group,* edited by Edward L. Bishop (1992)

11 *American Proletarian Culture: The Twenties and The Thirties,* edited by Jon Christian Suggs (1993)

12 *Southern Women Writers: Flannery O'Connor, Katherine Anne Porter, Eudora Welty,* edited by Mary Ann Wimsatt and Karen L. Rood (1994)

13 *The House of Scribner, 1846–1904,* edited by John Delaney (1996)

14 *Four Women Writers for Children, 1868–1918,* edited by Caroline C. Hunt (1996)

15 *American Expatriate Writers: Paris in the Twenties,* edited by Matthew J. Bruccoli and Robert W. Trogdon

Yearbooks

1980 edited by Karen L. Rood, Jean W. Ross, and Richard Ziegfeld (1981)

1981 edited by Karen L. Rood, Jean W. Ross, and Richard Ziegfeld (1982)

1982 edited by Richard Ziegfeld; associate editors: Jean W. Ross and Lynne C. Zeigler (1983)

1983 edited by Mary Bruccoli and Jean W. Ross; associate editor: Richard Ziegfeld (1984)

1984 edited by Jean W. Ross (1985)

1985 edited by Jean W. Ross (1986)

1986 edited by J. M. Brook (1987)

1987 edited by J. M. Brook (1988)

1988 edited by J. M. Brook (1989)

1989 edited by J. M. Brook (1990)

1990 edited by James W. Hipp (1991)

1991 edited by James W. Hipp (1992)

1992 edited by James W. Hipp (1993)

1993 edited by James W. Hipp, contributing editor George Garrett (1994)

1994 edited by James W. Hipp, contributing editor George Garrett (1995)

1995 edited by James W. Hipp, contributing editor George Garrett (1996)

1996 edited by Samuel W. Bruce and L. Kay Webster, contributing editor George Garrett (1997)

Concise Series

Concise Dictionary of American Literary Biography, 6 volumes (1988-1989): *The New Consciousness, 1941-1968; Colonization to the American Renaissance, 1640-1865; Realism, Naturalism, and Local Color, 1865-1917; The Twenties, 1917-1929; The Age of Maturity, 1929-1941; Broadening Views, 1968-1988.*

Concise Dictionary of British Literary Biography, 8 volumes (1991-1992): *Writers of the Middle Ages and Renaissance Before 1660; Writers of the Restoration and Eighteenth Century, 1660-1789; Writers of the Romantic Period, 1789-1832; Victorian Writers, 1832-1890; Late Victorian and Edwardian Writers, 1890-1914; Modern Writers, 1914-1945; Writers After World War II, 1945-1960; Contemporary Writers, 1960 to Present.*

American Travel Writers, 1776–1864

Dictionary of Literary Biography® • Volume One Hundred Eighty-Three

American Travel Writers, 1776–1864

Edited by
James Schramer
Youngstown State University
and
Donald Ross
University of Minnesota

A Bruccoli Clark Layman Book
Gale Research
Detroit, Washington, D.C., London

The paper used in this publication meets the minimum requirements
of American National Standard for Information Sciences–Permanence
Paper for Printed Library Materials, ANSI Z39.48-1984.

Library of Congress Cataloging-in-Publication Data

American travel writers, 1776–1864 / edited by James J. Schramer and Donald Ross.
   p. cm.–(Dictionary of literary biography; v. 183)
"A Bruccoli Clark Layman book."
Includes bibliographical references and index.
ISBN 0-7876-1072-0 (alk. paper)
1. Travelers' writings, American–Bio-bibliography–Dictionaries. 2. Americans–Travel–Foreign
countries–History–Dictionaries. 3. American prose literature–19th century–Bio-bibliography–
Dictionaries. 4. American prose literature–18th century–Bio-bibliography–Dictionaries. 5. Authors,
American–19th century–Biography–Dictionaries. 6. Authors, American–18th century–Biography–
Dictionaries. 7. Travelers–United States–Biography–Dictionaries. I. Schramer, James J. II. Ross,
Donald, 1941– . III. Series.
PS366.T73A44 1997
810.9'355–dc21
                                              97-26928
                                               CIP

10 9 8 7 6 5 4 3 2 1

To our students

Contents

Plan of the Series xiii

Introduction xv

John Adams (1735–1826)
Abigail Adams (1744–1818) 3
  Dennis R. Perry

John Woodhouse Audubon (1812–1862) 18
  Barbara J. Cicardo

Horatio Bridge (1806–1893) 27
  Allen Flint

William Wells Brown (circa 1813–1884) 35
  Brian D. Reed

Fanny Calderón de la Barca (1804–1882) 43
  Linda Ledford-Miller

James Fenimore Cooper (1789–1851) 48
  Jared Gardner

George Copway (circa 1818–1869) 68
  Timothy Sweet

David Crockett (1786–1836) 73
  Lane Stiles

Richard Henry Dana Jr. (1815–1882) 79
  Harold K. Bush Jr.

Amasa Delano (1763–1823) 90
  Richard V. McLamore

Ralph Waldo Emerson (1803–1882) 96
  Bruce A. Harvey

Benjamin Franklin (1706–1790) 103
  Donald A. Duhadaway Jr.

John Charles Frémont (1813–1890)
Jessie Benton Frémont (1834–1902) 115
  Karen M. Woods

Margaret Fuller (1810–1850) 126
  Jeffrey Steele

Josiah Gregg (1806–1850) 139
  Nancy Cook

Nathaniel Hawthorne (1804–1864)
Sophia Peabody Hawthorne (1809–1871) 148
  Laurie A. Sterling

Joel Tyler Headley (1813–1897) 162
  Paola Gemme

Washington Irving (1783–1859) 168
  Xavier Baron

Thomas Jefferson (1743–1826) 187
  Bryan F. Le Beau

George Jones (1800–1870) 197
  James A. Wren

Meriwether Lewis (1774–1809)
William Clark (1770–1838) 201
  Rob J. Brault

Alexander Slidell Mackenzie (1803–1848) 224
  Barbara Ryan

Francis Parkman (1823–1893) 231
  James L. Gray

Rembrandt Peale (1778–1860) 243
  Anita G. Gorman

Matthew Perry (1794–1858) 251
  Dorsey Kleitz

Zebulon Montgomery Pike (1779–1813)............259
  Linda Lincoln

David Porter (1780–1843)......................................268
  Udo Nattermann

James Riley (1777–1840) 273
  Paul Baepler

Catharine Maria Sedgwick (1789–1867) 278
  Stephanie A. Tingley

Lydia Howard (Huntley)
Sigourney (1791–1865) 285
  Laurie Delaney

Benjamin Silliman (1779–1864)............................292
  Anna E. Lomando

John Lloyd Stephens (1805–1852) 298
    Edward J. Gallagher

Henry David Thoreau (1817–1862) 305
    Stephen Adams

John Trumbull (1756–1843) 312
    Martha I. Pallante

Charles Wilkes (1798–1877) 316
    James J. Schramer

Nathaniel Parker Willis (1806–1867)....................332
    Karen Schramm

American Travel Writing (1776–1864) 342
Checklist of Further Reading 349
Contributors 352
Cumulative Index...355

Plan of the Series

The advisory board, the editors, and the publisher of the *Dictionary of Literary Biography* are joined in endorsing Mark Twain's declaration. The literature of a nation provides an inexhaustible resource of permanent worth. We intend to make literature and its creators better understood and more accessible to students and the reading public, while satisfying the standards of teachers and scholars.

To meet these requirements, *literary biography* has been construed in terms of the author's achievement. The most important thing about a writer is his writing. Accordingly, the entries in *DLB* are career biographies, tracing the development of the author's canon and the evolution of his reputation.

The purpose of *DLB* is not only to provide reliable information in a convenient format but also to place the figures in the larger perspective of literary history and to offer appraisals of their accomplishments by qualified scholars.

The publication plan for *DLB* resulted from two years of preparation. The project was proposed to Bruccoli Clark by Frederick C. Ruffner, president of the Gale Research Company, in November 1975. After specimen entries were prepared and typeset, an advisory board was formed to refine the entry format and develop the series rationale. In meetings held during 1976, the publisher, series editors, and advisory board approved the scheme for a comprehensive biographical dictionary of persons who contributed to North American literature. Editorial work on the first volume began in January 1977, and it was published in 1978. In order to make *DLB* more than a reference tool and to compile volumes that individually have claim to status as literary history, it was decided to organize volumes by

topic, period, or genre. Each of these freestanding volumes provides a biographical-bibliographical guide and overview for a particular area of literature. We are convinced that this organization—as opposed to a single alphabet method—constitutes a valuable innovation in the presentation of reference material. The volume plan necessarily requires many decisions for the placement and treatment of authors who might properly be included in two or three volumes. In some instances a major figure will be included in separate volumes, but with different entries emphasizing the aspect of his career appropriate to each volume. Ernest Hemingway, for example, is represented in *American Writers in Paris, 1920–1939* by an entry focusing on his expatriate apprenticeship; he is also in *American Novelists, 1910–1945* with an entry surveying his entire career, as well as in *American Short-Story Writers, 1910–1945, Second Series* with an entry concentrating on his short stories. Each volume includes a cumulative index of the subject authors and articles. Comprehensive indexes to the entire series are planned.

The series has been further augmented by the *DLB Yearbooks* (since 1981) which update published entries and add new entries to keep the *DLB* current with contemporary activity. There have also been *DLB Documentary Series* volumes which provide biographical and critical source materials for figures whose work is judged to have particular interest for students. One of these companion volumes is entirely devoted to Tennessee Williams.

We define literature as the *intellectual commerce of a nation:* not merely as belles lettres but as that ample and complex process by which ideas are generated, shaped, and transmitted. *DLB* entries are not limited to "creative writers" but extend to other figures who in their time and in their way influenced the mind of a people. Thus the series encompasses historians, journalists, publishers, book collectors, and screenwriters. By this means readers of *DLB* may be aided to perceive literature not as cult scripture in the keeping of intellectual high priests but firmly positioned at the center of a nation's life.

DLB includes the major writers appropriate to each volume and those standing in the ranks behind them. Scholarly and critical counsel has been sought in deciding which minor figures to include and how full their entries should be. Wherever possible, useful references are made to figures who do not warrant separate entries.

Each *DLB* volume has an expert volume editor responsible for planning the volume, selecting the figures for inclusion, and assigning the entries. Volume editors are also responsible for preparing, where appropriate, appendices surveying the major periodicals and literary and intellectual movements for their volumes, as well as lists of further readings. Work on the series as a whole is coordinated at the Bruccoli Clark Layman editorial center in Columbia, South Carolina, where the editorial staff is responsible for accuracy and utility of the published volumes.

One feature that distinguishes *DLB* is the illustration policy—its concern with the iconography of literature. Just as an author is influenced by his sur-roundings, so is the reader's understanding of the author enhanced by a knowledge of his environment. Therefore *DLB* volumes include not only drawings, paintings, and photographs of authors, often depicting them at various stages in their careers, but also illustrations of their families and places where they lived. Title pages are regularly reproduced in facsimile along with dust jackets for modern authors. The dust jackets are a special feature of *DLB* because they often document better than anything else the way in which an author's work was perceived in its own time. Specimens of the writers' manuscripts and letters are included when feasible.

Samuel Johnson rightly decreed that "The chief glory of every people arises from its authors." The purpose of the *Dictionary of Literary Biography* is to compile literary history in the surest way available to us—by accurate and comprehensive treatment of the lives and work of those who contributed to it.

The *DLB* Advisory Board

Introduction

THE UNITED STATES OF AMERICA
DEPARTMENT OF STATE

To all whom these presents shall come,
Greeting:

Know Ye, that the bearer hereof John
James Audubon, a distinguished naturalist and
native citizen of the United States, has made
known to me his intention of travelling on this
continent with the view principally of aiding the
cause by extending his researches and explorations in natural history, and as he is known to be
a man of character, and honor, and worthy of all
friendly offices, and of all personal regard—

These are, therefore to request all whom it
may concern, to permit him to pass freely without let or molestation, and to extend to him all
such friendly aid and protection as he may need,
and which becomes the hospitality of civilized
and friendly nations.

In testimony, etc. 24th day of July, A D.
1842

DAN'L WEBSTER

The United States Department of State and the
Passport Office from the beginning have followed a
liberal policy regarding travel within and outside
the United States. An 1898 pamphlet on passport
history and regulations issued by the State Department reads: "In times of peace a law abiding American citizen has always been free to leave the country
without the permission of the Government; and, under the same conditions, foreigners have always
been permitted to travel or sojourn within our
boundaries without a permissive document." During the nineteenth century the Department of State,
reflecting the patriarchal attitudes of the times, issued umbrella passports to male heads of households. The regulations then stipulated that "When
the applicant is to be accompanied by his wife, children, or servants, or females under his protection, it
will be sufficient to state the names and ages of such
persons and their relationship to the applicant, as
one passport may cover the whole." The Civil War
and changing American views on slavery accounted

for a shift in policy in 1862, when household passports were limited to husband, wife, and minor children. Although the government's liberal travel policy was temporarily suspended during the Civil
War—when travel into or out of the United States
was severely limited—after the war the prewar policy was restored, and servants (no longer implicitly
slaves) were again covered by a single family passport.

Although twentieth-century Americans would
certainly object to excluding women, children, and
servants from individual passport coverage, the
views of the mid-nineteenth-century American Department of State on a citizen's right to travel still
strike a responsive chord with a people who treasure freedom of movement. Americans have, after
all, inherited a legacy of exploration, immigration,
and migration. America is a nation of travelers, and
the county has come to signify the restlessness of the
human spirit.

From its entry into the European consciousness, America has occupied a textual as well as a
geographical space. Beginning with Columbus's dispatches, through John Smith's reports to Elizabethan England, to J. Hector St. John de Crèvecoeur's
Letters from an American Farmer (1782), Europeans and
European-Americans have read the New World
landscape as a text that could be realized more fully
if they wrote about it. They continued to revise and
edit their vision of America in the travel works they
produced as they settled and unsettled American
space. England and its colonies in North America
were involved in a fluid exchange of texts and travelers across the Atlantic as the colonists rode out the
English Civil War (1640s) and the Glorious Revolution (1689).

Neither British colonial North America nor
the subsequent republic were as detached from the
turmoil of Europe as many Americans liked to believe. If British colonists in North America wanted
to know for or against whom they were to fight in
the widening global conflict that Americans referred
to collectively as the French and Indian Wars, they
had to keep up with what was going on in England
and the rest of Europe. During the Revolutionary
and post-Revolutionary periods, influential Ameri-

cans traveled regularly to Europe. From the colonial period and into the era of nation-building and beyond, Americans have regarded their roots in the Old World as significant to their identities, and their hunger or need to represent in words the world outside the United States has continued to the present day.

Travel both within and outside the United States was deeply connected to Americans' search for a cultural identity. Americans traveled and wrote about those travels to discover who they were as a nation and as individuals. Whether they went west into what was once seen as the Great American Desert of the interior or sailed east on a reverse voyage of discovery back to Europe, Americans were often more interested in discovering themselves than they were in learning about others. The essays in *Dictionary of Literary Biography 183: American Travel Writers, 1776–1864* give the reader a series of hints about how American travelers from the Revolutionary period through the end of the Civil War saw, interpreted, and constructed themselves, America, and the world. To better understand these constructions within the context of the period, readers may find it worthwhile to consider the general perspectives and conditions that informed the views of nineteenth-century Americans and to reflect upon the rhetorical issues that enrich the modern reader's response to travel writing.

The travel literature genre for English-speaking people was well established from Queen Elizabeth's time on. The New World of the Americas as opened up by literarily self-conscious, voluntary travelers, beginning with Columbus and continuing with Elizabethan explorers such as John Smith and Sir Martin Frobisher. Jonathan Swift's remarkable parody *Gulliver's Travels* (1727) and Daniel Defoe's *Robinson Crusoe* (1719) attained popular success within a context of many famous travel accounts. The eighteenth century produced many lesser-known but influential travel books, many of which at the time were considered scientific.

Colonial American works such as William Byrd's *History of the Dividing Line* (manuscript 1728), J. Hector St. John de Crèvecoeur's *Letters from an American Farmer,* and William Bartram's *Travels* (1791) fit into this scientific tradition, as North Americans explored the natural world and the Native American cultures at the borders of the colonies. Thomas Jefferson's influential *Notes on the State of Virginia* (1785) set out criteria for a scientific study of a locale, including a range of information, from personal observations to statistical data and lists of cultivated crops.

Travel writing as a genre succeeded by its cumulative effect. There were hundreds of titles that dealt with treks over much of the globe by the start of the nineteenth century, and popular travel accounts were often quickly translated into major languages. Few individual titles were noteworthy, which may partly account for the relative absence of travel writing from the literary canons of most countries. As time went by, critical comments by Europeans such as Frances Trollope and Charles Dickens about their trips to the United States invited rebuttal from Americans such as James Fenimore Cooper and Nathaniel Hawthorne.

One distinctive area of American travel literature was Americans' exploration of newly acquired territory. The American horizon in the first half of the nineteenth century was widened as the Louisiana Purchase (1803), the Florida Purchase (1819), and the Mexican War (1846–1848) opened vast tracts of land to settlement by U.S. citizens. The Louisiana Purchase, which virtually doubled the country's size, was terra incognita to the majority of the population living near the East Coast. As Stephen E. Ambrose points out in *Undaunted Courage: Meriwether Lewis, Thomas Jefferson, and the Opening of the American West* (1996), at the time of the Louisiana Purchase the population of the United States was less than five and a half million people. Of that population, almost 20 percent were slaves, and fully two-thirds of Americans "lived within fifty miles of tidewater." Beginning with the expedition led by Meriwether Lewis and William Clark, the federal government sponsored expeditions to map and explore the territory. The men sent on these missions made systematic observations on the climate, geography, and geology as well as the plants, forests, animals, and peoples of the regions through which they traveled.

The man behind the Louisiana Purchase was President Thomas Jefferson, an American version of the Enlightenment ideal of the private scholar and public figure, who was captivated as much by the texts he read as the maps he contemplated. Among the books that influenced Jefferson's thinking was Alexander Mackenzie's *Voyages from Montreal, on the River St. Lawrence, Through the Continent of North America, to the Frozen and Pacific Ocean* (1801). Mackenzie's account moved Jefferson to action because it announced that the British were boldly staking their claim to the western expanses of their portion of North America. The work also influenced Jefferson's decision to mount a U.S. expedition because Mackenzie insisted that the way to the Pacific coast was unobstructed and relatively easy. Jefferson and Lewis, who imagined the Rockies as similar to the Appalachian chain, found the encouragement they so eagerly sought in Mackenzie's narrative.

In its later acquisition of Florida and two-fifths of what had been Mexico, the United States laid claim to lands that in comparison to the Louisiana Purchase were already known. Florida, having been settled by Europeans, had been well traveled. Still, until the Spanish presence had been replaced with Anglo colonization, it remained an exotic locale in the American imagination. Some of the lands obtained as part of the Mexican War conquest, especially Texas, had been extensively settled. California, which had been explored, gave the United States access to the Pacific. With the discovery of gold in California and news reports of the Gold Rush, more and more Americans traveled west, and the country as a whole began to become aware of the immense size of its possessions. The exploration and settlement of the West eventually led to the construction of the transcontinental railroad to tie the country together.

The publication of territorial travel narratives allowed educated citizens to get a feel for the opportunities for settlement and economic exploitation that were available. As M. H. Dunlop puts it in *Sixty Miles from Contentment: Traveling the Nineteenth-Century American Interior* (1995), they provided a "guide to the possibilities of emigration." The citizens of the United States were unusually mobile by European standards, and as the farming population on the Atlantic coast increased rapidly, the need to find new land when the old land played out also grew. Along with oral reports, books such as Francis Parkman's *The California and Oregon Trail* (1849) played an important role in encouraging migration along the Oregon Trail and other westward routes. The settlement patterns were often based on travel writings that followed the explorers.

The migration across the Rocky Mountains to Oregon and California occasioned a second wave of travel writing. Less oriented toward scientific observation of flora and fauna than the reports from expeditions early in the nineteenth century, this second wave of travel writers focused on the topography as a physical barrier to the movement of white settlers and the spread of their culture. Many of these narratives took the form of handbooks that offered practical advice for the immigrant.

Much early travel to the areas under U.S. control—the territories under various degrees of white settlement—fell into the general category of testing the new land to find out what it was like and what it was worth. The immigrant European-Americans found nomadic Indians in their way, so a good portion of the writing had to do with the resulting cultural conflicts.

An important theme of American ideology was that only through settlement and private ownership of land was the national title effectively confirmed. The doctrine of private ownership was the centerpiece of the argument against Native American rights or claims to land, for piece by piece the land that had once been a tribe's recognized heritage was claimed by whites. On their first exploratory contacts, whites viewed Native Americans either as noble or as primitive. As settlers began to take over the land of Native Americans, however, white attitudes toward Native Americans became more complex. Dunlop describes the ambivalence many western travelers felt: "Nineteenth-century [white] travelers wanted to wonder at, if not fear, Indians, wanted to see them in paint and tribal costume, wanted them to perform, wanted to buy at the lowest possible price everything they carried or wore, and then wanted to flee them." The ways of life of many Native American tribes were rapidly destroyed by the encroachment of white civilization as the issue soon became not who had a right to the land but who had the might to stay on that land.

Beyond the exploration of their own continent, Americans also traveled to other lands, including Asia, South America, and the Middle East, though travel to such exotic destinations was limited before 1865. Starting soon after the Treaty of Paris in 1783, American traders were on their way to Canton (1784–1785), chiefly to replace the British source for tea which was cut off. The era of the China clipper ships from the late 1840s to the early 1850s was the golden age of sailing. By the time Commodore Matthew Perry "opened" Japan to trade in 1854, America had gotten past the initial phase of exploration and developing markets in China and elsewhere on the Asian continent and was beginning to send out missionaries and to export the less tangible features of the Yankee culture. A few Americans visited South America in the 1820s to witness the revolutions that reshaped former Spanish and Portuguese colonies, but most American travelers to that continent were more interested in exporting goods and establishing trade than in revolution. Except for brushes with the Barbary pirates and commercial competition with the British trade in Egyptian cotton, the United States had few economic or cultural interests in the Moslem world, so travel accounts from the Middle East were few until after the Civil War, when Egypt and the Holy Land became tourist destinations.

By far the most common destination for the American traveler abroad was Europe, though

Americans often faced difficulties in traveling to the Old World. Tensions between the United States and Great Britain and European wars significantly affected American access to Europe during certain periods. During the years of the Revolutionary War, English navigation laws restricted travel. Travel to the continental European countries became highly restricted for some twenty years during the Napoleonic Wars and their generally successful blockades. The War of 1812 also complicated travel abroad. After the disruptions of the Napoleonic Wars, cholera epidemics in 1832–1833 and the revolutions of 1848 again limited travel to Europe. In all cases, following the unpleasantries, travel by Americans increased significantly. In the first decade of the nineteenth century fewer than one thousand U.S. passports were issued; the number rose to more than forty thousand in the 1850s. (These statistics understate the number of travelers, since one passport could cover an entire household, including servants or slaves, and since many traveled without official documents.)

The post-Napoleonic era, coinciding with the end of the War of 1812, significantly eased both travel and commercial interactions between America and Europe. Great Britain was the "old home" of many Americans whose ancestors had migrated from England, Scotland, and Wales. As an original ally in the Revolutionary War, France held a special appeal for American travelers to the Continent. Not-yet-unified Germany and Italy became choice places to visit for art and formal education. The Irish potato famine of the late 1840s and changing policies on the part of continental governments led not only to new waves of immigrants to the United States but also to an increased awareness of European travel possibilities on the part of Americans.

Until the travel boom of the post–Civil War period, the rest of Europe was little known to most Americans. As citizens of a nation that espoused the official separation of church and state, Americans viewed Catholic Europe, especially Spain and Italy, with distrust. The anti-Catholic bias of most American travelers showed in their frequently condescending attitudes toward these countries. It was not until after the Civil War that Americans began to travel Greece and Italy, viewing those countries as the cradles of their democratic culture. As immigrants came to America from European countries other than Great Britain, the possible sites of return increased. In addition to thinking of England as a collective "old home," newer generations of Americans began to visit ancestral homelands in Germany, Ireland, and Scandinavia.

Throughout the years from 1776 to 1864, travel was uncomfortable and often arduous. The early modes of transport were acutely sensitive to weather conditions. Small ships responded to every wave that crossed their bows; ground transportation was feasible only during the daytime, and roads were dusty in summer, muddy in spring and fall, and bumpy all year long. Before the railroad and steamship, carriage and sailing schedules were notoriously unreliable, and hiring a private coach was beyond the financial means of all but the wealthiest travelers. Because the means of transportation were slow and unpleasant, the traveler had an incentive to stay at each place for days or even weeks. Major improvements in sea and land transportation beginning in the second quarter of the nineteenth century made long-distance trips easier and cheaper. Travel handbooks such as John Murray's "Red Guides" (from 1836) and Karl Baedeker's (from 1835), originally covering Europe but later expanding across the globe, and packaged tours, starting with Thomas Cook's excursion train in England in 1841, helped the traveler find the best ways to move around and to find accommodations. Such changes also began to affect the rhythm of the trip abroad by raising the importance of "sights" and by tempting the traveler limited by time to keep on the move. Some Europeans saw the train as destroying the traveler's ability to appreciate the countryside and argued that the true traveler should revert to travel by foot or horseback. Few Americans expressed similar regrets.

Most American travelers abroad before 1865 can be arranged into six groups. Businessmen of various stripes—cotton exporters, importers of foreign goods, bankers—composed a prominent group. Evangelical zeal led Protestant congregations to send missionaries to non-Christian areas. These clergymen were often obliged to send letters back that would be published in a local newspaper, and accounts of missionary activities were frequently used to raise money to continue the work. Another growing group of Americans abroad were reporters sent by the larger newspapers and magazines, many of whom had roving international correspondents. Margaret Fuller, for example, was on a newspaper assignment (1847–1850) when she traveled to Europe. Many artists traveled, and some of them lived for several years abroad. In the late eighteenth century their destination was chiefly England; later, Italy was the main drawing card, since live models and skilled labor were cheap, as was Carrara marble. There were those who went abroad for medical reasons seeking relief or cures based on various claims about climate and atmosphere. Theodore

Parker sought a tuberculosis cure; Ralph Waldo Emerson's brother went to Puerto Rico for the same reason. Last, a few Americans in these early years went abroad just for leisure. In most cases, of course, those who traveled abroad were financially well-to-do, for spending months or years away from home was an expensive proposition.

In *The Fortunate Pilgrims* (1964), his influential study of American travelers to Italy from 1800 to 1860, Paul R. Baker classifies early American travel writers as belonging to one of four types: discoverers, explorers, romanticizers, or exoticizers—labels that may be usefully modified and applied to the more general discussion of the types of American travelers to Europe in the last years of the eighteenth century through the nineteenth century:

1. *Discoverers–1776-1820.* In the period after Independence, American artists, scientists, and public figures traveled to the Old World to discover what it could offer the new nation. Artists such as Rembrandt Peale went to complete their apprenticeships; scientist Benjamin Silliman went to bring back European science to Yale University; public figures such as John Adams, Benjamin Franklin, and Jefferson went to Europe as ambassadors.

2. *Explorers–1820-1840.* As travel to Europe became easier many Americans went to Europe to explore its social life and cultural institutions. Writers such as Washington Irving and James Fenimore Cooper spent years abroad writing about Europe for American audiences. Americans visiting Europe during these years often had done little background reading and were only vaguely familiar with the countries they were visiting.

3. *Romanticizers–by 1860.* Showing a maturing confidence in their own national identity, American travelers at mid century such as Nathaniel Hawthorne were mainly interested in exploring their cultural roots in the Europe of the past rather than in the present conditions of the Continent. Despite having a wealth of literary guides in hand, the romantic travelers saw themselves as wandering, finding and expressing freedom, rather than traveling with a purpose.

4. *Exotic Adventurers–by 1900.* When traveling to Italy and the rest of Europe had become commonplace, some Americans began to search out the picturesque or the bizarre in lesser known cultures. Baker sees these travel writers as "even more detached from ordinary life than the romanticizers had been."

Three more types of travelers and modes of travel discourse could be added to Baker's categories: scientific, economic, and cultural explorers.

In *Voyage into Substance: Art, Science, Nature, and the Illustrated Travel Account, 1760-1840* (1984), Barbara M. Stafford identifies a prescientific flurry of travel books from the early eighteenth century. These works glory in the picturesque and focus on landscapes, vistas, and other impressive natural phenomena; they describe flora, fauna, and Indians, often including appendices that catalogue new discoveries. While these travel writings are largely before the era covered by *DLB 183,* the scientific redefinition of the picturesque informs American travel writing into the early nineteenth century.

Scientific travel writing focused on the exploration of oceans, geology, and biological diversity. Mapping and charting were important activities, since they set up routes for future, routine travel. The instrumentation and apparatus for conducting science was inexpensive—in many cases, all one really needed was a note pad—so that amateur naturalists could make a genuine contribution to knowledge. Scientific societies sometimes fully endorsed and published the findings of amateurs. In the second half of the nineteenth century the standards of these societies changed as formal schooling became a prerequisite for serious, publishable scientific work. By then, biologists, geologists, and anthropologists usually published their work in professional journals. If they did travel writing at all, it tended to be on the scenic and personal aspects of the places visited.

A role frequently assumed by American travel writers was as an economic scout for their growing new nation. In *DLB 183* Charles Wilkes, Matthew Perry, and Amasa Delano are examples. Markets were needed for the surplus of food, timber, and other raw materials that had previously gone to the British Empire. The United States also sought replacements for British manufactured goods. The end of the Revolutionary War left the United States with a fleet of boats up and down the Atlantic coast, few trading partners, and high inflation. Vicissitudes in European trade owing to the break with England and the Napoleonic wars led the United States to look elsewhere. The turn away from England as the source of imports and destination for exports led to some opening of trade to the Mediterranean, and China became a significant trading partner.

Except for Niagara Falls, the Catskills, and a few other natural phenomena, the perception reigned, especially among the country's cultural elite, that there was "nothing to see" in America. Henry James in his 1879 biography of Nathaniel Hawthorne articulates this attitude nicely when he remarks that there were "no great things to look out at (save forests and rivers)." This limited perspective would probably obtain for most upper- and middle-class Americans who would not see it a great treat to go to New York City, Philadelphia, or Boston but who revered European fashion and culture.

American travelers in search of European culture generally avoided commenting on contemporary political and economic events in favor of the past or the picturesque, which they saw as America's birthright. Christopher Mulvey in *Anglo-American Landscapes: A Study of Nineteenth-Century Anglo-American Travel Literature* (1983) pays special attention to Americans' attitude toward England: "Americans of all dispositions made reference to their childhood as they approached and as they first explored England." They saw the country as a series of gardens, or as the scenes of poems and novels from works they read as children, or, even better, as a series of picturesque ruins. The literate and the privileged such as Ralph Waldo Emerson and Lydia Howard Sigourney managed to visit the homes of the aging writers of the Romantic age as well as some up-and-coming Victorians.

Travel writing often gave a mixed political message to the American audience by implicitly or explicitly contrasting the visited society with home. The introduction of different "models" of societies sometimes seems designed to promote change in America, as when Margaret Fuller suggests her country could profit by recapturing the idealism she found in Italy; however, most nineteenth-century travelers were enthusiastically patriotic. The intended rhetorical effect is usually the validation of American values and institutions, especially those institutions linked to democracy. In *Discovery of Europe: The Story of American Experience in the Old World* (1947) Philip Rahv asserts that Hawthorne, for example, "retained the elemental Americanism and natural democratic bias of the early years of the Republic." Americans, like other travelers, used their perceived domestic standards of morality for their touchstones. In his report on the reactions of Americans to Italy, Baker notes that many found the Italian family not tightly knit or home-centered enough. They were also appalled by the concept of the convent and objected to seeing women do heavy manual labor. Many travelers saw their efforts abroad and their writings for domestic readers as a means of spreading the secular gospel of American democracy and were critical of the class systems and titled nobility of European societies.

In most cases the American traveler in Europe was the first American the European host encountered. There was often an emotional imbalance in their relationship, since the American in Europe felt that he or she was going "home," even if that home was only a cultural conception of the Old World as the source of Western civilization. From books or oral accounts, the American arrived with a sense of what he or she expected to find, while most Europeans had no sense of whom they were greeting. In *Literary Pioneers: Early American Explorers of European Culture* (1935), Orie William Long documents the travels of Henry Wadsworth Longfellow, Edward Everett, George Ticknor, and others who studied in Germany from 1815 to the 1830s and who returned to America to be leaders in literature and higher education. During this period of increased travel to Europe, many literate American travelers were deeply influenced by attitudes arising from the Romantic movement in literature.

Concurrently with the early national period in America, British travel writing underwent a change from the scientific to the Romantic as represented in the narrative poems of George Gordon, Lord Byron, and the personal memoirs, including the sonnet sequences, of William Wordsworth. Such writings established the central importance of a subjective apprehension of European cities, ancient artifacts, and such natural scenery as the British countryside and the Alps. James Buzard in *The Beaten Track: European Tourism, Literature, and the Ways to Culture, 1800–1918* (1993) characterizes the change this way: "Scenes, situations, and characters from these texts became the appropriatable, exchangeable markers in a cultural economy in which 'travellers' competed for pre-eminence by displaying their imaginative capacities." Despite Byron's personal commitment to political idealism, the Byronic figure was depoliticized in travel literature. His strong opposition to the Ottoman rule of Greece and his generally liberal views were not carried over into the guidebooks that gave inspirational passages for the visitor to quote whilst looking at the Colosseum at midnight. Buzard discusses this "reconstructed Byron" at length.

The influence of the English Romantics on America took about a generation to be felt. The American romantic travel narrative generally shows up in the second wave of travel to and writing about a given place. The initial exploration had been, in most cases, formally documented by the end of the eighteenth century in scientific style and fashion. The second wave made personal impression the new style for travel writing. Stafford discusses the dilemma of the factual travel account, which only served well during the "era of primary discoveries." What Mary Louise Pratt in her article in *Race, Writing and Difference* (1986) calls the "scientistic, information-oriented branch" became boring and stale, and the Enlightenment's claim to universality no longer was seen as being desirable in the Romantic age.

Stafford observes that the instructive guides were "overshadowed by the sentimental, self-projecting, or autobiographical journey, tour, or circuit." The emphasis on individual impression rather than direct, empirical observation also fit into the way Americans celebrated Europe for its past rather than its present. In their attempts to represent the freshness of their personal view, the romantic travelers to Europe often chose not to admit that they knew anything about what inspired their emotions. Stafford sees this process as the "hegemony of the external" being displaced by the new emphasis on the imaginative and emotional, "the slighting of visual for psychological fact." Pratt notes that this shift in emphasis makes the traveler the focus of the narrative: "The traveler is the protagonist of the journey and the primary focus of the account."

Landscapes, both in the territories and in Europe, were frequently seen through a Romantic lens. Views were evaluated as to whether they were "sublime," "beautiful," or "picturesque" as defined by Edmund Burke and other late-eighteenth-century theorists. As the aesthetic language became more sophisticated, interest grew in "scenery," a highly selected subset of "nature." Travelers would describe scenes so that they would have a proper picturesque aura. This bias sometimes led to an aesthetic emphasis on the natural environment that rejected the importance of human culture. The history of Native Americans was generally erased or denied in this view of the country. As more travel accounts became available, the pressure for the travel writer to say something original intensified. As Stafford notes, "Landscapists can avoid being imitative only by retaining their individuality."

Like all other types of writing, travel writing sets up relations among the identity of the author—in this case the traveler—his or her personal interpretation of experience, and the reproduction of cultural values. As a genre, travel writing exists in the borderland between the social and the poetic, as the writer's primary concerns are typically description and personal expression. The social and linguistic processes involved in travel writing lead the writer to express not only a personal vision but also an evolving cultural ideology. This can be seen, for example, in the appropriation of British Romanticism by American travel writers for their own cultural puposes. Genres are value-laden and value-creating forms; they symbolize communal identity.

Even though most travel writing is in first person, it is best to think of it as having a biographical rather than an autobiographical focus. The traveler is certainly the main character, but the account is supposed to display the places visited, not the traveler's personal life. Robert Scholes and Robert Kellogg in *The Nature of Narrative* (1966) make the distinction "between the first-person speaker in empirical narrative (the eye-witness narrator or the autobiographical confessor) and the first-person speakers of fictional narrative (the characters who tell the primary author-narrators their stories, often leading to stories between stories)." They define travel writing as one of the "eye-witness narrative forms": the writer's voice is both personal and authoritative. Scholes and Kellogg would argue that the travel writer's first-person narrator "is not a character in narrative, but he is not exactly the author himself, either. He is a persona, a projection of the author's empirical virtues."

Travel writers select events to report on based on their perceptions of what matters to the readers. Usually, they adopt the attitude of "You are with me" or "You could do what I am describing." The reader often perceives their accounts as firsthand and nonfictional, though the implied objectivity is rarely claimed explicitly. Whether the surface form is a sustained narrative, journal, series of letters, or even a logbook, the reader is expected to recognize the writer's presence and personal involvement at the distant scene. By and large, the travelers present themselves as being alone (even when they were with friends and family, local hosts, and guides), and concerns about relative isolation and solitude are rhetorically part of the tale. The travel writer, as Eric J. Leed in *The Mind of the Traveler: From Gilgamesh to Global Tourism* (1991) describes the posture of writer Charles Moritz, often tries to present himself "as a solitary wanderer in a foreign land, from the perspective of his best friend at home." Percy G. Adams in *Travel Literature and the Evolution of the Novel* (1983) notes that the typical traveler returns "to scorn the ignorance of his untraveled acquaintances."

American travel writers often strive to portray themselves as representative or ordinary men and women, writing to peers in common or plain style. Despite their posture of intimacy with the reader, travel writers rarely reveal intensely personal experiences such as sexual encounters. The reader's response to the first person in travel writing is sometimes complicated by the celebrity of the author. Many travel writers have reputations apart from their travel writing. Readers have preconceptions about famous authors, such as Washington Irving, James Fenimore Cooper, and Catherine Maria Sedgwick, and important political figures, such as John Adams, Benjamin Franklin, and Thomas Jefferson.

Travel writers take on a variety of rhetorical postures, from the "gee whiz," naive tourist to the ironic, sophisticated traveler. The travel writer may present a visited place from the point of view of a stranger or from that of a temporary native. Under the sway of Romanticism in the first half of the nineteenth century, both readers and writers came to value the writer's voice and personality as much as the distant scene depicted. Later in the nineteenth century writers—especially those who wrote about Europe—increasingly tried to take on the role of knowledgeable expert. The emphasis shifted to the topic, the places and peoples visited, and the writer's personality slipped into the background. Pratt describes these later travelers this way: "[M]ost of them did not write themselves as heroes. Indeed, one of the most striking aspects of this informational branch of travel writing is the way it reverses and refuses heroic priorities: it narrates place and describes people." An important, didactic function of later travel writing by Americans was to break away from the British models and to try to create homegrown expectations for future travelers, traders, and tourists. The traveler's role is often symbolized by how much gear he or she brings along. Henry David Thoreau talked about himself as a "knight of the umbrella and bundle," and set his traveling style in contrast to those who brought along a full array of steamer trunks containing table settings and the like. Some chameleonlike travelers such as John Lloyd Stephens made a point of going "native" and affecting local dress and manners, while others held out, often trying to preserve their American ways with little success.

Of greater cultural significance was the issue of language acquisition for the traveler. Outside of Europe, Americans often followed the British lead and cultivated native interpreters, either bilingual or pidgin speakers. Sometimes travelers set themselves as being superior to others because of their proficiency with languages. Other Americans, shut out from direct communication with the natives, quietly ignored them and focused on landscapes and natural phenomena.

The attitudes of the natives were often crucial to the tone of the travel writing account. In *The Tourist: A New Theory of the Leisure Class* (1976) Dean McCannell explains the tourist's situation: "In the give-and-take of urban street life in tourist areas, the question of who is watching whom and who is responding to whom can be as complex as it is in the give-and-take between ethnographers and their respondents." In some texts—those that focus on architecture or other artworks or those that focus on nature—the natives may well become invisible. Where the natives are involved, they can see the traveler as an enemy, a potential trading partner, a hostage,

and, occasionally, as a friend. Travelers and natives frequently see one another as alien versions of themselves, which often results in the travel writer's missing subtleties that deserve notice and exaggerating the significance of differences.

It is worth noting that the traveler in undeveloped areas was often not as invisible as she or he might imply. The traveler could disrupt the lives of locals for better or worse. Travelers inevitably brought the modern world—both material goods and modern attitudes—to the villager or peasant. Often the implied conflict between the traveler and the native is denoted by the rhetoric of pronouns: "us" versus "them." Travelers who sojourned for long periods in alien cultures sometimes expressed a desire to get to know the natives, leading occasionally to resentment when the natives failed to include the visitor in their private lives.

Most Americans and Europeans who traveled in the eighteenth and nineteenth centuries were men. The cost of travel often led husbands to leave their wives behind when they needed to journey abroad. There were exceptions, of course—rich women, ambassadors' wives, and, later, female reporters. The male domination of travel writing, as Leed asserts, "describes the mobilities of men and assumes the sessility of women"; travel writing is "a male literature reflecting a masculine point of view." Feminist scholars and others have frequently pointed out that this reality has led metaphorically to frequent displays of "the male gaze and female landscape." Some women managed to edge into travel writing because—at least in the early nineteenth century—the genre allowed them to use the "letters from abroad" mode of discourse that was considered an acceptable form of female writing.

It is clear, often from explicit statements, that many travel writers believed that they could accurately represent what they observed and experienced. Others admitted that they were able only to illustrate experiences in the foreign country and only to suggest an aspect of reality. Scholes and Kellogg assert that "Traveler's tales in all countries are notoriously untrustworthy, and untrustworthy in proportion to the distance of the travels from familiar territory, just as ancient maps become less and less reliable toward their edges." On the other hand, Claude Lévi-Strauss in *Tristes Tropiques* (1975) defends the value of short glimpses of a world that is seen from a moving point of view as "the intense concentration forced upon one by the brevity of the stay." That the view is limited to surfaces and fleeting glimpses—the point of view of the passing stranger observing the world through a narrow carriage window—does not necessarily make it invalid.

In retrospect, with the aid of such penetrating critics as Pratt and Buzard, the reader can look beyond the travel writer's ideology and notice some of the cultural and political results of nineteenth-century writing about other cultures. Both the romantic and scientific approaches to travel writing ultimately had the effect of preparing a rhetorical vanguard for imperialism and the expansion of capitalism. While the ordinary family might see a description of a foreign country as providing guidance for the next summer's vacation, such information also helped governments and entrepreneurs prepare their plans for exploiting human and natural resources in a systematic way. As the disciplines of anthropology and ethnology entered the American academy, new claims were made about the carefully trained scientific observer's ability to use extensive observations and a detached attitude to bring a remote culture to life on the page. The *Oxford English Dictionary* traces the history of the term ethnology from its being a study of national differences and ancient practices within Europe (between the first use of the term in 1834 through the 1860s) to the "collection of ethnological curiosities" and "particular institutions and customs" among remote tribes. Buzard argues that an anthropologist and linguist such as Edward Sapir could understand the coherence of the tribe under study while the ordinary travel writer would not. Pratt in *Imperial Eyes: Studies in Travel Writing and Transculturation* (1992) comments extensively and less charitably on the vogue of "portraits of manners and customs" as a blind for the subjective or economic involvement of the traveler and the country he or she represents.

Another way to characterize the rhetoric of travel writing is to focus on metonymy as its central trope; in Leed's words, "Travel is a 'generalizing' activity." Thus, scientific writing depends on having the selected details stand for the entire landscape or culture. Stafford calls this "a commitment to cloaking ideas with bodies communicated in a mode that suppresses the exhibition of self to reveal the system of the other." Romantic writers rhetorically argued for the viewer to stand for other visitors. Pratt in her article frames part of her argument for the underlying imperialism of such writing in her discussion of "othering": "The people to be othered are homogenized into a collective 'they,' which is distilled further into an iconic 'he' (the standardized adult male specimen)."

Places are similarly construed. Buzard comments on "the totality 'Europe'" and points to the underlying absurdity of books from George Putnam's *The Tourist in Europe* (1838) to the twentieth-century's *Europe on Five Dollars a Day,* "guides which effectively reinforce the reified unity of 'Europe' and put the key to that unity in the carrier's hand—or on American shelves and coffee-tables." The symbols of successful travel, from artifacts and souvenirs to photographs, were seen as metonymically representing the places that had been visited.

Most readers appreciate travel writing that represents experience in what seems to be a transparent and truthful way. At a trivial level, the travel writer presents readers with an elegant postcard—the account puts a picturesque setting into perspective by providing a suitable frame. Travel accounts are judged good when they draw readers to interact with the visited place as if they were there and convey a sense of place that is different from the readers' ordinary experiences. At a deeper level, though, accounts of travel present the readers with the difficult problem of having to decide how far to trust the traveler's vision. One way to characterize the issue is to recall the long-standing tradition between expressive and mimetic theories of literature—metaphorically whether the visited place is observed with a "lens" or reflected passively with a "mirror."

Readers' responses to a particular travel narrative—the degree to which they view it as a lens or a mirror—probably turns on their expectations and reactions to the writer's persona. In the modern, poststructuralist age, where objectivity has been called into question, readers are likely to focus on the traveler's lens and to be aware of the ways that the traveler's contemporary culture has distorted or even created that lens. Modern readers often see narrators' attitudes in terms of ideology, which Suzanne Lanser in *The Narrative Act: Point of View in Prose Fiction* (1981) describes as "a nonconscious body of knowledge, values, and structures which represent the viewer's understanding of 'the world' and which may appear to him or her to be entirely natural and objective, but that impact of that nonconscious ideology may nonetheless be reflected in the stricture of the text."

Nineteenth-century travel writers expected their readers' ready acceptance of their claims, while readers expected writers to present an accurate and interesting account of their experiences. This implied contract between the writer and the audience was sometimes broken by knowledgeable readers or reviewers who chose to look behind or beyond the experience rendered on the page. Readers' own travels to the place described, whether before or after reading the text, might lead them to question the reality or objectivity of the writer's account and thus subvert the contract. Readers might also decide to break the contract if they perceived the writer as too personal or subjective, for they then might not be able to share an experience that is uniquely the writer's. Another strain on the contract could arise from a disagreement between the reader and writer on the fuction of the travel narrative: A reader might expect a prosaic account filled with information while the writer might have intended to provoke an aesthetic response by creating a poetic description.

In "good" travel narratives, readers and critics are often impressed by rhetorical and literary elements, suggesting that travel writing is typically judged by how close it mimics well-crafted fiction or the novel. Another criterion is tied to how persuasive an account is judged to be. Travel writers often had an explicit agenda—to change American architecture, improve American culture, alter marriage customs—and it is for the reader or the critic to decide how well the case was made.

Travel begets writing, which begets reading, which begets travel. Buzard neatly describes the relationship:

> Travel literature about the Continent seemed to grow in almost self-perpetuating fashion because it was both symptom and contributing cause of the new atmosphere of the crowd. Travelling and reading were seen to complement each other, constituting a cyclic ritual in which readers both shaped their expectations and relived their past travels through texts. It had long been true that preparatory readings—not only of travel books but of histories, poems, plays, novels—could help to establish future travelers' expectations; that travel could test those expectations; and that further reading could strengthen remembered expectations and experiences, recharging the reader's sense of having accomplished something meaningful by travelling.

As Walter J. Ong asserts in *Orality and Literacy: The Technologizing of the Word* (1982), writing is a technology, and as print technology improved, travel writing increasingly went beyond just words. Early books had maps and engravings; later ones had photographs. The picturesque rendering of landscapes through verbal description was often replaced by visual images. A good picture could, perhaps, substitute for the high moment in the picturesque, that time when the narrator can not even try to capture the scene in words. The images of foreign people and scenes—"The Zouave," "The Seraglio"—stood metonymically for the visited culture in ways that words could not.

If travel writing as a category were eliminated from libraries and bookstores, all the travel books would fit elsewhere—as memoir, as natural history, as ethnography. Alternatively, travel writing could be taken as including most books, for nearly all writing concerns place and setting to some degree. Travel writing as a genre shows what Mulvey terms "the chronic insecurity of the form." Buzard distinguishes "between the objective, informative 'guidebook' on the one hand and the impressionistic 'travel book' (or more tentative 'travel sketch') on the other," but between these poles there is room for endless variation. Words in book titles such as *journal, diary, letters,* and the noncommittal *account* are signs of the range of the genre. The structure of the account may or may not be the same as the structure of the journal. While most accounts switch between narration and exposition, the label does not suggest whether the work is the record of notes scribbled in the heat of the experience or the product of later reflection. Writing in epistolary, diary, or journal formats implies postponed judgments, while logs, chronicles, or annals suggest a lack of selectivity and often defy clearly defined plot movement. Labels such as *narrative, history,* and *autobiography* suggest the writer's attempt to control and shape her or his experience.

The travel narrative of adventure stands in marked contrast to the tourist's experiences, which are comfortable and predictable. While in some narratives the traveler seems always in control and knows where he or she is going, in others the traveler uses novelistic devices to create suspense and drama. At the extreme, there is the dangerous overland expedition or the naval voyage that is interrupted by pirates, war, or insurrection. But even when the experience is harrowing the traveler almost always returns home safely. In more subdued cases, the writer engages readers by confounding expectations, emphasizing the striking differences or suprising similarities between the distant culture and his or her own.

The journal or epistolary forms carry with them a promise of authenticity in that the traveler relates his or her experience soon after the fact. The presence of these forms brings to light how close much travel writing comes to memoir and autobiography, with all of the difficulties those genres have for readers to judge the balance among the self-serving, the authentic, and the unconsciously revealing. Adams argues that by the beginning of the nineteenth century, "throughout Europe the popular first-person travel accounts would necessarily affect not only the content but the form of autobiography and fiction and would not, in fact, be thought of as a genre separate from autobiography or, often, from fiction. For the personal, subjective nature of that literature has always been one of its chief and most endearing elements, no matter how often some readers and critics through the ages have tried to eliminate it from all travel accounts as undesirable." Travel writing in the form of letters usually points to a specific audience, whether an individual, an institution (such as the Congress or the president), or ordinary people back home. The presence of an explicit audience gives the reader a clear grasp of the context and may help establish the credibility of the writer's experience.

Travel narratives are like histories in being built around a story, in being situated in a specific place and time, and often in developing a theme. The presence of the narrating voice, however, tends to exclude them from proper history, at least when history is required to be objective and scientific. The final relation between these two types of writing is somewhat symbiotic, since travel writings are often seen as primary sources for later histories. Travel writing also often approaches other nonfiction genres such as journalism and anthropology.

Mulvey suggests the indeterminate nature of the genre has given travel writers an inferiority complex: "Travel writers feared that travel writing was artistically inferior to other genres. It was not given serious consideration by literary critics. Travel writers feared that travel writing was academically inferior to other sciences. It was not clearly an art or a science. It could be either, which was suspicious; it was frequently neither, which was shameful." In the midst of these insecurities, often articulated quite defensively by the authors themselves, deciding where to locate a particular text depends finally on the reader's judgment.

The difficulty of classifying travel literature is apparent in the classification system of the library. The subject headings for the Library of Congress include a variety of relevant subdivisions—"Description and travel," "Guidebooks," "Maps," "Pictorial works"—which can be used to bring out the travel-related genre aspect of works entered under the names of places (or, rarely, peoples, as in "Gypsy"). Similarly, ranges are identified in library classification systems that link travel writing about a place within a broader, geographical classification (the Library of Congress classification gathers travel writing about the United States as a whole within the larger classification of American history). These topic and genre classifications sometimes surprise readers who look for travel works by literary authors. For example, a librarian is more likely to place Henry James's *The American Scene* (1907) under "Atlantic States—Description and travel" instead of with James's other literary works. Practices vary among librarians, but there does seem to be a tendency to catalogue by place rather than by the people being observed (which might lead toward anthropology) and not to subdivide travel writing by its century (which might lead toward history).

The historical relation between travel writing and prose fiction has been explored in detail by Adams and others. Adams tries to redress the scholarly neglect of the influence of travel writing on the novel, a neglect that he traces chiefly to the exclusion of travel writing from the literary canon. He gives an account of the enormous body of travel writing that was available to the first European novelists and assesses its affect on novelists: "And no matter how fantastic or how believable the fiction was, no matter whether or not its title claimed some of the accoutrements of travel literature, writers who invented characters and sent them on journeys—and that means the great majority of epics, romances, historic and other long narratives—satirized the details of travelers, employed such details imaginatively, perhaps fantastically, or actually transferred real ones from travel books." Fiction written before 1630 attests "to the ancient and perennial thirst for exact details—whether recognizably real, merely marvelous, or obviously fantastic." In further exploring the "tension" between the romantic and realistic, he finds both drawing on a common tradition, "the journey plot, whether real or allegorical, is the most nearly basic in imaginative literature." Adams is less persuasive when he tries to link travel writing with the domestic narrative.

Although there are clear historical connections between travel writing and the novel, they remain distinct genres. The novel in its matured, nineteenth-century manifestations delves into the inner selves and motivations of characters. The basic mimetic impulse in travel writing is sociological or anthropological rather than psychological—a major difference between travel literature and the novel. In travel writing the visited people are characterized by their actions and sometimes by their words but almost never by their thoughts or unconscious motives. It is probably the focus in the novel on character that more than any other single factor distinguishes it from travel writing, which avoids the detailed treatment of any character other than the narrator. However, though travel writing can be said to lack the psychological sophistication of the novel, the writers profiled in *Dictionary of Literary Biography 183: American Travel Writers, 1776–1864* show that it is a rich, wide-ranging genre. At their best, American travel writers provided their audiences with important insights into foreign places and cultures through accounts that combine aesthetic pleasures with the excitement of discovery.

Acknowledgments

This book was produced by Bruccoli Clark Layman, Inc. Karen L. Rood is senior editor for the *Dictionary of Literary Biography* series. George P. Anderson was the in-house editor. He was assisted by Philip B. Dematteis.

Administrative support was provided by Ann M. Cheschi and Brenda A. Gillie.

Bookkeeper is Joyce Fowler.

Copyediting supervisor is Jeff Miller. The copyediting staff includes Phyllis A. Avant, Patricia Coate, Christine Copeland, Thom Harman, and William L. Thomas Jr. Freelance copyeditors include Rebecca Mayo and Jessica Rogers.

Editorial associates are Judith E. McCray and L. Kay Webster.

Layout and graphics staff includes Marie L. Parker and Janet E. Hill.

Office manager is Kathy Lawler Merlette.

Photography editors are Julie E. Frick and Margaret Meriwether. Photographic copy work was performed by Joseph M. Bruccoli.

Production manager is Samuel W. Bruce.

Software specialist is Marie L. Parker.

Systems manager is Chris Elmore.

Typesetting supervisor is Kathleen M. Flanagan. The typesetting staff includes Pamela D. Norton and Patricia Flanagan Salisbury. Freelance typesetters include Melody W. Clegg and Delores Plastow.

Walter W. Ross, Steven Gross, and Mark McEwan did library research. They were assisted by the following librarians at the Thomas Cooper Library of the University of South Carolina: Linda Holderfield and the interlibrary-loan staff; reference-department head Virginia Weathers; reference librarians Marilee Birchfield, Stefanie Buck, Stefanie DuBose, Rebecca Feind, Karen Joseph, Donna Lehman, Charlene Loope, Anthony McKissick, Jean Rhyne, and Kwamine Simpson; circulation-department head Caroline Taylor; and acquisitions-searching supervisor David Haggard.

American Travel Writers, 1776–1864

Dictionary of Literary Biography

John Adams
(19 October 1735 – 4 July 1826)

and

Abigail Adams
(11 November 1744 – 28 October 1818)

Dennis R. Perry
University of Missouri–Rolla

See also the John Adams entry in *DLB 31: American Colonial Writers, 1735–1781.*

John Adams

BOOKS: *Thoughts on Government: Applicable to the Present State of the American Colonies* (Philadelphia: Printed by John Dunlap, 1776);

Observations on the Commerce of the American States with Europe and the West Indies; Including the Several Articles of Import and Export. Also, An Essay on Canon and Feudal Law . . . (Philadelphia: Printed & sold by Robert Bell, 1783);

History of a Dispute with America, from its Origins in 1754. Written in 1774 (London: Printed for J. Stockdale, 1784); enlarged edition, in *Novanglus, and Massachusettensis; or, Political Essays, Published in the Years 1774 and 1775, On the Principle Points of Controversy, Between Great Britain and Her Colonies . . .*, by Adams, as Novanglus, and David Leonard, as Massachusettensis (Boston: Printed & published by Hews & Goss, 1819);

A Defence of the Constitutions of Government of the United States of America, volume 1 (London: Printed for C. Dilly, 1787; Philadelphia: Printed for Hall & Sellers, J. Crukshank, and Young & M'Colloch, 1787; New York: Printed & sold by H. Gaine, 1787); volumes 2–3 (London: Printed for C. Dilly & J. Stockdale, 1787–1788); volumes 1–3 (Philadelphia: Printed by Budd & Bartram for William Cobbett, 1797);

Discourses on Davila. A Series of Papers, on Political History: Written in the Year 1790, and then published in the Gazette of the United States (Boston: Printed by Russell & Cutler, 1805);

Diary of John Adams and *Autobiography,* in volumes 2 and 3 of *The Works of John Adams,* edited by Charles Francis Adams (Boston: Little, Brown, 1850–1851);

The Earliest Diary of John Adams, edited by L. H. Butterfield, Wendell D. Garrett, and Marc Friedlander (Cambridge, Mass.: Harvard University Press, 1966).

Collections: *The Works of John Adams,* 10 volumes, edited by Charles Francis Adams (Boston: Little, Brown, 1850–1856);

The Adams Papers, 26 volumes to date (Boston: Harvard University Press, 1961–   );

Legal Papers of John Adams, edited by L. Kinvin Wroth and Hiller B. Zobel (Cambridge, Mass.: Belknap Press, 1965).

OTHER: *A Dissertation on the Canon and Feudal Law,* by Adams, but attributed to Jeremy Gridley, in *The True Sentiments of America,* compiled by Thomas Hollis (London: Printed for I. Almon, 1768), pp. 111–143.

John Adams's travels extended from his journey in August 1774 to Philadelphia, where he spent much of the next two and a half years as a member

John and Abigail Adams, August 1766; portraits by Benjamin Blyth (Massachusetts Historical Society)

of the Continental Congress, through his years as a diplomat in Paris, Holland, and Great Britain, to his final return to his beloved Pens Hill in Braintree, Massachusetts, in June 1788. During these fourteen years he made his mark as a prominent statesman and helped establish the place of the newly independent United States in the world. The letters he exchanged with his wife, Abigail, during his time away from home rank with the great American literary correspondences. Both correspondents were remarkable individuals.

Descendant of a family that went back to the early days of Massachusetts, including a maternal ancestor from Plymouth colony, John Adams was the first to bring his family to national and international prominence. Born in Braintree, where his family had lived since 1639, John was the son of John Adams and Susanna Boylston Adams. A farmer, the elder Adams provided John with an example of public-mindedness, serving as constable, selectman, and lieutenant in the militia. His pious parents taught young Adams the value of hard work. He graduated from Harvard and then studied law, creating a successful practice in Boston. Adams became involved in colonial politics after the impo-

sition of the Stamp Act in 1765 and earned his countrymen's respect through his writings and his law practice. He returned from his travels to be elected the first vice president of the United States and to become the nation's second president.

Adams married Abigail Smith, daughter of a Congregational minister from Weymouth, on 25 October 1764. A frail child, Abigail grew up in her grandmother's house. With her natural gifts she made the most of her opportunities to hear intelligent conversation, read from her father's library, and learn of the world. She would become an effective and independent woman. Although Abigail never attended school, she was an astute observer and commentator on current affairs. Virtually single-handedly she raised the couple's four children during the stress of the Revolution and ran the family farm at Braintree during her husband's long absences.

John and Abigail's correspondence first became a national treasure when the letters were edited by their grandson Charles Francis Adams and published for the centennial year of the Declaration of Independence as *Familiar Letters of John Adams and His Wife, during the Revolution* (1876). As L. H. Butterfield notes in his introduction to *The Book of Abigail and John: Selected Letters of the Adams Family, 1762–1784* (1975), the initial enthusiasm for the letters was rooted in the way the Adamses epitomized the values of independence, sacrifice, and fortitude associated with revolutionary America. They seemed to become "*everybody's* grandparents." Today the letters are also valued for their candor, refreshing humor, and insights into a mature intimacy maintained and deepened under stress. In their letters the Adamses range broadly, covering topics as diverse as Puritan typology and Enlightenment wit, providing accurate descriptive details and philosophical generalizations about experience, commenting on the people they knew and the extraordinary times in which they lived. Lending all of this a timeless charm is each spouse's loving sensitivity to the other's situation, health, and feelings.

In addition to his correspondence with Abigail, Adams kept a detailed diary and later wrote his autobiography, both of which were first published in *The Works of John Adams (1850–1851)*, edited by C. F. Adams. While both of these works provide valuable insights into his life and travels, they tend to be overburdened with mundane detail, neither tapping his best literary nor best personal side. The *Diary* is a wonderful resource of historical information on people and ideas during the Revolutionary period, occasionally breaking into effective travel narrative that paints significant moments in the kind of detail Abigail always longed for (but rarely received) from her husband's letters. Adams's *Autobiography* reads as a formalized version of his *Diary*, endlessly detailed but without focus. His description of his first voyage to France takes twenty-six pages in volume four of *The Adams Papers* (1961–). A true traveler and travel writer at heart, Adams's streak of Puritan practicality may have prevented him from finding a completely satisfactory vehicle for literary pursuits. He always felt the pull of duty to concentrate on the political and diplomatic issues.

Adams's letters to Abigail bring out some of his best writing, wedding insight in personal and cultural matters to an engaging style. They had been married for only ten years when Adams embarked on his public role as a representative of Massachusetts; John was thirty-nine and Abigail twenty-nine. Since his public life was always fraught with controversy and misunderstanding, his letters to Abigail were his lifeline to a loving environment of acceptance and understanding, where lengthy apologies for his views and actions were not necessary. Her wit, charm, and practical good sense as both writer and audience encouraged her husband to take the time to express his thoughts and feelings. While she shared many of Adams's ideas, her lively take on life inevitably had a brightening influence on her husband's natural seriousness.

Other circumstances combined to make Adams's letters his most important travel writing. First, the danger of mail falling into the wrong hands during and after the Revolution was so great that Adams did not relate the details of government business or write much about the petty jealousies he felt. Second, his busy schedule kept his letters to Abigail concise, curtailing his propensity to overwrite. Third, because he was corresponding with his wife, he avoided the obsession to correct the perceived misrepresentations that particularly mar the *Autobiography*. As a result, what the letters lack in detail is more than made up for in their conciseness and liveliness.

Adams's travel writing phase began in the troubled years leading up to the Revolutionary War. The Boston Port Act and other coercive acts, which sealed up the city, were threats that the other colonies all felt, and they led to the formation of the First Continental Congress. As one of the elected delegates from Massachusetts, Adams and the other delegates from the colony began their journey to Philadelphia on 10 August 1774. Six days later he describes in his *Diary* their reception as they passed through New Haven, Connecticut. After being greeted by many carriages and horsemen, including the sheriff, the constable, and the justice of the peace, they were well received by the townsfolk: "as We came into the Town all the Bells in Town were sett to ringing, and the People Men, Women and Children were crouding at the Doors and Windows as if it was to see a Coronation. At Nine O Clock the Cannon were fired, about a Dozen Guns I think."

Once in Philadelphia, Adams wrote to Abigail of both the good and frustrating aspects of colonial politics. In his 8 September 1774 letter he notes the unity among the delegates: "Every Gentleman seems to consider the Bombardment of Boston, as the Bombardment, of the Capital of his own Province." Adams writes of how impressed he is with the Congress, characterizing it as "a Collection of the greatest Men upon this Continent, in Point of Abilities, Virtues and Fortunes." However, he soon realized the dangers of such an assembly, complaining in a 9 October letter of the necessity of each of these great men discoursing at length on every subject: "The Consequence of this is, that Business is drawn and spun out to an immeasurable Length." Such frustrations also bring out Adams's humorous side: "I believe if it was moved and seconded that We should come to a Resolution that Three and two make five We should be entertained with Logick

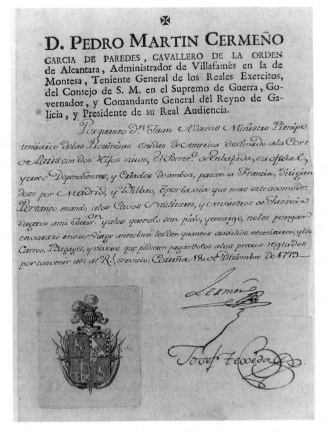

D. PEDRO MARTIN CERMEÑO

GARCIA DE PAREDES, CAVALLERO DE LA ORDEN de Alcantara, Administrador de Villafamès en la de Montesa, Teniente General de los Reales Exercitos, del Consejo de S. M. en el Supremo de Guerra, Governador, y Comandante General del Reyno de Galicia, y Presidente de su Real Audiencia.

Passport issued to John Adams and his party for their 1779 journey through Spain (Massachusetts Historical Society)

Œconomy, Parcimony must be our Refuge." Here he reflects the mood of resolutions made by the Congress urging restraint and prudence in all public behaviors, including at funerals and theaters.

Adams's letters show his continual concern for the home front, particularly Abigail's anxiety about the activities of British troops in Boston. He tried to maintain his role as father and husband despite distances, reassuring her in his letter of 28 August 1774 that "Prudence and Caution should be our Guides." Each spouse worried about the other's health and happiness. Abigail generally wrote chatty and earnest letters that evoke a sense of home, the progress of the children, friends, and of the farm. In her 16 October letter Abigail gives vent to her emotions, despite the dangers of postal theft: "The whole collected stock of ten weeks absence knows not how to brook any longer restraint, but will break forth and flow thro my pen. May the like sensations enter thy breast, and (in spite of all the weighty cares of State) Mingle themselves with those I wish to communicate. . . ." Adams, in his turn, also found the separation hard, as is clear from the opening of his letter of 29 September: "Sitting down to write to you, is a Scene almost too tender for my State of Nerves."

Adams returned to Braintree in late October 1774 after the Continental Congress claimed the rights due all British subjects in its *Declarations of Rights* and adjourned until the following May. In addition to his many other duties during this first session of Congress, Adams wrote a pamphlet advocating dominion status for the American colonies. Between sessions of Congress the colony moved inexorably closer to the more radical position of Adams and others; with the Battles of Lexington and Concord on 19 April 1775 war officially began.

When he returned to Philadelphia in May 1775 as a delegate to the Second Continental Congress, Adams was prepared to work hard and found himself doing committee work seven hours a day (eventually he was chair of twenty-five committees), in addition to the six-hour sessions of Congress. He made many significant contributions: he was instrumental in the appointment of George Washington as commander in chief; he led the way for the ratifying of the *Declaration of Independence*; and he helped create an American navy. The session was also the occasion of some rancor. Adams was particularly impatient with John Dickinson's desire to appease Great Britain. Privately envious of how much more glory military officers received than politicians, he also developed a petty jealousy of Washington's growing fame, which he felt was overrated.

For Abigail this was also a period of trial. Beyond the inconveniences and terrors of the war, she

and Rhetorick, Law, History, Politicks and Mathematicks, concerning the Subject for two whole Days, and then We should pass the Resolution unanimously in the Affirmative." While instances of humor are relatively rare in Adams's writings, its presence in the letters suggests that such light spirits may not have been uncommon for him.

Certain himself of the need for Congress to take decisive action in response to tyranny, he was impatient with its willingness to delay decisive action, particularly since his own province was the center of British hostilities. He complains of the necessary socializing in his 29 September letter, remarking that he fears he shall be "kill'd with Kindness"; he describes the continuous round of feasting "upon ten thousand Delicacies" and then going home "fatigued to death with Business, Company, and Care." Yet in the same letter Adams comments on the work of the Continental Congress in grand, visionary terms: "We have had as great Questions to discuss as ever engaged the Attention of Men." Such a sense of the importance of the cause led him to austere measures, as is evident in his 20 September letter to Abigail: "Frugality, my Dear, Frugality,

dealt with smallpox and dysentery in her home, had a stillborn baby, and felt keenly the absence of her husband's comforting presence. She often requested more and better letters, writing in a letter dated 16 June 1775 that "every line is like a precious Relict of the Saints." If anybody should have felt unfairly robbed of glory, certainly Abigail would have been a candidate. To his credit Adams seems to have appreciated, at least in part, her trials. He tried to sustain Abigail as much as his busy schedule and distracted mind enabled him, writing on 7 July 1775, "It gives me more Pleasure than I can express to learn that you sustain with so much Fortitude, the Shocks and Terrors of the Times."

Adams's volatile emotions, swinging between a selfless public-mindedness and a petty ambition for fame, are manifest. On the one hand, he wrote on 17 June 1775 of his hopes that the "People of our Province" will treat Washington, whom many regarded as an outsider taking over the management of their war, "with all that Confidence and Affection, that Politeness and Respect, which is due to one of the most important Characters in the World." On the other hand, Adams just six days later seemed to pity himself after accompanying Washington at the beginning of their journey toward Boston. The "Pride and Pomp of War" made him feel a "poor Creature, worn out with scribbling, for my Bread and my Liberty," regretful that he "must leave others to wear the Lawrells which I have sown; others, to eat the Bread which I have earned." Following Washington's success at the Battle of Trenton on 25 December 1776, Adams found it hard to grant him all of the credit he deserved. After a day of thanksgiving was appointed by Congress, Adams closed his 26 October 1777 letter with the remark that "Now We can allow a certain Citizen to be wise, virtuous, and good, without thinking him a Deity or a saviour." But Adams was nothing if not changeable. In a bout of homesickness on 16 March 1777 he claims to have "nothing of Caesars Greatness in my soul. Power has not my Wishes in her Train. . . . the Enjoyment of my Farm and Garden, would make me as happy as my Nature and State will bear."

Adams was a thoroughgoing New Englander who viewed the prospective nation and the world with a provincial eye. Although he gloried in the concept of a system of united states and saw many similarities among the various areas, Adams was mindful of his provincial prejudices. He admits to Abigail in his 29 October 1775 letter that his intense preference for New England over other areas of the colonies may be owing to an "Infirmity, in my own Heart" which he calls "partial Fondness." He writes

Adams in the month after he signed the treaty that ended the American Revolution; portrait by John Singleton Copley (Harvard University Portrait Collection; bequest of Ward Nicholas Boylston, 1828)

that he has been ridiculed for his beliefs that New Englanders are superior to other Americans for their "purer English Blood" deriving from people who immigrated in "purer Times than the present." He also admits that he finds advantages in the morals, education, and land distribution of New England. In a 14 April 1776 letter he asserts that among his southern colleagues an "Inequality of Property, gives an Aristocratical Turn to all their Proceedings, and occasions a strong Aversion in their Patricians, to Common Sense." Yet he believes the times are changing so that "the Spirit of these Barons, is coming down, and it must submit."

Adams's travels broadened him to the extent that he also saw shortcomings in New Englanders. In a 4 August 1776 letter he admits that "My Countrymen want Art and Address. They want Knowledge of the World. They want the exteriour and superficial Accomplishments of Gentlemen. . . ." He goes even further to note that "our N. England People are Aukward and bashfull; yet they are pert, ostentatious and vain, a Mixture which excites Ridicule and gives Disgust." He expresses the hope that they will develop such graces that, added to their native virtues and "solid Abilities," will enable New England to produce important leaders for the new nation.

Despite his provinciality, Adams loved to travel and see various manners and peoples. In the spring of 1777 he wrote to Abigail, "It is good to change Place—it promotes Health and Spirits." While going through Baltimore in February 1777 following a brief congressional recess, Adams relished the opportunity to inquire into all aspects of the city's culture, and he described in impressive detail the "perfection" of its mechanical arts, the economy of its public institutions, and the piety of its Lutheran religion. Adams had an insatiable appetite for knowledge and experience of all practical kinds, together with great stores of energy to pursue them when not ill or busy with other matters. After visiting a studio in Philadelphia, he wrote on 21 August 1776 that he wished he "had Leisure, and Tranquility of Mind to amuse myself with these Elegant, and ingenious Arts of Painting, Sculpture, Statuary, Architecture, and Musick." He often traveled with a purpose and wrote of wanting to improve New England by noting the finer accomplishments in other areas of the colonies. He was particularly inspired by Philadelphia's philosophical society and hoped to help establish one in New England.

Between bouts with sickness and the "continual alarms" of war, Abigail kept her husband well informed of the local scene, often becoming his chief source of solid information on the progress of the war in the Boston area. In one of the few times she ever appealed to him as a delegate and not as a husband, she broached the subject of women's rights. In a 31 March 1776 letter she asks that Congress "Remember the Ladies, and be more generous and favourable to them than your ancestors." She justifies her request by noting that men are "Naturally Tyrannical" and that laws should protect women from the "vicious and the Lawless." In his 14 April response Adams lightheartedly (and conventionally) asserts that "we know better than to repeal our Masculine systems" because men's power over women is "little more than Theory." If women were granted any more rights then they now enjoy, he maintains, it "would compleatly subject Us to the Despotism of the Peticoat." In her 7 May letter Abigail notes the irony of such a body of revolutionaries for freedom

maintaining "Arbitrary power" over their wives: "notwithstanding all your wise Laws and Maxims we have it in our power not only to free ourselves but to subdue our Masters." Hence Abigail Adams was at the forefront of another revolution, the seeds of which may well have been planted in the fertile soil of 1776.

In December 1777, during a leave from Congress, Adams's hard work and leadership were recognized with a commission to serve as minister to France. Although he balked at a dangerous winter passage and feared the possibility of capture en route, he recorded in his *Autobiography* his determination that his duty lay in carrying out the plans for foreign relations he had earlier promoted in Congress. He set sail with his son John Quincy, then ten years old, on the frigate *Boston* on 13 February 1778, beginning a ten-year period of almost continuous residence in Europe.

Father and son had a difficult but interesting voyage to Europe, most of which is recorded in Adams's *Autobiography,* which he wrote between 1802 and 1807. Possibly influenced by the wonderfully descriptive letters and diary of Abigail concerning her own 1784 voyage, Adams here reaches unusual levels of suggestive detail as a travel writer. For example, he paints an exciting picture of a storm: "The Wind blowing against the current, not directly, but in various Angles, produced a tumbling Sea, vast mountains of Water above Us, and as deep caverns below Us, the mountains sometimes dashing against each other, and sometimes piling up on one another like Pelion on Ossa, and not unfrequently breaking on the Ship threatened to bury Us all at once in the deep." He goes on to describe the "harsh musick" of the vibrating shrouds and ropes, creating a "hideous howl, of itself enough to deafen Us, added to this the howl and Whistle of the Winds, and incessant roar of the Ocean all in boiling rage and fury, white as Snow with foam through the whole Extent of the horrison. . . ." While the entire account of the voyage lacks a tight focus, encumbered by too many insignificant details, he includes a variety of interesting information about sailors' superstitions, a Portuguese man-of-war they caught, and amusements and trials on shipboard.

In March 1778 Adams arrived in Bordeaux, where he had his first shocking encounter with the distinctly un-Puritan French culture. As he delightfully records in his *Autobiography,* during dinner "one of the most elegant Ladies at Table, young and handsome," asked, since his name was Adams, how Adam and Eve "found out the Art of lying together." Prefacing his response by noting how he had been used to the "Modesty, Delicacy and Dig-

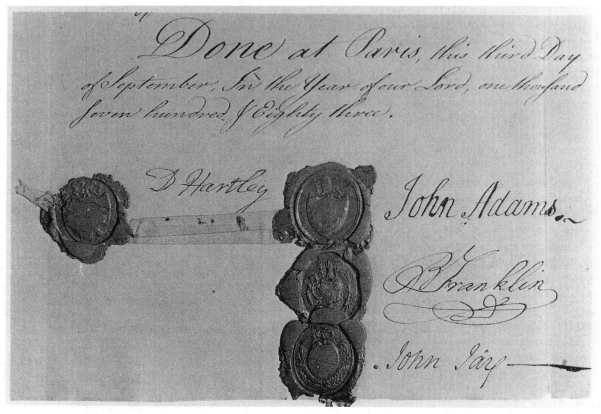

*Signatures and seals on Adams's duplicate copy of the 1783 peace treaty between the United States and Great Britain
(Massachusetts Historical Society)*

nity" of the ladies of America, he records his clever answer: "I rather thought it was by Instinct, for there was a Physical quality in Us resembling the Power of Electricity or of the Magnet, by which when a Pair approached within a striking distance they flew together like the needle to the Pole or like two Objects in electric Experiments." The exchange concludes when she replies that it was certainly a "very happy shock." Much about Adams's provincial mind is revealed in this account. While he is able to hold back his natural blush and enter into this playful, sexual banter in a manner not unworthy of Benjamin Franklin, he later cannot help but question whether he should "have added 'in a lawfull Way' after 'a striking distance.'" It may be just as well that he did not write of this encounter to Abigail.

Adams arrived in Paris on 8 April to find a disorderly foreign mission that lacked administrative records of any kind. Finding excessive quarreling among the members of the joint commission, Silas Deane, Arthur Lee, and Franklin, Adams made informal recommendations to Congress through his cousin Samuel Adams that only two ministers were necessary and that their duties should be divided be-

tween commerce and politics. These proposals were accepted, leaving Adams awkwardly out of a job, without the necessary formal release allowing him to return home. In his 28 February 1779 letter he complains to Abigail: "The Scaffold is cutt away, and I am left kicking and sprawling in the Mire, I think. It is hardly a state of Disgrace that I am in but rather of total Neglect and Contempt."

The increased difficulty of getting transatlantic mail safely back and forth understandably proved trying to Adams. In a 9 February 1779 letter to Abigail he writes, "God knows how much I suffer for Want of Writing to you. It used to be a cordial to my Spirits." Among the issues Adams would have loved to convey to his favorite confidante was his growing disaffection with Franklin. It was during this stay in France that Adams's once warm opinion of Franklin began to change from admiration to jealous contempt. He records in his autobiography that he and Franklin felt a special friendship when they first met in Passy, the result of working together in Congress for more than two years. However, he describes Franklin's life irritatedly as "a Scene of continual discipation," which left little time for the urgent business the earnest Adams felt needed attention. In part, at least, the growing disaffection on both sides was owing to a difference in diplomatic philosophy. While Franklin felt most comfortable making himself a charming figure by which to win French respect and love for himself and his country, Adams felt obligated to work hard at the process of making the relationship between the two countries totally explicit—and somewhat equal. In addition, the rift between them was the classic impasse between contrasting personalities: Adams as the straightforward, earnest Puritan and Franklin as the sophisticated man of the world. Also, Adams's increasing jealousy over Franklin's popular fame—which, like Washington's, he felt was overrated—became a factor in feeding his disdain.

During his stay in France the provincial Adams faced new challenges, and his candid accounts of his collisions with the liberal culture add a dimension to his portrait, revealing the conflict within his identity as both conservative New Englander and Enlightenment revolutionary. He is favorable to much he discovers in France. He wrote on 1 April 1778 in his diary that he found the opera "a very chearfull, sprightly Amusement, having never seen any Thing of the Kind before." In his 3 June 1778 letter to Abigail he compares the country to "one great Garden. Nature and Art have conspired to render every Thing here delightful." He notes in his 26 July letter that "every Thing that can sooth, charm and bewitch is here." He even gently taunts Abigail in his 25 April letter about how much he admires the French ladies for their education, brilliance, and accomplishments: "Don't be jealous. They are handsome, and very well educated."

But unlike Franklin or Thomas Jefferson, Adams would not permit himself to relax and fully enjoy the delights of this European wonderland. In the midst of splendors he dutifully talked himself out of enjoying them. In his letter of 12 April he despairs of describing the sights—"The Richness, the Magnificence, and Splendor, is beyond all Description"—but then claims to receive "but little Pleasure in beholding all these Things." He "cannot help suspecting that the more Elegance, the less Virtue." In his 3 June letter, after warning of the dangers of French luxury and hoping his own country escapes its "bewitching Charms," he humorously anticipates the reaction of American women to losing the fashionable benefits of luxury: "Oh the Tyrant! the American Ladies would say! What!—Ay, my dear Girls, these Passions of yours, which are so easily alarmed, and others of my own sex which are exactly like them, have done and will do the Work of Tyrants in all Ages." He reflects a conventional American fear of European decadence—a temptation to be avoided back home.

After hearing of the cultural superiority of France, especially concerning the education of French women, Abigail in her 30 June letter takes the opportunity again to assail her husband on the needs of women in America: "you need not be told how much female Education is neglected, nor how fashonable it has been to ridicule Female learning. . . ." She rejoices in the accomplishments of French women and goes on to paraphrase her reading on female education: "If women says the writer are to be esteemed our Enemies, methinks it is an Ignoble Cowardice thus to disarm them and not allow them the same weapons we use ourselves, but if they deserve the title of our Friends tis an inhumane Tyranny to debar them of priviliges of ingenious Education which would also render their Friendship so much the more delightfull to themselves and us." No record exists of John Adams's response.

With no official reason to be in France, Adams finally received his official release and returned to Boston in August 1779 after nearly one and one-half years away. While he succeeded in seeing the foreign mission reorganized, probably his major useful accomplishment was seeing a world unimaginably remote from Braintree. That experience would help prepare him for the diplomatic work yet to come as a representative of the new nation in the courts of kings.

Once at home Adams was elected from Braintree to help prepare a state constitution, which he drafted alone. It was later ratified by vote of the people and remains the basis of the commonwealth's law. While thus engaged he received another commission from Congress, as minister plenipotentiary to negotiate peace and trade with Great Britain. He was to go to France immediately and to stand by until the war was over. He accepted this latest difficult challenge as a stern but welcome duty to the country, and after being home for only three months he set sail on 13 November 1779 on the *La Sensible*. Recognizing the value of foreign travel, Adams brought along his sons John Quincy, now twelve, and Charles, nine. This mission would result in one of the most challenging periods of his life, keeping him from home for nine years, although Abigail would join him in 1784 and end the famous correspondence that their separation required.

After a difficult voyage, their leaky ship landed on the northern coast of Spain, forcing Adams and his sons to travel in cold weather a thousand miles, crossing the Pyrenees, to get to Paris. In a 12 December 1779 letter to his daughter "Nabby" before they had progressed far on the rigorous trip,

Adams expresses his wish that he could send over some lemons, oranges, and watermelons from Spain, as well as some chocolate, "which is the finest I ever saw." Although he says he is interested by the wonders he sees, he seems to have been ambivalent about the private value of travel: "But you must remember that my Voyages and Journeys are not for my private Information, Instruction, Improvement, Entertainment or Pleasure; but laborious and hazardous Enterprizes of Business." He also rightly prophesies that he "shall never be much polished, by Travel, whatever your Brothers may be." He goes on to hope his sons are improved and educated by their travels, but is not anxious that they be much polished. Expressing clearly priorities that his travels only solidified, Adams notes that although the arts should not be "wholly avoided or neglected especially by your Sex," they should take a backseat to those virtues that are more "useful and essential" to her roles as daughter, sister, wife, mother, and friend. Although Adams perceived dangers in the luxury and sophistication of Europe, he evidently also believed, as hinted by his desire to bring his sons along, that Massachussets needed some of the cultural enlightenment only available across the Atlantic.

During his journey through Spain, Adams wrote about cultural conditions of a less polished state than he had seen in either Paris or Braintree. To Abigail he suggests in his 16 December letter that "You would have been diverted to have seen Us all mounted upon our Mules and marching in Train." He records many fascinating details of the trip in his *Diary*. Of his accommodations on Spanish farms, he comments in a 28 December 1779 entry: "We have a Chamber, for seven of Us to lodge in. We shall lay our Beds upon Tables, Seats and Chairs, or the floor as last night. We have no Smoke and less dirt, but the floor was never washed I believe." He notes that the "Mules, Hogs, fowls and human Inhabitants" live together. Despite such hardships, Adams describes the trip enthusiastically, including the style of the saddles on which they ride, the contents of their saddlebags, and the cut of the mules' ears and tails, showing again the side of his personality that relished cultural contact for its own sake and enjoyed recording it in careful, specific detail. After a chilly, expensive journey, leaving Adams and his sons with violent colds, they finally arrived safely in Paris and took up lodgings in a hotel.

One of the major problems Adams faced—as well as created—during this period in Paris involved the Comte Charles Gravier de Vergennes, the French foreign minister. Wanting to control the peace process himself and to limit the trade agreements between the United States and England, Ver-

Abigail Adams in 1785, portrait by Mather Brown (New York State Historical Association, Cooperstown)

gennes advised Adams to keep his mission a secret officially and to be patient until further instructions would be given. As historian James Truslow Adams (not related to the family of John and Abigail Adams) remarks in *The Adams Family* (1930), Adams may not have been a gracious diplomat, but he was a "shrewd Yankee," and he recognized Vergennes's insulting high-handedness and his attempts to give France too much power over the new nation. Unfortunately, Adams made an enemy of Vergennes, nearly committing diplomatic suicide by providing unwanted advice to the French foreign minister while bypassing Franklin, the only recognized American official in France. One of his motives for these indiscretions was Adams's ongoing contempt for Franklin, who seemed to him careless and less concerned about the interests of the United States than in placating France.

After seeing some of the sights around Paris, John tried to describe to Abigail some of the beautiful gardens he had visited, but he laments revealingly in a 12 May 1780 letter that "I wish I had time to describe these objects to you in a manner, that I should have done, 25 Years ago, but my Head is too full of Schemes and my Heart of Anxiety. . . ." Here, perhaps, is the key to his diplomatic troubles. Whatever his qualifications for diplomacy with England whenever the war should end, he was not temperamentally suited for patient waiting. Even during this relatively quiet time he asserted that he must "study Politicks and War that my sons may have liberty to study Mathematicks and Philosophy." This sentiment opened up for him a practical vision of the progress of culture in the United States: "My sons ought to study Mathematicks and Philosophy, Geography, natural History, Naval Architecture, navigation, Commerce and Agriculture, in order to give their Children a right to study Painting, Poetry, Musick, Architecture, Statuary, Tapestry and Porcelaine." Whatever else may be said of Adams, none can doubt his loyalty to duty. He was not willing to enjoy himself at the nation's expense, as Franklin once suggested he should do until the war ended.

Back in Massachusetts, Abigail's firsthand observations of the war made her correspondence a kind of travel writing in its own right, for with Boston under siege, forcing her to share lodgings with refugees from the city, each day brought new sights. In addition to her endless orders for imported goods, which she sold for much-needed cash, and the homey news about which she so delightfully informed her husband, she described meeting the "Marquis de la Fayette" and her interest in the governor's race between favored but unsuccessful James Bowdoin and that "tinkleling cymball," John Hancock. She was particularly struck by the up-and-down nature of the conflict with England, and she penned what must have been an accurate description of the Revolutionary War experience of many Americans in her letter of 5 July 1780: "who ever takes a retrospective view of the war in which we are engaged, will find that Providence has so intermixed our successes, and our defeats, that on the one hand we have not been left to despond, nor on the other, to be unduely elated." But most of all she misses her husband and requests a miniature likeness be sent to her. She had had one made that she describes in a 24 July letter as "more the resemblance of a cloisterd Monk, than the Smileing Image of my Friend."

Recognizing the futility of his efforts in France, Adams left Paris on 27 July 1780 with John and Charles and went to the Netherlands on a "fishing expedition" to look into the potential for negotiating a Dutch loan for the United States. In September he received word from Congress empowering him to proceed officially. Adams's initiative was ultimately successful, for he was able to promote American interests by capitalizing on the growing animosity between Holland and England.

Adams wrote to Abigail from Amsterdam on 4 September 1780 of how impressed he was with Dutch frugality, industry, and cleanliness, noting that they "deserve the Imitation of my Countrymen." In correspondence dated 15 September he calls Holland "the greatest Curiosity in the World" because it is so little known by the other nations, though the Dutch carry "Learning and Arts I think to greater Extent" than either England or France. However, Adams became so incensed by the treatment of his sons in Amsterdam schools by the masters, whom he describes in a 18 December letter as "mean Spirited Writches, pinching, kicking, and boxing the Children," that he transfers them to Leiden. This and other experiences caused Adams to qualify his initial enthusiasm for Holland and to detect an "incessant Contemplation of Stivers and Doits [Dutch coins of little value], which pervades the whole People." While he was all for frugality, "Avarice, and Stingyness are not Frugality." This led to nearly a whole page in which he again contemplates the superior attitudes and opportunities of America, where "any Man with common Industry and Prudence may be independant." Despite these faults, Adams continued to look on Holland favorably, concluding from a typically American perspective that it is better to be too frugal than too decadent.

Forced to give advice to his sons from a distance, Adams broached subjects that he would not have thought to mention to Abigail. His 28 December 1780 letter to John Quincy again indicates his characteristic double vision. After telling his son that "Skating is a fine Art. It is not Simple Velocity or Agility that constitutes the Perfection of it but Grace," he goes on to clarify his feeling: "In Truth I care very little about any" of the arts of skating, dancing, or riding. What he was really interested in from John Quincy was information concerning every detail about the university's constitution, including the number of professors and their characters. As always, he deliberately reined in his natural interest in beauty and grace.

During the summer of 1781 Adams's problems with Vergennes finally exploded as Franklin sided with the French in questioning Adams's propriety in unofficially meddling in French-American relations. As a result of the controversy Adams lost his exclusive powers to negotiate peace with Great Britain and became only part of a joint commission that included John Jay, Henry Laurens, Jefferson, and, inevitably, Franklin. Adding insult to injury, Congress ordered the commission to be governed by the counsel of the French court. Soon after this news Adams came down with a "nervous fever," brought on perhaps only in part by the Dutch summer. He relates to Abigail in a letter of 9 October 1781 that the fever "seized upon my head, in such a manner that for five or six days I was lost, and so insensible to the Operations of the Physicians and surgeons, as to have lost the memory of them." Concerning the humiliating actions of Congress, Adams in a 2 December letter perhaps protests too much when he claims that those who wish to "injure me in the Estimation of my Countrymen . . . will never hurt your Husband, whose Character is fortified with a shield of Innocence and Honour ten thousandfold stronger than brass or Iron." Despite his disappointments, Adams never lost faith in his rightness and plans to "laugh before all Posterity at their impotent Rage and Envy. They could not help blushing themselves if they were to review their Conduct." In part he refers here to Franklin's role in pretending to Vergennes not to be aware of Adams's views and then to criticize and demean his countryman before a foreign power.

Having had only three months together at home between Adams's European assignments, both husband and wife keenly felt their separation. In his 25 September 1780 letter Adams admits that he can have no pleasures "except at the Foot of Pens hill—When Oh When shall I see the Beauties of that rugged Mountain!" He was evidently reluctant to express too much emotion, as when he closed his 9 October 1781 letter, "With Sentiments and Affections that I cannot express, Yours." But while Adams, supposedly fearing the embarrassment of having his letters captured and published, expressed his personal loneliness for Abigail through his longing for Pens Hill, Abigail was more freely emotive. "How tormenting is absence!" she exclaims in a letter dated 13 November 1780. Unable to conceal her concern for John's health and well-being, Abigail quotes Jean-Jacques Rousseau: "Nothing escapes the apprehension of those who have every thing to lose." Counting the days, Abigail often reminds her husband of how long it has been between letters, although she adds that she is sure he has written. In her 1 August 1781 letter she relates a dream in which he and her sons returned: "Cruel that I should wake only to experience a renual of my daily solicitude."

In a 14 May 1781 letter to John Quincy, Adams reveals his own loneliness indirectly as he anticipates that of his son. The exhorting father reveals how much English poetry has meant to him in passing weary hours: "You will never be alone with a Poet in your Poket." For Adams, art was most valuable when it fulfilled just such a utilitarian function. But poetry could not fill the void he increas-

ingly felt. In a 2 December 1781 letter to Abigail he remarks, "If God should please to restore me once more to your fireside, I will never again leave it without your Ladyships Company."

Since the Dutch had only recently surrendered the port of Saint Eustatius to the British in the West Indies, they were reluctant at first to anger Great Britain by recognizing the independence of the United States. Adams launched a propaganda campaign through the Dutch and British press. His most important work was *A Memorial to Their High Mightinesses* (1781), in which he compares the struggles of Holland and America for liberty. Within a year of publication his reputation blossomed, as the Netherlands recognized the United States on 19 April 1782. By October a treaty of amity and commerce was signed, dispelling the gloom of Adams's illness and of the Vergennes affair. His spirits rose as he was ceremonially received in the courts of the land. In a 1 July 1782 letter from The Hague, Adams tells Abigail that he "begins to be a Courtier," indulging in some rare self-mockery: "I assure you it is much wholesomer to be a complaisant, good humoured, contented Courtier, than a Grumbletonian Patriot, always whining and snarling." While apologizing for his vanity over his diplomatic triumph in the Netherlands, he exclaims nevertheless: "If this had been the only Action of my Life, it would have been a Life well spent." In a letter dated 15 August a month and a half later, he again characterizes his success in Holland "as the happiest Event, and the greatest Action of my Life past or future."

Despite his recurring fears that peace still remained years in the future, Adams returned to Paris for peace negotiations in October 1782. On the heels of his great work in Holland, Adams wrote his 12 October letter to Abigail in a lively spirit. Although he had endured trials and anticipated "another Furnace of Affliction" in Paris, he felt himself ready: "Yet I am very gay, more so than usual. I fear nothing. Why should I. I had like to have said nothing worse can happen." He tells his wife that he is sending some scarlet cloth, which he describes as "very Saucy." With the war winding down, the Adamses began to discuss the possibility of her coming over to be with him, though both realized it will be some time before his situation is certain enough to make final plans.

During the negotiations, far from resigning his position to Vergennes and Franklin, Adams found a powerful ally of his own in Jay. Together they insisted on treating Great Britain on an equal footing—and without advice from France. On this occasion Adams's and Jay's instincts proved right. Fortunately, their success ultimately enabled such a viola-

First page of "Travels and Negotiations," the second part of John Adams's Autobiography (Massachusetts Historical Society)

tion of their limited mandate from Congress. While Jay was the principal negotiator, Adams made important contributions, particularly in gaining the British merchants' acquiescence by adding a clause that the United States should not impede just payment of debts. While he knew not involving the French in these negotiations was a dangerous business, Adams moved forward as a man who felt his

position was probably lost anyway. In his 8 November 1782 letter, when considering the wisdom of Abigail's coming over, he wrote that "I do not expect to hold any Place in Europe longer than next Spring. Mr. Jay is in the same Predicament."

Despite his fears, Adams in a 22 January 1783 letter to Abigail reports the significant news that the "Preliminaries of Peace and an Armistice" were signed at Versailles: "Thus drops the Curtain upon this mighty Trajedy, it has unravelled itself happily for Us–and Heaven be praised." Abigail's reaction to the news in her letter dated 28 April displays her superior ability to describe momentous occasions. She writes metaphorically of how this peace is homegrown in America, raised "by the hard Labour and indefatigable industry and firmness of her Sons and water'd by the Blood of many of them. May its duration be in proportion to its value, and like the Mantle of the prophet descend with blessings to Generations yet to come."

Believing his work in Europe over, Adams turned his attention to his reunion with Abigail. One can sense the relaxation in his letters as he wrote in less-guarded words of his anxiety and loneliness, as in his 29 January 1783 letter: "A Packet from you is always more than I can bear. It gives me a great Pleasure, the highest Pleasure, and therefore makes me and Leaves me Melancholly, like the highest Strains in Music." He awaited congressional acceptance of his resignation and anticipated returning home immediately. However, he made it clear to Abigail that if Congress renewed his old commission to make a commercial treaty with Great Britain, "nothing but your Company will make it acceptable." Although Abigail begged him not to accept another assignment from Congress, he did accept an appointment as part of a commission to Great Britain. After the death of Abigail's father, she and Nabby began the journey to join John and John Quincy in London.

On 24 May 1784 Abigail and Nabby arrived in Boston to await passage to Europe, which they obtained on 20 June. Abigail thus began her own travel writings recorded in her diary and through letters to John and others, in which she paints a lively picture of life aboard ship and of the English countryside. Abigail proved to be her husband's superior as a recorder of her travels. As a sensitive but untraveled woman, she wrote with enthusiasm, sketching landscapes, people, events, and the feelings they engendered. She brought all of her intellectual energy, humor, and wit to bear on her experiences, recording her adventures with the immediacy of sparkling conversation.

Abigail had all along dreaded the rigors and dangers of a sea voyage, not to mention the painful separation from family and friends. She was particularly unhappy to find herself without a male companion or any acquaintance on board. In her diary of 20 June she recorded that her worst fears at departing friends and family were realized, describing the farewell gathering at her Boston home as "a house of mourning"; her friends "like a funeral procession, all come to wish me well and to pray for a speedy return.–Good heaven, what were my sensations?" Her most difficult ordeal was taking leave of John's mother, from whom she had kept her departure a secret, "knowing the agony she would be in." The fateful day was as bad as imagined, leaving Abigail in an "agony of distress." Theatrically rendered, Mother Adams's words are emotionally charged: "Fatal day! I take my last leave; I shall never see you again. Carry my last blessing to my son."

Once on board and under sail, Abigail discovered further maladies characteristic of sea travel. She recorded in her diary that "about 2 oclock we reached the light when the Capt. sent word to all the Ladies to put on their Sea cloaths and prepare for sickness. We had only time to follow his directions before we found ourselves all sick." She found this part of her voyage utterly disgusting, the nausea resulting from a combination of the smell of the cargo (potash and oil) and "the continual rolling, tossing and tumbling." In a letter to her sister, Elizabeth Smith Shaw, she describes a mild storm recently encountered after three weeks at sea: "We could not however sit without being held into our chairs, and every thing that was moveable was in motion, plates Mugs bottles all crashing to peices. . . ." While she generally used commas to separate items in a list, Abigail better suggests the chaos she endured by omitting them in the above list. She adds that during the storm, while confined in her cabin, everything was "wet, dirty and cold, ourselves Sick."

The voyage, however, was not without its compensations for Abigail. In the same letter to her sister she writes that the sea presents her mind with sublime ideas of the divine: "I have contemplated it in its various appearances since I came to Sea, smooth as a Glass, then Gently agitated with a light Brieze, then lifting wave upon wave, moveing on with rapidity, then rising to the Skyes, and in majestick force tossing our Ship to and fro, alternately riseing and sinking; in the Night I have behold it Blaizing and Sparkling with ten thousand Gems–untill with the devoute psalmist I have exclaimed, Great and Marvellous are thy Works, Lord God Almighty, In Wisdom hast thou made them all."

Another compensation for the arduous voyage was the friends she made with many in the same cabin, where lack of air required open doors except when dressing and undressing: "a sweet Situation for a delicate Lady," she remarks to Elizabeth. She was pleased with the attentive men in the cabin who treated the ladies like sisters, particularly a Dr. Clark, who even amused the unhappy teenager Nabby, who apparently traveled more out of duty than personal desire. Abigail found Dr. Clark's presence indispensable when she was seized with rheumatism: "I was very sick, full of pain, a good deal of fever and very lame, so that I could not dress myself, but good nursing and a good Physician, with rubbing, and flannel, has relieved me."

When finally feeling well, Abigail took charge of improving sanitary conditions. First, she supervised the cooking, claiming the steward had "no more knowledge of his Business than a Savage." In addition, since the cabin floors were so caked with filth that she "was daily obliged to send my Shoes upon deck to have them scraped," she had her man-servant and others "with Scrapers, mops, Brushes, infusions of vinegar &c." clean up. Describing their progress, she wryly notes, "in a few hours we found there *was Boards for a floor.*" Rarely has a writer brought to life the experience of sea travel with such specific and amusing details.

Abigail's arrival in England was no less an ordeal, the ship fighting high winds, dense fog, and heavy rain. Because of the continual high seas, it was decided to anchor the ship and put the women onshore in small boats, despite a six-foot surf. She describes in a 20 July letter to her sister Mary Smith Cranch how she "could keep myself up no other way than as one of the Gentleman stood braced up against the Boat, fast hold of me and I with both my Arms round him. The other ladies were held, in the same manner whilst every wave gave us a Broad Side, and finally a Wave landed us with the utmost force upon the Beach." She notes that, soaking wet and walking onto shore while sinking in the sand, they all looked "like a parcel of Naiades just rising from the Sea." On the way to London the next day, she was impressed with the fine roads ("a Stone a Novelty") and the vast fields of grain and beans. She comments critically on Gothic cathedrals generally after viewing Canterbury's famous cathedral: "with but few windows which are grated with large Bars of Iron, and look more like jails for criminals, than places designd for the worship of the deity, one would suppose from the manner in which they are Guarded, that they apprehend devotion would be Stolen." Like her husband, Abigail had little regard for the trappings of the European, High Church tradition.

Also like her spouse, Abigail found many opportunities to compare her life in America to life in England. She was impressed with the attentive and gracious service she received at the inns but was surprised by the commonness of robberies along the highway and then by the harsh treatment of captured criminals. She describes seeing a robber just caught: "the poor wretch gastly and horible, brought along on foot." Only about twenty years old, his pathetic aspect touched Abigail, and she remarks that "You can form some Idea of my feelings when they told him aya, you have but a short time, the assise set next Month, and then my Lad you Swing." She concludes that "tho every robber may deserve Death yet to exult over the wretched is what *our* Country is not accustomed to, long may it be free of such villainies and long may it preserve a commisiration for the wretched."

From London she wrote to Adams at The Hague, happily announcing in her 23 July 1784 letter that "what is past, and what we sufferd by sickness and fatigue, I will think no more of. It is all done away in the joyfull hope of soon holding to my Bosom the dearest best of Friends." Adams received her letter three days later; he remarks in his 26 July letter that he is the happiest man on earth: "I am twenty Years younger than I was Yesterday." Meanwhile, in letters to sisters Elizabeth and Mary, Abigail describes some of the sights of London, particularly how she enjoys long walks. John and Abigail were finally reunited in London on 7 August 1784. Neither recorded the anticipated event.

The Adamses' reunion ended the major phase of their travel writings, embodied in their correspondence and diaries. In February 1785 John Adams was appointed minister to England, but it turned out to be an unhappy assignment for the former rebel. He was treated coolly by the British, and he had trouble explaining why the poor and disorganized new nation he represented did not keep all of the terms of its treaty. During his time there he wrote his *Defence of the Constitutions of the United States of America* (1787). He finally resigned in 1788, returning home with his family in April.

The correspondence of John and Abigail Adams regularly finds its way into literary anthologies and promises to delight generations to come. Abigail's correspondence gave vent to her tender feelings as well as to her cogent ideas concerning American independence and New England values. As a travel writer she has many insightful and amusing remarks on English life, particularly in comparison to her American ideals. Her travels broadened and nurtured an already flowering woman.

John Adams's travel correspondence serves both to soften and complicate the reader's response to this dedicated founding father. While he reveals compassionate and appealing facets of his character, at times his candor shows pettiness and a consuming need for recognition and appreciation. The letters also reveal a torn man of the Enlightenment, with a natural love of artistic and novel experience, beauty, and amusement, and the stern descendant of Puritan forebears, always pushing himself to make practical use of each moment and opportunity to do good—in his case, for the benefit of the independent new nation he loved above all things.

Letters:

Letters of John Adams to Dr. Calkoen of Amsterdam, Written at Amsterdam, 1780 (London, 1786); republished as *Twenty-six Letters, upon Interesting Subjects, Respecting the Revolution of America* (New York: Printed by John Fenno, 1789);

The Correspondence of John Adams, . . . Concerning the British Doctrine of Impressment (Baltimore: H. Niles, 1804);

Correspondence between the Hon. John Adams and the Late Wm. Cunningham . . . (Boston: E. M. Cunningham, 1823);

Letters of Mrs. Adams, the Wife of John Adams (Boston: Little, Brown, 1840);

Letters of John Adams, Addressed to His Wife, edited by Charles Francis Adams (Boston: Little, Brown, 1841);

Familiar Letters of John Adams and His Wife, during the Revolution, edited by C. F. Adams (New York: Hurd & Houghton, 1876);

Correspondence between John Adams and Mercy Warren . . . , edited by C. F. Adams, in *Collections of the Massachusetts Historical Society,* fifth series 4 (1878): 315–511;

Warren-Adams Letters, Being Chiefly a Correspondence Among John Adams, Samuel Adams, and James Warren, edited by Worthington Chauncey Ford, *Collections of the Massachusetts Historical Society,* 72–73 (1917–1925);

Statesman and Friend, the Correspondence of John Adams with Benjamin Waterhouse 1784–1822, edited by Ford (Boston: Little, Brown, 1927);

New Letters of Abigail Adams, 1788–1801, edited by Stewart Michell (Boston: Houghton Mifflin, 1947);

The Adams-Jefferson Letters, 2 volumes, edited by Lester J. Cappon (Chapel Hill: University of North Carolina Press, 1959);

Adams Family Correspondence, volumes 1–2, edited by L. H. Butterfield, Wendell D. Garrett, and Marjorie E. Sprague (Cambridge, Mass.: Harvard University Press, 1963); volumes 3–4, edited by Butterfield and Marc Friedlander (Cambridge, Mass.: Harvard University Press, 1973);

The Spur of Fame: Dialogues of John Adams and Benjamin Rush, 1805–1813, edited by John A. Schutz and Douglas Adair (San Marino, Cal.: Huntington Library, 1966);

The Book of Abigail and John: Selected Letters of the Adams Family 1762–1784, edited by Butterfield, Friedlander, and Mary-Jo Kline (Cambridge, Mass.: Harvard University Press, 1975).

Bibliographies:

John W. Cronin and W. Harvey Wise Jr., *A Bibliography of John Adams and John Quincy Adams* (Washington, D.C.: Riverford Publishing, 1935);

John E. Ferling, *John Adams: A Bibliography* (Westport, Conn.: Greenwood Press, 1994).

Biographies:

Gilbert Chinard, *Honest John Adams* (Boston: Little, Brown, 1933);

Catherine Drinker Bowen, *John Adams and the American Revolution* (Boston: Little, Brown, 1950);

Page Smith, *John Adams,* 2 volumes (Garden City, N.Y.: Doubleday, 1962);

James Bishop Peabody, ed., *John Adams, A Biography in His Own Words* (New York: Newsweek, 1973);

Peter Shaw, *The Character of John Adams* (Chapel Hill: University of North Carolina Press, 1976);

Charles W. Akers, *Abigail Adams, an American Woman* (Boston: Little, Brown, 1980);

Lynne Whithey, *Dearest Friend: A Life of Abigail Adams* (New York: Free Press, 1981);

Phyllis Lee Levin, *Abigail Adams: A Biography* (New York: St. Martin's Press, 1987);

John E. Ferling, *John Adams: A Life* (Knoxville: University of Tennessee Press, 1992).

References:

Robert A. East, *John Adams* (Boston: Twayne, 1979);

Joseph J. Ellis, *Passionate Sage: The Character and Legacy of John Adams* (New York: Norton, 1993);

Zoltan Haraszti, *John Adams and the Prophets of Progress* (Cambridge, Mass.: Harvard University Press, 1952);

John R. Howe Jr., *The Changing Political Thought of John Adams* (Princeton: Princeton University Press, 1966);

Steven G. Kurtz, *The Presidency of John Adams* (Philadelphia: University of Pennsylvania Press, 1957).

Papers:

The bulk of the John Adams papers are housed at the Massachusetts Historical Society in Boston, where they are being edited for the Belknap Press of Harvard University.

John Woodhouse Audubon

(30 November 1812 – 21 February 1862)

Barbara J. Cicardo
University of Southwestern Louisiana

BOOKS: *Illustrated Notes of an Expedition through Mexico and California* (New York: Published by J. W. Audubon, 1852); republished with four color illustrations (Tarrytown, N.Y.: Reprinted by William Abbatt, 1915);
Audubon's Western Journal: 1849–1850. Being the MS record of a trip from New York to Texas, and an overland journey through Mexico and Arizona to the gold fields of California, edited by Maria G. Audubon and Frank Heywood Hodder (Cleveland: Arthur H. Clark, 1906).

OTHER: John James Audubon and John Bachman, *The Viviparous Quadrupeds of North America,* 3 folio volumes (Philadelphia: J. T. Bowen, 1845–1848)—includes seventy-two paintings by J. W. Audubon; revised as *The Quadrupeds of North America,* 3 octavo volumes (New York: V. G. Audubon, 1849–1854)—includes five additional paintings by J. W. Audubon;
The Drawings of J. W. Audubon (San Francisco: Book Club of California, 1957).

John Woodhouse Audubon, 1853

John Woodhouse Audubon's contribution to American art and natural history will always be measured against the accomplishments and reputation of his famous father, John James Audubon, the internationally acclaimed creator of *Birds of America* (1827–1838). Nevertheless, he can lay claim in his own right to an important position among travel writers in the tradition of the solitary woodsman-artist: the philosophically stoic man who is reflective in the solitude of the wilderness and an urbane cosmopolite in the salons of Europe and America.

The first outline of John Woodhouse Audubon's personality is drawn from brief references in the letters and journals of the elder Audubon. Evidently a youth of enthusiasm, wit, and good-natured mischief, he matured into a dedicated artist. His was a complex personality—witty and melancholy, confident and shy, sophisticated and rustic. Readers can become directly acquainted with him only through his letters to his family and the books based on his journal of his travels in the West: *Illustrated Notes of an Expedition through Mexico and California* (1852) and *Audubon's Western Journal: 1849–1850* (1906). The publication of the first part of Audubon's journal in 1852 established him as an important chronicler of the American westward expansion and gave him membership in the distinguished group of naturalist travel writers, including William Bartram, the eighteenth-century explorer of the Floridas; Thomas Horsfield, the first American naturalist in Indonesia; as well as his father. Even with the muting of his character in the longer narrative edited largely by his daughter, Maria G. Audubon, in 1906, he still emerges as a vibrant personality, unique in the tradition of rugged frontiersmen because he was both an expert woodsman and an accomplished artist. Audubon's fascination with painting, whether of people, landscapes, animals, or plants, combined with his interest in recording impressions of people and events of strange places, formed the basis for his success as a travel writer and secured his reputation.

John Woodhouse Audubon was born on 30 November 1812 in Henderson, Kentucky, the younger of the two sons born to John James Audubon and Lucy Bakewell Audubon. His older brother, Victor Gifford Audubon, was born on 12 June 1809 in Louisville. Failure of the elder Audubon's mercantile business forced the family's removal from the Kentucky frontier outside Louisville to the city, where John James taught drawing. Financial disasters during the family's stay in Kentucky (1807–1819) left a lasting impression on both boys.

The young Audubon consequently developed the frugality and tenacity in money matters quite evident in his journal, a good example of which is his persistence (from 13 to 23 March 1849) in tracking down and bringing to justice the two men who stole a large part of the money for his expedition to California. Such persistence also illustrates his conscientious stewardship of the expedition's resources and his ingrained sense of money as the necessary resource for success of his family's artistic projects. Indeed, the major reasons for his joining the expedition in 1849 were to mine gold in California in order to finance more of the elder Audubon's work, to secure a comfortable future for the entire Audubon family, and to chronicle the mores of the people and describe the flora and fauna of the places he saw on his travels. His entire education, both in school and experientially with his parents, prepared him for his career as woodsman and artist.

From 1819 to 1821 John James Audubon traveled up and down both the Ohio and the Mississippi Rivers to collect specimens of American birds, finally settling in New Orleans, where Lucy joined him on 18 December 1821 with their two sons. Both parents supported the family by painting portraits and teaching drawing; John Woodhouse would follow their example and become a portrait painter. Both Audubon sons frequently traveled with their father, but it was John Woodhouse who became his father's "right-hand man" in drawing the specimens they found; Victor became the business manager for the family. John Chancellor describes the relationship in his *Audubon: A Biography* (1978):

From the year 1832 until the senior Audubon's death, he and his two sons formed an impressive business trio. Victor was sent to England to superintend the engraving and colouring of the plates and to deal with financial and administrative matters such as the processing of subscriptions. John accompanied his father in the field, both collecting and drawing birds and backgrounds.

The Audubons supervised the education of their two sons from the beginning, stressing the development of their abilities in art and music, and encouraging them to explore new lands and peoples whenever the opportunity presented itself. The father's letters contain many references to his supervision of the artistic training of Victor and John, almost as a portent of the important roles they were to play in furthering his publications. On 1 September 1826 he writes to the seventeen-year-old Victor: "My dear son let me now request you to pay great attention to *music, drawing* in my style and to read as much as possible—talents are regarded more than wealth. . . ." In a letter written to Lucy on the same day, he admonishes her to make sure that fourteen-year-old John continue his studies: "do remember my Beloved wife to have the goodness to teach (no matter how unwilling he may be) our Johny the piano and see that his Drawing goes on regularly and well—If I was to receive a good specimen entirely his own I would send him a handsome reward."

In 1831 the nineteen-year-old John Woodhouse accompanied his father on an expedition to the Florida Keys. Two years later he again traveled with his father on a trip to Labrador (9 June–31 August 1833), where he gained not only artistic experience but also valuable survival techniques that were to serve him well in his later expeditions. In her biography *John James Audubon* (1964) Alice Ford describes one of the father's requirements of his son: "On wet, cold days—all too frequent—Audubon set the boys [John and his cousin] ashore while he drew birds beneath the glass-covered hatch by the hour. He would rouse John at dawn and put him to skinning the quarry of the day before." John James was pleased with his son's development both as an outdoorsman and as an artist and wrote to Lucy that he was producing creditable landscapes. They returned to New York City on 7 September 1833.

The young Audubon had obviously been tempered by his experiences in Labrador, but if Howard Corning, editor of *Letters of John James Audubon 1826–1840* (1930), is correct, he still retained a strong desire to please his father, a goal that his mother encouraged. Corning includes a letter to Victor, supposedly from his father, that he believes is a fraud. Corning notes that the letter "is not addressed and is incomplete, the last part being miss-

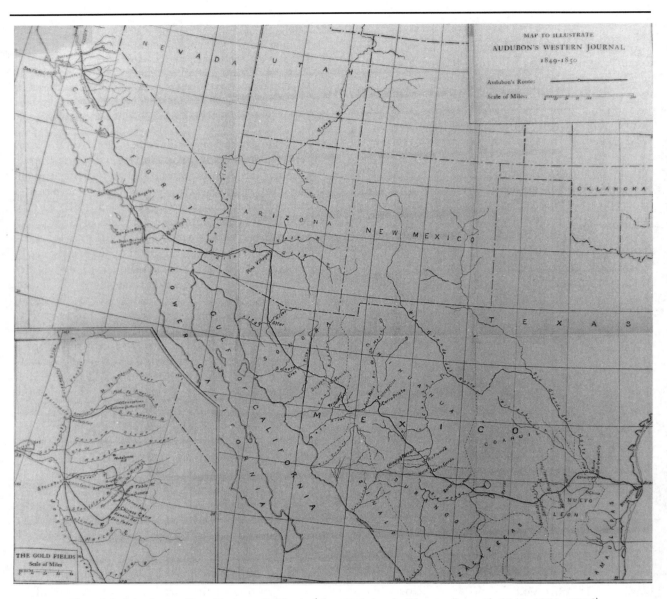

Map of Audubon's route from Mexico to California (from Audubon's Western Journal: 1849–1850, *1906)*

ing. It does not appear to be in Audubon's writing. Part looks like Mrs. Audubon's and part John's." One passage may be especially revealing, as it touches on John Woodhouse:

> I have been extremely pleased with his industry and loss of many boyish habits [tricks] indeed it was a great consolation to have him for my right hand man—on all occasions he lost no time when on this voyage. . . .

If John did indeed write this about himself, it is not only an example of his lifelong eagerness for his father's approval but also an early indication of the sometimes dry wit and sense of whimsy that appear in *Audubon's Western Journal*.

By October 1833 John James and his younger son were in Charleston, South Carolina, at the John Bachman residence, where John Woodhouse began coming to terms with his destiny. On 3 November 1833 he wrote to Victor, who was in England handling the family's financial matters and overseeing the publication of the *Birds of America:* "I am working that I may some day become a second Audubon not to make a fortune—my wish is that I may some day publish some Birds or quadrupeds and that my name may stand as does my Father's." Earlier in the letter he expresses his amazement at finding himself in Charleston drawing and painting for *Birds of America,* he "whose head was full of Steam Boats and Sail Boats." Wryly he accepts his destiny with a tinge of the fatalism that appears so frequently in his

Western Journal. "Well may the preachers say that 'Our ways are pointed by the Creator, and we follow his will and think it our own.'" The elder Audubon also wrote to Victor in 1833: "John [Woodhouse] has given you his own thoughts—I am delighted of late with his *industry* and his work. . . . With age I hope that he will become an excellent man."

According to Victor H. Cahalane in his introduction to *The Imperial Collection of Audubon Animals: The Quadrupeds of North America* (1967), John Woodhouse, called Johny (sometimes spelled *Johnny* by his father), was "quiet, sensitive, gruff with strangers, probably from shyness, but genial and a sparkling conversationalist among friends." He apparently had exuberant good spirits among his intimates and matured as he traveled with his father and undertook more responsibility in the family's efforts to publish the *Birds of America* and *The Viviparous Quadrupeds of North America* (1845–1848). John James included John Woodhouse in the trio largely responsible for the latter work. He gave him the nickname "Young Jostle." Audubon had written to Bachman of being "jostled" on his coach ride to Charleston. John James became "Old Jostle" and Bachman was "Jostle the Third."

The Audubon brothers were extremely close. Trained as artists and musicians, they were dedicated to the furthering of their father's work and their personalities and talents complemented each other. Both John Woodhouse and Victor were encouraged and even commanded by their father to travel widely to acquire urbanity and social grace, to observe and record their impressions, and to make connections that might be useful in the publication of the *Birds of America,* the obsession of the whole family. Consequently, they accompanied their father on his early expeditions and then, as they grew older, traveled on their own, together or separately. In 1836 they were sent by their father on a tour of the Continent. As John James wrote to John Bachman on 9 March 1836, "These and other circumstances . . . have induced Me to accept a very fair offer for John to go to the Mediterrean as far as Messina. . . . This I look forward to as an Immense benefit to our Sons as it might be a chance shot for them to see those Countries hereafter." Such preemptory ordering of his sons' lives was accepted behavior in the Audubon family.

On 2 August 1836 John James and John Woodhouse set sail for America, arriving at Staten Island on 4 September 1836. By December of that year John Woodhouse and Maria Martin (Bachman's sister-in-law) were deeply involved in completing the drawings of birds and plants. Seventy-six of the

drawings of this period are attributed to them. On 17 February 1837 he accompanied his father on an expedition from New Orleans to Houston and Galveston and back to New Orleans, observing and sketching birds and other animals of the coastal areas. Upon his return to Charleston he and Maria Bachman were married. They accompanied the senior Audubon back to New York, where the couple spent a brief honeymoon at Niagara Falls. They then set sail for Liverpool and London with John James. By September of 1839 Maria's failing health brought the couple back to New York and then to Charleston, where John became assistant artist, secretary, and general helper on *The Viviparous Quadrupeds of North America.*

By 1840 work on the seven-volume octavo edition of *Birds of America* was also well under way, and John James, Victor, and John Woodhouse completed the plan for *The Viviparous Quadrupeds of North America.* In autumn of that same year Victor married Eliza Bachman, John Bachman's other daughter, thus strengthening the ties between the two families. In 1841 the work of seeking subscribers for *The Viviparous Quadrupeds of North America* was proceeding with excursions by the senior Audubon into Canada and other parts of the United States to gain financial backing. Maria Bachman, John's wife, had died on 23 September 1840. After the mourning period was over, on 2 October 1841, John Woodhouse married Caroline Hall, "an English lady," who bore seven children, five of whom lived to maturity. In 1842 he returned to New York to the new family estate called Minnie's Land, or Minniesland, so named because John James had deeded it to Lucy Audubon, whom John Woodhouse and Victor called "Minnie," the Scottish diminutive for mother.

Meanwhile, the work on *The Viviparous Quadrupeds of North America* was progressing. The entire project took eleven years to complete, from 1840 to 1851. John James Audubon and his two sons, especially John Woodhouse, worked on the drawings while John Bachman wrote the accompanying text. Critics and art historians agree, however, that by 1846 John Woodhouse was doing most of the artwork. The three volumes of the work were published in 1845, 1846, and 1848; the volumes of an octavo edition were published in 1849, 1851, and 1854 as *The Quadrupeds of North America.* The Audubon sons, according to John Francis McDermott in the introduction to his *Audubon in the West* (1965), "collaborated on all the paintings in Volume III and much of the work in Volume II." In his introduction Cahalane states that John Woodhouse alone completed at least seventy-two of the 150 paintings in the imperial folio as well as the five "bonus" plates of the octavo edition.

The crediting of illustrations, furthermore, was not always rigorous. In the later octavo edition, some of the plates ascribed to John James Audubon in the imperial folio have been credited to John Woodhouse. One example concerns plate 120, a depiction of two lemmings. The folio edition credits the senior Audubon as the artist; however, the text states that the drawing was made in London by J. W. Audubon from museum skins obtained in Canada. In the octavo edition the text reads, "Drawn from nature by J. W. Audubon."

John Woodhouse, his wife Caroline, and his family had gone to England in June 1846 (after a fruitless expedition he had undertaken to Texas in 1845–1846) so that John could practice drawing mammals from museum specimens. He spent nearly a year painting mostly mammals of northern Canada in the British Museum and other institutions. As Cahalane describes, he was well prepared when he was left with the sole responsibility for the drawing or production of folio plates for *The Viviparous Quadrupeds of North America:*

> John Woodhouse took over the entire task of painting the mammals early in 1846. Unlike his father who had little formal instruction in art and worked chiefly with chalk, crayon and watercolors, John Woodhouse had the benefit of considerable training and painted almost entirely in oils. The style of the two men was similar, so alike, in fact, that in some instances it is not possible to credit the paintings with certainty. . . . Using his father's drawings from the Missouri Yellowstone trip (1843), the younger Audubon drew most of the larger mammals, as well as the small species of the far north. He redrew all of the imperial folio drawings for the "miniature" edition, a task which must have required many months.

Later biographers of John James Audubon as well as editors of *The Quadrupeds of North America* have recognized the immense contribution of John Woodhouse in completing the work. A 1967 edition gives him equal credit for the artwork. In his foreword to *Audubon's Animals: The Quadrupeds of North America,* compiled and edited by Alice Ford (1951) Thomas E. Gilliard notes that he "shouldered immense responsibilities both in the field and at the easel to bring the *Quadrupeds* to fruition. He strove valiantly to fulfill his father's aspirations. Indeed, at times, the paternal inspiration was of measure sufficient to make John Woodhouse Audubon gleam through his father's shadow." John James Audubon's distinctly American artistic idiom was so consciously developed that he was able to teach it to John Woodhouse so that their work was almost indistinguishable, although expert examination generally provides proper identification of the artist.

As his father became more feeble (the senior Audubon died in 1851), John Woodhouse assumed almost all of the artistic responsibility for their ongoing work, both *The Quadrupeds of North America* and new editions of *Birds of America*. On 31 January 1849, much against his own inclination but at his father's request, he set out for California. When he returned in 1850, he took up residence at Minniesland where he and Victor built two new houses. In 1853 Victor injured his spine in a fall, and for the next seven years he was an invalid. The greatly saddened John Woodhouse became the head of the family. Victor died in August 1860. John Woodhouse succumbed to a fever he had contracted a few days earlier on 21 February 1862.

While John Woodhouse Audubon's reputation as an artist was confirmed with the acknowledgment of his contributions to *The Viviparous Quadrupeds of North America,* his position among American travel writers rests mainly on the descriptions and drawings of his long trek from New York across Texas and northern Mexico to the California gold fields chronicled in *Illustrated Notes of an Expedition through Mexico and California* and *Audubon's Western Journal: 1849–1850*. In these works Audubon emerges as a complex man—good-humored, witty, and determined as well as cynical, depressed, and melancholy. These seemingly paradoxical traits set the tone and expand the meaning of the record of his western expedition.

The journal Audubon published as *Illustrated Notes of an Expedition through Mexico and California* has a controversial textual history because of the lack of availability of the original manuscripts and the role played by his daughter in the production of the 1906 version titled *Audubon's Western Journal: 1849–1850*. For the 1852 edition John Woodhouse Audubon's name appears on the title page as the publisher, with the address "34 Liberty Street" in New York as the location of the publication. This first edition is only forty-eight pages long and contains an authorial preface indicating that it is the first of "ten numbers" to be published monthly, should it meet with "the approbation of the writer's friends and the public."

Another version of these notes appeared in 1915, with an addition to the original title page stating that it was reprinted by William Abbatt in Tarrytown, New York, "Being Extra No. 41 of THE MAGAZINE OF HISTORY WITH NOTES AND QUERIES." Two other interesting changes occur in this edition: first, the "Editor's Preface" adds information about the original manuscript; second, at the

"A DRY GULCH" AT COLOMA, SUTTER'S MILLS
May 2, 1850

Two of Audubon's sketches from his journey: Jesus Maria, 20 July 1849, and Sutter's Mills, 2 May 1850 (from Audubon's
Western Journal: 1849–1850, *1906)*

end of page 48, appear the words "Here the original ends." Abbatt reports his belief that Audubon originally produced his works in two styles, one with plain illustrations and one with color, though he never was able to find the "plain" edition. He says that he was finally able to obtain a copy of the color edition "in the garret of an old-time dwelling, whose former occupants were personal friends of Mr. Audubon." The copy was "tucked under the rafters."

Publishing the work as a folio was too costly, so Abbatt produced a smaller version with the four drawings reproduced by photography and hand colored. He makes the claim that he is furnishing the public with "a very rare work, hitherto unattainable (no copy has been sold at auction in twenty years, and it is unknown to many collectors)." Finally, he alludes to the 1906 version of the journal edited by Maria G. Audubon and Frank Heywood Hodder, implying that it lacks the authenticity that he achieved: "It should be emphasized that the four plates cannot be found in *any other work* (in the only edition ever published, of the complete 'expedition,' they appear merely as insignificant, outline pencil sketches, *uncolored*." Abbatt's melodramatic and serendipitous finding of the early publication might invite skepticism among scholars; nevertheless, his edition does collate exactly with that of John Woodhouse's first publication. The same cannot be said of the 1906 version, the only purported "complete" edition of the *Journal*.

The 1852 *Illustrated Notes* ends at page 119 of *Audubon's Western Journal: 1849–1850,* which has an additional 124 pages, not including the index provided by Professor Frank Heywood Hodder. The difference in length does not necessarily suggest a problem, for one might assume that Audubon's daughter well could have had a copy of a more complete manuscript. What complicates the situation is the occurrence of major differences between the 1852 edition published under Audubon's supervision and the first portion of the 1906 edition despite both supposedly being based on the same original manuscript.

While John Woodhouse's original is a smooth, flowing narrative with some dates to locate the action, his daughter's edited version is organized into chapters, with dated entries as the primary ordering principle. These techniques help the reader to follow the complicated route of the expedition: chapter 1: "New York to Texas" (8 February–8 March 1849); chapter 2: "Disaster in the Valley of the Rio Grande" (13 March–23 March 1849); chapter 3: "Mexico from the Rio Grande to the Mountains" (28 April–27 June 1849); chapter 4: "Across the

Mexican Mountains to Altar" (28 June–9 September 1849); chapter 5: "Through Arizona to San Diego" (14 September–4 November 1849); chapter 6, "California from San Diego to San Francisco" (6 November–29 December 1849); and chapter 7, "A Tour of the Gold Fields" (2 January–6 May 1850). While the revised edition makes the path of the trip more readily accessible, a collation of the two works reveals other, more-problematic substantive differences.

The tone of the original is altered by the removal of emotionally charged comments on the character weaknesses of the men accompanying Audubon on his expedition. Audubon allows the reader to draw closer to him as narrator and to become acquainted with the whole man through his wry humor, candid acknowledgments of weaknesses, frustration, and even deep depression during the hardships that he and his fellow travelers endure. His daughter tends to gloss over and even entirely omit incidents that she apparently felt did not retain the factual tone of the narrative or that might have shown her father as less than the mythologized hero she presents in her short introductory biographical sketch. A few examples illustrate the point.

Toward the end of his narrative, Audubon recounts a particularly trying ascent in the Mexican mountains and the terrible cost in injured animals: "We were compelled to leave one mule in this pass, and shifting his pack to two or three others, released him to fatten—or feed buzzards—we scarcely cared which, so hard becomes the heart, when necessity drives one on." In the 1906 version the same incident is reported with no mention of the lack of sympathy created by the trials of the wilderness: "We were compelled to leave a mule here, and to divide his pack between two or three other animals."

Sometimes the 1906 edition clearly launders events or expressions of which the editor perhaps either personally disapproved or that might have shown Audubon in a light deemed "improper" for the audience. Thus, the 1906 version omits entirely the following humorous account:

> At twelve next morning we reached Tomochi, on a little river of the same name. The coral of the old mission, with the adobe sheds built against its walls on every side, and the "jacals" that made a little cluster round it, were occupied by about six hundred individuals of a splendid race of Indians; and eight or ten girls and women whom I saw bathing, were so beautiful, that, gentleman as I profess to be, I could not turn my head and look the other way; poor Acteon, cruel Diana! I thought, as I impatiently gave old Monterey the spur and dashed on to overtake my party.

Whether as an attempt at humor or realism or both, Audubon frequently used the idiom of the frontiersman, as in his long, detailed description of the eating schedule of the group: "Trask: impatiently, 'Is them plates clean,' Rhoades nonchalant, 'To be sure they is, did'nt we eat off 'em last night.'" Perhaps offended by the dialectal humor or seeking to keep a more formal tone, his daughter bowdlerizes the incident: "I hear Dr. Trask courteously ask: 'Are those plates clean?' and Rhoades's nonchalant answer: 'To be sure they are, didn't we eat off 'em last night.'"

The contrasting styles between the editions of John Woodhouse Audubon and his daughter point up both the complex character of the narrator and the richness and variety of his experiences. His smoother, more colloquial style and her stilted, more formal account, each containing different omissions and embellishments, make up the whole story of his remarkable journey. Ultimately, a study of both works reveals common threads of information and attitudes: the character of John Woodhouse; the valuable descriptions of the flora and fauna of the land he explored; the detailing of the characters of the men who made the westward trip; the observations on the strengths and weaknesses of humankind; and the expression of American chauvinism reflecting the isolationism and biased nationalism of the nineteenth century after the Mexican War.

Accounts in both editions as well as correspondence from members of the expedition attest to Audubon's leadership ability, unfailing determination, and unselfish care of his men. For his part he recounts the courage and endurance of the men amid great suffering and hardship. His detailed, often repetitive descriptions of laborious ascents and descents of the Mexican mountains, the sicknesses that decimated the group, and, at times, the shortage of supplies alternate with his lyric descriptions of panoramic views from mountain peaks and of exquisite birds and animals. Audubon's writing creates a sense of immediacy that involves the reader in an unfolding drama.

Humorous incidents break the narrative and on one occasion reveal an ethnic bias at odds with Audubon's generally humanitarian philosophy. When Audubon discovered that an enterprising young translator had embellished his message to the mayor of a small Mexican town, he threatened the boy "with a few superfluities (in the good old Saxon,) ending in the word thrashing, if he did not repeat word for word what I said. . . . The adroitness of the thieves here is almost equal to that of those at Naples." His daughter's edited version concludes similarly: "Upon matters being explained by a more trustworthy source, the Alcalde (mayor) was perfectly content, and bowed me out with much courtesy. . . . The adroitness of the Mexicans in thieving equals that of the rascals at Naples." Her version, though, removes the color from his text, illustrating the basic contrast in the tones of the two editions.

The differences in the editions underscore what Audubon wrote in the "Preface" to his 1852 publication. "To write a tale, however simple, and to tell one, are quite different things." He attempted to avoid the "literary" style "to tell a plain story of what I have done and seen, that may be interesting or instructive, I rely on the reader's generosity and lenity in criticising." Maria G. Audubon had a different goal in mind—to make of her father a gentleman hero. Both books place him in the tradition of the storytelling traveler who rises to the level of myth.

Audubon's "fragment" and his daughter's "entire" version of his trek to California establish him as a travel writer of importance, a chronicler of the zeitgeist of the westward expansion, and an example of the importance of the American frontier in the development of the national character. Audubon's journal also reveals that he recognized his position as a woodsman-artist, following the path that his father had taken and toward which he had been directed:

> I recollected my father's advice given some three years before, whilst in Texas,—"Push on to the West, even to California; you will find new animals at every change in the formation of country, and new birds from Central America will delight you." Can it be, that I, too, from long association with him, having been the companion of all his expeditions but one, since I was of age, had within me some little lurking spark of the noble desire for knowledge and love of nature, that for forty years had sent him wandering through her wildest scenes?

In his introduction to the 1906 edition Hodder notes that, up to that time, historians had neglected the importance of the westward movement, cataloguing what they perceived as more-significant historic events, such as the War of 1812. He recognizes Audubon's journal as an important work in rectifying this omission. "Not only does it reflect the energy and strength of character of the author but the glimpse it gives of the constancy of the greater part of his companions and of man's humanity to man under the most trying circumstances strengthens faith in the essential soundness of human nature." Audubon's journal sheds light on what was to become one of the determining factors in the search for a unique identity for the new nation.

Biography:

Maria G. Audubon, "Biographical Memoir," in *Audubon's Western Journal: 1849–1850. Being the MS record of a trip from New York to Texas, and an overland journey through Mexico and Arizona to the gold fields of California,* edited by Maria G. Audubon and Frank Heywood Hodder (Cleveland: Arthur H. Clark, 1906).

References:

William Abbatt, Preface to Audobon's *Illustrated Notes of an Expedition through Mexico and California* (Tarrytown, N.Y.: Reprinted by William Abbatt, 1915);

John James Audubon, *Letters of John James Audubon 1826–1840,* 2 volumes, edited by Howard Corning (Boston: Club of Odd Volumes, 1930);

Victor H. Cahalane, "New Text," in *The Imperial Collection of Audubon Animals: The Quadrupeds of North America,* edited by Cahalane (Maplewood, N.J.: Hammond, 1967);

John Chancellor, *Audubon: A Biography* (New York: Viking, 1978);

Thomas E. Gilliard, Foreword to *Audubon's Animals: The Quadrupeds of North America,* compiled and edited by Alice Ford (New York: Studio Publications in cooperation with Thomas Y. Crowell, 1951);

John Francis McDermott, Introduction to *Audubon in the West* (Norman: University of Oklahoma Press, 1965).

Papers:

The correspondence of John Woodhouse Audubon is scattered in private and public collections. There are holdings at the American Philosophical Society at Philadelphia, the Smithsonian Institution, the Alabama State Archives, and the Museum of Natural History.

Horatio Bridge

(8 April 1806 – 18 March 1893)

Allen Flint
University of Maine at Farmington

BOOKS: *Journal of an African Cruiser: Comprising Sketches of the Canaries, the Cape de Verds, Liberia, Madeira, Sierra Leone, and Other Places of Interest on the West Coast of Africa. By an Officer of the U.S. Navy,* edited by Nathaniel Hawthorne (New York & London: Wiley & Putnam, 1845);

Personal Recollections of Nathaniel Hawthorne (New York: Harper, 1893; London: Osgood, McIlvaine, 1893).

Horatio Bridge made a significant contribution to American literature by guaranteeing against loss the publication of *Twice-Told Tales* (1837), the second book of his former college classmate, Nathaniel Hawthorne, at a time when the struggling author was more than usually impecunious. Hawthorne's acknowledgment in his preface to *The Snow-Image, and Other Twice-Told Tales* (1851) of Bridge's financial assistance at a crucial time—"If anybody is responsible for my being at this day an author, it is yourself" and "For it was through your interposition . . . that your early friend was brought before the public, somewhat more prominently than theretofore, in the first volume of Twice-told Tales—is often quoted. (Hawthorne was later able to return the favor by extending loans to Bridge.) Another Bowdoin College classmate, President Franklin Pierce, promoted Bridge to chief of the Bureau of Provisions and Clothing, U.S. Navy in 1854. His navy career led to his first book, *Journal of an African Cruiser* (1845), and his friendship with Hawthorne led to his second, *Personal Recollections of Nathaniel Hawthorne* (1893). Both of Bridge's books are important, with *Journal of an African Cruiser* providing useful information about the slave trade as well as travel information about Africa.

Bridge was born in Augusta, Maine, on 8 April 1806 to wealthy, socially prominent, and politically important parents, Judge James Bridge and Hannah North Bridge. He graduated from Bowdoin College in the famous class of 1825 that included Henry Wadsworth Longfellow as well as Hawthorne. Pierce (Class of 1824), Hawthorne, and Jonathan Cilley

Horatio Bridge (Bowdoin College Museum of Art, Brunswick, Maine; gift of Marion Bridge Maurice)

were his closest friends at Bowdoin. When Cilley and Hawthorne wagered a barrel of wine that Hawthorne would be married by 14 November 1836, Bridge was entrusted with the notes they signed. Cilley lost the bet but was killed in a duel before he could pay.

Bridge read the law and was admitted to the bar in 1828, practicing briefly in Skowhegan and then in Augusta, Maine. As a holder of $40,000 to $50,000 worth of stock in the Kennebec Lock and Canal Company, he and others built a dam over the Kennebec River. In *Personal Recollections of Nathaniel Hawthorne* Bridge explains the failure of the dam during an 1839 flood:

The adventure turned out disastrously, for, after completing the work at a cost three times as great as the

27

original estimate, a freshet—higher, of course, "than was ever before known"—swept away the dam and the mills, cut a new channel for the river, swallowed up our paternal mansion and grounds near by, and ruined me financially.

In 1838 Bridge entered the U.S. Navy and was in the Mediterranean when disaster struck on the Kennebec. In 1843 he was assigned to the *Saratoga,* a ship in the antislaver squadron patrolling the west coast of Africa under the command of Commodore Matthew C. Perry, which gave rise to his *Journal of an African Cruiser.*

Although retrieving a sense of the flavor of Bridge's African writings and observations is possible from his original manuscript and notes, the main interest is in the published book, which had Hawthorne's name on its title page as the editor but not Bridge's as the author. Hawthorne's editing of Bridge's journal is discussed by Patrick Brancaccio in a 1980 essay in the *New England Quarterly* and by Thomas Woodson in the notes to Hawthorne's letters in *The Centenary Edition of the Works of Nathaniel Hawthorne* (1962–1988). Bridge evidently had his eye on publication as he began keeping a journal, and Hawthorne aided him at every step of the process.

In March 1843 Hawthorne wrote to Bridge suggesting that his letters from Africa might make up a volume. In May, before Bridge left New York, he wrote again offering advice about writing a journal:

> I would advise you not to stick too accurately to the bare fact . . . the result will be a want of freedom, that will deprive you of a higher truth than that which you strive to attain. Allow your fancy pretty free license, and omit no heightening touches merely because they did not chance to happen before your eyes. If they did not happen, they at least ought—which is all that concerns you. This is the secret of all entertaining travellers. . . . Begin to write always before the impression of novelty has worn off from your mind; else you will begin to think that the peculiarities, which at first attracted you, are not worth recording; yet these slight peculiarities are the very things that make the most vivid impression upon the reader. . . . After you have had due time for observation, you may then give grave reflections on national character, customs, morals, religion, the influence of peculiar modes of government etc. . . . All the merit will be your own; for I shall merely arrange them, correct the style, and perform other little offices as to which only a practised scribbler is *au fait.*

This passage reveals a great deal about Hawthorne's art as well as about his editing of *Journal of an African Cruiser.* Truth, for a romancer, is not in "bare fact" so much as in the writer's creation of what ought to happen. Character sketches such as fill the pages of Hawthorne's own journals appeal to readers' preference for gossip, just as "peculiarities" have value, Hawthorne arguing that such big themes as national character and morality can be dealt with later, *if at all* seemingly implied. Important also is Hawthorne's identification of himself as editor—a similarly worded disclaimer appears in the "Custom House" introduction to *The Scarlet Letter* (1850)—his insistence that he will "merely arrange" the facts and impressions. As he reminded Bridge in his May letter, Hawthorne was, on the basis of his work on the *American Magazine of Useful and Entertaining Knowledge,* an experienced editor.

Nearly a year later, in his 1 April 1844 letter, Hawthorne offers additional advice and reveals his feelings about the work at hand:

> A little of my professional experience will easily put it into shape; and I doubt not that the Harpers, or somebody else, will be glad to publish it either in the book or pamphlet form—or perhaps in both, so as to suit two different classes of readers. My name shall appear as editor, in order to give it what little vogue may be derived from thence—and its own merits will do the rest . . . Oh, it will be an excellent book!

Hawthorne described his editing of Bridge's journal in a letter written to E. A. Duyckinck on 2 March 1845:

> I have re-modelled the style, where it seemed necessary, and have developed his ideas, where he failed to do it himself, and have put on occasional patches of sentimental embroidery—at the same time avoiding to tamper with his facts, or to change the tenor of his observations upon them; so that the work has not become otherwise than authentic, in my hands.

A month later he wrote to Duyckinck, "My own share of it is so amalgamated with the substance of the work, that I cannot very well define what it is; but all the solid and material merit is due to my naval friend."

One instance of Hawthorne's apparent substitution of his own observation for that of his friend serves as an example of his "embroidery." James Mellow argues in *Nathaniel Hawthorne in His Times* (1980) that a reference to Fourierism is a "timely" addition by Hawthorne. In his *American Notebooks* (1932) for 27 July 1844 Hawthorne incudes a note on ants: "Here is a type of domestic industry—perhaps, too, something of municipal institutions—perhaps, likewise (who knows) the very model of a community which Fourierites and others are stumbling in pursuit of." While the manuscript of Bridge's journal has no entries for July 1844, the *Journal of an African Cruiser* does contain an entry dated 2 July 1844: "It would seem to be seriously worth while for the Fourierites to observe both the social economy and the modes of architecture of these African ants . . . Fourierites might stumble upon hints, in an ant-hill, for the convenient arrangement of . . . Phalanxteries." Perhaps the conclusive evidence is not so much in the general similarity of the passages as in Hawthorne's use of the word *stumbling* in his own journal and his parallel use of *stumble* in Bridge's text. In all likelihood, when Hawthorne read whatever Bridge wrote about ants, he reverted to his own recently written analogy.

As an account of a tour of duty in the anti-slaver squadron off West Africa in the 1840s, *Journal of an African Cruiser* has a place on the shelf of antislavery literature as well as travel literature, being cited or at least mentioned in serious works on the slave trade, especially works that focus on the suppression of such trade. The book's value as travel literature arises in part from the dearth of information about Africa. Although Bridge was not a great writer, he was intelligent and perceptive and was uniquely situated to observe and comment upon physical and social life on the so-called slave coast of Africa. He had no cause to plead and apparently had plenty of time on his hands. He was often included in parties that went ashore for various official and unofficial reasons. Further, this journal deals with his second trip to the area, the first occurring on the *Cyane* in 1838–1841. Bridge continued to read about Africa while experiencing life there, noting in one instance that Joseph Jenkins Roberts, the appointed governor and later elected president of Liberia, lent him Parliament's report on West Africa.

In his preface Bridge asserts that Africa is "so little seductive" that he kept a journal for the mental exercise of doing so. He recognized, though, that the west coast of Africa had been little visited or written about, providing a "fresher field" than other places for travel writing. He hopes the book will add at least "a trifle" to the knowledge of the area, but he disclaims any expertise. He later asserts in the book that spots so little visited are "worth describing," but in a telling revelation of the attitude he brought to the task, he condemns "uncouth and peculiar" native dancing, concluding that "A gracefully quiet dance is the latest flower of high refinement." In form the book is a journal with dated entries from 5 June 1843 to 15 October 1844, divided into twenty-two chapters.

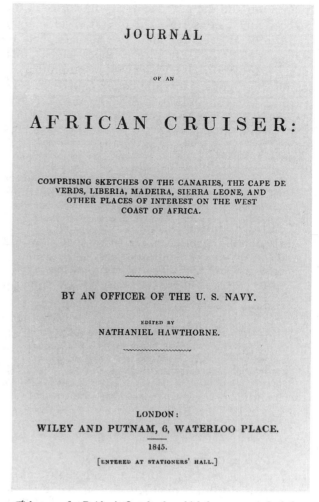

JOURNAL

OF AN

AFRICAN CRUISER:

COMPRISING SKETCHES OF THE CANARIES, THE CAPE DE VERDS, LIBERIA, MADEIRA, SIERRA LEONE, AND OTHER PLACES OF INTEREST ON THE WEST COAST OF AFRICA.

BY AN OFFICER OF THE U. S. NAVY.

EDITED BY
NATHANIEL HAWTHORNE.

LONDON:
WILEY AND PUTNAM, 6, WATERLOO PLACE.
1845.
[ENTERED AT STATIONERS' HALL.]

Title page for Bridge's first book, which he wrote at the behest of his friend Nathaniel Hawthorne

Near the conclusion of his first chapter, in which the ship sails from New York to the Canary Islands, Bridge observes the "loafers" who hang around seaports and tells an anecdote about a murderer among his own ship's crew. He does so, however, without indicating what action he took upon making the discovery. Bridge uses the incident to show the range of types among the crew and the "high romance" of their lives. In the last two paragraphs of the chapter he describes Grand Canary Island and its capital, Las Palmas, ending with a reference to cave dwellers—largely poor people and vagabonds. He observes that the climate of Teneriffe, the largest of the islands, is paradisaic but notes a shortage of water: the territory inland is "wild and bold, but sterile" and "barren, desolate, and unpromising."

Bridge often mentions economic and social matters. He remarks on an unsuccessful coffee plantation and the practice of drying coffee in the streets, and he describes the operation of a sugar cane mill. He reports that American exports to Africa include food, furniture, shoes, clocks, and other manufactured items as well as rum, tobacco, gunpowder, guns, pans, and cotton cloth, while African exports include camwood, palm oil, ivory, peanuts, gold dust, and gum. Trade with colonists and other non-natives is relatively easy, he maintains, because the rules are clear and there are products to trade; it is even easier to trade with slavers for they have money. Trading with natives is difficult, however, because it must be done according to their rules and customs.

Bridge's interests range from human sacrifice to Liberian independence. He writes that he would like "to witness the thrilling spectacle of a human sacrifice, which, being partly a religious rite, is an affair of a higher order than one of our civilized executions." Later he notes his disapproval of Liberia's breaking away from the American Colonization Society. The account of his travels includes the usual perils of life aboard ship and in a tropical area: illness, getting wet, drowning, poisonous insects, and sharks. Illness is presented as the result of breathing bad air, no doubt the conventional belief before the discovery of the germ theory of disease, for there is no mention of unclean food.

Two of the most important people mentioned in *Journal of an African Cruiser* are Joseph Jenkins Roberts and John Brown Russwurm. Roberts was president of Liberia from 1847 to 1855 and from 1871 to 1876, and Russwurm was governor of the colony of Maryland at Cape Palmas and was instrumental in uniting that colony with Liberia. Bridge first mentions them at the beginning of chapter 3 without providing their first names and without clarifying which of them governed which colony.

Bridge is unfailingly complimentary in his extensive discussions of Roberts. He reports on Roberts and Commodore Perry conducting a "palaver" with a native chief on the killing by natives of two seamen, the chief pleading the exigencies of war. He also describes the settlement of a dispute about land between natives and colonists. Bridge concludes that "Governor Roberts exhibited much sagacity and diplomatic shrewdness," even though Bridge thought that "in some points, the affair had remarkably the aspect of a forcible acquisition of territory by the colonists." Bridge ends his discussion of one meeting by praising Roberts as a "dignified, manly, and sensible person." (President Roberts happened to call on

Hawthorne in 1856 when the latter was consul at Liverpool. There is no indication in Hawthorne's journal account of the meeting that he remembered editing statements about Roberts ten years earlier. As Brancaccio notes, his attitude toward Roberts was "condescending." Hawthorne's reference to Roberts as a "mulatto man" is changed in his wife's editing to "negro" in the *English Notebooks*.)

Bridge's responses to Russwurm are equally favorable. One of the first blacks to graduate from an American college, he went on to edit a newspaper and was the first superintendent of schools in Liberia before becoming governor of the colony of Maryland at Cape Palmas. However, while it is noted early that Russwurm had a "collegiate education," *Journal of an African Cruiser* does not mention that he had graduated from Bowdoin in 1826 and that both Bridge and Hawthorne knew him there. Bridge praises the leadership of Russwurm and Commodore Perry for leading an attack on natives in an effort to protect colonists from invasion. He also notes that Russwurm tried in vain to convince natives to move their town to suit the convenience of the colonists.

Bridge inevitably encountered missionaries from various countries representing several denominations. Not unlike his Bowdoin friends Hawthorne and Pierce, Bridge gives little impression of more than a passing interest in or personal commitment to religion; hence his remarks tend to possess the advantage of being dispassionate. His coolness permits him to praise, for example, a bland preacher who gained respect for "his amiable, guileless disposition, and unassuming piety." But his lack of involvement perhaps also makes his observations seem a bit superficial, as when he castigates a priest who drowned while "on a drunken frolic, in company with some colored women" or when he reduces to simplistic terms the advantages (superiority of their system) and disadvantages (gaudy display and bribery) of Catholic over Protestant missionary efforts. In a relatively rare excursion into theology, Bridge reasons that God fit the climate to the people, not that people adapt to their environment, but he lapses into acceptance of racial stereotypes in doing so.

Bridge does address seriously several issues involving missionaries, as when he doubts "the expediency of sending missionary ladies to perish here . . . it may well be questioned whether a missionary ought . . . to be married . . . one great advantage the Catholic missionary possesses over the Protestant." While he generally praises missionaries and commends black priests, Bridge also notes that one source of tension in Liberia stems from the white missionaries' assumption of superiority over black colonists. According to Bridge, the missionaries "did not wish their affairs to be identified with those of the colonists." Bridge also suspects Protestant missionaries of being behind an effort to thwart French territorial expansion because they believe it will lead to the arrival of Catholic priests.

Bridge treats native religious customs as curiosities. He reports that at some funerals servants and other escorts are sacrificed to be buried with kings. Noting that some tribes worship monkeys, "the most ridiculous of animals," while others throw slaves to the sharks, he claims that native morality is superior to their religion. While natives are "not insensible to the advantages of education," Bridge asserts that they have mixed reactions to the educational efforts of missionaries. He believes that British money spent on religion has been "almost entirely thrown away," leading some missionaries to devote their attention to education.

Bridge makes frequent observations about women, often in the language and from the perspective of his time. He praises a sailor's nursing an ill mate "as tenderly as a woman," finds drunken women as shocking as a drunken priest, and describes "conjugal and other customs," apparel, work, respect for age, and punishments for unfaithful wives (without commenting on unfaithful husbands). There is considerable ogling, with frequent observations about scanty clothing (children tended to be naked, while adults usually wore only loincloths or skirts) and the lack of restraint in movement, as when viewing dark-skinned maidens dancing. A shawl, carelessly draped to conceal one breast while revealing the other, is notable, as is the native women's competent and practical assistance to his crew, especially by one tall girl whom Bridge imagines to be attracted to him. Women are listened to as peacemakers, but they also torture prisoners of war. After noting that native street vendors tend to be women he clearly shows his bias: "It would perhaps add to our manliness of character, if at least the minor departments of traffic were resigned to the weaker sex, among ourselves."

Given the assignment of the *Saratoga* and the establishment of Liberia and Sierra Leone as homes for freed slaves, Bridge predictably addresses the issues of abolition, slavery, and the slave trade. In his preface he professes his "freedom from partizan bias," insisting that he is "without prejudice" about abolition and colonization. Bridge's early expres-

sions, however, suggest that he shared the easy assumptions about race common to his time. He writes about "a little black fellow, whose sobriquet was Othello"; he says of the Portuguese that their claim to white blood is "not apparent in their complexions" (an observation not in the original journal); and he seems quick to characterize the behavior of natives as "intemperate, dissolute, and vile." He refers to the entertainment provided by "a negro band," after which Othello "played monkey" (whatever demeaning antic that might have been).

The implications of race are always present for Bridge. When "a large negro" loses his balance and drops Bridge while carrying him through the surf, he concludes, "An abolitionist, perhaps, might draw a moral from the story, and say that all, who ride on the shoulders of the African race, deserve nothing better than a similar overthrow" (an addition to his journal entry on the subject). After describing a woman dressed only in a loincloth who is "not a little attractive," he continues, "It is to be observed, however, that the sable hue is in itself a kind of veil, and takes away from that sense of nudity which would so oppress the eye, were a woman of our own race to present herself so scantily attired." This is a deeply embedded kind of racism in which color cloaks the humanity of the people deemed uncivilized.

Bridge categorizes people in a manner seemingly the product of bias, as when he distinguishes between "negroes and mulattoes." Although such distinctions are meaningful in the context of the nineteenth century, they also suggest something of a fascination with the making of distinctions. Bridge, though, sometimes appears to be self-conscious about using racial terms, as when he places quotation marks around "nigger." His sensitivity to the ways in which some people he meets are themselves sensitive about color (or at least he imagines them to be so) adds to the persistent attention given to race in the book. He asserts, "Most colored men avoid alluding to their hue, thus betraying a morbid sensibility upon the point, as if it were a disgraceful and afflicting dispensation."

Bridge always remarks on what he regards as evidence of refinement or civilization among Africans. He notes that the governor of the Dutch fort at Axim is "apparently a mulatto." When he meets a cultivated and well-dressed clerk, he writes, "It is interesting to meet the natives of Africa at so advanced a stage of refinement, yet retaining somewhat of their original habits and character, which is of course entirely lost in the Liberian colonists," who he believes lack refinement because

Bridge at the time of Personal Recollections of
Nathaniel Hawthorne

colonists will never recognize the natives otherwise than as heathen. Amalgamation is scarcely more difficult between the white and colored races in America, than it is in Africa, between the "black-white" colonist and the unadulterated native.

Bridge sees many reasons for conflict in Liberia. He notes that the country has a low percentage of arable land and that "most coastal areas have richer soil than Liberia." Further, Liberian sugar and coffee—the most likely exports—could not compete with Caribbean slave-labor products. Another of the "drawbacks of Colonization" is that there were relatively few employment opportunities for women, who outnumbered men three or four to one. Bridge also believes that recently freed slaves are "no better than mere children, as respects the conduct and economy of life" and that many colonists are ill-prepared for the difficulty of the work. Still, Bridge's earliest assessment is that the colonists are better off in Africa than in America, so important is freedom.

Among the most illuminating insights are those expressed late in the book when Bridge is offering summary speculations about colonization and Liberia. He believes Liberia is "a better country than America, for the colored race," but that its success depends on hard work. Blacks in Liberia have "their fair position in the comparative scale of mankind" because visitors must associate with colonists as equals, an impossibility in the United States. This above all else makes Liberia a better place for blacks, for they are "redeemed from ages of degradation" there. Blacks make laws that whites must obey. "When the white man sets his foot on the shore of Africa, he finds it necessary to throw off his former prejudices," Bridge writes. And Bridge does so, while admitting he is not sure he would be courageous enough to do so in any other place.

Bridge notes a huge discrepancy in reports of the number of slaves—from fifteen thousand to five hundred thousand—exported annually from Africa. The British, he observes, send freed slaves to virtual slavery in the British West Indies as well as dump the crews of slavers on the African coast, probably to starve to death. He believes the British could stop slave trade if they desired and denies the report that the Liberian colonists favor slave trade. He does believe the "natives are generally favorable to the slave trade," no doubt in part because slaves tend to be from the interior. Both British and American merchant traders inadvertently abet the slave trade by providing provisions for slave traders.

they had been slaves. Despite praise of black priests, he considers them "queer specimens." He cites the case of "Dr. Fergusson, a mulatto in color, but born in Scotland, and married to a white lady" (and educated at Edinburgh) as proof that "the African race may, with due advantages, be cultivated and refined so as to compare with the best specimens of white gentlemen."

Perhaps Bridge's most compelling reflection of the age's racism is in a judgment rendered early in the book, "So sensible are they of their own inferiority, that if a person looks sternly in the face of a native, when about to be attacked by him, and calls out to him loudly, the chances are ten to one that the native runs away. This effect is analogous to that which the eye of man is said to exert on the fiercest of savage beasts."

Trouble between natives and colonists occupies a great deal of Bridge's account. Bridge simplifies the contrast as one between civilized people and barbarians and perhaps exaggerates the level of civilized refinement brought by the colonists:

Many of the natives look with contempt on the colonists, and do not hesitate to tell them that they are merely liberated slaves. On the other hand, the

The next-to-last chapter is about Sierra Leone, Britain's sanctuary for black veterans and freed slaves. Bridge contrasts Sierra Leone unfavorably with Liberia, to the end of advancing the superiority of American over British philanthropy. His prediction of the imminent bankruptcy of Sierra Leone was not fulfilled. In his last chapter Bridge addresses the failure of his antislaver squadron to capture a single slave ship. He explains that the laws of the United States permitted the squadron to search and seize only American ships. The slavers chose to fly the flags of other nations, primarily Spain, Portugal, and Brazil.

Among the minor inconsistencies in the writing is Bridge's mentioning of "eatables and drinkables" without providing details, hence failing to render the scene but following with several pages of detailed description, as when he discusses the wines of Madeira. Some of his writing, though, can be touching in its coyness and indirection. He describes a prostitute, without using the term, as "a young girl, a mere rosebud of a woman . . . very thinly clad, and with her whole frame shivering, the poor thing assumed an airy and mirthful deportment, to attract us." In a rare use of irony Bridge writes, after complaining about being overcharged, "It is delightful, in these remote, desolate, and semi-barbarous regions, to meet with characteristics that remind us of a more polished and civilized land," but this passage is not in his original journal.

Several passages are interesting for being omitted from the *Journal of an African Cruiser* but included in Bridge's daily record. Missing is an entry about dining that is critical of Governor Roberts's wife for being "not well-versed in the honors of the table." Omitted also, following the description of a sixteen-year-old colonist girl, is a more intimate note: "She said she should like a companion, & I promised to bring a mulatto boy [servant] ashore for her," with "boy" crossed out and "servant" written in. Another passage was probably deleted because of Bridge's embarrassment that the captain "spoke plainly of the d-[amne]-d niggers" in the presence of Roberts and other blacks.

Bridge apparently decided that he would revise his book if he got the chance, as is clear from two entries in his 1846 journal. On both inside covers (he apparently turned the book over and began anew at the back) is inscribed: "In case of my death, I wish this manuscript and my copy of The Journal of an African Cruiser in which I have made memoranda, delivered to my friend Nath. Hawthorne, Esq. of Salem, to be used as he thinks fit. /

H.B. / Nov 12, 1846." Just beyond midway in the journal is the draft of an introduction to a revised book:

> When I returned from an African Cruise and gave my Journal and memoranda to an early friend & classmate to be edited and published, it was with little expectation of producing, by our joint labors, so successful a volume. From different causes, however, it proved one of the popular ephemerals of the time, and I came to regard it with more self-complacency than I had supposed it possible to entertain upon the subject, before the critics in England as well as America had placed upon the volume their stamp of approbation.

The introduction goes on to say that a new book or a new edition is necessary because he has taken another cruise to Africa and wants to correct "many errors of fact and some of opinion" and to restore much that had to be cut from the first edition.

Bridge married Charlotte Marshall in 1846; their daughter died at age three. He held the difficult position as chief of the Bureau of Provisions and Clothing for fifteen years, including the difficult time of the Civil War, after which he retired. His *Personal Recollections of Nathaniel Hawthorne* is a collection of anecdotes combined with passages of letters from Hawthorne. For example, it is Bridge to whom Hawthorne wrote on 4 February 1850 concerning *The Scarlet Letter:* "I finished my book only yesterday; one end being in the press in Boston, while the other was in my head here in Salem—so that, as you see, the story is at least fourteen miles long." Hawthorne was more open to Bridge than to others, owning, for example, "I have no kindred with, nor leaning towards, the Abolitionists," a position Bridge reiterated a few pages later. The correspondence makes clear that Hawthorne encouraged Bridge to take notes in a way that would lead to a book and that Hawthorne would be the sole financial beneficiary of whatever success the book came to enjoy.

One passage in *Personal Recollections of Nathaniel Hawthorne* touches on John Brown Russwurm, whom Bridge had highly praised in *Journal of an African Cruiser.* Just after relating a prank played on Calvin Stowe (for which Bridge assumed a black-faced disguise), he writes:

> Governor Russwurm . . . was a diligent student, but of no marked ability. He lived at a carpenter's house, just beyond the village limits, where Hawthorne and the writer called upon him several times, but his sensitiveness on account of his color prevented him from returning the calls. Twenty years later I renewed the acquaintance pleasantly in Africa, where—as Governor of Cape Palmas—he received, with dignity

and ease, the Commodore and officers of our squadron, myself all the more cordially because we had been college associates and fellow-Athenaeans.

Recollecting the black-face prank apparently led Bridge to think about the only black at Bowdoin during his time there. Bridge died in Athens, Pennsylvania, on 18 March 1893, the same year his book on Hawthorne was published.

References:

Patrick Brancaccio, "'The Black Man's Paradise': Hawthorne's Editing of *The Journal of an African Cruiser,*" *New England Quarterly,* 53 (March 1980): 23–41;

Wilmot Brookings Mitchell, *A Remarkable Bowdoin Decade, 1820–1830* (Brunswick, Maine: Bowdoin College, 1952).

Papers:

Bridge's journal for 5 June 1843 to 19 March 1844 is in the Berg Collection at the New York Public Library. His 1846 journal, a pocket diary, and a copy of *Journal of an African Cruiser* with his and John Roberts's marginal notes are at Bowdoin College.

William Wells Brown

(circa 1814 – 6 November 1884)

Brian D. Reed
Kent State–East Liverpool

See also *DLB 3: Antebellum Writers in New York and the South* and *DLB 50: Afro-American Writers Before the Harlem Renaissance.*

BOOKS: *Narrative of William W. Brown, A Fugitive Slave, Written by Himself* (Boston: Anti-Slavery Office, 1847; enlarged, 1848; London: Charles Gilpin, 1849);

A Lecture Delivered before the Female Anti-Slavery Society of Salem, at Lyceum Hall, Nov. 14, 1847 (Boston: Massachusetts Anti-Slavery Society, 1847);

A Description of William Wells Brown's Original Panoramic Views of the Scenes in the Life of an American Slave, from His Birth in Slavery to His Death or His Escape to His First Home of Freedom on British Soil (London: Charles Gilpin, 1849);

Three Years in Europe; or, Places I Have Seen and People I Have Met (London: Charles Gilpin, 1852); expanded as *The American Fugitive in Europe. Sketches of Places and People Abroad* (Boston: John P. Jewett / New York: Sheldon, Lamport & Blakemann, 1855);

Clotel; or, The President's Daughter: A Narrative of Slave Life in the United States (London: Partridge & Oakey, 1853); revised as *Clotelle: A Tale of Southern States* (Boston: J. Redpath / New York: H. Dexter Hamilton, 1864); revised as *Clotelle: or, The Colored Heroine; A Tale of the Southern States* (Boston: Lee, 1867);

St. Domingo: Its Revolutions and Its Patriots. A Lecture, Delivered before the Metropolitan Athenaeum, London, May 16 and at St. Thomas' Church, Philadelphia, December 20, 1854 (Boston: Bela Marsh, 1855);

The Escape; or, A Leap for Freedom. A Drama in Five Acts (Boston: R. F. Wallcut, 1858);

Memoir of William Wells Brown, an American Bondman. Written by Himself (Boston: Anti-Slavery Office, 1859);

The Anti-Southern Lecturer (London, 1862);

The Black Man; His Antecedents, His Genius, and His Achievements (New York: Thomas Hamilton /

Boston: R. F. Wallcut, 1863; revised and enlarged, 1863);

The Negro in the American Rebellion: His Heroism and His Fidelity (Boston: Lee & Shepard, 1867);

The Rising Son; or, The Antecedents and Advancement of the Colored Race (Boston: A. G. Brown, 1873);

My Southern Home: Or, The South and Its People (Boston: A. G. Brown, 1880).

Collections: *The Travels of William Wells Brown,* edited by Paul Jefferson (New York: Markus Wiener, 1991);

From Fugitive Slave to Freeman: The Autobiographies of William Wells Brown, edited by William L. Andrews (New York: Mentor, 1993).

OTHER: *The Anti-Slavery Harp; a Collection of Songs for Anti-Slavery Meetings. Compiled by William W. Brown* (Boston: Bela Marsh, 1848; Newcastle, U.K.: J. Blackwell, 1850).

William Wells Brown's chillingly realistic depictions of the horrors of slavery make him an important figure in American literature. Despite his wretched beginnings in bondage he rose to become the first African American novelist, playwright, and travel writer. The diversity of his talents as autobiographer, historian, writer, explorer, doctor, entrepreneur, sociologist, and orator for abolitionism and temperance are all the more remarkable for his being self-educated.

Brown was born a slave in the vicinity of Lexington, Kentucky, around 1814. His mother, Elizabeth, was a slave, and his father, George Higgins, was a slaveholder and a near relation of his first master, Dr. John Young. A member of the old Southern aristocratic Wickliffe family, Young was a wealthy plantation owner and cultivator of tobacco, hemp, flax, and feed corn. Although Young usually recorded the dates of birth of his slaves, there exists no such record for Brown. Biographer L. H. Whelchel Jr. asserts, "Brown must have been born in 1813," yet other scholars, notably Curtis W. Ellison and William Edward Farrison, put the year as 1814. Others argue that Brown was born much later.

The confusion about the date of Brown's birth is understandable because of his own statements. In *Narrative of William Wells Brown, A Fugitive* (1847) Brown states, "The man who stole me as a son as I was born, recorded the birth of all the infants which he claimed to be his property," but he gives no further information about the date. In legal documents Brown used a variety of dates. While he usually listed his birth year as 1814, he chose to use 1819 on his registration for his second marriage. In addition, slaveholders for many reasons found it beneficial to conceal a slave's age, so any documents created during Brown's early life are questionable.

In *Narrative of William Wells Brown, A Fugitive Slave* Brown relates in rich detail his early life in bondage, his attempts to gain freedom, and his final escape. Written from memory in 1846, Brown's travel-slave narrative was an immediate best-seller. It was often republished and sold more than nine thousand copies in a two-year period. Contemporary critics were as delighted as the public with Brown's original work, calling it "marvelous" and "almost as winning as that of Defoe's books." Brown's story was honed by years of retelling in lectures, and its publication may have been prompted by the success of *Narrative of the Life of Frederick Douglass, an American Slave* in 1845.

Brown suffered greatly in his childhood. One of his most vivid memories is the brutal treatment his mother received on Young's plantation:

> My mother was a field hand, and one morning was ten or fifteen minutes behind the others in getting into the field. As soon as she reached the spot where they were at work, the overseer commenced whipping her. She cried, "Oh! pray—Oh! pray—Oh! pray"—these are generally the words of slaves, when imploring mercy at the hands of their oppressors. . . . I could hear every crack of the whip, and every groan and cry of my poor mother.

Not only did Brown have to suffer the psychological and physical afflictions of slavery, but he also had the added indignity of not having a name. Slaves were not allowed surnames, possibly because so many were fathered by whites. All Brown had was his Christian name, William, and even that was taken away from him by the Youngs when they adopted a son with the same name. During the remainder of his time as Young's property Brown was known only as Sandford.

Young moved to Saint Charles County in the Missouri Territory in 1816 and later, when Brown was about ten years old, bought a large farm near Saint Louis. To help cover expenses Young began hiring out Brown and his mother in the city. Among other jobs, he worked as a tavern boy, a worker on a Mississippi River steamboat, and a servant to a hotel owner. Brown's service in the tavern under its owner, Major Freeland, gave him his first personal experience of particularly cruel treatment. Brown describes Freeland as a despicable "horse racer, cock-fighter, gambler, and withal an inveterate drunkard." After six months of continual brutality, Brown ducked into a nearby woods without any plan of escape. He was treed by vicious dogs used to hunt runaway slaves and soon apprehended, whipped, and "smoked"—a punishment in which the victim is tied in a smokehouse and forced to gasp for air as burning tobacco stems produce a choking atmosphere. Certainly, Brown's time in Freeland's employ greatly influenced his later push for both temperance and abolition.

Brown's desire for justice and freedom became even stronger when he was in the employ of a Northern slaveowner at the Missouri Hotel in Saint Louis, John Colburn—"a more inveterate hater

GREAT HOUSE AT POPLAR FARM.

LEAP OF THE FUGITIVE SLAVE.

Illustrations from Brown's last book, in which he compared the lives of African Americans before and after the Civil War

of the negro I do not believe ever walked God's green earth." Colburn would beat his slaves for any reason he could find, once subjecting a servant to "over fifty lashes on the bare back with a cow-hide" for setting the table with a knife that was "not as clean as it might have been." The man was whipped even more severely when he was so bold as to complain to the master who had hired him out to Colburn. Brown saw clearly that a slave did not have the right to complain of poor treatment or to defend himself lest he be beaten even more.

Brown's removal to Saint Louis was all the more bitter because of the strain it placed on his family. Two of his brothers had just died before he and his mother were sent away, and he also left behind three brothers and a sister, Elizabeth, at the Young farm. While Brown was working for Colburn, his mother and siblings, save for one brother, were sold to Isaac Mansfield, the owner of "a large manufacturing establishment," to cover debts. Even though this caused some separation, it temporarily kept Brown's remaining family close in the Saint Louis area.

In 1830 Brown finished his time with Colburn and was employed as an errand boy in the printing office of Reverend Elijah P. Lovejoy, a devout abolitionist and the editor of the *St. Louis Times*. Brown was able to start his own self-education by handling type and learning the workings of a newspaper. He described Lovejoy as "decidedly the best master that I had ever had" and stated that he was "indebted to him . . . for what little learning I

obtained while in slavery." Even so, after six months with Lovejoy, Brown was still mostly illiterate.

Brown's next job, his second as a steamboat worker, was as a waiter aboard the Saint Louis–based *Enterprise*. His work soon sharpened his desire for freedom:

> The situation was a pleasant one to me;—but in passing from place to place, and seeing new faces everyday, and knowing that they could go where they pleased, I soon became unhappy, and several times thought of leaving the boat at some landing-place, and trying to make my escape to Canada.

Brown, however, was unwilling to make the attempt and leave his mother and siblings behind in slavery.

While on one of its trips down the Mississippi, the *Enterprise* carried a cargo of slaves owned by James Walker, a ruthless slave trader who was impressed by Brown's efficiency as a waiter. After much insistence on Walker's part Young consented to hire Brown out to him in 1832. Most of *Narrative* is devoted to the time Brown spent with Walker, the gloomiest year of his life. Walker used Brown as a "custodian of slaves," a role he found depressing and demeaning. One of his duties was to get slaves ready for sale and to ensure that they would get a good price. Brown "was ordered to have the old men's whiskers shaved off, and the grey hairs plucked out where they were not too numerous." He also was required to encourage slaves to dance, sing, and play games to make them "appear cheerful and happy" so they would bring extra dollars. Brown recalls with horror that he "often set them to dancing when their cheeks were wet with tears."

The evils of slavery continued for Brown after his release from Walker's control. After a few failed agricultural ventures left him financially needy, Young decided to sell Brown, who was horrified at the prospect of losing touch with what was left of his already divided family. While Young would not allow him to buy his freedom, he did agree to let Brown search for his own purchaser in the Saint Louis region. This gave Brown the opportunity to scour the Saint Louis streets for his scattered family. When he found his sister in a jail waiting to be taken to Mississippi, Brown felt powerless to help but promised her he would escape slavery with their mother.

"After much persuasion" Brown convinced his mother to flee Saint Louis with him and set out for the Canadian border. Brown described their journey as difficult, but his memories of the cruelty of the slave life they were leaving gave him the strength to continue:

> As we travelled towards a land of liberty, my heart would at times leap for joy. At other times, being, as I was, almost constantly on my feet, I felt I could travel no further. But when the thought of slavery, with its democratic whips—its republican chains—its evangelical blood-hounds, and its religious slave-holders—when I thought of all this paraphernalia of American democracy and religion behind me, and the prospect of liberty before me, I was encouraged to press forward.

They were caught a week and a half after their escape. When his mother was forced to return to Mansfield, who was irate at the cost of her capture, Brown was overwhelmed with guilt. Despite their misfortune, Brown's mother encouraged her son to continue his own quest for freedom. Her final words to him—"You have ever said that you would not die a slave; that you would be a freeman. Now try to get your liberty!"—rang in Brown's ears until he achieved his goal. At a young age Brown had seen and experienced almost every agonizing aspect of slavery.

After Brown's recent attempt for freedom, a disgruntled Young sold him to Enoch Price to work on his steamboat, the *Chester*. By this time Brown had traveled extensively along the Mississippi between Saint Louis and New Orleans and become wise in the ways of travelers. Aware of Brown's desire to escape, Mrs. Price tried to get him interested in one of her slave girls as a means of ensuring that he would not wander far. "As she knew," asserts Farrison in his biography of Brown,

"a slave without local parental, filial, or marital attachments . . . was much less contented and much more likely to escape." Brown recognized the trap: "I determined never to marry any woman on earth until I should get my liberty." He feigned interest in marriage to ease the Prices' suspicions and allow himself some extra mobility. When the Prices had enough faith in Brown to let him accompany them on a trip up the river, he was ready to act. While docked in Cincinnati on New Year's Day 1834, Brown made a successful escape. Using the North Star as his guide, he took off across Ohio and headed for Canada.

Without an overcoat in the intense winter cold, Brown was in dire need of assistance. While hiding in some roadside bushes for a few nights without food or shelter, Brown realized that he must get help or die. He approached a white man who appeared to be a Good Samaritan and told him of his predicament. The man took Brown into his home, clothed and fed him, and made him feel, as Farrison describes, "a normal person among other normal persons." Brown's new friend was Wells Brown. Thinking this man had saved his life and feeling indebted and grateful to him, Brown honored him by taking his name. Henceforth, he called himself William Wells Brown.

With a new set of shoes, a sack of food, a small amount of money, and some better clothing, Brown again set out for Canada. Within four days he was halfway to Cleveland but out of food and miserably cold. Again Brown had to ask for charity, so he approached a pleasant-looking farmhouse, but this time the owner of the house refused to feed him. The farmer's wife asserted herself and pushed her husband aside to allow Brown to enter the dwelling and eat as much as he could. Brown exclaimed, "Ever since that act, I have been in favor of 'woman's rights.'" The woman presented Brown with a note to her friend who lived further north so that she would also give him some provisions, and in this "underground" fashion he arrived in Cleveland in three more days, at the end of January.

His frequent change of employment while a hired slave not only gave Brown insight into the evils of slavery and fodder for his literary works, but it also helped him attain many skills with which he could gain employment. When Brown reached Cleveland he began work as a handyman and became known as a clever jack-of-all-trades. One of his first purchases as a freedman was a spelling book. In a sketch of his life included in *Clotel; or, The President's Daughter: A Narrative of Slave Life in the United States* (1853) Brown relates that he learned to write by practicing with chalk on fences and then tricking white boys who came along into helping him with corrections. While this anecdote is not referred to in *Narrative* and may be contrived, it illustrates Brown's determination to educate himself.

In the summer of 1834 in Cleveland, Brown met and quickly married Elizabeth (Betsey) Schooner, a free woman. A longer courtship might have revealed some flaws in their relationship, but initially the couple was happy. Tensions grew in the relationship as Brown's tireless push for economic self-sufficiency and his time-consuming dedication to abolitionist causes gave the couple little time for solving their problems.

After the sudden death of the couple's first daughter and his being cheated out of his summer wages by the captain of a steamer, Brown moved his family from Cleveland to Monroe, Michigan, where he showed his entrepreneurial spirit. Brown opened a popular barbershop and a small banking business, and he returned to work as a seasonal steamboat steward for various employers on the Great Lakes. He also became more involved in abolitionist activities, assisting many fugitive slaves to freedom in Canada.

At the end of the summer of 1836 Brown moved his family to Buffalo because of its large African American population, its closeness to Canada, and its active steamboat port where he could obtain work and continue ferrying passengers to freedom. In his *Narrative* Brown states "In the year 1842, I conveyed, from the first of May to the first of December, sixty-nine fugitives over Lake Erie to Canada." Brown continued to be active in antislavery organizations, and he also organized a temperance society for freedmen. His time as president of the society afforded him much experience with parliamentary form and public speaking, which undoubtedly helped prepare him for his future life as a lecturer. Brown's antislavery activities soon gained the favorable attention of abolitionists aligned with William Lloyd Garrison, who hired him as a part-time lecturer for several of their antislavery societies.

Despite the birth of two daughters—Clarissa in 1836 and Josephine in 1839—Brown's activities often took him away from home. With his increased salary and fame Brown in 1840 made a lecture trip to Cuba and Haiti, where he was first able to observe blacks in other countries. He may have traveled to Haiti for the opportunity to see a society where blacks lived free, slavery having been abolished on the island nation in the revolution of 1801. While Brown sometimes mentioned spending time in Havana and in the West Indies, he wrote little about his first travels abroad. But surely this journey helped prepare him for his later ambitious travels and allowed him to compare American governmental policy toward Africans with policies and practices elsewhere.

Although his desire may not have been for travel, his need to supply the family with income and his dedication to abolitionist causes often drew Brown away from his home in Buffalo to the larger eastern cities, placing added strain on his marriage. His early days as a lecturer were filled with travel so that he could reach large audiences in New York, Ohio, and Massachusetts. Known for his wit, sarcasm, and ability to entertain, Brown often won audiences over with his talents as a singer and his abilities as a gifted storyteller. His widening popularity as a lecturer allowed him to meet important black scholars such as Frederick Douglass and Henry Highland Garnet and gave him reason to work on his literary skills. Brown's earliest published writing was a letter appearing in the 5 October 1843 *National Anti-Slavery Standard,* in which he appealed for a shift away from a focus on Washington politicians and toward a greater concern with persuading the public of the immorality of slavery.

Brown's call for a grassroots movement to abolish slavery furthered his effectiveness before the masses and increased the admiration of his superiors. By the end of 1843 Brown became a full-time lecturer for the Western New York Anti-Slavery Society. His constant travels on the lecture circuit led to the end of his marriage in 1847, when he discovered his lonely wife was having an affair. Brown separated from her and set up a residence with his two daughters in Boston. This hub of abolitionist scholarship would remain his base for the rest of his life.

Brown's literary career began the same year his marriage ended. His matter-of-fact style and reasonable tone in his *Narrative* made readers quickly sympathize with his ordeal. His style and concern for the sensibilities of his readers were often copied by future writers for the cause. Encouraged by his friends and motivated by his own success, Brown in 1848 published *The Anti-Slavery Harp,* a collection of abolitionist songs. As editor of the work Brown wisely chose pieces that did not belittle whites as oppressors but used emotional lyrics emphasizing the horrors of slavery and the need for reform. Brown included his own composition titled "Fling out the Anti-Slavery Flag."

Because of his notoriety and the growing interest in abolitionist concerns Brown was commissioned by the American Peace Society to be their representative at the Paris Peace Congress of 1849. This offer came at a perfect time for Brown because his old master, Enoch Price, was hot on his trail. In 1848 Price offered to sell Brown his freedom for $325, but Brown staunchly refused this offer and widely publicized the injustice of bought freedom. Because Brown refused to buy his own freedom and bounty hunters were known for violence, travel became a necessity. He accepted the Peace Society's offer and traveled to Paris as well as England to lecture and publish British editions of his *Narrative* and his anthology.

Brown's reception in France was enthusiastic. His address upon the American spirit (which allowed people to be held in bondage) created quite a sensation at the Paris Peace Congress and established his European reputation as a motivational lecturer. Brown traveled extensively in England, crisscrossing the country to deliver speeches before town meetings and college colloquiums. During this time he befriended Victor Hugo, who taught him French, and he co-founded the *Anti-Slavery Advocate,* a London abolitionist newspaper.

In the summer of 1850 Brown decided to carry out an idea that he had conceived while viewing a particularly tame Boston exhibition of Southern scenes in the fall of 1847. That exhibition, which offered romantic views of slavery upon the Mississippi, caused him to consider what a more factual artistic representation could achieve. Brown employed London artists to depict scenes of slavery that he recounted. By the end of the summer he had amassed twenty-four drawings and opened his own successful London exhibition. The accompanying forty-eight-page catalogue, *A Description of William Wells Brown's Original Panoramic Views of the Scenes in the Life of an American Slave, from His Birth in Slavery to His Death or Escape to His First Home of Freedom on British Soil* (1850), complete with drawings and original text, was both an appeal to the sympathies of the English and a means of thanking the country for its sanctuary. His continued success enabled Brown to bring his daughters Clarissa and Josephine to England to live with him.

During his five-year stay in England Brown published *Three Years in Europe; or, Places I Have Seen and People I Have Met* (1852), an epistolary travel narrative in which he relates his observations and experiences mostly among the English. Contemporary critics praised the book, one calling it "the best book yet written by a black American." While composing this narrative Brown traveled twenty thousand miles around Britain and Europe and gave more than a thousand speeches.

It is surprising that after such horrid treatment in the land of his birth Brown still feels such a closeness to America. At the beginning of *Three Years in Europe* Brown remarks on this curious attachment as he sets sail for the British Isles:

> I had supposed I would leave the country without any regret; but in this I was mistaken, for when I saw the last thread of communication cut off between me and the land, and the dim shores dying away in the distance, I almost regretted that I was not on shore.

Explaining that "the experience of above twenty years' travelling had prepared me to undergo what most persons must, in visiting a strange country," Brown quickly manages to adapt to the new country. But even while touring the countryside in England, he seems to recall his homeland fondly. In Aberdeen he finds that "the dwellings, being mostly of granite, remind one of Boston." The "dark days" of a foggy London seem to depress him when he thinks of the western sun.

Brown's knack for description is evident as he observes the landscape and records his reactions. He seems particularly enthralled with European architecture. He marvels while "reveling among the fountains and statues" at Versailles; he is awestruck by "the finest paintings in the world" at the Louvre; the "noble edifice" of Saint Patrick's in Dublin and the "towering" dome of Saint Paul's in London are all part of a brilliant scene that Brown describes with enthusiastic detail.

Brown is also interested in the sociological differences between the Old World and the New World. It is with hopeful reflection that Brown notices "the marked differences between the English and the Americans" when it comes to race: "The prejudice which I have experienced on all and every occasion in the United States . . . vanished as soon as I set foot on the soil of Britain. . . . I was recognized as a man, and an equal."

Shortly after his arrival in England Brown published his most famous work, *Clotel; or, The President's Daughter.* The central character of this successful first African American novel is based upon the supposed illegitimate slave daughter of Thomas Jefferson. Drawing liberally on his own memories of the evils he had experienced, Brown gave a haunting portrayal of American slavery that had never been seen before in such detail. Although critics have found it overly sentimental and criticized its structure, the importance of *Clotel* as a pioneering effort by an African American writer should not be overlooked. Certainly Brown paved the way for many talented writers who would follow.

On 7 July 1854, after long negotiations with Enoch Price, Brown's English friends purchased his freedom for the sum of $300—an event of no little importance to the American abolitionist movement. With no further need to remain abroad Brown returned to America that same year to continue his career as an orator, traveling through Pennsylvania and Ohio and later touring and lecturing with Susan B. Anthony in New York. Meanwhile Brown began his work as a dramatist, writing "Experience, or How to Give a Northern Man a Backbone"—a satirical response to Rev. Nehemiah Adam's proslavery book, *A South-Side View of Slavery* (1854), and *The Escape; or, A Leap for Freedom* (1858), the first play ever published by an African American.

Brown became even more intense in his attacks against slavery in the period immediately before the outbreak of the Civil War. As Farrison reports, Brown, in a 26 October 1860 speech in Boston responding to Alabama Sen. William L. Yancey's defense of slavery, maintained that whites were descendants of barbarians while blacks had superior roots in Ethiopian civilization, that ancient Africans were leaders of their own advanced civilizations. Brown argued that Britons and Anglo-Saxons had been enslaved races at different times in history and that the white man was presently enslaved in the South through his slave children. The speech marks the beginning of Brown's interest in documenting African American history.

Sometime in 1860 after the death of Betsey Schooner, Brown married Annie Elizabeth Gray, with whom he spent the rest of his life. Tragically both of their children, including a girl named Clotelle, died while quite young. During this period of misfortune Brown found time to study medicine, and by the end of the Civil War he became comfortable enough with his knowledge to write "MD" after his name. Brown's writing also seemed to change, shifting from the realm of literature to his new concerns with sociology and history. Possibly, Brown's most important accomplishment was as an early historian of African American culture.

Brown felt strongly about the importance of African Americans in American society, and he set out to dispel the false notion that Africans were naturally inferior to European races. In *The Black Man; His Antecedents, His Genius, and His Achievements* (1863), Brown highlights African Americans who were able to overcome their oppressive environment and rise to positions of prominence. After the end of the Civil War Brown pushed further for

African American representation in American history by publishing *The Negro in the American Revolution: His Heroism and His Fidelity* (1867) and what is perhaps his most important historical work, *The Rising Son; or, The Antecedents and Advancement of the Colored Race* (1873), which records the lives of over one hundred African Americans in short biographical form.

During his final years Brown continued to travel and write vigorously. He became intrigued with the recent changes in the South and in 1879 decided to visit the former slave states to compare the struggles of the Southern freedman with his recollections of slave life. His final published work, *My Southern Home: or, The South and Its People* (1880), is rich in poetry, folk songs, and etchings of Southern life and was popular with both critics and the public. The volume sold well and was in its fourth edition by 1884, keeping Brown in the public eye until his death. The first half of *My Southern Home* deals with Southern slave life, both as Brown had experienced it and as he had gleaned from his conversations with other slaves. While he repeats many of the stories from his previous works, Brown gives the reader a fuller historical context than he previously attempted. The final portion of the book is a critical account of Brown's visits to the South in the winter of 1879–1880, "where the incidents were jotted down at the time of their occurrence."

In *My Southern Home* Brown points out the unjust laws and government apathy that limited African Americans to a status similar to that under slavery. Conditions were often no better than when slaves had been working for a brutal master. A former slave from Arkansas told Brown how little African American workers could expect for their labor:

> Since about '68, we've been getting about two bits a day—that's twenty cents. Then there are some people that work by the month, and at the end of the month they are either put off or cheated out of their money entirely.

Others told him "the taxes and rent are so heavy that the children have to work when they are as young as ten years" and that they were kept from voting or from getting "any schooling from the public schools."

Brown, though, does not place the blame solely on the white oppressors. Although he sees many African American farmers in Alabama who settle their debt "the moment they are in a position to do sò" and many women who work hard to get ahead and save, Brown is dismayed by the many

African Americans who "never stop buying until their money is exhausted" and run "from store to store" squandering their funds on gaudy, "unserviceable" clothing. He calls for African Americans to "cultivate self-denial" and achieve "a higher standard of moral, social, and literary culture" so that a unified effort can "remove the dark shadow of ignorance that now covers the land." Brown did not think African Americans should flee the South to escape Southern oppression; instead, he believed the South was the home of African Americans "by common right." His call for a unified African American voice and purpose in *My Southern Home* is still considered by many the key to African American empowerment.

In late October 1884 Brown was confined to his home in Chelsea, where he died of a bladder tumor on the afternoon of 6 November. He had risen from slavery to become a tireless worker for the causes of abolition and prohibition and the first important African American historian, novelist, and travel writer. His long journey inspired many African Americans and opened the eyes of whites on two continents to the evils of slavery. His works provide an important perspective on American and European culture in the nineteenth century.

Biographies:

Josephine Brown, *Biography of an American Bondman, By His Daughter* (Boston: R. F. Walcutt, 1856);

William Edward Farrison, *William Wells Brown: Author and Reformer* (Chicago & London: University Press of Chicago, 1969);

L. H. Whelchel Jr., *My Chains Fell Off: William Wells Brown, Fugitive Abolitionist* (Lanham, Md.: University Press of America, 1985).

References:

William H. Andrews, "Mark Twain, William Wells Brown, and the Problem of Authority in New South Writing," in *Southern Literature and Literary Theory,* edited by Jefferson Humphries (Athens: University of Georgia Press, 1990), p.p. 1–21;

Curtis W. Ellison, *William Wells Brown and Martin R. Delany: A Reference Guide* (Boston: G. K. Hall, 1978);

J. Noel Heermance, *William Wells Brown and Clotelle: A Portrait of the Artist in the First Negro Novel* (Hamden, Conn.: Archon, 1969);

Vernon Loggins, *The Negro Author: His Development in America to 1900* (New York: New York University Press, 1971).

Papers:

Small collections of Brown's papers are located at George Arents Research Library at Syracuse University; Boston Public Library; Butler Library, Columbia University; Enoch Pratt Free Library in Baltimore; the Schomberg Center for Research in Black Culture of the New York Public Library; Houghton Library, Harvard University; the Historical Society of Pennsylvania; and the Passport Division, United States Department of State.

Fanny Calderón de la Barca

(23 December 1804 – 6 February 1882)

Linda Ledford-Miller
University of Scranton

BOOKS: *Life in Mexico during a Residence of Two Years in That Country,* 2 volumes (Boston: Little, Brown, 1843 / London: Chapman & Hall, 1843;

The Attaché in Madrid; or, Sketches of the Court of Isabella II. Translated from the German, anonymous (New York: Appleton, 1856).

Edition: *Life in Mexico: The Letters of Fanny Calderón de la Barca,* annotated (Garden City, N.Y.: Doubleday, 1966).

OTHER: "The Italian Drama," anonymous, *North American Review,* 39 (October 1834): 329–370.

Fanny Calderón de la Barca's renown rests upon a single book, *Life in Mexico during a Residence of Two Years in That Country* (1843). It is based on her experiences in Mexico when she accompanied her husband, Angel Calderón de la Barca, on his diplomatic mission from 1839 to 1842 as the first Spanish envoy after Mexico had won its independence from Spain in 1821. Guadalupe Appendini is one of many who consider it "el mejor libro que sobre Mexico haya escrito un extranjero" (the best book on Mexico written by a foreigner).

Born Frances Erskine Inglis on 23 December 1804 in Edinburgh, Scotland, Fanny was the fifth child of what was to be a family of ten children—six daughters and four sons. Her father, William Inglis, was a Writer to the Signet, a special branch of the legal profession in Scotland; her mother, Jane Stein, was an Erskine and consequently related to several noble Scottish families. Inglis's education included a thorough knowledge of French as well as travel in Italy.

When Inglis's father was forced to declare bankruptcy in 1828, the family moved to Normandy, where he died in 1830. His widow moved to Boston with four of her daughters, Fanny among them, and several grandchildren and opened a school. Owing perhaps to the reputation for excellence of Scottish schoolteachers, the school was

Fanny Calderón de la Barca

quite successful at first. It struggled after the appearance of an anonymous satire, purportedly coauthored by Inglis, that caricatured prominent Bostonians, who had sponsored an elaborate charity bazaar.

The family looked for a new location in which to earn their living and in 1835 moved to the village of New Brighton on Staten Island, where some time later Inglis met her future husband. Angel Calderón de la Barca was born in 1790 of Spanish parents in Buenos Aires, Argentina, then a Spanish colony. Educated in England from childhood, he was forty-

43

eight years old by the time he married Inglis (she was thirty-three), had been a prisoner of war of the French, and had served diplomatic missions in Germany and Russia. Married on 24 September 1838, they lived in Washington, where Angel Calderón was the Spanish minister to the United States during the presidency of Martin Van Buren (1837–1841).

The Calderóns together had a wide experience of different cultures. Each had negotiated daily life in more than one nonnative language prior to Angel Calderón's next assignment in the unknown country to the South. On 27 October 1839 the Calderóns set sail for Mexico, where Angel was to be Spain's first emissary to independent Mexico. On that same date Fanny Calderón's letters begin.

Life in Mexico during a Residence of Two Years in That Country is composed of fifty-four letters dated from 27 October 1839 to 28 April 1842. Written to friends and family without any intention of future publication, Calderón's letters are candid and charming and detail an important period in Mexican history. Indeed, the letters so impressed the Calderóns's friend William Hickling Prescott (known as the author of a well-received book on the Catholic sovereigns Ferdinand and Isabella) that he urged her to publish them. His subsequent book, *History of the Conquest of Mexico* (1843), profited from both Fanny Calderón's letters and the Calderóns' research efforts in Mexico on his behalf, as Prescott himself did not visit Mexico prior to publishing the book for which he is still best remembered.

The letters first appeared in 1843, published in nearly simultaneous editions in the United States and Britain. The British edition owes its appearance to the intervention of Prescott, who wrote to Charles Dickens asking for his help in finding a publisher for *Life in Mexico*. Dickens obliged by recommending it to his own publisher. Prescott not only wrote the preface to the book but also published a supportive review in the *North American Review*. Reception in the United States was highly favorable. One reviewer in the February 1843 issue of *The United States Magazine and Democratic Review* recommended the book as an antidote to American stereotypes of Mexicans: "[these letters] must and will be read, and so far as read will tend to dissipate many of our errors concerning our Mexican neighbors, whom we are in the ungenerous habit of under-rating, and increase our respect for them." Reception in Britain was also positive, although at least one reviewer accused the author of embroidering a tale and of never having been in Mexico at all.

A few copies of *Life in Mexico* were circulating in Mexico, and the *Siglo Diez y Nueve* newspaper announced that it would serialize a Spanish translation. Some were concerned that Calderón had been aided by her husband, who was privy to potential secrets of state. The first four letters translated into Spanish appeared over a period of four weeks between 28 April and 26 May 1843. The fourth letter, on Veracruz, caused one reviewer to complain of Calderón's criticism and insults of Mexicans from that city. The fifth letter would have touched upon Gen. Antonio López de Santa Anna, then president and de facto dictator of Mexico. It was never published. The first complete Spanish translation of *Life in Mexico* was not published until 1920.

Sensitive to her husband's political position, Calderón published *Life in Mexico* somewhat anonymously, listing herself only as "Mme. C-------------- De La B-------------." It was also typical of women authors of the period to use a pseudonym or embrace anonymity. Most Mexican residents referred to in her letters are similarly listed by title and the first initial of the surname, although sometimes the surname is entered by first and last letter: Señora C---------a, for example. Many of the figures thus protected would have been immediately recognizable to many Mexicans of the time, but the modern reader must depend on the comprehensiveness of annotated editions in Spanish and English.

Calderón's fifty-four letters trace her travels by sea from New York to Havana, Cuba, to her first sight of Mexico at the coastal town of Veracruz and her travels by land from Veracruz to Mexico (to Mexicans, "Mexico" means the capital city). She describes her settling in first one house, then another, and details every facet of her daily life and that of many around her. She describes her many journeys around the country, observes at close hand two *pronunciamentos* (pronouncements), or small revolutions, and the change of power from one president to another. She witnesses the copper monetary crisis caused by rampant counterfeiting and suffers the travails of travel on horseback or in a stagecoach, subject to the heat, thunderstorms, and scorpions of tropical Mexico and the dangers of highwaymen who rob and murder with relative freedom. She attends and participates in many social, cultural, and religious functions both in the capital and in smaller towns and villages. When her husband is to be replaced by a new emissary from Spain, she records their leave-takings and their journey back to Veracruz and Havana, ending her last letter with her imminent arrival in the United States. And at every turn she describes the people, places, landscape, customs, beliefs, and history of the Mexican people with a painter's eye, a naturalist's skill of observation, and a fine sense of humor.

Calderón's home in Mexico City

As a foreigner and the wife of an important diplomat, Calderón had access to the most influential members of Mexican society and politics and was allowed entry into areas denied to most, perhaps especially to women. By special permission of the archbishop she was allowed to visit two convents, even though convents in this period were strictly cloistered. The dictum that a nun, as the bride of Christ, became "dead to the world" was strictly enforced. Parents who offered their daughters to a convent from religious motives (usually paying a dowry for her care and to benefit the convent) could expect to see their daughter no more. Calderón witnessed the ceremony of convent entry of at least three young girls. She records of the second ceremony that she "saw another girl sacrificed." At the third she testifies to the sorrow of the mother parting from her daughter: "All the sweet ties of nature had been rudely severed, and she had been forced to consign her . . . to a living tomb."

A Protestant married to a Catholic, Calderón describes religious practice in a Catholic country with an outsider's candor. She notes that religion is invoked for any and all causes, right or wrong, citing as examples the pulque shops (pulque is an alcoholic beverage made from the native maguey, an important commercial product of the period) that call themselves "Pulquerias of the Most Holy Virgin" and the gambling event held annually at Easter.

She memorably describes the public penitence called *desagravios,* held during a thirty-five-day pe-riod in August and September. Men and women do penitence separately, so Calderón attended with the women. She records their penance of kneeling "for about ten minutes with their arms extended in the form of a cross, uttering groans." She is able to observe the men's penance as well, her disguised presence made possible by "certain means, private but powerful." With the church plunged into darkness, she is shocked to hear about 150 men scourging themselves in a medieval imitation of the scourging of Christ. She finds the activity "perfectly sickening" and only by holding "Señora ---'s" hand can she avoid feeling "transported into a congregation of evil spirits."

Calderón and her husband made many friends among the clergy and nuns, including the archbishop. Indeed, if she were to choose to be one from among all the well-to-do people she knows in Mexico, she would choose the archbishop's situation, she says, for "he is a pope without the trouble, or the tenth part of the responsibility. He is venerated more than the Holy Father is in enlightened Rome, and, like kings in the good old times, can do no wrong." His salary is high; his table filled with the sweets sent by nuns; he lives in a palace; and he rides in a comfortable carriage. "In fact, comfort, which is unknown amongst the profane of Mexico, has taken refuge with the archbishop; and though many drops of it are shed on the shavenheads of all bishops, curates, confessors, and friars, still in his illustrious person it concentrates as in a focus." De-

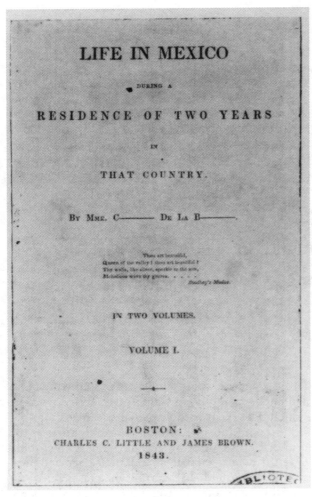

Title page for Calderón's first book, which includes her
commentary on Cuba as well as Mexico

spite both her overt and implied criticism of Catholicism, being steeped in the culture of a Catholic country surely had its effects, for on 10 May 1847 Calderón was accepted into the Catholic faith at Georgetown's Holy Trinity Church in Washington.

Calderón's letters relate much recent Mexican history. She comments that the revolutionary fervor that accompanied the declaration of independence led to the destruction of missions established by Jesuits (which were inherited by Dominicans after the Jesuits were expelled in 1767) and Franciscans. This action ultimately harmed its destroyers since the Indians who had once been governed by priests and friars were then free to invade Mexico's far-flung, unprotected borders. She explains the Plan of Iguala, which offered the three guarantees of "freedom, union, and religion . . . as security to the Spaniards," and lists the seventeen articles of the Treaty of Cordova, signed in 1821, creating the independent empire of Mexico headed by Augustín de Itur-

bide, whose empire was overthrown by army officers and replaced with a federal republic. She tells the story of La Malinche, Hernando Cortes's lover and interpreter, the first Christian in Mexico.

Calderón provides a brief history of Mexico's revolutions, beginning with the uprising of Dolores in 1810 and including the federalist revolution she witnessed in 1840 and Gen. Santa Anna's successful invasion of Mexico in 1842. Of the latter she says, "let them give everything whatever name is most popular, the government is now a military dictatorship." Gen. Santa Anna is "now Dictator or King, in all but name, [and] the conquerors and the conquered, those of the Progress, and those of the Dictatorship, seem all, barring a few noble exceptions, actuated by one motive; personal interest." She and her husband were personal friends of the ousted president, Anastasio Bustamente, but had no such friendship with Santa Anna.

Such openly expressed opinions would hardly have been popular in Mexico at the time. Antonio Acevedo Escobedo notes, "En todas las latitudes, los libros de memorias de viajeros de otra nacionalidad sobre determinado pais constituyen, de modo infalible, un depósito de materias inflamables, un motivo de scándalo" (At any latitude, memoirs by travelers of another nationality about a particular country infallibly constitute a reservoir of flammable material, a motive for scandal).

Responding to a relative's query, Calderón delineates the seven Mexican races which are supposed to be distinct: "lst, the Gapuchinos, or Spaniards born in Europe; 2nd, the Creoles, that is, whites of European family born in America; 3rd, the Mestizos [descendants of whites and Indians]; 4th, the Mulattoes, descendants of whites and negroes, of whom there are few; 5th, the Zambos, descendants of negroes and Indians, the ugliest race in Mexico; 6th, the Indians; and 7th, the remains of the African negroes." She attributes the sad state of the Indians to the conquest, in which most Indian nobles and priests were killed, leaving the remaining Indians to fall into "that state of ignorance and degradation, from which they have never emerged." Although maintaining class distinctions, Calderón was sympathetic to the plight of the poor. Obtaining special permissions, she visited a jail, a hospital, an insane asylum, and an orphanage. She believed that charity was practiced on a grander scale in Mexico than in any other country.

Calderón's letters reveal a Mexico seldom seen in the travel writings of others, and they reveal a woman who matures with her experiences. When she first encountered the typical Mexican hacienda, or ranch house, for example, she considered it a huge, empty structure. Not long before leaving Mexico she states that "the houses, which at first appeared gloomy, large, and comfortless, habit has reconciled us to, and experience has taught us that they are precisely suited to this climate of perpetual spring." She makes a similar remark about Veracruz's food and a more telling comment on the dangers of opinion: "Vera Cruz cookery, which two years ago I thought detestable, now appears to me delicious! . . . How necessary for a traveller to compare his judgments at different periods, and to correct them! First impressions are of great importance, if given only as such; but if laid down as decided opinions, how apt they are to be erroneous!"

Calderón spent the year following her Mexican sojourn in Europe visiting Scotland and living in Madrid until Angel Calderón was again appointed Spanish minister to the United States. After spending nine years in Washington the Calderóns returned to Madrid, where Angel was to be minister of foreign affairs. It was a period of political intrigue and upheaval that Fanny Calderón is said to have documented in *The Attaché in Madrid,* published in 1856 as the translation from German of the memoirs of an unnamed German diplomat.

The Calderóns were forced into exile in 1854, returning to Spain in 1856. Angel Calderón died in 1861, but Fanny Calderón continued her involvement in public life as the governess to the Infanta Isabel. She was rewarded with the title of Marquesa de Calderón de la Barca in 1876, in recognition of her husband's service as well as her own.

Calderón led an active life until the end; her death at the age of seventy-seven was swift and unexpected, the result of a cold that worsened rapidly. Though her marriage with Calderón was childless, *Life in Mexico during a Residence of Two Years in That Country* became her legacy and has been republished often. In 1959 a new Spanish translation became the first edition to be annotated. An extensively annotated and illustrated edition in English was published in 1966, and included new material taken from the two extant private journals of the three she had kept while in Mexico. Calderón's letters in *Life in Mexico* continue to provide the "rich stores of instruction and amusement" Prescott recommended to the reading public of 1843.

References:

Guadalupe Appendini, *La vida en México en 1840* (Mexico City: Departmento del Distrito Federal, Secretaria de Obras y Servicios, 1974);

Henry Baerlein, Introduction, in *Life in Mexico During a Residence of Two Years in That Country* (London: Dent; New York: Dutton, 1913), pp. vii–xxii;

Woodrow Borah, Introduction, in *Life In Mexico* (Berkeley: University of California Press, 1982), pp. 5–8;

Antonio Acevedo Escobedo, Prologue, in *La Vida en México* (Mexico City: Secretaria de Educación Pública, 1944);

Howard T. Fisher and Marion Hall Fisher, Introduction, and "First Appearance of Life in Mexico; Early Comments; Subsequent History," in *Life in Mexico: The Letters of Fanny Calderón de la Barca* (Garden City, N.Y.: Doubleday, 1966), pp. xxi–xxix, 629–636;

Sonja Karsen, "An Interpretation of Frances Calderón de la Barca's *Life in Mexico During a Residence of Two Years in That Country,*" *Revista Interamericana de Bibliografía/Inter-American Review of Bibliography,* 39, no. 2 (1989): 195–201;

Richard Sterne, "A Mexican Flower in Rappaccini's Garden: Madame Calderón de la Barca's *Life in Mexico* Revisited," *Nathaniel Hawthorne Journal,* 74 (1974): 277–279;

Felipe Teixidor, Prologue, in *La vida en México durante una residencia de dos años es ese país,* (Mexico City: Porrúa, 1967), pp. vii–lxvii;

Molly Marie Wood, "A Search for Identity: Frances Calderón de la Barca and *Life in Mexico.*" M.A. thesis, University of Richmond, 1992.

James Fenimore Cooper

(15 September 1789 – 14 September 1851)

Jared Gardner
Grinnell College

See also the Cooper entry in *DLB 3: Antebellum Writers in New York and the South.*

BOOKS: *Precaution,* anonymous, 2 volumes (New York: Goodrich, 1820; London: Colburn, 1821);

The Spy, anonymous, 2 volumes (New York: Wiley & Halstead, 1821; London: Whittaker, 1822);

The Pioneers, anonymous, 2 volumes (New York: Wiley / London: John Murray, 1823);

Tales for Fifteen, as Jane Morgan (New York: Wiley, 1823);

The Pilot, anonymous, 2 volumes (New York: Wiley, 1823; London: Miller, 1824);

Lionel Lincoln, anonymous, 2 volumes (New York: Wiley, 1824–1825);

The Last of the Mohicans, anonymous, 2 volumes (Philadelphia: Carey & Lea / London: Miller, 1826);

The Prairie, anonymous (3 volumes, London: Colburn / 2 volumes, Philadelphia: Carey, Lea & Carey, 1827);

The Red Rover, anonymous (3 volumes, Paris: Bossange / 2 volumes, London: Colburn, 1827; 2 volumes, Philadelphia: Carey, Lea & Carey, 1828);

Notions of the Americans, anonymous, 2 volumes (London: Colburn / Philadelphia: Carey, Lea & Carey, 1828);

The Borderers, anonymous, 3 volumes (London: Colburn & Bentley, 1829); republished as *The Wept of Wish-Ton-Wish,* 2 volumes (Philadelphia: Carey, Lea & Carey, 1829);

The Water-Witch, anonymous (3 volumes, Dresden: Walther / 2 volumes, London: Colburn & Bentley, 1830; 1 volume, Philadelphia: Carey & Lea, 1831);

The Bravo, anonymous (3 volumes, London: Colburn & Bentley / 2 volumes, Philadelphia: Carey & Lea, 1831);

James Fenimore Cooper in 1822, portrait by John W. Jarvis (Yale University Art Gallery; gift of Edward S. Harkness)

The Heidenmauer, anonymous (3 volumes, London: Colburn & Bentley / 2 volumes, Philadelphia: Carey & Lea, 1832);

The Headsman (3 volumes, London: Bentley / 2 volumes, Philadelphia: Carey, Lea & Blanchard, 1833);

A Letter to His Countrymen (New York: Wiley / London: Miller, 1834);

The Monikins, anonymous (3 volumes, London: Bentley / 2 volumes, Philadelphia: Carey, Lea & Blanchard, 1835);

Sketches of Switzerland (Philadelphia: Carey, Lea & Blanchard, 1836); republished as *Excursions in Switzerland* (London: Bentley, 1836);

A Residence in France; with an Excursion up the Rhine, and a Second Visit to Switzerland, 2 volumes (London: Bentley, 1836); republished as *Sketches of Switzerland . . . Part Second,* 2 volumes (Philadelphia: Carey, Lea & Blanchard, 1836);

Recollections of Europe, 2 volumes (London: Bentley, 1837); republished as *Gleanings in Europe,* 2 volumes (Philadelphia: Carey, Lea & Blanchard, 1837);

England, 2 volumes (London: Bentley, 1837); republished as *Gleanings in Europe. England,* 2 volumes (Philadelphia: Carey, Lea & Blanchard, 1837);

Excursions in Italy, 2 volumes (London: Bentley, 1838); republished as *Gleanings in Europe. Italy,* 2 volumes (Philadelphia: Carey, Lea & Blanchard, 1838);

The American Democrat (Cooperstown, N.Y.: H. & E. Phinney, 1838);

Homeward Bound, anonymous (3 volumes, London: Bentley / 2 volumes, Philadelphia: Carey, Lea & Blanchard, 1838);

Home as Found, 2 volumes (Philadelphia: Lea & Blanchard, 1838); republished as *Eve Effingham* (London: Bentley, 1838);

The Chronicles of Cooperstown (Cooperstown, N.Y.: H. & E. Phinney, 1838);

The History of the Navy of the United States of America, 2 volumes (Philadelphia: Lea & Blanchard / London: Bentley, 1839);

The Pathfinder, anonymous (3 volumes, London: Bentley / 2 volumes, Philadelphia: Lea & Blanchard, 1840);

Mercedes of Castille, anonymous, 2 volumes (Philadelphia: Lea & Blanchard, 1840; London: Bentley, 1841);

The Deerslayer, anonymous, 2 volumes (Philadelphia: Lea & Blanchard / London: Bentley, 1841);

The Two Admirals (3 volumes, London: Bentley / anonymous, 2 volumes, Philadelphia: Lea & Blanchard, 1842);

The Jack O'Lantern, 3 volumes (London: Bentley, 1842); republished as *The Wing-and-Wing,* anonymous, 2 volumes (Philadelphia: Lea & Blanchard, 1842);

Le Mouchoir (New York: Wilson, 1843); republished as *The French Governess* (London: Bentley, 1843);

The Battle of Lake Erie (Cooperstown: H. & E. Phinney, 1843);

Wyandotté (3 volumes, London: Bentley / anonymous, 2 volumes, Philadelphia: Lea & Blanchard, 1843);

Ned Myers (2 volumes, London: Bentley / Philadelphia: Lea & Blanchard, 1843);

Afloat and Ashore, anonymous (3 volumes, London: Bentley / 2 volumes, Philadelphia: Published by the Author, 1844);

Lucy Hardinge, 3 volumes (London: Bentley, 1844); republished as volumes 3 and 4 of *Afloat and Ashore* (Philadelphia: Published by the Author, 1844);

Satanstoe (3 volumes, London: Bentley / New York: Burgess, Stringer, 1845);

The Chainbearer, anonymous (3 volumes, London: Bentley / 2 volumes, New York: Burgess, Stringer, 1845);

Lives of Distinguished American Naval Officers, 2 volumes (Philadelphia: Carey & Hart, 1846);

Ravensnest, anonymous, 3 volumes (London: Bentley, 1846); republished as *The Redskins,* 2 volumes (New York: Burgess, Stringer, 1846);

Mark's Reef, anonymous, 3 volumes (London: Bentley, 1847); republished as *The Crater,* 2 volumes (New York: Burgess, Stringer, 1847);

Captain Spike, 3 volumes (London: Bentley, 1848); republished as *Jack Tier,* anonymous, 2 volumes (New York: Burgess, Stringer, 1848);

The Bee Hunter, anonymous, 3 volumes (London: Bentley, 1848); republished as *The Oak Openings,* 2 volumes (New York: Burgess, Stringer, 1848);

The Sea Lions, anonymous (3 volumes, London: Bentley / 2 volumes, New York: Stringer & Townsend, 1849);

The Ways of an Hour, anonymous (New York: Putnam / London: Bentley, 1850);

New York, edited by Dixon Ran Fox (New York: Payson, 1932);

The Lake Gun, edited by Robert E. Spiller (New York: Payson, 1932);

Early Critical Essays, 1820–1822, edited by James Franklin Beard (Gainesville, Fla.: Scholars' Facsimiles & Reprints, 1955).

Collection: *Cooper's Novels,* 32 volumes (New York: Townsend, 1859–1861).

James Fenimore Cooper sailed for Europe with his family on 1 June 1826 for a projected five-year visit. He left New York with the multiple aims of securing favorable European publication agreements for his works, furthering the education of his children, and recovering his health, which

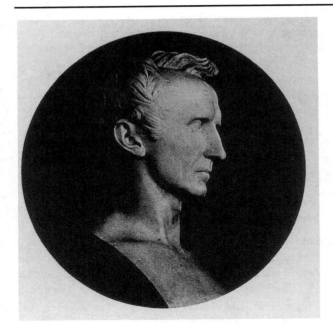

Bust of Cooper by P.J. David d'Angers, made in Paris in 1828

had been taxed by his grueling pace of production during the first half of the decade. On all of these scores his sojourn, which lasted seven years, proved successful, as he was able to negotiate with British, French, and German publishers for good terms for *The Prairie* (1827) and subsequent novels, find tutors for his children, and improve his constitution. Somewhat unexpectedly, he also found that his reputation had preceded him, and his successes as a novelist brought him into contact with European society to a degree unusual for Americans abroad. But Cooper's series of five travel books, which he wrote after his return to America, would ultimately contribute to the decline of his popular reputation at home and abroad.

James Cooper (he added his mother's maiden name in 1826) was born in Burlington, New Jersey, on 15 September 1789 to William Cooper and Elizabeth Fenimore Cooper. He was brought at the age of thirteen months to his family's manorial estate in Cooperstown, New York, a town founded on the shore of Otsego Lake by his father. Educated in Burlington, Cooperstown, and Albany, Cooper was thirteen when he entered Yale. He was dismissed from the school in his third year because of a prank and took to the sea, sailing to Europe before the mast in 1806–1807 and later serving several years in the U.S. Navy. Cooper married Susan Augusta Delancey on 1 January 1811; their seven children—five daughters and two sons—were born by the early 1820s. Cooper began his literary career in 1820 with *Precaution,* a novel of manners.

From 1821 to 1826 he established his reputation as a novelist of the American wilderness and the sea, publishing *The Spy* (1821), *The Pioneers* (1823), *The Pilot* (1824), *Lionel Lincoln* (1824–1825), and *The Last of the Mohicans* (1826).

Cooper found his European popularity both flattering and uncomfortable, as he was from the moment he left America's shores keenly aware of how easily his reputation might be besmirched by too much contact with European finery. He worked hard throughout his first residence in Paris from 1826 to 1828 to limit his encounters with society and thus maintain his reputation as a patriotic American, yet he would become increasingly involved in French life and culture during his two subsequent stays in the capital. During his European sojourn, Cooper would also visit England, Switzerland, Italy, and Germany. Throughout his time abroad Cooper worked hard at his profession, and the extent of his travels is all the more remarkable when one considers that his sightseeing was performed after long days' work on the books he wrote in whole or in part while in Europe, including *The Prairie, Notions of the Americans* (1828), *The Red Rover* (1828), *The Wept of Wish-Ton-Wish* (1829), *The Water-Witch* (1830), *The Bravo* (1831), *The Heidenmauer* (1832), and *The Headsman* (1833).

Early on, Cooper conceived of his travels in Europe as source material for future books, and two years after his return from Europe in 1833 he began the process of turning his journal notes into *Sketches of Switzerland* (1836), the first of five epistolary travel narratives that were published in the years 1836–1838. The book is a record of the family's travels in Switzerland between 14 July and 15 October 1828. Cooper's manifest intent is to create word paintings that capture the breathtaking beauty and effects of the Swiss mountains and landscape. The political and social theorizing that dominate the subsequent volumes is relatively muted in *Sketches of Switzerland,* and it is clearly with an eye toward making his own contribution to the picturesque tradition that Cooper devoted himself in inaugurating his series.

"I have no idea of boring mankind with statistics, and dry essays on Politics," Cooper wrote on 11 March 1828 to his American publishers, Carey, Lea and Carey, "but to give only, rapid sketches of what I shall see, with *American* eyes." Having purportedly written *Notions of the Americans* to educate Europeans on the "true" facts and conditions of America, he conceived of his series of travel books to make his own countrymen see clearly the conditions of Europe. In *Sketches of Switzerland* the education is primarily aesthetic as

Cooper guides his reader carefully through the proper responses and estimations of the natural world's beauties. This was to be Cooper's book from abroad written specifically "for America," "the first of a series written especially for my own Countrymen."

Cooper had been mistakenly optimistic about the success of *Notions of the Americans* in the United States. The long delay in publishing his travel narratives upon his return from Europe is accounted for in large measure by its failure as well as the hostile response of the conservative American Whig press to his European trilogy—*The Bravo, The Heidenmauer,* and *The Headsman*—all of which drew heavily on the historical and political landscapes of his travels. Cooper's studied avoidance of the topical and political in favor of the natural in *Sketches of Switzerland* can be seen as an attempt to recover a reputation he was beginning to find difficult to maintain, especially after the failure of his most recent fiction, the Swiftian satire *The Monikins* (1835), in which Cooper describes an imaginary journey among the sentient monkeys who inhabit the nations of Leaphigh and Leaplow, representing England and America, respectively. The novel is an extended and occasionally vicious attack on both British aristocracy and American boorishness.

As Cooper turned to his own travels for works of nonfiction on his return to New York, he had every reason to avoid political subjects. By the time he began publishing accounts of his travels he was feeling an increasing sense of alienation from his own country and, simultaneously, a deepening sense of his own antimonarchical political convictions as a result of his experiences abroad. In *Sketches of Switzerland* it is almost as if he wished to recapture the optimism and innocence lost in the political imbroglios that consumed much of his energy in the 1830s.

Despite the deliberate avoidance of controversy in *Sketches of Switzerland,* Cooper's correspondence from his 1828 Switzerland visit makes it clear that political issues, American and European, were very much on his mind. Writing to his longtime friend, Luther Bradish, on 16 August 1828 from his Bern residence before beginning his second trip into the countryside, Cooper discussed these concerns at length, noting the rising instability in Europe and worrying about the increasing threats of disunion at home, even speculating as to the English machinations in the recent tensions in South Carolina: "That England will, if she does not now, make powerful efforts in secret to divide the States, I think no man who calmly regards the question, and

remembers her uniform course of policy can doubt."

In the same letter Cooper spells out what would become the underlying aims of *Sketches of Switzerland* several years later, an agenda that was clearly on his mind from the start. Cooper believed that two of the greatest dangers facing the republic were the misconceptions of Europeans, especially the British, regarding the United States, and the misconceptions of Americans regarding Europe—especially European opinion *of* America. The first of these he hoped to have solved with *Notions of the Americans,* the fictional travels of a British bachelor who corrects the errors and prejudices of contemporary British narratives about the United States. Cooper hoped his own travels in Europe would allow him to correct the second of these dangers, which he saw as becoming more pressing every day:

> I wish to God that our countrymen . . . could get an opportunity of knowing the real opinion of these people . . . We never shall get to be the thoroughly manly people we ought to be and might be, until we cease to look to European opinions for anything except those which are connected with the general advancement of the race . . . This truckling to foreigners and eagerness to know what other nations think of us, is a fault that always disgusted me when at home, but it is a hundredfold more disgusting now that I know how utterly *worthless* are the opinions they republish.

Beginning with *Sketches of Switzerland,* Cooper worked to disabuse Americans of their flattering conception of their status in European eyes, pointing out that most Europeans conceive of Americans as little more than savages, criminals, or slaves.

Moreover—and it is here that Cooper began to find himself in trouble with his American readers—Cooper also wished to educate Americans about European landscape and aesthetics to convey a more worldly and *relative* appreciation of the merits and defects of the United States. At almost every turn in *Sketches of Switzerland* Cooper pauses to compare something Swiss—a mountain, an inn, and even the Swiss women of various cantons—to its American counterpart. His aim was twofold: first, to teach Americans how better to appreciate their own natural resources beyond mere utility and profit, and, second, to curb an unfortunate American tendency toward ignorant braggadocio as far as the rest of the "civilized world" was concerned.

For the most part Cooper's lessons are gentle and favorable to American pride. But as the book progresses, the tone of the lessons becomes somewhat overbearing. There is, as many readers of the time discerned, a tendency to repeat ad nauseam the terms of the cult of the picturesque, spelling out with a painful deliberation, as a reviewer in the 31 May 1836 issue of *Waldie's Journal of Belles Letters* put it, "what does or does not add to the picturesque." Cooper's enthusiasm for the landscape and the picturesque convention of bringing the painter's tools to the written description of landscape is everywhere apparent, and his attempt to educate his countrymen into the proper appreciation of the landscape and its effects is occasionally patronizing. By the second half of the volume, Cooper is finding less and less to compare favorably on behalf of things American, and he frequently vents his frustration about ignorance being so often mistaken for patriotism.

Sketches of Switzerland initially seems to have little in the way of narrative organization beyond the chronology of the four tours—the first two taken with his wife, his eldest daughter, Susan, and his nephew and secretary, William Cooper, and the last two accompanied only by a Swiss guide. Comparing the book to the journal entries he meticulously maintained during each trip shows that Cooper scarcely altered the chronology. Yet there is a larger shadow of a narrative, not present in the journal entries, which Cooper allowed to intrude into his book. The persona he creates moves from wide-eyed helplessness and wonder in the face of a nature more miraculous and awesome than any he had encountered before to a perspective more worthy of a worldly and independent explorer of the sublime. In addition there is a more surprising but significant shift in tone from the beginning to the end. As if foreshadowing a decline that awaited Cooper, Europe, and America, the landscape, which initially evokes emotions ranging from tearful wonder to sylvan delight, carries with it by the end, as the Coopers prepare for their autumn excursion into Italy (the subject of the fifth published volume), signals of a coming darkness and inevitable decay.

Such shifts in tone, however, are subtle at best, and Cooper's novel readers turning to his Switzerland volume for a compelling story were inevitably disappointed. Cooper wrote looking back on his journal entries, which were themselves sparse but regular, embellishing his descriptions and recovering his more poetic sensations through memory. His journal entry for 1 September 1828 is typical of the material he had to work from when he sat down to write the book seven years later:

Ascent. Rigi Staffe[l.]. Glorious view. Ascent. Fissure in the mountain. Prussian Nobleman 2 years ago. English servant, General &c–Rigi Kulm. Society. Auberge. Supper. Sheets. Blust[er]ing germans.

The published account of these scenes and events in *Sketches of Switzerland* takes up many pages, and what is in the journal described simply as "Glorious view" becomes one of the central scenes of the book:

> For myself, I can fairly say, that, the occasion of a total eclipse of the sun excepted, I never felt so deep a sentiment of admiration and awe, as at that exquisite moment. So greatly did reality exceed the pictures we had formed, that the surprise was as complete as if nothing had been expected. The first effect was really bewildering, leaving behind it a vague sensation, that the eye had strangely assembled the rarest elements of scenery, which were floating before it, without order, in pure wantonness. To this feeling, the indefinite form of the lake of Lucerne greatly contributed, for it stretches out its numerous arms in so many different directions, as, at first, to appear like water in the unreal forms of the fancy. Volumes of mist were rolling swiftly along it, at the height of about two thousand feet above its surface, and of as many below ourselves, allowing us to look through its openings, in a way to aid the illusion.

This description epitomizes Cooper's practice in *Sketches of Switzerland*. As the passage suggests he hungrily sought out among the Alps those scenes that lent themselves to a painterly approach and emphasized the effects of the landscape before its details. The concrete observations of the mist and the arms of the lake seem entirely in the service of the effects they produce in the viewer, "contribut[ing]" to the "feeling[s]" and "aid[ing]" the "illusion" being described. While Cooper was interested in creating a useful tool for subsequent travelers and included the results of his historical research and precise information about the conditions of inns and towns, his main intent was in providing a guide not to the best hotel but to the best effects—to where in this rugged landscape the proper combination of shapes, size, textures, and lights and darks might evoke the sublime or the picturesque. In recounting his surprise (or occasionally, his disappointment) in what he finds at a particular turn in the mountain roads Cooper was suggesting to his reader not only where these effects might be found but how they should be appreciated when discovered, whether in Switzerland or in Otsego County, New York.

Such moments are repeated throughout the book, and in each case Cooper carefully sets up the narrative—usually around an elaborate ascent—to emphasize dramatically the awe inspired by the scene. As he says in the preface, "The narrative form is the best for a book of travels, for, besides possessing the most interest, it enables the reader to understand the circumstances under which one, who appears as a witness, had obtained his facts." Taking the reader through a scene, Cooper used his narrative skills to transform his prosaic journal entries into scenes of picturesque tension in which the encounter with the scene provides the reader an experience corresponding to that of the narrator.

Cooper does strain himself somewhat in coming up with new ways of setting up these encounters as the book progresses, and he is aware that he risks losing the effect of subsequent picturesque passages because of the enthusiasm of those preceding: "You have read so much already of surprises and of the effects of the extraordinary and unexpected scenery, that I almost fear to recur to the subject," he writes his imaginary correspondent of the Brünig pass. "But the truth will not be said unless I tell you this was *the* surprise, before all others."

In addition to his primary task of instructing his reader in the picturesque worldview Cooper takes on some secondary roles, most prominent of which is that of the amateur ethnographer studying the differences in "national characteristics":

> During the drive back, I counted the proportion of light haired people again, including all whom we met or passed. The whole number was one hundred and ten. Of these ninety-seven had hair of the different shades that make auburn, from the very light brown to the very fair. None had red hair, and scarcely any black. In France, I still think the proportion would have been the other way.

Cooper is in part having some fun with the long tradition of European travels in America that sought to discover the peculiarities and national oddities of the "American people," as he turns some of these same terms back on his European hosts. Throughout this book and those following, nothing seems to motivate Cooper's ire more than the many scenes, recounted in painful detail, in which he encounters European misconceptions about who and what Americans are. The book abounds with accounts of the slights he experiences because of his national identity. He had come to Europe expecting that his American name would be a "passport" to European society and instead found it to be a kind of scarlet letter. Many of the scenes of European rudeness are meant to be humorous, as the several episodes in which he encounters the supposedly popular misconception that all Americans are "black as coal." But Cooper does not take these anti-American prejudices lightly, and he serves notice to his countrymen as to the true sentiments of Europe regarding them.

Cooper is also critical of his own country, especially of its commercialism, often focusing on scenes that remind him of a lost purity in America. He describes a Swiss tavern that recalls to him

> the old fashioned, quiet, Dutch inns that once existed on the Mohawk; and which were as much superior to their noisy, tobacco-chewing, whisky-drinking, dirty, Yankee successors, as cleanliness, stability, and sour-crout can be superior to the system in which a day may commence with a settlement, and end with a removal. How loathsome is a state of society that reduces the feelings of neighborhood, religion, veneration for the past, hopes for the future, country, kindred, and friends, to the level of a speculation!

Cooper's critique of the speculating spirit and particularly of the instability of American communities is consistent in this book, and indeed Cooper had registered such criticism as early as *The Pioneers*. But the sight in Switzerland of picturesque yeomen firmly rooted to the land brought Cooper's bitterness toward the new class of speculating "pioneers" to the surface with a peculiar vehemence. As he remarks about a particularly comfortable and affordable inn, "There is a satisfaction, in finding that a grasping cupidity has not penetrated to a spot like this, that has no connexion with the purse."

While the first half of *Sketches of Switzerland* records the innocence of the Swiss in their proper relation to the land and the unparalleled sublimity of the landscape, the second half reveals the signs of decay and desolation that intrude into the narrator's view, eventually driving him and his family from this Alpine wonderland into the more political world of the subsequent volumes. The beggars that begin appearing lead Cooper to comment "that the great influx of strangers is rapidly demoralizing the country. . . . Men are so constructed that they will turn the picturesque into profit, and even women too."

After Cooper strikes out on his own in his third and fourth trips, the sight of his fellow man brings him increasingly to despair: "I know not how it is, the littlenesses one meets with among these sublime mountains occasion more disgust than they do in tamer countries." He begins to find his fellow men repulsive. This feeling culminates in a disturbing encounter during the Coopers's exodus from Switzerland into Italy with a description of a "race of miserable objects called *Crétins,* beings possessing the most disgusting likeness to our species, of which they are physical abortions, but deprived in a great

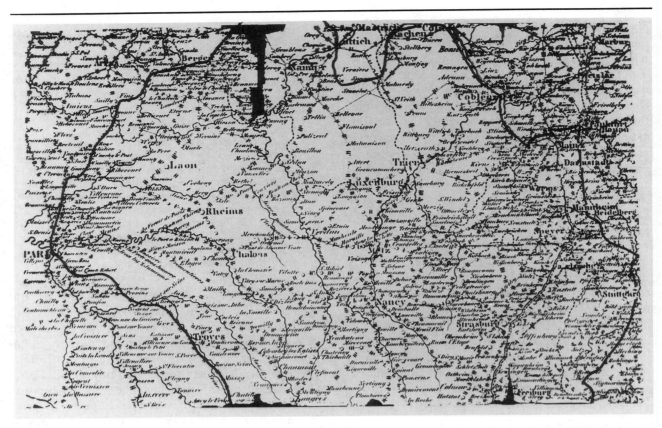

Cooper's travels in 1832, marked on a map from Julius Bernard Engelmann and Heinrich August Ottokar Reichard's Manuel pour les Voyageurs en Allemagne et dans les Pays Limitrophes *(1827), a guidebook Cooper carried with him in Europe*

degree of reason." Cooper's overwhelming disgust with the Crétins leads him to spell out a subtext for the whole book: anxiety over the potential degeneration of mankind.

Toward the end of the book the landscape also turns ominous, especially after Cooper encounters the desolation of Goldau, a Swiss village that had been destroyed in the collapse of two miles of mountain strata twenty years earlier. The tales of the destructive potential of the landscape bring about a notable shift in Cooper's attitude, as the scenes of wonder give way to a somewhat combative relation to the landscape. Cooper transforms himself in the final journey from a passive witness awed by the land to a pioneer striking out to conquer it: "I turned to my maps and guide books with a good deal of curiosity, in order to ascertain, if, after having reaped the honour of discovering a mountain, it was not now to be my good fortune to discover a country!"

Although he is playful in his references to himself as a pioneer, Cooper takes seriously his new role as pathfinder rather than follower in his fourth expedition into the "great nucleus of the Alps." As the narrator becomes an active agent, the first-person voice begins to dominate. When his solitary expedition comes to an end, Cooper describes seeing the Jungfrau, the unconquered mountain which had greeted him and his family on their entrance into Switzerland, now bearing a flag that indicates to the world that the "virgin mountain" had at last been conquered. This victory belongs to Swiss mountaineers, yet Cooper seems to invite the obvious association.

For all his shying away from politics in *Sketches of Switzerland,* Cooper found that much of the reviewers' attentions were devoted to the comparatively few pages in which he touched on such matters rather than the vast majority that concerns the natural world. In the book Cooper critiques the confederacy system of government and is critical of Federalism and all Americans who would return the nation to a monarchical system. But Cooper's emphasis on nature clearly is intended to diminish the central political debates of his day, including slavery. He describes two Englishmen debating West Indian slavery, one a "philanthropist" and the other an advocate of the slave system, setting the scene against the backdrop of the mountains to dismiss as ludicrous the debate that was at the time bringing his own country ever closer to civil war.

In the preface to *Sketches of Switzerland* Cooper seems to anticipate—and perhaps to have precipitated—the negative response of some American reviewers. He criticizes both parties in the United States, savages the press, and claims for himself the moral high ground from which to observe and write about the petty party politics of the day. It is certainly easy to see why the casual reader might be confused as to Cooper's political sensibilities. As in his novels he offers a fierce defense of democracy and a critique of aristocratic government at home and abroad, while at the same time he is fascinated by the nobility and the rites of European high society. This perceived contradiction fed the criticism of the book, and it was attacked both for its rabble-rousing democraticism and for its supposed worship of the modes of aristocratic government.

It was the double bind that Cooper found himself in with his tentative approach to the contemporary political scene that prompted him to undertake a more plainspoken political work in the second volume in the series, in which he recounted his travels on the Rhine and his second visit to Switzerland four years after the first. Although the travels described in Cooper's second volume, first published in Britain as *A Residence in France; with an Excursion up the Rhine, and a Second Visit to Switzerland* (1837) and then as *Sketches of Switzerland . . . Part Second* in America, were chronologically the last he completed before returning to America, Cooper had clear reasons for choosing to publish this account second in his series.

Beyond its obvious connection to the first book in the Swiss setting, the volume also allowed Cooper to return to the political scene after the tumultuous events of the 1830 July Revolution—which resulted in the abdication of Charles X and the ascension to the French throne of Louis Philippe—and to consider the changes that had been wrought in France and throughout Europe. Cooper had by this time become so deeply involved in European politics that he founded and chaired the American Polish Committee to aid the refugees fleeing the struggles in that country. And with the death of Cooper's idol and friend, General Lafayette, the book provided an opportunity to defend the general's reputation in the face of the widespread critique of his actions during and after the July Revolution. Cooper conceived his two Switzerland volumes as counterparts to each other, the first focusing on the natural world and the second on the political. Indeed, a full third of the book titled *Sketches of Switzerland . . . Part Second* in

America is devoted to his residence and political intrigues in Paris in the months following the July Revolution.

Along with the shift in subject between the two volumes there is a marked change in the narrator, who is transformed from the awestruck student of the picturesque into a savvy commentator on European society. The aftermath of the July Revolution brought many disappointments that profoundly affected Cooper's worldview during his last stay in Paris. Most significant among these was Lafayette's decision to turn down the presidency of a proposed republic and instead to work with Louis Philippe to create a constitutional monarchy—a compromise that Cooper believed was fatal to France's republican dreams and to Lafayette's political future. Cooper's close observation of the French Court's manipulation of the general was deeply painful for him, and the book as a whole stands as a testament to his hero's career and sacrifices on behalf of liberty as Cooper works to defend even those decisions of Lafayette that he clearly had a hard time understanding.

Cooper's feelings of loneliness and alienation in Paris in *Sketches of Switzerland . . . Part Second* are not surprising. In his first book on Switzerland he records many instances of French abuse of America, and Cooper clearly saw himself as the representative American. Perhaps such episodes were intended to prepare the reader for the proper reception of Cooper's experiences in Paris in his second book: alone, defending the honor of America against its many enemies, including the king of France. Cooper records extended debates in which he is forced to defend his nation against many charges.

For Cooper there seems to be only one other man in all of France who has remained loyal to the republican "experiment": Lafayette, the last of the Founding Fathers. In Cooper's third book on his travels he would record his feelings on learning of the deaths of John Adams and Thomas Jefferson in 1826, and it is clear from *Sketches of Switzerland . . . Part Second* that Lafayette served as the last living embodiment of the hero of Cooper's imagination and of much of his fiction—Harper, Effingham, Natty Bumppo, Hard-Heart, and Uncas—all wrapped up in one. Cooper's admiration for Lafayette borders on idolatry; he sees in the man a symbol of everything in the dream of America's founding that must be preserved at all costs.

Cooper's loyalty to Lafayette—whom he had also celebrated in *Notions of the Americans* on the occasion of the general's American visit—put him in a position to feel personally the fierce political winds

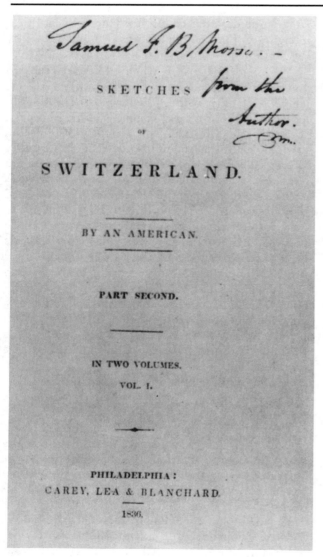

Title page from the copy of Cooper's second travel book that he presented to Samuel F. B. Morse (Collection of Robert B. Honeyman Jr.)

not only at war with the Court's ministers and the press, but also, to his great surprise, with agents of the United States. Cooper for the first time felt abandoned by his country, a sentiment from which he never entirely recovered.

At the same time that Cooper became a target of the doctrinaire forces of Louis Philippe's *juste milieu,* his fortunes as a novelist in Europe and in the United States took a decided and sudden turn for the worse. Since his arrival in 1826 Cooper's economic arrangements in Europe had been looking up, and Cooper associated, probably not incorrectly, the turn in the press with the influence of the agents of the monarchy arrayed against him. Most distressing for Cooper, however, was the failure of the American press and government to come to his support. When the critical reviews in New York started to look much like those appearing in Europe, Cooper saw in this evidence of the influence of Europe over American opinion. His bitterness is clear in *Sketches of Switzerland . . . Part Second:*

> Unsalaried and untrusted by my own government, opposed, in appearance at least, by its agents, I am thrown, for the vindication of truth, completely on my own resources, so far as any American succor has been furnished; and am reduced to the narrow consolation of making this simple record of the facts, which, possibly, at some future day, may answer the purpose of an humble protest in favour of the right.

Cooper's book must be understood not only as his vindication of Lafayette but also of himself. After having announced his "retirement" from fiction in the bitter *A Letter to His Countrymen* in 1834, Cooper here vividly portrays his loneliness and the political and even physical dangers he braved in defense of his country's reputation and honor, only to find himself abandoned when he most needed his nation's support.

Cooper begins *Sketches of Switzerland . . . Part Second* almost allegorically with a description of the descent of cholera upon Paris, painting a desolate cityscape reminiscent of that of Charles Brockden Brown's *Arthur Mervyn* (1799–1800). As if to underscore the connection of the pestilence to the political issues that dominate the book, Cooper recounts a story in which one of the Polish generals in exile predicted, some ten days before, the arrival of the disease after seeing "a hazy appearance in the atmosphere." Following the memoirs of the cholera, Cooper describes in detail his own involvement in the cost-of-government debate, thus inviting the reader to associate the bleak descriptions of deserted streets in the midst of the epidemic with his own psychic loneliness in the midst of the contro-

blowing at this time through France. At Lafayette's entreaty, Cooper in November 1831 agreed to write a refutation of an article by Louis-Sébastien Saulnier, who had argued that the cost of government in the United States far exceeded that of France and other monarchies. Cooper knew that the article was meant not only as a general attack on republicanism but also as a personal attack on the general, whose loyalty to the United States earned him the whispered slur of "l'Amérique" around the Court, and he willingly undertook the assignment in the defense of both Lafayette and his country. What must have at first appeared to be a fairly innocuous task, in which Cooper strongly believed all the facts were in his favor, turned into the first great political crisis of Cooper's career, in which he found himself

versy. Shortly thereafter Cooper recounts strolling to the Palais Royal only to discover it and all the surrounding streets completely deserted.

Cooper's account of the 1832 June Revolt is the most dramatic and carefully crafted part of the book. Using the techniques he had been developing in describing the mountains of Switzerland, he extends the picturesque style to the description of a city in the midst of political turmoil. Providing little context to orient the reader, Cooper emphasizes his own bewilderment at the occurrences he witnesses as he walks through the streets. He clearly wants the reader to feel the isolation from the scene that he felt in the midst of the revolt. Along with Cooper's family back at the hotel the reader feels suspense as the author wanders around the streets observing the movement of the guard, the mob, and the bystanders.

As the night deepens Cooper, finding himself alone on a bridge, realizes that events are occurring in the city that might well determine "the fate of not only France, but of all Europe." "Excited by these reflections," he continues, "I paused to contemplate the scene":

> I have told you how picturesque and beautiful Paris appears viewed from her bridges. . . . [T]he *Pont des Arts,* at night, . . . affords . . . striking glimpses of those ancient, tall, angular buildings along the river, that, but for their forms and windows, would resemble low rocky cliffs. In the center of this mass of dwellings, among its damp and narrow streets, into which the sun rarely penetrates, lay bodies of men, sleeping on their arms, or merely waiting for the dawn, to decide the fate of the country. It was carrying one back to the time of the "*League*" and the "*Fronde,*" and I involuntarily cast my eyes to that balconied window in the Louvre, where Charles IXth is said to have stood when he fired upon fleeing Protestants.

Here is the picturesque of the cityscape as the chiaroscuro of the city against the night sky leads to alternating associations, from the shapes of cliffs and mountains to the historical associations of France's long and checkered struggle with political and religious tyranny.

Cooper's easy shift into picturesque reverie shows that the shapes and effects of nature are not lost even here, just as he discovered by the end of the first *Sketches of Switzerland* that the shapes and effects of man were to be found even on top of the Jungfrau. Cooper's description of the streets of Paris between the forces of repression (the monarchy) and those of anarchy (the revolutionaries) plays out perfectly in the lights and darks of the scene he paints so carefully. The rest of the book is a search

for the necessary middle ground both in politics and in landscape. For Cooper this balance is embodied in Lafayette and his country estate at La Grange.

The political events of Paris serve as a frame for Cooper's account of his travels on the Rhine, but in some ways they so outweigh the travels in interest and energy as to make his observations on the landscape and the return to post-Revolution Switzerland seem like a digression. For Cooper, however, the travels into the countryside were an intense relief, an escape from the plagues—political and literal—of Paris. His interest in the picturesque did not diminish during the intervening years. The significant change, though, is that Cooper apparently no longer believed that one could or should attempt to separate the natural from the human world, and so what is developed is a more specific theory of the politics of the picturesque, just as earlier in the cityscapes one could say Cooper was searching for the picturesque in the political.

Cooper headed on his second trip into Switzerland less in search of the sublime landscape of the Alps than for the happy medium between the savage and the cultivated that has come to be his ideal, aesthetically, as it has long been politically. As he describes it, "Our tastes are certainly altering. . . . We are beginning to feel it is vulgar to be astonished, and even in scenery, I think we rather look for the features that fill up the keeping, and make the finish, than those which excite wonder." Even as he criticizes the French for their overcultivation and tyrannical ordering of the landscape, increasingly in this expedition Cooper expresses his displeasure with America's lack of civilized comforts and cultivation. "In America everything is so much reduced to the standard of the useful that little of the graceful has yet been produced," he remarks while contemplating a particularly fine hotel in Cologne.

The failure of America to landscape the White House gardens gives rise to anathemas against the lack of taste and gentility among his countrymen: it "goes to show either that we want the taste and habits necessary to appreciate the privation, (as is probably the case,) or the generosity to do a liberal act." The public promenade of Wiesbaden inspires still more violent expressions of frustration with American lack of cultivation:

> Ten years would suffice to bring such a promenade to perfection, and yet nothing like it exists in all America! One can surely smoke cigars, drink Congress water, discuss party politics and fancy himself a statesman, whittle, clean his nails in company and never out of it, swear things are good enough for him without having known any other state of society, squander dollars on discomfort and refuse cents to elegance and con-

venience, because he knows no better, and call the obliquity of taste patriotism. . . . He may . . . do all this, and so may an Esquimaux maintain that whale blubber is preferable to beef-steaks. I wonder that these dogged and philosophical patriots do not go back to warlocks, scalps and paint!

No charge could be more damning to his own countrymen than that of a lack of cultivation bordering on savagery, but Cooper's stay in Europe, and especially his experiences in Paris, had convinced him of the need to bring more graces into American society. His own fierce patriotism led him to his self-proclaimed role as tutor of taste for his American readers, and his frustration with his countrymen on this score was bringing him into a position of greater alienation from his land, even as his experiences abroad were convincing him more and more of the "superiority of his own free institutions over those of every other Christian nation."

Everywhere Cooper traveled in Germany and in Switzerland in 1832 conspiracy and political dangers seemed to lie waiting. Along the way he encountered agents of the Carlists, a foiled "counter-revolution" in Bern, political debates, and news of the growing tensions at home that threatened disunion. The last is brought up again during the author's final discussion with Lafayette upon the family's return from their travels in the countryside, as the general anxiously inquires as to Cooper's predictions regarding the eventual outcome of the present debate over union. The book ends with Cooper discoursing on the strengths of the union to Lafayette and with the general and his family giving a final lesson in gentility and deportment to Cooper and his American readers:

> Two capital mistakes exist in America on the subject of France. One regards its manners, and the other its kitchen. We believe that French deportment is superficial, full of action, and exaggerated. This would be truly a wonder in a people who possess a better tone of manners, perhaps than any other; for quiet and simplicity are indispensable to high breeding. The French of rank are perfect models of these excellencies. As to the *cuisine* we believe it highly seasoned. Nothing can be farther from the truth; spices of all sorts being nearly proscribed.

Thus Cooper ends his tribute to Lafayette not with a celebration of his political career but with a testament to the excellencies of his manners and the moderation of his cuisine. Lafayette represents for Cooper not a foreign influence to be feared but a model whose balance, poise, and patience are to be emulated in every aspect of contemporary American life, from the salon to the Congress.

Reviews of the two Switzerland volumes were largely favorable, although weariness with the subject matter was widely voiced. The books' weak sales in Europe and in the United States echoed the critical malaise with Swiss travels as a whole. The reviewer for the June 1836 *Athenaeum* applauded the first volume: "His descriptions have all the minuteness and reality of a Dutch picture; yet are massive and picturesque as the originals from which they are taken." But in the second volume the reviewer for the September 1836 issue found evidence of "a sore spirit" and advised the author to acquire "a calm patience of neglect and willful injustice."

The July 1836 *North American Review* applauded the books for their descriptions and commended Cooper for "his power of setting before his readers, with admirable distinctness, striking views of natural scenery." But the reviewer went on to criticize the turn toward politics in the second volume, bemoaning the fact that "Mr. Cooper's political mania breaks out in some places, to mar the beauty of the work. It is a profanation of the noble scenery to which the book is devoted, to intrude the passions of the politician, among the feelings such scenery is calculated to excite." This review represents the general consensus: the books were celebrated for their descriptions of nature (even as these descriptions are defined as being a dime a dozen) and castigated for the contamination of the natural world by political concerns. The September 1836 *American Quarterly Review* also complains of too many descriptions of this scenery in recent publications and then criticizes Cooper for his introduction of "party doctrine" in a book of travels through Switzerland. The reviewer prophesied little good would come for Cooper's reputation from his travel writings, a prediction that proved to be a great understatement.

Cooper chose to turn in his next book from the end of his travels in Europe back to the beginning, returning to his family's initial residence in France in the years preceding the July Revolution. Like the first two volumes of the travel series published in 1836, the third and fourth volumes that were brought out in 1837 were conceived of as a pair: *Recollections of Europe,* published in America as *Gleanings in Europe,* covered the period of the Coopers' residence in Paris from July 1826 through February 1828; *England,* published in America as *Gleanings in Europe. England,* was based on the Coopers' stay in London from March through May 1828. Quite different in many respects from the first two books, they focus almost entirely on social and political observations and anecdotes, with little of Cooper's energy given to the conventions of the picturesque or the natural world. The volumes resemble more in tone and style the travel literature about America published by Europeans in the 1820s and 1830s; Cooper, who disliked the tone of these studies of American manners and society, purposefully borrowed their critical stance and applied it with full force to the Old World.

This is not to say that these volumes were dominated by bitterness and bile toward Cooper's European hosts, although this was indeed a charge leveled against them by many reviewers. Cooper worked hard to achieve a position of critical and independent observer. Especially in regard to France he balances the number of subjects for positive and negative comparison to the United States. Since these books are first and foremost designed as a series of transatlantic comparisons, they lack the careful narrative organization of the first two volumes, and their more rapid composition is noticeable. Without the advantage of the journals that had provided the material for the Switzerland books Cooper instead relied primarily on his impressive memory, and there is correspondingly less detail in description and more in the way of anecdote and broad characterization.

The volumes shift somewhat in their organizational style, being ordered as a series of letters to actual friends and correspondents, though none of the chapters was actually sent as a letter. The conceit allows Cooper to move more freely and loosely from one subject of inquiry to another as his subjects are here dictated by the interests of his fictional correspondents. To Mrs. Jay, for example, he provides accounts of high society, while to Jacob Sutherland, a New York State Supreme Court Justice, he focuses his attention on the comparative legal systems of France and the United States.

The reception of the first two volumes at home and abroad and the increasingly violent attacks on Cooper's reputation from the Whig press in America led Cooper to see definitive evidence of what he had long believed to be the case: the United States was intellectually dependent on Europe, especially England, for all its opinions. Cooper believed that his reputation at home was suffering largely owing to the machinations of the French and British press, which had targeted him for especial malice because of his determined defense of republican institutions while abroad. His countrymen's inability to recognize themselves as dupes of these devices by coming to his defense disappointed him greatly.

In his 1836 books Cooper saw educating his countrymen about the true state of Europe's opinion of them and their institutions as a subsidiary task, but in 1837 he made this task his primary goal. As Cooper declares in the preface to *Gleanings in Europe. England:* "The American who should write a close, philosophical, just, popular, and yet comprehensive view of the fundamental differences that exist between the political and social relations of England and those of his own country, would confer on the latter one of the greatest benefits it has received since the memorable events of July 4, 1776." The Revolution, he argues, had given America only political independence, and its "mental emancipation" remains to be effected. Although Cooper stops short of making such revolutionary claims for his own work, it is clear that such was his ambition.

In the first book of the American-titled *Gleanings in Europe* series, Cooper examines the waning years of the Bourbons and Charles X. France during this period held for Cooper great interest, as a variety of political forces were carving up the Parisian political landscape and working to secure advantages against the coming storm. The Loyalists supporting the Bourbons, the Doctrinaires working for a constitutional monarchy, the Orleanists defending the interests of the bourgeoisie, and republicans seeking democracy all struggled for dominance. It was a veritable laboratory of political theory for Cooper, allowing him an excellent opportunity to discuss the best form of government. It also provides an important background for understanding the disappointments and disillusionment that followed the July Revolution as described in *Sketches of Switzerland . . . Part Second*.

Another important though largely unacknowledged reason for Cooper's choosing to remember Paris in 1826–1828 is nostalgia. France in those years provided Cooper's greatest surprise of his entire European sojourn: the discovery of his celebrity in Paris and his installation as a cornerstone of the romantic revolution, which was then combating the established forces of academic classicism. Each of his travel volumes must be understood against the backdrop of Cooper's dramatically declining reputation at home and abroad, and the return to the more pleasant memories of France in the late 1820s must have provided fond material for the beleaguered writer.

Cooper (and his publishers) knew the difficulties he would face with the volume. For all its play at immediacy through the use of the epistolary structure the book has a retrospective feel. As he writes in the preface, these episodes of the recent

Page from the manuscript for Gleanings in Europe. England (1837) (Paul Fenimore Cooper Jr.)

past "are the *gleanings* of *a harvest already gathered*," and the book describes a political landscape that must have appeared to many contemporary readers as yesterday's news. Cooper repeatedly describes scenes, such as the disrespectful reception of the royal family by their subjects during a horse race, designed to prophesy what was by then already a proven fact: that the Bourbon restoration was about to be undone. These predictions could not help but have the effect of twenty-twenty hindsight no matter how true they were to Cooper's perceptions at the time. The market, furthermore, was flooded with volumes on Paris, and nothing in his recent publishing history could have led Cooper to expect much from his latest travel narrative. Indeed, his price for these volumes had fallen considerably with his publishers in Britain and the United States, and, despite the bargain arrangements these houses secured, neither was able to report a profit on the publication.

For all their faults the 1837 travel books possess certain advantages over their predecessors. By his sustained focus primarily on the two capital cities, with only occasional excursions to the provinces, Cooper is able to dig deeper beneath the surface and show more attention to detail than he did in the first two volumes. Especially rewarding for a reader interested in Cooper, the books are much more conversational in tone and give a greater sense of access to the man than did the 1836 books. They move easily between discussions of grand political theory and the light, biting satire Cooper had shown himself capable of in *The Monikins*.

One of the striking features of both 1837 books is the droll humor that Cooper dishes out in regular doses, as when he describes the vain attempts of an American captain who speaks no French to teach his Parisian maid how to make cocoa. The chapter in which a famous hypnotist tries to convince Cooper of the virtues of animal magnetism proved to be a particularly popular episode. Cooper's memory of the hypnotist's efforts to enlist his subject's credulity is memorably phrased: "The doctor had not the smallest doubt of his ability to put me to sleep; an ability, so far as his theory went, I thought it was likely enough he might possess, though I greatly questioned his physical means."

Cooper keeps to his self-appointed role as tutor to Americans on issues of manners and gentility, and some of the lectures must have been particularly grating since he found much to admire in Paris. "We commit some mistakes on this side of the water," Cooper writes to his American readers, "in matters of taste and etiquette. A few words simply expressed . . . may serve to remove some errors." For example, Cooper lectures on the rules of precedence governing entrance to the dining room, and he especially would have the Americans learn to emulate French "laws of intercourse" governing the reception of strangers into town. A note to one chapter expresses his disappointment on his return to America to find "a vast expansion of mediocrity" in which "the towns increased, more tawdry than ever, but absolutely with less real taste than they had in my youth." As several British reviewers delighted in predicting, such frank sentiments were not likely to endear Cooper to his already alienated readership at home.

The bulk of the book, however, is a broad study of the main features of French society in which Cooper compares everything from justice and the military to the size and complexion of men and women on both sides of the Atlantic. This last subject is something of a burning concern for Cooper in both the French and English volumes, and he decides in both cases strongly in favor of the Americans. In fact, on most of these issues, Cooper proudly finds the American side of the question at least equal and often superior to its European counterpart. It is primarily in manners and in their lack of devotion to the arts and culture that Cooper finds his countrymen seriously underdeveloped.

The reception of this volume on both sides of the Atlantic was lukewarm, and for the most part profound disinterest was the dominant chord struck in the papers and magazines. The January 1837 *Athenaeum* predicted the book would not meet with much admiration in either Britain or America, but neither did it finally meet with much in the way of censure. The April 1837 *Knickerbocker Magazine* admired the book and commended Cooper for traveling with "the spirit of a true American" (which must have greatly pleased the author). The 4 March 1837 *New-York Mirror* found the work "entirely free from the objections that have been urged against Mr. Cooper's late writings." Other American magazines, such as the January 1838 *North American Review,* suggested that the book does not sustain the reader's interest and argued that Cooper carries too far his fierce republicanism. British reviews tended to follow the lead of the *Athenaeum* in damning the book with faint praise.

The Coopers left Paris in February 1828 for London, where they set up residence on Saint James Place. *Gleanings from Europe. England* begins conversationally but even more than its predecessor has serious political points of honor to settle with its subject. Indeed, Cooper seems to feel few compunctions about assaulting English institutions, social and political, on almost every score. While it is not at all unlikely that he saw in this stance a means of generating more attention, both at home and abroad, for his travel narratives, Cooper clearly felt the importance of his mission. In *Sketches of Switzerland . . . Part Second* he had called attention to the politics of travel writing by observing that during the government-cost controversy much of his opposition's statistics were drawn from a seemingly innocuous appendix to an Englishman's travels in America. But in his book on England, the dangers of foreign writings on America and the need to secure "mental emancipation" become points of real urgency.

In an extended diatribe on the need for laws to secure the copyrights of foreign authors in America—a debate in which Cooper briefly involved himself with his publishers on behalf of Walter Scott—he explains the need for such laws to discourage the piracy of British literature in the United States. The reasons that would make such steps necessary extend beyond the need for strong native literature; indeed, Cooper argues that the dangers posed by the pirating of British literature might well determine the fate of the nation. Because of the many similarities between the two nations England is a dangerous example: "It is the very points of resemblance that create the danger, for where there is so much that is alike, we run the risk of confounding principles." The discussion of the copyright law encompasses Cooper's larger anxieties about Americans' inability to appreciate justly the differences between English and American institutions—an inability owing in part to English literature's influence—and the resulting dangers to the nation: "It is high times, not only for the respectability, but for the *safety* of the American people, that they should promulgate a set of principles that are more in harmony with their facts."

Cooper even extends his anxiety to his rival, Scott: "These very works of Sir Walter Scott, are replete with one species of danger to the American readers. . . . The bias of his feelings, his prejudices, I might also say of his nature, is deference to hereditary rank. . . . This idea pervades his writings, not in professions, but in the deep insinuating current of feeling, and in a way, silently and stealthily, to carry with it the sympathies of the reader." As "the American Scott," a man whose own reputation at home and abroad had been largely defined in terms of his British counterpart, Cooper's focus on Scott here is especially poignant.

Although he developed a friendly relationship with Scott in Paris and later in London, Cooper maintained the need to distinguish himself from the man who had influenced him more than any other. And as they shared an American publisher, a publisher who was by this point becoming increasingly wary of the turn Cooper's writing and marketability had taken, Cooper must have felt the sting of the rivalry as he wrote these volumes, several years after Scott's death in 1832. Looking around for explanations as to his recent change of fortune, Cooper found in Scott a representative of all that stood against him. He complains that an American writer such as himself competing with "even a diminished Scott" on "American principles" would be almost "certain to fail . . . from the very circumstance that he would find the minds of his readers already occupied by . . . hostile notions."

Cooper resorts to a somewhat martial and even xenophobic rhetoric that is nonetheless quite heartfelt. He sees the two nations engaged in a cultural and intellectual war in which he stands as a lone bastion battling both the enemy abroad and the incursions of the enemy's agents at home. He works carefully to correct what he feels are some serious misconceptions about the British system at home and to point out the fundamental differences between the two systems of government, especially the dangerous hold of the aristocracy on all aspects of British life and the "system of exclusion" that it has created.

Cooper here begins to develop the theory of democracy that will be the focus of *The American Democrat* (1838). He objects not to the division of society into castes and classes, which he argues is the necessary condition of civilization in any form ("there can be no greater fallacy than to say, one man is as good as another, in all things") but to the failure to provide all castes with equal *political* rights. This distinction is one that Cooper would expand upon in *Gleanings in Europe. Italy* (1838), which was first published in England as *Excursions in Italy* (1838), and in all of his later political writings as he calls for less deference to one's superiors in Europe and more deference in the United States.

Not all of Cooper's memories and associations in this volume are bitter, and he clearly enjoys describing his literary encounters with the likes of William Godwin and Samuel Taylor Coleridge. For all he pretends to complain about he takes real pleasure in the society of London, although, owing to the recent death of his wife's father, Cooper made the social calls alone during the family's stay in England. And for all of Cooper's abiding antipathy toward the English as a whole, he expresses a recurring fascination with and admiration for the "Anglo-Saxon race." Early in his previous book on France, for example, he describes an English girl of particular delicacy and "spirit" whose features he defines as "quite peculiar to the Anglo-Saxon race." "The workings of such a countenance," he goes on, "are like the play of lights and shades in a southern sky." The scene clearly works to associate the features of Cooper's Anglo-Saxon ideal with the picturesque landscape epitomized by his beloved Italy. What England lacks in terms of landscape it makes up for, it would seem, in racial stock—an inheritance Cooper is quite willing to claim for the United States.

The critical reception of his book on England, as Cooper expected, was anything but tame, especially in the subject country. The October 1837 *Quarterly Review* led the charge against the book in a vindictive review reprinted widely by other magazines, claiming "so ill-written—ill-informed—ill-bred—ill-tempered, and ill-mannered a production it has never yet been our fortune to meet. . . . As a literary work it is really below contempt." *The Quarterly Review,* along with many other British magazines, condemned Cooper for his prejudices, his egotism, and his supposedly poor manners while a guest in London, facetiously retitling the work "*J. Fenimore Cooper, Esquire, in England, with Sketches of his Behaviour in the Metropolis.*" For many British reviewers in the Tory press the book constituted an extended insult. The August 1837 *Blackwood's* castigated Cooper as "a vulgar man, who . . . has unluckily imagined himself a genius." Even those inclined to be more sympathetic to Cooper's politics, such as *The Spectator,* found need to denigrate Cooper's avowed Anglophobia in its May 1837 issue. Nevertheless, as the *Athenaeum* judiciously pointed out in June, the sins of this book against England were no more than countless Britons had committed against the United States in their own travel narratives.

Such support, of course, is what Cooper must have expected and perhaps hoped for, seeking to inspire a national defense of his writing and American literature and principles in general against the influence of the British press. But such was not to be the case. Although Cooper would again blame the hostility toward the book largely on British influence, he had by this time also embroiled himself in an increasingly heated contest with the Whig press in America. His disputes with tenants in Cooperstown were only further fueling the hostile press against him.

The American reception was influenced by that in Britain from the beginning. Sympathetic reviewers, such as William Cullen Bryant writing for the 5 September 1837 *Evening Post,* cited favorable English responses, while those hostile turned to the negative reviews found in *Blackwood's* or *The Quarterly Review,* the latter being reprinted and discussed widely in the United States. The January 1838 *New-York Mirror* staged a valiant defense of Cooper against his British adversaries, but the majority of American reviewers found much to commend to their readers in the savaging of Cooper by *The Quarterly Review.* Even the *Knickerbocker Magazine,* which had been favorably inclined to the work in October 1837, published a second review in February of the next year largely agreeing with the response of *The Quarterly Review.* The failure of *Gleanings in Europe. England* in the United States disappointed Cooper greatly, as he believed it the best of his travel narratives, though he found good evidence of his claims for England's hold over American opinion in the manipulation of the critical reception by the British press.

Cooper performed something of an about-face in his final volume of travel writings, *Gleanings in Europe. Italy* in the United States, turning deliberately from the political toward the picturesque once again. With the poor reception of his recent books Cooper knew that his publishers in England and America were reluctant to print another volume of the travels. Carey, Lea & Blanchard purchased the book for only $200, so low had their faith in the profitability of Cooper's nonfiction fallen.

Italy served as Cooper's aesthetic ideal in almost every way, the perfect admixture of all he found ideal in nature and in man, and in recalling the experiences of his family in that country Cooper seems to recover the pleasures and even the indolence of the visit. His prose shifts dramatically from the combative and critical tone of the previous two travel books toward a pastoral nostalgia for a land and a time of perfect peace for him and his family. Unlike England, where they resided only a short time, the Coopers spent nineteen months in Italy, from June 1828 to May 1830, dividing the trip primarily between Florence, the Bay of Naples, and Rome, and concluding with a short visit to Venice.

Cooper, much to his surprise, found much to admire in the Italians and their country, including rare examples of respect for Americans. "There is a sleepy indolence in these Italians, that singularly suits my humour," he writes. "They seem too gentlemanlike to work, or to be fussy, but appear disposed to make a *siesta* of life, and to enjoy the passing moment." The language of *Gleanings in Europe. Italy* is indeed dreamy; the tone is unusually sensual; and the narrator retires to a position of sophisticated witness of the wonders of the land.

The first section of the book was greatly aided by Cooper's journal entries, which resemble his sketch-like entries he made in Switzerland. After Florence, however, Cooper turns from his own notes to guidebooks for his recollections, and the book suffers correspondingly in its forcefulness and cohesion. By the end it starts to resemble a conventional travel guide. Nevertheless, there is an intensity of description found in the best sketches that surpasses anything in the earlier books, and Cooper's Gothic fantasies and picturesque reveries are at times almost boyishly playful, in stark contrast to the disgruntled persona he had assumed in his recent works.

Although Cooper's decision to write a picturesque book once again might be seen as a return to the approach of his first travel book, his notion of the picturesque and his understanding of its significance had changed. The landscape here does not bring the narrator to his knees in awe; instead, Cooper works to paint elaborate panoramas that chart carefully the contrasts he finds everywhere in the landscape: "There is an admixture of the savage and the refined in the ragged ravines of the hills, the villas, the polished town, the cultivated plain, the distant and chestnut-covered peaks, the costumes, the songs of the peasants, the Oriental olive, the monasteries and churches, that keep the mind constantly attuned to poetry." The lights and darks of the mountainsides, the rudeness and the grace of the vistas, the simultaneous heat of the sun and the cool of ocean breezes all present themselves to Cooper as precisely the perfect balance, an aesthetic as well as a national ideal. His attempt to render the Italian chiaroscuro here is derived in part from earlier practitioners of the picturesque, most notably William Gilpin, but his ideas about the picturesque view of the landscape also show two other important influences.

The first of these is Cooper's discovery of Italian painting in 1828, when he had spent much of his time examining the art collections of the Louvre. His interest in painting and the visual arts—which in part was born out of his desire, shared by the Hudson River School of painters, to find a proper mode by which to comprehend the wonders of the American wilderness—is everywhere evident in this volume. For Cooper, Raphael had come to represent perfect appreciation for the delicacy of beauty, while Correggio and Titian expressed how the full power of lights and darks could be brought into harmony by a master. And though Cooper shies away from the open sexuality of much Baroque painting, its effects are also felt in the sensual pleasure Cooper allows himself here not only in the landscape, which he at one point likens to "an extremely fine woman," but also in the Italians themselves. Thanks in part to his application of the lessons of these and other masters, Cooper moved beyond Gilpin's appreciative terms for the picturesque and the sublime toward a greater range of responses, both emotional and intellectual, than he was able to produce in *Sketches of Switzerland*.

The second influence that took Cooper's conception of the picturesque in a new direction is the political concerns and critical debates generated by his earlier travel writings. But instead of further political preaching and complaining, Cooper devotes his attention primarily to the aesthetic as a political and intellectual ideal. Italy for much of the book serves as an ideal not in its politics or even in its society (although Cooper finds much to commend in the latter) but in its perfect balance. Cooper's interest in the aesthetic is not as an end in itself but as an ennobling force, his beau ideal of the graceful, the harmonious, the ordered, and the mannered—all qualities that he finds lacking in his own land. "I am far from underrating the importance of fine natural scenery to a nation," he writes; "I believe it not only aids character, but that it strengthens attachments. . . . There is, in America, enough beautiful nature, coupled with the moral advantages we enjoy, to effect all necessary ends." His account of the Italian landscape is not simply a guide to his fellow Americans to understanding the picturesque; Cooper suggests that the landscape offers a natural model of all he would wish for his country in society, government, and manners.

Cooper shies away from treating his Italian hosts in much detail, ignoring the intense political tensions of the day facing a divided Italy, much of which was at the time still under foreign control. His Italians tend to be caricatures—noble peasants, untrustworthy servants, cowardly boatsmen. The distance Cooper keeps from the Italian people is markedly greater than the distance he maintains from the French or the English in the previous two volumes.

Politically, Italy's "conquered" and divided state is offered as a warning for those Americans who spoke favorably of disunion. Cooper saw Italy, for all its wonders, as a nation that had seen its best days; America, on the other hand, was a land of limitless potential and possibility. He regarded the lessons of those who achieved the highest states of civilization in the past as crucial learning for those who would achieve the highest in the future.

Cooper spends less space than before in commenting on American principles, and he bravely applauds many features of the Italian landscape at the expense of their American counterparts. He even ridicules the conventional association of the New York Harbor with the Bay of Naples. Readers misunderstood the aim of much of his writing along these lines, seeing in it evidence of Cooper's supposed bile toward his native land. But Cooper believed that only by learning to see beyond provincial prejudices would America ever become a truly "manly" nation: "If it be patriotism to deem all our geese swans, I am no patriot." Cooper wished to make the Italian ideal available to his countrymen and tried to teach them to see it as he had.

Toward the end of the fifth volume in Cooper's travel series, his exhaustion and sense of failure to live up to his subject matter are evident. He felt that *Gleanings in Europe. Italy* was not as effective as its predecessors and was frustrated with critical responses that celebrated it at the expense of *Gleanings in Europe. England*. The reviews for the most part were muted, and few devoted more than a brief notice to the book. The July 1838 *American Monthly Magazine* applauded it for being less cranky and egotistical than its predecessors, and most reviews followed with similar negative praise for the book's merits in relation to the books on France and England. The critics, like the public, were tired of Cooper's travels, and all joined with his publishers in wishing him a speedy return to the task of fiction writing.

Cooper, however, was not yet ready to return to fiction. Instead, he produced more volumes of nonfiction, moving from travel writing to political theory and history with *The American Democrat* and *The Chronicles of Cooperstown* (1838). What would finally return him to fiction was the mounting crisis with his neighbors over property rights to Three Mile Point, a debate that would provide background for the Effingham novels of 1838, *Homeward Bound* and *Home as Found*. It was a debate that raged during the writing and publishing of the final volumes in his travel series, further eroding the novelist's reputation, but Cooper avoids its direct mention in his travel writings. Only once does he allude to the subject at all, when toward the end of *Gleanings in Europe. England* he writes of America as a land in which "all the local affections are sacrificed to the spirit of gain. The man who should defend the roof of his fathers, against an inroad of speculators, would infallibly make enemies, and meet with persecution." In the Three Mile Point controversy Cooper saw himself as vainly defending the land of his father, Judge William Cooper.

This mournful note of the betrayal, however, extends beyond his home in Otsego County to the nation as a whole. Returning from his years abroad, Cooper found himself more fiercely committed than before he left for Europe to the institutions and principles of the United States and believed that as a world traveler he was particularly qualified to defend them against their enemies at home and especially abroad. "Defend[ing] the roof of his fathers," however, he discovers, earns him only "persecution." "I know very well," he continues in *Gleanings in Europe. England,* "this is merely a consequence of a society in the course of establishing itself, but it shows how vulnerable is our happiness."

While *Gleanings in Europe. Italy* may have afforded Cooper a chance to recover briefly a moment of perfect happiness, its composition seems to have served only to harden the sense of isolation from his own land. Looking over his shoulder seven years later, Cooper still longs for this ideal, so lacking in his own life in Cooperstown, and he writes on 31 June 1838 to American sculptor Horatio Greenough, in the midst of the Three Mile Point controversy, "I could wish to die in Italy." Continuing in the same letter, Cooper writes:

> I have not done justice to Italy, or myself, in the book on that country—I did think to make it a pleasant book of its sort, but the failure is owing to circumstances I could not control. I wanted time to do what I think I could easily have done, with such a subject. I wrote the first part of Switzerland con amore, and I hope credibility, but the sale scarcely paying the expense of printing I got discouraged, and can not say I have tried since. . . . The fact that I am attached to the institutions of the country has completely annihilated me as a writer, here, for this is the most intolerant nation under the sun, and the *readers,* in their hearts, are deadly opposed to these ins[ti]tutions.

Although some of Cooper's major novels still lay ahead, including *The Pathfinder* (1840) and *The Deerslayer* (1841), he was never to recover entirely his optimism, reputation, energy, or the faith in his audience and his nation with which he set sail for Europe. At the beginning of *Recollections of Europe* an English traveler prophesied that Cooper would "never come back" to his native land after an absence of five years. Although Cooper there defined the Englishman as "a false prophet," one might see from the hindsight of literary history that perhaps the man was more right than either Cooper or his countrymen could have recognized at the time.

Letters:

Correspondence of James Fenimore Cooper, edited by James Fenimore Cooper, 2 volumes (New Haven: Yale University Press, 1922);

Letters and Journals of James Fenimore Cooper, edited by James Franklin Beard, 6 volumes (Cambridge: Harvard University Press, 1960–1968).

Bibliographies:

Robert E. Spiller and Philip C. Blackburn, *A Descriptive Bibliography of the Writings of James Fenimore Cooper* (New York: Bowker, 1934);

James F. Beard, "James Fenimore Cooper," in *Fifteen American Authors before 1900,* edited by Robert A. Rees and Earl N. Harbert (Madison: University of Wisconsin Press, 1971), pp. 63–96;

Alan Frank Dyer, ed., *James Fenimore Cooper: An Annotated Bibliography of Criticism* (New York: Greenwood Press, 1991).

Biographies:

Susan Fenimore Cooper, *Pages and Pictures from the Writings of James Fenimore Cooper* (New York: Townsend, 1861);

Thomas R. Lounsbury, *James Fenimore Cooper* (Boston: Houghton, Mifflin, 1882);

William Branford Shubrick Clymer, *James Fenimore Cooper* (Boston: Small, Maynard, 1900);

Ethel R. Outland, *The "Effingham Libels" of Cooper; a Documentary History* (Madison: University of Wisconsin Press, 1929);

Henry Walcott Boynton, *James Fenimore Cooper* (New York: Century, 1931);

James Grossman, *James Fenimore Cooper* (Stanford: Stanford University Press, 1949);

Donald A. Ringe, *James Fenimore Cooper* (New York: Twain, 1962; revised edition, Boston, 1988);

Stephen Railton, *Fenimore Cooper: A Study of His Life and Imagination* (Princeton: Princeton University Press, 1978).

References:

Charles Hansforth Adams, *"The Guardian of the Law": Authority and Identity in James Fenimore Cooper* (University Park: Penn State University Press, 1990);

Richard Chase, *The American Novel and Its Tradition* (Garden City: Doubleday Anchor, 1957), pp. 43–65;

John Conron and Constance Ayers Denne, "Historical Introduction," *Gleanings in Europe: Italy,* edited by Denne (Albany: State University of New York Press, 1981);

George Dekker, *James Fenimore Cooper: The American Scott* (New York: Barnes & Noble, 1967);

Leslie Fiedler, *Love and Death in the American Novel* (New York: Criterion, 1960), pp. 162–214;

Kay Seymour House, *Cooper's Americans* (Columbus: Ohio State University Press, 1966);

William P. Kelly, *Plotting America's Past: Fenimore Cooper and "The Leatherstocking Tales"* (Carbondale: Southern Illinois University Press, 1983);

D. H. Lawrence, *Studies in Classic American Literature* (New York: Seltzer, 1923), pp. 40–69;

R. W. B. Lewis, *The American Adam: Innocence, Tragedy, and Tradition in the Nineteenth Century* (Chicago: University of Chicago Press, 1955);

John P. McWilliams, *Political Justice in a Republic: James Fenimore Cooper's America* (Berkeley: University of California Press, 1972);

Blake Nevius, *Cooper's Landscapes: An Essay on the Picturesque Vision* (Berkeley: University of California Press, 1976);

Mark R. Patterson, *Authority, Autonomy, and Representation in American Literature, 1776–1865* (Princeton: Princeton University Press, 1988), pp. 81–136;

H. Daniel Peck, *A World By Itself: The Pastoral Moment in Cooper's Fiction* (New Haven: Yale University Press, 1977);

Thomas Philbrick, "Historical Introduction," *Gleanings in Europe: France,* edited by Philbrick and Denne (Albany: State University of New York Press, 1983);

Philbrick, *James Fenimore Cooper and the Development of American Sea Fiction* (Cambridge: Harvard University Press, 1961);

Geoffrey Rans, *Cooper's Leatherstocking Novels: A Secular Reading* (Chapel Hill: University of North Carolina Press, 1991);

Ernst Redekop and Maurice Geracht, "Historical Introduction," *Gleanings in Europe: The Rhine,* edited by Philbrick and Geracht (Albany: State University of New York Press, 1986);

Donald A. Ringe, *The Pictorial Mode: Space & Time in the Art of Bryant, Irving, & Cooper* (Lexington: University of Kentucky Press, 1971);

Ringe and Kenneth W. Staggs, "Historical Introduction," *Gleanings in Europe: England,* edited by James P. Elliott, Staggs, and Robert D. Madison (Albany: State University of New York Press, 1982);

John F. Ross, *The Social Criticism of Fenimore Cooper* (Berkeley: University of California Press, 1933);

Henry Nash Smith, *Virgin Land: The American West as Symbol and Myth* (Cambridge: Harvard University Press, 1950), pp. 59–70;

Robert R. Spiller, *Fenimore Cooper: Critic of His Times* (New York: Minton, Balch, 1931);

Spiller, Introduction to *Gleanings in Europe: France,* edited by Spiller (London: Oxford University Press, 1928);

Spiller and James F. Beard, "Historical Introduction," *Gleanings in Europe: Switzerland,* edited by Staggs and Elliot (Albany: State University of New York Press, 1980);

Jane Tompkins, *Sensational Designs: The Cultural Work of American Fiction* (New York: Oxford University Press, 1985), pp. 94–121;

James D. Wallace, *Early Cooper and His Audience* (New York: Columbia University Press, 1986).

Papers:

The main collection of Cooper's papers is in the Beinecke Rare Book Room and Manuscript Library, Yale University. The New York State Historical Association, at Cooperstown, has many items relating to the Cooper family.

George Copway
(Kah-ge-ga-gah-bowh)

(circa 1818 – January 1869)

Timothy Sweet
West Virginia University

See also the Copway entry in *DLB 175: Native American Writers of the United States.*

BOOKS: *The Life, History, and Travels of Kah-ge-ga-gah-bowh (George Copway), a Young Indian Chief of the Ojebwa Nation, a Convert to the Christian Faith and a Missionary to His People for Twelve Years; with a Sketch of the Present State of the Ojebwa Nation, in Regard to Christianity and Their Future Prospects. Also an Appeal; with All the Names of the Chiefs Now Living, Who Have Been Christianized, and the Missionaries Now Laboring among Them* (Albany, N.Y.: Printed by Weed & Parsons, 1847); revised and enlarged as *The Life, Letters and Speeches of Kah-ge-ga-gah-bowh, or George Copway, Chief of the Ojibway Nation* (New York: Benedict, 1850); republished as *Recollections of a Forest Life; or, The Life and Travels of Kah-ge-ga-gah-bowh, or George Copway, Chief of the Ojibway Nation* (London: Gilpin, 1850);

Organization of a New Indian Territory, East of the Missouri River. Arguments and Reasons Submitted to the Honorable the Members of the Senate and House of Representatives of the 31st Congress of the United States: by the Indian Chief Kah-ge-ga-gah-bouh, or Geo. Copway (New York: Benedict, 1850);

The Traditional History and Characteristic Sketches of the Ojibway Nation. By G. Copway, or Kah-ge-ga-gah-bowh, Chief of the Ojibway Nation (London: Gilpin, 1850; Boston: Mussey, 1851); republished as *Indian Life and Indian History, by an Indian Author. Embracing the Traditions of the North American Indians Regarding Themselves, Particularly of that Most Important of All the Tribes, the Ojibways* (Boston: Colby, 1858);

Running Sketches of Men and Places, in England, France, Germany, Belgium, and Scotland. By George Copway (Kah-ge-ga-gah-bowh) (New York: Riker, 1851).

Editions: *Recollections of a Forest Life* (Toronto: Canadiana, 1970);

George Copway (National Archives of Canada)

The Traditional History and Characteristic Sketches of the Ojibway Nation (Toronto: Coles, 1972);

Indian Life and Indian History (New York: AMS, 1978);

The Life, Letters and Speeches of Kah-ge-ga-gah-bowh, or G. Copway, Chief of the Ojibway Nation, edited by Donald B. Smith and A. LaVonne Brown Ruoff (Lincoln: University of Nebraska Press, 1997).

OTHER: Acts of the Apostles, translated by Copway and Sherman Hall as *Odizhijigeuiniua igou gaanoninjig* (Boston: Printed for the American Board of Commissioners for Foreign Missions by Crocker & Brewster, 1838);

Julius Taylor Clark, *The Ojibway Conquest: A Tale of the Northwest. By Kah-ge-ga-gah-bowh, or, G. Copway, Chief of the Ojibway Nation,* introduction, additional poem, and notes by Copway (New York: Putnam, 1850);

Copway's American Indian, edited by Copway (July–October 1851).

When George Copway was a boy the Great Spirit came to him in a dream, telling him, "You will travel much; the water . . . and the winds, will carry your canoe safely through the waves." Those words, from Copway's 1847 autobiography, *The Life, History, and Travels of Kah-ge-ga-gah-bowh,* would prove truer than he knew when he wrote them. He had already traveled extensively in the regions of the Great Lakes and upper Mississippi and on the eastern seaboard, and in 1850 he would travel to Europe.

Copway's description of his tour of England and the Continent, *Running Sketches of Men and Places* (1851), was the first travel book written by a Native American. While Native Americans' accounts of travels had been published earlier—such as Hendrick Aupaumut's record of political negotiations with various tribes, *A Short Narrative of My Last Journey to the Western Country* (1827), or Black Hawk's account of his tour of the East while prisoner of war, in *Life of Black Hawk* (1833)—Copway's is the first such book in which the experience of travel itself is the primary focus. In addition to his autobiography and travel book, Copway published an ethnohistory of the Ojibwas and a plan for the organization of a self-governing Indian territory, both in 1850, and edited a short-lived newspaper in 1851.

Kah-ge-ga-gah-bowh ("Standing Firm") was born in 1818 near the mouth of the Trent River, Canada West (now Ontario). His parents were of the Missasauga band of Ojibwa (Anishinaabeg), who had been living in the Rice Lake area, north of Cobourg, since the early 1700s. The band's totem was the Crane, a lineage that Kah-ge-ga-gah-bowh traces back as far as his great-grandfather, the first Ojibwa settler at Rice Lake. Cranes traditionally are noted for their skills as orators, interpreters, and chiefs, and perhaps this heritage contributed to Kah-ge-ga-gah-bowh's later success as a missionary, writer, and political activist.

Kah-ge-ga-gah-bowh was raised as a traditional Ojibwa, learning to hunt for the fur trade that provided the band's economic base. His parents converted to Christianity shortly after the first Methodist minister visited their settlement in 1827. In the summer after his mother's death in 1830, George Copway (as he was called after his parents' conversion) attended a Methodist camp meeting with his father and was converted. His dedication must have impressed the missionaries, for in 1834 at age sixteen he was one of four Missasauga Ojibwas chosen to be sent to the Lake Superior mission of the American Methodist Church. From 1834 through 1836 his missionary work took him among Ojibwas in the vicinities of Sault Sainte Marie, La Pointe, Lac Court Oreille, and Fort Snelling. As a reward for his devoted service his way was paid to Ebenezer Manual Labor School in Jacksonville, Illinois. Two years there comprised his only formal education. After graduation in 1839 he traveled home to Rice Lake by way of Chicago, Detroit, Buffalo, Rochester, Syracuse, Albany, New York, Newark, and Boston, all of which are mentioned in the autobiography.

In 1840 Copway married Elizabeth Howell, twenty-four-year-old daughter of Capt. Henry Howell, an English gentleman who owned a farm near Toronto. The couple immediately departed for missions among the Ojibwas in the Lake Superior and upper Mississippi region, where they would spend the next two years. They were eager to return to Rice Lake, however, and in 1842 were invited back to undertake various missionary and fund-raising tours. Copway's success in these causes is evidenced by his election as vice president of the Grand Council of Methodist Ojibwas of Upper Canada in 1845.

Overzealous in his work, Copway soon spent more than the council appropriated and was accused of embezzlement; at the same time, managing some business dealings for the Rice Lake band, he drew a small amount of money without the leaders' authorization. As a result he was imprisoned for several weeks. Charges were dropped and he was released, since the Indian Department saw little hope of recovering any money from the impoverished Copway; he was, however, expelled from the Methodist Church of Canada. Copway defended himself against the charges in his autobiography but never mentioned his time in prison or his expulsion from the church. Upon his release he and his wife went to Boston, hoping that Presbyterians or Congregationalists there would sponsor their return as missionaries to the Lake Superior region. They did not get such a post, but in the meantime Copway was lecturing in eastern cities on temperance and Indian topics and was writing his autobiography.

Copway published *The Life, History, and Travels of Kah-ge-ga-gah-bowh* in Albany. His popularity as a lecturer probably helped the book's sales; in any case it was highly successful, going through seven printings by the end of 1848. He revised the book for publication in 1850. A British edition titled *Recollections of a Forest Life* was published in 1850 and reprinted in 1851.

Details about the book's composition did not survive; however, a preface acknowledges the assistance of

> a friend, who has kindly corrected all *serious* grammatical errors, leaving the unimportant ones wholly untouched, that my own style may be exhibited as truly as possible. . . . The language (except in a few short sentences), the plan, and the arrangement are all my own; and I am wholly responsible for all the statements, and the remaining defects.

Donald Smith, who has written the most extensive biography of Copway to date, speculates that the friend was his wife, Elizabeth, and concludes from internal evidence that most of the content was provided by Copway. This collaborative pattern probably holds for *Running Sketches* as well, Smith suggests.

In the autobiography, accounts of travel are often subordinated to the narrative of mission work, yet there are occasional moments of adventure or reflection. Travel description plays a much larger part here than it does, for example, in William Apess's *A Son of the Forest* (1831), with which Copway's *Life* is sometimes compared. An unusual twist on the captivity narrative occurs during an 1836 canoe trip down the Mississippi to Prairie Du Chien and through Sioux territory. Where whites would have passed unmolested, Copway's party, being Ojibwas and thus enemies of the Sioux, are fired on and taken prisoner. They are released three days later only after they manage to communicate that they are Christian missionaries (and thus effectively "white"). Copway frequently reflects on the landscape. For example, en route to Sault Sainte Marie in 1835 he notices that one of the sand points of Grand Island has sunk and reports, according to the local Ojibwas:

> the Great Spirit had removed from under that point, to some other place, because the Methodist Missionaries had encamped there the previous fall, and had, by their prayers, driven the Spirit from under that point.

In his later travels in eastern cities Copway reflects upon his own sense of displacement. His picturesque description of the view from the top of the Boston State House, which implicitly celebrates industrial progress, partakes of what Leo Marx in *The Machine in the Garden* (1964) terms the rhetoric of the technological sublime. Copway sees the harbor filled with ships, "wharves . . . filled with merchandise," steamboats "breathing out fire and smoke," and to landward, steeples, factories, and railroad cars "whiz[zing] along the flats like a troop of runaway horses." At these signs of the "prosperity of the white man, . . . tears fill [his] eyes." His two responses to this scene remain unreconciled. First he gives a Christian moral of assimilation: "Happy art thou, O Israel, who is like unto thee." He then laments the terms of that assimilation in a poem:

> Once more I see my fathers' land,
>   Upon the beach, where oceans roar;
> Where whiten'd bones bestrew the sand,
>   Of some brave warrior of yore.
> The *groves*, where once my fathers roam'd—
>   The *river*, where the beaver dwelt—
> The *lakes*, where angry waters foam'd—
>   Their *charms*, with my fathers, have fled.
>
> O! Tell me, ye "pale faces," tell,
>   Where have my proud ancestors gone?
> Whose smoke curled up from every dale,
>   To what land have their free spirits flown?
> Whose wigwams stood where cities rise;
>   On whose war-path the steam horse flies;
> And ships, like mon-e-doos in disguise,
>   Approach the shore in endless files.

After the publication of his autobiography Copway continued on the lecture circuit. He became acquainted with literary figures interested in Indian matters such as Francis Parkman Jr. and Henry Wadsworth Longfellow (Copway evidently being the only Ojibwa the latter met before he published *The Song of Hiawatha* in 1855). He formulated a plan for a large Indian Territory, which would eventually qualify for statehood, to be located in what are now the eastern Dakotas; the official language of this territory was to be Ojibwa. This plan was published in a pamphlet, *Organization of a New Indian Territory* (1850), and was presented to Congress but never got to the floor. Returning to his writing after this brief foray into national politics, Copway published *The Traditional History and Characteristic Sketches of the Ojibway Nation* (1850). This book contains the clearest expression of his Ojibwa nationalism.

In August 1850 Copway was invited by Elihu Burritt, a leading peace activist, to attend the Fourth General Peace Congress at Frankfurt am Main as one of forty American delegates and the only Native

American. This trip provided him with the material for his travel book, *Running Sketches of Men and Places.* LaVonne Ruoff criticizes the book for being "padded with newspaper accounts of Copway's triumphal lecture tour through Great Britain and descriptions of places taken from current travel books." It is true that approximately one-sixth of the text consists of passages from guidebooks, particularly *Black's Picturesque Tourist and Road and Railway Guide Book Through England and Wales,* which had been available since the early 1840s. Copway had also quoted large extracts from other books, a practice not uncommon at the time, in writing his *Traditional History and Characteristic Sketches of the Ojibway Nation,* which contains a great deal of material credited to Gen. Lewis Cass and Ojibwa historian William Warren.

In *Running Sketches of Men and Places* Copway includes unattributed excerpts from biographical sketches of people with whom he conversed: Richard Cobden, British proponent of laissez-faire economics and fellow delegate to the Peace Congress; Rev. Edwin H. Chapin, celebrated preacher of "the doctrine of unlimited salvation"; and Ferdinand Freiligrath, a Prussian poet imprisoned for expressing republican sentiments. Also included are texts of three of the lectures Copway delivered in England and Scotland—on his plan for the organization of a self-governing Indian territory, Ojibwa legends (adventures of Nanabozho, the earth-diver story, and so forth), and the evangelization of the Indians—as well as newspaper clippings noting his reception in England and Germany.

Three of the twenty-three chapters concern the Peace Congress, Copway's reason for traveling. Copway introduced a resolution there that had particular relevance for the Ojibwas, whom the United States had recently forced into ceding large tracts of land: "This Congress, acknowledging the principle of non-intervention, recognizes it to be the sole right of every state to regulate its own affairs." A contemporary report on the Congress in *The Advocate of Peace* mentions Copway's attendance "as representative of his red brethren" and notes that Richard Cobden, pointing to Copway, argued that modern nations, in maintaining standing armies, are "greater savages than even the North American Indian tribes." Copway does not comment directly on such tokenism. He reports that he was "received with much enthusiasm" even though he gave his "poorest speech" ever, for he spoke at the end of the conference, following many great orators, when "the people had become tired of listening, and seemed to have no desire for anything new." He includes a newspaper clipping suggesting that the audience may have been more interested in his appearance than in anything he said: "The Frankforters are sorry that he wears a modern hat, instead of a cap with feathers." While two chapters describe the business of the Peace Congress, a third gives a sometimes satiric picture of Americans in Europe and characterizes oratorical styles by nationality.

Four chapters are devoted to London. Visiting the House of Commons, Copway was critical of the architecture but impressed by speakers such as Benjamin Disraeli and Cobden; he reports on the debate over whether Baron von Rothschild, a Jew, would be allowed to take the seat to which he was elected. (Rothschild's portrait provides the frontispiece to *Running Sketches;* Copway's own portrait does not appear until chapter 6.) He devotes an entire chapter to Jenny Lind, noting that he used his celebrity status to get a ticket to a sold-out performance. He remarks that her mouth "was like that of the Hon. Henry Clay," yet his enraptured description of her voice—"my soul, wrapt in ecstasy, seemed borne on to the garden of Eden"—hints at the infatuation that, as Donald Smith reports, would become evident when Lind toured the United States in 1851.

When not occupied with events in London, the Peace Congress, or his lectures, Copway found himself drawn to landscape views. In these passages his style is characteristically reflective or associational as it had been in the autobiography. A view of the Irish coast reminds him of the Irish immigrants to Canada with whom he and his father had often conversed; a view of the ocean recalls stories told by a sailor who spent four years living among the Rice Lake Ojibwa. Like most of his American contemporaries Copway prefers a picturesque or pastoral arrangement of landscape. He objects, for example, to the "sameness" of the Belgian landscape: "Nothing seems to be anywhere, which could give it the contrast" necessary for aesthetic affect; "All alike, the land is cultivated." In the Rhine Valley, however, he finds abundant picturesque scenes.

The English countryside, too, exhibits the complex harmony of the picturesque and prompts a reflection on the comparative "cultivation" of England and the United States:

Groups of trees, and cultivated fields spreading as far as the eye can reach, on both sides. Beautiful green hedges, and fields of grain, some being reaped, and some still standing, waving gracefully as if inviting reapers to the harvest. . . . How vastly superior in point of cultivation is this country to America! Were they as much superior in cultivation of mind, we might be ashamed of ourselves! Unfortunately, they who till the soil have generally little time, and still less opportunity, for mental improvement. Without this, all this landscape beauty is but an outside shell, and when our country shall have become as old as England is now, we may excell the English in cultivation and refinement.

In such passages Copway often positions himself as an American and not specifically as an Indian.

In the Boston State House passage of the autobiography, Copway had briefly engaged in the rhetoric of the technological sublime. Such rhetoric is again evident in Copway's description of the docks of Liverpool:

They are a piece of master workmanship—a noble monument of untiring industry. The tide brings in a hundred ships inside, and when it goes out, it takes as many more. There, within the reach of the streets which run from the town into the river, are hid secure the ships which have braved the oceans of all quarters of the world. Here, now, as if weary of wandering by sea, slumber the godlike instruments of navigation.

Elsewhere, however, Copway expresses ambivalence about the progress of industry and commerce. Summarizing his visit to the famous steel town of Birmingham, he writes that:

the steel which is made here will accomplish the double work of doing good and doing evil—good in the way of subduing the wilderness and causing it to minister to the life of man and evil in the way of destroying life and making the earth desolate. Implements of husbandry, and the arts on the one hand, and swords, knives, rifles and muskets on the other.

The destructive work of technology, of course, includes the European conquest of the American continent. Copway's attitude toward such scenes is ambivalent; he is torn between his Indian and Christian identifications.

Running Sketches was Copway's last book. Evidently, sales were poor, for it was never reprinted. It has received little critical attention, partly because it seldom directly addresses the issue of "Indian identity" with which scholars of Native American literature have been preoccupied. The only substantial discussion is found in Timothy Sweet's "Pastoral Landscape with Indians," which analyzes the treatment of pastoral motifs in all of Copway's works.

After the publication of *Running Sketches,* Copway started a newspaper, *Copway's American Indian,* but this was a financial failure and ceased publication after three months in 1851. He continued on the lecture circuit but had trouble drawing audiences as slavery eclipsed Native American issues in the public eye. In 1858 he was imprisoned for debt in Boston. After this the record is blank until 1864, when he worked to recruit Canadian Indians for the Union army. In 1867 he was in Detroit, where he and his brother advertised themselves as herbal healers. In 1868 he appeared at an Algonquin-Iroquois mission in Canada, announcing his intention to convert to Catholicism. He died before receiving his first communion.

The significance of Copway's travel writing consists in its amplification of themes found elsewhere in his works and in the works of his Native American contemporaries. The themes of greatest interest in his travel writing—his engagements with technology and the pastoral—reflect his political attempts to secure a place for his people in the face of an expanding American nation. These and other tensions in his texts emerge from tensions in his own life. A willing convert, Copway sought acceptance from the dominant culture, yet his writings contain evidence of a strong Ojibwa nationalism as well.

References:
"Fourth Peace Congress," *Advocate of Peace,* 10 (November–December 1850): 286–311;

A. LaVonne Brown Ruoff, "George Copway: Nineteenth-Century American Indian Autobiographer," *Auto/Biography,* 3 (Summer 1987): 6–17;

Donald B. Smith, "The Life of George Copway or Kah-ge-ga-gah-bowh (1818–1869)—and a review of his writings," *Journal of Canadian Studies,* 23 (Fall 1988): 5–38;

Timothy Sweet, "Pastoral Landscape with Indians: George Copway and the Political Unconscious of the American Pastoral," *Prospects,* 18 (1993): 1–27.

David Crockett

(17 August 1786 – 6 March 1836)

Lane Stiles
University of Minnesota

See also the Crockett entries in *DLB 3: Antebellum Writers in New York and the South* and *DLB 11: American Humorists, 1800–1950.*

BOOKS: *The Life and Adventures of Colonel David Crockett of West Tennessee,* attributed to Crockett but probably written by Mathew St. Claire Clarke (Cincinnati: Printed by E. Deming, 1833); republished as *Sketches and Eccentricities of Colonel David Crockett of West Tennessee* (New York: J. & J. Harper; London: J. Limbird, 1833);

A Narrative of the Life of David Crockett of the State of Tennessee, by Crockett and Thomas Chilton (Philadelphia & Baltimore: Carey & Hart / London: J. Limbird, 1834);

An Account of Col. Crockett's Tour to the North and Down East . . . , Written by Himself, attributed to Crockett but probably written by William Clark (Philadelphia & Baltimore: Carey & Hart, 1835);

The Life of Martin Van Buren, attributed to Crockett but probably written by Augustin Smith Clayton (Philadelphia: R. Wright, 1835);

Col. Crockett's Exploits and Adventures in Texas, attributed to Crockett but written by Richard Penn Smith (Philadelphia: T. K. & P. G. Collins, 1836; London: R. Kennett, 1837);

Edition and Collection: *The Autobiography of David Crockett,* edited with an introduction by Hamlin Garland (New York: Scribners, 1923), includes *The Narrative, An Account of Colonel Crockett's Tour,* and *Col. Crockett's Exploits and Adventures*;

A Narrative of the Life of David Crockett of the State of Tennessee, edited by Joseph John Arpad (New Haven, Connecticut: College and University Press, 1972); published as a facsimile, with introduction and annotations by James A. Shackford and Stanley J. Folmsbee (Knoxville: University of Tennessee Press, 1973).

Perhaps no American traveler of the first

David Crockett (Special Collections, Thomas Cooper Library, University of South Carolina)

half of the nineteenth century was better known to American audiences than David Crockett. Like Daniel Boone before him, "Davy" Crockett stood tall in the national imagination as a paradigm of the frontiersman, a popular type that appropriately had taken early form in travel books. Crockett's popularity and renown, however, far exceeded Boone's, driven by—and, in turn, driving—the production of an extraordinary body of myth-making literature that elevated Crockett into one of America's first and most enduring mass-culture heroes.

Although more literate than he pretended, Crockett the writer (as opposed to Crockett the self-promoter) played a limited role in the production of this literature. Of the various works attributed to him, all were to some extent ghost written, even his autobiography, *A Narrative of the Life of David Crockett of the State of Tennessee* (1834). Still, *A Narrative of the Life of David Crockett* is a significant historical and literary text—not only the most authentic record of Crockett the man but also one of the earliest and most notable examples of southwest humor and a unique document of frontier life and politics in the age of Andrew Jackson.

Crockett came by his pioneering spirit naturally. His paternal grandparents had pushed westward from North Carolina across the Appalachians at the beginning of the Revolutionary War. Both were killed by Indians in 1777, not long after settling in what is now eastern Tennessee. Their son John Crockett escaped the attack and around 1780 married Rebecca Hawkins, who gave birth to David on 17 August 1786 at the Crockett home in Greene County, Tennessee. The Crocketts were poor, even by rural standards, and the young Crockett, who had very little formal education, left home early to work and travel. On 14 August 1806, three days before his twentieth birthday, Crockett married Mary "Polly" Finley, with whom he had three children.

In 1811 Crockett moved his family from eastern to middle Tennessee—one of a series of westering migrations that would continue to the end of his life. (Like other poor backwoodsmen, Crockett moved as much out of economic need as wanderlust, repeatedly abandoning "sickly" or game-depleted land for newer and richer territories.) Two years later the Creek Indian War broke out, and Crockett volunteered to fight Indians under the command of Gen. Andrew Jackson. Shortly after his return from the war, in 1815, Polly Crockett died; within a year, Crockett married Elizabeth Patton, a widow with two children.

Crockett was elected to the Tennessee legislature in 1821, and two years later "the gentleman from the cane" (*cane* was short for *canebreak,* a rough thicket of canes, typical of the wilds of western Tennessee) was reelected after moving to a new district in the western part of the state. In 1827 Crockett was sent by Tennessee voters to Washington for the first of three nonconsecutive terms in the House of Representatives. Although elected as a Jacksonian, Crockett broke with the president over such issues as public land policy, Indian removal, and the Bank of the United States and soon found himself taken up by eastern Whigs as a conservative countersymbol to Jackson, although he was really more of an anti-Jacksonian than a Whig. After Crockett was defeated for reelection to Congress in 1835 he

promptly left Tennessee to explore Texas. On 6 March 1836 the forty-nine-year-old Crockett, who had by then joined the cause for Texas independence, was killed by Gen. Antonio López de Santa Anna's forces at the battle of the Alamo.

Crockett's autobiography recounts selected events of his life through his third term in Congress; one of its purposes was to support Crockett's campaign for reelection for a fourth term—and perhaps, although Crockett repeatedly denied it, a possible run for the presidency against Jackson's handpicked successor, Martin Van Buren, in 1836. Though rife with anti-Jackson sloganeering, *A Narrative of the Life of David Crockett* is, generally, as Crockett asserts in the preface, "a plain, honest, home-spun account" of his life. He does, however, like any good frontier storyteller, stretch the truth now and then.

Crockett claims, for example, that he writes his own story to correct the inaccuracies of an extremely popular biography released the previous year, *The Life and Adventures of Colonel David Crockett of West Tennessee* (1833), which was republished that same year as *Sketches and Eccentricities of Colonel David Crockett of West Tennessee.* Crockett protests that he does not know the biography's author. In truth, he not only knew but probably collaborated with the book's anonymous author, Mathew St. Clair Clarke—a clerk of the House of Representatives and an anti-Jacksonian ally of Nicholas Biddle of the Bank of the United States. Clarke had intended the biography to propagandize for Crockett's reelection, but by exaggerating Crockett's frontier idiom and demeanor he may have hurt as much as helped him—hence, Crockett's disavowal.

A Narrative of the Life of David Crockett promises a more authentic Crockett. "The whole book is my own," Crockett declares in the preface, "and every sentiment and sentence in it." Here again Crockett stretches the truth, for he wrote with the help of Thomas Chilton, a congressman from Kentucky, who, like Clarke, was allied with anti-Jacksonian interests and who, like Clarke (but to a much lesser degree), could not resist inflecting Crockett's voice with backwoods solecisms. On the whole, though, Crockett's voice dominates the book, and except for a politically expedient revision of his war record and some confused chronology, the autobiography fairly depicts his life and language (even as it reinforces his emerging legendary status).

As the autobiography of a type of American traveler, *A Narrative of the Life of David Crockett* inevitably involves itself in the discourse of American travel writing. Indeed, the most vividly rendered and carefully detailed passages of the book describe not Crockett's personal and familial life but his travels throughout the South and the West. These travels began early. At age twelve, Crockett was hired out by his father to accompany a cattle drive to Rockbridge County, Virginia. A year later Crockett ran away from home to avoid punishment for playing hooky, again hitching up with a drover headed toward Virginia.

He eventually landed in Baltimore, where in the manner of the young Benjamin Franklin, he booked passage to England. (Crockett's book evokes Franklin in a more general way as well—as an early work in the tradition, established by Franklin, of the autobiography of the self-made man.) Unlike Franklin, Crockett never set sail, and after an absence of two and one-half years, he returned home, so changed his family at first did not recognize him. Crockett narrates both of these early journeys largely in terms of relationships with his various employers—some of whom were considerate and ethical, and some, not—and the hardships he had to endure in these latter cases.

Domestic life intervened, and Crockett did not travel extensively again until he enlisted in the Tennessee militia after the Creek Indians massacred more than five hundred whites and blacks at Fort Mims in the summer of 1813. Crockett's military duty took him southward into Alabama and eventually as far south as Pensacola, Florida. The poorly supplied militia was constantly short on rations, and Crockett spent most of his time hunting and scavenging for food. There were also occasional encounters with Indians, both friendly and hostile.

The callousness of Crockett's accounts of his company's engagements with the Creeks belies the more sympathetic rhetoric that had been attributed to him a few years earlier in a speech opposing the Indian Removal Act of 1830. For example, Crockett describes what happened after a band of Creek warriors barricaded themselves in a house:

> We now shot them like dogs; and then set the house on fire, and burned it up with the forty-six warriors in it. I recollect seeing a boy who was shot down near the house. His arm and thigh was broken, and he was so near the burning house that the grease was stewing out of him. In this situation he was still trying to crawl along; but not a murmur escaped him, though he was only about twelve years old. So sullen is the Indian, when his dander is up, that he had sooner die than make a noise, or ask for quarters.

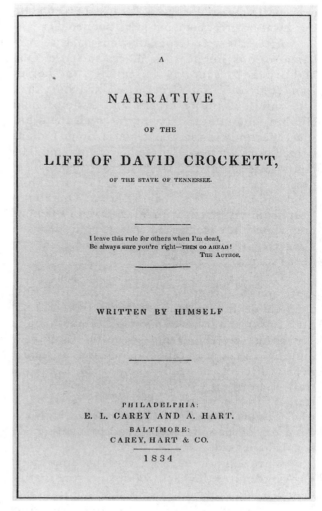

A

NARRATIVE

OF THE

LIFE OF DAVID CROCKETT,

OF THE STATE OF TENNESSEE.

I leave this rule for others when I'm dead,
Be always sure you're right—THEN GO AHEAD!
THE AUTHOR.

WRITTEN BY HIMSELF

PHILADELPHIA:
E. L. CAREY AND A. HART.
BALTIMORE:
CAREY, HART & CO.
1834

Title page for Crockett's autobiography, which he wrote with the help of Kentucky congressman Thomas Chilton

The next day the hungry troops found some potatoes in the cellar beneath the burned house and ate them, although, says Crockett, "I had a little rather not, if I could have helped it, for the oil of the Indians we had burned up on the day before had run down on them, and they looked like they had been stewed with fat meat."

For all their apparent racism these accounts do reveal Crockett's egalitarian tendencies. One incident in particular demonstrates his deep-seated distrust of rank and class pretension. Warned of an impending Indian attack, Private Crockett rushes to inform his commanding officer but to his consternation is ignored. The next day an officer arrives to relay exactly the same warning, and this time the commanding officer immediately musters the troops for a forced march. Complains Crockett: "[This] convinced me, clearly, of one of the hateful ways of the world. When I made my report, it wasn't believed, because I was no officer; I was no great man, but just a poor soldier."

After the war Crockett went back to Alabama to look for possible places to settle. One night, near present-day Tuscaloosa, the horses wandered away, and Crockett walked more than fifty miles, "wading creeks and swamps, and climbing mountains," trying to catch them but succeeded only in catching malaria. Some Indians helped him to a farm, where he recuperated. His family was astonished when he returned to Tennessee, for his fellow travelers had reported him dead and buried. With characteristic Old Southwest drollness (prefiguring Mark Twain's famous quip about the exaggerated reports of his demise), Crockett notes: "I know'd this was a whapper of a lie, as soon as I heard it."

Crockett's inveterate restlessness is nowhere more apparent than in the autobiography's final chapters dealing with his political career. He has little to say about his terms in office but much to say about electioneering for office and bear hunting while out of office. Crockett consistently depicts life on the trail—whether the campaign trail, the trail of wild game, an Indian trail, the trail of fortune, or the trail west—as a series of obstacles to overcome. Travel for Crockett is always a journey of the self: meeting and conquering personal challenges.

Throughout much of the autobiography, Crockett mutes the backwoods bragging that he believed had skewed Clarke's characterization of him, but at times, especially in the concluding chapters, something of the legendary, tall-tale Crockett can be glimpsed: the folksy stump orator verbally besting his more learned and better heeled opponents, the fearless hunter crawling blindly into a dark crevice to kill a bear with only a knife. Crockett's bear-hunting prowess, as described in an account of a particularly successful hunting trip to extreme western Tennessee, is so formidable that one suspects that Thomas Bangs Thorpe's Big Bear of Arkansas might have met a different end had Crockett crossed the Mississippi River. But even Crockett's liveliest hunting stories never sacrifice the simplicity, directness, and believability that firmly grounds the entire autobiography. (Testimonials from his contemporaries suggest that Crockett was as good a hunter as he claimed to be.)

The impression *A Narrative of the Life of David Crockett* leaves of its subject is, finally, one of an ingenuous, naturally heroic man of action, fully capable at age twelve of walking seven miles in two hours in knee-deep snow to escape an unscrupulous employer, or at sixteen of crossing a white-capped river in a borrowed canoe on a bitterly cold winter day to make his way home after a long absence, or at thirty-six of crossing a half-frozen, mile-wide flooded stream on foot in order to fetch a keg of powder so his family could have meat.

Generally ignored by critics on its release Crockett's *A Narrative of the Life of David Crockett* nonetheless proved popular with readers, both in the East and the West, selling out its first printing immediately and going into several reprintings in a matter of months, much to Crockett's delight.

Shortly after release of the book in February or March 1834, Crockett abandoned his congressional duties and set out on a tour of the North and the East. He claimed variously that the tour was to promote sales of the autobiography, to rehabilitate his health, or to study northern industrial culture, but the truth was that Crockett was fulfilling a political obligation to his powerful Whig supporters, who were hoping to exploit his rising national reputation. The tour lasted from 25 April to 13 or 14 May 1834 and included visits to Baltimore, Philadelphia, New York, Jersey City, Newport, Boston, Lowell, Providence, and Camden.

One of the results of Crockett's travels was a book-length assemblage of newspaper clippings, ghost-written speeches, and other documents of the carefully orchestrated tour, titled *An Account of Col. Crockett's Tour to the North and Down East . . . Written by Himself* and released in March 1835. Despite the claim of the subtitle Crockett's contribution was merely to collect these documents and pass them to the ghost writer, probably William Clark, a Whig congressman from Pennsylvania. What might have been a humorous inversion of the conventional narrative of the easterner traveling through the West was in the end little more than a propagandist anti-Jackson, pro-Bank campaign tract.

The Life of Martin Van Buren, another pro-Whig work attributed to Crockett, followed a couple of months later. This time Crockett's involvement did not extend past lending his name to the project; the caustic biography of Jackson's vice president was most likely written by Crockett's friend Augustin Smith Clayton of Georgia, another anti-Jacksonian congressman. Both *An Account of Col. Crockett's Tour* and *The Life of Martin Van Buren* fared poorly with the public as did Crockett's campaign: he lost his bid for reelection to the House of Representatives in August 1835. Shortly afterward on 1 November 1835 Crockett departed for Texas with three friends, traveling down the Mississippi River to the Arkansas River, then west to the Red River, and finally south to San Antonio.

Crockett's death at the Alamo in March 1836 effectively ended his usefulness to the Whig press, but it did not stop the publication of the works ostensibly or nominally written by him. One such narrative was commissioned by Crockett's publishers, Carey & Hart, in the hopes of salvaging the poor sales of *An Account of Col. Crockett's Tour*. The commissioned work—*Col. Crockett's Exploits and Adventures in Texas*—was supposedly based on a diary kept by Crockett that had been rescued from the Alamo, but except for elements from two of Crockett's letters the work was entirely fabricated. Published in early summer 1836, the book was ghostwritten (in a double sense, since Crockett was already dead) by Richard Penn Smith. As Carey and Hart hoped, public interest in Crockett increased dramatically after his martyrdom; the back stock of *An Account of Col. Crockett's Tour* was soon depleted, and *Col. Crockett's Exploits and Adventures in Texas* sold more than ten thousand copies in less than a year.

A series of first-person narratives written in Crockett's voice also found popular audiences after his death. These narratives were published in the Crockett almanacs, which began in 1835 while Crockett was still alive and continued for more than twenty years through 1856, more than forty-five issues in all. The Crockett almanacs were largely responsible for the creation of the tall-tale Crockett—the ring-tailed-roaring, backwoods-screaming half-man/half-alligator, yaller flower of the forest who could hunt bear, kill Indians, and fool Yankees better than any other frontiersman alive. Several of the initial tales in the almanacs were based on stories drawn from Clarke's *The Life and Adventures* and Crockett's *A Narrative of the Life of David Crockett;* for this reason it has often been thought that Crockett actually authored some of the tales, but this was not the case. Over time the tales became increasingly fantastic, and Crockett was transformed into a kind of mythic superhero. Through the almanacs, Crockett's travels continued posthumously; his adventures took him all over the United States and into Central and South America, the Pacific Islands, the Far East, and even outer space, where he saved the planet from destruction by ripping the tail off Halley's Comet.

The legend eventually displaced the man. When such writers as Walter Blair, Constance M. Rourke, and Richard M. Dorson began the twentieth-century reexamination of Crockett in the 1930s, it was quite naturally as a native comic legend and epic folk hero—a point of view that tended to value the tall tales over the autobiography. James Atkins Shackford's definitive biography *Davy Crockett: The Man and the Legend* (1956) did much to restore the historical Crockett and establish the historicity of *A Narrative of the Life of David Crockett*. More recently, scholars from many disciplines have been interested in the interplay between David Crockett the man and Davy Crockett the legend and in the various historical, cultural, and literary forces that have helped to construct and perpetuate the Crockett legend that now seems to have had more to do with print culture than with folk culture.

While popular interest in Crockett has declined considerably from its peak in the early 1950s, when nearly every young child in America owned a coonskin cap and could sing the words to Disney's "The Ballad of Davy Crockett," the Tennessean shows no signs of disappearing from the pantheon of American legends. *A Narrative of the Life of David Crockett* should remain an important work in the American literary canon for some time to come: as the prototype of an indigenous form of American humor; as a document of colloquial American dialect and usage; as one of the earliest American autobiographies (published only sixteen years after the first American edition of Franklin's autobiography); as a central cultural artifact in the construction of a national type; and as a historical record of the life and times of one of America's most popular heroes.

Bibliography:

Miles Tanenbaum, "Following Davy's Trail: A Crockett Bibliography," in *Crockett at Two Hundred,* edited by Michael A. Lofaro and Joe Cummings (Knoxville: University of Tennessee Press, 1989), pp. 192–241.

Biographies:

Edward Sylvester Ellis, *The Life of Colonel David Crockett* (Philadelphia: Porter & Coates, 1884);

Charles Fletcher Allen, *David Crockett, Scout, Small Boy, etc.* (Philadelphia: J. P. Lippincott, 1911);

Constance M. Rourke, *Davy Crockett* (New York: Harcourt, Brace, 1934);

Edwin Justice Mayer, *Sunrise in My Pocket: or The Last Days of Davy Crockett* (New York: Julian Messner, 1941);

Irwin Shapiro, *Yankee Thunder: The Legendary Life of Davy Crockett* (New York: Julian Messner, 1944);

Walter Blair, *Davy Crockett—Frontier Hero: The Truth as He Told It—The Legend as His Friends Built It* (New York: Coward-McCann, 1955); republished as *Davy Crockett: Legendary Frontier Hero* (Springfield, Illinois: Lincoln-Herndon Press, 1986);

James Atkins Shackford, *David Crockett: The Man and the Legend,* John B. Shackford, ed. (Chapel Hill: University of North Carolina Press, 1956).

References:

Walter Blair, "Six Davy Crocketts," *Southwest Review,* 25 (1940): 443–462;

Richard M. Dorson, ed., *Davy Crockett: American Comic Legend* (New York: Rockland Editions, 1939);

Richard Boyd Hauck, *Crockett: A Bio-Bibliography* (Westport, Connecticut: Greenwood Press, 1982); republished as *Davy Crockett: A Handbook* (Lincoln: University of Nebraska Press, 1986);

Dan Kilgore, *How Did Davy Die?* (College Station: Texas A&M University Press, 1978);

Michael A. Lofaro, ed., *Davy Crockett: The Man, The Legend, The Legacy, 1786–1986* (Knoxville: University of Tennessee Press, 1985);

Lofaro, ed., *The Tall Tales of Davy Crockett: The Second Nashville Series of Crockett Almanacs, 1839–1841,* facsimile edition (Knoxville: University of Tennessee Press, 1987);

Lofaro and Joe Cummings, eds., *Crockett at Two Hundred: New Perspectives on the Man and the Myth* (Knoxville: University of Tennessee Press, 1989);

Franklin J. Meine, ed., *The Crockett Almanacks: Nashville Series, 1835–1838* (Chicago: The Caxton Club, 1955).

Richard Henry Dana Jr.

(1 August 1815 – 6 January 1882)

Harold K. Bush Jr.
Michigan State University

See also the Dana entry in *DLB 1: The American Renaissance in New England.*

BOOKS: *Two Years Before the Mast: A Personal Narrative of Life at Sea,* anonymous (New York: Harper, 1840; revised edition, 1869; London: Moxon, 1841);

The Seaman's Friend; Containing a Treatise on Practical Seamanship (Boston: Little, Brown, 1841); republished as *The Seaman's Manual* (London: Moxon, 1841);

To Cuba and Back: A Vacation Voyage (Boston: Ticknor & Fields, 1859; London: Smith & Elder, 1859);

Speeches in Stirring Times and Letters to a Son, edited by Richard Henry Dana III (Boston & New York: Houghton Mifflin, 1910);

An Autobiographical Sketch (1815–1842), edited by Robert F. Metzdorf (Hamden, Conn.: Shoe String Press, 1953);

The Journal of Richard Henry Dana, Jr., edited by Robert F. Lucid (Cambridge, Mass.: Harvard University Press, 1968).

SELECTED PERIODICAL PUBLICATIONS–
UNCOLLECTED: "Journal of a Voyage from Boston to the Coast of California, by Richard Henry Dana, Jr.," edited by James Allison, *American Neptune,* 12 (July 1952): 177–186;

"Five Dana Letters," edited by Allison, *American Neptune,* 13 (July 1953): 162–176.

Richard Henry Dana Jr. in the early 1840s (Massachusetts Historical Society)

In 1834 a well-bred Harvard undergraduate from one of New England's most prominent literary families decided to leave that hallowed college for an extended voyage as a common sailor on a merchantman bound for Cape Horn and the nearly unknown California coast. It detracts not at all from his decision to note that he was forced to leave Harvard because of the weakness of his eyes. The young man's harrowing experiences on the high seas and grueling labor curing hides for export back to America resulted in his masterful *Two Years Before the Mast: A Personal Narrative of Life at Sea* (1840), a huge best-seller that was simultaneously a travel guidebook, a coming-of-age story, a realistic account of the day-to-day activities of merchant seamen, and a symbolic depiction of the death and rebirth of the tale's protagonist and narrator, Richard Henry Dana Jr.

While Dana was subsequently unable to match the greatness of his first book, *Two Years Before the Mast* is one of the most influential of all American tales of the sea, the prototype for a genre of fiction and nonfiction and the inspiration for

The Pilgrim, *Dana's first ship; painting by William S. Thompson (Santa Barbara Historical Society)*

scores of subsequent books. Dana should also be credited with pioneering the literary shift from romantic depictions of the sea to a more realistic view, although his book includes both romantic and realistic features. Finally, more than any other single work, Dana's tale initiated one of the most important trends of nineteenth-century American prose writing: quest or journey narratives, a mode of writing whose tone, content, and themes would influence such great works as Francis Parkman's *The Oregon Trail* (1849); Herman Melville's *Redburn* (1849), *White-Jacket* (1850), and *Moby-Dick* (1851); and Mark Twain's *Roughing It* (1871), *Old Times on the Mississippi* (1875), and *The Adventures of Huckleberry Finn* (1885).

Dana was born on 1 August 1815 in Cambridge, Massachusetts, the second of four children. His sister, Ruth, was one year older; a brother, Ned, was three years younger; and a sister, Susan, five years younger, died in infancy. To say that Dana's family had traditional roots and prestigious ties to the history of New England would be an understatement: Dana's first North American ancestor, also named Richard Dana, came to America in 1640; his grandfather Francis Dana (1743–1811) graduated from Harvard, was a delegate to the Continental Congress, served as an American representative to Russia in the Washington administration, and went on to become both U.S. congressman and justice of the Massachusetts Supreme Court. Dana's father,

Richard Henry Dana Sr. (1787–1879), made a name for himself as a poet, literary critic, early champion of his friend William Cullen Bryant, and editor of the *North American Review*. Dana's mother, Ruth Charlotte Smith Dana, died in 1822 when Dana was only six years old, and the loss of her took a tremendous toll upon her husband and children.

Not long after his mother died, Dana began attending one school after another in the areas surrounding Boston. His experience in these schools was almost entirely dreary and at times terrifying because of the various corporal punishments enacted by the instructors. There were only two teachers he remembers fondly in the extensive journal that he began keeping when he was twenty-seven. (It was published in 1968 as *The Journal of Richard Henry Dana, Jr.*) One of the exceptions was a young scholar Dana knew only briefly, who as he notes became "known as a writer and lecturer upon what is called the transcendental philosophy . . . a very pleasant instructor." This was, of course, Ralph Waldo Emerson, who, despite being mildly criticized by Dana for his unsystematic teachings and his loose discipline, was well liked by the students: "[there were none] so popular with us, nor perhaps so elevated in their habits of thought as Mr. E." The other teacher of note was the Reverend William H. Sandford, whom Dana credited as being the best teacher he ever encountered. Dana's school career before Harvard is also notable for the pranks and high jinks that he and his cohorts, including such students as James Russell Lowell and Thomas Wentworth Higginson, perpetrated on their instructors and fellow students. This facet of his schooling foreshadowed the far more serious disciplinary actions that he would face at Harvard.

In 1831 Dana entered Harvard College, whose president, Josiah Quincy, was mistrusted and disliked by most students, especially as he represented staid, traditional Christianity and had a stern, dogmatic view of discipline and punishment. When Dana and some of his classmates expressed public sympathy for a student who had been expelled by Quincy, they were suspended for six months from the college, beginning on 2 March 1831. He was then remarkably lucky to associate with a brilliant scholar, Leonard Woods Jr. of Andover Theological Seminary, under whom he studied Latin, Greek, German, and geometry. Woods's rather liberal approach proved to be a boon to the young Dana, so much so that upon his return to Harvard, he wrote in his diary, he felt like a "slave whipped to his dungeon."

Because of his intensive work with Woods, Dana began to excel in his Harvard classwork. However, during the summer vacation after his junior year he was afflicted severely by the measles, after which his failing eyesight caused him to leave Harvard until such time as he was physically capable of continuing. The attempts to treat his weakened eyes seemed useless, and after a lengthy stay at his home, he determined to sail as a regular seaman on a merchant ship. The decision to enter what amounted to a foreign world for the genteel Bostonian proved to be, as Bliss Perry puts it, "Dana's magical chance," providing him the opportunity to see the working life of a different class of citizens as well as to visit the opposite end of North America. To get there he would have to survive the stormy passage that links the Atlantic and Pacific Oceans, Cape Horn at the bottom of the South American continent.

Two Years Before the Mast, the preeminent autobiographical sea adventure, essentially begins and ends with Dana's voyage out of and his return to Boston Harbor. Dana boarded the *Pilgrim* on 14 August 1834 and returned on a larger ship, the *Alert,* on 20 September 1836. Although this is roughly a two-year span, the title—as has often been noted—is a bit deceiving, since Dana spent approximately sixteen months of the period on the California coast, principally in Santa Barbara, Monterey, San Diego, Los Angeles, and San Francisco, working principally at gathering and curing bullock hides (or "hide-droghing"). Nonetheless, much of the book

describes the difficult day-to-day tasks of sailors, the oppressive authority of the ship's captain and other officers, and the dangers facing sailors, especially those posed by the threatening conditions around the Cape. As the largely innocent protagonist thrust into a tough world of mindless servitude and lurking dangers, Dana survives and endures, his growth to manhood echoing some of the major strains of American fiction and autobiography before and since.

The book can easily be broken down according to a three-part structure: the voyage out from Boston, around Cape Horn, and to California (chapters 1–8); the period of work in California (chapters 9–28); and the difficult voyage home (chapters 29–36). It is symmetrically balanced in its allotment of chapters, with the twenty California chapters flanked on either side by eight chapters devoted to each voyage. Dana's struggles with his poor eyesight nicely dovetail into his book's central theme of one man's journey to enlightenment and a vision of the sublime. The actual names of the ships also serve Dana's purpose, the voyage out in the *Pilgrim* suggesting his role as seeker of truth, and his voyage back in the *Alert* denoting a person of intensive observational skills and perhaps even rarefied vision.

Perhaps the most striking feature of the narrative is the transformation of the protagonist from an awkward neophyte into a hardened veteran of the sea. Initially, Dana has a difficult time even understanding the orders that are being rapidly shouted from the officers to the men. One of the first memorable images of the book is that of Dana, ordered aloft before he has gained his "sea legs," bending over the rails to vomit into a churning sea. He regularly notes and evaluates the various skills of his fellow sailors, and it is obvious throughout that he is trying hard to measure up as a competent worker aboard the *Pilgrim.* His desire to match his shipmates was no doubt all the greater because of his obvious difference from them in class and education. He watches carefully when older sailors perform difficult tasks, telling the reader that he intends to be able to carry out the same task later in the voyage.

The reader is treated to detailed descriptions of life aboard the *Pilgrim*: the autocratic and sometimes vicious rulership of Captain Thompson; the painstaking maintenance of the ship, including long hours of scraping, painting, and various other menial tasks; the never-changing meals of biscuits, tea, and beef; and the sleeping in snatches when not on watch. As Dana records, "the discipline of the ship requires every man to be at work upon something

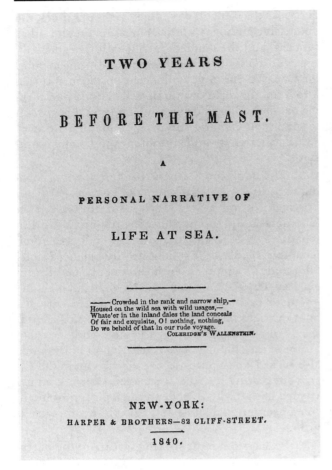

TWO YEARS

BEFORE THE MAST.

A

PERSONAL NARRATIVE OF

LIFE AT SEA.

—— Crowded in the rank and narrow ship,—
Housed on the wild sea with wild usages,—
Whate'er in the inland dales the land conceals
Of fair and exquisite, O! nothing, nothing,
Do we behold of that in our rude voyage.
COLERIDGE'S WALLENSTEIN.

NEW-YORK:
HARPER & BROTHERS—82 CLIFF-STREET.
1840.

*Title page for Dana's first book, in which he depicts the
life of a common seaman*

when he is on deck, except at night and on Sundays."

Dana occasionally refers to sailors as slaves and recognizes the captain as "lord paramount" who can without fear of retribution whip uncooperative seamen. He believes "There is nothing for Jack [the common sailor] to do but to obey orders" and on another occasion bluntly states, "Jack is a slave aboard ship." The climax of such slave imagery is the atrocious scene in which a seaman named Sam is flogged by Captain Thompson: "You've got a driver over you! Yes, a slave-driver—a negro driver! I'll see who'll tell me he isn't a negro slave!" After this horrible treatment, Dana remarks, "I thought of our situation, living under a tyranny; of the character of the country we were in; . . . and vowed that if God should ever give me the means, I would do something to redress the grievances and relieve the sufferings of that poor class of beings, of whom I then was one."

In the opening pages of the first chapter, Dana makes the case for the uniqueness of *Two Years Be-*

fore the Mast because of its point of view. He invokes the romantic sea novels of James Fenimore Cooper, in particular *The Pilot* (1824) and *The Red Rover* (1827), arguing that such popular books should be considered of a different sort of book from his own because they offer accounts by naval officers, each of whom goes to sea "as a gentleman, 'with his gloves on' (as the phrase is), and who associates only with his fellow-officers, and hardly speaks to a sailor except through a boatswain's mate." An officer inevitably has "a very different view of the whole matter from that which would be taken by a common sailor."

Dana claims a greater realism for his work than previously attained because prior to it, "A voice from the forecastle has hardly yet been heard." He asserts his "design is, and it is this which has induced [him] to publish the book, to present the life of a common sailor at sea as it really is—the light and the dark together." Dana's emphasis in seeking a lowly, common "voice" to speak for the plight of the everyday sailor and his desire to balance the more romantic and "lighter" view of sailing with the more realistic and "darker" view of the actual lives of seamen should be seen as one of the earliest and surely one of the most influential uses of realism in American literary prose.

This emphasis on the "real" experiences of sailors is occasionally reaffirmed by the authorial asides that regularly interrupt the story's main narrative: "I have here gone out of my narrative course in order that any who read this may form as correct an idea of a sailor's life and duty as possible. I have done it in this place because, for some time, our life was nothing but the unvarying repetition of these duties." Much later, in decrying the narrow visions of "those who have never lived anywhere but in their own homes, and never walked but in one line from their cradle to their graves," Dana provides an especially cogent articulation of the philosophy of the conscientious realist: "We must come down from our heights, and leave our straight paths, for the byways and low places of life, if we would learn truths by strong contrasts; and in hovels, in forecastles, and among our own outcasts of foreign lands, see what has been wrought upon our fellow-creatures by accident, hardship, or vice."

Dana, however, did not write only in a realistic mode. The many pastoral moments in the book reflecting the grandeur and at times sublimity of nature as well as the frequent allusions to and quotations from Romantic literature—the opening epigraph is from Samuel Taylor Coleridge's "The Piccolomini" and the final page of the "Concluding Remarks" quotes George Gordon, Lord Byron's

"Childe Harold's Pilgrimage"—betray Dana's affinities with the magic of the sea and his associations of the seafaring life with heroism and self-reliance. Dana's early description of the sunrise shows his romantic tendencies:

> There is something in the first grey streaks stretching along the eastern horizon and throwing an indistinct light upon the face of the deep, which combines with the boundlessness and unknown depth of the sea around you, and gives one the feeling of loneliness, of dread, and of melancholy foreboding, which nothing else in nature can give.

The cadence of the book of Genesis is noticeable in the phrase, "the face of the deep" (Gen. 1:2), and the sensations of both grandeur and dread bespeak the power of an encounter with the sublime in nature, a common feature of romantic thought.

Dana is mainly realistic in his lengthy descriptions of life in the nearly primeval lands along the California coast. The labor was dreadfully hard, and the sailors on land were worked much like slaves. The months in California were a monotonous succession of sailing up and down the coast in search of hides, some fifty-five thousand that required two vessels to ship to Boston. Dana's stay in California is remarkable for his close contact with workers from a variety of geographical backgrounds. In San Diego, where he spends about four months, four Hawaiians are part of his working group. Dana becomes close friends with these men and begins the task of learning their language and customs. Elsewhere, Dana acquired a solid knowledge of Spanish. He befriended Spaniards and Mexicans as well as Russians, Italians, and other ethnic groups, all of whom succeed in motivating Dana's curiosity about their languages and customs. Despite such curiosity, Dana's prejudice toward the local inhabitants perhaps betrays his staid Brahman background as he considers most Mexicans nothing more than "hungry, drawling, lazy half-breeds."

Upon the return voyage Dana returns to highly romantic storytelling. Perhaps the most powerfully romantic moment of the book is his representation of the encounter with a massive iceberg off of Cape Horn:

> All hands were soon on deck, looking at it, and admiring in various ways its beauty and grandeur. But no description can give any idea of the strangeness, splendor, and really, the sublimity, of the sight. Its great size;—for it must have been from two to three miles in circumference, and several hundred feet in height;—its slow motion, as its base rose and sank in the water, and its high points nodded against the clouds; the dashing of the waves upon it, which, breaking high with foam, lined its base with a white crust; and the thundering sound of the cracking of the mass, and the breaking and tumbling down of huge pieces; together with its nearness and approach, which added a slight element of fear,—all combined to give to it the character of true sublimity.

This may very well be the longest sentence in the entire book, and justifiably so, detailing as it does the sight that captures most fully the transcendent and the sublime, one of the surest stamps of the romantic spirit.

Perhaps the poetic cadence of the passage, its joining of "strangeness" with "splendor," "beauty and grandeur" with "fear," and its emphasis on sheer size and whiteness, caught the eye of the young Melville, who read *Two Years Before the Mast* and corresponded briefly with Dana about sea fiction. It was Dana who first suggested in a letter that Melville try writing about the lives of seamen on a whaler, a matter that Melville took up later in his classic novel *Moby-Dick,* whose description of the white whale can be related to Dana's iceberg. Like Melville, Dana is probably most accurately described as a writer who operates effectively in both romantic and realistic modes.

Dana's story has the resonance of myth, for in his odyssey he is tested, learns of his vulnerabilities and strengths, faces the prospect of death, and returns home a new man. Recognizing his ignorance of ship manners and language, Dana dies to his own pride on the voyage out. At the end of his stay in California, as he is longing to return home, Dana is ordered to stay for at least another year and return with the *Pilgrim*. This shocking news contradicts what he had earlier been told and brings Dana to despair. However, through his conniving and ultimately by getting another sailor to replace him, he is able to join the crew of the *Alert*. His closest encounter with death comes on the return voyage when the ship is stymied several times in its attempt to round stormy and abominably cold Cape Horn. To make matters worse Dana at the time is struck with a monstrous toothache that nearly kills him. After the ship negotiates the cape and begins its northward trek, he begins a slow recovery from the illness. The mythic hero is thus regenerated into an older and wiser spiritual being and returns home to declare publicly a newly restored "vision" engendered by his journey.

Two Years Before the Mast received excellent reviews heralding it as a singular contribution to American letters. William Cullen Bryant in the *Democratic Review,* for example, called it "a new thing in our literature," one marked by a "perfect verity." But though the book was long a best-seller, it made

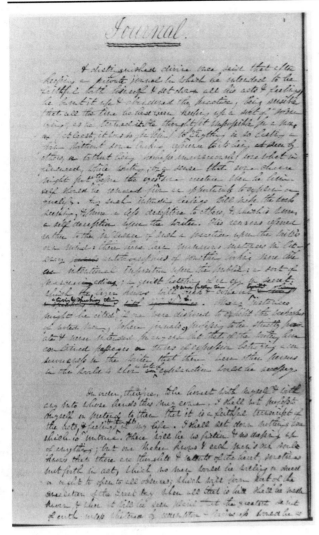

The first page of the journal Dana began keeping on 17 December 1842 (Massachusetts Historical Society)

tic style: *Ned Myers; or, A Life before the Mast* came out in 1843, and was soon followed by *Afloat and Ashore* and its sequel, *Miles Wallingford,* both published in 1844.

The most significant accomplishment by an author influenced by Dana's work was surely Melville's joining of realistic sea stories with a variety of mythic and romantic themes in his novels. Because of this connection in particular, *Two Years Before the Mast,* with its innovative and varied modes of discourse—realistic observer of everyday life, romantic poet of the sea, and inscriber of autobiographical self-searching—should be regarded as one of the more important shaping influences of the literary period that has come to be called the "American Renaissance" (1850–1855), the high point of which was, for many critics, Melville's great novel of the whale.

Dana graduated from Harvard in 1837 and entered Harvard's Dane Law School later in the same year; he was admitted to the bar and commenced his own law practice in 1840—all of which happened prior to the publication of *Two Years Before the Mast.* As his law practice burgeoned subsequent to the great success of his book, and with his marriage to Sarah Watson in 1841, with whom he would raise six children, Dana moved into a career and life that would engage him intensely for the rest of his days. Despite many distractions, though, Dana did write extensively in his journal, which he began on 17 December 1842 and kept for roughly twenty years.

The Journal of Richard Henry Dana, Jr. is a great treasure of information about the man and his travels. Included as a preface, *An Autobiographical Sketch (1815–1842)* (1953) offers a valuable look at Dana's life from birth through the date of its composition in 1842. The body of the *Journal* covers not only Dana's personal life and professional career but also provides the details of his reactions during his later travels: to England and France in 1856, to Cuba in 1859, and around the world in 1859–1860.

Shortly after his marriage Dana published *The Seaman's Friend* (1841), a book of practical seamanship and advice for seafarers, especially beginners. It includes a lengthy glossary of sea terms and delineates sea customs, legal codes, and the practical duties of mariners. Establishing Dana's expertise on maritime law and furthering his reputation as a spokesman for the common seaman and his rights, the book opened the way for him to become an advocate for many troubled sailors. He would not publish another book for the next eighteen years.

Settling into his law practice, Dana aspired to legal greatness, perhaps hoping to achieve high public office later in life. Evidently a workaholic, he

Dana little money. He had made a hasty and ill-advised arrangement with his publisher, the Harper brothers, that gave him only a single cash payment of $250 for the rights to the book for twenty-nine years. While the Harpers earned an estimated $10,000 from the book in its first two years, and possibly as much as $50,000 over the life of the agreement, Dana reaped only the emotional satisfaction of being recognized as the author of one of the widest-selling books of the era.

An immediate result of the success of Dana's book was the publication of many similar tales: Samuel Leech's *Thirty Years from Home, or A Voice from the Main Deck* (1843), Nicholas Isaac's *Twenty Years Before the Mast* (1845), and William Nevens's *Forty Years at Sea* (1845) are just three of the better-known volumes. Cooper also brought out sea novels that show the influence of Dana's more rigorously realis-

spent long hours in his office, regularly depriving himself of sufficient sleep and sometimes skipping meals to continue his work. In large part Dana's dedication stemmed from constant financial pressure: his legacy from his parents was negligible, and he felt burdened with the responsibility of providing for his growing family in a manner commensurate with the upper-class background he shared with his wife. The result of his years of physical neglect and stressful overwork were periods of physical exhaustion and collapse, which resulted in the prescription of voyages as medical and spiritual remedies.

Dana took an active interest in the political issues of the day and was much before the public. He was one of the initiators of the National Free Soil convention held in 1842 in Buffalo. He became involved in two of the notable cases that resulted from the notorious Fugitive Slave Act of 1850: he attempted to help the rescuers of the fugitive slave called Shadrach in 1851; he also came to the aid of fugitive slave Anthony Burns in 1854. Dana agreed to help in these cases because of his strong antislavery sentiment, and he did so without ever garnering legal fees. The defense of Burns, which did not succeed, brought about a physical assault upon Dana that nearly killed him. Dana also was a delegate to the Constitutional Convention of Massachusetts held in Boston in 1853, was appointed as U.S. district attorney for Massachusetts by Abraham Lincoln in 1861, and unsuccessfully ran for the U.S. Congress in 1868.

Dana also maintained a lasting connection with the important literary figures of the era. In 1855 he was a founding member of a literary fellowship called the "Saturday Club," which met regularly to dine at the Parker House, an elite establishment known throughout New England. The other members of the club included Oliver Wendell Holmes, James Russell Lowell, Henry Wadsworth Longfellow, Ralph Waldo Emerson, Louis Agassiz, John Lothrop Motley, Nathaniel Hawthorne, William Dean Howells, Henry James Sr., Francis Parkman, William Hickling Prescott, Charles Sumner, and John Greenleaf Whittier. These were the predominant literary names of the nineteenth century in New England, and Dana's close association with these refined gentlemen helped to assuage the growing stress that his career and financial concerns brought upon him.

In 1856, when his wife was pregnant with their sixth child and his law practice, as usual, was oppressively busy, Dana was able to fulfill a longtime dream of visiting Europe. He sailed from Boston on 2 July and returned from Liverpool about six weeks later, on 23 August. Most of his visit was spent in sightseeing in Great Britain, the land that he had come to associate most fully with his own personal and ideological roots. Thanks to introductory letters from his close friend Sumner, a famous American statesman who had visited Britain the year before, Dana was able to dine with royalty and important political and literary leaders.

Among the highlights of the trip Dana recorded in the *Journal* were his multiple visits to Westminster Abbey: "Oh, the ancient, the solemn grandeur of this place! The height of its roofs, the long perspective of its aisles, the deep sombre color of its walls, the accumulation of its monuments of all ages—there is but one thing to do, and that is to let the tears come." Architectural wonders such as this, according to Dana, were "not made for the luxury or pride of men, but [as] a grand dedication to the Glory of God." Regarding the British Museum, Dana claims that "it is quite out of the question to describe this noble institution. . . . [it contains] everything bearing upon everything."

Dana's description of his visit to Windsor again betrays his keen enjoyment. He recalls how his party "went off, through a beautiful country, past villages, churchyards, spires, rising above the woods, parks, villas, cultivated fields, hedgerows and green lanes, and were set down, in the ancient town of Windsor. . . . [It is] a true old English village, streets narrow and winding, houses old and quaint, . . . but the castle itself towers and dominates over the whole country, on its lofty site . . . and rises into majestic towers." Dana calls Windsor "beautiful beyond description" and the "greatest city of Christendom."

Dana also provides reverent impressions of the university towns of Cambridge and Oxford: "There is something about Oxford, which no other place in the world exactly equals. Antiquity, historical associations, venerable architecture . . . and the all pervasive presence of the means and appliances of learning, and over all, the religious nature of the institutions, give to this spot a character unlike that of any other place in Christendom." A prominent characteristic of Dana's comments throughout his stay is his obvious reverence for Great Britain as the cradle of American culture and as the preeminent exemplar of Christian thought in the modern world.

Dana clearly tried to see as much of the sites as he could, a task made more difficult because of a hectic social calendar. Dana gives detailed accounts of his scores of visits with royalty. On one occasion, near the end of his allotted time, he dined with author Thomas Babington Macaulay, who encouraged Dana to use his final week to explore Paris and parts of France. Partly as a result of Macaulay's advice, Dana embarked on a whirlwind tour of Paris: in his fifty-eight-hour visit to the French capital, Dana saw many of the most famous sights and felt satisfied to be able to sample French culture, even if briefly. While his excursions were "a full day's work," his impressions were favorable: "the several ideas remained of the nicest order, quiet, and taste, and a lavishness of expense, and a presence everywhere of the glories of France." The Louvre is a "stupendous affair," and those buildings leading away from it, including the "Place Carousel, the Tuilleries, the gardens of the Tuilleries, the Place de la Concorde, and the Avenue of the Champs Elysées, ending in the Arc de Triomphe," offer the "finest vista in any capitol in the world."

Upon his return to America, Dana continued his intensive public and legal careers. As his biographer Charles Francis Adams claimed, "it was during these years—the comparatively brief period between 1856 and 1860—that Dana's practice was largest and most absorbing. His forensic reputation then stood at its height. A harder life than he lived during these years, or one better calculated to develop any lurking weak centre in the physical nervous system it would have been difficult to devise. . . . The routine of his life during those years was as simple as it was killing."

Dana was given the chance to visit Cuba in February 1859, and though he planned to take the time to relax, he spent his brief visit in a frenzied attempt to see and do everything that could be done, much as he had done in Paris. Despite being immediately thrown back into the same hectic pace upon his return, Dana was somehow able to use his extensive notes from the journey to put together and publish a book, *To Cuba and Back: A Vacation Voyage* (1859). His great compulsion to produce is indicated by the book's being published and sold a mere two months after his return to Boston!

Given the speed of its composition, it is not surprising that *To Cuba and Back: A Vacation Voyage* is an inconsistent and spotty effort, though Dana does provide some memorable portraits of Cuban life and culture. Like *Two Years Before the Mast* the book is structured in three parts: the voyage to Cuba, the zealous and energetic chronological depiction of Dana's time on the island, and the return to Boston. Dana discusses Cuba's religion, natural beauty, politics, and perhaps most memorably its slave system. His depiction of the miserable circumstances of slave workers on the huge sugar plantation that he visited stays with the reader long after the majority of the book has been forgotten. Dana's description of the Cuban bullfights shows his sharp eye for detail and his natural artistic gift of expression along with a humorous vein.

Despite its unevenness, *To Cuba and Back: A Vacation Voyage* sold well, and by the end of the nineteenth century at least twenty editions had been published. Since it was almost the first detailed look at Cuba by an American, it became a common purchase as a sort of guidebook for those who would travel there.

The stress of his hectic life finally exhausted Dana, and in summer 1859 he suffered an almost total physical and emotional collapse. Upon the strong advice of his physician, Dana was convinced to leave Boston for an extended period of time. Hoping, as he had hoped more than twenty years before, that a long voyage would reinvigorate him, Dana in July 1859 departed on a round-the-world odyssey, not returning until late September 1860.

Dana's *Journal* contains a rich collection of brief sketches and episodes and is especially valuable for depicting a variety of places and cultures that few Americans before him had observed. Chronologically, Dana stopped in Cuba; Panama; California; the Sandwich Islands; California again; China, including Hong Kong, Canton, Shanghai, and Macao; Japan, including Nagasaki, Yokohama, Mount Fuji, and Hakodate; Penang; Ceylon; India; Egypt, including Cairo, the Pyramids, and Alexandria; Greece; Italy; Switzerland; Germany; Belgium; Britain; and New York. Perhaps the most compelling effect of Dana's writing is his tone, his utter delight in being set free from responsibilities and treated to an exciting montage of world culture.

Although Dana provides interesting information about American response to many exotic locales, his most extensive treatment is given to China and Japan, where his expressive ability seems to rise to the heights of his romantic appreciation. Upon his arrival in China, he is immediately struck by the intense activity and the awesome size of the population: "What a hive of industry is a Chinese town! No industry is so minute, constant & infinitesimally divided. China is an ant hill." Dana shows great interest in architecture and in religious ceremony, the latter suggested by his description of Nagasaki, Japan: "This is a great religious festival day, among the people. The temples are thronged, the women & children are dressed in their best, simple arches of bamboo dressed with leaves are thrown across the chief streets, lanterns are suspended from every available place, & transparencies prepared for the evening."

Dana is struck time and again by the foreignness of what he witnesses:

> How strange everything is! I am in the midst of China and Chinese, & from our windows & the balcony I look

Dana in middle age (National Park Service, Longfellow National Historic Site)

out upon this ancient river, literally alive with passing boats & junks, & cries as thick & fast as of birds in a forest! . . . . As we return, it is getting dusk, & the Chinese are lighting the lanterns in their boats. The river looks like a swamp of fire flies. Each boat, however small, has its little shrine, at wh. tapers or incense sticks are burned morning & night.

His feeling of unreality is again mentioned in his description of the busy market in Canton: "And, what a strange world, within! This long, narrow, winding alley—not over 4 feet wide, from house to house, crammed, jammed, brimming, overflowing, shops, shops, shops, men, men, men—a stream of life, drift-ing up, drifting down . . . ." Upon his return to New York, Dana doubtless found it odd that his long journey had come to an end: "This day opens in America—home. Been absent 433 days, of which spent about 233 on the water and 200 on land. New York completes the circumnavigation of the globe!"

Dana's world trip allowed him, for the first time since his youth, to spend a total of four weeks back in California, and he visited many of the scenes from *Two Years Before the Mast*. Dana's account of his reflections on the emergence of California as a potential world economic and cultural center were published as "Twenty-Four Years After" in the 1869 revised version of *Two Years Before the Mast,* which he published after the copyright had finally reverted back to him from the Harper brothers. In that and subsequent editions of the book for the rest of his life, Dana used the new addition to replace the "Concluding Chapter."

Dana describes a young and boisterous society that had changed radically from the near wilderness settings he had known. San Francisco, for instance, had become a city of one hundred thousand inhabitants, "one of the capitals of the American Republic, and the sole emporium of a new world, the awakened Pacific. . . . [When] I saw all these things, and reflected on what I once was and saw here, and what now surrounded me, I could scarcely keep my hold on reality at all, or the genuineness of anything, and seemed myself like one who had moved in 'worlds not realized.'" Santa Barbara is "now a seaport of the United States, a part of the enterprising Yankee nation, and not still a lifeless Mexican town."

Despite the halfhearted romantic tone of these remarks, it is clear that Dana was not altogether taken with the rapid evolution of the coast of California. He is nostalgic when he runs into a former acquaintance, Captain Wilson, who commanded the *Ayacucho* in 1835–1836: "How we walked the deck together, hour after hour, talking over the old times—the ships, the captains, the crews, the traders on shore, the ladies, the Missions, the southeasters! indeed, where could we stop?" Often he waxes eloquent about the vast changes in the landscape and the inevitability of destruction and death: "How softening is the effect of time! It touches us through the affections. I almost feel as if I were lamenting the passing away of something loved and dear—the boats, the Kanakas, the hides, my old shipmates! Death, change, distance, lend them a character which makes them quite another thing from the vulgar, wearisome toil of uninteresting, forced manual labor."

Dana seems highly ambivalent about the settlement and "Americanization" of California. His critical tone is probably somewhat a result of his own attitude about himself as a man at midcareer, uncertain about the value of his struggles, perhaps aware that his greatest achievement is twenty-four years in the past. Such a recognition is perhaps signaled by Dana's romanticizing his youth as carefree and adventurous. Dana seems to believe that both he and California seem to have moved from a romantic youth into a sort of midlife crisis.

Following his inauguration in March 1861, Abraham Lincoln appointed Dana the U.S. district attorney for the district of Massachusetts. In 1863 Dana represented the nation before the Supreme Court in the famous "Prize Cases." In 1866 it appeared that Dana's work as editor of the *Elements of International Law,* written by the famous lawyer Henry Wheaton, would add to his reputation; instead, he was sued as a plagiarist by the former editor, William Beach Lawrence. There followed a series of legal battles that would drag on for the next thirteen years, putting Dana in an unenviable legal and social position. Although he was found not to have pirated Lawrence's work, the accusation began a series of disappointments that marked the latter years of Dana's career.

Although Dana did win a seat in the Massachusetts legislature in the fall of 1866, his hopes for a more important post were never realized: he was defeated in his attempt at winning a seat in the U.S. Congress in 1868, and just when he was on the brink of being named U.S. ambassador to Great Britain under President Ulysses S. Grant in 1876, his enemies, led by Lawrence, defeated his nomination. Lawrence's depiction of Dana as a plagiarist and a cheat was apparently accepted by the influential members of the Senate Foreign Relations Committee, who held the power to accept or reject the nomination. For all practical purposes this episode marked the end of Dana's public career. He retired from active legal practice in 1878 with the goal of writing an extensive treatment of international law that he believed would be his greatest legal achievement. The book, however, was never to be published. Dana spent the closing years of his life in France, Italy, and Switzerland studying international law and working on the volume. He died in Rome on 6 January 1882 and was buried there by his wife.

In 1910 many of Dana's public speeches along with a selection of personal letters were edited by his son, Richard Henry Dana III, and published as *Speeches in Stirring Times and Letters to a Son.* In these letters, the only significant published collection of his correspondence, Dana appears as a learned, genteel father imparting stolid words of wisdom to a naive son. Of greater interest are the speeches, which reveal Dana's views on important fugitive slave issues and provide details of the many cases related to fugitive slaves with which he was involved. The book also offers a long "Introductory Sketch," written by a loving son about his famous father.

Dana's reputation as a writer rests almost entirely on *Two Years Before the Mast,* a book that reads as a compelling coming-of-age adventure story while standing as a groundbreaking travel narrative. Dana's masterpiece is a milestone of American literature in which one can detect the beginnings of the movement from romance to realism, a move that most critics see as defining American literature in the nineteenth century. Dana should be regarded as a literary pioneer and credited with the revolutionary qualities that permeate his greatest achievement.

Biographies:

Charles Francis Adams, *Richard Henry Dana: A Biography* (Boston: Houghton, Mifflin, 1891);

Richard Henry Dana III, "Introductory Sketch," in *Speeches in Stirring Times* (New York: Harper, 1910), pp. 1–63;

Samuel Shapiro, *Richard Henry Dana, Jr.: 1815–1882* (East Lansing: Michigan State University Press, 1961).

References:

Robert L. Gale, *Richard Henry Dana, Jr.* (New York: Twayne, 1969);

James D. Hart, "The Education of Richard Henry Dana, Jr.," *New England Quarterly,* 9 (1936): 3–25;

D. H. Lawrence, *Studies in Classic American Literature* (New York: Seltzer, 1923);

Robert F. Lucid, "The Influence of *Two Years Before the Mast* on Herman Melville," *American Literature,* 31 (1959): 243–256;

Lucid, "*Two Years Before the Mast* as Propoganda," *American Quarterly,* 12 (1960): 392–403;

Bliss Perry, "Dana's Magical Chance," in his *The Praise of Folly and Other Papers* (Boston: Houghton Mifflin, 1923);

Thomas Philbrick, *James Fenimore Cooper and the Development of American Sea Fiction* (Cambridge, Mass.: Harvard University Press, 1961);

Thomas Philbrick, introduction, in *Two Years Before the Mast* (New York: Penguin, 1981), pp. 7–30.

Papers:

The major Dana collections are at the Massachusetts Historical Society, Boston, and the Longfellow House, Cambridge, Massachusetts. Other important collections include those found at the Women's Archives, Cambridge, Massachusetts, and at the National Archives and the Library of Congress, both in Washington, D.C.

Amasa Delano
(21 February 1763 – 21 April 1823)

Richard V. McLamore
McMurry University

BOOK: *A Narrative of Voyages and Travels in the Northern and Southern Hemispheres: Comprising Three Voyages Round the World; Together with a Voyage of Survey and Discovery in the Pacific and Oriental Islands* (Boston: Printed for the author by E. G. House, 1817).

Characterizing himself as "a child of misfortune" drawn by ambition and curiosity to far-flung voyages and enterprises, Amasa Delano would have agreed ruefully with a reviewer's description of him in *The North-American Review and Miscellaneous Journal* for July 1817 as a "tempest-beaten mariner, who had made three or four voyages round the world, of three or four years each, with only the success of getting home again." A shipbuilder, ship's officer, captain, and owner of several vessels, Delano participated in voyages of commerce and discovery to China, India, the Pacific islands, and South America from 1789 to 1807 and wrote about them in *A Narrative of Voyages and Travels in the Northern and Southern Hemispheres: Comprising Three Voyages Round the World; Together with a Voyage of Survey and Discovery in the Pacific and Oriental Islands* (1817). The work is an account of his attempts to navigate the rapidly shifting currents of cultural contact, commercial competition, and political upheaval of the late eighteenth and early nineteenth centuries. He is, however, perhaps best known to modern readers through Herman Melville's contemptuous portrayal of him as an exemplar of morally blind and intellectually vapid American imperialism in the novella "Benito Cereno," first published in 1855 in *Putnam's Monthly* and collected in Melville's *The Piazza Tales* (1856).

Delano was born on 21 February 1763 in Duxbury, Massachusetts, to Samuel Delano and Abigail Drew Delano. In his book Delano frequently mentions his brothers, Samuel and William, as accompanying him on his voyages; his two sisters are referred to only in passing. The unidentified author of the biographical sketch that concludes *A Narrative of Voyages and Travels in the Northern and Southern Hemispheres* says that Delano's given name commemo-

Amasa Delano

rated his uncle, a lieutenant in Rogers's Rangers during the French and Indian Wars who was massacred by Indians in 1759 after being compelled by "the greatest necessity . . . to eat an Indian child which they met in the woods."

After returning from his own service in the colonial militia, Delano's father, a master shipbuilder, taught all of his sons shipbuilding and sailing. Avoiding school and study with an avidity he would later regret, Amasa Delano excelled in swimming, fishing, and hunting. He was an especially gifted swimmer, a skill that would not only earn him the admiration of many of the native peoples he would encounter during his travels but would also save his life on at least two occasions.

In 1772, assuming that the town's proximity to the colony's major port would provide more work for a shipbuilder, Delano's father moved the family to Braintree, Massachusetts. Samuel Delano could hardly have picked a less propitious time to move to the Boston vicinity: already notorious as the center of opposition to British imperial policies, Boston was already beginning to suffer from the restrictions that would, eventually, almost completely close the port. Within two years the family returned to Duxbury.

Even though anticolonial agitation had stymied his business plans, Samuel Delano, like virtually everyone else in Duxbury, supported the patriot cause, and he enlisted in the colonial army at Roxbury. In 1777, with Samuel languishing aboard the British prison ship *Rainbow,* the fourteen-year-old Amasa Delano heeded the call for recruits to join Gen. Horatio Gates in halting Gen. John Burgoyne's advance toward Albany. Mustered under the command of Capt. Joseph Wadsworth of Duxbury, he marched with the corps as far as Boston. On his arrival, however, Amasa met his father, who had recently been released from captivity. To Amasa's great annoyance, Samuel insisted that father and son return together to Duxbury.

Delano served in a militia company during the summer of 1778; the next summer he joined the crew of the privateer *Mars* for a miserable and unsuccessful nine months of cruising the waters between Boston and the West Indies. Delano recalled in *A Narrative of Voyages and Travels in the Northern and Southern Hemispheres:* "we beat about on the coast of America the greatest part of that terrible winter of 1779–1780, losing sails, rigging, spars, and men almost every day." In addition to contracting a variety of illnesses from which it took him months fully to recover, Delano acquired a lifelong aversion to the practice of privateering, which he describes as "entirely at variance with [the] first principle of honourable warfare. . . . would not say that all men engaged in this business are wicked and corrupt, but it is certainly true that few situations could be imagined where a man's conscience, his moral feelings, his sentiments of honour, and his generous ambition, would suffer more."

For the rest of the Revolutionary War Delano assisted his father in shipbuilding and sailed aboard various merchant vessels trading with the West Indies, Spain, and Portugal. During a voyage aboard the brig *Peacock,* built by Delano and his father, Delano was blown overboard in the middle of the night. Encumbered with a greatcoat and boots, his cries for help drowned out by the wind, he struggled for hours until he was able to reach the main chains of the ship and climb aboard. His adventures also included confrontations with vessels from the British fleet that scoured the coast attempting to cut off revolutionary supply lines.

After the cessation of hostilities Delano returned to shipbuilding in Duxbury and in Brunswick, Maine. In 1786 he went back to sea, making several successful voyages to the West Indies for his uncle Joseph Drew. In 1787 he took command of the *Jane,* bound for Cork, Ireland, and Saint Ubes, Portugal. Defrauded by the ship's owner and supercargo and vexed with many difficulties in carrying out his command, Delano found the voyage a succession of disasters. Finally, on 28 December 1788 the ship was wrecked off Cape Cod. Delano's bad luck continued in his next venture, a failed endeavor to raise and repair a vessel sunk in the Taunton River. "Mortified" by this failure, he considered abandoning "all enterprize of the sort" until he obtained the position of second officer aboard the *Massachusetts,* which was, at the time of her launch in September 1789, the largest merchant ship built in the United States and one of the first designed for the trade in silks, teas, spices, and other commodities with China, India, and the South Pacific.

The *Massachusetts* sailed from Boston on 28 March 1790, crossed the equator on 18 May, and reached Jakarta on 30 August. Although the ship's commander, Maj. Samuel Shaw of Boston, doubled as U. S. consul for India and China, they "found no favor in trade" in Jakarta "and were obliged to leave the port without selling any of our cargo, although it had been expressly laid in for this port." With the condition of the cargo rapidly deteriorating, they sailed for Canton on 7 September. After weathering a typhoon outside Canton Bay on 27 September they arrived in Canton to discover that Shaw's partner had run up large debts. Their cargo by this time was virtually worthless, and they lacked the funds to repair the ship or to lay in a new cargo. The *Massachusetts,* one of the few vessels in the area to survive the typhoon with only minor damage, was their only saleable commodity, and it was sold to the Danish East India Company for $65,000.

Making use of his skills as a master builder and assisted by his brother Samuel, who had also been on the crew of the *Massachusetts,* Delano undertook the repairs of a Danish ship that had been severely damaged in the typhoon. Around this time he met the British commodore John McClure, who, impressed with his skills as a sailor and shipwright, offered Delano a place on the HMS *Panther*'s mission of survey and discovery through the South Pacific. Delano, who had "a strong desire" for such service, boarded the *Panther* in Macau on 14 April 1791 as "a volunteer officer, doing duty as lieutenant, and subject to none but the Commodore's command."

Ostensibly freed from the mercenary responsibilities of commercial navigation, and surrounded by officers who "had not been exposed to any degradation of sentiment or moral feeling, by that miscellaneous intercourse with nations, in the pursuits of trade, which has too often corrupted the mind and character through the temptations of avarice and commercial policy," Delano delighted in realizing his early dreams of encountering seas, lands, and peoples unknown to other American sailors. He kept "minute and full [journals] upon whatever was extraordinary" on the voyage and also carried on a course of reading designed to make up for his earlier lack of education.

Playing on the credulity and greed that they took to be indelible American traits, Delano's English fellow officers aboard the *Panther* concocted a story about gold ore to be found in a river in one of the Babuyan Islands just north of Luzon in the Philippines. On 16 May 1791 Delano set off in pursuit of the gold, accompanied by a Malabar servant who had been instructed to point upriver whenever Delano asked him about the location of the precious metal. After six miles of tortuous hiking Delano realized that the boy had never ascended the river: "The trick was a severe one for me, but it had been well managed, and my ardor and credulity were fairly chargeable to myself. After a hard struggle with my mortification, I determined to take it in good part. . . . To relieve my mind, and to carry back something to check the force of the laugh against me, I employed myself in making observations upon the scenery, the soil, the products, the insects, and the reptiles about me." Delano and his comrade soon filled the bag that he had hoped to stuff with gold "with fowls of different kinds, and of a plumage surpassing in beauty and richness, the finest colours of the mineral kingdom." Aside from curing, for the moment, Delano's avarice, the incident taught him "how to judge of the sufferings and wants of men, whose spirits fail when they are at a distance from home, and appear to themselves to be cast out from the sympathies of the human family." Urging sympathy and understanding in place of dominance, Delano argues that commanders should recognize that "sailors, and all men, even of the meanest education, have the essential qualities of high minds, and are exalted and improved, at the same time that they are won by generosity and kindness."

The *Panther* left Port San Pio on 18 May and arrived at Palau—which Delano refers to as Pelew—on 10 June. The voyage appears to have been intended, at least in part, to counter Dutch control of the Indonesian islands by "extending," as Delano writes, "the blessings of civilization, agriculture, and Christianity among the Pelew islanders." In addi-

tion to surveying the islands to facilitate navigation and determine their productive capacities, McClure established livestock and plants such as nutmeg and clove in the Palauan agricultural system. Although Delano does not mention the fact, the introduction of nutmeg and clove to Palau was an act of economic piracy, since the Dutch, to maintain their monopoly, had ordered these plants destroyed on all but selected plantations on Ambon and Banda in the Spice Islands.

McClure also continued the English practice of maintaining a favored ruler in power against the claims of rival chiefs and factions. At Palau, therefore, Delano took part in a display of force designed to cower the other chiefs into submitting to the control of the English-backed Abba Thule. While this particular maneuver succeeded, in the long run the policy failed, as the rival chiefs also gained access to English weapons and influence. Delano was not completely cognizant of McClure's designs; nevertheless, he suspected McClure of harboring "the idea of becoming sovereign in this dominion, and of forming a people and their institutions after a model of his own."

During the sixteen days they spent on the Palau Islands, several members of the crew of the *Panther,* including Delano, helped Abba Thule quell an incipient rebellion on the island of Artingall. Delano confesses to being disconcerted by the benevolent manner in which these "pagans" conducted negotiations and prepared for war. Learning that Abba Thule had informed the rebel groups "that we should be there in three days for war," Delano, aghast at "this conduct on the part of the king," recommended "stratagems" and surprise tactics as part of "the acknowledged system of lawful and honourable warfare" practiced in "Christian nations." Abba Thule replied that while in general he thought highly of the English, he thought his own methods "more politic as well as more just." The king's opinion seemed to be borne out when the factions averted battle and settled their differences through negotiation. Holding up to his readers the example of Abba Thule's magnanimity and honesty, Delano asserts that "Christians might learn of Abba Thule a fair comment on the best principles of their own religion."

Reflecting later on "the unhappy alteration in the character and conduct of this people since they became acquainted with the Europeans," Delano decides "that the fire arms and ammunition which we had left with the Pelews had done them incalculable injury." At almost every stage of the voyage, in fact, Delano encounters evidence of the degradation of the natives caused by contact with Europeans. Dis-

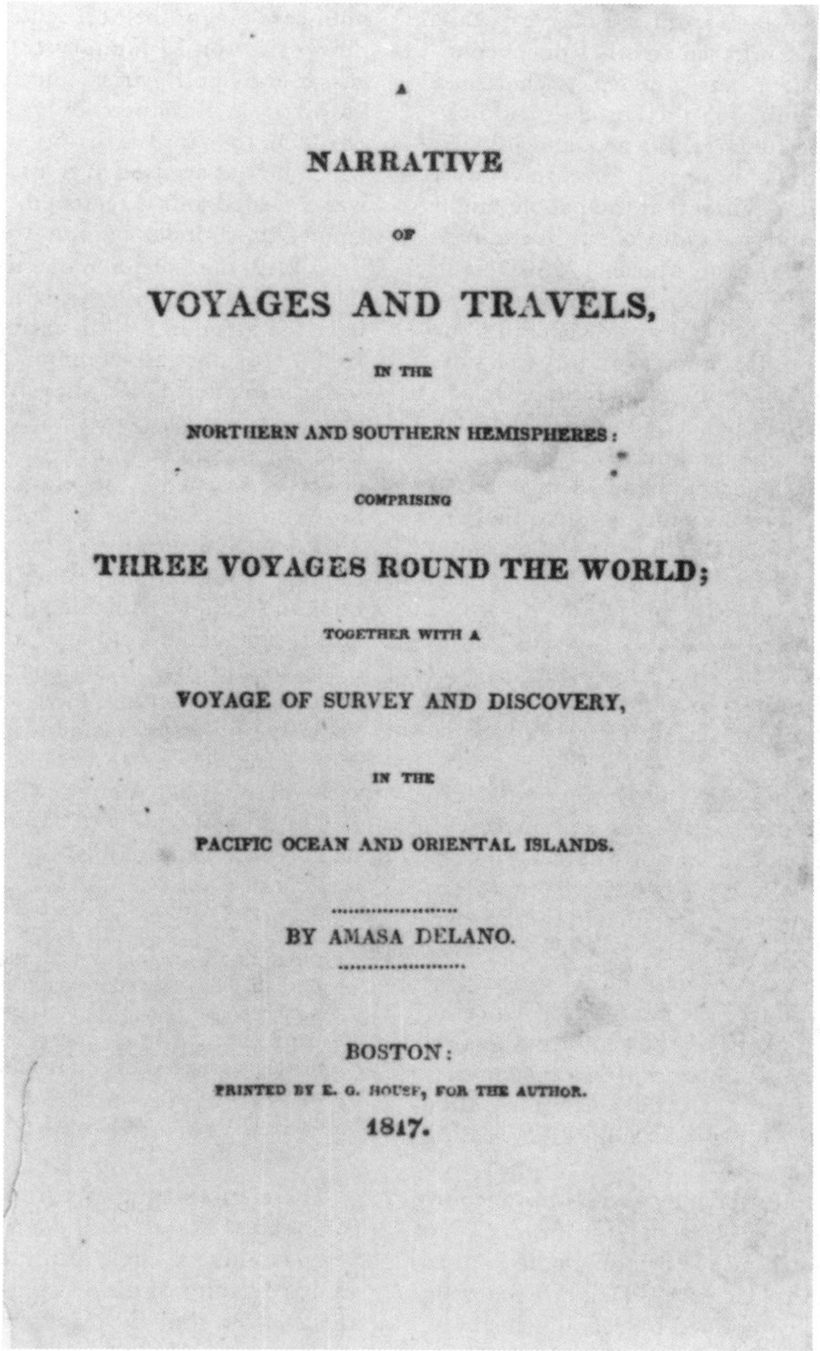

A

NARRATIVE

OF

VOYAGES AND TRAVELS,

IN THE

NORTHERN AND SOUTHERN HEMISPHERES:

COMPRISING

THREE VOYAGES ROUND THE WORLD;

TOGETHER WITH A

VOYAGE OF SURVEY AND DISCOVERY,

IN THE

PACIFIC OCEAN AND ORIENTAL ISLANDS.

BY AMASA DELANO.

BOSTON:
PRINTED BY E. G. HOUSE, FOR THE AUTHOR.
1817.

Title page for Delano's only book, in which he cites the deleterious influence of Europeans on less-developed cultures

possessed of their "early simplicity and goodness" without gaining "the intelligence and virtue of a civilized people," the Palau islanders cast doubt in Delano's mind about the wisdom and efficacy of the project of "civilization."

Leaving Palau on 27 June 1791, the *Panther* headed toward New Guinea to search for a passage through the southern part of the island. En route they visited several of the Dutch-controlled islands—most notably Ambon, which they reached on 28 September. After surveying the distillation procedures for extracting the essential oils of the clove and nutmeg and nearly creating a riot at a party given in their honor, they left for New Guinea on 10 November. Concluding that no strait was to be found, they set sail for Timor on 27 November after repelling a surprise attack from the natives, who, Delano confesses, had suffered greatly from encounters with previous Europeans. The *Panther* then set a return course for China via the Dutch- or Malay-controlled islands of Sumatra, Borneo, and Jolo. At all of these places McClure ordered his crew "to be generous in bestowing [gifts] that the people might have strong impressions in favour of our liberality."

Returning to Macau in March 1793, Delano took command of the *Eliza,* which proved to be leaky and "very dull in sailing." Reaching the French-held island of Mauritius on 10 July in a state of near exhaustion from continual pumping, Delano learned that France had beheaded Louis XVI; had declared itself a republic; had declared war on England, Spain, and Holland; and had laid an embargo on Mauritius. Maneuvering quickly and quietly to protect the interests of the Dutch owner of his cargo of sugar, Delano, in partnership with the American owner of the *Eliza,* sold the sugar and bought a larger vessel in hopes of profitably carrying cotton from Bombay to China. But "the whole project failed, and proved to be a total loss of all the capital." Delano was forced to accept free passage home in a friend's ship.

After spending five years as a master builder in Massachusetts, Delano returned to sea on 10 November 1799 at the helm of the aptly named *Perseverance,* built by Delano and his brother Samuel. For most of the next eight years Delano led the *Perseverance* and its sister ship, the *Pilgrim,* in sealing voyages off the coasts of South America and Australia. Delano was not particularly successful as a sealer; in one embarassing incident in 1804 his crew was reduced to battling a group of Australian convicts with "clubs, sticks, stones, and everything they could get hold of" for possession of a sealing ground.

Delano must thus have looked on his encounter with the Spanish ship *Tryal* on 20 February 1805 as a providential gift. In the episode, made famous in Melville's "Benito Cereno," Delano, realizing that the vessel was controlled by rebellious slaves, recaptured it. He apparently assumed that the captain, Benito Cereno, would reward him for his efforts; instead, Cereno accused Delano of attempting to steal his vessel. The dispute eventually involved the viceroy of Chile, Catholic Church officials, and representatives of the Chilean mercantile houses. Delano finally agreed to accept an $8,000 settlement and a testimonial of gratitude from the Spanish government.

After several more cruises of the sealing grounds, Delano reached Canton by way of Hawaii on 10 November 1806. He left China, which he pro-

nounces "one of the best regulated governments in the world," on 27 January 1807, stopped in Madagascar and South Africa, and returned to Boston on 26 July. He attempted only one more voyage, an 1810 trip to Saint Barthelmy in the West Indies, on which he was accused of smuggling. The *Perseverance* was boarded and threatened with seizure, and Delano escaped under cannon fire.

With the exception of a trip to Mount Vernon, Ohio, to visit relatives in 1811, Delano appears to have remained in Boston until his death on 21 April 1823. He married Hannah Appleton, a widow, sometime after 1812; they had no children. Still plagued by "misfortunes and embarrassments," Delano spent these years in obscurity and near poverty. Assisted by several unidentified "friends," he wrote *A Narrative of Voyages and Travels in the Northern and Southern Hemispheres* in 1816–1817. Although he says in the preface that he undertook the book to "obtain a competency to support myself and family through an old age" and to spend, "in a rational and profitable manner, a number of months which might otherwise have been left a prey to melancholy and painful meditations," it really represents a last, desperate attempt to rescue his sense of self-worth. When Delano assesses the undeserved fate of Eli Hayden, who had built the *Massachusetts,* he may well be thinking of his own career. Hayden, he says, was

> a man of abilities in his profession, and who deserved more than he received from the community.... His fate has been like that of too many others. After making many exertions in an honest and useful pursuit, and gaining a competency by his industry, he found himself circumvented and was obliged to retire with loss into the country.

Delano struggles throughout *A Narrative of Voyages and Travels in the Northern and Southern Hemispheres* to take his defeats philosophically. Summing up his account of his voyages on the *Massachusetts,* the *Panther,* and the *Eliza* from 1789 to 1794, he reminisces wistfully:

> At that period my mind was elastic and ready to draw every agreeable emotion from every companion, every object and every event. But trials and depressions which I have since met and endured have taken away this elasticity, and have left me with that kind of tranquility which always succeeds the permanent disappointment of high hopes, and which is some compensation for their loss. Chastised expectations, a sort of contentment with ordinary comforts, diminished activity, and the small, still pleasures of a life of peace without much responsibility remain.

Thus, as Melville perceived, *A Narrative of Voyages and Travels in the Northern and Southern Hemispheres* owes most of its interest to the psychological dramas and self-doubt with which Delano struggles throughout. Similarly, *The North-American Review,* observing "that a voyage round the world has got to be quite an every day affair," opined that "Whoever would wish to acquire a satisfactory knowledge of the ports and islands in these regions, the character, customs, and resources of their inhabitants, would doubtless look for it in some higher source, than this work." Like most travel writers of the period, Delano awkwardly attempts to blend a more or less chronologically accurate narrative of the interesting and important events he experienced with an impersonal catalogue of exotic people, places, and things and the moral and philosophical conclusions he derived from his travels. But Delano seems more concerned with demonstrating the worthiness of his own character and actions than with entertaining or instructing his readers. Like most contemporary accounts by American and European travelers and adventurers, *A Narrative of Voyages and Travels in the Northern and Southern Hemispheres* often moves abruptly from supposedly disinterested inquiry to the kind of economically motivated observation evident in McClure's "surveys." Yet Delano is by no means comfortable with the exploitation that he finds to have characterized most relationships between European and native peoples. Time and again he rails against the "un-Christian" and uncivilized manner in which Europeans "used their arts and force, as members of civilized society, to betray, to kidnap, or to seize openly and violently, the natives for the most selfish and inhuman purposes." In spite of the frequent episodes of greed and exploitation that Delano charges to his own account, he seems almost compelled to prove the worthiness of his own character as revealed in his encounters with alien cultures. Deprived of financial profits, he seeks to show that he has acquired cultural and moral capital and thereby to assert the intrinsic worth of his experiences. But, as Melville recognized, Delano's avaricious participation in reenslaving the Africans aboard the *Tryal* shows that *A Narrative of Voyages and Travels in the Northern and Southern Hemispheres* is a work of unintentional self-revelation.

References:
E. F. Carlisle, "Captain Amasa Delano: Melville's American Fool," *Criticism,* 7 (1965): 349–362;

Seymour L. Gross, ed., *A Benito Cereno Handbook* (Belmont, Cal.: Wadsworth, 1965);

Richard V. McLamore, "Narrative Self-Justification: Melville and Amasa Delano," *Studies in American Fiction,* 23 (Spring 1995): 35–54;

Herman Melville, "Benito Cereno," in his *The Piazza Tales* (New York: Dix & Edwards / London: Sampson Low, 1856), pp. 109–270;

Harold Scudder, "Melville's *Benito Cereno* and Captain Delano's *Voyages,* " *PMLA,* 43 (1928): 302–332;

Sterling Stuckey and Joshua Leslie, "Aftermath: Captain Delano's Claim against Benito Cereno," *Modern Philology,* 85 (February 1988): 265–287.

Ralph Waldo Emerson

(25 May 1803 – 27 April 1882)

Bruce A. Harvey
Florida International University

See also the Emerson entries in *DLB 1: The American Renaissance in New England; DLB 59: American Literary Critics and Scholars, 1800–1850;* and *DLB 73: American Magazine Journalists, 1741–1850.*

BOOKS: *Nature* (Boston: Munroe, 1836);
A Oration, Delivered before the Phi Beta Kappa Society, at Cambridge, August 13, 1837 (Boston: Munroe, 1837);
An Address Delivered before the Senior Class in Divinity College, Cambridge . . . 15 July 1838 (Boston: Munroe, 1841);
Essays [First Series] (Boston: Munroe, 1841; London: Fraser, 1841; expanded, Boston: Munroe, 1847);
Nature; An Essay, and Lectures on the Times (London: Clarke, 1844);
Orations, Lectures, and Addresses (London: Clarke, 1844);
Essays: Second Series (Boston: Munroe, 1844; London: Chapman, 1844);
Poems (London: Chapman, 1847; Boston: Munroe, 1847); revised and enlarged as *Selected Poems* (Boston: Osgood, 1876); revised and enlarged again as *Poems* (Boston & New York: Houghton, Mifflin, 1884 [volume 9, Riverside Edition]; London: Routledge, 1884; revised, Boston & New York: Houghton, Mifflin, 1904 [volume 9, Centenary Edition]);
Nature; Addresses, and Lectures (Boston & Cambridge: Munroe, 1849); republished as *Miscellanies; Embracing Nature, Addresses, and Lectures* (Boston: Phillips, Sampson, 1856); republished as *Miscellanies* (London: Macmillan, 1884);
Representative Men: Seven Lectures (Boston: Phillips, Sampson, 1850; London: Chapman, 1850);
English Traits (Boston: Phillips, Sampson, 1856; London: Routledge, 1856);
The Conduct of Life (Boston: Ticknor & Fields, 1860; London: Smith, Elder, 1860);

Ralph Waldo Emerson in 1847 (Concord Free Public Library)

May-Day and Other Pieces (Boston: Ticknor & Fields, 1867; London: Routledge, 1867);
Society and Solitude. Twelve Chapters (Boston: Fields, Osgood, 1870; London: Sampson, Low, Son & Marston, 1870);
Letters and Social Aims (Boston: Osgood, 1876; London: Chatto & Windus, 1876);
The Works of Ralph Waldo Emerson, 3 volumes (London: Bell, 1883);

Miscellanies (Boston: Houghton, Mifflin, 1884 [volume 11, Riverside Edition]; London: Routledge, 1884);

Lectures and Biographical Sketches (Boston & New York: Houghton, Mifflin, 1884; London: Routledge, 1884);

Natural History and Intellect and Other Papers (Boston & New York: Houghton, Mifflin, 1893 [volume 12, Riverside Edition]; London: Routledge, 1894);

Two Unpublished Essays: The Character of Socrates: The Present State of Ethical Philosophy (Boston & New York: Lamson, Wolffe, 1896);

The Journals of Ralph Waldo Emerson, 10 volumes, edited by Edward Waldo Emerson and Waldo Emerson Forbes (Boston & New York: Houghton, Mifflin, 1909–1914);

Uncollected Writings: Essays, Addresses, Poems, Reviews and Letters (New York: Lamb, 1912);

Young Emerson Speaks: Unpublished Discourses on Many Subjects, edited by Arthur Cushman McGiffert Jr. (Boston: Houghton, Mifflin, 1938);

The Early Lectures of Ralph Waldo Emerson, volume 1, edited by Stephen E. Whicher and Robert E. Spiller (Cambridge, Mass.: Harvard University Press, 1959); volume 2, edited by Whicher, Spiller, and Wallace E. Williams (Cambridge, Mass.: Harvard University Press, 1964); volume 3, edited by Spiller and Williams (Cambridge, Mass.: Harvard University Press, 1972);

The Journals and Miscellaneous Notebooks of Ralph Waldo Emerson, 16 volumes, edited by William H. Gilman and others (Cambridge, Mass.: Harvard University Press, 1960–1983).

Collections: *Emerson's Complete Works,* 12 volumes (Boston: & New York: Houghton, Mifflin, 1903–1904 [Centenary Edition]);

The Collected Works of Ralph Waldo Emerson, 5 volumes to date (Cambridge, Mass.: Harvard University Press, 1971–   ).

OTHER: Thomas Carlyle, *Sartor Resartus,* edited, with a preface, by Emerson (Boston: Munroe, 1836);

Memoirs of Margaret Fuller Ossoli, 2 volumes, written and edited by Emerson, William Henry Channing, and James Freeman Clarke (Boston: Phillips, Sampson, 1852); 3 volumes (London: Bentley, 1852);

Parnassus, edited by Emerson (Boston: Osgood, 1875).

Ralph Waldo Emerson, the most renowned New England Transcendentalist, stirred Victorian American audiences with his message of self-reliance, philosophical idealism, and forward-looking optimism. Emerson's one travel work and the only book-length volume he wrote, *English Traits* (1856), is, however, considerably less informed by his Transcendental philosophy than his other writings, either in terms of content or style. Indeed, many scholars hold that this work, a sophisticated appraisal of mid-nineteenth-century English national identity, is the least Emersonian of his publications. Rather than expanding upon abstract Idealist concepts (such as the "Over-Soul" or "Self-Reliance"), *English Traits* offers specific social observations, concrete details, abundant facts and statistics, and alternately admiring and satiric anecdotes about English literati and historical figures. Likewise, although the prose style is often allusive and aphoristic, it avoids the daunting ellipses of Emerson's more famous, visionary essays. The volume will seem less atypical, though, if the reader recognizes that it engages a basic theme that preoccupied Emerson throughout his career—the opposed claims, on the one side, of nature, potentiality, and liberty; and, on the other, culture, realized power, and tradition.

English Traits received mixed reviews in the contemporary British and American journals, but the volume sold well. It is judged to be one of the best travel works on England ever composed by an American. Part sociological treatise, historical survey, and travelogue, it has garnered high praise for its lively commentary on the rich contradictoriness of English society and culture during the Victorian era.

The incisiveness of Emerson's reflections are all the more striking when one realizes that he spent relatively little time abroad. Born in Boston on 25 May 1803, the fourth child of William and Ruth Haskins Emerson, Emerson led a conventional life as a devoted family man and respected citizen of Concord, with only his lectures and essays voicing his radical critique of the soul-stultifying materialism and propriety of mid-nineteenth-century American society. Emerson, his mother, and his siblings suffered genteel impoverishment after his father (pastor of Boston's First Church) died when Ralph Waldo was eight, but Emerson endured these early years of deprivation and graduated from Harvard in 1821, continuing to train for the ministry at Harvard's Divinity School. Upon becoming a minister, however, Emerson became dissatisfied on philosophical grounds with his chosen vocation and resigned his post in 1832 to embark on his lifelong career as a brilliant lecturer and leading light of the Transcendentalist movement.

Emerson's pamphlet *Nature* (1836) and formal addresses—*A Oration, Delivered before the Phi Beta Kappa Society, August 13, 1837* (1837), commonly titled "The American Scholar," and *An Address Delivered before the Senior Class in Divinity College, Cambridge . . . 15 July 1838* (1841), called "The Divinity School Address"—vigorously announced a program of spiritual and imaginative renewal, premised upon the potentiality of an institutionally independent self in tune with what Emerson called the cosmic "Over-Soul." His initial writings were rebuffed by Boston clergy and Harvard professors; but by the time the collection *Essays [First Series]* (1841) was published, Emerson's reputation was assured. By the end of the Civil War Emerson had become nationally revered and an internationally famous author. In the last two decades, critics and biographers have increasingly turned to Emerson's copious journals, which often record his personal anxieties and darker meditations and suggest that the optative mood of his published writings was maintained courageously rather than complacently. Emerson died of pneumonia, after a gradual waning of physical, literary, and oratorical power, on 27 April 1882.

Emerson first visited England and the Continent in 1832–1833 primarily for health reasons, but it was his second visit to England, from October 1847 to July 1848, to present a lecture series hosted by the Mechanics' Institutes in Lancashire and Yorkshire that led him to compose *English Traits*. Emerson planned to write the book while in England, yet it took him nearly a decade to complete it. His journal entries and letters home needed to be supplemented by extensive research (an approach at odds with Emerson's usual practice); moreover, his many lecture tours in the United States during the early 1850s frequently drew him away from the task of finishing the book.

Finally published in August 1856, *English Traits* immediately became one of Emerson's more popular works. The source of its popularity was threefold: Emerson had whetted his audience's appetite by offering more than forty lectures on England in lyceums from New England to Saint Louis; in an age of patriotic boosterism, his fellow citizens were curious to hear how the sage from Concord would describe the older, parent country; for those impatient with Emerson's more obscure Transcendental musings, the plain intelligibility of the subject promised to be a pleasant departure. The eagerly anticipated volume was widely reviewed on both sides of the Atlantic, with British reviewers either defending or attacking the author for perceived anti-English jabs and American reviewers complaining that, as one put it, Emerson had "laid it on pretty thick" in his adulation of the parent country.

English Traits occasionally situates Emerson as an embodied traveler in time and space—making the transatlantic journey, visiting country houses, inspecting the ruins of Stonehenge—but generally it is more a historical analysis of English character and culture than a travelogue recording scenery, memorable sites or monuments, and encounters with noteworthy individuals. Emerson rarely offers pictorial set pieces; instead, in each chapter he exemplifies a particular trait, ranging widely, in a pastiche fashion, through the present as well as the dense fabric of the British past.

In the first of his nineteen chapters, "First Visit to England," Emerson briefly recalls his journey to England in 1832 after a tour of Sicily, Italy, and France. He describes in thumbnail sketches interviews with Horatio Greenough (the American sculptor) and Walter Savage Landor in Florence and with Samuel Taylor Coleridge, Thomas Carlyle, and William Wordsworth in England. The sketches of the British authors, with the exception of Carlyle, are perfunctory and dismissive. Coleridge seemed to Emerson "old and preoccupied, and could not bend to a new companion and think with him." Wordsworth left him with the "impression of a narrow and very English mind; of one who paid for his rare elevation by general tameness and conformity." Intentionally or not, these sketches signal Emerson's resistance to the cultural and literary claims of the parent country. In contrast to such opinionated, stuffy British literary masters, Emerson delights in his countryman, Greenough, whose organic and functional theory of art won his approval. Emerson raises this tacit comparison—between the vital youth of the home country and the decrepit conventionality and arrogance of the older one—intermittently throughout the remainder of his study.

English Traits, proper, begins after Emerson's second chapter, in which he narrates the crossing from Boston to Liverpool and ponders good-humoredly the possibility of calamity and the overwhelming primal power of the sea. The remaining chapters may be divided into three sets. The first set, chapters 3 through 9, takes different slants upon English national identity, although each chapter actually overlaps the others considerably in content. The middle of the book, chapters 10 through 15, examines particular institutions or features of British culture and society. The last

Henry is quite unable to labor lately since his sickness, & so must resign the garden into other hands, but as Private Secretary to the President of the Dial, his works & fame may go out into all lands, and, as happens to great Premiers, quite extinguish the titular Master. My reading lately is to the subject of Poetry, which has at least this advantage over many others, that it pays the student well day by day, even if it should fail to reward his inquisition with one adequate perception after many days & nights. The Custom of that Enchanted hall I have often heard of, I have often experienced. The Muse receives you at the door with godlike hospitality, gives bread & wine & blandishment will turn the world for you into a ballad drives you mad with a ballad with a verse with a syllable, leaves you with that, & Behold! afar off shines the Muse &

A page from Emerson's 10 April 1842 letter to Margaret Fuller concerning his taking over the editorship of the Dial *(Ralph Waldo Emerson Memorial Association Collection, Houghton Library, Harvard University)*

chapters cover Emerson's visit with Carlyle (a respected friend and correspondent from the days of his first trip) and their tour of the ancient Druid ruins and environs, miscellaneous observations, and, last, a transcript of an address given in November 1847 to the Manchester Athenaeum.

The first major sequence begins with two chapters in which Emerson assesses the essential character of the English people. In chapter 3, "Land," he reviews climatic conditions, the island's advantageous location for international commerce, and its abundant natural resources, which make it a "miniature of Europe." This chapter, though, focuses less on the effect of topography on national character than on how national character has shaped the landscape. Emerson emphasizes, in particular, that "art" has "conquer[ed] nature" and "transform[ed] a rude, ungenial land into paradise of comfort and plenty"; the "fields have been combed and rolled till they appear to have been finished with a pencil instead of a plough." This ingenuity in transforming the natural environment, Emerson believes, has led to Britain's maturity as a nation and its global domination; yet further development seems unlikely: "British power has culminated, is in solstice, or [is] already declining." In the fourth chapter, "Race," Emerson indecisively ponders whether British ascendancy can be accounted for in terms of "blood or race." Emerson finds the notion of national-racial identity dubious but nonetheless devotes the last half of the chapter to describing typical English physiognomies and concludes that the English have "more constitutional energy than any other people."

Chapters 5 through 9–titled "Ability," "Manners," "Truth," "Character," and "Cockayne"–laud the English for their probity, sincerity, industry, and stamina. Invariably, however, Emerson qualifies his praise. Strength of character and utilitarian habits have given them "the leadership of the modern world," but they are also, he claims, "impatient of genius, or of minds addicted to contemplation." Although the country's technological wizardry is astounding, British workers have become mere appendages to their machinery–indeed, industry "give[s] a mechanical regularity to all the habit and action of men. A terrible machine has possessed itself of the ground, the air, the men and women, and hardly even thought is free." The English display remarkable civility; yet by this "Gibraltar of propriety, mediocrity gets intrenched, and consolidated, and founded in adamant." Emerson asserts that while "traditions and usages" of liberty are salutary, the Englishman is too inclined to "force his island

by-laws down the throat of great countries, like India, China, Canada, [and] Australia" and is given to smugness.

The next chapter sequence–"Wealth," "Aristocracy," "Universities," "Religion," "Literature," and "The 'Times'"–assesses English national identity by turning to more specific social or cultural institutions. Once again, Emerson expresses ambivalence. The aristocracy, a holdover from feudalism, "shocks republican nerves"; yet the same aristocracy, besides being known for good breeding and talented statesmen, preserves in mansions and palaces glorious art works and cultural artifacts. Oxford produces splendid regimens of well-heeled and well-educated gentlemen; yet its resistance to new ideas stifles imaginative enterprise. English literature, likewise, strikes Emerson as being mediocre, at best "common sense inspired"; in "the absence of the highest aims, of the pure love of knowledge and the surrender to nature, there is the suppression of the imagination, the priapism of the senses and the understanding." Emerson also rebukes *The London Times* as a guide of national opinion for being more facile than moral in the light it sheds on the country's affairs.

The final chapters are a miscellany, and few critics have been satisfied by them. In chapter 16, "Stonehenge," Emerson recollects his tour of the ancient ruins in the company of Carlyle. He dryly reduces the romantic mystery of the site, remarking that the difficulty of handling and carrying the stones presents no marvel: "the like is done in all cities, every day, with no other aid than horse-power." The chapter is notable, though, for containing Emerson's most succinct musing upon the essential contrast between America and England:

> I saw everywhere in the country proofs of sense and spirit, and success of every sort: I like the people: they are as good as they are handsome; they have everything, and can do everything: but meantime, I surely know, that, as soon as I return to Massachusetts, I shall lapse at once into the feeling, which the geography of America inevitably inspires, that we play the game with immense advantage; that there and not here is the seat and centre of the British race; and that no skill or activity can long compete with the prodigious natural advantages of that country, in the hands of the same race; and that England, an old and exhausted island, must one day be contented, like other parents, to be strong only in her children.

The idea of the movement of empire westward was a commonplace of the era; the latter part of the passage, which sounds a valedictory note upon

British culture as being nearly moribund, reflects Emerson's adoption of a cyclical theory of history, which he derived from the conclusions of Carlyle and German historians. While America, too, would be subject to the same cycles, Emerson believed it was just at the threshold of its emergence as a global power, still more aligned with the fertility of nature than with the artifice of nurture: "There, in that great sloven continent, in high Alleghany pastures, in the sea-wide, sky-skirted prairie, still sleeps and murmurs and hides the great mother, long since driven away from the trim hedge-rows and over-cultivated garden of England."

English Traits effectually ends at this point. The remaining three chapters—"Personal," "Result," and "Speech at Manchester"—are codas. "Personal" provides a list of various luminaries he met and those who offered him hospitality. "Result" concludes by condemning British imperialism, the inequality of property in a class society, and the overemphasis on "corporeal civilization," though Emerson concedes that England has long been the promoter of liberty and the principles of freedom. "Speech at Manchester" is a transcript of Emerson's address to the Manchester Athenaeum in November 1847, a panegyric on England's high sense of morality, national loyalty, and robustness.

Emerson is a skilled stylist throughout the volume. He excels in using piquant images and contrasts, as when he remarks on English thoroughness—"The Frenchman invented the ruffle, the Englishman added the shirt"—or reserve—"They do not wear their heart in their sleeve for daws to peck at." Emerson is also fond of the catalogue, a compiling of sundry examples after an abstract statement. His opinion that the "bias of the nation is a passion for utility," for instance, is followed by a list: "They love the lever, the screw, and pulley, the Flanders draught-horse, the waterfall, wind-mills, tide-mills; the sea and the wind to bear their freight ships." Another characteristic is Emerson's love of allusion. In each chapter he weaves together far-ranging historical allusions, from references to Norman chroniclers to anecdotes about Lord Elgin's tenacity in the salvaging of Greek ruins; his facts, episodes, and personalities from the past and the present echo each other to exemplify enduring English cultural traits.

Throughout *English Traits* Emerson remains ambivalent toward English society as he reflects upon the merits and deficiencies of the parent country in respect to his own. He tends to celebrate English individualism and solidity of character and yet criticizes overly entrenched tradition. Although

impressed by English industry and mechanical know-how, he condemns the alienation of the laborer and the inequities of a rigid class system. Extended comparisons to his own country are infrequent, but the subtext of *English Traits* is the younger nation's inevitable ascendancy over the older one. The spectacle of a country whose identity has matured fascinates Emerson precisely because his own country was as yet immature, unformed, with its future beckoning. Although *English Traits* is not considered to be among the best of Emerson's works, its content, inviting tone, and stylistic verve guarantee that it will continue to be deemed an important travel work of the nineteenth century.

Letters:
The Letters of Ralph Waldo Emerson, volumes 1–6 edited by Ralph L. Rust, volumes 7–8 edited by Eleanor M. Tilton (New York: Columbia University Press, 1939).

Biographies:
Gay Wilson Allen, *Waldo Emerson: A Biography* (New York: Viking, 1981);
Robert D. Richardson Jr., *Emerson: The Mind on Fire* (Berkeley: University of California Press, 1995).

References:
Richard Bridgman, "From Greenough to 'Nowhere': Emerson's *English Traits,*" *New England Quarterly,* 59 (December 1986): 469–485;
Robert E. Burkholder, "The Contemporary Reception of *English Traits,*" in *Emerson Centenary Essays,* edited by Joel Myerson (Carbondale: Southern Illinois University Press, 1982), pp. 156–172;
Benjamin Goluboff, "Emerson's *English Traits:* 'The Mechanics of Conversation,'" *American Transcendental Quarterly,* 3 (June 1989): 153–167;
Carl Hovde, "English and American Traits," in *Emerson and His Legacy: Essays in Honor of Quentin Anderson,* edited by Stephen Donadio, Stephen Railton, and Ormond Seavey (Carbondale: Southern Illinois University Press, 1986), pp. 66–83;
Philip L. Nicoloff, *Emerson on Race and History: An Examination of "English Traits"* (New York: Columbia University Press, 1961);
John Peacock, "Self-Reliance and Corporate Destiny: Emerson's Dialectic of Culture," *Emerson Society Quarterly,* 29, no. 2 (1983): 59–72;

Joel Porte, *Representative Man: Ralph Waldo Emerson in His Time* (New York: Oxford University Press, 1979; republished, with a new preface, New York: Columbia University Press, 1988);

William W. Stowe, "Ralph Waldo Emerson: the Reluctant Traveler," *Going Abroad: European Travel in Nineteenth-Century American Culture* (Princeton: Princeton University Press, 1994), pp. 72–101;

Donald Yannella, *Ralph Waldo Emerson* (Boston: Twayne, 1982);

Larzer Ziff, "Sloven Continent: Emerson and an American Ideal," *Literary Democracy: The Declaration of Cultural Independence in America* (New York: Penguin, 1982).

Papers:

The majority of Emerson's papers are held in the Ralph Waldo Emerson Memorial Association collection at the Houghton Library at Harvard University.

Benjamin Franklin

(17 January 1706 – 17 April 1790)

Donald A. Duhadaway Jr.
University of Delaware

See also the Franklin entries in *DLB 24: American Colonial Writers, 1606–1734; DLB 43: American Newspaper Journalists, 1690–1872;* and *DLB 73: American Magazine Journalists, 1741–1850.*

BOOKS: *A Dissertation on Liberty and Necessity, Pleasure and Pain . . .* (London, 1725);

A Modest Inquiry into the Nature and Necessity of Paper-Currency . . . (Philadelphia: Printed & sold at the New Printing-Office, 1729);

Poor Richard, 1733. An Almanack . . . , as Richard Saunders, Philom (Philadelphia: Printed & sold by B. Franklin, 1732);

Poor Richard, 1734. An Almanack . . . , as Saunders (Philadelphia: Printed & sold by B. Franklin, 1733);

Poor Richard, 1735. An Almanack . . . , as Saunders (Philadelphia: Printed & sold by B. Franklin, 1734);

Some Observations on the Proceedings against The Rev. Mr. Hemphill; with a Vindication of His Sermons (Philadelphia: Printed & sold by B. Franklin, 1735);

A Letter to a Friend in the Country, Containing the Substance of a Sermon Preach'd at Philadelphia, in the Congregation of The Rev. Mr. Hemphill, Concerning the Terms of Christian and Ministerial Communion (Philadelphia: Printed & sold by B. Franklin, 1735);

A Defense Of the Rev. Mr. Hemphill's Observations: or, An Answer to the Vindication of the Reverend Commission . . . (Philadelphia: Printed & sold by B. Franklin, 1735);

Poor Richard, 1736. An Almanack . . . , as Saunders (Philadelphia: Printed & sold by B. Franklin, 1735);

Poor Richard, 1737. An Almanack . . . , as Saunders (Philadelphia: Printed & sold by B. Franklin, 1736);

Poor Richard, 1738. An Almanack . . . , as Saunders (Philadelphia: Printed & sold by B. Franklin, 1737);

Benjamin Franklin, circa 1780; portrait by Rosalie Filleul (American Philosophical Society)

Poor Richard, 1739. An Almanack . . . , as Saunders (Philadelphia: Printed & sold by B. Franklin, 1738);

Poor Richard, 1740. An Almanack . . . , as Saunders (Philadelphia: Printed & sold by B. Franklin, 1739);

Poor Richard, 1741. An Almanack . . . , as Saunders (Philadelphia: Printed & sold by B. Franklin, 1740);

Poor Richard, 1742. An Almanack . . . , as Saunders (Philadelphia: Printed & sold by B. Franklin, 1741);

Poor Richard, 1743. An Almanack . . . , as Saunders (Philadelphia: Printed & sold by B. Franklin, 1742);

Poor Richard, 1744. An Almanack . . . , as Saunders (Philadelphia: Printed & sold by B. Franklin & Jonas Greene, 1743);

An Account Of the New Invented Pennsylvanian Fireplaces . . . (Philadelphia: Printed & sold by B. Franklin, 1744);

Poor Richard, 1745. An Almanack . . . , as Saunders (Philadelphia: Printed & sold by B. Franklin, 1744);

Poor Richard, 1746. An Almanack . . . , as Saunders (Philadelphia: Printed & sold by B. Franklin, 1745);

Poor Richard, 1747. An Almanack . . . , as Saunders (Philadelphia: Printed & sold by B. Franklin, 1746);

Plain Truth: or, Serious Considerations On the Present State of the City of Philadelphia, and Province of Pennsylvania, as A. Tradesman of Philadelphia (Philadelphia: Printed by B. Franklin, 1747);

Poor Richard improved: Being an Almanack and Ephemeris . . . For the Bissextile Year, 1748 . . . , as Saunders (Philadelphia: Printed & sold by B. Franklin & D. Hall, 1748);

Poor Richard improved: Being an Almanack and Ephemeris . . . For the Year of Our Lord 1749 . . . , as Saunders (Philadelphia: Printed & sold by B. Franklin & D. Hall, 1748);

Proposals Relating to the Education of Youth in Pensilvania (Philadelphia, 1749);

Poor Richard improved: Being an Almanack and Ephemeris . . . For the Year of Our Lord 1750 . . . , as Saunders (Philadelphia: Printed & sold by B. Franklin & D. Hall, 1749);

Poor Richard improved: Being an Almanack and Ephemeris . . . For the Year of Our Lord 1751 . . . , as Saunders (Philadelphia: Printed & sold by B. Franklin & D. Hall, 1750);

Experiments and Observations on Electricity, Made at Philadelphia in America . . . , part 1 (London: Printed & sold by E. Cave, 1751);

Poor Richard improved: Being an Almanack & Ephemeris . . . For the Year of Our Lord 1752 . . . , as Saunders (Philadelphia: Printed & sold by B. Franklin & D. Hall, 1751);

Poor Richard improved: Being an Almanack & Ephemeris . . . For the Year of Our Lord 1753 . . . , as Saunders (Philadelphia: Printed & sold by B. Franklin & D. Hall, 1752);

Supplemental Experiments and Observations on Electricity, Part II. Made at Philadelphia in America . . . (London: Printed and sold by E. Cave, 1753);

Poor Richard improved: Being an Almanack and Ephemeris . . . For the Year of Our Lord 1754, as Saunders (Philadelphia: Printed & sold by B. Franklin & D. Hall, 1753);

Some Account of the Pennsylvania Hospital . . . (Philadelphia: Printed by B. Franklin & D. Hall, 1754);

New Experiments and Observations on Electricity. Made at Philadelphia in America . . . , part 3 (London: Printed & sold by D. Henry & R. Cave, 1754);

Poor Richard improved: Being an Almanack and Ephemeris . . . For the Year of Our Lord 1755 . . . , as Saunders (Philadelphia: Printed & sold by B. Franklin & D. Hall, 1754);

Poor Richard improved: Being an Almanack and Ephemeris . . . For the Year of Our Lord 1756 . . . , as Saunders (Philadelphia: Printed & sold by B. Franklin & D. Hall, 1755);

Poor Richard improved: Being an Almanack and Ephemeris . . . For the Year of Our Lord 1757 . . . , as Saunders (Philadelphia: Printed & sold by B. Franklin & D. Hall, 1756);

Poor Richard improved: Being an Almanack and Ephemeris . . . For the Year of Our Lord 1758 . . . , as Saunders (Philadelphia: Printed & sold by B. Franklin & D. Hall, 1757);

Father Abraham's Speech To a great Number of People, at a Vendue of Merchant-Goods; Introduced to The Publick By Poor Richard (A Famous Pennsylvanian Conjuror and Almanack-Maker) . . . (Boston: Printed & sold by Benjamin Mecom, 1758); republished as *The Way to Wealth, as clearly shown in the Preface of An Old Pennsylvania Almanack, Intituled, Poor Richard Improved* (London: Printed & sold by H. Lewis: Printed & sold by R. Snagg, 1774);

The Interest of Great Britain Considered, With Regard to her Colonies, And the Aquisitions of Canada and Guadaloupe. To which are added, Observations concerning the Increase of Mankind, Peopling of Countries, &c. (London: Printed for T. Becket / Boston: Printed by B. Mecom, 1760);

A Narrative of the Late Massacres, in Lancaster County, of a Number of Indians, Friends of this Province, By Persons Unknown . . . (Philadelphia: Printed by Anthony Armbruster, 1764);

Cool Thoughts on the Present Situation of Our Public Affairs . . . (Philadelphia: Printed by W. Dunlap, 1764);

Remarks on a late Protest Against the Appointment of Mr. Franklin an Agent for this Province (Philadelphia: Printed by B. Franklin & D. Hall, 1764);

Oeuvres de M. Franklin, 2 volumes, edited by Jacques Barbeu-Duborg (Paris: Quillau, 1773);

Political, Miscellaneous, and Philosophical Pieces . . . , edited by Benjamin Vaughan (London: Printed for J. Johnson, 1779);

Observations on the Causes and Cure of Smokey Chimneys (London: Printed for J. Debrett, 1787);

Philosophical and Miscellaneous Papers. Lately written by B. Franklin, LL.D., edited by Edward Bancroft (London: Printed for C. Dilly, 1787);

Rules for Reducing a Great Empire to a Small One (London: Printed for James Ridgway, 1793);

Autobiography of Benjamin Franklin, first complete edition, edited by John Bigelow (Philadelphia: Lippincott / London: Trübner, 1868);

Benjamin Franklin Experiments. A New Edition of Franklin's Experiments and Observations on Electricity, edited by I. Bernard Cohen (Cambridge, Mass.: Harvard University Press, 1941);

Benjamin Franklin's Autobiographical Writings, edited by Carl Van Doren (New York: Viking, 1945);

Benjamin Franklin's Memoirs, Parallel Text Edition, edited by Max Farrand (Berkeley: University of California Press, 1949);

Benjamin Franklin: His Contribution to the American Tradition, edited by Cohen (New York: Bobbs-Merrill, 1953);

Franklin's Wit and Folly: The Bagatelles, edited by Richard E. Amacher (New Brunswick, N.J.: Rutgers University Press, 1953);

The Autobiography of Benjamin Franklin, edited by Leonard W. Labaree, Ralph L. Ketcham, and others (New Haven: Yale University Press, 1964);

The Political Thought of Benjamin Franklin, edited by Ketcham (Indianapolis: Bobbs-Merrill, 1965);

The Bagatelles from Passy by Benjamin Franklin, Text and Facsimile (New York: Eakins Press, 1967);

The Autobiography of Benjamin Franklin, A Genetic Text, edited by J. A. Leo Lemay and P. M. Zall (Knoxville: University of Tennessee Press, 1981).

Collections: *The Works of Dr. Benjamin Franklin,* 6 volumes, edited by William Duane (Philadelphia: Duane, 1808–1818);

Memoirs of the Life and Writings of Benjamin Franklin, 3 volumes, edited by William Temple Franklin (London: Henry Colburn, 1817–1818);

The Works of Benjamin Franklin, 10 volumes, edited by Jared Sparks (Boston: Hilliard, Gray, 1836–1840);

The Writings of Benjamin Franklin, 10 volumes, edited by Albert Henry Smyth (New York: Macmillan, 1905–1907);

The Papers of Benjamin Franklin, edited by Leonard W. Labaree, Whitfield J. Bell Jr., and others,

29 volumes to date (New Haven: Yale University Press, 1959–);

The Complete Poor Richard Almanacs Published by Benjamin Franklin, edited by Bell (Barre, Mass.: Imprint Society, 1970).

Benjamin Franklin—printer, scientist, inventor, author, philosopher, and statesman—was also one of the great travelers of the eighteenth century. Living in Europe for more than a quarter of a century, first as a young entrepreneur, then in service to colonial Pennsylvania, and finally as a representative of the United States, Franklin made the dangerous Atlantic crossing eight times. One of his great strengths, according to biographer Esmond Wright, was "his almost total freedom from the limits of his own environment" and the ease with which he assimilated into European life. Renowned and respected for his many accomplishments, Franklin was, arguably, America's premier diplomat during the eighteenth century, a role he played until he was nearly eighty years old.

"Travelling," Franklin observed in his papers, "is one Way of lengthening Life, at least in Appearance." Certainly, some of the most enduring images of Franklin the person are the result of his journeys. The young Franklin's escape from the overbearing mastership of his brother and his subsequent flight from Boston to Philadelphia was perhaps the most important trip he ever made. As depicted in the *Autobiography of Benjamin Franklin* (1868), his entry into Philadelphia with "three great puffy rolls" tucked under his arms is one of the most famous images in American history. Franklin's well-known—and self-styled—images as defender of American liberties, Enlightenment luminary, Bonhomme Richard, and ladies' man were all largely cultivated abroad.

Although he was a voluminous writer, Franklin was not a systematic chronicler of his journeys and did not produce a great travelogue. Wright attributes this paucity of travel accounts to Franklin's almost total lack of aesthetic response: "the assiduous letter-writer left no descriptions of scenery, of nature, or of buildings; travelling in Scotland thirteen years after Culloden, he made no reference to the Jacobites and mentioned not a mountain." Franklin, indeed, often seems to care little for details that other travelers might treasure:

Many people are fond of accounts of old Buildings and Monuments, but for me I confess that if I could find in my travels a receipt for Parmesan cheese, it would give me more satisfaction than a transcript from any inscription from any old Stone whatever.

But while Franklin's scattered observations on his travels must be gleaned from several sources, often his personal letters, they are all the more significant for their relative rarity.

The youngest son of the ten children born to Abigail Folger Franklin and Josiah Franklin (who had already fathered seven children in a previous marriage), Franklin was raised in humble circumstances and received only two years of formal education. He read widely, however, and modeled his writing on that of such authors as Joseph Addison, Daniel Defoe, and Jonathan Swift. Bored by the family business of making candles and boiling soap, twelve-year-old Franklin allowed his father to convince him to become an apprentice to his half brother, James, the owner of a print shop. He worked for his brother until he was seventeen, enjoying his first success as an author when he anonymously submitted a series of fourteen satiric essays—later known as the "Silence Dogood Papers"—to his brother's newspaper, *The New-England Courant.* Franklin's strained relationship with his brother eventually led him to leave Boston for Philadelphia, where he was able to establish himself as a skillful printer by working for Samuel Keimer.

Encouraged by Pennsylvania governor Sir William Keith, who promised letters of credit and introduction that would enable him to establish his own printing shop back in the colony, Franklin and a friend, James Ralph, embarked for England in November of 1724. As Franklin explained in his *Autobiography,* except for the companionship of Quaker merchant Thomas Denham, the "Voyage was otherwise not a pleasant one, as we had a great deal of bad Weather." Upon arriving in London on Christmas Eve, Franklin discovered that Keith had not carried through on his promises; consequently, he remained in England for eighteen months while he worked to save money for his passage back to Philadelphia.

Franklin departed for America on 22 July 1726 and landed in Philadelphia on 11 October. A voluminous writer, Franklin tended to keep a journal of events that interested him. His *Journal of a Voyage, 1726,* which has been published in *The Papers of Benjamin Franklin* (1959–), provides a glimpse of the rigors of the Atlantic crossing. Franklin had a lifelong interest and commitment to diet, exercise, and hygiene, and the long confinement proved especially taxing to the young man, who occasionally "leaped overboard and swam round the ship to wash myself." Franklin occupied his time, as he was to do on other trips across the Atlantic, by observing natural phenomena and social interaction and

with plans for his future conduct, the precursor to his later formula for moral perfection.

Franklin shows an acute interest in scientific observation, as many of the journal entries discuss weather and its effects on the voyage. He also notes the behavior of dolphins and other marine life. On 18 August he wrote: "Four dolphins followed the ship for some hours: we struck at them with the fizgig [harpoon], but took none." In another passage he described the dolphin "as beautiful and well shaped a fish as any that swims."

On 19 August, Franklin recorded a rough sample of ship justice when the passengers hung up a card cheater by the waist:

We let him hang, cursing and swearing for near a quarter of an hour; but at length he crying out Murder! and looking black in the face, the rope being overtort about his middle, we thought proper to let him down again; and our mess have excommunicated him till he pays his fine, refusing either to play, eat, drink or converse with him.

On 25 August, with a month and a half remaining in the journal, Franklin recorded the tedium of an ocean voyage:

What I have said may in a measure account for some particulars in my present way of living here on board. Our company is in general very unsuitably mixed, to keep up the pleasure and spirit of conversation: and if there are one or two pair of us that can sometimes entertain one another for half an hour agreeable, yet perhaps we are seldom in the humour for it together. I rise in the morning and read for an hour or two perhaps, and then reading grows tiresome. Want of exercise occasions want of appetite, so that eating and drinking affords but little pleasure. I tire myself with playing at draughts, then I go to cards; nay there is no play so trifling or childish, but we fly to it for entertainment. A contrary wind, I know not how, puts us all out of good humour; we grow sullen, silent and reserved, and fret at each other upon every little occasion. 'Tis a common opinion among the ladies, that if a man is ill-natured he infallibly discovers it when he is in liquor. But I, who have known many instances to the contrary, will teach them a more effectual method to discover the natural temper and disposition of their humble servants. Let the ladies make one long sea voyage with them, and if they have the least spark of ill nature in them and conceal it to the end of the voyage, I will forfeit all my pretensions to their favour.

A month later Franklin wrote: "All our discourse now is of Philadelphia, and we begin to fancy ourselves on shore already. Yet a small change of weather, attended by a westerly wind, is sufficient to blast all our blooming hopes, and quite spoil our present good humour."

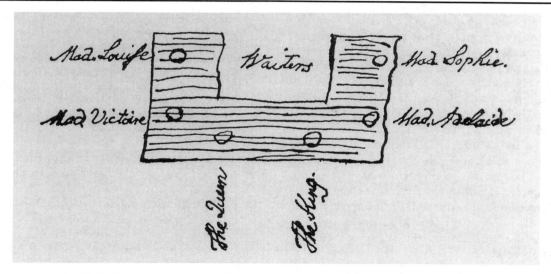

*Franklin's diagram of the seating of the French royal family at supper, which he included in his
14 September 1767 letter to Polly Stevenson (Library of Congress)*

Upon his return Franklin took up residence in Philadelphia, where he would remain for the next thirty-one years. He married Deborah Reed in 1730, with whom he had two children. His son, Francis Folger, was born in 1732 and died of smallpox in 1736; his daughter, Sarah, was born in 1743. Franklin's first child, William, born in 1730 or 1731, was illegitimate.

Resuming his printing trade, he soon owned his own press and published much of the colony's public printing as well as the *Pennsylvania Gazette* and *Poor Richard's Almanack*. So successful was this endeavor that Franklin could turn control of his enterprises over to a partner and retire in 1748 at age forty-two. Citizen Franklin served as clerk (1736–1751) and as member of the Pennsylvania Assembly (1751–1764), postmaster of Philadelphia (1737–1753), deputy postmaster general for the colonies (1753–1774), delegate to the Albany Congress (1754), and military leader in the Lehigh Valley. He played a key role in most of Philadelphia's civic improvements during the eighteenth century, helping establish a circulating library, the American Philosophical Society, and what would become the University of Pennsylvania. Franklin became the center of Philadelphia's scientific establishment and was an active participant and correspondent in the scientific endeavors of his day. When he journeyed abroad again Franklin was a wealthy, influential man, well known in Europe for his scientific accomplishments, particularly for his *Experiments and Observations on Electricity, made at Philadelphia in America* (1751), which within twenty years had gone through four English editions, three in French, and one each in German and Italian.

Franklin was the delegate the Pennsylvania Assembly chose as its representative before the king during the late 1750s and 1760s. In the summer of 1757 Franklin, accompanied by his son, William, embarked on his second voyage to England. He used the long sea journey to write "The Way to Wealth," the immensely successful preface to *Poor Richard improved: Being an Almanack and Ephemeris . . . For the Year of Our Lord 1758* (1757), a retrospective look at some of Poor Richard's advice culled from more than two decades. Franklin recounted in his *Autobiography* the near shipwreck they endured, the landing at Falmouth—"A most pleasing Spectacle to those who had been so long without any other Prospects, than the uniform View of a vacant Ocean!"—and their visit to "Stonehenge on Salisbury Plain, and Lord Pembroke's House and Gardens, with his very curious Antiquities at Wilton."

Franklin arrived in London on 27 July 1757 with the Assembly's instructions to petition the king for the right to tax proprietary estates. Owing partly to his attacks on the proprietors in the London press through such vehicles as *An Historical Review of the Constitution and Government of Pennsylvania* (1759), which he co-authored with Richard Jackson, an English lawyer, Franklin's diplomatic endeavors were a qualified success. His second stay in England lasted from 1757 to 1762.

These five years were among Franklin's happiest, for at least during this part of his life he loved England. On 6 September 1758 Franklin wrote to his wife, Deborah, detailing the trip he and his son made to Cambridge for commencement ceremonies and to the English countryside, where he met surviving members of both his and Deborah's families.

Franklin enjoyed the Cambridge activities, and he and his son "were present at all the ceremonies, dined every day in their halls, and my vanity was not a little gratified by the particular regard shown me by the chancellor and vice chancellor of the university and the heads of colleges." Viewing the ancestral family freehold at Ecton, Franklin noted that "the land is now added to another farm, and a school kept in the house: it is a decayed old stone building, but still known by the name of Franklin House." The parish rector "showed us the old church register, in which were the births, marriages, and burials of our ancestors for 200 years," and the rector's wife showed the Franklins gravestones of their ancestors. At Birmingham, Franklin met some of his wife's relatives.

Franklin also visited Scotland, Holland, and Belgium during these years. In 1759 he and his son journeyed to Scotland where he received a doctor of laws from the University of St. Andrews and began a warm friendship with Henry Home, Lord Kames, to whom Franklin wrote on 5 January 1760:

> On the whole, I must say I think the time we spent there was six weeks of the densest happiness I have met with in any part of my life; and the agreeable and instructive society we found there in such plenty has left so pleasing an impression on my memory that, did not strong connexions draw me elsewhere, I believe Scotland would be the country I should choose to spend the remainder of my days in.

Franklin discussed his trip to Flanders in a summer 1761 letter to Jared Ingersoll, a lawyer in Connecticut:

> When I travelled in Flanders, I thought of your excessively strict observation of Sunday; and that a man could hardly travel on that day among you upon lawful occasions without hazard of punishment; while, where I was, every one travelled, if he pleased, or diverted himself in any other way; and in the afternoon both high and low went to the play or to the opera, where there was plenty of singing, fiddling, and dancing. I looked round for God's judgments, but saw no signs of them. The cities were well built and full of inhabitants, the markets filled with plenty, the people well favoured and well clothed, the fields well tilled, the cattle fat and strong, the fences, houses, and windows all in repair, and no Old Tenor anywhere in the country; which would almost make one suspect that the Deity is not so angry at that offence as a New England justice.

Despite his five years' absence from Philadelphia and his family, Franklin regretted leaving England in 1762. On 17 August he wrote to Lord Kames from Portsmouth, England:

> I am now waiting here only for a wind to waft me to America, but cannot leave this happy Island and my Friends in it, without extream Regret, tho' I am going to a Country and a People that I love. I am going from the old World to the new, and I fancy I feel like those who are leaving this World for the next; Grief at the Parting; Fear of the Passage; Hope of the Future; those different Passions all affect their Minds at once; and these have tender'd me down exceedingly.

On 23 August, still in Portsmouth, Franklin wrote to his English friend William Strahan detailing his expectation to bring Deborah and "settle here for ever." Franklin left England before the end of the month in a convoy of ten merchant ships and a man-of-war. Franklin recalled his impression of Madeira in a letter to Lord Kames dated 2 June 1765:

> 'Tis a fertile Island, and the different Heights and Situations among its Mountains, afford such different Temperaments of Air, that all the Fruits of Northern and Southern Countries are produc'd there, Corn, Grapes, Apples, Peaches, Oranges, Lemons, Plaintains, Bananas, &c.

The remainder of the trip also passed pleasantly, with weather so fine that the passengers could visit from ship to ship and dine with each other, "which made the time pass agreably, much more so than when one goes in a single Ship, for this was like travelling in a moving Village, with all one's Neighbour's about one."

Even after his return to America, Franklin missed England. On 25 March 1763 he wrote to Polly Stevenson, the daughter of his London landlady, detailing his fondness for the English:

> Of all the enviable Things England has, I envy it most its People. Why should that petty Island, which compar'd to America is but like a stepping Stone in a Brook, scarce enough of it above Water to keep one's Shoes dry; why, I say, should that little Island, enjoy in almost every Neighbourhood, more sensible, virtuous and elegant Minds, than we can collect in ranging 100 Leagues of our vast Forests.

Franklin took up his old life in Philadelphia for the two years from 1762 to 1764 but then returned to England in service of the Assembly. His instructions for this second voyage on behalf of the colony were to petition the king to make Pennsylvania a royal possession. He was in England for more than a decade (1764–1775), but instead of securing the conversion of Pennsylvania into a royal holding, Franklin returned to the colonies embittered and convinced that America could no longer be joined with England. His changed feelings about the country are evident in his 25 February 1775 letter to Joseph Galloway, a Philadelphia lawyer and Assembly member:

> When I consider the extream Corruption prevalent among all Orders of Men in this old rotten State, and the glorious publick Virtue so predominant in our rising Country, I cannot but apprehend more Mischief than Benefit from a closer Union. I fear They will drag us after them in all the plundering Wars their desperate Circumstances, Injustice and Rapacity, may prompt them to undertake; and then wide-wasting Prodigality and Profusion a Gulph that will swallow up every Aid we may distress ourselves to afford them. Here Numberless and needless Places, enormous Salaries, Pensions, Perquisites, Bribes, groundless Quarrels, foolish Expeditions, false Accompts or no Accompts, Contracts and Jobbs devour all Revenue, and produce continual Necessity in the Midst of natural plenty. I apprehend therefore To unite us intimately, will only be to corrupt and poison us also.

For most of his ten-year stay, however, Franklin had been happy, a fact attested to by the publication of his daily "newspaper," *The Craven Street Gazette,* which Wright calls "his genial parody of royal gazettes." In *The Craven Street Gazette* Franklin recorded the daily happenings of his own London household by placing his own family members and friends as members of a royal entourage:

> This Morning Queen Margaret, accompanied by her first Maid of Honour, Miss Franklin, set out for Rochester. Immediately on their Departure, the whole street was in tears from a heavy Shower of Rain.
> ....
> This evening there was high Play at the Groom Porter's in Cravenstreet House. The Great Person [Franklin] lost Money. It is supposed the Ministers, as is usually supposed of all Ministers, shared the Emoluments among them.

Franklin also traveled extensively during these years in London. He visited other parts of England, including Twyford, where he began writing his *Autobiography* in 1771. He also journeyed to Hanover in 1766 and to Paris in 1767 and again in 1769, and he made a long excursion to Scotland and Ireland in 1771.

His first visit to France made quite an impression on Franklin; as was often the case, the only full account of this voyage appears in his correspondence, this time his 14 September 1767 letter to his friend Polly Stevenson. He discusses the "various imposition we suffer'd from Boat-men, Porters, &c. on both Sides of the Water. I know not which are most rapacious, the English or the French; but the latter have, with their Knavery the most Politeness." "The Roads," he wrote, "we found equally good

with ours in England." He comments on the lighter and darker complexions of women in different parts of France as well as on women's beauty secrets. The queen, he notes, does not use rouge, "having in the Serenity, Complacence and Benignity that shine so eminently in or rather through her Countenance, sufficient Beauty, tho' now an old Woman, to do extreamly well without it."

In the letter Franklin also reports attending court at Versailles with Sir John Pringle, a fellow member of the Royal Academy:

> We went to Versailles last Sunday, and had the Honour of being presented to the King, he spoke to both of us very graciously and chearfully, is a handsome Man, has a very lively Look, and appears younger than he is. In the Evening we were at the *Grand Couvert,* where the Family sup in Publick. . . . The King talk'd a great deal to Sir John [Pringle], asking many Questions about our Royal Family; and did me too the Honour of taking some Notice of me.

On this rare occasion Franklin also takes notice of the buildings and grounds:

> Versailles has had infinite Sums laid out in Building it and Supplying it with Water: Some say the Expence exceeded 80 Millions Sterling. The Range of Building is immense, the Garden Front most magnificent all of hewn Stone, the Number of Statues, Figures, Urns, &c in Marble and Bronze of exquisite Workmanship is beyond Conception. But the Waterworks are out of Repair, and so is great Part of the Front next the Town, looking with its shabby half Brick Walls and broken Windows not much better than the Houses in Durham Yard. There is, in short, both at Versailles and Paris, a prodigious Mixture of Magnificence and Negligence, with every kind of Elegance except that of Cleanliness, and what we call *Tidyness.*

Franklin believed that the French were extraordinarily polite, an impression he returned to time and again over the years:

> The Civilities we every where receive give us the strongest Impressions of the French Politeness. It seems to be a Point settled here universally that Strangers are to be treated with Respect, and one has just the same Deference shewn one here by being a Stranger as in England by being a Lady.

Visiting France was a delight to Franklin, as living there would be to him in the 1770s and 1780s: "It is but a Fortnight since we left London; but the Variety of Scenes we have gone through makes it seem equal to Six Months living in one Place."

Franklin in the fur hat he wore in France to affect the impression of a simple backwoodsman
(Yale University Art Gallery)

In a letter dated 6 February 1772 Franklin describes the social conditions he saw during his trip to Ireland and Scotland the previous year:

> My last Tour was thro' Ireland and Scotland. In Ireland I had a good deal of Conversation with the Patriots; they are all on the American side of the Question in which I endeavour'd to confirm them. The lower People in that unhappy Country, are in a most wretched Situation, thro' the Restraints on their Trade and Manufactures. Their Houses are dirty Hovels of Mud and Straw; their Clothing Rags, and their Food little beside Potatoes. Perhaps three fourths of the Inhabitants are in this Situation; . . . In Scotland things make a better Appearance, and seem on the mending Hand. Yet half the People there wear neither Shoes nor Stockings, or wear them only in Church; No wonder that Scotch Stockings are imported into America. The Gentry in both Countries live extreamly well, are a hospitable Friendly People to Strangers, and very sensible in Conversation. In many parts of England, too, the Working Poor are miserably fed, clothed and lodged. In short, I see no Country of Europe where there is so much general Comfort and Happiness as in America, Holland perhaps excepted.

Increasingly, Franklin's efforts and energy were dedicated to the political events of the 1760s and 1770s. Originally sent to England as agent for Pennsylvania, by 1770 he also acted as spokesman for Georgia, New Jersey, and Massachusetts in the growing friction between mother country and colonies. The Franklin who returned to Philadelphia in May of 1775 was a deeply saddened man, afflicted by the breakdown in relations between the colonies

*Franklin's 19 September 1785 letter to Jane Mecom, in which he announces his safe return
to America after nearly nine years in Europe (private collection)*

and England and the recent death of his wife, whom he had not seen in a decade.

Franklin was called upon in late 1776 to be a representative of the American people overseas. Active since his return the previous year, most notably in his work on the Pennsylvania Constitution of 1776 and the Declaration of Independence, Franklin was asked by Congress to join the delegation to France to negotiate for a treaty that would bring the French government into the war on the side of the United States. Franklin reached France with his two grandsons in December 1776, "safe after a Passage of 30 Days, somewhat fatigued and weakened by the Voyage, which was a rough one," as he wrote his sister Jane Mecom.

From the end of 1776 until September 1785, when he returned to Philadelphia, Franklin's was the most important American voice in France. He provided military intelligence to the colonies, played the dominant American role in enacting the

Treaty of Amity and Commerce with France in 1778, and, perhaps even more importantly for the financially strapped colonists, secured loan after loan from the near-bankrupt French government. Franklin also played a leading role in the Treaty of Paris, which ended the war in 1783. Faced with enormous obstacles and despite schisms within his own delegation, Franklin—already into his seventies—proved himself a masterful diplomat, skillfully using his reputation as an American sage and rustic in his efforts.

Franklin captivated the French. Known and revered for his science, for his creation of Poor Richard, and for being the emissary from a nation willing to oppose the British, the great Doctor Franklin was a celebrity during all of his stay in the country. Shortly after arriving Franklin commented on the hospitality accorded him in an 8 December 1776 letter to Mecom: "You can have no Conceptions of the Respect with which I am receiv'd and treated here by the first People, in my private Character: for as yet I have assumed no public One." He held court at Passy, just as he had in Craven Street. His contentment with life there is apparent in his 5 October 1777 letter to Mecom:

> I enjoy here an exceeding good state of Health.—I live in a fine airy House upon a Hill, which has a large Garden with fine Walks in it, about 1/2 an hours Drive from the City of Paris. I walk a little every Day in the Garden, have a good Appetite & sleep well.—I think the French Cookery agrees with me better than the English;—I suppose there is little or no Butter in their Sauces: for I have never once had the Heartburn since my being here tho' I eat heartily, which shows that my Digestion is good. I have got into a good Neighborhood, of very agreable People who appear very fond of me; at least they are pleasingly civil: so that upon the whole I live as comfortably as a Man can well do so far from his Home & his Family.

Franklin maintained a busy social life with the luminaries of French society, especially the ladies. Franklin clearly relished the attention that he received from French women, as is clear in his 11 October 1779 letter to Eliza Hubbard Partride, a stepniece:

> Somebody, it seems, gave it out that I lov'd Ladies; and then every body presented me their Ladies (or the Ladies presented themselves) to be embrac'd, that is to have their Necks kiss'd. For as to kissing of Lips or Cheeks it is not the Mode here, the first is reckon'd rude, & the other may rub off the Paint. The French Ladies have however 1000 other ways of rendering themselves agreable; by their various Attentions and Civilities, & their sensible Conversation. 'Tis a delightful People to live with.

Franklin became a close confidant to several women, maintained a flirtatious correspondence, and even asked Madame Helvetius to marry him; she politely declined.

While in France, Franklin kept up an active correspondence concerning scientific matters, writing even to acquaintances in England. He was witness to two of France's most exciting developments during the 1780s, the successful launch of the first hot air balloons and mesmerism. In a 16 January 1784 letter to John Ingenhousz, a Dutch physician, Franklin presents his estimate of the importance of balloons: "Five thousand balloons, capable of raising two men each, could not cost more than five ships of the line, and where is the prince who can afford so to cover his country with troops for its defence as that ten thousand men descending from the clouds might not in many places do an infinite deal of mischief before a force could be brought together to repel them?" He expresses his doubts about Friedrich Anton Mesmer and animal magnetism in a letter dated 19 March: "I cannot but fear that the expectation of great advantage from this new method of treating diseases will prove a delusion."

Franklin returned to Philadelphia in 1785. He used his last voyage across the Atlantic, as he had always done before, to observe and wonder, writing on this occasion about such topics as the Gulf Stream, the use of kayaks, and smoky chimneys. Though he spent many years abroad, as he wrote to Richard Jackson on 7 October 1755, "Pensilvania is my Darling." He lived out his remaining years in Philadelphia. Franklin's service to his nation was far from over, however; he served as chief executive of Pennsylvania and as an adviser to the Constitutional Convention before dying at home on 17 April 1790.

Letters:

Les Amitiés Américaines de Madame d'Houdetot, d'après sa Correspondance In èdite avec Benjamin Franklin et Thomas Jefferson, edited by Gilbert Chinard (Paris: E. Champion, 1924);

"My Dear Girl": The Correspondence of Benjamin Franklin, Polly Stevenson, Georgiana and Catherine Shipley, edited by James M. Stifler (New York: Doran, 1927);

The Letters and Papers of Benjamin Franklin and Richard Jackson, 1753–1785, edited by Carl Van Doren (Philadelphia: American Philosophical Society, 1947);

Benjamin Franklin and Catherine Ray Greene: Their Correspondence, edited by William G. Roelker (Philadelphia: American Philosophical Society, 1949);

Benjamin Franklin's Letters to the Press, 1758–1775, edited by Verner W. Crane (Chapel Hill: University of North Carolina Press, 1950);

"Franklin's Letters on Indians and Germans" and "Franklin and Jackson on the French War," edited by A. O. Aldridge, *American Philosophical Society Proceedings*, 94 (August 1950): 391–395, 396–397;

The Letters of Benjamin Franklin and Jane Mecom, edited by Van Doren (Princeton: Princeton University Press, 1950);

"'All Clear Sunshine!' New Letters of Franklin and Mary Stevenson Hewson," edited by Whitfield J. Bell Jr., *American Philosophical Society Proceedings*, 100 (December 1956): 521–536;

Mr. Franklin: A Selection from His Personal Letters, edited by Leonard W. Labaree and Bell (New Haven: Yale University Press, 1956).

Bibliographies:

Paul Leicester Ford, *Franklin Bibliography: A List of Books Written by, or Relating to, Benjamin Franklin* (Brooklyn: Historical Printing Club, 1889);

I. Minis Mays, *Calendar of the Papers of Benjamin Franklin in the Library of the American Philosophical Society,* 6 volumes (Philadelphia: University of Pennsylvania Press, 1908);

C. William Miller, *Benjamin Franklin's Philadelphia Printing, 1728–1766. A Descriptive Bibliography* (Philadelphia: American Philosophical Society, 1974).

Biographies:

James Parton, *Life and Times of Benjamin Franklin,* 2 volumes (Boston: Mason Brothers, 1864);

Carl Van Doren, *Benjamin Franklin* (New York: Viking, 1938);

Carl L. Becker, *Benjamin Franklin, A Biographical Sketch* (Ithaca: Cornell University Press, 1946);

A. Owen Aldridge, *Benjamin Franklin: Philosopher and Man* (Philadelphia: Lippincott, 1965);

Claude-Anne Lopez, *Mon Cher Papa: Franklin and the Ladies of Paris* (New Haven: Yale University Press, 1966);

Thomas Fleming, ed., *Benjamin Franklin: A Biography in His Own Words* (New York: Newsweek Book Division, 1972);

Catherine Drinker Bowen, *The Most Dangerous Man in America: Scenes from the Life of Benjamin Franklin* (Boston: Little, Brown, 1974);

Lopez and Eugenia W. Herbert, *The Private Franklin: The Man and His Family* (New York: Norton, 1975);

David Freeman Hawke, *Franklin* (New York: Harper & Row, 1976);

David Schoenbrun, *Triumph in Paris: The Exploits of Benjamin Franklin* (New York: Harper & Row, 1976);

Ronald W. Clark, *Benjamin Franklin: A Biography* (New York: Random House, 1983);

Esmond Wright, *Franklin of Philadelphia* (Cambridge, Mass.: Belknap Press of Harvard University Press, 1986);

Wright, ed., *Benjamin Franklin: His Life As He Wrote It* (Cambridge, Mass.: Harvard University Press, 1990);

Robert Middlekauf, *Benjamin Franklin and His Enemies* (Berkeley: University of California Press, 1996).

References:

F. B. Adams Jr., "Franklin and His Press at Passy," *Yale University Library Gazette,* 30 (April 1956): 133–138;

A. O. Aldridge, *Benjamin Franklin and Nature's God* (Durham: Duke University Press, 1967);

Aldridge, *Franklin and His French Contemporaries* (New York: New York University Press, 1957);

Richard E. Amacher, *Benjamin Franklin* (New York: Twayne, 1962);

Brian M. Barbour, ed., *Benjamin Franklin: A Collection of Critical Essays* (Englewood Cliffs, N.J.: Prentice-Hall, 1979);

Whitfield J. Bell, "Benjamin Franklin as an American Hero," *Association of American Colleges Bulletin,* 43 (March 1957): 121–132;

Melvin H. Buxbaum, *Critical Essays on Benjamin Franklin* (Boston: G. K. Hall, 1987);

Benjamin Franklin, ed., *Boston Printers, Publishers, and Booksellers, 1640–1800* (Boston: G. K. Hall, 1980);

Bruce I. Granger, *Benjamin Franklin, an American Man of Letters* (Ithaca: Cornell University Press, 1964);

Ralph W. Ketcham, *Benjamin Franklin* (New York: Twayne, 1965);

J. A. Leo Lemay, "Benjamin Franklin, Universal Genius," in *The Renaissance Man in the Eighteenth Century* (Los Angeles: William Andrews Clark Memorial Library, University of California, 1978), pp. 1–44;

Lemay, "Franklin's Suppressed 'Busy-Body,'" *American Literature,* 37 (November 1965): 307–311;

Lemay, ed., *The Oldest Revolutionary: Essays on Benjamin Franklin* (Philadelphia: University of Pennsylvania Press, 1976);

Lemay, ed., *Reappraising Benjamin Franklin: A Bicentennial Perspective* (Newark: University of Delaware Press, 1993);

Frank Lawrence Lucas, *The Art of Living: Four Eighteenth-Century Minds—Hume, Horace Walpole, Burke and Benjamin Franklin* (New York: Macmillan, 1959);

Dorothy Medlin, "Benjamin Franklin and the French Language," *French-American Review*, 1 (Fall 1977): 232–239;

Richard D. Miles, "The American Image of Benjamin Franklin," *American Quarterly*, 9 (Summer 1957): 117–143;

Antonio Pace, *Benjamin Franklin and Italy* (Philadelphia: American Philosophical Society, 1958);

Vernon L. Parrington, "Benjamin Franklin: Our First Ambassador," in his *Main Currents in American Thought: The Colonial Mind, 1620–1800,* volume 1 (New York: Harcourt, Brace, 1927), pp. 164–178;

Clinton Rossiter, "Benjamin Franklin," in his *Seedtime of the Republic* (New York: Harcourt, Brace, 1953), pp. 281–312;

Charles L. Sanford, ed., *Benjamin Franklin and the American Character* (Boston: Heath, 1955);

David Schoenbrun, *Triumph in Paris: The Exploits of Benjamin Franklin* (New York: Harper & Row, 1976);

Gerald Stourzh, *Benjamin Franklin and American Foreign Policy* (Chicago: University of Chicago Press, 1954);

Carl Van Doren, ed., *Meet Dr. Franklin* (Philadelphia: Franklin Institute, 1943).

Papers:
The largest collection of Franklin manuscripts is held by the American Philosophical Society Library, Philadelphia. Other important holdings include the Stevens Collections, Library of Congress; the University of Pennsylvania Library; the Library of the Historical Society of Pennsylvania; and Yale University.

John Charles Frémont
(21 January 1813 – 13 July 1890)
and
Jessie Benton Frémont
(31 May 1834 – 27 December 1902)

Karen M. Woods
University of Minnesota

John Charles Frémont

BOOKS: *Northern Boundary of Missouri,* 27th Congress, 3rd session, serial 420, House document 38 (Washington: Printed by order of the U.S. Congress, 1842);

A Report on an Exploration of the Country Lying between the Missouri River and the Rocky Mountains on the Line of the Kansas and Great Platte Rivers, 27th Congress, 3rd session, serial 416, Senate document 243 (Washington: Printed by order of the U.S. Senate, 1843);

Report of the Exploring Expedition to the Rocky Mountains in the Year 1842, and to Oregon and North California in the Years 1843–'44, 28th Congress, 2nd session, serial 461, Senate executive document 174 (Washington: Gales & Seaton, 1845); 28th Congress, House executive document 106 (Washington: Blair & Rives, 1845);

Geographical Memoir upon Upper California, in Illustration of His Map of Oregon and California, 30th Congress, 1st session, serial 511, Senate miscellaneous document 148 (Washington: Wendell & Van Benthuysen, 1848); 30th Congress, 2nd session, House miscellaneous document 5 (Washington: Tippin & Streeper, 1849);

Memoirs of My Life, volume 1 (Chicago & New York: Belford, Clarke, 1887).

Collection: *The Expeditions of John Charles Frémont,* 3 volumes, with supplement and map portfolio, edited by Donald Jackson and Mary Lee Spence (Urbana, Chicago & London: University of Illinois Press, 1970, 1973, 1984).

OTHER: "Central Railroad Route to the Pacific," *National Intelligencer* (June 1854); republished as "Central Railroad Route to the Pacific. Letter of J. C. Frémont to the Editors of the National Intelligencer . . .," 33rd Congress, 2nd session, House miscellaneous document 8 (Washington, 1854).

Jessie Benton Frémont

BOOKS: *The Story of the Guard: A Chronicle of the War* (Boston: Ticknor & Fields, 1863);

A Year of American Travel (New York: Harper, 1878);

How to Learn and Earn; or, Half Hours in Some Helpful Schools, by Frémont and others (Boston: D. Lothrop, 1884);

Souvenirs of My Time (Boston: D. Lothrop, 1887);

Far-West Sketches (Boston: D. Lothrop, 1890);

The Will and the Way Stories (Boston: D. Lothrop, 1891).

OTHER: "Biographical Sketch of Senator Benton in Connection with Western Expansion," in *Memoirs of My Life,* by John Charles Frémont (Chicago & New York: Belford, Clarke, 1887), pp. 1–17;

"The Origin of the Frémont Explorations," *Century Magazine,* 41 (March 1891): 766–771.

John Charles Frémont, "The Pathfinder," is generally remembered as a major explorer of the American West and as the conqueror of California. In a career marked by controversy he was one of the first senators elected from California, the first Republican presidential candidate, a mine and railroad developer, a Civil War general, and the governor of the Arizona Territory. His marriage to Jessie Anne Benton, daughter of expansionist Sen. Thomas Hart Benton, gave him access to political power and created a lifelong literary partnership. Donald Jackson and Mary Lee Spence write in their introduction to *The Expeditions of John Charles Frémont* (1970, 1973, 1984) that "the documentary history of these two persons is but a single subject of study."

John Charles Frémont (portrait by William S. Jewett, National Portrait Gallery, Smithsonian Institution) and Jessie Benton Frémont (portrait by T. Buchanan Read, Southwest Museum)

John Frémont was the child of a love affair between Anne Pryor of Richmond, who was trapped in a loveless marriage to an older man, and the French émigré Charles Frémon (it is unclear whether Anne or John Charles added the *t* to the surname). In July 1811 the lovers eloped, and moving south to escape the censure of Virginia society, lived as husband and wife. John Frémont was born in Savannah, Georgia, on 21 January 1813. The stigma of illegitimacy was to remain with him his entire life. The Frémons had three other children, Anne, Elizabeth, and Thomas (called Frank), and led a nomadic lifestyle. After Charles Frémon died in 1818, the family moved to Charleston, South Carolina.

In 1826 John Frémont went to work as a clerk for a lawyer, John W. Mitchell, who helped guide his education. Three years later he received a charity scholarship to the College of Charleston. In 1833 Joel Poinsett, a Jacksonian leader in the state, got him a position as a math instructor in the navy. By 1837 he had become an army engineer and led a squad of surveyors to map the Indian territory in South Carolina. He was appointed a second lieutenant in the Corps of Topographical Engineers in 1838. A crucial influence on his career and educa-

tion was his job as an assistant to Joseph Nicola Nicollet, the first systematic modern cartographer. His work with Nicollet taught him to use astronomy in mapmaking and laid the foundation for the explorations that would make him famous.

In April 1841 John Frémont met sixteen-year-old Jessie Anne Benton. She was the daughter of Thomas Hart Benton, one of Missouri's first senators, and Elizabeth McDowell of Virginia. Their attraction was obvious, but Jessie's parents disapproved of a match with a poor army officer who was twelve years her senior. Senator Benton used his influence as chair of the Senate Committee on Territories to send the dashing Frémont away. He was suddenly sent to survey the lower Des Moines River in Iowa Territory. His report, *Northern Boundary of Missouri,* was published by Congress in 1842. The survey, much to Senator Benton's dismay, put John Frémont in the national limelight and made him even more attractive to Jessie Benton. They continued to meet in secret and then eloped on 19 October 1841.

Their marriage led to a lifelong literary collaboration. Jessie Frémont was the amanuensis, editor, and secretary for the reports of John Frémont's expeditions and also worked on his memoir. Later,

The San Juan Mountains, engraving by Edward Kern, from Memoirs of My Life *(1887)*

when the Frémonts faced financial difficulties, Jessie Frémont wrote dozens of sketches of her American and European travels, which were later collected in her books. Critics have unfairly condemned Jessie's flair for the dramatic; they fail to recognize that it was her sense of drama that made the expedition reports such a success. As biographer Andrew Rolle explains in *John Charles Frémont: Character as Destiny* (1991) the two had complementary talents—John Frémont's was

scientific, Jessie Frémont's literary and artistic: "Disallowed a public image in her own right, she used her talents to promote her husband's, all the while trying to fuse her identity with his."

Following the success of his Des Moines River survey, John Frémont went on five major expeditions. On his first expedition (10 June–17 October 1842), under government auspices, he led a party of twenty-five that included Jessie's twelve-year-old brother Randolph to survey the lines of travel for military posts between the Missouri River and the Rocky Mountains. He describes the findings of this journey in *A Report on an Exploration of the Country Lying between the Missouri River and the Rocky Mountains on the Line of the Kansas and Great Platte Rivers* (1843). The party left Kansas City and followed the Kansas River northwest until they reached the Platte River in present-day Nebraska. From there they followed the South Platte River west to Saint Vrain's Fort in present-day Colorado. They then headed north to Fort Laramie on the North Platte River (today in Wyoming) and followed the river west through the South Pass, climbing to what they mistakenly believed was the highest peak of the Rocky Mountains. Owing to a severe shortage of supplies, they were forced to turn back, and returned east via the North Platte and Platte Rivers. The four-month exploration was just the first of John Frémont's many long absences from his wife; the couple would be separated for five of the first eight years of their marriage.

One of the surprises of John Frémont's reports is his many contacts with other travelers. He never personally claimed the title "Pathfinder," and as biographer Allan Nevins explains in *Frémont: Pathmarker of the West* (1939), he was really more of a "Pathmarker." On the first expedition Frémont followed three weeks behind a group of emigrants, admitting later that "Travelling on the fresh traces of the Oregon emigrants relieves a little of the loneliness of the road."

In his first report, as in the subsequent ones, Frémont describes travel over rough terrain in inclement weather, hunting buffalo, losing provisions, encounters with other travelers and Indians, and careful scientific observation. With the aid of his wife, Frémont produced not dry government documents but reports that read like epistolary adventure novels. He was always careful to justify his leadership decisions and to place himself in the best possible light. Some of his fellow travelers–S. N. Carvalho, Theodore Talbot, Charles Preuss, Christopher "Kit" Carson, James Milligan, and Edward and Richard Kern–also published books, and their accounts of controversial events sometimes contradict Frémont's view.

Frémont's account of this first major expedition is also sprinkled with romantic descriptions of nature and anecdotes of bravery and heroism. The 22 July 1842 depiction of the North Platte River, for example, is striking:

> Like the whole country, the scenery of the river had undergone an entire change, and was in this place the most beautiful I have ever seen. The breadth of the stream, generally near that of its valley, was from two to three hundred feet, with a swift current, occasionally broken by rapids, and the water perfectly clear. . . . Viewed in the sunshine of a pleasant morning, the scenery was of a most striking and romantic beauty, which arose from the picturesque disposition of the objects and the vivid contrast of colors. I thought with much pleasure of our approaching descent in the canoe through such an interesting place.

As the party pushed toward the Rocky Mountains, they encountered many Indians who told them stories of drought and starvation. The interpreter told John Frémont: "The best advice I can give you, is to turn back at once." Frémont gave his men the option of retreat, "But not a man flinched from the undertaking." Heroism combined with patriotism when Frémont unfurled the national flag on a peak of the Rocky Mountains on 15 August 1842 (probably either Garnett Peak or Woodrow Wilson Peak): "We had climbed the loftiest peak of the Rocky Mountains, . . . and standing where never human foot had stood before, felt the exultation of first explorers." After this triumph the party turned toward home.

Soon after the couple were reunited in Washington, Jessie Frémont gave birth to their daughter, Elizabeth (called Lilly), on 13 November 1842. The Frémonts then started working on the report of the expedition, which includes a plant catalogue and astronomical and meteorological tables. The report was an important geographical, political, and scientific document that included reliable maps and advice for settlers. Unlike the accounts of other explorers, the Frémonts' report was written with the grace of Washington Irving and included the observations of trained scientists. Senator Benton used it to promote Western expansion, as the United States raced Great Britain to settle the Oregon Territory.

Frémont's report of his second government-sponsored expedition was included with his first report and published as *Report of the Exploring Expedition to the Rocky Mountains in the Year 1842, and to Oregon and North California in the Years 1843–'44* (1845). For this expedition that would last more than fourteen months, from 29 May 1843 to 6 August 1844, Frémont was instructed "to connect the reconnoisance of 1842 . . . with the surveys of Commander Wilkes on the coast of the Pacific ocean, so as to give a connected survey of the interior of our continent." He was to map the area between Saint Louis and California, continuing the work of his first expedition which had stopped at the Rocky Mountains. The Frémont family left Washington for Saint Louis to prepare for his departure.

Jessie Frémont was again actively involved in her husband's work: she handled the mail, inventoried equipment, and interviewed members of the exploring party. She also used her authority to make a crucial decision. Fearing danger from Indians, John Frémont had asked the army for a twelve-pound howitzer cannon. Soon after the party had left, however, Jessie opened a letter from Washington questioning the use of a heavy weapon for a supposedly peaceful party. The letter ordered Frémont to return to Washington immediately and placed his men under a different command. Jessie was suspicious of the political machinations implicit in the letter; thus, instead of forwarding the letter to her husband, she sent him a mysterious note: "Do not delay another day. But trust and start at once." She saved the expedition but strained the relations between her father and husband and the military establishment in Washington.

The expedition took a slightly different route to the South Pass of the Rocky Mountains than the first expedition. The party went up the valley of the Kansas River to Saint Vrain's Fort (present-day northeastern Colorado) and then headed northwest to the South Pass. The real object of the trip would begin here, where the last expedition left off: to find a new road to Oregon and California. In the report John Frémont makes his typically thorough scientific observations: he constantly notes the temperature, altitude, longitude and latitude, and qualities of the land. After the South Pass the next point of interest was the Great Salt Lake. Frémont departs from his scientific voice to describe the "still and solitary grandeur" of the lake with romantic enthusiasm:

> It was one of the great points of the exploration; and as we looked eagerly over the lake in the first emotions of excited pleasure, I am doubtful if the followers of Balboa felt more enthusiasm when, from the heights of the Andes, they saw for the first time the great Western ocean. It certainly was a magnificent object and a noble *terminus* to this part of our expedition; and to travellers so long shut up among mountain ranges, a sudden view over the expanse of silent waters had in it something sublime.

Frémont biographer Rolle maintains that the explorer's description of Utah inspired Brigham Young to bring the Mormons there.

From the Great Salt Lake the party traveled northwest to the Columbia River in Oregon Territory, a region Frémont would strongly promote in the last section of his report:

> Commercially, the value of the Oregon country must be great, washed as it is by the north Pacific ocean—fronting Asia—producing many of the elements of commerce—mild and healthy in its climate—and becoming, as it naturally will, a thoroughfare for the East India and China trade.

After getting supplies from the Vancouver fort of the British Hudson's Bay Company, Frémont made the pivotal decision to return east by a new route: he would lead his expedition to the south and then turn eastward to explore the Great Basin between the Rocky Mountains and the Sierra Nevada, perhaps finding the mythical Buenaventura River, which early maps showed running from the Rocky Mountains to San Francisco Bay.

The narrative gains suspense as Frémont describes this arduous leg of the journey. Beginning their southward trek through Oregon on 18 November 1843, the expedition reached a crisis point on the eastern side of the Sierra Nevada by 3 January 1844. Hampered by snow and fog, their animals too weak to carry them, they were at the edge of the desert, unable to find the river and lakes for which they were bound. On 18 January Frémont decided to abandon the eastern course and cross the Sierra Nevada to the Sacramento Valley.

While Frémont describes the winter crossing of the mountains as the result of pressing circumstance, Jackson and Spence suggest that he may have intended to ignore his instructions and make such a crossing all along. Regardless of his motivation, the decision was a disaster: owing to the snow and lack of provisions it took the party five weeks to travel the seventy miles to Sutter's Fort. On 25 February the party split up: Frémont went ahead with a small group and planned to return with supplies and fresh animals. He arrived at Sutter's Fort on 6 March and the next day went back for the rest of his men, meeting them on 8 March: "a more forlorn and pitiable sight . . . cannot well be imagined." After rest and refitting Frémont and his men resumed their journey home on 24 March. Along the way the party helped some Mexicans in their battle with local Indians.

John Frémont arrived back in Saint Louis on 6 August 1844, and once again Jessie worked with him for several months on the report. After the account of the two expeditions was published by Congress, it was republished by trade publishers and became an instant success. Rolle observes that the maps, using astronomical observations, reached new levels of professionalism. The Frémonts' books became popular "trail bibles" because of their information about Indians, flora, fauna, and pioneers.

Kit Carson and Frémont at Taos, soon after an expedition in which eleven people died in the San Juan Mountains (Denver Public Library, Western History Department)

While Frémont's first two expeditions had made him a national hero, his last three would be controversial.

Frémont left on his third major expedition in the fall of 1845. His orders were to continue his survey of the Rockies, the Great Salt Lake region, and the Sierra Nevada, but biographers disagree over whether or not it was supposed to be a strictly scientific venture. Frémont claimed in *Memoirs of My Life* (1887) to have had secret instructions to continue to California and to guard U.S. interests in the event of war with Mexico. At any rate, Frémont's party of sixty armed men arrived in Monterey in March

1846. Liberally interpreting whatever orders he had, Frémont gave some support to the American dissidents who captured Sonoma and declared the Bear Flag Republic in June 1846. President Polk had declared war in May 1846, and when the news reached California, Commo. Robert F. Stockton made Frémont a major, and together their forces completed the conquest of California.

Frémont, however, was soon caught in a power play between Commodore Stockton and Gen. Stephen Watts Kearny of the army. While Commodore Stockton had appointed Frémont governor of California, General Kearny had been sent with orders to establish a government. Frémont sided with Commodore Stockton in the conflict of authority, so General Kearny had Frémont arrested on charges of disobedience and brought back to Washington. At his eighty-nine-day court-martial trial from 2 November 1847 to 31 January 1848, Frémont was found guilty and dismissed from the army. President Polk did not reverse the verdict but did overturn the dismissal. Senator Benton was infuriated by the proceedings and published a pamphlet supporting his son-in-law, *Defense of Lieut. Col. J. C. Frémont* (1848). Frémont would accept nothing less than complete vindication, so he resigned from the army on 19 February 1848. While the trial was devastating for his family, the court-martial heightened Frémont's national reputation as the conqueror of California.

Once John Frémont resigned from the army, he and Jessie got to work on the report of his third expedition, *Geographical Memoir upon Upper California in Illustration of His Map of Oregon and California* (1848). Unlike his first two reports, this was a brief sketch of his notes for a full report to be completed later. The *Geographical Memoir* does not have the adventure stories of the earlier writings; it mainly gives a fuller description of the areas included on the map. Frémont also acts as an advocate of California settlement. Calling it the "Italy of America," he claims that "Geographically, the position of this California is one of the best in the world; lying on the coast of the Pacific, fronting Asia, on the line of the American road to Asia, and possessed of advantages to give full effect to its grand geographical position." As usual he includes charts of his astronomical and meteorological observations. Unfortunately, the Frémonts never wrote the full report, and his field notes have been lost.

John Frémont was soon thereafter involved with his fourth expedition. This venture was privately sponsored by Senator Benton and several Saint Louis merchants who dreamed of a railroad to the Pacific along the thirty-eighth parallel that would make Saint Louis the gateway to California. Frémont's task was to find whether gaps in the southern Rockies were passable in the winter. Jessie, their six-year-old daughter Lilly, and their baby son, Benton (born 24 July 1848), accompanied John west to Saint Louis. Mother and children then were to return east and take a ship to California via Panama. Sadly, the baby did not live to make the trip, dying on 6 October 1848 of heart failure.

While no report was ever published on the expedition that left Kansas City on 20 October 1848, scholars have been able to learn about the journey by studying Frémont's manuscript of the unpub-

lished second volume of his memoirs. The party quickly proceeded west and reached Bent's Fort (present-day Colorado) on 16 November. There was already a foot of snow on the ground, a bad sign for a winter exploration. By 21 November, they reached Pueblo on the eastern edge of the Rocky Mountains and were warned by mountain men not to continue. But, characteristically, Frémont was determined to press on. This was a disastrous decision: the harsh winter conditions and mistakes in navigation put the lives of the party at risk.

With his men frostbitten and starving and their pack animals dying of exposure and hunger, Frémont in desperation finally decided to split up the party as he had in his third expedition. When he arrived in Taos on 21 January 1849, he was a physical and emotional wreck. Alexis Godey, a French-Canadian scout ever loyal to Frémont, went back to rescue the remainder of the party and found them on 28 January. Frémont was later accused of abandoning his men, and the expedition was also tainted by accusations of cannibalism. Eleven of the thirty-three members of the party died, and the survivors were walking skeletons. Because of his recklessness and poor judgment, Frémont bears the principal responsibility for this tragedy.

He soon continued to California, where he expected Jessie to meet him in March. They intended to settle on their Mariposa ranch, which had been bought for them accidentally by an agent who did not follow instructions. Jessie and Lilly, though, were undergoing a travel ordeal of their own. Having arrived in Panama, they had to cross the isthmus by boat and mule train under hazardous conditions. When they reached the Pacific side, the ship that was supposed to take them to California was nowhere to be found because the crew, hearing of the discovery of gold in California, had deserted. After a seven-week wait, Jessie and Lilly finally arrived in San Francisco on 4 June 1849. Ten days later the Frémonts were reunited.

The mistaken land purchase turned out to be a glorious error, as gold was discovered on the Mariposa property and the Frémonts turned their attention to mining their new-found fortune. In the excitement of the gold rush, California applied to be a free state, and John Frémont was elected one of the state's first two senators in December 1850. His career in the Senate was short-lived, however: his inattention to California's needs soon cost him his position. There were also additions to the Frémont family at this time. John Jr. was born on 19 April 1851, and Anne was born on 1 February 1853, although she died six months later on 12 July. The family

Jessie Benton Frémont at home in San Francisco (The Bancroft Library)

took an extended trip to Europe in 1852–1853, staying in London and Paris.

John Frémont left for his fifth and final expedition in 1853, another attempt to map the central transcontinental railroad that Senator Benton and the Frémonts still advocated. As in the fourth expedition, the party headed west to Bent's Fort on the Arkansas River. Leaving the fort on 25 November 1853, Frémont unrealistically hoped to reach California in sixty days. Again, travel was slow and difficult in the cold and snow. The party ran out of food and ate the horses as they died. One man died on the journey. They stumbled into the Mormon outpost Parowan on 8 February 1854, starving, frostbitten, and exhausted. After resting and obtaining supplies, the party continued to California, arriving in San Francisco on 16 April 1854. The expedition was an utter failure, and the proposed railroad route was never used. The only good news that spring was the birth of the Frémonts' fifth child, Frank, on 17 May 1854.

While a full report of the fifth expedition was never completed, John Frémont did write a seven-page letter to the *National Intelligencer* in June 1854 describing his exploration and advocating the central railroad route. The letter, titled "Central Railroad Route to the Pacific," was then published by Congress on 27 December 1854. Frémont provides a concise geographical description of the route, simi-

lar in form to his earlier *Geographical Memoir*. In describing the hazards of the expedition, he writes smoothly and with supreme confidence, seeing himself as an explorer-hero while never admitting responsibility for the disastrous results of his bad judgment.

Amazingly, he concludes that his last two failed expeditions proved the viability of the central route. Glossing over the fact that men starved and froze to death, he writes: "It is clearly established that the winter condition of the country constitutes no impediment." His concluding remarks show echoes of Jessie's flair and the Benton vision:

> It seems a treason against mankind and the spirit of our progress which marks the age, to refuse to put this one completing link to our national prosperity and the civilization of the world. Europe still lies between Asia and America; build this railroad, and things will have revolved about; America will lie between Asia and Europe.

Despite the failures of his last two expeditions, Frémont remained a national hero. In the summer of 1855 he was talked about as a potential Democratic presidential nominee but refused the nomination because of his antislavery beliefs. The following summer he became the first nominee of the new Republican Party. This was a difficult decision because it meant a break between the Frémonts and their southern family and friends. Frémont had the support of many writers and intellectuals, including John Greenleaf Whittier, Ralph Waldo Emerson, Bronson Alcott, Horace Greeley, Washington Irving, and Henry Ward Beecher. In a three-party race between the Democrat, the Republican, and the American parties, the Democratic candidate James Buchanan was the decisive victor, but Frémont came in second with 33.1 percent of the popular vote.

When the Civil War broke out in 1861 John Frémont was appointed a major general and put in charge of the Department of the West, headquartered at Saint Louis. On 31 August 1861 he issued his own emancipation proclamation for the region. President Abraham Lincoln was furious: he rescinded the order and reassigned Frémont. However, abolitionists were thrilled by this daring action and would nominate Frémont for president at the radical Republican convention in Cleveland. Frémont accepted the nomination in June 1864 but withdrew from the election in September to ensure a Republican victory.

After the war the Frémonts faced financial ruin owing to bad investments, legal entanglements, and extravagant spending. Jessie Frémont, like many other nineteenth-century women who turned to the pen to support the family in times of financial difficulty, began to sell her work, writing many stories and sketches for *Harper's Magazine* and the *New York Ledger* as well as juvenile journals *Wide Awake* and *The Will and the Way*. She drew material from her life experiences, especially her travels to California and Europe. In 1878, the year John Frémont became governor of the Arizona Territory, Jessie Frémont published *A Year of American Travel*. Only five inches tall and three inches wide and selling for twenty-five cents, the book tells the story of her 1848 trip to California to meet her husband and their return to Washington when he became senator.

Jessie Frémont recounts the grueling land and river journey across the hot and unhealthy climate of Panama. Although her escort was amazed by her fortitude, she explains that she felt no equanimity: "As there were no complaints or tears or visible breakdown, he gave me credit for high courage, while the fact was that the whole thing was so like a nightmare that one took it as a bad dream—in helpless silence." As so often happened to John Frémont on his journeys, people begged her to turn back at every point of the trip. In addition to the physical dangers of her journey, she became frantic when hearing the news of her husband's tragic third expedition.

Once the family was happily reunited, Jessie Frémont portrays their domestic and political life in California. She seems quite aware that a settled community had been living there before the United States took over, but her remarks have a touch of condescension: "Before we brought taxes and litigation upon them, the Californians were a wholesome and cheerful people." Perhaps the most interesting section of the book is where she describes the Frémonts' role in the organization of California as a free state. Their household served as an example of a graceful home without slavery. Jessie Frémont was becoming the guardian of the Benton and Frémont legends; in *A Year of American Travel* she works hard to preserve their reputations.

The sketches in Jessie Frémont's next collection, *Souvenirs of My Time* (1887), are divided into two sections, titled "American" and "Foreign Series." In the "American" section, she recounts her childhood in Washington and Saint Louis and tells the story of how she met John Frémont. She is well aware of the important connection she made between her father, the expansionist senator, and her husband, the explorer: "Was it not a good fortune that I should make the connecting link between my father's thought, and that thought made action by Mr. Frémont." She also repeats the account from her previous book about their adventures in Panama and California, showing again her awareness of the effects of American expansion on the residents: "It is not an honorable chapter in American history that records our dealings with weaker peoples. The Louisiana purchase brought upon its old settlers much of the same bad faith and injustice I have seen imposed upon the original holders of lands in California." Nevertheless, Frémont never doubts the rightness of Western expansion and always shows her father and her husband treating the residents of American acquisitions fairly.

In "Foreign Series" Jessie Frémont gives accounts of her family's European travels, focusing on the spring of 1852 to the spring of 1853. The Frémonts were acclaimed in Europe and were received at court and in the best society. Jessie was clearly dazzled by the historical monuments and Old World rituals she found there. However, she understood that she was not experiencing the life of everyday people: "For Paris is not France. Not any more than New York city is the United States. Although New Yorkers and foreigners think so, we know better, and that the Daisy Millers and their unhealthy sharp little brothers and feeble-minded mothers do *not* represent us all."

Also in 1887 the Frémonts published the first volume of John Frémont's *Memoirs of My Life*. As usual, the book was a family project, but John Frémont was given the sole credit. As Frémont writes in his introduction, the book was intended to have three main subjects: "the geographical explorations, made in the interest of Western expansion; the presidential campaign of 1856, made in the interest of an undivided country; and the civil war, made in the same interest." The book also includes a "Biographical Sketch of Senator Benton" for which Jessie Frémont gets the author's credit. Volume one concludes with the year 1847 and draws on his reports of the first three expeditions almost verbatim. Unfortunately, the first volume was also enormous and overpriced. It did not sell, and though Jessie would work on it after her husband's death, the projected second volume was never completed.

In late 1887 John Frémont became seriously ill with bronchitis. Doctors recommended a move to a warm climate, but the now-destitute Frémonts had no money for travel. Family friend and railroad magnate Collis P. Huntington responded to Jessie's request for aid with a private car to California. As Rolle reports in his biography of Frémont, Huntington told them: "Our road goes over your buried campfires and climbs many a grade you jogged over on a mule. I think we rather owe you this." With this generosity, the Frémonts retired in California.

Jessie Frémont's *Far-West Sketches*, published in early 1890, is a short volume of ten sketches mostly about her life and adventures in California in the 1850s. She gives a lively account of setting up housekeeping on the frontier and a description of social mores in the Old West. She shows some awareness of the problematic interaction between the races in California in her description of a misunderstanding in a Chinese village but claims success in her work with the local Indian girls. In language embarrassing to late-twentieth-century readers, she writes, "They looked a different race after they had seen the advantage of cleanliness . . . and the tidy club of plaited hair tied with a bright ribbon, made them into picturesque peasants." She also describes traveling in the Arizona Territory in the late 1870s, when her husband was appointed governor. She was shocked by her first views of the desert: "the tawny yellow of the sand-waste cut by the deep-rolling, dull-yellow waters of the Colorado; scattered about in irregular lines and groups the brown-yellow adobe houses, . . . over all the fierce red-yellow glare of sun-fire rather than sunshine. Not a tree, not a bush, nor a blade of grass."

On 13 July 1890 John Frémont died unexpectedly while in New York on business. Jessie Frémont would live the next twelve years in California with her daughter Lilly. Always the guardian of the Frémont reputation, she finished an article her husband had been writing for the March 1891 issue of *Century Magazine,* "The Origin of the Frémont Explorations," which recounts the first three successful expeditions and defends his place in history. With typical dramatic flair, she writes: "Though the pathfinders die, the paths remain open." Jessie continued her work on her husband's behalf until her death on 27 December 1902. Lilly later published a memoir of her life with her illustrious parents, *Recollections of Elizabeth Benton Frémont* (1912).

John Charles Frémont's controversial career was marked by triumph and disaster. His devoted wife, Jessie Benton Frémont, made the literary documentation of her husband's successes her life's work. Their collaboratively written books tell much of the history of American Western expansion and are still compelling narratives for late-twentieth-century readers. While he did not always cover new ground, John Frémont's excellent maps and reports facilitated the settlement of California and the Oregon Territory and made him one of the most enduring of explorers. Biographer Ferol Egan describes the Frémonts as "symbols of a national identity that no longer had to look back toward Europe for its cultural heroes." Through the reports of his exploits, John Frémont became America's epic hero and is a lasting figure in our history.

Letters:

The Letters of Jessie Benton Frémont, edited by Pamela Herr and Mary Lee Spence (Urbana & Chicago: University of Illinois Press, 1993).

Biographies:

John Bigelow, *Life of John Charles Frémont* (New York: Derby & Jackson, 1856);

Charles W. Epham, *The Life, Explorations, and Public Services of John Charles Frémont* (New York: Livermore & Rudd, 1856);

Samuel M. Smucker, *The Life of Col. John Charles Frémont and His Narrative of Explorations and Adventures in Kansas, Nebraska, Oregon, and California* (New York: Miller, Orton, & Mulligan, 1856);

Cardinal L. Goodwin, *John Charles Frémont, an Explanation of his Career* (Stanford University: Stanford University Press, 1930);

Catherine Coffin Phillips, *Jessie Benton Frémont: A Woman Who Made History* (San Francisco: John Henry Nash, 1935);

Allan Nevins, *Frémont: Pathmarker of the West* (New York & London: D. Appleton-Century, 1939);

Ferol Egan, *Frémont: Explorer for a Restless Nation* (Garden City, N.Y.: Doubleday, 1977);

Andrew Rolle, *John Charles Frémont: Character as Destiny* (Norman: University of Oklahoma, 1991).

References:

LeRoy Hafen and Ann W. Hafen, eds., *Frémont's Fourth Expedition: A Documentary Account of the Disaster of 1848–1849* (Glendale, Cal.: A. H. Clark, 1960);

Robert V. Hine and Savoie Lottinville, eds., *Soldier in the West: Letters of Theodore Talbot during His Services in California, Mexico, and Oregon, 1845–53* (Norman: University of Oklahoma Press, 1972);

Mark Stegmaier and David Miller, eds., *James F. Milligan: His Journal of Frémont's Fifth Expedition, 1853–1854* (Glendale, Cal.: A. H. Clark, 1988).

Papers:

The Frémont Collection in the Bancroft Library at the University of California, Berkeley, includes correspondence and the manuscript to the unfinished second volume of John Charles Frémont's memoirs. There are other collections at the Southwest Museum in Los Angeles and the Huntington Library in San Marino, California. The family papers of many Frémont contemporaries, including those of Montgomery Blair and Robert E. Lee, are held by the Library of Congress.

Margaret Fuller

(23 May 1810 – 19 July 1850)

Jeffrey Steele
University of Wisconsin–Madison

See also the Fuller entries in *DLB 1: The American Renaissance in New England; DLB 59: American Literary Critics and Scholars, 1800–1850;* and *DLB 73: American Magazine Journalists, 1741–1850.*

BOOKS: *Summer on the Lakes, in 1843* (Boston: Little, Brown / New York: C. S. Francis, 1844); enlarged as *Summer on the Lakes. With Autobiography . . . And Memoir,* by Ralph Waldo Emerson and others (London: Ward & Lock, 1861);

Woman in the Nineteenth Century (New York: Greeley & McElrath / London: Clarke, 1845); enlarged as *Woman in the Nineteenth Century, and Kindred Papers Relating to the Sphere, Condition, and Duties of Woman,* edited by Arthur B. Fuller (Boston: Jewett / Cleveland: Jewett, Proctor & Worthington / New York: Sheldon, Lamport, 1855);

Papers on Literature and Art, 2 volumes (New York & London: Wiley and Putnam, 1846); enlarged as *Art, Literature, and the Drama,* edited by Arthur B. Fuller (Boston: Brown, Taggard & Chase / New York: Sheldon / Philadelphia: Lippincott / London: Sampson Low, 1860);

Memoirs of Margaret Fuller Ossoli, edited, with contributions, by Emerson, James Freeman Clarke, and William Henry Channing (2 volumes, Boston: Phillips, Sampson, 1852; 3 volumes, London: Bentley, 1852);

At Home and Abroad, or Things and Thoughts in America and Europe, edited by Arthur B. Fuller (Boston: Crosby, Nichols / London: Sampson Low, 1856);

Life Without and Life Within; or, Reviews, Narratives, Essays, and Poems, edited by Arthur B. Fuller (Boston: Brown, Taggard & Chase / New York: Sheldon / Philadelphia: Lippincott / London: Sampson Low, 1860);

Margaret and Her Friends, or Ten Conversations with Margaret Fuller upon the Mythology of the Greeks and its Expression in Art, reported by Caroline W. Healey (Boston: Roberts Brothers, 1895).

Margaret Fuller in 1846

Editions and Collections: *The Writings of Margaret Fuller,* edited by Mason Wade (New York: Viking, 1941);

Margaret Fuller: American Romantic. A Selection from her Writings and Correspondence, edited by Perry Miller (Garden City, N.Y.: Anchor/Doubleday, 1963);

The Woman and the Myth: Margaret Fuller's Life and Writings, edited by Bell Gale Chevigny (Old Westbury, N.Y.: Feminist Press, 1976);

Margaret Fuller: Essays on American Life and Letters, edited by Joel Myerson (New Haven, Conn.: College & University Press, 1978);

"These Sad But Glorious Days": Dispatches from Europe, 1846–1850, edited by Larry J. Reynolds and

Susan Belasco Smith (New Haven & London: Yale University Press, 1991);

The Essential Margaret Fuller, edited by Jeffrey Steele (New Brunswick, N.J.: Rutgers University Press, 1992).

OTHER: Johann Eckermann, *Conversations with Goethe in the Last Years of His Life,* translated by Fuller (Boston: Hillard, Gray, 1839);

Günderode, translated by Fuller (Boston: E. P. Peabody, 1842).

SELECTED PERIODICAL PUBLICATIONS–
UNCOLLECTED: "Goethe," *Dial,* 2 (July 1841);

"The Great Lawsuit. Man *versus* Men. Woman *versus* Women,"*Dial,* 4 (July 1843);

"Emerson's Essays," *New-York Daily Tribune,* 7 December 1844;

"St. Valentine's Day–Bloomingdale Asylum for the Insane," *New-York Daily Tribune,* 22 February 1845;

"Our City Charities. Visit to Bellevue Alms House, to the Farm School, the Asylum for the Insane, and the Penitentiary on Blackwell's Island," *New-York Daily Tribune,* 19 March 1845;

"Prevalent Idea that Politeness is Too Great a Luxury to Be Given to the Poor," *New-York Daily Tribune,* 31 May 1845;

"Asylum for Discharged Female Convicts," *New-York Daily Tribune,* 19 June 1845;

"The Irish Character," *New-York Daily Tribune,* 28 June 1845;

"The Social Movement in Europe," *New-York Daily Tribune,* 5 August 1845;

"1st January, 1846," *New-York Daily Tribune,* 1 January 1846;

"Letters from England," *New-York Daily Tribune,* 24 September 1846;

"Things and Thoughts in Europe," *New-York Daily Tribune,* 29 September 1846–9 January 1850.

Best remembered as the author of *Woman in the Nineteenth Century* (1845), Margaret Fuller has been celebrated as one of the foremost social critics of her day. Her importance as a feminist theorist has doubtless contributed to her not being widely recognized as a pathbreaking travel writer. Her *Summer on the Lakes, in 1843* (1844)–which records her travels from Niagara Falls through the Great Lakes to Illinois and Wisconsin–helped to define American literary travel writing at the same time that it analyzed patterns of western settlement on the frontier. As a pioneering columnist for the *New-York Tribune* several years later, Fuller visited the city's asylums, prisons, and mental institutions. Her records of

these visits function as a kind of urban travel writing, analyzing the ways in which the inmates of various institutions had been viewed as tourist attractions analogous to the "picturesque" American Indians of Michigan and Wisconsin. Finally, Fuller's European dispatches, published under the heading "Things and Thoughts in Europe" in the *New-York Daily Tribune,* examined European culture at one of its pivotal moments–the years surrounding the revolutionary outbreaks of 1848.

Fuller scholars have begun to see that travel provided the impetus for much of her most important cultural criticism. In the nineteenth century many easterners saw frontier settlers, American Indians, and the urban poor as separate, as beings whose lives and interests were detached from their own. Highlighting the aestheticism of those who admired the "picturesque" beauty of the racially other or the poor, Fuller challenged her readers to become conscious of the ideological and social privileges that invested cultural otherness with such an allure.

Just as Fuller's feminist essays analyze the forces that had led to the objectification of women in American society, her travel writing examines the ways in which the objects of tourist attention were viewed as sources of pleasure or entertainment. At their root Fuller's travel texts dramatize a process of democratic acceptance in which many of the forgotten inhabitants of the United States make demands upon her readers' sympathy as individuals who cannot be easily pigeonholed or pushed away. When she traveled to Europe, Fuller extended her commitment to democracy to include French and Italian citizens laboring to overthrow forms of government that had deprived them of basic human rights.

Fuller's childhood and youth contributed to her political sensitivity. The eldest child of Margarett Crane and Timothy Fuller, she was born in Cambridgeport, Massachusetts, on 23 May 1810, on the margins of the rich intellectual and political worlds of Cambridge and Boston. During her youth her father–a four-term congressman who eventually served as chairman of the House Naval Committee–played a central role in her intellectual development. According to Fuller's later account in her unfinished autobiography, her father's early tutelage in Latin and history provided her with a rigorous but severe model of intellectual attainment. Such an education was not unusual for a boy in the opening decades of the nineteenth century, but–as the education of a girl–it provided a model of mental discipline that clashed with the gender roles of the time. At an age when most young women of Fuller's generation were trained for a life confined to marriage and child-raising, she was developing a voracious

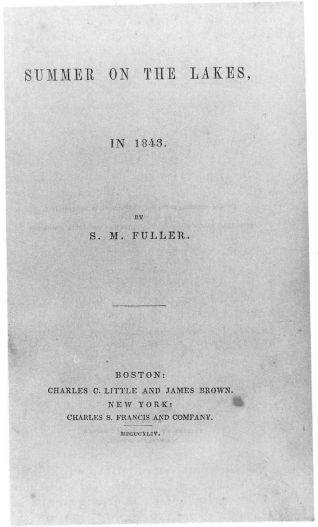

SUMMER ON THE LAKES,

IN 1843.

BY

S. M. FULLER.

BOSTON:
CHARLES C. LITTLE AND JAMES BROWN.
NEW YORK:
CHARLES S. FRANCIS AND COMPANY.
MDCCCXLIV.

Title page for Fuller's first book, in which she gives a sympathetic account of Native American culture

appetite for books and ideas. The eldest Fuller child by five years (since her sister Julia had died when eighteen months old), Margaret was encouraged by her father to supplement qualities of domesticity and submissiveness (expected of the "true woman") with literary ambition and intellectual pride.

Fuller's mother also had a profound influence on her daughter's development. In some of her writings, Fuller attributes to her mother traditional nurturing qualities, describing her as "one of those fair and flower-like natures" who exhibited "spontaneous love for every living thing." Her mother's garden provided a welcome refuge from the strain of academic recitation in her father's study; and, in later years, flowers became powerful maternal symbols in Fuller's essays and poetry.

Fuller did not fit easily into the female world or into the male world. She attempted to balance in herself qualities that had been coded both male and female in her culture, for both her father and mother were models she attempted to emulate. In her July 1843 *Dial* essay, "The Great Lawsuit. Man *versus* Men. Woman *versus* Women"—the nucleus of *Woman in the Nineteenth Century*—Fuller would argue that women (as well as men) should exhibit both "masculine" and "feminine" qualities: both critical self-consciousness and sympathy.

The circumstances of Fuller's life complicated her search for balance and harmony within herself. As an American woman who reached maturity in the 1830s, she was acutely aware of the ways in which her life was circumscribed by her gender. She lacked the opportunities for educational and professional advancement enjoyed by her male friends and by her younger brothers (three of whom eventually graduated from Harvard at a time when American colleges were closed to women). As she grew older Fuller found that her literary ambitions were difficult to reconcile with the domestic duties required of her as the family's eldest daughter. This situation was exacerbated by Timothy Fuller's decision in 1833, after his retirement from politics, to move his family from Cambridge to western Massachusetts. While Fuller's domestic responsibilities increased, her social and intellectual opportunities declined. Then, when her father died suddenly of cholera on 1 October 1835, Fuller found herself in the position of having to support her mother and younger siblings. An avid student of European literature, Fuller at the time had been making arrangements to travel to the Continent with her friends John and Eliza Farrar. Instead, during the next three years she bolstered her family's finances by teaching school, first in Boston and then in Providence. She contributed to the support of her family until her younger siblings matured.

Fuller's intellectual brilliance attracted the attention of Ralph Waldo Emerson, Henry David Thoreau, and the other members of the new Transcendentalist circle. In 1839 she agreed to become the first editor of the Transcendentalist journal *The Dial,* a position that gave her the opportunity to share her ideas with many of America's most advanced thinkers. Fuller also supported herself by offering a series of "Conversations," beginning on 6 November 1839, for the women of Boston and Cambridge. In this separate intellectual world she cemented her friendship with women such as Elizabeth Peabody, Lydia Maria Child, and Caroline Healey Dall, who later would rank among the most influential women in America. Fuller would become a frequent visitor at Brook Farm, a utopian community founded in April 1841 that adapted the radical social experiments of the French theorist Charles Fourier. Just as she gravitated back and forth between her father's library and her mother's garden, she moved easily in various social and intellectual settings—an ability that would enrich her travel writing.

By the summer of 1843 Fuller was ready for a change. In March 1842 Emerson had taken over her role as editor of *The Dial*. She had published her long-awaited essay on the writings of Johann Wolfgang von Goethe, "Goethe," in the July 1841 *Dial*, and her feminist manifesto, "The Great Lawsuit." Her brothers, in their late teens and early twenties, were becoming more self-sufficient, while her younger sister, Ellen, had been married for two years. Thus, when Fuller's friends Sarah Shaw and James Freeman Clarke offered to help finance a trip through the Great Lakes to Illinois and Wisconsin, she jumped at the chance to explore the western frontier.

From May to September 1843 Fuller's letters recorded her vivid impressions of the "great influences" at work in the West. Not surprisingly, she experienced at first a sense of dislocation as she encountered many men and women whose material goals and physical energy sharply contrasted with the intellectual world she had left behind in Massachusetts. In a 16 August letter to William Henry Channing she complained that she had lost her sense of "home"; while to Emerson she wrote on the next day, "I like not the petty intellectualities, cant, and bloodless theory there at home, but this merely instinctive existence . . . pleases me no better." In the months after her return Fuller analyzed this collision of viewpoints as she turned to writing *Summer on the Lakes, in 1843*. In November she began measuring her observations against those of previous Western travelers that she read in the Harvard College Library. (She was the first woman to gain admittance to this intellectual sanctum.)

Summer on the Lakes, in 1843—an extended prose narration of seven chapters—is one of the finest American examples of the literary excursion, a form more famously exemplified by Henry David Thoreau's *A Week on the Concord and Merrimack Rivers* (1849). Characterized by the heterogeneous mixture of genres, a literary excursion gains coherence to the extent that it exhibits the growth of its narrator's intellectual or cultural awareness. Some critics, such as William Stowe, have seen mostly disorder in Fuller's combination of descriptive sketches, literary extracts, dramatic dialogues, fiction, and poetry. But others, such as Christina Zwarg, have found a center of dramatic interest in the narrator's struggle

with the various cultural scripts of nineteenth-century America.

Describing her visit to Niagara Falls in the first chapter, Fuller shows her awareness of how individual perceptions have been affected by the ideologically laden representations of others. "Happy were the first discoverers of Niagara," she exclaimed, "those who could come unawares upon this view and upon that, whose feelings were entirely their own." Fuller knew that her visit to Niagara Falls was expected to replicate the cultural script of "sublimity," which had been popularized by the theories of Edmund Burke and Immanuel Kant as well as by many landscape paintings. The viewer of the sublime was expected to be overpowered by the grandeur of a scene that overloaded normal patterns of perception, allowing the release of deeply buried feelings from the unconscious. Since—for the Romantic artist—the unconscious was viewed as the site of transcendent power, experiences of sublimity were cultivated by Fuller's generation either as gateways to the divine or as expressions of the infinite potential of the human mind.

Fuller found the expected "grandeur" at Niagara, but the emphasis of her opening chapter is less on the experience of sublime transcendence than on a sense of vulnerability and "undefined dread." Fuller had expected to appropriate easily the aesthetic benefits of her travels. But instead of occupying a position of cultural mastery, she began to feel removed from the aesthetic viewpoint she had been taught to value. She identified more with the plight of an eagle chained near the Falls—a victim of cultural imperialism—than with the position of previous visitors, primarily men who had found that the script of the sublime reinforced their privileged sense of identity.

Fuller's movement from cultural privilege to political sympathy is most apparent in her encounters with white frontier women and American Indians. In the early chapters of *Summer on the Lakes*, she dramatizes herself as an Eastern "lady" discomfited by the squalor and hardships of the Illinois frontier. Exhibiting the familiar aestheticism of genteel urban travelers, she struggles to locate picturesque values—such as pleasing irregularity and quaint beauty—in the people and locales she visits. But this, as Martin Price observes, is exactly the great liability of the picturesque: its "dissociation of visual, pictorial, or generally aesthetic elements from other values in contemplating a scene." Fuller's search for the picturesque detaches her from persons or places, which are judged only as objects that provide visual pleasure, promoting the isolation of aesthetic enjoyment at the expense of possible moral or political involvement. The ugly, the vulgar, and the politically disturbing are either dismissed outright or appreciated for their "irregular" aesthetic qualities. The result—in the words of one of Fuller's characters—is the removal of details "from the demesne of coarse utilities into that of picture."

Such aestheticism motivates much of Fuller's narration in the second and third chapters, which detail her journey into the prairie west of Chicago. Evincing "distaste" at the confusion of western settlement, she attempts to look with "a poetic eye," while redeeming her image of the West with a "sweetness . . . shed over all thoughts." Fuller's tendency to resolve her descriptions into picturesque moments finally gives way in chapter 3 to sympathetic political engagement, when she considers the hardships experienced by white women who followed their husbands to the West. Such women, she observes, were initially trained to become "the ornaments of society." But on the frontier, their success depends upon their capacity to cast off the "fatal spirit of imitation" motivating them to display themselves as picturesque objects of male admiration (akin to a beautiful landscape). Like Fuller herself (who has been struggling with the cultural restrictions of picturesque values), they need a new way of imagining their lives. Many readers have noticed that such passages pick up Fuller's concerns in "The Great Lawsuit."

While they seem to stray from her travels, Fuller's next two chapters advance her interest in the plight of women in society by focusing on the lives of two extraordinary women: Mariana, the subject of an interpolated short story, and the Seeress of Prevorst, a famous mesmeric medium. Examining the fates of imaginative women who failed to achieve in their lives a "poise" between their creative impulses and social circumstances, these narratives together provide a striking counterpoint to Fuller's larger story. Trapped in a world that provides no satisfactory outlet for her brilliance, Mariana learns to cradle her grief, holding it "in the arms and to the heart, like a child which makes it wretched, yet is indubitably its own." Although the Seeress achieves a greater "harmony and clearness of the inward life," she too fails to find a stable balance between the "natural" and "spiritual" sides of her being.

Fuller's mourning of such losses contrasts with her earlier aestheticism. Rather than celebrating her own sense of cultural privilege, she sympathizes with those whose circumstances have prevented their achievement of a harmony of being. At this point she puts into place the model of response found in all of her mature travel writing: sublime appropriation and picturesque detachment give way to identification and politicized mourning. Grieving for the losses experienced by the different people she encounters, she shatters the complacency embraced by many of her genteel tourist contemporaries.

This transformation is most evident in Fuller's depiction in chapter 6 of the Chippewa and Ottawa encamped on Mackinaw Island. Fuller turns the chapter into an extended book review, citing many of the accounts of American Indian culture that her research unearthed. Although some of these texts provide glimpses of "beauty and grandeur" of Indian character, most of them—in Fuller's eyes—are skewed by prejudices that prevent their authors or readers from taking the "position of the Indians." Distinguishing her own sympathetic viewpoint from such cultural blindness, Fuller accumulates instances of Indian heroism, faith, nobility, and self-sacrifice, which she offers as "a collection of genuine fragments" that provide "a glimpse of what was great in Indian life and Indian character." The Indian, she concludes, must be "looked at by his own standard"—not through the eyes of "inherited prejudices" or from the perspective of an imperialistic "civilization." Fuller's sympathetic account of American Indian culture thus resists the appropriation of the picturesque gaze.

Completing *Summer on the Lakes* on her birthday, 23 May 1844, Fuller spent the next seven months expanding her essay "The Great Lawsuit" into *Woman in the Nineteenth Century*. This revision was shaped by Fuller's travels and her eventual move to New York, where she began to encounter the suffering of the women languishing in New York's mental institutions and prisons. Reflecting the interest of the new urban "moral reform" societies, she began to question the standards of a society that incarcerated female prostitutes and "vagrants" without addressing the social factors that contributed to their delinquency.

Several other female authors known for their travel writing were also drawn to the reform movements in New York in the 1840s and 1850s. In 1844, two years before she published *Life in Prairie Land,* Eliza Farnham became the matron of the women's division of Sing Sing state prison in Ossining, New York. In 1848 Catharine Sedgwick, the author of *Letters from Abroad to Kindred at Home* (1841), was selected the first director of the Women's Prison Association. In the 1850s Caroline Kirkland, known for *A New Home, Who'll Follow?* (1839), served on the executive committee of the Home for Discharged Female Convicts. To some degree all of these writers followed the trajectory of nineteenth-century reform movements, which were shifting from Boston to New York as the social problems of the modern metropolis began to attract attention.

As reformers began visiting the new penal and medical institutions, they journeyed to locales that probably seemed as foreign as the Western frontier. The disciplinary institutions of the burgeoning city had created a new kind of space that needed to be explored and charted. Along with other women, Fuller began questioning the social expense of incarcerating and cutting off from normal exchange the prisoners and inmates of newly constructed institutions. Accepting a position as book reviewer and social analyst for Horace Greeley's *New-York Tribune,* she published a series of sketches depicting her visits with women in Sing Sing and various other correctional institutions.

The most striking of these urban travel essays is Fuller's 19 March 1845 article titled "Our City Charities. Visit to Bellevue Alms House, to the Farm School, the Asylum for the Insane, and the Penitentiary on Blackwell's Island." This essay exemplifies the problem of moral response that had structured *Summer on the Lakes*—the conflict between a picturesque gaze imposing standards of middle-class respectability and a moral involvement with society's victims. The new urban correctional institutions were prominent tourist attractions, often visited by those who merely wanted to gawk at the poor, the insane, and the criminal. According to Fuller biographer Paula Blanchard, a "large proportion" of nineteenth-century New York's "'sights' were philanthropic institutions, many of which were housed in new buildings" and which were "prominently listed in the city's guidebooks."

The inmates of such establishments seemed to embody an urban picturesque whose aestheticized aura paralleled that of western settlers and Indians. Although Fuller admonished male visitors who examined nursing mothers with "careless scrutiny" and exposed newborn infants to the "gaze of the stranger," she herself succumbed to the temptation to see picturesque qualities in some of the inmates. In the Alms House, a Dutch girl with "ragged dark hair" and "a glowering wizard eye" looked "like a gnome"; while in the Asylum for the Insane, a Catholic woman who had "become insane while preparing to be a Nun" took on a "high poetical interest." But while Fuller aestheticized some of the inmates, she also attempted to shift public opinion in order to improve their living conditions. In "Prevalent Idea that Politeness is Too Great a Luxury to be Given to the Poor," published in the 31 May 1845 *New-York Daily Tribune,* she demanded from her readers a "genuine respect" and "courtesy" that rec-

ognized the human ties between themselves and the less fortunate members of society.

In 1846, after publishing over 250 articles in the *New-York Daily Tribune* in two years, Fuller once again took on wider travels. She had wanted to visit Europe since her childhood, and, when Marcus and Rebecca Spring offered to take her along with them as a companion, she was finally able to embark. She helped to defray her expenses with a series of travel dispatches which were published on the front page of the *Tribune* under the heading "Things and Thoughts in Europe." Because of the time delay in receiving mail from Europe, Fuller's dispatches were published four to six weeks after their date of composition. In 1991 they were collected and reprinted in *"These Sad But Glorious Days": Dispatches from Europe, 1846–1850,* a volume that charts Fuller's travels through Scotland and England, to Paris and Italy.

From a historical perspective Fuller could not have picked a more propitious moment to travel abroad. Europe was poised on the edge of revolution. France and the Italian states (as well as much of western Europe) were radically transformed by a series of revolutions in 1848, though Britain managed to avoid this social cataclysm. In Fuller's descriptions of England and Scotland one finds the obligatory sketches of the Lake District, castles, and various noted figures such as William Wordsworth and Thomas Carlyle. But paired with such standard tourist fare are accounts of new reform institutions, vivid descriptions of urban poverty, and reflections upon the effects of industrialization. Fuller found evidence of reform in the new Mechanics' Institutes of Manchester and Liverpool, which through schools and libraries provided educational opportunities for factory workers. But she was saddened by the "swarms of dirty women and dirtier children" that filled the streets of Liverpool, Glasgow, and London. It is "impossible," she exclaimed, "to forget the frightful inequalities between the lot of man and man, or believe that God can smile upon a state of things such as we find existent here."

Fuller's dispatches from Britain at times highlight the "interesting and pregnant associations" evoked by her reading. She measures the sights in Scotland against favorite passages in Sir Walter Scott's novels and recalls the vivid history of Mary, Queen of Scots. On occasion Fuller seems overwhelmed by the many travel accounts of previous visitors. Recounting her journey to Walter Scott's house in dispatch #6, a dispatch published in the *Tribune* on 23 December 1846, she complains that the "universal feeling . . . has made this pilgrimage so common that there is nothing left for me to say."

Fuller in Rome (engraving by M. Haider after a portrait by Thomas Hicks)

But while she seems disappointed to discover scenes she already knows—in Inverary, for example, "the position of every object the same as indicated" in one of Scott's novels—she uncovers an unwritten world in the urban landscape of Glasgow: "I saw here . . . persons, especially women, dressed in dirty, wretched tatters, worse than none, and with an expression of listless, unexpecting woe upon their faces, far more tragic than the inscription over the gate of Dante's *Inferno*."

Repeating the dramatic tensions of the opening chapters in *Summer on the Lakes,* Fuller in the early British dispatches attempts to locate a picturesque country while revealing a growing depth of political sympathy that threatens her aesthetic detachment. In London she makes the obligatory visits to museums and libraries, but her most striking commentary concerns the social inequalities behind such cultural displays. Such disparities, she maintains, recall "portentous times when empires and races have crumbled and fallen from inward decay." Sensing the revolutionary pressures that were building in Europe, she prays that "the needful changes in the conditions of this people may be effected by peaceful revolution."

Fuller's encounter in London with Italian nationalist Joseph Mazzini began to convince her that more radical measures than prayer were needed for reform to take place. Stirred by Mazzini's political idealism, she writes in a 19 Februayr 1847 dispatch that he and his compatriots demonstrate a "purity of impulse, warmth of sympathy, largeness and steadiness of view and fineness of discrimination which must belong to the legislator for a CHRISTIAN commonwealth." Such democratic idealism became the standard by which Fuller came to measure her experiences in France and Italy.

In Paris Fuller found an artistic world that seemed to have grown old and "degenerate." With a few notable exceptions, such as the actress Mademoiselle Rachel, she missed the "depth of soul" that for her Romantic generation signaled the presence of authentic motives. In her journey through France following her departure from Paris on 25 February 1847, she became more interested in the socialist doctrines of Fourier and in the work of reformers caring for the poor and downtrodden. Struck by the "terrible ills . . . infest[ing] the body politic of Europe," she became even more outspoken, writing in her 15 May 1847 dispatch that the time had come for "radical measures of reform."

In contrast to the ostentatious wealth and political corruption marking what would be the final year of Louis Philippe's reign, Fuller found in the new reform institutions of France pockets of "light" and "dark nooks . . . touched by a consoling ray." Such illumination, she showed her *New-York Tribune* readers, was needed by the sickly families of weavers crammed into a tenement in Lyons. Entire families, "from nine years old upward," ate and worked in their cramped rooms. When the work failed, many of the young women of this class were forced into prostitution. "To themselves be woe," Fuller indignantly exclaimed, echoing the words of the prophet Jeremiah, "who have eyes and see not, ears and hear not, the convulsions and sobs of injured Humanity!"

Arriving in Italy in March 1847, Fuller felt as if she had found a home. Traveling to Genoa, Naples, and then on to Rome, she quickly became immersed in a world that corresponded to her political convictions. Her friendship with Mazzini gave her entry into the inner circle of republican patriots who were attempting to unify the separate kingdoms and states of Italy. Many of the early dispatches from It-

aly capture the high note of enthusiasm that was beginning to mold the Italian people into coherent revolutionary parties. Fuller recorded the excitement of a "torch-bearing procession," "a river of fire" celebrating the first steps toward the establishment of a representative council. In October she described the people's "intoxication of joy" at reforms instituted by Pope Pius IX. As the spirit of reform spread, Fuller filled her writing with apocalyptic imagery that reflected her identification with the revolutionary fervor building throughout the Italian states. Events "tend to a great crisis, not merely to revolution but to radical reform," she observed in October, as she felt around her a renewed spirit of democracy. Several weeks later she declared that "all things bode and declare a new outbreak of fire, to destroy old palaces of crime!" Describing how she was "heated by enthusiasm" from the "first spark of Liberty" kindled in Italy, she waited for the people to burst into flame.

Fuller's ardent response to the Italian patriots was reinforced by her love affair with Giovanni Ossoli, one of Mazzini's followers and a member of the Roman Civic Guard. Her growing excitement at the political events unfolding around her was reinforced by her deep love for the man she met in Rome in April and who would become the father of her child. (Biographers continue to debate whether or not Fuller and Ossoli ever married, since the church records that would settle this question were destroyed during the bombing raids of World War II.) Although Fuller kept her involvement with Ossoli a secret from her friends back in America, the tone of her 1847 Italian dispatches betrays a depth of passion that must have surprised many of her readers.

Fuller's growing emotional commitment to Italy and the Italian people is apparent in several striking observations on tourists in Italy. Most travelers, she complained in May 1847, pass "along the beaten track" and see "the least possible of the country." It is "quite out of the question to know Italy," she remarks, "without long residence . . . and without an intimacy of feeling, an abandonment to the spirit of the place, impossible to most Americans." In her memorable dispatch #18, published in the 1 January 1848 *Tribune,* Fuller classifies Americans in Italy according to their capacity to empathize with the great events taking place around them. Escaping from self-absorption, the "thinking American"– Fuller's ideal traveler–is "a man who . . . does not wish one seed from the Past to be lost," a person able to comprehend and identify with the people and events he encounters.

Fuller's putative husband, Marchese Giovanni Angelo Ossoli (Houghton Library, Harvard University)

Placing herself in this ideal category, Fuller contrasts her involvement with the detachment of the typical tourist searching for the picturesque: "What was but picture to us becomes reality; remote allusions and derivations trouble no more; we see the pattern of the stuff, and understand the whole tapestry." As she had done in *Summer on the Lakes,* she differentiates political engagement from an aesthetic view that would turn the Italian people into tourist attractions. In contrast to "sight-seeing," she argues in a December dispatch published on 29 January 1848, it is necessary to cultivate "real knowledge, the recreative power induced by familiar love." Asserting her distance from the picturesque, she declares, "I cannot look merely with a pictorial eye." Instead, she claims to begin to be able "to see and feel the real Rome." Bell Chevigny argues in her 1986 article in *American Quarterly* that Fuller's experience in Italy became meaningful because she identified with a political cause that for her made the "world intelligible for her."

Fuller's political involvement carries over into some striking apostrophes to her readers back home. Seeing around her a spirit of democracy that recalls the "early hours" of the American republic, she hopes that her *New-York Tribune* dispatches will cultivate sympathy for the advocates of Italian unification. "This cause is OURS," she asserts, criticizing those complacent Americans who "talk about the corrupt and degenerate state of Italy as they do about that of our slaves at home." Fuller challenges her homeland, which was then at war with Mexico, with the events in Italy. "Must I not confess in my country," she complains in her eighteenth dispatch,

> to a boundless lust for gain? . . . Then there is this horrible cancer of Slavery, and this wicked War, that has grown out of it. How dare I speak of these things here? I listen to the same arguments against the emancipation of Italy, that are used against the emancipation of our blacks; the same arguments in favor of the spoliation of Poland as for the conquest of Mexico. I find the cause of tyranny and wrong everywhere the same—and lo! my Country the darkest offender.

In 1848, as the discontent in Europe broke out in widespread revolutions, Fuller became even more outspoken in her demand that the American people recognize the rebirth of the true spirit of democracy.

By the end of March 1848, just after the end of Carnival, news reached Rome that King Louis Philippe of France—and what Fuller called his "empire of sham"—had been overthrown. The response throughout Italy was electric, as many saw the revolution in France as a sign of their own capacity to defeat the despotic monarchies and autocratic states that had carved Italy into a political patchwork. In Rome regiments of the central Papal States rapidly formed, as the people "kindl[ed] into pure flame at the touch of a ray from the Sun of Truth." Filled with "sublime hopes of the Future," Fuller perceived in the moment the fulfillment of all her political idealism. When a provisional government was proclaimed at Milan, she described its leaders in her dispatch published 15 June 1848 as "men whose hearts glow with . . . generous ardor," a "wisdom from on high." But as the year progressed, Fuller's hopes were dampened by the hostility to reform shown by the monarchs of Naples and Sardinia and by the increasing resistance of Pius IX to any lessening of his power.

Fuller posted no dispatches between late April and early December 1848. She hid her pregnancy by leaving Rome in May, giving birth to her son, Angelo, in Rieti on 5 September. In mid November she left her son with a nurse so that she could return to Ossoli, who as an officer in the Civic Guard had been recalled to Rome. In August Austrian troops had invaded northern Italy to protect their territories and quell uprisings in Milan, Venice, and Lombardy. As they moved closer to Rome, the people eagerly awaited the Pope's response. Fuller captures the tense political situation in one of her finest dispatches, the twenty-sixth, written in Rome on 2 December 1848 and published in the *Tribune* on 26 January 1849.

Apologizing for—but not explaining—her "six months of seclusion," Fuller re-creates the moment when the Pope's power failed. On 16 September the Pope had appointed Pellegrino Rossi as prime minister of the Papal States. An ambassador of the deposed French king and a conservative statesman distrusted by the majority of the people, Rossi became for many a symbol of oppression. His repressive measures—which included restraining the press, arbitrary arrests, and exiling suspected dissidents—led to increasing discontent. As the rivers in Rome "burst their bounds" in fall floods, "the public indignation rose" to its highest level. Rossi was stabbed to death by an unknown assassin on 15 November while making his way into the Chamber of Deputies. Re-creating the moment, Fuller provides what seems to be an eyewitness account of the scene of Rossi's death and its aftermath, though she was not present. In the ensuing tumult, she recounts, the Pope's Swiss Guards opened fire on the people—an event that precipitated the flight of Pius IX from Rome a week later.

By 8 February 1849 a Constitutional Assembly of the Roman States was elected, and Rome declared itself an independent republic. French troops, under the command of Gen. Nicolas Oudinot, advanced on Rome to restore the Pope to power. Despite Fuller's continuing pleas for American assistance, it was soon apparent that the Roman Republic would stand alone, ringed by enemies. In a May dispatch published on 23 June 1849, as the French troops camped in the distance, she declared, "The struggle is now fairly, thoroughly commenced between the principle of Democracy and the old powers, no longer legitimate."

In contrast to most American writers of her generation, Fuller experienced firsthand the horrors of war. Accepting the directorship of the Hospital of the Fate Bene Fratelli (four years before Florence Nightingale directed her first hospital), she tended the wounded and dying. As the intensity of the French siege increased, she watched with horrified fascination the bombs coming over the city walls. "In the evening," she writes on 21 June 1849,

> 'tis pretty, though a terror, to see the bombs, fiery meteors, springing from the horizon line upon their bright path to do their wicked message. 'Twould not be so bad, meseems, to die of one of these, as wait to have every drop of pure blood, every child-like radiant hope, drained and driven from the heart by the betrayals of nations and of individuals.

On the fourth of July 1849 (a historical irony not lost on Fuller), the French troops breached the walls, entered the city, and commenced to slaughter all those who resisted them. Two days before, Giuseppe Garibaldi, accepting the inevitable defeat of

Fuller memorial in Cambridge, Massachusetts

Rome, had retreated with his surviving legions. "Never have I seen a sight so beautiful, so romantic and so sad," Fuller exclaims, fully sympathetic to the warriors who had already "sacrificed hecatombs of their best and bravest."

In many of the most profound moments in her writing Fuller casts herself in the role of mourner, lamenting the losses of the people she encounters, especially the sufferings of those whose lives were scarred by political oppression. In dramatizing her emotions at the fall of Rome, she turns the image of the grieving woman. "And Rome, anew the Niobe!" she exclaims in her dispatch written on 6 July, identifying herself with the mythical mother whose seven sons and seven daughters were slain by Latona because of her pride. Ovid's account of Niobe in book VI of the *Metamorphoses* concludes with the transformation of Niobe into a stone statue surrounded by the dead bodies of her children, and Fuller evokes a corresponding scene to summarize her helpless grief at the carnage:

> A contadini showed me where thirty-seven braves are buried beneath a heap of wall that fell upon them in the shock of one cannonade. A marble nymph, with broken arm, looked sadly that way from her sun-dried fountain, some roses were blooming still, some red oleanders amid the ruin. The sun was casting its last light on the mountains on the tranquil, sad Campagna, that sees one leaf turned more in the book of Woe.

Recalling the destruction of Rome and the death of its heroic youth in a letter to Ellen Fuller Channing dated 11 December 1849, Fuller casts herself as Mary weeping over the body of Christ: "But when I saw the beautiful fair young men bleeding to death, or mutilated for life, I felt all the woe of all the mothers who had nursed each to that full flower to see it thus cut down. I felt the consolation too for those youths died worthily. I was the Mater Dolorosa."

In her final Italian dispatches Fuller transforms her grief into inspiring prophecy. Larry J. Reynolds asserts that "her persona" takes on the lineaments of "Liberty in her martial pose." Viewing the defeated Roman republicans as political martyrs, she looks forward to the eventual and inevitable triumph of their ideals. The "falsehood of France," she writes,

> the inertia of England, the entrance of Russia into Hungary—all these steps tracked in blood, which cause so much anguish at the moment, Democracy ought in fact to bless. They insure her triumphs—there is no possible compromise between her and the Old.

Writing from Florence on 15 November 1849, she expresses the fervent hope that "immortal flowers bloom on the grave of all martyrs, and phoenix births rise from each noble sacrifice." In the economy of Fuller's creative rhythms, mourning always seems to lead to insight, defeat to a sense of victory. At various pivotal moments during her life, she transforms wrenching crisis into renewed energy.

In her last published work, the dispatch written 6 January and appearing in the *Tribune* on 13 February 1850, Fuller evokes the image of an apocalyptic fire that will burn away the "vast harvest of hatred and contempts sown over every inch of Roman ground." The "next revolution, here and elsewhere," she prophesies, "will be radical." Envisioning a future in which Christ's promise to the poor and downtrodden is answered by effective political reform, she looks forward to an "uncompromising revolution" in which "not only the Austrian, and every potentate of foreign blood, but every man who assumes an arbitrary lordship over fellow man, must be driven out."

While such radicalism may surprise Fuller's readers who are more used to the moderate tone of her *Dial* essays and of *Woman in the Nineteenth Century*, her belief in the socialist theories of her age had been growing for nearly a decade, since her visits to the utopian community at Brook Farm. As a journalist in New York, she became one of the first American writers to review the early works of Karl Marx. In Europe her friendships with Mazzini and the Polish patriot Adam Mickiewicz exposed her to many of the most advanced social theories of the day. Fuller's commitment to radical social change is often evident in her Italian dispatches. Addressing the people of America on the significance of the 1848 revolution in France in her dispatch published on 4 May 1848, she cautioned them to learn the "real meaning of the words FRATERNITY, EQUALITY." "You may in time," she prayed, "learn to reverence, learn to guard, the true aristocracy of a nation, the only real noble—the LABORING CLASSES." Several weeks later, she cryptically alluded "to that of which the cry of Communism, the systems of Fourier, &c. are but the forerunners." In the dispatch published on January 1850 she declared her commitment to socialism:

> I believed before I came to Europe in what is called Socialism, as the inevitable sequence to the tendencies and wants of the era, but I did not think that these vast changes in modes of government, education and daily life, would be effected as rapidly as I now think they will, because they must. The world can no longer stand without them.

Many of Fuller's fréends back in Boston and New York must have been shocked by such sentiments, which seemed strangely out of place for a nation settling into its new role as the military leader of North America.

Fresh from its victory over Mexico and pushing westward through the domains of Indian tribes visited by Fuller in 1843, the United States was not ready for the radical message of Margaret Fuller, who on 19 April 1848 made a scathing comparison between the New World and the Old:

> My country is at present spoiled by prosperity, stupid with the lust of gain, soiled by crime in its willing perpetuation of Slavery, shamed by an unjust war, noble sentiments much forgotten even by individuals, the aims of politicians selfish or petty, the literature frivolous or venal. In Europe, amid the teachings of adversity a nobler spirit is struggling—a spirit which cheers

and animates mine. I hear earnest words of pure faith and love.

As she watched the events of 1848 and 1849, Fuller had been writing a history of the Italian revolutions. Returning to America with her family in 1850, she carried with her the book that was to show America the significance of the events she had recently lived through. But that dream was not to be fulfilled. On 19 July 1850, battered in a storm off Fire Island, New York, her ship, the *Elizabeth,* ran aground and was wrecked. Refusing to abandon Giovanni Ossoli or their child, Fuller drowned with her family in sight of the land she had left four years before.

During the next several years, Fuller's friends worked to secure her literary reputation and to repair any social damage caused by her relationship with Ossoli. The resulting text, *The Memoirs of Margaret Fuller Ossoli,* appeared in 1852. Presenting Fuller as a safely married woman, the New England editors—Ralph Waldo Emerson, James Freeman Clarke, and William Henry Channing—stressed her early years when they knew her best. Fuller's travel writing was given short shrift. Critics are still coming to terms with the significance of these texts—the site where Fuller came closest to presenting her ideal of a just society in which all people might realize their dreams.

In contrast to many nineteenth-century women abroad, whose works are represented in Mary Schriber's anthology *Telling Travels* (1995), Fuller resisted the impulse to replicate the "discourse of colonialism." She argued instead for viewpoints that crossed the lines of cultural difference. Near the end of her life Fuller felt that the promise of democratic equality had begun to disappear in America. She had to travel to Italy and live through the horrors of a revolution to find a place where her political ideals could be realized, if only for a brief moment in time.

Letters:
The Letters of Margaret Fuller, edited by Robert N. Hudspeth (Ithaca, N.Y.: Cornell University Press, 1983–1994).

Bibliography:
Joel Myerson, *Margaret Fuller: A Descriptive Bibliography* (Pittsburgh: University of Pittsburgh Press, 1978).

Biographies:
Joseph Jay Deiss, *The Roman Years of Margaret Fuller* (New York: Crowell, 1969);
Paula Blanchard, *Margaret Fuller: From Transcendentalism to Revolution* (New York: Dell, 1979);
Charles Capper, *Margaret Fuller: An American Romantic Life, The Private Years* (New York & Oxford: Oxford University Press, 1992).

References:
Stephen Adams, "'That Tidiness We Always Look For in Woman': Fuller's *Summer on the Lakes* and Romantic Aesthetics," *Studies in the American Renaissance* (1987): 247–264;
Margaret Vanderhaar Allen, *The Achievement of Margaret Fuller* (University Park: Pennsylvania State University Press, 1979);
Bell Gale Chevigny, "To the Edges of Ideology: Margaret Fuller's Centrifugal Evolution," *American Quarterly,* 38 (1986): 173–201;
Chevigny, *The Woman and the Myth: Margaret Fuller's Life and Writings* (Old Westbury, N.Y.: Feminist Press, 1976);
Julie Ellison, *Delicate Subjects: Romanticism, Gender, and the Ethics of Understanding* (Ithaca, N.Y. & London: Cornell University Press, 1990);
Annette Kolodny, *The Land Before Her: Fantasy and Experience of the American Frontiers, 1630–1860* (Chapel Hill: University of North Carolina Press, 1984);
Joel Myerson, *Critical Essays on Margaret Fuller* (Boston: G. K. Hall, 1980);
Larry J. Reynolds, *European Revolutions and the American Literary Renaissance* (New Haven & London: Yale University Press, 1988);
Susan Belasco Smith, "*Summer on the Lakes*: Margaret Fuller and the British," *Resources for American Literary Study,* 18 (1991): 191–207;
Jeffrey Steele, "The Call of Eurydice: Mourning and Intertextuality in Margaret Fuller's Writing," in *Influence and Intertextuality in Literary History,* edited by Eric Rothstein and Jay Clayton (Madison: University of Wisconsin Press, 1991);
William Stowe, "Conventions and Voices in Margaret Fuller's Travel Writing," *American Literature,* 63 (1991): 242–262;
Christina Zwarg, *Feminist Conversations: Fuller, Emerson, and the Play of Reading* (Ithaca, N.Y. & London: Cornell University Press, 1995).

Josiah Gregg

(19 July 1806 – 25 February 1850)

Nancy Cook
University of Rhode Island

BOOK: *Commerce of the Prairies: or, The Journal of a Santa Fé Trader, During Eight Expeditions across the Great Western Prairies, and a Residence of Nearly Nine Years in Northern Mexico,* 2 volumes (New York: H. G. Langley / London: Wiley & Putnam, 1844); enlarged, 2 volumes (New York: J. & H. G. Langley, 1845); republished as *Scenes and Incidents in the Western Prairies: During Eight Expeditions, and including a Residence of Nearly Nine Years in Northern Mexico* (Philadelphia: J. W. Moore, 1856).

Edition: *Commerce of the Prairies,* edited by Max L. Moorhead (Norman: University of Oklahoma Press, 1954).

Josiah Gregg

Although he published only one book, Josiah Gregg created what several historians and literary critics have called a classic. Gregg's *Commerce of the Prairies* (1844) not only influenced and guided scores of travelers during the 1840s and 1850s but also has provided reliable information for historians, ethnographers, botanists, geographers, and other scholars from the mid nineteenth century to the present. While *Commerce of the Prairies* remains among the most useful contemporary narratives for scholars of the Southwest, the Mexican War, and the Santa Fe trade, it has gradually claimed a place as a literary classic as well. Scholarship on Gregg has been greatly aided by the work of Maurice Garland Fulton, who discovered Gregg's diary and letters and published the two-volume *Diary and Letters of Josiah Gregg* (1941–1944). Biographical information about Gregg prior to the publication of Fulton's work was both limited and largely undocumented.

Born in Overton County, Tennessee, on 19 July 1806, Gregg was the youngest of seven children born to Harmon Gregg and Suzannah Smelser Gregg. Descended from Scots who came to America in the seventeenth century, Gregg came from a restless family. His father was born in Kentucky and moved several times before settling in Missouri in 1812. He grew up on the frontier, moving from Tennessee to Illinois to Cooper's Fort, Missouri, by age six. In 1814 he survived an Indian attack in which his uncle was killed and a cousin captured. Such a life offered little opportunity for formal schooling. In a diary entry Gregg claims that his education "had been received in the woods in a round log cabin."

As a child of delicate health Gregg never shared in the heaviest labor of farm life. He read everything he could find and was soon tutoring others in mathematics in the makeshift school in Cooper's Fort. He taught himself French, Italian, some Greek and German, and surveying; he also began a lifelong habit of keeping notebooks, jotting down scientific measurements and personal observations. At eighteen he opened a school near Liberty, Missouri, but lasted only a year as a schoolmaster. He hoped to study medicine, but when he was denied an apprenticeship under the respected physician Dr. John Sappington of Saline, Missouri, Gregg turned to the study of law. As he later admitted to his brother John, law was the only study he had ever undertaken in which he did not make reasonable progress. He continued with law until forced to quit in 1830 due to illness.

Some scholars, pointing to Gregg's description of his illness in the preface to *Commerce of the Prairies,* have suggested that he suffered from hypochondria. But whether physiological or psychological in origin, Gregg's illness spurred his introduction to the West:

> For some months preceding the year 1831, my health had been gradually declining under a complication of chronic diseases, which defied every plan of treatment that the sagacity and science of my medical friends could devise. This morbid condition of my system, which originated in the familiar miseries of dyspepsia and its kindred infirmities, had finally reduced me to such a state, that, for nearly a twelve-month, I was not only disqualified for any systematic industry, but so debilitated as rarely to be able to extend my walks beyond the narrow precincts of my chamber. In this hopeless condition, my physicians advised me to take a trip across the Prairies, and, in the change of air and habits which such an adventure would involve, to seek that health which their science had failed to bestow. I accepted their suggestion, and, without hesitation, proceeded at once to make the necessary preparations for joining one of those spring Caravans which were annually starting from the United States, for Santa Fé.

When the merchant caravan left Independence, Missouri, in May 1831, Gregg's friends had to lift him into the wagon. After two weeks of travel on the prairie, Gregg was out of the wagon and astride his pony, no longer an invalid.

Since two of his brothers had made the trip west as traders, Gregg must have left having some knowledge of the trade in the area of Santa Fe, a crossroads for Indian, Spanish, and American cultures. He put the six weeks of travel to good use, for he hired on as a bookkeeper to Jesse Sutton, one of the merchants, and learned Spanish. This preparation led him naturally to his calling as a Santa Fe trader. He plied his trade for the next nine years, crossing the Plains on four trips from 1831 to 1840. He returned to Independence in the fall of 1833 but set out again for Santa Fe as Sutton's partner in the spring of 1834. On this second trip he traveled further into Mexico, returning to the United States in the fall of 1836. He left again the following spring, staying until the fall of 1838. On his final trading trip in the spring of 1839, Gregg blazed a new trail to Santa Fe. His more southerly trail was favored for its earlier spring pasturage, allowing Gregg's group of traders to arrive in Santa Fe sooner and get a jump on the competition using the older route. The Santa Fe trade declined through the late 1830s, and Gregg's profits declined despite his new route. He returned from this last trip to Santa Fe in the spring of 1840 but continued to travel the borderlands of the frontier for the next few years.

The rough prairie life suited him. He writes in the preface that the first journey served "to beget a passion for Prairie life which I never expected to survive." Indeed, Gregg seems to have been happy and healthy as long as he remained away from cities and towns. He disliked meeting people: his modesty prevented him from engaging much with those he felt his intellectual superiors, and he had no tolerance for those whom he felt his inferiors. He never married, and his letters suggest that he avoided romantic relations with women. On his travels he could put his skills as a linguist, a surveyor, and a cartographer to use.

In reflecting on the last trip in *Commerce of the Prairies* Gregg's longing for his former life is evident:

> Since that time I have striven in vain to reconcile myself to the even tenor of civilized life in the United States; and have sought in its amusements and its society a substitute for those high excitements which have attracted me so strongly to Prairie life. Yet I am almost ashamed to confess that scarcely a day passes without my experiencing a pang of regret that I am not now roving at large upon those western plains.

He shows a fierce individualism in his love for "the wild, unsettled and independent life of the Prairie trader," which

> makes perfect freedom from nearly every kind of social dependence an absolute necessity of his being. He is in daily, nay, hourly exposure of his life and property, and in the habit of relying upon his own arm and his own gun both for protection and support.

COMMERCE OF THE PRAIRIES:

OR THE

Journal of a Santa Fé Trader,

DURING

EIGHT EXPEDITIONS ACROSS

THE GREAT WESTERN PRAIRIES,

AND

A RESIDENCE OF NEARLY NINE YEARS

IN

NORTHERN MEXICO.

Illustrated with Maps and Engravings.

BY JOSIAH GREGG.

IN TWO VOLUMES.

VOL. I.

NEW YORK:
HENRY G. LANGLEY, 8 ASTOR HOUSE.
M DCCC XLIV.

Title page for Gregg's only book, in which he shows a deep appreciation for the freedom of frontier life

No court or jury is called to adjudicate upon his disputes or his abuses, save his own conscience; and no powers are invoked to redress them, save those with which the God of Nature has endowed him. He knows no government—no laws, save those of his own creation and adoption. He lives in no society which he must look up to or propitiate.

He seems incredulous that he or anyone would willingly give up such freedom:

The exchange of this untrammelled condition—this sovereign independence, for a life in civilization, where both his physical and moral freedom are invaded at every turn, by the complicated machinery of social institutions, is certainly likely to commend itself to but few,—not even to all those who have been educated to find their enjoyments in the arts and elegancies peculiar to civilized society;—as is evinced by the frequent instances of men of letters, of refinement and of wealth, voluntarily abandoning society for a life upon the Prairies, or in the still more savage mountain wilds.

Despite his love for such a life, Gregg was never again able to spend an extended period on the prairies.

Gregg did not settle down after his last trip to Santa Fe. He made the family farm in Jackson County, Missouri, his home base in 1840 but made a visit to his brother John in Arkansas. In the more settled area, John Gregg found his brother "restless. There nothing seemed suited to his taste–nothing adapted to his genius." Gregg sojourned in Indian Territory during the summer and in 1841 went to Texas to trade mules and purchase land. He continued his habit of observing and recording the details of the country. The notes from his Texas trip show his remarkable range: from comments on the shabby state of Texas politics and the qualities and defects of the people to observations on flora, water quality, soil composition, and topography.

Gregg earned a living in various ways, including as a surveyor and as a merchant in partnership with his brother John and George Pickett, John's brother-in-law. By the end of 1842 he had begun to organize and prepare his notes "for the compilation of a work on Santa Fé and the Prairies." The timing of the publication of *Commerce of the Prairies* would be propitious, for the Southwest was becoming the focus of national attention. Santa Fe trade was stopped by Mexican Gen. Antonio López de Santa Anna in 1843, and tensions between Mexico and the United States were building toward war. Gregg's book would help the American public understand the importance of the territory and trade in the region.

Although his book was far from finished Gregg went to Philadelphia in July 1843 to buy goods for another trip west and to find a publisher. He did not fare well in the city. He was distracted, uncomfortable, and then ill. He moved frequently in search of a quiet place to live and work. His illness worsened, and his hair "commenced shedding as fast as a horse in the spring," so he began to wear a toupee. He discovered that writing a book was hard work and complained to brother John that the "job is surely ten times more tedious and laborious than I had supposed–had I anticipated it, I would hardly have undertaken–but my motto is 'Go ahead.'"

By November Gregg felt ready to seek out a publisher. He first approached Harper and Brothers, the publishers of Richard Henry Dana's *Two Years Before the Mast* (1840), but they rejected his manuscript. D. Appleton and Company accepted it, subject to editing, choosing a self-titled Irish count named Louis Fitzgerald Tasitro, a sometime actor and translator, to work with Gregg to prepare the work for publication. The pairing was a disaster. Gregg, a stickler for facts and the unvarnished truth, balked at Tasitro's flowery language and disregard for details. Gregg broke with Tasitro and sought the advice of William Cullen Bryant, who had edited Dana's

manuscript. Bryant recommended a lawyer with literary ambitions, John Bigelow. Bigelow, who went on to a distinguished career as a diplomat, a historian, and an author, proved amenable to Gregg's literary aims and they set to work.

At various times there have been claims that Bigelow was the true author of *Commerce of the Prairies*. He would later coedit the *New York Evening Post,* discover and edit Benjamin Franklin's *Autobiography* (1868), and write many volumes of history. Gregg, on the other hand, was often assumed to be an untutored and poorly educated plainsman. The biographical research of Maurice Garland Fulton, however, has shown that despite his modest formal education Gregg was a learned and talented man. Bigelow has claimed only a modest influence on *Commerce of the Prairies*. Fifty years after his work with Gregg, Bigelow reflected, "Whatever the value his book possesses–and as a history of the trans-Mississippi commerce before the invasion of the railway, it has, I think, great and enduring value–was due to him and him only. My laundry work added no more value to the washing of it than the washing and ironing adds to the value of a new garment."

In March 1844 Gregg and the Appleton company canceled their contract, and Gregg arranged to have the book published by H. G. Langley. *Commerce of the Prairies* was published by Langley in July 1844, in two duodecimo volumes with engravings and maps. The first edition of two thousand copies sold well, and by fall he was preparing a second edition with minor corrections, a new preface, a glossary of Spanish words, and an index. Gregg had a series of problems with Langley, which went into bankruptcy in 1846, and it seems unlikely that he made any money from his book despite its popularity. Other editions were published in the United States and England, and the book was also translated into German. The definitive edition of Gregg's classic work, edited and introduced by Max L. Moorhead, was published by University of Oklahoma Press in 1954.

Commerce of the Prairies offers a mixture of scientific observation, history, and personal narrative gathered during Gregg's extensive travels in the Southwest. Gregg begins his book with a brief history of the Santa Fe trade, which he follows with his account of a trip along the Santa Fe Trail. He then offers a history of New Mexico with an extended description of life and customs there, which is followed by his personal experiences as a trader in New Mexico and northern Mexico. He recounts a trip back to the

Page from Gregg's diary (from Diary & Letters of Josiah Gregg, *1941–1944)*

United States, discusses the decline of Santa Fe trade, and concludes with several chapters describing the prairies; their geography, flora and fauna; and the aboriginal people who inhabit them.

While Gregg was able to prepare a broadside of abridged notices for advertising purposes that praised *Commerce of the Prairies* as a literary work and for its veracity, no-nonsense tone, and comprehensiveness, he was generally not pleased with the perceptiveness of reviewers or in many cases with their appropriation of his book for political purposes. Some reviewers, believing that Gregg's book proved the crucial value of the Santa Fe region for American interests, made *Commerce of the Prairies* a weapon for the cause of manifest destiny. In Gregg's eyes one of the worst offenders was his editor. In a June 1844 review in the *Democratic Review* Bigelow asked, "Who can doubt but that civilization and trade, those ancient allies whose union has been cemented by a duration of so many hundred years, are destined to enter into and possess the whole of that unreclaimed region which now remains in the undisturbed possession of the buffalo and the wild horse, and the yet wilder Indian?" As Edward Halsey Foster notes, Bigelow's "article had as much to do with expansionist politics as with *Commerce of the Prairies*."

By the spring of 1846 Gregg's book was becoming what he resolutely hoped it would not—a guidebook for the hordes about to descend on New Mexico and northern Mexico. Gregg's maps were the most accurate available, and the U.S. Army, then advancing to engage Mexican troops, used them extensively. *Commerce of the Prairies* also soon became required reading for the immigrants to the West. There are echoes of Gregg's book in *The California and Oregon Trail* (1849), as E. N. Feltskog notes in his 1969 edition of Francis Parkman's classic, and many other narratives from this period quote extensively from *Commerce of the Prairies*. Gregg's readers learned a great deal about the route they traveled, whom they might encounter, what they would see, and where they would find water and feed for livestock. Gregg also provided the immigrants an advance glimpse of the natives of the region they were soon to invade. Gregg's often unfavorable descriptions of New Mexicans may have had a profound influence on Anglo-Hispanic relations at a crucial moment in their development.

Interest in *Commerce of the Prairies* revived in the early twentieth century when Reuben Gold Thwaites included it as volume nineteen of his influential reprint series *Early Western Travels 1748–1846* (1904–1907). Thwaites found that "as a contribution to the history and development of the far Southwest, Gregg's *Commerce of the Prairies* stands without a rival and is indispensable to a full knowledge of the American past." Scholars of the time followed Thwaites's lead and valued Gregg's book for its historical documentation.

In *Rio Grande* (1933), his classic history of the Southwest, Harvey Fergusson focuses on Gregg, reading his book as revealing a quintessential American type: "In Gregg more than any other man I know of, the American pioneer became articulate." Gregg captured the sense of freedom that prairie life afforded but also, according to Fergusson, revealed his sense of isolation, "the terrible loneliness of those who never find their peers and cannot tolerate their inferiors." Fergusson believed Gregg was better read and more thoughtful than most pioneers and noted that he seemed uncommonly sensitive to such frontier practices as the slaughter of the buffalo. Gregg presented an American "tragic dilemma": the "contradiction between his love of the United States as an abstraction and his contempt for it as a social reality. . . . For the country he loved and longed to serve was killing the wilderness he loved and lived in. . . . Surely there was never a more complete revelation of that impulse of social avoidance which drove men into the wilderness to subdue it." Such a reading places Gregg in the company of more famous pioneers such as Daniel Boone and James Fenimore Cooper's fictional pioneer, Natty Bumppo.

Since the 1930s a steady stream of Gregg scholarship has appeared, and one finds Gregg mentioned in most books on Southwestern history and literature. In the 1940s James Frank Dobie called *Commerce of the Prairies* "one of the classics of bedrock Americana." In *Josiah Gregg and His Vision of the Early West* (1979) Paul Horgan argues that Gregg "fashioned, with his literary skill, the ablest account we have of the westward adventure." Henry Nash Smith pronounced that *Commerce of the Prairies* "ranks with the Lewis and Clark narrative as a literary monument of the westward movement." While some modern critics have criticized the structure of *Commerce of the Prairies,* arguing that the rigid separation between personal narrative and factual information makes it disjointed, Gregg has been universally praised for his scrupulous attention to detail, his pioneering research on the history of New Mexico and many Native American tribes, and his frank accounts of his own travels and experiences.

After he completed *Commerce of the Prairies* Gregg continued his notebook-keeping, with an eye toward publication of a sequel for which he offered the tentative title "Roving Abroad." He left the East for Shreveport, Louisiana, where his brother John had moved. He tried to regain his health with a bee hunt on the prairies, but as soon as he returned to his brother's home he fell ill again. He made a quick trip to New York to work on the second edition of *Commerce of the Prairies,* then again went to Shreveport. Restless, he decided to pursue his old dream of medical study and in the autumn of 1845 went to Louisville, Kentucky, to attend medical lectures at the Medical Institute of Louisville, now part of the University of Louisville.

He hoped to attend the six one-hour lectures per day and take the degree in the spring of 1846, but again his health failed him. Though he missed many classes, his professors awarded him an honorary degree in March 1846. While frustrated by his failure to perform to his own exacting standards, Gregg left Louisville entitled to call himself Dr. Gregg. But he told his brother that he never intended to use the title unless he practiced medicine. His brother John remembers: "He read medicine and attended the Lectures, not with a

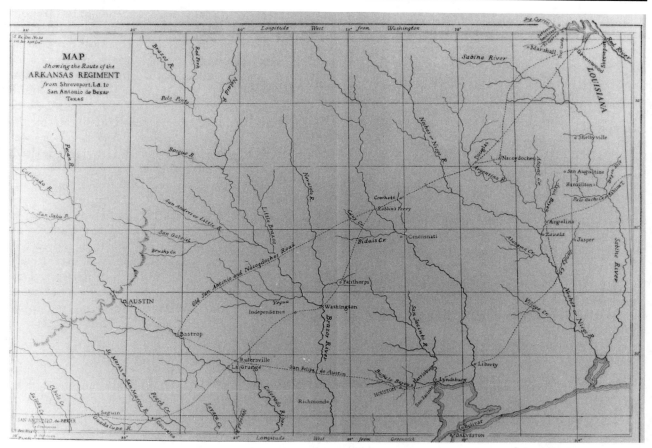

Gregg's map of the route of the Arkansas Regiment (from Diary & Letters of Josiah Gregg)

view of ever practicing; but to gratify his passion for science; and in the belief that it might add to his standing in Mexico, where he intended traveling."

In the spring of 1846—a banner year for westward travel because of the resumption of trade in the Southwest and the troop movement toward Mexico as well as the immigration to California and Oregon—Gregg made arrangements to join a caravan for Santa Fe. All along the border, large regiments of volunteers were forming to fight in the war with Mexico. Gregg's caravan was soon overtaken by a messenger from Senator Sevier of Arkansas, who requested that Gregg serve as guide and translator for the Arkansas volunteer regiment marching to Chihuahua with Gen. John Ellis Wool.

Gregg took a few of his things and returned to Missouri to await a commission, but when none came he started south anyway, making the twelve-hundred-mile trip to San Antonio on horseback. On his arrival he found no one could clarify his position, and he began to file articles with several western newspapers as a war correspondent. He served the military unofficially as a cartographer, a guide, and an interpreter but became a thorn in the side of military leaders, challenging many of their procedures and decisions and revealing their shortcomings in his newspaper dispatches. He was an eyewitness to the battle of Buena Vista, and although he found that in battle the rough American soldiers "fought bravely," he was at times disgusted by their behavior toward the Mexicans. He deplored that "our troops had destroyed and stolen immense amounts of property from the Mexicans which had not been compensated for." He found the American medical corps indifferent to the sufferings of Mexican officers and asserted that the admirable behavior of many Mexicans toward their invaders was rewarded by outrages against their persons, property, and customs.

Although Gregg was unhappy, he stayed with General Wool's army until they reached Saltillo, Mexico, where he left Wool to join Colonel Doniphan in Chihuahua. His situation continued to be uncomfortable, for the leaders disliked him for his critical stories and he did not fit in with the men in the ranks. They found Gregg priggish, and he quickly became the butt of their pranks and jokes. In turn he found them to be ignorant and crude. Since he was "constantly engaged in botanical specimens," Gregg found the soldiers an interference: "they must needs know every particular about them—what the plant was good for—if for 'greens'—for medicine, etc. often accompanied by taunting and insulting expressions: so that the naturalist has to pass an ordeal in laboring among ignorant people, who are wholly unable to comprehend the utility of his collections."

There is no doubt that Gregg was easy to ridicule. Fergusson recounts Gregg's behavior when he suffered from the heat while riding with Doniphan's army across the desert of northern Mexico: "He procured a huge red umbrella and rode along holding it above his head. When the soldiers began to laugh at him he was so incensed that he rode the whole length of the army with his sunshade defiantly aloft and lodged a complaint with the commanding general."

Gregg reclaimed his personal belongings that had come with the caravan of merchants to Chihuahua, then returned to Saltillo with Doniphan's army. Santa Fe trader Samuel Magoffin and his young bride, Susan, were among the merchants traveling with Doniphan, and he and Gregg agreed to be partners on a trading venture. Although the war was not yet over, Gregg was still serving unofficially, so he was able to leave his things in Saltillo and travel to Philadelphia and New York to buy goods. While Gregg purchased goods in New York, Magoffin sent word that the situation in northern Mexico was too volatile for trade, and the partnership was ended. Annoyed and disappointed, Gregg went to Washington, hoping to secure some sort of government appointment from President Polk. He met with Polk and found it "remarkable that a man so short of intellect should have been placed in the executive chair!"

Gregg returned to Saltillo not as a government appointee or a trader but as a physician and scientist. When he arrived in the autumn of 1847, the army of occupation was still in the city; he offered Spanish lessons to American officers but attracted few students. He had more success with medicine, for although he charged considerably less than his competition he nevertheless found his medical practice lucrative. He was again restless, however, and by the spring of 1848 he had left his practice and embarked on an extended field trip.

He planned a botanical expedition first to Mexico City, then to the west coast of Mexico, and then on to California, and possibly Oregon. Gregg had collected botanical specimens for years and had received the encouragement of Dr. George Engelmann, a physician and botanist in Saint Louis. Gregg corresponded with Engelmann and forwarded specimens to him. Gregg's contribution to botanical taxonomy was significant, and his name was twice proposed for a genus of plants by the American Botanical Society. Although he was denied that honor because an older *Greggia* existed, twenty-three plant species are designated *greggii*.

In Mexico City he examined maps in the national archives, with a plan to publish the most accurate map of the day. He then made his way to Mazatlán, where he abandoned his plan for an overland trip to California. He traveled to San Francisco by sea, where he left his Mexican field notes with Jesse Sutton, his former partner in the Santa Fe trade. He instructed Sutton to forward his papers to John Gregg should anything happen to him and set out for the gold country of California.

In October 1849 Gregg wrote to his brother John from Rich Bar, a mining camp on the Trinity River. He had been commissioned to lead an expedition to search for a port more convenient to the northern mining camps than San Francisco. Winter had set in by the time the seven-man expedition was ready to start, and they took a month to make the trip to the coast that Indians had told them could be made in as few as eight days in good weather. By the time they reached the coast the men were exhausted, hungry, and combative. Several of their pack animals had died on the journey; they had run out of supplies; and their leader, "the old gentleman," as they called the forty-four-year-old Gregg, had slowed their pace with his frequent stops for scientific observation and measurement. As they headed south toward San Francisco along the coast they were repeatedly aided by local Indian tribes but continued to quarrel bitterly. One particularly violent disagreement between Gregg and his men has been memorialized in the name of the Mad River.

At last they stumbled onto the bay they sought, naming it Trinity Bay (a maritime expedition later gave it its present name, Humboldt Bay). Gregg's party rested, then continued south, crossing and naming the Van Duzen and Eel rivers. Again they argued, and the group split into two, each following different routes. Gregg's group headed down the coast but turned inland, hoping for an easier route. In a published account one member of the expedition,

Lewis K. Wood, wrote that Gregg suffered a fall from his horse on 25 February 1850 and died from starvation and exhaustion. According to Wood, Gregg was buried near Clear Lake, California, on that date. Since this remains the only known account of Gregg's death, biographers have generally accepted both the cause of death and the date. Howard T. Dimick, however, casts doubt on Wood's account. Dimick argues that the evidence provided is inconsistent with death by starvation and that Wood was not a reliable source, for he was not among the party with Gregg at the time of his death.

Regardless of the circumstances of his death Gregg died before he was able to compile his notes into the projected volume, "Rovings Abroad," leaving only *Commerce of the Prairies* as the enduring measure of his work. Although Gregg once remarked that he had "no desire to be considered an odd fish," he was certainly an eccentric—but it was in part his eccentricity that led him to create a classic American travel narrative and make lasting contributions to botany, cartography, ethnography, history, and literature.

Letters:

New Found Letters of Josiah Gregg, edited by John Thomas Lee (Worcester, Mass.: The Society, 1931);

Josiah Gregg and Dr. George Engelmann, edited by Lee (Worcester, Mass.: The Society, 1932);

Diary & Letters of Josiah Gregg, 2 volumes, edited by Maurice Garland Fulton (Norman: University of Oklahoma Press, 1941–1944).

Biography:

Paul Horgan, *Josiah Gregg and His Vision of the Early West* (New York: Farrar, Straus & Giroux, 1979).

References:

Howard T. Dimick, "Reconsideration of the Death of Josiah Gregg," *New Mexico Historical Review,* 22 (July 1947): 274–285;

Harvey Fergusson, *Rio Grande* (New York: Knopf, 1933), pp. 158–183;

Edward Halsey Foster, *Josiah Gregg and Lewis H. Garrard,* Western Writers series, no. 28 (Boise, Idaho: Boise State University, 1977);

Lawrence Clark Powell, *Southwest Classics* (Los Angeles: Ward Richie Press, 1974), pp. 13–24;

Ralph Emerson Twitchell, *Dr. Josiah Gregg, Historian of the Santa Fe Trail* (Santa Fe: Historical Society of New Mexico, 1924).

Papers:

Josiah Gregg's diaries are held by the Thomas Gilcrease Institute of American History and Art in Tulsa, Oklahoma.

Nathaniel Hawthorne
(4 July 1804 – 19 May 1864)

and

Sophia Peabody Hawthorne
(21 September 1809 – 26 February 1871)

Laurie A. Sterling
King's College

See also the Nathaniel Hawthorne entries in *DLB 1: The American Renaissance in New England* and *DLB 74: American Short-Story Writers Before 1880.*

Nathaniel Hawthorne

BOOKS: *Fanshawe, A Tale* (Boston: Marsh & Capem, 1828);

Twice-Told Tales (1 volume, Boston: American Stationers' Company, 1837; revised and enlarged edition, 2 volumes, Boston: Munroe, 1842; abridged edition, 1 volume, London: Kent & Richards, 1849);

Peter Parley's Universal History, on the Basis of Geography, by Hawthorne and Elizabeth Hawthorne (Boston: American Stationers' Company / London: Parker, 1837); republished, abridged, and modified as *Peter Parley's Common School of History* (Boston: American Stationers' Company, 1838);

The Sister Years: Being the Carrier's Address, to the Patrons of the Salem Gazette, for the First of January, 1839 (Salem, 1839);

Grandfather's Chair: A History for Youth (Boston: E. P. Peabody / New York: Wiley & Putnam, 1841; revised and enlarged edition, Boston: Tappan & Dennet, 1842); republished in *Historical Tales for Youth,* 2 volumes (Boston, 1842) and *True Stories from History and Biography* (Boston: Ticknor, Reed & Fields, 1851; London: Low, 1853);

Famous Old People: Being the Second Epoch of Grandfather's Chair (Boston: E. P. Peabody, 1841); republished in *Historical Tales for Youth* (1842) and *True Stories from History and Biography* (1851);

Liberty Tree: With the Last Words of Grandfather's Chair (Boston: E. P. Peabody, 1841); republished in

Historical Tales for Youth (1842) and *True Stories from History and Biography* (1851);

Biographical Stories for Children (Boston: Tappan & Dennet, 1842; London: Sonnenschein, 1898); republished in *Historical Tales for Youth* (1842) and *True Stories from History and Biography* (1851);

The Celestial Rail-Road (Boston: Wilder, 1843; London: Houlston & Stoneman, 1844);

Mosses from an Old Manse, 2 volumes (New York & London: Wiley & Putnam, 1846; revised and enlarged edition, Boston: Ticknor & Fields, 1854);

The Scarlet Letter, A Romance (Boston: Ticknor, Reed & Fields, 1850; London: Bogue/Hamilton/Johnson & Hunter/Washbourne/Edinburgh: Johnston & Hunter/Oliver & Boyd / Dublin: M'Glashan, 1851);

The House of the Seven Gables, A Romance (Boston: Ticknor, Reed & Fields / London: Bohn, 1851);

A Wonder-Book for Girls and Boys (Boston: Ticknor, Reed & Fields, 1852 [i.e., 1851]; London: Bohn, 1852);

The Snow-Image, and Other Twice-Told Tales (Boston: Ticknor, Reed & Fields, 1852 [i.e., 1851]; London: Bohn, 1851);

The Blithedale Romance (2 volumes, London: Chapman & Hall / 1 volume, Boston: Ticknor, Reed & Fields, 1852);

Life of Franklin Pierce (Boston: Ticknor, Reed & Fields, 1852; London: Routledge, 1853);

Tanglewood Tales, for Girls and Boys: Being a Second Wonder-Book (London: Chapman & Hall / Boston: Ticknor, Reed & Fields, 1853);

Transformation; or, The Romance of Monte Beni, 3 volumes (London: Smith, Elder, 1860); repub-

Nathaniel and Sophia Peabody Hawthorne (left: portrait by Charles Osgood, Essex Institute, Salem, Massachusetts)

lished as *The Marble Faun; or, The Romance of Monte Beni,* 2 volumes (Boston: Ticknor & Fields, 1860);

Our Old Home: A Series of English Sketches (1 volume, Boston: Ticknor & Fields / 2 volumes, London: Smith, Elder, 1863);

Pansie: A Fragment (London: Hotten, 1864);

Passages from the American Note-Books, 2 volumes, edited by Sophia Peabody Hawthorne (Boston: Ticknor & Fields, 1868; London: Smith, Elder, 1868);

Passages from the English Note-Books, 2 volumes, edited by Sophia Peabody Hawthorne (Boston: Fields, Osgood / London: Strahan, 1870);

Passages from the French and Italian Note-Books, 2 volumes, edited by Sophia Peabody Hawthorne (London: Strahan, 1871; Boston: Osgood, 1872);

Septimus, A Romance, edited by Una Hawthorne and Robert Browning (London: King, 1872); republished as *Septimus Felton; or The Elixir of Life* (Boston: Osgood, 1872);

Fanshawe and Other Pieces (Boston: Osgood, 1876);

The Dolliver Romance and Other Pieces (Boston: Osgood, 1876);

Doctor Grimshawe's Secret, A Romance, edited by Julian Hawthorne (Boston: Osgood / London: Longmans, Green, 1883);

Alice Doane's Appeal, Chiefly about War Matters, and Life of Franklin Pierce, volume 24 of the *Wayside Edition* (Boston & New York: Houghton, Mifflin, 1884);

The Ghost of Doctor Harris (N.p., 1900);

Twenty Days with Julian and Little Bunny (New York: Privately printed, 1904);

The American Notebooks, edited by Randall Stewart (New Haven: Yale University Press, 1932);

The English Notebooks, edited by Stewart (New York: Modern Language Association of America, 1941);

Hawthorne as Editor; Selections from the Writings in the American Magazine of Useful and Entertaining Knowledge, edited by Arlin Turner (Baton Rouge: Louisiana State University Press, 1941);

The American Notebooks, edited by Claude M. Simpson, volume 8 of *The Centenary Edition of the Works of Nathaniel Hawthorne* (Columbus: Ohio State University Press, 1973);

The Snow Image and Uncollected Tales, edited by J. Donald Crowley and Fredson Bowers, volume 11 of *The Centenary Edition of the Works of Na-*

thaniel Hawthorne (Columbus: Ohio State University Press, 1974);

The American Claimant Manuscripts: The Ancestral Footstep, Etherege, Grimshawe, edited by Edward H. Davidson, Simpson, and L. Neal Smith, volume 12 of *The Centenary Edition of the Works of Nathaniel Hawthorne* (Columbus: Ohio State University Press, 1977);

The Elixir of Life Manuscripts: Septimus Felton, Septimus Norton, and The Dolliver Romance, edited by Davidson, Simpson, and Smith, volume 13 of *The Centenary Edition of the Works of Nathaniel Hawthorne* (Columbus: Ohio State University Press, 1977);

Hawthorne's Last Notebook, 1835–1841, edited by Hyatt H. Waggoner and Barbara S. Mouffe (University Park: Pennsylvania State University Press, 1978);

The French and Italian Notebooks, edited by Thomas Woodson, volume 14 of *The Centenary Edition of the Works of Nathaniel Hawthorne* (Columbus: Ohio State University Press, 1980).

Collection: *The Centenary Edition of the Works of Nathaniel Hawthorne,* 20 volumes (Columbus: Ohio State University Press, 1962–1988).

OTHER: *Journal of an African Cruiser; Comprising Sketches of the Canaries, the Cape de Verds, Liberia, Madeira, Sierra Leone, and Other Places of Interest on the West Coast of Africa. By an Officer of the U.S. Navy* [Horatio Bridge]. *Edited by Nathaniel Hawthorne* (New York & London: Wiley & Putnam, 1845).

Sophia Peabody Hawthorne

BOOKS: *Notes in England and Italy* (New York: Putnam, 1869);

The Cuba Journal, 1833–1835, facsimile, edited by Claire Badaracco (Ann Arbor, Mich.: University Microfilms, 1985).

On 9 July 1842 Nathaniel Hawthorne and Sophia Peabody were married in a simple ceremony that capped a courtship of nearly five years. Thus Hawthorne, at the age of thirty-eight, assumed his role as head of a domestic circle that grew to include three children: Una, Julian, and Rose. Hawthorne's own childhood was unsettled. He was born on 4 July 1804 in Salem, Massachusetts, to Nathaniel and Elizabeth Manning Hathorne (he added the *w* to the spelling years later). His father, a ship's captain, died when he was four, and Hawthorne's youth was spent between Salem and the Manning home in Maine. He attended Bowdoin College from 1821 to 1825, returning to his mother's home in Salem to begin writing in earnest.

Sophia Peabody was born in Salem to Eliza and Nathaniel Peabody on 21 September 1809. Much of her education was guided by her sister Elizabeth, and Peabody proved a good student with an interest in transcendentalism and art. At the age of eighteen she began to manifest an acute sensitivity to noise, the cause of violent headaches from which she was to suffer throughout her life. Her health precarious, she was soon labeled an invalid and considered too delicate and frail to marry. From 1828 to 1833, her "invalid years," Peabody was confined in the upstairs of her Salem home. During this time she directed her energies toward her own education, which was enriched by many of Salem's intellectuals, including her cousins Walter and William Channing, Francis Graeter, and Thomas Doughty.

Well before Nathaniel Hawthorne and Sophia Peabody met, she was—like her husband to be—a writer. Throughout their years together she was a journal keeper and, like him, recorded much of their family life and their travels. Eventually a large portion of Nathaniel Hawthorne's notebooks would find its way into the public eye. Sophia Hawthorne's writing, on the other hand, remained strictly private until after her husband's death. Her observations on England and Italy did become public when she needed money after her husband's death, but what the public saw in 1869 was but a small sample of her writing.

While neither Hawthorne is particularly remembered for travel writing, both wrote volumes about their travels. In these later writings from Europe one sees a particular concern for the American values that sustained them throughout their marriage. But in the early 1830s, well before their marriage, both produced material that could be classified under the rubric "travel literature," although the forms and intent of their writings differed greatly. Hawthorne toured New England and upstate New York in 1832 gathering material and experiences for his writing. Meanwhile, Peabody, placed in the role of a nineteenth-century invalid woman, traveled to Cuba in hopes of restoring her health.

In 1833 Mary Peabody went to Cuba to be a governess and tutor to the children of Dr. Richard and Laurete Morrell in San Marcos; Sophia Peabody accompanied her sister and was to teach the children drawing as her health permitted. Her substantial education in Salem guided her writing, and she kept an artist's journal in the form of letters sent back to Massachusetts. Her journal was a project in

The city of Rochester, on the Upper Falls of the Genesee River, the setting for Hawthorne's "Sketches from Memory. By a Pedestrian. No. II" (lithograph by J. H. Bufford)

self-education and improvement, and she wrote three times daily; the result was three volumes about her experiences in Cuba from December 1833 through April 1835. A facsimile edition, *The Cuba Journal, 1833–1835,* was edited by Claire Badaracco and published in 1985.

While the Cuba journal was not published in her lifetime, Peabody's writings did have more than a strictly private audience. Her letters were circulated or read aloud to her sister Elizabeth's circle in Boston, after which they were sent to Salem where her mother probably shared them with others, including Bronson Alcott. According to Badaracco, Peabody's work was much praised and was clearly shaped by the diverse expectations of her audience—some wanted an artist's journal, some wanted travel accounts and descriptions, while others wanted "an invalid's prayerbook." Apparently Elizabeth wrote to advise her sister on content, stressing that she should document her own progress in Spanish and art and avoid discussions of slavery. In many ways Peabody's Cuba journal is clearly the product of a young artist schooled in observing natural detail. She writes enthusiastically of the scenery and the flora, frequently describing paintings and sketches that she evidently sent along with her text. She repeatedly sketches the scenery with her words, trying to re-create for her readers in Massachusetts the tropical lushness that surrounds her.

Typical of such sketches is the description of a neighboring estate that she sent to her mother on 12 February 1834:

> Yesterday afternoon we all went to the Poutou estate. & I must try to give you some idea of its marvellous beauty. We entered through an avenue of orange & mango trees, very, very wide, & so arranged that the foliage gradually rose to a great hieght. The orange trees are uncommonly tall & are planted within the rows of mangos which are much taller & the golden fruit in the midst of the deep green has a beautiful effect.

Such bucolic descriptions contrast starkly with her description of Havana.

Bustling with commerce, Havana is noisy and not at all the place where the invalid would find relief from her headaches. Taking a scene that, had it been in an American city, her future husband might have presented as a sign of the city's prosperity, Peabody writes of an invalid's hell:

> The never ceasing song of the negroes as they raise the sugar and coffee into the ships is enough to create a slow fever. The street cries of men and women with fruits upon their heads, the squalls of children, the continuous stream of talk from groups all about, uttered in the highest key, the monotonous hammering of coopers

and tinkers the screams of macaws & parrots and all the unmusical birds . . . put me beside myself. Add to that this gale . . . and you will have some idea of the physical comfort to be found in Havana. . . . O, I forgot the bells! the bells! They are never Still. Tinkle, tinkle, bang bang, squeak, squeak from morning till night from night till morning, and at dawn a drum goes round . . . which sets every nerve on edge. The Spaniards worship noise. It is the god of their Idolatry, together with dirt—[.]

Perhaps the most interesting parts of Peabody's account occur when she disregards Elizabeth's injunctions and comments on slavery. Watching the slaves return from their labors in the field to receive their orders for the next day, Peabody remarks, "It is a very picturesque sight—yet it seems a sad mockery to extract any thing that has any relation to beauty or enjoyment from the poor wretches whose bondage is more & more oppressive to me every day." But despite her professed abhorrence for slavery Peabody reveals an ambivalence that may have been typical of white, middle-class women from New England.

At times her observations show her wariness of these "poor creatures" so different from herself and an awe of the institutions that can tame and control them. Commenting on the treatment of the "miserable wretches" working on a neighboring estate, Peabody says, "It made my heart sick to look at them," but then immediately describes one man who appears especially powerful and threatening:

One with his fierce eye and brow, and brawny black and blue limbs looked like the very spirit of evil; yet even *he* was courteous. . . . He looked like the untamable *obliged* to *appear* tame, while he was furious for revenge.

While she stresses his courtesy and his "gentle movement," it is his apparent fierceness and "untamable" nature that lies beneath his demeanor that is most strikingly evoked. Later, as she rides by a group of slaves in the coca groves, Peabody comments on their courtesy and then remarks, "There are two or three very stately forms among them—w'h look as powerful as Samson—& not at all bowed by their condition. What a power is that w'h enchains such with slavery—!"

An unspoken fear of these powerful yet submissive men seems to lie behind the procedures that follow the drowning of a slave boy, whom Peabody apparently believes will receive a reward in heaven:

I am glad for the child; but it was a great loss to the estate, besides that the expenses attending such an accident are immense—The Justicia must all go there & it will cost an hundred dollars. . . . But all this ceremony & enquiry is to prevent any dark proceedings among the slaves—The death of each one must be satisfactorily accounted for.

The child's death quickly becomes a matter of economic concern, and the elaborate investigation suggests the anxiety of the rulers to maintain order.

Earlier Peabody had commented that there were two reasons that she would not "allow [herself] to dwell upon slavery." Not only would such rumination "counter the beneficent influences" she had "left home and country to court" but also it would affront her faith in God, her assurance that "he makes up to every being the measure of happiness which he loses thro' the instrumentality of others." She then resolves to "lose" herself in other thoughts. The view that slavery was more God's business than humanity's is similar to the attitude her future husband would express years later in his biography of Franklin Pierce. Hawthorne saw slavery as "one of those evils which divine Providence does not leave to be remedied by human contrivances, but which, in its own good time . . . [will] vanish like a dream." Such a philosophy allowed Peabody to disavow the institution that she found both a moral bugbear and a security blanket.

While Peabody's early writings generally avoid political content, Hawthorne's American travel writings, drawn from his 1832 tour of New England and upstate New York and published between 1835 and 1837, had a clear political and cultural agenda. Originally Hawthorne had planned for these sketches to be part of a longer framed narrative called "The Story Teller," in which his semi-autobiographical narrator, Oberon, would interweave travel observations with fictional tales. Hawthorne never carried the project through to completion, though some sketches initially intended for the volume were published in journals between 1835 and 1837: "Sketches from Memory. By a Pedestrian. No. I," "Sketches from Memory. By a Pedestrian. No. II," "An Ontario Steam Boat," "My Visit to Niagara," "Fragments From the Journal of a Solitary Man," and "Old Ticonderoga. A Picture of the Past."

Although Hawthorne writes through the voice of Oberon, a persona, these sketches reveal much about his own travels and observations. They show Hawthorne not so much as a tourist but as a chronicler of America and American prosperity. Alfred Weber argues that Hawthorne undertook his tour to "gather material for a national literature," and indeed, the author's democratic agenda is clear through the portrait he draws of the country and its inhabitants, holding up its economic prosperity as a hope for the future.

In "Sketches from Memory. By a Pedestrian. No. II" Hawthorne's goal is apparent in his depic-

Page from Nathaniel Hawthorne's notebooks (MA569, Pierpont Morgan Library)

tion of Rochester, New York, a rapidly developing town on the Erie Canal, which, as Weber indicates, Americans saw as a symbol of the country's burgeoning economic prosperity. As the canal boat approaches the city the narrator comments that "The town had sprung up like a mushroom, but no presage of decay could be drawn from its hasty growth. Its edifices are of dusky brick, and of stone that will not be grayer in a hundred years than now. . . . Its attributes of youth are the activity and eager life with which it is redundant." He moves on to describe a bustling and active commercial scene, not dissimilar from that which his future wife found so troubling in Havana. Hawthorne, though, finds in the noise and activity a sense of excitement, a pride in the city's prosperity. "In short," he concludes, "everybody seemed to be there and all had something to do, and were doing it with all their might."

His final image is that of the only idle individuals on this busy street. Commenting first upon "a party of drunken recruits for the western military posts, principally Irish and Scotch, though they wore uncle Sam's gray jacket and trowsers," he then spies "one other idle man. He carried a rifle on his shoulder and a powder-horn across his breast, and appeared to stare about him with confused wonder, as if, while he was listening to the wind among the forest boughs, the hum and bustle of an instantaneous city had surrounded him." In *Hawthorne's American Travel Sketches* (1989), edited by Weber, Beth L. Lueck, and Dennis Berthold, Berthold recognizes this character as the "stereotypical American woodsman." Clearly the scene suggests that progress has left this symbol of America's frontier confused and dazed. He has been replaced by the new settler of the frontier, commercial enterprise, which seems to build cities almost instantaneously.

The drunken men in the scene point to Hawthorne's preoccupation with proper American values in these travel sketches. He presents the Irish and Scotch almost as imposters, as foreigners in American uniforms. Eager to assert the promise of his country's democratic project, Hawthorne here and in other sketches subtly defines the "true" American character, suggesting that only those who uphold the proper values—democracy, productivity, domesticity—are fit to be called "Americans."

In "The Canal Boat," from "Sketches from Memory . . . No. II," Hawthorne draws a contrast between two vessels. One boat, laden with American-made goods —"lumber, salt from Syracuse, or Genessee flour"—seems a horn of plenty that demonstrates the country's bounty. Through its window the narrator asks his reader to note a cozy domestic scene that even the rapid expansion of commercialism cannot disturb:

> a woman . . . at her house-hold work, with a little tribe of children, who perhaps had been born in this strange dwelling and knew no other home. Thus, while the husband smoked his pipe at the helm, and the eldest son rode one of the horses, on went the family, traveling hundreds of miles in their own house, and carrying their fireside with them.

Later the narrator describes "a boat, of rude construction, painted all in gloomy black, and manned by three Indians, who gazed at us in silence and with a singular fixedness of eye." These threatening Native Americans, who "had attempted to derive benefit from the white man's mighty projects, and float along the current of his enterprise," seem unlikely to share in the future prosperity of the nation.

In "The Ontario Steam-Boat" Hawthorne begins by observing the social stratification of the passengers on the boat: "there were three different orders of passenger;—an aristocracy, in the grand cabin and ladies' saloon; a commonality in the forward cabin; and, lastly, a male and female multitude on the forward deck, constituting as veritable a Mob, as could be found in any country." At first viewing this stratification as artificial, Hawthorne muses on the perceived fluidity of the class system in Jacksonian America, insisting that in actuality "the different ranks melt and mingle into one another, so that it is as impossible to draw a decided line between any two contiguous classes, as to divide a rainbow accurately into its various hues." In this instance, though, he insists that the citizens "classified themselves," finding in their arrangement "something analogous to that picturesque state of society, in other countries and earlier times, when each upper class excluded every lower one from its privileges." In viewing the separation of the different classes as the result of freely made choices, Hawthorne ignores the economic circumstances that brought the divisions about.

In his language Hawthorne further exposes his own class biases. Those of the middle "class" on the boat he calls "honest yeomen" and "thrifty citizens," while those on the forward deck he twice refers to as a "mob." He asserts that the people on the deck "Did not belong to that proud and independent class, among our native citizens who chance, in the present generation, to be at the bottom of the body politic; they were the exiles of another clime—the scum which every wind blows off the Irish shores—the pauper-dregs which England flings out upon America." Like the drunken soldiers on the Rochester street, these people are somehow impos-

Hawthorne in 1857

tors, not true Americans. While poorer "native" citizens find themselves in their social position by "chance," clearly these foreigners bear the blame for their circumstances.

As Hawthorne's description continues the reason for the culpability of the mob becomes clear: these foreigners do not share the values of domesticity and decorum that Hawthorne finds representative of America. As the men and women arrange themselves for sleep, Hawthorne records a scene he clearly finds indecorous, men and women "laying aside their upper garments," their bodies "strewn at random." Finally he observes, "some laws of mutual

aid and fellowship had necessarily been established—yet each individual was lonely and selfish. Even domestic ties did not invariably retain their hallowed strength." For these masses Hawthorne seems unable to envision any happy resolution. He predicts that they will be left homeless, not in an American city, but "upon the wharves of Quebec and Montreal."

It is unsurprising that the one hope Hawthorne finds in this mass of men and women resides in a family. Distinct from the selfish individuals of the mob, they show a "moral strength" that makes them look "precisely like the members of a comfortable household, sitting in the glow of their own fireside." Unlike the rest of the people whom Hawthorne condemns to homeless wandering in Canada, this group, he says, "were always at home, for domestic love . . . gave them a home in one another's hearts; and whatever sky might be above them, that sky was the roof over their home." By virtue of their cozy domesticity the author might even envision this group settling in his America, for their decency, like the bustle of commercial America, "was . . . a sure prophecy of better days to come."

Although Hawthorne shows he is quick to judge individuals based on their appearance and suitability as Americans, in "The Canal Boat" he fears that another may too harshly judge his fellow citizens. Noticing an English traveler who also seems to be observing people and writing, Hawthorne imagines that the Englishman is taking notes for a future travelogue and fears he "would hold up an imaginary mirror, wherein our reflected faces would appear ugly and ridiculous, yet still retain an undeniable likeness to the originals. Then . . . he would make these caricatures the representatives of great classes of countrymen."

While Hawthorne identifies several types that may serve as fodder for the foreigner's pen, he seems most fearful of the portrait that will be painted of the "Detroit merchant." He envisions the Englishman's words:

> In this sharp-eyed man, this lean man, of wrinkled brow, we see daring enterprise and close-fisted avarice combined; here is the worshipper of Mammon at noonday; here is the three-times bankrupt, richer after every ruin; here, in one word, (Oh wicked Englishman to say it!) here is the American.

There is a playfulness in the voice here—Hawthorne admits that his own speculations are the result of "an evil spirit in me"—but clearly he is worried that the Englishman will pervert the commercial spirit of America that he finds so progressive. Perhaps through the encounter the self-consciously ambiguous Hawthorne wants his reader to contemplate the subjectivity of the observer, to question the worth of observations made by one who stands apart and judges, with an unsympathetic eye.

Hawthorne's next foray into travel writing, *Our Old Home: A Series of English Sketches* (1863), came almost three decades after his first. In the interim he had achieved both domestic happiness and his peak commercial success. In the early 1850s he published three of his four major romances: *The Scarlet Letter* (1850), *The House of the Seven Gables* (1851), and *The*

Blithedale Romance (1852). In July 1853 the Hawthornes sailed to England, where he served as the United States consul for Liverpool. Hawthorne resigned his post on 13 February 1857, after his friend Franklin Pierce lost the U.S. presidency, and the family traveled through France to Italy, where they stayed until May 1859. Returning to England in June 1859, Hawthorne worked on *The Marble Faun* (1860), which was originally published as *Transformation; or, The Romance of Monte Beni*. In June of 1860 the Hawthorne family sailed back to the United States. Back in Concord, working from the notebooks he kept during his time in England, he wrote the sketches that would become *Our Old Home*.

Most of the sketches in *Our Old Home* were first published in periodicals, mainly in the *Atlantic Monthly* between October 1860 and August 1863. At the urging of William Ticknor and James Fields, the periodical sketches, along with two pieces that were composed solely for the planned collection and begin the collection, were published as a book in September 1863. The thirteen sketches are "To a Friend," "Consular Experiences," "Leamington Spa," "About Warwick," "Recollections of a Gifted Woman," "Lichfield and Uttoxeter," "Pilgrimage to Old Boston," "Near Oxford," "Some of the Haunts of Burns," "A London Suburb," "Up the Thames," "Outside Glimpses of English Poverty," and "Civic Banquets." In *Our Old Home*, just as in his American travel sketches, Hawthorne's main concern is American culture. His examination of the political institutions in England and their connection to American institutions is part of his larger interest in the relationship between America and its European foundations that becomes even clearer in *The French and Italian Notebooks* (1980).

In *Our Old Home* Hawthorne comments upon the ability of the English to build the new upon the old, upon "what such a people as ourselves would destroy." In Britain things new "derive a massive strength from their deep and immemorial foundations, though with such limitations and impediments as only an Englishman could endure." London, like Rome, engenders a "home-feeling" in Hawthorne: "As long as either of those two great cities shall exist, the cities of the Past and of the Present, a man's native soil may crumble beneath his feet without leaving him altogether homeless." But while the rich past provides a stable foundation for American values, Hawthorne asserts that Americans use this past differently than do the English. In contrast to the hidebound Englishman, the American "willingly accepts growth and change as the law of his own national and private existence." Though he "has a singular tenderness for the stone-encrusted institutions of the mother country," he "recognizes the tendency of these hardened forms to stiffen her joints and fetter her ancles."

While Hawthorne sometimes sounds like a tour guide in his descriptions of the picturesque English countryside, finding even the cottages of the "poorest order" attractive, he is less taken with the country's inhabitants. Ironically, in these sketches Hawthorne could justly be accused of being the unsympathetic observer that he feared the English traveler from "The Canal Boat" might become:

> an American is not very apt to love the English people, as a whole, on whatever length of acquaintance. . . . Therefore . . . an American seldom feels quite as if he were at home among the English people. If he do so, he has ceased to be an American. But it requires no long residence to make him love their island.

He finds in the English an "insular narrowness" that is "exceedingly queer and of very frequent occurrence" in "men of education and culture, as of clowns."

To Hawthorne's eyes the English are ruder, simpler, and more indecorous than Americans. He dwells upon their "large physical endowments" and in an oft-quoted passage unleashes a surprisingly venomous attack on a dowager whom he observes at Leamington. Describing her as a type that has no equivalent "among our own ladies," Hawthorne asserts that the English lady at fifty

> has an awful ponderosity of frame . . . massive with solid beef and streaky tallow; so that (though struggling manfully against the idea) you inevitably think of her as made up of steaks and sirloins. When she walks, her advance is elephantine. . . . She imposes awe and respect by the muchness of her personality, to such a degree that you probably credit her with far greater moral and intellectual force than she can fairly claim. . . . she has the effect of a seventy-four gun ship in time of peace; for, while you assure yourself that there is no real danger, you cannot help thinking how tremendous would be her onset, if pugnaciously inclined, and how futile the effort to inflict any counter injury.

After continuing to speculate on this "spectacle to howl at," Hawthorne questions, "I wonder whether a middle-aged husband ought to be considered as legally married to all the accretions that have overgrown the slenderness of his bride, since he led her to the altar, and which make her so much more than he ever bargained for! Is it not a sounder view of the case, that the matrimonial bond cannot be held to include the three-fourths of the wife that had no existence when the ceremony was performed?"

Later, as he comments on a fair, Hawthorne notices "a great many portable weighing-machines, the owners of which cried out . . . 'Come, know your weight!'" and a "multitude of people, mostly large in the girth," who answered these calls:

> I know not whether they valued themselves on their beef, and estimated their standing, as members of society, at so much a pound; but I shall set it down as a national peculiarity, and a symbol of the prevalence of the earthly over the spiritual element, that Englishmen are wonderfully bent on knowing how solid and physically ponderous they are.

It is not surprising that these biting descriptions drew a good deal of indignation and criticism in the British press, though some publications tried to ascribe Hawthorne's bitterness to his feelings about the Civil War. Hawthorne, for his part, felt that he had been more critical of the American character than of the English. He wrote to Fields in October of 1863: "The English critics seem to think me very bitter against their countrymen, and it is perhaps natural that they should, because their self-conceit can accept nothing short of indiscriminate adulation; but I really think that Americans have more cause than they to complain of me. Looking over the volume, I am rather surprised to find whenever I draw a comparison between the two peoples, I almost invariably cast the balance against ourselves."

The social system of Britain did not fare much better than its people in Hawthorne's estimation. One of the most powerful of the sketches in *Our Old Home* is "Outside Glimpses of English Poverty." Turning off the busier streets, Hawthorne discovers a world that reminds him of "some of Dickens's grimiest pages . . . a sort of sombre phantasmagoric spectacle, exceedingly undelightful to behold, yet involving a singular interest and even fascination in its ugliness." He stresses that such poverty is "a monstrosity unknown on our side of the Atlantic."

Hawthorne reports the strain such poverty puts on domestic relationships. While he sees hope in the sight of older children supervising younger children at play and is touched by the "gaunt and ragged mother priding herself on the pretty ways of her ragged and skinny infant," he speaks of the "squalid rooms" where "families and neighborhoods together" seek shelter from the elements. He recalls how "a mother (drunken, I sincerely hope) snatched her own imp out of a group of pale, half-naked, humor-eaten abortions . . . [and] brought down her heavy hand on its poor little tenderest part and let it go again with a shake."

NOTES

IN

ENGLAND AND ITALY.

By MRS. HAWTHORNE.

NEW YORK:
G. P. PUTNAM & SON.
1869.

*Title page for Sophia Peabody Hawthorne's first book, which
she chose not to publish during her husband's lifetime*

The hope Hawthorne sees for the future of the British poor in the almshouse he visits is uncertain. While he is "glad to observe how unexceptionably all the parts of the establishment were carried on, and what an orderly life, full-fed, sufficiently reposeful, and undisturbed by the arbitrary exercise of authority, seemed to be led here," he notes "that there must be insuperable difficulties, for the majority of the poor, in the way of getting admittance to the almshouse." Nor are the inhabitants of the almshouse uniformly well cared for. Upon entering the children's ward Hawthorne encounters a "wretched, pale, half-torpid little thing, (about six years old, perhaps, but I know not whether a girl or a boy), with a humor in its eyes and face, which the governor said was the scurvy." In a disturbing description, he tells how the child "prowled about [the governor] like a pet kitten, brushing against his legs, following everywhere at his heels, pulling at his coat-tail, and, at last, . . . got directly before him and held forth its arms, mutely insisting on being taken up." Hawthorne is interested

in the governor's reaction because he perceives him as a typical Englishman with a "distaste for whatever was ugly." When the man takes the child up into his arms, Hawthorne asserts that "the child's mission in reference to our friend was to remind him that he was responsible, in his degree, for all the sufferings and misdemeanors of the world in which he lived."

Hawthorne notes that the disparity in the treatment of the sexes in the wider society hinders the prospects of the women in the almshouse. While the men can be taught trades and sent into the world to earn a livelihood, the women are not so lucky: "They can only go to service, and are invariably rejected by families of respectability on account of their origin, and for the better reason of their unfitness to fill satisfactorily even the meanest situations in a well-ordered English household." The result is that these women find work in households of a lower class where they "endure harsh treatment . . . and finally drop into the slough of evil." Hawthorne finally lays the blame for all this poverty on the organization of English society: "Is, or is not, the system wrong?" he asks. "One day or another, safe as they deem themselves, and safe as the hereditary temper of the people tends to make them, the gentlemen of England will be compelled to face this question."

At the same time Hawthorne was recording his observations about England, Sophia Hawthorne was also making a personal record of her experiences. Both Hawthornes kept journals, and both wrote volumes of personal notes while abroad. In a 5 June 1857 letter to Ticknor, Hawthorne admits, "Mrs. Hawthorne altogether excels me as a writer of travels. Her descriptions are the most perfect pictures that ever were put on paper." He then continues, "it is a pity they cannot be published; but neither she nor I would like to see her name on your list of female authors." When Fields asked that Sophia Hawthorne publish part of her journals for publication, her husband wrote to Francis Bennoch on 29 November that "she positively refuses to be famous, and contents herself with being the best wife and mother in the world." Years later, living in Dresden after her husband's death and in need of money, Sophia Hawthorne would publish excerpts from her journal as *Notes in England and Italy* (1869).

In her book Sophia Hawthorne also comments on the human conditions of England. In Lancashire she remarks on the manufacturing towns, likening one to a monument to "the Smoke-Demon." Unlike her husband, though, Sophia Hawthorne seems to feel some moral culpability for the appalling living conditions she witnesses. "Dear me!" she exclaims, "at what a cost come forth, so clean and splendid, all our pretty prints, and silks, and velvets! How is it that the grimness of the workmen and of the atmosphere never sullies them?"

Nathaniel Hawthorne's concern with the sanctity of the domestic circle and issues of home continued in *The French and Italian Notebooks* (1980), which he wrote during the family's stay in Italy in 1858 and 1859. While these notebooks were not published in his lifetime, much of his last completed romance, *The Marble Faun,* was drawn from the observations first recorded here. In both the notebooks and *The Marble Faun* Hawthorne dwells on the uncanniness of his relation to Rome. The city is both unhomelike and strangely homelike at the same time. Entering the city after an absence, he comments, "I hate the Roman atmosphere; indeed, all my pleasure in getting back—all my home-feeling has already evaporated, and what now impresses me, as before is the languor of Rome,—its weary pavements, its little life, pressed down by a weight of death." But a few months later, from France, he writes that "no place ever seemed so close to me and so strangely familiar. I seem to know it better than my birthplace, and to have known it longer; and though I have been very miserable there . . . I still cannot say I hate it, perhaps might fairly own a love for it."

Hawthorne's deep feelings for Rome seem attributable to its rich history. In the notebooks and in *The Marble Faun* he figures Rome as the foundation, albeit an unstable one, upon which America is built. He finds America's lineage in the city's ruins: "these remains do not make that impression of antiquity upon me, which Gothic ruins do. Perhaps it is so because they belong to quite another system of society and epoch of time, and in view of them, we forget all that has intervened betwixt them and us." Observing Capitoline Hill, he remarks, "the remains of the ancient Capitol, which form the foundation of the present edifice . . . will make a sure basis for as many edifices as posterity may choose to rear upon it, till the end of the world. It is wonderful, the solidity with which those old Romans built; one would suppose they contemplated the whole course of Time as the only limit of their individual life." Rome was strangely homelike to Hawthorne because he keenly felt its historical legacy and especially its significance for his country.

Perhaps Sophia Hawthorne viewed Rome's kinship with America with a greater sense of foreboding than did her husband. Toward the end of their visit she reassesses her opinions of Rome, realizing that at first her views had been colored with mid-century American preconceptions: "I then devoutly believed that a Roman was a cunning composition of perfect honor, bravery, and virtue . . . I thought a Roman never ate. . . . I supposed he lived on glory, a kind of whip syllabub." But her experience of the city had brought her to a new understanding: "My eyes were holden, so that I could not see the sin or shame. . . . I review history now, and perceive the truth better. . . . Yet history might never have destroyed my fancies, if I had not come to Rome." She seems to have misgivings about America's descent from the Roman republic. In a section that she edited from the published version of her journal, she speculates that "when America has fulfilled its destiny," it, like Rome, might "also bow her beaming forehead to the mire."

Before the end of his sojourn in Italy, Hawthorne, like Kenyon, the artist hero of *The Marble Faun,* would declare himself ready to return to the domestic comfort of America. The stay in Rome had not been a happy one for the Hawthornes, in large part because their daughter Una had suffered a bout of "Roman fever" that nearly cost her life and permanently affected her physical and emotional health. But even before Una's illness, Hawthorne, unlike his wife, had not found Italy congenial. Perhaps much of his attitude is explained by an early passage in his notebook: "There was never any idea of domestic comfort, or of what we include in the name of home, at all implicated in [Roman palaces], they being generally built by wifeless and childless churchmen for the display of pictures and statuary in galleries and long suites of rooms."

Hawthorne repeatedly mentions the Catholic church and its dissociation from the admirable qualities upon which it was founded, remarking on his distrust of the celibates who run the institution: "I heartily wish the priests were better men, depended upon for a constant supply and succession of good and pure ministers, their religion has so many admirable points." After a particularly trying episode with customs when he found himself obliged to resort to bribes, he comments that the unsavory official with whom he dealt was "of aspect very suitable to the agent of a government of priests."

Even the art of the Catholic church seems to come up short in its portrayals of the domestic ties upon which Hawthorne's Christianity is founded. He resents that church officials "interfere with the great purposes for which their churches were built" by hanging curtains around famous paintings and charging fees for viewing them. Commenting on the representations of the Madonna in Italian art, he asserts that the "the early faces of the Madonna are especially stupid . . . a sort of face such as one might carve on a pumpkin, representing a heavy, sulky, phlegmatic woman." The depictions lack the look of motherhood that Hawthorne found so comforting even among the lower classes of the English.

Much of the art that the Hawthornes and other Americans visited Rome to see challenged their sense of decorum and values. As biographer T. Walter Herbert notes, Hawthorne was distressed by the sensuality of Italian art, but his response was complicated. For example, Hawthorne calls Titian's *Magdalen* "very coarse and sensual, with only an impudent assumption of penitence" and then immediately remarks, "but it is a splendid picture, nevertheless, with those naked, lifelike arms, and the hands that press the rich locks about her, and so carefully permit those voluptuous breasts to be seen." In his response to sculptor Hiram Powers's *Washington,* Hawthorne feels Powers had shown "contempt" for the eighteenth-century garb that he felt compelled to place upon his statue. Hawthorne comments that Powers, like many artists in Italy, was "especially fond of nudity," finally remarking with some humor: "Did anybody ever see Washington nude? It is inconceivable. He had no nakedness, but I imagine he was born with his clothes on, and his hair powdered."

The Hawthornes' reactions to fine art reveal their aesthetic differences, for Sophia Hawthorne was more enchanted with the works of the "great masters" than was her husband. Before Una's illness temporarily stopped the pen of both parents, Sophia, a painter herself, raved about the works she saw and occasionally engaged in criticism. With uncharacteristic humor she said, "Rubens, must sometimes have taken beer-barrels for models, and touched them off with armes and heads and legs." Her husband, on the other hand, wrote that Rubens and other Dutch painters "were like bread and beef and ale, after having been fed too long on made dishes." Indeed, the "made dishes" they were viewing drew much less enthusiasm from him, as Hawthorne repeatedly complained in his journal of weariness and boredom. The amount of art was overwhelming, and very little, he felt, was truly worthy of praise. Arriving at the Sciarra Palace he commented, "It has (Heaven be praised!) but four rooms of pictures."

Just as the Hawthornes' reactions to art differed so did their response to travel abroad. Sounding much like Hilda, the American artist in *The Marble Faun,* she found the opportunity to view the work of the great masters practically the only reason for travel: "How could Mr. E. say such a preposterous thing as that it was just as well *not* to travel as to travel! . . . No, indeed; it would be better if every man could look upon these wonders of genius, and grow thereby." Nathaniel Hawthorne, though, grew tired of life abroad, once remarking, "Travelling with a family is a bore beyond anything that can be preconceived." Clearly, his time abroad had caused him to feel uncentered. Like Kenyon, he was longing for home and the "actualities" of America. Yet, as their time abroad ended, he expressed in his letters both a desire to be home and a certain fear. Earlier in his journals he had said that only a sense of homelessness could ever cause him to find a home in Italy. Fittingly, his *French and Italian Notebooks* close as he contemplates home. He longs to return to Concord but clearly fears that he will not find the comfort he longs for. On 22 June 1859 he writes that in a week or two he will see Concord, "there to enjoy (if enjoyment it prove) a little rest, and sense that we are home."

Letters:

Letters of Hawthorne to William D. Ticknor, 1851–1864, 2 volumes (Newark, N.J.: Carteret Book Club, 1910);

The Letters, 1813–1843, edited by Thomas Woodson, L. Neal Smith, and Norman Holmes Pearson, volume 15 of *The Centenary Edition of the Works of Nathaniel Hawthorne* (Columbus: Ohio State University Press, 1984);

The Letters, 1843–1853, edited by Woodson, Smith, and Pearson, volume 16 of *The Centenary Edition of the Works of Nathaniel Hawthorne* (Columbus: Ohio State University Press, 1985);

The Letters, 1853–1856, edited by Woodson, Smith, and Pearson, volume 17 of *The Centenary Edition of the Works of Nathaniel Hawthorne* (Columbus: Ohio State University Press, 1987);

The Letters, 1857–1864, edited by Woodson, Smith, and Pearson, volume 18 of *The Centenary Edition of the Works of Nathaniel Hawthorne* (Columbus: Ohio State University Press, 1987).

Bibliographies:

Beatrice Ricks, Joseph D. Adams, and Jack O. Hazlerig, *Nathaniel Hawthorne: A Reference Bibliography, 1900–1971, with Selected Nineteenth-Century Materials* (Boston: G. K. Hall, 1972);

C. E. Frazer Clark Jr., *Nathaniel Hawthorne: A Descriptive Bibliography* (Pittsburgh: University of Pittsburgh Press, 1978).

Biographies:

Julian Hawthorne, *Nathaniel Hawthorne and His Wife,* 2 volumes (Boston: Osgood, 1884);

Horatio Bridge, *Personal Recollections of Nathaniel Hawthorne* (New York: Harper, 1893);

Rose Hawthorne Lathrop, *Memories of Hawthorne* (Boston: Houghton, Mifflin, 1897);

Julian Hawthorne, *Hawthorne and His Circle* (New York: Harper, 1903);

Randall Stewart, *Nathaniel Hawthorne: A Biography* (New Haven: Yale University Press, 1948);

Raymona E. Hull, *Nathaniel Hawthorne; The English Experience 1853–1864* (Pittsburgh: University of Pittsburgh Press, 1980);

James R. Mellow, *Nathaniel Hawthorne in His Times* (Boston: Houghton Mifflin, 1980);

Edwin Haviland Miller, *Salem is My Dwelling Place: A Life of Nathaniel Hawthorne* (Iowa City: University of Iowa Press, 1991);

T. Walter Herbert, *Dearest Beloved: The Hawthornes and the Making of the Middle-Class Family* (Berkeley: University of California Press, 1993).

References:

Newton Arvin, *Hawthorne* (Boston: Little, Brown, 1929);

Nina Baym, *The Shape of Hawthorne's Career* (Ithaca, N.Y.: Cornell University Press, 1976);

Michael Davitt Bell, *Hawthorne and the Historical Romance of New England* (Princeton: Princeton University Press, 1971);

Milicent Bell, *Hawthorne's View of the Artist* (Albany: State University of New York Press, 1962);

Richard Broadhead, *Hawthorne, Melville, and the Novel* (Chicago: University of Chicago Press, 1973);

Evan Carton, *The Rhetoric of American Romance: Dialectic and Identity in Emerson, Dickinson, Poe, and Hawthorne* (Baltimore: Johns Hopkins University Press, 1985);

Michael J. Colacurcio, *The Province of Piety: Moral History in Hawthorne's Early Tales* (Cambridge: Harvard University Press, 1984);

Frederick C. Crews, *The Sins of the Fathers: Hawthorne's Psychological Themes* (New York: Oxford University Press, 1966);

Kenneth Dauber, *Rediscovering Hawthorne* (Princeton: Princeton University Press, 1977);

Neal F. Doubleday, *Hawthorne's Early Tales: A Critical Study* (Durham, N.C.: Duke University Press, 1972);

Edgar Dryden, *Nathaniel Hawthorne: The Poetics of Enchantment* (Ithaca, N.Y.: Cornell University Press, 1977);

Gloria C. Erlich, *Family Themes and Hawthorne's Fiction: The Tenacious Web* (New Brunswick, N.J.: Rutgers University Press, 1984);

Richard Harter Fogle, *Hawthorne's Fiction: The Light and the Dark* (Norman: University of Oklahoma Press, 1952);

Robert Fossom, *Hawthorne's Inviolable Circle: The Problem of Time* (De Land, Fla.: Everett/Edwards, 1972);

Michael T. Gilmore, *American Romanticism and the Marketplace* (Chicago: University of Chicago Press, 1985);

Henry James, *Hawthorne* (New York: Harper, 1879);

Roy R. Male, *Hawthorne's Tragic Vision* (Austin: University of Texas Press, 1957);

Terence Martin, *Nathaniel Hawthorne,* revised edition (Boston: Twayne, 1983);

F. O. Matthiessen, *American Renaissance: Art and Expression in the Age of Emerson and Whitman* (New York: Oxford University Press, 1941);

Hugo McPherson, *Hawthorne as Myth-Maker: A Study in Imagination* (Toronto: University of Toronto Press, 1969);

Roy Harvey Pearce, ed., *Hawthorne Centenary Essays* (Columbus: Ohio State University Press, 1964);

Arlin Turner, *Nathaniel Hawthorne: An Introduction and Interpretation* (New York: Barnes & Noble, 1961);

Mark Van Doren, *Nathaniel Hawthorne* (New York: Sloane, 1949);

Edward Charles Wagenknecht, *Nathaniel Hawthorne: Man and Writer* (New York: Oxford University Press, 1961);

Hyatt H. Waggoner, *Hawthorne: A Critical Study,* revised edition (Cambridge: Harvard University Press, 1963);

Alfred Weber, Beth L. Lueck, and Dennis Berthold, eds., *Hawthorne's American Travel Sketches* (Hanover: University Press of New England, 1989).

Papers:
Major collections of Nathaniel Hawthorne's papers are at the Berg Collection of the New York Public Library, Boston Public Library, Bowdoin College Library, Essex Institute, Henry E. Huntington Library, and Pierpont Morgan Library. Six volumes of Sophia Peabody Hawthorne's journals are held by the New York Public Library.

Joel Tyler Headley

(30 December 1813 – 16 January 1897)

Paola Gemme
Pennsylvania State University

See also the Headley entries in *DLB 30: American Historians, 1607–1865* and *DS 13: The House of Scribner, 1846–1904.*

BOOKS: *Italy and the Italians, in a Series of Letters* (New York: Platt, 1844); revised and enlarged as *Letters from Italy* (New York: Wiley & Putnam, 1845);

The Alps and the Rhine; a Series of Sketches (New York: Wiley & Putnam, 1845); republished as *Travels in Italy: The Alps and the Rhine* (Dublin: M'Glashan, 1849);

Napoleon and His Marshals, 2 volumes (New York: Baker & Scribner, 1846); republished as *The Distinguished Marshals of Napoleon* (New York: Taylor, 1850); republished as *The Imperial Guard of Napoleon: From Marengo to Waterloo* (New York: Scribner, 1851);

The One Progressive Principle (New York: Taylor, 1846);

The Sacred Mountains (New York: Baker & Scribner, 1847);

Washington and His Generals, 2 volumes (New York: Baker & Scribner, 1847);

The Life of Oliver Cromwell (New York: Baker & Scribner, 1848; Dublin: M'Glashan, 1849);

The Adirondack; or, Life in the Woods (New York: Baker & Scribner, 1849); republished as *Life in the Woods . . .* (Dublin: M'Glashan, 1850); revised and enlarged (New York: Scribner, 1864);

The Miscellaneous Works of the Reverend J. T. Headley, with a Biographical Sketch, 2 volumes (New York: Taylor, 1849);

Luther and Cromwell (New York: Taylor, 1850);

Rambles and Sketches (New York: Taylor, 1850);

The Power of Beauty (New York: Taylor, 1850);

History of the Persecutions and Battles of the Waldenses (New York: Taylor, 1850);

Sacred Scenes and Characters (New York: Baker & Scribner, 1850);

The Beauties of J. T. Headley; with a Sketch of His Life (New York: Taylor, 1851);

The Lives of Winfield Scott and Andrew Jackson (New York: Scribner, 1852);

The Second War with England (New York: Scribner, 1853);

The Life of George Washington (New York: Scribner, 1856);

The Life of General H. Havelock (New York: Scribner, 1859);

The Chaplains and Clergy of the Revolution (Springfield, Mass.: G. & F. Bill, 1861);

The Great Rebellion; a History of the Civil War in the United States, 2 volumes (Hartford, Conn.: Hurlbut & Williams, 1863–1866);

Grant and Sherman; Their Campaigns and Generals (New York: Treat, 1865);

Farragut, and Our Naval Commanders (New York: Treat, 1867);

The Life of Ulysses S. Grant (New York: Treat, 1868);

Sacred Heroes and Martyrs (New York: Treat, 1870);

The Great Riots of New York, 1712 to 1873 (New York: Treat, 1873);

The Achievements of Stanley and Other African Explorers (Philadelphia: Hubbard, 1878);

Stanley's Adventures in the Wilds of Africa (Philadelphia: College Library Publishing, 1881);

Our Army in the Great Rebellion. Heroes and Battles of the War, 1861–1865 (New York: Treat, 1891).

Joel Tyler Headley is best known as the prolific author of histories, especially *Napoleon and His Marshals* (1846) and *Washington and His Generals* (1847). Their exceptional popularity with mid-nineteenth-century American readers is generally attributed to the public's appetite for pictures of military valor during the war between Mexico and the United States (1846–1848). While Headley's accounts of his travels in Europe and America have been largely ignored by critics, these books were also best-sellers and played on the same nationalistic sentiments as did his histories. Headley the traveler often gratified the patriotism of his readers by favorably comparing the landscape, people, and institutions of the United States with those of the countries he visited. Thus, Headley's travel writing, like his histories, can be seen as documents of American nationalism.

Headley was born on 30 December 1813 in Walton, Delaware County, New York, into a wealthy family that boasted aristocratic English ancestors. His father, the Presbyterian minister Isaac Headley, was the descendant of an English baronet who had emigrated to America in 1665. His mother, Irene Benedict, was also from an old and prominent New York family. Like his father, Headley decided to pursue the ministry and attended Auburn Theological Seminary. The poor health that was to plague him throughout his life, however, soon interfered with his ambitions, and, unable to sustain the heavy workload of a parish minister, he abandoned the religious office forever. Although he renounced the ministry for a career as a writer, Headley's religious formation was to profoundly influence his work.

In an attempt to restore his health, Headley in 1842 left for a long European tour that provided him with material for a series of successful travel books. Upon his return to the United States, Headley published a brief memoir of his travels in Italy, *Italy and the Italians* (1844). The success of his first publication induced him to expand the account of his Italian adventures into *Letters from Italy* (1845). The book, with its stories of unfortunate lovers turned insane and assassins armed with deadly stilettos, catered to the reading public's taste for the Gothic, but no doubt its strong anti-Catholicism also greatly contributed to its appeal. Headley represents Italy as a once prosperous country ruined by a corrupt and tyrannical church. In *Letters from Italy* priests stage fake miracles to ensure the respect and obedience of the faithful, sell their services to lovers who need an unsuspected messenger to reach their beloved, and maybe even protect murderers, as the horrified Headley suggests after discovering in the cathedral of Florence the skeleton of a man who had been "built up alive" in one of the side walls.

Even more than for their immorality, Headley censures the Catholic clergy for their exploitation of the people. In his rendition of Catholicism in Italy, the church first feeds upon the people by imposing exorbitant taxes and then attempts to allay their discontent by staging religious pageants that further drain their resources. Observing the celebrations held in Rome for Easter, Headley severely criticizes their extravagance, from the rich attires and the cardinals' carriages "half covered with gold" to the "peacock feathers" used to fan the Pope. His scathing comments on the annual illumination of the exterior of Saint Peter, for him a "costly amusement [that] robbed hundreds of mouths of their daily bread," are representative of his indictment of the policies of the church:

> It is an operation of great expense, and attended with much danger. It is caused by suspending *four thousand four hundred lanterns* upon [St. Peter], covering it from the dome down. To accomplish this, men have to be let down with ropes, over every part of the edifice, and left dangling there for more than an hour. . . . The eighty men employed in it always receive extreme unction before they attempt it. . . . The Pope must amuse the people, and glorify his reign, though he hazard human life in doing it. But he has the magnanimity to secure the sufferer from evil in the next world. . . . This is very kind of the Pope.

Headley concludes that the decline of Italy is a direct consequence of the rise of Catholicism: "A weak and imbecile pope tells his beads and 'patters prayer' where the Caesars trod! And the triumphant processions of the empire are changed into long trains of superstitious monks."

Headley's exposé of the Catholic church in Italy was bound to interest an American audience preoccupied with the rise of Catholicism in America. The exodus of impoverished farmers from Ireland in the 1830s and 1840s had greatly augmented the

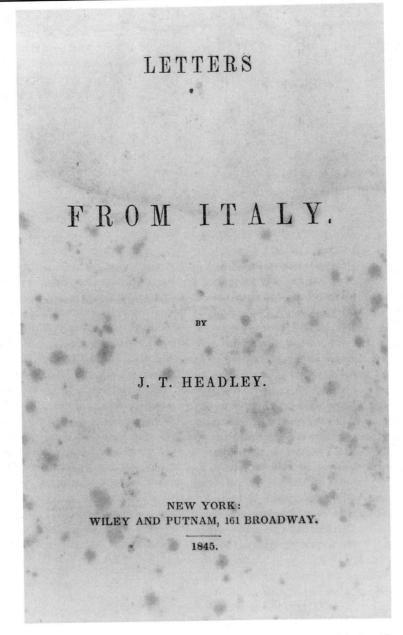

Title page for the enlarged edition of Headley's first book, in which he harshly criticizes the Catholic Church

number of Catholics in the United States, especially in the cities of the Northeast. This wave of immigration had initially been welcomed as supplying labor for an expanding economy, but the financial crisis of the late 1830s made it impossible to absorb the incoming workers, causing a turnabout in the public attitude toward immigrants as the Irish were perceived as a burden on the economy rather than an asset. Hostility against them often focused on the characteristic that made them most foreign—their religion. Many argued that Irish Catholic immigrants were subject to the despotism of the Church and unable to adapt to democratic institutions.

Headley insisted on the despotic nature of Catholicism in an essay on the newly elected Pope Pius IX included in *Rambles and Sketches* (1850). Pius IX had awakened the hopes of liberals in Italy and abroad with a series of reforms, especially his granting a general amnesty to all political offenders in his kingdom. Americans had joined in the celebration of the Pope, most notably by organizing a public meeting in New York in 1847 to express their sympathy with him and their hopes for Italy. Headley raised a dissenting voice, arguing that the new Pope had introduced reforms out of a desire to keep his throne rather than to delegate power to his subjects:

> the Pope has done much; but, with all his reforms, his government is still a despotic one. A criminal code is there in force, and municipal and provincial laws, and a censorship of the press, and an exercise of arbitrary power, which, if applied even to the monarchy of England, would cause a revolution that all the standing armies of the world could not arrest. To read some of the papers in this country, and listen to some of the public speeches, one would imagine that Pius IX wished of all things to establish a republican form of government, and lacked only the ability; while in truth, I suppose there is not a government on the earth for which he has such a supreme and hearty contempt as for this same republic of the United States.

Such an assessment served to warn Americans of the threat posed by Catholicism to their republican government.

A few years after the publication of this essay, Headley took a more active role in opposing the spread of Catholicism in America by becoming a member of the antialien Know-Nothing Party, among whose goals were the restriction of immigration and the modification of the existing naturalization laws to prevent immigrants from voting and holding public office. In 1855 Headley was elected secretary of state in New York on the Know-Nothing ticket, a position which he held until 1858.

As a travel writer Headley comments more often on social institutions than on tourist sights. In Italy the wealth of religious shrines prompted him to condemn the Catholic Church. In France the sites that had witnessed the unfolding of the Revolution and then the rise and demise of Napoleon occasioned an extended meditation on the future of democracy and the differences among nations.

In the essays devoted to France in *Rambles and Sketches* Headley provides an interpretation of the history of the Revolution and the Empire. He disagreed with the historiographic tradition that censured the Revolution as an episode of unjustifiable popular violence, instead identifying its cause in the oppression of the people by the aristocracy and the clergy. As he puts it, "it is time tyranny and the Catholic religion, refusing month after month, and year after year, the humble and earnest prayer of a perishing people, were called to account for the horrors of the French Revolution, and not the excited, maddened populace." For Headley, moreover, the

Revolution, including its bloodiest episodes, was crucial in leading Europe to more enlightened forms of government. He argues that "convulsions like those which rocked France and sunk her in a sea of blood, were necessary to disrupt and upheave the iron-like feudal system that had been cemented, and strengthened, and rusted together for centuries." Headley's seemingly radical interpretation of the Revolution as a rightful rebellion of the oppressed is tempered, however, by his narrative depicting Napoleon's rise to absolute power as a necessary measure against revolutionaries who had gone too far and rejected God as well as their king. In this reconstruction of the events, Bonaparte is seen as the savior of France from political disorder rather than as the undoer of the Republic.

Headley's representation of republican uprisings in Europe, from the French Revolution at the end of the eighteenth century to the contemporary insurrections in Italy, are characterized by a tension between the celebration of democracy as a form of government destined to spread to the entire world and a fundamental skepticism regarding the ability of non–Anglo Americans to achieve and preserve a republican system. While he calls democracy "the one progressive principle" and writes that "the people are yet to have the power, and . . . it requires only the ear of reason to hear the sound of falling thrones in the future," Headley also maintains that not all peoples are fit for self-rule. He characterizes the French as "atheistic and insulting anarchists" whose lack of religious faith weakened the social structure and caused the fall of the Republic. And he believes that "the love of pleasure and its pursuit take from the Italian character the manliness . . . necessary to a republican form of government." The contradictions in Headley's representation of republican experiments in Europe, however, find a solution in an exalted image of the United States. By representing democracy as the universal goal of political evolution and by faulting the ability of other peoples to attain it, Headley implicitly celebrated America above all others.

Headley's contemporaries, both his admirers and his detractors, identified the nationalistic nature of his writing as one of the main reasons for his popularity. Critic Rufus Wilmot Griswold, who thought him "one of the most promising of the youthful writers of this country," praised his *Letters from Italy* because they equated America with innocence and youth and Europe with corruption and decay. Commenting on the same work, writer Henry T. Tuckerman agreed with Griswold on Headley's strategy, but disagreed on the truthfulness of the opposition: "when Mr. Headley thought of his country . . . its image did not rise before him as embodied in rail-road cars, steamboats and hotels, but rather under the guise of some domestic Eden, whose secluded loveliness it had been his privilege familiarly to know." For Tuckerman it was Headley's construction of a flattering image of the nation that made his works "very winning to the self-love of American readers." Edgar Allan Poe probably put it best when he wrote of Headley in the October 1850 issue of the *Southern Literary Messenger* that "the thing that he 'does' especially well is the public."

After his European trip failed to restore his health, Headley began spending long periods of time in the Adirondacks, a region in upstate New York which, when he visited it in the 1840s, was still for the most part unsettled. As in his account of his travels in Europe, in *The Adirondack; or Life in the Woods* (1849) Headley told his readers the tale they wanted to hear, namely that the forests and ridges of America were just as beautiful as those of Italy, France, and Germany. The Alps are always present as the epitome and paragon of natural beauty in Headley's description of the sights he encounters. A mountain chain, for instance, is said to "rise and sink along the horizon in such colossal proportions that one imagines himself in the Alps." Similarly, to emphasize the grandiosity of a cliff, Headley comments that he "never saw but one precipice that impressed [him] so, and that was in the Alps, in the pass of the Grand Scheideck."

Behind Headley's celebration of the wild regions of North America, however, lies more than nationalistic pride. Headley argues not only that the scenery of America is as attractive as that of Europe, but that the natural landscape is superior to the urban one. *The Adirondack* opens with an encounter between Headley and an old friend of his who had been ruined by the economic crash of 1837 and had repaired to the country to become a farmer. Asked how his new life compared with his past one in New York, the former dandy responds, "I am happier here. I prefer this life to that in the city." This early episode sets the tone for the entire narrative, which reflects throughout the mid nineteenth century America's anxiety about the course of civilization.

As tides of immigration filled cities with a frequently destitute population and as industrial complexes were erected within urban precincts to employ the newly available labor force, appalled middle-class Americans had begun to perceive the wilderness as a refuge from the evils of modernity rather than as an obstacle to progress. Headley and his contemporaries expressed their uneasiness with urbanization and industrialization by reading na-

ture as the prime manifestation of the deity. His contemplation of nature throughout is an intensely spiritual, even mystical experience: "I believe that every man degenerates without frequent communion with nature. It is one of the open books of God, and more replete with instruction than anything ever penned by man. A single tree standing alone, and waving all day long its green crown to the summer wind, is to me fuller of meaning and instruction than the crowded mart or gorgeously built town."

By far the most popular and most often anthologized passage of *The Adirondack* deals not with the discovery of God in the wilderness but with the disappearance of its native inhabitants, the St. Regis tribe. The episode relates Headley's encounter with an old Indian and his daughter, whom he calls the "relics" of a "now nearly extinct" tribe. In his description of the couple as they leave the camp, Headley predicts that even these last two surviving members of a once powerful tribe will soon perish:

> I watched as they receded in the distance, with emotions of pity and admiration. Some night that old hunter would lie down by his camp fire, never to rise again, and that young Indian girl watch beside him alone. Thus in the still forest would she see him die, without one heart to sympathize with her, or one voice to cheer her solitude, then drag his lifeless form to the canoe, and seek with it the graves of her tribe.

The significance of this passage lies in its representation of the extinction of the native tribe as a natural phenomenon, not as a direct consequence of the whites' appropriation of Indian territory or warfare against them. To hear that "the doom of the red man of this continent" was to "gradually melt away like the snows of spring"—a common euphemism for the extermination of Native American tribes among Anglo writers—must no doubt have anesthetized the conscience of Headley's white readers, especially at a time when the Western tribes were being removed to reservations. In *The Adirondack* Headley recasts a history of genocide into a melancholy tale of the inevitable demise of Native American tribes.

Headley recounted not only his own travels in Europe and the United States but also reported secondhand on the more sensational ones of African explorers in the 1850s and 1860s. Although he wrote about several British adventurers, the bulk of his work is devoted to the American Henry Morton Stanley. Once again, Headley had correctly estimated his readers' nationalistic pride, and new editions of his *The Achievements of Stanley and Other African Explorers* (1878) were published until the end of the century.

Part of the reason for the book's popularity was commercial. Americans had always had an enormous economic interest in Africa, had at one time held intensive commercial relations with the coastal tribes of East Africa, and were now eager to assess their business opportunities in the hitherto unexplored interior of the continent. In the year Headley's writings on Africa were first published, Commodore Robert W. Shufeld was sent on an official mission to explore the basin of the Congo and establish commercial relations with the local populations. *The Achievements of Stanley,* with its representation of Africa as a land of "untold wealth waiting the enterprising hand of commerce" and its long, detailed lists of its products—"sugar-cane, cotton, coffee, oil palm, tobacco, spices, timber, rice, wheat, Indian corn, India rubber, copal, hemp, ivory, iron, copper, silver, gold and various other articles of commerce"—both echoed and contributed to the climate of commercial interest in the African continent in postbellum America.

Headley overtly tells a tale not of economics but of philanthropy, stating in the introduction that "all the explorations have tended to one great end—the civilization and Christianization" of Africa. But Headley ties Africa's supposed lack of civilization to its poor economic development, describing the people as savages because of their supposed failure to use the resources of the land. The economic exploitation by the white West is seen as a benevolent gesture, a push toward the future. Africa, according to Headley, "contains almost everything that civilization needs, and in the future . . . will be traversed by railroads and steamboats, and the solitudes that have echoed for thousands of years to the howl of wild beasts, and yells of equally wild men, will resound with the hum of peaceful industry and the rush and roar of commerce."

While the barbarism of Africa is represented by its untamed forests, Headley finds that its un-Christian sinfulness lies in the perpetuation of slavery. Headley describes the slave trade as being practiced by Africans upon Africans only. He does not discuss the historic involvement of the Western powers and is conspicuously silent on the complicity of the United States in the commerce of slaves from colonial times until the beginning of the nineteenth century. With total disregard for the role of the whites' demand for human chattel in creating and perpetuating the slave trade, Headley depicts the African slave dealers as embodiments of evil and exalts the American explorers who fought against them as heroic "deliverer[s] to the down-trodden inhabitants." As in *The Adirondack,* where the disturbing reality of genocide was hidden under the tale of the natural extinction of Native Americans, *The Achievements of Stanley* offers readers an appealing story of generous Western intervention in the affairs of inferior peoples that masks the reality of economic imperialism and ignores the horrific history of the transatlantic slave trade.

As one of the most prolific and popular historians of nineteenth-century America, Headley in his historical writings is as usefully read for what his constructions of history reveal about the attitudes of his own time as they are for the history they purportedly record. In this regard Headley's travel writings are an important complement to his work as a historian, for they more directly show how Headley and his American audience chose to view themselves. The America that emerges from Headley's travels is a country that wished to continue dreaming of greatness, expansion and righteousness without acknowledging its troubling nightmares of ethnic conflict, urban squalor, and racial oppression.

References:

Rufus Wilmot Griswold, *The Prose Writers of America* (Philadelphia: Carey & Hart, 1847), pp. 540–542;

Thomas Rose and James Rodgers, Introduction, *The Great Riots of New York, 1712–1873* (New York: Bobbs-Merrill, 1970), pp. v–xxx;

Philip G. Terry, Introduction, *The Adirondack; or, Life in the Woods* (Harrison, N.Y.: Harbor Hill, 1982), pp. 5–22;

Henry T. Tuckerman, "A Word for Italy," *Democratic Review,* 17 (1845): 203–212.

Washington Irving

(3 April 1783 – 28 November 1859)

Xavier Baron
University of Wisconsin–Milwaukee

See the Irving entries in *DLB 3: Antebellum Writers in New York and the South; DLB 11: American Humorists, 1800–1950; DLB 30: American Historians, 1607–1865; DLB 59: American Literary Critics and Scholars, 1800–1850; DLB 73: American Magazine Journalists, 1741–1850;* and *DLB 74: American Short-Story Writers Before 1880.*

BOOKS: *Salmagundi; or, the Whim-whams and Opinions of Launcelot Langstaff, Esq. & Others,* by Irving, William Irving, and James Kirke Paulding, 20 parts, republished in 2 volumes (New York: Printed and published by D. Longworth, 1807–1808; London: Printed for J. M. Richardson, 1811; revised edition, New York: D. Longworth, 1814; revised by Irving, Paris: Galignani, 1824; Paris: Baudry, 1824);

A History of New York, from the Beginning of the World to the End of the Dutch Dynasty. Containing Among many Surprising and Curious Matters, the Unutterable Ponderings of Walter the Doubter, the Disastrous Projects of William the Testy, and the Chivalric Achievements of Peter the Headstrong, the three Dutch Governors of New Amsterdam; being the only Authentic History of the Times that ever hath been, or ever will be Published, as Diedrich Knickerbocker, 2 volumes (New York & Philadelphia: Inskeep & Bradford / Boston: M'Ilhenny / Baltimore: Coale & Thomas / Charleston: Morford, Willington, 1809; revised edition, New York & Philadelphia: Inskeep & Bradford, 1812; London: John Murray, 1820); republished as volume 1 of *The Works of Washington Irving* (New York & London: Putnam, 1848; revised edition, 2 volumes, New York: Printed for the Grolier Club, 1886);

The Sketch Book of Geoffrey Crayon, Gent., as Geoffrey Crayon, 7 parts (New York: Printed by C. S. Van Winkle, 1819–1820); revised edition, 2 volumes (volume 1, London: John Miller, 1820; volume 2, London: John Murray, 1820); revised edition (Paris: Baudry & Didot, 1823);

Washington Irving (Library of Sleepy Hollow Restorations)

republished as volume 2 of *The Works of Washington Irving* (New York & London: Putnam, 1848);

Bracebridge Hall, or the Humourists. A Medley, as Geoffrey Crayon, 2 volumes (New York: Printed by C. S. Van Winkle, 1822; London: John Murray, 1822); republished as volume 6 of *The Works of Washington Irving* (New York & London: Putnam, 1849);

Letters of Jonathan Oldstyle, Gent., as The Author of *The Sketch Book* (New York: Clayton, 1824; London: Wilson, 1824);

Tales of a Traveller, as Geoffrey Crayon, 2 volumes (London: John Murray, 1824; abridged edition, Philadelphia: Carey & Lea, 1824; unabridged edition, New York: Printed by C. S. Van Winkle, 1825); republished as volume 7 of *The Works of Washington Irving* (New York & London: Putnam, 1849);

The Miscellaneous Works of Oliver Goldsmith, with an Account of His Life and Writings, 4 volumes (Paris: Galignani/Didot, 1825); biography revised in *The Life of Oliver Goldsmith, with Selections from His Writings,* 2 volumes (New York: Harper, 1840); biography revised and enlarged as *Oliver Goldsmith: A Biography,* volume 11 of *The Works of Washington Irving* (New York: Putnam / London: John Murray, 1849);

A History of the Life and Voyages of Christopher Columbus (4 volumes, London: John Murray, 1828; 3 volumes, New York: G & C. Carvill, 1828; revised, 2 volumes, 1831); republished in *The Life and Voyages of Christopher Columbus; to Which Are Added Those of His Companions,* volumes 3–5 of *The Works of Washington Irving* (New York & London: Putnam, 1848–1849);

A Chronicle of the Conquest of Granada, as Fray Antonio Agapida, 2 volumes (Philadelphia: Carey, Lea & Carey, 1829; London: John Murray, 1829); republished as volume 14 of *The Works of Washington Irving* (New York: Putnam / London: John Murray, 1850);

Voyages and Discoveries of the Companions of Columbus (London: John Murray, 1831; Philadelphia: Carey & Lea, 1831); republished in *The Life and Voyages of Christopher Columbus; to Which Are Added Those of His Companions,* volumes 3–5 of *The Works of Washington Irving* (New York & London: Putnam, 1848–1849);

The Alhambra, as Geoffrey Crayon, 2 volumes (London: Colburn & Bentley, 1832); as The Author of *The Sketch Book,* 2 volumes (Philadelphia: Carey & Lea, 1832); revised as *The Alhambra: A Series of Sketches of the Moors and Spaniards by the Author of "The Sketch Book"* (Philadelphia: Carey, Lea & Blanchard, 1836); revised as volume 15 of *The Works of Washington Irving* (New York: Putnam, 1851);

A Tour on the Prairies, number 1 of *Miscellanies,* as The Author of *The Sketch Book* (London: John Murray, 1835); republished as number 1 of *The Crayon Miscellany* (Philadelphia: Carey, Lea & Blanchard, 1835); republished in *The Crayon Miscellany,* volume 9 of *The Works of Washington Irving* (New York & London: Putnam, 1849);

Abbotsford and Newstead Abbey, number 2 of *Miscellanies,* as The Author of *The Sketch Book* (London: John Murray, 1835); republished as number 2 of *The Crayon Miscellany* (Philadelphia: Carey, Lea & Blanchard, 1835); republished in *The Crayon Miscellany,* volume 9 of *The Works of Washington Irving* (New York & London: Putnam, 1849);

Legends of the Conquest of Spain, number 3 of *Miscellanies,* as The Author of *The Sketch Book* (London: John Murray, 1835); republished as number 3 of *The Crayon Miscellany* (Philadelphia: Carey, Lea & Blanchard, 1835); republished in *The Crayon Miscellany,* volume 9 of *The Works of Washington Irving* (New York & London: Putnam, 1849);

Astoria, or, Enterprise Beyond the Rocky Mountains, 3 volumes (London: Bentley, 1836); republished as *Astoria, or Anecdotes of an Enterprise Beyond the Rocky Mountains,* 2 volumes (Philadelphia: Carey, Lea & Blanchard, 1836); revised as volume 8 of *The Works of Washington Irving* (New York: Putnam, 1849);

Adventures of Captain Bonneville, or, Scenes beyond the Rocky Mountains of the Far West, 3 volumes (London: Bentley, 1837); republished as *The Rocky Mountains: Or, Scenes, Incidents, and Adventures in the Far West; Digested from the Journal of Captain B. L. E. Bonneville, of the Army of the United States, and Illustrated from Various Other Sources,* 2 volumes (Philadelphia: Carey, Lea & Blanchard, 1837); republished as *The Adventures of Captain Bonneville, U.S.A., in the Rocky Mountains and the Far West* as volume 10 of *The Works of Washington Irving* (New York & London: Putnam, 1849);

Biography and Poetical Remains of the Late Margaret Miller Davidson (Philadelphia: Lea & Blanchard, 1841; London: Tilt & Bogue, 1843);

Mahomet and His Successors, volumes 12 and 13 of *The Works of Washington Irving* (New York: Putnam, 1850); republished as *Lives of Mahomet and His Successors,* 2 volumes (London: John Murray, 1850);

Chronicles of Wolfert's Roost and Other Papers (Edinburgh: Constable, Low / London: Hamilton, Adams / Dublin: M'Glashan, 1855); republished as *Wolfert's Roost and Other Papers,* volume 16 of *The Works of Washington Irving* (New York: Putnam, 1855);

Life of George Washington, 5 volumes (New York: Putnam, 1855–1859; London: Bohn, 1855–1859);

Spanish Papers and Other Miscellanies, Hitherto Unpublished or Uncollected, edited by Pierre M. Irving, 2 volumes (New York: Putnam/Hurd & Houghton, 1866; London: Low, 1866); republished as *Biographies and Miscellaneous Papers by*

Washington Irving (London: Bell & Daldy, 1867).

Journals and Notebooks: 5 volumes, edited by Natalia Wright, Walter A. Reichart, Lillian Schlissel, Wayne R. Kime, and Andrew B. Myers (Madison: University of Wisconsin Press / Boston: Twayne, 1969–1985).

Collection: *The Complete Works of Washington Irving*, edited by Richard Dilworth Rust and others, 30 volumes (Madison: University of Wisconsin Press / Boston: Twayne, 1969–1988).

OTHER: "The Catskill Mountains," in the *Home Book of the Picturesque* (New York: Putnam, 1852), pp. 71–78.

Washington Irving, America's first successful professional man of letters, was an essayist, humorist, historian, literary critic, antiquarian scholar, magazine journalist, and short-story writer. In addition, he wrote charming, observant travel pieces. The variety of Irving's accomplishments as a writer stem from his wide reading, for he often chose to try his hand at what he read. Like most travelers, Irving wrote about the places and people he experienced, but his responses were extraordinarily literary. He often reflected on places associated with famous writers, parading his extensive reading in "learned" quotations from and allusions to the reactions of his models.

Because of his penchant for imitation, Irving in his travel writing often loses freshness and becomes clichéd. British author William Hazlitt criticized him in *The Spirit of the Age* (1825) for producing "literary anachronisms": "He comes to England for the first time, and being on the spot, fancies himself in the midst of those characters and manners which he had read in the *Spectator* and other approved authors, and which were the only idea he had hitherto formed of the parent country. Instead of looking round to see what *we are,* he sets to work to describe us as *we were*—at second hand." Often, however, Irving gently mocks his sources as he copies them.

In his writing Irving—especially in the persona of his surrogate, Geoffrey Crayon, Gent., through whom much of his experience and imagination is transparently filtered—is part old-fashioned patrician essayist and part romantic seeker after the picturesque and sentimental. Because his characterization of Crayon is inconsistent, Irving appears to the reader to be caught between the Old World and the New. He avoids facing his conflicting attractions to both cultures by turning to mockery or fantasy. But Irving also surely realized that his unresolved am-

bivalence appealed to a young, restless, unconfident nation, doubtful about its identity and ready to be entertained. Irving personalized the increasingly popular documentary magazine travel sketch by adding emotion and imagination. He had a natural affinity for caricature—apparent in his drawings included in his notebooks and journals—and unsupported generalization, both staples of travel writing. He was also fond of the miscellany form, and his eclectic mixture of description, observation, narrative, and reportage seemed to fit the randomness of travel.

Most of his travel writing about Europe, especially Great Britain and Spain, is intended to introduce American readers to the wonders of the old world and its largely peasant folkways and customs. Irving takes the tone of a stable middle-class observer reporting on exotic adventures. He followed the same approach in the books he wrote on the American West after his return to the United States in 1832. He does not examine controversial issues, ignoring contemporary European politics, imperialism, mercantilism, the expansive growth of industrial cities with their increasing pollution and mechanization, just as he overlooks the exploitation of the American West. More often than not the actual is passed over for the safety of the picturesque and the stereotypical. Irving's nostalgic love of the antiquarian past and escapist love of nature characterized Romanticism's confrontation with industrialization.

The youngest of eleven children, Washington Irving was born in New York City on 3 April 1783, the day the American Revolution officially ended, to the former Sarah Sanders and William Irving, a moderately successful importer. New York was rapidly becoming the young country's major city, its chief port, and the premier entry point of European culture and ideas. Irving had a melancholy temperament and throughout his life suffered from recurring bouts of depression. All of Irving's siblings became prominent in business, political, and literary circles. Two brothers went to Columbia College, while Irving, an indifferent student, had just eight years of formal education.

Irving's informal education was enriched by his reading of the western European canon. He was attracted to the social satire of Miguel de Cervantes, François Rabelais, and Henry Fielding. His favorite reading material included ancient and modern travel books, which often mixed geography and history, inventively handling fact and fiction. He was most influenced by the English eighteenth-century periodical essayists centered in cosmopolitan Lon-

Irving's letter home at the beginning of his European tour in 1804 (New York Public Library; Astor, Lenox and Tilden Foundations)

don: Joseph Addison, Richard Steele, Jonathan Swift, and Oliver Goldsmith.

Irving's first published work was a series of nine periodical essays presented as "Letters to the Editor" of the *Morning Chronicle* in 1802–1803. He created the persona of "Jonathan Oldstyle, Gent." to criticize the roughness of the current scene in contrast to a more refined past. The preoccupation of the essays with typical amusements and burlesques of early American theatrical life presaged his frequent playgoing during his first visit to Europe in 1804–1806, which interrupted both his position as "candidate attorney" in the law office of Josiah Hoff-

man and his budding romance with Hoffman's daughter Matilda.

Provided with many letters of introduction, he had access to the crumbling European aristocracy. As his letters and journals reveal, his travels to France, Spain, Italy, the Netherlands, the Germanies, and England at the time of Napoleon's conquest of Europe inspired and invigorated his natural talents of observation. While Irving was keen to present himself as clever and cosmopolitan, he shows a tendency toward the effete and the unoriginal, as is evidenced by his clichéd remarks about lusty Italian women and superstitious Catholics. His early, firsthand experience of the Old World fed his natural conservatism and reenforced his preference for traditional, neoclassical reading and culture.

When Irving returned to New York he joined his brother William and William's brother-in-law, James Kirke Paulding, in writing and publishing *Salmagundi* (1807–1808), a comic series of twenty periodical pamphlets that spoof eighteenth-century periodicals such as Goldsmith's *The Bee*. Several numbers contain parodies of travel writing. In the fourth issue Irving shows his thorough knowledge of the clichés of the genre, written by

> travel-mongers, who write whole volumes about themselves, their horses and their servants, interspersed with anecdotes of inn-keepers–droll sayings of stage-drivers, and interesting memoirs of the lord knows who. They will give you a full account of a city, its manners, customs, and manufactures, though perhaps all their knowledge of it was obtained by a peep from their inn-windows, and an interesting conversation with the landlord or waiter.

Six chapters follow from the notebooks of Jeremy Cockloft, the Younger about his trip to New Jersey. The tenth issue presents notes in a similar vein from a trip to Pennsylvania; the twelfth contains "A Tour in Broadway"; the fourteenth features Launcelot Langstaff's description of Cockloft-Hall; the fifteenth includes "Sketches from Nature by Anthony Evergreen, Gent."; and the seventeenth offers Langstaff's account of the library of Cockloft-Hall and its resident visiting antiquarian, Will Wizard, who presents to him "the Chronicles of the Renowned and Ancient City of Gotham."

Irving made use of many of the devices he mocked in *Salmagundi* in his later works, including his first full-length book, *A History of New York, from the Beginning of the World to the End of the Dutch Dynasty* (1809). A comic, fantastic parody of Samuel L. Mitchill's *The Picture of New York* (1807)–a work of boosterism and dry statistics–Irving's book and its pseudonymous historian Diedrich Knickerbocker indicate his antiquarian interests, which had been nurtured by his experiences in Europe. The Dutch, whose obsessive cleanliness and other quirks Irving had noted while on his travels, are the butts of what Irving scholar William Bedford Clark calls an "extended ethnic joke." Critic Martin Roth argues that Irving mocks European customs in order to clear the way for a new American culture. But regardless of any deeper purpose, Irving displays a flair for the picturesque landscape as when he describes "the island of Manna-hata, spread wide before them, like some sweet vision of fancy, or some fair creation of industrious magic." He used this talent, sometimes

sincerely, sometimes mockingly, throughout his career.

Writing *A History of New York* served in part to distract Irving from his grief over the death on 26 April 1809 of Matilda Hoffman, probably the great love of his life. After his book's completion and success Irving edited the *Analectic Magazine,* writing a few original essays (two of which, "Philip of Pokanoket" and "Traits of Indian Character" appeared later in *The Sketch Book)* and reprinting pieces from literary journals. During the War of 1812 he was aide-de-camp with the rank of lieutenant colonel to New York governor Daniel Tompkins.

After the return of peace Irving turned his attentions to his family's troubled export-import business and sailed to England in 1815. Despite desperate efforts, he was unable to save the business, which went bankrupt in 1818. During this period the strain of his brother Peter's poor health was compounded by the news of his mother's death on 9 April 1817. He experienced a sense of profound failure which manifested itself as "a melancholy that corrodes the spirit & seems to rust all the springs of mental energy." His two passions, travel and writing, provided relief. Along with visits to his sister Sally's family, the Van Warts, in Birmingham, he traveled to Wales, and to his father's native Scotland, where he was warmly greeted by Sir Walter Scott. When his brother's health improved he moved to London, the literary capital of the English speaking world.

Irving's financial straits led him to write his most famous work, *The Sketch Book of Geoffrey Crayon, Gent.,* which appeared in seven paper-bound installments in the United States (1819–1820) and in two clothbound volumes in Great Britain (1820), with slightly different contents for the audiences of the two countries. *The Sketch Book* presents his most important travel writing. The quotation from John Lyly's *Euphues* (1578–1580) which opens "The Author's Account of Himself," underscores the loss of identity and home that the traveler to a foreign country both suffers and enjoys. The epigraph also initiates a tone of apology since Irving places Europe's "charms of storied and poetical association" above America's "charms of nature." Crayon, a thinly disguised Irving, longs for an older world–"to escape in short, from the commonplace realities of the present, and lose myself among the shadowy grandeurs of the past."

Perhaps Irving's melancholy during the years immediately preceding *The Sketch Book* is evidenced in the first sketch, "The Voyage." It is dominated by the image of a ghost ship floating without a clear direction, an emblem of the traveler who is "cast loose from the secure anchorage of settled life and sent adrift upon a doubtful world." But the voyage also allows and induces Irving's narrator "to gaze upon the piles of golden clouds just peering above the horizon; fancy them some fairy realms and people them with a creation of my own." Irving's imagination, partaking of both the Romantic and the Gothic, is often in evidence in the volume.

Upon his arrival Crayon sees "the moldering ruin of an abbey over run with ivy, and the taper spire of a village church rising from the brow of a neighbouring hill—all were characteristic of England," but though most of the thirty-two sketches concern the observations of an American visitor in England, the lack of narrative connection between them soon becomes apparent. The second sketch, "Roscoe"—titled after historian William Roscoe, a habitué of the Athenæum in Liverpool—celebrates books, which unlike fickle friends "only continue the unaltered countenance of happier days, and cheer us with that true friendship which never deceived hope nor deserted sorrow." The next sketch, "The Wife," which has no particular setting, signals a shift away from travel writing to personal anecdote and reflects Irving's sentimentality about virtuous young women. In "Rip Van Winkle," the first of six pieces in the volume set in his native country, Irving's depiction of Rip's termagant wife implies a kind of consolation for the bachelor who admired the young wife in the previous sketch.

The shifting pattern of the miscellany continues in "English Writers on America," which, despite self-serving special pleading and insecure bragging, is imbued with a resolute and eloquent conviction of the importance and lasting value of writing and English writers in particular: "We are a young people, necessarily an imitative one, and must take our examples and models, in a great degree, from the existing nations of Europe. There is no country more worthy of our study than England." (Such sentiments are greatly expanded, with additional emphasis on American sensitivities to British criticism, in the 1848 preface to the revised edition of *The Sketch Book*.) Athough his sketches lack narrative coherence, Irving often creates interesting juxtapositions, as when his tribute to English writing follows what is often cited as the first American short story, "Rip Van Winkle."

In "Rural Life in England," one of his many travel pieces that show Irving's penchant for intuitive generalization, he associates the English gift for "rural feeling" with their love of urban gardens. "Even those less fortunate individuals, who are doomed to pass their lives in the midst of din and

Page from Irving's diary, May 1805, Paris (from Stanley T. Williams's The Life of Washington Irving, *1935)*

traffic, contrive to have something that shall remind them of the green aspect of nature." Contrasting "the cold formalities and negative civilities of the town" with the "natural feelings" the Englishman enjoys in the country, where he "becomes joyous and freehearted," Irving implies that English "country life" is similar to that of rural America. Irving, "the country squire," can be cloying in his condescending sentimentality when he writes about "the peasantry in their best finery, with ruddy faces and modest cheerfulness, thronging tranquilly along the green lanes to church," but there is genuine feeling for the "sweet home feeling; this settled repose of affection in the domestic scene" that he observes later that evening.

Irving's visit to the "The Boar's Head Tavern" is an example of the literary past and "sweet Jack Falstaff" influencing his appreciation of the present. His visit to the site in the City of London of Falstaff's favorite haunt in Shakespeare's history plays inspires a sustained and complex piece of travel writing. It succeeds as a combination of the actual experience enriched by references to historical figures such as Jack Cade, Wat Tyler, and William Walworth. The heritage of Shakespeare's Henry plays is delightfully mixed with the more immediate atmosphere of tobacco, porter, and breast of lamb, presided over by Dame Honeyball, a real-life descendant of Shakespeare's Mistress Quickly.

The writing in "Westminster Abbey" is accomplished, as Irving attends to atmosphere and narrative progression while observing both panoramic and specific detail. The past and present intrude upon each other: "wandering about these gloomy vaults and silent aisles, studying the records of the dead, the sound of busy existence from without occasionally reaches the ear." His descriptions of Henry VII's chapel, the tomb of Edward the Confessor, and Poet's Corner are reverent and yet attentive to telling details. Even the antiquarian notes toward the end are instructive without being obtrusive, preceded as they are by thoughts on mutability and followed by observations of the special atmosphere of the Abbey by candle and moonlight.

The Sketch Book also contains five Christmas sketches, which are presented as a travel memoir, with an introductory essay on "Christmas" that emphasizes the persistence and timeless charm of English rural folk customs. In "The Stage Coach" Irving describes the trip to Yorkshire. The warmth, conviviality, and food of the village inn presage that of the Bracebridge country estate in northern rural England, the setting for "Christmas Eve," "Christmas Day," and "The Christmas Dinner." The narrative and details of these sketches support the generalizations of the introductory essay. These sketches, although they include jibes at the Puritans who remain as intent as ever on abolishing the "rites and ceremonies of Christmas," were unobjectionable to contemporary readers and achieved popular success. Their most interesting figure is Squire Bracebridge, whose lament over the passing of so many customs and observances among the peasantry is contrasted with his preservation of Christmas traditions. But the squire also reveals a conservative, and troubling, lack of compassion for the peasants when he complains that they "have become too knowing, and begin to read newspapers, listen to ale house politicians, and talk of reform."

The bookish Irving and the romantic lover of the countryside come together in Irving's most impressive travel piece in *The Sketch Book,* "Stratford-on-Avon," in which his appreciation of Shakespeare and the world that inspired him are interdependent. The abundance of quotations is finely tuned to the narration and description, which are structured as a visitor's itinerary, passing from inn, to birthplace, to

church and tomb. Words and scenes become present experiences, as the brilliant past of the greatest English writer is contrasted to the prosaic and rather phony present. Irving shows he is "completely possessed by the imaginary scenes and characters connected with" Shakespeare's plays.

Throughout *The Sketch Book* Irving indulges in generalizations about national or ethnic character, which reach a crescendo in "John Bull," an essay that distills Irving's version of the English national character. Irving is aware that such a figure is more caricature than characterization but claims that he is only doing what the English themselves do. Irving's John Bull, although admirable in his plain, unromantic, good-tempered ways, has fallen on bad times. Irving wishfully speculates that he may quit meddling in the affairs of others "by dint of the cudgel" so that he may "renew the jovial scenes of ancient prosperity." Read as political allegory, this may be a comment about English imperialism, or, perhaps, the recent War of 1812.

The immediately enthusiastic reception on both English-speaking sides of the Atlantic to *The Sketch Book* was largely attributable to Irving's ability to appeal to the tastes of a variety of readers: the miscellany had something for everyone. The best travel pieces, "Westminster Abbey" and "Stratford-on-Avon," were especially attractive to American readers, eager in their young country for some traditions to savor. They whetted the appetite of the traveler eager to visit what Nathaniel Hawthorne called "Our Old Home" and pleased those who stayed home with a visit they could re-create in their imaginations.

Having learned a bitter financial lesson when he gave up the United States copyright of *Salmagundi* to his publisher and lost his profits, Irving had become a shrewd professional man of letters. The two versions of *The Sketch Book* had separate but closely coordinated publication dates in the United States and in Great Britain, so that he was doubly protected from literary piracy. Irving earned some $9,000 in American profits in 1820–1821, some three times what he earned in 1809 for his popular *A History of New York* and almost double the $5,000 James Fenimore Cooper was paid for *The Last of the Mohicans* (1826).

Irving attempted to capitalize on the success of the Christmas pieces in *The Sketch Book* by expanding and elaborating his treatment of rural life in *Bracebridge Hall, or The Humourists. A Medley* (1822), a miscellany of two volumes in fifty-one parts that contains some sketches set in France, Spain, and the United States. In his introductory essay, "The Author," Irving as Geoffrey Crayon promises a travel book, impressed as he was on coming to England where

> every thing was full of matter; the footsteps of history were every where to be traced; and poetry had breathed over and sanctified the land. . . . Such too was the odd confusion of associations that kept breaking upon me as I first approached London. One of my earliest wishes had been to see this great metropolis. I had read so much about it in the earliest books that had been put into my infant hands; and I had heard so much about it from those around me who had come from the "old countries," that I was familiar with the names of its streets and squares, and public places, before I knew those of my native city. It was, to me, the great centre of the world, round which every thing seemed to revolve. . . . I shall continue on . . . looking at things poetically, rather than politically; describing them as they are, rather than pretending to point out how they should be; and endeavouring to see the world in as pleasant a light as circumstances will permit.

Irving in 1809, portrait by John Wesley Jarvis

But Irving does not write much about London, and the volume contains little travel writing. The bulk of the work is a nostalgic presentation of a privileged rural way of life that was becoming increasingly rare in England but increasingly popular with American Anglophiles.

The conservative Irving shows affection for the admirable landowner and the long-owned ancestral estate. Servants, relics, trees, and family traditions are given superficial treatment in the first volume, while "English Country Gentlemen," the loss of English merriment, "Gipsies," May Day celebrations, and a family wedding are among the subjects of the second volume. Although some readers enjoyed the diversity of comic types Irving depicts, only "The Stout Gentleman" can be labeled an unqualified success, perhaps because it was based on actual experience, his pleasurable evenings spent listening to Sir Walter Scott's stories. Most of the pieces are derived from caricatures and generalizations from Irving's eclectic reading and fondness for the writers of the eighteenth century.

In the summer of 1822 Irving started an elaborate tour of the Continent, visiting for the first time the Rhine valley, the Black Forest, the Bavarian mountains, Salzburg, and Vienna. In midautumn he settled in Dresden, where he remained for the better part of a year, probably because he fell in love with eighteen-year-old Emily Foster, whose aristocratic family were visitors from England. Only a limited friendship resulted, and in the summer of 1823, Irving resettled in Paris, where for several years he was primarily preoccupied with dramatic adaptations and largely unsuccessful theatrical adventures

with a fellow New Yorker—feckless actor and failed businessman, John Howard Payne.

Irving's next book, *Tales of a Traveller* (1824), was wholly fiction and received mixed reviews. The ideas for the stories and sketches were gathered during his European travels, and most were derived from German writing. The volume is divided into four parts, the first three of which are set in Europe: the pieces in "Strange Stories by a Nervous Gentlemen" are parodies of Gothic literature; "Buckthorne and His Friends" contains depictions of the catty life of literary London; and "The Italian Banditti," a derivative and overwritten collection of stereotypes, focuses on instances of crime in Italy. In the last section, titled "The Money Diggers," Irving resurrects Diedrich Knickerbocker as the historian of buried-treasure legends in New York. The poor sales of the book likely contributed to his turning from fiction to biography and history.

Irving was living in Bordeaux with his elder brother, fellow bachelor and frequent traveling companion, Peter, when he accepted the offer of a diplomatic passport from Alexander H. Everett, the American minister in Madrid, to travel to Spain. He and his brother arrived in the Spanish capital in February 1826, where he remained until 1829, officially as the attaché to the American legation, but at Everett's suggestion working on the translation of the documents collected and published by Spanish historian Martin Fernández de Navarrete. Visitors such as Henry Wadsworth Longfellow found Irving in 1827 working with great energy and discipline to absorb the scholarship of Navarrete and the government documents provided by Obadiah Rich, an American consul, who also helped with Irving's housing and living arrangements. His position and work led to the publication in 1828 of *A History of the Life and Voyages of Christopher Columbus,* based on the work of Navarrete and other unpublished sources. Irving's dramatic narrative of the controversial Columbus soon lost favor and was seldom taken seriously by later historians.

In his research at the library of the Jesuits' College of Madrid and at the Biblioteca Real, in which he was assisted by his brother, Irving became interested in the Christian conquest of Moorish Granada, which was completed in the winter of 1491–1492, just before Columbus sailed to the Caribbean. The resulting book, *A Chronicle of the Conquest of Granada* (1829) is a fictitious account of the battles that led to the end of the centuries-old Muslim control of much of Spain, told by Fray Antonio Agapida, a fictitious scholarly friar, pedant, and bigot. With this fictional mask Irving could use the facts of the conflict—as they were then understood—to appeal to the historically minded, while also imagining the actions and events so as to satisfy a popular audience. Drawing from and variously combining a variety of biased and often unreliable sources, Irving produced a romantic narrative that most critics consider a failed experiment. Irving's work was appreciated in Spain, however, and in 1829 he was made a corresponding member of the Royal Academy of History in Madrid.

In 1829 President Andrew Jackson appointed Irving the first secretary to the American legation in London. He held a position with the legation for two years, resigning his post in late September 1831 to devote himself to writing. During his time in England, Irving received a Gold Medal as a historian from the Royal Society of Literature in London (1830) and was given an honorary Doctor of Civil Laws by Oxford University (1831). He continued to write of Spain, titling his next book, *The Alhambra* (1832), after the Moorish citadel and palace that dominates the city of Granada. Irving had first visited the province and city in March 1828 and had taken notes during his stay at the palace during May and June 1829.

In *The Alhambra* Irving follows the same formula that served him so well in *The Sketch Book,* mixing picturesque descriptions, anecdotal essays, and folktales, emphasizing even more the bittersweet experience of a lost, brilliant past. The first sketch, "The Journey," is an effective evocation of the south of Spain, "for the greater part a stern melancholy country, with rugged mountains and long sweeping plains, destitute of trees, and indescribably silent and lonesome, partaking of the savage and solitary character of Africa." The account of the five-day journey is enriched with details of each day's progress, lunches and siestas, distant views of Moorish ruins, stories and legends from the people, and in Loxa, descriptions of the Corona inn and its beautiful hostess, assorted guests, and the Andalusians he watches from his window. Upon his party's arrival in the city Irving finds that their guide "had decoyed [them] into one of the shabbiest posadas in Granada." Irving thus suggests the criminality of the natives through an anecdote, a commonly used yet most unfair ploy among travel writers.

Irving's experience serves to justify his initial distrust of the "son of the Alhambra," the shabby Mateo Ximenes, in the second sketch, "Palace of the Alhambra." It presents some of Irving's finest travel writing, a deft mixture of succinct history, clear description and explanation invigorated with Mateo's tales, all presented in a tone of wonder and excitement. "I now perceived I had made an invaluable acquaintance in this son of the Alhambra, one who knew all the apocryphal history of the place and firmly believed in it, and whose memory was stuffed with a kind of knowledge for which I have a lurking fancy, but which is too apt to be considered rubbish by less indulgent philosophers." The sketch, which Irving calls a "general introduction," concludes with a "Note on Morisco Architecture" and its "fairy tracery."

Irving's account of the palace and its legends is sometimes marred by his condescension—as when he grandly rationalizes that "there are none who understand the art of doing nothing and living upon nothing, better than the poor classes of Spain"—but at his best Irving is able to infuse his descriptions with enthusiasm and insight. In "The Hall of the Ambassadors" he contrasts the "light, elegant, and voluptuous character" of "this Moorish pile" and the "gloomy solemnity of the Gothic." Each, he suggests, bespeaks "the opposite and irreconcilable natures of the two warlike peoples who so long battled." In "The Mysterious Chambers" he blends description with a sense of the dangerous unknown and romantic melancholy as he tells of the rooms and gardens identified with Elizabetta of Farnese and the "fair Lindaraxa," where he determines to live despite his servants' fears:

> Even the thoughts of the fair Elizabetta and the beauties of her court, who had once graced these chambers, now, by a perversion of fancy, added to the gloom. Here was the scene of their transient gayety and loveliness; here were the very traces of their elegance and en-

Page from a draft for "Local Traditions," a sketch in The Alhambra *(New York Public Library; Astor, Lenox and Tilden Foundations)*

joyment; but what and where were they?—Dust and ashes! tenants of the tomb! phantoms of the memory!

Irving's narrative is replete with "long buried superstitions," bats, shrieks in the night, and eerie moonlight.

Irving's talent as a storyteller is both his strength and his weakness as a travel writer. The stories and anecdotes he introduces provide depth to his depiction of the present as places call forth tales. "The peculiar charm of this old dreamy palace," Irving writes, "is its power of calling up vague reveries and picturings of the past, and thus clothing naked realities with the illusions of memory and the imagination." But Irving's intrusions into his descriptions and his use of stories often leave the reader unsure of the line between illusion and reality. Irving's celebration of "the Alhambra—a Moslem pile in the midst of a Christian land, an Oriental palace amidst the Gothic edifices of the West, an elegant memento of a brave, intelligent, and graceful people who conquered, ruled and passed away"—shows he is interested in the past, not the present, in the story more than the reality. In contrast, in the "Author's Farewell to Granada" Irving seemingly discounts the "tales and gossip and local knowledge" of Mateo Ximenes and ends with an apologetic tone, calling his experience in the Alhambra "one of the pleasantest dreams of a life, which the reader perhaps may think has been too much made up of dreams."

As a whole *The Alhambra* is Irving's most attractive romantic work, free of feeble comic wit and the bigoted condemnation of the Muslims evident in *A Chronicle of the Conquest of Granada*. While it was not as successful in Irving's lifetime as *The Sketch Book,* it has survived as an important part of his canon. The charms and mysteries of *The Alhambra,* made convincing by Irving's evident affection for his subject, still enchant.

In the spring of 1832 Irving returned from seventeen years abroad to great acclaim in his homeland, including banquets in New York and honorary degrees from Columbia and Harvard Universities. With friends such as Charles Joseph Latrobe from England, Count Albert-Alexandre de Pourtalés from Switzerland, and James Kirke Paulding, he traveled up the Hudson and throughout upper New York State and New England. In September, with Indian Commissioner Henry Ellsworth, Irving, Latrobe, and Pourtalés went on a trip down the Ohio, Mississippi, and Missouri Rivers and frontiers beyond, as far west as present-day Norman, Oklahoma. All four wrote accounts of the expedition.

Irving's record of the trip was published as *A Tour on the Prairies* (1835), planned as the first in a series of travel sketches of American and European places. *Abbotsford and Newstead Abbey* and *Legends of the Conquest of Spain,* which were mined from his Scottish and Spanish notebooks, were published separately that same year. When George P. Putnam published the revised edition of Irving's complete works in 1849, the three sections were combined as *The Crayon Miscellany,* an apt title since the three works vary in locale and treatment. Only the first two can be called travel literature, being based on personal experience and with a sense of place.

The introduction to *A Tour on the Prairies* has an apologetic tone that suggests Irving's sensitivity to the charge that he prized Europe more than his homeland. It is one of the few times that the work—a rather flat, reportorial narrative—takes on a personal accent. Irving went to the Indian territories expressly to get material for a book, which traces a month-long trek on horseback through the Indian territory of eastern Oklahoma. Irving offers a collection of briefly sketched scenes and episodes, variously described.

In *A Tour on the Prairies* Irving shows a cosmopolitan's culture shock at encountering the rough and harsh West. Mildly incensed at the hatred and distrust shown by some of the white settlers for the Indians, the narrator acknowledges the inaccuracy of "poetic" descriptions, arguing that "the Indian of poetical fiction is like the shepherd of pastoral romance, a mere personification of imaginary attributes." While he sometimes describes the Indians with condescension—he remarks, for example, that they exhibit "a gipsey fondness for brilliant colours"—Irving more often admires them for being "perfectly independent of the world, and competent to self protection and self maintenance."

Just as he did in the opening chapter of *The Sketch Book,* Irving contrasts the natural beauty of America to the cultural splendor of Europe. His many references to the Continent, though, often indicate that he views the landscape through European preconceptions:

> We were overshadowed by lofty trees, with straight smooth trunks, like stately columns, and as the glancing rays of the sun shone through the transparent leaves, tinted with the many coloured hues of autumn, I was reminded of the effect of sunshine among the stained windows and clustering columns of a Gothic cathedral. Indeed there is a grandeur and solemnity in some of our spacious forests of the West that awaken in me the same feeling I have experienced in those vast and venerable piles, and the sound of the wind sweeping through them, supplies occasionally the deep breathings of the organ.

While Irving can praise the high spirits and "manliness, simplicity and self dependence" of young mountain men and even condemn the sending of "our youth abroad to grow luxurious and effeminate in Europe," his most facile reference points are to his experience of European culture. "The foliage had a yellow autumnal tint," he observes, "which gave to the sunny landscape the golden tone of one of the landscapes of Claude Lorrain."

Perhaps the overarching weakness of *A Tour on the Prairies* is that Irving does not seem convincingly interested in the West he describes. The search for buffalo herds on the vast prairies carries the narrative forward, but most of the pages of the account deal with the hunt for daily food—deer, turkey and the prized elk—and the generalized details of twelve-to-fifteen-mile daily rides and the routines of camp life. Irving breaks the main story line with digressions about bees, Indian stories and burial customs, and wild horses. He also weaves in accounts of the boastful and cocky Frenchman, Antoine "Tonish" Deshetres, and the erratic but daring Pierre Beattie of "French-Osage" parentage. In one chapter he describes a dramatic prairie thunderstorm and in general is more effective in evoking the weather than in presenting the landscape.

The climax of *A Tour on the Prairies* occurs when Irving's horse is attacked by a charging buffalo. He manages to escape but finds himself separated from his companions and alone on the barren prairie:

> To one unaccustomed to it there is something inexpressibly lonely in the solitude of a prairie. The loneliness of a forest seems nothing to it. There the view is shut in by trees, and the imagination is left free to picture some livelier scene beyond. But here we have an immense extent of landscape without a sign of human existence. We have the consciousness of being far, far beyond the bounds of human habitation; we feel as if moving in the midst of a desert world.

Irving's book generally communicates the message that the West belongs to the animals and not to man, at least not to the white man who has seen Europe.

The exploring party returns home hungry, weary, and discouraged after a relatively uneventful adventure into the Pawnee Hunting Ground. The rather abrupt ending seems a confirmation of William Bedford Clark's view that *A Tour on the Prairies* is really a farcical chronicle of eastern naiveté confronting frontier realities and failing to overcome them. Perhaps Irving's work is most charitably read as a satire of western expansion, mocking the absurdity of the American myth of so-called progress. Irving's account shows that America had not yet tamed the West.

Although published in one volume, Irving's pieces on Abbotsford and Newstead Abbey are the result of visits to the homes of two great writers under quite different circumstances some fifteen years apart. In 1817 an insecure Irving was graciously received by Sir Walter Scott at Abbotsford for an extended visit. In 1832 Irving slept in George Gordon, Lord Byron's bed at Newstead Abbey seven years after the poet's death and shortly before

Irving's triumphant return to his own country. Although readers in the twentieth century have generally ignored Irving's last travel pieces about the literary British Isles, *Abbotsford* and *Newstead Abbey,* like most of Irving's works, were warmly received by contemporary Americans, who were proud of the country's first internationally recognized author.

Irving considered Scott the equal of Shakespeare and was flattered when the established author praised *A History of New York* in 1813. *Abbotsford* is based on only a four-day visit, but Irving's affection for Scott, who died in 1832, and his appreciation for the Scottish writer's work enabled him to expand his notebook accounts believably. As travel literature the account wavers and perhaps slides into literary anecdote, but for Irving it is the account of one of his most rewarding experiences. Irving was able to provide his readers a thrill that many travelers desire: a long, friendly encounter with a celebrity.

After modestly apologizing for his faulty memory, Irving begins his remembrance with effective descriptions of Scott's home as he waits outside and then of the novelist and his family. The next day he sets out for his visit to Melrose Abbey, generously quoting from the "Lay of the Last Minstrel" while his guide, Johnny Bowers, points out scenes from the poem alternating with anecdotes about the "affability of Scott." Remembering his walk later that day with Scott, Irving focuses on Scott's love for his dogs and his sense of their personalities as vivid and distinct as those of his neighbors.

Irving skillfully presents Scott's love of the popular songs and stories of his country, not as sometime entertainment but as necessary threads in the tapestry of his Scottish experience: "'They are part of our national inheritance,' said he; 'and something that we may truly call our own. They have no foreign taint; they have the pure breath of the heather and the mountain breeze.'" Obviously affected by Scott's love for Scottish folklore and his love for his native country, Irving is prompted to make a similar declaration of his own and then discusses "the poetic materials furnished by American scenery."

Irving records the many turns of the two men's conversation during the visit. Scott speaks of domestic concerns and remarks on the Scottish character as exemplified in "the quiet, orderly, honest conduct of his neighbors" and the continuing "ancient jealousy between the Highlanders and the Lowlanders." While eating or on walks, Scott tells tales about local sites and their people. On the third day the men, accompanied by Scott's daughters,

Irving's view from his rooms in the Alhambra (photograph by Mary Lee R. Williams)

journey to Dryburgh Abbey, near where Scott's grandfather had lived, where Scott as a child had "first imbibed his passion for legendary tales, border traditions, and old national songs and ballads." Irving emphasizes Scott's fondness for "a sly and quiet humour" and a "beneficent spirit which gives such an air of bonhommie to Scott's humour throughout all his works," not unlike Irving's own.

Abbotsford thus records a meeting of similar temperaments and is suggestive of how Irving might have been influenced by the older man. It is plausible that Irving's technique in his travel works of starting with a place and then presenting some of the stories connected with it is derived from Scott's example. Similarly, Irving's love for a warm and interesting country home such as Abbotsford is clear in his own Sunnyside, the cottage and land he bought in 1835 near Tarrytown along the Hudson River. Finally, the example Scott gave of using and developing local anecdotes and traditions, rather than English ones, perhaps inspired Irving to continue to do the same with American materials.

Newstead Abbey is based on three visits Irving made to Byron's ancestral home in late 1831 and early 1832, the last with future president Martin Van Buren and his son. Working from the notes and observations he made at the time, Irving produced a book that is both antiquarian and literary. Its emphasis throughout is on the past, and it contains dozens of quotations that show the writer's considerable familiarity with Byron's poetry.

The opening "Historical Notice" situates the abbey in the Sherwood Forest of Robin Hood and tells of its founding by Henry II in the twelfth century to expiate the murder of Saint Thomas à Becket. The abbey was dissolved in the sixteenth century by Henry VIII and given to Sir John Byron, whose ghost supposedly still haunts the residence. In 1765 "The Wicked Lord Byron," the poet's great uncle, won a duel in London but was convicted of manslaughter and retired to the abbey. By the time the nineteenth-century poet lived there in 1808, Newstead Abbey was in disrepair, desolate and melancholy, as Byron records in his poems, which are generously quoted by Irving. Byron sold it in 1817 to Colonel Wildman, a hero of Waterloo, who had begun extensive repairs when Irving arrived. The spirit of the place and the restoring and rebuilding that was going on may, like Abbotsford, have inspired Irving to buy the cottage that he later named Sunnyside.

In a tour of the building conducted by the old chamberlain, Irving intersperses his descriptions of the restored rooms with quotations from Byron's *Don Juan* (1819–1824) and other poems. He gives special attention to "The Abbey Garden," the former haunt of the long-dispersed monks, and its grove, "The Devil's Wood," which was one of several spots where Byron walked with his sister. Irving is charmed by the continuity of the past, remarking that "in crossing the Trent one seems to step back into old times" for "everything has a quaint and antiquated air." The anecdotes told in the chapter titled "Old Servants" prompt Irving to seek out Nanny Smith, Byron's "quondam housekeeper," and record her stories about the poet and the abbey. Such reminiscences give Irving the opportunity to retell a ghost story or two. In the book's longest chapter, "Annesley Hall," Irving describes the home of the Chaworths (one of whose ancestors Byron's great uncle killed in a duel) and the young Miss Chaworth, with whom Byron fell in love at age fifteen. Irving identifies with the smitten but unloved poet as he tells his story and illustrates the tour of the house with liberal quotations from Byron's "Dream," and other poems.

Inspired by the spirit of Newstead Abbey and its surroundings, Irving spends several chapters on the legends of Sherwood Forest and Robin Hood.

Irving notes that one of "the earliest books that captivated my fancy when a child was a collection of Robin Hood ballads." In separate chapters he focuses on ancient trees: the "Pilgrim Oak," saved by the local people from the destructive intent of "old Lord Byron," the "Ravenshead Oak," and "Parliament Oak." In contemplating these ancient trees Irving imagines a colorful and fanciful past firmly rooted in the recalled experiences of his boyhood reading and fancies.

In the concluding chapter, "The Little White Lady," Irving narrates the encounters of Colonel Wildman and his family with a strange, reclusive, deaf and dumb young woman, who, rather like Irving, visits Newstead Abbey out of devotion to Byron and his poetry. She is supported by the family, is lent copies of Byron's poems, and writes her own poems to the poet whom she had never met. Irving quotes not only the poems but also long letters in which she describes her destitution, melancholy, and appreciation for Byron's work. He ends the book abruptly with the report that she was killed by a rapidly driven cart as she was traveling to London to better her situation.

While Irving's *Astoria, or, Anecdotes of an Enterprise Beyond the Rocky Mountains* (1836) is primarily a history of the establishment of John Jacob Astor's commercial colony, the first permanent United States settlement on the Pacific coast, it is notable as travel literature for its descriptions of the western terrain and its people. His goal, as expressed in a 29 October 1834 letter to Pierre M. Irving, was to go beyond history to present:

> a body of information concerning the whole region beyond the Rocky Mountains, on the borders of Columbia River, comprising the adventures, by sea and land, of traders, trappers, Indian warriors, hunters, &c.; their habits, characters, persons, costumes, &c.; descriptions of natural scenery, animals, plants, &c., &c. I think, in this way, a rich and varied work may be formed, both entertaining and instructive, and laying open scenes in the wild life of that adventurous region which would possess the charm of freshness and novelty.

Astor had decided to establish an outpost at the mouth of the Columbia River after the expedition led by Meriwether Lewis and William Clark had suggested the opportunities for the fur trade there. He allowed Irving access to his company's documents and arranged interviews with men who had participated in the expeditions. Able to draw somewhat on his own experience of the land west of the Mississippi and provided with a mass of secondary materials organized by his nephew Pierre, Irving was able to create some compelling accounts of the disappearing world of the Old West and its explorers, fur traders, and mountain men.

After a brief account of competing fur trading companies, Irving begins with the sea expedition of the *Tonquin,* the ship Astor equipped to help establish his outpost. The ship, with a crew of twenty, set sail from New York on 8 September 1810, reached the Falkland Islands by 4 December, Cape Horn by Christmas Day, and Hawaii by 11 February 1811. Irving devotes a chapter to describing the customs and dress of the inhabitants of Hawaii and the Sandwich Islands. The *Tonquin* finally arrived at the Columbia River on 22 March 1811. Irving based his report on the fishing and other practices of the Indians on Ross Cox's *Adventures on the Columbia River* (1831), a principal source for *Astoria,* as are Gabriel Franchère's *Narrative of a Voyage to the Northwest Coast of America* (1820) and Robert Stuart's *Discovery of the Oregon Trail* (1812–1813). Irving concludes the maritime part of his narrative with descriptions of the loss of the *Tonquin* to Indians near Vancouver Island, the preparation of the Indians for winter, and the celebration of "the New Year's festival of 1812 at the infant colony of Astoria."

Irving then begins a second narrative, tracing the journey of Astor's first transcontinental expedition. The expedition of ten men started from Montreal in July 1810 in a long canoe, reaching Mackinac Island on 22 July. By way of the Fox, Wisconsin, and Mississippi Rivers the men reached Saint Louis on 3 September and began making their way up the Missouri on 21 October. For this leg of the journey Irving only briefly describes the "motley populations" of Mackinac Island and Saint Louis. As he continues to report the expedition's push west in the spring of the following year, Irving often interrupts his narrative to provide background material concerning the rival fur-trading companies and to relate stories of fearless explorer-trappers such as John Colter, who once escaped from Blackfeet warriors.

By July 1811, a year after their departure, the party was trading with the Arikaras in the far north of present-day South Dakota. As the expedition prepares to head directly west, Irving reflects on

> the nature of this immense wilderness of the Far West; which apparently defies cultivation, and the habitation of civilized life. Some portions of it along the rivers may partially be subdued by agriculture, others may form vast pastoral tracts, like those of the east; but it is to be feared that a great part of it will form a lawless interval between the abodes of civilized man, like the wastes of the ocean or the deserts of Arabia; and, like them, be subject to the depredations of the marauder.

A pencil sketch made by Irving during his western travels in 1832 (New York Public Library; Astor, Lenox and Tilden Foundations)

Irving uses such "excursive speculations" and his descriptions of the ferocious Blackfeet tribe to build suspense.

Along with descriptions of the monotonous landscape and the grandeur of the skies, Irving incorporates details about the buffalo, lost hunters, and grizzly bears; however, the farther west the expedition travels the less Irving is able to draw on personal experience. He offers anecdotes about Indian tribes and records the travails of the expedition as it takes a disastrous turn on the Snake River, losing a canoe and one man in the rapids. Forced to store its goods in caches, the expedition split into two groups and barely survived the winter of 1811 before finally reaching Astoria. In the spring of the next year various expeditions were sent out to retrieve the goods and to search for survivors.

In the last section of his book Irving writes of Astoria and its failure to fend off hostile Indians. The outbreak of the War of 1812 led Astor to sell his fort to the British in 1813. Irving laments seeing "a grand and beneficial stroke of genius fail of its aim; but we regret the failure of this enterprise in a national point of view; for, had it been crowned with success, it would have redounded greatly to the advantage and extension of our commerce." Astoria, however, was restored to the United States in 1818 and grew to play an important role in trade in the region, although that trade was controlled not by Astor but by the British into the 1840s. Irving's assessment seems more concerned with the interests of Astor than with the interests of the nation.

Irving's next book, *Adventures of Captain Bonneville, or, Scenes beyond the Rocky Mountains of the Far West* (1837) is based on the amateur "travelling notes" of Captain Bonneville, an American fur trader and army captain, the leader of a three-year expedition (1832–1835). Without the original manuscript, scholars have been unable to determine Irving's exact contribution to the work. While the sublime and the picturesque in the western landscape are often noted as Captain Bonneville leads his party along the Vermillion, South Platte, and North Platte Rivers in western Nebraska, the descriptive passages are invariably short on specific details. The book includes perfunctory sketches of the Rocky Mountains, the Salmon and Snake Rivers, and Great Salt and Bear Lakes. By the conclusion of the account, Irving has provided very few of the "scenes, incidents, and adventures" promised in the American title of the work.

In *Adventures of Captain Bonneville,* as in *Astoria,* Irving largely ignores the exploitation of the western lands and their native peoples. The thoroughly middle-class Irving turned a blind eye to the robberies and brutalities committed by land speculators and other developers in the middle and far West, as is shown in his 10 January 1838 letter to his lifelong friend, Gouverneur Kemble:

> The late land speculations, so much deprecated, though ruinous to many engaged in them, have forced agriculture and civilization into the depths of the wilderness; have laid open the recesses of the primeval forests; made us acquainted with the most available points of our immense interior; have cast the germs of future towns and cities and busy marts in the heart of the savage solitudes, and studded our vast rivers and internal seas with ports that will soon give activity to a vast internal commerce. Millions of acres which might otherwise have remained idle and impracticable wastes, have been brought under the dominion of the plough, and hundreds of thousands of industrious yeomen have been carried into the rich but remote depths of our immense empire, to multiply and spread out in every direction, and give solidity and strength to our confederacy. All this has in a great measure been effected by the extravagant schemes of land speculators.

Critic Peter Antelyes, however, perceives a paradox in Irving's writing, asserting that he endorses "expansionism while noting the dangers posed to American society by that expansion."

Irving's descriptions of the American West seem generally devoid of enthusiasm. His western books, especially *Bonneville,* ring false because they lack the affection for the subject that suffuses *The Alhambra* and the personal experience that informs *The Sketch Book.* Vernon Louis Parrington, referring to Irving's first name for his Sunnyside estate, pointed out the problem in 1927: "The atmosphere of the Snake River could not be created in the quiet study at the 'Roost'; it needed the pen of a realist to capture the romance of those bitter wanderings in mountain and sagebrush." Even in *A Tour on the Prairies* the presentation of the landscape is simplistic compared to the richness of his European books, where Irving expands the perception and experience of the present by looking beyond the moment, usually into the fictional past. The West as Irving knew it had no past that appealed to his imagination.

Irving continued to write but produced no more major works of travel writing. He served as minister to Spain from 1842 to 1846 but was exhausted by the strained relations between Spain and the United States over Cuba and resigned the office to practice law on Wall Street. In 1848 he prepared a revised edition of his writing in *The Works of Washington Irving.* It was the first time an American had undertaken such a project, and it made both Irving and his publisher, George P. Putnam, wealthy.

One of Irving's best travel essays, titled "The Catskill Mountains," was first published in *The Home Book of the Picturesque* (1851). His affection for the mountains where he set his most famous stories is obvious: "Their detached position, overlooking a wide lowland region with the majestic Hudson rolling through it, has given them a distinct character; and rendered them at all times a rallying point for romance and fable."

Chronicles of Wolfert's Roost and Other Papers (1855), a collection of sketches and stories previously published in *Knickerbocker Magazine* (1837–1839) and elsewhere, was published as volume 15 of Putnam's edition of *The Works of Washington Irving* and included several travel pieces. "The Creole Village: A Sketch from a Steamboat" (1837) stresses the Indian, Spanish, and mainly French ancestry of a river town in Louisiana. "Sketches in Paris in 1825" contains observations recorded in his journals that are often derived from friends such as actor Francois-Joseph Talma. In "The Parisian Hotel" he tells of his elderly neighbor, "a little antique Frenchman" with regular habits, and a crusty Englishman, in Paris to save money, who "will not admit that Paris has any advantage over London." This leads to a general essay on "English and French Character," much indebted to Talma, and a comparison of the "Tuilleries and Windsor Castle": "The Tuilleries, outwardly a peaceful palace, is in effect a swaggering military hold; while, the old castle, on the contrary, in spite of its bullying look, is completely under petticoat government."

Irving died at Sunnyside on 28 November 1859, eight months after completing his five-volume biography of George Washington, *Life of George Washington* (1855–1859). He was respected by his readers for his polished, traditional style as well as his personal modesty. Irving is a pioneer in American literature, whose success and travels made him an ambassador for the literature of the New World. As his travel writing shows, Irving, like other Americans of his era, was fascinated by his cultural roots in Europe even as he was insecure about his natural roots in America.

Letters:

Letters, 4 volumes, edited by Ralph M. Aderman, Herbert L. Klienfield, and Jenifer S. Banks (Boston: Twayne, 1978–1982).

Bibliographies:

William R. Langfeld and Philip C. Blackburn, *Washington Irving: A Bibliography* (New York: New York Public Library, 1933);

Stanley T. Williams and Mary A. Edge, *A Bibliography of the Writings of Washington Irving* (New York: Oxford University Press, 1936);

Sunnyside, Irving's home in Tarrytown, New York

Haskell S. Springer, *Washington Irving: A Reference Guide* (Boston: G. K. Hall, 1976);

Springer and Raylene Penner, "Washington Irving: A Reference Guide Updated," *Resources for American Literary Study,* 11 (1981): 257–279;

James W. Tuttleton, "Washington Irving," in *Fifteen American Authors before 1900: Bibliographical Essays on Research and Criticism,* edited by Earl N. Harbert and Robert A. Rees (Madison: University of Wisconsin Press, 1984), pp. 330–356;

Edwin T. Bowden, *Washington Irving: Bibliography* (Boston: Twayne, 1989);

Biographies:

Pierre M. Irving, *The Life and Letters of Washington Irving,* 4 volumes (New York: Putnam, 1862–1864);

Stanley T. Williams, *The Life of Washington Irving,* 2 volumes (New York: Oxford University Press, 1935);

Claude G. Bowers, *The Spanish Adventures of Washington Irving* (Boston: Houghton Mifflin, 1940).

References:

Ralph Aderman, ed., *Critical Essays on Washington Irving* (Boston: G. K. Hall, 1990);

Aderman, ed., *Washington Irving Reconsidered* (Hartford, Conn.: Transcendental Books, 1969);

Peter Antelyes, *Tales of Adventurous Enterprise: Washington Irving and the Poetics of Western Expansion* (New York: Columbia University Press, 1990);

Brigitte Bailey, "Irving's Italian Landscapes: Skepticism and the Picturesque Aesthetic," *Emerson Society Quarterly,* 32 (1986): 1–22;

Michael Davitt Bell, "Feelings and Effects: Washington Irving," in his *The Development of American Romance* (Chicago: University of Chicago Press, 1980), pp. 63–85;

Mary Weatherspoon Bowden, *Washington Irving* (Boston: Twayne, 1981);

Malcolm Bradbury, "Storied Associations: Washington Irving goes to Europe," in his *Dangerous Pilgrimages: Transatlantic Mythologies and the Novel* (New York: Viking, 1996), pp. 53–83;

Stanley Browdin, ed., *The Old World and New World Romanticism of Washington Irving* (Westport, Conn.: Greenwood Press, 1986);

Heiner Bus, *Studien zur Reiseprosa Washington Irvings* (Frankfurt Am Main: Verlag Peter Lang, 1982);

James Buzard, *The Beaten Track. European Tourism, Literature, and the Ways of Culture, 1800–1918* (Oxford: Oxford University Press, 1992);

Terry Caesar, *Forgiving the Boundaries: Home as Abroad in American Travel Writing* (Athens: University of Georgia Press, 1995);

James T. Callow, *Kindred Spirits: Knickerbocker Writers and American Artists, 1807–1974* (Chapel Hill: University of North Carolina Press, 1967);

William Bedford Clark, "How the West Won: Irving's Comic Inversion of the Westering Myth in *A Tour on the Prairies,*" *American Literature,* 50 (1978): 335–347;

Ross Cox, *The Columbia River,* edited by Edgar I. Stewart and Jane R. Stewart (Norman: University of Oklahoma Press, 1957);

Martha Dula, "Audience Response to *A Tour on the Prairies in 1835,*" *Western American Literature,* 8 (1973): 67–74;

M. H. Dunlop, *Sixty Miles from Contentment: Traveling the Nineteenth-Century American Interior* (New York: Basic Books, 1995);

Hugh Egan, "The Second-Hand Wilderness: History and Art in Irving's *Astoria,*" *American Transcendental Quarterly,* 2 (1988): 253–270;

Henry Leavitt Ellsworth, *Washington Irving on the Prairie or A Narrative of a Tour of the Southwest in the Year 1832,* edited by Stanley T. Williams and Barbara D. Simison (New York: American Book Company, 1937);

Wayne Franklin, "The Misadventures of Irving's Bonneville: Trapping and Being Trapped in the Rocky Mountains," in *The Westering Experience in American Literature: Bicentennial Essays,* edited by Merrill Lewis and L. L. Lee (Bellingham: Bureau for Faculty Research, Western Washington University, 1977), pp. 122–128;

Hans Galinsky, "Exploring the 'Exploration Report' and Its Image of the Overseas World: Spanish, French, and English Variants of a Common Form Type in Early American Literature," *Early American Literature,* 12 (1977): 5–24;

Emilio Goggio, "Washington Irving and Italy," *Romanic Review,* 21 (1930): 25–33;

Bruce Greenfield, "Washington Irving: Historian of American Discovery," in his *Narrating Discovery: The American Explorer in American Literature, 1790–1855* (New York: Columbia University Press, 1992), pp. 113–163;

Allen Guttmann, "Washington Irving and the Conservative Imagination," *American Literature,* 26 (1964): 165–173;

Judith G. Haig, "Washington Irving and the Romance of Travel: Is There an Itinerary in *Tales of a Traveller?,*" in *The Old and New World Romanticism of Washington Irving,* edited by Stanley Brodwin (New York: Greenwood Press, 1986), pp. 61–68;

William L. Hedges, *Washington Irving: An American Study, 1802–1832* (Baltimore: Johns Hopkins University Press, 1965);

Hedges, "Washington Irving: Nonsense, the Fat of the Land and the Dream of Indolence," in *The Chief Glory of Every People,* edited by Matthew J. Bruccoli (Carbondale: Southern Illinois University Press, 1973), pp. 141–160;

George S. Hellman, *Washington Irving Esquire: Ambassador at Large from the New World to the Old* (New York: Knopf, 1925);

John Joseph, "I-tinerary: the Romantic Travel Journal after Chateaubriand," *South Central Review,* 1 (1984): 38–51;

Joy S. Kasson, "Washington Irving: The Citadel Within," in her *Artistic Voyagers: Europe and the American Imagination in the Works of Irving, Allston, Cole, Cooper, and Hawthorne.* (Westport, Conn.: Greenwood Press, 1982), pp. 6–42;

Wayne R. Kime, "The Completeness of Washington Irving's *A Tour of the Prairies,*" *Western American Literature,* 8 (1973): 55–65;

Kime, "Washington Irving and The Empire of the West," *Western American Literature,* 5 (1971): 277–285;

Kris Lackey, "Eighteenth-Century Aesthetic Theory and the Nineteenth Century Traveler in Trans-Allegheny America," *American Studies,* 32 (1991): 33–48;

Allison Lockwood, *Passionate Pilgrims: The American Traveler in Great Britain, 1800–1914* (New York: Cornwall Books, 1981);

Thomas J. Lyon, "Washington Irving's Wilderness," *Western American Literature,* 1 (Fall 1966): 167–174;

Ahmend M. Metwalli, "Americans Abroad: The Popular Art of Travel Writing in the Nineteenth Century," in *America: Exploration and Travel,* edited by Steven E. Kagel (Bowling Green, Ohio: Bowling Green State University Popular Press, 1979), pp. 68–82;

Bruno Montfort, "Washington Irving et le pittoresque post-romantique," *Revue Française d'Études Américaines,* no. 42 (1989): 439–453;

Christopher Mulvey, *Transatlantic Manners: Social Patterns in Nineteenth-century Anglo-American Travel Literature* (New York: Cambridge University Press, 1990);

Andrew B. Myers, ed., *A Century of Commentary on the Works of Washington Irving, 1860–1974* (Tarrytown, N.Y.: Sleepy Hollow Restorations, 1976);

Myers, ed., *Washington Irving: A Tribute* (Tarrytown, N.Y.: Sleepy Hollow Restorations, 1972);

Vernon Louis Parrington, *The Romantic Revolution in America 1800–1860* (New York: Harcourt, Brace, 1927);

Thomas H. Pauly, "The Literary Sketch in Nineteenth Century America," *Texas Studies in Literature and Language,* 17 (1975): 489–503;

Henry A. Pochmann, "Irving's German Tour and Its Influence on His Tales," *PMLA,* 45 (1930): 1150–1187;

Pochmann, "Washington Irving: Amateur or Professional?," in *Essays on American Literature in Honor of Jay B. Hubbell,* edited by Clarence Gohdes (Durham: Duke University Press, 1967), pp. 63–76;

Walter A. Reichart, *Washington Irving and Germany* (Ann Arbor: University of Michigan Press, 1957);

Reichart, "Washington Irving's Reise durch Österreich," *Jahrbuch des Wiener Goethevereins,* 66 (1962): 120–126;

Donald A. Ringe, *The Pictorial Mode: Space and Time in the Art of Bryant, Irving and Cooper* (Lexington: University of Kentucky Press, 1971);

Martin Roth, *Comedy in America: The Lost World of Washington Irving* (Port Washington, N.Y.: Kennikat Press, 1976);

Jeffrey Rubin-Dorsky, *Adrift in the Old World: The Psychological Pilgrimage of Washington Irving* (Chicago: University of Chicago Press, 1988);

Rubin-Dorsky, "*The Alhambra:* Washington Irving's House of Fiction," *Studies in American Fiction,* 11 (1983): 171–188;

Rubin-Dorsky, "Washington Irving and the Genesis of the Fictional Sketch," *Early American Literature,* 21 (1986–1987): 226–247;

J. A. Russell, "Irving: Recorder of Indian Life," *Journal of American History,* 25 (1931): 185–195;

William C. Spengemann, *The Adventurous Muse: The Poetics of American Fiction, 1789–1900* (New Haven: Yale University Press, 1977);

Robert E. Spiller, *The American in England in the First Half Century of Independence* (New York: Henry Holt, 1926);

William W. Stowe, *Going Abroad: European Travel in Nineteenth-century American Culture* (Princeton: Princeton University Press, 1994);

Cushing Strout, *The American Image of the Old World* (New York: Harper & Row, 1963);

Robert Thacker, *The Great Prairie Fact and the Literary Imagination* (Albuquerque: University of New Mexico Press, 1989);

Edgeley W. Todd, "Washington Irving Discovers the Frontier," *Western Humanities Review,* 11 (1957): 29–39;

James W. Tuttleton, ed., *Washington Irving: The Critical Reaction* (New York: AMS Press, 1993);

Francis H. Underwood, "Washington Irving and Scotland," *Blackwood's Edinburgh Magazine,* 266 (1949): 257–263;

James W. Webb, "Irving and His 'Favorite Author,'" *Mississippi Studies in English,* 3 (1962): 61–74;

Stanley T. Williams, *The Spanish Background of American Literature,* 2 volumes (New Haven: Yale University Press, 1955);

Nathalia Wright, "The Influence of Their Travels on the Writers of the American Renaissance," *Emerson Society Quarterly,* 42 (1966): 12–17;

Wright, "Irving's Use of His Italian Experiences in *Tales of a Traveller:* The Beginning of an American Tradition," *American Literature,* 31 (1959): 191–196;

Wright, "The Untrammeled Life," in *American Novelists in Italy* (Philadelphia: University of Pennsylvania Press, 1965), pp. 34–114;

Waldemar Zacharasiewicz, "Skizzen eines Reisenden: Bemarkungen zu einem bestimmenden Thema in Werk Washington Irving," in *Essays in Honor of Professor Tyrus Hillway,* edited by Erwin A. Stürzl (Salzburg: Salzburg Studies in English Literature, 1977), pp. 296–325.

Papers:

The New York Public Library holds the most substantial collection of Irving's papers. Other collections include Historic Hudson Valley, the Carl H. Pforzheimer Library, the Huntington Library, and the university libraries of Virginia, Columbia, Yale, and Harvard. See H. L. Kleinfield, "A Census of Washington Irving Manuscripts," *Bulletin of the New York Public Library,* 68 (1964): 13–32.

Thomas Jefferson
(13 April 1743 – 4 July 1826)

Bryan F. Le Beau
Creighton University

See also the Jefferson entry in *DLB 31: American Colonial Writers, 1735–1781.*

BOOKS: *A Summary View of the Rights of British America* . . . (Williamsburg, Va.: Printed for Clementina Rind / London: Printed for G. Kearsly, 1774);

Notes on the State of Virginia . . . (Paris: Privately printed, 1785; London: J. Stockdale, 1787; Philadelphia: Printed & sold by Pritchard & Hall, 1788);

A Manual of Parliamentary Practice For Use in the Senate of the United States (Washington, D.C.: Published by Joseph Milligan, 1812);

The Autobiography of Thomas Jefferson, in volume 1 of *Memoirs, Correspondence and Miscellanies from the Papers of Thomas Jefferson,* 4 volumes, edited by Thomas Jefferson Randolph (Charlottesville, Va.: F. Carr, 1829); republished as *Memoirs, Correspondence and Private Papers of Thomas Jefferson* (London: Colburn & Bentley, 1829);

An Essay Towards Facilitating Instruction in the Anglo Saxon and Modern Dialects of the English Language . . . (New York: Printed by J. F. Trow for the Trustees of the University of Virginia, 1851);

The Life and Morals of Jesus of Nazareth [English text only] (Saint Louis, Chicago & New York: N. D. Thompson, 1902); [Greek, Latin, French, and English texts] (Washington, D.C.: U.S. Government Printing Office, 1904);

The Commonplace Book of Thomas Jefferson, edited by Gilbert Chinard (Baltimore: Johns Hopkins University Press / Paris: Presses Universitaires de France, 1926);

The Literary Bible of Thomas Jefferson: His Commonplace Book of Philosophers and Poets, edited by Chinard (Baltimore: Johns Hopkins University Press / Paris: Presses Universitaires de France, 1928);

Thomas Jefferson's Garden Book, 1766–1824, edited by Edwin Morris Betts (Philadelphia: American Philosophical Society, 1944);

Thomas Jefferson's Farm Book, edited by Betts (Princeton: Princeton University Press, 1953).

Thomas Jefferson, portrait by Rembrandt Peale, 1805 (The New York Historical Society, New York City; gift of Thomas J. Bryan)

Editions and Collections: *The Writings of Thomas Jefferson,* edited by Henry A. Washington, 9 volumes (Washington, D.C.: Taylor & Maury, 1853–1854);

The Writings of Thomas Jefferson, edited by Andrew A. Lipscomb and Albert Ellery Bergh, 20 volumes (Washington, D.C.: Thomas Jefferson Memorial Association, 1903–1904);

The Works of Thomas Jefferson, edited by Paul Leiscester Ford, 12 volumes (New York: Putnam, 1904–1905);

Autobiography, edited by Ford (New York: Putnam, 1914);

The Declaration of Independence, edited by Julian P. Boyd, revised edition (Princeton: Princeton University Press, 1945);

The Papers of Thomas Jefferson, first series, edited by Boyd and others, 20 volumes (Princeton: Princeton University Press, 1953–1982); second series, edited by Charles T. Cullen and others, 1 volume to date (Princeton: Princeton University Press, 1983–   );

Notes on the State of Virginia, edited by William Peden (Chapel Hill: University of North Carolina Press, 1954);

Thomas Jefferson: Writings, edited by Merrill D. Peterson (New York: Library of America, 1984).

Thomas Jefferson traveled abroad only once, from 1784 to 1789, and during his lifetime he never published any of the voluminous letters, papers, and notes he compiled while abroad. If he had, they would have rivaled the best travel literature of the day for both their wealth of information and perceptiveness. Jefferson went to Europe on government business, but at that he was only modestly successful. His travels, though, provided him with knowledge of France and other European countries second to none among his American contemporaries; lent substance to his already pronounced affection for France; positioned him for a much valued perspective on the two key historical events of the decade, the American Constitutional Convention and the French Revolution; and underscored his conviction that the future of the world belonged to the United States, not Europe.

Jefferson was born in what is now Albemarle County, Virginia, on 13 April 1743. He was the first son, the third of ten children, of Peter Jefferson, a surveyor, landowner, and magistrate, and Jane Randolph, a member of the most prominent family of Virginia. He was given a classical education through private tutoring and then attended the College of William and Mary, where he studied law. When he turned twenty-one, Jefferson inherited 2,750 acres from the estate of his father, who had died in 1757. He began a successful law practice following his admission to the bar in 1767, and two years later he designed and began building his home, Monticello, atop a mountain on part of his father's original landholdings. He would tinker with the design of his home throughout his life.

Jefferson married Martha Wayles Skelton on New Year's Day 1772. The couple's first child, Martha (called Patsy), was born later that year on 27 September. She would be Jefferson's only child to outlive him. Just one of the couple's five other children, Mary (called Maria or Polly), who was born on 1 August 1778, lived to adulthood. In 1773 Jefferson inherited 11,000 acres and 135 slaves from his father-in-law, but he also incurred enormous debts with which he would struggle for the rest of his life. In 1782 the death of his wife, who had been in poor health since the birth of her sixth child, affected Jefferson deeply. Despite his private troubles, Jefferson excelled in public life. Before he departed for Europe the forty-one-year-old Jefferson had served in the Virginia legislature, in the Continental Congress, and as Virginia's governor and had authored the Declaration of Independence. Upon his return to the United States he served successively as secretary of state, vice president, and president.

On 7 May 1784 Congress appointed Jefferson to a two-year term as Minister Plenipotentiary. His task was to collaborate with John Adams, then in The Hague, and Benjamin Franklin, in Paris, in negotiating as many treaties of amity and commerce with European nations as possible. From Boston Jefferson sailed with his daughter Martha for England on 5 July, leaving his two younger daughters behind (Mary would join him in 1787). The crossing took only nineteen days and, as young Martha reported in a 24 August 1785 letter to Elizabeth House Trist, was unusually pleasant: "We had a lovely passage in a beautiful new ship, that had made but one passage before. There were only six passengers, all of whom Papa knew, and a fine sunshine all the way, with a sea which was as calm as a river." Jefferson made his way to France on 31 July.

Of all the world's capitals Paris fascinated Jefferson most. Several times larger than Philadelphia, the largest American city, graced by some of the world's most beautiful boulevards, parks, palaces, and rivers, and inhabited by many of the most influential artists and thinkers of the day, Paris offered the cultivated Jefferson a veritable cornucopia of opportunities. To an extent he never anticipated, however, it also bore witness to the grinding poverty, debilitating social inequality, and political tyranny of a nation on the verge of revolution.

Jefferson often found official duties trying even when, as was the case in Paris, they were not demanding. This continued to be true after Franklin retired in the spring of 1785 and Jefferson succeeded him as minister to France. Jefferson was concerned with freeing American commerce from the myriad of restrictions placed upon it by the nations of Europe. Britain in particular excluded America from many of its lucrative ports, especially in the West Indies. The United States had signed treaties of amity and commerce with France in 1778, the Netherlands in 1782, and Sweden in 1783, but provisions therein were limited, and nearly three-quarters of the newly independent nation's exports continued to go to England, a situation Jefferson considered unhealthy. Jefferson concluded a

Jefferson's residence (left, front) on the Champs-Elysées in Paris from 1785 to 1789; engraving by François Nicolas Martinet (1779)

treaty with Prussia in 1785 and expanded various commercial agreements with France and the Netherlands, but he accomplished little else.

Jefferson initially took apartments near the Palais Royal and in the Rue des Petits Augustins, but he soon moved to a house at the corner of the Grande Route des Champs Élysées and the Rue Neuve de Berry. Jefferson placed his daughter in a convent, the Abbaye Royale de Panthémont, which had been recommended by one of the Marquis de Lafayette's "lady friends" as the best and most genteel school in Paris, whether or not one was Roman Catholic.

At first Jefferson's social life revolved around his American colleagues Franklin and Adams, but within a matter of months Lafayette and Franklin presented Jefferson to the highest circles of Parisian society. Lafayette introduced him to the Duc de la Rochefoucauld and the Marquis de Condorcet. Through Franklin he met the Contesse d'Houdetot and visited the salon of Madame Helvetius at Auteuil. Thereafter, according to Merrill Peterson, "the cup of [Jefferson's] happiness gradually filled, not with work only, but with the infinitely varied pleasures of mind and spirit."

It was in this polite society that Jefferson fell in love again. In 1786 he had a brief, apparently uncon-summated affair with Maria Cosway, a twenty-seven-year-old painter of miniatures whose husband, Richard Cosway, also painted miniatures. Although she was an Englishwoman, Cosway had lived on the Continent for most of her life, and Jefferson probably met her in a Paris salon. As Jefferson was quite reticent on the subject, little is known of their relationship, which cooled when Cosway, after only a few months, returned to England. For a time, though, Jefferson was uncharacteristically overcome with emotion. He sent Cosway a poignant Wertherian dialogue titled "My Head and My Heart" in October 1786. His opening lines read: "Having performed the last sad office of handling you into your carriage . . . and seen the wheels get actually into motion, I turned on my heel and walked, more dead than alive. . . . Oh, my friend," he continued, "I am rent into fragments by the force of my grief!"

As a product of the Enlightenment, Jefferson was committed to the promotion of what was good and useful for mankind. Even before he left America, Jefferson was knowledgeable in painting, literature, music, sculpture, and architecture. For a lover of fine art and literature such as Jefferson, Europe was a paradise, and he took full advantage of the cultural opportunities to evolve, in George Shackelford's words,

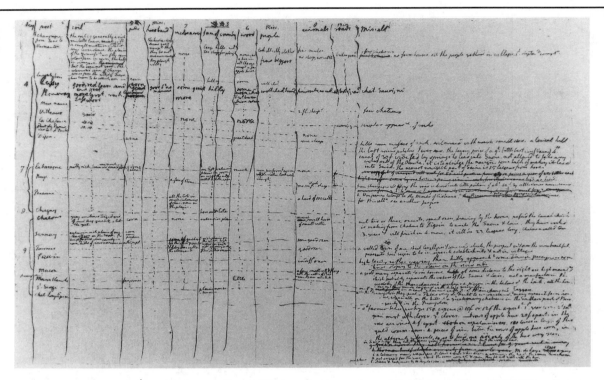

Page from Jefferson's notes on his journey through Champagne, Burgundy, and Beaujolais in June 1887 (Massachusetts Historical Society)

from "talented provincial to traveled sophisticate." For example, in architecture, which he considered the most important of the fine arts, Jefferson had developed a stylistic preference for symmetry and formality. He had studied the sixteenth-century Italian architect Andrea Palladio and much admired the Palace of Versailles. After a few years in Europe, however, he found that style too grand, and he began to favor simpler designs. As Shackelford explains, Jefferson came to prefer the less ornate style that flourished during the reign of Louis XVI to that of Louis XIV, the work of the contemporary French architect Charles Louis Clérisseau, who aided Jefferson with his design of the Virginia state capitol, to that of Palladio. He expanded his cultural vision, and he returned to the United States as a connoisseur and patron of the arts.

Nevertheless, as important as the arts were to Jefferson personally, he did not believe they should be the new nation's first priority, and most of his observations concern what he called "science," which might more accurately be called technology. Upon his arrival in Europe, Jefferson was disappointed with the science he found, initially concluding that contrary to what he expected, France lagged behind the United States. Although he would later revise his assessment, Jefferson's failure to appreciate the more advanced French scientific community was in part owing to his lack of understanding of its more theoretical concerns and also a reflection of his preference for "things useful."

Although he purchased and sent back to the United States many of the latest European scientific publications—including the two dozen or so volumes in print of *Encyclopédie Méthodique*—Jefferson spent much of his time gathering an extensive collection and creating detailed records of the many useful items he observed. Because he thought it undesirable and also believed that circumstances rendered it unlikely that the United States would become a manufacturing nation in the near future, Jefferson made relatively few comments on manufacturing. Instead, he made notes on bridges, boats, canal locks, phosphoric matches, hot-air balloons, a newly invented cylinder lamp which burned olive oil, and a wide range of agricultural products.

In March 1786 Jefferson visited England to aid John Adams, who had been reassigned to that country, in negotiating a treaty with the minister of Tripoli. The negotiations failed, but Jefferson took advantage of his visit to sample British hospitality, society, and culture, little of which impressed him. His visit began on a sour note when he was snubbed at court by George III. "On my presentation," he wrote in a 28 March 1786 letter to William Short, "it was impossible for anything to be more ungracious than their [the

King and Queen's] notice of Mr. Adams and myself. I saw at once that the ulcerations in the narrow mind of that mulish being left nothing to be expected on the subject of my attendance." He nevertheless resolved to tour the countryside.

Since the days of the American Revolution, Jefferson had developed a distaste for England, but he did manage to find much in the country to admire. He concluded that the British monarchy did not oppress its people to the degree that the French monarchy did. He commented favorably on the nation's mechanical arts and its gardens, which were less formal than their French counterparts. Jefferson was impressed by gristmills, thermometers, protractors, globe telescopes, solar microscopes, hydrometers, harpsichords, and portable copying presses. He visited sixteen English gardens, including those at Chiswick, Hampton Court, Stowe, and Blenheim, before returning to Paris on 3 May.

In March of the following year Jefferson took leave of his responsibilities in Paris to tour southern France and northern Italy for three months. In part, he wanted a break from his diplomatic duties as well as seeking the regenerative and reinvigorating powers of the warmer climate, but he also wished to learn what those regions had to offer. The journey was one of the highlights of his European stay, and his notebook observations run to fifty-four printed pages.

Although he was clearly taken by the region's architecture, painting, sculpture, and antiquities, he devoted most of his comments to its agricultural products. Passing through Burgundy, Jefferson made the first of his extensive observations on the wine industry. All along his route he visited vineyards and made notes on the processes involved. In the end, however, he did not commend the industry to his countrymen. He concluded that it was not the best use to which the land might be put, and that it seemed to be the "parent of misery," because those who cultivated the vine in France were always poor.

In Beaujolais Jefferson was struck by Michael Angelo Slodtz's classic sculpture "Diana and Endymion" (1740). As he continued on his travels, he was even more taken by the Roman antiquities he saw. At Nîmes, for example, Jefferson visited the Maison Carrée, which he and Clérisseau had used as a model for the Virginia state capitol in Richmond, thereby providing a major impetus for the classical revival in the United States. When actually in the presence of the Roman artifact, Jefferson was even more impressed by its grandeur. On 20 March 1787 he wrote to his Parisian friend Madame de Tesse: "Here I am, Madam, gazing whole hours at the Maison Quarrée, like a lover at his mistress."

Reports of his aesthetic delights notwithstanding, Jefferson reported to John Jay on 4 May 1787 that his principal reason for visiting Nîmes was to speak to a Brazilian living in the area who had written to him the previous autumn about the possibilities of revolution in that South American country, a colony of Portugal. Jefferson told this unnamed Brazilian that the United States was not in any position to get involved in any way, and, moreover, that it was interested in cultivating the friendship of Portugal for commercial reasons.

Arriving at Aix on 25 March, Jefferson bathed for four days in its famed waters in an unsuccessful attempt to ease the pain of a dislocated wrist. He found Provence beautiful and commented favorably on the softness of the region's language, as compared to Parisian French, but his main interest was in Marseilles and the status of American commerce. His inquiry led him to conclude that the extent of American shipping in area ports was entirely unsatisfactory, largely because of the disruptive actions of Algerine pirates.

Jefferson had found that two varieties of rice were sold in France—Carolina rice from America and Piedmont rice from the border area of Italy, France, and Switzerland—and that the latter was preferred because its grains were less broken. The common assumption was that the European rice was superior because of a better husking machine. When Jefferson was unable to find out anything about this technology while he was in Marseilles, he decided to travel to see an actual husking machine in the Piedmont, only to find that the rice named for the region was actually cultivated and husked in Lombardy. Thus, Jefferson came to celebrate his forty-fourth birthday on muleback crossing the Alps to Italy, a trip he found enchanting.

En route from Marseilles to Italy Jefferson visited Toulon, where he sampled capers; Hyères, where he made notes on an orange grove; and Nice, where he studied olive and fig trees. In Turin Jefferson favorably reviewed in his notes a new wine, the "red wine of Nebiule," but his first order of business in Lombardy remained the region's rice. Finally being able to observe the husking process, Jefferson realized that the difference between Carolina and Piedmont rice was not in its husking, as the American and Italian machines were quite similar, but in the rice. He then hired a muleteer to smuggle samples of the unprocessed rice out of Italy.

Jefferson proceeded to Milan and its vicinity, where he visited Lake Como and the celebrated church of Certosa. Similarly, he saw the cathedral at Milan and other Italian churches and concluded that they were perfect examples of the misuse of money. Jefferson had little use for Gothic architecture and believed—perhaps in an anticlerical vein—that such churches resulted more in economic oppression than spiritual elevation.

Although tempted to venture further into Italy, duty beckoned, and Jefferson left Milan for Paris. He made stops at Genoa, Marseilles, and Nîmes, and he traveled along the Languedoc Canal, a plan of which he purchased in Marseilles, to Toulouse. Jefferson stopped in Bordeaux, where he inquired into the wines of the region, as well as its Roman ruins. He explored Brittany as far east as L'Orient, where he investigated opportunities for the importation of American fish oil, but from there he returned directly to Paris.

Jefferson valued little the results of the official business he conducted during his trip. Of more importance to him were his agricultural observations. He was proud of solving the riddle of Piedmont rice and also wrote enthusiastically of shipping olive trees to the United States. Of all God's gifts to man, he explained in a 30 July 1787 letter to William Drayton olives were the second most precious, bread being the first. Upon his return to America he resolved to begin the cultivation of olives. Although he succeeded in having about five hundred trees planted in South Carolina and Georgia, he went to his grave seeing little more accomplished.

In March 1788 Jefferson left Paris for a seven-week trip to the Low Countries and western Germany, a route seldom taken by Americans but that had been recommended to Jefferson by the American artist John Trumbull. Jefferson stopped in The Hague, where he and Adams, who had been recalled and was preparing to depart for home, engaged in diplomacy. When his business was completed, Jefferson moved on to Amsterdam, Utrecht, and points east. As he had all along, Jefferson made notes of what he observed, including a drop-leaf table, diamond-shaped house joists, wind sawmills, Dutch wheelbarrows, a machine that drew boats over a dam, two drawbridges, and a hexagonal lantern. Jefferson took a two-week trip up the Rhine to Strassburg, where he proclaimed the cathedral steeple the highest and handsomest in the world. He returned to Paris via Alsace, Lorraine, and Champaigne, which he declared the most picturesque leg of his journey.

As was his habit Jefferson spent more of his time making notes on practical matters than on aesthetic concerns. He declared Düsseldorf's art gallery sublime but saw no need to describe it, while he wrote at length about the hogs of Westphalia. He bought maps of all the important towns he encountered and described their commerce. He tasted Rhône and Moselle wines; he saw for the first time the rudiments of central heating; and he made note of a folding ladder he would later replicate for Monticello. Jefferson found

the Dutch pleasantly prosperous but the Prussian people poor, and, because he believed they shared the same soil and climate, he attributed the difference to their respective governments, the Dutch government seeming comparatively free and responsible when compared to the Prussian administration.

Jefferson returned in late April 1787 to Paris, his point of observation for the U.S. Constitutional Convention and the first stages of the French Revolution. Neither event changed to any considerable extent Jefferson's political philosophy, but they did force him to apply and adjust it. Later, during his presidency, Jefferson's political opponents would use his initial unfavorable comments on the Constitution against him and negatively exaggerate his role in the French Revolution.

If Jefferson had not been in France, he would have been in Philadelphia among the fifty-five men who drafted the U.S. Constitution, but in Paris he was relegated to the role of interested outside observer. In preparation for the Constitutional Convention, Jefferson shipped nearly two hundred books to Madison, but given the distance involved and the rudimentary lines of communication, he could do little else. As was the case with many Americans in 1787, Jefferson was ambivalent about adopting a new constitution. After spending most of his years abroad attempting to secure treaties of commerce with nations convinced that the sovereignty of the states would undermine the authority of the American Confederation Congress to either conclude or enforce such agreements, he had come to favor Federalist reform. At the same time his living in France had made him more than ever committed to republican government. He wrote to George Washington on 2 May 1788 that as a result of his years spent in Europe, he had become ten thousand times more the enemy of monarchy than he had ever been. He believed that there was scarcely an evil in Europe that could not be traced to that institution and, similarly, scarcely any good that could not be derived from its "small fibres of republicanism."

Perhaps because of his distance from the event, Jefferson was far less alarmed by Shay's Rebellion (1785–1786)—an uprising led by Daniel Shay in which impoverished farmers in Massachusetts prevented the courts from sitting—than were men such as Washington and Madison. He stood virtually alone among American leaders in minimizing the dangers of the disturbance. When Jefferson first received reports of the rebellion, he was embarrassed, for he had placed his faith for the future of the new republic in just such independent farmers, and their actions served to confirm reports circulating in Europe of American disorder. His regret concerning its effect on opinion abroad soon gave way to some enthusiasm for the idea of re-

A 9 October 1787 letter to the Comte de Moustier, in which Jefferson characterizes the relationships of the United States to France and England (private collection)

belliousness. He sent what were to become his best-known comments on the subject to Abigail Adams and to William S. Smith. To Adams he wrote on 22 February 1787 that "the spirit of resistance to government is so valuable on certain occasions, that I wish it to be always kept alive. It will often be exercised when wrong, but better so than not to be exercised at all. I like a little rebellion now and then. It is like a storm in the atmosphere." In his 13 November letter to Smith he was even more sanguine: "God forbid that we should ever be twenty years without such a rebellion. . . . What signify a few lives lost in a century or two? The tree of liberty must be refreshed from time to time with the blood of patriots and tyrants. It is its natural manure."

Jefferson had not been certain that a new constitution, instead of an amended Articles of Confederation, was necessary, but he found much in the new document that he liked. He was critical, however, of its lack of a bill of rights, which he insisted in a 20 December 1787 letter to Madison "is what the people are entitled to against every government on earth, general or particular, and what no just government should refuse, or rest on inferences." But once he received assurances that a bill of rights would be added, he favored ratification.

As was appropriate for someone with official diplomatic status, Jefferson actually played no direct role in the French Revolution. But that is not to suggest that he was unsympathetic, or that he did not let his sentiments be known. Horrified by the plight of France's poor, Jefferson blamed their poverty on the concentration of property in the hands of the few and on the absolute monarchy and privileged aristocracy that perpetuated the situation. Nevertheless, he did not see either the immediate radical redistribution of property or toppling the French monarchy as practical solutions. He realized that, although its goals and accomplishments could set the tone for political reform, the American revolutionary model was not immediately useful for the French. Every society, he came to believe, begins at a different point and must follow its own path to liberty. To the French he recommended as a short-term model the British constitutional monarchy.

Jefferson was pleased with the pace of reform in France in 1787, but thereafter it moved more rapidly than he expected or welcomed. In 1788 he applauded Louis XVI's call for the assembly of the Estates General for the next year. In a 9 August letter to James Monroe he concluded that it was probable that within two or three years France would enjoy a "tolerably free constitution" without loss of a drop of blood. When the Estates General reached no compromise with the king, Jefferson grew alarmed and blamed the king for his support of a hereditary aristocracy. On 17 June 1789 those pressing for radical reforms defied the king and proclaimed themselves the National Assembly.

During the summer of 1789 Lafayette and other members of the National Assembly were charged with preparing a bill of rights and sought Jefferson's advice, sending him three consecutive drafts for his comments. Jefferson made note that he offered some advice on wording, but in the absence of any detailed records it is difficult to say exactly how much of the final formulation of the Declaration of the Rights of Man can be attributed to Jefferson.

While Jefferson took little pleasure in the storming of the Bastille and the humiliation of Louis XVI, he was consoled by the king's apparent submission to the call for a new constitution. Once again Jefferson was consulted as the chairman of the National Assembly's Constitutional Committee wrote seeking his advice. Jefferson offered the committee sincere best wishes, but, as ambassador, he declined to respond.

When the committee reached an impasse, however, Lafayette once again sought Jefferson's advice. Lafayette requested and received permission from Jefferson to bring a small group from the Constitutional Committee to dinner. After dinner the group spent some six hours discussing the proposed constitution, but there is no record of what, if any, contributions Jefferson offered. In his notes Jefferson simply remarks that he was a sympathetic but silent observer.

Jefferson left France before the worst excesses of the French Revolution occurred. He was able to depart believing it represented a victory of reason over ignorance, superstition, and hereditary privilege. The revolution marked the adoption by the French of principles that might be called American—which Jefferson had played no small role in formulating—but to him it was not a triumph of American ideology. Instead, Jefferson saw the popular revolt as signaling the recognition of eternal truths that would thereafter be realized throughout Europe.

In addition to his duties Jefferson took it upon himself while abroad to correct erroneous reports and impressions of the United States. Jefferson found newspapers, especially English ones, most egregious and blatant in their misrepresentations, but over them he had little influence. Instead, he focused on French books and literary journals, few of which were actually hostile, but several of which were misinformed. Notable among his efforts was his extensive rewriting of Jean-Nicolas Démeunier's long article, "États Unis," for the *Encyclopédie Méthodique*.

Jefferson began *Notes on the State of Virginia* (1785), the only book he published, in response to a request from the secretary of the French legation,

Passports issued to Jefferson during the French Revolution by Louis XVI and by Lafayette
(Library of Congress TJ Papers, 52:8824,8863; Library of Congress)

François de Barbé-Marbois, for information on the state. He completed this treatise on the rivers and mountains, flora and fauna, and laws and institutions of his country in 1781. Jefferson's book was first published in 1785 in a private printing of some two hundred copies; the first publication for the public was made in 1787.

A modern reader might see *Notes on the State of Virginia* as a glorified guidebook, but the eighteenth-century reader regarded it as a work of natural and civil history. It was the product of both patriotic and scientific impulses, which are evident in Jefferson's response to European theories of New World degeneracy. The Comte de Buffon, perhaps the greatest naturalist of his time, had written in *Histoire naturelle* (1749) that the New World exhibited fewer and smaller species than the Old; that the American environment was inferior to that of Europe, in its being cooler, wetter, and newer (in geologic time); and that in this abandoned condition, "everything languishes, corrupts, and proves abortive." Abbé Raynal reached the same conclusion in *Histoire philosophique et politque des éstablissements et du commerce des Européens dans les deux Indes* (1770) concerning Native Americans and Europeans

living in America. Jefferson counters such charges point by point. In response to Raynal's further criticism that the United States was yet to produce a great poet, an able mathematician, or a man of genius in any art or science, Jefferson asserts that the country is young and has a small population when compared to European nations. He also cites such figures as Washington and Franklin as men of genius.

Beginning in early 1788, Jefferson asked Congress for a five- or six-month leave from his duties to return to Virginia to tend to personal affairs and to take his daughters home. (Patsy had recently expressed interest in joining the convent at which she was a student, perhaps persuading Jefferson that it was time to take her back to Protestant, republican Virginia.) It was only with the inauguration of Washington, however, that he received permission. On 26 September 1789, amidst at least eighty-six cases and containers of books, works of art, and various sample species of plants and animals, Jefferson left Paris. He departed from Le Havre, France, on 8 October, cleared Yarmouth on 22 October, and arrived at Norfolk, Virginia, on 23 November.

Jefferson, then forty-six, fully intended to return to France within a matter of months, if only for a brief time, after which he planned to retire to his beloved Monticello. Upon his arrival, though, he learned that the president had nominated him to be the nation's first secretary of state. Jefferson would never leave the United States again.

Jefferson apparently never came to a settled opinion on whether travel abroad would serve to corrupt Americans or lead them to value their country even more. But in *The Autobiography of Thomas Jefferson* (1829) he recalled his years in France with great fondness:

> A more benevolent people, I have never known, nor greater warmth and devotedness in their select friendships. Their kindness and accommodation to strangers is unparalleled, and the hospitality of Paris beyond anything I had conceived to be practicable in a large city.

Jefferson praised the "politeness of their general manner" and "the ease and vivacity of their conversation," all of which gave "a charm to their society to be found nowhere else." And, he concluded, if he were to be asked in what country other than his own he would prefer to live, it would be France.

Letters:

Gilbert Chinard, *Jefferson et les Ideologues, d'après sa correspondance inedité avec Destutt de Tracy Cabanis J.-B. Say et Auguste Comte* (Baltimore: Johns Hopkins University Press / Paris: Presses Universitaires de France, 1925);

The Letters of Lafayette and Jefferson, edited by Chinard (Baltimore: Johns Hopkins University Press / Paris: "Les Belles Lettres," 1929);

The Correspondence of Jefferson and Du Pont de Nemours, edited by Chinard (Baltimore: Johns Hopkins University Press / Paris: "Les Belles Lettres," 1931);

The Adams-Jefferson Letters, 2 volumes, edited by Lester J. Cappon (Chapel Hill: University of North Carolina Press, 1959);

The Family Letters of Thomas Jefferson, edited by Edwin Morris Betts and James Adams Bear Jr. (Columbia: University of Missouri Press, 1966);

The Republic of Letters: The Correspondence between Thomas Jefferson and James Madison, 1776–1826, 3 volumes, edited by James Morton Smith (New York: Norton, 1995).

Bibliographies:

E. Millicent Sowerby, *Catalogue of the Library of Thomas Jefferson,* 5 volumes (Washington, D.C.: Library of Congress, 1952–1959);

William B. O'Neal, *Jefferson's Fine Arts Library: His Selections for the University of Virginia Together with His Own Architectural Books* (Charlottesville: University Press of Virginia, 1976);

Eugene L. Huddleston, *Thomas Jefferson: A Reference Guide* (Boston: Hall, 1982);

Frank Shuffleton, *Thomas Jefferson, 1981–1990: An Annotated Bibliography* (New York: Garland, 1992).

Biographies:

George Tucker, *The Life of Thomas Jefferson,* 2 volumes (Philadelphia: Carey, Lea & Blanchard, 1837);

Henry S. Randall, *The Life of Thomas Jefferson,* 3 volumes (New York: Derby & Jackson, 1858);

Sarah N. Randolph, *The Domestic Life of Thomas Jefferson* (New York: Harper, 1871);

Gilbert Chinard, *Thomas Jefferson: The Apostle of Americanism* (Boston: Little, Brown, 1929; revised 1939);

Dumas Malone, *Jefferson and His Times,* 6 volumes (Boston: Little, Brown, 1948–1981);

Merrill D. Peterson, *Thomas Jefferson and the New Nation: A Biography* (New York: Oxford University Press, 1970);

Fawn Brodie, *Thomas Jefferson: An Intimate History* (New York: Norton, 1974);

Virginius Dabney, *The Jefferson Scandals: A Rebuttal* (New York: Dodd, Mead, 1981);

Joseph J. Ellis, *American Sphinx: The Character of Thomas Jefferson* (New York: Knopf, 1997).

References:

William Howard Adams, *The Eye of Thomas Jefferson* (Washington, D.C.: National Gallery of Art, 1976);

Marie Kimball, *Jefferson: The Scene of Europe, 1784–1789* (New York: Coward-McCann, 1950);

Howard C. Rice Jr., *Thomas Jefferson's Paris* (Princeton: Princeton University Press, 1926);

George G. Shackelford, *Thomas Jefferson's Travels in Europe, 1784–1789* (Baltimore: Johns Hopkins University Press, 1995).

Papers:

Major collections of Jefferson's papers are held at the Library of Congress, the Massachusetts Historical Society, the University of Virginia, the Missouri Historical Society, and the Henry E. Huntington Library.

George Jones

(30 July 1800 – 22 January 1870)

James A. Wren
Niigata University

BOOKS: *Sketches of Naval Life with Notices of Men, Manners and Scenery on the Shores of the Mediterranean in a Series of Letters from the* Brandywine *and* Constitution *Frigates,* 2 volumes, as "A Civilian" (New Haven: Howe, 1829);

Excursions to Cairo, Jerusalem, Damascus, and Balbec from the United States Ship Delaware, *during Her Recent Cruise: With an Attempt to Discriminate between Truth and Error in Regard to the Sacred Places of the Holy City* (New York: Van Nostrand & Dwight, 1836);

United States Japan Expedition: Observations on the Zodiacal Light, from April 2, 1853, to April 22, 1855, Made Chiefly on Board the United States Steam-Frigate Mississippi, *during Her Late Cruise in Eastern Seas, and Her Voyage Homeward. With Conclusions from the Data Obtained,* volume 3 of *Narrative of the Expedition of an American Squadron to the China Seas and Japan, Performed in the Years 1852, 1853, and 1854, under the Command of Commodore M. C. Perry, United States Navy, by Order of the Government of the United States. Compiled from the Original Notes and Journals of Commodore Perry and His Officers, at His Request and under His Supervision,* 3 volumes, edited by Francis L. Hawks (Washington, D.C.: Published by order of the Congress of the United States, A. O. P. Nicholson, printer, 1856);

Life-Scenes from the Four Gospels (New York: Pratt, 1865);

Life-Scenes from the Old Testament (Philadelphia: Garrigues, 1868).

From 1851 to 1856 the Reverend George Jones accompanied Commodore Matthew C. Perry on the American expedition to open isolationist Japan to foreign trade. Although he is self-effacing in his report on the mission, his participation contributed in no small measure to its success.

Jones was born on a farm near York, Pennsylvania, on 30 July 1800 to Robert and Elizabeth Dunnman Jones. After graduating from Yale College in 1823, he taught for two years at a school he organized in Washington, D.C. The call of the sea proved too strong to resist, and in 1825 he became secretary to Commodore Charles Morris, commander of the U.S. Navy frigate *Brandywine*. He also taught navigation to the midshipmen aboard the ship. After transporting the Revolutionary War hero Marquis de Lafayette home to France from a visit to the United States, the *Brandywine* sailed to the Mediterranean. There Jones transferred to another frigate, the *Constitution*. At the end of his commission in 1828 he returned to Yale as a tutor, publishing *Sketches of Naval Life with Notices of Men, Manners and Scenery on the Shores of the Mediterranean in a Series of Letters from the* Brandywine *and* Constitution *Frigates* in 1829.

In 1830 Jones was ordained and made rector of the Episcopal Church in Middletown, Connecticut. After a year he resigned and took an outdoor job in Indiana for health reasons. In 1832 he became acting chaplain aboard the frigate *United States,* the flagship of the Mediterranean Squadron. He was commissioned chaplain on 20 April 1833 and transferred to the *Delaware* in March 1834. In February 1836 he became chaplain at the Norfolk Navy Yard in Virginia. He published an account of his second voyage to the Mediterranean as *Excursions to Cairo, Jerusalem, Damascus, and Balbec from the United States Ship* Delaware, *during Her Recent Cruise: With an Attempt to Discriminate between Truth and Error in Regard to the Sacred Places of the Holy City* (1836). In correspondence with naval officers, a meeting with the secretary of the navy, and an article in the *Naval Magazine* (May 1836) he agitated for the establishment of a naval school. In 1837 he married Mary Amelia Sullivan. From 1840 to 1845 he served as chaplain aboard the frigates *Macedonian, Columbus, Constitution,* and *Brandywine.* In September 1845 he became head of the English department at the United States Naval School in Annapolis, Maryland, which had recently been established partly in response to his urgings. The school was reorganized as the United

George Jones as portrayed by a Japanese observer

States Naval Academy in October 1850, and in February 1851 Jones became its first chaplain.

In March 1852 President Millard Fillmore ordered Commodore Perry to negotiate a commercial treaty with Japan. On 24 November the *Mississippi* departed from Norfolk; at Perry's invitation, Jones was on board as chaplain. A fleet of five ships was assembled along the way. The voyage proved to be most arduous, and it fell largely to Jones to hold the crew of the *Mississippi* together during times of difficulty.

Arriving in Shanghai on 4 May 1853, the expedition was met by a state of political unrest—although American expatriates in the area, sensing the economic utility of having a U.S. man-of-war in port, may have exaggerated the danger of their situation. Torn between his commitment to his mission and his duty to protect American interests, Perry instructed the *Plymouth* to remain behind to assist the foreign community should the crisis escalate. After recovering from an outbreak of dysentery, the rest of the squadron departed Shanghai on 17 May, anchoring at Napha (present-day Naha, Okinawa) in the Lew Chew Islands on 26 May. The following morning two groups were assigned to explore the coast of the main island; a third group, including Jones, went into the interior to collect specimens of animals, minerals, and vegetables. Jones functioned as the expedition's naturalist; much of what was learned about the Okinawan interior resulted from his observations. A week of grueling investigations ended with the presentation of gifts, including handkerchiefs of Canton silk from Jones, to an elderly Lew Chew statesman who had assisted them in their endeavors—and, most likely, was spying on them for the shogun.

After establishing relations with the southern islands the squadron reached Uraga, a small city on the west side of Yedo Bay (present-day Tokyo Bay), on 8 July. As the four huge black ships—two of them steam powered—arrived, the Japanese draped the coastline in banners; the Americans never learned whether the banners were intended to conceal the interior from the foreigners' gaze or to give the im-

UNITED STATES JAPAN EXPEDITION.

OBSERVATIONS

ON

THE ZODIACAL LIGHT,

FROM

APRIL 2, 1853, TO APRIL 22, 1855,

MADE CHIEFLY ON BOARD

THE UNITED STATES STEAM-FRIGATE MISSISSIPPI,

DURING HER LATE CRUISE IN EASTERN SEAS, AND HER VOYAGE HOMEWARD:

WITH

CONCLUSIONS FROM THE DATA THUS OBTAINED;

BY

REV. GEORGE JONES, A. M.,

CHAPLAIN UNITED STATES NAVY.

"Je ne comprends pas par quel sort un objet [la Lumière Zodiacale], qui touche de si près l'astronomie moderne et la physique céleste, a été négligé jusqu'à ce point par les astronomes et par les auteurs météorologiques."—MAIRAN.

VOLUME III.

WASHINGTON:
BEVERLEY TUCKER, SENATE PRINTER.
1856.

Facsimile title page for Jones's account of his voyage to Japan, published as volume three of Matthew Perry's Narrative of the Expedition of an American Squadron to the China Seas and Japan

pression that troops were hidden behind them. In a last-minute attempt to avert an invasion by the "barbarians" the Japanese delivered a document in French ordering the ships to depart. Perry convinced the shogun that resistance would be futile, and an official reception was held on 12 July. When Perry's request to speak directly with the emperor was denied, he asked that a letter from President Fillmore be forwarded to the emperor. With three hundred American servicemen, in full ceremonial regalia, in attendance, the shogun took delivery of the letter, encased in a gold-inscribed rosewood box, on 14 July. The letter explained that the purpose of the American visit was to secure "friendship, commerce, a supply of coal and provisions, and protection for our shipwrecked people." The squadron departed from Yedo Bay three days later, after Perry informed the shogun of his intention to return the following spring for the emperor's positive response. "With all of these ships?" inquired the interpreter. "Probably with more," Perry replied.

The squadron returned to Napha on 25 July. There the commodore told the Lew Chew government that if he did not receive satisfactory responses to his demands by noon the following day he would land two hundred men, march to Shui, and occupy the palace. Several concessions were thus obtained from the Okinawans, and the squadron departed from Napha for Hong Kong on 1 August. On 20 January 1854 Perry returned to Napha aboard the *Susquehanna* and was informed that the Japanese emperor had died shortly after reading the president's letter. The success of the mission was thrown into doubt by this setback, but the commodore—fortified by inspirational words from his chaplain—remained resolute. At the end of February, Perry ordered the fleet to the coastal village of Yoku-hama (the present-day city of Yokohama). On 9 March, Jones led a funeral prossession ashore to lay the body of a sailor to rest at what would become the landmark Foreign Cemetery. The solemn tone of the ceremony and its dual meaning, commemorating the emperor's death as well as that of the sailor, were not wasted on the large crowd of Japanese who had gathered out of curiosity.

The Japanese-American Friendship and Trade Treaty was signed on 21 March. Written in English, Japanese, Dutch, and Chinese, the treaty granted to the United States trading rights in the ports of Hakodate and Shimoda and provided for the establishment of an American consulate in the latter city. On 11 July, Perry signed a compact between the United States and the Kingdom of Lew Chew with essentially the same provisions as the treaty with Japan. The fleet left Napha on 17 July; it stopped at Kelung, Formosa (present-day Taiwan), where a party led by Jones undertook a search for coal. The ships reached the Brooklyn Navy Yard on 23 April 1855. The following day, with all crew members present, the commodore lowered the American flag, officially bringing the mission to an end.

Perry ordered Jones to remain in New York to help in preparing the official report of the expedition. *Narrative of the Expedition of an American Squadron to the China Seas and Japan, Performed in the Years 1852, 1853, and 1854, under the Command of Commodore M. C. Perry, United States Navy, by Order of the Government of the United States. Compiled from the Original Notes and Journals of Commodore Perry and His Officers, at His Request and under His Supervision*, edited by Francis L. Hawks, was printed in three volumes in 1856. Jones was the author of the third volume, the 705-page *Observations on the Zodiacal Light, from April 2, 1853, to April 22, 1855, Made Chiefly on Board the United States Steam-Frigate* Mississippi, *during Her Late Cruise in Eastern Seas, and Her Voyage Homeward. With Conclusions from the Data Obtained*. A commercial edition of the report, published by D. Appleton and Company of New York and London, appeared in 1857; it comprised only the material in the first volume of the government edition.

After completing the report Jones was granted a one-year leave of absence from the navy; he spent seven months of it in Quito, Ecuador, making further observations of the zodiacal light. He returned to his post of chaplain at the Naval Academy in the spring of 1857. After a brief term of service on the U.S.S. *Minnesota* in the Atlantic, he retired from the navy in July 1862. During the Civil War he served on a volunteer basis in military hospitals in Washington, D.C., and Annapolis, at times as a chaplain but much more frequently as a nurse. After the war he wrote two more books, *Life-Scenes from the Four Gospels* (1865) and *Life-Scenes from the Old Testament* (1868). He died in Philadelphia, where he was serving as chaplain of the United States Naval Asylum, on 22 January 1870.

References:

William Heine, *With Perry to Japan: A Memoir*, translated by Frederic Trautmann (Honolulu: University of Hawaii Press, 1990);

Edward Yorke McCauley, *With Perry in Japan: The Diary of Edward Yorke McCauley*, edited by Allan B. Cole (Princeton: Princeton University Press, 1942);

Katherine Plummer, *The Shogun's Reluctant Ambassadors: Sea Drifters* (Tokyo: Lotus Press, 1985);

Arthur Walworth, *Black Ships off Japan* (Hamden, Conn.: Archon, 1966).

Meriwether Lewis
(18 August 1774 – 11 October 1809)

and

William Clark
(1 August 1770 – 1 September 1838)

Rob J. Brault
University of Minnesota

BOOKS: *History of the Expedition under the Command of Captains Lewis and Clark, to the Sources of the Missouri, thence Across the Rocky Mountains and down the River Columbia to the Pacific Ocean. Performed during the years 1804–5–6. By Order of the Government of the United States,* 2 volumes, by Nicholas Biddle, edited by Paul Allen (Philadelphia: Bradford & Inskeep / New York: Abm. H. Inskeep, J. Maxwell, printer, 1814); published as *Travels to the Source of the Missouri River and Across the American Continent to the Pacific Ocean. Performed by Order of the Government of the United States, in the Years 1804, 1805, and 1806,* edited by Thomas Rees (London: Longman, Hurst, Rees, Orme & Brown, 1814);

The Original Journals of the Lewis and Clark Expedition, 1804–1806; Printed from the Original Manuscripts in the Library of the American Philosophical Society and by Direction of its Committee on Historical Documents, together with Manuscript Material of Lewis and Clark from Other Sources, including Note-Books, Letters, Maps, etc., and the Journals of Charles Floyd and Joseph Whitehouse, Now for the First Time Published in Full and Exactly as Written, 8 volumes, edited by Reuben Gold Thwaites (New York: Dodd, Mead, 1904–1905);

The Journals of Captain Meriwether Lewis and Sergeant John Ordway, Kept on the Expedition of Western Exploration, 1803–1806, edited by Milo M. Quaife (Madison, Wis.: The Society, 1916);

Westward with Dragoons; the Journal of William Clark on his Expedition to Establish Fort Osage, August 25 to September 22, 1808; a Description of the Wilderness, an Account of the Building of the Fort, Treaty-Making with the Osages and Clark's Return to St. Louis, edited by Kate L. Gregg (Fulton, Mo.: Ovid Bell, 1937).

Editions: *History of the Expedition under the Command of Lewis and Clark, to the Sources of the Missouri River, thence Across the Rocky Mountains and down the Columbia River to the Pacific Ocean, Performed during the years 1804–5–6, by Order of the Government of the United States,* 4 volumes, edited by Elliott Coues (New York: Harper, 1893);

Lewis and Clark in North Dakota; the Original Manuscript Journals and the Text of the Biddle Edition during the Time the Expedition Remained in North Dakota (Bismarck: State Historical Society of North Dakota, 1947–1948);

The Journals of Lewis and Clark, edited by Bernard De Voto (Boston: Houghton Mifflin, 1953);

The Lewis and Clark Expedition, facsimile of 1814 edition edited by Archibald Hanna (Philadelphia: Lippincott, 1961);

The Journals of the Lewis and Clark Expedition, 8 volumes, edited by Gary Moulton (Lincoln: University of Nebraska Press, 1983).

In 1803 the United States doubled in size as the result of the Louisiana Purchase. A year later the dominant movement in American society of the nineteenth century, westward expansion, originated with the men that President Thomas Jefferson sent out to explore the newly won territory, the famous expedition led by Meriwether Lewis and William Clark. Together the two men actively contributed to only one book, *History of the Expedition under the Command of Captains Lewis and Clark, to the Sources of the Missouri, thence Across the Rocky Mountains and down the River Columbia to the Pacific Ocean* (1814), which was published five years after Lewis's death. But there are few schoolchildren in the United States who have not heard some version of their story. The significance of their success in American his-

William Clark and Meriwether Lewis, portraits by Charles Willson Peale (Independence National Historical Park Collection, Philadelphia)

tory is undeniable. As Archibald Hanna states in his introduction to the 1961 edition, Lewis and Clark started "the westward procession, first of trappers, then of settlers, that was the really decisive factor in making Oregon American rather than British."

While a northwest water passage to the Pacific had been sought for more than three hundred years, there were still huge blank spaces in the maps of North America at the time of the expedition. There was no water route through the Spanish territory to the south, and Alexander Mackenzie's voyage from Lake Athabasca to the Pacific in 1792–1793 proved there was none to the north in Canada. If there was to be a Northwest Passage, it had to involve the Missouri, which flowed east from the mountains and into the Mississippi, and the Columbia, which flowed west out of the mountains and into the Pacific. Confident that the headwaters of the two rivers must be fairly close together since the Indians spoke of crossing between them, Jefferson commissioned a government-financed expedition to claim those headwaters. In his biography of Lewis that was published in the 1814 *History of the Expedition*, Jefferson urged the nation to recognize the explor-

er's "sufferings and successes, in endeavoring to extend for them the boundaries of science, and to present to their knowledge that vast and fertile country, which their sons are destined to fill with arts, with science, with freedom and happiness."

Meriwether Lewis was born on 18 August 1774 to William and Lucy Lewis, whose maiden name was Meriwether. The Lewises, who had four more children after Meriwether, lived in the prominent society of the Albemarle district of Virginia, near Charlottesville, and were near neighbors of the Jeffersons and the Madisons. William and his brother Charles both fought in the Revolutionary War, and his brother Nicholas served in a 1776 expedition against the Cherokees. After William, who served as a lieutenant at Yorktown, died of pneumonia in 1779 shortly after the battle, Nicholas became Meriwether's guardian.

From his guardian Lewis gained a hatred for the British, a desire to join the military, and a strong streak of self-reliance. The Albermarle district was a hunter's paradise, and when his mother remarried to Capt. John Marks, a wealthy landowner from northeastern Georgia, in 1780, Meriwether continued his outdoor pursuits in even rougher country. By the age of eight he was spending nights out alone hunting raccoon and opossum, and as a young teen he gained a reputation for having a cool head in a crisis. On one occasion he found himself facing a charge from an enraged bull. Instead of fleeing, he calmly aimed his flintlock rifle and dropped the animal with the single shot he had.

When he was about thirteen Lewis returned to Albemarle and with help from his Uncle Nicholas began managing his father's thousand-acre farm. Here he began his schooling in Latin, mathematics, and rudimentary science under local tutors. When his stepfather died in 1792, Meriwether brought his mother and the rest of his family home from Georgia and truly took over as head of the family.

While the life of a farmer was more interesting to Lewis than the life of a scholar, he jumped at the chance of adventure in 1794, joining the militia to suppress the Whiskey Rebellion. The action was over before he reached the field, but Lewis loved the military, and, when he was eligible for discharge, chose instead to be transferred to the regular army, becoming an ensign in May 1795. Serving under Gen. "Mad Anthony" Wayne, he saw the chiefs of several Indian nations sign the Treaty of Greenville on 3 August 1795, his first of many encounters with Indians.

That same year he was court-martialed on charges of insubordination and conduct unbecoming of an officer brought by a Lieutenant Eliott. According to Lewis's biographer Richard Dillon, he was "acquitted with honor," but General Wayne had him reassigned to the Chosen Rifle Company under the command of William Clark to ensure no further conflict. In their eight months together Clark and Lewis became good friends, but Clark resigned from the army on 1 July 1796 to aid in a family financial crisis involving his brother, Revolutionary War general George Rogers Clark.

By 1799 Lewis was serving on the Indian frontier at Detroit and was promoted to lieutenant. In December 1800 the twenty-three-year-old Lewis was promoted to captain and became the regimental paymaster. Then, in February 1801, Lewis's career took a turn into higher circles of power when he received, through his commanding officer, a letter from the new president, Thomas Jefferson, asking Lewis to serve as his secretary while retaining his military standing. According to Jefferson, Lewis had the requisite knowledge of the military and of the western regions of the country, and he knew from personal acquaintance that Lewis was the right man for the job. In 1802 Jefferson and Lewis began planning the western expedition the president had long

dreamed of, and the Corps of Discovery was born. As preparations were under way in 1803, Lewis wrote a letter asking William Clark to be his second in command for the upcoming expedition.

William Clark was born on 1 August 1770 to John and Ann Clark in Caroline County, Virginia. He was the ninth of ten children, and his five brothers, all older than he, served as officers in the Revolutionary War. Jonathan Clark, the eldest, was granted a gold medal by Gen. George Washington; George Rogers Clark gained fame for winning the Ohio Valley to the Revolutionary cause, and John Clark died from tuberculosis as a prisoner aboard a British ship. Like Lewis, William Clark developed a love for the military and a hatred of the British at an early age.

In 1784, when William was thirteen, the Clark family moved to Kentucky. Although all of his older brothers had been educated, the lack of formal schooling on the frontier required Clark to teach himself with his brothers' aid. While he distinguished himself as a diligent student of natural history, science, math, architecture, navigation, and land surveying, his language skills suffered greatly, and his writing was filled with spelling and grammatical errors. According to biographer Jerome Steffen, Clark claimed that "Learning does not consist in the knowledge of languages, but in the knowledge of things to which language gives names. Science and Philosophy."

In 1789 Clark finally got his chance to join the army and fight against the British when he signed up under Maj. John Hardin. He participated in the destruction of Indian villages along the Wabash River, whose warriors had been conspiring with the British to keep the Ohio Valley out of the control of the United States. In 1791 he became an acting lieutenant in Gen. Charles Scott's campaign north of the Ohio River. When the war against the Indians bogged down, Washington put Gen. "Mad Anthony" Wayne in charge, and Clark remained under his command for the rest of his military career. Serving as a fort engineer, an escort for supply trains, and on intelligence and diplomatic missions throughout the Ohio Valley campaigns, Clark gained a reputation as intrepid, resourceful, and responsible.

Although he did well in the military, Clark chafed under the interminable delays of military expeditions and what he regarded as his slow rate of promotion. He retired from the army to help his family deal with the tangled financial affairs of his elder brother, George Rogers Clark, whose personal expenses in fighting the Revolutionary War were disallowed by the state of Virginia in 1792, re-

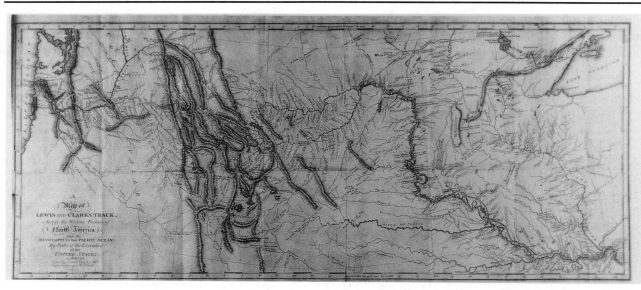

Map of Lewis and Clark's expedition route, included as the frontispiece in some copies of their History of the Expedition *(1814)*

sulting in massive debts and angry creditors who had provided military supplies. Thomas Jefferson, angered by such shabby treatment shown to a patriot, pushed for and gained him a grant of land in Indiana, but George Rogers Clark eventually gave his land to William to shield it from creditors. When their father, John Clark, died in 1799, the bulk of the estate went to William, again as a dodge to avoid creditors. On paper William Clark owned more than eighty thousand acres of land, but he viewed this legacy as a family responsibility and managed it with this burden in mind.

His Indian war experiences had convinced Clark of the power of commerce in diplomacy, and he felt that developing trade was a good way to help his country outside the military. In 1799 his brother George initiated a scheme to build a canal that would allow ships to avoid the falls on the Ohio River, but a spate of lawsuits engaged the attention of both brothers for years, and when the furor settled down, William spent much of 1800 and 1801 visiting Meriwether Lewis in Washington. He never did realize his business dreams, for on 19 June 1803 he received the letter from Lewis asking him to join the Corps of Discovery, an offer he eagerly accepted. For bureaucratic reasons he was recommissioned as a first lieutenant, but Lewis regarded him as an equal, and all of the company's men agreed and deferred to Captain Clark throughout the expedition.

Jefferson, a Democratic Republican who believed that the future of the United States lay to the west, faced opposition from the Federalists, who argued that adding new territories and states, espe-

cially such large ones, would pull the new, fragile republic apart. As early as 1783 Jefferson was sounding out George Rogers Clark about an expedition to explore the West. In 1786, while serving as ambassador to France, he met John Ledyard, who wanted to walk from Europe to North America's east coast by way of Siberia, the Bering Strait (presumably in a native's boat), and western North America. In 1789 Ledyard got as far as Kamchatka before Russian empress Catherine the Great decided to rescind her permission and had him arrested and expelled to Poland.

The frustrated Jefferson knew the British were expanding their trade westward through Canada and that no one then knew how far south Canada would extend. The race to find a northwest water route to the Pacific gained urgency in 1792, when American captain Robert Gray discovered the Columbia River while exploring the Pacific coast. In 1793 Jefferson commissioned André Michaux, a French botanist, to undertake the exploration, but Michaux was revealed as a spy, working with the French revolutionary minister to the U.S., Edmond-Charles-Édouard Genet, who was known as Citizen Genet, and an embarrassed Jefferson canceled the commission. In 1794 Mackenzie pioneered the overland route across the Canadian Rockies to the Pacific, and, while he failed to find a Northwest Passage, his recommendations to the British regarding the fur trade made the need for speed all the more obvious.

All of these exploration attempts were envisioned while the West nominally belonged to Spain, which was relatively weak, and Jefferson had little difficulty gaining permission for a "scientific" expedition. This changed in 1800 with the Treaty of San Ildefonso, which gave the Louisiana Territory and the Caribbean island of Santo Domingo to France. France already owned New Orleans, which gave it de facto control of traffic up the Mississippi, the only practical link between the eastern states and the new states west of the Appalachian Mountains, a stretch of wilderness at least one hundred miles wide that required weeks of arduous travel.

Napoleon Bonaparte had designs on a French empire in North America, but in 1802 the French needed troops for their renewed war with Great Britain and abandoned their eleven-year campaign in Hispaniola as their losses to yellow fever, more than to rebel activities, continued to mount. To end the French threat Jefferson wanted to buy New Orleans and send Lewis up the Missouri, since international law agreed that whoever claimed the headwaters of a river deserved free access for the river's entire length. In January 1803 Jefferson asked Congress for a secret expedition whose ostensible purpose was to renew the trading agreements with the Indians but whose true goals included claiming the Oregon Territory through a link between the Missouri and the Columbia Rivers and winning Indian support of American interests.

In April 1803 Napoleon, seeking to cut his losses in North America, instructed his minister, Charles-Maurice de Talleyrand Périgord, who was negotiating the sale of New Orleans, to offer the entire territory for sale while it was still France's to sell. American ambassador Robert Livingston, unable to consult with his superiors, gambled on the purchase and made what has been called the sweetest real estate deal in history: nearly a million square miles for $15 million. Although the Lewis expedition was already outfitting and preparing, the new political situation dramatically altered its legal status, and on 20 June Jefferson issued his official instructions to Captain Lewis.

Jefferson's instructions, which he reproduced in his biography of Lewis, were lengthy, explicit, and demanding. His first priority was discovering a water route to the Pacific, and the expedition was to note the latitude and longitude of "durable" landmarks for later navigators. Of particular importance was the portage between the headwaters of the two known rivers. Jefferson requested several copies of all maps and specified that one of these should be on birchbark so as to be waterproof. All of this information was to be forwarded to the war office upon Lewis's return, perhaps because this office had the best cartographers or perhaps because Jefferson anticipated British counterclaims to the vast western territories.

In addition to mapping the water route Lewis was to learn as much as possible about the people he met for the sake of future commerce. Jefferson wanted to know about their names, territories, relationships with other peoples, language, culture, agriculture, ways of waging war, modes of hunting or fishing, food, diseases, possible trade goods, religious beliefs, morals, and any "peculiarities" of their laws and customs. These exhaustive ethnographies would eventually aid commerce with the Indians and "those who may endeavor to civilize and instruct them." Lewis and his men were to act as ambassadors, foster peace between the tribes, and to invite their chiefs to visit Washington at the government's expense. Jefferson also suggested that Lewis take some kinepox and teach the Indians how to use it against smallpox.

On top of all this, Jefferson wanted other information regarding the soil, vegetation, animals, mineral deposits, "volcanic appearances," climate, and the seasonal appearances of plants, animals, and insects. In addition to mapping his own route, Lewis was to gather information about other branches of the Missouri and the Columbia and any other rivers that might prove navigable. In particular Jefferson wanted to learn about the northern source of the Mississippi and its position relative to the Lake of the Woods, as well as the disposition of any Canadian traders.

Since no one knew quite what to expect from the Indians or from other governments with interests in North America, Jefferson explicitly left it up to Lewis to decide if the trip must be abandoned, since they might well meet with superior hostile forces. Jefferson wanted to learn about the fur trade in particular, and whether the trade now traveling by sea around the Cape of Good Hope or Cape Horn might be redirected to a land route through the United States. He provided generous letters of credit (which proved useless) and left it up to Lewis whether to return all or part of the company by sea or to return along their land route, making corrections to their maps along the way.

Lewis and Clark chose their men deliberately. Although the expedition required military status and discipline, simply being a good soldier was not enough, and they sought men who could withstand the rigors of such a long and arduous journey. In the winter of 1803–1804 the selected men trained for the mission at Fort Massac, their camp upstream from Saint Louis in Illinois. The company consisted of nine young men from Kentucky, handpicked by Lewis and Clark and sworn into the army as pri-

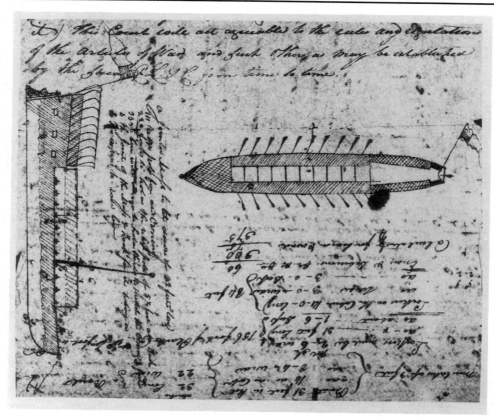

Clark's sketches of the expedition keelboat, circa 21 January 1804 (Field Notes [Dubois Journal], document 7, Frederick W. and Carrie S. Beinecke Collection of Western Americana, Yale University)

vates; fourteen regular army privates, three of whom were promoted to sergeant; Clark's black servant (actually a slave), York; Lewis's dog, a Newfoundland named Scammon; and two woodsmen, or, as Lewis called them, "French watermen," who would serve as hunters and interpreters. One of these was George Drouillard, or Drewer as he was called, a half French Canadian, half Shawnee whose hunting skills would prove invaluable. The other was Toussaint Chaboneau, whose best claim to fame was his Shoshone wife, Sacajawea, the only woman on the expedition, who proved invaluable as a liaison with other Indians. For the first leg of the voyage up the Missouri, Lewis and Clark also took a corporal, six privates, and nine French engagés hired as boatmen, interpreters, and hunters. These men went as far as Fort Mandan, and then returned to Saint Louis when the expedition started up portions of the Missouri that were still unknown to western cartographers.

Considering the length and difficulty of the whole expedition, it is remarkable that there were only two defections and one death. Two men—an engagé named La Liberté and a Private Reed—deserted early on. While Reed was captured, dismissed from the army, and sent back to Saint Louis, La Liberté was never seen again. The only casualty was Sgt. Charles Floyd, who died on 20 August 1804 of a "bilious cholic," probably appendicitis. In the official account Lewis and Clark note that Floyd "died with a composure" that displayed his "firmness and good conduct." While hunters and scouts continually left the main party, sometimes disappearing for days longer than expected, the company somehow managed to keep all of its members alive and together until 15 August 1806, when John Colter requested and received early dismissal so he could embark on a trapping venture rather than return to Saint Louis.

Throughout the voyage Lewis and Clark praised the skill, the strength, the endurance, and especially the morale of their company, as again and again the men's fortitude under arduous conditions was tested. Swarms of mosquitoes were often so thick as to preclude sleep, and once were so bad that Lewis's dog was reduced to howling and the men were coughing and spitting out the insects that entered their throats while they breathed. When it rained the men slept in the water, or, if it became too deep, had to spend the night upright. On at least one occasion they were pelted to the ground by hail-stones. One night on a hunting trip, Clark spent the night out in temperatures that reached 10° below zero with only a blanket and a few buffalo hides. When a campsite on the coast was overrun by the tide and high winds, the company spent the night struggling to protect the boats and all their cargo from being destroyed in the waves. Most of their route was covered by boat, and they experienced many mishaps. Half of their river travel, of course, was upstream, and they had to haul boats up rapids with towlines made of elk skin. When their route in the mountain plains was thickly covered with prickly pear cactus, Clark once pulled seventeen spines from his feet when he finally quit walking. They also faced snow-covered, exposed trails where one slip meant a fall over a precipice. On the return trip especially they suffered from exhaustion and hunger. They were threatened by wild animals, including grizzlies, and sometimes by unfriendly Indians. And yet the captains maintained that the party always pushed on uncomplainingly and "with great cheerfulness."

The Corps of Discovery left Saint Louis on 21 May 1804, proceeding up the lower Missouri River on a fifty-five-foot keelboat powered by twenty-two oars and two smaller open boats, or *periogues,* of six and seven oars. From the first Lewis and Clark never forgot what they were supposed to be learning. Trade was uppermost in their minds, and, in addition to mapping the route carefully, they noted locations for future trading establishments and the forts necessary to protect them. The land around modern-day Council Bluffs, Iowa, was "exceedingly favourable for a fort and trading factory, as the soil is well calculated for bricks, and there is an abundance of wood in the neighbourhood." The text rarely sounds like typical nature writing, for while Lewis and Clark often refer to a scene as "beautiful," their descriptions were often prosaic, if not downright mercantile: "Our camp is in a beautiful plain, with timber thinly scattered for three quarters of a mile, and consisting chiefly of elm, cottonwood, some ash of an indifferent quality, and a considerable amount of a small species of white oak."

While the expedition would succeed only because of the aid of various Indian tribes, tensions sometimes arose between the whites and Indians throughout the trip. The first serious threat of violence came along the Missouri in late September among the Teton Sioux, who, dissatisfied with the gifts of the explorers, attempted to keep their boats from departing by sitting on the mooring lines. When Clark threatened the displeasure of "our great father, who could in a moment exterminate

them," the chief of the Sioux said that he also had warriors, and in a moment Clark, who had drawn his sword, was surrounded by Sioux warriors who "drew arrows from their quivers and were bending their bows, when the swivel in the boat was instantly pointed towards them, and twelve of our most determined men jumped into the periogue and joined captain Clarke." The standoff ended when the Sioux chief called on his warriors to withdraw, and the party was able to continue.

Since Lewis and Clark faced the challenge of leading their expedition into territory that no one had explored and written about, they were always in need of good guides—many of them, since no one person or group of people had ever made the entire trip. No white people knew the land beyond the Missouri's bend to the west in present-day North Dakota, and the Indians who served as guides only knew relatively small portions of the party's route. The captains' desperation for information is shown by the tidbits they gathered on other rivers from the traders and trappers they met as they traveled up the familiar reaches of the Missouri: on 12 June 1804 a Mr. Durion, who had spent twenty years among the Sioux, gave them a description of the Little Sioux River; on 2 October a Mr. Valle told them of the Cheyenne River under the Black Mountains; and on 3 November a "Canadian Frenchman" who had been down the Little Missouri shared what he knew.

Some passages in the journals are lyrical in their celebration of natural beauty. One sight that had nothing to do with exploration or the thrill of the "first white man" trope was the aurora borealis, the northern lights, a spectacle that many have attempted to describe and few so successfully:

> After glittering for some time its colours would be overcast, and almost obscured, but again it would burst out with renewed beauty; the uniform colour was pale light, but its shapes were various and fantastic: at times the sky was lined with light coloured streaks rising perpendicularly from the horizon, and gradually expanding into a body of light in which we could trace the floating columns sometimes advancing, sometimes retreating and shaping into infinite forms, the space in which they moved.

Like the Romantics, Lewis and Clark described cliffs in terms of architecture, especially in images of ancient ruins:

> In trickling down the cliffs, the water has worn the soft sandstone into a thousand grotesque figures, among which with a little fancy may be discerned elegant ranges of freestone buildings, with columns variously sculptured, and supporting long and elegant galleries,

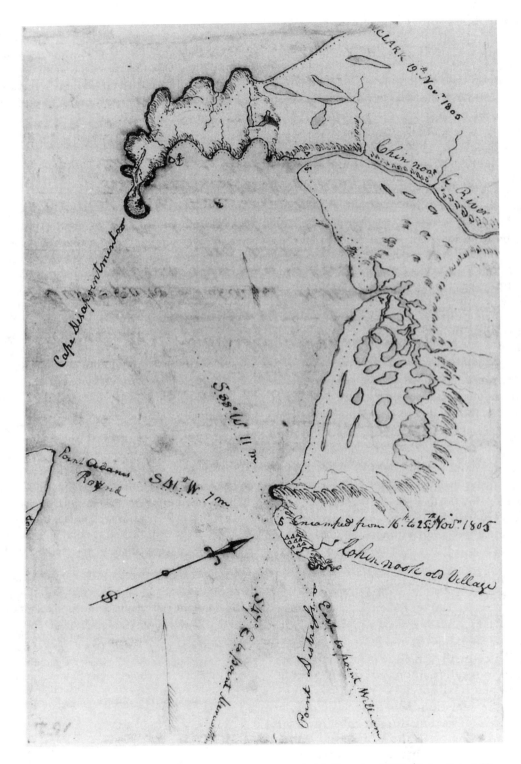

Clark's map of the mouth of the Columbia River, circa 16–25 November 1805 (Codex I, p. 152;
American Philosophical Society, Philadelphia)

while the parapets are adorned with statuary: on a nearer approach they represent every form of elegant ruins; columns, some with pedestals and capitals entire, others mutilated and prostrate, and some rising pyramidally over each other till they terminate in a sharp point. These are varied by niches, alcoves, and the customary appearances of desolated magnificence. . . . As we advance there seems no end to the visionary enchantment which surrounds us.

But unlike the Romantics, they went on to describe the stones' composition (earth, sand, and quartz) and structure ("almost invariably regular parallelipeds of unequal sizes"). While joy and excitement are sometimes revealed, the overall tone is official, as befitted the text that contained the most valuable item Lewis and Clark brought back from their travels: knowledge of the American West.

By the end of October they were looking for a good spot to spend the winter among the Mandans in what is now North Dakota. By mid November Fort Mandan was completed, and the company spent the winter of 1804–1805 in councils with the Indians, from whom they were able to procure corn by trading blacksmith work, and in meetings with British-backed traders in the area. Jefferson had been concerned about trade competition from the British, and he had reason to be. The company labored to show their regard to the Mandans, who compared them to the generous British traders from the north. When Chaboneau went out to visit with the Minnetarees, he heard that the North West Company agents, who ran a trading establishment only 150 miles away on the Assiniboine River, were circulating rumors disparaging the Americans and intended to build a fort among the Mandans. One of these traders, a Mr. Laroche, even asked to join the expedition west, but the captains refused, for obvious reasons. On 11 February 1805 Sacajawea gave birth to a son who would accompany them for the rest of the expedition. On 7 April the company left Fort Mandan in six canoes and the two periogues, sending the keelboat back to Saint Louis. By mid April they were entering territory never before seen by white people, and their dependence on information from the Indians became acute.

The captains took their duties as natural historians seriously. Early in their travels when the party heard of an animal that the French traders and trapper called the "petit chien"–the prairie dog–they went to work to obtain a specimen, pouring barrels of water down one burrow and attempting to dig up one of the animals with shovels. Eventually they caught one, which they described as resembling a small dog, but with some resemblance to a squirrel. Later, in his description of a rattlesnake, Lewis

counted "one hundred and seventy-six scuta [scales] on the belly, and seventeen on the tail" after listing its general dimensions and coloration. With a scientist's love for quantifiable data, Lewis measured the leaps of a hare species at eighteen to twenty-one feet.

The animal that received the most attention in the text was initially called the "white" bear, even though it was yellowish brown in color. This bear was clearly different from the familiar black bear in anatomical details such as overall size, position and placement of the testes, and the size of its teeth and claws, but the difference that most impressed Lewis and Clark was its ferocity. While black bears consistently fled humans, the grizzly bear of the plains was more likely to attack than to flee. One bear took ten bullets, five of these through the lungs, yet swam to a sandbar more than halfway across the Missouri and survived twenty minutes before dropping. It weighed between five hundred and six hundred pounds, was eight feet seven inches long, five feet ten inches around its breast, and had claws, or "talons," four and three-eighths inches long.

In another encounter, a bear that had been shot through the lungs chased its hunter for half a mile, then ran back on its trail for another mile, dug a trench two feet deep and five feet long, and survived another two hours. After this the company only hunted bear in large groups, but even a party of six had its hands full. Four hunters once fired on a bear at a range of forty paces; all four bullets hit and two of them passed through the lungs. When the bear charged its attackers, the two hunters who had reserved their fire shot; one bullet broke the bear's shoulder. This still did not stop the charging bear: the hunters scattered and each frantically reloaded and fired whenever the bear was chasing someone else, but additional bullets only enraged the bear and directed its attention toward the latest to fire. Two men, trapped and unable to reload, were sprinting toward the river with the bear only a few feet behind when another hunter finally managed to bring the bear down with a bullet to the head. With the difficulty of making a killing shot, owing to the structure and density of the bear's skull and the animal's tremendous vitality even when mortally wounded, the men decided such formidable prey was not worth the risk of hunting. There were many situations, however, when an aggressive grizzly forced the issue.

During their return voyage Lewis and Clark interviewed the Chopunnish about the relationship between the different bears they had encountered. The Chopunnish distinguished between the "hohhost" and the smaller "yackkah" on the basis of the

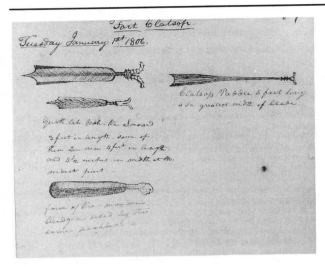

Lewis's sketch of two swords, a bludgeon, and a paddle, 1 January 1806 (Codex J, p. 1; American Philosophical Society, Philadelphia)

same size and temperament differences that Lewis and Clark had noted, regardless of color. While later zoologists would agree with the Chopunnish regarding the black bear and the brown, or grizzly, bear, Lewis and Clark decided there were three species, with a smaller black and reddish brown bear that was smaller than the "white or grizly," but clearly not the common black bear of both coasts, which they said was uniformly black.

In addition to detailing new species, Lewis and Clark counted the numbers of familiar and economically important animals such as the beaver, and noted how its home and dam building created new islands and widened riverbeds that might someday be crucial for the water routes of the fur trade. In the case of the buffalo that would feed so many settlers and was the foundation of the economy and culture of so many Indian nations, Lewis and Clark were astonished at their numbers. At one point during their return trip down tèe Missouri a herd that was fording the river was so long that neither end of the line was in sight when they came around a bend and so thick that the party had to wait for an hour to let the buffalo finish the crossing.

The Missouri, which at first glance would seem the easiest part of their voyage, became an ever more challenging river of shifting sandbars and collapsing banks. One night the guard awakened them all with the news that the sandbar on which they had camped was sinking. The river was carving it away, and the company barely loaded their gear into the boats and pulled away before the bank under which they had kept the boats collapsed. By the time they reached shore the sandbar was com-

pletely gone. Through it all, they pressed onward. When Lewis and a small party were wading down part of the Missouri, they had to carve footholds in the bank with their knives, and the journal complains that they "made only eighteen miles." Almost any daily mileage total less than twenty occasioned an apology, and days spent traveling downstream might cover more than eighty miles.

One day while Clark was scouting with Chaboneau, Sacajawea, and their son, they were nearly caught in a flash flood:

> Captain Clarke fortunately saw it a moment before it reached them, and springing up with his gun and shot-pouch in his left hand, with his right he clambered up the steep bluff, pushing on the Indian woman with her child in her arms; her husband too had seized her hand, and was pulling her up the hill, but he was so terrified at the danger that but for captain Clarke, himself and his wife and child would have been lost. So instantaneous was the rise of the water, that before captain Clarke had reached his gun and began to ascend the bank, the water was up to his waist, and he could scarce get up faster than it rose, till it reached the height of fifteen feet with a furious current, which had they waited a moment longer would have swept them into the river just above the great falls, down which they must inevitable have been precipitated . . . the Indian woman had just time to grasp her child, before the net in which it lay at her feet was carried down the current.

Aboard the boats, deft handling by the men was crucial in order to avoid disaster. The near capsize of a canoe on the Missouri near the Yellowstone (not far from the present-day border between North Dakota and Montana) in May 1805 almost finished the expedition before it ever reached the mountains, as it contained all of the instruments, medicines, and papers that had been generated on the trip. In the whitewater of the mountains, one of the men was thrown from a canoe, which then passed over him. If the water level had been two inches lower, he would have been crushed, but he escaped with a bruised leg. During their return voyage, the party lost a canoe on the Columbia and a raft with the last of their food and trade goods while crossing a mountain stream, and they were reduced to cutting the buttons from their clothes for trade.

The need for guides became more acute as the party followed the Missouri west into present-day Montana. Their first real crisis came in early June 1805 when they had to decide which of two large channels represented the true Missouri. The right choice would take them into the mountains and bring them close to the suspected source of the Columbia, which the Plains Indians had heard about but had never seen. Indian descriptions had not mentioned the river that appeared to head off to the north, which most resembled the lower Missouri in color, the southern branch being much clearer. After six days of scouting both branches and realizing that direction alone could not determine their choice since they could not see the course of either branch for a sufficient distance, Lewis and Clark decided that the colors indicated that the southern branch was more likely to be their desired route, as it probably flowed down out of the mountains, while the muddier north branch probably flowed through more open country and would not lead them to the mountainous source of the Columbia. The rest of the company favored the northern branch, since it was larger and looked more like the river they were on. They also argued that the Indians surely would have mentioned such a dramatic change in the river's appearance.

The captains were hesitant to impose their will by pulling rank, but on 9 June they did just that, arguing that the north branch was probably not worth mentioning in the Indians' view and that the direction of the south branch was more likely to fit their description, using the sunset as a reference point, of the location of a great waterfall on the Missouri. For five anxious days Lewis and Clark hoped they were not leading their men up a pointless creek they would have to retrace and worried about morale. Then on 14 June Lewis found the great waterfall that matched the Indians' description, right down to the position of a huge eagle's nest.

The description of that famous archetype from Romantic literature, the waterfall, begins with an elevated sentiment—"sublime spectacle . . . this stupendous object which since creation had been lavishing its magnificence upon the desert, unknown to civilization"—but these few lines are followed by pages of precise dimensions: "gathering strength from its confined channel, which is only two hundred and eighty yards wide, [the water] rushes over the fall to the depth of eighty-seven feet and three quarters of an inch." The most important descriptions of all for official purposes were of their position: "The latitude of our camp below the entrance of Portage creek, was found to be 47° 7' 10" 3, as deduced from meridian altitude of the sun's lower limb taken with octant by back observation giving 53° 10'." Descriptions of the grand views from bluffs or mountaintops become exercises in triangulation, with mountains described by their directions and positions as compass headings measured in degrees from the observer's position: "the direction of the first [mountain] chain was from south 20° east to north 20° west; of the second, from south 45° east to north 45° west." Clearly, Lewis and Clark viewed the mountains with a cartographer's eye and saw the "durable" landmarks that Jefferson had desired.

Making progress often meant improvising the means of pushing forward and enduring disappointments. The company managed to portage their equipment and supplies around the falls on wagons whose wheels they cut from a cottonwood tree twenty-two inches in diameter and whose axles were made from the mast of one of the periogues. Despite frequent breakdowns they reached the Missouri above the falls. They then spent the rest of June and part of July trying to make a skin cover, using twenty-eight elk skins and four buffalo skins, for an iron boat frame that Lewis had designed and built. They caulked the seams with a mixture of charcoal, beeswax, and tallow, but the stuff would not adhere to the elk skin and the frame was abandoned. Since water often damaged their equipment, the men came up with an ingenious way to protect their gunpowder on rivers and in caches; they made hollow canisters for the powder from the lead they would eventually melt down for bullets. Some difficulties could not be anticipated, however, as when a group of men driving a herd of ponies purchased from the Indians toward one of the rendezvous points discovered that the ponies were so used to hunting buffalo that they would take off after any that they saw. To keep their horses together, the men had to ride out ahead and drive any buffalo from the party's path.

In mid July they gave up on the skin boat and settled for two canoes, twenty-five and thirty feet long, carved out of cottonwood, which proved as brittle and fragile as the cottonwood wheels. On 15 July they were back on the river but soon were having to choose between several branches of the upper Missouri. By 18 July they were worried and expressed their need to meet some Shoshones or Snakes to gain necessary information about the rivers. On 22 July Sacajawea, who as a young girl had been captured from her Shoshone tribe by the Mandan and later sold to Chaboneau, began recognizing some of the country from her childhood. From 25 July to 6 August the company explored the three upper branches of the Missouri, and on 7 August they decided that the middle branch, which they named the Jefferson River, would take them near the source of the Columbia.

By 9 August Lewis and Clark realized that they needed guidance to find a practical route through the mountains to the Columbia River and anxiously searched for a Shoshone Indian to show them the way. By 11 August the party knew that Shoshones were in the area but were avoiding them, probably out of fear of their being a raiding party. One Indian in particular allowed Lewis, who was

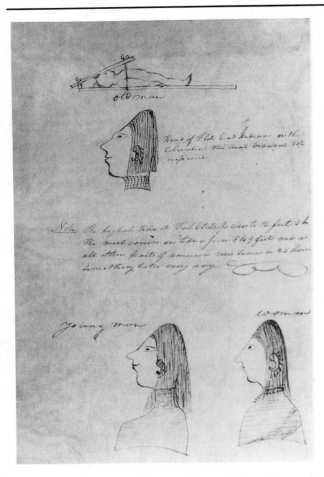

Clark's drawings of flat-head Indians, circa 30 January 1806
(Voorhis No. 2; Eleanor Glasgow Voorhis Memorial Collection,
Missouri Historical Society, Saint Louis)

scouting ahead, to approach within a hundred paces as he held out trinkets and raised his sleeve to show his white skin but fled when the two men with Lewis kept advancing. On 12 August, following the Shoshone's trail toward his people's encampment, Lewis and his party crossed the continental divide (the border of present-day Montana and Idaho) through Lemhi Pass and first tasted the headwaters of the Columbia. On 13 August, after Lewis encountered some Indian women who were too slow to escape and gave them gifts, the other Shoshones were soon convinced of the whites' peaceful intentions. The next day they saw their first salmon in a river, a sign that it eventually led to the sea.

The company still needed horses and guidance to find a navigable portion of the Columbia. The expedition represented the government of the United States, and it clearly rankled Lewis when he recognized the "necessity of requesting" horses and guides from the Indians, but without Shoshone aid the expedition might never have made it out of the

mountains. Although they had not crossed the mountains themselves, the Shoshones had talked with other nations from the west and advised that the trail that was apparently most direct was too rough, while the easier route which led further to the south could not be attempted until the following spring. From this point on the company was always in contact with one or another group of Indians until they reached the Pacific.

Finally a friendly old man agreed to accompany them. He insisted that the direct water route was too rough, but Clark insisted on the several days of travel it took to see it for himself. By 23 August Clark was satisfied that the old man was correct, and, after purchasing horses to carry their instruments, supplies, and trade goods, the party set out along an "Indian road" that eventually would lead to a navigable fork to the north. They continued overland into September, traveling among the Shoshones and the Chopunnish. Lewis and Clark saw ermine and speculated that the Indians could be encouraged to develop that trade. Later, when the Shoshones were reluctant to accompany the expedition out of fear of being ambushed by enemies, Lewis challenged their courage, and eventually induced them to come along.

During most of the twenty-eight months spent in the wilderness, the company's skilled hunters were usually able to provide the expedition with plentiful meat. Most of the land through which they traveled teemed with game, including buffalo, beaver, elk, deer, wolves, and grizzly bears. On one foray Clark's men provided three thousand pounds of meat, including thirty-six deer, fourteen elk, and one wolf. A day's fishing in the mountains once produced 528 fish, mostly trout. But the amount of food required to feed the party of thirty-two people was enormous; the captains estimated they needed "four deer, or an elk and a deer, or one buffaloe every twenty-four hours." The party did sometimes go hungry when game was scarce, and the captains complained when reduced to a vegetable diet, which they considered unhealthy for their men. It was in the mountains that the party faced the worst privations. Some of the Indians they met either could not or would not trade their food. When the Columbia River became navigable, many of the men were too sick with dysentery to help in the construction of canoes, and the party was reduced to butchering colts and some of the horses that had gotten them over the mountains.

On 7 September they took to the canoes they had just finished building and proceeded down the Columbia River. They saw the first tidewater on 2 November, and reached the Pacific Ocean on 14 November. As they entered and crossed the mountains, the company had seen fewer and fewer signs of trade with whites, but as soon as they began descending the Columbia they quickly saw trade goods that had come up from the coast. When they reached the coast, they saw an Indian woman with the name of a trader, "J. Bowen," tattooed on her arm, and the coastal Indians knew more than a dozen white traders by name who came annually in three- and four-masted oceangoing vessels. The rest of November was spent searching for a good wintering site, and on 7 December they began building Fort Clatsop.

The winter months were occupied in councils with the Indians and in hunting. While trading off the coast was already dependable and profitable, the explorers had learned that any land route for trade would depend on the Indians. In an appendix that was unfinished, trailing off into outline form, yet still published, Lewis made recommendations for trading with them. The Spanish traders had established a precedent for giving away goods when threatened by the Indians of the Plains, so that the Kansas and the Sioux claimed that "white men are like dogs, the more you beat them and plunder them, the more goods they will bring you, and the cheaper they will sell them." Lewis believed that American traders would need to work from protected forts. Also, the competing British were so well established that Lewis urged the government to begin excluding the Hudson Bay Company from trading in U.S. territory.

Although the possibility of trade was a short-term advantage, Lewis and Clark clearly saw that the destiny of the United States involved settling the West. On many occasions the account notes positions "well calculated" for settlement: "The hills or rather high grounds . . . are composed of a good rich black soil, which is perfectly susceptible of cultivation. . . . high open plains . . . are on both sides sufficiently fertile, but the south has the advantage of better streams of water, and may therefore be considered as preferable for settlements." A valley in the mountains along the Columbia was "the only desirable situation for a settlement on the western side of the Rocky Mountains, and being naturally fertile, would, if properly cultivated, afford subsistence for forty or fifty thousand souls." The captains pointed out an onion species which, because it "bears a large quantity to the square foot, and stands the rigours of the climate . . . will no doubt be an acquisition to the settlers." After an extensive description of the soil and climate of the lands along the Rocky Mountains, the account summarizes: "In short, this district affords many advan-

tages to the settlers, and if properly cultivated, would yield every object necessary for the subsistence and comfort of civilized man." Unfortunately, this region was already populated by the Shoshones and the Chopunnish, who are then described in detail without a trace of irony or conflict.

Fulfilling Jefferson's directive to catalogue the plants and animals they encountered for the education and preparation of those who would follow, Lewis and Clark appeared to focus on plants with economic uses and gave detailed descriptions of how they differed from closely related species already known in the United States. A new thistle received extensive and detailed description: "The cauline life . . . is simple, crenate, and oblong; rather more obtuse at its apex than at its insertion, which is decurrent, and its position declining; whilst the margin is armed with prickles, and its disk is hairy." Lewis also described its taste and how the Indians used it for food. Edible ferns, rushes, tubers, and berries received similar treatment.

When examining trees Lewis clearly saw lumber; he noted that "the coast is supplied with great quantities of excellent timber." Once again, detailed scientific descriptions focused on the differences from familiar plants, as in the case of a fir closely resembling the Canadian balsam but reaching heights up to one hundred feet: "The stem is simple, branching, and proliferous: its leaves are sessile, acerous, one eighth of an inch in length, and one sixteenth in width, thickly scattered on the twigs, and adhere to the three under sides only; gibbous, a little declining, obtusely pointed, soft, and flexible."

On 23 March 1806 the Lewis and Clark expedition left the coast and began their journey back up the Columbia River. By April food supplies were running low, and the local Indians, who were awaiting the return of the salmon in May, had none to spare, yet all went well until they reached the limits of boat travel in the mountains. On 24 April they left their canoes and took to horses they purchased from the Skilloots and the Eneeshurs. They proceeded up the Kooskooskee River, a branch of the Columbia, in search of the Chopunnish, with whom they had left their horses the previous winter. In early May the company had to choose between conflicting information from the Chopunnish and the Wollawollahs, but eventually decided to follow the advice of Weahkoonut, a Chopunnish chief, who led them to Twistedhair, the Chopunnish chief who had agreed to tend their horses over the winter until the company's return. By 9 May they had regained most of the horses they had left in the care of the tribe.

Pages from Lewis's journal with his drawings of the sage grouse, 2 March 1806, and the coho salmon,
16 March 1806 (left, Voorhis No. 2; Elanor Glasgow Voorhis Memorial Collection, Missouri
Historical Society, Saint Louis, and right, Codex J, p. 133; American Philosophical
Association, Philadelphia)

the rocks. the shell is thin and consists of one valve.
a small circular apperture is formed in the center of
the under shell. the animal is soft & boneless. —

The white salmon Trout which we had previously
seen only at the great falls of the Columbia has
now made its appearance in the creeks near
this place. one of them was brought us to
day by an Indian who had just
taken it with his gig. this is a
likeness of it; it was 2 feet 8 Inches
long, and weighed 10 lbs. the eye
moderately large. the pupple
with a small admixture of yellow, and
and iris of a silvery white,
terbid near it's border with
brown. the position
may be seen from
they are small
to the fish. the fins
pointed except the
which are a
back fin and
tain each
gills
twelve,
near the
rays, but
covered with
proportion
the tongue
with

it mo
black
is a little
a yellowis
of the fins
the drawing,
in proportion
are boney but not
tail and back fin
little so. the prim
ventaal ones, con
ten rays; those of the
thirteen, that of the tail
and the small fin placed
tail above has no bony
is a tough flexable substance
smooth skin. it is thicker in
to its width than the salmon.
is thick and firm beset on each border
small subulate teeth in a single series.
the teeth of the mouth are as before dis=
cribed. neither this fish nor the salmon
are caught with the hook, nor do I know
on what they feed. ————

The party had first begun to utilize the dog as a major food item when they first reached the mountains on the outward trip. Although some bands of the Sioux had served the party fat, "well-flavoured" dog on a few ceremonial occasions, they "could as yet partake but sparingly" owing to their repugnance at the idea of eating a dog, perhaps especially because Lewis had brought his own pet dog along. In the mountains, however, the cultural prohibitions reversed, and Lewis and Clark began to purchase dogs on a regular basis from the Chopunnish, who ridiculed them for eating dog while continuing to offer them in trade. By the time they were returning up the Columbia into the mountains, dog had become their preferred food, since the men were obviously healthier on this diet than on deer, elk, or horse.

The company's taste for dog led to some dangerous incidents. Although the Indians continued to trade dogs, on one occasion a Chopunnish tossed a "poor half-starved puppy almost into captain Lewis's plate" as an insult. Lewis responded by throwing it back in the Indian's face, drawing his tomahawk, and threatening violence for any further insult. Among the Wahclellahs, one of the men who had purchased a dog had to draw his knife and attack two Indians who tried to take it from him. On another occasion, three armed men had to retrace their trail in chase after some of the Wahclellahs who stole Lewis's pet dog, which they recovered when the Indians fled. The party saw such incidents not as the result of the Indians attempting to rescue dogs from consumption but as calculated insults from potential enemies who were testing the white men for weakness.

Since the Chopunnish were not ready to cross the mountains, Lewis and Clark decided to proceed without them, but by 17 June they realized they could not find their route through the high passes that were still buried in deep snow. The company turned back on 21 June, retracing their steps for the first and only time. In their entry for 27 June 1806, the captains admitted: "From this elevated spot we have a commanding view of the surrounding mountains, which so completely inclose us, that although we have once passed them, we almost despair of ever escaping from them without the assistance of the Indians." Morale was low, but after replenishing their supplies by hunting in the Quamash Flats, they found some Indians to guide them and spent five days on high, exposed trails that the snow made especially treacherous for loaded horses. Their guides moved with "instinctive sagacity; they never hesitat[ed], they [were] never embarrassed."

On 30 June the party reached the mouth of Traveler's Rest Creek, on the Kooskooskee River in the Bitterroot Mountains. Three days later they split up to explore different options for the portage between the two great rivers. Captain Clark took most of the men and Sacajawea to find the headwaters of the Jefferson River. At that point his party split again, some of the men returning along the known route down the Jefferson to the Missouri while Clark led a search for the Yellowstone River, which they took to its confluence with the Missouri. Sacajawea was helpful in guiding Clark through the mountains to the Yellowstone. On two occasions when the trail they were following faded out, she directed the party over gaps in the mountains by relying on her childhood memories.

Captain Lewis led a small party of nine men on the most direct overland route to the great falls of the Missouri. There he left three men to build canoes while he explored along the Maria River, which on the outward journey he had named after his cousin, Maria Wood. This excursion led to the only confrontation with Indians in which shots were fired.

While exploring the Maria, Lewis sent George Drouillard, one of the company's best hunters, out to explore a river valley. The party then noticed a group of Indians in the distance, apparently staring down into the valley where Drouillard had departed. Outnumbered and on bad horses, Lewis's party nevertheless set out to overtake the Indians before they might fall on the unsuspecting Drouillard, and a standoff ensued. Fearing that these were the "infamous" Minnetarees, or Blackfeet Indians, who would probably rob them, Lewis was "determined to die, rather than lose his papers and instruments," and advised his men "to resist to the last extremity." The two parties eventually agreed to talk, and the missing Drouillard was retrieved. An uneasy peace followed, during which Lewis gave presents to the men designated as chiefs. Satisfied that they could defend themselves against the Indians, who only had two firearms, the party agreed to camp with them.

Trouble began the next morning when one of the Blackfeet snatched up the rifles of one J. Fields and his brother, R. Fields, who had been asleep. The Fields brothers overtook him, and in the ensuing scuffle R. Fields stabbed the Indian through the heart. At the same time two other Indians were trying to take the rifles from Drouillard and Lewis. Drouillard leaped up and wrestled his rifle back from the thief. Lewis was awakened by the noise and, seeing his rifle missing, followed the Indian and ordered him to lay it down. He complied, and

Lewis ordered his men to refrain from killing him, but when he and some of the other Blackfeet began to drive off the explorers' horses, Lewis took off in pursuit, without his shot pouch, and threatened to shoot if they did not halt. When they turned, Lewis shot one in the belly, but the Blackfeet returned fire before crawling behind a rock. Lewis "was bare-headed," and "felt the wind of the ball very distinctly." Unable to reload, Lewis withdrew, and in the end the Blackfeet left behind four of their own horses and got away with only one from the explorers. This was the only exchange of gunfire on the expedition, for, although another group of Indians stole twenty-four horses from Clark's party, pursuit was fruitless, and the Indians got away cleanly.

After the skirmish with the Blackfeet, Lewis was eager to overtake other parties of the company that were exploring around the Maria River. They fought in the morning, made sixty-three miles by 3:00 P.M., rested an hour and a half, covered another seventeen miles, stopped to kill a buffalo and rest for two hours, then went on for twenty more miles by moonlight before they quit at 2:00 A.M. They met up with some of the men at the mouth of the Maria River and rested the next day, resolving to cover the remaining eighty-three miles to the Yellowstone in one more day. They made it by 4:00 in the afternoon. Before they made their rendevous with Clark and the others, Lewis's party suffered one more mishap when Lewis was shot by one of his own men, Cruzatte, who mistook him for an elk. The ball passed through Lewis's left thigh, grazing his right, and gave the captain considerable pain.

The parties rejoined on 12 August at the junction of the Yellowstone and Missouri Rivers and the next day set out down the lower Missouri. When the expedition met up with a Captain M'Clellan during their trip down the Missouri, he informed them that the general opinion in the United States was that they had been lost. In light of how narrowly they had so often escaped disaster, the surmise of the nation was not without likelihood. On the last leg of their journey their pace was rapid. They reached Saint Louis and "civilization" on 23 September 1806. On their journey out to the Pacific they traveled a total of 4,134 miles; their best return route, plotted directly from Traveler's Rest Creek on the Kooskooskee River to the falls of the Missouri, saved 579 miles.

Aside from a few incidents, the explorers had enjoyed friendly relations with the Indians they met. This was both fortunate and ironic, since they could never have completed their mission without the guidance and hospitality of the very people who would be displaced by the settling of the West, which the Lewis and Clark expedition helped initiate. Regarding their indebtedness to Indian assistance, Lewis and Clark offered the following, more belligerent attitude as their voyage drew to a close in the land of the Kansa: "we held ourselves in readiness to fire upon any Indians who should offer us the slightest indignity, as we no longer needed their friendship."

Throughout their accounts the explorers rhetorically justified what was ahead for the Indians whose friendship would soon be deemed no longer necessary. Their references to the violent and nomadic histories of the Indians show that they considered their decline inevitable. Thus, the history of the Cheyennes was "the short and melancholy relation of the calamities of almost all Indians." Similarly, the "history of the Mandans . . . illustrates more than any other nation the unsteady movements and the tottering fortunes of the American nations." The ability of Lewis and Clark and the government they represented to see lands populated with Indians as open to white settlement spelled out the future of the West, as it was the settlers who eventually sealed the doom of so many Indian nations by the simple expedient of taking their land and making it private property. Time after time those nations closest to whites adopted their weapons and their vices and were destroyed from within even as they drove those nations who lacked firearms onto the least desirable land and into poverty. The time of the Indians was drawing to a close, and the destiny of the American West lay with the trapper and eventually the settler.

While Lewis and Clark were envisioning the future of the West in trade and settlement, they were also preparing a careful ethnography of the peoples whose help had often saved the expedition. Jefferson had demanded extensive information of the culture and politics of the Indians, and Lewis and Clark collected a wealth of detailed observations that reveal not only the Indian cultures and their values, but also the values of the ethnographers themselves. When describing the Kaninaviesch, for example, Lewis and Clark supposed that the tribe was an offshoot of the Pawnees. Showing their bias against nomadic tribes, the captains write that the Kaninaviesch had "degenerated from the improvements of the parent tribe, and no longer live in villages, but rove through the plains." Clearly, people living in settlements, as white people did, were more civilized than nomads. Such people were also more likely to be amenable to the commercial and political relationships that Jefferson, Lewis, and Clark envisioned.

The explorers also placed great value in honesty, and praised the actions of a Shoshone who, during the return trip through the mountains, returned a tomahawk that had been missing since the previous passage. This integrity was apparent even in the most trying situations. When the explorers brought down a deer, some of the Shoshones, who had not eaten for days, threw themselves on the entrails that one of the hunters had discarded. One of them was eating pieces of intestine, chewing at one end while he squeezed the contents out the other. The whites were disgusted:

> It was indeed impossible to see these wretches ravenously feeding on the filth of animals, and the blood streaming from their mouths, without deploring how nearly the condition of savages approaches that of the brute creation: yet though suffering with hunger they did not attempt, as they might have done, to take by force the whole deer, but contented themselves with what had been thrown away by the hunter.

It should come as no surprise that Lewis and Clark consistently offered their highest praise for those people that were the most helpful, especially those who gave them food. After the party left the Wollawollahs, who had freely shared what little food they had and apologized for not offering more, three young men followed the expedition to its next campsite to return a steel trap that had been left behind, reinforcing the high opinion the company held of their people: "We may, indeed, justly affirm, that of all the Indians whom we have met since leaving the United States, the Wollawollahs were the most hospitable, honest and sincere."

Despite their admiration for certain individuals or tribes, Lewis and Clark clearly viewed all of the Indians through a lens obscured by racial assumptions. They often referred to "the treacherous character of Indians in general" as a reason for the company to maintain its vigilance. On a trek with the Shoshones, the whites were astonished when one of the women dropped out of the group to give birth and caught up with the party within an hour, where they had stopped to rest. The captains surmised, "This wonderful facility with which the Indian women bring forth their children, seems rather some benevolent gift of nature . . . than any result of habit." They offered, as supporting evidence, the observation that when the father was white, labor was more difficult, indicating that "the easy delivery of the Indian women is wholly constitutional." In almost any account of their councils with the Indians, the explorers consistently referred to "our red children" who would, if sufficiently wise, submit to the will and protection of their "great father" in the East, President Jefferson.

Although Lewis and Clark considered themselves naturally more advanced, there were moments when they realized that what they found strange about the Indians was no stranger than some civilized practices. After noting that the coastal Indians would trade items of incredible value for what the whites considered cheap blue beads, they acknowledged that "if the example of civilized life did not completely vindicate their choice, we might wonder at their infatuated attachment to a bauble in itself so worthless," and that, in terms of carrying out commerce, the beads worked just as well as any precious metals. In fact, when they took to horseback in the mountains around the Columbia River, they ended up accepting these same blue beads in trade for the canoes they were leaving behind.

When the Shoshones finally allowed the party to approach and share a pipe, they all sat down and removed their moccasins, a custom indicating that they would go barefoot if they ever failed their word, an impressive offer in country thick with prickly pear. "It is not unworthy to remark the analogy which some of the customs of those wild children of the wilderness bear to those recorded in holy writ. Moses is admonished to pull off his shoes, for the place on which he stood was holy ground." A custom which the explorers found less appealing was the segregation of menstruating women to separate living quarters, which they compared to Jewish customs, but without going into detail: "It is scarcely necessary to allude more particularly to the uncleanness of Jewish females and rites of purification."

Many Indian behaviors and customs, of course, sharply contrasted with those of white society, and the explorers were captivated by what they considered bizarre. They recorded the ethic of a Yankton warrior society whose members vowed never to retreat, show fear, or deviate from their course of action. When a line of them began crossing the ice on the Missouri, their leader refused to change his course to avoid a hole in the ice, and plunged through. His fellows would have followed for honor's sake, if not forcibly detained by their village. The captains ridiculed the music of the Tetons, which "does not appear to be any thing more than a confusion of noises. . . . Sometimes . . . the women raise their voices and make a music more agreeable, that is, less intolerable than that of the musicians." They were amused by the improvident Mandan who, to show his trust in his "medicine," released his horses, which represented all of his wealth, to

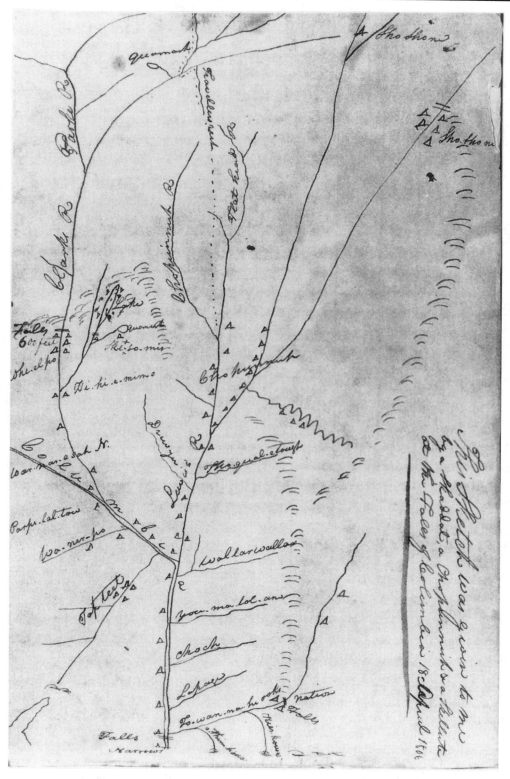

Clark's sketch of the Columbia River and its tributaries, circa 18–20 April 1806 (Voorhis No. 3;
Eleanor Glasgow Voorhis Memorial Collection, Missouri Historical Society, Saint Louis)

roam the plains: "The horses less religious took care of themselves, and the pious votary travelled home on foot." They also ridiculed the Mandans' and Minnetarees' belief in oracle stones, before which they would pray and smoke, then "retire to an adjoining wood for the night, during which it may be safely presumed that all the embassy do not sleep; and in the morning they read the destinies of the nation in the white marks on the stone, which those who made them are at no loss to decypher." When the religious customs were more familiar and similar to their own, such as those of the coastal Indians who placed their dead in canoes with their belongings, the explorers were more respectful, and noted the parallels between the Indians' and their belief in the afterlife.

A custom the expedition found among several nations was the granting of sexual favors, either as an item of commerce or as a sign of friendship. When the travelers refused, which they did not always do, the men making the offer (any activity that a woman initiated without consent of her husband or father was adultery) were offended, as were the women who "seemed to be much incensed at our indifference about their favours." Such offers were more often refused among the coastal Indians: "Their broad flat foreheads, their falling breasts, their ill-shaped limbs, the aukwardness of their positions, and the filth which intrudes through their finery; all these render a Chinnook or Clatsop beauty in full attire, one of the most disgusting objects in nature." On the other hand, among the Ricaras, where the women were "handsome and lively," the men's moral reluctance was less resolute.

The status of women in various Indian societies received attention in several passages, and Lewis and Clark tried to construct a pattern that would account for the variations they eventually noted. During their first mountain crossing they explained that among the Shoshones, "the mass of the females are condemned, as among all savage nations, to the lowest and most laborious drudgery." By the time they reached the coast, they had seen that the "savage nations" were not interchangeable, and began to question their assumptions about the links between the perceived morality of a society and the status of its women: "The treatment of women is often considered as the standard by which the moral qualities of savages are to be estimated. Our own observation, however, induced us to think that the importance of the female in savage life, has no necessary relation to the virtues of the men, but is regulated wholly by their capacity to be useful." Societies that most respected women and their opinions were "by no means the most distinguished for their virtues," while "the tribes among whom the women are very much debased, possess the loftiest sense of honor, the greatest liberality, and all the good qualities of which their situation demands the exercise."

Lewis and Clark came to understand that the treatment of women and other groups within Indian societies often depended on their perceived importance in the organization of a particular tribe. In societies where hunting was the chief source of subsistence, the primacy of men was unquestioned. In societies that depended to a greater extent on fish and on gathered plants, such as the Chinook and the Clatsops, women could and did hold power equal to the men. The explorers saw a similar pattern in the treatment of the elderly. Nomadic societies that depended on the chase would often abandon their elderly when they could no longer keep up, while those nations that lived in villages treated their elders with kindness and respect.

Upon their return to the United States, Lewis and Clark knew that their official duty was not complete. They still had to share the knowledge they had gathered with the government and eventually the public. Lewis, Clark, and the three sergeants had all kept journals and throughout their journey had often compared notes. The captains expected to profit from the publication of their story as well as their scientific knowledge. Lewis was chosen to prepare the final version for publication, but he never completed the task.

While early letters and announcements described the journey and its dangers, Lewis withheld most of the details for what he considered their proper publication. First to come was the bad news: there was no easy route to the Pacific. Instead, the portage was 340 miles, with 140 miles of treacherous mountain country that was still snowbound in late June. The good news, according to Lewis, was the chance for profit and influence in the fur trade, which was increasingly being dominated by the British.

After celebrations in Saint Louis, the captains were feted most of the way to Washington, D.C. They arrived in the capital in December 1806 and began their debriefing with Jefferson, which lasted into February. In addition to their official pay, the captains received sixteen hundred acres of land each and federal appointments. Lewis was appointed governor of the Louisiana Territory, commander in chief of its militia, and superintendent of Indian affairs, and Clark was appointed Indian agent and brigadier general of the Louisiana Militia.

Louisiana had to wait until March 1808 for its governor to arrive, for Lewis spent more than a year in Washington and Philadelphia. He attended Burr's trial for treason, shared the specimens of the expedition with the American Philosophical Society, and worked on the journals. He attempted to administer the territory through correspondence with the secretary for Louisiana, Frederick Bates, who had been appointed by Jefferson. This arrangement failed, and Lewis and Bates ended up arguing over who was at fault for the mismanagement of Indian affairs.

Lewis had insisted on having strict control over which whites were allowed to trade with the Indians, because he felt that a government monopoly was the only way both to protect the traders and to prevent them from abusing the Indians through dishonesty and alcohol. Bates granted Robert Dickson a trading license, but Dickson turned out to be a British agent who worked to unite Indian nations against the United States, and the lucrative fur trade that Lewis had envisioned was imperiled. Fearing a war with the Indians, Lewis tried to control white settlers' access to Indian territory, ordering federal troops and spending money without approval from Congress or informing Washington about his plans. In the territory popular opinion favored free trade and free access for settlers, and in Washington the army was more concerned with the threat of the British in the Great Lakes region.

When William Eustis became secretary of war, he became famous for cutting budgets, and he called Lewis to task for his expenditures, including over $7,000 spent to return the Mandan chief Shahaka, or Big White, who had visited Washington, to his people. In August 1809 Lewis received a letter from Eustis denying Lewis's bill for unapproved expenditures and making him personally responsible for the debts. Secretary Bates was openly discrediting the governor, and many in Saint Louis were sure that Lewis would lose his position. A depressed Lewis set out for Washington to argue his case before President James Madison and to visit Jefferson, who was impatient for publication of the journals.

Lewis traveled down the Mississippi, intending to take a ship from New Orleans to Washington. He stopped at Fort Pickering, the present-day site of Memphis, Tennessee, where he spent two weeks ill and under close guard to prevent suicide, which the crew of the boat said he had twice attempted. Captain Russell, commander of the fort, convinced Lewis to proceed by land instead of continuing down the river, since the British were expected to take New Orleans. Russell sent Maj. James Neelly and his servant to accompany Lewis

and his servant over the Natchez Trace, which was little more than a footpath in places.

Leaving on 29 September 1809, they crossed the Tennessee River on 8 October. Their horses, which were carrying Lewis's precious journals and accounts, escaped, and Neelly went to track them down. Lewis said he would stop and wait at the first settler's house and spent the night at Robert Grinder's cabin. He was away, but Mrs. Grinder gave the sleeping room to Lewis and slept in the kitchen while the two servants slept in the barn. During the night two shots were heard, and Mrs. Grinder heard Lewis crying out for help, but no one investigated the disturbance.

At daybreak, three hours after the shots were heard, the servants found Lewis with a bullet wound in his side and half of his forehead blown away. He lasted three more hours before dying. The circumstances were muddled at best. Witnesses said that the wounds were in the wrong position to be self-inflicted and that the body bore no powder burns. Mrs. Grinder's story was wild and inconsistent. Nevertheless, the official version, promoted by Jefferson, who cited the explorer's hypochondria and melancholy, was that Lewis had committed suicide. Neelly recovered the packhorses, and the journals, seven written by Lewis and six by Clark, were delivered to Washington and then to William Clark.

Since Lewis had promised to complete the editing and share any profit from publication, Clark had not intended to take any part in this task. Lewis had written a prospectus for three volumes but apparently had done little or no work before his death. Clark began searching for an editor who knew how to get the journals published and turned his and Lewis's journals, along with the diary of Sgt. John Ordway, over to Nicholas Biddle, a well-known lawyer in Philadelphia. Biddle hired private George Shannon, a member of the expedition, to help and consulted Dr. Benjamin Smith Burton of the University of Pennsylvania on the scientific data. Biddle also worked with Paul Allen, a Philadelphia journalist, in the preparation of the final draft. Both Biddle and Allen claimed they had done little but combine, correlate, and check for spelling and grammar and that the text truly represented the work of Lewis and Clark, claims supported by most critics and historians.

Biddle used the editorial *we* throughout, even when the narrative follows only one of the captains who was leading a group apart from the main company. Although Lewis did not read or write Latin, a handicap that prevented official, scientific recognition of the many discovered species until their later "rediscovery," one passage regarding the winter at Fort Mandan appears entirely in Latin. Apparently Biddle saw fit to place the passage, which described the sexual acts performed by the Mandans as a ritual to ensure hunting success, in a language that would only be read by the educated. The official version of the expedition was finally published on 20 February 1814 without any scientific information, maps, or sketches. The most complete version of the journals, including material that had surfaced in years after the 1814 edition, was edited in eight volumes by Reuben Gold Thwaites as *The Original Journals of the Lewis and Clark Expedition, 1804–1806* (1904–1905).

Unlike his cocaptain, Clark lived a long life and had a full career beyond his famous expedition. In 1808 he married Julia Hancock, and together they had four children, though only two sons, Meriwether Lewis Clark and George Rogers Hancock Clark, survived their parents. When Clark was appointed Indian agent in 1807, he saw it as his personal and public duty to assist in the assimilation of the Indians into the United States through trading and by treaty, realizing that the process would entail economic conflict, at least, with Britain. In 1809 he helped form the Missouri Fur Company, which undertook the delivery of Shahaka to the Mandans, but the company broke up in 1814 owing to lack of capital and the uncertainty created by the war with Britain that began in 1812.

In 1813 the Missouri Territory was created, and President Madison appointed Clark its governor and added Indian affairs to the office. In June 1814 Clark led an expedition to take the fort at Prairie du Chien (in present-day Wisconsin). Finding that the British and most of their Indian allies had just left, Clark left the fort under the command of Maj. Zachary Taylor. In July an Indian force of twelve to fifteen hundred men retook the fort, humiliating Clark and ending his hopes for keeping the peace among the Indian nations.

While Clark wanted to assimilate the Indians through trade and diplomacy, the settlers wanted vengeance and free access to Indian land, and Clark's policies became increasingly unpopular. His 1815 peace conference with the Indians, which focused on the fur trade, was seen as self-serving. In the 1816 election for the delegate to Congress for the territory, Clark declared his choice, John Scott, the winner before an official count could be taken. In the rescheduled election Clark was accused of sending the infantry to bully voters at polling places, but a court of inquiry dismissed the charges and Scott was declared the winner.

Clark was reappointed 21 June 1817 and again 10 February 1820, but in March 1820 Missouri drafted its own constitution and state government and held an election for governor. At the time Clark was accompanying his ill wife back to her family in Virginia, where she died on 27 June 1820, and barely campaigned for the office. His critics scorned him for his absence at such a crucial time, his friendship with the Indians, and his high-handed approach to elections and the drafting of the state constitution. He lost the election, but was still Indian agent until 1821, when Missouri became a state. Clark married Hariet Kennerly, a cousin of his first wife, in 1821; they had one son, Jefferson Kennerly Clark.

In 1822 Congress created the office of superintendent of Indian affairs and appointed Clark. He gained a reputation as a gifted and hardworking public servant as he carried out the official policy of Indian removal, though he still disagreed with the prevailing sentiment that the only goal was to drive out the Indians, an inferior race, as quickly as possible. Clark worked to make the removals gradual and to aid the Indians in the shift to a settled, agrarian lifestyle. He contended that the government bore responsibility to provide aid to Indians during their assimilation. In 1828, however, Andrew Jackson, a virulent Indian hater, won the presidential election. The next year Clark's departmental budget was cut.

Although the government ignored most of his advice, Clark continued to work in what he considered the Indians' best interests. His recommendations regarding government control of trade and liquor in the Indian territories eventually became part of the Indian Trade and Intercourse Act and the Indian Reorganization Act, both passed in 1834. However, the tide of white settlers into Indian lands was too great to permit successful regulation, and the abuse of the Indians went on essentially unimpeded. Clark died on 1 September 1838 and was lionized by the press and the government, including many who had earlier criticized him.

While the Lewis and Clark expedition may be said to have failed in its immediate goal—the discovery of a Northwest Passage—its long-term importance was historic, as the explorers began the westward movement of the American population. In reading their journals, though, one feels sure that had he lived Lewis would have joined Clark in criticizing and resisting the worst excesses and abuses of the movement they initiated. Their journals represent a wealth of scientific data that was unappreciated for too long, an often stirring narrative of adventure and hardships bravely faced, and the opening of the frontier that would define American life and politics in the nineteenth century.

Letters:

Donald Dean Jackson, ed., *Letters of the Lewis and Clark Expedition, with related documents, 1783–1854,* second edition (Urbana: University of Illinois Press, 1978).

Biographies:

Thomas Jefferson, "Life of Captain Lewis," in *The Lewis and Clark Expedition,* edited by Archibald Hanna (Philadelphia: Lippincott, 1961), pp. xv–xxviii;

Richard Dillon, *Meriwether Lewis: A Biography* (New York: Coward-McCann, 1965);

Jerome O. Steffen, *William Clark: Jeffersonian Man on the Frontier* (Norman: University of Oklahoma Press, 1977);

Stephen E. Ambrose, *Undaunted Courage: Meriwether Lewis, Thomas Jefferson, and the Opening of the American West* (New York: Simon & Schuster, 1996).

References:

Frank Bergon, "The Journals of Lewis and Clark: An American Epic," in *Old West–New West: Centennial Essays,* edited by Barbara Howard Meldrum (Moscow: University of Idaho Press, 1993), pp. 133–145;

Donald Barr Chidsey, *Lewis and Clark: The Great Adventure* (New York: Crown, 1970);

Paul Russell Cutright, *A History of the Lewis and Clark Journals* (Norman: University of Oklahoma Press, 1976);

Bruce Greenfield, "The Problem of the Discoverer's Authority on Lewis and Clark's Expedition," in *History: Macropolitics of Nineteenth Century Literature,* edited by Jonathan Arac and Harriet Ritvo (Philadelphia: University of Pennsylvania Press, 1991), pp. 12–36;

James P. Ronda, *Lewis and Clark among the Indians* (Lincoln: University of Nebraska Press, 1984);

J. Golden Taylor, "Across the Wide Missouri: The Adventure Narrative from Lewis and Clark to Powell," in *A Literary History of the American West,* edited by Max Westbrook and James H. Maguire (Fort Worth: Texas Christian University Press, 1987), pp. 71–103.

Papers:

The major collections of manuscripts by Lewis and Clark are at the Missouri Historical Society, Saint Louis; the State Historical Society of Missouri, Columbia; the State Historical Society of Wisconsin, Madison; the Academy of Natural Science and the American Philosophical Society, Philadelphia; the Newberry Library, Chicago; and at Yale University.

Alexander Slidell Mackenzie

(6 April 1803 – 13 September 1848)

Barbara Ryan
Michigan Society of Fellows

BOOKS: *A Year in Spain, by a Young American,* anonymous, 2 volumes (Boston: Hilliard, Gray, Little & Wilkins, 1829; London: John Murray, 1831; enlarged edition, 3 volumes, New York: Harper, 1836);

Popular Essays on Naval Subjects, anonymous (New York: Dearborn, 1833);

The American in England, anonymous, 2 volumes (New York: Harper, 1835; London: Bentley, 1836);

Spain Revisited, anonymous, 2 volumes (New York: Harper, 1836); republished as *Two Years in Spain, by a Young American* (London: Bentley, 1839);

The Life of Commodore Oliver Hazard Perry, 2 volumes (New York: Harper, 1840);

The Life of Paul Jones, 2 volumes (Boston: Hilliard, Gray, 1841; Aberdeen: Clark / London: Brittain, 1848);

Proceedings of the Naval Court Martial in the Case of Alexander Slidell Mackenzie, a Commander in the Navy of the United States, &c. Including the Charges and Specifications of Charges, Preferred against Him by the Secretary of the Navy. To Which Is Annexed, an Elaborate Review, by James Fennimore Cooper (New York: Langley, 1844);

Life of Stephen Decatur, a Commodore in the Navy of the United States (Boston: Little, Brown, 1846).

SELECTED PERIODICAL PUBLICATIONS–
UNCOLLECTED: "Thoughts on the Navy," *Naval Magazine,* 2 (January 1837): 2–42;

"Cooper's Naval History," *North American Review,* 49 (October 1839): 432–467.

Although his travel books were actually written–anonymously–by Alexander Slidell, the author's books and papers are catalogued under his mother's maiden name, Mackenzie, which he legally adopted to assure himself of an inheritance from a maternal uncle. Such a change was unusual but not unique; James Fenimore Cooper, his neighbor in

Alexander Slidell Mackenzie in 1842, portrait by R. Roberts (American Antiquarian Society)

Tarrytown, New York, had already done the same thing. The two men were initially cordial, but they came into conflict when Cooper blamed the failure of his history of the United States Navy on the publication at about the same time of Mackenzie's biography of a naval hero. Cooper exacted his revenge when Mackenzie was court-martialed in 1842 for executing aboard ship, without trial, three young sailors whom Mackenzie believed to be plotting a mutiny. The proceedings caused a sensation because the supposed ringleader, and the only crew member against whom any evidence had been found, was the youngest son of the secretary of war. Delighted with the scandal, Cooper heaped scorn on Mackenzie's contention that those executed aboard the *Somers* had planned to turn the vessel into a pirate ship. The deposition that Mackenzie prepared as the cornerstone of his defense was published as part of the court-martial proceedings that Americans followed avidly. But it was hardly Mackenzie's best work; indeed, critics suggested that the deposition was unconvincing because literary ambitions had gone to the beleaguered writer's head.

Born in New York City on 6 April 1803, Alexander Slidell was one of ten children of Margery Mackenzie Slidell and John Slidell, who had risen from tallow chandler to a merchant, banker, and shipowner. Alexander Slidell, who would describe himself in his first travel book as "no student and not at all precocious," ended his formal education at eleven. Joining the navy on 1 January 1815, he sailed to Algiers on the brig *Chippewa* and then in 1816 to the Mediterranean on the *Java*, commanded by a hero of the War of 1812, Oliver Hazard Perry. Perry was also Slidell's brother-in-law, since Perry's brother Matthew C. Perry, who would "open" Japan to the West in 1853, was married to Slidell's sister Jane.

Slidell served on the brig *Enterprise* and then on the voyage of the *Macedonian* to the west coast of South America. By 1824 he was hunting Caribbean pirates on the sloop *Terrier,* a quest that ended abruptly when he caught yellow fever and was granted two years' leave. Taking advantage of the respite, he traveled with his friend Henry Wadsworth Longfellow to Spain, a country that seemed to many Americans exotic, medieval, and half barbaric.

In *A Year in Spain, by a Young American* (1829) Slidell reports conversations he overheard in stagecoaches and hostelries; describes magnificent landscapes and regional customs, speech, clothing, and attitudes; and comments on the bloodthirstiness of highwaymen, matadors, and the Spanish legal system. He also displays a willingness to expose himself to the Spanish way of life with humorous zest. In one episode he tries to eat eggs cooked "in a sea of oil" at a roadside hostelry. The food was not poor, Slidell reports, but cutlery was scant:

> The bread and wine gave us no trouble, but the eggs were as much beyond our reach as fishes that you see in the water but have no means of catching; in vain did we ask for a spoon or a fork—our hostess only regretted that she could do nothing for us. Until a week before, she had two wooden spoons and one horn for the accommodation of cavaliers who did not carry their own utensils; but some quintas, or conscripts, had passed by on their way to the frontiers of Portugal, and halted during the heat of the day at her house, since then, she had seen nothing either of her horn spoon or of the two wooden ones, and she never meant to buy another. As our invention was sharpened by our hunger, Jose and I bethought ourselves to cut the bread into slices, and to use two pieces as chop-sticks, after the manner of the Chinese. In this way, and by lending each other occasional assistance in catching a refractory egg, we were enabled to drive them, one by one, into a corner, and draw them out, until nothing remained but the oil.

Chuckling half enviously over such episodes, Longfellow praised Slidell's book with a tinge of self-reproach. *A Year in Spain,* he wrote to Slidell in October 1829, "makes me . . . very melancholy when I read it, for open where I will, I find something unknown to me before. I was as long in Spain as you were—enjoyed the same advantages whilst there—and now having before my eye a record of what you did, and the information you collected there, I feel rather sad that I should have effected so little, where you have effected so much."

Washington Irving, who had lived in Spain, contributed an admiring review of Slidell's book to the London *Quarterly Review* (January 1831) in which he commented on the "considerable accuracy" with which the young writer reported on Spanish life, legends, and scenery. Irving's review also revealed Slidell's authorship of the work, which had been published anonymously, and called for "further and still more copious extracts from our gay and shrewd Lieutenant's log-book." Slidell evidently listened to this advice, since in 1836 he republished *A Year in Spain* with material about Gibraltar and Spain's southern coast that he had deleted from the first edition. This enlarged account, like all of the works Mackenzie wrote after the first edition of *A Year in Spain,* was criticized for verbosity. It would appear, then, that Irving's call for "more copious extracts" was unfortunate, especially as Irving himself had pruned *A Year in Spain* for its British edition; in fact, it was his own edition that Irving praised in the *Quarterly Review,* although he did not inform readers of the English journal of that fact.

More disinterested reviewers also praised Slidell's first book. The *Monthly Review* (April 1831) said that *A Year in Spain* had "the essential merit of truth and nature. . . . We own that we were at first inclined to doubt whether the lieutenant had not drawn a little upon his imagination" to describe an attack by Spanish bandits, the reviewer says, but concludes that "there is not a syllable of exaggeration in any part of the narrative." The *Southern Review* (November 1831) assured readers that the

THE

AMERICAN IN ENGLAND.

BY

THE AUTHOR OF " A YEAR IN SPAIN."

" If we may judge of what has been wrote on these things, by all who have wrote and galloped, or galloped and wrote, from the great Addison, who galloped with a satchel of books hanging at his tail, and galling his beast's crupper at every stroke, there is not a galloper of us all, who might not have gone on ambling quietly over his own ground, in case he had any, and have wrote all he had to write dry shod as well as not."

Sterne.

IN TWO VOLUMES.

VOL. I.

NEW-YORK:

HARPER & BROTHERS, 82 CLIFF-STREET.

1835.

Title page for Mackenzie's third book, in which he criticizes English society and weather

don's Saint James's Park for a statue of the Duke of York:

> I could not help asking myself what the Duke of York had done for England, that she should thus commemorate him. Will not posterity be disposed to ask the same question, and to wonder to what achievement of his inglorious career, conspicuous only for ignominious failure as a general, for base and infamous collusion as a commander-in-chief—to what act of a life passed in dishonourable neglect of the common honesty which enjoins the scrupulous payment of one's debts, and in low debauchery as a man, he is indebted for this honour, hitherto reserved as the noblest meed of heroes and patriots!

Observing members of the working class at midnight on the London streets, he avers with almost palpable distaste that laborers are "nothing pleasing, or even picturesque." To Slidell,

> All seemed in search of food, of the means of intemperance, and of gratifying low and brutal passions. The idea of amusement had evidently no place. The streets swarmed with abandoned women, filthy in their dress, open, brutal, and indecent in their advances.
>
> In the place of the guitar, the serenade, the musical cries of chestnut-women, lemonade-sellers, and watermen, the sound[s] here were harsh and grating; uttered in words ill pronounced and nasally prolonged, or in an unintelligible and discordant slang, which I no longer recognised as belonging to my own language.

The *Southern Literary Messenger* (February 1836) disparaged "Mr. Slidell's mechanical style," noting sentences "overloaded with verbiage" and containing uncertain antecedents. Nevertheless, the reviewer found *The American in England* "excellent in spite of its style" because of Slidell's meticulous fidelity to observation and lack of fustian. The *Monthly Review* (March 1836), however, catalogued Slidell's "hasty and erroneous views" of English institutions, customs, and physiognomies.

Slidell set off for Spain again in January 1834 as an official courier, responsible for delivering dispatches to the American minister in Madrid. His first book had angered members of the Spanish royal family, and King Ferdinand VII had ordered the writer barred from reentering the country. By this time, however, Ferdinand was dead, and his heirs were engaged in a civil war over the succession to the throne. Slidell's *Spain Revisited* (1836) records Spanish citizens' perspectives on the strife, noting that Spanish muleteers at an inn in the Pyrenees

> spoke of the difficulty a peaceable man experienced in following his occupations and passing from place to place without being compromised, and expressed a

young American "views things with an impartial eye."

Such comments promoted Slidell's reputation at home and abroad, and in short order, the new author was fielding requests from publishers for more travel narratives. He was also asked to write on shipping and navigation for *The Encyclopedia Americana;* the encyclopedia entries were republished as *Popular Essays on Naval Subjects* in 1833.

After serving on the frigate *Brandywine,* Slidell was granted another leave of absence in 1833 and went to England with another travel book in mind. The work that resulted, *The American in England* (1835), was not as lighthearted as his book on Spain. Slidell found that he did not like the English weather or the English people. In a typical passage he views the column that has been prepared in Lon-

hope that the combatants would speedily fall to in earnest, cut each other's throats, and settle the matter once and for ever. One fellow, seated very comfortably in an arm-chair, gravely and sententiously gave it as his opinion, that the best thing a quiet and well-intentioned person could do, in these times, was to betake himself to a good inn, light his cigar, and be silent—*lo mejor es quedar en una buena posada, echar su cigarillo y callar;* and, as he ended the sentence, he took out his paper and tobacco, and proceeded to suit the action to the word.

Slidell's real agenda in the work seems to have been to attack the Spanish clergy, who, he thought, "had mainly contributed to excite this civil war, with a view to prop their tottering estate." He muses about whether democracy can or should be established in a nation long accustomed to monarchial rule and decides that the country would not benefit from such a change: laws succeed when they express the will of the people they rule, and the king and clergy have corrupted the citizenry so grievously that any attempt to establish democracy would be doomed. Commenting on a guerrilla band that controlled a mountain pass, Slidell describes its leader as "a scoundrel" and thus "a genuine specimen of a class of men in Spain that grow up about the government, and are debased by its vile system and humiliating functions." Not all of his comments are as scathing, yet few aspects of this work recall the youthful lieutenant who had lightheartedly shared his Spanish experiences in his first book. The main problem with the book for the *Southern Literary Messenger* (May 1836) was "very bad grammar and a superabundance of gross errors." On the other hand the review noted that Slidell was gifted in "picturesque and vigorous description."

On 1 October 1835 Slidell married Catherine Alexander Robinson in New York City. The couple settled in Tarrytown and had four children; two of their three sons would become naval officers like their father; the third would join the cavalry.

Slidell's article "Thoughts on the Navy," which appeared in *Naval Magazine* in January 1837, discussed such innovations as the rank of admiral and a streamlined system of active duty that would allow younger officers to win commands. He also insisted on better control over the admission, training, and discipline of younger seamen. Admission was especially important, for at present, Slidell wrote, too many young recruits were "unsuitable materials" who could only be drummed out "after much trouble and disorder." He proposed a proud and efficient training ship "which would of course be ably commanded," with everything "done in the best manner" and "discipline . . . rendered both milder and more perfect." Although he was a strong be-

liever in the need to produce hardy and hierarchical crews—"there should be no difference of discipline between times of peace and war"—Slidell argued that punishments should be fair: "Discipline cannot be efficient until the punishment of delinquency shall be in all cases inevitable, freed from the prospect of evasion and restoration to rank, through the interference of influential friends." This program must have sounded right-minded to many readers, even if it struck old-timers as, at best, naive.

In 1837–1838 Slidell visited Russia aboard the *Independence;* he was then given command of the USS *Dolphin* and later of the steam sloop *Missouri*. In 1838 he legally added Mackenzie to his name so as to be eligible for a legacy left by a maternal uncle who did not want the name to die out.

Searching for new topics and audiences to increase his income as the children began to arrive, Mackenzie turned to biography and won acclaim. Written with a good deal of help from the Perry family, *The Life of Commodore Oliver Hazard Perry* (1840) helped Mackenzie's finances considerably, and *The Life of Paul Jones* (1841) was republished in London and Aberdeen in 1848. The only drawback to this solid achievement was that Mackenzie's Perry biography came into competition with Cooper's *The History of the Navy of the United States of America* (1839). The two writers had tackled different projects—Mackenzie had written only a life of his friend and relative, while Cooper's work was a compendious history of the navy since its formation—but that divergence added to Cooper's bile when Mackenzie's more specialized book proved to be the more successful of the two. The failure of Cooper's history owed a good deal to his treatment of the American victory on Lake Erie in 1813 during the War of 1812. The battle was a subject of controversy when he and Mackenzie wrote because Perry's second in command, Jesse Duncan Elliott, was claiming the credit for one of Great Britain's most ignominious naval defeats. To support his case, Elliott had pointed to a testimonial in which Perry said that his fellow officer had performed ably; but Perry had retracted the tribute, explaining that he had decided to overlook Elliott's cowardice in the battle because he had not wanted to single out one officer for reproach. Perry had also told of finding Elliott depressed and repentant for losing his great chance to earn honor and renown. Modern historians believe that Elliott was at best deluded. But this judgment was not available to Cooper when he wrote his history, and, familiar with current libel laws, he elected to bypass the dispute. Mackenzie took the other tack: pro-Perry to the core, he treated the Battle of Lake Erie at length and promoted the idea that

Philip Spencer, the leader of the three men Mackenzie hanged for mutiny in 1842

Perry had won it virtually singlehanded. This version won the support of John Canfield Spencer, the New York secretary of state, who supervised the libraries in the state's common schools; Spencer rejected Cooper's book as "controversial." Spencer's imprimatur won Mackenzie's Perry biography healthy sales; Cooper's reaction to the failure of his own book was to revile the reviewers. He was especially incensed by Mackenzie's commentary in the influential *North American Review* (October 1839): the poorly schooled Mackenzie called the acclaimed novelist's style "incorrect and inelegant" (albeit "strong"). More galling still, Mackenzie used the review to promote naval reforms that had nothing to do with Cooper's history.

Matters might have ended there if Mackenzie's naval career had not taken a disastrous turn. By August 1842 Spencer had become secretary of war. In that month his eighteen-year-old son Philip was assigned as a midshipman to the *Somers,* a new training ship commanded by Mackenzie. Most of the seamen aboard the *Somers* were in their teens, and even Mackenzie's fellow officers—several of whom were his nephews—were unusually young. Mackenzie

tried to remove the unruly Philip Spencer from duty when he learned of the young man's participation in a drunken brawl. When that request was denied, almost certainly because of Spencer's father's position, Mackenzie warned his junior officers to shun Spencer for their own good. Mackenzie knew and had lamented that fathers and judges sometimes used the navy as a substitute for the penitentiary; Philip's powerful father had done exactly that when he packed his son off to the navy rather than prosecute the boy for stealing $300 from Philip's mother. On the other hand, having read Mackenzie's remarks on discipline in "Thoughts on the Navy," Secretary Spencer may have believed that his son might straighten out if he were assigned to Mackenzie's ship.

After a shakedown cruise to Puerto Rico, the *Somers* set sail for Africa on 13 September 1842. On the return voyage Mackenzie had Philip Spencer and two other sailors, Elisha Small and Samuel Cromwell, hanged without trial on charges of plotting a mutiny. After the ship reached port Mackenzie himself was court-martialed on charges of unnecessary cruelty, conduct unbecoming an officer, and murder. One of the most shocking aspects of the "*Somers* tragedy" was the logbook's evidence that whippings of varying severity were daily occurrences on the ship, sometimes for minor offenses. Mackenzie's defense, and his sole testimony, consisted of a lengthy written deposition that was published as *Proceedings of the Naval Court Martial in the Case of Alexander Slidell Mackenzie, a Commander in the Navy of the United States, &c. Including the Charges and Specifications of the Charges, Preferred Against Him by the Secretary of the Navy* (1844). He pointed out that Spencer had maligned his captain as "a damned old granny" and in defiance of Mackenzie's orders had curried favor with the crew of the *Somers* by supplying them with tobacco, liquor, and small change. These actions were mere pranks in comparison to Spencer's mysterious references to captaining his own ship in the near future—highly unlikely, in the normal course of events, for a midshipman of eighteen. The problem was that none of the boy's acts or comments added up to a plot of mutiny. None of the executed men had confessed, nor did any of the other accused mutineers confess after watching their mates being hanged. One crew member did testify that Spencer had sounded him out as a comutineer, and a piece of paper was found in Spencer's locker bearing a Greek-based cipher that listed members of the crew of the *Somers* as "Doubtful," "Certain," or "To be kept, nolens volens," for qualities not specified. The secret tally was alarming; yet it was evidence against Spencer alone and not against the men

The first of three pages of notes Mackenzie took on his interview with Spencer before his execution (National Archives and Records Service)

who died at his side. Mackenzie seemed to have given little thought before ordering their deaths. Nor did he consider, as John Spencer charged that he should have, the possibility that the alleged conspiracy was a young man's fantasy that a wise commander would refuse to take seriously. In his deposition, Mackenzie said he decided to hang Spencer "because if he took him to the United States he would escape punishment, for everybody got clear who had money and friends"; he did not explain why he had not dropped his prisoners at Antigua or Martinique to await a trial.

Why had Mackenzie decided that Spencer and his two shipmates had to die? This question lay at the heart of the court-martial, and it was not answered by Mackenzie's diffuse deposition. In fact, as several onlookers remarked at the time, that wordy treatise looked like a travel narrative that lacked an editor's guiding hand. The vindictive Cooper wrote a lengthy rebuttal and critique of Mackenzie's deposition that was published along with the text. Even Mackenzie's supporters were dismayed by his minute rendering of shipboard scenes. Philip Hone, who had been friendly with Mackenzie's father and was soon to be a Perry in-law, wrote in his diary in late December 1842: "well would it have been for him if it had never seen the light. 'Oh that mine enemy should write a book!'" Hone lamented that "instead of a concise, manly statement of his proceeding on the discovery of the mutiny . . . we have a long rigmarole story" that betrays "the pride of authorship." On the other hand, in a situation in which he could have lost his freedom or even his life, Mackenzie may have had good reason to try to recapture "the microscopic minuteness" that had won him praise in his travel books.

In spite of the ineptitude of his defense, Mackenzie was acquitted of all charges. The uproar over the case led to sweeping changes in discipline and training of recruits in the navy. Mackenzie would have applauded such progressive measures if he had lived to see them. Instead, during the last years of his life he grieved that the voyage of the *Somers*, planned as a model of modern naval training, had resulted in a debacle that blighted the service's reputation. According to a biographical sketch by his wife, during the last few years of his life Mackenzie endured "a personal suffering such as few could know because few have the capacity so keenly to feel."

After the trial Mackenzie retired to his home in Tarrytown and wrote a third biography, *Life of Stephen Decatur, a Commodore in the Navy of the United States* (1846). Summoned back into naval service, he went to Cuba in 1846 on a secret mission for President James K. Polk. Ostensibly assigned to monitor privateers, Mackenzie actually negotiated the return to Mexico of Gen. Antonio López de Santa Anna in an attempt to end a border war. The desired peace did not come to pass, and Mackenzie soon joined Matthew Perry in blockading Mexican ports. In 1847 he acted as interpreter at the surrender of Veracruz and commanded artillery at the attack on Tabasco. In 1847–1848 he served as commander on the steamer *Mississippi*.

Mackenzie returned home in April 1848. For the next few months he spent the mornings working on a manuscript for a work about Ireland; in the afternoons he rode through the countryside around Tarrytown on his horse. On one such ride on 13 September 1848, he suffered a fatal heart attack. It was six years to the day since the *Somers* had weighed anchor on its ill-fated voyage to Africa.

Mackenzie's travel narratives are little read today, but they provide useful information on early-nineteenth-century Americans' perceptions of Spain and England and about the development of the genre of travel writing. In addition, they illuminate the deposition that Mackenzie wrote during the *Somers* trial. They thereby offer evidence concerning the values that resulted in one of the worst scandals in the history of the United States Navy.

References:
Harrison Hayford, *The Somers Mutiny Affair* (Englewood Cliffs, N.J.: Prentice-Hall, 1959);

Philip Hone, *The Diary of Philip Hone 1828–1851,* 2 volumes, edited by Bayard Tuckerman (New York: Dodd, Mead, 1889);

Philip McFarland, *Sea Dangers: The Affair of the Somers* (New York: Schocken, 1985);

Frederic Van de Water, *The Captain Called It Mutiny* (New York: Washburn, 1954).

Papers:
Scattered letters and the deposition presented at Alexander Slidell Mackenzie's court-martial are in the Library of Congress's Naval Historical Foundation Collection, the Massachusetts Historical Collection, the Houghton Library at Harvard University, the New York Historical Society, the New York Public Library, and the University of Michigan. Catherine Mackenzie's biographical sketch of her husband is in the Duyckinck Family Papers at the New York Public Library. Henry Wadsworth Longfellow's letters to Mackenzie are in the Longfellow Papers, Houghton Library, Harvard University.

Francis Parkman

(16 September 1823 – 8 November 1893)

James L. Gray
Indiana University of Pennsylvania

See also the Parkman entries in *DLB 1: The American Renaissance in New England* and *DLB 30: American Historians, 1607–1865.*

BOOKS: *The California and Oregon Trail . . .* (New York & London: Putnam, 1849); republished as *Prairie and Rocky Mountain Life: or, The California and Oregon Trail* (New York: Putnam, 1852); revised as *The Oregon Trail . . .* (Boston: Little, Brown, 1892);

The History of the Conspiracy of Pontiac and the Indian War After the Conquest of Canada (Boston: Little, Brown / London: Richard Bentley, 1851); revised and enlarged as *The Conspiracy of Pontiac and the Indian War after the Conquest of Canada,* 2 volumes (Boston: Little, Brown, 1870; revised edition, 1893);

Vassall Morton: A Novel (Boston: Phillips, Sampson, 1856);

Pioneers of France in the New World . . . , part one of *France and England in North America. A Series of Historical narratives* (Boston: Little, Brown, 1865; London: Routledge, 1868; revised and enlarged edition, Boston: Little, Brown, 1885; London, 1885);

The Book of Roses . . . (Boston: J. E. Tilton, 1866);

The Jesuits in North America in the Seventeenth Century, part two of *France and England in North America* (Boston: Little, Brown, 1867; London: Routledge, 1868);

The Discovery of the Great West . . . , part three of *France and England in North America . . .* (Boston: Little, Brown / London: John Murray, 1869); revised and enlarged as *La Salle and the Discovery of the Great West* (Boston: Little, Brown, 1879);

The Old Régime in Canada . . . , part four of *France and England in North America* (Boston: Little, Brown, 1874; revised and enlarged, Boston: Little, Brown, 1894);

Count Frontenac and New France under Louis XIV, part four of *France and England in North America* (Boston: Little, Brown, 1877);

Montcalm and Wolfe, 2 volumes, part seven of *France and England in North America* (Boston: Little, Brown / London: Macmillan, 1884);

A Half-Century of Conflict, 2 volumes, part six of *France and England in North America . . .* (Boston: Little, Brown / London: Macmillan, 1892);

The Journals of Francis Parkman, 2 volumes, edited by Mason Wade (New York: Harpers, 1947).

Edition: *The Oregon Trail,* edited by E. N. Felskog (Madison: University of Wisconsin Press, 1969).

Francis Parkman's importance as a travel writer has long rested on a single classic book, *The Oregon Trail* (1872), which was first published as *The California and Oregon Trail* (1849). It appeared at virtually the best possible time and under the best possible circumstance to ensure its immediate and continued success. Reflecting the interest in the exotic and the unknown which had been exploited by Richard Henry Dana's *Two Years Before The Mast* (1842) and Herman Melville's *Typee* (1846), as well as by the volumes in John Murray's Home and Colonial Library and many other adventurous travel narratives, it describes the American West at a time when gold in California, settlement in Oregon, and the war with Mexico were on the nation's mind. Parkman had several advantages over the others who wrote, some perhaps better than he, at almost the same time about the area he traveled. He had been there, and some of them had not; he had actually lived with the Indians and hunted buffalo, and as a scion of the New England patriarchy, he could show literate easterners—still the nation's opinion-makers—how they were to understand this largely unknown area, the Indians who lived there, and the immigrants who were fast laying claim to it.

Parkman's adventures, his New Englandness, and what was seen as his appropriately literary style made *The Oregon Trail* a popular text for generations, especially in high schools. Probably Parkman's magisterial tone—the sure and confident opinions and judgments of a young man about all he saw and experienced—contributed directly to both the immediate and the long-term success of *The Oregon Trail*. Its New England qualities and attitudes also made Parkman's book the classic work on the West for students of history and literature—the book they read and for which they had to account when they wrote about the American West. The continuing dominance of New England in education and literary study meant that this book would continue to be central to such study. Whatever the reasons for its popularity, *The Oregon Trail* is a major achievement for a man who celebrated his twenty-third birthday on the trip. Ironically, Parkman did not go to the West to gather material for a book about it—he went to restore his health and to gather material for his projected history of the French and Indian War—so the most famous book about the American West is almost an afterthought.

Francis Parkman was the first child of the Reverend Francis Parkman and his second wife, Caroline Hall Parkman. He had a half sister from his father's first marriage, three younger sisters, and one younger brother. The sisters were to be devoted to him throughout his life. On either side of his ancestry Parkman could be assured that he descended from the most respectable people. His father was minister of the New North Church in Boston for more than thirty years, his grandfather one of Boston's wealthiest merchants, and his great-grandfather the nearly legendary minister of Westborough, where he served for almost sixty years. His mother could trace her ancestry to the Cottons and the Brookses, and through her Parkman was second cousin to Henry Adams. He would never forget or ignore the position such a family gave him.

A somewhat sickly child, Parkman spent much of his youth on the farm of his grandfather Nathaniel Hall exploring a semiwild area called the Fells and attending a nearby school. It is generally agreed that he gained his taste for the wilderness there. At thirteen he returned to live with his parents and attend school in Boston. He entered Harvard in the fall of 1840, graduating four years later, and then entered Harvard Law School, apparently at his father's behest. It was immediately after completing law school that he embarked on the trip which led to *The Oregon Trail*.

That trip was not the beginning of Parkman's travels, however; more accurately, it was the last of several journeys, all but one noticeably shorter. Parkman had spent much of every summer after entering Harvard on exploring trips, most of them in New England but some extending as far west as Michigan. He had also spent several months in Europe. These travels both provided him with an opportunity to explore and made it possible for him to gather material for the history of the French and Indian War, which he had begun planning as early as 1841. Although Parkman, with the exception of some stories and an essay or two, did not publish accounts of these travels, he wrote letters to family members and kept extensive journals, which he clearly prepared with the assumption that they would be read by others.

The Journals of Francis Parkman (1947), published as two volumes, provides one sort of account of Parkman as traveler. As a whole these writings demonstrate little change in Parkman's purposes and attitudes toward what and whom he saw. First, Parkman sought adventure and was willing to push himself to the limits of his endurance in order to test himself against the environment and against others. Second, he thought little of those who could not or would not keep up with him and was characteristically not a pleasant traveling companion. Third, he usually adopted a class attitude toward those whom he met and tended to

First page of Parkman's 28 June 1846 letter to his father (Massachusetts Historical Society)

sneer at persons unlike himself. Fourth, especially in the later American journals, he attempted to gain as much historical knowledge as possible, responding most positively to those persons who had information for him. Fifth, he frequently practiced his ability to write picturesque scenes.

On the first of these trips, 19 July–13 August 1841, Parkman traversed much of the relatively unexplored parts of the White Mountains and Maine. He began, however, by visiting three sites that were already tourist attractions–Mount Washington, the site of the Willey slide in 1826, and the Flume. Parkman, in a blacked-out passage, apparently expressed his regret that he was accompanied only by Daniel Slade–a second companion, James Tower, having become ill the day they left. Tower's presence, Parkman believed,

would have allowed him to leave the other two when he wished. The first few days are characterized by Parkman's impatience with Slade, his objections to the wilderness being cleared for farming, and by his desire to keep pushing on.

Parkman's first major adventure occurred on 24 July: "This afternoon I achieved the most serious adventure it was ever my lot to encounter." In an act of bravado Parkman attempted to prove that he could climb rotting precipices which he mistakenly believed Professor Benjamin Silliman had found impossible to climb a year or two earlier. Parkman graphically describes becoming trapped and almost falling, finally opening his jackknife with his teeth and digging out hollows in the loose rock, by which he was able to reach the top. Parkman's description emphasizes the adventure and the danger but asserts his confidence under stress. "During the whole time of climbing, I felt perfectly cool, but when fairly up, I confess I shuddered as I looked down at the gulf I had escaped." Later he "astonished the company [at the tavern] with a recital of my adventure" and records that a young lady, apparently a Miss Prentiss, wrote an account in her journal. Parkman is here the adventurous hero, basking in the admiration of those around him, pleased that he had surpassed a Yale professor in courage and daring, and preening a bit for the family who would eventually read his account in Boston.

The next day he was part of a party of ten who climbed Mount Washington. Parkman makes a clear effort to describe the scene in striking terms—"wilder," "picturesque," and "sublime," among others. This first effort to write the picturesque scene succeeds rather well, as Parkman effectively combines visual and auditory images with references to the cold. And he points out that he walked most of both ways "from choice." Four days later when he sees the Flume, he describes it in terms that befit the landscape of a Gothic novel.

When Parkman reached the unexplored area of his journey, his first journal entry is grandiose:

> We left Colebrook and civilization this morning, and now a new epoch of this interesting history commences. Our journey lieth not, henceforward, through pleasant villages and cultivated fields, but through the wild forest and among lakes and streams which have borne no bark but the canoe of the Indian or the hunter. This is probably the last night for some time which we shall spend under a roof.

Parkman always enjoyed the idea that he was the first "civilized" person in an area; he would use similar terms at the beginning of *The Oregon Trail*. The trip was difficult, even after the two acquired a guide. On 6 August they turned back, partly because of a lack of food and blankets, partly because Slade refused to go further. Parkman writes: "My chief object in coming so far was merely to have a taste of the half-savage kind of life necessary to be led, and to see the wilderness where it was as yet un-invaded by the hand of man. I had had some hope of shooting a moose." While he did manage to shoot a moose, the rest of the trip was relatively uneventful.

The extensive trip Parkman planned for 1842 would first have explored several battlefield sites from the Seven Years' War in New York with a return via the relatively unexplored area around Mount Katahdin in Maine, but the return was redirected when his companion, Henry Orne White, ran out of money and desire. Late on the trip Parkman would condemn White with words that revealed as much about himself as about his traveling companion: "White paddled lazily and unskillfully, and showed much of that kind of resignation which consists in abandoning one's self to fate, instead of fighting with it."

Parkman's strong, sure reactions to his experiences are always evident. Often peevish, he uses heavy irony as a literary mode, shows significant class consciousness, especially about the Irish, and feels insulted when he is mistaken first for a crew member on a steamboat and later for an Indian. He particularly detests the train travel with which the trip began because it kept him from seeing the scenery, and he reserves his heaviest irony for Albany and Schenectady as cities. But he is fascinated by the battle sites, enjoys talking with those who have stories to tell about the battles, and approves of a minister whose text is "The Lord is a man of War." Rambling over the countryside at every opportunity, he goes on a rattlesnake hunt and provides a good description of being in a thunderstorm.

The most interesting person Parkman meets is a frontiersman named Abbot who surprises him by being erudite and a Whig. "I learned more from his conversation about the manners and customs of the semi-barbarians he lives among, than I could have done from a month's living among them." But the eighteen-year-old Parkman confidently orders Abbot, twice his age, around, and as arrogantly analyzes him: "Our guide is a remarkably intelligent fellow; has astonishing information for one of his condition; is resolute and as independent as the wind. Unluckily, he is rather too conscious of his superiority in these respects, and likes too well to talk of his own achievements. He is coarse and matter-of-fact to a hopeless extremity, self-willed and self-confident as the devil." Parkman's sure sense of superiority, criticizing in others as "inferior" many of those characteristics he admires in himself, identifies the New England Brahman who in a few years would demonstrate the same attitude in the West.

The year 1843 was an important one for Parkman's education as a traveler. Although he was plagued by illness during his summer trip, in which he specifically sought information for his projected history, his more important journal writing of that year concerned his European trip beginning in the fall. This journal is one and a half times the length of the previous three combined. Mason Wade, the editor of the journals, believes that the European trip was intended both to be a remedy "for the nervous exhaustion which was [the] chief symptom"

Illustrations for the first installment of the serial publication of Parkman's first book in Knickerbocker
Magazine, *15 February 1847*

of his bad health and to "round out his education, so far somewhat unduly provincial in character."

Parkman demonstrates early the affection for gratuitous violence that seemed to mark his character. The lone passenger on the ship, he is particularly drawn to Mr. Hansen, the second mate, who had been to the Rockies and talks vigorously. "Would that we had a consumptive minister, with his notions of peace, philanthropy, Christian forgiveness, and so forth, on board with us! It would be sport of the first water to set Mr. Hansen talking at him, and see with what grace the holy man would listen to his backwoods ideas of retributive justice and a proper organization of society." In one characteristic action Parkman, who had so desired to shoot a moose in Maine, saw a group of porpoises and sought a musket with which to shoot them.

Landing at Gibraltar, Parkman promptly describes the "motley population," admiring the Moors but not the Jews. He reacts to the rock itself as an effusive tourist. He then travels to Malta on a government steamer, commenting positively on a religious service in the midst of weapons of war:

> Above all there is no canting of peace. A wholesome system of coercions manifest in all directions– thirty-two-pounders looking over the bows–piles of balls on deck–muskets and cutlasses hung up below–the red jackets of marines–and the honest prayer that success should crown all these warlike preparations, yesterday responded to by fifty voices. There was none of the new-fangled suspicion that such belligerent petitions might be averse to the spirit of a religion that inculcates peace as its foundation. And I firmly believe that there was as much hearty faith and worship in many of those men as in any feeble consumptive wretch at home, who when smitten on one cheek literally turns the other likewise–instead of manfully kicking the offender into the gutter.

In Malta he exhibits the same attitude, saying at the tomb of one knight: "He looked like a gallant soldier, who had done good service to Christianity by dealing death to its enemies."

Such reflections fade from the rest of the journal. Parkman, who gives most of his space to Sicily and Italy, often sounds like the tourist he is, sometimes a bit homesick but always ready for a new adventure to push physical limits and usually ready to be critical of what he sees, especially the poor. The reader also senses that he feels more free because he has no permanent traveling companion. Thus, while he can accompany or is accompanied by others (Don Mateo Lopez, Theodore Parker and his wife, the brothers William Morris Hunt and John Hunt, even his disgraced uncle Samuel Parkman) for short periods of time, he can go where he wishes and do as he wishes. The most interesting parts of the rest of the journal fit into four broad groupings: his occasional indefatigable tourism; his appreciation for natural scenery, especially wild and desolate scenes which reminded him of the American wilderness; his continuing distaste for what he regarded as the lower classes, especially the poor and the wretched; and his ambivalent and shifting attitudes toward Catholicism.

Parkman did many of the things a tourist would be expected to do, often characteristically taking his actions to extremes in ways that belied the idea that he was in Europe to recover health. In one instance he attempts to acquire a souvenir from a bush at Virgil's tomb and is restrained forcibly by the guides who think his effort to climb to it is foolhardy. In another he goes as close to Vesuvius as possible with Theodore Parker, even setting fire to his cane by thrusting it down into cracks. In Scotland he asserts that for three days he walked for sixteen hours a day, by which means he "managed to see almost every spot of note for eight or ten miles round."

Natural scenery consistently drew a more positive response from Parkman than did the more conventional tourist sites. His comments on them frequently emphasize a memory of American scenes, experienced or imagined. Thus, he can say that Lake Como reminds him of Lake George but Lake Como suffers because it is "like a finished picture," whereas Lake George is characterized by a "shaggy, untamed aspect" and a "certain savage character." Another time he writes that a herd of oxen "was like the lodge of an Indian–and the cattle were like a herd of buffalo; I could have thought myself on the prairies." Parkman had not yet been on the prairies and must have been thinking of the fiction of James Fenimore Cooper or possibly Washington Irving's *A Tour on the Prairie* (1835). Near Andeer in eastern Switzerland he describes a mountain stream that clearly reminds him in a positive way of New England and of Cooper. He both mentions Cooper and describes himself sitting on a rock "fancying myself again in the American woods with an Indian companion," a fancy that is closer to Natty Bumppo and Chingachgook than it is to Parkman's personal experience. For Parkman, natural scenery, especially that which was wild and desolate and which reminded him of the United States, was much more important than art, architecture, and similar tourist attractions.

Parkman's most negative comments are about lower class or poorer Europeans, at whom he sneers from the time he lands at Gibraltar until he leaves Liverpool. Early on, *motley* becomes a favorite word to describe such persons, but such phrases as "scum of humanity," "dregs of humanity," "a throng of dirty men, women, and children," "gang of ragamuffins," and "beggars and other vermin," sprinkle the pages. His sense of the disorderliness of such persons particularly offends him. On a steamer from Glasgow to Liverpool he is offended when asked to move in order that a father may be near his son, whom Parkman calls a "brat," a "porpoise," and a "cub." The reader of this journal, as of earlier Parkman journals, cannot be surprised by several expressions of similar attitudes in *The Oregon Trail.*

During Parkman's lifetime his attitude toward Catholicism was a subject of significant debate, and the attitude in this journal is sufficiently ambivalent that it cannot resolve the question. He likens priests to "tall pig-weed flourish[ing] on a dunghill" at one point; in another instance he says that Holy Week in Rome is interesting only because of the people who come; and yet another time he asserts that he has come to despise priests. On the other hand, the Benedictines lead him from "reverence" for "the religion of generations of brave and great men" to an ability to "honor it [Catholicism] for itself." He is struck positively by the learning of the Jesuits, has persons try to convert him, and spends a week in a convent. One major biographer, Howard Doughty, thinks he may well have been tempted to convert. Many years later Parkman was to say that his time in the convent was intended for research in the same way that his time in the Indian village in *The Oregon Trail* was intended. But he does not suggest such a primary purpose in the journal. Certainly the journal indicates significant, though ambivalent, interest in Catholicism from this descendant of Puritans who had seldom before had even the briefest contact with Catholics.

Before his Oregon Trail adventure Parkman made two more extended trips, one to the Berkshire Hills in western Massachusetts and one to the Old Northwest to gather material for his projected book on Pontiac, an Ottawa Indian chief who fought against the British in pre-Revolution America. The journals for both trips are not particularly well developed, often seeming as though Parkman was taking notes that he planned to expand later. Wade believes that they show a new appreciation for America as compared to Europe. The first shows an interest in rustic style and language, sometimes seeming almost a folk study. The second, as Wade notes, reflects Parkman's unhappiness about himself and consequent criticism of those around him. Parkman had always inclined in his journals to denigrate those he saw and those who accompanied him. This might easily have become his most critical and bitter journal had he taken time to develop it.

The two trips just described seem almost a pause as Parkman gathered his physical and psychological strength for his big adventure, the most important journey of his writing career and one of the most important in American literature. In 1846 Parkman spent some five months in the West, much of it on the Oregon Trail and some on the Santa Fe Trail. He spent three weeks with the Sioux. His account of his adventures became easily the most famous of travelers' accounts of the American West. There are, in fact, five somewhat separable accounts of the journey: Parkman's journal; the *Knickerbocker Magazine* version, which resulted in Parkman's first popularity when it appeared between 1847 and 1849; the 1849 book edition; the 1872 revision; and another revision in 1892.

Wade argues strongly for the superiority of the journal. He accuses Charles Eliot Norton, who volunteered to help Parkman turn the magazine version into a book, of bowdlerizing "much anthropological data and many insights into Western life which seemed too crude to his delicate taste." Even more seriously Norton encouraged Parkman "to make literature out of history, at the expense of the latter." As a consequence Wade believes that much valuable material about the West, about pioneers, and about Indians was lost in the book versions. Wade believes Norton's and Parkman's companion on the trip, Quincy Shaw, kept the book from becoming the historical account it might have been and which Parkman has been blamed for not writing. Others, Wilbur R. Jacobs among them, believe that Parkman had significantly more control over what he published and that the 1849 text does represent his intentions. Parkman was an inveterate reviser; the 1872 and 1892 versions demonstrate this, especially the 1872 version, which tones down both the adventure and the contrast between West and East; E. N. Feltskog believes that in it Parkman wishes to emphasize more his study of the Indians than he does the adventure. (The quotations cited below, unless otherwise noted, are from the edition Feltskog produced in 1969, which is based upon the 1892 book. The points, though, generally hold for all of the editions of Parkman's classic.)

Parkman came to the West not only as a Boston Brahman but also as an avid reader of Cooper and Irving—whose *Astoria* (1836) he mentions—both of whom had painted the region as yet too wild for white settlers. He was reasonably certain of what he would see before he saw it. The first part of the book is marked by frequent references to leaving civilization behind, and the contrast between "civilization" and "savagery" is a constant theme. Thus, "jumping off" meant leaving "the principles of Blackstone's Commentaries" behind. Parkman was also recounting an adventure, and his emphasis on a difficult and dangerous landscape could only underline his heroism. The result was a book that made much of the wild and picturesque scene but that also underlined and reinforced attitudes that Parkman shared with other easterners.

The prairie may be pleasing to the eye, but Parkman found that its mud made for difficult travel and that it provided little game. He itemizes the "varmints" that plague the traveler: wolves (a label he also uses for coyotes), badgers, frogs, snakes, mosquitoes, and tadpoles in the drinking water. Early, he discusses in detail attempting to take a bath in muddy water among frogs, snakes, and mosquitoes and then returning to the camp to encounter a dorbug (dung beetle) invasion and a thunderstorm. The attention paid to such pesky problems leads to subsequent considerations of the land, as when on his first buffalo hunt Parkman becomes lost and has some difficulty finding his way back to the camp. Sometimes the landscape and the weather seem almost to conspire to make life difficult for Parkman and his companions; he recounts thunderstorms and sleet storms, asserting that the climate is even worse than that of New England. No matter what Parkman is doing, he is always aware of the landscape and the plants, animals, and insects on it, especially the cacti, lizards, wolves (coyotes), and flowers.

Even the flowers tend to be harsh and forbidding; when Parkman sees beautiful flowers, he is reminded of New England and its "powerful and ennobling influences." Parkman's evaluation of the Platte River Valley is revealing. He says the valley lacks picturesqueness, beauty, or grandeur. Its sole virtues are solitude and wildness; only lizards move across the landscape. But the valley also signals a return to those primeval values Parkman consistently seeks in his travel: "[H]ere each man lives by the strength of his arm and the valor of his heart. Here society is reduced to its original elements, the whole fabric of art and conventionality is struck rudely to pieces, and men find themselves suddenly brought back to the wants and resources of their original natures."

The tension between the repulsive quality of the landscape and the positive test of manhood it provides characterizes much of Parkman's attitude toward the landscape and by extension its human and animal inhabitants. If the land is so desolate and cruel that most civilized men should avoid it, it is appropriate for the strong and adventurous. The same Parkman who in his journal had gleefully recounted climbing a cliff he believed a Yale professor had declared unclimbable and who later declared his frustration that he was not permitted to climb to a bush near Virgil's tomb describes in *The Oregon Trail* climbing a mountain on his hands and knees when he is too sick to ride. The landscape, by testing Parkman, allows him to show himself superior to it.

The Parkman of *The Oregon Trail* often reminds the reader of the Parkman of the earlier journals. One obvious resemblance lies in his attitude toward the people he meets. Early in the first chapter he describes a grouping of several "dark slavish-looking Spaniards, gazing stupidly," some "crouching" Indians, two French hunters, and "three men," one of whom, "a tall, strong figure, with a clear blue eye and an open, intelligent face, might very well represent that race of restless and intrepid pioneers whose axes and rifles have opened a path from the Alleghanies to the western prairies." The ethnic and racial identification of the first three groups, contrasted to the "men" who are admirable pioneers, is clear.

Often the immigrants are not treated nearly so positively. In a closely following passage Parkman pictures at some length the "great confusion" of the many immigrants at Westport, Missouri, "holding meetings, passing resolutions, and drawing up regulations, but unable to unite in the choice of leaders to conduct them across the prairie." While he notes "healthy children's faces," a "buxom damsel," and "sober-looking countrymen . . . discussing the doctrine of regeneration," he emphasizes that among them are "some of the vilest outcasts in the country."

He professes himself unable to understand the causes of this "strange migration," but suggests "an insane hope" to improve their lives, a wish to "shak[e] off the restraints of law and society," or "restlessness." Most, he contends, will "bitterly repent the journey." This attitude prevails virtually every time Parkman reports meetings with pioneers. He finds them unattractive, often obscene, filled with "fear and dissension," usually envious of the freedom of his party, uncouth, prying, small-minded, and cowardly in the presence of Indians. Mormons are as unappealing. He refers to them as "these fanatics."

On two occasions Parkman's generalizations about the immigrants suggest his view of the human toll of the migration. After having been visited by a group of men whose oxen had been stolen by

Illustrations by Frederic Remington for an 1892 edition of The Oregon Trail

Indians and whom he describes as descendants of those Germanic tribes who had overrun Europe and destroyed the Roman Empire, Parkman comments on the accoutrements of civilization that have by necessity been left behind when it was no longer possible to transport them: "the shattered wrecks of ancient claw-footed tables, . . . or massive bureaus of carved oak . . . no doubt the relics of ancestral prosperity." They may have been carried along to earlier frontiers as their owners dropped in status; but here in this land they are "flung out to scorch and crack upon the hot prairie."

Visiting another group of immigrants at Fort Laramie, he describes them as "totally out of their element," men who are "bewildered and amazed," "lost" because the forest, not the prairie, is the home of the backwoodsman; further, Parkman finds they know nothing of the country, had "already experienced much misfortune, and had never put their own resources to the test." Simply put, he seems to believe that they lack the experience, intelligence, and moral courage to succeed. The effect of the point of both instances is not only that the immigrants are themselves failures generally but also that the experience of the prairie has made this failure even more apparent to themselves. He sees the landscape as defeating these people, as it might beat anyone less determined than what Parkman conceives himself to be. Parkman suggests a virtual breakdown of civilization as people move west of the frontier.

Parkman is even less sympathetic to ethnic groups other than those of European origin, sometimes indulging in gratuitous attacks. He refers to "swarthy ignoble Mexicans," with "brutish faces." With the exception of Henry Chatillon—a guide whom Parkman found loyal, courageous, and capable—French Canadians fare little better at Parkman's hands. It is interesting to note, however, that while Parkman in his journal observes a group of African American slaves and sees their actions as proof they are of an inferior race, he does not mention the scene in *The Oregon Trail*. He probably omitted the incident because it occurred at the end of his trip and had little to do with the journey itself.

Parkman frequently seems ambivalent about the Indians he came to see, and often is disparaging. His first encounter is with the "dregs of the Kanzas nation," whom he finds "all . . . alike squalid and wretched," with "snake-eyed children," and girls characterized by "native ugliness." The Pawnees are "treacherous, cowardly banditti." "Squalid," "motley," and "savage" are common descriptive terms for Parkman.

But Parkman also desires to pay homage to the Indian. His ambivalence is particularly evident in his extended description of a meeting along the Platte. First, he describes minutely the appearance, dress, and equipage of a single young mounted Dakota warrior in terms that are clearly admiring. Then he moves to what is intended as a picturesque scene of the other Dakota, dominated by the chief "Old Smoke" and his "youngest and favorite squaw," but with a miscellaneous assortment of men, women, and children in the background. What has been a "wild and striking scene" begins to appear chaotic and disordered, with hundreds of dogs running around and lodgepoles "scattered every where around, among weapons, domestic utensils, and the rude harness of mules and horses," all dominated by the "old women, ugly as Macbeth's witches, with their hair streaming loose in the wind." To one side Parkman notes a procession of immigrants who will "sweep from the face of the earth" the Indians. His last reference is to the "whole Indian rabble." In another passage, after describing Mato-Tatonka with great admiration for his simplicity of manner and attire, his warlike ability, his "statue-like form limbed like an Apollo of Bronze," and his impressive voice, Parkman writes, "Yet after all, he was but an Indian."

While such a dismissive movement from admiration of the individual to a rejection of the "rabble" does not appear in his every description of Indians, Parkman clearly has difficulty speaking positively of Indians without at the same time noting that they are but Indians. He twice indicates that his main purpose is to study Indians before they disappear, but the reader cannot believe that Parkman especially regrets the disappearance of those who to him are objects of study, not really persons. He is so unaware of himself that he can childishly reveal his own petulance about never getting to see Indians in a battle in the same paragraph that he refers to the Indians as "ungoverned children."

Despite all he experiences with the Indians, Parkman is always a hostile critic, remote from the culture he would observe. He argues that Indians quarrel too much and lack the unity to survive. He asserts that they raise their children badly by giving them too much freedom and are too savage to learn from "contact with civilization." Parkman at one point remarks on a tree, whose trunk was "on one side marked by a party of Indians with various inexplicable hieroglyphics." The Indians he would study never become more than "inexplicable hieroglyphics" to this Bostonian who could not accept those who did not share his values.

About halfway through the book Parkman sees an old Indian, who looks like a turkey buzzard perched in a tree, and is tempted to shoot him. "Surely, I thought, there could be no more harm in shooting such a hideous old villain, to see how ugly he would look when he was dead, than in shooting the detestable vulture which he resembled." That Parkman would think of an Indian as a repulsive bird is no more surprising than that his first impulse would be to shoot. Lucy Maddox uses this statement to tie Parkman's attitude toward Indians to his attitude toward buffalo, especially in their ugliness, and to suggest that when Parkman kills buffalo, he is symbolically killing Indians.

Certainly, the Parkman whose great pleasure on his first extended trip was that he shot a moose took equal pleasure in shooting buffalo. And the pleasure seems to lie primarily in seeing them dead. At first there is the adventure of the chase, and Parkman's first effort to kill buffalo is unsuccessful—a wild gallop to no effect except getting him lost. Parkman's second effort is in conjunction with the Indians with whom he is staying, and this time he does kill buffalo.

Parkman's longest discussion of buffalo hunting comes near the end of the book, on the return trip. He begins the section by talking about the high adventure of chasing down bison on horseback—"of all American wild sports this is the wildest"—leading to a moment of high emotional excitement and concentration: "The hunter . . . dashes forward in utter recklessness and self-abandonment. He thinks of nothing, cares for nothing but the game; his mind is stimulated to the highest pitch, yet intensely concentrated on one object." This running of buffalo to kill them is the moment in which Parkman as adventurer finds himself most fully living. But Parkman does most of his buffalo hunting on foot and takes an almost sadistic pleasure in killing: "At first sight of him every feeling of sympathy vanishes; no man who has not experienced it, can understand with what keen relish one inflicts his death wound, with what profound contentment of mind he beholds him fall." And kill them Parkman did, far beyond any need for meat. "'You are too ugly to live,' thought I; and aiming at the ugliest, I shot three of them in succession."

In this attitude toward the buffalo Parkman perhaps sums up all the ambivalences and contradictions of his experience on the Oregon Trail. Foreshadowed in his earlier journals, Parkman's attraction to wilderness and his desire to destroy its features remains a paradox which neither he nor his readers resolved: the journey to the uncivilized made him keenly aware of the primal within him. "We had seen life under a new aspect; the human biped had been reduced to his primitive condition," he claims.

But Parkman never desired a permanent wilderness condition; the wilderness and its inhabitants were too disorderly. He recognized the passing of what he saw; but he knew that what he considered "savagery" was inferior to what he considered "civilization" and did not lament the passing.

About two-thirds of the way through the book, in a famous passage not anticipated by the journal, Parkman observes small fishes in a pool, seemingly playing together but actually "engaged in cannibal warfare among themselves," until the "tyrant of the pool" appears and frightens them away. "'Soft-hearted philanthropists,' thought I, 'may sigh long for their peaceful millennium; for from minnows up to men, life is an incessant battle.'" The Darwinian Parkman seems to have seen his time on the prairie as part of this battle. Though the adventure tested and proved his strength, the site of the adventure began to lose meaning. The adventure was everything.

The Oregon Trail and Francis Parkman have remained popular subjects, with new biographies and critical studies appearing regularly in the twentieth century. Perhaps because the book is so obviously central to the evolving cultural view of the American West, students of literature and history have been obliged to come to terms with it. Bernard DeVoto has argued that Parkman missed the significance of the westward movement. R. W. B. Lewis emphasized the degree to which he opposed progress. Historians such as Wade have criticized its failures as history and as an ethnography of Native Americans. More recent cultural critics object to Parkman's treatment of Native Americans or of others on the plains. He has, for them, become the conservative spokesman for the Anglo-Saxon hierarchy. David Leverenz in *Manhood and the American Renaissance* (1989) argues that Parkman is committed to a cult of masculinity. But no serious student of American culture can or should dismiss him or *The Oregon Trail*. The book that first taught New Englanders how to understand the West remains central to that understanding, even for those who find it profoundly mistaken.

Letters:

Letters of Francis Parkman, 2 volumes, edited by Wilbur R. Jacobs (Norman: University of Oklahoma Press, 1960).

Biographies:

Charles H. Farnham, *A Life of Francis Parkman* (Boston: Little, Brown, 1900);

Henry Dwight Sedgwick, *Francis Parkman* (Boston: Houghton Mifflin, 1904);

Mason Wade, *Francis Parkman: Heroic Historian* (New York: Viking, 1942).

References:

Bernard DeVoto, *The Year of Decision: 1846* (Boston: Little, Brown, 1943);

Howard Doughty, *Francis Parkman* (New York: Macmillan, 1962);

E. N. Feltskog, Introduction to Parkman's *The Oregon Trail,* edited by Feltskog (Madison: University of Wisconsin, 1969), pp. 11a–75a;

Robert L. Gale, *Francis Parkman* (New York: Twayne, 1973);

Martin Green, "Parkman's *The Oregon Trail,*" in his *The Great American Adventure* (Boston: Beacon, 1984), pp. 101–115;

Wilbur R. Jacobs, *Francis Parkman, Historian as Hero: The Formative Years* (Austin: University of Texas Press, 1991);

David Leverenz, "Hard, Isolate, Ruthless, and Patrician: Dana and Parkman," in his *Manhood and the American Renaissance* (Ithaca: Cornell University Press, 1989), pp. 205–226;

David Levin, "Francis Parkman: *The Oregon Trail,*" in *Landmarks of American Writing,* edited by Hennig Cohen (New York: Basic Books, 1969), pp. 79–89;

R. W. B. Lewis, "The Function of History: Bancroft and Parkman," in his *The American Adam: Innocence, Tragedy, and Tradition in the Nineteenth Century* (Chicago: University of Chicago Press, 1955), pp. 159–173;

Lucy Maddox, "Points of Departure: Fuller, Thoreau, and Parkman," in her *Removals: Nineteenth-Century American Literature and the Politics of Indian Affairs* (New York: Oxford University Press, 1991), pp. 131–169;

Phillip G. Terrie, "The Other Within: Indianization on *The Oregon Trail,*" *New England Quarterly,* 64 (September 1991): 376–392.

Papers:

Parkman's historical papers are held by the Massachusetts Historical Society and his library and maps by Harvard University.

Rembrandt Peale
(22 February 1778 – 3 October 1860)

Anita G. Gorman
Slippery Rock University

BOOKS: *Account of the Skeleton of the Mammoth: A Non-Descript Carnivorous Animal of Immense Size, Found in America* (London: E. Lawrence, 1802);

An Historical Disquisition on the Mammoth, or, Great American Incognitum, an Extinct, Immense, Carnivorous Animal, Whose Fossil Remains Have Been Found in North America (London: Printed for E. Lawrence, by C. Mercier, 1803);

Notes on Italy, Written during a Tour in the Years 1829 and 1830 (Philadelphia: Carey & Lea, 1831);

Graphics: A Manual of Drawing and Writing, for the Use of Schools and Families (New York: J. P. Peaslee, 1835); republished as *Graphics: A Popular System of Drawing and Writing, for the Use of Schools and Families* (Philadelphia: C. Sherman, 1841);

Portfolio of an Artist (Philadelphia: Henry Perkins / Boston: Perkins & Marvin, 1839);

The Introduction to Peale's Graphics: A Popular System of Drawing and Writing Illustrated with Numerous Progressive Diagrams Calculated for the Use of the Public Schools (Philadelphia: C. Sherman, 1842);

Graphics: First Book of Drawing for the Use of Public Schools with Second Book of Drawing (Philadelphia: C. Sherman, 1843);

Introduction to the Study of Graphics: A Manual Exercise for the Education of the Eye, Auxiliary to the Employment of the Pencil and Pen; Arranged for the Primary Schools (Philadelphia: Edward C. Biddle, 1844);

Graphics, The Art of Accurate Delineation: A System of School Exercise, for the Education of the Eye and the Training of the Hand, as Auxiliary to Writing, Geography, and Drawing (Philadelphia: E. C. & J. Biddle, 1845).

Like his famous father, Charles Willson Peale, Rembrandt Peale engaged in wide-ranging pursuits including painting, natural history, and business; he was also instrumental in founding the Pennsylvania Academy of Fine Arts, the Philadelphia Society of American Artists, and the Peale Museum in

Rembrandt Peale, portrait by his father, Charles Willson Peale (National Portrait Gallery, Smithsonian Institution; gift of Donald Hamilton Workman)

Baltimore. Although he never approached his father's renown as an artist, Rembrandt Peale's many achievements mark him as a key figure in nineteenth-century America. Many of his portraits are masterpieces; his textbooks on graphics were used in schools for many years; and his *Notes on Italy* (1831), a record of an extensive European tour, remains valuable for its descriptions of contemporary European civilization and art and its delineation of American artistic perceptions and aspirations in the nineteenth century.

The seventh child, second son, and third surviving child of Charles Willson Peale and Rachel Brewer Peale, Rembrandt Peale was proud to have been born on 22 February 1778, the birthday of his hero George Washington, although according to the old Julian calendar (superseded by the Gregorian calendar in 1751), Washington's birthday was actually February 11. Peale's birth occurred at the Van Arsdalen farm near Richboro, Bucks County, Pennsylvania, where his father had found a refuge for the family while the British were occupying Philadelphia. According to C. Edwards Lester in *The Artists of America* (1846), Peale was told that his birth was supposed to take place in Philadelphia: "my father had raised a volunteer company, of which he was made captain, and being under Washington's command with the army, my mother, alarmed by the approach of the British troops, sought refuge at a farm-house twenty miles from the city, where I was born on the 22d of February, 1778."

His father's favorite student, Peale devoted himself to art more than did any other child of this large and highly artistic clan. He began drawing at the age of eight and is said to have become interested in his vocation when his father exhibited to the public over one hundred old Italian paintings imported by a local businessman. William Dunlap claims in his *History of the Rise and Progress of the Arts of Design in the United States* (1834) that he once heard Peale remark on his impatience with the time eating took from his art, "that so great was his love of the occupation, that he injured his health by swallowing his food without chewing, and laid the foundation of illness in after life." Peale was so precocious that, when he copied his sister Angelica's drawings, his remarkable efforts caused her to relinquish her own artistic ambitions.

Confident in his superiority to other students his age in school, Peale boasted of his interest in literature and the writing of poetry, and, when only thirteen, painted his self-portrait in oils, a pleasing work that demonstrates his prodigious talent. Soon after, he executed a self-portrait illuminated by candlelight, a tour de force he followed by rendering the burning of the Zion Lutheran Church in Philadelphia. During this period Peale experimented with various sources of light—day, moon, lamp, candle, fire—to determine their visual effects and also taught a young boy first to draw and then to write. This was the first practical application of Peale's belief that drawing and writing were connected, a theory he later propounded in his textbooks on graphics.

In 1794 Charles Willson Peale founded the Columbianum, the American Academy of Painting, Sculpture, and Architecture, largely for his second son's benefit; it did not last. In September 1795,

when Rembrandt was seventeen, his father used his influence to persuade George Washington, who was posing for the elder Peale for the last time, to sit for the young Rembrandt as well. Three other family members were involved in the sitting, a phenomenon that led the painter Gilbert Stuart to remark to Mrs. Washington that George was being "Pealed all around." Rembrandt took this portrait of Washington to Charleston, South Carolina, where he painted ten copies, as well as portraits of historian Dr. David Ramsay, General Gadsden, and General Sumter.

In 1796 Peale and his older brother Raphaelle (the first four sons in the family were named after famous painters—Raphaelle, Rembrandt, Titian Ramsay, and Rubens) started a gallery in Baltimore to show their original paintings as well as their copies of portraits painted by their father. The brothers also exhibited items of interest to the field of natural history; the gallery remained open for three years.

On 12 June 1798, when he was only twenty, Peale married Eleanor May Short, the daughter of his parents' housekeeper. Although he decided in 1800, perhaps in jest, to use only the name Rembrandt, he later changed his mind about identifying so closely with the Dutch master. With other members of the family Peale engaged in the 1801 unearthing of mastodon skeletons in Ulster and Orange Counties, New York, the first found in America.

Also in 1801 he painted what in the twentieth century has become an extremely valuable piece (it was sold in 1985 for $4,070,000), *Rubens Peale with a Geranium,* one of the most original American paintings of the period. Peale's work was as much a portrait as a still life, with equal attention paid to the face and upper body of the human subject and the flowering plant with its leaves near to or touching his head. The painting was thought for a time to represent the first geranium cultivated in America; Rubens Peale's daughter, Mary Jane Peale, in her 1883 will refers to "*The Portrait* of Father with the Geranium, the first brought to this country, and painted on account of the plant which shows that it was in the studio being a little withered." Although historians have concluded that geraniums were grown in America prior to the date of the painting, Rubens's plant still ranks among the first in America to bloom from seed.

In 1802–1803 Peale made the first of his trips to Europe. In England he exhibited one of the mastodon skeletons, which did not yield much profit, and painted portraits of such subjects as the president of the Royal Society, Sir Joseph Banks, and the poet Robert Bloomfield. He also published a pamphlet based on the excavations in New York, *Account of the Skeleton of the Mammoth: A Non-Descript Carnivorous Animal of Immense Size, Found in America* (1802), as well as a second book, *An Historical Disquisition on the Mammoth, or, Great American Incognitum* (1803).

Unable to exhibit their skeleton in Paris because of the war between England and France, the brothers traveled back to America in 1803. In 1804 Peale created a painting room in the State House at Philadelphia where the legislature had granted Charles Willson Peale space for a museum and gallery. As his father's associate, Peale painted portraits, including one of Thomas Jefferson done in 1805 from life and considered by many to be his masterpiece. That same year the artist was instrumental in helping to establish the Pennsylvania Academy of Fine Arts and also exhibited thirty portrait paintings.

In spring 1808, on his first visit to Paris, Peale painted for his father's collection portraits of such famous Frenchmen as Jean-Antoine Houdon, Abbé Huay, Count Rumford, Jacques-Louis David, Dominique-Vivant Denon, and Bernardin de St. Pierre. Although Denon, the director-general of French museums, offered him a paid position, Peale chose to return to America in October to be with his family in a more stable political climate. However, he returned to Paris the following year for more painting. He often used an encaustic technique, mixing pigment in wax rather than oil, which he learned in France. He would later become one of the earliest American lithographers, taking up the medium of "stone printing" circa 1825. In C. Edwards Lester's 1846 book *The Artists of America* Peale describes himself as the first lithographer in the nation.

During his 1809–1810 stay in France, Peale decided to concentrate on historical paintings. He later claimed he had been asked to work as a court painter for Napoleon, a position he did not accept. Nevertheless, influenced by French neoclassicism, he executed a portrait of Bonaparte on horseback. During his sojourns in France, Peale met such artists as Jacques-Louis David and François-Pascal-Simon Gérard. After viewing Napoleon's impressive art collection at the Louvre, he wrote in a letter Paul Rubens, Raphael, Titian, and Sir Anthony Van Dyck, reporting that he had "selected their beauties, noticed their defects, methodised their systems," and forged a "Union of their various excellencies in the *Picture of my Brain,* which is still to be my model, assisted by Nature—which I believe is sufficiently beautiful in America."

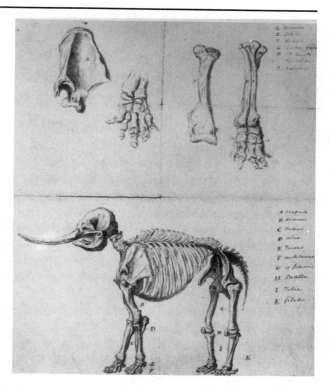

Peale's working sketch of the mastadon, 1801 (American Philosophical Society Library, Philadelphia)

In November 1810 Peale returned to Philadelphia, later exhibiting his equestrian painting of Napoleon, which was shown in Baltimore and Philadelphia and praised by the critic John Neal though disparaged by the architect Benjamin Henry Latrobe. Now convinced that he should create large historical views, Peale opened in Baltimore the Apollodorian Gallery of Paintings, a gallery and museum where he could show such work and through which he could encourage other painters. He was unable, though, to carry through his plan of establishing an academy for teaching fine arts at the gallery.

Peale's painting of *The Roman Daughter* (circa 1810–1812) evoked criticism from those scandalized by its depiction of a woman offering a man nourishment from her naked breast. Pavel Svinin, secretary to the Russian consul and himself an artist, labeled this a copy of a Gérard painting and also disparaged Peale's portrait of Napoleon, charges the artist vigorously opposed. When Peale and a friend, the painter Thomas Sully, confronted Svinin, the Russian retracted his charge, saying that he had misjudged *The Roman Daughter.* Two of Peale's better works followed: a portrait of Stephen Decatur, and a well-crafted study of Maximilian Godefroy.

The criticism of *The Roman Daughter* discouraged Peale from painting for a time, and he did not regain his enthusiasm for his vocation until 1820, when he painted the *Court of Death,* a large (twelve feet by twenty-four feet) canvas that was taken on tour for more than a year, advertised as "The Great Moral Painting," and viewed by an estimated thirty-two thousand people, earning its painter close to $9,000. Suggesting the styles of Benjamin West, Angelica Kauffmann, and the followers of Jacques-Louis David, the painting, according to Lester's *Artists of America,* was described by the artist as a "picture twenty-four feet long, consisting of twenty-three figures—a pictorial discourse on life and death, being an attempt by *personification* to show the reality and necessity of death, and the charms of virtue, contrasted with vice and intemperance, and the horrors of war."

In a letter Peale wrote that although he took the idea for the painting from a poem on death by Bielby Porteus, bishop of London, he "imagined a more original, impressive style of personification, at once philosophical and popular, and had the satisfaction to find, that it was equally understood and appreciated by the ignorant and the learned." Peale called his effort "the first attempt, in modern times, to produce moral impressions on the ancient Greek plan, without the aid of mythology, or conventional allegory, being as readily understood by the ignorant as the learned; and was the first public appeal in favor of temperance, before the establishment of societies for its promotion." A detailed account of the history of the painting's execution appears in a "Notes and Queries" column, written by Peale, in the September 1857 issue of *The Crayon.*

Peale's ethical concerns are also shown in his behavior during the War of 1812. In an August 1814 letter to his brother Rubens, he asserted that he could not take up arms and shoot another human being; therefore, he could not help defend his country. When the Battle of Baltimore was won by the Americans, the city celebrated a day of thanksgiving on 28 October 1814, and Peale made a large donation to a relief fund. The same year Peale and Rubens began Peale's Baltimore Museum and Gallery of Fine Arts.

In the ensuing years Peale became involved in a business venture designed to provide gaslight for the streets of Baltimore, the Gas Light Company of Baltimore. Although America's vast gas industry had its beginnings with this enterprise, the company failed to provide Peale with the profits he expected. In 1820, frustrated by his own perhaps too varied professional interests, Peale confessed in a letter to his brother Titian that he, along with his father, now considered natural history and painting incompatible pursuits. In 1821, tired from his frustrating work with the gas company and the museum and in debt to his brother, Peale offered his museum to Rubens. In 1822 Peale and his family moved to New York City where in 1825 he succeeded John Trumbull as president of the American Academy of Fine Arts (founded in 1802 as the New York Academy of Fine Arts).

Peale made sixty (perhaps more) copies of one of his most successful portraits, the 1824 *National Portrait and Standard Likeness of Washington,* known both as *Patriae Pater* (the phrase appears in the painting) and as the *Porthole Portrait* because of the painted circle of stones surrounding the head of the first president. Peale describes this portrait in *Notes on Italy* as "my portrait of Washington, which represents him as seen through a perforated screen of ornamented stone work, beneath the Phidian head of Jupiter." The public came to call the portrait "Peale's Washington," and to the painter it eventually bore the title, "My Washington." The portrait is emblematic of Peale's last years, largely spent promoting homage to George Washington by lecturing on the first president, illustrating those lectures with his own paintings, and billing himself as "the only living painter who ever saw Washington." Late in 1825 Thomas Jefferson rejected Peale's application to teach landscape painting at the University of Virginia on the grounds that Peale was overqualified for the position. In early 1826 Peale, along with twenty-nine others, founded the National Academy of Design.

Peale's various activities as museum director, researcher in pigments, teacher of graphics, writer, painter, and gaslight entrepreneur reveal a man interested and competent in a wide array of disciplines; they also show a man who needed money to support his family and fame to ply his ego. His frequent trips to Europe demonstrate a restlessness, a recognition that Europe's long artistic tradition provided a more hospitable environment for a painter than did America's nascent one. This recognition is clear in a letter he wrote to Jefferson on 17 December 1800, in which Peale discussed his art and the superiority of France over Italy as a place to study, and gaining financial support for his family while he studied art in Europe. When Peale in 1823 decided he needed to travel to London because artists were more fully supported in England than in America, his father did not offer him financial support and worried that friends would consider his son a rootless wanderer.

Peale crossed the Atlantic for the fourth time in 1828, sojourning for two years in Italy, France, and England. His 1829–1830 tour of the Continent formed the basis for his substantial memoir, *Notes on Italy*. Prior to the trip, Peale made plans to finance his journey by taking orders for copies of the works of old masters, but only seven potential patrons showed interest. He was able to secure the necessary funds for his trip—on which he was accompanied by his son, Michael Angelo—by borrowing from family members and friends and offering a lottery (with his work as prizes).

At the outset Peale states that *Notes on Italy* is essentially a journal, the entries written soon after the observations. He explains his need to return to Europe: his previous trips had not taken him to Italy, largely because of political reasons, and as an artist he needed to visit that treasure of art history. Peale's tour began in Le Havre, then moved to Paris, Lyons, Marseilles, Naples, Pompeii, Rome, Florence, Venice, and other centers of art. The author's eye is keen, his observations detailed, and his perspective largely positive.

Not content to report only on art, Peale also observes people, church services, and customs. In Naples, Peale reports on the pasta (he calls it macaroni) hanging out to dry:

> The filthy streets and houses in which this singular, tough, wire-drawn tubular dough was thus exposed, effectually suppressed all desire to eat of it myself, but I was amused in seeing it eaten in the streets at stalls, where it is cooked and given out in platters to humble purchasers, who take it up with their fingers; and, stretching out their necks, with open mouth suck it in, in a most amusing manner.

He sees beggars and "wretchedness" in the city, but he admires an institution providing housing and education for poor children and adults.

Peale's sharp mind, clear writing style, and penchant for detail make his descriptions of houses, roads, towns, customs, and people vivid and seemingly accurate. The modern reader will find the volume a resource for information not only on the art treasures of Italy and France but also on the status of ancient buildings, towns, and ruins. Peale also finds folk customs worth reporting. For example, he notes the lacrymatories, glass vials intended to catch "the tears of grief" in order to "disturb the sentiment and restrain the flood." Peale comments that "it is much more reasonable to believe that these little vessels, whether of glass or earthenware, which are found in sepulchral vases, were used for odoriferous liquids."

Peale's final arrival at Rome captures the wonder of the first-time visitor:

> Having at last arrived in Rome; breathed its mild air; eaten of its excellent food, prepared by the cunning of a French cook, and presented in all the ceremony of successive courses, as prescribed by the gourmand code; and tasted, not to say drunk, of its pleasant wine—it only remained to sleep in Rome, to lie on beds of wool, and over mattresses filled with corn-husks, elevated on an iron bedstead; to think, if not to dream, of its ancient glories; and wake to the wonders of art which render it the centre of attraction to artists, and to the curious of all nations.

Peale delights in the colorful beauty of Rome and its endless variety.

Although he usually confines himself to factual description, Peale occasionally draws a conclusion about Roman society, as when he relates that "the women in humble life are often degraded by the most servile slavery, whilst their lazy husbands are basking in the sun, or engaged in idle gossip." As Paul R. Baker reports in *The Fortunate Pilgrims: Americans in Italy 1800–1860* (1964), several nineteenth-century American travelers, convinced that women were more highly valued in America than in Italy, made similar observations. On the other hand, Peale applauds the Italian custom "of servant women riding in open carriages with their mistresses, especially on holidays, even when they have not the charge of nursing; it indicates domestic harmony and great kindness of heart," here echoing the praise that fellow American James Fenimore Cooper bestowed on the Italian upper classes.

Peale gives detailed descriptions of theatrical events as well as of ceremonies occasioned by the death of Pope Leo XII and the election and coronation of Pope Pius VIII. He is unhappy with the condition of some of the art he views, lamenting, for example, the "difficult and painful" task of perceiving the composition of Michelangelo's *Last Judgment,* "in the dark, stained with damp and mould, and blackened by smoke," a work now celebrated, he believes, only for its antiquity, no longer for its artistry. Nathaniel Hawthorne, who some years later was also to remark at the "ruined splendor" of the Sistine Chapel, took time to comment on the theology of *The Last Judgment,* which his New England mentality found harsh. In contrast with Hawthorne and his dark ruminations, Peale examines Italian art from the perspective of an artist without a tendency toward theological polemic. Peale finds much to wonder at in Rome, including Michelangelo's *Pietà,* which he considers an awe-inspiring work.

Notes on Italy details Peale's visits to the studios of painters and sculptors and his efforts at copying various masterpieces. He freely engages in art

Peale's painting of Niagara Falls, 1831 (Lowe Art Museum, University of Miami, Coral Gables, Florida; gift of Allan Gerdau)

criticism, saying of Raphael that he "was not singular in drawing well":

> it was the distinction of the school in which he was educated; but he had the good sense to design his groups with few figures, which were carefully studied, according to the best principles then known; and he particularly succeeded in giving them grace, propriety of action, and expression.

Stating that Raphael, were he alive, would "applaud" many contemporary painters, Peale certainly seems to be referring here to himself, among others.

Having spent almost six months in Rome, Peale traveled to Florence, a city he preferred for its cleanliness and greater prosperity. From there he went to Leghorn, Pisa, Massa, Spezzia, Genoa, Parma, Bologna, Ferrara, Francolino, and Venice. In "Leaving Milan" he writes:

> I may bid farewell to the arts of Italy! An Italian, not exempted from bigotry, discovered a new world for the emancipation of man. May America in patronising the arts, receive them as the offspring of enlightened Greece, transmitted through Italy, where their miraculous powers were nourished in the bondage of mind. Let them in turn be emancipated and their persuasive and fascinating language be exalted to the noblest purposes, and be made instrumental to social happiness and national glory.

Lillian B. Miller argues that during this extensive journey "Rembrandt acquired all the information and experiences he believed were necessary to free himself from what he later referred to as his obsession with Italy. In future years Paris and London would continue to invite him, but this one concentrated visit cured his Italian fever: he would never again feel the same desire to return to the country of his youthful dreams." Rembrandt Peale's fifth and final trip to Europe occurred between 1831 and 1834. The trips were financed partly by his painting of copies of Italian masters, which he felt free to modify as he worked.

Peale believed that writing involves drawing "the forms of letters," that "Drawing is little more than writing the forms of objects. Every one that can learn to write is capable of learning to draw; and every one should know how to draw, that can find advantage in writing." To demonstrate his conviction that competent handwriting could be taught and that writing skill is the foundation of drawing, Peale published *Graphics: A Manual of Drawing and Writing, for the Use of Schools and Families* (1835), a book that he brought out in at least four different versions during the next decade. These books stayed in print for thirty years.

Peale's graphics textbooks were popular, though controversial. In 1843 the controllers of the public schools of the First District of Pennsylvania passed resolutions approving of Peale's system, recommending "a continuance of the course of Instruction in Drawing, as taught in the High School by Professor Peale" (Peale taught for a time at Central High School in Philadelphia) and thanking him for "his zealous efforts tending to the introduction of Drawing as a Branch of General Education." Peale's belief that handwriting and drawing are related and teachable is imbued with a positive, holistic attitude; he argues that students should "cultivate the Ear" and also "the Eye by the exact analysis and delineation of forms; not only for its collateral aid in Writing and other branches of Education, and its acknowledged utility in every manufacture and situation in life,—but also for its constant influence in the cause of morals, by its refinement of the public taste, and the variety of occupation it affords."

A man who read widely and pursued many interests, Peale published in 1839 his *Portfolio of an Artist,* a collection of writings that appealed to him and also includes some of his own poems. His preface includes a paean to visual perception:

> The beautiful creations of this wonderful world are chiefly manifested through the sense of sight, and especially all that relates to form and colour, distance, light, and shade; with every variation incidental to night and day; through mist and fog; in the dim twilight; by the lamp's mellow beam; the cool reflection of the moon; or the copious outpourings of the glorious sun.

The other senses, the painter asserted, "however highly they may be prized, are productive of inferior enjoyments, though essential to existence."

His first wife having died on 3 April 1836, Peale married Harriet Cany on 6 November 1840. She was involved in her family's fancy-goods business and shared his interest in painting. Peale's wife joined him in copying paintings, including the *Porthole Portrait.*

Most critics assert that Peale, despite his early promise and his great gifts, failed to achieve the financial success, fame, and lasting reputation he so ardently desired. Unable to vary the subject matter

of his paintings substantially, Peale was caught between the schools of neoclassicism and romanticism, and his later portraits failed to excite his viewers. From the 1830s until his death he was considered one of the old masters of America's Golden Age, an anachronism to a public and to artists intent on exploring new techniques and subject matter.

Between 1855 and 1858 Peale published articles on art called "Reminiscences" in *The Crayon;* he also lectured on "Washington and his Portraits" in New York, Boston, and Philadelphia between 1857 and 1860 and published the lecture in *The Crayon.* He died on 3 October 1860 in Philadelphia, praised as the venerable patriarch among American artists. His life's work includes more than eight hundred portraits and landscapes, some of which have not been identified or found. He actively participated in the life of the young republic, and his varied enterprises reflect the activity and vitality of the new nation. Rembrandt Peale's volume of travel literature, *Notes on Italy,* though not an exciting work, provides the twentieth-century reader with a veritable catalogue of nineteenth-century Italian art, a detailed view of Italian life, and analyses of the state of artistic development in America and the relationship between American and European art by one whose life and work contributed to the formation of American culture.

References:

William T. Alderson, ed., *Mermaids, Mummies, and Mastodons: The Emergence of the American Museum* (Washington, D.C.: American Association of Museums, 1992);

Paul R. Baker, *The Fortunate Pilgrims: Americans in Italy 1800–1860* (Cambridge, Mass.: Harvard University Press, 1964);

Catalogue of an Exhibition of Portraits by Charles Willson and James Peale and Rembrandt Peale (Philadelphia: Pennsylvania Academy of the Fine Arts, 1923);

William Dunlap, *History of the Rise and Progress of the Arts of Design in the United States* (New York, 1834); edited by Alexander Wyckoff, with notes and additions by Frank W. Bayley and Charles Goodspeed (New York: Benjamin Blom, 1965);

Four Generations of Commissions: The Peale Collection of the Maryland Historical Society March 3, 1975–June 29, 1975 (Baltimore: Maryland Historical Society, 1975);

Carol Eaton Hevner, "Lessons from a Dutiful Son: Rembrandt Peale's Artistic Influence on His Father, Charles Willson Peale," in *New*

Perspectives on Charles Willson Peale: A 250th Anniversary Celebration, edited by Lillian B. Miller and David C. Ward (Pittsburgh: University of Pittsburgh Press, 1991);

C. Edwards Lester, *The Artists of America: A Series of Biographical Sketches of American Artists; with Portraits and Designs on Steel* (New York: Baker & Scribner, 1846);

Maryland Heritage: Five Baltimore Institutions Celebrate the American Bicentennial (Baltimore: Maryland Historical Society, 1976);

Lillian B. Miller, *In Pursuit of Fame: Rembrandt Peale, 1778–1860* (Washington, D.C.: National Portrait Gallery, Smithsonian Institution / Seattle: University of Washington Press, 1992);

Miller, ed., *The Selected Papers of Charles Willson Peale and His Family* (New Haven: Yale University Press, 1983);

Rembrandt Peale, 1776–1860, A Life in the Arts: An Exhibition at the Historical Society of Pennsylvania, February 22, 1985 to June 28, 1985 (Philadelphia: Historical Society of Pennsylvania, 1985);

John Wilmerding, *Essays on American Art* (Princeton: Princeton University Press, 1991).

Papers:

The papers of Rembrandt Peale and other members of the Peale family are housed in several institutions, including the American Philosophical Society, the Historical Society of Pennsylvania, the Library Company of Philadelphia, the Peale Museum Archives in Baltimore, and the Maryland Historical Society.

Matthew Perry

(10 April 1794 – 4 March 1858)

Dorsey Kleitz
Tokyo Woman's Christian University

BOOKS: *Narrative of an Expedition of an American Squadron to the China Seas and Japan, Performed in the Years 1852, 1853, and 1854, under the Command of Commodore M. C. Perry, United States Navy, by Order of the Government of the United States. Compiled from the Original Notes and Journals of Commodore Perry and His Officers, at His Request, and under His Supervision, by Francis L. Hawks, D.D., L.L.D.,* 3 volumes (Washington, D.C.: A. O. P. Nicholson, 1856); volume 1 published with same title (Washington, D.C.: Beverly Tucker, 1856; New York: D. Appleton / London: Trubner, 1856);

The Japan Expedition, 1852–1854: The Personal Journal of Matthew C. Perry, edited by Roger Pineau (Washington, D.C.: Smithsonian, 1968).

Editions: *The Americans in Japan: An Abridgment of the Government Narrative of the U.S. Expedition to Japan, under Commodore Perry,* edited by Robert Tomes (New York: D. Appleton, 1857);

Japan Opened: Compiled Chiefly from the Narrative of the American Expedition to Japan, in the Years 1852–3–4, anonymous (London: Religious Tract Society, 1858);

Narrative of an Expedition of an American Squadron to the China Seas and Japan under the Command of Commodore M. C. Perry . . . , abridged and edited by Sidney Wallach (New York: Coward-McCann, 1952; London: Macdonald, 1954).

American naval officer Matthew Calbraith Perry was the commander of the expedition of "black ships" that opened Japan to the West in 1854 after more than two hundred years of isolation. Often confused with his eldest brother, Oliver Hazard Perry, the hero of the Battle of Lake Erie, the younger Perry served in the War of 1812 early in his distinguished career and was active in the cause against the slave trade. During the Mexican War he was commodore of the Gulf Squadron, winning a decisive victory at Veracruz. He was also a naval reformer who advocated a steam navy and the

Matthew Perry after his return from the 1853 visit to Japan (photograph by Mathew Brady)

establishment of a naval academy for officers and the better training of crews. Perry was fifty-eight years old when he was selected to lead the naval mission to Japan. His account of that expedition, the massive three-volume *Narrative of an Expedition of an American Squadron to the China Seas and Japan* (1856), ranks with Richard Henry Dana's *Two Years Before the Mast* (1840) and Elisha Kent Kane's *Arctic Explorations* (1856) as a classic narrative of nineteenth-century American sea adventure and exploration and is a key document in the history of American expansion in the Pacific.

Born and raised in Newport, Rhode Island, to a seafaring family with strong Quaker roots, Matthew

Perry was the fourth of eight children. His father, Christopher Perry, fought in the American Revolution both as a soldier and a sailor and was captured three times. While on parole from an Irish prison where his wartime service aboard a privateer had landed him, Christopher Perry met his future wife, Sarah Alexander Wallace. Newport at the turn of the century was a cosmopolitan town with good private schools that gave Matthew Perry a solid understanding of mathematics and a taste for literature. His first active duty was in 1809 when he served as a midshipman aboard the armed schooner *Revenge,* commanded by his eldest brother. Two years later, after being transferred to the *President,* Perry was slightly wounded by an exploding gun during the first naval engagement of the War of 1812 against H.M.S. *Belvidera.* On Christmas Eve of 1814 he married Jane Slidell, a devoted wife who bore him ten children and allied Perry with her wealthy, influential New York family.

In 1820 Perry served as executive officer on the *Cyane* when that vessel helped found Liberia as a refuge for former black slaves from America. It was Perry who suggested the site for what later became Monrovia, which became the capital of the country. In a transaction similar to the purchase of Manhattan Island, the land for the city was bought with an assortment of axes, cloth, and other trading goods. The following year at his own request Perry returned to Africa, this time in the *Shark,* his first command. His orders were to take Rev. Eli Ayers to Africa as U.S. commissioner for the Negro colony and to patrol the coast in search of slavers. It was during this voyage that Perry first established his reputation for running a tight ship. Perry's goal was to keep the men healthy and occupied. He missed no opportunity to procure fresh vegetables, allowed a minimum of shore leave, and employed corporal punishment. Perry's strict discipline and deep growling voice earned him a nickname that stuck with him throughout his life: "Old Bruin."

Perry spent most of the next ten years in the West Indies and the Mediterranean. In 1826 he was promoted to the grade of master commandant. In 1830 he was put in charge of the warship *Concord* and given the mission of conveying the brilliant southern orator John Randolph to his new post as American envoy in Russia. Randolph, whose eccentricity bordered on insanity, pushed Perry's patience to its limit. The envoy criticized Perry's disciplinary measures and soon after arriving in Russia decided that Saint Petersburg was too hot and dusty and that Perry should take him to London. Exercising the utmost self-restraint, Perry finally delivered his disagreeable passenger to England in late September.

In 1833 Perry began a decade of shore duty in New York working on various schemes to reform the navy. During this time he helped organize the Naval Lyceum to promote the education of naval officers. Dissatisfied with the haphazard, learn-by-doing method of educating midshipmen, he also drew up plans for a naval apprentice system, an idea that ultimately led to the founding of the Naval Academy at Annapolis in 1845. Sometimes called the father of the steam navy, Perry in 1837 was placed in charge of the *Fulton,* one of the pioneer naval steamships, and worked tirelessly to promote this new technology.

In 1841 Perry was made commandant of the New York Navy Yard; because he was in command of all the naval vessels in New York harbor, he acquired the courtesy title of commodore. During the next few years he became involved in the *Somers* mutiny, one of the key incidents behind Herman Melville's *Billy Budd* (1924). Built under Perry's supervision at the Brooklyn Navy Yard, the man-of-war brig U.S.S. *Somers* was one of the fastest ships in the navy. Perry chose as its commander his brother-in-law, Master Commandant Alexander Slidell Mackenzie, who had established a literary reputation with several biographies and *A Year in Spain,* a travel book that won him the friendship of Henry Wadsworth Longfellow and Washington Irving. Two of Commodore Perry's sons were also on board: twenty-one-year-old Lieutenant Matthew C. Perry Jr. and seventeen-year-old Oliver H. Perry II. Lieutenant Perry's immediate commanding officer was First Lieutenant Guert Gansevoort, Melville's cousin.

The trouble began when Midshipman Philip Spencer—son of John Canfield Spencer, secretary of war in President John Tyler's cabinet—was assigned to the *Somers.* Spencer was a spoiled college dropout with a bad reputation. Commander Mackenzie refused to accept him, but Spencer went over his head to Commodore Perry, who, hoping Spencer would reform or possibly to please the Tyler administration, reinstated him. In September 1842 the *Somers* sailed for Africa carrying dispatches for the *Vandalia.* On the return passage Spencer and two other sailors were arrested for plotting to mutiny. Spencer admitted discussing mutiny and drawing up a list of crew members who might support the uprising but insisted it was all an elaborate joke. Mackenzie, however, was not convinced. All three sailors were tried by a drumhead court, which included Lieutenants Gansevoort and Perry, and then hanged from the yardarm.

The ensuing controversy was probably the most severe trial of Perry's life. Anticipating that

The landing of Perry's squadron at Kurihama, 14 July 1853; contemporary painting by Kyukisai Unra (Shiryo Hensanjo, Tokyo)

Secretary Spencer would go after Mackenzie, Perry wrote his congressman in Washington on 27 December 1842: "No man is fit for the navy if he is not ready at all times to interpose his life in the preservation of the integrity of the American flag and the safety of the vessel entrusted to his and their charge." A naval court of inquiry supported Mackenzie, but that did not end the matter. Commander Mackenzie requested to be tried by court-martial in order to clear his name. Under vigorous cross-examination, Lieutenant Gansevoort defended Mackenzie's actions, and on the charge of murder the court voted for acquittal. Although Perry was pleased that his brother-in-law had been exonerated, he was deeply shaken. James Fenimore Cooper kept the event in the public eye with his eighty-one-page *Review of the Proceedings of the Naval Court Martial* (1844), in which he accused Mackenzie of being an incompetent martinet and, in an especially pointed criticism, called the *Somers* a "family yacht" rather than a man-of-war.

In 1843 Perry was back at sea commanding the African Squadron, charged with suppressing the slave trade under the provisions of the Webster-Ashburton Treaty and protecting the colony of freed slaves. His next important service was performed during the Mexican War. In 1847 he commanded the naval forces in the siege of Veracruz and with Gen. Winfield Scott was credited with the capture of the city. On his return to New York at the end of the war there was a civic reception at which Perry was given the key to the city. At age fifty-four he was receiving public recognition for his contribution to the manifest destiny of the United States. The idea of a western empire involving the Pacific islands and countries in Asia was beginning to come into popular focus.

In January 1852 Perry was selected to undertake the most important diplomatic mission ever entrusted to an American naval officer: he was sent to Japan, a country which had virtually sealed itself against contact with the West, to negotiate a treaty allowing a limited opening to the United States. American trade with Asia was growing. Salem, Boston, New York, and Philadelphia had a thriving commerce with China, protected by the U.S. Navy. With the end of the Mexican War, the United States acquired ports in San Diego and San Francisco, and settlement in the Oregon Territory was bringing more shipping to Portland and Seattle. American business was beginning to look to the Orient, and Perry, although he had never seen the Pacific, was put in charge of the East India Squadron that guarded American interests in Asia. In accepting the mission Perry was farsighted enough to realize that the United States had an important stake in the opening of Japan. In a 14 December 1852 letter to Navy Secretary J. P. Kennedy in Washington he wrote that the people of Japan, "if treated with strict justice and gentle kindness, will render confidence for confidence, and . . . the Japanese will learn to consider us their friends."

In 1638, at the height of the Age of Exploration, Japan expelled all Europeans except for a few Dutch cooped up on a tiny island off Nagasaki and entered a two-hundred-year period of isolation. Its people were forbidden to leave, and Japanese fishermen shipwrecked on foreign shores were not allowed to return. Based in Edo (now Tokyo), the xenophobic Tokugawa shogunate reigned over an independent, peaceful, prosperous nation in which artists and artisans flourished. Previous attempts by European countries to breach Japan's isolation had only deepened the Japanese fear of foreigners. The Opium War in China in 1840 demonstrated the ruthlessness of European expansion. The United States, on the other hand, may have seemed less threatening. It lacked Europe's tradition of imperialism and colonialism and was more open to ethnic pluralism and religious freedom.

In mounting the expedition Perry had to use all of his talents. In Japan he would have to be both ambassador and commodore, and months of planning, organizing, and hard work were required. As ambassador Perry collected a shipload of various items that displayed America's achievements in industry and the arts as gifts for the Japanese. A telegraph and a quarter-scale railroad, complete with poles, wires, rails, ties, locomotive, and passenger car, were loaded on board along with a case of Samuel Colt firearms and a daguerreotype camera. Folio engravings of John James Audubon's *Birds of America* (1827–1838) and *Quadrupeds of North America* (1842–1845) were purchased for $1,000 each. To provide the Japanese with entertainment Perry brought along a French chef, an Italian bandmaster, and a Negro minstrel show.

As commodore, Perry needed the best ships he could get and reliable sailor-commanders to serve under him. He took as his flagship the steam frigate *Mississippi*, which had been built at his order and had been his during the Mexican War. Complementing this was the *Susquehanna*, another war steamer he had used as a flagship from time to time. For his closest officers he chose men he knew and trusted. Henry A. Adams, commander of the *Mississippi*, was also captain of the fleet; Franklin Buchanan was picked as

commander of the *Susquehanna*. Both men had served under Perry during the Mexican War, and Buchanan had also been the Naval Academy's first commandant.

Perry saw his mission as having scientific as well as diplomatic objectives. By the 1850s there were ample precedents for such missions. In the eighteenth century Capt. James Cook had led several expeditions to the Pacific that included scientists and artists. On a grander scale Napoleon in 1798–1799 had combined a military campaign and a scientific expedition in Egypt. There an officer of the engineers discovered the Rosetta Stone and the French army's scientific contingent amassed volumes on the antiquities, geography, and natural history of Egypt. Perry's friend Commodore Charles Wilkes had also included artists and scientists on his Pacific Exploring Expedition of 1838. As is clear from his journal– published as *The Japan Expedition, 1852–1854: The Personal Journal of Matthew C. Perry* (1968)–Perry, although on an errand of "naval and diplomatic character," expected his officers to contribute "to the general mass of information which it is desirable to collect." The catch was that Perry was determined to control how this information would be given to the world.

During Perry's assignments in Africa and Mexico he had been annoyed by occasional malicious articles and letters in the American press. Now, on a delicate diplomatic voyage to Japan, Perry imposed a press blackout. His General Order No. 1 prohibited officers and men from sending home notes, drawings, journals, curiosities, and specimens without his permission. Further, these items were all declared the property of the Navy Department and had to be surrendered to Perry at the end of the expedition. Letters, also, were not allowed to be given to newspapers. Perry wanted no civilians on board–men who would clutter the ship, disregard authority, and subvert the official mission–yet some had to be included. Perry needed a qualified agriculturalist, a sinologist, and interpreters. He chose Bayard Taylor, the noted poet and journalist, to dispatch the authorized communiqués to the press and write accounts of the expedition, but only after Taylor agreed to join the navy temporarily as master's mate. For graphic documentation Perry added Eliphalet M. Brown Jr. as photographer and William Heine as chief artist.

In September 1852 Perry left New York on the *Mississippi* for Japan via Africa, the Indian Ocean, and China. He had been promised thirteen ships, but when the *Mississippi* arrived in Hong Kong in April 1853 to rendezvous with the rest of the expedition, only three were waiting: the storeship *Supply* and the aging war sloops *Saratoga* and *Plymouth*. Though these were not the smoke-belching, roaring behemoths Perry had wanted to have to overawe the Japanese, he pushed on to the Lew Chew Islands (Ryukyu Islands), which were nominally controlled by the Japanese and the Chinese. Here the skeleton fleet was joined by the *Susquehanna*. On Great Lew Chew Island (Okinawa), the largest island, Perry established a base with the *Supply* and explored the countryside, testing out on a small scale what he hoped to do in Japan. Perry also spent a week in the Bonin Islands (Ogasawara Islands) purchasing land for a whaling station and charting the islands. On 2 July 1853, with the *Mississippi* and the *Susquehanna* towing the two war sloops, Perry finally set sail from Okinawa for Japan.

The expedition anchored off Uraga, a town well fortified to protect the capital, Edo, further up Edo Bay. The steamships, moving without sails against wind and tide, caused much excitement and curiosity. The Japanese called them *Kurofune* (black ships) because of their dark hulls, black guns, and gushing smoke. The squadron remained idle for several days as the Japanese mobilized their defenses and prepared to respond to the unexpected threat. They instructed Perry to go to Nagasaki, the traditional port of contact with foreign ships. Perry, however, was firm: he had a letter explaining his mission from President Millard Fillmore for the emperor, and his orders were for him to deliver it personally. Should the emperor refuse to accept this "letter of friendship," it would be taken as an insult with consequences that could not be gauged. With almost a thousand men and sixty-six guns the Americans were a force to be reckoned with. The Japanese brought out their muskets, pistols, swords, and spears but there was no violence. Officials discussed and debated while diplomats prepared to meet the Americans and negotiate. On 14 July, Perry and a delegation of naval officers and crewmen landed at Nagahama, remaining long enough to deliver the letter from the president to an imperial emissary and to obtain assurances that they could return in the future for an answer. Perry then steamed off toward Hong Kong and other Asian ports to wait.

Perry's allowing the Japanese time to consider their options was a masterly stroke of diplomacy. Having familiarized himself with Japanese history and religion and having talked with missionaries and whaling captains who had knowledge of the Japanese character, Perry was well prepared to meet the Japanese on their own terms. They were averse to change and needed time to evaluate the letter properly, and Perry was patient and amenable.

President Fillmore's letter requested limited but specific advantages for American commercial ships. The effect of the initiative was to throw the government into turmoil. Japan in the mid 1800s had a dual system of governance: the emperor was the country's conscience and soul, while the shogun was its political and military head.

Already weakened by infighting, corruption, and nepotism, the shogun Ieyasu was forced to seek counsel from the daimyos who ruled Japan's regional domains. The daimyo of Mito circulated a letter urging war against the Americans and blaming the shogun for the crisis. The letter also suggested reinvesting the emperor with his traditional military authority, thus beginning the struggle that eventually led to the Meiji Restoration in 1868. Ultimately the confusion in the ruling structure of Japan benefited Commodore Perry's expedition. Because the Japanese were unable to agree on a definite course of action, Perry was able to push hard in the negotiations and generally get his way.

In February 1854 Perry returned to Japan ready to talk. In the seven months since he had left, his fleet had grown to nine ships, including three steam frigates, four sloops of war, and two storeships. The first formal meeting between the Americans and the imperial commissioners took place on 8 March at Kanagawa, a village near Yokohama. Perry had written in his personal journal that when dealing "with people of forms it is necessary either to set all ceremony aside, or to out-Herod Herod in assumed personal consequence and ostentation." Thus, his landing, choreographed to present the commodore and the country he represented as strong and confident, left little doubt about which side was in control. As the band played "The Star-Spangled Banner," the commodore led three hundred of his officers and staff in a procession flanked by two rows of armed, flag-bearing, uniformed soldiers in starched white slacks and gloves. Watching from the bay was a phalanx of boats bristling with weaponry.

It was gunboat diplomacy at its finest, and it worked. Over the next three weeks the two parties met several times, exchanging gifts and discussing details of the treaty. The American presents—$20,000 worth—attracted crowds of officials from Edo. The Japanese gifts, with the exception of the three imperial spaniels for the president, were generally considered rather ordinary by the Americans. They included silks, brocades, lacquerware, fans, writing tables, porcelain, pipes, sixty umbrellas, and two hundred bags of rice. Perry and his officers were treated to a sumo exhibition and responded by entertaining the Japanese on board the ships. Finally, on 31 March, eight and a half months after Perry's

Perry's delivery of President Millard Fillmore's letter to the emperor of Japan accepted by the emperor's emissary; illustration from Narrative of an Expedition of an American Squadron to the China Seas and Japan *(1856)*

first landing in Japan, the Treaty of Kanagawa was signed.

For Perry the treaty was not essentially a commercial compact but one of amity and friendly exchange. Shimoda, on the Izu Peninsula, was immediately opened for the purchase of supplies. Hakodate, in Hokkaido, was to be opened after a year. No other ports were to be entered except by ships in distress. Shipwrecked sailors were not to be confined in Japan and were to be taken to either Shimoda or Hakodate for repatriation. Supplies were to be procured only through the agency of Japanese officials. Most-favored-nation status, providing that any rights granted to other nations would be given to the United States, was granted. And finally, an American consul could be appointed to reside at Shimoda within eighteen months after the signing of the treaty.

American newspapers were generally enthusiastic at the official news of the expedition's success. In the *New York Tribune* (14 June 1854) Horace Greeley singled out Perry for high praise: "This memorable success is undoubtedly due to the line of conduct adopted by Commodore Perry—a mixture of prudence, caution, and inflexible determination,

which led him surely, step by step, to the end he had in view." James Gordon Bennett's prediction in the *New York Herald* (13 June 1854) that "intercourse with Japan will in reality do more for the people of that empire than for us" seems especially accurate in light of post–World War II economic history.

Perry returned to Lew Chew where a similar treaty was signed with the local authorities. At Okinawa, Perry also had to investigate the death of William Board, an American sailor who had gotten drunk and attempted to rape a young girl. Her neighbors stoned him and chased him to the shore where he apparently fell in the water and drowned. This seems to have been the only act of violence against the local population by a member of the expedition.

Commodore Perry, worn out and arthritic, left the expedition at Hong Kong and returned to the United States by way of Suez, Europe, and the Atlantic. In England he visited Nathaniel Hawthorne, who was serving as American consul in Liverpool. Perry was looking for someone to write a comprehensive account of all of the Japan expedition's activities, and he hoped the famous author would be interested. Hawthorne, however, turned Perry down, claiming that his official duties to the United States prevented him from taking on the project. He described Perry in his journal as "a brisk, gentlemanly, off-hand (but not rough), unaffected, and sensible man, looking not so elderly as he ought, on account of a very well-made wig. . . . I seldom meet with a man who puts himself more immediately on conversible terms than the Commodore." Hawthorne was right about everything except the wig—Perry had his own full head of dark hair. Hawthorne recommended his friend Herman Melville, who was at loose ends following the recent commercial and critical failure of *Moby-Dick* (1851) and other novels, but Perry ignored the suggestion. "It would be a desirable labor for a young literary man," Hawthorne wrote, "or, for that matter, an old one; for the world can scarcely have in reserve a less hackneyed theme than Japan."

Oddly, although Perry's achievement was hailed throughout Europe, in the United States there was little fanfare. There were speeches, presentations, and thanks from the Congress, but in 1852 the election Millard Fillmore, Perry's sponsor, had been replaced by Franklin Pierce, and Americans were now focused on the explosive issue of slavery. The *Mississippi* arrived in New York in April 1855 carrying the memorabilia, logs, and other records of the expedition to Japan to a modest welcoming crowd. Perry rented two rooms from the American Bible Society to work on his account of the expedition and hired the Reverend Francis L. Hawks as author-editor. Hawks, rector of Calvary Church in New York, was a popular sermonizer and orator who had written books on religious history, ancient Egypt, and Peruvian antiquities.

Perry and Hawks's work on the narrative sparked a rush to publish other books about Japan. Bayard Taylor, although unable to retrieve his journal from the Navy Department, published *A Visit to India, China, and Japan in the Year of 1853* (1855), and J. W. Spalding, the purser's assistant aboard the *Mississippi,* came out with *The Japan Expedition: Japan and Around the World, An Account of Three Visits to the Japanese Empire* (1855). Through news accounts of the expedition the public's appetite had been whetted; now anyone with information on Japan was busy writing an article or book. After Perry made several visits to Washington to plead for financial support, Congress promised $400,000 to publish thirty-four thousand copies of what was to be a three-volume work. Volume one, a narrative account of the Japan expedition, was published by the government in the spring of 1856 and was followed several months later by a trade edition. The government then brought out the subsequent volumes, which were not published commercially.

In the prefatory note to the first volume Perry credited his officers for their many contributions to the expedition, and in a footnote he acknowledged his debt to the journals and artwork of individuals he specifically named. Perry also declared that his "highest ambition" was to tell the story of the expedition "in such a manner as would not only present a true picture, but also keep alive the interest of the reader; his wish was to make a book that might furnish information without being wearisome." The first volume of the *Narrative* combines a history of previous voyages to Japan; a study of Japanese, Okinawan, and to some extent Chinese society; and a careful account of the American expedition. It is beautifully illustrated with full-color plates and lithographs made by William Heine either from life or from daguerreotypes that were unfortunately destroyed by a fire. Probably owing to Perry's and Hawks's strong religious beliefs as well as the tenor of the times, the *Narrative* takes a Protestant-moralist stand on ethics and chastity, and reveals a horror of lewdness and intemperance.

The second volume contains essays on different aspects of the expedition written by officers and enlisted men who accompanied Perry. Chaplain George Jones writes on the geology of Okinawa; Bayard Taylor on its botany; Joel Abbot, captain of the corvette *Macedonia,* on the west coast of Japan; and Junius J. Boyle on Volcano Bay in Hokkaido. Besides these essays Perry and Hawks enlisted specialists in the United States to evaluate the notes taken by members of the expedition and write reports. Thus, John Cassin reports on birds; James C. Brevoort on fish; and Dr. John C. Jay on shells. All three essays include many beautiful color illustrations based on paintings made on the spot by William Heine and Bayard Taylor. The third volume is devoted to a study of zodiacal light by Chaplain Jones and is full of star charts. Zodiacal light, a faint glow along the horizon caused by the reflection of sunlight before sunrise and after sunset, was carefully studied by scientists in the nineteenth century but is of little scientific interest today.

Taken in its entirety, Perry's three-volume *Narrative* is a fascinating work, much more satisfying than the subsequent one-volume versions, which either present only the first third of the work or an abridgment of the whole. Most of the text is in third person, but there are large chunks taken directly from sources other than Perry's journal that are told in first person. The sections dealing with the exploration of Okinawa and the Bonin Islands, for example, come largely from Bayard Taylor's journal and are quoted verbatim. Thus, although the *Narrative* has a veneer of dry objectivity similar to any government report, on close examination it is an anthology of journals, all dealing with the same event, carefully stitched together by Perry and Hawks.

This is not to say that the *Narrative* tells the whole story. Perry was fair and just, but he had a sizable ego. He oversaw Hawks's work, making sure everything was presented as *couleur de rose*. Although Perry's name is not on the title page as author or editor, the reality is that the *Narrative* is his book, a tale of how the generally upstanding representatives of a young democratic nation pressured the semibarbaric people of an old authoritarian empire to open their borders. Perry's critics were quick to point out that the opening was barely a crack. What was needed was a commercial treaty with Japan, and the commodore had failed to obtain this. The treaty he had returned with was a limited diplomatic pact, not the trade agreement many had expected.

The critical response to the *Narrative* was positive but qualified. A reviewer for the April 1856 issue of the *North American Review* wrote that the details of the story are "so curious, the event itself so significant, and the scenes so unique, that the whole narrative, though given in a matter-of-fact and simple style, has a romantic charm parallel with its scientific and diplomatic interest." In the next issue, however, another reviewer took exception to Hawks's eulogy of Perry and tone of national congratulation: "When the laudation passes beyond the Commodore to extol the character of the American people, it seems to us not in good taste for a government publication. It is the people who publish it. It scarcely becomes them to blow their own trumpets."

In February 1858, while he was waiting for his next assignment, Perry caught a severe cold, which, aggravated by his arthritis, lasted for weeks and finally led to his death on 4 March. The funeral was a civic event, a grand pageant with five hundred men from the Seventh Regiment, two hundred officers from the First Division of the New York State Militia, and a uniformed contingent of men and officers who had served under Perry on the Japan expedition. Reverend Hawks assisted in the service at Saint Mark's in the Bowery where Perry's coffin was deposited in the Slidell family vault. Eight years later, as Commodore Perry had requested, his body was moved to Island Cemetery in Newport near his parents.

Commodore Matthew C. Perry was the guiding force in American commercial and military expansion in the Pacific in the nineteenth century. He was a no-nonsense man of thought and action who laid the foundation for the future relationship between America and Japan. Today, Commodore Perry and his black ships are still the central metaphor used to describe the complicated relationship between these two countries and peoples. In 1945 when the Japanese signed the unconditional surrender that brought World War II to an end, they did it aboard the U.S.S. *Missouri* anchored off Yokohama, not far from where Perry's *Mississippi* had anchored ninety-two years earlier. Brought over especially for the occasion and displayed on board the *Missouri* was the tattered American flag with thirty-two stars that had flown from the commodore's ship. In his speech following the ceremony Gen. Douglas MacArthur said that Perry's "purpose was to bring to Japan an era of enlightenment and progress, by lifting the veil of isolation to the friendship, trade, and commerce of the world."

Letters:
Correspondence Relative to the Naval Expedition to Japan (Washington, D.C., 1854?).

Biography:
Samuel Eliot Morison, *"Old Bruin": Commodore Matthew Calbraith Perry* (New York: Little, Brown, 1967).

References:
William Heine, *With Perry to Japan, a Memoir by William Heine,* translated by Frederic Trautmann (Honolulu: University of Hawaii Press, 1990);
Arthur Walworth, *Black Ships off Japan: The Story of the Opening up of Japan by Commodore Perry in 1853* (New York: Knopf, 1946);
Peter Booth Wiley, *Yankees in the Land of the Gods: Commodore Perry and the Opening of Japan* (New York: Viking, 1990).

Papers:
Significant collections of Perry's manuscripts and correspondence are held by the Beinecke Library at Yale University, the Library of Congress, the National Archives, and the U.S. Naval Academy Museum. Other important repositories are at the Alderman Library at the University of Virginia, the New York Historical Society, the Chrysler Museum, and the Smithsonian Institution.

Zebulon Montgomery Pike

(5 January 1779 – 27 April 1813)

Linda Lincoln
University of Minnesota

BOOKS: *An Account of Expeditions to the Sources of the Mississippi, and through the Western Parts of Louisiana, to the Sources of the Arkansaw, Kans, La Platte, and Pierre Jaun, Rivers; Performed by Order of the Government of the United States during the Years 1805, 1806, and 1807. And a Tour through the Interior Parts of New Spain, When Conducted through These Provinces, by Order of the Captain-General in the Year 1807* (Philadelphia: C. & A. Conrad, 1810); republished as *Exploratory Travels through the Western Territories of North America: Comprising a Voyage from St. Louis, on the Mississippi, to the Source of That River, and a Journey though the Interior of Louisiana, and the North-Easter Provinces of New Spain* (London: Longman, Hurst, Rees, Orme & Brown, 1811);

The Journals of Zebulon Montgomery Pike, 2 volumes, edited by Donald Jackson (Norman: University of Oklahoma Press, 1966).

Edition: *The Expeditions of Zebulon Montgomery Pike, to Headwaters of the Mississippi River, through Louisiana Territory, and in New Spain, During the Years 1805–6–7,* 3 volumes, edited by Elliott Coues (New York: F. P. Harper, 1895); republished as 2 volumes (Mineola, N.Y.: Dover, 1984).

OTHER: "Papers of Zebulon M. Pike, 1806–1807," edited by Henry E. Bolton, *American Historical Review,* 13 (July 1908): 798–827.

The life of Zebulon Montgomery Pike was short—just thirty-four years—but it was intense and dramatic. Driven by honor, ambition, and patriotism, Pike devoted his life to the military service of his young country, carrying out his orders with single-minded zeal. For most of his career Pike operated on the frontiers of the United States, leading the two expeditions that he described in *An Account of Expeditions to the Sources of the Mississippi, and through the Western Parts of Louisiana . . . And a Tour through the Interior Parts of New Spain . . .* (1810). Pike

Zebulon Montgomery Pike soon after returning from his western expeditions, portrait by Charles Willson Peale (Independence National Historical Park Collection)

describes his expeditions to find the sources of the Mississippi and Arkansas Rivers; in addition, he includes a third section describing his experience in Mexico after he was taken captive by the Spaniards in what is now Colorado.

Published four years before *History of the Expedition under the Command of Captains Lewis and Clark* (1814), Pike's work provided the American public with its first information about the trans-Mississippi territory that had been acquired in the Louisiana Purchase. His account generated intense interest in this new territory, both among Americans and Europeans; an English edition was published in 1811, followed by translations in French, Dutch, and German. Although Pike was later suspected of being involved with Aaron Burr and Gen. James Wilkinson in their conspiracy to establish an empire in the Southwest, he successfully defended his innocence, continuing to rise through the military ranks until he was killed in battle in 1813.

Zebulon Montgomery Pike was born on 5 January 1779 in Somerset County, New Jersey, to Zebulon and Isabella (née Brown) Pike. His father had served in the Revolutionary War, rising to the rank of captain. Isabella Brown was the daughter of James Brown, who had also served as an officer in the Revolutionary War and later became a prominent landholder. When the war ended and Pike's father was discharged, he moved his family to Pennsylvania, first to a farm in Bucks County and then to land on Bald Eagle Creek. No records exist of Pike's school attendance during his childhood years, though some scholars have suggested that he attended school and received private lessons from a mathematician named Mr. Wall in Bucks County. Finding it difficult to support his growing family, Pike's father reenlisted as a captain in the army in 1792 and was transferred to Pittsburgh. His division was soon ordered down the Ohio River to defend Fort Washington in Cincinnati against Indian attacks. Isabella and the Pike children—Zebulon Montgomery, then fourteen; James, eight; Maria Herriot, four; and George Washington, a newborn—went with him to this frontier outpost.

Fort Washington was commanded by General Wilkinson, who would strongly influence Pike's military career and later become notorious for his suspected machinations with Aaron Burr. In 1794 fifteen-year-old Pike enlisted in the army, joining his father's company as a cadet. His early years in the military were unremarkable. From 1794 to 1795 Pike transported supplies from Fort Washington to the various army garrisons along the Miami River. After American troops defeated the local Indian tribes in August 1795, forcing them to give up their Ohio country and parts of eastern Indiana, Pike was sent further west and spent the next five years distributing supplies to forts along the Ohio and Mississippi Rivers. By March 1799 Pike was made a second lieutenant, and by November of the same year he became a first lieutenant. In these years he also worked to improve his meager education, studying mathematics, French, and Spanish. In 1801 he married his cousin Clarissa (Clara) Brown, from Sugar Grove, Kentucky. During the early years of their marriage, the Pikes were assigned to various frontier outposts including Fort Knox and Kaskaskia, both in Indiana.

In 1805 Wilkinson, then governor of the new Louisiana Territory, chose Pike to lead a party in the exploration of the northern reaches of the region and to locate the source of the Mississippi River. The United States had concluded the Louisiana Purchase in 1803, and President Thomas Jefferson was eager for information about the acquired lands, having already sent an expedition led by Meriwether Lewis and William Clark to search for a northwest river passage to the Pacific coast in 1804. Pike was also charged with the tasks of selecting sites for military posts, establishing peace between the Sioux and Ojibway tribes, and gathering information about the activities of British traders in the area.

On 9 August 1805 Pike left Saint Louis on a seventy-foot keelboat, accompanied by twenty men and four months' worth of provisions. As Elliott Coues points out in the biographical introduction to his edition of Pike's expedition, the young explorer's responsibilities on the expedition were extensive, as he records how he served as "astronomer, surveyor, commanding officer, clerk, spy, guide, and hunter." Frequently, Pike says, he "preced[ed] the party for miles in order to reconnoiter . . . returning in the evening, hungry and fatigued, to sit down in the open air, by firelight, to copy the notes and plot the courses of the day."

The little time and energy Pike had left for writing at the end of each day is clear from the style and content of the journal he kept during this expedition. His daily entries are factual, terse, and spare, containing such details as distances traveled, weather conditions, and geographical features. Pike shows little taste for romantic scenery or the drama of exploring new territory; his observations are those of a military man recording facts and concrete details, a truth Pike acknowledges in his preface: "As a military man—as a soldier from the time I was able to bear arms—it cannot be expected that a production of my pen can stand the test of criticism."

In one area, though, Pike's account takes on considerably more interest and drama, and that is in his descriptions of the interactions his party had with the native peoples living along the river. Pike goes into more depth and detail in his reports of these encounters, providing intriguing firsthand accounts of Indian speeches, ceremonies, feasts, and games. When visiting a Sioux village, for example, Pike is fascinated by the "many curious maneuvers" of a village dance in which men and women, "all dressed in the gayest manner," run up and blow on each other, at which point "the person blown at, whether man or woman, would fall, and appear to

who returned the compliment (on the 10.
of Aug't.) by killing 10 Sioux at the entrance
of the St Peters. Also that a war party composed
of the Sacks, Reynards and Puants of 200
Warriors had embarked on an expedition
against the Sauteaux. but that they had
heard that the Chief having had an unfa
-vourable dream persuaded the party to
return. and that I would meet them on my
voyage.

Here I was introduced to a Chief
called the Raven of the Reynards. remarke
a very Flowery speech on the occasion; which
I returned in a few words, accompanied by
a small present.

I was about embarking
and sweing my two men over by I was when
a pedogue arrived in which was a Mr Blondeau,
two Frenchmen, and my two such, whom the above
named Gentleman had engaged at the
little Town above the Rapids of Stony
river; They had been six days without
any thing to eat except muscles when they
met Mr Fanecz Read whose humanity,
and attention to them, partly restored their
strength, and Spirits, and enabled them
to reach the Reynard Village where they met
Mr Blondeau. The Indian Chief furnished
them with Corn and showed in
Friendship by every possible attention.
Immediately discharged the hire of the Indians
and send Mr Blondeau a bye the
Prairie des Chiens. Rain the wind
at pat of. Distance 25 miles.

Page from Pike's journal for 1 September 1805 (American Philosophical Society, Philadelphia)

be almost lifeless, or in great agony; but would recover slowly, rise, and join in the dance. This they called their great medicine; or, as I understood the word, dance of religion." In another instance, Pike observes a lively game of lacrosse played between a team of Sioux and a team made up of Puants and Reynards. He explains how the game is played, as well as the strategies and skills required. In the game he watched, Pike says, "the Sioux were victorious—more, I believe, from the superiority of their skill in throwing the ball than by their swiftness, for I thought the Puants and Reynards the swiftest runners."

Pike's mission was not to act as ethnographer but to assert the interests and authority of the United States over the territory and its inhabitants, and in this task he met with mixed results. While his attempt to persuade representatives of the warring tribes to come with him to Saint Louis to negotiate a peace treaty failed completely, as not a single person agreed to go with him, Pike believed that he did manage to achieve a permanent peace between the Sioux and the Ojibway. In his journal he asks, "If a subaltern with but 20 men, at so great a distance from the seat of his government could effect so important a change in the minds of those savages, what might not a great and independent power effect, if, instead of blowing up the flames of discord, they exerted their influence in the sacred cause of peace?"

Pike did gain one important concession from the Indians, persuading the Sioux near the present site of Saint Paul, Minnesota, to trade approximately one hundred thousand acres of land along the river, reaching from the confluence of the Saint Croix and Mississippi Rivers to just above Saint Anthony Falls, the present site of Minneapolis. Pike viewed this land as the best site for the garrison that was later to become Fort Snelling, an important western outpost for the United States Army. As he wrote to General Wilkinson, he was able to acquire this tract "for a song," trading presents worth $200 for land valued at $200,000. He did have some trouble persuading the Sioux chiefs to sign the treaty, recording that "they conceived their word of honor should be taken for the grant without any mark"; Pike says he convinced them, however, that "it was not on their account, but my own, that I wished them to sign it."

Pike was unable to locate the true source of the Mississippi, and the expedition collected little valuable new information about the region. He came within twenty-five miles of the actual source of the Mississippi, Lake Itasca, but followed the wrong fork of the river to Leech Lake, which he took to be the river's source. In his entry for 1 February, Pike records his "success": "I will not attempt to describe my feelings on the accomplishment of my voyage, for this is the main source of the Mississippi." With this statement Pike was echoing what many already believed true about the source of the Mississippi; like most of his other observations about the land through which he passed, Pike was largely recording information that was already known to Europeans from the travels and descriptions of French and British fur traders.

Throughout the course of his expedition, Pike failed to identify a single new stream or lake, and his maps and notes are often inaccurate and unclear. The limited achievements, however, may well have been due to his lack of reliable scientific equipment. In defending the information he collected, Pike says he had "no instruments proper for celestial observations . . . nor had I proper time-pieces or instruments for meteorological observations." With his many responsibilities, Pike says, he also had little leisure for recording scientific data. "My thoughts," he says, "were too much engrossed in making provision for the exigencies of the morrow to attempt a science which requires time, and a placidity of mind which seldom fell to my lot." His daily journal entries were "written at night, frequently by firelight, when extremely fatigued, and the cold so severe as to freeze the ink in my pen."

As these words reflect, Pike's mission to the source of the Mississippi was long and arduous; the expedition ended up taking more than double the planned four months, placing the poorly equipped party in northern Minnesota for the entire winter. Two factors that contributed to the slow progress Pike and his men made were the difficulty of negotiating the Mississippi and the unexpected challenges of winter weather, which forced the party to travel with sleds and snowshoes rather than boats and canoes. Pike and his men eventually returned safely to Saint Louis on 30 April 1806, eight months and twenty-two days after they had set out. He believed he had successfully accomplished the mission's goals, but the goals he claimed to have accomplished would unravel with time. What Pike did not know is that he had misidentified the river's source, that the Sioux and Ojibway would soon begin fighting again, that the Indian tribes would side with the British in the War of 1812, and that British traders in the area would continue their activities despite his warnings. What Pike did gain, though, was the opportunity to lead another expedition, as General Wilkinson immediately selected him to lead an exploratory mission through the southwestern parts of the Louisiana territory.

Pike's ostensible objectives for this second mission were several. He was to begin by escorting a party of Osage Indians who had been taken prisoner by the Potawatomis back to their homes on the Grand Osage River and then continue west to negotiate a peace between the Kansas and the Osage tribes. Moving still further west he was to establish contact with the Comanches, who were considered a threat because of their close association with the Spanish in the Southwest. These tasks accomplished, he was to explore the Arkansas River to its source and return via the Red River to the U.S. post at Natchitoches, in what is now the state of Louisiana.

In addition to these documented objectives, Pike also likely had instructions from General Wilkinson to collect information about the activities of the Spanish in the poorly defined western regions of the Louisiana territory. The Spanish had been upset about France's sale of the territory to the United States. In 1806 war between Spain and the United States was widely expected, and Secretary of War Henry Dearborn had instructed Wilkinson to conduct intelligence operations in the area to determine the nature and extent of Spanish activities. Pike was evidently instructed to collect this information, which Wilkinson may well have been interested in for his own purposes of establishing a rival empire in the region with the help of Aaron Burr. That Pike was aware of Wilkinson's treasonous activities is now doubted by historians.

Even more so than his voyage up the Mississippi, Pike's expedition to the source of the Arkansas was long, difficult, and perilous, particularly because the party took no winter clothing with them, as Pike had not expected to encounter the sort of winter weather he had faced in Minnesota. As it turned out, the winter endured in the Rockies was much worse, and Pike and his men suffered severe hardships, including some cases of permanent physical damage due to frozen limbs and near starvation. Before enduring the winter, however, Pike and his men had to suffer through the heat of a Missouri summer, with the party leaving Saint Louis on 15 July 1806, less than three months after Pike had returned from his previous mission. He was accompanied by twenty men, eighteen of whom had taken part in his Mississippi expedition, as well as the fifty-one Osage prisoners who were being escorted back to their villages. Pike and his men sailed in two large riverboats up the Missouri and Osage Rivers, while the Osages walked and rode beside them onshore. By 20 August the party reached the Osage villages in the area that is now western Missouri; here Pike and his men rested and negotiated the purchase of a few horses before resuming their journey on 1 September.

The party then turned northwest, toward the Pawnee Indians living on the Republican River in what is now northeastern Kansas. Pike's goals were to solicit the Pawnees' allegiance to the United States and to acquire horses and an interpreter from them, which he needed to establish contact with the Comanches to the west. Pike acquired few horses and no interpreters from the Pawnees, but he did achieve a temporary victory in persuading the Pawnee chiefs to lower the Spanish flag they had been flying and replace it with the American standard. Pike acknowledged that his request was a bold one, writing that "[t]his probably was carrying the pride of nations a little too far, as there had so lately been a large force of Spanish cavalry at the village, which had made a great impression on the minds of the young men, as to their power, consequence, etc., which my appearance with 20 infantry was by no means calculated to remove." Nevertheless, Pike insisted to the chiefs "that it was impossible for the nation to have two fathers; that they must either be the children of the Spaniards, or acknowledge their American father." When an old man silently lowered the Spanish flag and laid it at Pike's feet, Pike relented, praising the Pawnees for "show[ing] themselves dutiful children in acknowledging their great American father," returning the Spanish flag to them on the condition that it should not be raised again during his stay.

From the Pawnee villages Pike's party traveled southwest, reaching the Arkansas River, where on 28 October Lt. James Wilkinson (the general's son) and five soldiers proceeded down the river while Pike and the rest of his men headed upriver, following the trail recently left by Spanish troops across Kansas, and into the present state of Colorado. It was not long before Pike recognized that, as with his previous expedition, he would not be able to accomplish his goals in the time allotted. He decided to push on nevertheless, writing in his journal on 11 November, "I determined to spare no pains to accomplish every object, even should it oblige me to spend another winter in the desert."

A few days later, on 15 November, Pike made an encouraging discovery. Noting what at first looked like "a small blue cloud," Pike and his men soon "with one accord gave three cheers to the Mexican mountains." Pike's understanding of the size of the Rocky Mountains and thus the party's distance from them was distorted, however. On 17 November he noted that although they had "pushed on with an idea of arriving at the mountains," they "found at night no visible difference in their appearance from what we did yesterday." On 23 November, Pike thought they were close enough that it would take no more than a day's march to ascend the high point he had been viewing; from this pinnacle, he writes, the party would be "in a defensible situation" and able "to lay down the various branches and positions of the country."

Accompanied by three of his men, Pike began the journey to the top of what would become known as Pikes Peak, but again he was frustrated by the slow progress. Pike and his men marched on for several days, over slow and dangerous terrain; he writes that they found the climb "very difficult, being obliged to climb up rocks, sometimes almost perpendicular; and after marching all day we encamped in a cave, without blankets, victuals, or water." Finally, after four days of climbing left them halfway up the peak with little if anything to eat, Pike gave up, writing that "I believe no human being could have ascended to its pinical." Pike has become well known for the inaccuracy of this prediction, which was disproved in 1820 when Dr. Edwin James and his party reached the summit. In fairness to Pike it should be noted that his wording leaves it unclear whether he meant that it was impossible to ascend the peak or whether it was impossible for anyone in the condition of his party to do so. He does add that his decision to desist was influenced by "the condition of my soldiers, who had only light overalls on, no stockings, and were in every way ill provided to endur the inclemency of the region."

Pike rejoined the rest of his party, but his problems were only beginning, as bad maps and worse weather left him and his men hungry, sick, and lost. Relying on a map drawn by Alexander von Humboldt that was only partially correct, Pike's party wandered about through bitter cold and deep snow, mistaking the foot of Royal Gorge for the source of the Arkansas River. They lost the Spanish trail and followed the South Platte River. When they came again to the Arkansas, Pike mistook it for the Red River, which he believed would take them back to civilization. All the while he and his men suffered tremendously; a few had to be left behind, their feet having become frozen and gangrenous. Pike promised they would be rescued as soon as possible, which did not stop the men from later sending a desperate message to him containing "some of the bones taken out of their feet . . . conjur[ing] me, by all that was sacred, not to leave them to perish far from the civilized world."

Pike and the rest of the party continued their misguided peregrinations, crossing the Sangre de Cristo range before constructing a stockade on what they believed was the Red River. When a party of Spanish soldiers came to interrogate them, however, Pike and his men found that they were camped not on the Red River, and thus within United States territory, but on the Rio Grande, placing them well within enemy Spanish territory. Pike records his reaction to this news in his journal entry for 26 February: "I immediately ordered my flag to be taken down and rolled up, feeling how sensibly I had committed myself in entering their territory, and conscious that they must have positive orders to take me in."

One question that has dogged Pike scholars is whether the explorer was really lost when he entered Spanish territory. His writings indicate that he was eager to collect information about Spanish activities in the area, and a letter he wrote to General Wilkinson seems to imply a possible plan to wander into Spanish territory and pretend that he was lost. On 22 July 1806 Pike had written the following to Wilkinson:

> With respect to the Tetaus [Comanches], the general may rest assured I shall use every precaution previous to trusting them; but as to the mode of conduct to be pursued towards the Spaniards I feel more at a loss, as my instructions lead me into the country of the Tetaus, part of which is no doubt claimed by Spain . . . in consequence of which, should I encounter a party from the villages near Santa Fe, I have thought it would be good policy to give them to understand, that we were about to join our troops near Natchitoches, but had been uncertain about the headwaters of the rivers over which we passed.

Pike continues by suggesting the possibility that he and his men might be taken captive by the Spanish and brought to Santa Fe; "[T]his if acceded to," he writes, "would gratify our most sanguine expectations."

That Pike was eager to collect information about the Spanish is clear; that he was only pretending to be lost is much less so. Analyzing this question, Pike scholar Donald Jackson concludes that Pike was indeed lost when he encamped upon the Rio Grande. To accept the theory that he was not, Jackson says:

> [W]e must believe that Pike knew there was no Red River as far west as the Rockies, despite the information he had from such authorities as Baron von Humboldt; that when he and his men were freezing and starving . . . he was engaging in deliberate subterfuge, and that when he was confronted by a Spanish officer and was told he was encamped on the west side of the Rio Grande, his plea of ignorance was a long-planned lie. Given the

Pikes Peak, which the explorer failed to conquer

faulty knowledge of the West that Pike possessed, the thing is impossible.

Jackson argues that even Pike's letter to Wilkinson does not prove that he planned to "lose" himself in Spanish territory. Rather, "it only projected a plan to *pretend* he was lost if the need should arise." "When the time came," Jackson asserts, "he actually *was* lost."

After being discovered on the Rio Grande, Pike and his men were taken captive by the Spanish and escorted to Santa Fe, where Pike was questioned and most of his papers confiscated; he was able to retain some of his more important papers, having distributed them among his men to wear under their clothing. Pike was then sent to Chihuahua, where the case, considered a border violation, could be handled by Gen. Nemesio Salcedo, commandant general of the Interior Provinces of New Spain. Unwilling to risk a confrontation with the United States, Salcedo negotiated with U.S. officials for Pike's release, and on 28 April, Pike began the final leg of his journey, being escorted from Chihuahua to the U.S. border post at Natchitoches, where he finally arrived on 30 June 1807, nearly a year after he had set out from Saint Louis.

During the several months he spent in Mexico, Pike took extensive notes on his observations and experiences, although he was instructed by the Spanish authorities not to do so. As with his other journal entries Pike's Mexican writings are short, straightforward, and plain—hastily written before being hidden in clothes and gun barrels. Pike was particularly interested in the ways and manners of the Mexican people, the role of the Catholic clergy, and the activities of American expatriates in Mexico. These writings also show that Pike was well treated in Mexico, being frequently invited to partake in dinners, festivals, and other social activities. Pike recorded his pleasure at such treatment in his journal: "I think proper to bear testimony to the politeness, civility, and attention of all the officers who at different periods and in different provinces commanded my escort."

When Pike finally reached Natchitoches, he was no doubt pleased to be back on U.S. soil, but he soon discovered that he had returned right in the middle of Aaron Burr's celebrated trial for treason and that his name was linked with those of Burr and Wilkinson. Pike was horrified by this implication, voicing his anger and indignation in the preface to his published account:

There have not been wanting persons of various ranks who have endeavored to infuse the idea into the minds of the public that the last voyage was undertaken through some sinister designs of General Wilkinson . . . I cannot forbear, in this public manner, declaring the insinuation to be a groundless calumny, arising from the envenomed breasts of persons who, through enmity to the general, would, in attempting his ruin, hurl destruction on all those who, either through their official stations or habits of friendship, ever had any connection with that gentleman.

What Pike did not know, and which would be discovered later, is that Wilkinson had been on the Spanish payroll for several years, enriching himself through favorable trade agreements; evidence now shows that he was likely a central figure in Burr's scheme, turning against him only when it became necessary to save his own skin.

Although scholars in the past have suggested that Pike may have been involved in Wilkinson's schemes, historians now agree that Pike was likely no more than an innocent dupe of the general, collecting information that would benefit both the U.S. government and Wilkinson himself. Donald Jackson concludes that there simply is not sufficient evidence to implicate Pike in Wilkinson's activities: "His vigorous denials, upon returning from the West, seem to have sprung from a genuine ignorance of the Burr-Wilkinson plan. There is no evidence that he knew of the conspiracy." Moreover, the personality that emerges from Pike's writings is almost naively patriotic—simple, honest, and wholly dedicated to the service of his country. As Jackson writes, "Pike was not a complicated man. His faith in Wilkinson was childlike and naive; his unmistakable courage was often foolhardy. . . . He was unashamedly patriotic, openly sentimental." If Pike was guilty of anything, it was of being too loyal to his superior officer and zealous in his efforts to serve his country and rise in the military ranks.

Pike spent the next few years serving in various peacetime posts and preparing his journals for publication. These journals, published by C. and A. Conrad and Company of Philadelphia, were well received by the public, but Pike himself made little money from them because the publisher went bankrupt soon after. Pike's desire for promotion was also unmet for several years, until he was finally made a colonel in July 1812 and a brigadier general on 5 April 1813. Three weeks later on 27 April, Pike was killed leading his troops in an assault on the British fort at York (now Toronto), Canada. He was mortally wounded when a British magazine containing hundreds of barrels of gunpowder and other ammunition exploded, killing or wounding some 250 American soldiers. Before being carried away, Pike urged his men to victory, charging them to "Push on my brave fellows and avenge your general." He died a few hours later, his head resting on a captured British flag. Pike is believed to be buried in the cemetery at Sackets Harbor, New York. He was survived by his wife, Clara, and one child, a daughter also named Clara.

Biographies:

William Eugene Hollon, *The Lost Pathfinder* (Norman: University of Oklahoma Press, 1949);

John Upton Terrell, *Zebulon Pike: The Life and Times of an Adventurer* (New York: Weybright & Talley, 1968);

Elliott Coues, "Memoir of Zebulon Montgomery Pike," in his *The Expeditions of Zebulon Montgomery Pike,* volume 1 (Mineola, N.Y.: Dover, 1987), pp. xix–cxiii.

References:

Donald Jackson, "How Lost Was Zebulon Pike?," *American Heritage,* 16 (February 1965): 10–14, 75–80;

Jackson, "Zebulon Pike and Nebraska," *Nebraska History,* 47 (December 1966): 355–369;

Jackson, "Zebulon Pike 'Tours' Mexico," *American West,* 3 (Summer 1966): 64–71, 89–93.

David Porter

(1 February 1780 – 3 March 1843)

Udo Nattermann
University of Indianapolis

BOOKS: *Journal of a Cruise Made to the Pacific Ocean, by Captain David Porter, in the United States Frigate Essex, in the Years 1812, 1813, 1814. Containing Descriptions of the Cape de Verd Islands, Coasts of Brazil, Pangonia, Chili, and Peru, and of the Gallapagos Islands,* 2 volumes (Philadelphia: Bradford & Inskip, 1815); enlarged as *Journal of a Cruise Made to the Pacific Ocean. . . . Second Edition, To Which Is Now Added . . . an Introduction, in Which the Charges Contained in the Quarterly Review, of the First Edition of this Journal, Are Examined, and the Ignorance, Prejudice, and Misrepresentations of the Reviewer Exposed,* 2 volumes (New York: Wiley & Halstead, 1822); abridged as *A Voyage in the South Seas* (London: Sir R. Phillips, 1823);

An Exposition of the Facts and Circumstances which Justified the Expedition to Foxardo, and the Consequences Thereof. Together with the Proceedings of the Court of Inquiry Theron, Held by Order of the Hon. Secretary of the Navy (Washington, D.C.: Davis & Force, 1825);

Constantinople and Its Environs. In a Series of Letters, Exhibiting the Actual State of the Manners, Customs, and Habits of the Turks, Armenians, Jews, and Greeks, as Modified by the Policy of Sultan Mahmoud. By an American, Long Resident at Constantinople, 2 volumes (New York: Harper, 1835).

David Porter, portrait by Charles Willson Peale (Independence National Historical Park)

David Porter was a naval officer and a diplomat, not a professional writer; he wrote *Journal of a Cruise Made to the Pacific Ocean* (1815) and *Constantinople and Its Environs* (1835) at his friends' insistence, not to fulfill his literary aspiration. Yet his travel narratives have merit. Well received at the time of its publication, *Journal of a Cruise Made to the Pacific Ocean* is a document of early American nationalism and of American rivalry with Great Britain, an important chapter in the War of 1812. Porter's *Constantinople and Its Environs,* a loose compilation of letters he wrote to James Kirke Paulding, has remained largely unknown, though its multiplicity of voices and themes makes it a kind of precursor of Mark Twain's *The Innocents Abroad* (1869). If Porter was not blessed with great literary talent, he was at least lucky enough to be among the first Americans who would bring home to their countrymen detailed accounts of South Pacific and Middle Eastern cultures.

Born in Boston to Rebecca Henry Porter and David Porter, a veteran of the American Revolution, David Porter was raised in Baltimore and early introduced to the life of the navy. He became a midshipman in 1798 during the undeclared naval war with France and, proving himself able and courageous, rose rapidly in rank, serving as lieutenant on several ships engaged in fighting the Barbary pirates. Assigned in 1803 to the *Philadelphia* under Capt. William Bainbridge, Porter and the ship's crew were captured by Tripolitan forces and imprisoned for more than one and a half years. After his release Porter was made captain, and in 1806 he was promoted to master commandant.

Back in the United States, Porter befriended Washington Irving and became a member of his drinking club, the "Lads of Kilkenny." In 1808 Porter served as judge on four court-martial cases and married Evalina Anderson of Chester, Pennsylvania, where the couple set up residence. Though the marriage was a troubled one from the start, the Porters had ten children, one of whom was David Dixon Porter, later a famous naval officer himself and his father's biographer. It is worth noting that another member of the family, Porter's foster son, David Glasgow Farragut, also successfully pursued a military career, becoming the first admiral of the United States Navy.

Professional duties separated Porter from his wife soon after their wedding. For the next two years he was in charge of the naval station in New Orleans, overseeing ship repairs, material supplies, recruitments, and legal affairs; his military tasks were the enforcement of President Thomas Jefferson's Embargo Act and the suppression of the international slave trade. But the Louisiana experience was mostly frustrating: his father died; he came down with yellow fever; he quarreled with a superior; and he lost opportunities of improving his poor finances. Porter greatly welcomed the change that came in summer 1811 when he was given command of the frigate *Essex*, knowing that—with tensions between the United States and Great Britain growing—his chance of winning glory for himself and his country had come.

The first cruise of the *Essex* lasted a short two months, from July to September 1812. Yet Porter not only successfully intercepted several British merchant ships in the Atlantic but also captured the *Alert*, the first British warship to fall into American hands in the War of 1812. The second voyage of the *Essex*, commenced in the fall of the same year and terminated in the spring of 1814, made Porter a national hero. Assigned to harass British trade further, he sailed from Delaware Bay to the Cape Verde Islands, then along the Brazilian coast and around Cape Horn; in the South Pacific he journeyed north along the Chilean and Peruvian coasts to the Galápagos Islands, then west to the Marquesas Islands and back to Chile. There, in the port of Valparaiso, the *Essex* met her doom in bloody battle with the British frigate *Phoebe*. Though finally losing his ship to the enemy, Porter was able to do considerable economic damage to the British, for all practical purposes wiping out their whale fishery. President James Madison praised his accomplishments; Washington Irving memorialized him in the *Analectic Magazine;* and Philip Freneau eulogized the heroic battle of the *Essex* in his *Collection of Poems on American Affairs* (1815).

Journal of a Cruise Made to the Pacific Ocean chronicles the events of this voyage with an abundance of nautical and naval details, geographic and biological descriptions, as well as ethnographic and cultural observations. Yet behind the narrative's rhetoric of objectivity lurks the ever-present state of war. Porter's personal dislike of the British, his professional hostility toward their imperial force, and his political opposition to their monarchical system color his narrative. When he has the opportunity of flaunting his political predilections, Porter exploits it, boasting, for instance, how well he treated the British prisoners of war and how much they liked being under American command.

Porter treats his adventures as a test in which he has to prove his worthiness as seaman, soldier, and gentleman vis-à-vis the British—a fact that may account for some of the tediousness of his descriptions (for example, he catalogues virtually every item with which he outfitted his ship). The rounding of Cape Horn is also given considerable space in the book, perhaps justifiably so, for the *Essex* was the first American warship to attempt the feat, the first ever to show the American colors in the Pacific. The frigate's battles with and capture of British merchantmen are often related, almost anticlimactically, in relatively few words, compared to which the sum total of the financial damage done to the British is calculated in some detail. Upon arrival in Chile he rejoices in the revolutionary mood of the people and welcomes the newly established anti-Spanish regime of the Carrera brothers, to whom he would lend active support in future years. Through his writing Porter tries to create a stylized image of himself as commodore: he is not merely an officer in charge of a ship but a careful craftsman, an educated statesman, and a proud patriot.

The greatest portion of *Journal of a Cruise Made to the Pacific Ocean* concerns the exploratory activity of the *Essex*, her cruise to and through the South Pacific islands, which is illustrated by Porter's excellent drawings of, among other things, the Galápagos turtle, the breadfruit, and Polynesian

Porter's drawing of the Battle of Valparaiso, in which his ship, the Essex, *was destroyed by the British frigate* Phoebe

natives and artifacts. While the Galápagos Islands serve Porter primarily as a reservoir of provisions—the crew slaughters hundreds of tortoises, iguanas, seals, and shags—the Marquesas Islands become the locus of an unsettling cross-cultural encounter. In the text seemingly objective ethnographic accounts of the islanders' mode of warfare and fishery, religious notions and ceremonies, and system of government and customs stand next to Porter's declaration of his official goal: to use the aborigines for his own purposes.

Porter's announcement to his crew signals his attitude: "'We are bound to the Western islands, with two objects in view: Firstly, that we may put the ship in a suitable condition to enable us to take advantage of the most favourable season for our return home: Secondly, I am desirous that you should have some relaxation and amusement after being so long at sea, as from your late good conduct you deserve it.'" But repairing the ship and indulging in sexual pleasures might prove difficult, Porter warns, because the natives are "'much addicted to thieving, treacherous in their proceedings, whose conduct is governed only by fear, and regulated by views to their interest.'" That Porter ascribed his own motives to the Polynesians becomes obvious in the book: it is the Americans who try to get something for nothing by paying for valuable provisions and sexual favors with worthless scraps of iron.

Porter bluntly states that his "aim was to render all the tribes subservient," an objective he could finally achieve only at the cost of interfering in intertribal hostilities. Staying in the Marquesas Islands to prepare the *Essex* for her return required, according to Porter, that the natives be pacified, so he waged two wars in order to achieve "the utmost harmony." The second war, against the Typee, had disastrous consequences, for the American troops not only killed many natives but also utterly devastated their capital—an act for which Herman Melville would harshly criticize Porter in his novel *Typee* (1846). But for Porter military exigencies had priority over moral considerations. He was under orders, and if those orders made it necessary to impose his will on some weak foreigners, he would do so, even though he regretted harming people whose virtues and beauty he admired. Eventually, through an official declaration, Porter took formal possession of the Marquesas Islands for the United States and gave the landing place of the *Essex* American names, Massachusetts Bay and Madisonville. The act elicited from his critics his title as the first American imperialist.

Journal of a Cruise Made to the Pacific Ocean ends with a short description of the defeat of the *Essex*.

On his return trip to the United States, Porter stopped at Valparaiso, where his frigate was blockaded by two British warships, the *Phoebe,* under Capt. James Hillyar, and the *Cherub.* After an unsuccessful escape attempt the *Essex* was shot to pieces by the *Phoebe,* leaving almost half of her crew killed or wounded. Porter was arrested but was soon sent home to New York.

In the years following the war with Great Britain, Porter became a commissioner in charge of arbitrating jurisdictional disputes in the United States Navy. He remained involved in Latin American politics, helping the Carrera brothers with their fight for Chilean independence, and also wrote the two editions of his *Journal of a Cruise Made to the Pacific Ocean.* The first edition drew heavy criticism from a British critic, William Gifford, who in the *Quarterly Review* accused Porter of inaccuracy, tastelessness, and cruelty. Gifford took offense at Porter's assessment of his accomplishments as navigator and ship captain, his depiction of nude human bodies, and his warfare against the Typee. To defend his honor Porter revised *Journal of a Cruise Made to the Pacific Ocean,* providing a detailed account of the events subsequent to his departure from the Marquesas Islands, where he had left a few of his crew with the natives.

He also added a minute description of the circumstances surrounding the battle at Valparaiso, justifying his actions and accusing Captain Hillyar of improper conduct. He prefaced his revised narrative with a step-by-step refutation of Gifford's charges, pointing out that his descriptions were truthful, that his behavior in the Marquesas Islands was less cruel than that of Lord Anson and Capt. James Cook in their respective encounters with other cultures, and that Polynesian sexual mores ought not be judged by American or European standards. Ironically, Porter's call for a liberal view of sexuality was not heeded by his publisher, who omitted the allegedly obscene passages from the second edition.

Hard-pressed for money, Porter sought a more lucrative position than that of navy commissioner and took over the command of the West India Squadron, whose task was the suppression of Spanish and Latin American piracy. This assignment led to the most disgraceful event of his life. In November 1824, having learned that pirates were supposedly hiding in Fajardo, Puerto Rico, Porter sent a search group ashore; its members were first insulted and then arrested by local officials. Considering American national honor violated, Porter and two hundred of his men invaded the Spanish island to force the officials to apologize.

When his behavior became known in Washington he was called back to the United States and investigated on charges of disobedience and insubordination.

His case pending, Porter made the mistake of publicly defending his actions in a pamphlet, *An Exposition of the Facts and Circumstances which Justified the Expedition to Foxardo* (1825), which was regarded as yet another proof of his recalcitrance. He was court-martialed, found guilty, and suspended from his duties for six months. In spite of the lenient sentence he felt deeply humiliated, left the United States, and accepted an appointment as commander of the Mexican navy. In this position, which he held from 1826 to 1829, Porter met with more disappointment and failure as he was faced with mutinous crews, declining funds for his office, and even two attempts on his life. Full of hatred for the Mexicans, he returned to his mother country.

Continuing his life in exile, Porter briefly became consul general to the Barbary States in Algiers before accepting in 1831 the post of U.S. chargé d'affaires to the Ottoman Empire in Constantinople, a position upgraded in 1839 to minister resident. Except for his participation in negotiating an American-Turkish trade agreement, Porter's tenure, which lasted until his death, was a rather uneventful one. He annoyed the administrations in Washington with many insignificant dispatches, but his epistolary élan also resulted in his last literary production, *Constantinople and Its Environs.*

A sequence of letters addressed to a friend, the book resembles a diary recording Porter's activities and impressions. He calls it a "salmagundi"–a colorful prose mixture written in the tradition of Irving and Paulding–combining private reminiscence with public commentary on political issues, subjective satire with objective scholarship, and a traveler's fleeting observations with systematic instructions for the tourist. Although loose in structure and sometimes repetitive, *Constantinople and Its Environs* is given a measure of cohesion through a framing device, the editor's preface and Porter's last chapter, which state the reason the book deserves the attention of the American public: recently reformed, democratized, and modernized by Sultan Mahmoud, Turkey has become equal to the United States and therefore ought to be her political and economic partner. Porter emphasizes that his perspective is not that of the historian dealing with the past but that of the traveler concerned with the present, the here and now, wherein, he asserts, lies the truthfulness of his account. Thus, his book offers not so much a series of analyses as an abundance of descriptions of facets of Ottoman society: its infrastructure and industry, its political leadership and military system, its women and ethnic groups, its language and religious customs, and its famous tourist sites and other attractions.

Perhaps the most curious feature of *Constantinople and Its Environs* is Porter's ambiguous attitude toward the different groups of people he meets. His views can be boldly racist, particularly with respect to Jews, but also liberally cosmopolitan, as when he declares that Turks "have their customs, we have ours." He can praise the virtues of the Armenians, their hospitality and the beauty of their women, but also ridicule an Armenian man by calling him "old Tiger-cat." At times Porter uses an arrogant tone anticipatory of that of Twain, betraying a kind of Yankee impatience with the allegedly less enlightened and less rational members of mankind. Yet Porter's irony, like Twain's, does not stop here but turns self-critical, attacking the foreigners residing in Turkey and especially the diplomatic corps for their stupidity and provincialism. Thus, Porter's narrative borders on the satiric, presenting a diplomat's attempt at undermining his own professional endeavor.

The self-loathing occasionally expressed in *Constantinople and Its Environs* mirrors Porter's state of mind, for he came to regard his life and career as a failure. Filled with a high sense of personal honor and a longing for glory, he could not but look upon his achievements with bitterness. His family life was not happy, and his financial situation was always precarious; his reputation as an accomplished ship captain had been destroyed by his court-martial; and his professional life ended in relative obscurity. As a naval officer he had often had to contend with bureaucratic obstacles and the animosity of his peers. But it is only fair to add that Porter frequently had only himself to blame for the ill luck he met. He could be a cavalier but also a crank, a relativist but also a racist. The last decade of his life was overshadowed by illnesses, which made him an early invalid; nursed by a daughter and her husband during his final years, Porter died after a series of heart attacks.

Biographies:

David Dixon Porter, *Memoir of Commodore David Porter, of the United States Navy* (Albany, N.Y.: J. Munsell, 1875);

Archibald Douglas Turnbull, *Commodore David Porter, 1780–1843* (New York & London: Century, 1929);

David F. Long, *Nothing Too Daring: A Biography of Commodore David Porter, 1780–1843* (Annapolis, Md.: United States Naval Institute, 1970).

References:

William Gifford, *Quarterly Review* (London), 13 (July 1815): 352–383;

T. Walter Herbert Jr., "Educating Nature's Children," in his *Marquesan Encounters: Melville and the Meaning of Civilization* (Cambridge: Harvard University Press, 1980), pp. 78–117.

Papers:

The major Porter collections are held by the Library of Congress and the William L. Clements Library in Ann Arbor, Michigan. Other collections are held by the Historical Society of Pennsylvania, the New York Historical Society, and the United States Naval Academy Museum in Annapolis, Maryland.

James Riley

(27 October 1777 – 15 March 1840)

Paul Baepler
University of Minnesota

BOOKS: *An Authentic Narrative of the Loss of the American Brig* Commerce, *Wrecked on the Western Coast of Africa, in the Month of August, 1815: With an Account of the Sufferings of Her Surviving Officers and Crew, Who Were Enslaved by the Wandering Arabs on the Great African Desart, or Zahahrah; and Observations Historical, Geographical, &c., Made during the Travels of the Author, While a Slave to the Arabs, and in the Empire of Morocco. . . . Preceded by a Brief Sketch of the Author's Life; and Concluded by a Description of the Famous City of Tombuctoo, on the River Niger, and of Another Large City, Far South of It, Called Wassanah; Narrated to the Author at Mogadore, by Sidi Hamet, the Arabian Merchant. With an Arabic and English Vocabulary* (Hartford, Conn.: Published by the author, 1817); republished as *Loss of the American Brig* Commerce, *Wrecked on the Western Coast of Africa, in the Month of August, 1815: With an Account of Tombuctoo, and of the Hitherto Undiscovered Great City of Wassanah,* edited by Anthony Bleecker (London: John Murray, 1817); enlarged as *An Authentic Narrative of the Loss of the American Brig* Commerce, *Wrecked on the Western Coast of Africa, in the Month of August, 1815: With an Account of the Sufferings of Her Surviving Officers and Crew, Who Were Enslaved by the Wandering Arabs on the Great African Desart, or Zahahrah; and Observations Historical, Geographical, &c., Made during the Travels of the Author, While a Slave to the Arabs, and in the Empire of Morocco. . . . Preceded by a Brief Sketch of the Author's Life; and Concluded by a Description of the Famous City of Tombuctoo, on the River Niger, and of Another Large City, Far South of It, Called Wassanah; Narrated to the Author at Mogadore, by Sidi Hamet, the Arabian Merchant. With a New, Valuable, and Interesting Appendix* (New York: Published by the author, 1818; revised edition, New Haven, Conn.: Andrus, 1829); revised as *What He Saw and Did in Africa: Being a Narrative of the Loss of the American Brig* Commerce,

James Riley

Wrecked on the Western Coast of Africa: With an Account of the Sufferings of the Surviving Officers and Crew, Who Were Enslaved by the Wandering Arabs, on the African Desart, or Zahahrah; and Observations Historical, Geographical, etc., Made during the Travels of the Author, While a Slave to the Arabs and in the Empire of Morocco (New York: World, 1876);

Sequel to Riley's Narrative: being a sketch of interesting incidents in the life, voyages and travels of Capt. James Riley, from the period of his return to his native land, after his shipwreck, captivity and sufferings among the Arabs of the desert, as related in his narrative, until his death. Compiled Chiefly from the Original Journal and Manuscripts Left at His Death in the Possession of His Son, edited by William Willshire Riley

(Columbus, Ohio: G. Brewster / Springfield: A. R. Wright, 1851).

Edition: *Sufferings in Africa: Captain Riley's Narrative; An Authentic Narrative of the Loss of the American Brig* Commerce, *Wrecked on the Western Coast of Africa, in the Month of August, 1815. With an Account of the Sufferings of Her Surviving Officers and Crew, Who Were Enslaved by the Wandering Arabs on the Great African Desert, or Zahahrah, and Observations Historical, Geographical, &c., Made during the Travels of the Author While a Slave to the Arabs, and in the Empire of Morocco,* edited by Gordon H. Evans (New York: Potter, 1965).

With nearly a million copies in circulation, Capt. James Riley's narrative of his two months in captivity in the Sahara Desert, first published in 1817, was one of the best-selling books of the nineteenth century. Its original popularity can probably be traced to America's growing nationalism after the Tripolitan War (1801–1805) and the country's skirmish with Algeria in 1815. It remained in print until the middle of the century, a time when the country was divided over the issue of slavery, probably because of public fascination with the idea of a white man held as a slave by Africans. Abraham Lincoln read Riley's narrative as a child, and it has been suggested that it was one of the principal influences that formed Lincoln's stance on slavery.

Riley was born in Middletown, Connecticut, on 27 October 1777, one of thirteen children of Asher and Rebecca Sage Riley. He left school at age eight, when he was hired out by his parents to neighboring farmers. At fifteen Riley shipped out on his first voyage to the West Indies. In the ensuing five years he rose from cabin boy to cook, seaman, second mate, and chief mate; he then moved to New York City and accepted the first of many commands. In 1808 his ship, the *Two Marys,* was captured by the French, and he lost everything he owned. He got married and fathered five children, one of whom would be named after the man who redeemed Riley from slavery.

The events described in Riley's narrative began with his departure from New Orleans in June 1815 on the brig *Commerce.* He took on a cargo of brandy and wine in Gibraltar and set sail along the African coast for the Cape Verde Islands, planning to round out his lading with a store of salt. At about 10:00 P.M. on 28 August the *Commerce* ran aground in the fog, and Riley gave the command to abandon the sinking brig. Landing at a place Riley would later identify as Cape Barbas, the mariners encountered a group of bedouins. Fearing enslavement, Riley and his men rowed their longboat back into

the surf. With only a single water keg, a few pieces of salt pork, and a pig, the eleven men survived for nine days until, dehydrated and starving, they rowed to shore again on 10 September.

The crew had no choice but to deliver themselves to a group of nearby Arabs. The sailors were stripped naked and split into two groups. With little to wear, eat, or drink, and suffering capricious abuse from their master, Riley and the four other men in his group dragged themselves through the scorching desert. Riley wept for joy when he was bought by a more kindly trader, Sidi Hammet, who promised to take Riley and two of his companions to Mogadore, Morocco, and sell them to the British consul, William Willshire. After a lengthy march Riley, Aaron Savage, and Savage's son Horace reached their destination on 7 November and were redeemed for $1,852.45. Achieving a safe haven at last, Riley finally buckled. As he would later write: "My mind . . . could no longer sustain me. . . . I had remained continually bathed in tears, and shuddering at the sight of every human being, fearing I should again be carried into slavery." Riley remained insensible for three days. Nursed back to health by Willshire, he was placed aboard the *Rapid,* bound for New York, arriving in early 1816.

In 1821 Riley moved his family to Van Wert County, Ohio, where he founded the town of Willshire. His account of his experiences, *An Authentic Narrative of the Loss of the American Brig* Commerce, *Wrecked on the Western Coast of Africa, in the Month of August, 1815: With an Account of the Sufferings of Her Surviving Officers and Crew, Who Were Enslaved by the Wandering Arabs on the Great African Desert, or Zahahrah; and Observations Historical, Geographical, &c., Made during the Travels of the Author, While a Slave to the Arabs, and in the Empire of Morocco,* was published the following year. He had first written his account "entirely from memory, unaided by notes or any journal" while he recovered with the British Consul. He then verified his recollections by comparing them with his comrades.

Riley's tale is the most popular of a group of travel accounts known as Barbary captivity narratives. Since the sixteenth century Europe and North Africa had waged war against each other, capturing and enslaving thousands of prisoners. It is estimated that as many as twenty-seven thousand white captives were held in Algiers during the 1630s, and at least as many Muslims were chained aboard European galleys. Harrowing stories of North African captivity found their way into European literature as survivors began to record their experiences. Richard Hakluyt's *The Principall Navigations, Voiages and Discoveries of the English Nation* (1589), the first

Illustration for Riley's 1817 book

major anthology of travel narratives in English, includes several early captivity narratives. Miguel de Cervantes, who was himself a captive, wrote two plays about Barbary captivity; Molière's *Les Fourberies de Scapin* (1671; translated as *The Cheats of Scabin*, 1677) is based on the same situation, as are several scenes in Voltaire's *Candide* (1759).

In 1625–just five years after the establishment of the Plymouth settlement–Anglo-Americans became North African captives for the first time. The earliest American Barbary captivity narrative to survive was written by Joshua Gee in 1687. (It was published in 1943 as *Narrative of Joshua Gee of Boston, Mass., while he was captive in Algeria of the Barbary pirates, 1680–1687.)* In the late eighteenth and early nineteenth centuries many works had Barbary captivity themes, including Susanna Rowson's play *Slaves in Algiers* (1794) and Royall Tyler's novel *The Algerine Captive* (1797). Riley's shipwreck narrative, along with *The Narrative of Robert Adams, a Sailor, Who Was Wrecked on the Western Coast of Africa, in the Year 1810, Was Detained Three Years in Slavery by the Arabs of the Great Desert, and Resided Several Months in the City of Tombuctoo* (1816), Riley's shipmate Archibald Robbins's *A Journal, Comprising an Account of the Loss of the Brig* Commerce, *of Hartford (Con.) James Riley, Master, upon the Western Coast of Africa, August 28th, 1815; Also of the Slavery and Sufferings of the Author and the Rest of the Crew upon the Desert of Zahara, in the Years 1815, 1816, 1817; With Accounts of the*

Manners, Customs, and Habits of the Wandering Arabs; Also, A Brief Historical and Geographical View of the Continent of Africa (1817), and Judah Paddock's *A Narrative of the Shipwreck of the Ship* Oswego, *on the Coast of South Barbary, and of the Sufferings of the Master and Crew While in Bondage among the Arabs* (1818) became popular near the end of the period of interest in the Barbary Coast. By this time European countries had begun systematically to colonize North Africa, and Americans had begun to examine the question of slavery within their own borders.

In many early Puritan tales of captivity by Indians, such as Mary White Rowlandson's *The Soveraignty & Goodness of God, Together with the Faithfulness of His Promises Displayed; Being a Narrative of the Captivity and Restauration of M$^{rs.}$ Mary Rowlandson* (1682), the narrator casts himself or herself as a dutiful penitent who is chosen by God to undergo a litany of sufferings not unlike those visited upon Job. The narrator's endurance of these trials and eventual rescue proves his or her worthiness, and he or she becomes an exemplar for the community. A trace of this Puritan impulse remains in Riley's narrative as he admits that he cannot understand God's master plan: "Thy ways, great Father of the universe, are wise and just, and what am I! an atom of dust, that dares to murmur at thy dispensations." At the conclusion of his story he affirms that God had "snatched" him from the "jaws of destruction." He also takes the opportunity to descant on the civility of the United States, "whose political and moral institutions are in themselves the very best of any that prevail in the civilized portions of the globe." Riley's liberation marks not only God's triumph but also the triumph of civilization over barbarity. This duality structures the entire narrative.

As a mariner Riley had probably read or heard exaggerated tales of the Barbary Coast, and his ethnographic passages often echo those earlier descriptions. This feature is clear from the outset as he makes contact with the Arabs. He initially describes the first of his Arab captors in familiar terms, as having a complexion between that of an "Indian" and a "negro." As his portrait evolves, however, Riley's imagination becomes excited:

> His hair was long and bushy, resembling a *pitch mop*, sticking out every way six or eight inches from his head; his face resembled that of an ourang-outang more than a human being; his eyes were red and fiery; his mouth, which stretched nearly from ear to ear, was well lined with sound teeth; and a long curling beard, which depended from his upper lip and chin down upon his breast, gave him altogether a most horrid appearance, and I could not but imagine that those well set teeth were sharpened for the purpose of devouring human flesh!

Cannibalism marked the greatest division between a civilized world and a barbarous one, so it comes as no surprise that Riley's Arab has teeth sharpened for "devouring human flesh!" Soon Riley begins to fear that those teeth will be used on him: "I concluded my last moments had come, and that my body was doomed to be devoured by these beings, whom I now considered to be none other than Cannibals, that would soon glut their hungry stomachs with my flesh."

As the narrative proceeds, however, and Riley and his men grow more abject in their slavery, they become so hungry that the taboo against eating human meat begins to erode:

> Hunger, that had preyed upon my companions to such a degree as to cause them to bite off the flesh from their arms, had not the same effect on me. I was forced in one instance to tie the arms of one of my men behind him, in order to prevent his gnawing his own flesh; and in another instance, two of them having caught one of the boys, a lad about four years old, out of sight of the tents, were about dashing his brains out with a stone, for the purpose of devouring his flesh, when luckily at that instant I came up and rescued the child, with some difficulty, from their voracity.

At the last moment Riley is able to convince his crew that it would be more manly to die by hunger than to degrade themselves in this way. By recounting this crisis in such vivid detail, Riley illustrates the triumph of honor and self-restraint—hallmarks of an enlightened civilization—over the constant temptation to lapse into barbarism.

Throughout his account Riley describes the landscape in which he finds himself. The desert terrain is brutal to his shoeless feet, and the blowing sand scours his skin; yet he has enough detachment to make scientific speculations, theorizing that the sea once covered the desert. The towering Atlas Mountains in the distance fill him with awe. Later, "Notwithstanding my frame was literally exhausted, yet my imagination transported me back to a time when this region might have been inhabited by men in a higher state of civilization, and when it was probably one of the fairest portions of the African continent."

The situation of an American held in bondage on the continent from which the United States had imported its own slaves must have made some of Riley's readers question the institution of slavery. Riley's narrative is listed in John Locke Scripps's campaign biography of Lincoln (1860), which Lincoln himself revised, as one of the books that the young Lincoln owned. In 1934 the scholar R. Gerald McMurtry credited Riley with influencing Lincoln's antislavery position.

Although the entire narrative could be regarded as a consideration of slavery, Riley confronts the issue explicitly in only a few passages. Early in their captivity, Riley and his men encounter a "negro slave," Boireck, who makes constant fun of the Americans: "He would poke our sore flesh with a sharp stick, to make sport, and show the Arabs what miserable beings we were, who could not even bear the rays of the sun (the image of God, as they term it) to shine upon us." One of the crew can hardly contain his anger, but Riley admonishes him: " 'Let the negro laugh if he can take any pleasure in it; I am willing he should do so, even at my expense: he is a poor slave himself, naked and destitute, far from his family and friends, and is only trying to gain the favour of his masters and mistresses, by making sport of us, whom he considers as much inferior to him as he is to them.' "

By the conclusion of the narrative Riley's sufferings have convinced him of the immorality of all slaveholding: "I have now learned to look with compassion on my enslaved and oppressed fellow creatures, and my future life shall be devoted to their cause:—I will exert all my remaining faculties to redeem the enslaved, and to shiver in pieces the rod of oppression." This magnanimous sentiment, however, is tempered by a greater fear:

I am far from being of the opinion that they should all be emancipated immediately, and at once. I am aware that such a measure would not only prove ruinous to great numbers of my fellow citizens, who are at present slave holders, and to whom this species of property descended as an inheritance; but that it would also turn loose upon the face of a free and happy country, a race of men incapable of exercising the necessary occupations of civilized life, in such a manner as to ensure to themselves an honest and comfortable subsistence.

Because the Arabs separated the crew of the *Commerce,* Riley could recount only the experiences of his own party. Robbins, who served aboard the brig as an able seaman, traveled with the other band of captives; his narrative went through thirty editions. Robbins, who languished in captivity far longer than his captain, faulted Riley for choosing an unfamiliar route to the Cape Verde Islands, for ignoring the mate's warning that the ship was venturing too near the coast, and for encouraging the crew to stuff their clothing full of money—which only incited the Arabs to treat the men more cruelly.

Another edition of Riley's narrative, with a new appendix, was published in 1818. He was elected to the Ohio legislature in 1823. In January 1828 he wrote a continuation of his life story, which was published in a revised edition of his narrative in 1829. Riley returned to the sea in 1831, continuing to trade between Morocco and various American ports. He died aboard his brig, the *William Tell,* on 15 March 1840. In 1851 his son William Willshire

Riley published *Sequel to Riley's Narrative;* compiled from journals and manuscripts James Riley had left behind at his death, it tells the story of his life subsequent to the captivity. Eight more editions of Riley's original narrative appeared between his death and the beginning of the Civil War; it then went out of print until 1965, when the Clarkson N. Potter firm brought out the first half of the account. Though highly popular in its day, Riley's narrative has been virtually forgotten. It is, however, important not only as a document of how nineteenth-century Americans imagined Africa but also for its effect on how people conceived of slavery in their own country.

References:

R. Gerald McMurtry, "The Influence of Riley's *Narrative* upon Abraham Lincoln," *Indiana Magazine of History,* 30 (June 1934): 133–138;

Archibald Robbins, *A Journal, Comprising an Account of the Loss of the Brig* Commerce, *of Hartford (Con.) James Riley, Master, upon the Western Coast of Africa, August 28th, 1815; Also of the Slavery and Sufferings of the Author and the Rest of the Crew upon the Desert of Zahara, in the Years 1815, 1816, 1817; With Accounts of the Manners, Customs, and Habits of the Wandering Arabs; Also, A Brief Historical and Geographical View of the Continent of Africa* (Hartford, Conn.: Printed by F. D. Bolles, 1817);

John Locke Scripps, *Tribune Tracts—No. 6: Life of Abraham Lincoln* (New York: Greeley, 1860).

Catharine Maria Sedgwick

(28 December 1789 – 31 July 1867)

Stephanie A. Tingley
Youngstown State University

See also the Sedgwick entries in *DLB 1: The American Renaissance in New England* and *DLB 74: American Short-Story Writers Before 1880.*

BOOKS: *A New-England Tale; or, Sketches of New-England Character and Manners* (New York: Bliss & White, 1822; London: Miller, 1822); enlarged as *A New England Tale and Miscellanies* (New York: Putnam, 1852);

Mary Hollis: An Original Tale (New York: New York Unitarian Book Society, 1822);

Redwood: A Tale, 2 volumes (New York: Bliss & White, 1824);

The Travellers: A Tale, Designed for Young People (New York: Bliss & White, 1825);

The Deformed Boy (Brookfield: E. G. Merriam, 1826);

Hope Leslie; or, Early Times in Massachusetts, 2 volumes (New York: White, Gallaher & White, 1827);

A Short Essay to Do Good (Stockbridge: Webster & Stanley, 1828);

Clarence; or, A Tale of Our Own Times, 2 volumes (Philadelphia: Carey & Lea, 1830; London: Colburn & Bentley, 1830; revised edition, New York: Putnam, 1849);

Home (Boston: Munroe, 1835; London: Simpkin Marshall, 1836);

The Linwoods: or, "Sixty Years Since" in America, 2 volumes (New York: Harper, 1835; London: Churton, 1835);

Tales and Sketches (Philadelphia: Carey, Lea & Blanchard, 1835);

The Poor Rich Man, and The Rich Poor Man (New York: Harper, 1836; London: Tegg, 1837);

Live and Let Live; or, Domestic Service Illustrated (New York: Harper, 1837; London: Green, 1837);

A Love Token for Children (New York: Harper, 1838);

Means and Ends; or, Self-Training (Boston: March, Capen, Lyon & Webb, 1839);

Stories for Young Persons (New York: Harper, 1841; London: Tilt & Bogue, 1841);

Catharine Maria Sedgwick, engraving after a portrait by Charles C. Ingham

Letters from Abroad to Kindred at Home, 2 volumes (London: Moxon, 1841; New York: Harper, 1841);

Tales and Sketches: Second Series (New York: Harper, 1844);

Morals or Manners; or, Hints for Our Young People (New York: Wiley & Putnam, 1846; London: Wiley, 1846);

Facts and Fancies for School-Day Reading (New York & London: Wiley & Putnam, 1848);

The Boy of Mount Rhigi (Boston: C. H. Pierce, 1848);

Tales of City Life. I. The City Clerk. II. "Life Is Sweet" (Philadelphia: Hazard & Mitchell, 1850);

Married or Single? (1 volume, London: Knight, 1857; 2 volumes, New York: Harper, 1857);

Memoir of Joseph Curtis, a Model Man (New York: Harper, 1858);

The Power of Her Sympathy: The Autobiography and Journal of Catharine Maria Sedgwick, edited by Mary Kelley (Boston: Massachusetts Historical Society, 1993).

Edition: *Hope Leslie; or, Early Times in Massachusetts,* edited by Mary Kelley (New Brunswick, N.J.: Rutgers University Press, 1987).

OTHER: "Le Bossu," in *Tales of Glauber-Spa,* 2 volumes, edited by William Cullen Bryant (New York: Harper, 1832), I: 25–108;

"A Memoir of Lucretia Maria Davidson," in *Lives of Sir William Phips, Israel Putnam, Lucretia Maria Davidson, and David Rittenhouse,* volume 7 of *The Library of American Biography,* edited by Jared Sparks (Boston: Hilliard, Gray / London: Kennett, 1837), pp. 219–294.

SELECTED PERIODICAL PUBLICATIONS– UNCOLLECTED: "The Irish Girl," *United States Magazine and Democratic Review,* 10 (February 1842): 129–140;

"A Huguenot Family," *Godey's Lady's Book,* 25 (September 1842): 144–148, 189–193;

"Imelda of Bologna," *Columbia Lady's and Gentleman's Magazine,* 5 (1846): 153–161;

"Owasonook," *Sartain's Union Magazine,* 6 (June 1850): 399–407.

Catharine Maria Sedgwick enjoyed both critical and popular acclaim during her lifetime for her novels, short stories, sketches, and advice manuals as well as for her sole contribution to the genre of travel literature: *Letters from Abroad to Kindred at Home* (1841). Critics in her own day praised Sedgwick's use of American history, characters, and settings as well as her investigation of American manners, morals, values, and ideals, and beginning in 1822 with the publication of her first novel, *A New-England Tale,* they regularly listed Sedgwick as one of the founders of American literature, a group that included Washington Irving, James Fenimore Cooper, and William Cullen Bryant. Since Sedgwick's work was rediscovered in the 1970s most of the critical attention has been paid to her novels, especially the historical novel *Hope Leslie* (1827), reprinted in 1987 as part of the Rutgers University Press American Women Writers series, which deals with attitudes in Puritan New England toward religion, women's roles, and relationships between whites and Native Americans. In contrast, little has been written about the nonfiction prose—mostly didactic—on which she

focused during the last half of her long career as a professional writer.

In *Woman's Fiction* (1978) Nina Baym points out that Sedgwick's career was atypical because, unlike most female writers of her time, she "turned to writing as diversion and psychological therapy rather than for economic reasons." Her family strongly and consistently supported her literary efforts. During the first half of her career Sedgwick spent most of her energy on fiction; after 1835 she turned largely to various kinds of nonfiction prose: moral tales, pieces to teach lessons to children or to be read in Sunday school, etiquette books, and essays.

The didactic purpose that dominates her later writing is evident in her earlier fiction as well, for as Mary Kelley notes, "from the beginning of her career . . . the aesthetic and the moral were joined." Sedgwick herself makes the utilitarian and didactic purposes of her writing explicit in a letter to her friend, the Reverend Dr. William Ellery Channing dated 24 August 1837: "When I feel that my writings have made any one happier or better, I feel an emotion of gratitude to Him who has made me the medium of any blessing to my fellow creatures."

Born in Stockbridge, Massachusetts, on 28 December 1789, Sedgwick was the third daughter and sixth of seven children of Theodore Sedgwick and his second wife, Pamela Dwight Sedgwick. Sedgwick's father, a leading Massachusetts Federalist, served in both houses of the legislature and later in the United States Senate and House of Representatives. She enjoyed the educational and social benefits that her family's prominence provided. Although she says in her autobiography, *The Power of Her Sympathy* (1993), " 'Education' in the common sense I had next to none, but there was much chance seed dropped in the fresh furrow, and some of it was good seed, and some of it, I may say, fell on good ground," she in fact attended the local district schools and, later, prestigious boarding schools for young ladies in Albany, New York City, and Boston. She also grew up in a rich intellectual environment. In her autobiography she recalls: "I was reared in an atmosphere of high intelligence. My father had uncommon mental vigor. So had my brothers. Their daily habits, and pursuits, and pleasures were intellectual, and I naturally imbibed from them a kindred taste." The Sedgwick household was filled with cultivated guests who talked articulately and energetically about art, politics, literature, and theology. As an adult she would be part of a Unitarian circle that included such Boston luminaries as the Channings and the Peabodys.

The Sedgwick home in Stockbridge, Massachusetts

Sedgwick wrote often about the need for women to be self-sufficient, and her novels are rich with women characters who are active, independent, strong, and articulate. Yet rather than argue for equal rights, she advocated the notion of separate spheres, believing that women could achieve the most in their traditional roles as the spiritual and moral centers of their families and communities. Sedgwick never married, although she turned down several marriage proposals, and after her father's death in 1813 she spent much of her adult life in her brothers' homes: winters at Robert's home in New York City and summers at Charles's home in Lenox, Massachusetts. Her decision to remain single was unusual in her time, for nine out of ten nineteenth-century women married. Her last novel, *Married or Single?* (1857), pokes fun at the stereotype of the spinster as homely, pitiful, and unhappy and argues that remaining single was preferable to being in a bad marriage. In an 18 May 1828 entry in her private journal, however, Sedgwick expresses ambivalence about her choice and her circumstances: "From my own experience I would not advise any one to remain unmarried. . . ." In an 1854 entry she writes, "I certainly think a happy marriage the happiest condition of human life," yet "it is the high opinion

of its capabilities which has perhaps kept me from adventuring in it." In place of a family of her own Sedgwick developed close relationships with her brothers and their families; she considered her nieces and nephews—especially her namesake, Kate—her surrogate children.

In addition to her yearly trips to New York City, Sedgwick undertook excursions to Niagara Falls, Canada, and Virginia; went on an extensive tour of the western United States that included a boat trip down the Mississippi River; and made one extended journey to Europe. Nevertheless, she repeatedly insisted that she preferred staying at home in the familiar environs of the Berkshires. In an 1821 letter from Lake Champlain, Canada, to her sister-in-law she says:

> I begin to snuff my native air, and feel its inspiration warming my heart with the anticipated delight of home faces and home scenes. I begin to suspect that I am quite too national for this philosophic age, but would not, if I could, be cured of my prejudices in favor of my own people.

Similarly, Sedgwick in 1821 before she traveled abroad resists her friend Mrs. Frank Channing's suggestion that she go to Europe:

LETTERS FROM ABROAD

TO

KINDRED AT HOME.

"Well, John, I think we must own that God Almighty had a hand in making
other countries besides ours."—*The Brothers.*

BY THE AUTHOR OF

"HOPE LESLIE," "POOR RICH MAN AND THE RICH POOR MAN,"
"LIVE AND LET LIVE," &c., &c.

IN TWO VOLUMES.

VOL. I.

NEW-YORK:

HARPER & BROTHERS, 82 CLIFF-STREET.

1841.

*Title page for Sedgwick's only travel book, in which she views Europe with
"The eye of a denizen of the New World"*

I am not at all prepared for many of the advantages that might be reaped from a voyage to Europe, and as to happiness, I have had such an old-fashioned bringing up that there is no equivalent for me for the pleasures of home. . . . There is nothing distant and foreign that has such charms to my imagination as the haunts about my own home, a chase along the banks of our little stream with the children, breaking willow sticks for the boys, helping the girls to get the flowers, and devising and leading their sports. . . .

Sedgwick regularly incorporates details from her travels into her novels, making most frequent use of the rural landscapes and small villages of her native Berkshire region. In *Hope Leslie,* for example, Hope and Mr. Fletcher climb Mount Holyoke, near Northampton, and Sedgwick describes the magnificent views of the Connecticut Valley from the summit. An 1821 letter in which she describes her trip to Niagara Falls and Canada becomes part of a key scene in *Clarence* (1830); chapter 14 of *Married or Single?* includes an elegant extended description of Mapleton as a typical New England village. Edward

Halsey Foster notes that Sedgwick's descriptions have much in common with James Fenimore Cooper's novels and the paintings of the Hudson River School: "The characters are shown surrounded by a vast landscape," and a contrast or tension is often set up between civilization and wilderness.

Sedgwick's fictional narrators regularly stop the story to comment on Americans' reasons for traveling and to offer a critique of their behavior as tourists. In chapter 15 of *Clarence* the narrator notes acerbically:

> Nothing is more characteristic of our country than the business-like way in which pleasure is pursued. . . . The host of travellers who run away from their offices, counters, and farms, for a few hot weeks in mid-summer, hurry from post to post, as if they were in truth "following the business of travelling for a living."

Sedgwick often poses as an outsider describing and analyzing American society, much as an anthropologist might. In an 11 May 1833 journal entry she asks herself: "Let me see how I would describe the society of New York if I were writing to a correspondent abroad. . . . This is not easy to give with truth." Sedgwick is particularly fascinated with how values and behavior reflect a national identity that champions democracy and celebrates individuality.

Sedgwick employs a similar didactic tone in her comments on proper behavior for travelers in the advice manuals and other nonfiction prose she wrote later in her career. In *Morals or Manners; or, Hints for Our Young People* (1846) she says that "manners are a most important distinction where all are born to equal rights, and where the highest places are open to all." She admonishes her young readers:

> Remember that among strangers, good breeding is the stamp that marks you. If you are in a steamer, a railroad car, or even an omnibus, be observant of others, and unselfish—do not in any way annoy them. Do not eagerly look out for the best seat. Do not, in a steamer, if you happen to be sleepless at night, talk aloud to the disturbance of those who can sleep, and fain would.

Like other travelers in nineteenth-century America, she spends pages railing against her countrymen's habit of chewing tobacco and spitting.

In *Means and Ends; or, Self-Training* (1839), an advice manual for those entering careers in domestic service, she celebrates the ways travel equalizes and enriches Americans of differing backgrounds and financial means:

> The habit of travelling that prevails and is increasing among our people, is favorable to good manners. In our steamboats and rail-road cars, the humblest, and hitherto most sequestered individual, sits side by side, eats at the same table, and sleeps in the same apartment, with the most highly educated and polished. Very dull must those be who cannot, if they will, profit by a good model.

Sedgwick recommends that her readers further improve themselves by reading good travel writing:

> You may lack money and opportunity to travel twenty miles from home, when, for one or two dollars, you may buy a book that will take you with a well-instructed and all-observing companion half over the world. Or, if you cannot expend the cost of the book you may get it from a society, or district-library; or borrow it from some kindly-disposed person.

In her own contribution to the travel-literature genre, the two-volume *Letters from Abroad to Kindred at Home,* Sedgwick shows how travel can contribute to an individual's education and compares the New World with the Old World. In 1839 and 1840 she toured England, Belgium, Germany, Switzerland, France, and Italy with her brother Robert, his wife, her favorite niece, and their eldest daughter, Kate. Robert had suffered a stroke in the mid 1830s, and his family hoped that European touring would restore his health. The improvement Robert enjoyed was only temporary; he died a few months after their return to the United States.

Sedgwick's travel essays are written in the form of letters to the daughter of her brother Charles. In the preface to the first volume she alludes only obliquely to the personal context of her trip, writing apologetically:

> Of *my friends,* then, I ask indulgence for the following pages. . . . Our tour was made under circumstances which forbade any divergence from the highway of all the travelling world, and, consequently, we passed over a field so thoroughly reaped that not an ear, scarcely a kernel, remains for the gleaner. In addition to this, and to painful anxieties and responsibilities that accompanied us at every step, we were followed by intelligence of deep domestic calamity. On this subject I need not enlarge; the disqualifying influence of these circumstances will be comprehended without my opening the sanctuary of private griefs.

It is not known what the "domestic calamities" might have been. Sedgwick also does not mention that as a famous American writer she was treated as a celebrity in Europe. She met some of the most prominent people on the Continent, including royalty, writers, and artists.

Sedgwick's allusion to fields "so thoroughly reaped that not an ear, scarcely a kernel, remains for the gleaner" reveals that she is aware that her travel book is joining countless others. She says that she has tried to avoid tedious repetition of the same material:

I was aware that our stayers-at-home had already something too much of churches, statues, and pictures, and yet that they cannot well imagine how much they make up the existence of tourists in the Old World. I have sedulously avoided this rock, and must trust for any little interest my book may possess to the honesty with which I have recorded my impressions, and to the fresh aspect of familiar things to the eye of a denizen of the New World. The fragmentary state in which my letters appear is owing to my fear of wearying readers less interested than my own family by prolonged details or prosing reflections, or disgusting them with the egotism of personal experience.

Sedgwick's primary interest is in comparing Europe with America and trying to tell her readers "truly what I see and hear," looking with fresh American eyes on foreign scenes while avoiding the conventional long-winded, detailed descriptions of guidebooks. She tries to demonstrate that for the most part American scenery, mores, and ideals are better than European ones: "We passed villages [on the way to Liège] at short intervals, not bearing the smallest resemblance to a new-England village, for there is nothing that bears the name in Europe so beautiful. I may say this without presumption after having seen the English villages." Later she writes, "My dear C., it is worth the trouble of a pilgrimage to the Old World to learn to feel—to *realize* our political blessings and our political exemptions."

Sedgwick's perceptions of Europe are often colored by her reading. On her way to Florence, she notes, she was "amid scenery so wild and solitary that it recalled my earliest ideas of Italy got from Mrs. Radcliffe's romances." In London she is reminded of Charles Dickens's *Pickwick Papers* (1836–1837): "And, by-the-way, the passing equipages appear to us the originals of Cruikshank's illustrations, and the parties driving them facsimiles of Pickwick (the modern Don Quixote) and his club." Somewhat contradictorily, Sedgwick is annoyed by Europeans who draw stereotypical impressions about America from literature:

"I took him for an American," said one of my companions, with perfect nonchalance. "Pray tell me why." "He looks so like the picture in Mrs. Trollope's book." It is true, this was a secluded young person in a provincial town, but I felt mortified that in one fair

young mind Mrs. Trollope's vulgar caricatures should stand as the type of my countrymen.

Later, she complains:

I have heard persons repeatedly expressing a desire to visit America—for what? "To see a prairie"—"to see Niagara"—"to witness the manner of the help to their employers; it must be so very comical!" but, above all, "to eat canvass-back ducks!" The canvass-backs are in the vision of America what St. Peter's is in the view of Rome.

Sedgwick confesses, "With my strong American feelings, and my love of home so excited that my nerves were all on the outside, I was a good deal shocked to find how very little interest was felt about America in the circles I chanced to be in."

There are, however, passages in which Sedgwick reports being swept away by the beauties of the European landscape. Her most ecstatic response comes when she first glimpses the Alps:

We have heard of the Alps all our lives. We have read descriptions of them in manuscript and print, in prose and poetry; we knew their measurement; we have seen sketches, and paintings, and models of them; and yet, I think, if we had looked into the planet Jupiter, we could scarcely have felt a stronger emotion of surprise. In truth, up, up, where they hung and shone, they seemed to belong to heaven rather than earth; and yet, such is the mystery of the spirit's kindred with the effulgent beauty of God's works, that they seemed: A part of me and my soul, as I of them.

A pioneering work in a field American women writers were just beginning to enter, Sedgwick's *Letters from Abroad to Kindred at Home* was reviewed enthusiastically and became a best-seller in America. Sedgwick was cared for during the last few years of her life by her niece Kate, in whose home in West Roxbury, Massachusetts, she died on 31 July 1867.

Letters:
Life and Letters of Catharine M. Sedgwick, edited by Mary E. Dewey (New York: Harper, 1871).

References:
Nina Baym, *Woman's Fiction: A Guide to Novels by and about Women in America, 1820–1870* (Ithaca, N.Y.: Cornell University Press, 1978), pp. 53–63;
Gladys Brooks, *Three Wise Virgins* (New York: Dutton, 1957), pp. 180–210;
Lee Virginia Chambers-Schiller, *Liberty a Better Husband: Single Women in America. The*

Generations of 1780–1840 (New Haven: Yale University Press, 1984);

Edward Halsey Foster, *Catharine Maria Sedgwick* (New York: Twayne, 1974);

Mary Kelley, "*Legacy* Profile: Catharine Maria Sedgwick (1789–1867)," *Legacy,* 6 (Fall 1989): 43–50;

Kelley, "Negotiating a Self: The Autobiography and Journals of Catharine Maria Sedgwick," *New England Quarterly,* 66 (1993): 366–398;

Kelley, *Private Woman, Public Stage: Literary Domesticity in Nineteenth-Century America* (New York: Oxford University Press, 1984), pp. 199–206, 236–246;

Kelley, "A Woman Alone: Catharine Maria Sedgwick's Spinsterhood in Nineteenth-Century America," *New England Quarterly,* 51 (June 1978): 209–225;

Sister Mary Michael Welsh, *Catharine Maria Sedgwick: Her Position in the Literature and Thought of Her Time up to 1860* (Washington, D.C.: Catholic University of America Press, 1937).

Papers:
Catharine Maria Sedgwick's letters, diaries, and journals are at the Massachusetts Historical Society, Boston. Although most of her papers are located in the Catharine Maria Sedgwick Papers, some of her letters are in the Sedgwick Family Papers.

Lydia H. Sigourney

(1 September 1791 – 10 June 1865)

Laurie Delaney
University of Cincinnati

See also the Sigourney entries in *DLB 1: The American Renaissance in New England, DLB 42: American Writers for Children Before 1900,* and *DLB 73: American Magazine Journalists, 1741–1850.*

BOOKS: *Moral Pieces, in Prose and Verse* (Hartford, Conn.: Sheldon & Goodwin, 1815);

The Square Table, anonymous (Hartford, Conn.: Goodrich, 1819);

No. II. The Square Table, or the Meditations of Four Secluded Maidens Seated around It, anonymous (Hartford, Conn., 1819);

Traits of the Aborigines of America: A Poem, anonymous (Cambridge, Mass.: Harvard University Press, printed by Hilliard & Metcalf, 1822);

Sketch of Connecticut, Forty Years Since, anonymous (Hartford, Conn.: Cooke, 1824);

Poems (Boston: Goodrich / Hartford, Conn.: Huntington, 1827);

Female Biography; Containing Sketches of the Life and Character of Twelve American Women, anonymous (Philadelphia: American Sunday-School Union, 1829);

Biography of Pious Persons: Abridged for Youth, 2 volumes, anonymous (Springfield, Mass.: Merriam, 1832);

Evening Readings in History: Comprising Portions of the History of Assyria, Egypt, Tyre, Syria, Persia, and the Sacred Scriptures; With Questions, Arranged for the Use of the Young, and of Family Circles, anonymous (Springfield, Mass.: Merriam, 1833; London, 1834);

Letters to Young Ladies, anonymous (Hartford, Conn.: Printed by P. Canfield, 1833; London: Simpkin, Marshall, 1835; revised edition, Hartford, Conn.: Watson, 1835; enlarged edition, New York: Harper, 1837; enlarged again, London: Jackson & Walford / Edinburgh: Innes, 1841; New York: Harper, 1842);

The Farmer and the Soldier: A Tale, as L. H. S. (Hartford, Conn.: Printed by J. Hubbard Wells, 1833);

Lydia H. Sigourney (Connecticut Historical Society)

Memoir of Phebe P. Hammond, a Pupil in the American Asylum at Hartford (New York: Sleight & Van Norden, 1833);

The Intemperate, and the Reformed: Shewing the Awful Consequences of Intemperance and the Blessed Effects of the Temperance Reformation (Boston: Bliss, 1833);

Sketches (Philadelphia: Key & Biddle, 1834; London: Rich, 1834);

Poetry for Children (Hartford, Conn.: Robinson & Pratt, 1834); enlarged as *Poems for Children* (Hartford, Conn.: Canfield & Robbins, 1836);

Poems (Philadelphia: Key & Biddle, 1834); enlarged as *Select Poems* (Philadelphia: Greenough, 1838;

enlarged edition, Philadelphia: Biddle, 1842; enlarged again, 1845);

Lays from the West, edited by Joseph Belcher (London: Ward, 1834);

Tales and Essays for Children (Hartford, Conn.: Huntington, 1835);

Memoir of Margaret and Henrietta Fowler, anonymous (Boston: Perkins, Marvin / Philadelphia: Perkins, 1835); republished as *The Lovely Sisters, Margaret and Henrietta* (Hartford, Conn.: Parsons, 1845); republished as *Margaret and Henrietta* (New York: American Tract Society, 1852);

Zinzendorff, and Other Poems (New York: Leavitt, Lord / Boston: Crocker & Brewer, 1835);

History of Marcus Aurelius, Emperor of Rome (Hartford, Conn.: Belknap & Hamersley, 1836);

Olive Buds (Hartford, Conn.: Watson, 1836);

Stories for Youth: Founded on Fact (Hartford, Conn.: Watson, 1836);

The Girl's Reading-Book: In Prose and Poetry, for Schools (New York: Taylor, 1838; revised, 1839); republished as *The Book for Girls* (New York: Taylor, 1844);

Letters to Mothers (Hartford, Conn.: Hudson & Skinner, 1838; London: Wiley & Putnam, 1839; enlarged edition, New York: Harper, 1839);

The Boy's Reading-Book: In Prose and Poetry, for Schools (New York: Taylor, 1839); enlarged as *The Boy's Book* (New York: Turner, Hughes & Hayden / Raleigh, N.C.: Turner & Hughes, 1843);

Memoir of Mary Anne Hooker (Philadelphia: American Sunday-School Union, 1840);

Pocahontas, and Other Poems (London: Tyas, 1841; revised edition, New York: Harper, 1841);

Poems, Religious and Elegiac (London: Tyas, 1841);

Pleasant Memories of Pleasant Lands (Boston: Munroe, 1842; London: Tilt & Bogue, 1843; revised and enlarged, Boston: Munroe, 1844);

Poems (Philadelphia: Locken, 1842);

The Pictorial Reader, Consisting of Original Articles for the Instruction of Young Children (New York: Turner & Hayden, 1844); republished as *The Child's Book: Consisting of Original Articles, in Prose and Poetry* (New York: Turner & Hayden, 1844);

Scenes in My Native Land (Boston: Munroe, 1845; London: Wiley & Putnam, 1845);

Poetry for Seamen (Boston: Munroe, 1845); enlarged as *Poems for the Sea* (Hartford, Conn.: Parsons, 1850); republished as *The Sea and the Sailor* (Hartford, Conn.: Brown, 1857);

The Voice of Flowers (Hartford, Conn.: Parsons, 1846);

Myrtis, with Other Etchings and Sketchings (New York: Harper, 1846);

The Weeping Willow (Hartford, Conn.: Parsons, 1847);

Water-Drops (New York & Pittsburgh: Carter, 1848);

Illustrated Poems . . . With Designs by Felix O. C. Darley (Philadelphia: Carey & Hart, 1849);

Whisper to a Bride (Hartford, Conn.: Parsons, 1850);

The Poetical Works of Mrs. L. H. Sigourney, edited by F. W. N. Bayley (London: Routledge, 1850);

Examples of Life and Death (New York: Scribner, 1851);

Letters to My Pupils: With Narrative and Biographical Sketches (New York: Carter, 1851);

Olive Leaves (New York: Carter, 1852);

The Faded Hope (New York: Carter, 1853); republished as *Faded Hopes* (London: Nisbet, 1853);

Memoir of Mrs. Harriet Newell Cook (New York: Carter, 1853);

The Western Home, and Other Poems (Philadelphia: Parry & McMillan, 1854);

Past Meridian (New York: Appleton / Boston: Jewett, 1854; London: Hall, 1855; enlarged edition, Hartford, Conn.: Brown, 1856; revised and enlarged edition, Hartford, Conn.: Brown & Gross, 1864);

Sayings of the Little Ones, and Poems for Their Mothers (Buffalo: Phinney / New York: Ivison & Phinney, 1855);

Examples from the Eighteenth and Nineteenth Centuries (New York: Scribner, 1857);

Lucy Howard's Journal (New York: Harper, 1858; London: Low, 1858);

The Daily Counsellor (Hartford, Conn.: Brown & Gross, 1859);

Gleanings (Hartford, Conn.: Brown & Gross / New York: Appleton, 1860);

The Man of Uz, and Other Poems (Hartford, Conn.: Williams, Wiley & Waterman, 1862);

The Transplanted Daisy: A Memoir of Frances Racillia Hackley (New York: Printed by Sanford, Harroun, 1865);

Letters of Life (New York: Appleton, 1866);

Great and Good Women: Biographies for Girls (Edinburgh: Nimmo, 1866).

OTHER: *The Writings of Nancy Maria Hyde, of Norwich, Conn. Connected with a Sketch of Her Life,* edited anonymously by Sigourney (Hartford, Conn.: Printed by Russell Hubbard, 1816);

The Religious Souvenir, for MDCCCXXXIX, edited by Sigourney (New York: Scofield & Voorhies, 1839);

The Religious Souvenir, edited by Sigourney (New York: Scofield & Voorhies, 1839); republished as *The*

Frontispiece depicting Sir Walter Scott's home and the title page for Sigourney's first travel book
(courtesy of Special Collections, Ohio University)

Christian Keepsake: A Christmas & New Year's Gift (New York: Leavitt & Allen, 1856);

Selections from Various Sources, edited by Sigourney (Worcester, Mass.: Turnes, 1863).

In a review of her *Zinzendorff, and Other Poems* (1835) in the January 1836 *Southern Literary Messenger,* Edgar Allan Poe criticized Lydia H. Sigourney's writing as derivative and said that she benefited from the company of other writers who had "manufactured for themselves a celebrity." Six years later, however, he solicited her work for *Graham's Magazine,* and he retracted his earlier criticism in the January 1842 issue of *Graham's* while reviewing her *Pocahontas, and Other Poems* (1841): "We have accused her of imitation of Mrs. Hemans—but this imitation is no longer apparent." The most popular American poet of her time, Sigourney was memorialized by John Greenleaf Whittier and parodied by Mark Twain. She was rarely openly criticized, and most criticisms that did appear were qualified with excuses for her. Her sentimental works disappeared from the canon of American literature shortly after her death, and, despite the efforts of a few critics—primarily feminist scholars—since the 1970s, students of American letters generally remain unacquainted with her writing.

The daughter of Ezekiel Huntley and his second wife, Zerviah Wentworth Huntley, Lydia Howard Huntley was born on 1 September 1791 in Norwich, Connecticut. Throughout her childhood she was encouraged to read by Mrs. Jerusha Lathrop, for whom her father worked as a gardener. After Lathrop's death in 1805, Huntley was so grief-stricken that a physician recommended a change of scene. Huntley went to Hartford to stay with Mrs. Jeremiah Wadsworth and her son, Daniel, who were relatives of Lathrop's. An entry in Sigourney's journal about her trip to Hartford, her earliest travel writing, appears in her 1866 autobiography, *Letters of Life.*

After a two-week visit with the Wadsworths, Huntley returned to Norwich and tried to open a school. The enterprise was unsuccessful, so she went back to Hartford with her friend Nancy Maria Hyde to learn embroidery, painting, and other arts for young ladies. In 1811 the two started a school in Norwich that remained open for more than a year. In 1814 Huntley visited the Wadsworths again, and Daniel Wadsworth helped her and Hyde open a school for girls in Hartford. Huntley designed a curriculum that emphasized reading, writing, history, geography, philosophy, and mathematics. In 1815 Wadsworth arranged for the publication of Huntley's first collection of poetry, *Moral Pieces, in Prose and Verse.* All of the poems in the volume are emblematic of Christian piety, a dominant theme in all of her work.

In 1819 Huntley left teaching to marry Charles Sigourney, a banker and hardware store owner. Charles Sigourney was a widower with three children; he and Lydia had five children, of whom only the last two—Mary, born in 1827, and Andrew, born in 1831—survived infancy. In keeping with the custom of the time, Charles Sigourney believed that writing should be no more than a pastime for his wife. Thus, although she wrote prolifically and published her work in periodicals as well as in book form, using the income to support her aging parents, her writings appeared anonymously during the early years of her marriage. By 1833, however, Charles's business interests were failing to provide for the family in the manner to which they were accustomed, and Lydia began to take public credit for her work. *The Farmer and the Soldier: A Tale* (1833) was published under her initials, while the works that followed, with a few exceptions, appeared under her name. From this period Sigourney aggressively built her reputation and increased the fees she charged for her writing. She edited the annual *Religious Souvenir* in 1838 and 1839. From 1839 to 1842 she was listed on the title page as an editor of *Godey's Lady's Book,* but it appears that she did little editorial work; her name was used for the prestige it conferred on the periodical.

In 1840, on the advice of her doctor, Sigourney went on a tour of Great Britain and Paris. "Modified from the notes of a Journal regularly kept," Sigourney's *Pleasant Memories of Pleasant Lands* was published in 1842. The book is organized chronologically around Sigourney's almost daily journal entries. Each section begins with a poem, followed by a few paragraphs of prose. As the title suggests, and as Sigourney states in her preface, her objective was to focus on the pleasant aspects of her journey rather than on the "dark shades" and "blemishes." The book begins, however, on a somber note with the poem "To a Land Bird at Sea," which had originally appeared in the January 1842 issue of *Graham's Magazine.* She recounts the arrival of a land bird on the ship on the eighth day of the voyage, praises the bird's courage, and mourns after the exhausted creature dies. She then retells the tale in prose. The next two poems, "A Sabbath at Sea" and "The Rose Geranium," added in the second edition (1844), describe a service praising God for preserving the passengers against the "monstrous tide" and depict the death of an infant on board, respectively. It is clear that Sigourney was not fond of ocean travel, as she continues in a grave tone for the next few sections to explain, in often melodramatic terms, the dangers and discomforts of the voyage.

Schools, hospitals, prisons, and asylums were some of Sigourney's favorite places to visit in

SCENES IN MY NATIVE LAND,
BY
Mrs. L. H. Sigourney.

Ruins of Church at Jamestown

Title page for Sigourney's second travel book, which includes the history of many of the sites she visited

England, and her descriptions of these institutions provide lessons in Christian behavior: for example, her account of the Liverpool Church and School for the Blind reminds the reader of the importance of charity. She expresses pity for the poor and disenfranchised and points out the importance of the teaching of both practical skills and the word of God to make such people productive members of society.

Sigourney also loved to visit old homes, castles, churches, graveyards, and memorials. Throughout *Pleasant Memories of Pleasant Lands* one hears little about the living; Great Britain provides Sigourney with the opportunity to give her readers history lessons. Many of her poems describe battles or the overthrowing of monarchs; Roman ruins are reminders of an ancient,

civilized ancestry. She has sympathy for Anne Boleyn and, on her visit to Paris, for Josephine, women who were treated heinously by their husbands, Henry VIII and Napoleon Bonaparte, respectively. (The poem about Boleyn is only slightly revised from one in her 1827 *Poems*.)

Another victim of intemperate power is Mary, Queen of Scots. Perhaps because of Sigourney's Scottish heritage she feels warmly toward the Scots, and throughout the portion of the book dedicated to her Scottish tour she seems to favor them over the English. She criticizes the "greedy" English guide who showed her the former home of Sir Walter Scott: "It is desirable that a spot like Abbotsford, one of the 'Mecca-shrines' of Scotland, should be exhibited to pilgrims either by a native of its clime, or at least by one not deficient in the common courtesy of a guide." She also notes that the gypsies, whom she compares to American Indians, are treated better by the Scots than by the English.

Later, however, Sigourney softens her criticism of the English. In the section "March, at Denmark Hill" she writes:

> I think the English are true friends. They are not assiduous to put forth their best virtues at first sight, nor to overwhelm a stranger with courtesies, nor to run risks, like king Hezekiah, by the display of their most sacred treasures to foreign eyes. They make no protestations beyond what they feel, and are willing to embody in deeds.
>
> A similar principle of integrity seems to pervade social intercourse. They speak what they conceive to be truth, whether it is likely to render them popular or not, whether it coincides or not with the opinions and prejudices of those with whom they converse.
>
> They are also distinguished by a love of order. The ranks are clearly defined, and are not ambitious to encroach on established boundaries.

While Sigourney values the wild quality of America, viewing untamed nature as a symbol of the power and greatness of the country, she also wishes that America shared more of the English sense of orderliness. She bemoans the way nature is treated as a resource in America and the way Americans, busy building a country and making their livings from the land, do not take the time to decorate their towns with flowers and trees as the English do. Such symbols of leisure appeal to Sigourney's class-consciousness: although she longs for home throughout her travels and constantly reminds her audience that she is a republican, the idea of aristocracy fascinates her. She also laments the lack of loyal and efficient servants in America. (It was important to Sigourney to be perceived as comfortably middle class. In her autobiography she describes her childhood home as a mansion, and, although she acknowledges that her family were "tenants," she describes her father's role in the widow Lathrop's household as "indispensable"; she never refers to him as a gardener, his actual position.)

Finally, Sigourney expresses her appreciation for the fondness many British people seemed to feel for America:

> Indeed friendly feelings towards our country seemed prevalent among all with whom we associated in Great Britain. Symptoms of disaffection or hostility between the nations were deprecated by the wisest and best, as unnatural, inexpedient, and unchristian. It was freely acknowledged that whatever promoted amity between two nations, united by the ties of an active commerce, common language, and kindred origin, was highly desirable.

England provides America with a link to Europe and a sense of history and permanence, and Sigourney emphasizes the need to nurture what she often calls the mother/daughter relationship between the two nations.

Sigourney used her trip to try to tie herself firmly into the English literary tradition. She visited William Wordsworth, Joanna Baillie, Samuel Rogers, Mr. and Mrs. S. C. Hall, and Maria Edgeworth, as well as the graves of Scott and William Shakespeare. She frequently mentions and quotes the English author Felicia Hemans, as if to remind her audience that she has been called "the American Mrs. Hemans." Sigourney's literary name-dropping backfired, however, when she was criticized for including in her book passages from letters from Edgeworth, the novelist Caroline Anne Bowles Southey (the poet laureate Robert Southey's second wife), and Mary Russell Mitford that created the impression that she had close friendships with the authors. The *Story Teller* accused Sigourney of embellishing the letters, and the *London Athenaeum* commented in the 15 April 1843 issue, "The real question is the moral wrong in publishing a private letter at all." In the second edition of *Pleasant Memories of Pleasant Lands* Sigourney eliminated the quotations from the letters of Mrs. Southey, Edgeworth, Mitford, and Mrs. Hall and noted that she had not visited the Southeys because "the call of a stranger might be deemed intrusive."

In 1843–1844 Sigourney was listed as editor of the *Ladies' Companion,* although, again, she probably did little if any editorial work for the magazine. Her second travel book, *Scenes in My Native Land* (1845), describes locations in Connecticut, Massachusetts, New York, and Pennsylvania; in some cases Sigourney had visited the places herself, while in other cases she drew on accounts by others. The work is similar in many ways to *Pleasant Memories of Pleasant Lands:* each section comprises a poem followed by a short prose piece; Sigourney uses her visits to churches, graveyards, hospitals, asylums, and prisons to provide lessons in rehabilitation, Christian charity, and pious duty; and she quotes liberally from other writers, particularly Wordsworth, Hemans, Scott, Catharine Maria Sedgwick, Lydia Maria Child, and Harriet Beecher Stowe. She also devotes much space to accounts of historical events, especially violent confrontations; instead of the contests for the throne that were dispersed throughout her travelogue of Great Britain, however, here she relates battles from the Revolutionary War and skirmishes between whites and American Indians. Though she believes in the superiority of "the Saxon race, whose birth-right is to rule," she also accepts the stereotype of the noble savage and abhors the un-Christian treatment the Indians received at the hands of whites. She praises William Penn for forming the only treaty with the Indians that was not broken and condones the "sense of equity, which often marked similar transactions with the natives" when whites purchased land rather than stealing it. Her poem "Vale of Wyoming" is the tale of a young girl who is captured by Indians; her family searches for her for more than fifty years, but when they find her she refuses to return to white society:

> "Hate they not
> The red man in their heart? Smooth christian words
> They speak, but from their touch, we fade away,
> As from the poisonous snake."

Unlike her earlier travel book, this one is not based on a specific journey; hence, it is not organized chronologically. Sigourney begins and ends the book with sections on Niagara Falls, which she had visited with her son in June 1844; the falls are her favorite symbol for the power of nature and of God. The book draws heavily on her earlier publications: for example, "First Church at Jamestown" is retitled and republished from the 1827 *Poems,* and several other verses are adapted from the same collection. In addition, Sigourney takes material from her magazine pieces and from the biographical sketch she wrote for *The Writings of Nancy Maria Hyde* (1816), which she edited the year of her friend's death. She also presents the history of the Wadsworth family in great detail throughout the text. The work sold poorly in the United States but did well in England; exactly the opposite had been true of her first travel book.

Like *Scenes in My Native Land,* much of Sigourney's later work—such as *The Voice of Flowers* (1846), *The Weeping Willow* (1847), and *Poetry for Seamen* (1845; enlarged as *Poems for the Sea,* 1850)—was compiled from her earlier publications. New works from her later career include *The Faded Hope* (1853), a memoir of her son Andrew, who had died of consumption at nineteen in 1850; *Past Meridian* (1854), a collection of essays on old age; *The Western Home, and Other Poems* (1854), about Aaron Burr's adventures in Ohio; and *Lucy Howard's Journal* (1858), the fictional diary of a young girl's education. Charles Sigourney died in

1854; Lydia Sigourney died on 10 June 1865. Her autobiography, *Letters of Life,* was completed by her daughter with a maudlin description of Sigourney's last hours.

Biography:

Gordon Sherman Haight, *Mrs. Sigourney: The Sweet Singer of Hartford* (New Haven: Yale University Press, 1930).

References:

Nina Baym, "Reinventing Lydia Sigourney," in her *Feminism and American Literary History* (New Brunswick, N.J.: Rutgers University Press, 1992), pp. 151–166;

Mary De Jong, "*Legacy* Profile: Lydia Howard Huntley Sigourney," *Legacy: A Journal of American Women Writers,* 5 (Spring 1988): 35–43;

Annie Finch, "The Sentimental Poetess in the World: Metaphor and Subjectivity in Lydia Sigourney's Nature Poetry," *Legacy: A Journal of American Women Writers,* 5 (Fall 1988): 3–18;

Rufus W. Griswold, *The Female Poets of America* (Philadelphia: Carey & Hart, 1849);

Griswold, *Poets and Poetry in America* (Philadelphia: Carey & Hart, 1842);

Patricia Okker, "Sarah Joseph Hale, Lydia Sigourney, and the Poetic Traditions in Two Nineteenth-Century Women's Magazines," *American Periodicals: A Journal of History, Criticism, and Bibliography,* 3 (1993): 32–42;

Ann Douglas Wood, "Mrs. Sigourney and the Sensibility of Inner Space," *New England Quarterly,* 45 (June 1972): 163–181;

Sandra A. Zagarell, "Expanding 'America': Lydia Sigourney's *Sketch of Connecticut,* Catherine Sedgwick's *Hope Leslie,*" *Tulsa Studies in Women's Literature,* 6 (Fall 1987): 225–245.

Papers:

Lydia H. Sigourney's papers are at the Connecticut Historical Society, the Connecticut State Library, and Trinity College, all in Hartford; the Henry E. Huntington Memorial Library, San Marino, California; the Schlesinger Library, Radcliffe College; Yale University Library; the New York Historical Society; and the Boston Public Library.

Benjamin Silliman
(8 August 1779 – 24 November 1864)

Anna E. Lomando
Pennsylvania State University, New Kensington Campus

BOOKS: *Letters of Shahcoolen, a Hindu Philosopher, Residing in Philadelphia; to His Friend El Hassan, an Inhabitant of Delhi* (Boston: Russell & Cutler, 1802);

A Journal of Travels in England, Holland, and Scotland, and of Two Passages over the Atlantic, in the Years 1805 and 1806, 2 volumes (New York: E. Sargeant, 1810); revised edition, 3 volumes (New Haven: S. Converse, 1820);

Remarks, Made on a Short Tour, Between Hartford and Quebec, in the Autumn of 1819 (New Haven: S. Converse, 1820; revised edition, 1824); republished as *A Tour to Quebec, in the Autumn of 1819* (London: Sir Richard Phillips, 1822);

Outline of the Course of Geological Lectures Given in Yale College (New Haven: H. Howe, 1829);

Elements of Chemistry in the Order of the Lectures Given in Yale College, 2 volumes (New Haven: H. Howe, 1830–1831);

Peculiarities of the Shakers, Described in a Series of Letters from Lebanon Springs, in the Year 1832, Containing an Account of the Origin, Worship, and Doctrines, of the Shakers' Society (New York: J. K. Porter, 1832);

Consistency of the Discoveries of Modern Geology with the Sacred History of the Creation and the Deluge (London: J. S. Hodson, 1837); republished as *Suggestions Relative to the Philosophy of Geology, as Deduced from the Facts and to the Consistency of Both the Facts and Theory of This Science with Sacred History* (New Haven: B. L. Hamlen, 1839);

A Visit to Europe in 1851, 2 volumes (New York: Putnam, 1853; London: S. Low, Son, 1854).

Edition: *Letters of Shahcoolen, a Hindu Philosopher, Residing in Philadelphia; to His Friend El Hassan, an Inhabitant of Delhi, with an Introduction by Ben Harris McClary* (Gainesville, Fla.: Scholars Facsimiles & Reprints, 1962).

OTHER: William Henry, *An Epitome of Experimental Chemistry, in Three Parts,* second American edition, edited by Silliman (Boston: William Andrews, 1810);

Benjamin Silliman in 1825, portrait by Samuel F. B. Morse (Yale University Art Gallery; gift of Bartlett Arkell to Silliman College)

American Journal of Science, edited by Silliman, first series, 1 (July 1818); second series, 10 (November 1850);

Robert Baker, *An Introduction to Geology,* second American edition, edited by Silliman (New Haven: H. Howe, 1833).

SELECTED PERIODICAL PUBLICATIONS–UNCOLLECTED: "Sketches of a Tour in the Counties of New-Haven and Litchfield in Connecticut, with Notices of the Geology, Mineralogy and Scenery," *American Journal of Science,* 2 (November 1820): 201–235;

"Notes on a Journey from New-Haven, Conn. to Mauch Chunck and other Anthracite regions of Pennsylvania," *American Journal of Science,* 19 (January 1831): 1–21;

"Notice of a Fountain of Petroleum Called the Oil Spring," *American Journal of Science,* 23 (January 1833): 97–102;

"Lowell: Geological Facts," *American Journal of Science,* 27 (July 1835): 340–347;

"Remarks on Some of the Gold Mines, and on Parts of the Gold Region of Virginia Founded on Personal Observations, Made in the Months of August and September, 1836," *American Journal of Science,* 32 (July 1837): 98–130.

Although he is remembered primarily for his contributions to scientific education and for offering the first course in geology in the United States, Benjamin Silliman wrote three major works of travel literature and frequently included scenic descriptions in his professional writing. At Yale his talent as a teacher, an editor, and a popularizer of science helped the university become one of the important centers for scientific education in New England. Often, Silliman's travel was in the service of science even when he traveled for personal reasons. For example, a journal he kept during a trip to regain his health contains meticulously detailed descriptions of geological formations. Perhaps because his interests were wide, Silliman lacked the focus to make original contributions to scientific knowledge he might otherwise have made, but his curiosity about the world and his ability to communicate made him an engaging travel writer. Through his writings one meets an intelligent, well-educated nineteenth-century American traveler at home and abroad.

Benjamin Silliman was born to Mary Fish Silliman and Gold Selleck Silliman on 8 August 1779, while his father was a prisoner of the British Army. He was privately educated and entered Yale at age thirteen. After completing his studies at Yale in September 1796 Silliman helped his mother on the family farm for a year. He taught at a private school for another year before deciding to study law. In 1799 he was offered a position as a tutor at Yale and for the next three years was both tutor and law student.

In July 1801 the president of Yale, Dr. Timothy Dwight, asked Silliman, who knew little of either subject, to become the college's first professor of chemistry and natural history. On 7 September 1802, after successfully completing his law examinations, he accepted the formal offer of the Yale Corporation. He embarked on the study of the sciences in Philadelphia in 1802. With this brief introduction Silliman began to teach chemistry at

Yale in April 1804. When he learned that the Yale Corporation planned to spend $9,000 to purchase scientific books and apparatus, Silliman suggested to President Dwight that he be sent to Europe not only to acquire the equipment and books but also to further his education by attending lectures and demonstrations unavailable in the United States. Convinced that Silliman's proposal was in the best interest of the institution, President Dwight and the Yale officials gave their approval. In April 1805 Silliman was on his way to England, Holland, and Scotland.

The record of this journey, *A Journal of Travels in England, Holland, and Scotland, and of Two Passages over the Atlantic in the Years 1805 and 1806* (1810), was published three years after Silliman's return. He intially kept the journal so that he might share his experiences with his brother and a select circle of friends, but the circle widened, and he was persuaded to publish his book. The published work is a guidebook written by an observant, if naive, young man. His description of icebergs to an audience unlikely to have seen such an awe-inspiring sight is illustrative of his style. After explaining that "so peculiar was their appearance, that it is not easy to compare them to any thing but themselves," he does find a way to help his reader visualize the sight by comparing the structure to a "lofty palace" in ruins and the material to "white marble. . . . They resembled most some ancient venerable ruin, while the beauty and splendor of the materials made them look like a work of art."

Silliman was captivated by the majesty of nature and man's attempts to harness its energy. His enthusiasm for his subject and his development as a scientific observer are plain in the accounts of his frequent trips to the mines of Great Britain. From his first venture into a mine in Derbyshire, where he admits to a "secret joy" on reentering the light, to his depiction of the wonders and terrors of the Owdin mine, to his detailed description of the largest copper mine in Cornwall, Silliman shows an increasing confidence in his ability to depict the underground scenes and explain the methods used to mine and remove ore. By the time he arrives in New Castle and the most modern mines he can explain intelligibly to the lay person the steam-powered elevator that transports the miners into the depths of the mine and the system used to vent gasses safely.

Silliman's fascination with machinery was not confined to mining, for he toured many factories. Journeying through the south of England, he visited the factories where fine cloth, glass, brass, and pins were manufactured. His interest extended to all

Title pages for the two volumes of Silliman's last book, in which he comments on the changes he noticed in Europe since his previous visit forty-five years before

kinds of machinery, for he also describes in minute detail the machine used to clean the streets of London and the apparatus used for illuminating with gas light, commenting on its beauty, danger, and limits.

A preoccupation of Silliman's with the practical uses of scientific discoveries is in keeping with the nineteenth-century concern with improving the quality of life, but as an American he also has a special interest in having his country fulfill its destiny. Thus, while he is impressed with Oxford and its history he saves his deepest admiration for Cambridge, where there is more interest in the workings of this new technology. He declares their chemistry laboratories the finest because they have a steam engine and a paper mill.

Although Silliman spends much of his time studying technological improvements and attending lectures, he also finds time to see the countryside and take in a fine view or two. When he is forced to travel at night he is sorry to miss the lovely scenery. In one instance he placed himself in danger by climbing a steep hill as night fell. Precariously, he descended the hill only to discover that the only available inn was filled. Because of his insistence, he was given a bed in the public room. And the next morning, not to be denied his view, he returned to the hill.

Throughout his journey Silliman collected geological specimens and admired the collections of others. Unfortunately, because of the difficulty of gaining admittance to the British Museum and the insufficient time he was allowed to spend there, he was unable to examine its splendid mineral collection as closely as he wished. He was; however, able to see a few of the other displays and was interested in the manuscript of Alexander Pope's translations of Homer and a copy of the Magna Carta. Some of the displays at the British Museum and at other sites prompted Silliman to muse on man's futile desire to find immortality in memorials and mummification, which he concludes failed to protect man from his ultimate return to dust. Despite his American ideals he confesses some awe at the tombs of monarchs, especially those of Elizabeth I; Mary, Queen of Scots; and the Henrys.

Silliman's Puritan roots and provincialism are often apparent in his reaction to British social life. Determined to sample the public entertainments available in England, he attends the theater, dancing at Vauxhall, and the opera. Most of these experiences, though, leave him unimpressed and disapproving, especially of the roles women assume and the costumes they wear. He detests opera, declaring it to be the province of the rich. Silliman further betrays his lack of worldliness in his account of the courtesans he encounters in his rambles. His usual clear, careful descriptions become vague, and the reader is left to wonder what he discovered about the seamier side of London. Silliman is, however, direct and plain in his depiction and condemnation of those few clergymen in whom he discovered a taste for strong drink, gambling, or a tendency to swear.

After crossing the channel and traveling at great personal risk on the Continent, which was much disturbed by the Napoleonic Wars, Silliman was bitterly disappointed at being denied permission to continue his journey to Paris. Disgruntled, he returned to Britain and traveled to Edinburgh, where he spent the remainder of his time abroad studying and planning for his return to Yale. In the spring he returned to the United States, where he was overwhelmed by the beauty of the land in bloom. Clearly, Silliman wants to impress his reader with the significance of the journey ending at a time when all the earth is filled with promise.

Silliman soon resumed his teaching duties and became engrossed by professional concerns as well as his personal life. In 1809 he married Harriet Trumball, daughter of the governor of Connecticut, and during the first six years of their marriage the couple had two daughters and two sons. In 1810 Silliman was one of the founders of the Medical Institution of Yale College, which accepted its first students in the fall of 1813. The publication of *A Journal of Travels* also broadened Silliman's horizons. Fellow scientists and educators wrote to him, and he commenced some lifelong correspondences as a result. His professional stature continued to grow, and in July 1818 he began the *American Journal of Science.* He was the only editor of this important journal until 1837, when his son Benjamin joined him as an associate editor.

The added stress of initiating the journal took its toll on Silliman's health, which was also probably weakened by family tragedy. In 1819 his eldest son, Jonathan Trumball, died; a daughter who was born shortly after his death survived for only two months. A journey to restore his health was proposed, and in the fall of 1819 Silliman and his brother-in-law, Daniel Wadsworth, took a trip to Quebec.

This excursion resulted in *Remarks, Made on a Short Tour, Between Hartford and Quebec* (1820), a book that runs to 407 pages. In contrast to his first travel book, in which he integrated geological and scenic descriptions, Silliman separated his subjects, clearly labeling the sections on geology for the convenience of his readers. Silliman's tone is also different from that of his previous book, for his intent is to educate the reader. The voice of the first journal was that of a student; this voice is unmistakably that of a teacher.

Silliman again shows an interest in landscape. He writes of the clarity of Lake George and the beauty of the mountains surrounding the lake, waxing poetic at his first glimpse of Quebec. But Silliman's control of his material is surer than in *A Journal of Travels*. He uses selective description in a purposeful fashion. When he depicts the domestic activity on the Saint Lawrence River—carts loading fuel in the water, women washing clothes on the shore, and small craft on the river—he explains that the scenes are "trivial, but still, they tend to characterize the country and its inhabitants."

Silliman found lessons in the history of the areas through which he traveled. Referring to Wolfe's papers and letters and Tobias Smollet's *History of England,* he ponders the consequences of the struggle between France and England in the New World and notes the destructive effect on Europe of the continued enmity of these two powers. Most of the history that he cites is anecdotal and honors national efforts. But on occasion a particular site will prompt Silliman to meditate on "the mutability of power and the fluctuations of empire." At Fort Ticonderoga he observes that the often bitterly contested fortification has become a cattle pasture.

Traveling on the inland waterways and lakes allowed Silliman to study the steam trade in Canada and the United States. Although he admired the modern technology, he considered the river steamers dangerous because of the fire in the "bowels" of the craft and because the crews were often careless with combustibles stored too near the boilers. He pronounces the Canadian vessels "steadier" than American steamships and their meals "luxurious."

Although he denied that he had written a travel book, Silliman does offer some advice and guidance to the tourist. Based on his understanding of the differences in the ways inns are run in England and America, he advises English travelers on how to behave so that they will receive good treatment in American establishments. He advises caution in diet because he found the water and food, especially the unpalatable bread, hard to digest. Silliman describes the common people as cheerful, polite, and kind to strangers and dogs. Noting that despite the British victory the people mainly speak French, Silliman declares: "Indeed to have seen Quebec and Montreal, and the intervening and surrounding country, is, in some degree, a substitute for a visit to Europe."

Silliman returned to more personal suffering. In 1820 and 1821 the Sillimans' two infant sons died, making four children they had lost in three years. Silliman also continued to be plagued by health problems. His personal troubles did not, however, derail his professional success. Silliman's account of the spectacular Weston meteor and his work with Robert Hare's oxyhydrogen blowpipe gained fame for Yale, which became an acknowledged leader in chemistry, geology, and mineralogy. In 1830 and 1831 he published the two volumes of his *Elements of Chemistry*.

Many of Silliman's students went on to distinguished careers. Edward Hitchcock taught at Amherst, and Oliver Hubbard went to Dartmouth. Amos Eaton founded Rensselaer, which later became Rensselaer Polytechnic Institute. Not only did Silliman teach science to the students of Yale, he also introduced science to the general public with a series of lectures. In the spring of 1834 Silliman traveled to Hartford to deliver his first talk. Encouraged by his warm reception, he became an important popularizer of science.

Silliman maintained an active professional life for fifteen more years. In August 1849 he asked to retire at commencement in 1850. But when his wife died in 1850 he decided to stay at the university, hoping the work would help fill the empty place in his life. In 1851 Silliman asked for a leave of absence in order to return to Europe. Accompanied by his son, Benjamin Jr., his daughter-in-law, her sister, his oldest grandson, and a student from the school of Applied Chemistry, Silliman traveled to the Continent. He claimed he was traveling for his son's benefit; however, Silliman had some unfulfilled desires, and the political climate of the Continent was now such that he could visit Paris. The record of this journey became *A Visit to Europe in 1851* (1853).

Referring to his previous travels as "those of my youth," Silliman's tone is often nostalgic, although he remains vigorous at seventy. If he declines the opportunity to descend into a mine in England, claiming to have had enough subterranean adventures forty-six years earlier—before many of his party were born—he does arise at 2:00 A.M. to begin a two-day climb of Mount Etna. His exhausting 11,000-foot climb is rewarded by splendid views of the Val del Bove and Mount Rossi. While it was Silliman's interest in science that drew him to Italy, where he examined Mount Vesuvius and Mount Etna for evidence of the physical origins of the earth, he never doubted that the ultimate reality was spiritual. Indeed, his appendix to Robert Baker's *An Introduction to Geology* (1833)—published separately as *Consistency of the Discoveries of Modern Geology with the Sacred History of the Creation and the Deluge* (1837)—was an attempt to square geology with Genesis. Those narratives of the sites Silliman chose not to visit would be written by the younger men of the party and included in his journal.

Although Silliman tended to be circumspect in his public statements, *A Visit to Europe in 1851* is filled with frank evaluations of the European political situation. He is especially critical of the king of Naples, describing him as a "detested" monarch who, afraid to reside in the city he governs, must live sixteen miles from Naples. Silliman notes that the king had earned his reputation because he had delivered his own people into the hands of their enemies.

Silliman made many comparisons between the England of his first and second visits. He approved of the new and more open admissions policies of the British Museum. But the most poignant comparisons concern some of the great men whom he saw during his first trip. Considering the statues in Westminster Abbey and St. Paul's church, he stops at one and declares: "Mr. Pitt, whose voice I heard in the House of Commons, now appears in his mute statue, with outstretched arms, as if about to speak."

The journey home to the United States gave Silliman an opportunity to use his sea legs during a period of rough weather. Although he sympathized with the weaker members of the party, he could not resist the temptation to brag at his own hardiness. When the ship arrived in port Silliman described a spectacular evening sky. He finds the beautiful sunset that appears during an electrical storm a fitting display for a man who took his first voyage in "the morning of life" and his second "in its sober evening." Silliman remarried in 1851, retired in 1853, and after a brief illness died on 24 November 1864. Silliman's travel writings provide the reader with a uniquely American perspective and response to Europe in a period when the country was finding its place in the world. Even though dated in some respects, many of Silliman's observations are acute, and the work may still be read with pleasure.

Biographies:

George P. Fisher, *Life of Benjamin Silliman,* 2 volumes (New York: Scribner, 1866);

John F. Fulton and Elizabeth H. Thomson, *Benjamin Silliman: Pathfinder in American Science* (New York: Henry Schuman, 1947);

Chandros Michael Brown, *Benjamin Silliman: A Life in the Young Republic* (Princeton, N.J.: Princeton University Press, 1989).

References:

Francis Parsons, ed., *Six Men of Yale* (New Haven: Yale University Press, 1939), pp. 65–84;

Leonard G. Wilson, ed., *Benjamin Silliman and His Circle: Studies on the Influence of Benjamin Silliman on Science in America* (New York: Science History Publications, 1979).

Papers:

The major collections of Silliman's papers are in the Sterling Memorial and Beinecke Libraries of Yale University. Other collections are held by the Pennsylvania Historical Society, Philadelphia; the American Philosophical Society, Philadelphia; the Library Company, Philadelphia; and the New York Historical Society. The correspondence of Silliman and Daniel Wadsworth is at Trinity College in Hartford.

John Lloyd Stephens

(28 November 1805 – 13 October 1852)

Edward J. Gallagher
Lehigh University

BOOKS: *Incidents of Travel in Egypt, Arabia Petræa, and the Holy Land,* 2 volumes as "an American" (New York: Harper, 1837; London: Bentley, 1838);

Incidents of Travel in Greece, Turkey, Russia, and Poland, 2 volumes, anonymous (New York: Harper, 1838); republished as *Incidents of Travel in the Russian and Turkish Empires* (London: Bentley, 1839);

Incidents of Travel in Central America, Chiapas, and Yucatan, 2 volumes (New York: Harper, 1841; London: John Murray, 1841);

Incidents of Travel in Yucatan, 2 volumes (New York: Harper, 1843; London: John Murray, 1843).

Edition: *Incidents of Travel in Central America, Chiapas, and Yucatan,* 2 volumes, edited by Richard L. Predmore (New Brunswick, N.J.: Rutgers University Press, 1949).

SELECTED PERIODICAL PUBLICATION–
UNCOLLECTED: "An Hour with Alexander Von Humboldt," *Living Age,* 15 (October–December 1847): 151–153.

Dubbed "The American Traveler," John Lloyd Stephens explored both the Old and New Worlds between 1835 and 1843; he later dedicated his life to the travel of others as an officer in steamboat and railroad companies. Today he is best known as "The Discoverer of the Mayas." Assessing the ruins of Copán, Stephens wrote: "America, say historians, was peopled by savages; but savages never reared these structures, savages never carved these stones." His adventurous, relatively inexpensive, profusely illustrated books on Central America and Yucatán were designed to reach a mass audience; they virtually invented American archaeology.

Stephens was born on 28 November 1805 in Shrewsbury, New Jersey, to Benjamin and Clemence Lloyd Stephens. The family moved to New York City in 1806. Stephens entered public school in 1812, the Classical School in 1815, and Columbia

John Lloyd Stephens at age forty

College in 1818; at Columbia he studied with the celebrated classicist Charles Anthon and graduated at the head of his class in 1822. From 1822 to 1824 he studied at the Tapping Reeve Law School in Litchfield, Connecticut. In 1824, with his cousin Charles Hendrickson, Stephens began his traveling career by visiting his Aunt Helena in the Illinois Territory, continuing on to Saint Louis and New Orleans and returning to New York in February 1825. He passed the bar in 1827. An ardent Jacksonian, he became known as the "pet speaker" of

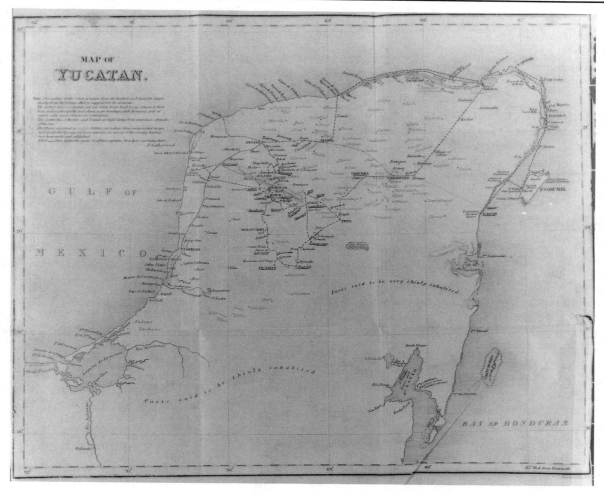

Map from Stephens's Incidents of Travel in Yucatan *(1843)*

Tammany Hall. In the fall of 1834, struggling with a strep throat that was aggravated by his public speaking, he embarked on a tour of England, France, Italy, Greece, Turkey, Russia, and Poland to regain his health.

"I have just arrived at this place, and I live to tell it": in his first published words one can sense the roguish, irreverent, self-mocking voice of the typical American with which Stephens captivated masses of readers. Charles Fenno Hoffman started Stephens's career as a travel writer by publishing his often outrageous April 1835 letters from Smyrna (today Izmir, Turkey), without Stephens's knowledge, as "Scenes in the Levant" in the *American Monthly Magazine* in October, November, and December 1835 and November 1836; the letters were later included verbatim in Stephens's *Incidents of Travel in Greece, Turkey, Russia, and Poland* (1838). Stephens, in the first of his many descriptions of ruins, creates a haunting picture of a paradisiacal Greek village transformed by "accursed Turks" into a "city of the

dead," and this down-to-earth "straggler from a busy, money-getting land" is completely spellbound at the Temple of Ephesus. What one remembers most, however, are his lack of creature comforts; his ode to his pantaloons, which "*parted from*" him; a comparison of Greek and Turkish bedbugs; and what a camel's face looks like to a man dying of thirst. Feeling, on the last day of his visit to Athens, that "his blood was up" among the "enduring witnesses of the Athenian glory," Stephens re-creates the battle of Salamis. He goes "to work systematically" and fights "the whole battle through," giving "the Persians ten to one," "making the Greeks fight like devils," and finally sending the defeated Persians scampering off to the tune of "devil take the hindmost." After meditating on the throne of Xerxes, "as pretty a place as a man could have selected to see his friends whipped and keep out of harm's way himself," he is preparing "to do something" at the tomb of Themistocles—only to have his eyes "blasted with the sight" of the grave of the "unclassical" John Johnson. "Why didn't they bury him in a dunghill?" he rails, and dashes back to his ship having completely desacralized a chapter of the Western classical heritage.

Unable to get sea passage home from Paris in November 1835, Stephens read Léon de Laborde's *Voyage de l'Arabie Petrée* (1830; translated as *Journey through Arabia Petræa to Mount Sinai,* 1836), and by December he was in plague-stricken Alexandria preparing for his second Old World journey. He completed the trip in the latter part of 1836, and in May 1837 the firm of Harper and Brothers announced the publication of his *Incidents of Travel in Egypt, Arabia Petræa, and the Holy Land.* The book was an immediate popular and critical success and went through ten editions before the end of the decade.

From Alexandria, Stephens moves past spectacles "of misery and wretchedness" to Cairo, where hideous slave markets, vicious whippings of criminals, guides clamoring for "backsheesh," and an audience with the pasha of Egypt deconstruct the romantic "Cairo of the Caliphs" of the Arabian Nights tales. On New Year's Day 1836 he starts up the Nile with Paul, his Maltese "dragoman," in a hired boat protected by an American flag made by an Arabian tailor. The irreverent Stephens buys a stuffed crocodile to send home as a joke, and more than a hundred Arabs escort the ancient river god on board "with a pomp and circumstance worthy of his better days." The Nile commands no worship from the American traveler: the Cataracts, fabled as terrors, fall a mere two feet; Sam Patch, the notorious Niagara-jumper, would have "turned up his nose in scorn." Thebes, Karnak, and Luxor are less noteworthy than the Irish stew Paul cooks for a party of Western travelers. All that Stephens brings back from his voyage are the clothes he buys off the back of a nubile Nubian and a piece of a skull he dashes against a stone to get "a memorial of a king."

After Egypt, Stephens sets out for the Holy Land on an "entirely new" route through bedouin country to "the long-lost city of Petra," the Edom cursed in the Bible. The world's most "curious and wonderful remains" have been "buried from the eyes of mankind" for more than a thousand years in this "city excavated from solid rock." The highlight of his journey is a momentary spiritual transcendence on Mount Sinai that, "half-unconscious," he shatters by shooting at a partridge. On the dangerous last leg of the journey Stephens dons pistols and saber and disguises himself as Abdel Hasis, "a merchant of Cairo." Claiming to be the first man to cross this cursed land, he proudly writes the first American name on the wall of the "delicate and limpid" temple in Petra. Even a skeptic who would not believe the Bible, he says, must believe "the handwriting of God himself in the desolation and eternal ruin" before his very eyes.

"One by one I had seen the many illusions of my waking dreams fade away," says Stephens in Hebron, the first city he visits in the Holy Land. The greedy and gluttonous bedouins are so far from being admirable "children of Nature," he says, that his "fellow-citizens and fellow-worshippers of mammon" may hold up their heads. The Christian will suffer "many grievous disappointments" at hallowed sites that have been decorated "as if intentionally and impiously to destroy all resemblance" to Scripture by the "false but well-meaning piety of Christians" such as Empress Helena. In Bethlehem, where most holy places have "no better claim to authenticity than the credulity of a weak and pious old woman," we must "give ourselves up to the illusion" and be ready "to believe that we are indeed standing where Christ was born." But crass reality constantly assaults cherished religious illusions. In the Holy Sepulchre during Easter season Stephens says that it would take "a warmer imagination than mine" to see sincere piety "in the fierce struggling of these barefooted pilgrims." Finding the "display of gold" and the "tinsel and show" inconsistent with the humble foot-washing ceremony, he encounters "pure faith and worship" in the home of an American missionary with the family Bible open on the table and the missionary's wife and two schoolchildren as the congregation. Stephens yearns to find Sodom and Gomorrah, the "monuments" of God's "fearful anger"; but, fleeing "an Old Italian quack" after a physical breakdown in Beirut, he ends his travels in the East.

His reviewers thought that it was good that Stephens was not a scientist, artist, architect, or antiquarian but simply an enterprising and spirited traveler recording what readers would see "on the spot" and making them feel as though they were his companions. Edgar Allan Poe praised Stephens in the October 1837 *New York Review* as a "man of good sense and sound feeling" who had "utter absence of pretension" and was free of the "exaggerated sentimentality of Chateaubriand," "the *too French* enthusiasm of Lamartine," and a "degrading spirit of utilitarianism." Another reviewer noted that the wide public acceptance of Stephens's book indicated a preference for American over British literature, just as the book itself contrasts American energy with the fading kingdoms of the Old World.

Incidents of Travel in Egypt, Arabia Petræa, and the Holy Land was so popular that a reviewer suggested "another set of volumes from the same pen," and in 1838 *Incidents of Travel in Greece, Turkey, Russia, and*

Poland, the complete record of his first Old World trip, appeared. Stephens's first port of call on this trip is Missolonghi, where he meets the "stately" widow of the Greek war hero Marco Bozzaris; perhaps it was she, Stephens speculates romantically, who ignited Bozzaris's revolutionary fervor. After viewing the contemporary ruins at Scio and the classical ruins at Corinth and at Athens—where the American missionary school is the "only door of instruction" in the "city which surpassed all the world in learning"—and almost ruining himself by indulging in such Turkish luxuries as coffee, cigars, and baths, Stephens proceeds to Russia.

Russia makes a fascinating comparison with America: "We are both young, and both marching with gigantic strides to greatness, yet we move by different roads"—individual enterprise versus "a gigantic government" that simply says "*Let there be a city!*" Traveling several thousand miles through the desolate Russian interior with his virtually toothless French guide (and adding first American in Kiev to his list of firsts), Stephens is appalled by horrors such as a village where the serfs are literally starving in the streets. On the other hand, while travel usually confirmed Stephens of his patriotism, this time he does not hesitate to say that "abroad, slavery stands as a dark blot upon our national character . . . it will not admit of any palliation." Less seriously, but no less characteristically, Stephens's tall tale of mock near-death at the hands of a "tormentor" at a Moscow bath that was so hot that he understands why Russians roll themselves in mid-winter snow, caused a reviewer for the April 1839 issue of *Dublin Magazine* to speculate that Stephens was raised in Kentucky, a state associated with fanciful tales.

Poland, like Greece, had recently undergone a revolution, and Stephens includes a moving eyewitness account of the "battle of Grokow" by a boy whose brother was killed in it. Poland, however, had a far greater concentration of Jews than any other country in Europe, and Stephens's description of them is rather unflattering. While sensitive to the history of oppression from which the Jews "found rest" in Poland, Stephens finds them "far from being an interesting people. . . . They swarm about the villages and towns, intent on gain. . . . Outward degradation has worked inward on their minds . . . and the despised have become despicable." His health fails in Warsaw, another ruined city, in August 1835. After pushing on to the Vistula salt mines, where he corrects previous "glowing accounts" of subterranean colonies, Stephens returns to Paris. Like his first travel book, *Incidents of Travel in Greece, Turkey, Russia, and Poland*

was well received and had gone into a seventh edition by 1839.

In 1836, while waiting in London to return to New York after his Holy Land trip, Stephens had met the English artist, architect, and archaeologist Frederick Catherwood, who was exhibiting the painting *Panorama of Jerusalem.* Catherwood brought to Stephens's attention a book by Felix de Cabrera on the ruins of Palenque in Guatemala. In New York a bookshop owner, John Russell Bartlett, provided Stephens with the few accounts available of New World travel. In 1837 Catherwood moved to New York, and he and Stephens made plans for a trip to Central America. At that point President Martin Van Buren appointed Stephens minister to the war-torn Central American Federation; his mission was to close the American legation, find the established government, and secure an agreement with it. On 3 October 1839 Stephens and Catherwood set out for Belize on a trip that would produce what many commentators have called the richest contribution ever made to the study of Ancient America: *Incidents of Travel in Central America, Chiapas, and Yucatan* (1841).

Belize, says Stephens, has all the comforts of "the last place made," a place only the runaway slave from Maryland whom Stephens meets there could appreciate. "Armed with a brace of pistols and a large hunting knife," Stephens heads into a country distracted by revolution, where he is prey to malarial fevers and the bites and stings of the indefatigable *niguas* and *garrapatas*. These experiences are nothing like the romantic associations with the adventures of Christopher Columbus that he invokes at the threshold of the jungle. On the way to his first destination, Copán, he is forced to bluff and bluster his way out of arrest by ragtag soldiers who at home "would have been turned out of any decent state prison lest they contaminate the other boarders."

At Copán a square stone column fourteen feet high and three feet on each side proves to him that "the people who once occupied the American continents were not savages." The beauty, desolation, and mystery of Copán create "an interest higher, if possible, than I had ever felt among the ruins of the Old World." Harassed by the owner of the property, Stephens, with classic Yankee audacity, buys Copán for fifty dollars, planning to transport the ruins to an American antiquities museum he would found in New York City. The owner could not have been "more surprised than if I had asked to buy his poor old wife . . . to practice medicine upon." There follows, to the utter incomprehension of the natives, a detailed surveying of the ruins, "my first essay in

Frontispiece and illustrations from Stephens's Incidents of Travel in Yucatan

engineering." Stephens also plays the role of "proprietor of the city," showing visitors "all the lions as the cicerone does in the Vatican or the Pitti Palace." But, unable to read the hieroglyphics of this lost civilization, he cannot say what it all means or who the people were.

Saying that he would trade his diplomatic honors for the nearness of a beautiful woman and his chance at the sublime for a good macadamized road, Stephens leaves Catherwood to finish up in

Copán while he tries to complete his political mission. "Where was my government?" he asks several times, but the question is not easily answered in a land wracked by savage conflict. Stephens provides portraits of the rival leaders, Rafael Carrera and Francisco Morazan, noting that he shook hands and sat side by side with men "thirsting for each other's blood." His war stories, especially those dramatizing the danger in which he found himself, contribute significantly to his book's appeal. Once he fakes energetic partisan support to avoid being shot on the spot: "I have never passed through a more trying ordeal. . . . It would have been a fearful thing to fall into the hands of such men, with their passions roused by resistance and bloodshed." On another occasion he is saved by the lucky memory of a mob member whom he had earlier treated to breakfast. Through all the military madness, though, Stephens still has the comic sensibility to find that insects make him forget an earthquake, the crudeness to judge that a volcano is wasted without the hotel on its summit that it would have at home, the business sense to start investigating a canal route, and the philosophical detachment to listen in "profound silence" to the "waves of the great south ocean . . . rolling from the creation for more than five thousand years, unknown to civilized man" as he realizes that he has "crossed the Continent of America."

On 7 April 1840 Stephens and Catherwood set off on a one-thousand-mile journey, passing through Quiragua—where, unfortunately, French speculators have driven up the selling price of ruins—to Palenque, which they approach, literally, on the backs of Indians. Covering perhaps sixty square miles, Palenque, says Stephens's wife with some exaggeration, is "entirely unknown; there is no mention of it in any book, and no tradition that it had ever been. To this day it is not known by what name it was called." Stephens provides a detailed survey of the ruins, "without speculation or comment." Only at the end does he resurrect imaginatively those "cultivated, polished, and peculiar people" whose "once great and lovely city, overturned, desolate, and lost . . . was a mourning witness to the world's mutations." Stephens toys with the idea of getting married so that he may legally buy the ruins; but he cannot choose between two sisters, and he leaves Palenque on 1 June. His final stop is Uxmal in Yucatán, the site of a cenote more beautiful than any a Greek poet had ever imagined, before returning to New York City, where he arrives—after being eyed by sharks while becalmed—at the end of July 1840.

At the conclusion of the book Stephens lays out what Victor Wolfgang von Hagen calls his "archaeological Monroe Doctrine": the ruins in Central America

> are different from the works of any other known people . . . are of a new order . . . entirely and absolutely anomalous . . . they stand alone. . . . not derived from the Old World, but originating and growing up here, without models or masters, having a distinct, separate, independent existence: like the plants and fruits of the soil, indigenous.

Incidents of Travel in Central America, Chiapas, and Yucatan received laudatory reviews. In the August 1841 *Graham's Magazine* Poe said: "The work is certainly a magnificent one—perhaps the most interesting book of travel ever published." Although George Jones devoted eighty pages of his *History of Ancient America* (1843) to arguing, against Stephens, that New World natives were Tyrians and Israelites, William Hickling Prescott, on the verge of completing his magisterial *Conquest of Mexico* (1843), agreed in his 2 August 1841 letter to Stephens with his conclusions and praised him for opening the way to future researches. Stephens's book was in its twelfth edition by 1842.

Stephens, Catherwood, and the surgeon and ornithologist Dr. Samuel Cabot left for Yucatán in October 1841 after Stephens declined Secretary of State Daniel Webster's offer of the post of secretary of the U.S. legation in Mexico. The opening of Stephens's account of the trip, *Incidents of Travel in Yucatan* (1843), has comic elements as Stephens roguishly decides to make daguerreotypes only of women as practice for recording the ruins, and as the trio is besieged by cross-eyed natives wanting Cabot to operate on them for strabismus. The first main stop on the forty-four-city trek is a six-week stop at Uxmal. From Kabah, a magnificent ruin unknown even to the people of Yucatán, Stephens sends carved five-hundred-pound doorjambs back to New York City to form the basis of his projected Museum of American Antiquities. Especially memorable on this trip are the underground explorations: the Wells of Bolinchen are the subject of a well-known Catherwood illustration; Stephens takes a bath 1,400 feet from the mouth of a cave and 450 feet below the surface of the earth. Disregarding the natives' superstition about the place, Stephens explores the "Labyrinth" with pistol in one hand, candle in the other, and twine tied to his wrists, braving the bats, twisting corridors, and airless narrows until he stands thwarted before a blank wall. Desperately desiring to capture the secret of the place that he tastes tantalizingly just ahead, Stephens wants to dig through the wall; but he finally has to bow to reality and turn back in a "state of utter disappointment." In another impenetrable chamber Stephens drives the natives and himself until he collapses with fever. He wants to "unravel all mystery, and establish a connecting link between the past and present," perhaps even finding a lost civilization where Indians now live "as they did before the discovery of America." Stephens reaffirms, with evidence from dozens more sites, his previous conclusion that there was a distinctly American civilization in existence at the time of the

Conquest. These ancient builders "rise like skeletons from the grave, wrapped in their burial shrouds: claiming no affinity with the works of any known people, but a distinct, independent, and separate existence." Stephens and his party left Yucatán in June 1842. In a fire on 31 July, Stephens lost virtually everything he had sent back to New York City for his Museum of American Antiquities.

In June 1846 Stephens served as a delegate to the New York Constitutional Convention for both the Whig and Democratic Parties. In June 1847 he sailed, as vice president of the Ocean Steam Navigating Company, to Bremerhaven on the maiden voyage of the SS *Washington*. This trip gave him the opportunity to fulfill his "special desire" to visit Alexander von Humboldt, the world-renowned authority on Mexico. As Stephens recounted in *Living Age* in 1847, Humboldt received him at the Royal Palace in Potsdam with the "flattering greeting that no letter of introduction was necessary." Their common interest, "the ruined cities of America," was their first topic of conversation, but they went on to talk of steam transportation, the political reform movement in Germany, and the war in Mexico, which, more than all the fruits of peace, raised America to the rank of "first-rate power" in Old World eyes. To such words "no American could listen without feeling pride," and Stephens took away Humboldt's autograph as "a memento of one of my most interesting incidents of travel."

Anticipating a demand for transportation to the West after gold was discovered in California in 1848, Stephens, William H. Aspinwall, and Henry Chauncey incorporated the Panama Railroad Company in April 1849 with Stephens first as vice president and later as president. Despite a crippling fall from a mule, Stephens was a driving on-site administrator, carrying out negotiations in Bogotá and overseeing the engineering of the undertaking. His health undermined by malaria, he was found unconscious in 1852 under the "Stephens Tree," a huge ceiba that he had saved from destruction by slightly altering the railroad's course. He was taken to New York City, where he died on 13 October—three weeks after the Panama Mail Steamship Company christened the SS *John L. Stephens*. He is buried in Marble Cemetery.

Along with Heinrich Schliemann—whom Stephens met in Panama before Schliemann began his excavations at Troy—Stephens is one of a handful of explorers who have discovered the remnants of lost civilizations. But his major significance today is as a target of critiques of imperialism. The artist Robert Smithson's "Incidents of Mirror-Travel in the Yucatan," mimics the title of Stephens's book; Smithson placed mirrors at nine "non-sites" in Yucatán, photographed them, and then dismantled them so that "Yucatan is elsewhere." Since 1984 the Argentine artist Leandro Katz has been attempting to reappropriate Mayan sites from their representation by Stephens and Catherwood by combining his photographs with Catherwood's illustrations. David E. Johnson presents a powerful critique of *Incidents of Travel in Central America, Chiapas, and Yucatan* and *Incidents of Travel in Yucatan,* arguing that Stephens devalues native knowledge so that he can "discover" ruins, imagine them in a European framework, and then make knowledge of Central America the property of foreigners and a commodity for export. Such critiques are themselves significant testimony for the claim by Van Wyck Brooks that Stephens is "the greatest of American travel-writers."

References:

Van Wyck Brooks, *The World of Washington Irving* (New York: Dutton, 1944), pp. 491–498;

David E. Johnson, " 'Writing in the Dark': The Political Fictions of American Travel Writing," *American Literary History,* 7 (Spring 1995): 1–27;

George Jones, *History of Ancient America* (London: Longman, Brown, Green, and Longmans, 1843; New York: Harper, 1843);

Leandro Katz, *The Catherwood Project: Robert B. Menschel Photography Gallery, January 15–March 10, 1992* (Syracuse: Robert B. Menschel Photography Gallery, 1992);

Rajeev S. Patke, "Stevens and Stephens: A Possible Source," *American Literature,* 53 (May 1981): 306–313;

Keith Robinson, "The Archaeological Image of Mexico in the Nineteenth Century: Verbal and Visual Discourses in the Works of Stephens and Catherwood, Charnay and Maudslay," dissertation, University of Essex, 1994;

Robert Smithson, "Incidents of Mirror-Travel in Yucatan," *Artforum,* 9 (September 1969): 28–33;

Victor Wolfgang von Hagen, *Maya Explorer: John Lloyd Stephens and the Lost Cities of Central America and Yucatan* (Norman: University of Oklahoma Press, 1947).

Papers:

The John Lloyd Stephens Correspondence and Papers collection is at the Bancroft Library of the University of California at Berkeley.

Henry David Thoreau
(12 July 1817 – 6 May 1862)

Stephen Adams
University of Minnesota–Duluth

See also the Thoreau entry in *DLB 1: The American Renaissance in New England.*

BOOKS: *A Week on the Concord and Merrimack Rivers* (Boston & Cambridge: Munroe, 1849);

Walden; Or Life in the Woods (Boston: Ticknor & Fields, 1854);

Excursions, edited by Ralph Waldo Emerson (Boston: Ticknor & Fields, 1863);

The Maine Woods, edited by William E. Channing and Sophia Thoreau (Boston: Ticknor & Fields, 1864);

Cape Cod, edited by Channing and Sophia Thoreau (Boston: Ticknor & Fields, 1865);

Letters to Various Persons, edited by Emerson (Boston: Ticknor & Fields, 1865);

A Yankee in Canada, with Anti-Slavery and Reform Papers, edited by Channing and Sophia Thoreau (Boston: Ticknor & Fields, 1866);

Early Spring in Massachusetts, edited by H. G. O. Blake (Boston: Houghton, Mifflin, 1881);

Summer, edited by Blake (Boston & New York: Houghton, Mifflin, 1884);

Winter, edited by Blake (Boston & New York: Houghton, Mifflin, 1888);

Autumn, edited by Blake (Boston & New York: Houghton, Mifflin, 1892);

The Writings of Henry David Thoreau, 10 volumes (Boston & New York: Houghton, Mifflin, 1894);

Familiar Letters, edited by Frank B. Sanborn (Boston & New York: Houghton, Mifflin, 1894);

Poems of Nature, edited by Henry S. Salt and Sanborn (London: Lane / Boston & New York: Houghton, Mifflin, 1895);

The Service, edited by Sanborn (Boston: Goodspeed, 1902);

Sir Walter Releigh, edited by Henry Aiken Metcalf (Boston: Bibliophile Society, 1905);

The First and Last Journeys of Thoreau, 2 volumes, edited by Sanborn (Boston: Bibliophile Society, 1905);

Henry David Thoreau (Concord Free Public Library)

The Writings of Henry David Thoreau, 20 volumes (Boston & New York: Houghton, Mifflin, 1906);

The Moon (Boston & New York: Houghton Mifflin, 1927);

The Transmigration of the Seven Brahmans, edited by Arthur Christy (New York: Rudge, 1931);

Collected Poems of Henry Thoreau, edited by Carl Bode (Chicago: Packard, 1943; enlarged edition, Baltimore: Johns Hopkins University Press, 1964);

Consciousness in Concord The Text of Thoreau's Hitherto "Lost Journal," edited by Perry Miller (1840–1841) (Boston: Houghton Mifflin, 1958);

The Writings of Henry D. Thoreau, 12 volumes to date (Princeton: Princeton University Press, 1971–   );

Faith in a Seed: The Dispersion of Seeds and Other Late Natural History Writings, edited by Bradley P. Dean (Washington, D.C. & Covelo, Cal.: Island Press/Shearwater Books, 1993).

John Aldrich Christie best captures the paradoxes and contradictions in Henry David Thoreau's treatment of travel. He characterizes Thoreau as "a man who on the one hand reiterates his disdain for travel and on the other peppers his writings with its products; a writer who urges his readers to concentrate upon a knowledge of their own local plot of ground at the same time that he makes sure in his writing that their acquaintance with the world be nothing less than global; the seemingly contented provincial who is all the while devouring the accounts of other men's furthest travels." Thoreau is best known for his works of domestic travel: *A Week on the Concord and Merrimack Rivers* (1849), *The Maine Woods* (1864), *Cape Cod* (1865); the shorter essays in *Excursions* (1863), and even *Walden* (1854), which can profitably be read as a voyage—after traveling a good deal in Concord Thoreau sojourns in a place "as far off as many a region viewed nightly by astronomers . . . a withdrawn, but forever new and unprofaned, part of the universe."

Thoreau's one account of travel outside the United States is "An Excursion to Canada," a work that grew out of an organized trip that the Fitchburg Railroad ran as a promotion in 1850. Thoreau called the work "insignificant"; he commented in a 27 February 1853 letter to his friend Harrison Blake, "I do not wonder that you do not like my Canada story. It concerns me but little, and probably is not worth the time it took to tell it. Yet I had absolutely no design whatever in my mind, but simply to report what I saw. I have inserted all of myself that was implicated or made the excursion." Since Thoreau's own disparaging remarks, most critics have ignored or have commented briefly, mostly unfavorably, upon the work. Walter Harding in *The New Thoreau Handbook* (1980), for example, calls it "one of Thoreau's least inspired 'excursions.' . . . The entire essay seems out of character." William Howarth writes, "'Canada' has a crabbed and peckish hu-mor, clumsy interpolations of guidebook lore, and a didactic air." Robert D. Richardson Jr. adds, "In general, Thoreau's account of what he saw on this trip is thin, uninspired, complaining." Critics Sidney Poger, Edmund Berry, Max Cosman, Barrie Davies, Sherman Paul, and Stephen Adams and Donald Ross Jr. find greater value in the piece, finding connections with Thoreau's other, more highly regarded works.

Born 12 July 1817 in Concord, Massachusetts, Thoreau was the third of four children of Cynthia Dunbar Thoreau and John Thoreau, a farmer and store manager. His family moved about when Thoreau was a child, living in Chelmsford, a village ten miles from Concord, from 1818 to 1821 and then moving to Boston, where his father taught school, before returning to Concord. Thoreau in 1822 enrolled in the Concord Academy, a private school founded by prominent townspeople. Because his parents, who could afford to send only one son to college, thought him the most scholarly of their children, Thoreau entered Harvard in 1833. He graduated in 1837 and that same year, on 22 October, began his voluminous journal. He also became associated with the "Hedge Club," an informal group of New England Transcendentalists that included Ralph Waldo Emerson, Orestes Brownson, Margaret Fuller, Frederic Henry Hedge, George Ripley, Jones Very, Elizabeth Peabody, Bronson Alcott, and Theodore Parker. He contributed poems to *The Dial,* a Transcendentalist organ, throughout its four-year existence (1840–1844).

After Thoreau left college, he engaged in a variety of jobs in his father's pencil factory and in the community as a teacher, surveyor, builder, and repairman. Thoreau lived what Nathaniel Hawthorne characterized as "a sort of Indian life among civilized men—an Indian life, I mean, as respects the absence of any systematic effort for a livelihood." Thoreau's response to the tenth-anniversary questionnaire from his Harvard class reveals his varied occupations: "I am a Schoolmaster—a private Tutor, a Surveyor—a Gardener, a Farmer—a Painter, I mean a House Painter, a Carpenter, a Mason, a Day-Laborer, a Pencil-Maker, a Glasspaper Maker, a Writer, and sometimes a Poetaster." The most celebrated period of his life was his twenty-six-month sojourn on Walden Pond, from 4 July 1845 to 6 September 1847. Living in the tiny cabin he built himself, Thoreau wrote all of *A Week on the Concord and Merrimack Rivers* and much or all of the first version of *Walden.*

Despite his radical individualism, Thoreau never tried to live apart from the cares or the affections of the world. In the 1840s he suffered the deaths of his brother John from lockjaw and his sister Helen from tuberculosis. His opposition to slavery led him to refuse to pay the poll tax, and he would have spent more than one night in jail had not his tax been paid anonymously. Thoreau also took trips that would provide the basis for much of his thinking and his writing. In 1843 he went to Staten Island, New York, to serve as tutor to the children of Emerson's brother William and found New York City "a thousand times meaner than I could have imagined." He traveled with his friend William Ellery Channing, a poet who would become Thoreau's editor and biographer, through the Berkshires and Catskills in 1844 and to Cape Cod in 1849. In 1846 he and his cousin George Thatcher climbed Mount Katahdin in Maine.

Thoreau's September 1850 trip to Canada was different than any other trip he had ever taken because it was rigidly structured. He, his friend Channing, and fifteen hundred "fellow-travelers" paid for a weeklong tour of eastern Canada. Eighty-four pages of Thoreau's journal are missing just after the notation "Left Concord Wednesday morning Sep 25th '50 for Quebec. Fare $7.00 to and fro. Obliged to leave Montreal on return as soon as Friday Oct 4th." He used these journal entries (and extensive notes from his reading about Canada after the trip) to write a narrative of the excursion that he tapped for lectures in early 1852. In March of that year he gave a manuscript of the narrative to Horace Greeley, who sometimes acted as his literary agent. Greeley reported in a 25 June letter that several magazines "have refused it on the ground of its length" before he finally placed the work.

In 1853 *Putnam's Monthly Magazine* published most of the first three chapters in its January, February, and March issues under the title "An Excursion to Canada." But Thoreau stopped publication when the editor, George William Curtis, censored an acerbic comment about religion. Thoreau withdrew the manuscript, as he wrote to Blake on 27 February, "because the editor Curtis requires the liberty to omit the heresies without consulting me—a privilege California is not rich enough to bid for." Thoreau eventually added some sentences and footnotes to the piece, but he did not revise extensively. The complete text was published with other material after Thoreau's death as *A Yankee in Canada, with Anti-Slavery and Reform Papers* (1866). Under the title *A*

Yankee in Canada it appeared in the *Excursions* volume of the 1906 *The Writings of Henry David Thoreau,* the standard edition for many years. Under Thoreau's original title, "An Excursion to Canada," it will appear in the *Excursions* volume of the new standard edition, the Princeton University Press's *The Writings of Henry D. Thoreau.*

"An Excursion to Canada" is structured conventionally enough as a voyage out and back, from Concord to Montreal by rail and steamboat (chapter 1); to Quebec and the falls of Montmorenci (chapter 2); to the falls of Saint Anne, Thoreau's farthest point down the Saint Lawrence (chapter 3); to the falls of Chaudière and back to Quebec (chapter 4). The narrative concludes with more remarks on Quebec and a summary of information about the Saint Lawrence as Thoreau returns to Montreal and then Concord (chapter 5). Along the way he comments extensively on the history and present state of Canada.

Thoreau begins, "I fear that I have not got much to say about Canada, not having seen much; what I got by going to Canada was a cold." The curmudgeonly opening sets the tone for the rest of "An Excursion to Canada," which is pervaded by Thoreau's dry satiric humor. But why did he not see much, and why was not more of himself "implicated" in this trip, when his other travels proved so engaging and fruitful? The main reason is that the itinerary and schedule were mostly out of Thoreau's control. Instead of setting his own leisurely pace, with plenty of time for the meditative "sauntering" and close observation of nature that he so loved, Thoreau was "whirled rapidly along" on a timetable dictated by the tour's promoters.

In his journal for 22 August 1851 he drafted what became the initial sentence of the work, with an explanation later omitted: "I fear that I have not got much to say not having seen much—for the very rapidity of the motion had a tendency to keep my eye lids closed—." His journal describes how the tourists were treated as a commodity: "while it was understood that the freight was not to be willfully & intentionally debarred from seeing the country if it had eyes," the important thing for the railroad was delivering this cargo "at the right place & time." Beside the disadvantages of speed, much of the travel occurred in the dark. Thoreau caught "only a glimpse" of Lake Champlain as he was forced to "rush to a wharf and go on board a steamboat . . . too late to see the lake." Steaming down the Saint Lawrence from Montreal to Quebec, he missed most of the scenery because "the daylight now

Thoreau in his traveling outfit, sketch made by Daniel Ricketson in 1854 (from Daniel Ricketson and His Friends, *1902)*

render Canada backward, undemocratic, and hostile to individual freedom. Because of its intrusive presence, the British army is the most prominent of these institutions. Thoreau frequently pokes fun at the omnipresent British soldiers, who are useful mainly "for music and entertainment"; the sentries are of no use at all "unless to hinder a free circulation of the air." He sees the soldiers not as individuals but as "one vast centipede of a man . . . the imperfect tools of an imperfect and tyrannical government"; "all true manhood was in the process of being drilled out of them." The repressive British military is most evident at the walled fortress that is Quebec, which Thoreau denounces as "a 'folly,'—England's folly,—and, in more senses than one, a castle in the air." "Such works do not consist with the development of the intellect," he insists, "huge stone structures of all kinds, both in their erection and by their influence when erected, rather oppress than liberate the mind. They are tombs for the souls of men, as frequently for their bodies also."

The Catholic Church, too, becomes a regular target of Thoreau's sharp commentary as he satirizes useless, effeminate priests, tearful nuns, and gullible, oxlike worshipers. In the passage that Curtis censored, Thoreau wrote, "I am not sure but this Catholic religion would be an admirable one if the priest were quite omitted. I think that I might go to church myself some Monday, if I lived in a city where there was such a one to go to." Thoreau may be indulging in the anticatholicism common to his day, but his remarks relate to crucial concerns in "An Excursion." He did not see much on his trip because oppressive social institutions did not allow him to. If walls and military guards physically restrict what people can see in Canada, the church erects more subtle but equally dangerous barriers to perception. Thoreau passes a schoolhouse that "appeared like a place where the process, not of enlightening, but of obfuscating the mind was going on, and the pupils received only so much light as could penetrate the shadow of the Catholic Church." He cannot see the Canadian countryside clearly because the "saintly names" given to towns, mountains, villages, and everything else "veiled the Indian and the primitive forest, and the woods toward Hudson's Bay were only as the forests of France and Germany."

"In short," Thoreau writes, "the inhabitants of Canada appeared to be suffering between two fires,—the soldiery and the priesthood." Seeing both as remnants of a feudal system that keeps

failed us, and we went below." The return trip took Thoreau in one night through territory that Cartier called "'full of the most beautiful trees in the world,' which he goes on to describe. But we merely slept and woke again to find that we had passed through all that country which he was eight days in sailing through."

But even more important for Thoreau's perceptions and state of mind were the social forces everywhere in evidence—forces that distracted him from his usually inspiring explorations of nature. Although he pays fairly cursory attention to the Saint Lawrence River and three of its waterfalls, Thoreau keeps focusing on institutions that

Canada hopelessly backward, Thoreau stresses the anachronistic nature of the country. Although the Old World considers Canada new, "it appeared as old as Normandy itself, and realized much that I had heard of Europe and the Middle Ages." He calls the walled city of Quebec "a relic of antiquity and barbarism.... Those who built this fort, coming from Old France with the memory and tradition of feudal days and customs weighing on them, were unquestionably behind their age; and those who now inhabit and repair it are behind their ancestors or predecessors. Those old chevaliers thought that they could transplant the feudal system to America. It has been set out, but it has not thriven." The omnipresent fortifications in Canada "carry us back to the Middle Ages, the siege of Jerusalem, and St. Jean d'Acre, and the days of the Bucaniers."

Thoreau saw all these throwbacks not as quaint but as tragic. Canada's feudal tenure afflicts its citizens with "a poverty which not even its severity of climate and ruggedness of soil will suffice to account for." He notes that the people of Montmorenci County do not take advantage of their government's attempt to "provide for the extinction of feudal and seigniorial rights and burdens . . . and for the gradual conversion of those tenures into the tenure of free and common socage." Thoreau concludes, "Why should Canada, wild and unsettled as it is, impress us as an older country than the States, unless because her institutions are old? All things appeared to contend there, as I have implied, with a certain rust of antiquity, such as forms on old armor and iron guns,—the rust of conventions and formalities."

He directs his criticism at both the French and British in Canada. While he admires the heroes that he has been reading about (Samuel de Champlain, Jacques Cartier, Pehr Kalm, Pierre-François-Xavier de Charlevoix, and others—"The Canadians of those days, at least, possessed a roving spirit of adventure"), he dismisses contemporary French Canada as "a nation of peasants." These people "appeared very inferior, intellectually and even physically, to that of New England. In some respects, they were incredibly filthy.... The impression made on me was that the French Canadians were even sharing the fate of the Indians, or at least gradually disappearing in what is called the Saxon current." But neither is Thoreau impressed by the Saxon line in Canada. While the typical Yankee "is fully resolved to better his condition essentially," the Englishman's virtue "consists in merely maintaining his ground or condi-

tion." He shares with his French counterpart a debilitating stasis or backwardness.

The praise that Thoreau lavished on the people of the United States, as he compares them favorably with Canadians, also differentiates "An Excursion in Canada" from Thoreau's other works. While he does include Yankees—and himself—among his many satiric targets in the piece, Thoreau spares his fellow citizens the attacks prominent in other compositions from the same period—especially *Walden* and the antislavery essays. At times he sounds chauvinistic, as if he were deliberately paying back French and British visitors for their critical accounts of travel in the United States. But even this boosterism is related to Thoreau's central concern for the dangers that institutions pose to the free individual. He writes, "It was evident that, both on account of the feudal system and the aristocratic government, a private man was not worth so much in Canada as in the United States; and, if your wealth in any measure consists in manliness, in originality and independence, you had better stay here."

Echoing "Resistance to Civil Government" and other reform essays, Thoreau writes, "What makes the United States government, on the whole, more tolerable—I mean only for us lucky white men—is the fact that there is so much less government with us." This theme links "An Excursion to Canada" with Thoreau's other contemporary writing. In "Slavery in Massachusetts," too, for example, political repression affects Thoreau's perception of and relation to nature. Because of its cooperation with slaveholders, Massachusetts changes in Thoreau's vision from a fertile wonderland to "part of the empire of hell":

> I walk toward one of our ponds, but what signifies the beauty of nature when men are base? We walk to lakes to see our serenity reflected in them; when we are not serene, we go not to them. Who can be serene in a country where both the rulers and the ruled are without principle? The remembrance of my country spoils my walk. My thoughts are murder to the State, and involuntarily go plotting against her.

In the same way, Canada's "imperfect and tyrannical government" prevents Thoreau from dwelling on and appreciating the Canadian landscape as he otherwise would. There is, then, some logic to the 1866 edition that included "A Yankee in Canada" with the reform essays, even if subsequent editors have placed it with Thoreau's shorter excursions.

All in all, his Canada trip was frustrating for Thoreau. He concludes the account by hoping for a more fruitful tour in the future: "I should still like right well to make a longer excursion on foot through the wilder parts of Canada, which perhaps might be called *Iter Canadense*." At the end of his life Thoreau did travel briefly once more in Canada on his way to and from Minnesota, which had become a state three years earlier. His doctor sent him west in a futile effort to improve his health, which was rapidly failing from tuberculosis. Thoreau spent a little time on the Canadian side of Niagara Falls in mid May 1861 and then traveled briefly by rail in Canada (Goderich, Stratford, and Toronto) on his way back from Minnesota to Concord in late June. But he left only brief field notes, chiefly botanical, about this visit. These notes were excerpted by Frank B. Sanborn in *The First and Last Journeys of Thoreau* and published in 1962 by Walter Harding as *Thoreau's Minnesota Journey: Two Documents*. Thoreau died on 6 May 1862.

Letters:

The Correspondence of Henry David Thoreau, edited by Walter Harding and Carl Bode (New York: New York University Press, 1958);

Kenneth Walter Cameron, *Companion to Thoreau's Correspondence* (Hartford, Conn.: Transcendental Books, 1964);

Cameron, *Over Thoreau's Desk: New Correspondence* (Hartford, Conn.: Transcendental Books, 1965).

Bibliographies:

Francis H. Allen, *A Bibliography of Henry David Thoreau* (Boston: Houghton Mifflin, 1908);

William White, *A Henry David Thoreau Bibliography* (Boston: Faxon, 1939);

Philip E. Burnham and Carvel Collins, "Contributions toward a Bibliography of Thoreau, 1938–1945," *Bulletin of Bibliography,* 19 (September–December 1946, January–April 1947): 16–19, 37–39;

Walter Harding, *A Centennial Check-list of the Editions of Henry David Thoreau's Walden* (Charlottesville: University Press of Virginia, 1954);

Harding, *Thoreau's Library* (Charlottesville: University Press of Virginia, 1957);

Christopher A. Hildenbrand, *A Bibliography of Scholarship about Henry David Thoreau 1940–1967* (Hays, Kans.: Fort Hays State College, 1967);

A Bibliography of the Thoreau Society Bulletin Bibliographies 1941–1969 (Troy, N.Y.: Whitston, 1971);

Lewis Leary, "Henry David Thoreau," in *Eight American Authors: A Review of Research and Criticism,* edited by James Woodress (New York: Norton, 1971);

Annette M. Woodlief, "Walden: A Checklist of Literary Criticism through 1973," *Resources for American Literary Study,* 5 (Spring 1975): 15–58;

Jeanetta Boswell and Sarah Crouch, *Henry David Thoreau and the Critics* (Metuchen, N.J.: Scarecrow Press, 1981);

Raymond R. Borst, *Henry David Thoreau: A Descriptive Bibliography* (Pittsburgh: University of Pittsburgh Press, 1982);

Michael Meyer, "Henry David Thoreau," in *The Transcendentalists: A Review of Research and Criticism,* edited by Joel Myerson (New York: Modern Language Association, 1984);

Raymond R. Borst, *Henry David Thoreau: A Reference Guide, 1875–1899* (Boston: G. K. Hall, 1987);

Robert Sattelmeyer, *Thoreau's Reading: A Study in Intellectual History with Bibliographical Catalogue* (Princeton: Princeton University Press, 1988);

Boswell, "Henry David Thoreau," in *The American Renaissance and the Critics: The Best of a Century of Criticism* (Wakefield, N.H.: Longwood Academic, 1990);

Gary Scharnhorst, *Henry David Thoreau: An Annotated Bibliography of Comment and Criticism Before 1900* (Hamden, Conn.: Garland, 1992).

Biographies:

William Ellery Channing, *Thoreau: the Poet-Naturalist* (Boston: Roberts, 1873; revised edition, Boston: Charles E. Goodspeed, 1902);

Frank B. Sanborn, *Henry D. Thoreau* (Boston: Houghton, Mifflin, 1882);

Henry S. Salt, *The Life of Henry David Thoreau* (London: Bentley, 1890; revised edition, London: Walter Scott, 1896);

Annie Russell Marble, *Thoreau: His Home, Friends and Books* (New York: Crowell, 1902);

Edward Emerson, *Henry Thoreau as Remembered by a Young Friend* (Boston: Houghton Mifflin, 1917);

Henry Seidel Canby, *Thoreau* (Boston: Houghton Mifflin, 1939);

Sherman Paul, *The Shores of America: Thoreau's Inward Exploration* (Urbana: University of Illinois Press, 1958);

Richard Bridgman, *Dark Thoreau* (Lincoln: University of Nebraska Press, 1962);

Milton Meltzer and Walter Harding, *A Thoreau Profile* (New York: Crowell, 1962);

Walter Harding, *The Days of Henry Thoreau* (New York: Knopf, 1965; enlarged and corrected edition, New York: Dover, 1992);

Joel Porte, *Emerson and Thoreau* (Middletown, Conn.: Wesleyan University Press, 1966);

Richard Lebeaux, *Young Man Thoreau* (Amherst: University of Massachusetts Press, 1977);

Edward Wagenknecht, *Henry David Thoreau: What Manner of Man?* (Amherst: University of Massachusetts Press, 1981);

William L. Howarth, *The Book of Concord: Thoreau's Life as a Writer* (New York: Viking, 1982);

Richard Lebeaux, *Thoreau's Seasons* (Amherst: University of Massachusetts Press, 1984);

Robert D. Richardson, *Thoreau: A Life of the Mind* (Berkeley: University of California Press, 1986);

Walter Harding, ed., *Thoreau As Seen by His Contemporaries* (New York: Dover, 1989);

Raymond R. Borst, *The Thoreau Log: A Documentary Life of Henry David Thoreau, 1817–1862* (New York: G. K. Hall, 1992).

References:

Stephen Adams and Donald Ross Jr., *Revising Mythologies: The Composition of Thoreau's Major Works* (Charlottesville: University Press of Virginia, 1988);

Edmund Berry, "Thoreau in Canada," *Dalhousie Review,* 23 (1943): 68–74;

John Aldrich Christie, *Thoreau as World Traveler* (New York: Columbia University Press, 1965);

Max Cosman, "A Yankee in Canada," *Canadian Historical Review,* 25 (1944): 33–37;

Barrie Davies, "Sam Quixote in Lower Canada," *Bulletin de L'Association canadienne des Humanités,* 20 (1969): 67–78;

Walter Harding, *Thoreau's Minnesota Journey: Two Documents,* Thoreau Society Booklet no. 16 (Geneseo, N.Y.: Thoreau Society, 1962);

Harding and Michael Meyer, *The New Thoreau Handbook* (New York: New York University Press, 1980);

William L. Howarth, *The Book of Concord: Thoreau's Life as a Writer* (New York: Viking, 1982);

Joel Myerson, *The Cambridge Companion to Henry David Thoreau* (Cambridge: Cambridge University Press, 1995);

Sidney Poger, "Thoreau as Yankee in Canada," *American Transcendental Quarterly,* 14 (1972): 174–177;

Robert D. Richardson Jr., *Henry Thoreau: A Life of the Mind* (Berkeley: University of California Press, 1986).

Papers:

The major collections of Henry David Thoreau's manuscripts are held by the Pierpont Morgan Library, New York City; the Berg Collection at the New York Public Library; the Houghton Library at Harvard University; the Henry E. Huntington Library; the C. Waller Barrett Library at the University of Virginia; the Abernethy Library at Middlebury College; and the Concord Free Public Library. See William L. Howarth's *The Literary Manuscripts of Henry David Thoreau* (Columbus: Ohio State University Press, 1974).

John Trumbull

6 June 1756 – 10 November 1843)

Martha I. Pallante
Youngstown State University

BOOK: *Autobiography, Reminiscences and Letters by John Trumbull from 1756 to 1841* (New York, London & New Haven, 1841).

Edition: *The Autobiography of Colonel John Trumbull: Patriot-Artist, 1756–1843,* edited by Theodore Sizer (New Haven: Yale University Press, 1953).

Artists and historians since the mid nineteenth century have acknowledged John Trumbull as the United States' premier "patriot-artist" of the early national period and have recognized his artistic contributions to that era and to modern perceptions of it. Frequently overlooked, however, is his one literary work, *Autobiography, Reminiscences and Letters by John Trumbull from 1756 to 1841* (1841). Much of this memoir deals with his experiences in Europe between 1780 and 1815.

Trumbull was born on 6 June 1756 in Lebanon, Connecticut, the last of six children. His father, Jonathan Trumbull, served as a representative to the Connecticut General Assembly and later as the colony's governor; his mother, Faith Robinson Trumbull, was descended from a spiritual leader of the Pilgrims, John Robinson. In 1761 Trumbull suffered a head injury that left him blind in his left eye. At a local school run by Nathan Tisdale, one of the finest tutors in the colony, Trumbull showed a remarkable facility for languages and drawing. His artistic ability would take him to Europe in search of training and an audience, while his flair for languages would enable him to converse with Europeans in their own idiom.

By the time he was fifteen Trumbull had decided to become a painter, but his father wanted him to pursue a career in the law or the ministry. Thus, in 1771 Trumbull dutifully entered Harvard College, where, he claims in his autobiography, his extracurricular activities paid the greatest returns. From a family of Acadian refugees he learned French, "which in after life was of eminent utility." He spent the time he could appropriate from his official studies copying works of art. In 1773 he "graduated without applause" and without the prospect of employment.

John Trumbull; self-portrait, probably painted circa 1804 (Yale University Art Gallery)

In 1775 Trumbull served as an adjutant for Gen. Joseph Spencer of the First Connecticut Militia Regiment. After the Battle of Bunker Hill he received an appointment as second aide-de-camp to George Washington, who took advantage of Trumbull's ability to draw battlefields and troop deployments. In 1777 he resigned over an error in the wording of his commission and moved to Boston to resume his artistic pursuits. Frustrated by the lack of qualified instruction there, he moved to London in 1780 to study in Benjamin West's studio. Trumbull did not see why the fact that Great Britain was at war with some of its colonies should be an impediment to his pursuing his studies in London; he says in his autobiography that when British officials arrested him, a "thunderbolt falling at my feet, would not have been more astounding. . . . I had become as confident of safety in

Trumbull's drawing Paris as Seen from the House of the Abbé Chalut, *1786*
(Susan Silliman Pearson, New Haven)

London as I should have been in Lebanon." Paroled in 1781, he returned to his family home in Connecticut.

In 1784 Trumbull again embarked for Europe; this time he had letters of introduction to government officials from his father, whom he had finally persuaded to support his artistic endeavors. He continued his studies at West's studio in London, where he completed the first of his major historic works, *The Battle of Bunker Hill,* in 1786. Later that year Thomas Jefferson invited him to visit Paris. Trumbull spent the next three years there viewing the works of the European masters. During this period he began the twofold artistic career that he would pursue for the rest of his life: portraits would support him financially, while historical paintings would be his passion. In Paris he completed his widely acclaimed work *The Declaration of Independence.*

Returning to the United States in November 1789, Trumbull entered into a love affair with Harriet Wadsworth that was cut short by her death. He went back to London in 1794 as a secretary to John Jay, who was negotiating a peace treaty with Britain. He married Sarah Hope Harvey, an Englishwoman thirteen years his junior, who was considered by most of his acquaintances to be a social liability. He took into his household his illegitimate son, John Trumbull Ray, whom he passed off as his nephew. He observed the French Revolution, the rise of Napoleon Bonaparte, and the deterioration of the United States' relationship with Great Britain. Although he wanted to return to America, he was forced to remain in England during the War of 1812. His frustrations increased with the knowledge that his son had joined the British army.

After the war Trumbull and his wife took up residence in New York City. Trumbull affiliated himself with the American Academy of Fine Arts and accepted a commission to decorate the Capitol building in Washington, D.C. In 1817 he was elected president of the academy; he would serve in that capacity for nineteen years. His wife died in April 1824.

As Trumbull passed his seventieth year he became increasingly beleaguered by debt, and in 1830 he entered into an arrangement with Yale College that would support him in his later years: in exchange for the right to hold permanently the fifty-five of his paintings then in Trumbull's possession, Yale agreed to construct a gallery of Trumbull's design for their exhibition and to pay him an annual stipend of $1,000. He explained in his autobiography that he had made the same offer to his alma mater, Harvard; only after Harvard rejected it did he turn to Yale. In 1837 Trumbull moved to New Haven to live with his nephew-in-law, Benjamin Silliman, at whose suggestion he began to write his autobiography. After its publication Trumbull returned to New York City, where he died on 10 November 1843.

The same attention to detail and the acute sense of place that earned praise for Trumbull's historical paintings are found in his autobiography. Irma Jaffe

Trumbull's painting Caerphilly Castle in South Wales, *1803 (private collection)*

says that Trumbull went about preparing the materials for his memoirs in the same way he readied himself to paint one of his historical works: "He gathered the factual materials [letterbooks and diaries], arranged the research, made an outline, and filled in the composition."

The most successful—and certainly the lengthiest—part of the autobiography is the central section, which deals with Trumbull's European travels. According to Silliman's preface these chapters, which are based largely on his diary, have the "flavor and excitement of youth." While Trumbull spent only twenty of his more than eighty years abroad, he devotes nearly 60 percent of his autobiography to his travels in Europe.

Europe both fascinated and repulsed Trumbull. Recounting his first trip there, he says, "I was very much struck with the total dissimilitude to the shores of America; there all is new, here all things bore the marks of age." On 18 September 1786, while touring along the Rhine, Trumbull commented in his diary—which he includes, virtually unaltered, in his autobiography—on the social and political inequities in central Europe: "It would give great pleasure to see rising upon the ruins of war, the habitations of peace and industry; but such pleasure is not to be expected in a country like this." He observes that although the land produced abundantly,

"in the midst of plenty, inhabitants, although merry, appear to be wretched . . . with their needs sacrificed to support the pride and pomp of one family." Describing the shortcomings of the French Revolution, as compared with that of the United States, he says: "The calm splendor of our own Revolution, comparatively rational and beneficial as it had been, was eclipsed in the meteoric glare and horrible blaze of glory of republican France; and we, who in our own case, had scarcely stained the sacred robe of rational liberty with a single drop of blood unnecessarily shed, learned to admire that hideous frenzy which made the very streets of Paris flow with blood."

Trumbull's descriptions of the places he visited have the same clarity and accuracy that characterize his painting and prints. He reveals a hierarchy of interests: first come works of art, then churches, fortifications, and other structures; he generally devotes the least amount of attention to the people he encountered. For example, he rhapsodizes: "The Gardens of Versailles must be seen; they cannot be described," but he makes only cursory comments about the people he encountered at court. The Louvre he calls "*very fine* indeed, the best thing which I have yet seen," while the Tuileries are "the vilest possible jumble of antique and Gothic, perfectly, utterly bad." In his account of a festival at Saint Cloud in 1784 he describes, in great detail, "a very beautiful stone bridge": "the floor of this bridge is horizontal; it consists of seven arches, which have a beautiful degree of lightness; these arches, which in fact are hemispherical, are sloped from one fourth of the piers on each side to the outer face." At Aix-la-Chapelle (Aachen) "a most fertile valley," dividing "the town into two large and several small parts," is "crossed by one long bridge of six arches and several small ones."

The later chapters of Trumbull's autobiography deal with a span of nearly thirty years but contain little more than mentions of legal or contract negotiations, lists of artworks he completed, and descriptions of the places where he lived. Only when he discusses the creation of the Trumbull Gallery at Yale College and his decision to write his reminiscences does the work regain some of its earlier excitement or sense of purpose.

The autobiography was not a success. In a 25 July 1845 letter to Jabez Huntington, Silliman said that "the book was a loss to the publishers and disappointed the distinguished author." He ascribes the work's failure to "the perverted taste of the age . . . not in harmony with the sober realities of life." He suggests that if Trumbull had been less scrupulous and had included more innuendo and gossip, the book might have appealed more to its crass audience. Theodore Sizer says in the preface to his 1953 edition of the autobiography that Trumbull's cantankerous nature and old-fashioned formality made him less than accessible in the "rough-and-tumble, democratic 19th century." Trumbull's early biographers, however, used large portions of the autobiography in their works: C. Edwards Lester in *The Artists of America* (1846) and John F. Weir in *John Trumbull: A Brief Sketch of His Life, to Which Is Added a Catalogue of His Works* (1901) rely heavily on Trumbull's own words. Sizer gave up the idea of writing a biography of Trumbull in favor of editing the autobiography when he realized that he could tell the story no better than Trumbull had. Written in the age of Alexis de Toqueville and J. Hector St. John Crèvecoeur's commentaries on the United States, Trumbull's work provides an American's view of Europe.

Biographies:

C. Edwards Lester, "John Trumbull," in his *The Artists of America: A Series of Biographical Sketches of American Artists with Portraits and Designs on Steel* (New York: Baker & Scribner, 1846), pp. 135–171;

John F. Weir, *John Trumbull: A Brief Sketch of His Life, to Which Is Added a Catalogue of His Works* (New York: Scribners, 1901);

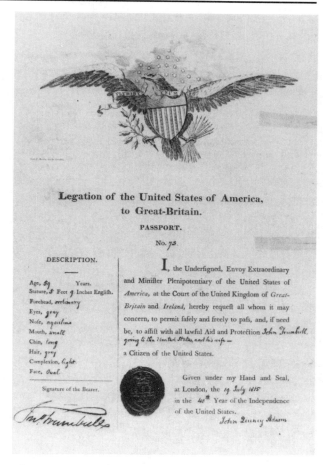

Passport used by Trumbull to return to the United States from England in 1815 (Benjamin Franklin Collection, Yale University Library)

Irma Jaffe, *John Trumbull: Patriot-Artist of the American Revolution* (Boston: New York Graphic Society, 1975);

Helen A. Cooper, *John Trumbull, The Hand: Spirit of a Painter* (New Haven: Yale University Art Gallery, 1982).

References:

John H. Morgan, *Painting by John Trumbull at Yale University* (New Haven: Yale University Press, 1926);

Theodore Sizer, "A Early Check List of the Paintings of John Trumbull," *Yale University Library Gazette,* 22 (April 1948): 116–123;

Sizer, "Trumbull's Troubles: An Omitted Chapter of the Artist's Life," *Yale University Library Gazette,* 25 (October 1950): 43–59;

Sizer, "Who Was The Colonel's Lady? The Strange Case of Mrs. John Trumbull," *New York Historical Quarterly,* 36 (October 1952): 410–429;

Sizer, *The Works of Colonel John Trumbull* (New Haven: Yale University Press, 1950; revised, 1967).

Charles Wilkes
(3 April 1798 – 8 February 1877)

James J. Schramer
Youngstown State University

BOOKS: *Synopsis of the Cruise of the U.S. Exploring Expedition, during the Years, 1838, '39, '40, '41 & '42: Delivered before the National Institute, by Its Commander, Charles Wilkes, Esq., on the Twentieth of June 1842: To Which Is Added a List of Officers and Scientific Corps Attached to the Expedition* (Washington, D.C.: Printed by P. Force, 1842);

The Narrative of the United States Exploring Expedition: During the Years 1838, 1839, 1840, 1841, 1842, 5 volumes (Philadelphia: Printed by C. Sherman, 1844; London: Wiley & Putnam, 1845); abridged by Wilkes as *Voyage round the World, Embracing the Principal Events of the Narrative of the United States Exploring Expedition,* 1 volume (Philadelphia: Gorton, 1849);

Western America, Including California and Oregon, with Maps of those Regions, and of "the Sacramento Valley" (Philadelphia: Lea & Blanchard, 1849);

Meteorology (Philadelphia: Printed by C. Sherman, 1851);

Theory of the Winds: Read before the American Scientific Association of Providence, August 20th, 1855. Accompanied by a Map of the World, Showing the Extent and Direction of the Winds. To Which Is Added, Sailing Directions for a Voyage around the World (Philadelphia, 1856; London: Trübner, 1860);

Theory of the Zodiacal Light: Read before the Meeting of the American Association for the Advancement of Science, at Montreal, August 1857 (Philadelphia: Printed by C. Sherman, 1857);

Hydrography, 3 volumes (Philadelphia: Printed by C. Sherman, 1858–1861);

Report on the Examination of the Deep River District, North Carolina, U.S. 35th Congress, second session, Senate, Ex. Doc. no. 26 (Washington, D.C., 1859);

Autobiography of Rear Admiral Charles Wilkes, U.S. Navy 1798–1877, edited by William J. Morgan, David B. Tyler, Joye L. Leonhart, and Mary F. Loughlin (Washington, D.C.: Naval

Charles Wilkes; portrait by Thomas Sully (U.S. Naval Academy Museum)

History Division, Department of the Navy, 1978).

In the first half of the nineteenth century the United States government sponsored two highly significant exploring expeditions. From 1803 to 1806 Meriwether Lewis and William Clark led an expedition through the interior of North America to the Pacific coast. A little more than thirty years later Lt. Charles Wilkes of the United States Navy captained an oceanic expedition that produced the first clear evidence that Antarctica was a continent, charted hundreds of South Pacific islands, and mapped the northwestern coast of North America. Most Americans have heard of the exploits of Lewis and Clark, but few know about the four-year voyage of Wilkes and his squadron. Wilkes, who served in the navy for more than fifty years and faced two courts-martial for his headstrong actions and his unguarded opinions of his superiors, deserves more attention than he has received from scholars. He provides a fascinating example of nineteenth-century American optimism in the face of adversity.

Wilkes was born on 3 April 1798 to John De Ponthieu Wilkes, a businessman involved in the import trade, and Mary Seton Wilkes. Wilkes's grandmother Elizabeth Ann Seton founded the Sisters of Charity; his grandfather Andrew Seton was a successful Manhattan banker who had become a friend and father figure to John De Ponthieu Wilkes after the young Englishman arrived in New York in the 1760s. The Wilkes family was staunchly Tory but was not without its rebels: John De Ponthieu Wilkes's uncle, also named John, had published a libelous attack on King George III in his newly founded newspaper, *The North Briton,* in 1762. When John De Ponthieu Wilkes came to the colonies, he learned that in America his uncle was seen as a radical hero on par with Thomas Paine. One Pennsylvania town went so far in its admiration that it renamed itself Wilkes-Barre in honor of the editor and his friend Issac Barre, a member of Parliament and champion of the colonies.

After Mary Wilkes died in 1801 Charles was raised by his sister Eliza, his maternal grandmother, and a nursemaid. He attended a series of boarding schools with his brothers, as well as the preparatory school for Columbia. Already developing a reputation for stubbornness, however, Wilkes decided that instead of attending college he preferred to learn about the world of work as a clerk in his father's office and then secure an appointment as a midshipman in the navy.

After months of what one might suppose was inspired wheedling from Wilkes, his father wrote the secretary of the navy to inquire about the possibility of his son's being accepted as a midshipman. The secretary replied that no slots were available at that time, but if the young man would serve an apprenticeship in the merchant marine the Navy Department would look on that time favorably when it considered its next round of applicants. Thinking that a strong taste of what Charles most wanted would cure him of his taste for the sea, his father secured a berth for him aboard the *Hibernia.* In 1815 Wilkes sailed from New York for La Havre, France.

In his autobiography (1978) Wilkes, looking back on these early years, would recall that "Humanity did not exist on the great deep and petty tyranny

was Rampant." Despite the hardships and maltreatment, Wilkes remained determined to enter naval service. After his first voyage Wilkes sailed to Wilmington, North Carolina, on the *Calpi* and then to La Havre again on the *Emulation.* On 1 January 1818 he became a midshipman in the United States Navy. His happiness was undercut by the death of his father a month later.

In July 1818 Wilkes made his first cruise aboard a navy ship, the *Independence,* where, he recalled in his autobiography, the conditions were just as harsh as those in the merchant marine: "A midshipman's life on board a [*sic*] American Man of War was a dog's life, and in many respects acts of tyranny and a total disregard to the feelings of young officers were lost sight of." To secure a better berth Wilkes asked for and received a transfer to the *Guerriere,* which was sailing to the Mediterranean. Of his new quarters, Wilkes would write in his autobiography: "We were assigned the Cockpit for our mess, which was on the deck below the steerage. It was but 4 1/2 feet high between decks, and as we were all of almost grown size, rather an inconvenient one; but as to space, we had plenty of room." On this cruise Wilkes sailed to Naples, Minorca, and Saint Petersburg. In his autobiography Wilkes describes the Russian capital as having a "pleasing effect upon a first visit. It is built of yellow or rather Cream coloured brick and would on sight be called a city of extended palaces as far as its outward show gives the impression." On closer inspection, however, he sees that "it wants the life of a city and the movement and stir of an active population. This is entirely wanting. There does not appear to be any work or employment going on." The city reminds Wilkes of a dreary military camp: "Each block of houses has its guard house and guard for any and all officers who may happen to pass, and this gives a kind of military despotism feeling to the stranger." Wilkes concludes that Saint Petersburg "may be called a phlegmatic city; it cloys and there is no desire left to again visit it."

Wilkes completed his Mediterranean cruise in early 1821; on 26 May he departed for South America aboard the *Franklin,* under Capt. Charles Stewart. When the *Franklin* arrived in Valparaiso, Chile, Wilkes accepted an unusually demanding assignment for a young midshipman. The captain of the *O'Cain,* a merchantman engaged in the fur-seal trade, had died on the voyage back from the Falklands, and the American consul requested that one of the naval officers in port take command of the ship. Stewart recommended Wilkes for the position. As an added inducement, Wilkes was promised a share of the money from the sale of the cargo

Wilkes's illustration of two ships in his United States Exploring Expedition, the Porpoise *and the* Sea-Gull, *battling fog, high seas, and icebergs near Antarctica in March 1839 (from Wilkes's* The Narrative of the United States Exploring Expedition, *1844)*

once the *O'Cain* reached Boston. Taking command of the *O'Cain* on 3 March 1823, Wilkes made record time on the final leg of the run from Bermuda to Boston and earned $8,000, a considerable sum at the time.

Wilkes was promoted to lieutenant on 28 April 1826, two days after he and Jane Renwick were married in New York City. Their son John was born on 31 March 1827.

On 15 July 1828 Wilkes requested assignment to the proposed United States Exploring Expedition to the South Seas; it would, however, be ten years before his request was granted. In the early 1800s John Cleves Symmes Jr. had proposed that the interior of the earth was hollow and could be reached by entering through a hole in the South Pole. Although Edgar Allan Poe would use the "Holes in the Poles Theory" as the basis for *The Narrative of Arthur Gordon Pym, of Nantucket* (1838), few believed in Symmes's ideas. Owners of whaling and sealing ships looking for fresh hunting grounds, however, saw that Symmes could help them convince Congress to support an expedition to the South Seas. President John Quincy Adams, eager to leave his mark on history by authorizing a grand exploration, as Thomas Jefferson had

done with Lewis and Clark twenty-five years earlier, pushed for a congressional resolution authorizing an expedition. Congress was unenthusiastic, however, and Andrew Jackson, who succeeded Adams in 1829, had no interest in the idea.

On 3 January 1829 Wilkes's daughter Jane was born. On 21 April 1830 Wilkes began a Mediterranean cruise on the *Boston*. Among the assignments for this cruise was to take Commo. David Porter to his post as chargé d'affaires in Turkey. Wilkes spent his brief shore time during the cruise visiting historical sites in North Africa. In his autobiography he recalls his impressions of Algiers, which he visited soon after the French occupied the city, and the ruins of ancient Carthage. He returned from the cruise in 1831 and began an extensive period of shore duty in Washington, D.C. A son, Edmund, was born to the Wilkeses on 4 February 1833. In 1834 Wilkes received permission from the Board of Naval Commissioners to erect, at his own expense and on his own Capitol Hill property, a building to house the first United States naval observatory. That same year the Board of Naval Commissioners appointed him head of the Depot of Charts and Instruments.

It was also in 1834 that President Jackson re-

Drawing by Lt. George F. Emmons of the Peacock, *its rudder damaged, working its way out of the ice during the expedition's second approach to Antarctica in January 1840 (Beinecke Rare Book and Manuscript Library, Yale University)*

versed his previous opposition to the polar expedition and appointed Capt. Thomas Caresby Jones, who had served with him in the Battle of New Orleans, to command the squadron. Wilkes was selected as purchasing agent for the expedition, and on 8 August 1836 he left from New York City to buy instruments and books in Europe.

Jackson had wanted the expedition to sail in October 1836, but problems with the ships delayed its departure. Eventually, Jackson had to replace Jones as commander because the naval commissioners objected to the extravagant scale of his plans. Martin Van Buren became president in 1838; his secretary of war, Joel R. Poinsett, an amateur botanist (the poinsettia was named after him), wanted the expedition to go forward. Impressed with Wilkes's scientific background and his reputation as the most knowledgeable hydrographer in the navy, Poinsett appointed Wilkes the expedition's commander.

On 18 August 1838–a month after Wilkes's second daughter, Eliza, was born on 19 July–the United States Exploring Expedition sailed from Norfolk, Virginia. The squadron consisted of Wilkes's flagship, the sloop *Vincennes;* the sloop *Peacock;* the brig *Porpoise;* the supply ship *Relief;* and two tenders, the *Flying-Fish* and the *Sea-Gull.* The ships' crews were drawn from the ranks; Wilkes chose most of the squadron's officers, including his nephew, Wilkes Henry. In addition to the naval personnel, the expedition's roster included nine scientists, all civilians.

The squadron arrived in Rio de Janeiro in late November for reconditioning and reprovisioning. As two of the squadron's young officers ruefully discovered, Wilkes held his men to a high standard of scientific accuracy even in port. When Lieutenants George F. Emmons and Joseph Underwood climbed to the top of Sugar Loaf Mountain, they expected their exploit to be greeted with praise. Instead, Wilkes wrote to Emmons's commanding officer: "Sir I learn with surprise that an officer of your ship made an excursion to an important height in this vicinity without obtaining the necessary instruments for its correct admeasurement; as it results only in the idle & boastful saying that its summit has been reached, instead of an excursion which might have been useful to the expedition." Within a few days Emmons and Underwood repeated their climb, this time lugging the proper measuring devices to the top.

The squadron departed from Rio on 6 January 1839 and anchored in Orange Harbor, Tierra del Fuego, on 18 February. Wilkes's official report, *The Narrative of the United States Exploring Expedition. During the Years 1838, 1839, 1840, 1841, 1842* (1844), describes the topography of Orange Harbor in precise detail:

The whole coast has the appearance of being of recent volcanic rocks, but all our investigations tended to prove to the contrary. We nowhere found any cellular lava, pumice, or obsidian, nor was there any granite, or other primitive rock seen though reported by Captain King as existing.

Wilkes's description of some Petcherai Indians who visited the squadron reflects the racist attitudes of the time:

> It is impossible to imagine any thing in human nature more filthy. They are an ill-shapen and ugly race. They have little or no idea of the relative value of articles, even those that one would suppose were of the utmost use to them, such as iron and glassware.

The Indians wore little or no clothing, despite temperatures that were no higher than 46° Fahrenheit. The Americans shared their discarded clothes with the natives, with comical results:

> The most difficult fit, and the one which produced the most merriment, was that of a woman to whom an old coat was given. This she concluded belonged to her nether limbs, and no signs, hints, or shouts, could correct her mistake. Her feet were thrust through the sleeves, and after hard squeezing she succeeded in drawing them on. With the skirts brought up in front, she took her seat in the canoe with great satisfaction, amid a roar of laughter from all who saw her.

Although the expedition gathered significant information about the native population during its stay at Orange Harbor, Wilkes was eager to proceed south: "Although the season was late, I at least anticipated getting some experience among the ice; and I supposed the lateness of the season would have allowed it to detach itself from the shores of Palmer's Land, and would permit us as near an approach as possible to its main body or barrier in the vicinity of Cook's Ne Plus Ultra." Leaving the *Vincennes* and the *Relief* in port, Wilkes boarded the *Porpoise* on 25 February 1839 and sailed, along with the *Sea-Gull,* for Antarctica; the *Peacock* and *Flying-Fish* followed behind. According to Wilkes's report:

> At daylight on the 1st of March we had snow in flurries, and the first ice islands were made. They excited much curiosity, and appeared to have been a good deal worn, as though the sea had been washing over them for some time. They were of small size in comparison to those we afterwards saw, but being unused to the sight, we thought them magnificent.

On 3 March the four ships headed to Palmer's Land. By early morning they found their course blocked by icebergs and decided they could sail no further. Wilkes recalled the scene in his report: "I have rarely seen a finer sight. The sea was literally studded with these beautiful masses, some of pure white, others showing all the shades of opal, others emerald green, and occasionally here and there some of deep black, forming a strong contrast to the pure white." As the expedition sailed further south it encountered its first exposure to the rigors of the Antarctic climate. Wilkes, in a remark that would be echoed by later American and British polar expeditions, complains in his report about the poor quality of the equipment issued to his crews:

> The men were suffering, not only from the want of sufficient room to accommodate the numbers in the vessel, but from the inadequacy of clothing with which they had been supplied. Although purchased by the government at great expense, it was found to be entirely unworthy the service, and inferior in every way to the samples exhibited.

The men's misery, along with increasing gales, constant fog, and multiplying icebergs, forced Wilkes to return to Orange Harbor with the *Porpoise* and the *Sea-Gull.* The *Peacock* and the *Flying-Fish,* still in Antarctic waters, met with no better conditions than had the other two ships: "The weather, during the cruise south, was exceedingly unfavourable," Wilkes says in his report; "for, with few exceptions, during their stay in the Antarctic Circle, they were enveloped in dense fogs, or found only occasional relief from them in falls of snow." The season for Antarctic exploration was over for the year.

The *Relief,* carrying most of the scientists, did not return to Orange Harbor but, unknown to Wilkes, sailed directly to Valparaiso, Chile, arriving on 13 April. On 17 April, Wilkes, ordering the *Sea-Gull* and the *Flying-Fish* to remain in port for ten days to await the *Relief,* boarded the *Vincennes* and, along with the *Porpoise,* sailed for Valparaiso. On 28 April the *Sea-Gull* and the *Flying-Fish* weighed anchor and set sail for Chile. During the evening the two ships became separated in a fierce gale off False Cape Horn. The *Vincennes* and the *Porpoise* arrived at Valparaiso on 15 May; on 19 May the *Flying-Fish* sailed into Valparaiso harbor alone. At first Wilkes was not alarmed; the squadron had been sailing in groups of two and three for some four months, and the ships had often been out of each other's sight. But by early June it was obvious that the *Sea-Gull* had been lost. Wilkes's remarks in his report reflect his restrained demeanor and rigid sense of mission:

> The time has since elapsed, and the careful search that was made, leaves no doubt of her loss, and a strong belief that all on board perished in that gale. Nothing since that time has been heard of her. How, or in what way, disaster happened to her, it is impossible to conjecture. I had the greatest confidence in the officers who had charge of

Illustration by Wilkes of some of his crew members on an ice island mear Antarctica, with his flagship, the
Vincennes, *anchored nearby (from Wilkes's* The Narrative of the United States
Exploring Expedition)

her; they were both well acquainted with the management of the vessel. Their loss and that of the vessel, were a great disadvantage to the Expedition, which was felt by me during the remainder of the cruise.

Typical of naval officers of his day, he cites the loss of Passed Midshipmen Frederick A. Bacon and John Reid, two officers aboard the *Sea-Gull,* but makes no specific mention of any of the fifteen enlisted men.

Valparaiso was a welcome relief from overcrowded quarters and the fierce Antarctic weather. Some of the crew members soon found their way to what Wilkes calls in his report the "well-known hills to the south of the port, called the 'Main and Fore Top,' " where the grog shops were located. Wilkes says that the "females, remarkable for their black eyes and red 'bayettas,' are an annoyance to the authorities, the trade, and commanders of vessels, and equally so to the poor sailors, who seldom leave this port without empty pockets and injured health." Meanwhile, some of the scientists made an excursion into the interior, visiting the copper mines near San Felipe operated by Henry Newman, an Englishman. Wilkes says in his report: "The manner of labour in the mines is in as rude a state as it was found in the agricultural branches of industry. A clumsy pick-axe, a short crowbar, a stone-cutter's chisel, and an enormous oblong iron hammer, of twenty-five pounds weight, were the only tools." The miners, he says,

are allowed as rations for breakfast four handfuls of dried figs, and the same of walnuts: value about three cents. For dinner they have bread, and fresh beef or pork. Small stores, as sugar and tea, they find for themselves. One of the greatest inconveniences, and which is attended with some expense, is the supply of the miners with water, which has to be brought up the mountains.

Like the agricultural and mining operations in Chile, the Americans found the religious and political institutions in the country to be backward. Although Wilkes remarks that the established Catholic religion is "so far enlightened as to tolerate that of the Protestant Episcopal form," he concludes: "The people may generally be called bigoted, and under the control of the priests." On the country's politics, to which he devotes an entire chapter of his report, Wilkes finds much to admire in the example of Bernardo O'Higgins, the dictator who ruled Chile from 1817 to 1823, peacefully surrendered when he was deposed, and went into comfortable exile in Peru.

The squadron sailed on 6 June for Callao, Peru. En route they stopped at San Lorenzo Island to smoke an infestation of rats out of the *Relief.* While the squadron was anchored at San Lorenzo, Captain McKeever of the *Falmouth* brought in three deserters from Wilkes's crew. The ringleaders, Blake and Lester, had incited a riot when they broke into the whiskey stores for the other ships and had gotten the marine guards drunk. Wilkes ordered that the usual punishment of twelve lashes be doubled to twenty-four for the third man, while Blake and Lester were to receive thirty-six and forty-one, respectively. In his report Wilkes justifies his decision:

> This was awarding to each about one-tenth of what a court-martial would have inflicted; yet it was such an example as thoroughly convinced the men that they could not offend with impunity. This was, I am well satisfied, considered at the time as little or no punishment for the crimes of which they had been guilty; but I felt satisfied that the prompt and decided manner in which it was administered, would have the desired effect of preserving the proper discipline, and preventing its recurrence. In this I was not disappointed.

Wilkes concludes by citing his instructions from Secretary of the Navy John K. Paulding to let "necessity" be his guide.

The expedition arrived in Callao on 30 June. As they had in Chile, the expedition members traveled inland from the coast. Wilkes describes Lima as a "declining city," much altered from his first visit on his 1821 voyage: "The neglected walls and ruined tenements, the want of stir and life among the people, are sad evidences of this decay." He finds the cathedral remarkable not only for its size but also for the "bad taste" of its ornamentation. When his party visits a crypt under the great altar, they find that many of the coffins are open and that the sacristan is willing to part with remnants of the "saints" for a trifling sum. Wilkes offhandedly remarks, "Two skulls and a hand were obtained."

The scientists traveled into the Andes to gather botanical samples. Near the source of the Amazon they reached Casa Cancha, which was little more than a mule drivers' rendezvous. As "a special mark of distinction" they were given a small room that adjoined the hut in which the meals were prepared. The evening meal consisted of a charred quarter of mutton that the landlady, lacking a knife, tore into small chunks. "Our gentlemen remonstrated, but nothing would stop her until nearly every morsel of it had passed through her dirty hands. This, added to her state of intoxication, caused some of them to lose their supper from sheer disgust, though all agreed that she tore it into pieces in a most dexterous manner." Suffering from their meal and altitude sickness, the scientists passed an uneasy night, but they recovered sufficiently to visit some of the nearby mines. As was the case in Chile, many of the mines were run by English companies. At one of the mines the English superintendent explained that "the old Spaniards had worked the mines cheaper than any one has been able to do since. They were large landholders, and contrived to keep themselves in debt to their tenants;

this they always paid in manufactured goods, very much in demand with the Indians who worked the mines, thus making a double profit on the wages." The Spanish example is not lost on the Americans. According to Wilkes, "The great error committed by all the English companies established in 1825, for working mines in Spanish America, was in saddling themselves with great numbers of people, engaged at high salaries, and workmen at extravagant wages; the expenses attending this force swallowed up much of the funds before any work was begun." In this passage, as in his remarks about the cheap provisions given the Chilean miners, Wilkes dislays little compassion for the plight of the underpaid workers. Linking economic development to political stability, Wilkes concludes that "little capital will be invested" in Peru until the political upheavals of the past twenty years are put to rest. According to Wilkes, Simón Bolívar represented both the promise and the problems of South American leadership. Despite his early success and his obvious talent, Bolívar's "desire of personal aggrandizement caused him to forget that he set out to promote the welfare and the happiness of his country." Wilkes finds it "remarkable, that not one of the men that the revolutions in South America have brought forth, appears to have been influenced by the feeling that he was serving his country." Wilkes's comments about what he sees as a lack of patriotism show how greatly he and his countrymen misunderstood the effects of three hundred years of Spanish colonial rule on South America. The borders of the newly emerging countries were arbitrary constructs, as was the concept of national loyalty. Bolívar had wanted to unite the whole of South America and, therefore, saw himself as a continental rather than a national figure.

Wilkes concludes his chapter on Peru with observations on the opportunities for trade that Peru and Chile offer the United States:

> These countries offer a large market for our domestic cottons; and if the prices can be maintained, the United States will supply the most of the coarser kinds used there. I have it from the best authority, that the consumption of these goods is now double what it was five years ago, and it is still increasing.

On 13 July the squadron sailed from Callao for the Paumotu group of islands (present-day Tuamotu) in the vicinity of the Society Islands and Tahiti. On 13 August they arrived at Clermont de Tonnerre, or Minerva Island (now Reao Island), the first coral island the expedition members had seen. Wilkes says in his report:

We had pictured them to ourselves as being a kind of fairy-land, and therefore looked for them with some anxiety. At first sight the island appeared much like a fleet of vessels at anchor, nothing but the trees being seen in the distance, and as the ship rises and sinks with the swell of the ocean, these are alternately seen and lost sight of. On a nearer approach, the whole white beach was distinctly seen, constituting a narrow belt of land, of a light clay colour, rising out of the deep ocean, the surf breaking on its coral reefs, surrounding a lagoon of a beautiful blue tint, and perfectly smooth.

On Minerva the expedition had its first encounter with South Seas natives. Using a "New Zealander"–probably a Maori–named John Sac as an interpreter, Wilkes attempted to come ashore, but the natives cried out, "Go to your own land; this belongs to us, and we do not want anything to do with you." Convinced that he could get the natives to accept the trinkets that the expedition had brought along, one of the scientists, the conchologist Joseph P. Couthouy, swam ashore, only to be chased off at spear-point by the native chief. To show the natives that he had the means to meet their challenge, Wilkes had his men load their pieces with mustard seed and fire at the legs of the islanders. After this display of gunboat diplomacy the Americans were allowed to land, but Wilkes ordered his men to remain on the beach and to avoid contact with the natives. At Serle Island (now Pukarua) the natives were friendlier, and Wilkes planned to land the next day. During the night, however, the *Porpoise* and the *Vincennes* collided, damaging both ships and causing them to lose their position for a morning landing. Wilkes set a course northward for Dog Island (now Pukapuka), which proved to be uninhabited. If their first encounter with a coral island had produced visions of an earthly paradise, Dog Island quickly dispelled such illusions: there was no fresh water, and the lagoon was filled with sharks, "which were so ravenous that they bit the oars." Wilkes goes on:

> The landing on a coral island effectually does away with all preconceived notions of its beauty, and any previous ideas formed in its favour are immediately put to flight. The verdure which seemed from a distant view to carpet the whole island, was in reality but a few patches of wiry grass, obstructing the walking, and offering neither fruit nor flowers to view; it grew among the rugged coral debris, with a little sand and vegetable earth.

The island did, however, prove to be an excellent collection ground. The nesting birds were so tame that the naturalists could capture them by hand or lift them off their nests to gather their eggs for specimens.

Peaceful contact with island natives finally took place on Wytoohee (present-day Napuka), one of the Disappointment Islands. Wilkes reported: "The color of these natives was much darker than those seen before; in some the hair was inclined to frizzle, and the beard curly. All the grown men that I saw had mustaches; their features were strongly marked with a good-humoured expression of countenance; they wore the maro, and some had a few feathers in their hair." These are the happy natives of the European and American imagination: "They had no idea of the principle of barter, and allowed any thing to be taken without opposition, receiving any articles in return with delight and gratitude." When Wilkes's men asked why there were no women present, they discovered that there were limits to the natives' generosity. The natives replied that they had discovered the reason for this visit to their island: "That as we inhabited an island without any women, we wanted to have some." In contrast to the trusting natives of Wytoohee, the inhabitants of the other Disappointment Island, Otooho (present-day Tepoto), chased the expedition's naturalists into the water. From Otooho, Wilkes set a course for Raraka, where, he observes:

> Nothing could be more striking than the difference that prevailed between these natives and those of the Disappointment Islands, which we had just left. The half-civilization of the natives of Raraka was very marked, and it appeared as though we had issued out of darkness into light. . . . We were not long at a loss as to what to ascribe it; the missionary had been at work here, and his exertions had been based on a firm foundation; the savages had been changed to a reasonable creature.

Wilkes's uncritical acceptance of the missionaries' work seems naive today, but he thought that the results warranted the intrusion into a society's way of life: "Here all the shipwrecked mariners would be sure of kind treatment, and a share of the few comforts these people possess. No savage mistrust and fear were seen here."

The squadron's next stop, on 10 September 1839, was Tahiti. Observing the island from a distance, Wilkes is unimpressed:

> The beauty of the distant view of Tahiti has been celebrated by all navigators, but I must confess that it disappointed me. The entire outline of the island was visible for too short a time and at too great a distance to permit its boasted features to be distinctly seen. Upon a second and nearer view, its jagged peaks and rugged inaccessible mountains were visible, but we looked in vain for the verdant groves which are said by all writers to clothe it. These indeed exist, but are confined to a narrow belt of low land, lying between the mountains and the shore, and being unseen at a distance, the general aspect of the

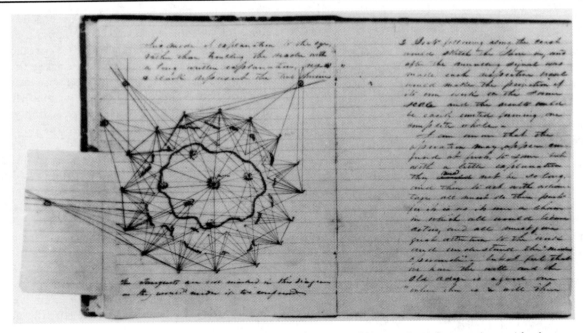

Pages from Wilkes's instructions for his officers, with a diagram of his procedures for surveying an island
(Manuscript Division, Library of Congress)

island is that of a land recently thrown up by volcanic activity.

But when Wilkes compares Tahiti, where the greenery seems to rush down from the mountains to the water, to the "barren coast of Peru," the island does begin to appear to be a paradise. He decides that his initial "disappointment probably arose in part from finding every thing more diminutive than I had been led to imagine from the highly-wrought descriptions I had been perusing only a few days before."

Wilkes is more critical of the missionaries in Tahiti than he is of those in Raraka. Noting that the missionaries have done nothing to promote the mechanical arts, he argues that the introduction of simple machines such as the hand loom, the spinning wheel, and the plow would have laid the groundwork for further industry. He also observes that the missionaries' introduction of European dress has adversely affected native handcrafts: "While they wore their native tapa, the fabric, though of little value, gave employment to numbers of women; and this change of dress, intended as an advance in civilization, has had the effect of superseding employments which formerly engaged their attention, and occupied their time." The missionaries had also brought in a foreign plant that had taken over vast areas of the landscape: "Ten years prior to our visit, about which time the guava was introduced by the missionaries, the plain from the sea to the base of the hills was covered with verdure; and now it is overrun with an almost impenetrable thicket, before which all vegetation disappears."

On 29 September the squadron sailed for Samoa, arriving on 7 October. There Wilkes notes a dichotomy among the natives:

> There is already a great difference, not only in dress but in appearance, between those who have adopted Christianity, and those who adhere to heathenism. The latter have a wild look, to which their long hair, tied in a bunch behind, adds not a little; and when going to war they let it hang down in wild confusion, which increases their savage appearance.

The Christians, on the other hand, "crop their hair short,—a fashion that was introduced by the missionaries." Dress, or the lack thereof, also separates the two groups: "In the heathen villages the dress of the Samoans is to be seen in its primitive simplicity. It is no more than the titi, which is a short apron and girdle of the ti (Draecaena), tied around the loins and falling down to the thighs." The women in these villages "do not show the least sign of feminine bashfulness, while those of the Christian villages cover their bosoms, and exhibit as much modesty as those of any country." Wilkes found much to admire in the Samoans, a people of regular habits who held women "in much consideration" and treated them "with great attention."

After staying in Samoa for six weeks, the squadron sailed to New South Wales, Australia, to prepare for its second Antarctic cruise. Even at this relatively early stage of white settlement, Wilkes notes, the aboriginal population of New South Wales was "fast disappearing," and he forecasts a grim future for them: "The ravages of intoxication and disease, combined with the occasional warfare, will readily account for the rapid disappearance of the native population; and but a few more years will suffice for the now scanty population to become extinct." Their treatment of women distinguishes the aborigines of New South Wales from the Samoans whom Wilkes admired:

> Polygamy exists, and they will frequently give one of their wives to a friend who may be in want of one; but notwithstanding this laxity they are extremely jealous, and are very prompt to resent any freedom taken with their wives. Their quarrels for the most part are occasioned by the fair sex, and being the cause, they usually are the greatest sufferers; for the waddy is applied to their heads in a most unmerciful style.

To acquaint his readers with New South Wales, a country that "is known in the United States almost by its name alone," Wilkes sketches the history of the convict colony of Botany Bay. The first convicts arrived in 1788, the first free settlers in 1794. In the early 1800s Gov. Lachlan Macquarie extended the "privileges and immunities" of the free settlers to emancipated convicts. "This policy soon had its effect at home, where it is said that crimes were committed in the hope of being sentenced to transportation; and it is asserted that the emancipated convicts, known as ticket-of-leave men, were much more desirably situated than honest persons of their own rank of life in the mother country." The result of what Wilkes considers an overly liberal policy was to produce an enmity between the free settlers and the emancipated convicts that "remains unbroken to the present day, and affects even the third and fourth generation." Wilkes's opinions may have been influenced by the problems he was having in controlling his crew: during the squadron's stay in New South Wales five men deserted from the *Flying-Fish* and nine from the *Peacock.* Wilkes concludes about New South Wales: "Notwithstanding I have mentioned many things that have struck us as requiring great reform, yet the whole impression left on my mind is, that it is a glorious colony, which the mother country, and the whole Anglo-Saxon race, may well be proud of."

The expedition departed Sydney Harbor on 26 December for its second Antarctic cruise, leaving the scientists behind to explore New South Wales and New Zealand. For the first five days the weather was mild; but Wilkes, anticipating that his men would later have to come up from the warmth belowdecks

Expedition artist Alfred T. Agate's portrait of King Tanoa of Ambau, the most powerful Fiji chief (from Wilkes's The Narrative of the United States Exploring Expedition)

to freezing conditions, kept the temperature inside the *Vincennes* to 50°. By 1 January 1840 the weather had begun to change:

> The sea was smooth and placid, but the sky was in places lowering, and had a wintry cast, to which we had long been strangers; the temperature began to fall, the breeze to increase, and the weather to become misty. In a few hours we were sailing rapidly through the water, with a rising sea, and by midnight it was reported that the *Flying-Fish* was barely visible.

Soon the *Vincennes* crew lost sight of the *Flying-Fish;* when it did not reappear, they were sure that it had met the same fate as the *Sea-Gull.*

On 16 January "appearances believed at the time to be land were visible from all the three vessels [the *Porpoise,* the *Peacock,* and the *Vincennes*], and the comparison of the three observations, when taken in connexion with the more positive proofs of its existence afterwards obtained, has left no doubt that the appearance was not deceptive." Wilkes's tortured prose means that the squadron had sighted the landmass of Antarctica. In his entry for 19 January Wilkes's narrative style takes on an almost poetic quality:

> We had a beautiful and unusual sight presented to us this night: the sun and moon both appeared above the horizon at the same time, and each throwing its light abroad. The latter was nearly full, the former illuminated the icebergs and distant continent with his deep golden rays; while the latter, in the opposite horizon, tinged with silvery light the clouds in its immediate neighborhood. There now being no doubt in any mind of the discovery of land, it gave an exciting interest to the cruise, that appeared to set aside all thought of fatigue, and to make every one willing to encounter any difficulty to effect a landing.

On 23 January the *Vincennes* found what appeared to be a relatively clear path through the ice fields, but by midnight icebergs had cut off all approaches to land:

> I was, therefore, reluctantly compelled to return, not a little vexed that we were again foiled in our endeavor to reach the Antarctic Continent. This was a deep indentation in the coast, about twenty-five miles wide: we explored it to the depth of about fifteen miles, and did not reach its termination. This bay I have called Disappointment Bay.

Wilkes's retreat from Disappointment Bay took six days. On 29 January the *Vincennes* battled through a gale and dodged ice islands. When the sun broke through the next morning the men looked back: "No straight line could have been drawn from us in any direction, that would not have cut a dozen icebergs in the same number of miles, and the wondering exclamations of the officers and crew were oft repeated,—'How could we have passed through them unharmed? . . . What a lucky ship!' "

The *Peacock* had not been so lucky. On 24 January it collided with an ice island in Disappointment Bay, twisting the rudder, and became caught in the ice. The crew faced "the melancholy alternative . . . of being frozen to death one after the other, or perishing in a body by the dissolving of the iceberg on which they should take refuge, should the vessel sink." The ship squeezed through a passage between two icebergs, timbers groaning, as the crew pushed against the bergs with poles. By the afternoon of 25 January, Capt. William L. Hudson decided that there was "no other course but to drive her out." He ordered all available canvas to be set, and by the next morning the crew "found themselves in clear water, without a rudder, the gripe gone, and, as was afterwards found, the stem ground down to within an inch and a half of the woodends." The rudder was re-

paired, but Hudson decided that it would not hold up against further collisions with the ice. He ordered the ship back to Sydney, where it arrived on 22 February. Illness and fatigue forced the rest of the ships also to abandon the cruise. The *Flying-Fish,* which had not perished after all, turned back on 5 February after the crew wrote a petition asking Capt. Robert F. Pinkney to consider their weakened condition and "relieve us from what must terminate in our death." It reached the Bay of Islands in New Zealand on 10 March. The *Porpoise* turned back on 14 February and arrived at the Bay of Islands on 26 March. The *Vincennes* did not turn back until 21 February; it reached Sydney on 11 March and left for New Zealand on 19 March.

The next major cruise for the expedition was to Tonga and Fiji. On 6 April the *Vincennes,* the *Porpoise,* and the *Flying-Fish* sailed from New Zealand; the *Peacock* had sailed from Sydney on 30 March. Of the Fijians, Wilkes writes: "None of them equal the natives of Tonga in beauty of person." He is also critical of their character: "They tell a falsehood in preference, when the truth would be better to their purpose; and, in conversing with them, the truth can only be obtained, by cautioning them not to talk like a Feejee man, or, in other words, not to tell any lies." Their greatest flaw is their covetousness: "a white man might travel with safety from one end of the island to the other, provided he had nothing about him to excite their desire of acquisition." Although the Fijians believe in an afterlife, this "belief in a future state, guided by no just notions of religion or moral obligation, is the source of many abhorrent practices. Among these are the custom of putting their parents to death when they are advanced in years; suicide; the immolation of wives at the funeral of their husbands, and human sacrifices."

Wilkes reserves his most vivid descriptions for that most talked about and expected of "savage" practices, cannibalism:

> Formal human sacrifices are frequent. The victims are usually taken from a distant tribe, and when not supplied by war or violence, they are at times obtained by negotiation. After being selected for this purpose, they are often kept for a time to be fattened. When about to be sacrificed, they are compelled to sit upon the ground, with their feet drawn under their thighs, and their arms placed close before them. In this posture they are bound so tightly that they cannot stir, or move a joint. They are then placed in the usual oven, upon hot stones, and covered with leaves and earth, where they are roasted alive. When the body is cooked, it is taken from the oven, and the face painted black, as is done by the natives on festal occasions.

There is no evidence that Wilkes personally witnessed such a ceremony; he is relying mainly on the testimony of David Whippy, who had deserted a ship eighteen years earlier after being mistreated by his commander and had become "the principal man among the whites" in Fiji. Wilkes thought Whippy a "prudent trustworthy person"; a footnote in the narrative notes that Whippy "has, since our return, been appointed vice-consul for the Feejee Group." Wilkes goes on:

> Whippy told me that he saw, on one occasion, upwards of twenty men cooked; and several of the white residents stated that they have seen bodies brought from such a distance as to be green from putrescence, and to have the flesh dropping from the bones, which were, notwithstanding, eaten with greediness and apparent pleasure.

Wilkes adds that the "cannibal propensity is not limited to enemies or persons of a different tribe, but they will banquet on the flesh of their dearest friends, and it is even related, that in times of scarcity, families will make an exchange of children for this horrid purpose." He then voices his real concern:

> When they set so little value on the lives of their own countrymen, it is not to be expected that they should hold in much regard those of foreigners. It is necessary, therefore, while holding intercourse with them, to be continually guarded against their murderous designs, which they are always meditating for the sake of the property about the person, or to obtain the body for food.

On 3 July the crew of the *Peacock* came face to face with the reality of cannibalism. Anchored in Noloa Bay, the crew found themselves in the midst of a tribal war. Wilkes reports that "a canoe came alongside, bringing the skull yet warm from the fire, much scorched, and marked with the teeth of those who had eaten of it." As one of the officers was negotiating "with the natives for the purchase of the skull for a fathom of cloth," another native came up to him "holding something in his right hand, which he soon applied to his mouth, and began to eat." The astonished Americans "discovered it to be the eye of the dead man, which the native had plucked from the skull a few moments before." Wilkes goes on to make a horrifying pun: if the men had doubted the existence of Fijian cannibalism up to then, he says, "this ocular proof of their cannibal propensities fully satisfied them." He concludes:

> Previous to this occurrence, no one in the squadron could say that he had been an eye-witness to cannibalism, though few doubted its practice, but the above transaction placed it beyond all doubt, and we now have the very skull which was bought from those who were picking and eating it, among our collections.

Less than a month later two of Wilkes's officers—Lieutenant Underwood and Midshipman Henry, Wilkes's nephew—were killed by Fijians on a small island near Malolo: "One of the victims was my own near relation, confided to my care by a widowed mother; I had therefore more than the ordinary degree of sorrow, which the loss of promising and efficient officers must cause in the breast of every commander, to oppress me." Convinced that "the blood of the slain imperatively called for retribution, and the honour of our flag demanded that the outrage upon it should not remain unpunished," Wilkes decided to attack two Fijian towns. He wanted the attack to serve as a "salutary lesson" to the natives, and he planned it carefully to "avoid, as far as possible, the risk of losing other valuable lives." The "valuable lives" were, of course, those of his own men, not of the people in the villages.

Before exacting his revenge, Wilkes buried his dead. Though relieved that the "bodies had been rescued from the shambles of these odious cannibals," Wilkes was concerned that "even the grave might not be held sacred from their hellish appetites." Ultimately convinced that a "secluded sand-island" was "far enough removed from these condor-eyed savages to permit them to be entombed in the earth, without risk of exhumation," he set out on the funeral detail:

> Only twenty sailors (all dressed in white), and myself and officers, landed to pay this last mark of affection and respect to those who had gone through so many toils, and shared so many dangers with us, and of whom we had so suddenly been bereaved. The quiet of the scene, the solemnity of the occasion, and the smallness of the number who assisted, were all calculated to produce an unbroken silence. The bodies were quietly taken up and borne along to the centre of the island, where stood a grove of ficus trees, whose limbs were entwined in all directions by running vines. It was a lonely and a suitable spot that had been chosen, in a shade so dense that scarce a ray of the sun could penetrate it.

Wilkes's desciption of the ceremony is meant to be contrasted with his account of the hideous practices of the cannibals and, thus, to bring home to the reader the distance separating the civilized from the uncivilized world.

After this pastoral interlude Wilkes describes the destruction of the towns of Arro and Sualib. Because most of the native men had left to defend Sualib, Wilkes encountered no opposition in Arro, and he had the village burned. Sualib was protected by a ditch and a palisade, and a line of skirmishers

Drawing by Emmons of the burning of a village on the Fijian island of Malolo (Beinecke Rare Book and Manuscript Library, Yale University)

blocked the approach to the town; but "our men spread out so as to outflank the skirmishers, and by a few rockets and a shower of balls showed them that they had different enemies from Feejee men to deal with." Having pushed the skirmishers into the fort, Wilkes reduced it with rocket fire: "A rocket, of which several had already been tried without visible effect, now struck one of the thatched roofs; a native sprang up to tear it off, but that moment was his last, and the roof immediately burst into flames." Within an hour the "whole town was reduced to ashes." Summing up the results of the attack, in which more than eighty natives were killed, Wilkes eerily foreshadows his twentieth-century successors expostulating on the "surgical" use of military force:

> The blow that I inflicted not only required to be done promptly and effectually, as a punishment for the murder of my officers, but was richly deserved for other outrages. It could not have fallen upon a place where it could have produced as much effect, in impressing the whole group with a full sense of our power and determination to punish such aggressions.
>
> Such has been its effect on the people of Malolo, that they have since been found the most civil, harmless, and well-disposed natives of the group.

Departing from the Fiji Islands on 11 August, the *Vincennes* reached Honolulu on 24 September; the rest of the squadron arrived over the next several weeks. Wilkes's orders were to survey the northwest

coast of the United States after the ships were refitted in Hawaii, but he determined that it was too late in the year to begin those operations. Instead, he ordered the *Peacock* to return to Samoa, along with the *Flying-Fish;* the *Porpoise* was sent back to the Paumotu Group. The *Vincennes* began exploring the Hawaiian Islands on 3 December.

Among the achievements of the *Vincennes* crew was the establishment of an observatory at the edge of the crater on the summit of Mauna Loa. It was a formidable undertaking; the sailors had to battle cold and altitude sickness while carrying the heavy scientific gear. The first night on the summit was 25 December; the temperature was 22°. "No very merry Christmas for us cold, wet & with everything to discourage me," Wilkes noted.

On 19 March 1841 the *Vincennes* returned to Honolulu to get ready for its cruise to the Columbia River; the *Porpoise* arrived on 24 March. On 5 April the two ships sailed for the northwestern coast of the United States, arriving at Cape Disappointment on 28 April. Unable to spot a channel in the roiling waters at the mouth of the Columbia River, Wilkes turned north and proceeded through the Strait of Juan de Fuca, stopping at Port Townsend and Port Lawrence before anchoring on 11 May at Fort Nisqually, an outpost of the British Hudson's Bay Company at the southern end of Puget Sound near present-day Tacoma, Washington. From Fort Nisqually, Wilkes and his men traveled overland, ford-

One of more than twenty-eight hundred pages of the manuscript for Wilkes's autobiography that
he completed before failing health forced him to stop work
(Manuscript Division, Library of Congress)

ing the Nisqually River, paddling down the Cowlitz River to its juncture with the Columbia and from there to Astoria, then back upriver to Vancouver and south to the American settlements in the Willamette Valley; finally, they returned to Fort Nisqually. Another party, led by Lt. Robert E. Johnson and including the naturalist Edward Charles Pickering and the botanist William D. Brackenridge, made an even longer overland trip, crossing the Cascades, using gum-rubber rafts to cross the swollen Yakima River, following the Columbia north through the Grand Coulee country to Fort Colville, and then traveling south along the Colville River to Spokane. Proceeding south from Spokane, they engaged some Indians to ferry them across the Snake River and traveled to Fort Walla Walla; from there they made their way back to the Yakima, followed it back to the Cascades, recrossed the mountains, and arrived at Fort Nisqually, after a two-month journey, on 15 July. Of the lands east of the Cascades, which were generating so much interest in Washington that the United States was about to go to war with Britain over the boundary issue, Brackenridge wrote: "It appears to me, that we must certainly have viewed it in a very different light from the Majority of the Writers that have come out so boldly in its favour." The botanist saw the dry coulee lands as an unpromising site for agricultural ventures.

On 27 July Wilkes learned that the *Peacock* had been wrecked at the mouth of the Columbia on 18 July. No lives had been lost, and the crew had set up an encampment at Astoria. The *Flying-Fish* was awaiting the *Vincennes* and the *Porpoise* when they arrived at Astoria on 7 August. Before his arrival Wilkes had sent orders ahead for a party led by Lieutenant Emmons and including Brackenridge, the artist Alfred T. Agate, the mineralogist James Dwight Dana, the botanist William Rich, and the naturalist Titan R. Peale to journey overland to San Francisco. Amazingly, considering the distance and the difficulties, this party, like the one that had surveyed the eastern regions of what is now Washington State, completed its mission and arrived on time.

On 31 October 1841 the *Vincennes*, the *Porpoise*, the *Flying-Fish*, and the *Oregon*, which Wilkes had purchased to replace the *Peacock*, sailed from San Francisco, arriving in Honolulu on 17 November. Wilkes sent the *Porpoise* and the *Oregon* on a west-northwest course from Hawaii to Singapore; the *Vincennes* and the *Flying-Fish* sailed to Singapore via Manila and Ascension Island. Fearing that the *Flying-Fish* might not survive a trip around the Cape of Good Hope in the approaching hurricane season, Wilkes sold it in Singapore. The remaining ships left on 26 February 1842 and arrived in New York City on 10 June.

It was a bittersweet return. Rather than the public acclaim to which Wilkes and his men felt entitled, the expedition members received an indifferent reception. The public seemed unaware of their accomplishments; Congress was upset over the cost of the expedition (the original congressional act had authorized the expenditure of $300,000; the final cost was $928,183.62, a considerable sum for the time but still a modest investment for the scientific return); and the scientific community was already disputing Wilkes's claim that the expedition was the first to establish that Antarctica was a continent. Furthermore, within six weeks of his return Wilkes was court-martialed. Among the charges was that his actions at Arro and Sualib, coupled with his earlier burning of a village on the island of Venna Lebra in retaliation for an attack on a shore party and the capture of one of the squadron's cutters, had violated his orders to treat the natives with kindness. His junior officers brought several other charges against Wilkes, but the only one that the court upheld was that he had acted with undue severity by giving out more lashes to insubordinate seamen and marines than were allowed

under naval regulations. His punishment was a public reprimand from Secretary of the Navy Abel P. Upshur on 22 September 1842:

> The country which honored you with a command far above the just claims of your rank in the navy, had a right to expect that you would, at least, pay a scrupulous respect to their laws. The rebuke, which by the judgment and advice of your own associates in the service, she now gives you of having violated these laws in an important particular, involving the rights of her citizens, will be regarded by all, as the mildest form in which she could express her displeasure.

It was a light punishment, but the proud Wilkes took it as a stinging insult. One of the court's members, Lt. Samuel F. du Pont, wrote that Wilkes's "extreme arrogance & conviction that he would not only be acquitted, but that it would be accompanied with a flourish of trumpets & a swipe at his accusers, has thus rendered his sentence doubly severe to himself." To add to Wilkes's humiliation, Lieutenant Hudson, whom he considered responsible for the wreck of the *Peacock*, was promoted before him. Wilkes had to wait until July 1843 to achieve the rank of commander.

Using the massive notes and journals that he and his colleagues had compiled during their four-year mission, Wilkes prepared the five-volume *Narrative of the United States Exploring Expedition*. Although his work was unacknowledged in America, in 1848 the Royal Geographical Society awarded him its Founder's Medal for the "zeal and intelligence with which he carried out the scientific exploring expedition intrusted to him . . . and for the volumes which he has published, detailing the narrative of that expedition." On the basis of the expedition's findings he also wrote *Western America, Including California and Oregon, with Maps of those Regions, and of "the Sacramento Valley"* (1849), *Meteorology* (1851), and *Hydrography* (1858–1861). His wife had died in August 1848; in 1854 he married Mary Lynch Bolton. They had a daughter, Mary, in 1859.

Political opposition and his work on the expedition's papers kept Wilkes from receiving a military assignment during the Mexican War. He did, however, serve in the Civil War, and it is for an incident in that war that he may be best remembered today. On 14 May 1861 he assumed command of the *San Jacinto* off the coast of Africa. On 8 November, while cruising near the Panama channel, he ordered the boarding of the British steamer *Trent* and the removal of Confederate commissioners James Mason and John Slidell to the *San Jacinto*. The *Trent* affair set off an international incident that almost led to war with Great Britain. Although many in the North saw him as a hero, the Lincoln administration, to placate the British, officially disapproved of his actions. On 30 November Wilkes was removed from the command of the *San Jacinto*. He commanded a squadron in the West Indies in 1862–1863. On 27 February 1864 court-martial proceedings began against Wilkes for the second time, and on 26 April he was found guilty of disobedience of orders and insubordination for his actions in the *Trent* affair. He was given a public reprimand and a three-year suspension. Despite these setbacks, on 6 August 1866 he was promoted to rear admiral on the retired list. In 1870 he was recalled to duty to continue work on the expedition's publications; he served in this capacity until his release from duty on 17 March 1873.

Wilkes began writing his autobiography in 1871; failing health forced him to stop work in September 1875. He had completed more than twenty-eight hundred manuscript pages. He died at his Washington home on 8 February 1877 and was buried at Oak Hill Cemetery in Washington. His obituary mentioned only that he had established an observatory on land attached to his home; his voyages to the South Seas, his surveying of the Pacific Northwest coast, and his discovery that Antarctica was a continent were overlooked. The *New York Tribune* said that he "was a brave and fearless officer, and though severe in discipline was admired for his courage and heroic deeds." On 17 August 1909 his remains were reinterred in Arlington National Cemetery.

On 12 August 1912 Sen. Elihu Root, supporting a recommendation before Congress to place a memorial to Wilkes in Arlington, noted that Wilkes had not only been the first to determine that Antarctica was a continent but had also made charts of more than fifteen hundred miles of the Antarctic coast. In 1940 the American Philosophical Society of Philadelphia and the American Geographical Society of New York observed the centenary of the Exploring Expedition. The navy published his autobiography in 1978; in the introduction Rear Adm. John D. Kane notes that the manuscript's length and Wilkes's "horrendous handwriting" had kept the work from being published for a century after Wilkes' death. On 13 November 1985 "Magnificent Voyagers," an exhibition of the works and collections produced by the Exploring Expedition, opened at the Smithsonian Institution.

From the evidence supplied by his junior officers at his court-martial it seems clear that Wilkes was a rigid disciplinarian, an often vain martinet convinced of his right to command but insecure about his position in the naval hierarchy. Yet one has to admire his iron will and his stubborn determination not only to see the Exploring Expedition through to completion but also to see its records brought to publication. Without Wilkes's resolve, the story of the last great circumnavigation of the globe by sailing vessels might never have seen print.

Bibliography:
Daniel C. Haskell, *The United States Exploring Expedition 1838–1842 and Its Publications 1844–1874* (New York: New York Public Library, 1942).

Biography:
Daniel Henderson, *The Hidden Coast: A Biography of Admiral Charles Wilkes* (New York: Sloane, 1953).

References:
Harley Harris Bartlett, "The Reports of the Wilkes Expedition, and the Work of the Specialists in Science," *Proceedings of the American Philosophical Society,* 82 (1940): 601–705;
Daniel C. Gilman, *The Life of James Dwight Dana* (New York & London: Harper, 1899);
Jessie Poesch, *Titian Ramsay Peale 1799–1885 and His Journals of the Wilkes Expedition* (Philadelphia: American Philosophical Society, 1961);
William Jones Rhees, ed., *The Smithsonian Institution: Documents Relative to Its Origin and History, 1835–1851,* volume 1 (Washington, D.C.: U.S. Government Printing Office, 1901);
William Stanton, *The Great United States Exploring Expedition of 1838–1842* (Berkeley, Los Angeles & London: University of California Press, 1975);
David B. Tyler, *The Wilkes Expedition, the First United States Exploring Expedition (1838-1842)* (Philadelphia: American Philosophical Society, 1968);
Herman J. Viola and Carolyn Margolis, eds., *Magnificent Voyagers: The U.S. Exploring Expedition, 1838–1842* (Washington, D.C.: Smithsonian Institution Press, 1985).

Papers:
The Charles Wilkes Family Papers, including the manuscript for Wilkes's autobiography, are in the Manuscript Division of the Library of Congress. The Hull Collection of Wilkes Papers is also in the Library of Congress. Ships' journals of the United States Exploring Expedition are in the National Archives, although the Mariner's Museum and Library in Newport News, Virginia, holds the ship's journal of Lt. James Alden, executive officer of Wilkes's flagship. The Wilkes Family Papers are in the Manuscript Department of Duke University Library; the Papers of Charles Wilkes, 1837–1847, are in the Kansas State Historical Society, Topeka.

Nathaniel Parker Willis

(20 January 1806 – 20 January 1867)

Karen Schramm
Camden County College

See also the Willis entries in *DLB 3: Antebellum Writers in New York and the South; DLB 59: American Literary Critics and Scholars, 1800–1850;* and *DLB 73: American Magazine Journalists, 1741–1850.*

BOOKS: *Sketches* (Boston: S. G. Goodrich, 1827);

Fugitive Poetry (Boston: Pierce & Williams, 1829);

Poem, Delivered before the Society of United Brothers, at Brown University on the Day Preceding Commencement, September 6, 1831, with Other Poems (New York: Harper, 1831);

Melanie and Other Poems (London: Saunders & Otley, 1835; enlarged edition, New York: Saunders & Otley, 1837);

Pencillings by the Way (3 volumes, London: Macrone, 1835; 2 volumes, Philadelphia: Carey, Lea & Blanchard, 1836);

Inklings of Adventure (3 volumes, London: Saunders & Otley, 1836; 2 volumes, New York: Saunders & Otley, 1836);

A l'abri; or, The Tent Pitch'd (New York: Colman, 1839); republished as *Letters from under a Bridge* (London: Virtue, 1840; New York: Morris, Willis, 1844);

Bianca Visconti; or, the Heart Overtasked (New York: Colman, 1839);

Tortesa; or, the Usurer Matched (New York: Colman, 1839);

American Scenery; or, Land, Lake, and River: Illustrations of Transatlantic Nature, 2 volumes (London: Virtue, 1840);

The Romance of Travel (New York: Colman, 1840); republished as *Loiterings of Travel* (London: Longman, Orme, Brown, Green & Longmans, 1840);

Canadian Scenery Illustrated from Drawings by W. H. Bartlett, 2 volumes (London: Virtue, 1842);

The Sacred Poems of N. P. Willis (New York: Morris, Willis, 1843);

The Lady Jane, and Other Humorous Poems (New York: Morris, Willis, 1844);

Nathaniel Parker Willis

The Poems, Sacred, Passionate, and Humorous (New York: Clark & Austin, 1844);

Letters on Fashion (New York: Mirror Library, 1844);

Dashes at Life with a Free Pencil (1 volume, New York: Burgess, Stringer, 1845; 3 volumes, London: Longman, Brown, Green & Longmans, 1845);

Rural Letters and Other Records of Thought at Leisure (New York: Baker & Scribner, 1849);

People I Have Met; or, Pictures of Society and People of Mark, Drawn under a Thin Veil of Fiction (Auburn, N.Y.: Alden, Beardsley, 1849; London: Bohn, 1850);

Life Here and There (New York: Baker & Scribner, 1850);

Hurry-graphs; or, Sketches of Scenery, Celebrities & Society, Taken from Life (Auburn, N.Y. & Rochester: Alden & Beardsley, 1851);

Summer Cruise in the Mediterranean (Auburn, N.Y.: Alden & Beardsley, 1853; London: Nelson, 1853);

Fun-Jottings; or, Laughs I Have Taken a Pen To (New York: Scribner, 1853);

Health Trip to the Tropics (New York: Scribner, 1853; London: Sampson, Low, 1854);

Famous Persons and Places (New York: Scribner, 1854; London: Ward & Lock, 1854);

Out-Doors at Idlewild; or, The Shaping of a Home on the Banks of the Hudson (New York: Scribner, 1855);

The Rag-Bag, A Collection of Ephemera (New York: Scribner, 1855);

Paul Fane; or, Parts of a Life Else Untold (New York: Scribner / Boston: Williams, 1857; London: Clarke, 1857);

The Convalescent (New York: Scribner, 1859).

Collections: *The Complete Works of N. P. Willis* (New York: Redfield, 1846);

The Prose Works of N. P. Willis (Philadelphia: Carey & Hart, 1849);

Poems of Nathaniel Parker Willis, edited, with a memoir, by H. L. Williams (New York: Hurst, 1882);

The Poetical Works of N. P. Willis (London: Routledge, 1888).

PLAY PRODUCTIONS: *Bianca Visconti; or, the Heart Overtasked,* New York, Park Theatre, 25 August 1837;

The Betrothal, 29 November 1837;

Tortesa the Usurer, New York, National Theatre, 8 April 1839.

OTHER: *The Legendary, Consisting of Original Pieces, Principally Illustrative of American History, Scenery, and Manners,* 2 volumes, edited by Willis (Boston: S. G. Goodrich, 1828);

The Token: A Christmas and New Year's Present, edited by Willis (Boston: S. G. Goodrich, 1829);

The Opal: A Pure Gift for the Holy Days, edited by Willis (New York: J. C. Riker, 1844);

The Prose and Poetry of Europe and America, compiled by Willis and George Pope Morris (New York: Leavitt & Allen, 1845);

The Gem of the Season, for 1850, edited by Willis (New York: Leavitt, Trow, 1850);

Memoranda of the Life of Jenny Lind, edited by Willis (Philadelphia: Peterson, 1851);

Trenton Falls, Picturesque and Descriptive, edited by Willis (New York: Putnam, 1851).

SELECTED PERIODICAL PUBLICATION—UNCOLLECTED: "Death of Edgar A. Poe," *Home Journal* (30 October 1849).

A popular and prolific travel writer—as well as a poet, dramatist, short-story writer, novelist, and editor—Nathaniel Parker Willis was a keen observer of natural and social scenes. A darling of society, Willis relished elegant appearances, dressing his long frame to foppish perfection. In many ways his writing mirrors his social pose: it is often charming, witty, and graceful but is occasionally somewhat artificial. He toured the United States, Canada, Europe, and Asia and recorded his impressions not only in travel works such as *Pencillings by the Way* (1835) but throughout all the literary genres in which he worked. His fame in his day may be gauged by the fact that virtually everyone of any importance had something to say about him, whether laudatory or derogatory. Today, however, he is largely—and undeservedly—forgotten.

Willis was born in Portland, Maine, the second of nine children of Nathaniel and Hannah Parker Willis. On the paternal side he came from a long line of printers, editors, and publishers. His great-grandfather was a printer in Boston. His grandfather established the Boston Whig paper, the *Independent Chronicle,* in 1776 and published it until 1784; edited the Martinsburg, Virginia, *Potomac Guardian* from 1790 to 1796; and published the *Sciota Gazette,* the first newspaper in Ohio, in 1796. Willis's father established the *Eastern Argus* in Portland in September 1803 and founded the *Boston Recorder,* the first religious newspaper in the country (he insisted that it was the first one in the world), in January 1816 and *The Youth's Companion,* the first children's magazine ever published, in 1827. Two of Willis's siblings also achieved literary fame. His sister, Sarah Willis Payson, the witty "Fanny Fern," was a successful writer of children's stories and social commentary; his youngest brother, Richard Storrs Willis, the editor of the *New York Musical World* and *Once a Week,* was known for his poetry and musical compositions.

In 1812 Willis's family moved to Boston. Willis briefly attended school in Concord, New Hampshire, then returned home to attend the Boston Latin School and, in 1821, Phillips Academy in Andover, New Hampshire. Though he was not a particularly diligent student, he read widely and showed promise as a writer, keeping a diary and writing poetry. While attending Yale University he found an outlet for his verse in his father's *Boston Recorder* and *The Youth's Companion;* he wrote blank-verse paraphrases of familiar passages from Scrip-

View of Mount Jefferson from Mount Washington, New Hampshire; illustration by William Henry Bartlett for Willis's
American Scenery *(1840)*

ture under the pen name "Roy." Finding his work eagerly received by readers, Willis submitted his poems to other publications and won a fifty-dollar prize from *The Album,* an illustrated annual. He thereby achieved national prominence, and his poetry was frequently quoted and anthologized.

Willis's youthful poetry is important not so much for its style—it is, as Edgar Allan Poe pronounced it, "tame" and "merely paraphrastic"—but for its literary settings. Although his scriptural poetry is an early indication of Willis's use of exotic locales for his compositions, the verses are unexciting. He had not been to the Holy Land and was thus describing scenes at second hand; consequently, his poems lack the sparkle of his later works. Yet they are valuable as a harbinger of his most successful genre, travel writing.

Before graduating from Yale, Willis spent a summer touring New York, New England, and Canada. Among the products of this sojourn is "Leaves from a Colleger's Album," an amusing sketch of a trip on the Erie Canal. He continued writing and publishing verses, generally using the pseudonym "Cassius," but he turned increasingly to secular subject matter. In 1827, the year he graduated from Yale, his poetry collection *Sketches* was published in Boston by Samuel Griswold Goodrich. He received offers to write for such magazines as the Philadel-

phia *Atlantic Souvenir;* William Cullen Bryant's new publication, the *New York Review and Athenaeum Magazine;* and Goodrich's annual, *The Token.*

Settling in Boston, Willis was hired by Goodrich as editor of *The Legendary* in 1828; he moved to Goodrich's *The Token* in 1829. He established his own magazine, the *American Monthly,* in April 1829 and published it until August 1831. It included tales, poems, book reviews, essays, and travel sketches. He was simultaneously publishing articles in other journals, including the *New York Mirror.* In September 1829 his collection *Fugitive Poetry* appeared. He continued to write prose pieces as well, developing a graceful style characterized by clarity and wit.

Though he was, as his biographer Henry A. Beers says, "the favorite periodical writer of his day," Willis had many detractors. Goodrich observes in his autobiography, *Recollections of a Lifetime* (1856), that Willis was "more written about than any other literary man in our history." Tall, handsome, and with luxuriant wavy hair, rosy cheeks, and an aristocratic mein, "natty Natty," as he was called, was a dandy and a social poseur. Poe declared that his success was "to be attributed, one-third to his mental ability and two-thirds to his physical temperament." He enjoyed gossip, which he called "the undress of the mind," and he included it in his magazine in a breezy, playful style. Such juicy banter was, however, not to the taste of everyone in Puritan Boston, and Willis received anonymous letters calling him a "puppy," a "rake," and other insulting names. He was harassed in the newspapers for his foppish dress, his apparent frivolity, and his conceit. Although by the accounts of colleagues Willis was kind, gracious, and helpful, he seemed to have a flair for bringing out the snide, petty side in critics. Even his sister, "Fanny Fern," would become so disgusted with his status as social pet that she would satirize him in her scurrilous novel *Ruth Hall* (1855).

In the summer of 1831 Willis moved to New York City and merged his magazine into the weekly *New York Mirror*, a journal of literature, the fine arts, and society edited by Theodore S. Fay and George Pope Morris of "Woodman, Spare That Tree" fame.

Because of the increasing number of Americans traveling to Europe, Americans were voracious readers of travel accounts: 1,822 travel books were published by Americans before 1900, 691 of them between 1800 and 1868. Newspapers and magazines were filled with travel articles and reviews of travel books, frequently reprinting large excerpts of articles that had appeared in London journals. Before the merger Willis had announced in the *American Monthly* that he intended to travel to Europe for a two-year sojourn and send back travel and social sketches, but financial difficulties had forced him to abandon the plan. After the merger he persuaded his coeditors to send him to Europe as a "foreign correspondent"; he would receive $500 for expenses and $10 for each letter he sent back to the *Mirror*. Cortland P. Auser notes: "Until 1831, no journalist who had gone to Europe had been paid solely by one periodical to send copy back to the States for publication."

Before leaving for Europe Willis toured Philadelphia; Baltimore; Washington, D.C.; and Mount Vernon, writing sketches, or "Pencillings," of them for the *Mirror;* for good measure, he jotted down his impressions of New York City. He finally sailed in October, arriving at Le Havre, France, on 3 November. His expense money only went so far, and he received the ten-dollar payments irregularly. Still, with typical aplomb, he always managed to dine and be entertained handsomely. He obtained many letters of introduction, and he also got himself attached to the American legation in Paris, headed by William Cabell Rives, thereby gaining admittance into virtually all of fashionable European society. His extraordinary panache is indicated by the lord lieutenant of Ireland's description of the suave travel writer as "an eminent young American likely to attain the Presidency."

The first of Willis's 139 travel letters—"notes written on the road, and dispatched without a second perusal"—appeared in the *Mirror* on 13 February 1832; they would be collected as *Pencillings by the Way* but were titled "First Impressions of Europe" in the magazine. In his letters Willis practiced what he had preached in his review of Henry E. Dwight's *Travels in the North of Germany in the Years 1825 and 1826* in the *American Monthly* (July 1829): the travel writer should not rely on dry, tedious statistics about people and places but should be something of a Renaissance man, broadly familiar with all aspects of a civilization's culture; he should "not confine himself to things about him" but should "give us the impressions they make upon himself." The writer had to be capable of stimulating the reader's imagination, so as to make the reader feel as if he or she were accompanying the writer on his travels: "A book without this quality gives us the same idea of a country that a skeleton does of the human figure, or a chalk outline of a landscape in June." Although Willis frets in one letter that "writing and sending off unrevised is the worst thing in the world for one's reputation," the hasty composition is actually part of the letters' appeal. Beers says that "Willis's rapid sketches were capital writing of their kind, and the work of a born 'foreign correspondent.' He was a quick and sympathetic, though not subtle observer, had an eye for effect, and a journalist's instinct for seizing the characteristic features of a scene and leaving out the lumber. Few of his letters were in the least guide-bookish." Though the letters were supposed to be weekly efforts, transmission delays made their publication in the periodical erratic; but this irregular appearance, by heightening readers' anticipation, only made the letters more popular. Morris claimed that the "pencillings" were reprinted by five hundred newspapers.

Willis was charmed by Paris, with its museums, gardens, fancy balls, and fine restaurants: "Paris is a world for research. . . . One might live a life of novelty without crossing the barrier." Whether strolling in the gardens of the Tuileries with James Fenimore Cooper, meeting the king (thanks to Rives), or circulating in fashionable society, Willis was having the time of his life. He also enjoyed his rambles about the countryside; as he says in a letter from Marseilles, dated 28 April 1832, "It is like an intoxication to travel in Europe. I feel no annoyance, grumble at no imposition, am never out of temper. . . . I feel every day that my mind is opening and laying up material which I could get nowhere else." As enchanting as France was, however, its society seemed artificial. While the traveling American has "the independent, self-possessed

The United States Capitol, Washington, D.C.; illustration by Bartlett for Willis's American Scenery

bearing of a man unused to look upon anyone as his superior in rank, united to the inquisitive, sensitive, communicative expression which is the index to our national character," in the pretentious world of French high society "everything gets travestied. . . . The general ambition seemed to be to appear that which one is not." Of course, as Beers points out, Willis himself was practicing such deception: "Few of the people whom he met in society suspected what thin ice he was skating on, or dreamed for an instant that the dashing young *attache* was dependent for his bread and butter on weekly letters to a newspaper."

After approximately six months in France, Willis moved on to Italy. Spending nearly a year in Florence, Rome, and Naples, he met the grand duke of Tuscany and was invited to ducal balls and other social events. He stayed in a palazzo with the American sculptor Horatio Greenough and took the opportunity to dabble in clay molding, an interest that he would develop creatively in various stories and in his only novel, *Paul Fane; or Parts of a Life Else Untold* (1857). The art, architecture, and scenery of Italy awed him: "I . . . have felt so unequal to the description that but for my promise I should never write a line about them." Describing the sun's effect on the interior of a cathedral, Willis notes that "the checkered pavement seems trembling with a quiver-

ing radiance, the altar is far and indistinct, and the lamps burning over the tomb of San Carlo, shine out from the centre like gems glistening in the midst of some enchanted hall."

Invited on a six-month cruise of the Mediterranean on the frigate *Constellation,* Willis departed on 3 June 1833 and saw Elba, Naples, Sicily, Trieste, Vienna, the Ionian Islands, Greece, the Dardanelles, and the Levant. He spent five weeks in Constantinople, which he calls the "fairest metropolis of the Mahomets" and "Paradise transcended"; he repeatedly used Asia Minor as a setting for his fiction. He remained there for five weeks.

After his cruise Willis made his way to England; on the way he stopped in Fiesole to visit Walter Savage Landor, who gave him letters of introduction to the author and renowned hostess Marguerite, Countess of Blessington. He arrived at Dover on 1 June 1834. In England he explored castles, country houses, parks, and, of course, Almack's, the fashionable establishment for well-heeled socialites. England appeared to bring out the dapper journalist's social aspirations to the utmost. In a personal letter to his sister Julia he gushed, "All the best society of London exclusives is now open to me—*me!* a sometime apprentice at setting types—me! . . . Thank heaven, there is not a countryman of mine, except Washington Irving, who has even the standing in England which I have got in *three days* only." Exultingly, Willis described the endless round of "dinners, balls, soirees, garden parties and the opera" in which he participated. In turn, British society adored the witty young gentleman from the United States. Through Lady Blessington he was introduced to Benjamin Disraeli, Edward Bulwer-Lytton, Charles Lamb, and one of his favorite authors, Barry Cornwall, and he gained admittance to the fashionable Travellers' Club.

Deluged with offers from English periodicals at high rates of pay, Willis began contributing clever sketches to *Blackwood's,* the *New Monthly,* the *Court Magazine,* and the *Metropolitan Monthly* under the pseudonym "Philip Slingsby"; the pieces were later collected in *Inklings of Adventure* (1836). Stories such as "Incidents on the Hudson," "By a Here and Thereian," and "Larks in Vacation" depict American life as well as travels throughout Italy and the Near East. The sketches appeared at the same time in the *Mirror* and were also published in German periodicals.

Although Willis's travel letters were popular with the public, they were were attacked by many critics because of their indiscretion in making public the private conversations, connections, and characteristics of socially prominent individuals. In the September 1835 *London Quarterly* review of the original *Mirror* letters John Gibson Lockhart called Willis an "animal." Perhaps the most bitingly critical British review appeared in *Fraser's* (February 1836), where Willis's work was dubbed the "book of a goose." "There is not a single idea in it, from the first page to the last," the reviewer fulminated, "beyond what might germinate in the brain of a washerwoman." Willis was called a "lickspittle," a "beggarly skittler," a "jackass," a "ninny," a "haberdasher," a "namby-pamby writer in twaddling albums," a "fifty-fifth rate scribbler of gripe-visited sonnets," a "windygutted visitor," and a "sumph." Years later, in her autobiography (1877), the English travel writer Harriet Martineau would cast doubt on Willis's accuracy: "His countrymen and countrywomen accept, in simplicity, his accounts of our aristocracy as from the pen of one of their own coterie; and they may as well have the opportunity of judging for themselves whether their notorious 'Penciller' is qualified to write of Scotch dukes and English marquises and European celebrities of all kinds in the way he has done." In America he was censured by the *Morning Courier and New York Enquirer* (29 April 1835), the *National Intelligencer* (6 May 1835), and the *New York Evening Post* (7 May 1835), which accused him of "open violation of the laws of good breeding." Morris declined to defend

his coeditor, saying that he could not be held responsible for Willis's social gaffes.

On 1 October 1835, after a short courtship, Willis married an Englishwoman, Mary Leighton Stace; the couple honeymooned in Paris for two weeks. In November the first edition of *Pencillings by the Way* was published in London; it included only seventy-nine of the letters, which were still appearing in the *Mirror*. In the preface to this edition Willis noted by way of apology that "from the distance of America and the ephemeral nature and usual obscurity of periodical correspondence," he had thought the letters would give no offense. His final letter for the *Mirror* appeared on 14 January 1836, and the first American edition of *Pencillings by the Way* was published later that year. The book was in its seventh British edition by 1863. Willis estimated that he made approximately $5,000 from the work. Bayard Taylor, who would establish a thirty-year career as a travel writer, observed in his *Views A-Foot* (1846) that "when a young boy of ten years" he had read *Pencillings by the Way* "as they appeared from week to week in the country newspaper, and the contemplation of those charming pictures of scenery and society filled me with a thousand dreams and aspirations."

In May 1836 Willis and his wife left England for America, where Willis tried unsuccessfully to secure a diplomatic post in Saint Petersburg, Russia. On 20 September he signed an agreement with the London publisher George Virtue to provide the texts for two illustrated gift books: Willis would travel to popular destinations in the northeastern United States and Canada and describe them, offering information on history, legends, and folklore associated with the region; the English artist William Henry Bartlett would accompany him and supply engravings of the places. The project was designed to appear in monthly installments, each comprising eight pages of text and four plates. For his efforts Willis would receive "fifteen guineas a number." In the autumn he went to Niagara Falls and then to Washington, D.C., where he spent the winter and early spring. In the summer of 1837 he and Bartlett traveled the area around the Susquehanna River. During this trip Willis bought a two-hundred-acre garden estate near Oswego, New York, that he named Glenmary in honor of his wife. The Willises settled there later that year.

As *The New York Times* would say in his obituary, at Glenmary, Willis "did as all literary farmers do—waste money." To boost his finances, he tried writing dramas. The five-act verse tragedy *Bianca Visconti; or the Heart Overtasked,* was composed in competition for a prize offered by the actress Jose-

Idlewild, Willis's home near Cornwall-on-the-Hudson, New York

phine Clifton for the play best suited to her acting skills; it was first performed at the Park Theatre in New York City on 25 August 1837 and was published in 1839. On 29 November 1837 Clifton produced a comedy by Willis, *The Betrothal,* but it was not successful and was never published. Another comedy, *Imei, the Jew,* was never finished. More successful was his comic Florentine play, *Tortesa the Usurer* (1839), which was produced at the National Theatre in New York City on 8 April 1839.

Willis severed relations with Morris and the *Mirror* in January 1839 because of a controversy resulting from some sarcastic society articles, signed "Veritas," that were published in "New Series of Letters from London," a travel series begun on 26 October 1838. Willis joined Dr. T. O. Porter in establishing a weekly, the *Corsair,* on 16 March. Willis left the affairs of the *Corsair* almost totally in Porter's hands while he and his wife went to England on business in the summer of 1839.

Arriving in England, the Willises learned that Mrs. Willis's father had died a week earlier. In London Willis published several of his poems, Italian romances, and European travel essays under the title *Loiterings of Travel* (1840), which was published in the U.S. as *The Romance of Travel.* The section "Sketches of Travel" deals with his trips to the British Isles and includes discussions of topics ranging from William Shakespeare to traffic jams on Bond Street. Also included in *Loiterings of Travel* are his letters to the *Corsair,* "Jottings Down in London,"

which explore such subjects as London railroad stations and the Bedlam insane asylum. For his British audience he describes Washington, D.C., noting that "within a half hour's gallop, you have a sylvan retreat of every variety of beauty, and in almost any direction. . . . That which makes the charm of a city, and that from which we seek the country, are equally here, and the penalties of both are removed."

Willis and Bartlett's two-volume, 246-page *American Scenery; or, Land, Lake, and River Illustrations of Transatlantic Nature* appeared in 1840. It was aimed at the armchair traveler: its stated purpose was to permit "those whose lot is domestic and retired" to "travel" vicariously "at little cost and pains." According to Beers, Willis's contribution was "hack work," composed of hastily written passages, scraps of his earlier writing, paraphrases of other travelers' accounts, and sections of a friend's diary. Similarly, in the companion book, the two-volume, 244-page *Canadian Scenery Illustrated from Drawings by W. H. Bartlett* (1842), Willis took virtually all of his material from travel narratives by other writers, giving credit to his sources at the outset. The most effective passages in *American Scenery* describe places Willis had actually visited: Niagara Falls, the Palisades, the Hudson River, Trenton Falls, Saratoga, and Virginia's Natural Bridge. He also comments on famous sites such as the White House, Mount Vernon, the Erie Canal, Bunker Hill, and Yale University. Willis's Canadian text, regardless of its provenance, is still of interest for its information on settlement history, Canadian lifestyles, and Indian legends and superstitions.

Throughout these texts Willis is participating in a nationalistic movement to defend and glorify the American landscape. A long-standing complaint by those who had traveled to Europe, or at least had read about it, was that American scenery could not measure up to European in grandeur or in literary associations. Endowed with majestic snow-capped mountains, deep and beautiful lakes, and other natural wonders, Europe was a fabled land; by comparison, America seemed hardly fit for comment. But some American writers, including Willis, believed that the American landscape did have aesthetic value, and they tried to locate scenes in America that could equal those of Europe in magnificence or literary associations.

When they compared American to European scenery, American writers both condemned and condoned their country's landscape, practically in the same breath. In *American Scenery* Willis proclaims America to be woefully in need of "finish." A young country in the throes of expansion, settlement, and exploitation, it is full of "blemishes" such as "girdled trees . . . drowned woods, burnt or fallen stumps, rough enclosures, and stony land." Still, America possesses a vitality that Europe lacks; it is imbued with the spirit of progress. Future directed, the American "looks upon all external objects as exponents of the future. In Europe they are only exponents of the past." The "blemishes" reflect a nation in progress, not the dull, overfinished, tradition-bound landscape Europe offers.

America's landscape is fresh and diversified; it can be approached with no tedious preconceptions, commented on with no slavish imitation of others' hackneyed responses. It possesses scenes, according to Willis, "which history . . . has not yet found leisure to put into form, and which romance and poetry . . . have not yet appropriated." And while Europe has awesome mountains, lakes, and ruins, America has its own scenic wonders, such as Niagara Falls. "Unquestionably," Niagara is "the sublimest thing in nature," Willis opines in *American Scenery.*

When Willis returned to New York in the spring of 1840 he discovered that his coeditor, Porter, had abandoned the *Corsair* in discouragement over its insolvency. Its last issue was slated for 7 March. The news came at a bad time for Willis. His articles, stories, and poems were being published in magazines such as *Graham's, Godey's Lady's Book, The Ladies' Companion,* and *Brother Jonathan,* and he received high pay for them—fifty dollars per article in

Godey's, for instance; Beers characterizes him as "beyond a doubt, the most popular, best paid, and in every way most successful magazinist that America had yet seen." Yet his finances were strained. He had expected some money from his father-in-law's estate, but he received nothing. Most sadly for him, he had insufficient funds to keep his beloved Glenmary, where his daughter Imogene was born on 20 June 1842. In the *Godey's* of December 1842 he announced that he would be leaving Glenmary.

Willis reestablished his partnership with Morris. The *Mirror* had ceased publication in early 1843, so in April they began the weekly *New Mirror.* Although the periodical was an immediate success, they were soon forced to end its publication because of increases in the cost of postage. They then started a newspaper, the daily *Evening Mirror,* on 7 October 1844. As the director of the journal's literary department, Willis placed several of his stories, poems, and miscellaneous papers in its pages and hired Poe as literary critic and "paragraphist." Willis was also the New York City correspondent for the Washington, D.C., *National Intelligencer.* He edited an annual, the *Opal,* for 1844, and published *Lectures on Fashion* (1844), *The Poems Sacred, Passionate, and Humorous* (1844), and *Dashes at Life with a Free Pencil* (1845), which was divided into three sections: "High Life in Europe and American Life," "Inklings of Adventure," and "Loiterings of Travel."

Willis's youngest sister, Ellen, died in February 1844, and his mother died in March. His wife died in childbirth on 25 March 1845; the baby girl was stillborn. Overworked and grieving, Willis sailed to England in the early summer of 1845 with his three-year-old daughter, Imogene. In England he suffered from an attack of "brain fever" that persisted for two weeks. To recuperate he left his daughter with her aunt and traveled to Germany to visit his brother Richard, who was studying music in Leipzig. Falling ill again, he returned to England, and from there to America in the spring of 1846. While Willis had been in Europe, Morris had withdrawn from the *Evening Mirror* and had begun the weekly *National Press;* on his return to America, Willis joined his coeditor in the new project. Eventually they changed the magazine's name to the *Home Journal,* for many people had interpreted the earlier title as signifying a political newspaper. The *Home Journal* was a successful enterprise, and Willis and Morris would edit it until their deaths.

On 1 October 1846 Willis married Cornelia Grinnell of New Bedford, Massachusetts, who was nearly twenty years his junior. She gave birth to a son, Grinnell, on 28 April 1848. Willis spent the summer of 1848 at Sharon Springs recuperating from an attack of rheumatic fever. As his biographer notes, Willis was "never really a well man" after his 1845 illness. On 27 April 1850 his wife gave birth to a daughter, Lilian. Also in 1850 Willis became involved in the divorce case of his friend, the actor Edwin Forrest. Forrest accused his wife of having an affair with another actor; various literati took strong sides in the matter, and Willis defended Mrs. Forrest. Forrest had someone send an anonymous letter to Mrs. Willis, accusing her husband of having an affair with Mrs. Forrest; he also attacked Willis with a whip. Willis sued Forrest for assault, and Forrest sued him for libel.

In 1851 Willis published *Hurry-graphs; or, Sketches of Scenery, Celebrities & Society, Taken from Life,* a collection of travel essays and society sketches he had written for the *Home Journal* on various places in New England, including Cape Cod, Plymouth, New Bedford, the regions around the new Erie Road, Lake Mahopic, Greenwood Lake, Ramapo, and Westchester.

In the spring of 1852 Willis was diagnosed with lung disease. With his father-in-law he went on a restorative trip that included a cruise to Bermuda and the West Indies and visits to Charleston, Savannah, New Orleans, Mammoth Cave, and Harrodsburg Springs. Though ill, he wrote travel essays on these places for the *Home Journal;* they were collected as *Health Trip to the Tropics* (1853).

Willis's doctor told him to leave New York City for his health, and in 1852 the Willises settled on a fifty-acre tract near Cornwall-on-the-Hudson. There they built a large gabled cottage they named Idlewild, moving into the new house on 26 July 1853. Washington Irving was their neighbor at Sunnyside and paid frequent visits. The Willises' guests also included Bayard Taylor, Charles A. Dana, Theodore Fay, and James Thomas Fields. Another daughter, Edith, was born on 28 September 1853 and a son, Bailey, on 31 May 1857.

In June 1858 Willis and some fifty other writers and artists went on a five-day rail trip from Baltimore to Wheeling arranged by the Baltimore and Ohio Railroad. Willis reported on the journey for the *Home Journal,* as he did his three-week trip in July 1860 to Yellow Springs, Ohio; Chicago; Madison, Wisconsin; Saint Louis; Cincinnati; and Pittsburgh. His final book, *The Convalescent* (1859), includes narratives of trips to Nantucket, the Rappahannock, and a horse fair in Springfield, Massachusetts. Even if it does not measure up to the splendid *Pencillings by the Way,* Willis's later travel writing is always pleasant. People continued to read his works: no matter how much old material he included in his volumes, he always found a ready market.

In May 1861 Willis became a war correspondent for the *Home Journal.* He was based in Washington, D.C., where he became a great favorite of Mary Todd Lincoln's, but he ventured outside the city and was nearly captured by Confederate troops near Mount Vernon. His duties, which lasted for more than a year, exhausted him. The Civil War also took its toll on the *Home Journal* as many of its Southern readers cancelled their subscriptions.

Strapped for funds, Willis had to rent out Idlewild; his family took up residence at New Bedford with his father-in-law. Willis lived mainly in New York, believing that he had to stay in the city to do his job because Morris was growing feeble. In the autumn of 1863, against the wishes of her proud husband, Cornelia Willis opened a girls' school to bring in extra money. Morris died in July 1864; ill himself, and suffering from epileptic seizures, Willis continued his editorial duties alone. By November 1866 Willis was so weak and had fainted in the street so often that he was brought home to Idlewild. He died on 20 January 1867. He was buried at Mount Auburn; his pallbearers included Henry Wadsworth Longfellow, Charles A. Dana, Oliver Wendell Holmes, and James Russell Lowell.

As a writer Willis was not without his faults; digressiveness, frivolity, and a tendency toward stylistic fluff are the most notable of them. His digressions, however, are part of his charm, and in his travel writing they permit him to exercise his powers of scenic description. As Beers notes, however, Willis's talents were often "wasted on dissertations upon the cut of a beard or the fashion of a coat." His society gossip, fashion sketches, and other journalistic trivialities detracted from his professionalism as a travel writer.

Willis understood the demands of the nineteenth-century literary marketplace. The public craved exotic adventures filled with sumptuous description of foreign locales, and Willis delivered scores of sketches of cosmopolitan travel. His travelogues are never mere guidebooks; he had a remarkable ability to capture the essence of a scene, and through his lavish "pencillings" the reader partakes of the sights, sounds, smells, tastes, and textures of distant lands. In his sparkling travel writing Nathaniel Parker Willis remains, even today, largely unmatched.

Biography:

Henry A. Beers, *Nathaniel Parker Willis,* American Men of Letters Series (Boston: Houghton, Mifflin / Cambridge, Mass.: Riverside Press, 1885).

References:

Cortland P. Auser, *Nathaniel Parker Willis* (New York: Twayne, 1969);

James T. Callow, *Kindred Spirits: Knickerbocker Writers and American Artists, 1807–1855* (Chapel Hill: University of North Carolina Press, 1967);

Harriet Martineau, *Harriet Martineau's Autobiography, with Memorials by Maria Weston Chapman,* 3 volumes (London: Smith, Elder, 1877);

Edgar Allan Poe, "N. P. Willis," in his *Essays and Reviews,* edited by G. R. Thompson (New York: Library of America, 1984), pp. 1123–1130;

Robert E. Spiller, *The American in England* (New York: Holt, 1926);

William W. Stowe, *Going Abroad: European Travel in Nineteenth-Century American Culture* (Princeton: Princeton University Press, 1994);

Bayard Taylor, *Views A-Foot; or, Europe Seen with Knapsack and Staff* (New York: Wiley & Putnam, 1846).

Papers:

Nathaniel Parker Willis's letters are at the Yale University Library. A fragmentary diary is in the public library in Morristown, New Jersey.

American Travel Writing, 1776–1864

This checklist of selected primary sources is designed to provide some idea of the vast range of American travel writing during the period from 1776 to 1864. It is intended as a supplement to the entries in this volume and as a guide to further research.

Adams, John Quincy. *Letters on Silesia, Written during a Tour through That Country in the Years 1800, 1801.* London: Budd, 1804.

Adams. *Memoirs of John Quincy Adams, Comprising Portions of His Diary from 1795 to 1848,* 12 volumes, edited by Charles Francis Adams. Philadelphia: Lippincott, 1874–1877.

Allen, Grant. *The European Tour: A Handbook for Americans and Colonists.* London: Richards, 1899; New York: Dodd, Mead, 1899.

Allen, Harriet Trowbridge. *Travels in Europe and the East: During the Years 1858–59 and 1863–64.* New Haven: Tuttle, Morehouse & Taylor, 1879.

Allen, Zachariah. *The Practical Tourist; or, Sketches of the State of the Useful Arts, and of Society, Scenery, &c. &c. In Great-Britain, France and Holland,* 2 volumes. Providence, R.I.: Beckwith, 1832.

Brace, Charles Loring. *Home-Life in Germany.* New York: Scribner, 1853.

Brace. *Hungary in 1851; With an Experience of Austrian Police.* New York: Scribner, 1852.

Brace. *The Norse-Folk; or, a Visit to the Homes of Norway and Sweden.* New York: Scribner, 1857.

Brackenridge, Henry Marie. *South America: A Letter on the Present State of That Country, to James Monroe, President of the United States.* Washington, D.C.: Office of the National Register, 1817.

Brackenridge. *Voyage to South America, Performed by Order of the American Government in the Years 1817 and 1818, in the Frigate* Congress, 2 volumes. Baltimore: Published by the author, printed by John D. Toy, 1819; London: Printed for J. Miller, 1820.

Bridgman, Eliza Jane (Gillett). *Daughters of China; or, Sketches of Domestic Life in the Celestial Empire.* New York: Carter, 1853.

Browne, John Ross. *An American Family in Germany.* New York: Harper, 1866.

Browne. *Etchings of a Whaling Cruise, with Notes of a Sojourn on the Island of Zanzibar.* New York: Harper, 1846.

Browne. *The Land of Thor.* New York: Harper, 1867.

Browne. *Yusef; or, the Journey of the Frangi: A Crusade in the East.* New York: Harper, 1853.

Bullard, Anne Tuttle Jones. *Sights and Scenes in Europe: A Series of Letters from England, France, Germany, Switzerland, and Italy, in 1850.* Saint Louis: Chambers & Knapp, 1852.

Burritt, Elihu. *A Walk from London to John O'Groat's, with Notes by the Way.* London: Low, Son & Marston, 1864.

Burritt. *A Walk from London to Land's End and Back, with Notes by the Way.* London: Low, 1865.

Burritt. *Walks in the Black Country and Its Green Border-Land.* London: Low, 1868.

Calvert, George Henry. *First Years in Europe.* Boston: Spencer, 1866.

Calvert. *Scenes and Thoughts in Europe,* as an American. New York: Wiley & Putnam, 1846.

Calvert. *Scenes and Thoughts in Europe,* second series. New York: Putnam, 1852.

Calvert. *Travels in Europe: Its People and Scenery, Embracing Graphic Descriptions of Its Principal Cities, Buildings, Scenery, and Most Notable People in England and the Continent.* Boston: Cottrell, 1860.

Cazneau, Mrs. William Leslie. *Eagle Pass; or, Life on the Border,* as Cora Montgomery. New York: Putnam, 1852.

Cazneau. *Our Winter Eden: Pen Pictures of the Tropics.* New York: Authors' Publishing Co., 1878.

Cheever, Henry Theodore. *The Island World of the Pacific: Being the Personal Narrative and Results of Travel through the Sandwich or Hawaiian Islands and Other Parts of Polynesia.* New York: Harper, 1851.

Cheever. *Life in the Sandwich Islands; or, the Heart of the Pacific as It Was and Is.* New York: Barnes / Cincinnati: Derby, 1851.

Cheever. *The Whale and His Captors; or, The Whaleman's Adventures and the Whale's Biography as Gathered on the Homeward Cruise of the "Commodore Preble."* New York: Harper, 1850 [i.e., 1849].

Clarke, James Freeman. *Eleven Weeks in Europe; and What May Be Seen in That Time.* Boston: Ticknor, Reed & Fields, 1852.

Colton, Walter. *Deck and Port; or, Incidents of a Cruise in the United States Frigate* Congress *to California. With Sketches of Rio Janeiro, Valparaiso, Lima, Honolulu, and San Francisco.* New York: Barnes / Cincinnati: Derby, 1850.

Colton. *The Sea and the Sailor: Notes on France and Italy, and Other Literary Remains.* New York: Barnes / Cincinnati: Derby, 1851.

Colton. *Ship and Shore; or, Leaves from the Journal of a Cruise to the Levant.* New York: Leavitt, Lord, 1835.

Colton. *Visit to Constantinople and Athens.* New York: Leavitt, Lord / Boston: Crocker & Brewster, 1836.

Crèvecoeur, J. Hector St. John de. *Letters from an American Farmer: Describing Certain Provincial Situations, Manners, and Customs, Not Generally Known; and Conveying Some Idea of the Late and Present Interior Circumstances of the British Colonies in North America. Written for the Information of a Friend in England, by J. Hector St. John, a Farmer in Pennsylvania.* London: Printed for Thomas Davies & Lockyer Davis, 1782; Philadelphia: From the press of Mathew Carey, 1793.

Cross, Joseph. *The American Pastor in Europe,* edited by John Cumming. London: Bentley, 1860.

Cross. *Edens of Italy.* New York: Whittaker, 1883.

Cross. *A Year in Europe.* Nashville: Southern Methodist Publishing House, 1858.

Cushing, Caroline Elizabeth Wilde. *Letters, Descriptive of Public Monuments, Scenery, and Manners in France and Spain,* 2 volumes. Newburyport, Mass.: Printed by E. W. Allen & Co., 1832.

Delaplain, Sophia. *A Thrilling and Exciting Account of the Sufferings and Horrible Tortures Inflicted on Mortimer Bowers and Miss Sophia Delaplain, by the Spanish Authorities, for the Supposed Participation with Gen. Lopez in the Invasion of Cuba; Together with the Plan of Campaign of Lopez.* Charleston, S.C.: E. E. Barclay/M. B. Crosson & Co., 1851.

Dewey, Orville. *The Old World and the New; or, A Journal of Reflections and Observations, Made on a Tour in Europe,* 2 volumes. New York: Harper, 1836.

Ditson, George Leighton. *Circassia; or, A Tour to the Caucasus.* New York: Stringer & Townsend, 1850.

Ditson. *The Crescent and French Crusaders.* New York: Derby & Jackson, 1859.

Ditson. *The Para Papers on France, Egypt and Ethiopia.* Paris: Fowler / New York: Mason, 1858.

Dorr, David F. *A Colored Man round the World: By a Quadroon.* Cleveland: Printed for the author, 1858.

Dwight, Theodore. *A Journal of a Tour in Italy, in the Year 1821. With a Description of Gibraltar,* as an American. New York: Printed for the author by A. Paul, 1824.

Dwight. *The Northern Traveller: Containing the Routes to Niagara, Quebec, and the Springs; with Descriptions of the Principal Scenes, and Useful Hints to Strangers.* New York: Wilder & Campbell, 1825.

Eames, Jane Anthony. *Another Budget; or, Things Which I Saw in the East.* Boston: Ticknor & Fields, 1855.

Eames. *The Budget Closed.* Boston: Ticknor & Fields, 1860.

Eames. *A Budget of Letters; or, Things Which I Saw Abroad.* Boston: Ticknor, 1847.

Eames. *Letters from Bermuda.* Concord, N.H.: Printed by the Republican Press Association, 1875.

Earle, Pliny. *European Institutions for Idiots.* Utica, N.Y.: Saunderson, printer, 1852.

Earle. *Institutions for the Insane, in Prussia, Austria and Germany.* Utica: Printed at the New York State Lunatic Asylum, 1853.

Earle. *A Visit to Thirteen Asylums for the Insane in Europe: To Which Are Added a Brief Notice of Similar Institutions in Transatlantic Countries and in the United States, and an Essay on the Causes, Duration, Termination and Moral Treatment of Insanity. With Copious Statistics.* Philadelphia: Dobson, 1841.

Fiske, Samuel Wheelock. *Mr. Dunn Browne's Experiences in Foreign Parts.* Boston: Jewett, 1857.

Flagg, Edmund. *Venice: The City of the Sea, from the Invasion by Napoléon in 1797 to the Capitulation of Radetzky, in 1849,* 2 volumes. New York: Scribner, 1853.

Forbes, Mrs. E. A. *A Woman's First Impressions of Europe: Being Wayside Sketches Made during a Short Tour in the Year 1863.* New York: Derby & Miller, 1865.

Furniss, William. *The Land of the Caesar and Doge: Historical and Artistic; Incidental, Personal, and Literary.* New York: Cornish, Lamport, 1853.

Furniss. *Landvoieglee; or, Views across the Sea.* New York: D. Appleton / Philadelphia: G. S. Appleton, 1850.

Furniss. *Waraga; or, The Charms of the Nile.* New York: Baker & Scribner, 1850.

Gibson, James. *A Journal of the Late Siege by the Troops from North America, against the French at Cape Breton, the City of Louisbourg, and the Territories Thereunto Belonging. Surrendered to the English, on the 17th of June, 1745, after a Siege of Forty-eight Days.* London: Printed for J. Newbery, 1745. Republished as *A Boston Merchant of 1745; or, Incidents in the Life of James Gibson, a Gentleman Volunteer at the Expedition to Louisbourg; with a Journal of That Siege, Never Before Published in This Country. By One of His Descendants,* edited by Lorenzo D. Johnson. Boston: Redding, 1947.

Haight, Mrs. Sarah Rogers. *Letters from the Old World by a Lady of New York,* 2 volumes. New York: Harper, 1839.

Haight. *Over the Ocean; or, Glimpses of Travel in Many Lands.* New York: Paine & Burgess, 1846.

Hall, Fanny W. *Rambles in Europe; or, A Tour through France, Italy, Switzerland, Great Britain, and Ireland, in 1836,* 2 volumes. New York: French, 1838.

Hastings, Susannah Willard Johnson. *A Narrative of the Captivity of Mrs. Johnson, Containing an Account of Her Sufferings, during Four Years with the Indians and the French.* Walpole, N.H.: Carlisle, 1796.

Kirkland, Caroline M. *Holidays Abroad; or, Europe from the West,* 2 volumes. New York: Baker & Scribner, 1849.

Lanman, Charles. *Adventures in the Wilds of the United States and British American Provinces,* 2 volumes. Philadelphia: Moore, 1856.

Lanman. *Haw-ho-noo; or, Records of a Tourist.* Philadelphia: Lippincott, Grambo, 1850.

Lanman. *A Summer in the Wilderness: Embracing a Canoe Voyage up the Mississippi and around Lake Superior.* New York: D. Appleton / Philadelphia: G. S. Appleton, 1847.

Lanman. *A Tour to the River Saguenay, in Lower Canada.* Philadelphia: Carey & Hart, 1848.

LeVert, Octavia Walton. *Souvenirs of Travel,* 2 volumes. New York & Mobile, Ala.: Goetzel, 1857.

Lippincott, Sara Jane Clarke. *Haps and Mishaps of a Tour in Europe,* as Grace Greenwood. Boston: Ticknor, Reed & Fields, 1854.

Lippincott. *Merrie England: Travels, Descriptions, Tales and Historical Sketches,* as Greenwood. Boston: Ticknor & Fields, 1855.

Lippincott. *Stories and Sights of France & Italy,* as Greenwood. Boston: Ticknor & Fields, 1867.

Longfellow, Henry Wadsworth. *Outre-Mer: A Pilgrimage beyond the Sea,* 2 volumes. Volume 1, Boston: Hilliard, Gray, 1833; volume 2, Boston: Lilly, Wait, 1834; enlarged edition, 2 volumes, New York: Harper, 1835; London: Bentley, 1835.

Lynch, William Francis. *Narrative of the United States' Expedition to the River Jordan and the Dead Sea.* Philadelphia: Lee & Blanchard, 1849.

Lynch. *Naval Life; or, Observations Afloat and on Shore. The Midshipman.* New York: Scribner, 1851.

Lynch. *Official Report of the United States' Expedition to Explore the Dead Sea and the River Jordan.* Baltimore: Murphy, 1852.

Malcom, Howard. *Travels in South-Eastern Asia, Embracing Hindustan, Malaya, Siam, and China; with Notices of Numerous Missionary Stations, and a Full Account of the Burman Empire,* 2 volumes. Boston: Gould, Kendall & Lincoln, 1839.

Marcy, Randolph Barnes. *The Prairie Traveler: A Handbook for Overland Expeditions, with Maps, Illustrations, and Itineraries of the Principal Routes between the Mississippi and the Pacific.* New York: Harper, 1859.

Miller, Anna C. Johnson. *The Cottages of the Alps; or, Life and Manners in Switzerland.* New York: Scribner, 1860.

Miller. *Peasant Life in Germany.* New York: Scribner, 1858.

Morrell, Abby Jane Wood. *Narrative of a Voyage to the Ethiopic and South Atlantic Ocean, Indian Ocean, Chinese Sea, North and South Pacific Ocean, in the Years 1829, 1830, 1831.* New York: Harper, 1833.

Nordhoff, Charles. *Nine Years a Sailor: Being Sketches of Personal Experience in the United States Naval Service, the American and British Merchant Marine, and the Whaling Service.* Cincinnati: Moore, Wilstach, Keys, 1857.

Nordhoff. *Northern California, Oregon, and the Sandwich Islands.* New York: Harper, 1874.

Nordhoff. *Peninsular California: Some Account of the Climate, Soil, Productions, and Present Condition Chiefly of the Northern Half of Lower California.* New York: Harper, 1888.

Nordhoff. *Stories of the Island World.* New York: Harper, 1857.

Norman, Benjamin Moore. *Rambles by Land and Water; or, Notes of Travel in Cuba and Mexico: Including a Canoe Voyage up the River Panuco, and Researches among the Ruins of Tamaulipas.* New York: Paine & Burgess / New Orleans: Norman, 1845.

Norman. *Rambles in Yucatan; or, Notes of Travel through the Peninsula, Including a Visit to the Remarkable Ruins of Chi-Chen, Kabah, Zayi, and Uxmal.* New York: Langley / Philadelphia: Thomas, Cowperthwait / New Orleans: Norman, Steel, 1843.

Olin, Stephen. *Greece and the Golden Horn.* New York: Derby / Boston: Phillips, Sampson, 1854.

Olin. *The Life and Letters of Stephen Olin . . . Late President of the Wesleyan University,* 2 volumes, edited by John McClintock and others. New York: Harper, 1853.

Olin. *Travels in Egypt, Arabia Petræa, and the Holy Land,* 2 volumes. New York: Harper, 1843.

Paine, Caroline. *Tent and Harem: Notes of an Oriental Trip.* New York: Appleton, 1859.

Palmer, John Williamson. *The Golden Dragon; or, Up and down the Irrawaddi: Being Passages of Adventure in the Burman Empire,* as an American. New York: Dix, Edwards, 1856. Revised as *Up and down the Irrawaddi; or, The Golden Dragon: Being Passages of Adventure in the Burman Empire.* New York: Rudd & Carleton, 1859.

Palmer. *The New and the Old; or, California and India in Romantic Aspects.* New York: Rudd & Carleton, 1859.

Palmer, Phoebe Worrell. *Four Years in the Old World; Comprising the Travels, Incidents, and Evangelistic Labors of Dr. and Mrs. Palmer in England, Ireland, Scotland and Wales,* third edition. New York: Foster & Palmer, 1866.

Putnam, George Palmer. *The Tourist in Europe; or, A Concise Summary of the Various Routes, Objects of Interest, &c. in Great Britain, France, Switzerland, Italy, Germany, Belgium and Holland; with Hints on Time, Expenses, Hotels, Conveyances, Passports, Coins, &c.: Memoranda during a Tour of Eight Months in Great Britain and on the Continent, in 1836.* New York: Wiley & Putnam, 1838.

Robinson, Edward, and Eli Smith. *Biblical Researches in Palestine, and in the Adjacent Regions: A Journal of Travels in the Year 1838. Drawn up from the Original Diaries, with Historical Illustrations by Edward Robinson,* 3 volumes. Boston: Crocker & Brewster, 1856.

Robinson and Smith. *Biblical Researches in Palestine, Mount Sinai, and Arabia Petræa: A Journal of Travels in the Year 1838,* 3 volumes. Boston: Crocker & Brewster / New York: Leavitt, 1841.

Rush, Richard. *Memoranda of a Residence at the Court of London, Comprising Incidents Official and Personal, from 1819 to 1825: Including Negotiations on the Oregon Question, and Other Unsettled Questions between the United States and Great Britain.* Philadelphia: Lea & Blanchard, 1845.

Rush. *Occasional Productions, Political, Diplomatic, and Miscellaneous. Including, among Others, a Glance at the Court and Government of Louis Phillippe and the French Revolution of 1848, While the Author Resided as Envoy Extraordinary and Minister Plenipotentiary from the United States at Paris,* edited by Benjamin Rush and James Murray Rush. Philadelphia: Lippincott, 1860.

Sansom, Joseph. *Letters from Europe, during a Tour through Switzerland and Italy, in the Years 1801 and 1802,* 2 volumes, as a Native of Pennsylvania. Philadelphia: Printed for the author by A. Bartram, sold by T. Dobson, 1805. Republished as *Travels from Paris through Switzerland and Italy, in the Years 1801 and 1802: With Sketches of the Manners and Characters of the Respective Inhabitants,* 1 volume. London: Printed for R. Phillips, 1808.

Sansom. *Sketches of Lower Canada, Historical and Descriptive: with the Author's Recollections of the Soil, and Aspect; the Morals, Habits, and Religious Institutions, of That Isolated Country; during a Tour to Quebec, in the Month of July, 1817.* New York: Printed for Kirk & Mercein, 1817. Republished as *Travels in Lower Canada, with the Author's Recollections of the Soil, and Aspect: the Morals, Habits, and Religious Institutions, of That Country.* London: Printed for S. R. Phillips & Co., 1820.

Schriber, Mary Suzanne, ed. *Telling Travels: Selected Writings by Nineteenth-Century American Women Abroad.* De Kalb: Northern Illinois University Press, 1995.

Scott, Anna M. Steele. *Day Dawn in Africa; or, Progress of the Protestant Episcopal Mission at Cape Palmas, West Africa.* New York: Protestant Episcopal Society for the Promotion of Evangelical Knowledge, 1858.

Scott. *Rome as It Is: Being Reminiscences of a Visit to the "City of the Cæsars."* Philadelphia: Lippincott, 1874.

Shuck, Henrietta Hall. *Scenes in China; or, Sketches of the Country, Religion, and Customs, of the Chinese.* Philadelphia: American Baptist Publication Society, 1852.

Smith, Abigail Adams. *Journal and Correspondence of Miss Adams, Daughter of John Adams, Second President of the United States. Written in France and England in 1785,* 2 volumes, edited by Caroline Amelia Smith De Windt. New York: Wiley & Putnam, 1841–1842.

Stewart, Charles Samuel. *Brazil and La Plata: The Personal Record of a Cruise.* New York: Putnam, 1856.

Stewart. *Private Journal of a Voyage to the Pacific Ocean, and Residence at the Sandwich Islands, in the Years 1822, 1823, 1824 and 1825.* New York: Haven, 1828.

Stewart. *Sketches of Society in Great Britain and Ireland,* 2 volumes. Philadelphia: Carey, Lea & Blanchard, 1834.

Stewart. *A Visit to the South Seas, in the U.S. Ship* Vincennes, *during the Years 1829 and 1830: With Scenes in Brazil, Peru, Manilla, the Cape of Good Hope, and St. Helena,* 2 volumes. New York: Haven, 1831.

Sweat, Margaret Jane Massey. *Highways of Travel; or, A Summer in Europe.* Boston: Walker, Wise, 1859.

Taylor, Fitch Waterman. *The Broad Pennant; or, A Cruise in the United States Flag Ship of the Gulf Squadron, during the Mexican Difficulties: Together with the Sketches of the Mexican War, from the Commencement of Hostilities to the Capture of the City of Mexico.* New York: Leavitt, Trow, 1848.

Taylor. *The Flag-Ship; or, a Voyage around the World, in the United States Frigate* Columbia; *Attended by Her Consort, the Sloop of War* John Adams, *and Bearing the Broad Pennant of Commodore George C. Read,* 2 volumes. New York: Appleton, 1840.

Thomas, Mrs. Susan Brewer. *Travels in Europe, Egypt, and Palestine.* Philadelphia: Lippincott, 1860.

Train, George Francis. *An American Eagle in a British Cage; or, Four Days in a Felon's Cell. By a Prisoner of State.* Cork: Cotter, 1868.

Train. *An American Merchant in Europe, Asia, and Australia: A Series of Letters from Java, Singapore, China, Bengal, Egypt, the Holy Land, the Crimea and Its Battlegrounds, England, Melbourne, Sidney, Etc.* New York: Putnam, 1857. Republished as *Young America Abroad, in Europe, Asia, and Australia: A Series of Letters.* London: Low, 1857.

Tuckerman, Henry Theodore. *Isabel; or, Sicily: A Pilgrimage.* Philadelphia: Lea & Blanchard, 1839. Republished as *Isabel; or, A Pilgrimage in Sicily.* London: Bruce, 1844.

Tuckerman. *The Italian Sketch Book,* as an American. Philadelphia: Key & Biddle, 1835.

Tuckerman. *A Month in England.* New York: Redfield, 1853.

Wallis, Mary Davis Cook. *Life in Feejee; or, Five Years among the Cannibals,* as a Lady. Boston: Heath, 1851.

Warren, John Esaias. *Notes of an Attaché in Spain in 1850.* London: Bentley, 1851. Republished as *Vagamundo; or, The Attaché in Spain: Including a Brief Excursion into the Empire of Morocco.* New York: Scribner, 1851.

Warren. *Para; or, Scenes and Adventures on the Banks of the Amazon.* New York: Putnam, 1851.

Wikoff, Henry. *The Adventures of a Roving Diplomatist.* New York: Fetridge, 1857. Republished as *A New Yorker in the Foreign Office, and His Adventures in Paris.* London: Trübner, 1858.

Wikoff. *My Courtship and Its Consequences.* New York: Derby / Boston: Phillips, Samson, 1855.

Wikoff. *Napoleon Louis Bonaparte, First President of France: Biographical and Personal Sketches, Including a Visit to the Prince at the Castle of Ham.* New York: Putnam / London: Chapman, 1849.

Wikoff. *The Remembrances of an Idler.* New York: Fords, Howard & Hulbert, 1880.

Willard, Emma Hart. *Journal and Letters, from France and Great-Britain.* Troy, N.Y.: N. Tuttle, printer, 1833.

Winchester, Charles Wesley. *The Gospel of Foreign Travel.* Rochester, N.Y.: Press of Democrat & Chronicle, 1891.

Checklist of Further Readings

Adams, Percy G. *Travel Literature and the Evolution of the Novel.* Lexington: University of Kentucky Press, 1983.

Adler, Judith, "Origins of Sightseeing." *Annals of Tourism Research,* 16 (1989): 7–29.

Andrews, Malcolm. *The Search for the Picturesque: Landscape Aesthet–ics and Tourism in Britain, 1760–1800.* Stanford: Stanford University Press, 1989.

Baker, Paul R. *The Fortunate Pilgrims: Americans in Italy, 1800–1860.* Cambridge, Mass.: Harvard University Press, 1964.

Behdad, Ali. *Belated Travelers: Orientalism in the Age of Colonial Dissolution.* Durham, N.C. & London: Duke University Press, 1994.

Bowen, Frank C. *A Century of Atlantic Travel: 1830–1930.* Boston: Little, Brown, 1930.

Brooks, Van Wyck. *The Dream of Arcadia: American Writers and Artists in Italy, 1760–1915.* New York: Dutton, 1958; London: Dent, 1959.

Buzard, James. *The Beaten Track: European Tourism, Literature and the Ways to Culture, 1800–1918.* Oxford: Clarendon Press/Oxford University Press, 1993.

Caesar, Terry. " 'Counting the Cats in Zanzibar': American Travel Abroad in American Travel Writing to 1914," *Prospects,* 13 (1989): 95–134.

Clifford, James. "Notes on Theory and Travel," *Inscriptions,* 5 (1989): 177–188.

Cole, Garold L. "The Travel Account as a Social Document: A Survey of Recent Journal Articles," *Exploration: Journal of the MLA Special Session on the Literature of Exploration and Travel,* 7 (1979): 42–55.

Culler, Jonathan. "Semiotics of Tourism," *American Journal of Semiotics,* 1 (1981): 127–140.

Dulles, Foster Rhea. *Americans Abroad: Two Centuries of European Travel.* Ann Arbor: University of Michigan Press, 1964.

Dulles, *The Old China.* Boston: Houghton Mifflin, 1930.

Dunlop, Mary Helen. *Sixty Miles from Contentment: Traveling the Nineteenth-Century American Interior.* New York: Basic Books, 1995.

Earnest, Ernest. *Expatriates and Patriots: American Artists, Scholars, and Writers in Europe.* Durham, N.C.: Duke University Press, 1968.

Lanser, Suzanne. *The Narrative Act: Point of View in Prose Fiction.* Princeton: Princeton University Press, 1981.

Leed, Eric J. *The Mind of the Traveler: From Gilgamesh to Global Tourism.* New York: Basic Books, 1991.

Lochsberg, Winifred. *History of Travel.* Leipzig: Edition Leipzig, 1979.

Lockwood, Allison. *The Passionate Pilgrims: The American Traveler in Great Britain, 1800–1914.* Rutherford, N.J.: Fairleigh Dickinson University Press, 1981.

Long, Orie William. *Literary Pioneers: Early American Explorers of European Culture.* Cambridge, Mass.: Harvard University Press, 1935.

MacCannell, Dean. *Empty Meeting Grounds: The Tourist Papers.* London & New York: Routledge, 1992.

MacCannell. *The Tourist: A New Theory of the Leisure Class.* New York: Schocken, 1976.

Memmi, Albert. *The Colonizer and the Colonized.* New York: Orion Press, 1965.

Metualli, A. M. "Americans Abroad: The Popular Art of Travel Writing in the Nineteenth Century," *Exploration: Journal of the MLA Special Session on the Literature of Exploration and Travel,* 4 (1976): 115–124.

Mills, Sara. *Discourses of Difference: An Analysis of Women's Travel Writing and Colonialism.* New York & London: Routledge, 1991.

Mulvey, Christopher. *Anglo-American Landscapes: A Study of Nineteenth-Century Anglo-American Travel Literature.* London: Cambridge University Press, 1983.

Mulvey. *Transatlantic Manners: Social Patterns in Nineteenth-Century Anglo-American Travel Literature.* London: Cambridge University Press, 1990.

Ong, Walter J. *Orality and Literacy: The Technologizing of the Word.* London & New York: Methuen, 1982.

Passport Office, United States Department of State. *The United States Passport: Past, Present, Future.* Washington, D.C.: U.S. Department of State, 1976.

Pratt, Mary Louise. *Imperial Eyes: Studies in Travel Writing and Transculturation.* New York & London: Routledge, 1992.

Pratt. "Scratches on the Face of the Country; or, What Mr. Barrow Saw in the Face of the Bushman," in *"Race," Writing, and Difference,* edited by Henry Louis Gates Jr. Chicago: University of Chicago Press, 1986, pp. 138–162.

Rahv, Philip, ed. *Discovery of Europe: The Story of American Experience in the Old World.* Boston: Houghton Mifflin, 1947; revised edition, Garden City, N.Y.: Doubleday, 1960.

Rice, Warner G., ed. *Literature as a Mode of Travel.* New York: New York Public Library, 1963.

Said, Edward. *Culture and Imperialism.* New York: Knopf, 1993.

Said. *Orientalism.* New York: Pantheon, 1979.

Salomone, A. William. "The Nineteenth-Century Discovery of Italy: An Essay in American Cultural History. Prolegomena to a Historiographical Problem," *American Historical Review,* 73 (1968): 1359–1391.

Schivelsbusch, Wolfgang. *The Railway Journey: The Industrialization of Time and Space in the Nineteenth Century.* Berkeley: University of California Press, 1986.

Scholes, Robert, and Robert Kellogg. *The Nature of Narrative.* London & New York: Oxford University Press, 1966.

Sears, John. *Sacred Places: American Tourist Attractions in the Nineteenth Century.* New York: Oxford University Press, 1989.

Smith, Harold F. *American Travellers Abroad: A Bibliography of Accounts Published before 1900.* Carbondale: Library of Southern Illinois University, 1969.

Spurr, David. *The Rhetoric of Empire: Colonial Discourse in Journalism, Travel Writing, and Imperial Administration.* Durham, N.C.: Duke University Press, 1993.

Stafford, Barbara M. *Voyage into Substance: Art, Science, Nature, and the Illustrated Travel Account, 1760–1840.* Cambridge, Mass.: MIT Press, 1984.

Swinglehurst, Edmund. *Cook's Tours: The Story of Popular Travel.* Poole, Dorset: Blandford, 1982.

Trease, Robert G. *The Grand Tour.* London: Heinemann, 1967.

U.S. Department of State. *The American Passport: Its History and a Digest of Laws, Rulings, and Regulations Governing Its Issuance by the Department of State.* Washington, D.C.: Government Printing Office, 1898.

White, Hayden. *Tropics of Discourse: Essays in Cultural Criticism.* Baltimore: Johns Hopkins University Press, 1978.

Contributors

Stephen Adams...*University of Minnesota–Duluth*
Paul Baepler...*University of Minnesota*
Xavier Baron...*University of Wisconsin–Milwaukee*
Rob J. Brault..*University of Minnesota*
Harold K. Bush Jr. ....*Michigan State University*
Barbara J. Cicardo...*University of Southwestern Louisiana*
Nancy Cook ....*University of Rhode Island*
Laurie Delany ....*University of Cincinnati*
Donald A. Duhadaway Jr. ....*University of Delaware*
Allen Flint..*University of Maine at Farmington*
Edward J. Gallagher...*Lehigh University*
Jared Gardner ....*Grunnell College*
Paola Gemme ....*Pennsylvania State University*
Anita G. Gorman ....*Slippery Rock University*
James L. Gray ....*Indiana University of Pennsylvania*
Bruce A. Harvey ....*Florida International University*
Dorsey Kleitz...*Tokyo Women's Christian University*
Bryan F. Le Beau ....*Creighton University*
Linda Ledford-Miller..*University of Scranton*
Linda Lincoln ....*University of Minnesota*
Anna E. Lomando...*Pennsylvania State University*
Richard V. McLamore ....*McMurry University*
Udo Nattermann...*University of Indianapolis*
Martha I. Pallante..*Youngstown State University*
Dennis R. Perry...*University of Missouri–Rolla*
Brian D. Reed ....*Kent State–East Liverpool*
Barbara Ryan ....*Michigan Society of Fellows*
James J. Schramer..*Youngstown State University*
Karen Schramm...*Camden County College*
Jeffrey Steele...*University of Wisconsin–Madison*
Laurie A. Sterling..*King's College*
Lane Stiles...*University of Minnesota*
Timothy Sweet...*West Virginia University*
Stephanie A. Tingley...*Youngstown State University*
Karen M. Woods...*University of Minnesota*
James A. Wren..*Nügata University*

Cumulative Index

Dictionary of Literary Biography, Volumes 1-183
Dictionary of Literary Biography Yearbook, 1980-1996
Dictionary of Literary Biography Documentary Series, Volumes 1-15

Cumulative Index

DLB before number: *Dictionary of Literary Biography,* Volumes 1-183
Y before number: *Dictionary of Literary Biography Yearbook,* 1980-1996
DS before number: *Dictionary of Literary Biography Documentary Series,* Volumes 1-15

A

Abbey Press DLB-49

The Abbey Theatre and Irish Drama,
1900-1945 . . . . DLB-10

Abbot, Willis J. 1863-1934 . . . . DLB-29

Abbott, Jacob 1803-1879 . . . . DLB-1

Abbott, Lee K. 1947- DLB-130

Abbott, Lyman 1835-1922 . . . . DLB-79

Abbott, Robert S. 1868-1940 . . . . DLB-29, 91

Abe, Kōbō 1924-1993 . . . . DLB-182

Abelard, Peter circa 1079-1142 . . . . . DLB-115

Abelard-Schuman DLB-46

Abell, Arunah S. 1806-1888 . . . . DLB-43

Abercrombie, Lascelles 1881-1938 . . . . DLB-19

Aberdeen University Press
Limited DLB-106

Abish, Walter 1931- DLB-130

Ablesimov, Aleksandr Onisimovich
1742-1783 . . . . DLB-150

Abraham à Sancta Clara
1644-1709 . . . . DLB-168

Abrahams, Peter 1919- DLB-117

Abrams, M. H. 1912- DLB-67

Abrogans circa 790-800 . . . . DLB-148

Abschatz, Hans Aßmann von
1646-1699 . . . . DLB-168

Abse, Dannie 1923- DLB-27

Academy Chicago Publishers DLB-46

Accrocca, Elio Filippo 1923- DLB-128

Ace Books DLB-46

Achebe, Chinua 1930- DLB-117

Achtenberg, Herbert 1938- DLB-124

Ackerman, Diane 1948- DLB-120

Ackroyd, Peter 1949- DLB-155

Acorn, Milton 1923-1986 . . . . DLB-53

Acosta, Oscar Zeta 1935?- DLB-82

Actors Theatre of Louisville DLB-7

Adair, James 1709?-1783? DLB-30

Adam, Graeme Mercer 1839-1912 . . . . DLB-99

Adame, Leonard 1947- DLB-82

Adamic, Louis 1898-1951 . . . . DLB-9

Adams, Alice 1926- Y-86

Adams, Brooks 1848-1927 . . . . DLB-47

Adams, Charles Francis, Jr.
1835-1915 . . . . DLB-47

Adams, Douglas 1952- Y-83

Adams, Franklin P. 1881-1960 . . . . . DLB-29

Adams, Henry 1838-1918 . . . . . DLB-12, 47

Adams, Herbert Baxter 1850-1901 . . . . DLB-47

Adams, J. S. and C.
[publishing house] DLB-49

Adams, James Truslow 1878-1949 . . . . DLB-17

Adams, John 1735-1826 . . . . . . DLB-31, 183

Adams, John 1735-1826 and
Adams, Abigail 1744-1818 . . . . . DLB-183

Adams, John Quincy 1767-1848 . . . . . DLB-37

Adams, Léonie 1899-1988 . . . . DLB-48

Adams, Levi 1802-1832 . . . . DLB-99

Adams, Samuel 1722-1803 . . . . . DLB-31, 43

Adams, Thomas
1582 or 1583-1652 . . . . DLB-151

Adams, William Taylor 1822-1897 . . . . DLB-42

Adamson, Sir John 1867-1950 . . . . . DLB-98

Adcock, Arthur St. John
1864-1930 . . . . DLB-135

Adcock, Betty 1938- DLB-105

Adcock, Betty, Certain Gifts DLB-105

Adcock, Fleur 1934- DLB-40

Addison, Joseph 1672-1719 . . . . . . DLB-101

Ade, George 1866-1944 . . . . . . DLB-11, 25

Adeler, Max (see Clark, Charles Heber)

Adonias Filho 1915-1990 . . . . DLB-145

Advance Publishing Company DLB-49

AE 1867-1935 . . . . DLB-19

Ælfric circa 955-circa 1010 . . . . . . DLB-146

Aeschines circa 390 B.C.-circa 320 B.C.
. . . . DLB-176

Aeschylus
525-524 B.C.-456-455 B.C. DLB-176

Aesthetic Poetry (1873), by
Walter Pater DLB-35

After Dinner Opera Company Y-92

Afro-American Literary Critics:
An Introduction DLB-33

Agassiz, Jean Louis Rodolphe
1807-1873 . . . . DLB-1

Agee, James 1909-1955 . . . . . DLB-2, 26, 152

The Agee Legacy: A Conference at
the University of Tennessee
at Knoxville Y-89

Aguilera Malta, Demetrio
1909-1981 . . . . DLB-145

Ai 1947- DLB-120

Aichinger, Ilse 1921- DLB-85

Aidoo, Ama Ata 1942- DLB-117

Aiken, Conrad 1889-1973 . . . . . DLB-9, 45, 102

Aiken, Joan 1924- DLB-161

Aikin, Lucy 1781-1864 . . . . . . DLB-144, 163

Ainsworth, William Harrison
1805-1882 . . . . DLB-21

Aitken, George A. 1860-1917 . . . . . . DLB-149

Aitken, Robert [publishing house] DLB-49

Akenside, Mark 1721-1770 . . . . DLB-109

Akins, Zoë 1886-1958 . . . . DLB-26

Akutagawa, Ryūnsuke
1892-1927 . . . . DLB-180

Alabaster, William 1568-1640 . . . . . DLB-132

Alain-Fournier 1886-1914 . . . . DLB-65

Alarcón, Francisco X. 1954- DLB-122

Alba, Nanina 1915-1968 . . . . DLB-41

Albee, Edward 1928- DLB-7

Albert the Great circa 1200-1280 . . . . DLB-115

Alberti, Rafael 1902- DLB-108

Albertinus, Aegidius
circa 1560-1620 . . . . DLB-164

Alcaeus born circa 620 B.C. DLB-176

Alcott, Amos Bronson 1799-1888 . . . . DLB-1

Alcott, Louisa May
1832-1888 . . . . . . DLB-1, 42, 79; DS-14

Alcott, William Andrus 1798-1859 . . . . DLB-1

Alcuin circa 732-804 . . . . DLB-148

Alden, Henry Mills 1836-1919 . . . . . DLB-79

Alden, Isabella 1841-1930 . . . . DLB-42

Alden, John B. [publishing house] DLB-49

Alden, Beardsley and Company DLB-49

Aldington, Richard
1892-1962 . . . . . . DLB-20, 36, 100, 149

Aldis, Dorothy 1896-1966 . . . . DLB-22

Aldiss, Brian W. 1925- DLB-14

Aldrich, Thomas Bailey
     1836-1907 . . . . DLB-42, 71, 74, 79

Alegría, Ciro 1909-1967 . . . . DLB-113

Alegría, Claribel 1924- DLB-145

Aleixandre, Vicente 1898-1984 . . . . . DLB-108

Aleramo, Sibilla 1876-1960 . . . . DLB-114

Alexander, Charles 1868-1923 . . . . . . DLB-91

Alexander, Charles Wesley
     [publishing house] DLB-49

Alexander, James 1691-1756 . . . . . . DLB-24

Alexander, Lloyd 1924- DLB-52

Alexander, Sir William, Earl of Stirling
     1577?-1640 . . . . DLB-121

Alexie, Sherman 1966- DLB-175

Alexis, Willibald 1798-1871 . . . . DLB-133

Alfred, King 849-899 . . . . DLB-146

Alger, Horatio, Jr. 1832-1899 . . . . . . DLB-42

Algonquin Books of Chapel Hill DLB-46

Algren, Nelson 1909-1981 . . . . . DLB-9; Y-81, 82

Allan, Andrew 1907-1974 . . . . DLB-88

Allan, Ted 1916- DLB-68

Allbeury, Ted 1917- DLB-87

Alldritt, Keith 1935- DLB-14

Allen, Ethan 1738-1789 . . . . DLB-31

Allen, Frederick Lewis 1890-1954 . . . . DLB-137

Allen, Gay Wilson
     1903-1995 . . . . DLB-103; Y-95

Allen, George 1808-1876 . . . . DLB-59

Allen, George [publishing house] DLB-106

Allen, George, and Unwin
     Limited DLB-112

Allen, Grant 1848-1899 . . . . . DLB-70, 92, 178

Allen, Henry W. 1912- Y-85

Allen, Hervey 1889-1949 . . . . DLB-9, 45

Allen, James 1739-1808 . . . . DLB-31

Allen, James Lane 1849-1925 . . . . . . DLB-71

Allen, Jay Presson 1922- DLB-26

Allen, John, and Company DLB-49

Allen, Paula Gunn 1939- DLB-175

Allen, Samuel W. 1917- DLB-41

Allen, Woody 1935- DLB-44

Allende, Isabel 1942- DLB-145

Alline, Henry 1748-1784 . . . . DLB-99

Allingham, Margery 1904-1966 . . . . . DLB-77

Allingham, William 1824-1889 . . . . . DLB-35

Allison, W. L.
     [publishing house] DLB-49

The *Alliterative Morte Arthure* and
     the *Stanzaic Morte Arthur*
     circa 1350-1400 . . . . DLB-146

Allott, Kenneth 1912-1973 . . . . DLB-20

Allston, Washington 1779-1843 . . . . . DLB-1

Almon, John [publishing house] DLB-154

Alonzo, Dámaso 1898-1990 . . . . DLB-108

Alsop, George 1636-post 1673 . . . . . DLB-24

Alsop, Richard 1761-1815 . . . . DLB-37

Altemus, Henry, and Company DLB-49

Altenberg, Peter 1885-1919 . . . . DLB-81

Altolaguirre, Manuel 1905-1959 . . . . . DLB-108

Aluko, T. M. 1918- DLB-117

Alurista 1947- DLB-82

Alvarez, A. 1929- DLB-14, 40

Amadi, Elechi 1934- DLB-117

Amado, Jorge 1912- DLB-113

Ambler, Eric 1909- DLB-77

*America: or, a Poem on the Settlement of the
     British Colonies* (1780?), by Timothy
     Dwight DLB-37

American Conservatory Theatre DLB-7

American Fiction and the 1930s DLB-9

American Humor: A Historical Survey
     East and Northeast
     South and Southwest
     Midwest
     West DLB-11

The American Library in Paris Y-93

American News Company DLB-49

The American Poets' Corner: The First
     Three Years (1983-1986) Y-86

American Proletarian Culture:
     The 1930s DS-11

American Publishing Company DLB-49

American Stationers' Company DLB-49

American Sunday-School Union DLB-49

American Temperance Union DLB-49

American Tract Society DLB-49

The American Trust for the
     British Library Y-96

The American Writers Congress
     (9-12 October 1981) Y-81

The American Writers Congress: A Report
     on Continuing Business Y-81

Ames, Fisher 1758-1808 . . . . DLB-37

Ames, Mary Clemmer 1831-1884 . . . . DLB-23

Amini, Johari M. 1935- DLB-41

Amis, Kingsley 1922-1995
     . . . . DLB-15, 27, 100, 139, Y-96

Amis, Martin 1949- DLB-14

Ammons, A. R. 1926- DLB-5, 165

Amory, Thomas 1691?-1788 . . . . DLB-39

Anaya, Rudolfo A. 1937- DLB-82

Ancrene Riwle circa 1200-1225 . . . . . DLB-146

Andersch, Alfred 1914-1980 . . . . DLB-69

Anderson, Margaret 1886-1973 . . . . DLB-4, 91

Anderson, Maxwell 1888-1959 . . . . . . DLB-7

Anderson, Patrick 1915-1979 . . . . . . DLB-68

Anderson, Paul Y. 1893-1938 . . . . . . DLB-29

Anderson, Poul 1926- DLB-8

Anderson, Robert 1750-1830 . . . . . . DLB-142

Anderson, Robert 1917- DLB-7

Anderson, Sherwood
     1876-1941 . . . . DLB-4, 9, 86; DS-1

Andreae, Johann Valentin
     1586-1654 . . . . DLB-164

Andreas-Salomé, Lou 1861-1937 . . . . DLB-66

Andres, Stefan 1906-1970 . . . . DLB-69

Andreu, Blanca 1959- DLB-134

Andrewes, Lancelot
     1555-1626 . . . . DLB-151, 172

Andrews, Charles M. 1863-1943 . . . . . DLB-17

Andrews, Miles Peter ?-1814 . . . . . . DLB-89

Andrian, Leopold von 1875-1951 . . . . DLB-81

Andrić, Ivo 1892-1975 . . . . DLB-147

Andrieux, Louis (see Aragon, Louis)

Andrus, Silas, and Son DLB-49

Angell, James Burrill 1829-1916 . . . . . DLB-64

Angell, Roger 1920- DLB-171

Angelou, Maya 1928- DLB-38

Anger, Jane flourished 1589 . . . . DLB-136

Angers, Félicité (see Conan, Laure)

Anglo-Norman Literature in the
     Development of Middle English
     Literature DLB-146

The Anglo-Saxon Chronicle
     circa 890-1154 . . . . DLB-146

The "Angry Young Men" DLB-15

Angus and Robertson (UK)
     Limited DLB-112

Anhalt, Edward 1914- DLB-26

Anners, Henry F.
     [publishing house] DLB-49

Annolied between 1077
     and 1081 . . . . DLB-148

Anselm of Canterbury
     1033-1109 . . . . DLB-115

Anstey, F. 1856-1934 . . . . DLB-141, 178

Anthony, Michael 1932- DLB-125

Anthony, Piers 1934- DLB-8

Anthony Burgess's *99 Novels:*
     An Opinion Poll Y-84

Antin, David 1932- DLB-169

Antin, Mary 1881-1949 . . . . Y-84

Anton Ulrich, Duke of Brunswick-Lüneburg
     1633-1714 . . . . DLB-168

Antschel, Paul (see Celan, Paul)

Anyidoho, Kofi 1947- DLB-157

Anzaldúa, Gloria 1942- DLB-122

Anzengruber, Ludwig
     1839-1889 . . . . DLB-129

Apess, William 1798-1839 . . . . DLB-175

Apodaca, Rudy S. 1939- DLB-82

Apollonius Rhodius third century B.C.
. . . . DLB-176

Apple, Max 1941- DLB-130

Appleton, D., and Company DLB-49

Appleton-Century-Crofts. DLB-46

Applewhite, James 1935- DLB-105

Apple-wood Books DLB-46

Aquin, Hubert 1929-1977 . . . . DLB-53

Aquinas, Thomas 1224 or
1225-1274 . . . . DLB-115

Aragon, Louis 1897-1982 . . . . DLB-72

Aralica, Ivan 1930- DLB-181

Aratus of Soli circa 315 B.C.-circa 239 B.C.
. . . . DLB-176

Arbor House Publishing
Company DLB-46

Arbuthnot, John 1667-1735 . . . . . . DLB-101

Arcadia House. DLB-46

Arce, Julio G. (see Ulica, Jorge)

Archer, William 1856-1924 . . . . DLB-10

Archilochhus mid seventh century B.C.E.
. . . . DLB-176

The Archpoet circa 1130?-? DLB-148

Archpriest Avvakum (Petrovich)
1620?-1682 . . . . DLB-150

Arden, John 1930- DLB-13

Arden of Faversham DLB-62

Ardis Publishers. Y-89

Ardizzone, Edward 1900-1979 . . . . . DLB-160

Arellano, Juan Estevan 1947- DLB-122

The Arena Publishing Company DLB-49

Arena Stage DLB-7

Arenas, Reinaldo 1943-1990 . . . . . . DLB-145

Arensberg, Ann 1937- Y-82

Arguedas, José María 1911-1969 . . . . DLB-113

Argueta, Manilio 1936- DLB-145

Arias, Ron 1941- DLB-82

Arishima, Takeo 1878-1923 . . . . . . DLB-180

Aristophanes circa 446 B.C.-circa 446 B.C.-
circa 386 B.C. DLB-176

Aristotle 384 B.C.-322 B.C. DLB-176

Ariyoshi, Sawako 1931-1984 . . . . . DLB-182

Arland, Marcel 1899-1986 . . . . DLB-72

Arlen, Michael
1895-1956 . . . . DLB-36, 77, 162

Armah, Ayi Kwei 1939- DLB-117

Der arme Hartmann
?-after 1150 . . . . DLB-148

Armed Services Editions DLB-46

Armstrong, Richard 1903- DLB-160

Arndt, Ernst Moritz 1769-1860 . . . . . DLB-90

Arnim, Achim von 1781-1831 . . . . . DLB-90

Arnim, Bettina von 1785-1859 . . . . . DLB-90

Arno Press DLB-46

Arnold, Edwin 1832-1904 . . . . DLB-35

Arnold, Edwin L. 1857-1935 . . . . . DLB-178

Arnold, Matthew 1822-1888 . . . . DLB-32, 57

Arnold, Thomas 1795-1842 . . . . DLB-55

Arnold, Edward
[publishing house] DLB-112

Arnow, Harriette Simpson
1908-1986 . . . . DLB-6

Arp, Bill (see Smith, Charles Henry)

Arpino, Giovanni 1927-1987 . . . . . DLB-177

Arreola, Juan José 1918- DLB-113

Arrian circa 89-circa 155 . . . . DLB-176

Arrowsmith, J. W.
[publishing house] DLB-106

Arthur, Timothy Shay
1809-1885 . . . . . . DLB-3, 42, 79; DS-13

The Arthurian Tradition and Its European
Context DLB-138

Artmann, H. C. 1921- DLB-85

Arvin, Newton 1900-1963 . . . . DLB-103

As I See It, by
Carolyn Cassady DLB-16

Asch, Nathan 1902-1964 . . . . DLB-4, 28

Ash, John 1948- DLB-40

Ashbery, John 1927- DLB-5, 165; Y-81

Ashendene Press DLB-112

Asher, Sandy 1942- Y-83

Ashton, Winifred (see Dane, Clemence)

Asimov, Isaac 1920-1992 . . . . . DLB-8; Y-92

Askew, Anne circa 1521-1546 . . . . . DLB-136

Asselin, Olivar 1874-1937 . . . . DLB-92

Asturias, Miguel Angel
1899-1974 . . . . DLB-113

Atheneum Publishers DLB-46

Atherton, Gertrude 1857-1948 . . . . DLB-9, 78

Athlone Press DLB-112

Atkins, Josiah circa 1755-1781 . . . . . DLB-31

Atkins, Russell 1926- DLB-41

The Atlantic Monthly Press DLB-46

Attaway, William 1911-1986 . . . . . . DLB-76

Atwood, Margaret 1939- DLB-53

Aubert, Alvin 1930- DLB-41

Aubert de Gaspé, Phillipe-Ignace-François
1814-1841 . . . . DLB-99

Aubert de Gaspé, Phillipe-Joseph
1786-1871 . . . . DLB-99

Aubin, Napoléon 1812-1890 . . . . . . DLB-99

Aubin, Penelope 1685-circa 1731 . . . . DLB-39

Aubrey-Fletcher, Henry Lancelot
(see Wade, Henry)

Auchincloss, Louis 1917- DLB-2; Y-80

Auden, W. H. 1907-1973 . . . . . . DLB-10, 20

Audio Art in America: A Personal
Memoir Y-85

Audubon, John Woodhouse
1812-1862 . . . . DLB-183

Auerbach, Berthold 1812-1882 . . . . . DLB-133

Auernheimer, Raoul 1876-1948 . . . . . DLB-81

Augustine 354-430 . . . . DLB-115

Austen, Jane 1775-1817 . . . . DLB-116

Austin, Alfred 1835-1913 . . . . DLB-35

Austin, Mary 1868-1934 . . . . DLB-9, 78

Austin, William 1778-1841 . . . . DLB-74

Author-Printers, 1476–1599 . . . . . . DLB-167

The Author's Apology for His Book
(1684), by John Bunyan DLB-39

An Author's Response, by
Ronald Sukenick Y-82

Authors and Newspapers
Association DLB-46

Authors' Publishing Company DLB-49

Avalon Books DLB-46

Avancini, Nicolaus 1611-1686 . . . . . DLB-164

Avendaño, Fausto 1941- DLB-82

Averroëö 1126-1198 . . . . DLB-115

Avery, Gillian 1926- DLB-161

Avicenna 980-1037 . . . . DLB-115

Avison, Margaret 1918- DLB-53

Avon Books DLB-46

Awdry, Wilbert Vere 1911- DLB-160

Awoonor, Kofi 1935- DLB-117

Ayckbourn, Alan 1939- DLB-13

Aymé, Marcel 1902-1967 . . . . DLB-72

Aytoun, Sir Robert 1570-1638 . . . . . DLB-121

Aytoun, William Edmondstoune
1813-1865 . . . . DLB-32, 159

B

B. V. (see Thomson, James)

Babbitt, Irving 1865-1933 . . . . DLB-63

Babbitt, Natalie 1932- DLB-52

Babcock, John [publishing house] DLB-49

Babrius circa 150-200 . . . . DLB-176

Baca, Jimmy Santiago 1952- DLB-122

Bache, Benjamin Franklin
1769-1798 . . . . DLB-43

Bachmann, Ingeborg 1926-1973 . . . . DLB-85

Bacon, Delia 1811-1859 . . . . DLB-1

Bacon, Francis 1561-1626 . . . . DLB-151

Bacon, Roger circa
1214/1220-1292 . . . . DLB-115

Bacon, Sir Nicholas
circa 1510-1579 . . . . DLB-132

Bacon, Thomas circa 1700-1768 . . . . . DLB-31

Badger, Richard G.,
and Company. DLB-49

Bage, Robert 1728-1801. . . . . DLB-39

Bagehot, Walter 1826-1877. . . . . . . DLB-55

Bagley, Desmond 1923-1983 . . . . . . DLB-87

Bagnold, Enid 1889-1981 . . . . . DLB-13, 160

Bagryana, Elisaveta 1893-1991 . . . . . DLB-147

Bahr, Hermann 1863-1934 . . . . . DLB-81, 118

Bailey, Alfred Goldsworthy
1905- DLB-68

Bailey, Francis
[publishing house]. DLB-49

Bailey, H. C. 1878-1961 . . . . DLB-77

Bailey, Jacob 1731-1808. . . . . DLB-99

Bailey, Paul 1937- DLB-14

Bailey, Philip James 1816-1902 . . . . . DLB-32

Baillargeon, Pierre 1916-1967 . . . . . . DLB-88

Baillie, Hugh 1890-1966 . . . . DLB-29

Baillie, Joanna 1762-1851 . . . . DLB-93

Bailyn, Bernard 1922- DLB-17

Bainbridge, Beryl 1933- DLB-14

Baird, Irene 1901-1981 . . . . DLB-68

Baker, Augustine 1575-1641 . . . . . . DLB-151

Baker, Carlos 1909-1987 . . . . DLB-103

Baker, David 1954- DLB-120

Baker, Herschel C. 1914-1990 . . . . . DLB-111

Baker, Houston A., Jr. 1943- DLB-67

Baker, Samuel White 1821-1893 . . . . DLB-166

Baker, Walter H., Company
("Baker's Plays") DLB-49

The Baker and Taylor
Company DLB-49

Balaban, John 1943- DLB-120

Bald, Wambly 1902- DLB-4

Balde, Jacob 1604-1668 . . . . DLB-164

Balderston, John 1889-1954. . . . . . . DLB-26

Baldwin, James
1924-1987 . . . . DLB-2, 7, 33; Y-87

Baldwin, Joseph Glover
1815-1864 . . . . DLB-3, 11

Baldwin, Richard and Anne
[publishing house] DLB-170

Baldwin, William
circa 1515-1563 . . . . DLB-132

Bale, John 1495-1563 . . . . DLB-132

Balestrini, Nanni 1935- DLB-128

Ballantine Books. DLB-46

Ballantyne, R. M. 1825-1894 . . . . . . DLB-163

Ballard, J. G. 1930- DLB-14

Ballerini, Luigi 1940- DLB-128

Ballou, Maturin Murray
1820-1895 . . . . DLB-79

Ballou, Robert O.
[publishing house] DLB-46

Balzac, Honoré de 1799-1855. . . . . DLB-119

Bambara, Toni Cade 1939- DLB-38

Bancroft, A. L., and
Company DLB-49

Bancroft, George
1800-1891 . . . . DLB-1, 30, 59

Bancroft, Hubert Howe
1832-1918 . . . . DLB-47, 140

Bangs, John Kendrick
1862-1922 . . . . DLB-11, 79

Banim, John
1798-1842. . . . . DLB-116, 158, 159

Banim, Michael 1796-1874. . . . . DLB-158, 159

Banks, John circa 1653-1706 . . . . . . DLB-80

Banks, Russell 1940- DLB-130

Bannerman, Helen 1862-1946 . . . . . . DLB-141

Bantam Books. DLB-46

Banti, Anna 1895-1985 . . . . DLB-177

Banville, John 1945- DLB-14

Baraka, Amiri
1934- DLB-5, 7, 16, 38; DS-8

Barbauld, Anna Laetitia
1743-1825 . . . . . DLB-107, 109, 142, 158

Barbeau, Marius 1883-1969. . . . . . . DLB-92

Barber, John Warner 1798-1885 . . . . . DLB-30

Bàrberi Squarotti, Giorgio
1929- DLB-128

Barbey d'Aurevilly, Jules-Amédée
1808-1889 . . . . DLB-119

Barbour, John circa 1316-1395 . . . . . DLB-146

Barbour, Ralph Henry
1870-1944 . . . . DLB-22

Barbusse, Henri 1873-1935 . . . . . . DLB-65

Barclay, Alexander
circa 1475-1552 . . . . DLB-132

Barclay, E. E., and Company DLB-49

Bardeen, C. W.
[publishing house]. DLB-49

Barham, Richard Harris
1788-1845 . . . . DLB-159

Baring, Maurice 1874-1945 . . . . DLB-34

Baring-Gould, Sabine 1834-1924 . . . . DLB-156

Barker, A. L. 1918- DLB-14, 139

Barker, George 1913-1991 . . . . . . DLB-20

Barker, Harley Granville
1877-1946 . . . . DLB-10

Barker, Howard 1946- DLB-13

Barker, James Nelson 1784-1858 . . . . DLB-37

Barker, Jane 1652-1727 . . . . . . DLB-39, 131

Barker, Lady Mary Anne
1831-1911 . . . . DLB-166

Barker, William
circa 1520-after 1576 . . . . DLB-132

Barker, Arthur, Limited DLB-112

Barkov, Ivan Semenovich
1732-1768 . . . . DLB-150

Barks, Coleman 1937- DLB-5

Barlach, Ernst 1870-1938 . . . . . DLB-56, 118

Barlow, Joel 1754-1812 . . . . DLB-37

Barnard, John 1681-1770 . . . . DLB-24

Barne, Kitty (Mary Catherine Barne)
1883-1957 . . . . DLB-160

Barnes, Barnabe 1571-1609 . . . . . . DLB-132

Barnes, Djuna 1892-1982. . . . . . DLB-4, 9, 45

Barnes, Jim 1933- DLB-175

Barnes, Julian 1946- Y-93

Barnes, Margaret Ayer 1886-1967. . . . DLB-9

Barnes, Peter 1931- DLB-13

Barnes, William 1801-1886 . . . . . . DLB-32

Barnes, A. S., and Company. DLB-49

Barnes and Noble Books. DLB-46

Barnet, Miguel 1940- DLB-145

Barney, Natalie 1876-1972 . . . . DLB-4

Barnfield, Richard 1574-1627 . . . . . DLB-172

Baron, Richard W.,
Publishing Company DLB-46

Barr, Robert 1850-1912. . . . . . . DLB-70, 92

Barral, Carlos 1928-1989 . . . . DLB-134

Barrax, Gerald William
1933- DLB-41, 120

Barrès, Maurice 1862-1923 . . . . . . DLB-123

Barrett, Eaton Stannard
1786-1820 . . . . DLB-116

Barrie, J. M. 1860-1937 . . . . DLB-10, 141, 156

Barrie and Jenkins. DLB-112

Barrio, Raymond 1921- DLB-82

Barrios, Gregg 1945- DLB-122

Barry, Philip 1896-1949 . . . . DLB-7

Barry, Robertine (see Françoise)

Barse and Hopkins DLB-46

Barstow, Stan 1928- DLB-14, 139

Barth, John 1930- DLB-2

Barthelme, Donald
1931-1989 . . . . DLB-2; Y-80, 89

Barthelme, Frederick 1943- Y-85

Bartholomew, Frank 1898-1985 . . . . . DLB-127

Bartlett, John 1820-1905 . . . . DLB-1

Bartol, Cyrus Augustus 1813-1900 . . . . DLB-1

Barton, Bernard 1784-1849 . . . . DLB-96

Barton, Thomas Pennant
1803-1869 . . . . DLB-140

Bartram, John 1699-1777 . . . . DLB-31

Bartram, William 1739-1823 . . . . DLB-37

Basic Books DLB-46

Basille, Theodore (see Becon, Thomas)

Bass, T. J. 1932- Y-81

Bassani, Giorgio 1916- DLB-128, 177

Basse, William circa 1583-1653 . . . . DLB-121

Bassett, John Spencer 1867-1928 . . . . . DLB-17

Bassler, Thomas Joseph (see Bass, T. J.)

Bate, Walter Jackson
1918- DLB-67, 103

Bateman, Christopher
[publishing house] DLB-170

Bateman, Stephen
circa 1510-1584 . . . . DLB-136

Bates, H. E. 1905-1974 . . . . DLB-162

Bates, Katharine Lee 1859-1929 . . . . . DLB-71

Batsford, B. T.
[publishing house] DLB-106

Battiscombe, Georgina 1905- DLB-155

The Battle of Maldon circa 1000 . . . . DLB-146

Bauer, Bruno 1809-1882 . . . . DLB-133

Bauer, Wolfgang 1941- DLB-124

Baum, L. Frank 1856-1919 . . . . DLB-22

Baum, Vicki 1888-1960 . . . . DLB-85

Baumbach, Jonathan 1933- Y-80

Bausch, Richard 1945- DLB-130

Bawden, Nina 1925- DLB-14, 161

Bax, Clifford 1886-1962 . . . . . . DLB-10, 100

Baxter, Charles 1947- DLB-130

Bayer, Eleanor (see Perry, Eleanor)

Bayer, Konrad 1932-1964 . . . . DLB-85

Baynes, Pauline 1922- DLB-160

Bazin, Hervé 1911- DLB-83

Beach, Sylvia 1887-1962 . . . . . DLB-4; DS-15

Beacon Press DLB-49

Beadle and Adams DLB-49

Beagle, Peter S. 1939- Y-80

Beal, M. F. 1937- Y-81

Beale, Howard K. 1899-1959 . . . . . . DLB-17

Beard, Charles A. 1874-1948 . . . . . . DLB-17

A Beat Chronology: The First Twenty-five
Years, 1944-1969 . . . . DLB-16

Beattie, Ann 1947- Y-82

Beattie, James 1735-1803 . . . . DLB-109

Beauchemin, Nérée 1850-1931 . . . . . . DLB-92

Beauchemin, Yves 1941- DLB-60

Beaugrand, Honoré 1848-1906 . . . . . DLB-99

Beaulieu, Victor-Lévy 1945- DLB-53

Beaumont, Francis circa 1584-1616
and Fletcher, John 1579-1625 . . . . DLB-58

Beaumont, Sir John 1583?-1627 . . . . DLB-121

Beaumont, Joseph 1616–1699 . . . . . DLB-126

Beauvoir, Simone de
1908-1986 . . . . DLB-72; Y-86

Becher, Ulrich 1910- DLB-69

Becker, Carl 1873-1945 . . . . DLB-17

Becker, Jurek 1937- DLB-75

Becker, Jurgen 1932- DLB-75

Beckett, Samuel
1906-1989 . . . . DLB-13, 15; Y-90

Beckford, William 1760-1844 . . . . . . DLB-39

Beckham, Barry 1944- DLB-33

Becon, Thomas circa 1512-1567 . . . . DLB-136

Bećković, Matija 1939- DLB-181

Beddoes, Thomas 1760-1808 . . . . . DLB-158

Beddoes, Thomas Lovell
1803-1849 . . . . DLB-96

Bede circa 673-735 . . . . DLB-146

Beecher, Catharine Esther
1800-1878 . . . . DLB-1

Beecher, Henry Ward
1813-1887 . . . . DLB-3, 43

Beer, George L. 1872-1920 . . . . . . DLB-47

Beer, Johann 1655-1700 . . . . DLB-168

Beer, Patricia 1919- DLB-40

Beerbohm, Max 1872-1956 . . . . DLB-34, 100

Beer-Hofmann, Richard
1866-1945 . . . . DLB-81

Beers, Henry A. 1847-1926 . . . . . . DLB-71

Beeton, S. O.
[publishing house] DLB-106

Bégon, Elisabeth 1696-1755 . . . . . . DLB-99

Behan, Brendan 1923-1964 . . . . . . DLB-13

Behn, Aphra
1640?-1689 . . . . DLB-39, 80, 131

Behn, Harry 1898-1973 . . . . DLB-61

Behrman, S. N. 1893-1973 . . . . . DLB-7, 44

Belaney, Archibald Stansfeld (see Grey Owl)

Belasco, David 1853-1931 . . . . DLB-7

Belford, Clarke and Company DLB-49

Belitt, Ben 1911- DLB-5

Belknap, Jeremy 1744-1798 . . . . . DLB-30, 37

Bell, Clive 1881-1964 . . . . DS-10

Bell, Gertrude Margaret Lowthian
1868-1926 . . . . DLB-174

Bell, James Madison 1826-1902 . . . . . DLB-50

Bell, Marvin 1937- DLB-5

Bell, Millicent 1919- DLB-111

Bell, Quentin 1910- DLB-155

Bell, Vanessa 1879-1961 . . . . DS-10

Bell, George, and Sons DLB-106

Bell, Robert [publishing house] DLB-49

Bellamy, Edward 1850-1898 . . . . . . DLB-12

Bellamy, John [publishing house] DLB-170

Bellamy, Joseph 1719-1790 . . . . . . DLB-31

Bellezza, Dario 1944- DLB-128

La Belle Assemblée 1806-1837 . . . . . . DLB-110

Belloc, Hilaire
1870-1953 . . . . . DLB-19, 100, 141, 174

Bellow, Saul
1915- DLB-2, 28; Y-82; DS-3

Belmont Productions DLB-46

Bemelmans, Ludwig 1898-1962 . . . . . DLB-22

Bemis, Samuel Flagg 1891-1973 . . . . . DLB-17

Bemrose, William
[publishing house] DLB-106

Benchley, Robert 1889-1945 . . . . . . DLB-11

Benedetti, Mario 1920- DLB-113

Benedictus, David 1938- DLB-14

Benedikt, Michael 1935- DLB-5

Benét, Stephen Vincent
1898-1943 . . . . DLB-4, 48, 102

Benét, William Rose 1886-1950 . . . . . DLB-45

Benford, Gregory 1941- Y-82

Benjamin, Park 1809-1864 . . . . DLB-3, 59, 73

Benlowes, Edward 1602-1676 . . . . . DLB-126

Benn, Gottfried 1886-1956 . . . . . . DLB-56

Benn Brothers Limited DLB-106

Bennett, Arnold
1867-1931 . . . . DLB-10, 34, 98, 135

Bennett, Charles 1899- DLB-44

Bennett, Gwendolyn 1902- DLB-51

Bennett, Hal 1930- DLB-33

Bennett, James Gordon 1795-1872 . . . . DLB-43

Bennett, James Gordon, Jr.
1841-1918 . . . . DLB-23

Bennett, John 1865-1956 . . . . DLB-42

Bennett, Louise 1919- DLB-117

Benoit, Jacques 1941- DLB-60

Benson, A. C. 1862-1925 . . . . DLB-98

Benson, E. F. 1867-1940 . . . . . DLB-135, 153

Benson, Jackson J. 1930- DLB-111

Benson, Robert Hugh
1871-1914 . . . . DLB-153

Benson, Stella 1892-1933 . . . . . DLB-36, 162

Bent, James Theodore
1852-1897 . . . . DLB-174

Bent, Mabel Virginia Anna ?-? DLB-174

Bentham, Jeremy
1748-1832 . . . . DLB-107, 158

Bentley, E. C. 1875-1956 . . . . DLB-70

Bentley, Richard
[publishing house] DLB-106

Benton, Robert 1932- and Newman,
David 1937- DLB-44

Benziger Brothers DLB-49

Beowulf circa 900-1000
or 790-825 . . . . DLB-146

Beresford, Anne 1929- DLB-40

Beresford, John Davys
1873-1947 . . . . DLB-162; 178

Beresford-Howe, Constance
1922- DLB-88

Berford, R. G., Company DLB-49

Berg, Stephen 1934- DLB-5

Bergengruen, Werner 1892-1964 . . . . . DLB-56

Berger, John 1926- DLB-14

Berger, Meyer 1898-1959 . . . . DLB-29

Berger, Thomas 1924- DLB-2; Y-80

Berkeley, Anthony 1893-1971 . . . . . DLB-77

Berkeley, George 1685-1753 . . . . DLB-31, 101

The Berkley Publishing
Corporation DLB-46

Berlin, Lucia 1936- DLB-130

Bernal, Vicente J. 1888-1915 . . . . . . DLB-82

Bernanos, Georges 1888-1948 . . . . . DLB-72

Bernard, Harry 1898-1979 . . . . DLB-92

Bernard, John 1756-1828 . . . . DLB-37

Bernard of Chartres
circa 1060-1124? DLB-115

Bernari, Carlo 1909-1992 . . . . DLB-177

Bernhard, Thomas
1931-1989 . . . . DLB-85, 124

Bernstein, Charles 1950- DLB-169

Berriault, Gina 1926- DLB-130

Berrigan, Daniel 1921- DLB-5

Berrigan, Ted 1934-1983 . . . . . . DLB-5, 169

Berry, Wendell 1934- DLB-5, 6

Berryman, John 1914-1972 . . . . DLB-48

Bersianik, Louky 1930- DLB-60

Berthelet, Thomas
[publishing house] DLB-170

Berto, Giuseppe 1914-1978 . . . . . . DLB-177

Bertolucci, Attilio 1911- DLB-128

Berton, Pierre 1920- DLB-68

Besant, Sir Walter 1836-1901 . . . . . DLB-135

Bessette, Gerard 1920- DLB-53

Bessie, Alvah 1904-1985 . . . . DLB-26

Bester, Alfred 1913-1987 . . . . DLB-8

The Bestseller Lists: An Assessment Y-84

Betham-Edwards, Matilda Barbara (see Edwards,
Matilda Barbara Betham-)

Betjeman, John 1906-1984 . . . . . DLB-20; Y-84

Betocchi, Carlo 1899-1986 . . . . DLB-128

Bettarini, Mariella 1942- DLB-128

Betts, Doris 1932- Y-82

Beveridge, Albert J. 1862-1927 . . . . . DLB-17

Beverley, Robert
circa 1673-1722 . . . . DLB-24, 30

Beyle, Marie-Henri (see Stendhal)

Bianco, Margery Williams
1881-1944 . . . . DLB-160

Bibaud, Adèle 1854-1941 . . . . DLB-92

Bibaud, Michel 1782-1857 . . . . DLB-99

Bibliographical and Textual Scholarship
Since World War II Y-89

The Bicentennial of James Fenimore
Cooper: An International
Celebration Y-89

Bichsel, Peter 1935- DLB-75

Bickerstaff, Isaac John
1733-circa 1808 . . . . DLB-89

Biddle, Drexel [publishing house] DLB-49

Bidermann, Jacob
1577 or 1578-1639 . . . . DLB-164

Bidwell, Walter Hilliard
1798-1881 . . . . DLB-79

Bienek, Horst 1930- DLB-75

Bierbaum, Otto Julius 1865-1910 . . . . DLB-66

Bierce, Ambrose
1842-1914? DLB-11, 12, 23, 71, 74

Bigelow, William F. 1879-1966 . . . . . DLB-91

Biggle, Lloyd, Jr. 1923- DLB-8

Bigiaretti, Libero 1905-1993 . . . . . . DLB-177

Biglow, Hosea (see Lowell, James Russell)

Bigongiari, Piero 1914- DLB-128

Billinger, Richard 1890-1965 . . . . . . DLB-124

Billings, John Shaw 1898-1975 . . . . . DLB-137

Billings, Josh (see Shaw, Henry Wheeler)

Binding, Rudolf G. 1867-1938 . . . . . DLB-66

Bingham, Caleb 1757-1817 . . . . DLB-42

Bingham, George Barry
1906-1988 . . . . DLB-127

Bingley, William
[publishing house] DLB-154

Binyon, Laurence 1869-1943 . . . . . . DLB-19

Biographia Brittanica DLB-142

Biographical Documents I Y-84

Biographical Documents II Y-85

Bioren, John [publishing house] DLB-49

Bioy Casares, Adolfo 1914- DLB-113

Bird, Isabella Lucy 1831-1904 . . . . . DLB-166

Bird, William 1888-1963 . . . . . DLB-4; DS-15

Birken, Sigmund von 1626-1681 . . . . DLB-164

Birney, Earle 1904- DLB-88

Birrell, Augustine 1850-1933 . . . . . . DLB-98

Bisher, Furman 1918- DLB-171

Bishop, Elizabeth 1911-1979 . . . . DLB-5, 169

Bishop, John Peale 1892-1944 . . . DLB-4, 9, 45

Bismarck, Otto von 1815-1898 . . . . . DLB-129

Bisset, Robert 1759-1805 . . . . DLB-142

Bissett, Bill 1939- DLB-53

Bitzius, Albert (see Gotthelf, Jeremias)

Black, David (D. M.) 1941- DLB-40

Black, Winifred 1863-1936 . . . . DLB-25

Black, Walter J.
[publishing house] DLB-46

The Black Aesthetic: Background DS-8

The Black Arts Movement, by
Larry Neal DLB-38

Black Theaters and Theater Organizations in
America, 1961-1982:
A Research List DLB-38

Black Theatre: A Forum
[excerpts] DLB-38

Blackamore, Arthur 1679-? DLB-24, 39

Blackburn, Alexander L. 1929- Y-85

Blackburn, Paul 1926-1971 . . . . DLB-16; Y-81

Blackburn, Thomas 1916-1977 . . . . . DLB-27

Blackmore, R. D. 1825-1900 . . . . . . DLB-18

Blackmore, Sir Richard
1654-1729 . . . . DLB-131

Blackmur, R. P. 1904-1965 . . . . DLB-63

Blackwell, Basil, Publisher DLB-106

Blackwood, Algernon Henry
1869-1951 . . . . DLB-153, 156, 178

Blackwood, Caroline 1931- DLB-14

Blackwood, William, and
Sons, Ltd. DLB-154

Blackwood's Edinburgh Magazine
1817-1980 . . . . DLB-110

Blair, Eric Arthur (see Orwell, George)

Blair, Francis Preston 1791-1876 . . . . . DLB-43

Blair, James circa 1655-1743 . . . . . . DLB-24

Blair, John Durburrow 1759-1823 . . . . DLB-37

Blais, Marie-Claire 1939- DLB-53

Blaise, Clark 1940- DLB-53

Blake, Nicholas 1904-1972 . . . . DLB-77
(see Day Lewis, C.)

Blake, William
1757-1827 . . . . DLB-93, 154, 163

The Blakiston Company DLB-49

Blanchot, Maurice 1907- DLB-72

Blanckenburg, Christian Friedrich von
1744-1796 . . . . DLB-94

Blaser, Robin 1925- DLB-165

Bledsoe, Albert Taylor
1809-1877 . . . . DLB-3, 79

Blelock and Company DLB-49

Blennerhassett, Margaret Agnew
1773-1842 . . . . DLB-99

Bles, Geoffrey
[publishing house] DLB-112

Blessington, Marguerite, Countess of
1789-1849 . . . . DLB-166

The Blickling Homilies
circa 971 . . . . DLB-146

Blish, James 1921-1975 . . . . DLB-8

Bliss, E., and E. White
[publishing house] DLB-49

Bliven, Bruce 1889-1977 . . . . DLB-137

Bloch, Robert 1917-1994 . . . . DLB-44

Block, Rudolph (see Lessing, Bruno)

Blondal, Patricia 1926-1959 . . . . DLB-88

Bloom, Harold 1930- DLB-67

Bloomer, Amelia 1818-1894 . . . . . . DLB-79

Bloomfield, Robert 1766-1823 . . . . . DLB-93

Bloomsbury Group DS-10

Blotner, Joseph 1923- DLB-111

Bloy, Léon 1846-1917 . . . . DLB-123

Blume, Judy 1938- DLB-52

Blunck, Hans Friedrich 1888-1961 . . . . DLB-66

Blunden, Edmund
1896-1974 . . . . DLB-20, 100, 155

Blunt, Lady Anne Isabella Noel
1837-1917 . . . . DLB-174

Blunt, Wilfrid Scawen
1840-1922 . . . . DLB-19, 174

Bly, Nellie (see Cochrane, Elizabeth)

Bly, Robert 1926- DLB-5

Blyton, Enid 1897-1968 . . . . DLB-160

Boaden, James 1762-1839 . . . . DLB-89

Boas, Frederick S. 1862-1957 . . . . . DLB-149

The Bobbs-Merrill Archive at the
Lilly Library, Indiana University Y-90

The Bobbs-Merrill Company DLB-46

Bobrov, Semen Sergeevich
1763?-1810 . . . . DLB-150

Bobrowski, Johannes 1917-1965 . . . . . DLB-75

Bodenheim, Maxwell 1892-1954 . . . DLB-9, 45

Bodenstedt, Friedrich von
1819-1892 . . . . DLB-129

Bodini, Vittorio 1914-1970 . . . . . . DLB-128

Bodkin, M. McDonnell
1850-1933 . . . . DLB-70

Bodley Head DLB-112

Bodmer, Johann Jakob 1698-1783 . . . . DLB-97

Bodmershof, Imma von 1895-1982 . . . DLB-85

Bodsworth, Fred 1918- DLB-68

Boehm, Sydney 1908- DLB-44

Boer, Charles 1939- DLB-5

Boethius circa 480-circa 524 . . . . . . DLB-115

Boethius of Dacia circa 1240-? DLB-115

Bogan, Louise 1897-1970 . . . . . . DLB-45, 169

Bogarde, Dirk 1921- DLB-14

Bogdanovich, Ippolit Fedorovich
circa 1743-1803 . . . . DLB-150

Bogue, David [publishing house] DLB-106

Böhme, Jakob 1575-1624 . . . . DLB-164

Bohn, H. G. [publishing house] DLB-106

Bohse, August 1661-1742 . . . . DLB-168

Boie, Heinrich Christian
1744-1806 . . . . DLB-94

Bok, Edward W. 1863-1930 . . . . . . DLB-91

Boland, Eavan 1944- DLB-40

Bolingbroke, Henry St. John, Viscount
1678-1751 . . . . DLB-101

Böll, Heinrich 1917-1985 . . . . . Y-85, DLB-69

Bolling, Robert 1738-1775 . . . . DLB-31

Bolotov, Andrei Timofeevich
1738-1833 . . . . DLB-150

Bolt, Carol 1941- DLB-60

Bolt, Robert 1924- DLB-13

Bolton, Herbert E. 1870-1953 . . . . . DLB-17

Bonaventura DLB-90

Bonaventure circa 1217-1274 . . . . . . DLB-115

Bonaviri, Giuseppe 1924- DLB-177

Bond, Edward 1934- DLB-13

Bond, Michael 1926- DLB-161

Bonnin, Gertrude Simmons (see Zitkala-Ša)

Boni, Albert and Charles
[publishing house] DLB-46

Boni and Liveright DLB-46

Robert Bonner's Sons DLB-49

Bonsanti, Alessandro 1904-1984 . . . . DLB-177

Bontemps, Arna 1902-1973 . . . . . DLB-48, 51

The Book Arts Press at the University
of Virginia Y-96

The Book League of America DLB-46

Book Reviewing in America: I Y-87

Book Reviewing in America: II Y-88

Book Reviewing in America: III Y-89

Book Reviewing in America: IV Y-90

Book Reviewing in America: V Y-91

Book Reviewing in America: VI Y-92

Book Reviewing in America: VII Y-93

Book Reviewing in America: VIII Y-94

Book Reviewing in America and the
Literary Scene Y-95

Book Reviewing and the
Literary Scene Y-96

Book Supply Company DLB-49

The Book Trade History Group Y-93

The Booker Prize Y-96

The Booker Prize
Address by Anthony Thwaite,
Chairman of the Booker Prize Judges
Comments from Former Booker
Prize Winners Y-86

Boorde, Andrew circa 1490-1549 . . . . DLB-136

Boorstin, Daniel J. 1914- DLB-17

Booth, Mary L. 1831-1889 . . . . DLB-79

Booth, Philip 1925- Y-82

Booth, Wayne C. 1921- DLB-67

Borchardt, Rudolf 1877-1945 . . . . . . DLB-66

Borchert, Wolfgang
1921-1947 . . . . DLB-69, 124

Borel, Pétrus 1809-1859 . . . . DLB-119

Borges, Jorge Luis
1899-1986 . . . . DLB-113; Y-86

Börne, Ludwig 1786-1837 . . . . DLB-90

Borrow, George
1803-1881 . . . . DLB-21, 55, 166

Bosch, Juan 1909- DLB-145

Bosco, Henri 1888-1976 . . . . DLB-72

Bosco, Monique 1927- DLB-53

Boston, Lucy M. 1892-1990 . . . . . . DLB-161

Boswell, James 1740-1795 . . . . . DLB-104, 142

Botev, Khristo 1847-1876 . . . . DLB-147

Bote, Hermann
circa 1460-circa 1520 . . . . DLB-179

Botta, Anne C. Lynch 1815-1891 . . . . . DLB-3

Bottomley, Gordon 1874-1948 . . . . . . DLB-10

Bottoms, David 1949- DLB-120; Y-83

Bottrall, Ronald 1906- DLB-20

Boucher, Anthony 1911-1968 . . . . . . DLB-8

Boucher, Jonathan 1738-1804 . . . . . . DLB-31

Boucher de Boucherville, George
1814-1894 . . . . DLB-99

Boudreau, Daniel (see Coste, Donat)

Bourassa, Napoléon 1827-1916 . . . . . DLB-99

Bourget, Paul 1852-1935 . . . . DLB-123

Bourinot, John George 1837-1902 . . . . DLB-99

Bourjaily, Vance 1922- DLB-2, 143

Bourne, Edward Gaylord
1860-1908 . . . . DLB-47

Bourne, Randolph 1886-1918 . . . . . . DLB-63

Bousoño, Carlos 1923- DLB-108

Bousquet, Joë 1897-1950 . . . . DLB-72

Bova, Ben 1932- Y-81

Bovard, Oliver K. 1872-1945 . . . . . . DLB-25

Bove, Emmanuel 1898-1945 . . . . . . DLB-72

Bowen, Elizabeth 1899-1973 . . . . DLB-15, 162

Bowen, Francis 1811-1890 . . . . . . DLB-1, 59

Bowen, John 1924- DLB-13

Bowen, Marjorie 1886-1952 . . . . . . DLB-153

Bowen-Merrill Company DLB-49

Bowering, George 1935- DLB-53

Bowers, Claude G. 1878-1958 . . . . . DLB-17

Bowers, Edgar 1924- DLB-5

Bowers, Fredson Thayer
1905-1991 . . . . DLB-140; Y-91

Bowles, Paul 1910- DLB-5, 6

Bowles, Samuel III 1826-1878 . . . . . DLB-43

Bowles, William Lisles 1762-1850 . . . . DLB-93

Bowman, Louise Morey
1882-1944 . . . . DLB-68

Boyd, James 1888-1944 . . . . DLB-9

Boyd, John 1919- DLB-8

Boyd, Thomas 1898-1935 . . . . DLB-9

Boyesen, Hjalmar Hjorth
1848-1895. . . . . DLB-12, 71; DS-13

Boyle, Kay
1902-1992 . . . . . DLB-4, 9, 48, 86; Y-93

Boyle, Roger, Earl of Orrery
1621-1679 . . . . DLB-80

Boyle, T. Coraghessan 1948- Y-86

Božić, Mirko 1919- DLB-181

Brackenbury, Alison 1953- DLB-40

Brackenridge, Hugh Henry
1748-1816. . . . . DLB-11, 37

Brackett, Charles 1892-1969 . . . . DLB-26

Brackett, Leigh 1915-1978 . . . . . . DLB-8, 26

Bradburn, John
[publishing house]. DLB-49

Bradbury, Malcolm 1932- DLB-14

Bradbury, Ray 1920- DLB-2, 8

Bradbury and Evans. DLB-106

Braddon, Mary Elizabeth
1835-1915 . . . . DLB-18, 70, 156

Bradford, Andrew 1686-1742 . . . . DLB-43, 73

Bradford, Gamaliel 1863-1932 . . . . . . DLB-17

Bradford, John 1749-1830. . . . . DLB-43

Bradford, Roark 1896-1948. . . . . . . DLB-86

Bradford, William 1590-1657 . . . . DLB-24, 30

Bradford, William III
1719-1791. . . . . DLB-43, 73

Bradlaugh, Charles 1833-1891 . . . . . DLB-57

Bradley, David 1950- DLB-33

Bradley, Marion Zimmer 1930- DLB-8

Bradley, William Aspenwall
1878-1939. . . . . DLB-4

Bradley, Ira, and Company DLB-49

Bradley, J. W., and Company DLB-49

Bradstreet, Anne
1612 or 1613-1672 . . . . DLB-24

Bradwardine, Thomas circa
1295-1349 . . . . DLB-115

Brady, Frank 1924-1986. . . . . DLB-111

Brady, Frederic A.
[publishing house]. DLB-49

Bragg, Melvyn 1939- DLB-14

Brainard, Charles H.
[publishing house]. DLB-49

Braine, John 1922-1986 . . . . . DLB-15; Y-86

Braithwait, Richard 1588-1673 . . . . DLB-151

Braithwaite, William Stanley
1878-1962. . . . . DLB-50, 54

Braker, Ulrich 1735-1798. . . . . DLB-94

Bramah, Ernest 1868-1942 . . . . . . DLB-70

Branagan, Thomas 1774-1843 . . . . . DLB-37

Branch, William Blackwell
1927- DLB-76

Branden Press. DLB-46

Brant, Sebastian 1457-1521 . . . . . DLB-179

Brassey, Lady Annie (Allnutt)
1839-1887 . . . . DLB-166

Brathwaite, Edward Kamau
1930- DLB-125

Brault, Jacques 1933- DLB-53

Braun, Volker 1939- DLB-75

Brautigan, Richard
1935-1984 . . . . DLB-2, 5; Y-80, 84

Braxton, Joanne M. 1950- DLB-41

Bray, Anne Eliza 1790-1883. . . . . DLB-116

Bray, Thomas 1656-1730. . . . . . . DLB-24

Braziller, George
[publishing house] DLB-46

The Bread Loaf Writers'
Conference 1983 . . . . Y-84

The Break-Up of the Novel (1922),
by John Middleton Murry. DLB-36

Breasted, James Henry 1865-1935 . . . . DLB-47

Brecht, Bertolt 1898-1956. . . . . DLB-56, 124

Bredel, Willi 1901-1964. . . . . DLB-56

Breitinger, Johann Jakob
1701-1776. . . . . DLB-97

Bremser, Bonnie 1939- DLB-16

Bremser, Ray 1934- DLB-16

Brentano, Bernard von
1901-1964. . . . . DLB-56

Brentano, Clemens 1778-1842 . . . . . DLB-90

Brentano's DLB-49

Brenton, Howard 1942- DLB-13

Breton, André 1896-1966. . . . . DLB-65

Breton, Nicholas
circa 1555-circa 1626 . . . . DLB-136

The Breton Lays
1300-early fifteenth century DLB-146

Brewer, Warren and Putnam DLB-46

Brewster, Elizabeth 1922- DLB-60

Bridge, Horatio 1806-1893. . . . . . . DLB-183

Bridgers, Sue Ellen 1942- DLB-52

Bridges, Robert 1844-1930 . . . . . DLB-19, 98

Bridie, James 1888-1951. . . . . DLB-10

Bright, Mary Chavelita Dunne
(see Egerton, George)

Brimmer, B. J., Company DLB-46

Brines, Francisco 1932- DLB-134

Brinley, George, Jr. 1817-1875 . . . . DLB-140

Brinnin, John Malcolm 1916- DLB-48

Brisbane, Albert 1809-1890. . . . . . . DLB-3

Brisbane, Arthur 1864-1936. . . . . . DLB-25

British Academy DLB-112

The British Library and the Regular
Readers' Group Y-91

The British Critic 1793-1843. . . . . . DLB-110

The British Review and London
Critical Journal 1811-1825 . . . . . DLB-110

Brito, Aristeo 1942- DLB-122

Broadway Publishing Company DLB-46

Broch, Hermann 1886-1951. . . . . DLB-85, 124

Brochu, André 1942- DLB-53

Brock, Edwin 1927- DLB-40

Brockes, Barthold Heinrich
1680-1747 . . . . DLB-168

Brod, Max 1884-1968. . . . . DLB-81

Brodber, Erna 1940- DLB-157

Brodhead, John R. 1814-1873 . . . . . DLB-30

Brodkey, Harold 1930- DLB-130

Broeg, Bob 1918- DLB-171

Brome, Richard circa 1590-1652 . . . . DLB-58

Brome, Vincent 1910- DLB-155

Bromfield, Louis 1896-1956 . . . DLB-4, 9, 86

Broner, E. M. 1930- DLB-28

Bronk, William 1918- DLB-165

Bronnen, Arnolt 1895-1959 . . . . . DLB-124

Brontë, Anne 1820-1849 . . . . DLB-21

Brontë, Charlotte 1816-1855 . . . . DLB-21, 159

Brontë, Emily 1818-1848. . . . . . DLB-21, 32

Brooke, Frances 1724-1789 . . . . DLB-39, 99

Brooke, Henry 1703?-1783. . . . . . . DLB-39

Brooke, L. Leslie 1862-1940 . . . . . DLB-141

Brooke, Margaret, Ranee of Sarawak
1849-1936 . . . . DLB-174

Brooke, Rupert 1887-1915 . . . . . . DLB-19

Brooker, Bertram 1888-1955 . . . . . DLB-88

Brooke-Rose, Christine 1926- DLB-14

Brookner, Anita 1928- Y-87

Brooks, Charles Timothy
1813-1883. . . . . DLB-1

Brooks, Cleanth 1906-1994 . . . . DLB-63; Y-94

Brooks, Gwendolyn
1917- DLB-5, 76, 165

Brooks, Jeremy 1926- DLB-14

Brooks, Mel 1926- DLB-26

Brooks, Noah 1830-1903. . . . . DLB-42; DS-13

Brooks, Richard 1912-1992. . . . . . . DLB-44

Brooks, Van Wyck
1886-1963. . . . . . . DLB-45, 63, 103

Brophy, Brigid 1929- DLB-14

Brossard, Chandler 1922-1993 . . . . DLB-16

Brossard, Nicole 1943- DLB-53

Broster, Dorothy Kathleen
1877-1950 . . . . DLB-160

Brother Antoninus (see Everson, William)

Brougham and Vaux, Henry Peter
Brougham, Baron
1778-1868. . . . . DLB-110, 158

Brougham, John 1810-1880. . . . . . DLB-11

Broughton, James 1913- DLB-5

Broughton, Rhoda 1840-1920 . . . . . DLB-18

Broun, Heywood 1888-1939 . . . . DLB-29, 171

Brown, Alice 1856-1948. . . . . DLB-78

Brown, Bob 1886-1959 . . . . DLB-4, 45

Brown, Cecil 1943- DLB-33

Brown, Charles Brockden
1771-1810. . . . . DLB-37, 59, 73

Brown, Christy 1932-1981 . . . . DLB-14

Brown, Dee 1908- Y-80

Brown, Frank London 1927-1962 . . . . DLB-76

Brown, Fredric 1906-1972 . . . . DLB-8

Brown, George Mackay
1921- DLB-14, 27, 139

Brown, Harry 1917-1986 . . . . DLB-26

Brown, Marcia 1918- DLB-61

Brown, Margaret Wise
1910-1952 . . . . DLB-22

Brown, Morna Doris (see Ferrars, Elizabeth)

Brown, Oliver Madox
1855-1874 . . . . DLB-21

Brown, Sterling
1901-1989. . . . . DLB-48, 51, 63

Brown, T. E. 1830-1897 . . . . DLB-35

Brown, William Hill 1765-1793 . . . . DLB-37

Brown, William Wells
1814-1884. . . . . DLB-3, 50, 183

Browne, Charles Farrar
1834-1867 . . . . DLB-11

Browne, Francis Fisher
1843-1913 . . . . DLB-79

Browne, Michael Dennis
1940- DLB-40

Browne, Sir Thomas 1605-1682 . . . . DLB-151

Browne, William, of Tavistock
1590-1645 . . . . DLB-121

Browne, Wynyard 1911-1964 . . . . . DLB-13

Browne and Nolan DLB-106

Brownell, W. C. 1851-1928 . . . . . . DLB-71

Browning, Elizabeth Barrett
1806-1861 . . . . DLB-32

Browning, Robert
1812-1889 . . . . DLB-32, 163

Brownjohn, Allan 1931- DLB-40

Brownson, Orestes Augustus
1803-1876 . . . . DLB-1, 59, 73

Bruccoli, Matthew J. 1931- DLB-103

Bruce, Charles 1906-1971. . . . . DLB-68

Bruce, Leo 1903-1979. . . . . DLB-77

Bruce, Philip Alexander
1856-1933 . . . . DLB-47

Bruce Humphries
[publishing house] DLB-46

Bruce-Novoa, Juan 1944- DLB-82

Bruckman, Clyde 1894-1955 . . . . . . DLB-26

Bruckner, Ferdinand 1891-1958 . . . . DLB-118

Brundage, John Herbert (see Herbert, John)

Brutus, Dennis 1924- DLB-117

Bryant, Arthur 1899-1985 . . . . DLB-149

Bryant, William Cullen
1794-1878 . . . . DLB-3, 43, 59

Bryce Echenique, Alfredo
1939- DLB-145

Bryce, James 1838-1922 . . . . DLB-166

Brydges, Sir Samuel Egerton
1762-1837 . . . . DLB-107

Bryskett, Lodowick 1546?-1612 . . . . . DLB-167

Buchan, John 1875-1940 . . . . DLB-34, 70, 156

Buchanan, George 1506-1582 . . . . . DLB-132

Buchanan, Robert 1841-1901. . . . . DLB-18, 35

Buchman, Sidney 1902-1975 . . . . . . DLB-26

Buchner, Augustus 1591-1661. . . . . DLB-164

Büchner, Georg 1813-1837 . . . . . . DLB-133

Bucholtz, Andreas Heinrich
1607-1671 . . . . DLB-168

Buck, Pearl S. 1892-1973. . . . . . DLB-9, 102

Bucke, Charles 1781-1846. . . . . . . DLB-110

Bucke, Richard Maurice
1837-1902 . . . . DLB-99

Buckingham, Joseph Tinker 1779-1861 and
Buckingham, Edwin
1810-1833 . . . . DLB-73

Buckler, Ernest 1908-1984 . . . . . . DLB-68

Buckley, William F., Jr.
1925- DLB-137; Y-80

Buckminster, Joseph Stevens
1784-1812 . . . . DLB-37

Buckner, Robert 1906- DLB-26

Budd, Thomas ?-1698 . . . . DLB-24

Budrys, A. J. 1931- DLB-8

Buechner, Frederick 1926- Y-80

Buell, John 1927- DLB-53

Buffum, Job [publishing house]. DLB-49

Bugnet, Georges 1879-1981. . . . . . DLB-92

Buies, Arthur 1840-1901 . . . . DLB-99

Building the New British Library
at St Pancras Y-94

Bukowski, Charles
1920-1994 . . . . DLB-5, 130, 169

Bulatović, Miodrag 1930-1991. . . . . DLB-181

Bulger, Bozeman 1877-1932. . . . . . DLB-171

Bullein, William
between 1520 and 1530-1576. . . . DLB-167

Bullins, Ed 1935- DLB-7, 38

Bulwer-Lytton, Edward (also Edward Bulwer)
1803-1873 . . . . DLB-21

Bumpus, Jerry 1937- Y-81

Bunce and Brother DLB-49

Bunner, H. C. 1855-1896 . . . . . DLB-78, 79

Bunting, Basil 1900-1985 . . . . DLB-20

Bunyan, John 1628-1688 . . . . DLB-39

Burch, Robert 1925- DLB-52

Burciaga, José Antonio 1940- DLB-82

Bürger, Gottfried August
1747-1794 . . . . DLB-94

Burgess, Anthony 1917-1993 . . . . . . DLB-14

Burgess, Gelett 1866-1951 . . . . DLB-11

Burgess, John W. 1844-1931 . . . . . . DLB-47

Burgess, Thornton W.
1874-1965 . . . . DLB-22

Burgess, Stringer and Company DLB-49

Burick, Si 1909-1986. . . . . DLB-171

Burk, John Daly circa 1772-1808 . . . . DLB-37

Burke, Edmund 1729?-1797. . . . . . DLB-104

Burke, Kenneth 1897-1993 . . . . . DLB-45, 63

Burlingame, Edward Livermore
1848-1922 . . . . DLB-79

Burnet, Gilbert 1643-1715 . . . . . . DLB-101

Burnett, Frances Hodgson
1849-1924 . . . . . DLB-42, 141; DS-13, 14

Burnett, W. R. 1899-1982 . . . . DLB-9

Burnett, Whit 1899-1973 and
Martha Foley 1897-1977 . . . . . . DLB-137

Burney, Fanny 1752-1840 . . . . DLB-39

Burns, Alan 1929- DLB-14

Burns, John Horne 1916-1953. . . . . . . Y-85

Burns, Robert 1759-1796 . . . . DLB-109

Burns and Oates. DLB-106

Burnshaw, Stanley 1906- DLB-48

Burr, C. Chauncey 1815?-1883 . . . . . DLB-79

Burroughs, Edgar Rice 1875-1950. . . . DLB-8

Burroughs, John 1837-1921. . . . . . . DLB-64

Burroughs, Margaret T. G.
1917- DLB-41

Burroughs, William S., Jr.
1947-1981 . . . . DLB-16

Burroughs, William Seward
1914- DLB-2, 8, 16, 152; Y-81

Burroway, Janet 1936- DLB-6

Burt, Maxwell S. 1882-1954 . . . . . . DLB-86

Burt, A. L., and Company. DLB-49

Burton, Hester 1913- DLB-161

Burton, Isabel Arundell
1831-1896 . . . . DLB-166

Burton, Miles (see Rhode, John)

Burton, Richard Francis
1821-1890 . . . . DLB-55, 166

Burton, Robert 1577-1640. . . . . . . DLB-151

Burton, Virginia Lee 1909-1968 . . . . . DLB-22

Burton, William Evans
1804-1860 . . . . DLB-73

Burwell, Adam Hood 1790-1849 . . . . . DLB-99

Bury, Lady Charlotte
1775-1861 . . . . DLB-116

Busch, Frederick 1941- DLB-6

Busch, Niven 1903-1991 . . . . DLB-44

Bushnell, Horace 1802-1876 . . . . DS-13

Bussieres, Arthur de 1877-1913 . . . . . DLB-92

Butler, Juan 1942-1981 . . . . DLB-53

Butler, Octavia E. 1947- DLB-33

Butler, Robert Olen 1945- DLB-173

Butler, Samuel 1613-1680 . . . . . DLB-101, 126

Butler, Samuel 1835-1902 . . . . DLB-18, 57, 174

Butler, William Francis
1838-1910 . . . . DLB-166

Butler, E. H., and Company. DLB-49

Butor, Michel 1926- DLB-83

Butter, Nathaniel
[publishing house] DLB-170

Butterworth, Hezekiah 1839-1905 . . . . DLB-42

Buttitta, Ignazio 1899- DLB-114

Buzzati, Dino 1906-1972. . . . . DLB-177

Byars, Betsy 1928- DLB-52

Byatt, A. S. 1936- DLB-14

Byles, Mather 1707-1788 . . . . DLB-24

Bynneman, Henry
[publishing house] DLB-170

Bynner, Witter 1881-1968 . . . . DLB-54

Byrd, William circa 1543-1623 . . . . . DLB-172

Byrd, William II 1674-1744 . . . . DLB-24, 140

Byrne, John Keyes (see Leonard, Hugh)

Byron, George Gordon, Lord
1788-1824 . . . . DLB-96, 110

C

Caballero Bonald, José Manuel
1926- DLB-108

Cabañero, Eladio 1930- DLB-134

Cabell, James Branch
1879-1958 . . . . DLB-9, 78

Cabeza de Baca, Manuel
1853-1915 . . . . DLB-122

Cabeza de Baca Gilbert, Fabiola
1898- DLB-122

Cable, George Washington
1844-1925. . . . . DLB-12, 74; DS-13

Cabrera, Lydia 1900-1991 . . . . DLB-145

Cabrera Infante, Guillermo
1929- DLB-113

Cadell [publishing house] DLB-154

Cady, Edwin H. 1917- DLB-103

Caedmon flourished 658-680 . . . . . DLB-146

Caedmon School circa 660-899 . . . . DLB-146

Cafés, Brasseries, and Bistros. DS-15

Cahan, Abraham
1860-1951 . . . . DLB-9, 25, 28

Cain, George 1943- DLB-33

Caldecott, Randolph 1846-1886 . . . . . DLB-163

Calder, John
(Publishers), Limited. DLB-112

Calderón de la Barca, Fanny
1804-1882 . . . . DLB-183

Caldwell, Ben 1937- DLB-38

Caldwell, Erskine 1903-1987 . . . . DLB-9, 86

Caldwell, H. M., Company DLB-49

Calhoun, John C. 1782-1850 . . . . DLB-3

Calisher, Hortense 1911- DLB-2

A Call to Letters and an Invitation
to the Electric Chair,
by Siegfried Mandel DLB-75

Callaghan, Morley 1903-1990 . . . . . . DLB-68

Callahan, S. Alice 1868-1894 . . . . . DLB-175

Callaloo Y-87

Callimachus circa 305 B.C.-240 B.C.
. . . . DLB-176

Calmer, Edgar 1907- DLB-4

Calverley, C. S. 1831-1884 . . . . DLB-35

Calvert, George Henry
1803-1889 . . . . DLB-1, 64

Cambridge Press DLB-49

Cambridge Songs (Carmina Cantabrigensia)
circa 1050 . . . . DLB-148

Cambridge University Press. DLB-170

Camden, William 1551-1623 . . . . . DLB-172

Camden House: An Interview with
James Hardin. Y-92

Cameron, Eleanor 1912- DLB-52

Cameron, George Frederick
1854-1885 . . . . DLB-99

Cameron, Lucy Lyttelton
1781-1858 . . . . DLB-163

Cameron, William Bleasdell
1862-1951 . . . . DLB-99

Camm, John 1718-1778. . . . . DLB-31

Campana, Dino 1885-1932 . . . . . . DLB-114

Campbell, Gabrielle Margaret Vere
(see Shearing, Joseph, and Bowen, Marjorie)

Campbell, James Dykes
1838-1895 . . . . DLB-144

Campbell, James Edwin
1867-1896 . . . . DLB-50

Campbell, John 1653-1728 . . . . DLB-43

Campbell, John W., Jr.
1910-1971 . . . . DLB-8

Campbell, Roy 1901-1957 . . . . DLB-20

Campbell, Thomas
1777-1844 . . . . DLB-93, 144

Campbell, William Wilfred
1858-1918 . . . . DLB-92

Campion, Edmund 1539-1581 . . . . . DLB-167

Campion, Thomas
1567-1620 . . . . DLB-58, 172

Camus, Albert 1913-1960. . . . . DLB-72

The Canadian Publishers' Records
Database Y-96

Canby, Henry Seidel 1878-1961 . . . . . DLB-91

Candelaria, Cordelia 1943- DLB-82

Candelaria, Nash 1928- DLB-82

Candour in English Fiction (1890),
by Thomas Hardy DLB-18

Canetti, Elias 1905-1994. . . . . . . DLB-85, 124

Canham, Erwin Dain
1904-1982 . . . . DLB-127

Canitz, Friedrich Rudolph Ludwig von
1654-1699 . . . . DLB-168

Cankar, Ivan 1876-1918. . . . . DLB-147

Cannan, Gilbert 1884-1955. . . . . . . DLB-10

Cannell, Kathleen 1891-1974. . . . . . . DLB-4

Cannell, Skipwith 1887-1957 . . . . . . DLB-45

Canning, George 1770-1827. . . . . . DLB-158

Cannon, Jimmy 1910-1973 . . . . . . DLB-171

Cantwell, Robert 1908-1978 . . . . DLB-9

Cape, Jonathan, and Harrison Smith
[publishing house]. DLB-46

Cape, Jonathan, Limited. DLB-112

Capen, Joseph 1658-1725. . . . . DLB-24

Capes, Bernard 1854-1918. . . . . . . DLB-156

Capote, Truman 1924-1984 . . DLB-2; Y-80, 84

Caproni, Giorgio 1912-1990. . . . . . DLB-128

Cardarelli, Vincenzo 1887-1959 . . . . DLB-114

Cárdenas, Reyes 1948- DLB-122

Cardinal, Marie 1929- DLB-83

Carew, Jan 1920- DLB-157

Carew, Thomas
1594 or 1595-1640 . . . . DLB-126

Carey, Henry
circa 1687-1689-1743 . . . . DLB-84

Carey, Mathew 1760-1839 . . . . . DLB-37, 73

Carey and Hart. DLB-49

Carey, M., and Company DLB-49

Carlell, Lodowick 1602-1675 . . . . . DLB-58

Carleton, William 1794-1869 . . . . . DLB-159

Carleton, G. W.
[publishing house]. DLB-49

Carlile, Richard 1790-1843 . . . . DLB-110, 158

Carlyle, Jane Welsh 1801-1866. . . . . DLB-55

Carlyle, Thomas 1795-1881. . . . . DLB-55, 144

Carman, Bliss 1861-1929 . . . . DLB-92

Carmina Burana circa 1230 . . . . . DLB-138

Carnero, Guillermo 1947- DLB-108

Carossa, Hans 1878-1956. . . . . DLB-66

Carpenter, Humphrey 1946- DLB-155

Carpenter, Stephen Cullen ?-1820? . . . DLB-73

Carpentier, Alejo 1904-1980. . . . . . DLB-113

Carrier, Roch 1937- DLB-53

Carrillo, Adolfo 1855-1926 . . . . . . DLB-122

Carroll, Gladys Hasty 1904- DLB-9

Carroll, John 1735-1815 . . . . DLB-37

Carroll, John 1809-1884 . . . . DLB-99

Carroll, Lewis
   1832-1898 . . . . DLB-18, 163, 178

Carroll, Paul 1927- DLB-16

Carroll, Paul Vincent 1900-1968 . . . . DLB-10

Carroll and Graf Publishers DLB-46

Carruth, Hayden 1921- DLB-5, 165

Carryl, Charles E. 1841-1920 . . . . . DLB-42

Carswell, Catherine 1879-1946 . . . . . DLB-36

Carter, Angela 1940-1992 . . . . DLB-14

Carter, Elizabeth 1717-1806 . . . . . . DLB-109

Carter, Henry (see Leslie, Frank)

Carter, Hodding, Jr. 1907-1972 . . . . DLB-127

Carter, Landon 1710-1778 . . . . DLB-31

Carter, Lin 1930- Y-81

Carter, Martin 1927- DLB-117

Carter and Hendee DLB-49

Carter, Robert, and Brothers DLB-49

Cartwright, John 1740-1824 . . . . . . DLB-158

Cartwright, William circa
   1611-1643 . . . . DLB-126

Caruthers, William Alexander
   1802-1846 . . . . DLB-3

Carver, Jonathan 1710-1780 . . . . . . DLB-31

Carver, Raymond
   1938-1988 . . . . DLB-130; Y-84, 88

Cary, Joyce 1888-1957 . . . . . . DLB-15, 100

Cary, Patrick 1623?-1657 . . . . DLB-131

Casey, Juanita 1925- DLB-14

Casey, Michael 1947- DLB-5

Cassady, Carolyn 1923- DLB-16

Cassady, Neal 1926-1968 . . . . DLB-16

Cassell and Company DLB-106

Cassell Publishing Company DLB-49

Cassill, R. V. 1919- DLB-6

Cassity, Turner 1929- DLB-105

Cassius Dio circa 155/164-post 229
   . . . . DLB-176

Cassola, Carlo 1917-1987 . . . . DLB-177

The Castle of Perseverance
   circa 1400-1425 . . . . DLB-146

Castellano, Olivia 1944- DLB-122

Castellanos, Rosario 1925-1974 . . . . DLB-113

Castillo, Ana 1953- DLB-122

Castlemon, Harry (see Fosdick, Charles Austin)

Čašule, Kole 1921- DLB-181

Caswall, Edward 1814-1878 . . . . . . DLB-32

Catacalos, Rosemary 1944- DLB-122

Cather, Willa
   1873-1947 . . . . DLB-9, 54, 78; DS-1

Catherine II (Ekaterina Alekseevna), "The
   Great," Empress of Russia
   1729-1796 . . . . DLB-150

Catherwood, Mary Hartwell
   1847-1902 . . . . DLB-78

Catledge, Turner 1901-1983 . . . . . . DLB-127

Cattafi, Bartolo 1922-1979 . . . . DLB-128

Catton, Bruce 1899-1978 . . . . DLB-17

Causley, Charles 1917- DLB-27

Caute, David 1936- DLB-14

Cavendish, Duchess of Newcastle,
   Margaret Lucas 1623-1673 . . . . DLB-131

Cawein, Madison 1865-1914 . . . . . . DLB-54

The Caxton Printers, Limited DLB-46

Caxton, William
   [publishing house] DLB-170

Cayrol, Jean 1911- DLB-83

Cecil, Lord David 1902-1986 . . . . . . DLB-155

Celan, Paul 1920-1970 . . . . DLB-69

Celaya, Gabriel 1911-1991 . . . . DLB-108

Céline, Louis-Ferdinand
   1894-1961 . . . . DLB-72

The Celtic Background to Medieval English
   Literature DLB-146

Celtis, Conrad 1459-1508 . . . . DLB-179

Center for Bibliographical Studies and
   Research at the University of
   California, Riverside Y-91

The Center for the Book in the Library
   of Congress Y-93

Center for the Book Research Y-84

Centlivre, Susanna 1669?-1723 . . . . . DLB-84

The Century Company DLB-49

Cernuda, Luis 1902-1963 . . . . DLB-134

Cervantes, Lorna Dee 1954- DLB-82

Chacel, Rosa 1898- DLB-134

Chacón, Eusebio 1869-1948 . . . . . . DLB-82

Chacón, Felipe Maximiliano
   1873-? DLB-82

Chadwyck-Healey's Full-Text Literary Data-bases:
   Editing Commercial Databases of
   Primary Literary Texts Y-95

Challans, Eileen Mary (see Renault, Mary)

Chalmers, George 1742-1825 . . . . . . DLB-30

Chaloner, Sir Thomas
   1520-1565 . . . . DLB-167

Chamberlain, Samuel S.
   1851-1916 . . . . DLB-25

Chamberland, Paul 1939- DLB-60

Chamberlin, William Henry
   1897-1969 . . . . DLB-29

Chambers, Charles Haddon
   1860-1921 . . . . DLB-10

Chambers, W. and R.
   [publishing house] DLB-106

Chamisso, Albert von
   1781-1838 . . . . DLB-90

Champfleury 1821-1889 . . . . DLB-119

Chandler, Harry 1864-1944 . . . . . . DLB-29

Chandler, Norman 1899-1973 . . . . . DLB-127

Chandler, Otis 1927- DLB-127

Chandler, Raymond 1888-1959 . . . . . DS-6

Channing, Edward 1856-1931 . . . . . DLB-17

Channing, Edward Tyrrell
   1790-1856 . . . . DLB-1, 59

Channing, William Ellery
   1780-1842 . . . . DLB-1, 59

Channing, William Ellery, II
   1817-1901 . . . . DLB-1

Channing, William Henry
   1810-1884 . . . . DLB-1, 59

Chaplin, Charlie 1889-1977 . . . . . . DLB-44

Chapman, George
   1559 or 1560 - 1634 . . . . . DLB-62, 121

Chapman, John DLB-106

Chapman, William 1850-1917 . . . . . DLB-99

Chapman and Hall DLB-106

Chappell, Fred 1936- DLB-6, 105

Chappell, Fred, A Detail
   in a Poem DLB-105

Charbonneau, Jean 1875-1960 . . . . . DLB-92

Charbonneau, Robert 1911-1967 . . . . DLB-68

Charles, Gerda 1914- DLB-14

Charles, William
   [publishing house] DLB-49

The Charles Wood Affair:
   A Playwright Revived Y-83

Charlotte Forten: Pages from
   her Diary DLB-50

Charteris, Leslie 1907-1993 . . . . . . DLB-77

Charyn, Jerome 1937- Y-83

Chase, Borden 1900-1971 . . . . DLB-26

Chase, Edna Woolman
   1877-1957 . . . . DLB-91

Chase-Riboud, Barbara 1936- DLB-33

Chateaubriand, François-René de
   1768-1848 . . . . DLB-119

Chatterton, Thomas 1752-1770 . . . . . DLB-109

Chatto and Windus DLB-106

Chaucer, Geoffrey 1340?-1400 . . . . . DLB-146

Chauncy, Charles 1705-1787 . . . . . . DLB-24

Chauveau, Pierre-Joseph-Olivier
   1820-1890 . . . . DLB-99

Chávez, Denise 1948- DLB-122

Chávez, Fray Angélico 1910- DLB-82

Chayefsky, Paddy
   1923-1981 . . . . DLB-7, 44; Y-81

Cheever, Ezekiel 1615-1708 . . . . . . DLB-24

Cheever, George Barrell
   1807-1890 . . . . DLB-59

Cheever, John
1912-1982 . . . . . . DLB-2, 102; Y-80, 82

Cheever, Susan 1943- Y-82

Cheke, Sir John 1514-1557 . . . . . . DLB-132

Chelsea House DLB-46

Cheney, Ednah Dow (Littlehale)
1824-1904 . . . . DLB-1

Cheney, Harriet Vaughn
1796-1889 . . . . DLB-99

Cherry, Kelly 1940 . . . . Y-83

Cherryh, C. J. 1942- Y-80

Chesnutt, Charles Waddell
1858-1932 . . . . DLB-12, 50, 78

Chester, Alfred 1928-1971 . . . . DLB-130

Chester, George Randolph
1869-1924 . . . . DLB-78

The Chester Plays circa 1505-1532;
revisions until 1575 . . . . DLB-146

Chesterfield, Philip Dormer Stanhope,
Fourth Earl of 1694-1773 . . . . . DLB-104

Chesterton, G. K. 1874-1936
. . . . . DLB-10, 19, 34, 70, 98, 149, 178

Chettle, Henry
circa 1560-circa 1607 . . . . DLB-136

Chew, Ada Nield 1870-1945 . . . . . DLB-135

Cheyney, Edward P. 1861-1947 . . . . . DLB-47

Chiara, Piero 1913-1986 . . . . . DLB-177

Chicano History DLB-82

Chicano Language DLB-82

Child, Francis James
1825-1896 . . . . DLB-1, 64

Child, Lydia Maria
1802-1880 . . . . DLB-1, 74

Child, Philip 1898-1978 . . . . DLB-68

Childers, Erskine 1870-1922 . . . . . DLB-70

Children's Book Awards
and Prizes DLB-61

Children's Illustrators,
1800-1880 . . . . DLB-163

Childress, Alice 1920-1994 . . . . DLB-7, 38

Childs, George W. 1829-1894 . . . . . DLB-23

Chilton Book Company DLB-46

Chinweizu 1943- DLB-157

Chitham, Edward 1932- DLB-155

Chittenden, Hiram Martin
1858-1917 . . . . DLB-47

Chivers, Thomas Holley
1809-1858 . . . . DLB-3

Chopin, Kate 1850-1904 . . . . . DLB-12, 78

Chopin, Rene 1885-1953 . . . . DLB-92

Choquette, Adrienne 1915-1973 . . . . DLB-68

Choquette, Robert 1905- DLB-68

The Christian Publishing
Company DLB-49

Christie, Agatha 1890-1976 . . . . . DLB-13, 77

Christus und die Samariterin
circa 950 . . . . DLB-148

Chulkov, Mikhail Dmitrievich
1743?-1792 . . . . DLB-150

Church, Benjamin 1734-1778 . . . . . DLB-31

Church, Francis Pharcellus
1839-1906 . . . . DLB-79

Church, William Conant
1836-1917 . . . . DLB-79

Churchill, Caryl 1938- DLB-13

Churchill, Charles 1731-1764 . . . . DLB-109

Churchill, Sir Winston
1874-1965 . . . . DLB-100

Churchyard, Thomas
1520?-1604 . . . . DLB-132

Churton, E., and Company DLB-106

Chute, Marchette 1909-1994 . . . . DLB-103

Ciardi, John 1916-1986 . . . . . DLB-5; Y-86

Cibber, Colley 1671-1757 . . . . . . DLB-84

Cima, Annalisa 1941- DLB-128

Čingo, Živko 1935-1987 . . . . . . DLB-181

Cirese, Eugenio 1884-1955 . . . . DLB-114

Cisneros, Sandra 1954- DLB-122, 152

City Lights Books DLB-46

Cixous, Hélène 1937- DLB-83

Clampitt, Amy 1920-1994 . . . . . . DLB-105

Clapper, Raymond 1892-1944 . . . . DLB-29

Clare, John 1793-1864 . . . . . . DLB-55, 96

Clarendon, Edward Hyde, Earl of
1609-1674 . . . . DLB-101

Clark, Alfred Alexander Gordon
(see Hare, Cyril)

Clark, Ann Nolan 1896- DLB-52

Clark, C. M., Publishing
Company DLB-46

Clark, Catherine Anthony
1892-1977 . . . . DLB-68

Clark, Charles Heber
1841-1915 . . . . DLB-11

Clark, Davis Wasgatt 1812-1871 . . . . DLB-79

Clark, Eleanor 1913- DLB-6

Clark, J. P. 1935- DLB-117

Clark, Lewis Gaylord
1808-1873 . . . . DLB-3, 64, 73

Clark, Walter Van Tilburg
1909-1971 . . . . DLB-9

Clark, William (see Lewis, Meriwether)

Clarke, Austin 1896-1974 . . . . . DLB-10, 20

Clarke, Austin C. 1934- DLB-53, 125

Clarke, Gillian 1937- DLB-40

Clarke, James Freeman
1810-1888 . . . . DLB-1, 59

Clarke, Pauline 1921- DLB-161

Clarke, Rebecca Sophia
1833-1906 . . . . DLB-42

Clarke, Robert, and Company DLB-49

Clarkson, Thomas 1760-1846 . . . . . DLB-158

Claudius, Matthias 1740-1815 . . . . . DLB-97

Clausen, Andy 1943- DLB-16

Claxton, Remsen and
Haffelfinger DLB-49

Clay, Cassius Marcellus
1810-1903 . . . . DLB-43

Cleary, Beverly 1916- DLB-52

Cleaver, Vera 1919- and
Cleaver, Bill 1920-1981 . . . . . . DLB-52

Cleland, John 1710-1789 . . . . . . DLB-39

Clemens, Samuel Langhorne
1835-1910 . . . . . DLB-11, 12, 23, 64, 74

Clement, Hal 1922- DLB-8

Clemo, Jack 1916- DLB-27

Cleveland, John 1613-1658 . . . . . DLB-126

Cliff, Michelle 1946- DLB-157

Clifford, Lady Anne 1590-1676 . . . . DLB-151

Clifford, James L. 1901-1978 . . . . DLB-103

Clifford, Lucy 1853?-1929 . . . . DLB-135, 141

Clifton, Lucille 1936- DLB-5, 41

Clode, Edward J.
[publishing house] DLB-46

Clough, Arthur Hugh 1819-1861 . . . DLB-32

Cloutier, Cécile 1930- DLB-60

Clutton-Brock, Arthur
1868-1924 . . . . DLB-98

Coates, Robert M.
1897-1973 . . . . DLB-4, 9, 102

Coatsworth, Elizabeth 1893- DLB-22

Cobb, Charles E., Jr. 1943- DLB-41

Cobb, Frank I. 1869-1923 . . . . . . DLB-25

Cobb, Irvin S.
1876-1944 . . . . DLB-11, 25, 86

Cobbett, William 1763-1835 . . . . DLB-43, 107

Cobbledick, Gordon 1898-1969 . . . . DLB-171

Cochran, Thomas C. 1902- DLB-17

Cochrane, Elizabeth 1867-1922 . . . . DLB-25

Cockerill, John A. 1845-1896 . . . . . DLB-23

Cocteau, Jean 1889-1963 . . . . . . DLB-65

Coderre, Emile (see Jean Narrache)

Coffee, Lenore J. 1900?-1984 . . . . . DLB-44

Coffin, Robert P. Tristram
1892-1955 . . . . DLB-45

Cogswell, Fred 1917- DLB-60

Cogswell, Mason Fitch
1761-1830 . . . . DLB-37

Cohen, Arthur A. 1928-1986 . . . . . DLB-28

Cohen, Leonard 1934- DLB-53

Cohen, Matt 1942- DLB-53

Colden, Cadwallader
1688-1776 . . . . DLB-24, 30

Cole, Barry 1936- DLB-14

Cole, George Watson
1850-1939 . . . . DLB-140

Colegate, Isabel 1931- DLB-14

Coleman, Emily Holmes
1899-1974. . . . . DLB-4

Coleman, Wanda 1946- DLB-130

Coleridge, Hartley 1796-1849. . . . . . DLB-96

Coleridge, Mary 1861-1907 . . . . . DLB-19, 98

Coleridge, Samuel Taylor
1772-1834 . . . . DLB-93, 107

Colet, John 1467-1519 . . . . DLB-132

Colette 1873-1954 . . . . DLB-65

Colette, Sidonie Gabrielle (see Colette)

Colinas, Antonio 1946- DLB-134

Collier, John 1901-1980 . . . . DLB-77

Collier, Mary 1690-1762 . . . . DLB-95

Collier, Robert J. 1876-1918 . . . . . . DLB-91

Collier, P. F. [publishing house] DLB-49

Collin and Small DLB-49

Collingwood, W. G. 1854-1932. . . . . DLB-149

Collins, An floruit circa 1653 . . . . . DLB-131

Collins, Merle 1950- DLB-157

Collins, Mortimer 1827-1876. . . . DLB-21, 35

Collins, Wilkie 1824-1889 . . . DLB-18, 70, 159

Collins, William 1721-1759 . . . . . . DLB-109

Collins, William, Sons and
Company DLB-154

Collins, Isaac [publishing house] DLB-49

Collyer, Mary 1716?-1763? DLB-39

Colman, Benjamin 1673-1747 . . . . . DLB-24

Colman, George, the Elder
1732-1794 . . . . DLB-89

Colman, George, the Younger
1762-1836 . . . . DLB-89

Colman, S. [publishing house] DLB-49

Colombo, John Robert 1936- DLB-53

Colquhoun, Patrick 1745-1820 . . . . DLB-158

Colter, Cyrus 1910- DLB-33

Colum, Padraic 1881-1972 . . . . DLB-19

Colvin, Sir Sidney 1845-1927 . . . . . DLB-149

Colwin, Laurie 1944-1992 . . . . Y-80

Comden, Betty 1919- and Green,
Adolph 1918- DLB-44

Comi, Girolamo 1890-1968 . . . . . . DLB-114

The Comic Tradition Continued
[in the British Novel] DLB-15

Commager, Henry Steele
1902- DLB-17

The Commercialization of the Image of
Revolt, by Kenneth Rexroth. DLB-16

Community and Commentators: Black
Theatre and Its Critics DLB-38

Compton-Burnett, Ivy
1884?-1969 . . . . DLB-36

Conan, Laure 1845-1924 . . . . DLB-99

Conde, Carmen 1901- DLB-108

Conference on Modern Biography Y-85

Congreve, William
1670-1729 . . . . DLB-39, 84

Conkey, W. B., Company DLB-49

Connell, Evan S., Jr. 1924- DLB-2; Y-81

Connelly, Marc 1890-1980 . . . . . DLB-7; Y-80

Connolly, Cyril 1903-1974 . . . . DLB-98

Connolly, James B. 1868-1957 . . . . . DLB-78

Connor, Ralph 1860-1937 . . . . DLB-92

Connor, Tony 1930- DLB-40

Conquest, Robert 1917- DLB-27

Conrad, Joseph
1857-1924. . . . . . . DLB-10, 34, 98, 156

Conrad, John, and Company DLB-49

Conroy, Jack 1899-1990 . . . . Y-81

Conroy, Pat 1945- DLB-6

The Consolidation of Opinion: Critical
Responses to the Modernists DLB-36

Constable, Henry 1562-1613 . . . . . DLB-136

Constable and Company
Limited. DLB-112

Constable, Archibald, and
Company DLB-154

Constant, Benjamin 1767-1830 . . . . DLB-119

Constant de Rebecque, Henri-Benjamin de
(see Constant, Benjamin)

Constantine, David 1944- DLB-40

Constantin-Weyer, Maurice
1881-1964 . . . . DLB-92

Contempo Caravan: Kites in
a Windstorm Y-85

A Contemporary Flourescence of Chicano
Literature Y-84

The Continental Publishing
Company DLB-49

A Conversation with Chaim Potok Y-84

Conversations with Editors. Y-95

Conversations with Publishers I: An Interview
with Patrick O'Connor Y-84

Conversations with Publishers II: An Interview
with Charles Scribner III Y-94

Conversations with Publishers III: An Interview
with Donald Lamm Y-95

Conversations with Publishers IV: An Interview
with James Laughlin Y-96

Conversations with Rare Book Dealers I: An
Interview with Glenn Horowitz. . . . Y-90

Conversations with Rare Book Dealers II: An
Interview with Ralph Sipper Y-94

Conversations with Rare Book Dealers
(Publishers) III: An Interview with
Otto Penzler Y-96

The Conversion of an Unpolitical Man,
by W. H. Bruford DLB-66

Conway, Moncure Daniel
1832-1907. . . . . DLB-1

Cook, Ebenezer
circa 1667-circa 1732 . . . . DLB-24

Cook, Edward Tyas 1857-1919. . . . . DLB-149

Cook, Michael 1933- DLB-53

Cook, David C., Publishing
Company DLB-49

Cooke, George Willis 1848-1923. . . . . DLB-71

Cooke, Increase, and Company DLB-49

Cooke, John Esten 1830-1886 . . . . . . DLB-3

Cooke, Philip Pendleton
1816-1850 . . . . DLB-3, 59

Cooke, Rose Terry
1827-1892. . . . . DLB-12, 74

Cook-Lynn, Elizabeth 1930- DLB-175

Coolbrith, Ina 1841-1928 . . . . DLB-54

Cooley, Peter 1940- DLB-105

Cooley, Peter, Into the Mirror DLB-105

Coolidge, Susan (see Woolsey, Sarah Chauncy)

Coolidge, George
[publishing house]. DLB-49

Cooper, Giles 1918-1966 . . . . DLB-13

Cooper, James Fenimore
1789-1851 . . . . DLB-3, 183

Cooper, Kent 1880-1965 . . . . DLB-29

Cooper, Susan 1935- DLB-161

Cooper, William
[publishing house] DLB-170

Coote, J. [publishing house]. DLB-154

Coover, Robert 1932- DLB-2; Y-81

Copeland and Day DLB-49

Ćopić, Branko 1915-1984 . . . . DLB-181

Copland, Robert 1470?-1548 . . . . . DLB-136

Coppard, A. E. 1878-1957 . . . . . . DLB-162

Coppel, Alfred 1921- Y-83

Coppola, Francis Ford 1939- DLB-44

Copway, George (Kah-ge-ga-gah-bowh)
1818-1869. . . . . DLB-175, 183

Corazzini, Sergio 1886-1907. . . . . . DLB-114

Corbett, Richard 1582-1635. . . . . . DLB-121

Corcoran, Barbara 1911- DLB-52

Corelli, Marie 1855-1924 . . . . . DLB-34, 156

Corle, Edwin 1906-1956 . . . . Y-85

Corman, Cid 1924- DLB-5

Cormier, Robert 1925- DLB-52

Corn, Alfred 1943- DLB-120; Y-80

Cornish, Sam 1935- DLB-41

Cornish, William
circa 1465-circa 1524 . . . . DLB-132

Cornwall, Barry (see Procter, Bryan Waller)

Cornwallis, Sir William, the Younger
circa 1579-1614 . . . . DLB-151

Cornwell, David John Moore
(see le Carré, John)

Corpi, Lucha 1945- DLB-82

Corrington, John William 1932- DLB-6

Corrothers, James D. 1869-1917 . . . . . DLB-50

Corso, Gregory 1930- DLB-5, 16

Cortázar, Julio 1914-1984 . . . . DLB-113

Cortez, Jayne 1936- DLB-41

Corvinus, Gottlieb Siegmund
1677-1746 . . . . DLB-168

Corvo, Baron (see Rolfe, Frederick William)

Cory, Annie Sophie (see Cross, Victoria)

Cory, William Johnson
1823-1892 . . . . DLB-35

Coryate, Thomas
1577?-1617 . . . . DLB-151, 172

Ćosić, Dobrica 1921- DLB-181

Cosin, John 1595-1672. . . . . DLB-151

Cosmopolitan Book Corporation DLB-46

Costain, Thomas B. 1885-1965 . . . . . DLB-9

Coste, Donat 1912-1957 . . . . DLB-88

Costello, Louisa Stuart 1799-1870 . . . DLB-166

Cota-Cárdenas, Margarita
1941- DLB-122

Cotter, Joseph Seamon, Sr.
1861-1949 . . . . DLB-50

Cotter, Joseph Seamon, Jr.
1895-1919 . . . . DLB-50

Cottle, Joseph [publishing house] DLB-154

Cotton, Charles 1630-1687 . . . . DLB-131

Cotton, John 1584-1652. . . . . DLB-24

Coulter, John 1888-1980 . . . . DLB-68

Cournos, John 1881-1966. . . . . DLB-54

Cousins, Margaret 1905- DLB-137

Cousins, Norman 1915-1990 . . . . . DLB-137

Coventry, Francis 1725-1754 . . . . . . DLB-39

Coverdale, Miles
1487 or 1488-1569 . . . . DLB-167

Coverly, N. [publishing house]. DLB-49

Covici-Friede. DLB-46

Coward, Noel 1899-1973 . . . . DLB-10

Coward, McCann and
Geoghegan DLB-46

Cowles, Gardner 1861-1946 . . . . . . DLB-29

Cowles, Gardner ("Mike"), Jr.
1903-1985. . . . . DLB-127, 137

Cowley, Abraham
1618-1667. . . . . DLB-131, 151

Cowley, Hannah 1743-1809 . . . . . . DLB-89

Cowley, Malcolm
1898-1989. . . . . . . DLB-4, 48; Y-81, 89

Cowper, William
1731-1800. . . . . DLB-104, 109

Cox, A. B. (see Berkeley, Anthony)

Cox, James McMahon
1903-1974 . . . . DLB-127

Cox, James Middleton
1870-1957 . . . . DLB-127

Cox, Palmer 1840-1924. . . . . DLB-42

Coxe, Louis 1918-1993. . . . . DLB-5

Coxe, Tench 1755-1824 . . . . DLB-37

Cozzens, James Gould
1903-1978. . . . . DLB-9; Y-84; DS-2

Crabbe, George 1754-1832 . . . . DLB-93

Crackanthorpe, Hubert
1870-1896 . . . . DLB-135

Craddock, Charles Egbert
(see Murfree, Mary N.)

Cradock, Thomas 1718-1770. . . . . . DLB-31

Craig, Daniel H. 1811-1895 . . . . . . DLB-43

Craik, Dinah Maria
1826-1887 . . . . DLB-35, 136

Cranch, Christopher Pearse
1813-1892 . . . . DLB-1, 42

Crane, Hart 1899-1932 . . . . DLB-4, 48

Crane, R. S. 1886-1967. . . . . DLB-63

Crane, Stephen 1871-1900. . . . DLB-12, 54, 78

Crane, Walter 1845-1915 . . . . DLB-163

Cranmer, Thomas 1489-1556. . . . . DLB-132

Crapsey, Adelaide 1878-1914. . . . . . DLB-54

Crashaw, Richard
1612 or 1613-1649 . . . . DLB-126

Craven, Avery 1885-1980 . . . . DLB-17

Crawford, Charles
1752-circa 1815 . . . . DLB-31

Crawford, F. Marion 1854-1909 . . . . DLB-71

Crawford, Isabel Valancy
1850-1887 . . . . DLB-92

Crawley, Alan 1887-1975. . . . . DLB-68

Crayon, Geoffrey (see Irving, Washington)

Creamer, Robert W. 1922- DLB-171

Creasey, John 1908-1973 . . . . DLB-77

Creative Age Press DLB-46

Creech, William
[publishing house] DLB-154

Creede, Thomas
[publishing house] DLB-170

Creel, George 1876-1953 . . . . DLB-25

Creeley, Robert 1926- DLB-5, 16, 169

Creelman, James 1859-1915 . . . . . . DLB-23

Cregan, David 1931- DLB-13

Creighton, Donald Grant
1902-1979 . . . . DLB-88

Cremazie, Octave 1827-1879 . . . . . . DLB-99

Crémer, Victoriano 1909?- DLB-108

Crescas, Hasdai
circa 1340-1412? DLB-115

Crespo, Angel 1926- DLB-134

Cresset Press DLB-112

Cresswell, Helen 1934- DLB-161

Crèvecoeur, Michel Guillaume Jean de
1735-1813 . . . . DLB-37

Crews, Harry 1935- DLB-6, 143

Crichton, Michael 1942- Y-81

A Crisis of Culture: The Changing Role
of Religion in the New Republic
. . . . DLB-37

Crispin, Edmund 1921-1978 . . . . . . DLB-87

Cristofer, Michael 1946- DLB-7

"The Critic as Artist" (1891), by
Oscar Wilde DLB-57

"Criticism In Relation To Novels" (1863),
by G. H. Lewes DLB-21

Crnjanski, Miloš 1893-1977 . . . . . . DLB-147

Crockett, David (Davy)
1786-1836. . . . . DLB-3, 11, 183

Croft-Cooke, Rupert (see Bruce, Leo)

Crofts, Freeman Wills
1879-1957 . . . . DLB-77

Croker, John Wilson
1780-1857 . . . . DLB-110

Croly, George 1780-1860 . . . . DLB-159

Croly, Herbert 1869-1930 . . . . DLB-91

Croly, Jane Cunningham
1829-1901 . . . . DLB-23

Crompton, Richmal 1890-1969 . . . . DLB-160

Crosby, Caresse 1892-1970. . . . . . . DLB-48

Crosby, Caresse 1892-1970 and Crosby,
Harry 1898-1929. . . . . . . DLB-4; DS-15

Crosby, Harry 1898-1929. . . . . DLB-48

Cross, Gillian 1945- DLB-161

Cross, Victoria 1868-1952. . . . . DLB-135

Crossley-Holland, Kevin
1941- DLB-40, 161

Crothers, Rachel 1878-1958 . . . . . . DLB-7

Crowell, Thomas Y., Company DLB-49

Crowley, John 1942- Y-82

Crowley, Mart 1935- DLB-7

Crown Publishers DLB-46

Crowne, John 1641-1712 . . . . DLB-80

Crowninshield, Edward Augustus
1817-1859 . . . . DLB-140

Crowninshield, Frank 1872-1947. . . . DLB-91

Croy, Homer 1883-1965. . . . . DLB-4

Crumley, James 1939- Y-84

Cruz, Victor Hernández 1949- DLB-41

Csokor, Franz Theodor
1885-1969 . . . . DLB-81

Cuala Press. DLB-112

Cullen, Countee 1903-1946 . . . . DLB-4, 48, 51

Culler, Jonathan D. 1944- DLB-67

The Cult of Biography
Excerpts from the Second Folio Debate:
"Biographies are generally a disease of

English Literature" – Germaine Greer,
Victoria Glendinning, Auberon Waugh,
and Richard Holmes Y-86

Cumberland, Richard 1732-1811 . . . . . DLB-89

Cummings, Constance Gordon
1837-1924 . . . . DLB-174

Cummings, E. E. 1894-1962 . . . . . DLB-4, 48

Cummings, Ray 1887-1957 . . . . DLB-8

Cummings and Hilliard DLB-49

Cummins, Maria Susanna
1827-1866 . . . . DLB-42

Cundall, Joseph
[publishing house] DLB-106

Cuney, Waring 1906-1976 . . . . . . DLB-51

Cuney-Hare, Maude 1874-1936 . . . . . DLB-52

Cunningham, Allan
1784-1842 . . . . DLB-116, 144

Cunningham, J. V. 1911- DLB-5

Cunningham, Peter F.
[publishing house] DLB-49

Cunquiero, Alvaro 1911-1981 . . . . . DLB-134

Cuomo, George 1929- Y-80

Cupples and Leon DLB-46

Cupples, Upham and Company DLB-49

Cuppy, Will 1884-1949 . . . . DLB-11

Curll, Edmund
[publishing house] DLB-154

Currie, James 1756-1805 . . . . DLB-142

Currie, Mary Montgomerie Lamb Singleton,
Lady Currie (see Fane, Violet)

Cursor Mundi circa 1300 . . . . DLB-146

Curti, Merle E. 1897- DLB-17

Curtis, Anthony 1926- DLB-155

Curtis, Cyrus H. K. 1850-1933 . . . . DLB-91

Curtis, George William
1824-1892 . . . . DLB-1, 43

Curzon, Robert 1810-1873 . . . . . . DLB-166

Curzon, Sarah Anne 1833-1898 . . . . DLB-99

Cynewulf circa 770-840 . . . . DLB-146

Czepko, Daniel 1605-1660 . . . . . . DLB-164

D

D. M. Thomas: The Plagiarism
Controversy Y-82

Dabit, Eugène 1898-1936 . . . . DLB-65

Daborne, Robert circa 1580-1628 . . . . DLB-58

Dacey, Philip 1939- DLB-105

Dacey, Philip, Eyes Across Centuries:
Contemporary Poetry and "That
Vision Thing" DLB-105

Dach, Simon 1605-1659 . . . . DLB-164

Daggett, Rollin M. 1831-1901 . . . . . DLB-79

D'Aguiar, Fred 1960- DLB-157

Dahl, Roald 1916-1990 . . . . DLB-139

Dahlberg, Edward 1900-1977 . . . . . . DLB-48

Dahn, Felix 1834-1912 . . . . DLB-129

Dale, Peter 1938- DLB-40

Daley, Arthur 1904-1974 . . . . DLB-171

Dall, Caroline Wells (Healey)
1822-1912 . . . . DLB-1

Dallas, E. S. 1828-1879 . . . . DLB-55

The Dallas Theater Center DLB-7

D'Alton, Louis 1900-1951 . . . . DLB-10

Daly, T. A. 1871-1948 . . . . DLB-11

Damon, S. Foster 1893-1971 . . . . . . DLB-45

Damrell, William S.
[publishing house] DLB-49

Dana, Charles A. 1819-1897 . . . . DLB-3, 23

Dana, Richard Henry, Jr.
1815-1882 . . . . DLB-1, 183

Dandridge, Ray Garfield DLB-51

Dane, Clemence 1887-1965 . . . . . . DLB-10

Danforth, John 1660-1730 . . . . . . DLB-24

Danforth, Samuel, I 1626-1674 . . . . . DLB-24

Danforth, Samuel, II 1666-1727 . . . . . DLB-24

Dangerous Years: London Theater,
1939-1945 . . . . DLB-10

Daniel, John M. 1825-1865 . . . . . . DLB-43

Daniel, Samuel
1562 or 1563-1619 . . . . DLB-62

Daniel Press DLB-106

Daniells, Roy 1902-1979 . . . . DLB-68

Daniels, Jim 1956- DLB-120

Daniels, Jonathan 1902-1981 . . . . . DLB-127

Daniels, Josephus 1862-1948 . . . . . DLB-29

Dannay, Frederic 1905-1982 and
Manfred B. Lee 1905-1971 . . . . . DLB-137

Danner, Margaret Esse 1915- DLB-41

Danter, John [publishing house] DLB-170

Dantin, Louis 1865-1945 . . . . DLB-92

Danzig, Allison 1898-1987 . . . . . . DLB-171

D'Arcy, Ella circa 1857-1937 . . . . . DLB-135

Darley, George 1795-1846 . . . . . . DLB-96

Darwin, Charles 1809-1882 . . . . DLB-57, 166

Darwin, Erasmus 1731-1802 . . . . . DLB-93

Daryush, Elizabeth 1887-1977 . . . . . DLB-20

Dashkova, Ekaterina Romanovna
(née Vorontsova) 1743-1810 . . . . DLB-150

Dashwood, Edmée Elizabeth Monica
de la Pasture (see Delafield, E. M.)

Daudet, Alphonse 1840-1897 . . . . DLB-123

d'Aulaire, Edgar Parin 1898- and
d'Aulaire, Ingri 1904- DLB-22

Davenant, Sir William
1606-1668 . . . . DLB-58, 126

Davenport, Guy 1927- DLB-130

Davenport, Robert ?-? DLB-58

Daves, Delmer 1904-1977 . . . . . . DLB-26

Davey, Frank 1940- DLB-53

Davidson, Avram 1923-1993 . . . . . . DLB-8

Davidson, Donald 1893-1968 . . . . . DLB-45

Davidson, John 1857-1909 . . . . . . DLB-19

Davidson, Lionel 1922- DLB-14

Davie, Donald 1922- DLB-27

Davie, Elspeth 1919- DLB-139

Davies, Sir John 1569-1626 . . . . . . DLB-172

Davies, John, of Hereford
1565?-1618 . . . . DLB-121

Davies, Rhys 1901-1978 . . . . DLB-139

Davies, Robertson 1913- DLB-68

Davies, Samuel 1723-1761 . . . . . . DLB-31

Davies, Thomas 1712?-1785 . . . . DLB-142, 154

Davies, W. H. 1871-1940 . . . . . DLB-19, 174

Davies, Peter, Limited DLB-112

Daviot, Gordon 1896?-1952 . . . . . . DLB-10
(see also Tey, Josephine)

Davis, Charles A. 1795-1867 . . . . . . DLB-11

Davis, Clyde Brion 1894-1962 . . . . . . DLB-9

Davis, Dick 1945- DLB-40

Davis, Frank Marshall 1905-? DLB-51

Davis, H. L. 1894-1960 . . . . DLB-9

Davis, John 1774-1854 . . . . DLB-37

Davis, Lydia 1947- DLB-130

Davis, Margaret Thomson 1926- DLB-14

Davis, Ossie 1917- DLB-7, 38

Davis, Paxton 1925-1994 . . . . Y-94

Davis, Rebecca Harding
1831-1910 . . . . DLB-74

Davis, Richard Harding
1864-1916 . . . . DLB-12, 23, 78, 79; DS-13

Davis, Samuel Cole 1764-1809 . . . . . DLB-37

Davison, Peter 1928- DLB-5

Davys, Mary 1674-1732 . . . . DLB-39

DAW Books DLB-46

Dawson, Ernest 1882-1947 . . . . . . DLB-140

Dawson, Fielding 1930- DLB-130

Dawson, William 1704-1752 . . . . . . DLB-31

Day, Angel flourished 1586 . . . . . . DLB-167

Day, Benjamin Henry 1810-1889 . . . . DLB-43

Day, Clarence 1874-1935 . . . . DLB-11

Day, Dorothy 1897-1980 . . . . DLB-29

Day, Frank Parker 1881-1950 . . . . . DLB-92

Day, John circa 1574-circa 1640 . . . . . DLB-62

Day, John [publishing house] DLB-170

Day Lewis, C. 1904-1972 . . . . DLB-15, 20
(see also Blake, Nicholas)

Day, Thomas 1748-1789 . . . . DLB-39

Day, The John, Company DLB-46

Day, Mahlon [publishing house] DLB-49

Dazai, Osamu 1909-1948 . . . . DLB-182

Deacon, William Arthur
  1890-1977 . . . . DLB-68

Deal, Borden 1922-1985 . . . . DLB-6

de Angeli, Marguerite 1889-1987 . . . . . DLB-22

De Angelis, Milo 1951- DLB-128

De Bow, James Dunwoody Brownson
  1820-1867 . . . . DLB-3, 79

de Bruyn, Günter 1926- DLB-75

de Camp, L. Sprague 1907- DLB-8

The Decay of Lying (1889),
  by Oscar Wilde [excerpt] DLB-18

Dedication, Ferdinand Count Fathom (1753),
  by Tobias Smollett DLB-39

Dedication, The History of Pompey the Little
  (1751), by Francis Coventry DLB-39

Dedication, Lasselia (1723), by Eliza
  Haywood [excerpt] DLB-39

Dedication, The Wanderer (1814),
  by Fanny Burney. DLB-39

Dee, John 1527-1609. . . . . DLB-136

Deeping, George Warwick
  1877-1950 . . . . DLB 153

Defense of Amelia (1752), by
  Henry Fielding DLB-39

Defoe, Daniel 1660-1731 . . . . DLB-39, 95, 101

de Fontaine, Felix Gregory
  1834-1896 . . . . DLB-43

De Forest, John William
  1826-1906 . . . . DLB-12

DeFrees, Madeline 1919- DLB-105

DeFrees, Madeline, The Poet's Kaleidoscope:
  The Element of Surprise in the Making
  of the Poem DLB-105

de Graff, Robert 1895-1981 . . . . Y-81

de Graft, Joe 1924-1978 . . . . DLB-117

De Heinrico circa 980? DLB-148

Deighton, Len 1929- DLB-87

DeJong, Meindert 1906-1991 . . . . . . DLB-52

Dekker, Thomas
  circa 1572-1632 . . . . DLB-62, 172

Delacorte, Jr., George T.
  1894-1991 . . . . DLB-91

Delafield, E. M. 1890-1943 . . . . DLB-34

Delahaye, Guy 1888-1969 . . . . DLB-92

de la Mare, Walter
  1873-1956 . . . . DLB-19, 153, 162

Deland, Margaret 1857-1945 . . . . . . DLB-78

Delaney, Shelagh 1939- DLB-13

Delano, Amasa 1763-1823. . . . . . . DLB-183

Delany, Martin Robinson
  1812-1885 . . . . DLB-50

Delany, Samuel R. 1942- DLB-8, 33

de la Roche, Mazo 1879-1961 . . . . . DLB-68

Delbanco, Nicholas 1942- DLB-6

De León, Nephtal 1945- DLB-82

Delgado, Abelardo Barrientos
  1931- DLB-82

De Libero, Libero 1906-1981 . . . . . DLB-114

DeLillo, Don 1936- DLB-6, 173

de Lisser H. G. 1878-1944 . . . . . . DLB-117

Dell, Floyd 1887-1969 . . . . DLB-9

Dell Publishing Company DLB-46

delle Grazie, Marie Eugene
  1864-1931 . . . . DLB-81

Deloney, Thomas died 1600 . . . . . DLB-167

Deloria, Ella C. 1889-1971 . . . . . . DLB-175

Deloria, Vine, Jr. 1933- DLB-175

del Rey, Lester 1915-1993 . . . . DLB-8

Del Vecchio, John M. 1947- DS-9

de Man, Paul 1919-1983 . . . . DLB-67

Demby, William 1922- DLB-33

Deming, Philander 1829-1915 . . . . . DLB-74

Demorest, William Jennings
  1822-1895 . . . . DLB-79

De Morgan, William 1839-1917 . . . . DLB-153

Demosthenes 384 B.C.-322 B.C. DLB-176

Denham, Henry
  [publishing house] DLB-170

Denham, Sir John
  1615-1669 . . . . DLB-58, 126

Denison, Merrill 1893-1975 . . . . DLB-92

Denison, T. S., and Company DLB-49

Dennie, Joseph
  1768-1812 . . . . DLB-37, 43, 59, 73

Dennis, John 1658-1734 . . . . DLB-101

Dennis, Nigel 1912-1989 . . . . . . DLB-13, 15

Dent, Tom 1932- DLB-38

Dent, J. M., and Sons DLB-112

Denton, Daniel circa 1626-1703 . . . . DLB-24

DePaola, Tomie 1934- DLB-61

De Quincey, Thomas
  1785-1859. . . . . DLB-110, 144

Derby, George Horatio
  1823-1861 . . . . DLB-11

Derby, J. C., and Company DLB-49

Derby and Miller DLB-49

Derleth, August 1909-1971 . . . . DLB-9

The Derrydale Press DLB-46

Derzhavin, Gavriil Romanovich
  1743-1816 . . . . DLB-150

Desaulniers, Gonsalve
  1863-1934 . . . . DLB-92

Desbiens, Jean-Paul 1927- DLB-53

des Forêts, Louis-Rene 1918- DLB-83

Desnica, Vladan 1905-1967 . . . . . . DLB-181

DesRochers, Alfred 1901-1978 . . . . . DLB-68

Desrosiers, Léo-Paul 1896-1967 . . . . DLB-68

Dessì, Giuseppe 1909-1977 . . . . . . DLB-177

Destouches, Louis-Ferdinand
  (see Céline, Louis-Ferdinand)

De Tabley, Lord 1835-1895 . . . . . . DLB-35

Deutsch, Babette 1895-1982. . . . . . DLB-45

Deutsch, Niklaus Manuel (see Manuel, Niklaus)

Deutsch, André, Limited DLB-112

Deveaux, Alexis 1948- DLB-38

The Development of the Author's Copyright
  in Britain. DLB-154

The Development of Lighting in the Staging
  of Drama, 1900-1945 . . . . DLB-10

The Development of Meiji Japan. . . . DLB-180

de Vere, Aubrey 1814-1902 . . . . . . DLB-35

Devereux, second Earl of Essex, Robert
  1565-1601 . . . . DLB-136

The Devin-Adair Company DLB-46

De Voto, Bernard 1897-1955 . . . . . . DLB-9

De Vries, Peter 1910-1993 . . . . DLB-6; Y-82

Dewdney, Christopher 1951- DLB-60

Dewdney, Selwyn 1909-1979 . . . . . DLB-68

DeWitt, Robert M., Publisher DLB-49

DeWolfe, Fiske and Company. DLB-49

Dexter, Colin 1930- DLB-87

de Young, M. H. 1849-1925 . . . . . . DLB-25

Dhlomo, H. I. E. 1903-1956 . . . . . DLB-157

Dhuoda circa 803-after 843 . . . . . . DLB-148

The Dial Press DLB-46

Diamond, I. A. L. 1920-1988 . . . . . DLB-26

Di Cicco, Pier Giorgio 1949- DLB-60

Dick, Philip K. 1928-1982 . . . . DLB-8

Dick and Fitzgerald DLB-49

Dickens, Charles
  1812-1870 . . . . . DLB-21, 55, 70, 159, 166

Dickinson, Peter 1927- DLB-161

Dickey, James
  1923-1997 . . . . . . DLB-5; Y-82, 93; DS-7

James Dickey, American Poet Y-96

Dickey, William 1928-1994 . . . . . . DLB-5

Dickinson, Emily 1830-1886 . . . . . . DLB-1

Dickinson, John 1732-1808 . . . . . . DLB-31

Dickinson, Jonathan 1688-1747 . . . . DLB-24

Dickinson, Patric 1914- DLB-27

Dickinson, Peter 1927- DLB-87

Dicks, John [publishing house] DLB-106

Dickson, Gordon R. 1923- DLB-8

Dictionary of Literary Biography
  Yearbook Awards Y-92, 93

The Dictionary of National Biography
  . . . . DLB-144

Didion, Joan 1934- DLB-2, 173; Y-81, 86

Di Donato, Pietro 1911- DLB-9

Die Fürstliche Bibliothek Corvey Y-96

Diego, Gerardo 1896-1987 . . . . DLB-134

Digges, Thomas circa 1546-1595 . . . . DLB-136

Dillard, Annie 1945- Y-80

Dillard, R. H. W. 1937- DLB-5

Dillingham, Charles T.,
  Company DLB-49

The Dillingham, G. W.,
  Company DLB-49

Dilly, Edward and Charles
  [publishing house] DLB-154

Dilthey, Wilhelm 1833-1911 . . . . . . DLB-129

Dimitrova, Blaga 1922- DLB-181

Dimov, Dimitŭr 1909-1966 . . . . . . DLB-181

Dingelstedt, Franz von
  1814-1881 . . . . DLB-133

Dintenfass, Mark 1941- Y-84

Diogenes, Jr. (see Brougham, John)

Diogenes Laertius circa 200 . . . . . . DLB-176

DiPrima, Diane 1934- DLB-5, 16

Disch, Thomas M. 1940- DLB-8

Disney, Walt 1901-1966 . . . . DLB-22

Disraeli, Benjamin 1804-1881 . . . . DLB-21, 55

D'Israeli, Isaac 1766-1848 . . . . . . DLB-107

Ditzen, Rudolf (see Fallada, Hans)

Dix, Dorothea Lynde 1802-1887 . . . . . DLB-1

Dix, Dorothy (see Gilmer,
  Elizabeth Meriwether)

Dix, Edwards and Company DLB-49

Dixie, Florence Douglas
  1857-1905 . . . . DLB-174

Dixon, Paige (see Corcoran, Barbara)

Dixon, Richard Watson
  1833-1900 . . . . DLB-19

Dixon, Stephen 1936- DLB-130

Dmitriev, Ivan Ivanovich
  1760-1837 . . . . DLB-150

Dobell, Sydney 1824-1874 . . . . DLB-32

Döblin, Alfred 1878-1957 . . . . DLB-66

Dobson, Austin
  1840-1921 . . . . DLB-35, 144

Doctorow, E. L.
  1931- DLB-2, 28, 173; Y-80

Documents on Sixteenth-Century
  Literature DLB-167, 172

Dodd, William E. 1869-1940 . . . . . . DLB-17

Dodd, Anne [publishing house] DLB-154

Dodd, Mead and Company DLB-49

Doderer, Heimito von 1896-1968 . . . DLB-85

Dodge, Mary Mapes
  1831?-1905 . . . . DLB-42, 79; DS-13

Dodge, B. W., and Company DLB-46

Dodge Publishing Company DLB-49

Dodgson, Charles Lutwidge
  (see Carroll, Lewis)

Dodsley, Robert 1703-1764 . . . . DLB-95

Dodsley, R. [publishing house] DLB-154

Dodson, Owen 1914-1983 . . . . DLB-76

Doesticks, Q. K. Philander, P. B.
  (see Thomson, Mortimer)

Doheny, Carrie Estelle
  1875-1958 . . . . DLB-140

Domínguez, Sylvia Maida
  1935- DLB-122

Donahoe, Patrick
  [publishing house] DLB-49

Donald, David H. 1920- DLB-17

Donaldson, Scott 1928- DLB-111

Doni, Rodolfo 1919- DLB-177

Donleavy, J. P. 1926- DLB-6, 173

Donnadieu, Marguerite (see Duras,
  Marguerite)

Donne, John 1572-1631 . . . . . DLB-121, 151

Donnelley, R. R., and Sons
  Company DLB-49

Donnelly, Ignatius 1831-1901 . . . . . . DLB-12

Donohue and Henneberry DLB-49

Donoso, José 1924- DLB-113

Doolady, M. [publishing house] DLB-49

Dooley, Ebon (see Ebon)

Doolittle, Hilda 1886-1961 . . . . . . DLB-4, 45

Doplicher, Fabio 1938- DLB-128

Dor, Milo 1923- DLB-85

Doran, George H., Company DLB-46

Dorgelès, Roland 1886-1973 . . . . . . DLB-65

Dorn, Edward 1929- DLB-5

Dorr, Rheta Childe 1866-1948 . . . . . DLB-25

Dorris, Michael 1945-1997 . . . . . . DLB-175

Dorset and Middlesex, Charles Sackville,
  Lord Buckhurst,
  Earl of 1643-1706 . . . . DLB-131

Dorst, Tankred 1925- DLB-75, 124

Dos Passos, John
  1896-1970 . . . . DLB-4, 9; DS-1, 15

John Dos Passos: A Centennial
  Commemoration Y-96

Doubleday and Company DLB-49

Dougall, Lily 1858-1923 . . . . DLB-92

Doughty, Charles M.
  1843-1926 . . . . DLB-19, 57, 174

Douglas, Gavin 1476-1522 . . . . . DLB-132

Douglas, Keith 1920-1944 . . . . DLB-27

Douglas, Norman 1868-1952 . . . . . . DLB-34

Douglass, Frederick
  1817?-1895 . . . . . . DLB-1, 43, 50, 79

Douglass, William circa
  1691-1752 . . . . DLB-24

Dourado, Autran 1926- DLB-145

Dove, Rita 1952- DLB-120

Dover Publications DLB-46

Doves Press DLB-112

Dowden, Edward 1843-1913 . . . . DLB-35, 149

Dowell, Coleman 1925-1985 . . . . . DLB-130

Dowland, John 1563-1626 . . . . . . DLB-172

Downes, Gwladys 1915- DLB-88

Downing, J., Major (see Davis, Charles A.)

Downing, Major Jack (see Smith, Seba)

Dowriche, Anne
  before 1560-after 1613 . . . . . . DLB-172

Dowson, Ernest 1867-1900 . . . . DLB-19, 135

Doxey, William
  [publishing house] DLB-49

Doyle, Sir Arthur Conan
  1859-1930 . . . . . . DLB-18, 70, 156, 178

Doyle, Kirby 1932- DLB-16

Drabble, Margaret 1939- DLB-14, 155

Drach, Albert 1902- DLB-85

Dragojević, Danijel 1934- DLB-181

The Dramatic Publishing
  Company DLB-49

Dramatists Play Service DLB-46

Drant, Thomas
  early 1540s?-1578 . . . . DLB-167

Draper, John W. 1811-1882 . . . . . . DLB-30

Draper, Lyman C. 1815-1891 . . . . . . DLB-30

Drayton, Michael 1563-1631 . . . . . DLB-121

Dreiser, Theodore
  1871-1945 . . . . DLB-9, 12, 102, 137; DS-1

Drewitz, Ingeborg 1923-1986 . . . . . . DLB-75

Drieu La Rochelle, Pierre
  1893-1945 . . . . DLB-72

Drinkwater, John 1882-1937
  . . . . DLB-10, 19, 149

Droste-Hülshoff, Annette von
  1797-1848 . . . . DLB-133

The Drue Heinz Literature Prize
  Excerpt from "Excerpts from a Report
  of the Commission," in David
  Bosworth's *The Death of Descartes*
  An Interview with David
  Bosworth Y-82

Drummond, William Henry
  1854-1907 . . . . DLB-92

Drummond, William, of Hawthornden
  1585-1649 . . . . DLB-121

Dryden, Charles 1860?-1931 . . . . . DLB-171

Dryden, John 1631-1700 . . . DLB-80, 101, 131

Držić, Marin circa 1508-1567 . . . . . DLB-147

Duane, William 1760-1835 . . . . . . DLB-43

Dubé, Marcel 1930- DLB-53

Dubé, Rodolphe (see Hertel, François)

Dubie, Norman 1945- DLB-120

Du Bois, W. E. B.
  1868-1963 . . . . DLB-47, 50, 91

Du Bois, William Pène 1916- DLB-61

Dubus, Andre 1936- DLB-130

Ducharme, Réjean 1941- DLB-60

Dučić, Jovan 1871-1943 . . . . DLB-147

Duck, Stephen 1705?-1756 . . . . DLB-95

Duckworth, Gerald, and
    Company Limited DLB-112

Dudek, Louis 1918- DLB-88

Duell, Sloan and Pearce DLB-46

Duerer, Albrecht 1471-1528 . . . . DLB-179

Duff Gordon, Lucie 1821-1869 . . . . . DLB-166

Duffield and Green DLB-46

Duffy, Maureen 1933- DLB-14

Dugan, Alan 1923- DLB-5

Dugard, William
    [publishing house] DLB-170

Dugas, Marcel 1883-1947 . . . . DLB-92

Dugdale, William
    [publishing house] DLB-106

Duhamel, Georges 1884-1966 . . . . . . DLB-65

Dujardin, Edouard 1861-1949 . . . . . . DLB-123

Dukes, Ashley 1885-1959 . . . . DLB-10

Du Maurier, George
    1834-1896 . . . . DLB-153, 178

Dumas, Alexandre, père
    1802-1870 . . . . DLB-119

Dumas, Henry 1934-1968 . . . . DLB-41

Dunbar, Paul Laurence
    1872-1906 . . . . DLB-50, 54, 78

Dunbar, William
    circa 1460-circa 1522 . . . . . DLB-132, 146

Duncan, Norman 1871-1916 . . . . DLB-92

Duncan, Quince 1940- DLB-145

Duncan, Robert 1919-1988 . . . . . DLB-5, 16

Duncan, Ronald 1914-1982 . . . . DLB-13

Duncan, Sara Jeannette
    1861-1922 . . . . DLB-92

Dunigan, Edward, and Brother DLB-49

Dunlap, John 1747-1812 . . . . DLB-43

Dunlap, William
    1766-1839 . . . . DLB-30, 37, 59

Dunn, Douglas 1942- DLB-40

Dunn, Stephen 1939- DLB-105

Dunn, Stephen, The Good,
    The Not So Good DLB-105

Dunne, Finley Peter
    1867-1936 . . . . DLB-11, 23

Dunne, John Gregory 1932- Y-80

Dunne, Philip 1908-1992 . . . . DLB-26

Dunning, Ralph Cheever
    1878-1930 . . . . DLB-4

Dunning, William A. 1857-1922 . . . . . DLB-17

Duns Scotus, John
    circa 1266-1308 . . . . DLB-115

Dunsany, Lord (Edward John Moreton
    Drax Plunkett, Baron Dunsany)
    1878-1957 . . . . DLB-10, 77, 153, 156

Dunton, John [publishing house] DLB-170

Dupin, Amantine-Aurore-Lucile (see Sand, George)

Durand, Lucile (see Bersianik, Louky)

Duranty, Walter 1884-1957 . . . . DLB-29

Duras, Marguerite 1914- DLB-83

Durfey, Thomas 1653-1723 . . . . DLB-80

Durrell, Lawrence
    1912-1990 . . . . DLB-15, 27; Y-90

Durrell, William
    [publishing house] DLB-49

Dürrenmatt, Friedrich
    1921-1990 . . . . DLB-69, 124

Dutton, E. P., and Company DLB-49

Duvoisin, Roger 1904-1980 . . . . DLB-61

Duyckinck, Evert Augustus
    1816-1878 . . . . DLB-3, 64

Duyckinck, George L. 1823-1863 . . . . DLB-3

Duyckinck and Company DLB-49

Dwight, John Sullivan 1813-1893 . . . . DLB-1

Dwight, Timothy 1752-1817 . . . . DLB-37

Dybek, Stuart 1942- DLB-130

Dyer, Charles 1928- DLB-13

Dyer, George 1755-1841 . . . . DLB-93

Dyer, John 1699-1757 . . . . DLB-95

Dyer, Sir Edward 1543-1607 . . . . . . DLB-136

Dylan, Bob 1941- DLB-16

E

Eager, Edward 1911-1964 . . . . DLB-22

Eames, Wilberforce 1855-1937 . . . . . DLB-140

Earle, James H., and Company DLB-49

Earle, John 1600 or 1601-1665 . . . . . DLB-151

Early American Book Illustration,
    by Sinclair Hamilton DLB-49

Eastlake, William 1917- DLB-6

Eastman, Carol ?- DLB-44

Eastman, Charles A. (Ohiyesa)
    1858-1939 . . . . DLB-175

Eastman, Max 1883-1969 . . . . DLB-91

Eaton, Daniel Isaac 1753-1814 . . . . . DLB-158

Eberhart, Richard 1904- DLB-48

Ebner, Jeannie 1918- DLB-85

Ebner-Eschenbach, Marie von
    1830-1916 . . . . DLB-81

Ebon 1942- DLB-41

Ecbasis Captivi circa 1045 . . . . DLB-148

Ecco Press DLB-46

Eckhart, Meister
    circa 1260-circa 1328 . . . . DLB-115

The Eclectic Review 1805-1868 . . . . . DLB-110

Edel, Leon 1907- DLB-103

Edes, Benjamin 1732-1803 . . . . DLB-43

Edgar, David 1948- DLB-13

Edgeworth, Maria
    1768-1849 . . . . DLB-116, 159, 163

The Edinburgh Review 1802-1929 . . . . DLB-110

Edinburgh University Press DLB-112

The Editor Publishing Company DLB-49

Editorial Statements DLB-137

Edmonds, Randolph 1900- DLB-51

Edmonds, Walter D. 1903- DLB-9

Edschmid, Kasimir 1890-1966 . . . . . DLB-56

Edwards, Amelia Anne Blandford
    1831-1892 . . . . DLB-174

Edwards, Jonathan 1703-1758 . . . . . DLB-24

Edwards, Jonathan, Jr. 1745-1801 . . . . DLB-37

Edwards, Junius 1929- DLB-33

Edwards, Matilda Barbara Betham-
    1836-1919 . . . . DLB-174

Edwards, Richard 1524-1566 . . . . . . DLB-62

Edwards, James
    [publishing house] DLB-154

Effinger, George Alec 1947- DLB-8

Egerton, George 1859-1945 . . . . . . DLB-135

Eggleston, Edward 1837-1902 . . . . . DLB-12

Eggleston, Wilfred 1901-1986 . . . . . . DLB-92

Ehrenstein, Albert 1886-1950 . . . . . . DLB-81

Ehrhart, W. D. 1948- DS-9

Eich, Günter 1907-1972 . . . . DLB-69, 124

Eichendorff, Joseph Freiherr von
    1788-1857 . . . . DLB-90

1873 Publishers' Catalogues DLB-49

Eighteenth-Century Aesthetic
    Theories DLB-31

Eighteenth-Century Philosophical
    Background DLB-31

Eigner, Larry 1927- DLB-5

Eikon Basilike 1649 . . . . DLB-151

Eilhart von Oberge
    circa 1140-circa 1195 . . . . DLB-148

Einhard circa 770-840 . . . . DLB-148

Eisenreich, Herbert 1925-1986 . . . . . DLB-85

Eisner, Kurt 1867-1919 . . . . DLB-66

Eklund, Gordon 1945- Y-83

Ekwensi, Cyprian 1921- DLB-117

Eld, George
    [publishing house] DLB-170

Elder, Lonne III 1931- DLB-7, 38, 44

Elder, Paul, and Company DLB-49

Elements of Rhetoric (1828; revised, 1846),
    by Richard Whately [excerpt] DLB-57

Elie, Robert 1915-1973 . . . . DLB-88

Elin Pelin 1877-1949 . . . . DLB-147

Eliot, George 1819-1880 . . . . . DLB-21, 35, 55

Eliot, John 1604-1690 . . . . DLB-24

Eliot, T. S. 1888-1965 . . . . DLB-7, 10, 45, 63

Eliot's Court Press DLB-170

Elizabeth I 1533-1603 . . . . DLB-136

Elizabeth of Nassau-Saarbrücken
    after 1393-1456 . . . . DLB-179

Elizondo, Salvador 1932- DLB-145

Elizondo, Sergio 1930- DLB-82

Elkin, Stanley 1930- DLB-2, 28; Y-80

Elles, Dora Amy (see Wentworth, Patricia)

Ellet, Elizabeth F. 1818?-1877 . . . . . DLB-30

Elliot, Ebenezer 1781-1849 . . . . DLB-96

Elliot, Frances Minto (Dickinson)
    1820-1898 . . . . DLB-166

Elliott, George 1923- DLB-68

Elliott, Janice 1931- DLB-14

Elliott, William 1788-1863 . . . . DLB-3

Elliott, Thomes and Talbot DLB-49

Ellis, Edward S. 1840-1916 . . . . DLB-42

Ellis, Frederick Staridge
    [publishing house] DLB-106

The George H. Ellis Company DLB-49

Ellison, Harlan 1934- DLB-8

Ellison, Ralph Waldo
    1914-1994 . . . . DLB-2, 76; Y-94

Ellmann, Richard
    1918-1987 . . . . DLB-103; Y-87

The Elmer Holmes Bobst Awards in Arts
    and Letters Y-87

Elyot, Thomas 1490?-1546 . . . . DLB-136

Emanuel, James Andrew 1921- DLB-41

Emecheta, Buchi 1944- DLB-117

The Emergence of Black Women
    Writers DS-8

Emerson, Ralph Waldo
    1803-1882 . . . . DLB-1, 59, 73, 183

Emerson, William 1769-1811 . . . . . . DLB-37

Emin, Fedor Aleksandrovich
    circa 1735-1770 . . . . DLB-150

Empedocles fifth century B.C. DLB-176

Empson, William 1906-1984 . . . . . . DLB-20

Enchi, Fumiko 1905-1986 . . . . DLB-182

Encounter with the West DLB-180

The End of English Stage Censorship,
    1945-1968 . . . . DLB-13

Ende, Michael 1929- DLB-75

Endō, Shūsaku 1923-1996 . . . . DLB-182

Engel, Marian 1933-1985 . . . . DLB-53

Engels, Friedrich 1820-1895 . . . . . . DLB-129

Engle, Paul 1908- DLB-48

English Composition and Rhetoric (1866),
    by Alexander Bain [excerpt] DLB-57

The English Language:
    410 to 1500 . . . . DLB-146

The English Renaissance of Art (1908),
    by Oscar Wilde DLB-35

Enright, D. J. 1920- DLB-27

Enright, Elizabeth 1909-1968 . . . . . . DLB-22

L'Envoi (1882), by Oscar Wilde DLB-35

Epictetus circa 55-circa 125-130 . . . . DLB-176

Epicurus 342/341 B.C.-271/270 B.C.
    . . . . DLB-176

Epps, Bernard 1936- DLB-53

Epstein, Julius 1909- and
    Epstein, Philip 1909-1952 . . . . . . DLB-26

Equiano, Olaudah
    circa 1745-1797 . . . . DLB-37, 50

Eragny Press DLB-112

Erasmus, Desiderius 1467-1536 . . . . DLB-136

Erba, Luciano 1922- DLB-128

Erdrich, Louise 1954- DLB-152, 178

Erichsen-Brown, Gwethalyn Graham
    (see Graham, Gwethalyn)

Eriugena, John Scottus
    circa 810-877 . . . . DLB-115

Ernest Hemingway's Toronto Journalism
    Revisited: With Three Previously
    Unrecorded Stories Y-92

Ernst, Paul 1866-1933 . . . . . . DLB-66, 118

Erskine, Albert 1911-1993 . . . . Y-93

Erskine, John 1879-1951 . . . . . DLB-9, 102

Ervine, St. John Greer 1883-1971 . . . . DLB-10

Eschenburg, Johann Joachim
    1743-1820 . . . . DLB-97

Escoto, Julio 1944- DLB-145

Eshleman, Clayton 1935- DLB-5

Espriu, Salvador 1913-1985 . . . . . . DLB-134

Ess Ess Publishing Company DLB-49

Essay on Chatterton (1842), by
    Robert Browning DLB-32

Essex House Press DLB-112

Estes, Eleanor 1906-1988 . . . . DLB-22

Estes and Lauriat DLB-49

Etherege, George 1636-circa 1692 . . . DLB-80

Ethridge, Mark, Sr. 1896-1981 . . . . . DLB-127

Ets, Marie Hall 1893- DLB-22

Etter, David 1928- DLB-105

Ettner, Johann Christoph
    1654-1724 . . . . DLB-168

Eudora Welty: Eye of the Storyteller . . . Y-87

Eugene O'Neill Memorial Theater
    Center DLB-7

Eugene O'Neill's Letters: A Review Y-88

Eupolemius
    flourished circa 1095 . . . . DLB-148

Euripides circa 484 B.C.-407/406 B.C.
    . . . . DLB-176

Evans, Caradoc 1878-1945 . . . . . . DLB-162

Evans, Donald 1884-1921 . . . . DLB-54

Evans, George Henry 1805-1856 . . . . DLB-43

Evans, Hubert 1892-1986 . . . . DLB-92

Evans, Mari 1923- DLB-41

Evans, Mary Ann (see Eliot, George)

Evans, Nathaniel 1742-1767 . . . . . . DLB-31

Evans, Sebastian 1830-1909 . . . . . . DLB-35

Evans, M., and Company DLB-46

Everett, Alexander Hill
    790-1847 . . . . DLB-59

Everett, Edward 1794-1865 . . . . . DLB-1, 59

Everson, R. G. 1903- DLB-88

Everson, William 1912-1994 . . . . . DLB-5, 16

Every Man His Own Poet; or, The
    Inspired Singer's Recipe Book (1877),
    by W. H. Mallock DLB-35

Ewart, Gavin 1916- DLB-40

Ewing, Juliana Horatia
    1841-1885 . . . . DLB-21, 163

The Examiner 1808-1881 . . . . DLB-110

Exley, Frederick
    1929-1992 . . . . DLB-143; Y-81

Experiment in the Novel (1929),
    by John D. Beresford DLB-36

von Eyb, Albrecht 1420-1475 . . . . . DLB-179

Eyre and Spottiswoode DLB-106

Ezzo ?-after 1065 . . . . DLB-148

F

"F. Scott Fitzgerald: St. Paul's Native Son
    and Distinguished American Writer":
    University of Minnesota Conference,
    29-31 October 1982 . . . . Y-82

Faber, Frederick William
    1814-1863 . . . . DLB-32

Faber and Faber Limited DLB-112

Faccio, Rena (see Aleramo, Sibilla)

Fagundo, Ana María 1938- DLB-134

Fair, Ronald L. 1932- DLB-33

Fairfax, Beatrice (see Manning, Marie)

Fairlie, Gerard 1899-1983 . . . . DLB-77

Fallada, Hans 1893-1947 . . . . DLB-56

Falsifying Hemingway Y-96

Fancher, Betsy 1928- Y-83

Fane, Violet 1843-1905 . . . . DLB-35

Fanfrolico Press DLB-112

Fanning, Katherine 1927- DLB-127

Fanshawe, Sir Richard
    1608-1666 . . . . DLB-126

Fantasy Press Publishers DLB-46

Fante, John 1909-1983 . . . . . . DLB-130; Y-83

Al-Farabi circa 870-950 . . . . DLB-115

Farah, Nuruddin 1945- DLB-125

Farber, Norma 1909-1984 . . . . DLB-61

Farigoule, Louis (see Romains, Jules)

Farjeon, Eleanor 1881-1965 . . . . DLB-160

Farley, Walter 1920-1989 . . . . DLB-22

Farmer, Penelope 1939- DLB-161

Farmer, Philip José 1918- DLB-8

Farquhar, George circa 1677-1707 . . . . DLB-84

Farquharson, Martha (see Finley, Martha)

Farrar, Frederic William
1831-1903 . . . . DLB-163

Farrar and Rinehart. DLB-46

Farrar, Straus and Giroux DLB-46

Farrell, James T.
1904-1979 . . . . DLB-4, 9, 86; DS-2

Farrell, J. G. 1935-1979 . . . . DLB-14

Fast, Howard 1914- DLB-9

Faulkner, William 1897-1962
. . . . . . DLB-9, 11, 44, 102; DS-2; Y-86

Faulkner, George
[publishing house] DLB-154

Fauset, Jessie Redmon 1882-1961 . . . . DLB-51

Faust, Irvin 1924- DLB-2, 28; Y-80

Fawcett Books. DLB-46

Fearing, Kenneth 1902-1961 . . . . DLB-9

Federal Writers' Project. DLB-46

Federman, Raymond 1928- Y-80

Feiffer, Jules 1929- DLB-7, 44

Feinberg, Charles E. 1899-1988 . . . . . . Y-88

Feind, Barthold 1678-1721. . . . . DLB-168

Feinstein, Elaine 1930- DLB-14, 40

Feldman, Irving 1928- DLB-169

Felipe, Léon 1884-1968 . . . . DLB-108

Fell, Frederick, Publishers. DLB-46

Felltham, Owen 1602?-1668 . . . . DLB-126, 151

Fels, Ludwig 1946- DLB-75

Felton, Cornelius Conway
1807-1862. . . . . DLB-1

Fennario, David 1947- DLB-60

Fenno, John 1751-1798 . . . . DLB-43

Fenno, R. F., and Company DLB-49

Fenoglio, Beppe 1922-1963 . . . . DLB-177

Fenton, Geoffrey 1539?-1608 . . . . . . DLB-136

Fenton, James 1949- DLB-40

Ferber, Edna 1885-1968 . . . . . DLB-9, 28, 86

Ferdinand, Vallery III (see Salaam, Kalamu ya)

Ferguson, Sir Samuel 1810-1886 . . . . . DLB-32

Ferguson, William Scott
1875-1954 . . . . DLB-47

Fergusson, Robert 1750-1774 . . . . . . DLB-109

Ferland, Albert 1872-1943 . . . . DLB-92

Ferlinghetti, Lawrence 1919- DLB-5, 16

Fern, Fanny (see Parton, Sara Payson Willis)

Ferrars, Elizabeth 1907- DLB-87

Ferré, Rosario 1942- DLB-145

Ferret, E., and Company. DLB-49

Ferrier, Susan 1782-1854 . . . . DLB-116

Ferrini, Vincent 1913- DLB-48

Ferron, Jacques 1921-1985 . . . . DLB-60

Ferron, Madeleine 1922- DLB-53

Fetridge and Company DLB-49

Feuchtersleben, Ernst Freiherr von
1806-1849 . . . . DLB-133

Feuchtwanger, Lion 1884-1958 . . . . . DLB-66

Feuerbach, Ludwig 1804-1872. . . . . . DLB-133

Fichte, Johann Gottlieb
1762-1814 . . . . DLB-90

Ficke, Arthur Davison 1883-1945 . . . . DLB-54

Fiction Best-Sellers, 1910-1945 . . . . . . DLB-9

Fiction into Film, 1928-1975: A List of Movies
Based on the Works of Authors in
British Novelists, 1930-1959 . . . . . . DLB-15

Fiedler, Leslie A. 1917- DLB-28, 67

Field, Edward 1924- DLB-105

Field, Edward, The Poetry File. DLB-105

Field, Eugene
1850-1895 . . . . . DLB-23, 42, 140; DS-13

Field, John 1545?-1588. . . . . DLB-167

Field, Marshall, III 1893-1956. . . . . . DLB-127

Field, Marshall, IV 1916-1965 . . . . . . DLB-127

Field, Marshall, V 1941- DLB-127

Field, Nathan 1587-1619 or 1620 . . . . DLB-58

Field, Rachel 1894-1942 . . . . DLB-9, 22

A Field Guide to Recent Schools of American
Poetry. Y-86

Fielding, Henry
1707-1754 . . . . DLB-39, 84, 101

Fielding, Sarah 1710-1768. . . . . DLB-39

Fields, James Thomas 1817-1881 . . . . . DLB-1

Fields, Julia 1938- DLB-41

Fields, W. C. 1880-1946 . . . . DLB-44

Fields, Osgood and Company DLB-49

Fifty Penguin Years. Y-85

Figes, Eva 1932- DLB-14

Figuera, Angela 1902-1984 . . . . DLB-108

Filmer, Sir Robert 1586-1653 . . . . . . DLB-151

Filson, John circa 1753-1788 . . . . . . DLB-37

Finch, Anne, Countess of Winchilsea
1661-1720 . . . . DLB-95

Finch, Robert 1900- DLB-88

Findley, Timothy 1930- DLB-53

Finlay, Ian Hamilton 1925- DLB-40

Finley, Martha 1828-1909. . . . . DLB-42

Finn, Elizabeth Anne (McCaul)
1825-1921 . . . . DLB-166

Finney, Jack 1911- DLB-8

Finney, Walter Braden (see Finney, Jack)

Firbank, Ronald 1886-1926. . . . . . . DLB-36

Firmin, Giles 1615-1697. . . . . DLB-24

Fischart, Johann
1546 or 1547-1590 or 1591 . . . . DLB-179

First Edition Library/Collectors'
Reprints, Inc. Y-91

First International F. Scott Fitzgerald
Conference Y-92

First Strauss "Livings" Awarded to Cynthia
Ozick and Raymond Carver
An Interview with Cynthia Ozick
An Interview with Raymond
Carver Y-83

Fischer, Karoline Auguste Fernandine
1764-1842 . . . . DLB-94

Fish, Stanley 1938- DLB-67

Fishacre, Richard 1205-1248. . . . . . . DLB-115

Fisher, Clay (see Allen, Henry W.)

Fisher, Dorothy Canfield
1879-1958. . . . . DLB-9, 102

Fisher, Leonard Everett 1924- DLB-61

Fisher, Roy 1930- DLB-40

Fisher, Rudolph 1897-1934 . . . . . DLB-51, 102

Fisher, Sydney George 1856-1927 . . . . DLB-47

Fisher, Vardis 1895-1968. . . . . DLB-9

Fiske, John 1608-1677. . . . . DLB-24

Fiske, John 1842-1901 . . . . DLB-47, 64

Fitch, Thomas circa 1700-1774. . . . . . DLB-31

Fitch, William Clyde 1865-1909. . . . . . DLB-7

FitzGerald, Edward 1809-1883 . . . . . DLB-32

Fitzgerald, F. Scott
1896-1940. . . DLB-4, 9, 86; Y-81; DS-1, 15

F. Scott Fitzgerald Centenary
Celebrations. Y-96

Fitzgerald, Penelope 1916- DLB-14

Fitzgerald, Robert 1910-1985. . . . . . . Y-80

Fitzgerald, Thomas 1819-1891 . . . . . . DLB-23

Fitzgerald, Zelda Sayre 1900-1948 . . . . . Y-84

Fitzhugh, Louise 1928-1974. . . . . . . DLB-52

Fitzhugh, William
circa 1651-1701 . . . . DLB-24

Flanagan, Thomas 1923- Y-80

Flanner, Hildegarde 1899-1987 . . . . . DLB-48

Flanner, Janet 1892-1978 . . . . DLB-4

Flaubert, Gustave 1821-1880 . . . . . . DLB-119

Flavin, Martin 1883-1967 . . . . DLB-9

Fleck, Konrad (flourished circa 1220)
. . . . DLB-138

Flecker, James Elroy 1884-1915 . . . DLB-10, 19

Fleeson, Doris 1901-1970. . . . . DLB-29

Fleißer, Marieluise 1901-1974 . . . . DLB-56, 124

Fleming, Ian 1908-1964 . . . . DLB-87

Fleming, Paul 1609-1640 . . . . DLB-164

The Fleshly School of Poetry and Other
Phenomena of the Day (1872), by Robert
Buchanan DLB-35

The Fleshly School of Poetry: Mr. D. G.
Rossetti (1871), by Thomas Maitland
(Robert Buchanan) DLB-35

Fletcher, Giles, the Elder
1546-1611 . . . . DLB-136

Fletcher, Giles, the Younger
1585 or 1586-1623 . . . . DLB-121

Fletcher, J. S. 1863-1935 . . . . DLB-70

Fletcher, John (see Beaumont, Francis)

Fletcher, John Gould 1886-1950 . . . DLB-4, 45

Fletcher, Phineas 1582-1650 . . . . . . DLB-121

Flieg, Helmut (see Heym, Stefan)

Flint, F. S. 1885-1960 . . . . DLB-19

Flint, Timothy 1780-1840 . . . . DLB-73

Florio, John 1553?-1625 . . . . DLB-172

Foix, J. V. 1893-1987 . . . . DLB-134

Foley, Martha (see Burnett, Whit, and
Martha Foley)

Folger, Henry Clay 1857-1930 . . . . . DLB-140

Folio Society DLB-112

Follen, Eliza Lee (Cabot) 1787-1860 . . . DLB-1

Follett, Ken 1949- Y-81, DLB-87

Follett Publishing Company DLB-46

Folsom, John West
[publishing house] DLB-49

Folz, Hans
between 1435 and 1440-1513 . . . . DLB-179

Fontane, Theodor 1819-1898 . . . . . DLB-129

Fonvisin, Denis Ivanovich
1744 or 1745-1792 . . . . DLB-150

Foote, Horton 1916- DLB-26

Foote, Samuel 1721-1777 . . . . DLB-89

Foote, Shelby 1916- DLB-2, 17

Forbes, Calvin 1945- DLB-41

Forbes, Ester 1891-1967 . . . . DLB-22

Forbes and Company DLB-49

Force, Peter 1790-1868 . . . . DLB-30

Forché, Carolyn 1950- DLB-5

Ford, Charles Henri 1913- DLB-4, 48

Ford, Corey 1902-1969 . . . . DLB-11

Ford, Ford Madox
1873-1939 . . . . DLB-34, 98, 162

Ford, Jesse Hill 1928- DLB-6

Ford, John 1586-? DLB-58

Ford, R. A. D. 1915- DLB-88

Ford, Worthington C. 1858-1941 . . . . DLB-47

Ford, J. B., and Company DLB-49

Fords, Howard, and Hulbert DLB-49

Foreman, Carl 1914-1984 . . . . DLB-26

Forester, Frank (see Herbert, Henry William)

Fornés, María Irene 1930- DLB-7

Forrest, Leon 1937- DLB-33

Forster, E. M.
1879-1970 . . . DLB-34, 98, 162, 178; DS-10

Forster, Georg 1754-1794 . . . . DLB-94

Forster, John 1812-1876 . . . . DLB-144

Forster, Margaret 1938- DLB-155

Forsyth, Frederick 1938- DLB-87

Forten, Charlotte L. 1837-1914 . . . . . DLB-50

Fortini, Franco 1917- DLB-128

Fortune, T. Thomas 1856-1928 . . . . . DLB-23

Fosdick, Charles Austin
1842-1915 . . . . DLB-42

Foster, Genevieve 1893-1979 . . . . . DLB-61

Foster, Hannah Webster
1758-1840 . . . . DLB-37

Foster, John 1648-1681 . . . . DLB-24

Foster, Michael 1904-1956 . . . . DLB-9

Foulis, Robert and Andrew / R. and A.
[publishing house] DLB-154

Fouqué, Caroline de la Motte
1774-1831 . . . . DLB-90

Fouqué, Friedrich de la Motte
1777-1843 . . . . DLB-90

Four Essays on the Beat Generation,
by John Clellon Holmes DLB-16

Four Seas Company DLB-46

Four Winds Press DLB-46

Fournier, Henri Alban (see Alain-Fournier)

Fowler and Wells Company DLB-49

Fowles, John 1926- DLB-14, 139

Fox, John, Jr. 1862 or
1863-1919 . . . . DLB-9; DS-13

Fox, Paula 1923- DLB-52

Fox, Richard Kyle 1846-1922 . . . . . DLB-79

Fox, William Price 1926- DLB-2; Y-81

Fox, Richard K.
[publishing house] DLB-49

Foxe, John 1517-1587 . . . . DLB-132

Fraenkel, Michael 1896-1957 . . . . . . DLB-4

France, Anatole 1844-1924 . . . . . . DLB-123

France, Richard 1938- DLB-7

Francis, Convers 1795-1863 . . . . DLB-1

Francis, Dick 1920- DLB-87

Francis, Jeffrey, Lord 1773-1850 . . . . DLB-107

Francis, C. S. [publishing house] DLB-49

François 1863-1910 . . . . DLB-92

François, Louise von 1817-1893 . . . . DLB-129

Franck, Sebastian 1499-1542 . . . . . . DLB-179

Francke, Kuno 1855-1930 . . . . DLB-71

Frank, Bruno 1887-1945 . . . . DLB-118

Frank, Leonhard 1882-1961 . . . . . DLB-56, 118

Frank, Melvin (see Panama, Norman)

Frank, Waldo 1889-1967 . . . . . . DLB-9, 63

Franken, Rose 1895?-1988 . . . . Y-84

Franklin, Benjamin
1706-1790 . . . . DLB-24, 43, 73, 183

Franklin, James 1697-1735 . . . . DLB-43

Franklin Library DLB-46

Frantz, Ralph Jules 1902-1979 . . . . . . DLB-4

Franzos, Karl Emil 1848-1904 . . . . . DLB-129

Fraser, G. S. 1915-1980 . . . . DLB-27

Fraser, Kathleen 1935- DLB-169

Frattini, Alberto 1922- DLB-128

Frau Ava ?-1127 . . . . DLB-148

Frayn, Michael 1933- DLB-13, 14

Frederic, Harold
1856-1898 . . . . DLB-12, 23; DS-13

Freeling, Nicolas 1927- DLB-87

Freeman, Douglas Southall
1886-1953 . . . . DLB-17

Freeman, Legh Richmond
1842-1915 . . . . DLB-23

Freeman, Mary E. Wilkins
1852-1930 . . . . DLB-12, 78

Freeman, R. Austin 1862-1943 . . . . . DLB-70

Freidank circa 1170-circa 1233 . . . . . DLB-138

Freiligrath, Ferdinand 1810-1876 . . . . DLB-133

Frémont, John Charles 1813-1890
and Frémont, Jessie Benton
1834-1902 . . . . DLB-183

French, Alice 1850-1934 . . . . . DLB-74; DS-13

French, David 1939- DLB-53

French, James [publishing house] DLB-49

French, Samuel [publishing house] DLB-49

Samuel French, Limited DLB-106

Freneau, Philip 1752-1832 . . . . . DLB-37, 43

Freni, Melo 1934- DLB-128

Freshfield, Douglas W.
1845-1934 . . . . DLB-174

Freytag, Gustav 1816-1895 . . . . . . DLB-129

Fried, Erich 1921-1988 . . . . DLB-85

Friedman, Bruce Jay 1930- DLB-2, 28

Friedrich von Hausen
circa 1171-1190 . . . . DLB-138

Friel, Brian 1929- DLB-13

Friend, Krebs 1895?-1967? DLB-4

Fries, Fritz Rudolf 1935- DLB-75

Fringe and Alternative Theater
in Great Britain DLB-13

Frisch, Max 1911-1991 . . . . . . DLB-69, 124

Frischlin, Nicodemus 1547-1590 . . . . DLB-179

Frischmuth, Barbara 1941- DLB-85

Fritz, Jean 1915- DLB-52

Fromentin, Eugene 1820-1876 . . . . . DLB-123

From *The Gay Science,* by
E. S. Dallas DLB-2ĉ

Frost, A. B. 1851-1928 . . . . DS-13

Frost, Robert 1874-1963 . . . . . DLB-54; DS-7

Frothingham, Octavius Brooks
1822-1895 . . . . DLB-1

Froude, James Anthony
1818-1894 . . . . DLB-18, 57, 144

Fry, Christopher 1907- DLB-13

Fry, Roger 1866-1934 . . . . DS-10

Frye, Northrop 1912-1991 . . . . . DLB-67, 68

Fuchs, Daniel
1909-1993 . . . . DLB-9, 26, 28; Y-93

Fuentes, Carlos 1928- DLB-113

Fuertes, Gloria 1918- DLB-108

The Fugitives and the Agrarians:
The First Exhibition Y-85

Fulbecke, William 1560-1603? DLB-172

Fuller, Charles H., Jr. 1939- DLB-38

Fuller, Henry Blake 1857-1929 . . . . . DLB-12

Fuller, John 1937- DLB-40

Fuller, Margaret (see Fuller, Sarah Margaret,
Marchesa D'Ossoli)

Fuller, Roy 1912-1991 . . . . DLB-15, 20

Fuller, Samuel 1912- DLB-26

Fuller, Sarah Margaret, Marchesa
D'Ossoli 1810-1850 . . . DLB-1, 59, 73, 183

Fuller, Thomas 1608-1661 . . . . DLB-151

Fullerton, Hugh 1873-1945 . . . . DLB-171

Fulton, Len 1934- Y-86

Fulton, Robin 1937- DLB-40

Furbank, P. N. 1920- DLB-155

Furman, Laura 1945- Y-86

Furness, Horace Howard
1833-1912 . . . . DLB-64

Furness, William Henry 1802-1896 . . . . DLB-1

Furthman, Jules 1888-1966 . . . . DLB-26

Furui, Yoshikichi 1937- DLB-182

Futabatei, Shimei (Hasegawa Tatsunosuke)
1864-1909 . . . . DLB-180

The Future of the Novel (1899), by
Henry James DLB-18

Fyleman, Rose 1877-1957 . . . . DLB-160

G

The G. Ross Roy Scottish Poetry
Collection at the University of
South Carolina Y-89

Gadda, Carlo Emilio 1893-1973 . . . . DLB-177

Gaddis, William 1922- DLB-2

Gág, Wanda 1893-1946 . . . . DLB-22

Gagnon, Madeleine 1938- DLB-60

Gaine, Hugh 1726-1807 . . . . DLB-43

Gaine, Hugh [publishing house] DLB-49

Gaines, Ernest J.
1933- DLB-2, 33, 152; Y-80

Gaiser, Gerd 1908-1976 . . . . DLB-69

Galarza, Ernesto 1905-1984 . . . . . . DLB-122

Galaxy Science Fiction Novels DLB-46

Gale, Zona 1874-1938 . . . . DLB-9, 78

Galen of Pergamon 129-after 210 . . . DLB-176

Gall, Louise von 1815-1855 . . . . . . DLB-133

Gallagher, Tess 1943- DLB-120

Gallagher, Wes 1911- DLB-127

Gallagher, William Davis
1808-1894 . . . . DLB-73

Gallant, Mavis 1922- DLB-53

Gallico, Paul 1897-1976 . . . . . . DLB-9, 171

Galsworthy, John
1867-1933 . . . . DLB-10, 34, 98, 162

Galt, John 1779-1839 . . . . DLB-99, 116

Galton, Sir Francis 1822-1911 . . . . . DLB-166

Galvin, Brendan 1938- DLB-5

Gambit DLB-46

Gamboa, Reymundo 1948- DLB-122

Gammer Gurton's Needle DLB-62

Gannett, Frank E. 1876-1957 . . . . . DLB-29

Gaos, Vicente 1919-1980 . . . . DLB-134

García, Lionel G. 1935- DLB-82

García Lorca, Federico
1898-1936 . . . . DLB-108

García Márquez, Gabriel
1928- DLB-113

Gardam, Jane 1928- DLB-14, 161

Garden, Alexander
circa 1685-1756 . . . . DLB-31

Gardiner, Margaret Power Farmer (see
Blessington, Marguerite, Countess of)

Gardner, John 1933-1982 . . . . . . DLB-2; Y-82

Garfield, Leon 1921- DLB-161

Garis, Howard R. 1873-1962 . . . . . DLB-22

Garland, Hamlin
1860-1940 . . . . DLB-12, 71, 78

Garneau, Francis-Xavier
1809-1866 . . . . DLB-99

Garneau, Hector de Saint-Denys
1912-1943 . . . . DLB-88

Garneau, Michel 1939- DLB-53

Garner, Alan 1934- DLB-161

Garner, Hugh 1913-1979 . . . . DLB-68

Garnett, David 1892-1981 . . . . DLB-34

Garnett, Eve 1900-1991 . . . . DLB-160

Garraty, John A. 1920- DLB-17

Garrett, George
1929- DLB-2, 5, 130, 152; Y-83

Garrick, David 1717-1779 . . . . DLB-84

Garrison, William Lloyd
1805-1879 . . . . DLB-1, 43

Garro, Elena 1920- DLB-145

Garth, Samuel 1661-1719 . . . . DLB-95

Garve, Andrew 1908- DLB-87

Gary, Romain 1914-1980 . . . . DLB-83

Gascoigne, George 1539?-1577 . . . . . DLB-136

Gascoyne, David 1916- DLB-20

Gaskell, Elizabeth Cleghorn
1810-1865 . . . . DLB-21, 144, 159

Gaspey, Thomas 1788-1871 . . . . . . DLB-116

Gass, William Howard 1924- DLB-2

Gates, Doris 1901- DLB-22

Gates, Henry Louis, Jr. 1950- DLB-67

Gates, Lewis E. 1860-1924 . . . . DLB-71

Gatto, Alfonso 1909-1976 . . . . DLB-114

Gaunt, Mary 1861-1942 . . . . DLB-174

Gautier, Théophile 1811-1872 . . . . . DLB-119

Gauvreau, Claude 1925-1971 . . . . . . DLB-88

The *Gawain*-Poet
flourished circa 1350-1400 . . . . . DLB-146

Gay, Ebenezer 1696-1787 . . . . DLB-24

Gay, John 1685-1732 . . . . DLB-84, 95

The Gay Science (1866), by E. S. Dallas [excerpt]
. . . . DLB-21

Gayarré, Charles E. A. 1805-1895 . . . . DLB-30

Gaylord, Edward King
1873-1974 . . . . DLB-127

Gaylord, Edward Lewis 1919- DLB-127

Gaylord, Charles
[publishing house] DLB-49

Geddes, Gary 1940- DLB-60

Geddes, Virgil 1897- DLB-4

Gedeon (Georgii Andreevich Krinovsky)
circa 1730-1763 . . . . DLB-150

Geibel, Emanuel 1815-1884 . . . . . . DLB-129

Geiogamah, Hanay 1945- DLB-175

Geis, Bernard, Associates DLB-46

Geisel, Theodor Seuss
1904-1991 . . . . DLB-61; Y-91

Gelb, Arthur 1924- DLB-103

Gelb, Barbara 1926- DLB-103

Gelber, Jack 1932- DLB-7

Gelinas, Gratien 1909- DLB-88

Gellert, Christian Füerchtegott
1715-1769 . . . . DLB-97

Gellhorn, Martha 1908- Y-82

Gems, Pam 1925- DLB-13

A General Idea of the College of Mirania (1753),
by William Smith [excerpts] DLB-31

Genet, Jean 1910-1986 . . . . DLB-72; Y-86

Genevoix, Maurice 1890-1980 . . . . . DLB-65

Genovese, Eugene D. 1930- DLB-17

Gent, Peter 1942- Y-82

Geoffrey of Monmouth
    circa 1100-1155 . . . . DLB-146

George, Henry 1839-1897 . . . . DLB-23

George, Jean Craighead 1919- DLB-52

Georgslied 896? DLB-148

Gerhardie, William 1895-1977 . . . . . DLB-36

Gerhardt, Paul 1607-1676 . . . . DLB-164

Gérin, Winifred 1901-1981 . . . . DLB-155

Gérin-Lajoie, Antoine 1824-1882 . . . . . DLB-99

German Drama 800-1280 . . . . DLB-138

German Drama from Naturalism
    to Fascism: 1889-1933 . . . . DLB-118

German Literature and Culture from
    Charlemagne to the Early Courtly
    Period DLB-148

German Radio Play, The DLB-124

German Transformation from the Baroque
    to the Enlightenment, The DLB-97

The Germanic Epic and Old English Heroic
    Poetry: *Widseth, Waldere,* and *The
    Fight at Finnsburg* DLB-146

Germanophilism, by Hans Kohn DLB-66

Gernsback, Hugo 1884-1967 . . . . DLB-8, 137

Gerould, Katharine Fullerton
    1879-1944 . . . . ; . DLB-78

Gerrish, Samuel [publishing house] . . . DLB-49

Gerrold, David 1944- DLB-8

The Ira Gershwin Centenary Y-96

Gersonides 1288-1344 . . . . DLB-115

Gerstäcker, Friedrich 1816-1872 . . . . DLB-129

Gerstenberg, Heinrich Wilhelm von
    1737-1823 . . . . DLB-97

Gervinus, Georg Gottfried
    1805-1871 . . . . DLB-133

Geßner, Salomon 1730-1788 . . . . . . DLB-97

Geston, Mark S. 1946- DLB-8

Al-Ghazali 1058-1111 . . . . DLB-115

Gibbon, Edward 1737-1794 . . . . . . DLB-104

Gibbon, John Murray 1875-1952 . . . . DLB-92

Gibbon, Lewis Grassic (see Mitchell,
    James Leslie)

Gibbons, Floyd 1887-1939 . . . . DLB-25

Gibbons, Reginald 1947- DLB-120

Gibbons, William ?-? DLB-73

Gibson, Charles Dana 1867-1944 . . . . DS-13

Gibson, Charles Dana 1867-1944 . . . . DS-13

Gibson, Graeme 1934- DLB-53

Gibson, Margaret 1944- DLB-120

Gibson, Margaret Dunlop
    1843-1920 . . . . DLB-174

Gibson, Wilfrid 1878-1962 . . . . DLB-19

Gibson, William 1914- DLB-7

Gide, André 1869-1951 . . . . DLB-65

Giguère, Diane 1937- DLB-53

Giguère, Roland 1929- DLB-60

Gil de Biedma, Jaime 1929-1990 . . . . DLB-108

Gil-Albert, Juan 1906- DLB-134

Gilbert, Anthony 1899-1973 . . . . . . DLB-77

Gilbert, Michael 1912- DLB-87

Gilbert, Sandra M. 1936- DLB-120

Gilbert, Sir Humphrey
    1537-1583 . . . . DLB-136

Gilchrist, Alexander
    1828-1861 . . . . DLB-144

Gilchrist, Ellen 1935- DLB-130

Gilder, Jeannette L. 1849-1916 . . . . . DLB-79

Gilder, Richard Watson
    1844-1909 . . . . DLB-64, 79

Gildersleeve, Basil 1831-1924 . . . . . . DLB-71

Giles, Henry 1809-1882 . . . . DLB-64

Giles of Rome circa 1243-1316 . . . . DLB-115

Gilfillan, George 1813-1878 . . . . . . DLB-144

Gill, Eric 1882-1940 . . . . DLB-98

Gill, William F., Company DLB-49

Gillespie, A. Lincoln, Jr.
    1895-1950 . . . . DLB-4

Gilliam, Florence ?-? DLB-4

Gilliatt, Penelope 1932-1993 . . . . . . DLB-14

Gillott, Jacky 1939-1980 . . . . DLB-14

Gilman, Caroline H. 1794-1888 . . . . DLB-3, 73

Gilman, W. and J.
    [publishing house] DLB-49

Gilmer, Elizabeth Meriwether
    1861-1951 . . . . DLB-29

Gilmer, Francis Walker
    1790-1826 . . . . DLB-37

Gilroy, Frank D. 1925- DLB-7

Gimferrer, Pere (Pedro) 1945- DLB-134

Gingrich, Arnold 1903-1976 . . . . . . DLB-137

Ginsberg, Allen 1926- DLB-5, 16, 169

Ginzburg, Natalia 1916-1991 . . . . . . DLB-177

Ginzkey, Franz Karl 1871-1963 . . . . . DLB-81

Gioia, Dana 1950- DLB-120

Giono, Jean 1895-1970 . . . . DLB-72

Giotti, Virgilio 1885-1957 . . . . DLB-114

Giovanni, Nikki 1943- DLB-5, 41

Gipson, Lawrence Henry
    1880-1971 . . . . DLB-17

Girard, Rodolphe 1879-1956 . . . . . . DLB-92

Giraudoux, Jean 1882-1944 . . . . DLB-65

Gissing, George 1857-1903 . . . . DLB-18, 135

Giudici, Giovanni 1924- DLB-128

Giuliani, Alfredo 1924- DLB-128

Gladstone, William Ewart
    1809-1898 . . . . DLB-57

Glaeser, Ernst 1902-1963 . . . . DLB-69

Glancy, Diane 1941- DLB-175

Glanville, Brian 1931- DLB-15, 139

Glapthorne, Henry 1610-1643? DLB-58

Glasgow, Ellen 1873-1945 . . . . . . DLB-9, 12

Glaspell, Susan 1876-1948 . . . . DLB-7, 9, 78

Glass, Montague 1877-1934 . . . . . . DLB-11

The Glass Key and Other Dashiell Hammett
    Mysteries Y-96

Glassco, John 1909-1981 . . . . DLB-68

Glauser, Friedrich 1896-1938 . . . . . . DLB-56

F. Gleason's Publishing Hall DLB-49

Gleim, Johann Wilhelm Ludwig
    1719-1803 . . . . DLB-97

Glendinning, Victoria 1937- DLB-155

Glover, Richard 1712-1785 . . . . DLB-95

Glück, Louise 1943- DLB-5

Glyn, Elinor 1864-1943 . . . . DLB-153

Gobineau, Joseph-Arthur de
    1816-1882 . . . . DLB-123

Godbout, Jacques 1933- DLB-53

Goddard, Morrill 1865-1937 . . . . . . DLB-25

Goddard, William 1740-1817 . . . . . . DLB-43

Godden, Rumer 1907- DLB-161

Godey, Louis A. 1804-1878 . . . . . . DLB-73

Godey and McMichael DLB-49

Godfrey, Dave 1938- DLB-60

Godfrey, Thomas 1736-1763 . . . . . . DLB-31

Godine, David R., Publisher DLB-46

Godkin, E. L. 1831-1902 . . . . DLB-79

Godolphin, Sidney 1610-1643 . . . . . DLB-126

Godwin, Gail 1937- DLB-6

Godwin, Mary Jane Clairmont
    1766-1841 . . . . DLB-163

Godwin, Parke 1816-1904 . . . . . . DLB-3, 64

Godwin, William
    1756-1836 . . . . DLB-39, 104, 142, 158, 163

Godwin, M. J., and Company DLB-154

Goering, Reinhard 1887-1936 . . . . . . DLB-118

Goes, Albrecht 1908- DLB-69

Goethe, Johann Wolfgang von
    1749-1832 . . . . DLB-94

Goetz, Curt 1888-1960 . . . . DLB-124

Goffe, Thomas circa 1592-1629 . . . . . DLB-58

Goffstein, M. B. 1940- DLB-61

Gogarty, Oliver St. John
    1878-1957 . . . . DLB-15, 19

Goines, Donald 1937-1974 . . . . DLB-33

Gold, Herbert 1924- DLB-2; Y-81

Gold, Michael 1893-1967 . . . . . . DLB-9, 28

Goldbarth, Albert 1948- DLB-120

Goldberg, Dick 1947- DLB-7

Golden Cockerel Press DLB-112

Golding, Arthur 1536-1606 . . . . . . DLB-136

Golding, William 1911-1993 . . . . DLB-15, 100

Goldman, William 1931- DLB-44

Goldsmith, Oliver
    1730?-1774. . . . DLB-39, 89, 104, 109, 142

Goldsmith, Oliver 1794-1861 . . . . . . DLB-99

Goldsmith Publishing Company DLB-46

Gollancz, Victor, Limited DLB-112

Gómez-Quiñones, Juan 1942- DLB-122

Gomme, Laurence James
    [publishing house]. DLB-46

Goncourt, Edmond de 1822-1896 . . . DLB-123

Goncourt, Jules de 1830-1870 . . . . . DLB-123

Gonzales, Rodolfo "Corky"
    1928- DLB-122

González, Angel 1925- DLB-108

Gonzalez, Genaro 1949- DLB-122

Gonzalez, Ray 1952- DLB-122

González de Mireles, Jovita
    1899-1983 . . . . DLB-122

González-T., César A. 1931- DLB-82

Goodbye, Gutenberg? A Lecture at
    the New York Public Library,
    18 April 1995 . . . . Y-95

Goodison, Lorna 1947- DLB-157

Goodman, Paul 1911-1972 . . . . DLB-130

The Goodman Theatre DLB-7

Goodrich, Frances 1891-1984 and
    Hackett, Albert 1900- DLB-26

Goodrich, Samuel Griswold
    1793-1860 . . . . DLB-1, 42, 73

Goodrich, S. G. [publishing house] . . . DLB-49

Goodspeed, C. E., and Company DLB-49

Goodwin, Stephen 1943- Y-82

Googe, Barnabe 1540-1594 . . . . . . DLB-132

Gookin, Daniel 1612-1687 . . . . . . DLB-24

Gordon, Caroline
    1895-1981 . . . . . . DLB-4, 9, 102; Y-81

Gordon, Giles 1940- DLB-14, 139

Gordon, Lyndall 1941- DLB-155

Gordon, Mary 1949- DLB-6; Y-81

Gordone, Charles 1925- DLB-7

Gore, Catherine 1800-1861 . . . . . . DLB-116

Gorey, Edward 1925- DLB-61

Gorgias of Leontini circa 485 B.C.-376 B.C.
    . . . . DLB-176

Görres, Joseph 1776-1848 . . . . DLB-90

Gosse, Edmund 1849-1928 . . . . DLB-57, 144

Gosson, Stephen 1554-1624 . . . . . . DLB-172

Gotlieb, Phyllis 1926- DLB-88

Gottfried von Straßburg
    died before 1230 . . . . DLB-138

Gotthelf, Jeremias 1797-1854 . . . . . . DLB-133

Gottschalk circa 804/808-869 . . . . . DLB-148

Gottsched, Johann Christoph
    1700-1766 . . . . DLB-97

Götz, Johann Nikolaus
    1721-1781 . . . . DLB-97

Gould, Wallace 1882-1940 . . . . DLB-54

Govoni, Corrado 1884-1965 . . . . . . DLB-114

Gower, John circa 1330-1408 . . . . . DLB-146

Goyen, William 1915-1983 . . . . . DLB-2; Y-83

Goytisolo, José Augustín 1928- DLB-134

Gozzano, Guido 1883-1916 . . . . . . DLB-114

Grabbe, Christian Dietrich
    1801-1836 . . . . DLB-133

Gracq, Julien 1910- DLB-83

Grady, Henry W. 1850-1889 . . . . . . DLB-23

Graf, Oskar Maria 1894-1967 . . . . . DLB-56

Graf Rudolf between circa 1170
    and circa 1185 . . . . DLB-148

Grafton, Richard
    [publishing house] DLB-170

Graham, George Rex
    1813-1894 . . . . DLB-73

Graham, Gwethalyn 1913-1965 . . . . . DLB-88

Graham, Jorie 1951- DLB-120

Graham, Katharine 1917- DLB-127

Graham, Lorenz 1902-1989 . . . . . . DLB-76

Graham, Philip 1915-1963 . . . . . . DLB-127

Graham, R. B. Cunninghame
    1852-1936 . . . . . . DLB-98, 135, 174

Graham, Shirley 1896-1977 . . . . . . DLB-76

Graham, W. S. 1918- DLB-20

Graham, William H.
    [publishing house] DLB-49

Graham, Winston 1910- DLB-77

Grahame, Kenneth
    1859-1932 . . . . DLB-34, 141, 178

Grainger, Martin Allerdale
    1874-1941 . . . . DLB-92

Gramatky, Hardie 1907-1979 . . . . . . DLB-22

Grand, Sarah 1854-1943 . . . . DLB-135

Grandbois, Alain 1900-1975 . . . . . . DLB-92

Grange, John circa 1556-? DLB-136

Granich, Irwin (see Gold, Michael)

Grant, Duncan 1885-1978 . . . . DS-10

Grant, George 1918-1988 . . . . DLB-88

Grant, George Monro 1835-1902 . . . . DLB-99

Grant, Harry J. 1881-1963 . . . . DLB-29

Grant, James Edward 1905-1966 . . . . . DLB-26

Grass, Günter 1927- DLB-75, 124

Grasty, Charles H. 1863-1924 . . . . . DLB-25

Grau, Shirley Ann 1929- DLB-2

Graves, John 1920- Y-83

Graves, Richard 1715-1804 . . . . DLB-39

Graves, Robert
    1895-1985 . . . . DLB-20, 100; Y-85

Gray, Asa 1810-1888 . . . . DLB-1

Gray, David 1838-1861 . . . . DLB-32

Gray, Simon 1936- DLB-13

Gray, Thomas 1716-1771 . . . . DLB-109

Grayson, William J. 1788-1863 . . . . DLB-3, 64

The Great Bibliographers Series Y-93

The Great War and the Theater, 1914-1918
    [Great Britain] DLB-10

Greeley, Horace 1811-1872 . . . . . . DLB-3, 43

Green, Adolph (see Comden, Betty)

Green, Duff 1791-1875 . . . . DLB-43

Green, Gerald 1922- DLB-28

Green, Henry 1905-1973 . . . . DLB-15

Green, Jonas 1712-1767 . . . . DLB-31

Green, Joseph 1706-1780 . . . . DLB-31

Green, Julien 1900- DLB-4, 72

Green, Paul 1894-1981 . . . . . DLB-7, 9; Y-81

Green, T. and S.
    [publishing house] DLB-49

Green, Timothy
    [publishing house] DLB-49

Greenaway, Kate 1846-1901 . . . . . . DLB-141

Greenberg: Publisher DLB-46

Green Tiger Press DLB-46

Greene, Asa 1789-1838 . . . . DLB-11

Greene, Benjamin H.
    [publishing house] DLB-49

Greene, Graham 1904-1991
    . . . DLB-13, 15, 77, 100, 162; Y-85, Y-91

Greene, Robert 1558-1592 . . . . . DLB-62, 167

Greenhow, Robert 1800-1854 . . . . . DLB-30

Greenough, Horatio 1805-1852 . . . . . DLB-1

Greenwell, Dora 1821-1882 . . . . . . DLB-35

Greenwillow Books DLB-46

Greenwood, Grace (see Lippincott, Sara Jane
    Clarke)

Greenwood, Walter 1903-1974 . . . . . DLB-10

Greer, Ben 1948- DLB-6

Greflinger, Georg 1620?-1677 . . . . . DLB-164

Greg, W. R. 1809-1881 . . . . DLB-55

Gregg, Josiah 1806-1850 . . . . DLB-183

Gregg Press DLB-46

Gregory, Isabella Augusta
    Persse, Lady 1852-1932 . . . . . . DLB-10

Gregory, Horace 1898-1982 . . . . . . DLB-48

Gregory of Rimini
    circa 1300-1358 . . . . DLB-115

Gregynog Press DLB-112

Greiffenberg, Catharina Regina von
    1633-1694 . . . . DLB-168

Grenfell, Wilfred Thomason
    1865-1940 . . . . DLB-92

Greve, Felix Paul (see Grove, Frederick Philip)

Greville, Fulke, First Lord Brooke
1554-1628 . . . . DLB-62, 172

Grey, Lady Jane 1537-1554 . . . . DLB-132

Grey Owl 1888-1938 . . . . DLB-92

Grey, Zane 1872-1939 . . . . DLB-9

Grey Walls Press DLB-112

Grier, Eldon 1917- DLB-88

Grieve, C. M. (see MacDiarmid, Hugh)

Griffin, Bartholomew
flourished 1596 . . . . DLB-172

Griffin, Gerald 1803-1840 . . . . DLB-159

Griffith, Elizabeth 1727?-1793 . . . . DLB-39, 89

Griffith, George 1857-1906 . . . . . . DLB-178

Griffiths, Trevor 1935- DLB-13

Griffiths, Ralph
[publishing house] DLB-154

Griggs, S. C., and Company DLB-49

Griggs, Sutton Elbert
1872-1930 . . . . DLB-50

Grignon, Claude-Henri 1894-1976 . . . . DLB-68

Grigson, Geoffrey 1905- DLB-27

Grillparzer, Franz 1791-1872 . . . . . DLB-133

Grimald, Nicholas
circa 1519-circa 1562 . . . . DLB-136

Grimké, Angelina Weld
1880-1958 . . . . DLB-50, 54

Grimm, Hans 1875-1959 . . . . DLB-66

Grimm, Jacob 1785-1863 . . . . DLB-90

Grimm, Wilhelm 1786-1859 . . . . DLB-90

Grimmelshausen, Johann Jacob Christoffel von
1621 or 1622-1676 . . . . DLB-168

Grimshaw, Beatrice Ethel
1871-1953 . . . . DLB-174

Grindal, Edmund
1519 or 1520-1583 . . . . DLB-132

Griswold, Rufus Wilmot
1815-1857 . . . . DLB-3, 59

Gross, Milt 1895-1953 . . . . DLB-11

Grosset and Dunlap DLB-49

Grossman Publishers DLB-46

Grosseteste, Robert
circa 1160-1253 . . . . DLB-115

Grosvenor, Gilbert H. 1875-1966 . . . . DLB-91

Groth, Klaus 1819-1899 . . . . DLB-129

Groulx, Lionel 1878-1967 . . . . DLB-68

Grove, Frederick Philip 1879-1949 . . . DLB-92

Grove Press DLB-46

Grubb, Davis 1919-1980 . . . . DLB-6

Gruelle, Johnny 1880-1938 . . . . . . DLB-22

von Grumbach, Argula
1492-after 1563? DLB-179

Grymeston, Elizabeth
before 1563-before 1604 . . . . . . DLB-136

Gryphius, Andreas 1616-1664 . . . . . DLB-164

Gryphius, Christian 1649-1706 . . . . DLB-168

Guare, John 1938- DLB-7

Guerra, Tonino 1920- DLB-128

Guest, Barbara 1920- DLB-5

Guèvremont, Germaine
1893-1968 . . . . DLB-68

Guidacci, Margherita 1921-1992 . . . . DLB-128

Guide to the Archives of Publishers, Journals, and
Literary Agents in North American Libraries
. . . . Y-93

Guillén, Jorge 1893-1984 . . . . DLB-108

Guilloux, Louis 1899-1980 . . . . . . DLB-72

Guilpin, Everard
circa 1572-after 1608? DLB-136

Guiney, Louise Imogen 1861-1920 . . . DLB-54

Guiterman, Arthur 1871-1943 . . . . . DLB-11

Günderrode, Caroline von
1780-1806 . . . . DLB-90

Gundulić, Ivan 1589-1638 . . . . DLB-147

Gunn, Bill 1934-1989 . . . . DLB-38

Gunn, James E. 1923- DLB-8

Gunn, Neil M. 1891-1973 . . . . DLB-15

Gunn, Thom 1929- DLB-27

Gunnars, Kristjana 1948- DLB-60

Günther, Johann Christian
1695-1723 . . . . DLB-168

Gurik, Robert 1932- DLB-60

Gustafson, Ralph 1909- DLB-88

Gütersloh, Albert Paris 1887-1973 . . . DLB-81

Guthrie, A. B., Jr. 1901- DLB-6

Guthrie, Ramon 1896-1973 . . . . . . DLB-4

The Guthrie Theater DLB-7

Guthrie, Thomas Anstey (see Anstey, FC)

Gutzkow, Karl 1811-1878 . . . . DLB-133

Guy, Ray 1939- DLB-60

Guy, Rosa 1925- DLB-33

Guyot, Arnold 1807-1884 . . . . DS-13

Gwynne, Erskine 1898-1948 . . . . . . DLB-4

Gyles, John 1680-1755 . . . . DLB-99

Gysin, Brion 1916- DLB-16

H

H. D. (see Doolittle, Hilda)

Habington, William 1605-1654 . . . . . DLB-126

Hacker, Marilyn 1942- DLB-120

Hackett, Albert (see Goodrich, Frances)

Hacks, Peter 1928- DLB-124

Hadas, Rachel 1948- DLB-120

Hadden, Briton 1898-1929 . . . . . . DLB-91

Hagedorn, Friedrich von
1708-1754 . . . . DLB-168

Hagelstange, Rudolf 1912-1984 . . . . DLB-69

Haggard, H. Rider
1856-1925 . . . . . . DLB-70, 156, 174, 178

Haggard, William 1907-1993 . . . . . . Y-93

Hahn-Hahn, Ida Gräfin von
1805-1880 . . . . DLB-133

Haig-Brown, Roderick 1908-1976 . . . DLB-88

Haight, Gordon S. 1901-1985 . . . . . DLB-103

Hailey, Arthur 1920- DLB-88; Y-82

Haines, John 1924- DLB-5

Hake, Edward
flourished 1566-1604 . . . . DLB-136

Hake, Thomas Gordon 1809-1895 . . . . DLB-32

Hakluyt, Richard 1552?-1616 . . . . . DLB-136

Halbe, Max 1865-1944 . . . . DLB-118

Haldane, J. B. S. 1892-1964 . . . . . DLB-160

Haldeman, Joe 1943- DLB-8

Haldeman-Julius Company DLB-46

Hale, E. J., and Son DLB-49

Hale, Edward Everett
1822-1909 . . . . DLB-1, 42, 74

Hale, Janet Campbell 1946- DLB-175

Hale, Kathleen 1898- DLB-160

Hale, Leo Thomas (see Ebon)

Hale, Lucretia Peabody
1820-1900 . . . . DLB-42

Hale, Nancy 1908-1988 . . . . DLB-86; Y-80, 88

Hale, Sarah Josepha (Buell)
1788-1879 . . . . DLB-1, 42, 73

Hales, John 1584-1656 . . . . DLB-151

Haley, Alex 1921-1992 . . . . DLB-38

Haliburton, Thomas Chandler
1796-1865 . . . . DLB-11, 99

Hall, Anna Maria 1800-1881 . . . . . DLB-159

Hall, Donald 1928- DLB-5

Hall, Edward 1497-1547 . . . . DLB-132

Hall, James 1793-1868 . . . . . . DLB-73, 74

Hall, Joseph 1574-1656 . . . . . DLB-121, 151

Hall, Samuel [publishing house] DLB-49

Hallam, Arthur Henry 1811-1833 . . . . DLB-32

Halleck, Fitz-Greene 1790-1867 . . . . DLB-3

Haller, Albrecht von 1708-1777 . . . . DLB-168

Hallmann, Johann Christian
1640-1704 or 1716? DLB-168

Hallmark Editions DLB-46

Halper, Albert 1904-1984 . . . . . . DLB-9

Halperin, John William 1941- DLB-111

Halstead, Murat 1829-1908 . . . . . . DLB-23

Hamann, Johann Georg 1730-1788 . . . DLB-97

Hamburger, Michael 1924- DLB-27

Hamilton, Alexander 1712-1756 . . . . DLB-31

Hamilton, Alexander 1755?-1804 . . . . DLB-37

Hamilton, Cicely 1872-1952 . . . . . . DLB-10

Hamilton, Edmond 1904-1977 . . . . . . DLB-8

Hamilton, Elizabeth 1758-1816 . . . . DLB-116, 158

Hamilton, Gail (see Corcoran, Barbara)

Hamilton, Ian 1938- DLB-40, 155

Hamilton, Patrick 1904-1962 . . . . . . DLB-10

Hamilton, Virginia 1936- DLB-33, 52

Hamilton, Hamish, Limited DLB-112

Hammett, Dashiell 1894-1961 . . . . DS-6

Dashiell Hammett:
An Appeal in *TAC* Y-91

Hammon, Jupiter 1711-died between
1790 and 1806 . . . . DLB-31, 50

Hammond, John ?-1663 . . . . DLB-24

Hamner, Earl 1923- DLB-6

Hampton, Christopher 1946- DLB-13

Handel-Mazzetti, Enrica von
1871-1955 . . . . DLB-81

Handke, Peter 1942- DLB-85, 124

Handlin, Oscar 1915- DLB-17

Hankin, St. John 1869-1909 . . . . . . DLB-10

Hanley, Clifford 1922- DLB-14

Hannah, Barry 1942- DLB-6

Hannay, James 1827-1873 . . . . DLB-21

Hansberry, Lorraine 1930-1965 . . . . DLB-7, 38

Hapgood, Norman 1868-1937 . . . . . DLB-91

Happel, Eberhard Werner
1647-1690 . . . . DLB-168

Harcourt Brace Jovanovich DLB-46

Hardenberg, Friedrich von (see Novalis)

Harding, Walter 1917- DLB-111

Hardwick, Elizabeth 1916- DLB-6

Hardy, Thomas 1840-1928 . . . . DLB-18, 19, 135

Hare, Cyril 1900-1958 . . . . DLB-77

Hare, David 1947- DLB-13

Hargrove, Marion 1919- DLB-11

Häring, Georg Wilhelm Heinrich (see Alexis, Willibald)

Harington, Donald 1935- DLB-152

Harington, Sir John 1560-1612 . . . . DLB-136

Harjo, Joy 1951- DLB-120, 175

Harlow, Robert 1923- DLB-60

Harman, Thomas
flourished 1566-1573 . . . . DLB-136

Harness, Charles L. 1915- DLB-8

Harnett, Cynthia 1893-1981 . . . . . . DLB-161

Harper, Fletcher 1806-1877 . . . . DLB-79

Harper, Frances Ellen Watkins
1825-1911 . . . . DLB-50

Harper, Michael S. 1938- DLB-41

Harper and Brothers DLB-49

Harraden, Beatrice 1864-1943 . . . . . DLB-153

Harrap, George G., and Company
Limited DLB-112

Harriot, Thomas 1560-1621 . . . . . . DLB-136

Harris, Benjamin ?-circa 1720 . . . . DLB-42, 43

Harris, Christie 1907- DLB-88

Harris, Frank 1856-1931 . . . . DLB-156

Harris, George Washington
1814-1869 . . . . DLB-3, 11

Harris, Joel Chandler
1848-1908 . . . . . DLB-11, 23, 42, 78, 91

Harris, Mark 1922- DLB-2; Y-80

Harris, Wilson 1921- DLB-117

Harrison, Charles Yale
1898-1954 . . . . DLB-68

Harrison, Frederic 1831-1923 . . . . . . DLB-57

Harrison, Harry 1925- DLB-8

Harrison, Jim 1937- Y-82

Harrison, Mary St. Leger Kingsley (see Malet, Lucas)

Harrison, Paul Carter 1936- DLB-38

Harrison, Susan Frances
1859-1935 . . . . DLB-99

Harrison, Tony 1937- DLB-40

Harrison, William 1535-1593 . . . . . DLB-136

Harrison, James P., Company DLB-49

Harrisse, Henry 1829-1910 . . . . DLB-47

Harsdörffer, Georg Philipp
1607-1658 . . . . DLB-164

Harsent, David 1942- DLB-40

Hart, Albert Bushnell 1854-1943 . . . . DLB-17

Hart, Julia Catherine 1796-1867 . . . . DLB-99

The Lorenz Hart Centenary Y-95

Hart, Moss 1904-1961 . . . . DLB-7

Hart, Oliver 1723-1795 . . . . DLB-31

Hart-Davis, Rupert, Limited DLB-112

Harte, Bret 1836-1902 . . . . DLB-12, 64, 74, 79

Harte, Edward Holmead 1922- DLB-127

Harte, Houston Harriman 1927- DLB-127

Hartlaub, Felix 1913-1945 . . . . DLB-56

Hartlebon, Otto Erich
1864-1905 . . . . DLB-118

Hartley, L. P. 1895-1972 . . . . . DLB-15, 139

Hartley, Marsden 1877-1943 . . . . . . DLB-54

Hartling, Peter 1933- DLB-75

Hartman, Geoffrey H. 1929- DLB-67

Hartmann, Sadakichi 1867-1944 . . . . DLB-54

Hartmann von Aue
circa 1160-circa 1205 . . . . DLB-138

Harvey, Gabriel 1550?-1631 . . . . . . DLB-167

Harvey, Jean-Charles 1891-1967 . . . . DLB-88

Harvill Press Limited DLB-112

Harwood, Lee 1939- DLB-40

Harwood, Ronald 1934- DLB-13

Haskins, Charles Homer
1870-1937 . . . . DLB-47

Hass, Robert 1941- DLB-105

The Hatch-Billops Collection DLB-76

Hathaway, William 1944- DLB-120

Hauff, Wilhelm 1802-1827 . . . . DLB-90

A Haughty and Proud Generation (1922),
by Ford Madox Hueffer DLB-36

Haugwitz, August Adolph von
1647-1706 . . . . DLB-168

Hauptmann, Carl
1858-1921 . . . . DLB-66, 118

Hauptmann, Gerhart
1862-1946 . . . . DLB-66, 118

Hauser, Marianne 1910- Y-83

Hawes, Stephen
1475?-before 1529 . . . . DLB-132

Hawker, Robert Stephen
1803-1875 . . . . DLB-32

Hawkes, John 1925- DLB-2, 7; Y-80

Hawkesworth, John 1720-1773 . . . . . DLB-142

Hawkins, Sir Anthony Hope (see Hope, Anthony)

Hawkins, Sir John
1719-1789 . . . . DLB-104, 142

Hawkins, Walter Everette 1883-? DLB-50

Hawthorne, Nathaniel
1804-1864 . . . . DLB-1, 74, 183

Hawthorne, Nathaniel 1804-1864 and
Hawthorne, Sophia Peabody
1809-1871 . . . . DLB-183

Hay, John 1838-1905 . . . . DLB-12, 47

Hayashi, Fumiko 1903-1951 . . . . . . DLB-180

Hayden, Robert 1913-1980 . . . . . DLB-5, 76

Haydon, Benjamin Robert
1786-1846 . . . . DLB-110

Hayes, John Michael 1919- DLB-26

Hayley, William 1745-1820 . . . . DLB-93, 142

Haym, Rudolf 1821-1901 . . . . DLB-129

Hayman, Robert 1575-1629 . . . . . . DLB-99

Hayman, Ronald 1932- DLB-155

Hayne, Paul Hamilton
1830-1886 . . . . DLB-3, 64, 79

Hays, Mary 1760-1843 . . . . . DLB-142, 158

Haywood, Eliza 1693?-1756 . . . . . . DLB-39

Hazard, Willis P. [publishing house] DLB-49

Hazlitt, William 1778-1830 . . . . DLB-110, 158

Hazzard, Shirley 1931- Y-82

Head, Bessie 1937-1986 . . . . DLB-117

Headley, Joel T.
1813-1897 . . . . DLB-30, 183; DS-13

Heaney, Seamus 1939- DLB-40

Heard, Nathan C. 1936- DLB-33

Hearn, Lafcadio 1850-1904 . . . . . DLB-12, 78

Hearne, John 1926- DLB-117

Hearne, Samuel 1745-1792 . . . . DLB-99

Hearst, William Randolph
1863-1951 . . . . DLB-25

Hearst, William Randolph, Jr
1908-1993 . . . . DLB-127

Heath, Catherine 1924- DLB-14

Heath, Roy A. K. 1926- DLB-117

Heath-Stubbs, John 1918- DLB-27

Heavysege, Charles 1816-1876 . . . . . DLB-99

Hebbel, Friedrich 1813-1863 . . . . . . DLB-129

Hebel, Johann Peter 1760-1826 . . . . . DLB-90

Hébert, Anne 1916- DLB-68

Hébert, Jacques 1923- DLB-53

Hecht, Anthony 1923- DLB-5, 169

Hecht, Ben 1894-1964
. . . . DLB-7, 9, 25, 26, 28, 86

Hecker, Isaac Thomas 1819-1888 . . . . . DLB-1

Hedge, Frederic Henry
1805-1890 . . . . DLB-1, 59

Hefner, Hugh M. 1926- DLB-137

Hegel, Georg Wilhelm Friedrich
1770-1831 . . . . DLB-90

Heidish, Marcy 1947- Y-82

Heißenbüttel 1921- DLB-75

Hein, Christoph 1944- DLB-124

Heine, Heinrich 1797-1856 . . . . DLB-90

Heinemann, Larry 1944- DS-9

Heinemann, William, Limited DLB-112

Heinlein, Robert A. 1907-1988 . . . . . . DLB-8

Heinrich Julius of Brunswick
1564-1613 . . . . DLB-164

Heinrich von dem Türlîn
flourished circa 1230 . . . . DLB-138

Heinrich von Melk
flourished after 1160 . . . . DLB-148

Heinrich von Veldeke
circa 1145-circa 1190 . . . . DLB-138

Heinrich, Willi 1920- DLB-75

Heiskell, John 1872-1972 . . . . DLB-127

Heinse, Wilhelm 1746-1803 . . . . DLB-94

Heinz, W. C. 1915- DLB-171

Hejinian, Lyn 1941- DLB-165

Heliand circa 850 . . . . DLB-148

Heller, Joseph 1923- DLB-2, 28; Y-80

Heller, Michael 1937- DLB-165

Hellman, Lillian 1906-1984 . . . . . DLB-7; Y-84

Hellwig, Johann 1609-1674 . . . . DLB-164

Helprin, Mark 1947- Y-85

Helwig, David 1938- DLB-60

Hemans, Felicia 1793-1835 . . . . DLB-96

Hemingway, Ernest 1899-1961
. . . . DLB-4, 9, 102; Y-81, 87; DS-1, 15

Hemingway: Twenty-Five Years
Later Y-85

Hémon, Louis 1880-1913 . . . . DLB-92

Hemphill, Paul 1936- Y-87

Hénault, Gilles 1920- DLB-88

Henchman, Daniel 1689-1761 . . . . . DLB-24

Henderson, Alice Corbin
1881-1949 . . . . DLB-54

Henderson, Archibald
1877-1963 . . . . DLB-103

Henderson, David 1942- DLB-41

Henderson, George Wylie
1904- DLB-51

Henderson, Zenna 1917-1983 . . . . . . DLB-8

Henisch, Peter 1943- DLB-85

Henley, Beth 1952- Y-86

Henley, William Ernest
1849-1903 . . . . DLB-19

Henniker, Florence 1855-1923 . . . . . DLB-135

Henry, Alexander 1739-1824 . . . . . . DLB-99

Henry, Buck 1930- DLB-26

Henry VIII of England
1491-1547 . . . . DLB-132

Henry, Marguerite 1902- DLB-22

Henry, O. (see Porter, William Sydney)

Henry of Ghent
circa 1217-1229 - 1293 . . . . . . DLB-115

Henry, Robert Selph 1889-1970 . . . . DLB-17

Henry, Will (see Allen, Henry W.)

Henryson, Robert
1420s or 1430s-circa 1505 . . . . DLB-146

Henschke, Alfred (see Klabund)

Hensley, Sophie Almon 1866-1946 . . . DLB-99

Henson, Lance 1944- DLB-175

Henty, G. A. 1832?-1902 . . . . . DLB-18, 141

Hentz, Caroline Lee 1800-1856 . . . . . DLB-3

Heraclitus flourished circa 500 B.C.
. . . . DLB-176

Herbert, Agnes circa 1880-1960 . . . . DLB-174

Herbert, Alan Patrick 1890-1971 . . . . DLB-10

Herbert, Edward, Lord, of Cherbury
1582-1648 . . . . DLB-121, 151

Herbert, Frank 1920-1986 . . . . DLB-8

Herbert, George 1593-1633 . . . . . . DLB-126

Herbert, Henry William
1807-1858 . . . . DLB-3, 73

Herbert, John 1926- DLB-53

Herbert, Mary Sidney, Countess of Pembroke
(see Sidney, Mary)

Herbst, Josephine 1892-1969 . . . . . . DLB-9

Herburger, Gunter 1932- DLB-75, 124

Hercules, Frank E. M. 1917- DLB-33

Herder, Johann Gottfried
1744-1803 . . . . DLB-97

Herder, B., Book Company DLB-49

Herford, Charles Harold
1853-1931 . . . . DLB-149

Hergesheimer, Joseph
1880-1954 . . . . DLB-9, 102

Heritage Press DLB-46

Hermann the Lame 1013-1054 . . . . . DLB-148

Hermes, Johann Timotheus
1738-1821 . . . . DLB-97

Hermlin, Stephan 1915- DLB-69

Hernández, Alfonso C. 1938- DLB-122

Hernández, Inés 1947- DLB-122

Hernández, Miguel 1910-1942 . . . . . DLB-134

Hernton, Calvin C. 1932- DLB-38

"The Hero as Man of Letters: Johnson,
Rousseau, Burns" (1841), by Thomas
Carlyle [excerpt] DLB-57

The Hero as Poet. Dante; Shakspeare (1841),
by Thomas Carlyle DLB-32

Herodotus circa 484 B.C.-circa 420 B.C.
. . . . DLB-176

Heron, Robert 1764-1807 . . . . DLB-142

Herrera, Juan Felipe 1948- DLB-122

Herrick, Robert 1591-1674 . . . . . . DLB-126

Herrick, Robert 1868-1938 . . . . DLB-9, 12, 78

Herrick, William 1915- Y-83

Herrick, E. R., and Company DLB-49

Herrmann, John 1900-1959 . . . . DLB-4

Hersey, John 1914-1993 . . . . DLB-6

Hertel, François 1905-1985 . . . . DLB-68

Hervé-Bazin, Jean Pierre Marie (see Bazin, Hervé)

Hervey, John, Lord 1696-1743 . . . . . DLB-101

Herwig, Georg 1817-1875 . . . . DLB-133

Herzog, Emile Salomon Wilhelm (see Maurois, André)

Hesiod eighth century B.C. DLB-176

Hesse, Hermann 1877-1962 . . . . DLB-66

Hessus, Helius Eobanus
1488-1540 . . . . DLB-179

Hewat, Alexander
circa 1743-circa 1824 . . . . DLB-30

Hewitt, John 1907- DLB-27

Hewlett, Maurice 1861-1923 . . . . DLB-34, 156

Heyen, William 1940- DLB-5

Heyer, Georgette 1902-1974 . . . . . . DLB-77

Heym, Stefan 1913- DLB-69

Heyse, Paul 1830-1914 . . . . DLB-129

Heytesbury, William
circa 1310-1372 or 1373 . . . . . . DLB-115

Heyward, Dorothy 1890-1961 . . . . . . DLB-7

Heyward, DuBose
1885-1940 . . . . DLB-7, 9, 45

Heywood, John 1497?-1580? DLB-136

Heywood, Thomas
1573 or 1574-1641 . . . . DLB-62

Hibbs, Ben 1901-1975 . . . . DLB-137

Hichens, Robert S. 1864-1950 . . . . . DLB-153

Hickman, William Albert
1877-1957 . . . . DLB-92

Hidalgo, José Luis 1919-1947 . . . . . . DLB-108

Hiebert, Paul 1892-1987 . . . . DLB-68

Hieng, Andrej 1925- DLB-181

Hierro, José 1922- DLB-108

Higgins, Aidan 1927- DLB-14

Higgins, Colin 1941-1988 . . . . DLB-26

Higgins, George V. 1939- DLB-2; Y-81

Higginson, Thomas Wentworth
1823-1911 . . . . DLB-1, 64

Highwater, Jamake 1942?- DLB-52; Y-85

Hijuelos, Oscar 1951- DLB-145

Hildegard von Bingen
1098-1179 . . . . DLB-148

Das Hildesbrandslied circa 820 . . . . . DLB-148

Hildesheimer, Wolfgang
1916-1991 . . . . DLB-69, 124

Hildreth, Richard
1807-1865 . . . . DLB-1, 30, 59

Hill, Aaron 1685-1750 . . . . DLB-84

Hill, Geoffrey 1932- DLB-40

Hill, "Sir" John 1714?-1775 . . . . . . DLB-39

Hill, Leslie 1880-1960 . . . . DLB-51

Hill, Susan 1942- DLB-14, 139

Hill, Walter 1942- DLB-44

Hill and Wang DLB-46

Hill, George M., Company DLB-49

Hill, Lawrence, and Company,
Publishers DLB-46

Hillberry, Conrad 1928- DLB-120

Hilliard, Gray and Company DLB-49

Hills, Lee 1906- DLB-127

Hillyer, Robert 1895-1961 . . . . DLB-54

Hilton, James 1900-1954 . . . . . DLB-34, 77

Hilton, Walter died 1396 . . . . DLB-146

Hilton and Company DLB-49

Himes, Chester
1909-1984 . . . . DLB-2, 76, 143

Hindmarsh, Joseph
[publishing house] DLB-170

Hine, Daryl 1936- DLB-60

Hingley, Ronald 1920- DLB-155

Hinojosa-Smith, Rolando
1929- DLB-82

Hippel, Theodor Gottlieb von
1741-1796 . . . . DLB-97

Hippocrates of Cos flourished circa 425 B.C.
. . . . DLB-176

Hirabayashi, Taiko 1905-1972 . . . . . DLB-180

Hirsch, E. D., Jr. 1928- DLB-67

Hirsch, Edward 1950- DLB-120

The History of the Adventures of Joseph Andrews
(1742), by Henry Fielding
[excerpt] DLB-39

Hoagland, Edward 1932- DLB-6

Hoagland, Everett H., III 1942- DLB-41

Hoban, Russell 1925- DLB-52

Hobbes, Thomas 1588-1679 . . . . . . DLB-151

Hobby, Oveta 1905- DLB-127

Hobby, William 1878-1964 . . . . . . DLB-127

Hobsbaum, Philip 1932- DLB-40

Hobson, Laura Z. 1900- DLB-28

Hoby, Thomas 1530-1566 . . . . DLB-132

Hoccleve, Thomas
circa 1368-circa 1437 . . . . DLB-146

Hochhuth, Rolf 1931- DLB-124

Hochman, Sandra 1936- DLB-5

Hodder and Stoughton, Limited DLB-106

Hodgins, Jack 1938- DLB-60

Hodgman, Helen 1945- DLB-14

Hodgskin, Thomas 1787-1869 . . . . . DLB-158

Hodgson, Ralph 1871-1962 . . . . . . DLB-19

Hodgson, William Hope
1877-1918 . . . . . DLB-70, 153, 156, 178

Hoffenstein, Samuel 1890-1947 . . . . . DLB-11

Hoffman, Charles Fenno
1806-1884 . . . . DLB-3

Hoffman, Daniel 1923- DLB-5

Hoffmann, E. T. A. 1776-1822 . . . . . DLB-90

Hoffmanswaldau, Christian Hoffman von
1616-1679 . . . . DLB-168

Hofmann, Michael 1957- DLB-40

Hofmannsthal, Hugo von
1874-1929 . . . . DLB-81, 118

Hofstadter, Richard 1916-1970 . . . . . DLB-17

Hogan, Desmond 1950- DLB-14

Hogan, Linda 1947- DLB-175

Hogan and Thompson DLB-49

Hogarth Press DLB-112

Hogg, James 1770-1835 . . . . DLB-93, 116, 159

Hohberg, Wolfgang Helmhard Freiherr von
1612-1688 . . . . DLB-168

von Hohenheim, Philippus Aureolus
Theophrastus Bombastus (see Paracelsus)

Hohl, Ludwig 1904-1980 . . . . DLB-56

Holbrook, David 1923- DLB-14, 40

Holcroft, Thomas
1745-1809 . . . . DLB-39, 89, 158

Holden, Jonathan 1941- DLB-105

Holden, Jonathan, Contemporary
Verse Story-telling DLB-105

Holden, Molly 1927-1981 . . . . DLB-40

Hölderlin, Friedrich 1770-1843 . . . . . DLB-90

Holiday House DLB-46

Holinshed, Raphael died 1580 . . . . . DLB-167

Holland, J. G. 1819-1881 . . . . DS-13

Holland, Norman N. 1927- DLB-67

Hollander, John 1929- DLB-5

Holley, Marietta 1836-1926 . . . . DLB-11

Hollingsworth, Margaret 1940- DLB-60

Hollo, Anselm 1934- DLB-40

Holloway, Emory 1885-1977 . . . . . DLB-103

Holloway, John 1920- DLB-27

Holloway House Publishing
Company DLB-46

Holme, Constance 1880-1955 . . . . . . DLB-34

Holmes, Abraham S. 1821?-1908 . . . . DLB-99

Holmes, John Clellon 1926-1988 . . . . . DLB-16

Holmes, Oliver Wendell
1809-1894 . . . . DLB-1

Holmes, Richard 1945- DLB-155

Holroyd, Michael 1935- DLB-155

Holst, Hermann E. von
1841-1904 . . . . DLB-47

Holt, John 1721-1784 . . . . DLB-43

Holt, Henry, and Company DLB-49

Holt, Rinehart and Winston DLB-46

Holthusen, Hans Egon 1913- DLB-69

Hölty, Ludwig Christoph Heinrich
1748-1776 . . . . DLB-94

Holz, Arno 1863-1929 . . . . DLB-118

Home, Henry, Lord Kames (see Kames, Henry
Home, Lord)

Home, John 1722-1808 . . . . DLB-84

Home, William Douglas 1912- DLB-13

Home Publishing Company DLB-49

Homer circa eighth-seventh centuries B.C.
. . . . DLB-176

Homes, Geoffrey (see Mainwaring, Daniel)

Honan, Park 1928- DLB-111

Hone, William 1780-1842 . . . . . DLB-110, 158

Hongo, Garrett Kaoru 1951- DLB-120

Honig, Edwin 1919- DLB-5

Hood, Hugh 1928- DLB-53

Hood, Thomas 1799-1845 . . . . DLB-96

Hook, Theodore 1788-1841 . . . . . . DLB-116

Hooker, Jeremy 1941- DLB-40

Hooker, Richard 1554-1600 . . . . . . DLB-132

Hooker, Thomas 1586-1647 . . . . . . DLB-24

Hooper, Johnson Jones
1815-1862 . . . . DLB-3, 11

Hope, Anthony 1863-1933 . . . . DLB-153, 156

Hopkins, Gerard Manley
1844-1889 . . . . DLB-35, 57

Hopkins, John (see Sternhold, Thomas)

Hopkins, Lemuel 1750-1801 . . . . . . DLB-37

Hopkins, Pauline Elizabeth
1859-1930 . . . . DLB-50

Hopkins, Samuel 1721-1803 . . . . . . DLB-31

Hopkins, John H., and Son DLB-46

Hopkinson, Francis 1737-1791 . . . . . DLB-31

Horgan, Paul 1903- DLB-102; Y-85

Horizon Press DLB-46

Horne, Frank 1899-1974 . . . . DLB-51

Horne, Richard Henry (Hengist)
1802 or 1803-1884 . . . . DLB-32

Hornung, E. W. 1866-1921 . . . . . . DLB-70

Horovitz, Israel 1939- DLB-7

Horton, George Moses
1797?-1883? DLB-50

Horváth, Ödön von
1901-1938 . . . . DLB-85, 124

Horwood, Harold 1923- DLB-60

Hosford, E. and E.
[publishing house]. DLB-49

Hoskyns, John 1566-1638 . . . . DLB-121

Hotchkiss and Company DLB-49

Hough, Emerson 1857-1923 . . . . DLB-9

Houghton Mifflin Company DLB-49

Houghton, Stanley 1881-1913 . . . . . DLB-10

Household, Geoffrey 1900-1988 . . . . DLB-87

Housman, A. E. 1859-1936. . . . . . . DLB-19

Housman, Laurence 1865-1959. . . . . DLB-10

Houwald, Ernst von 1778-1845 . . . . DLB-90

Hovey, Richard 1864-1900 . . . . DLB-54

Howard, Donald R. 1927-1987 . . . . . DLB-111

Howard, Maureen 1930- Y-83

Howard, Richard 1929- DLB-5

Howard, Roy W. 1883-1964 . . . . . . DLB-29

Howard, Sidney 1891-1939 . . . . . DLB-7, 26

Howe, E. W. 1853-1937 . . . . . . DLB-12, 25

Howe, Henry 1816-1893 . . . . DLB-30

Howe, Irving 1920-1993 . . . . DLB-67

Howe, Joseph 1804-1873 . . . . DLB-99

Howe, Julia Ward 1819-1910 . . . . . . DLB-1

Howe, Percival Presland
1886-1944 . . . . DLB-149

Howe, Susan 1937- DLB-120

Howell, Clark, Sr. 1863-1936. . . . . . DLB-25

Howell, Evan P. 1839-1905 . . . . DLB-23

Howell, James 1594?-1666. . . . . DLB-151

Howell, Warren Richardson
1912-1984 . . . . DLB-140

Howell, Soskin and Company DLB-46

Howells, William Dean
1837-1920 . . . . DLB-12, 64, 74, 79

Howitt, William 1792-1879 and
Howitt, Mary 1799-1888 . . . . . DLB-110

Hoyem, Andrew 1935- DLB-5

Hoyers, Anna Ovena 1584-1655 . . . . DLB-164

Hoyos, Angela de 1940- DLB-82

Hoyt, Palmer 1897-1979. . . . . DLB-127

Hoyt, Henry [publishing house] DLB-49

Hrabanus Maurus 776?-856. . . . . . . DLB-148

Hrotsvit of Gandersheim
circa 935-circa 1000 . . . . DLB-148

Hubbard, Elbert 1856-1915. . . . . . . DLB-91

Hubbard, Kin 1868-1930 . . . . DLB-11

Hubbard, William circa 1621-1704. . . . DLB-24

Huber, Therese 1764-1829 . . . . DLB-90

Huch, Friedrich 1873-1913 . . . . DLB-66

Huch, Ricarda 1864-1947. . . . . DLB-66

Huck at 100: How Old Is
Huckleberry Finn? Y-85

Huddle, David 1942- DLB-130

Hudgins, Andrew 1951- DLB-120

Hudson, Henry Norman
1814-1886 . . . . DLB-64

Hudson, W. H.
1841-1922 . . . . DLB-98, 153, 174

Hudson and Goodwin DLB-49

Huebsch, B. W.
[publishing house]. DLB-46

Hughes, David 1930- DLB-14

Hughes, John 1677-1720 . . . . DLB-84

Hughes, Langston
1902-1967 . . . . . . DLB-4, 7, 48, 51, 86

Hughes, Richard 1900-1976. . . . . DLB-15, 161

Hughes, Ted 1930- DLB-40, 161

Hughes, Thomas 1822-1896 . . . . DLB-18, 163

Hugo, Richard 1923-1982 . . . . DLB-5

Hugo, Victor 1802-1885. . . . . DLB-119

Hugo Awards and Nebula Awards DLB-8

Hull, Richard 1896-1973 . . . . DLB-77

Hulme, T. E. 1883-1917 . . . . DLB-19

Humboldt, Alexander von
1769-1859 . . . . DLB-90

Humboldt, Wilhelm von
1767-1835 . . . . DLB-90

Hume, David 1711-1776 . . . . DLB-104

Hume, Fergus 1859-1932 . . . . DLB-70

Hummer, T. R. 1950- DLB-120

Humorous Book Illustration DLB-11

Humphrey, William 1924- DLB-6

Humphreys, David 1752-1818 . . . . . DLB-37

Humphreys, Emyr 1919- DLB-15

Huncke, Herbert 1915- DLB-16

Huneker, James Gibbons
1857-1921 . . . . DLB-71

Hunold, Christian Friedrich
1681-1721 . . . . DLB-168

Hunt, Irene 1907- DLB-52

Hunt, Leigh 1784-1859 . . . . DLB-96, 110, 144

Hunt, Violet 1862-1942 . . . . DLB-162

Hunt, William Gibbes 1791-1833 . . . . DLB-73

Hunter, Evan 1926- Y-82

Hunter, Jim 1939- DLB-14

Hunter, Kristin 1931- DLB-33

Hunter, Mollie 1922- DLB-161

Hunter, N. C. 1908-1971. . . . . DLB-10

Hunter-Duvar, John 1821-1899 . . . . . DLB-99

Huntington, Henry E.
1850-1927 . . . . DLB-140

Hurd and Houghton DLB-49

Hurst, Fannie 1889-1968 . . . . DLB-86

Hurst and Blackett. DLB-106

Hurst and Company DLB-49

Hurston, Zora Neale
1901?-1960 . . . . DLB-51, 86

Husson, Jules-François-Félix (see Champfleury)

Huston, John 1906-1987 . . . . DLB-26

Hutcheson, Francis 1694-1746 . . . . . DLB-31

Hutchinson, Thomas
1711-1780. . . . . DLB-30, 31

Hutchinson and Company
(Publishers) Limited DLB-112

von Hutton, Ulrich 1488-1523 . . . . . DLB-179

Hutton, Richard Holt 1826-1897. . . . . DLB-57

Huxley, Aldous
1894-1963 . . . . DLB-36, 100, 162

Huxley, Elspeth Josceline 1907- DLB-77

Huxley, T. H. 1825-1895. . . . . DLB-57

Huyghue, Douglas Smith
1816-1891 . . . . DLB-99

Huysmans, Joris-Karl 1848-1907 . . . . DLB-123

Hyman, Trina Schart 1939- DLB-61

I

Iavorsky, Stefan 1658-1722 . . . . DLB-150

Ibn Bajja circa 1077-1138 . . . . DLB-115

Ibn Gabirol, Solomon
circa 1021-circa 1058 . . . . DLB-115

Ibuse, Masuji 1898-1993. . . . . DLB-180

The Iconography of Science-Fiction
Art DLB-8

Iffland, August Wilhelm
1759-1814 . . . . DLB-94

Ignatow, David 1914- DLB-5

Ike, Chukwuemeka 1931- DLB-157

Iles, Francis (see Berkeley, Anthony)

The Illustration of Early German
Literary Manuscripts,
circa 1150-circa 1300 . . . . DLB-148

Imbs, Bravig 1904-1946 . . . . DLB-4

Imbuga, Francis D. 1947- DLB-157

Immermann, Karl 1796-1840 . . . . . DLB-133

Inchbald, Elizabeth 1753-1821 . . . . DLB-39, 89

Inge, William 1913-1973 . . . . DLB-7

Ingelow, Jean 1820-1897 . . . . . DLB-35, 163

Ingersoll, Ralph 1900-1985 . . . . . . DLB-127

The Ingersoll Prizes Y-84

Ingoldsby, Thomas (see Barham, Richard
  Harris)

Ingraham, Joseph Holt 1809-1860 . . . . . DLB-3

Inman, John 1805-1850 . . . . DLB-73

Innerhofer, Franz 1944- DLB-85

Innis, Harold Adams 1894-1952 . . . . . DLB-88

Innis, Mary Quayle 1899-1972 . . . . . . DLB-88

Inoue, Yasushi 1907-1991 . . . . DLB-181

International Publishers Company DLB-46

An Interview with David Rabe Y-91

An Interview with George Greenfield,
  Literary Agent Y-91

An Interview with James Ellroy Y-91

An Interview with Peter S. Prescott Y-86

An Interview with Russell Hoban Y-90

An Interview with Tom Jenks Y-86

Introduction to Paul Laurence Dunbar,
  Lyrics of Lowly Life (1896),
  by William Dean Howells DLB-50

Introductory Essay: Letters of Percy Bysshe
  Shelley (1852), by Robert
  Browning DLB-32

Introductory Letters from the Second Edition
  of Pamela (1741), by Samuel
  Richardson DLB-39

Irving, John 1942- DLB-6; Y-82

Irving, Washington 1783-1859
  . . . . . DLB-3, 11, 30, 59, 73, 74, 183

Irwin, Grace 1907- DLB-68

Irwin, Will 1873-1948 . . . . DLB-25

Isherwood, Christopher
  1904-1986 . . . . DLB-15; Y-86

Ishikawa, Jun 1899-1987 . . . . DLB-182

The Island Trees Case: A Symposium on
  School Library Censorship
  An Interview with Judith Krug
  An Interview with Phyllis Schlafly
  An Interview with Edward B. Jenkinson
  An Interview with Lamarr Mooneyham
  An Interview with Harriet
  Bernstein Y-82

Islas, Arturo 1938-1991 . . . . DLB-122

Ivanišević, Drago 1907-1981 . . . . . . DLB-181

Ivers, M. J., and Company DLB-49

Iwano, Hōmei 1873-1920 . . . . DLB-180

Iyayi, Festus 1947- DLB-157

Izumi, Kyōka 1873-1939 . . . . DLB-180

J

Jackmon, Marvin E. (see Marvin X)

Jacks, L. P. 1860-1955 . . . . DLB-135

Jackson, Angela 1951- DLB-41

Jackson, Helen Hunt
  1830-1885 . . . . DLB-42, 47

Jackson, Holbrook 1874-1948 . . . . . . DLB-98

Jackson, Laura Riding 1901-1991 . . . . DLB-48

Jackson, Shirley 1919-1965 . . . . DLB-6

Jacob, Piers Anthony Dillingham (see Anthony,
  Piers)

Jacobi, Friedrich Heinrich
  1743-1819 . . . . DLB-94

Jacobi, Johann Georg 1740-1841 . . . . . DLB-97

Jacobs, Joseph 1854-1916 . . . . DLB-141

Jacobs, W. W. 1863-1943 . . . . DLB-135

Jacobs, George W., and Company . . . DLB-49

Jacobson, Dan 1929- DLB-14

Jaggard, William
  [publishing house] DLB-170

Jahier, Piero 1884-1966 . . . . DLB-114

Jahnn, Hans Henny
  1894-1959 . . . . DLB-56, 124

Jakes, John 1932- Y-83

James, C. L. R. 1901-1989 . . . . . . DLB-125

James, George P. R. 1801-1860 . . . . . DLB-116

James, Henry
  1843-1916 . . . . . DLB-12, 71, 74; DS-13

James, John circa 1633-1729 . . . . . . DLB-24

The James Jones Society Y-92

James, M. R. 1862-1936 . . . . DLB-156

James, P. D. 1920- DLB-87

James Joyce Centenary: Dublin, 1982 . . . . Y-82

James Joyce Conference Y-85

James VI of Scotland, I of England
  1566-1625 . . . . DLB-151, 172

James, U. P. [publishing house] DLB-49

Jameson, Anna 1794-1860 . . . . . DLB-99, 166

Jameson, Fredric 1934- DLB-67

Jameson, J. Franklin 1859-1937 . . . . . DLB-17

Jameson, Storm 1891-1986 . . . . DLB-36

Jančar, Drago 1948- DLB-181

Janés, Clara 1940- DLB-134

Janevski, Slavko 1920- DLB-181

Jaramillo, Cleofas M. 1878-1956 . . . . DLB-122

Jarman, Mark 1952- DLB-120

Jarrell, Randall 1914-1965 . . . . . DLB-48, 52

Jarrold and Sons DLB-106

Jasmin, Claude 1930- DLB-60

Jay, John 1745-1829 . . . . DLB-31

Jefferies, Richard 1848-1887 . . . . . DLB-98, 141

Jeffers, Lance 1919-1985 . . . . DLB-41

Jeffers, Robinson 1887-1962 . . . . . . DLB-45

Jefferson, Thomas 1743-1826 . . . . DLB-31, 183

Jelinek, Elfriede 1946- DLB-85

Jellicoe, Ann 1927- DLB-13

Jenkins, Elizabeth 1905- DLB-155

Jenkins, Robin 1912- DLB-14

Jenkins, William Fitzgerald (see Leinster,
  Murray)

Jenkins, Herbert, Limited DLB-112

Jennings, Elizabeth 1926- DLB-27

Jens, Walter 1923- DLB-69

Jensen, Merrill 1905-1980 . . . . DLB-17

Jephson, Robert 1736-1803 . . . . DLB-89

Jerome, Jerome K.
  1859-1927 . . . . DLB-10, 34, 135

Jerome, Judson 1927-1991 . . . . DLB-105

Jerome, Judson, Reflections: After a
  Tornado DLB-105

Jerrold, Douglas 1803-1857 . . . . DLB-158, 159

Jesse, F. Tennyson 1888-1958 . . . . . . DLB-77

Jewett, Sarah Orne 1849-1909 . . . . DLB-12, 74

Jewett, John P., and Company DLB-49

The Jewish Publication Society DLB-49

Jewitt, John Rodgers 1783-1821 . . . . DLB-99

Jewsbury, Geraldine 1812-1880 . . . . . DLB-21

Jhabvala, Ruth Prawer 1927- DLB-139

Jiménez, Juan Ramón 1881-1958 . . . . DLB-134

Joans, Ted 1928- DLB-16, 41

John, Eugenie (see Marlitt, E.)

John of Dumbleton
  circa 1310-circa 1349 . . . . DLB-115

John Edward Bruce: Three
  Documents DLB-50

John O'Hara's Pottsville Journalism Y-88

John Steinbeck Research Center Y-85

John Webster: The Melbourne
  Manuscript Y-86

Johns, Captain W. E. 1893-1968 . . . . DLB-160

Johnson, B. S. 1933-1973 . . . . . DLB-14, 40

Johnson, Charles 1679-1748 . . . . . . DLB-84

Johnson, Charles R. 1948- DLB-33

Johnson, Charles S. 1893-1956 . . . DLB-51, 91

Johnson, Denis 1949- DLB-120

Johnson, Diane 1934- Y-80

Johnson, Edgar 1901- DLB-103

Johnson, Edward 1598-1672 . . . . . . DLB-24

Johnson E. Pauline (Tekahionwake)
  1861-1913 . . . . DLB-175

Johnson, Fenton 1888-1958 . . . . . DLB-45, 50

Johnson, Georgia Douglas
  1886-1966 . . . . DLB-51

Johnson, Gerald W. 1890-1980 . . . . . DLB-29

Johnson, Helene 1907- DLB-51

Johnson, James Weldon
  1871-1938 . . . . DLB-51

Johnson, John H. 1918- DLB-137

Johnson, Linton Kwesi 1952- DLB-157

Johnson, Lionel 1867-1902 . . . . DLB-19

Johnson, Nunnally 1897-1977 . . . . . DLB-26

Johnson, Owen 1878-1952 . . . . Y-87

Johnson, Pamela Hansford
1912- DLB-15

Johnson, Pauline 1861-1913. . . . . . . DLB-92

Johnson, Ronald 1935- DLB-169

Johnson, Samuel 1696-1772. . . . . . . DLB-24

Johnson, Samuel
1709-1784 . . . . . . DLB-39, 95, 104, 142

Johnson, Samuel 1822-1882 . . . . DLB-1

Johnson, Uwe 1934-1984 . . . . DLB-75

Johnson, Benjamin
[publishing house]. DLB-49

Johnson, Benjamin, Jacob, and
Robert [publishing house] DLB-49

Johnson, Jacob, and Company DLB-49

Johnson, Joseph [publishing house] DLB-154

Johnston, Annie Fellows 1863-1931 . . . DLB-42

Johnston, Basil H. 1929- DLB-60

Johnston, Denis 1901-1984 . . . . DLB-10

Johnston, George 1913- DLB-88

Johnston, Sir Harry 1858-1927 . . . . DLB-174

Johnston, Jennifer 1930- DLB-14

Johnston, Mary 1870-1936 . . . . DLB-9

Johnston, Richard Malcolm
1822-1898 . . . . DLB-74

Johnstone, Charles 1719?-1800? DLB-39

Johst, Hanns 1890-1978 . . . . DLB-124

Jolas, Eugene 1894-1952 . . . . DLB-4, 45

Jones, Alice C. 1853-1933 . . . . DLB-92

Jones, Charles C., Jr. 1831-1893 . . . . . DLB-30

Jones, D. G. 1929- DLB-53

Jones, David 1895-1974 . . . . . . DLB-20, 100

Jones, Diana Wynne 1934- DLB-161

Jones, Ebenezer 1820-1860 . . . . DLB-32

Jones, Ernest 1819-1868. . . . . DLB-32

Jones, Gayl 1949- DLB-33

Jones, George 1800-1870 . . . . DLB-183

Jones, Glyn 1905- DLB-15

Jones, Gwyn 1907- DLB-15, 139

Jones, Henry Arthur 1851-1929 . . . . . DLB-10

Jones, Hugh circa 1692-1760 . . . . . . DLB-24

Jones, James 1921-1977 . . . . DLB-2, 143

Jones, Jenkin Lloyd 1911- DLB-127

Jones, LeRoi (see Baraka, Amiri)

Jones, Lewis 1897-1939 . . . . DLB-15

Jones, Madison 1925- DLB-152

Jones, Major Joseph (see Thompson, William Tappan)

Jones, Preston 1936-1979 . . . . DLB-7

Jones, Rodney 1950- DLB-120

Jones, Sir William 1746-1794 . . . . . DLB-109

Jones, William Alfred 1817-1900 . . . . . DLB-59

Jones's Publishing House DLB-49

Jong, Erica 1942- DLB-2, 5, 28, 152

Jonke, Gert F. 1946- DLB-85

Jonson, Ben 1572?-1637 . . . . . . DLB-62, 121

Jordan, June 1936- DLB-38

Joseph, Jenny 1932- DLB-40

Joseph, Michael, Limited DLB-112

Josephson, Matthew 1899-1978 . . . . . DLB-4

Josephus, Flavius 37-100 . . . . DLB-176

Josiah Allen's Wife (see Holley, Marietta)

Josipovici, Gabriel 1940- DLB-14

Josselyn, John ?-1675 . . . . DLB-24

Joudry, Patricia 1921- DLB-88

Jovine, Giuseppe 1922- DLB-128

Joyaux, Philippe (see Sollers, Philippe)

Joyce, Adrien (see Eastman, Carol)

Joyce, James
1882-1941 . . . . DLB-10, 19, 36, 162

Judd, Sylvester 1813-1853 . . . . DLB-1

Judd, Orange, Publishing
Company DLB-49

Judith circa 930 . . . . DLB-146

Julian of Norwich
1342-circa 1420 . . . . DLB-1146

Julian Symons at Eighty Y-92

June, Jennie (see Croly, Jane Cunningham)

Jung, Franz 1888-1963 . . . . DLB-118

Jünger, Ernst 1895- DLB-56

Der jüngere Titurel circa 1275 . . . . . DLB-138

Jung-Stilling, Johann Heinrich
1740-1817 . . . . DLB-94

Justice, Donald 1925- Y-83

The Juvenile Library (see Godwin, M. J., and
Company)

K

Kacew, Romain (see Gary, Romain)

Kafka, Franz 1883-1924 . . . . DLB-81

Kahn, Roger 1927 . . . . DLB-171

Kaikō, Takeshi 1939-1989 . . . . DLB-182

Kaiser, Georg 1878-1945 . . . . DLB-124

Kaiserchronik circca 1147 . . . . DLB-148

Kaleb, Vjekoslav 1905- DLB-181

Kalechofsky, Roberta 1931- DLB-28

Kaler, James Otis 1848-1912 . . . . . . DLB-12

Kames, Henry Home, Lord
1696-1782 . . . . DLB-31, 104

Kandel, Lenore 1932- DLB-16

Kanin, Garson 1912- DLB-7

Kant, Hermann 1926- DLB-75

Kant, Immanuel 1724-1804 . . . . DLB-94

Kantemir, Antiokh Dmitrievich
1708-1744 . . . . DLB-150

Kantor, Mackinlay 1904-1977 . . . . DLB-9, 102

Kaplan, Fred 1937- DLB-111

Kaplan, Johanna 1942- DLB-28

Kaplan, Justin 1925- DLB-111

Kapnist, Vasilii Vasilevich
1758?-1823 . . . . DLB-150

Karadžić, Vuk Stefanović
1787-1864 . . . . DLB-147

Karamzin, Nikolai Mikhailovich
1766-1826 . . . . DLB-150

Karsch, Anna Louisa 1722-1791 . . . . DLB-97

Kasack, Hermann 1896-1966 . . . . . . DLB-69

Kasai, Zenzō 1887-1927 . . . . DLB-180

Kaschnitz, Marie Luise 1901-1974 . . . DLB-69

Kaštelan, Jure 1919-1990 . . . . DLB-147

Kästner, Erich 1899-1974 . . . . DLB-56

Kattan, Naim 1928- DLB-53

Katz, Steve 1935- Y-83

Kauffman, Janet 1945- Y-86

Kauffmann, Samuel 1898-1971 . . . . DLB-127

Kaufman, Bob 1925- DLB-16, 41

Kaufman, George S. 1889-1961 . . . . . DLB-7

Kavanagh, P. J. 1931- DLB-40

Kavanagh, Patrick 1904-1967 . . . . DLB-15, 20

Kawabata, Yasunari 1899-1972 . . . . DLB-180

Kaye-Smith, Sheila 1887-1956 . . . . . DLB-36

Kazin, Alfred 1915- DLB-67

Keane, John B. 1928- DLB-13

Keary, Annie 1825-1879 . . . . DLB-163

Keating, H. R. F. 1926- DLB-87

Keats, Ezra Jack 1916-1983 . . . . DLB-61

Keats, John 1795-1821 . . . . . . DLB-96, 110

Keble, John 1792-1866 . . . . . . DLB-32, 55

Keeble, John 1944- Y-83

Keeffe, Barrie 1945- DLB-13

Keeley, James 1867-1934 . . . . DLB-25

W. B. Keen, Cooke
and Company. DLB-49

Keillor, Garrison 1942- Y-87

Keith, Marian 1874?-1961 . . . . DLB-92

Keller, Gary D. 1943- DLB-82

Keller, Gottfried 1819-1890 . . . . . . DLB-129

Kelley, Edith Summers 1884-1956 . . . . DLB-9

Kelley, William Melvin 1937- DLB-33

Kellogg, Ansel Nash 1832-1886 . . . . . DLB-23

Kellogg, Steven 1941- DLB-61

Kelly, George 1887-1974 . . . . DLB-7

Kelly, Hugh 1739-1777 . . . . DLB-89

Kelly, Robert 1935- DLB-5, 130, 165

Kelly, Piet and Company DLB-49

Kelmscott Press DLB-112

Kemble, Fanny 1809-1893 . . . . DLB-32

Kemelman, Harry 1908- DLB-28

Kempe, Margery circa 1373-1438 . . . . DLB-146

Kempner, Friederike 1836-1904 . . . . . DLB-129

Kempowski, Walter 1929- DLB-75

Kendall, Claude [publishing company] . DLB-46

Kendell, George 1809-1867 . . . . DLB-43

Kenedy, P. J., and Sons DLB-49

Kennedy, Adrienne 1931- DLB-38

Kennedy, John Pendleton 1795-1870 . . . . DLB-3

Kennedy, Leo 1907- DLB-88

Kennedy, Margaret 1896-1967 . . . . . DLB-36

Kennedy, Patrick 1801-1873 . . . . . . DLB-159

Kennedy, Richard S. 1920- DLB-111

Kennedy, William 1928- DLB-143; Y-85

Kennedy, X. J. 1929- DLB-5

Kennelly, Brendan 1936- DLB-40

Kenner, Hugh 1923- DLB-67

Kennerley, Mitchell
   [publishing house] DLB-46

Kenny, Maurice 1929- DLB-175

Kent, Frank R. 1877-1958 . . . . DLB-29

Kenyon, Jane 1947- DLB-120

Keough, Hugh Edmund 1864-1912 . . . DLB-171

Keppler and Schwartzmann DLB-49

Kerner, Justinus 1776-1862 . . . . DLB-90

Kerouac, Jack 1922-1969 . . . . DLB-2, 16; DS-3

The Jack Kerouac Revival Y-95

Kerouac, Jan 1952- DLB-16

Kerr, Orpheus C. (see Newell, Robert Henry)

Kerr, Charles H., and Company DLB-49

Kesey, Ken 1935- DLB-2, 16

Kessel, Joseph 1898-1979 . . . . DLB-72

Kessel, Martin 1901- DLB-56

Kesten, Hermann 1900- DLB-56

Keun, Irmgard 1905-1982 . . . . DLB-69

Key and Biddle DLB-49

Keynes, John Maynard 1883-1946 . . . DS-10

Keyserling, Eduard von 1855-1918 . . . DLB-66

Khan, Ismith 1925- DLB-125

Khaytov, Nikolay 1919- DLB-181

Khemnitser, Ivan Ivanovich
   1745-1784 . . . . DLB-150

Kheraskov, Mikhail Matveevich
   1733-1807 . . . . DLB-150

Khristov, Boris 1945- DLB-181

Khvostov, Dmitrii Ivanovich
   1757-1835 . . . . DLB-150

Kidd, Adam 1802?-1831 . . . . DLB-99

Kidd, William
   [publishing house] DLB-106

Kiely, Benedict 1919- DLB-15

Kieran, John 1892-1981 . . . . DLB-171

Kiggins and Kellogg DLB-49

Kiley, Jed 1889-1962 . . . . DLB-4

Kilgore, Bernard 1908-1967 . . . . . . DLB-127

Killens, John Oliver 1916- DLB-33

Killigrew, Anne 1660-1685 . . . . . . DLB-131

Killigrew, Thomas 1612-1683 . . . . . DLB-58

Kilmer, Joyce 1886-1918 . . . . DLB-45

Kilwardby, Robert
   circa 1215-1279 . . . . DLB-115

Kincaid, Jamaica 1949- DLB-157

King, Clarence 1842-1901 . . . . DLB-12

King, Florence 1936 . . . . Y-85

King, Francis 1923- DLB-15, 139

King, Grace 1852-1932 . . . . . . DLB-12, 78

King, Henry 1592-1669 . . . . DLB-126

King, Stephen 1947- DLB-143; Y-80

King, Thomas 1943- DLB-175

King, Woodie, Jr. 1937- DLB-38

King, Solomon [publishing house] DLB-49

Kinglake, Alexander William
   1809-1891 . . . . DLB-55, 166

Kingsley, Charles
   1819-1875 . . . . . . DLB-21, 32, 163, 178

Kingsley, Mary Henrietta
   1862-1900 . . . . DLB-174

Kingsley, Henry 1830-1876 . . . . . . DLB-21

Kingsley, Sidney 1906- DLB-7

Kingsmill, Hugh 1889-1949 . . . . . . DLB-149

Kingston, Maxine Hong
   1940- DLB-173; Y-80

Kingston, William Henry Giles
   1814-1880 . . . . DLB-163

Kinnell, Galway 1927- DLB-5; Y-87

Kinsella, Thomas 1928- DLB-27

Kipling, Rudyard
   1865-1936 . . . . . . DLB-19, 34, 141, 156

Kipphardt, Heinar 1922-1982 . . . . . DLB-124

Kirby, William 1817-1906 . . . . DLB-99

Kircher, Athanasius 1602-1680 . . . . . DLB-164

Kirk, John Foster 1824-1904 . . . . . . DLB-79

Kirkconnell, Watson 1895-1977 . . . . DLB-68

Kirkland, Caroline M.
   1801-1864 . . . . . . DLB-3, 73, 74; DS-13

Kirkland, Joseph 1830-1893 . . . . . . DLB-12

Kirkman, Francis
   [publishing house] DLB-170

Kirkpatrick, Clayton 1915- DLB-127

Kirkup, James 1918- DLB-27

Kirouac, Conrad (see Marie-Victorin, Frère)

Kirsch, Sarah 1935- DLB-75

Kirst, Hans Hellmut 1914-1989 . . . . DLB-69

Kiš, Danilo 1935-1989 . . . . DLB-181

Kita, Morio 1927- DLB-182

Kitcat, Mabel Greenhow
   1859-1922 . . . . DLB-135

Kitchin, C. H. B. 1895-1967 . . . . . . DLB-77

Kizer, Carolyn 1925- DLB-5, 169

Klabund 1890-1928 . . . . DLB-66

Klaj, Johann 1616-1656 . . . . DLB-164

Klappert, Peter 1942- DLB-5

Klass, Philip (see Tenn, William)

Klein, A. M. 1909-1972 . . . . DLB-68

Kleist, Ewald von 1715-1759 . . . . . . DLB-97

Kleist, Heinrich von 1777-1811 . . . . . DLB-90

Klinger, Friedrich Maximilian
   1752-1831 . . . . DLB-94

Klopstock, Friedrich Gottlieb
   1724-1803 . . . . DLB-97

Klopstock, Meta 1728-1758 . . . . . . DLB-97

Kluge, Alexander 1932- DLB-75

Knapp, Joseph Palmer 1864-1951 . . . DLB-91

Knapp, Samuel Lorenzo
   1783-1838 . . . . DLB-59

Knapton, J. J. and P.
   [publishing house] DLB-154

Kniazhnin, Iakov Borisovich
   1740-1791 . . . . DLB-150

Knickerbocker, Diedrich (see Irving,
   Washington)

Knigge, Adolph Franz Friedrich Ludwig,
   Freiherr von 1752-1796 . . . . DLB-94

Knight, Damon 1922- DLB-8

Knight, Etheridge 1931-1992 . . . . . . DLB-41

Knight, John S. 1894-1981 . . . . DLB-29

Knight, Sarah Kemble 1666-1727 . . . . DLB-24

Knight, Charles, and Company DLB-106

Knight-Bruce, G. W. H.
   1852-1896 . . . . DLB-174

Knister, Raymond 1899-1932 . . . . . . DLB-68

Knoblock, Edward 1874-1945 . . . . . DLB-10

Knopf, Alfred A. 1892-1984 . . . . Y-84

Knopf, Alfred A.
   [publishing house] DLB-46

Knorr von Rosenroth, Christian
   1636-1689 . . . . DLB-168

Knowles, John 1926- DLB-6

Knox, Frank 1874-1944 . . . . DLB-29

Knox, John circa 1514-1572 . . . . . . DLB-132

Knox, John Armoy 1850-1906 . . . . . DLB-23

Knox, Ronald Arbuthnott
   1888-1957 . . . . DLB-77

Kobayashi, Takiji 1903-1933 . . . . . . DLB-180

Kober, Arthur 1900-1975 . . . . DLB-11

Kocbek, Edvard 1904-1981 . . . . . . DLB-147

Koch, Howard 1902- DLB-26

Koch, Kenneth 1925- DLB-5

Kōda, Rohan 1867-1947. . . . . DLB-180

Koenigsberg, Moses 1879-1945 . . . . . DLB-25

Koeppen, Wolfgang 1906- DLB-69

Koertge, Ronald 1940- DLB-105

Koestler, Arthur 1905-1983 . . . . Y-83

Kokoschka, Oskar 1886-1980 . . . . . DLB-124

Kolb, Annette 1870-1967 . . . . DLB-66

Kolbenheyer, Erwin Guido
    1878-1962 . . . . DLB-66, 124

Kolleritsch, Alfred 1931- DLB-85

Kolodny, Annette 1941- DLB-67

Komarov, Matvei
    circa 1730-1812 . . . . DLB-150

Komroff, Manuel 1890-1974 . . . . DLB-4

Komunyakaa, Yusef 1947- DLB-120

Koneski, Blaže 1921-1993 . . . . DLB-181

Konigsburg, E. L. 1930- DLB-52

Konrad von Würzburg
    circa 1230-1287 . . . . DLB-138

Konstantinov, Aleko 1863-1897 . . . . DLB-147

Kooser, Ted 1939- DLB-105

Kopit, Arthur 1937- DLB-7

Kops, Bernard 1926?- DLB-13

Kornbluth, C. M. 1923-1958 . . . . . . DLB-8

Körner, Theodor 1791-1813 . . . . . DLB-90

Kornfeld, Paul 1889-1942 . . . . DLB-118

Kosinski, Jerzy 1933-1991 . . . . . DLB-2; Y-82

Kosmač, Ciril 1910-1980 . . . . DLB-181

Kosovel, Srečko 1904-1926 . . . . . . DLB-147

Kostrov, Ermil Ivanovich
    1755-1796 . . . . DLB-150

Kotzebue, August von 1761-1819 . . . . DLB-94

Kotzwinkle, William 1938- DLB-173

Kovačić, Ante 1854-1889 . . . . DLB-147

Kovič, Kajetan 1931- DLB-181

Kraf, Elaine 1946- Y-81

Kranjčević, Silvije Strahimir
    1865-1908. . . . . DLB-147

Krasna, Norman 1909-1984 . . . . . . DLB-26

Kraus, Karl 1874-1936. . . . . DLB-118

Krauss, Ruth 1911-1993 . . . . DLB-52

Kreisel, Henry 1922- DLB-88

Kreuder, Ernst 1903-1972. . . . . . . DLB-69

Kreymborg, Alfred 1883-1966 . . . . DLB-4, 54

Krieger, Murray 1923- DLB-67

Krim, Seymour 1922-1989 . . . . DLB-16

Krleža, Miroslav 1893-1981 . . . . . DLB-147

Krock, Arthur 1886-1974 . . . . DLB-29

Kroetsch, Robert 1927- DLB-53

Krutch, Joseph Wood 1893-1970 . . . . DLB-63

Krylov, Ivan Andreevich
    1769-1844 . . . . DLB-150

Kubin, Alfred 1877-1959 . . . . DLB-81

Kubrick, Stanley 1928- DLB-26

Kudrun circa 1230-1240 . . . . DLB-138

Kuffstein, Hans Ludwig von
    1582-1656 . . . . DLB-164

Kuhlmann, Quirinus 1651-1689 . . . . DLB-168

Kuhnau, Johann 1660-1722 . . . . . . DLB-168

Kumin, Maxine 1925- DLB-5

Kunene, Mazisi 1930- DLB-117

Kunikida, Doppo 1869-1908. . . . . . DLB-180

Kunitz, Stanley 1905- DLB-48

Kunjufu, Johari M. (see Amini, Johari M.)

Kunnert, Gunter 1929- DLB-75

Kunze, Reiner 1933- DLB-75

Kupferberg, Tuli 1923- DLB-16

Kurahashi, Yumiko 1935- DLB-182

Kürnberger, Ferdinand
    1821-1879 . . . . DLB-129

Kurz, Isolde 1853-1944 . . . . DLB-66

Kusenberg, Kurt 1904-1983. . . . . . DLB-69

Kuttner, Henry 1915-1958 . . . . DLB-8

Kyd, Thomas 1558-1594 . . . . DLB-62

Kyffin, Maurice
    circa 1560?-1598 . . . . DLB-136

Kyger, Joanne 1934- DLB-16

Kyne, Peter B. 1880-1957 . . . . DLB-78

L

L. E. L. (see Landon, Letitia Elizabeth)

Laberge, Albert 1871-1960 . . . . DLB-68

Laberge, Marie 1950- DLB-60

Lacombe, Patrice (see Trullier-Lacombe,
    Joseph Patrice)

Lacretelle, Jacques de 1888-1985 . . . . DLB-65

Lacy, Sam 1903- DLB-171

Ladd, Joseph Brown 1764-1786 . . . . . DLB-37

La Farge, Oliver 1901-1963 . . . . DLB-9

Lafferty, R. A. 1914- DLB-8

La Flesche, Francis 1857-1932 . . . . . DLB-175

La Guma, Alex 1925-1985 . . . . DLB-117

Lahaise, Guillaume (see Delahaye, Guy)

Lahontan, Louis-Armand de Lom d'Arce,
    Baron de 1666-1715? DLB-99

Laing, Kojo 1946- DLB-157

Laird, Carobeth 1895- Y-82

Laird and Lee DLB-49

Lalić, Ivan V. 1931-1996 . . . . DLB-181

Lalić, Mihailo 1914-1992 . . . . DLB-181

Lalonde, Michèle 1937- DLB-60

Lamantia, Philip 1927- DLB-16

Lamb, Charles
    1775-1834 . . . . DLB-93, 107, 163

Lamb, Lady Caroline 1785-1828 . . . . DLB-116

Lamb, Mary 1764-1874 . . . . DLB-163

Lambert, Betty 1933-1983 . . . . DLB-60

Lamming, George 1927- DLB-125

L'Amour, Louis 1908?- Y-80

Lampman, Archibald 1861-1899 . . . . DLB-92

Lamson, Wolffe and Company DLB-49

Lancer Books DLB-46

Landesman, Jay 1919- and
    Landesman, Fran 1927- DLB-16

Landolfi, Tommaso 1908-1979 . . . . . DLB-177

Landon, Letitia Elizabeth 1802-1838 . . . DLB-96

Landor, Walter Savage
    1775-1864 . . . . DLB-93, 107

Landry, Napoléon-P. 1884-1956 . . . . . DLB-92

Lane, Charles 1800-1870 . . . . DLB-1

Lane, Laurence W. 1890-1967 . . . . . DLB-91

Lane, M. Travis 1934- DLB-60

Lane, Patrick 1939- DLB-53

Lane, Pinkie Gordon 1923- DLB-41

Lane, John, Company DLB-49

Laney, Al 1896-1988 . . . . DLB-4, 171

Lang, Andrew 1844-1912 . . . . . . DLB-98, 141

Langevin, André 1927- DLB-60

Langgässer, Elisabeth 1899-1950 . . . . DLB-69

Langhorne, John 1735-1779 . . . . . . DLB-109

Langland, William
    circa 1330-circa 1400 . . . . DLB-146

Langton, Anna 1804-1893 . . . . DLB-99

Lanham, Edwin 1904-1979 . . . . DLB-4

Lanier, Sidney 1842-1881 . . . . DLB-64; DS-13

Lanyer, Aemilia 1569-1645 . . . . . . DLB-121

Lapointe, Gatien 1931-1983 . . . . . . DLB-88

Lapointe, Paul-Marie 1929- DLB-88

Lardner, John 1912-1960 . . . . DLB-171

Lardner, Ring
    1885-1933 . . . . DLB-11, 25, 86,171

Lardner, Ring, Jr. 1915- DLB-26

Lardner 100: Ring Lardner
    Centennial Symposium. Y-85

Larkin, Philip 1922-1985 . . . . DLB-27

La Roche, Sophie von 1730-1807 . . . . DLB-94

La Rocque, Gilbert 1943-1984 . . . . . DLB-60

Laroque de Roquebrune, Robert (see Roquebrune,
    Robert de)

Larrick, Nancy 1910- DLB-61

Larsen, Nella 1893-1964 . . . . DLB-51

Lasker-Schüler, Else
    1869-1945 . . . . DLB-66, 124

Lasnier, Rina 1915- DLB-88

Lassalle, Ferdinand 1825-1864. . . . . . DLB-129

Lathrop, Dorothy P. 1891-1980 . . . . . DLB-22

Lathrop, George Parsons
1851-1898 . . . . DLB-71

Lathrop, John, Jr. 1772-1820 . . . . . . DLB-37

Latimer, Hugh 1492?-1555 . . . . DLB-136

Latimore, Jewel Christine McLawler
(see Amini, Johari M.)

Latymer, William 1498-1583 . . . . . . DLB-132

Laube, Heinrich 1806-1884 . . . . DLB-133

Laughlin, James 1914- DLB-48

Laumer, Keith 1925- DLB-8

Lauremberg, Johann 1590-1658 . . . . . DLB-164

Laurence, Margaret 1926-1987 . . . . . DLB-53

Laurentius von Schnüffis
1633-1702 . . . . DLB-168

Laurents, Arthur 1918- DLB-26

Laurie, Annie (see Black, Winifred)

Laut, Agnes Christiana 1871-1936 . . . . DLB-92

Lavater, Johann Kaspar 1741-1801. . . . DLB-97

Lavin, Mary 1912- DLB-15

Lawes, Henry 1596-1662 . . . . DLB-126

Lawless, Anthony (see MacDonald, Philip)

Lawrence, D. H.
1885-1930 . . . . . DLB-10, 19, 36, 98, 162

Lawrence, David 1888-1973 . . . . DLB-29

Lawrence, Seymour 1926-1994. . . . . . . Y-94

Lawson, John ?-1711 . . . . DLB-24

Lawson, Robert 1892-1957 . . . . DLB-22

Lawson, Victor F. 1850-1925. . . . . . . DLB-25

Layard, Sir Austen Henry
1817-1894 . . . . DLB-166

Layton, Irving 1912- DLB-88

LaZamon flourished circa 1200. . . . . DLB-146

Lazarević, Laza K. 1851-1890 . . . . . . DLB-147

Lea, Henry Charles 1825-1909. . . . . . DLB-47

Lea, Sydney 1942- DLB-120

Lea, Tom 1907- DLB-6

Leacock, John 1729-1802 . . . . DLB-31

Leacock, Stephen 1869-1944 . . . . . . DLB-92

Lead, Jane Ward 1623-1704 . . . . . . DLB-131

Leadenhall Press DLB-106

Leapor, Mary 1722-1746 . . . . DLB-109

Lear, Edward 1812-1888 . . . DLB-32, 163, 166

Leary, Timothy 1920-1996 . . . . DLB-16

Leary, W. A., and Company DLB-49

Léautaud, Paul 1872-1956 . . . . DLB-65

Leavitt, David 1961- DLB-130

Leavitt and Allen DLB-49

Le Blond, Mrs. Aubrey
1861-1934 . . . . DLB-174

le Carré, John 1931- DLB-87

Lécavelé, Roland (see Dorgeles, Roland)

Lechlitner, Ruth 1901- DLB-48

Leclerc, Félix 1914- DLB-60

Le Clézio, J. M. G. 1940- DLB-83

Lectures on Rhetoric and Belles Lettres (1783),
by Hugh Blair [excerpts]. DLB-31

Leder, Rudolf (see Hermlin, Stephan)

Lederer, Charles 1910-1976. . . . . . . DLB-26

Ledwidge, Francis 1887-1917. . . . . . . DLB-20

Lee, Dennis 1939- DLB-53

Lee, Don L. (see Madhubuti, Haki R.)

Lee, George W. 1894-1976. . . . . DLB-51

Lee, Harper 1926- DLB-6

Lee, Harriet (1757-1851) and
Lee, Sophia (1750-1824) DLB-39

Lee, Laurie 1914- DLB-27

Lee, Li-Young 1957- DLB-165

Lee, Manfred B. (see Dannay, Frederic, and
Manfred B. Lee)

Lee, Nathaniel circa 1645 - 1692 . . . . DLB-80

Lee, Sir Sidney 1859-1926. . . . . DLB-149

Lee, Sir Sidney, "Principles of Biography," in
Elizabethan and Other Essays. DLB-149

Lee, Vernon
1856-1935. . . . DLB-57, 153, 156, 174, 178

Lee and Shepard DLB-49

Le Fanu, Joseph Sheridan
1814-1873 . . . . . . DLB-21, 70, 159, 178

Leffland, Ella 1931- Y-84

le Fort, Gertrud von 1876-1971 . . . . DLB-66

Le Gallienne, Richard 1866-1947 . . . . DLB-4

Legaré, Hugh Swinton
1797-1843 . . . . DLB-3, 59, 73

Legaré, James M. 1823-1859. . . . . . DLB-3

The Legends of the Saints and a Medieval
Christian Worldview DLB-148

Léger, Antoine-J. 1880-1950. . . . . . . DLB-88

Le Guin, Ursula K. 1929- DLB-8, 52

Lehman, Ernest 1920- DLB-44

Lehmann, John 1907- DLB-27, 100

Lehmann, Rosamond 1901-1990 . . . . . DLB-15

Lehmann, Wilhelm 1882-1968 . . . . . DLB-56

Lehmann, John, Limited. DLB-112

Leiber, Fritz 1910-1992. . . . . DLB-8

Leibniz, Gottfried Wilhelm
1646-1716 . . . . DLB-168

Leicester University Press DLB-112

Leinster, Murray 1896-1975 . . . . . . DLB-8

Leisewitz, Johann Anton
1752-1806 . . . . DLB-94

Leitch, Maurice 1933- DLB-14

Leithauser, Brad 1943- DLB-120

Leland, Charles G. 1824-1903 . . . . . . DLB-11

Leland, John 1503?-1552 . . . . DLB-136

Lemay, Pamphile 1837-1918 . . . . . . DLB-99

Lemelin, Roger 1919- DLB-88

Lemon, Mark 1809-1870 . . . . DLB-163

Le Moine, James MacPherson
1825-1912 . . . . DLB-99

Le Moyne, Jean 1913- DLB-88

L'Engle, Madeleine 1918- DLB-52

Lennart, Isobel 1915-1971 . . . . DLB-44

Lennox, Charlotte
1729 or 1730-1804 . . . . DLB-39

Lenox, James 1800-1880. . . . . DLB-140

Lenski, Lois 1893-1974 . . . . DLB-22

Lenz, Hermann 1913- DLB-69

Lenz, J. M. R. 1751-1792 . . . . DLB-94

Lenz, Siegfried 1926- DLB-75

Leonard, Elmore 1925- DLB-173

Leonard, Hugh 1926- DLB-13

Leonard, William Ellery
1876-1944 . . . . DLB-54

Leonowens, Anna 1834-1914 . . . . DLB-99, 166

LePan, Douglas 1914- DLB-88

Leprohon, Rosanna Eleanor
1829-1879 . . . . DLB-99

Le Queux, William 1864-1927 . . . . . . DLB-70

Lerner, Max 1902-1992 . . . . DLB-29

Lernet-Holenia, Alexander
1897-1976 . . . . DLB-85

Le Rossignol, James 1866-1969. . . . . . DLB-92

Lescarbot, Marc circa 1570-1642 . . . . DLB-99

LeSeur, William Dawson
1840-1917 . . . . DLB-92

LeSieg, Theo. (see Geisel, Theodor Seuss)

Leslie, Frank 1821-1880 . . . . DLB-43, 79

Leslie, Frank, Publishing House DLB-49

Lesperance, John 1835?-1891 . . . . . . DLB-99

Lessing, Bruno 1870-1940 . . . . DLB-28

Lessing, Doris 1919- DLB-15, 139; Y-85

Lessing, Gotthold Ephraim
1729-1781 . . . . DLB-97

Lettau, Reinhard 1929- DLB-75

Letter from Japan. Y-94

Letter from London Y-96

Letter to [Samuel] Richardson on Clarissa
(1748), by Henry Fielding DLB-39

Lever, Charles 1806-1872. . . . . DLB-21

Leverson, Ada 1862-1933 . . . . DLB-153

Levertov, Denise 1923- DLB-5, 165

Levi, Peter 1931- DLB-40

Levi, Primo 1919-1987 . . . . DLB-177

Levien, Sonya 1888-1960 . . . . DLB-44

Levin, Meyer 1905-1981 . . . . DLB-9, 28; Y-81

Levine, Norman 1923- DLB-88

Levine, Philip 1928- DLB-5

Levis, Larry 1946- DLB-120

Levy, Amy 1861-1889 . . . . DLB-156

Levy, Benn Wolfe
1900-1973 . . . . DLB-13; Y-81

Lewald, Fanny 1811-1889 . . . . DLB-129

Lewes, George Henry
1817-1878 . . . . DLB-55, 144

Lewis, Agnes Smith 1843-1926 . . . . DLB-174

Lewis, Alfred H. 1857-1914 . . . . DLB-25

Lewis, Alun 1915-1944 . . . . . . DLB-20, 162

Lewis, C. Day (see Day Lewis, C.)

Lewis, C. S. 1898-1963 . . . . DLB-15, 100, 160

Lewis, Charles B. 1842-1924 . . . . . . DLB-11

Lewis, Henry Clay 1825-1850 . . . . . . DLB-3

Lewis, Janet 1899- Y-87

Lewis, Matthew Gregory
1775-1818 . . . . DLB-39, 158, 178

Lewis, Meriwether 1774-1809 and
Clark, William 1770-1838 . . . . . DLB-183

Lewis, R. W. B. 1917- DLB-111

Lewis, Richard circa 1700-1734 . . . . DLB-24

Lewis, Sinclair
1885-1951 . . . . DLB-9, 102; DS-1

Lewis, Wilmarth Sheldon
1895-1979 . . . . DLB-140

Lewis, Wyndham 1882-1957 . . . . . . DLB-15

Lewisohn, Ludwig
1882-1955 . . . . DLB-4, 9, 28, 102

Lezama Lima, José 1910-1976 . . . . . DLB-113

The Library of America DLB-46

The Licensing Act of 1737 . . . . . . DLB-84

Lichfield, Leonard I
[publishing house] DLB-170

Lichtenberg, Georg Christoph
1742-1799 . . . . DLB-94

Lieb, Fred 1888-1980 . . . . DLB-171

Liebling, A. J. 1904-1963 . . . . . . DLB-4, 171

Lieutenant Murray (see Ballou, Maturin
Murray)

Lighthall, William Douw
1857-1954 . . . . DLB-92

Lilar, Françoise (see Mallet-Joris, Françoise)

Lillo, George 1691-1739 . . . . DLB-84

Lilly, J. K., Jr. 1893-1966 . . . . DLB-140

Lilly, Wait and Company DLB-49

Lily, William circa 1468-1522 . . . . . DLB-132

Limited Editions Club DLB-46

Lincoln and Edmands DLB-49

Lindsay, Jack 1900- Y-84

Lindsay, Sir David
circa 1485-1555 . . . . DLB-132

Lindsay, Vachel 1879-1931 . . . . DLB-54

Linebarger, Paul Myron Anthony (see Smith,
Cordwainer)

Link, Arthur S. 1920- DLB-17

Linn, John Blair 1777-1804 . . . . . . DLB-37

Lins, Osman 1924-1978 . . . . DLB-145

Linton, Eliza Lynn 1822-1898 . . . . . DLB-18

Linton, William James 1812-1897 . . . DLB-32

Lintot, Barnaby Bernard
[publishing house] DLB-170

Lion Books DLB-46

Lionni, Leo 1910- DLB-61

Lippincott, Sara Jane Clarke
1823-1904 . . . . DLB-43

Lippincott, J. B., Company DLB-49

Lippmann, Walter 1889-1974 . . . . . DLB-29

Lipton, Lawrence 1898-1975 . . . . . DLB-16

Liscow, Christian Ludwig
1701-1760 . . . . DLB-97

Lish, Gordon 1934- DLB-130

Lispector, Clarice 1925-1977 . . . . . DLB-113

*The Literary Chronicle and Weekly Review
1819-1828* DLB-110

Literary Documents: William Faulkner
and the People-to-People
Program Y-86

Literary Documents II: *Library Journal*
Statements and Questionnaires from
First Novelists Y-87

Literary Effects of World War II
[British novel] DLB-15

Literary Prizes [British] DLB-15

Literary Research Archives: The Humanities
Research Center, University of
Texas Y-82

Literary Research Archives II: Berg
Collection of English and American
Literature of the New York Public
Library Y-83

Literary Research Archives III:
The Lilly Library Y-84

Literary Research Archives IV:
The John Carter Brown Library Y-85

Literary Research Archives V:
Kent State Special Collections Y-86

Literary Research Archives VI: The Modern
Literary Manuscripts Collection in the
Special Collections of the Washington
University Libraries Y-87

Literary Research Archives VII:
The University of Virginia
Libraries Y-91

Literary Research Archives VIII:
The Henry E. Huntington
Library Y-92

"Literary Style" (1857), by William
Forsyth [excerpt] DLB-57

Literatura Chicanesca: The View From Without
. . . . DLB-82

Literature at Nurse, or Circulating Morals (1885),
by George Moore DLB-18

Littell, Eliakim 1797-1870 . . . . DLB-79

Littell, Robert S. 1831-1896 . . . . . DLB-79

Little, Brown and Company DLB-49

Little Magazines and Newspapers DS-15

The Little Review 1914-1929 . . . . . . DS-15

Littlewood, Joan 1914- DLB-13

Lively, Penelope 1933- DLB-14, 161

Liverpool University Press DLB-112

The Lives of the Poets DLB-142

Livesay, Dorothy 1909- DLB-68

Livesay, Florence Randal
1874-1953 . . . . DLB-92

Livings, Henry 1929- DLB-13

Livingston, Anne Howe
1763-1841 . . . . DLB-37

Livingston, Myra Cohn 1926- DLB-61

Livingston, William 1723-1790 . . . . . DLB-31

Livingstone, David 1813-1873 . . . . . DLB-166

Liyong, Taban lo (see Taban lo Liyong)

Lizárraga, Sylvia S. 1925- DLB-82

Llewellyn, Richard 1906-1983 . . . . . DLB-15

Lloyd, Edward
[publishing house] DLB-106

Lobel, Arnold 1933- DLB-61

Lochridge, Betsy Hopkins (see Fancher, Betsy)

Locke, David Ross 1833-1888 . . . . DLB-11, 23

Locke, John 1632-1704 . . . . . . DLB-31, 101

Locke, Richard Adams 1800-1871 . . . . DLB-43

Locker-Lampson, Frederick
1821-1895 . . . . DLB-35

Lockhart, John Gibson
1794-1854 . . . . DLB-110, 116 144

Lockridge, Ross, Jr.
1914-1948 . . . . DLB-143; Y-80

Locrine and *Selimus* DLB-62

Lodge, David 1935- DLB-14

Lodge, George Cabot 1873-1909 . . . . DLB-54

Lodge, Henry Cabot 1850-1924 . . . . DLB-47

Lodge, Thomas 1558-1625 . . . . . . DLB-172

Loeb, Harold 1891-1974 . . . . DLB-4

Loeb, William 1905-1981 . . . . . . DLB-127

Lofting, Hugh 1886-1947 . . . . DLB-160

Logan, James 1674-1751 . . . . . DLB-24, 140

Logan, John 1923- DLB-5

Logan, William 1950- DLB-120

Logau, Friedrich von 1605-1655 . . . . DLB-164

Logue, Christopher 1926- DLB-27

Lohenstein, Daniel Casper von
1635-1683 . . . . DLB-168

Lomonosov, Mikhail Vasil'evich
1711-1765 . . . . DLB-150

London, Jack 1876-1916 . . . . . DLB-8, 12, 78

The London Magazine 1820-1829 . . . . . DLB-110

Long, Haniel 1888-1956 . . . . DLB-45

Long, Ray 1878-1935 . . . . DLB-137

Long, H., and Brother DLB-49

Longfellow, Henry Wadsworth
   1807-1882 . . . . DLB-1, 59

Longfellow, Samuel 1819-1892. . . . . . DLB-1

Longford, Elizabeth 1906- DLB-155

Longinus circa first century DLB-176

Longley, Michael 1939- DLB-40

Longman, T. [publishing house] DLB-154

Longmans, Green and Company DLB-49

Longmore, George 1793?-1867 . . . . . DLB-99

Longstreet, Augustus Baldwin
   1790-1870 . . . . DLB-3, 11, 74

Longworth, D. [publishing house] DLB-49

Lonsdale, Frederick 1881-1954 . . . . . DLB-10

A Look at the Contemporary Black Theatre
   Movement. DLB-38

Loos, Anita 1893-1981. . . . . DLB-11, 26; Y-81

Lopate, Phillip 1943- Y-80

López, Diana (see Isabella, Ríos)

Loranger, Jean-Aubert 1896-1942. . . . . DLB-92

Lorca, Federico García 1898-1936 . . . DLB-108

Lord, John Keast 1818-1872 . . . . . . DLB-99

The Lord Chamberlain's Office and Stage
   Censorship in England DLB-10

Lorde, Audre 1934-1992 . . . . DLB-41

Lorimer, George Horace
   1867-1939 . . . . DLB-91

Loring, A. K. [publishing house]. DLB-49

Loring and Mussey DLB-46

Lossing, Benson J. 1813-1891 . . . . . . DLB-30

Lothar, Ernst 1890-1974 . . . . DLB-81

Lothrop, Harriet M. 1844-1924 . . . . DLB-42

Lothrop, D., and Company DLB-49

Loti, Pierre 1850-1923 . . . . DLB-123

Lotichius Secundus, Petrus
   1528-1560 . . . . DLB-179

Lott, Emeline ?-? DLB-166

The Lounger, no. 20 (1785), by Henry
   Mackenzie DLB-39

Lounsbury, Thomas R. 1838-1915. . . . DLB-71

Louÿs, Pierre 1870-1925 . . . . DLB-123

Lovelace, Earl 1935- DLB-125

Lovelace, Richard 1618-1657 . . . . . . DLB-131

Lovell, Coryell and Company DLB-49

Lovell, John W., Company DLB-49

Lover, Samuel 1797-1868 . . . . DLB-159

Lovesey, Peter 1936- DLB-87

Lovingood, Sut (see Harris,
   George Washington)

Low, Samuel 1765-? DLB-37

Lowell, Amy 1874-1925 . . . . . . DLB-54, 140

Lowell, James Russell
   1819-1891 . . . . DLB-1, 11, 64, 79

Lowell, Robert 1917-1977 . . . . . DLB-5, 169

Lowenfels, Walter 1897-1976 . . . . . . DLB-4

Lowndes, Marie Belloc 1868-1947 . . . . DLB-70

Lownes, Humphrey
   [publishing house] DLB-170

Lowry, Lois 1937- DLB-52

Lowry, Malcolm 1909-1957 . . . . . . DLB-15

Lowther, Pat 1935-1975. . . . . DLB-53

Loy, Mina 1882-1966 . . . . DLB-4, 54

Lozeau, Albert 1878-1924. . . . . . . DLB-92

Lubbock, Percy 1879-1965 . . . . . . DLB-149

Lucas, E. V. 1868-1938 . . . . DLB-98, 149, 153

Lucas, Fielding, Jr.
   [publishing house]. DLB-49

Luce, Henry R. 1898-1967 . . . . DLB-91

Luce, John W., and Company. DLB-46

Lucian circa 120-180. . . . . DLB-176

Lucie-Smith, Edward 1933- DLB-40

Lucini, Gian Pietro 1867-1914 . . . . . DLB-114

Luder, Peter circa 1415-1472 . . . . . . DLB-179

Ludlum, Robert 1927- Y-82

Ludus de Antichristo circa 1160 . . . . . DLB-148

Ludvigson, Susan 1942- DLB-120

Ludwig, Jack 1922- DLB-60

Ludwig, Otto 1813-1865. . . . . DLB-129

Ludwigslied 881 or 882 . . . . DLB-148

Luera, Yolanda 1953- DLB-122

Luft, Lya 1938- DLB-145

Luke, Peter 1919- DLB-13

Lupton, F. M., Company DLB-49

Lupus of Ferrières
   circa 805-circa 862. . . . . DLB-148

Lurie, Alison 1926- DLB-2

Luther, Martin 1483-1546 . . . . DLB-179

Luzi, Mario 1914- DLB-128

L'vov, Nikolai Aleksandrovich
   1751-1803 . . . . DLB-150

Lyall, Gavin 1932- DLB-87

Lydgate, John circa 1370-1450 . . . . . DLB-146

Lyly, John circa 1554-1606 . . . . . DLB-62, 167

Lynch, Patricia 1898-1972 . . . . DLB-160

Lynch, Richard
   flourished 1596-1601 . . . . DLB-172

Lynd, Robert 1879-1949 . . . . DLB-98

Lyon, Matthew 1749-1822 . . . . DLB-43

Lysias circa 459 B.C.-circa 380 B.C.
   . . . . DLB-176

Lytle, Andrew 1902-1995 . . . . . DLB-6; Y-95

Lytton, Edward (see Bulwer-Lytton, Edward)

Lytton, Edward Robert Bulwer
   1831-1891 . . . . DLB-32

M

Maass, Joachim 1901-1972 . . . . DLB-69

Mabie, Hamilton Wright
   1845-1916 . . . . DLB-71

Mac A'Ghobhainn, Iain (see Smith, Iain
   Crichton)

MacArthur, Charles
   1895-1956 . . . . DLB-7, 25, 44

Macaulay, Catherine 1731-1791 . . . . DLB-104

Macaulay, David 1945- DLB-61

Macaulay, Rose 1881-1958 . . . . . . DLB-36

Macaulay, Thomas Babington
   1800-1859 . . . . DLB-32, 55

Macaulay Company. DLB-46

MacBeth, George 1932- DLB-40

Macbeth, Madge 1880-1965 . . . . . . DLB-92

MacCaig, Norman 1910- DLB-27

MacDiarmid, Hugh 1892-1978 . . . . . DLB-20

MacDonald, Cynthia 1928- DLB-105

MacDonald, George
   1824-1905 . . . . DLB-18, 163, 178

MacDonald, John D.
   1916-1986 . . . . DLB-8; Y-86

MacDonald, Philip 1899?-1980 . . . . . DLB-77

Macdonald, Ross (see Millar, Kenneth)

MacDonald, Wilson 1880-1967. . . . . DLB-92

Macdonald and Company
   (Publishers). DLB-112

MacEwen, Gwendolyn 1941- DLB-53

Macfadden, Bernarr
   1868-1955 . . . . DLB-25, 91

MacGregor, John 1825-1892 . . . . . . DLB-166

MacGregor, Mary Esther (see Keith, Marian)

Machado, Antonio 1875-1939 . . . . . DLB-108

Machado, Manuel 1874-1947 . . . . . DLB-108

Machar, Agnes Maule 1837-1927 . . . DLB-92

Machen, Arthur Llewelyn Jones
   1863-1947 . . . . DLB-36, 156, 178

MacInnes, Colin 1914-1976. . . . . . . DLB-14

MacInnes, Helen 1907-1985 . . . . . . DLB-87

Mack, Maynard 1909- DLB-111

Mackall, Leonard L. 1879-1937 . . . . DLB-140

MacKaye, Percy 1875-1956 . . . . . . DLB-54

Macken, Walter 1915-1967 . . . . . . DLB-13

Mackenzie, Alexander 1763-1820. . . . DLB-99

Mackenzie, Alexander Slidell
   1803-1848 . . . . DLB-183

Mackenzie, Compton
   1883-1972 . . . . DLB-34, 100

Mackenzie, Henry 1745-1831 . . . . . . DLB-39

Mackey, Nathaniel 1947- DLB-169

Mackey, William Wellington
1937- DLB-38

Mackintosh, Elizabeth (see Tey, Josephine)

Mackintosh, Sir James
1765-1832 . . . . DLB-158

Maclaren, Ian (see Watson, John)

Macklin, Charles 1699-1797 . . . . DLB-89

MacLean, Katherine Anne 1925- DLB-8

MacLeish, Archibald
1892-1982 . . . . DLB-4, 7, 45; Y-82

MacLennan, Hugh 1907-1990 . . . . . . DLB-68

Macleod, Fiona (see Sharp, William)

MacLeod, Alistair 1936- DLB-60

Macleod, Norman 1906-1985 . . . . . . DLB-4

Macmillan and Company DLB-106

The Macmillan Company DLB-49

Macmillan's English Men of Letters,
First Series (1878-1892) DLB-144

MacNamara, Brinsley 1890-1963 . . . . DLB-10

MacNeice, Louis 1907-1963 . . . . DLB-10, 20

MacPhail, Andrew 1864-1938 . . . . . DLB-92

Macpherson, James 1736-1796 . . . . . DLB-109

Macpherson, Jay 1931- DLB-53

Macpherson, Jeanie 1884-1946 . . . . . DLB-44

Macrae Smith Company DLB-46

Macrone, John
[publishing house] DLB-106

MacShane, Frank 1927- DLB-111

Macy-Masius. DLB-46

Madden, David 1933- DLB-6

Maddow, Ben 1909-1992 . . . . DLB-44

Maddux, Rachel 1912-1983 . . . . Y-93

Madgett, Naomi Long 1923- DLB-76

Madhubuti, Haki R.
1942- DLB-5, 41; DS-8

Madison, James 1751-1836 . . . . DLB-37

Maginn, William 1794-1842 . . . . DLB-110, 159

Mahan, Alfred Thayer 1840-1914 . . . . DLB-47

Maheux-Forcier, Louise 1929- DLB-60

Mahin, John Lee 1902-1984 . . . . . . DLB-44

Mahon, Derek 1941- DLB-40

Maikov, Vasilii Ivanovich
1728-1778 . . . . DLB-150

Mailer, Norman
1923- DLB-2, 16, 28; Y-80, 83; DS-3

Maillet, Adrienne 1885-1963 . . . . . . DLB-68

Maimonides, Moses 1138-1204 . . . . . DLB-115

Maillet, Antonine 1929- DLB-60

Maillu, David G. 1939- DLB-157

Main Selections of the Book-of-the-Month
Club, 1926-1945 . . . . DLB-9

Main Trends in Twentieth-Century Book Clubs
. . . . DLB-46

Mainwaring, Daniel 1902-1977 . . . . . DLB-44

Mair, Charles 1838-1927 . . . . DLB-99

Mais, Roger 1905-1955 . . . . DLB-125

Major, Andre 1942- DLB-60

Major, Clarence 1936- DLB-33

Major, Kevin 1949- DLB-60

Major Books DLB-46

Makemie, Francis circa 1658-1708 . . . . DLB-24

The Making of a People, by
J. M. Ritchie DLB-66

Maksimović, Desanka 1898-1993 . . . . DLB-147

Malamud, Bernard
1914-1986 . . . . . DLB-2, 28, 152; Y-80, 86

Malet, Lucas 1852-1931 . . . . DLB-153

Malleson, Lucy Beatrice (see Gilbert, Anthony)

Mallet-Joris, Françoise 1930- DLB-83

Mallock, W. H. 1849-1923 . . . . . DLB-18, 57

Malone, Dumas 1892-1986 . . . . DLB-17

Malone, Edmond 1741-1812 . . . . . DLB-142

Malory, Sir Thomas
circa 1400-1410 - 1471 . . . . DLB-146

Malraux, André 1901-1976 . . . . DLB-72

Malthus, Thomas Robert
1766-1834. . . . . DLB-107, 158

Maltz, Albert 1908-1985 . . . . DLB-102

Malzberg, Barry N. 1939- DLB-8

Mamet, David 1947- DLB-7

Manaka, Matsemela 1956- DLB-157

Manchester University Press DLB-112

Mandel, Eli 1922- DLB-53

Mandeville, Bernard 1670-1733 . . . . . DLB-101

Mandeville, Sir John
mid fourteenth century DLB-146

Mandiargues, André Pieyre de
1909- DLB-83

Manfred, Frederick 1912-1994 . . . . . . DLB-6

Mangan, Sherry 1904-1961 . . . . DLB-4

Mankiewicz, Herman 1897-1953 . . . . DLB-26

Mankiewicz, Joseph L. 1909-1993 . . . . DLB-44

Mankowitz, Wolf 1924- DLB-15

Manley, Delarivière
1672?-1724 . . . . DLB-39, 80

Mann, Abby 1927- DLB-44

Mann, Heinrich 1871-1950 . . . . . DLB-66, 118

Mann, Horace 1796-1859 . . . . DLB-1

Mann, Klaus 1906-1949. . . . . DLB-56

Mann, Thomas 1875-1955 . . . . DLB-66

Mann, William D'Alton
1839-1920 . . . . DLB-137

Manning, Marie 1873?-1945 . . . . . . DLB-29

Manning and Loring DLB-49

Mannyng, Robert
flourished 1303-1338 . . . . DLB-146

Mano, D. Keith 1942- DLB-6

Manor Books DLB-46

Mansfield, Katherine 1888-1923 . . . . DLB-162

Manuel, Niklaus circa 1484-1530 . . . . DLB-179

Manzini, Gianna 1896-1974 . . . . . . DLB-177

Mapanje, Jack 1944- DLB-157

March, William 1893-1954 . . . . . DLB-9, 86

Marchand, Leslie A. 1900- DLB-103

Marchant, Bessie 1862-1941 . . . . . . DLB-160

Marchessault, Jovette 1938- DLB-60

Marcus, Frank 1928- DLB-13

Marden, Orison Swett
1850-1924 . . . . DLB-137

Marechera, Dambudzo
1952-1987 . . . . DLB-157

Marek, Richard, Books DLB-46

Mares, E. A. 1938- DLB-122

Mariani, Paul 1940- DLB-111

Marie-Victorin, Frère 1885-1944 . . . . DLB-92

Marin, Biagio 1891-1985. . . . . DLB-128

Marincovioe, Ranko 1913- DLB-147

Marinetti, Filippo Tommaso
1876-1944 . . . . DLB-114

Marion, Frances 1886-1973 . . . . DLB-44

Marius, Richard C. 1933- Y-85

The Mark Taper Forum DLB-7

Mark Twain on Perpetual Copyright Y-92

Markfield, Wallace 1926- DLB-2, 28

Markham, Edwin 1852-1940 . . . . . . DLB-54

Markle, Fletcher 1921-1991 . . . . DLB-68; Y-91

Marlatt, Daphne 1942- DLB-60

Marlitt, E. 1825-1887 . . . . DLB-129

Marlowe, Christopher 1564-1593 . . . . . DLB-62

Marlyn, John 1912- DLB-88

Marmion, Shakerley 1603-1639 . . . . . DLB-58

Der Marner
before 1230-circa 1287 . . . . DLB-138

The *Marprelate Tracts* 1588-1589 . . . . DLB-132

Marquand, John P. 1893-1960 . . . . DLB-9, 102

Marqués, René 1919-1979 . . . . DLB-113

Marquis, Don 1878-1937 . . . . . . DLB-11, 25

Marriott, Anne 1913- DLB-68

Marryat, Frederick 1792-1848 . . . . DLB-21, 163

Marsh, George Perkins
1801-1882 . . . . DLB-1, 64

Marsh, James 1794-1842 . . . . DLB-1, 59

Marsh, Capen, Lyon and Webb DLB-49

Marsh, Ngaio 1899-1982 . . . . DLB-77

Marshall, Edison 1894-1967 . . . . . . DLB-102

Marshall, Edward 1932- DLB-16

Marshall, Emma 1828-1899 . . . . . . DLB-163

Marshall, James 1942-1992 . . . . DLB-61

Marshall, Joyce 1913- DLB-88

Marshall, Paule 1929- DLB-33, 157

Marshall, Tom 1938- DLB-60

Marsilius of Padua
circa 1275-circa 1342 . . . . DLB-115

Marson, Una 1905-1965 . . . . DLB-157

Marston, John 1576-1634 . . . . . DLB-58, 172

Marston, Philip Bourke 1850-1887 . . . . DLB-35

Martens, Kurt 1870-1945 . . . . DLB-66

Martien, William S.
[publishing house] DLB-49

Martin, Abe (see Hubbard, Kin)

Martin, Charles 1942- DLB-120

Martin, Claire 1914- DLB-60

Martin, Jay 1935- DLB-111

Martin, Johann (see Laurentius von Schnüffis)

Martin, Violet Florence (see Ross, Martin)

Martin du Gard, Roger 1881-1958 . . . DLB-65

Martineau, Harriet
1802-1876 . . . . DLB-21, 55, 159, 163, 166

Martínez, Eliud 1935- DLB-122

Martínez, Max 1943- DLB-82

Martyn, Edward 1859-1923 . . . . DLB-10

Marvell, Andrew 1621-1678 . . . . . . DLB-131

Marvin X 1944- DLB-38

Marx, Karl 1818-1883 . . . . DLB-129

Marzials, Theo 1850-1920 . . . . DLB-35

Masefield, John
1878-1967 . . . . . . DLB-10, 19, 153, 160

Mason, A. E. W. 1865-1948 . . . . . . DLB-70

Mason, Bobbie Ann
1940- DLB-173; Y-87

Mason, William 1725-1797 . . . . . . DLB-142

Mason Brothers DLB-49

Massey, Gerald 1828-1907 . . . . DLB-32

Massinger, Philip 1583-1640 . . . . . . DLB-58

Masson, David 1822-1907 . . . . DLB-144

Masters, Edgar Lee 1868-1950 . . . . . DLB-54

Mastronardi, Lucio 1930-1979 . . . . . DLB-177

Matevski, Mateja 1929- DLB-181

Mather, Cotton
1663-1728 . . . . DLB-24, 30, 140

Mather, Increase 1639-1723 . . . . . . DLB-24

Mather, Richard 1596-1669 . . . . DLB-24

Matheson, Richard 1926- DLB-8, 44

Matheus, John F. 1887- DLB-51

Mathews, Cornelius
1817?-1889 . . . . DLB-3, 64

Mathews, John Joseph
1894-1979 . . . . DLB-175

Mathews, Elkin
[publishing house] DLB-112

Mathias, Roland 1915- DLB-27

Mathis, June 1892-1927 . . . . DLB-44

Mathis, Sharon Bell 1937- DLB-33

Matković, Marijan 1915-1985 . . . . . DLB-181

Matoš, Antun Gustav 1873-1914 . . . . DLB-147

Matsumoto, Seichō 1909-1992 . . . . . DLB-182

The Matter of England
1240-1400 . . . . DLB-146

The Matter of Rome
early twelfth to late fifteenth
century DLB-146

Matthews, Brander
1852-1929 . . . . DLB-71, 78; DS-13

Matthews, Jack 1925- DLB-6

Matthews, William 1942- DLB-5

Matthiessen, F. O. 1902-1950 . . . DLB-63

Maturin, Charles Robert
1780-1824 . . . . DLB-178

Matthiessen, Peter 1927- DLB-6, 173

Maugham, W. Somerset
1874-1965 . . . . . DLB-10, 36, 77, 100, 162

Maupassant, Guy de 1850-1893 . . . . DLB-123

Mauriac, Claude 1914- DLB-83

Mauriac, François 1885-1970 . . . . . DLB-65

Maurice, Frederick Denison
1805-1872 . . . . DLB-55

Maurois, André 1885-1967 . . . . DLB-65

Maury, James 1718-1769 . . . . DLB-31

Mavor, Elizabeth 1927- DLB-14

Mavor, Osborne Henry (see Bridie, James)

Maxwell, William 1908- Y-80

Maxwell, H. [publishing house] . . . DLB-49

Maxwell, John [publishing house] DLB-106

May, Elaine 1932- DLB-44

May, Karl 1842-1912 . . . . DLB-129

May, Thomas 1595 or 1596-1650 . . . . DLB-58

Mayer, Bernadette 1945- DLB-165

Mayer, Mercer 1943- DLB-61

Mayer, O. B. 1818-1891 . . . . DLB-3

Mayes, Herbert R. 1900-1987 . . . . . DLB-137

Mayes, Wendell 1919-1992 . . . . . . DLB-26

Mayfield, Julian 1928-1984 . . . . . DLB-33; Y-84

Mayhew, Henry 1812-1887 . . . . . DLB-18, 55

Mayhew, Jonathan 1720-1766 . . . . . DLB-31

Mayne, Jasper 1604-1672 . . . . DLB-126

Mayne, Seymour 1944- DLB-60

Mayor, Flora Macdonald
1872-1932 . . . . DLB-36

Mayrocker, Friederike 1924- DLB-85

Mazrui, Ali A. 1933- DLB-125

Mažuranić, Ivan 1814-1890 . . . . . . DLB-147

Mazursky, Paul 1930- DLB-44

McAlmon, Robert
1896-1956 . . . . DLB-4, 45; DS-15

McArthur, Peter 1866-1924 . . . . DLB-92

McBride, Robert M., and
Company DLB-46

McCaffrey, Anne 1926- DLB-8

McCarthy, Cormac 1933- DLB-6, 143

McCarthy, Mary 1912-1989 . . . . DLB-2; Y-81

McCay, Winsor 1871-1934 . . . . DLB-22

McClane, Albert Jules 1922-1991 . . . . DLB-171

McClatchy, C. K. 1858-1936 . . . . . . DLB-25

McClellan, George Marion
1860-1934 . . . . DLB-50

McCloskey, Robert 1914- DLB-22

McClung, Nellie Letitia 1873-1951 . . . . DLB-92

McClure, Joanna 1930- DLB-16

McClure, Michael 1932- DLB-16

McClure, Phillips and Company DLB-46

McClure, S. S. 1857-1949 . . . . DLB-91

McClurg, A. C., and Company DLB-49

McCluskey, John A., Jr. 1944- DLB-33

McCollum, Michael A. 1946- Y-87

McConnell, William C. 1917- DLB-88

McCord, David 1897- DLB-61

McCorkle, Jill 1958- Y-87

McCorkle, Samuel Eusebius
1746-1811 . . . . DLB-37

McCormick, Anne O'Hare
1880-1954 . . . . DLB-29

McCormick, Robert R. 1880-1955 . . . . DLB-29

McCourt, Edward 1907-1972 . . . . . . DLB-88

McCoy, Horace 1897-1955 . . . . DLB-9

McCrae, John 1872-1918 . . . . DLB-92

McCullagh, Joseph B. 1842-1896 . . . . DLB-23

McCullers, Carson
1917-1967 . . . . DLB-2, 7, 173

McCulloch, Thomas 1776-1843 . . . . . DLB-99

McDonald, Forrest 1927- DLB-17

McDonald, Walter
1934- DLB-105, DS-9

McDonald, Walter, Getting Started:
Accepting the Regions You Own—
or Which Own You DLB-105

McDougall, Colin 1917-1984 . . . . . . DLB-68

McDowell, Obolensky DLB-46

McEwan, Ian 1948- DLB-14

McFadden, David 1940- DLB-60

McFall, Frances Elizabeth Clarke
(see Grand, Sarah)

McFarlane, Leslie 1902-1977 . . . . . . DLB-88

McFee, William 1881-1966 . . . . DLB-153

McGahern, John 1934- DLB-14

McGee, Thomas D'Arcy
1825-1868 . . . . DLB-99

McGeehan, W. O. 1879-1933 . . . DLB-25, 171

McGill, Ralph 1898-1969 . . . . DLB-29

McGinley, Phyllis 1905-1978 . . . . . DLB-11, 48

McGirt, James E. 1874-1930 . . . . . . DLB-50

McGlashan and Gill DLB-106

McGough, Roger 1937- DLB-40

McGraw-Hill DLB-46

McGuane, Thomas 1939- DLB-2; Y-80

McGuckian, Medbh 1950- DLB-40

McGuffey, William Holmes
1800-1873 . . . . DLB-42

McIlvanney, William 1936- DLB-14

McIlwraith, Jean Newton
1859-1938 . . . . DLB-92

McIntyre, James 1827-1906 . . . . DLB-99

McIntyre, O. O. 1884-1938 . . . . . . DLB-25

McKay, Claude
1889-1948 . . . . DLB-4, 45, 51, 117

The David McKay Company DLB-49

McKean, William V. 1820-1903 . . . . DLB-23

The McKenzie Trust Y-96

McKinley, Robin 1952- DLB-52

McLachlan, Alexander 1818-1896 . . . . DLB-99

McLaren, Floris Clark 1904-1978 . . . . DLB-68

McLaverty, Michael 1907- DLB-15

McLean, John R. 1848-1916 . . . . . . DLB-23

McLean, William L. 1852-1931 . . . . DLB-25

McLennan, William 1856-1904 . . . . . DLB-92

McLoughlin Brothers DLB-49

McLuhan, Marshall 1911-1980 . . . . . DLB-88

McMaster, John Bach 1852-1932 . . . . DLB-47

McMurtry, Larry
1936- DLB-2, 143; Y-80, 87

McNally, Terrence 1939- DLB-7

McNeil, Florence 1937- DLB-60

McNeile, Herman Cyril
1888-1937 . . . . DLB-77

McNickle, D'Arcy 1904-1977 . . . . . DLB-175

McPherson, James Alan 1943- DLB-38

McPherson, Sandra 1943- Y-86

McWhirter, George 1939- DLB-60

McWilliams, Carey 1905-1980 . . . . . DLB-137

Mead, L. T. 1844-1914 . . . . DLB-141

Mead, Matthew 1924- DLB-40

Mead, Taylor ?- DLB-16

Meany, Tom 1903-1964 . . . . DLB-171

Mechthild von Magdeburg
circa 1207-circa 1282 . . . . DLB-138

Medill, Joseph 1823-1899 . . . . DLB-43

Medoff, Mark 1940- DLB-7

Meek, Alexander Beaufort
1814-1865 . . . . DLB-3

Meeke, Mary ?-1816? DLB-116

Meinke, Peter 1932- DLB-5

Mejia Vallejo, Manuel 1923- DLB-113

Melanchton, Philipp 1497-1560 . . . . DLB-179

Melançon, Robert 1947- DLB-60

Mell, Max 1882-1971 . . . . DLB-81, 124

Mellow, James R. 1926- DLB-111

Meltzer, David 1937- DLB-16

Meltzer, Milton 1915- DLB-61

Melville, Elizabeth, Lady Culross
circa 1585-1640 . . . . DLB-172

Melville, Herman 1819-1891 . . . . DLB-3, 74

Memoirs of Life and Literature (1920),
by W. H. Mallock [excerpt] DLB-57

Menander 342-341 B.C.-circa 292-291 B.C.
. . . . DLB-176

Menantes (see Hunold, Christian Friedrich)

Mencke, Johann Burckhard
1674-1732 . . . . DLB-168

Mencken, H. L.
1880-1956 . . . . DLB-11, 29, 63, 137

Mencken and Nietzsche: An Unpublished Excerpt
from H. L. Mencken's *My Life
as Author and Editor* Y-93

Mendelssohn, Moses 1729-1786 . . . . DLB-97

Méndez M., Miguel 1930- DLB-82

The Mercantile Library of
New York Y-96

Mercer, Cecil William (see Yates, Dornford)

Mercer, David 1928-1980 . . . . DLB-13

Mercer, John 1704-1768 . . . . DLB-31

Meredith, George
1828-1909 . . . . DLB-18, 35, 57, 159

Meredith, Louisa Anne
1812-1895 . . . . DLB-166

Meredith, Owen (see Lytton, Edward Robert Bulwer)

Meredith, William 1919- DLB-5

Mergerle, Johann Ulrich
(see Abraham ä Sancta Clara)

Mérimée, Prosper 1803-1870 . . . . . DLB-119

Merivale, John Herman
1779-1844 . . . . DLB-96

Meriwether, Louise 1923- DLB-33

Merlin Press DLB-112

Merriam, Eve 1916-1992 . . . . DLB-61

The Merriam Company DLB-49

Merrill, James
1926-1995 . . . . DLB-5, 165; Y-85

Merrill and Baker DLB-49

The Mershon Company DLB-49

Merton, Thomas 1915-1968 . . . . DLB-48; Y-81

Merwin, W. S. 1927- DLB-5, 169

Messner, Julian [publishing house] DLB-46

Metcalf, J. [publishing house] DLB-49

Metcalf, John 1938- DLB-60

The Methodist Book Concern DLB-49

Methuen and Company DLB-112

Mew, Charlotte 1869-1928 . . . . . DLB-19, 135

Mewshaw, Michael 1943- Y-80

Meyer, Conrad Ferdinand 1825-1898 . . . DLB-129

Meyer, E. Y. 1946- DLB-75

Meyer, Eugene 1875-1959 . . . . DLB-29

Meyer, Michael 1921- DLB-155

Meyers, Jeffrey 1939- DLB-111

Meynell, Alice
1847-1922 . . . . DLB-19, 98

Meynell, Viola 1885-1956 . . . . DLB-153

Meyrink, Gustav 1868-1932 . . . . . . DLB-81

Michaels, Leonard 1933- DLB-130

Micheaux, Oscar 1884-1951 . . . . . . DLB-50

Michel of Northgate, Dan
circa 1265-circa 1340 . . . . DLB-146

Micheline, Jack 1929- DLB-16

Michener, James A. 1907?- DLB-6

Micklejohn, George
circa 1717-1818 . . . . DLB-31

Middle English Literature:
An Introduction DLB-146

The Middle English Lyric DLB-146

Middle Hill Press DLB-106

Middleton, Christopher 1926- DLB-40

Middleton, Richard 1882-1911 . . . . . DLB-156

Middleton, Stanley 1919- DLB-14

Middleton, Thomas 1580-1627 . . . . . DLB-58

Miegel, Agnes 1879-1964 . . . . DLB-56

Mihailović, Dragoslav 1930- DLB-181

Mihalić, Slavko 1928- DLB-181

Miles, Josephine 1911-1985 . . . . . . DLB-48

Miliković, Branko 1934-1961 . . . . . DLB-181

Milius, John 1944- DLB-44

Mill, James 1773-1836 . . . . . . DLB-107, 158

Mill, John Stuart 1806-1873 . . . . . DLB-55

Millar, Kenneth
1915-1983 . . . . DLB-2; Y-83; DS-6

Millar, Andrew
[publishing house] DLB-154

Millay, Edna St. Vincent
1892-1950 . . . . DLB-45

Miller, Arthur 1915- DLB-7

Miller, Caroline 1903-1992 . . . . DLB-9

Miller, Eugene Ethelbert 1950- DLB-41

Miller, Heather Ross 1939- DLB-120

Miller, Henry 1891-1980 . . . . . DLB-4, 9; Y-80

Miller, J. Hillis 1928- DLB-67

Miller, James [publishing house] DLB-49

Miller, Jason 1939- DLB-7

Miller, May 1899- DLB-41

Miller, Paul 1906-1991. . . . . DLB-127

Miller, Perry 1905-1963 . . . . DLB-17, 63

Miller, Sue 1943- DLB-143

Miller, Vassar 1924- DLB-105

Miller, Walter M., Jr. 1923- DLB-8

Miller, Webb 1892-1940 . . . . DLB-29

Millhauser, Steven 1943- DLB-2

Millican, Arthenia J. Bates
1920- DLB-38

Mills and Boon DLB-112

Milman, Henry Hart 1796-1868 . . . . . DLB-96

Milne, A. A.
1882-1956 . . . . . . DLB-10, 77, 100, 160

Milner, Ron 1938- DLB-38

Milner, William
[publishing house] DLB-106

Milnes, Richard Monckton (Lord Houghton)
1809-1885 . . . . DLB-32

Milton, John 1608-1674 . . . . . DLB-131, 151

Minakami, Tsutomu 1919- DLB-182

The Minerva Press DLB-154

Minnesang circa 1150-1280 . . . . . . DLB-138

Minns, Susan 1839-1938. . . . . DLB-140

Minor Illustrators, 1880-1914 . . . . . DLB-141

Minor Poets of the Earlier Seventeenth
Century DLB-121

Minton, Balch and Company DLB-46

Mirbeau, Octave 1848-1917. . . . . . DLB-123

Mirk, John died after 1414? DLB-146

Miron, Gaston 1928- DLB-60

A Mirror for Magistrates. DLB-167

Mishima, Yukio 1925-1970 . . . . . . DLB-182

Mitchel, Jonathan 1624-1668 . . . . . . DLB-24

Mitchell, Adrian 1932- DLB-40

Mitchell, Donald Grant
1822-1908 . . . . DLB-1; DS-13

Mitchell, Gladys 1901-1983. . . . . . . DLB-77

Mitchell, James Leslie 1901-1935. . . . DLB-15

Mitchell, John (see Slater, Patrick)

Mitchell, John Ames 1845-1918 . . . . DLB-79

Mitchell, Joseph 1908-1996. . . . . Y-96

Mitchell, Julian 1935- DLB-14

Mitchell, Ken 1940- DLB-60

Mitchell, Langdon 1862-1935 . . . . . . DLB-7

Mitchell, Loften 1919- DLB-38

Mitchell, Margaret 1900-1949 . . . . . . DLB-9

Mitchell, W. O. 1914- DLB-88

Mitchison, Naomi Margaret (Haldane)
1897- DLB-160

Mitford, Mary Russell
1787-1855. . . . . DLB-110, 116

Mittelholzer, Edgar 1909-1965. . . . . DLB-117

Mitterer, Erika 1906- DLB-85

Mitterer, Felix 1948- DLB-124

Mitternacht, Johann Sebastian
1613-1679 . . . . DLB-168

Miyamoto, Yuriko 1899-1951 . . . . . DLB-180

Mizener, Arthur 1907-1988 . . . . . . DLB-103

Modern Age Books. DLB-46

"Modern English Prose" (1876),
by George Saintsbury DLB-57

The Modern Language Association of America
Celebrates Its Centennial Y-84

The Modern Library DLB-46

"Modern Novelists – Great and Small" (1855), by
Margaret Oliphant DLB-21

"Modern Style" (1857), by Cockburn
Thomson [excerpt] DLB-57

The Modernists (1932), by Joseph Warren Beach
DLB-36

Modiano, Patrick 1945- DLB-83

Moffat, Yard and Company DLB-46

Moffet, Thomas 1553-1604 . . . . . . DLB-136

Mohr, Nicholasa 1938- DLB-145

Moix, Ana María 1947- DLB-134

Molesworth, Louisa 1839-1921 . . . . . DLB-135

Möllhausen, Balduin 1825-1905 . . . . . DLB-129

Momaday, N. Scott 1934- DLB-143, 175

Monkhouse, Allan 1858-1936. . . . . . DLB-10

Monro, Harold 1879-1932 . . . . . . DLB-19

Monroe, Harriet 1860-1936 . . . . . DLB-54, 91

Monsarrat, Nicholas 1910-1979. . . . DLB-15

Montagu, Lady Mary Wortley
1689-1762 . . . . DLB-95, 101

Montague, John 1929- DLB-40

Montale, Eugenio 1896-1981 . . . . . DLB-114

Monterroso, Augusto 1921- DLB-145

Montgomerie, Alexander
circa 1550?-1598 . . . . DLB-167

Montgomery, James
1771-1854 . . . . DLB-93, 158

Montgomery, John 1919- DLB-16

Montgomery, Lucy Maud
1874-1942 . . . . DLB-92; DS-14

Montgomery, Marion 1925- DLB-6

Montgomery, Robert Bruce (see Crispin, Edmund)

Montherlant, Henry de 1896-1972 . . . . DLB-72

The Monthly Review 1749-1844 . . . . . DLB-110

Montigny, Louvigny de 1876-1955 . . . DLB-92

Montoya, José 1932- DLB-122

Moodie, John Wedderburn Dunbar
1797-1869 . . . . DLB-99

Moodie, Susanna 1803-1885 . . . . . . DLB-99

Moody, Joshua circa 1633-1697 . . . . DLB-24

Moody, William Vaughn
1869-1910 . . . . DLB-7, 54

Moorcock, Michael 1939- DLB-14

Moore, Catherine L. 1911- DLB-8

Moore, Clement Clarke 1779-1863 . . . DLB-42

Moore, Dora Mavor 1888-1979 . . . . . DLB-92

Moore, George
1852-1933. . . . . . . DLB-10, 18, 57, 135

Moore, Marianne
1887-1972 . . . . DLB-45; DS-7

Moore, Mavor 1919- DLB-88

Moore, Richard 1927- DLB-105

Moore, Richard, The No Self, the Little Self,
and the Poets DLB-105

Moore, T. Sturge 1870-1944 . . . . . . DLB-19

Moore, Thomas 1779-1852 . . . . . DLB-96, 144

Moore, Ward 1903-1978. . . . . DLB-8

Moore, Wilstach, Keys and
Company DLB-49

The Moorland-Spingarn Research
Center DLB-76

Moorman, Mary C. 1905-1994 . . . . . DLB-155

Moraga, Cherríe 1952- DLB-82

Morales, Alejandro 1944- DLB-82

Morales, Mario Roberto 1947- DLB-145

Morales, Rafael 1919- DLB-108

Morality Plays: *Mankind* circa 1450-1500 and
Everyman circa 1500 . . . . DLB-146

Morante, Elsa 1912-1985 . . . . DLB-177

Morata, Olympia Fulvia
1526-1555 . . . . DLB-179

Moravia, Alberto 1907-1990. . . . . . DLB-177

Mordaunt, Elinor 1872-1942 . . . . . . DLB-174

More, Hannah
1745-1833 . . . . . . DLB-107, 109, 116, 158

More, Henry 1614-1687. . . . . DLB-126

More, Sir Thomas
1477 or 1478-1535 . . . . DLB-136

Moreno, Dorinda 1939- DLB-122

Morency, Pierre 1942- DLB-60

Moretti, Marino 1885-1979 . . . . . . DLB-114

Morgan, Berry 1919- DLB-6

Morgan, Charles 1894-1958. . . . . DLB-34, 100

Morgan, Edmund S. 1916- DLB-17

Morgan, Edwin 1920- DLB-27

Morgan, John Pierpont
1837-1913 . . . . DLB-140

Morgan, John Pierpont, Jr.
1867-1943 . . . . DLB-140

Morgan, Robert 1944- DLB-120

Morgan, Sydney Owenson, Lady
1776?-1859 . . . . DLB-116, 158

Morgner, Irmtraud 1933- DLB-75

Morhof, Daniel Georg
1639-1691 . . . . DLB-164

Mori, Ōgai 1862-1922 . . . . DLB-180

Morier, James Justinian
1782 or 1783?-1849 . . . . DLB-116

Mörike, Eduard 1804-1875 . . . . . . DLB-133

Morin, Paul 1889-1963 . . . . DLB-92

Morison, Richard 1514?-1556 . . . . . DLB-136

Morison, Samuel Eliot 1887-1976 . . . . DLB-17

Moritz, Karl Philipp 1756-1793 . . . . . DLB-94

Moriz von Craûn
circa 1220-1230 . . . . DLB-138

Morley, Christopher 1890-1957 . . . . . DLB-9

Morley, John 1838-1923 . . . . . DLB-57, 144

Morris, George Pope 1802-1864 . . . . . DLB-73

Morris, Lewis 1833-1907 . . . . DLB-35

Morris, Richard B. 1904-1989 . . . . . DLB-17

Morris, William
1834-1896 . . . . . DLB-18, 35, 57, 156, 178

Morris, Willie 1934- Y-80

Morris, Wright 1910- DLB-2; Y-81

Morrison, Arthur 1863-1945 . . . . DLB-70, 135

Morrison, Charles Clayton
1874-1966 . . . . DLB-91

Morrison, Toni
1931- DLB-6, 33, 143; Y-81

Morrow, William, and Company DLB-46

Morse, James Herbert 1841-1923 . . . . DLB-71

Morse, Jedidiah 1761-1826 . . . . DLB-37

Morse, John T., Jr. 1840-1937 . . . . . . DLB-47

Morselli, Guido 1912-1973 . . . . . . DLB-177

Mortimer, Favell Lee 1802-1878 . . . . DLB-163

Mortimer, John 1923- DLB-13

Morton, Carlos 1942- DLB-122

Morton, John P., and Company DLB-49

Morton, Nathaniel 1613-1685 . . . . . . DLB-24

Morton, Sarah Wentworth
1759-1846 . . . . DLB-37

Morton, Thomas
circa 1579-circa 1647 . . . . DLB-24

Moscherosch, Johann Michael
1601-1669 . . . . DLB-164

Moseley, Humphrey
[publishing house] DLB-170

Möser, Justus 1720-1794 . . . . DLB-97

Mosley, Nicholas 1923- DLB-14

Moss, Arthur 1889-1969 . . . . DLB-4

Moss, Howard 1922-1987 . . . . DLB-5

Moss, Thylias 1954- DLB-120

The Most Powerful Book Review in America
[*New York Times Book Review*] Y-82

Motion, Andrew 1952- DLB-40

Motley, John Lothrop
1814-1877 . . . . DLB-1, 30, 59

Motley, Willard 1909-1965 . . . . DLB-76, 143

Motte, Benjamin Jr.
[publishing house] DLB-154

Motteux, Peter Anthony
1663-1718 . . . . DLB-80

Mottram, R. H. 1883-1971 . . . . . . DLB-36

Mouré, Erin 1955- DLB-60

Mourning Dove (Humishuma)
between 1882 and 1888?-1936 . . . . DLB-175

Movies from Books, 1920-1974 . . . . . DLB-9

Mowat, Farley 1921- DLB-68

Mowbray, A. R., and Company,
Limited DLB-106

Mowrer, Edgar Ansel 1892-1977 . . . . DLB-29

Mowrer, Paul Scott 1887-1971 . . . . . DLB-29

Moxon, Edward
[publishing house] DLB-106

Moxon, Joseph
[publishing house] DLB-170

Mphahlele, Es'kia (Ezekiel)
1919- DLB-125

Mtshali, Oswald Mbuyiseni
1940- DLB-125

Mucedorus DLB-62

Mudford, William 1782-1848 . . . . . DLB-159

Mueller, Lisel 1924- DLB-105

Muhajir, El (see Marvin X)

Muhajir, Nazzam Al Fitnah (see Marvin X)

Mühlbach, Luise 1814-1873 . . . . . . DLB-133

Muir, Edwin 1887-1959 . . . . . . DLB-20, 100

Muir, Helen 1937- DLB-14

Mukherjee, Bharati 1940- DLB-60

Mulcaster, Richard
1531 or 1532-1611 . . . . DLB-167

Muldoon, Paul 1951- DLB-40

Müller, Friedrich (see Müller, Maler)

Müller, Heiner 1929- DLB-124

Müller, Maler 1749-1825 . . . . DLB-94

Müller, Wilhelm 1794-1827 . . . . . . DLB-90

Mumford, Lewis 1895-1990 . . . . . . DLB-63

Munby, Arthur Joseph 1828-1910 . . . . DLB-35

Munday, Anthony 1560-1633 . . . . DLB-62, 172

Mundt, Clara (see Mühlbach, Luise)

Mundt, Theodore 1808-1861 . . . . . DLB-133

Munford, Robert circa 1737-1783 . . . . DLB-31

Mungoshi, Charles 1947- DLB-157

Munonye, John 1929- DLB-117

Munro, Alice 1931- DLB-53

Munro, H. H. 1870-1916 . . . . . DLB-34, 162

Munro, Neil 1864-1930 . . . . DLB-156

Nabl, Franz 1883-1974 . . . . DLB-81

Nabokov, Vladimir
1899-1977 . . . . . DLB-2; Y-80, Y-91; DS-3

Nabokov Festival at Cornell Y-83

The Vladimir Nabokov Archive
in the Berg Collection Y-91

Nafis and Cornish DLB-49

Nagai, Kafū 1879-1959 . . . . DLB-180

Naipaul, Shiva 1945-1985 . . . . DLB-157; Y-85

Naipaul, V. S. 1932- DLB-125; Y-85

Nakagami, Kenji 1946-1992 . . . . . . DLB-182

Nancrede, Joseph
[publishing house] DLB-49

Naranjo, Carmen 1930- DLB-145

Narrache, Jean 1893-1970 . . . . . . DLB-92

Nasby, Petroleum Vesuvius (see Locke, David
Ross)

Nash, Ogden 1902-1971 . . . . DLB-11

Nash, Eveleigh
[publishing house] DLB-112

Nashe, Thomas 1567-1601? DLB-167

Nast, Conde 1873-1942 . . . . DLB-91

Nastasijević, Momčilo 1894-1938 . . . . DLB-147

Nathan, George Jean 1882-1958 . . . . DLB-137

Nathan, Robert 1894-1985 . . . . DLB-9

The National Jewish Book Awards Y-85

The National Theatre and the Royal
Shakespeare Company: The
National Companies DLB-13

Natsume, Sōseki 1867-1916 . . . . . . DLB-180

Naughton, Bill 1910- DLB-13

Naylor, Gloria 1950- DLB-173

Nazor, Vladimir 1876-1949 . . . . . . DLB-147

Ndebele, Njabulo 1948- DLB-157

Neagoe, Peter 1881-1960 . . . . DLB-4

Neal, John 1793-1876 . . . . DLB-1, 59

Neal, Joseph C. 1807-1847 . . . . DLB-11

Neal, Larry 1937-1981 . . . . DLB-38

The Neale Publishing Company DLB-49

Neely, F. Tennyson
[publishing house] DLB-49

Negri, Ada 1870-1945 . . . . DLB-114

"The Negro as a Writer," by
G. M. McClellan DLB-50

"Negro Poets and Their Poetry," by
Wallace Thurman DLB-50

Neidhart von Reuental
circa 1185-circa 1240 . . . . DLB-138

Neihardt, John G. 1881-1973 . . . . . DLB-9, 54

Neledinsky-Meletsky, Iurii Aleksandrovich
1752-1828 . . . . DLB-150

Nelligan, Emile 1879-1941 . . . . DLB-92

Nelson, Alice Moore Dunbar
1875-1935 . . . . DLB-50

Nelson, Thomas, and Sons [U.S.] DLB-49

N

Nelson, Thomas, and Sons [U.K.] . . . DLB-106

Nelson, William 1908-1978 . . . . DLB-103

Nelson, William Rockhill
1841-1915 . . . . DLB-23

Nemerov, Howard 1920-1991 . . . DLB-5, 6; Y-83

Nesbit, E. 1858-1924 . . . . . DLB-141, 153, 178

Ness, Evaline 1911-1986 . . . . DLB-61

Nestroy, Johann 1801-1862 . . . . DLB-133

Neukirch, Benjamin 1655-1729 . . . . . DLB-168

Neugeboren, Jay 1938- DLB-28

Neumann, Alfred 1895-1952 . . . . DLB-56

Neumark, Georg 1621-1681 . . . . DLB-164

Neumeister, Erdmann 1671-1756 . . . . DLB-168

Nevins, Allan 1890-1971 . . . . DLB-17

Nevinson, Henry Woodd
1856-1941 . . . . DLB-135

The New American Library DLB-46

New Approaches to Biography: Challenges
from Critical Theory, USC Conference
on Literary Studies, 1990 . . . . Y-90

New Directions Publishing
Corporation DLB-46

A New Edition of *Huck Finn* Y-85

New Forces at Work in the American Theatre:
1915-1925 . . . . DLB-7

New Literary Periodicals:
A Report for 1987 . . . . Y-87

New Literary Periodicals:
A Report for 1988 . . . . Y-88

New Literary Periodicals:
A Report for 1989 . . . . Y-89

New Literary Periodicals:
A Report for 1990 . . . . Y-90

New Literary Periodicals:
A Report for 1991 . . . . Y-91

New Literary Periodicals:
A Report for 1992 . . . . Y-92

New Literary Periodicals:
A Report for 1993 . . . . Y-93

The New Monthly Magazine
1814-1884 . . . . DLB-110

The New *Ulysses* Y-84

The New Variorum Shakespeare Y-85

A New Voice: The Center for the Book's First
Five Years Y-83

The New Wave [Science Fiction] DLB-8

New York City Bookshops in the 1930s and
1940s: The Recollections of Walter
Goldwater Y-93

Newbery, John
[publishing house] DLB-154

Newbolt, Henry 1862-1938 . . . . DLB-19

Newbound, Bernard Slade (see Slade, Bernard)

Newby, P. H. 1918- DLB-15

Newby, Thomas Cautley
[publishing house] DLB-106

Newcomb, Charles King 1820-1894 . . . . DLB-1

Newell, Peter 1862-1924 . . . . DLB-42

Newell, Robert Henry 1836-1901 . . . . DLB-11

Newhouse, Samuel I. 1895-1979 . . . . DLB-127

Newman, Cecil Earl 1903-1976 . . . . . DLB-127

Newman, David (see Benton, Robert)

Newman, Frances 1883-1928 . . . . Y-80

Newman, John Henry
1801-1890 . . . . DLB-18, 32, 55

Newman, Mark [publishing house] DLB-49

Newnes, George, Limited DLB-112

Newsome, Effie Lee 1885-1979 . . . . . DLB-76

Newspaper Syndication of American
Humor DLB-11

Newton, A. Edward 1864-1940 . . . . . DLB-140

Ngugi wa Thiong'o 1938- DLB-125

Niatum, Duane 1938- DLB-175

The *Nibelungenlied* and the *Klage*
circa 1200 . . . . DLB-138

Nichol, B. P. 1944- DLB-53

Nicholas of Cusa 1401-1464 . . . . . DLB-115

Nichols, Dudley 1895-1960 . . . . DLB-26

Nichols, Grace 1950- DLB-157

Nichols, John 1940- Y-82

Nichols, Mary Sargeant (Neal) Gove 1810-11884
. . . . DLB-1

Nichols, Peter 1927- DLB-13

Nichols, Roy F. 1896-1973 . . . . DLB-17

Nichols, Ruth 1948- DLB-60

Nicholson, Norman 1914- DLB-27

Nicholson, William 1872-1949 . . . . . DLB-141

Ní Chuilleanáin, Eiléan 1942- DLB-40

Nicol, Eric 1919- DLB-68

Nicolai, Friedrich 1733-1811 . . . . . DLB-97

Nicolay, John G. 1832-1901 and
Hay, John 1838-1905 . . . . DLB-47

Nicolson, Harold 1886-1968 . . . DLB-100, 149

Nicolson, Nigel 1917- DLB-155

Niebuhr, Reinhold 1892-1971 . . . . . DLB-17

Niedecker, Lorine 1903-1970 . . . . . DLB-48

Nieman, Lucius W. 1857-1935 . . . . . DLB-25

Nietzsche, Friedrich 1844-1900 . . . . DLB-129

Niggli, Josefina 1910- Y-80

Nightingale, Florence 1820-1910 . . . . DLB-166

Nikolev, Nikolai Petrovich
1758-1815 . . . . DLB-150

Niles, Hezekiah 1777-1839 . . . . DLB-43

Nims, John Frederick 1913- DLB-5

Nin, Anaïs 1903-1977 . . . . . . DLB-2, 4, 152

1985: The Year of the Mystery:
A Symposium Y-85

Nissenson, Hugh 1933- DLB-28

Niven, Frederick John 1878-1944 . . . . DLB-92

Niven, Larry 1938- DLB-8

Nizan, Paul 1905-1940 . . . . DLB-72

Njegoš, Petar II Petrović
1813-1851 . . . . DLB-147

Nkosi, Lewis 1936- DLB-157

Nobel Peace Prize

The 1986 Nobel Peace Prize
Nobel Lecture 1986: Hope, Despair and Memory
Tributes from Abraham Bernstein,
Norman Lamm, and
John R. Silber Y-86

The Nobel Prize and Literary Politics . . . Y-86

Nobel Prize in Literature

The 1982 Nobel Prize in Literature
Announcement by the Swedish Academy
of the Nobel Prize Nobel Lecture 1982:
The Solitude of Latin America Excerpt
from *One Hundred Years of Solitude* The
Magical World of Macondo A Tribute
to Gabriel García Márquez Y-82

The 1983 Nobel Prize in Literature
Announcement by the Swedish Academy Nobel Lecture 1983 The Stature of
William Golding Y-83

The 1984 Nobel Prize in Literature
Announcement by the Swedish Academy
Jaroslav Seifert Through the Eyes of the
English-Speaking Reader
Three Poems by Jaroslav Seifert Y-84

The 1985 Nobel Prize in Literature
Announcement by the Swedish Academy
Nobel Lecture 1985 . . . . Y-85

The 1986 Nobel Prize in Literature
Nobel Lecture 1986: This Past Must Address
Its Present Y-86

The 1987 Nobel Prize in Literature
Nobel Lecture 1987 . . . . Y-87

The 1988 Nobel Prize in Literature
Nobel Lecture 1988 . . . . Y-88

The 1989 Nobel Prize in Literature
Nobel Lecture 1989 . . . . Y-89

The 1990 Nobel Prize in Literature
Nobel Lecture 1990 . . . . Y-90

The 1991 Nobel Prize in Literature
Nobel Lecture 1991 . . . . Y-91

The 1992 Nobel Prize in Literature
Nobel Lecture 1992 . . . . Y-92

The 1993 Nobel Prize in Literature
Nobel Lecture 1993 . . . . Y-93

The 1994 Nobel Prize in Literature
Nobel Lecture 1994 . . . . Y-94

The 1995 Nobel Prize in Literature
Nobel Lecture 1995 . . . . Y-95

Nodier, Charles 1780-1844 . . . . DLB-119

Noel, Roden 1834-1894 . . . . DLB-35

Nogami, Yaeko 1885-1985 . . . . DLB-180

Nogo, Rajko Petrov 1945- DLB-181

Nolan, William F. 1928- DLB-8

Noland, C. F. M. 1810?-1858 . . . . . . DLB-11

Noma, Hiroshi 1915-1991 . . . . DLB-182

Nonesuch Press DLB-112

Noonday Press DLB-46

Noone, John 1936- DLB-14

Nora, Eugenio de 1923- DLB-134

Nordhoff, Charles 1887-1947 . . . . DLB-9

Norman, Charles 1904- DLB-111

Norman, Marsha 1947- Y-84

Norris, Charles G. 1881-1945 . . . . . . DLB-9

Norris, Frank 1870-1902 . . . . DLB-12

Norris, Leslie 1921- DLB-27

Norse, Harold 1916- DLB-16

North, Marianne 1830-1890 . . . . . . DLB-174

North Point Press DLB-46

Nortje, Arthur 1942-1970 . . . . DLB-125

Norton, Alice Mary (see Norton, Andre)

Norton, Andre 1912- DLB-8, 52

Norton, Andrews 1786-1853 . . . . DLB-1

Norton, Caroline 1808-1877 . . . . DLB-21, 159

Norton, Charles Eliot 1827-1908 . . . DLB-1, 64

Norton, John 1606-1663 . . . . DLB-24

Norton, Mary 1903-1992 . . . . DLB-160

Norton, Thomas (see Sackville, Thomas)

Norton, W. W., and Company DLB-46

Norwood, Robert 1874-1932 . . . . . . DLB-92

Nosaka, Akiyuki 1930- DLB-182

Nossack, Hans Erich 1901-1977 . . . . DLB-69

Notker Balbulus circa 840-912 . . . . DLB-148

Notker III of Saint Gall
circa 950-1022 . . . . DLB-148

Notker von Zweifalten ?-1095 . . . . . DLB-148

A Note on Technique (1926), by
Elizabeth A. Drew [excerpts] DLB-36

Nourse, Alan E. 1928- DLB-8

Novak, Slobodan 1924- DLB-181

Novak, Vjenceslav 1859-1905 . . . . . DLB-147

Novalis 1772-1801 . . . . DLB-90

Novaro, Mario 1868-1944 . . . . DLB-114

Novás Calvo, Lino 1903-1983 . . . . . DLB-145

"The Novel in [Robert Browning's] 'The Ring
and the Book'" (1912), by
Henry James DLB-32

The Novel of Impressionism,
by Jethro Bithell DLB-66

Novel-Reading: *The Works of Charles Dickens,
The Works of W. Makepeace Thackeray*
(1879), by Anthony Trollope DLB-21

The Novels of Dorothy Richardson (1918),
by May Sinclair DLB-36

Novels with a Purpose (1864), by
Justin M'Carthy DLB-21

Noventa, Giacomo 1898-1960 . . . . . DLB-114

Novikov, Nikolai Ivanovich
1744-1818 . . . . DLB-150

Nowlan, Alden 1933-1983 . . . . DLB-53

Noyes, Alfred 1880-1958 . . . . DLB-20

Noyes, Crosby S. 1825-1908 . . . . . . DLB-23

Noyes, Nicholas 1647-1717 . . . . DLB-24

Noyes, Theodore W. 1858-1946 . . . . . DLB-29

N-Town Plays circa 1468 to early
sixteenth century DLB-146

Nugent, Frank 1908-1965 . . . . DLB-44

Nugent, Richard Bruce 1906- DLB-151

Nušić, Branislav 1864-1938 . . . . . . DLB-147

Nutt, David [publishing house] DLB-106

Nwapa, Flora 1931- DLB-125

Nye, Edgar Wilson (Bill)
1850-1896 . . . . DLB-11, 23

Nye, Naomi Shihab 1952- DLB-120

Nye, Robert 1939- DLB-14

O

Oakes, Urian circa 1631-1681 . . . . . DLB-24

Oates, Joyce Carol
1938- DLB-2, 5, 130; Y-81

Ōba, Minako 1930- DLB-182

Ober, William 1920-1993 . . . . Y-93

Oberholtzer, Ellis Paxson
1868-1936 . . . . DLB-47

Obradović, Dositej 1740?-1811 . . . . . DLB-147

O'Brien, Edna 1932- DLB-14

O'Brien, Fitz-James 1828-1862 . . . . . DLB-74

O'Brien, Kate 1897-1974 . . . . DLB-15

O'Brien, Tim
1946- DLB-152; Y-80; DS-9

O'Casey, Sean 1880-1964 . . . . DLB-10

Occom, Samson 1723-1792 . . . . . . DLB-175

Ochs, Adolph S. 1858-1935 . . . . . . DLB-25

Ochs-Oakes, George Washington
1861-1931 . . . . DLB-137

O'Connor, Flannery
1925-1964 . . . . . DLB-2, 152; Y-80; DS-12

O'Connor, Frank 1903-1966 . . . . . . DLB-162

Octopus Publishing Group DLB-112

Oda, Sakunosuke 1913-1947 . . . . . . DLB-182

Odell, Jonathan 1737-1818 . . . . . . DLB-31, 99

O'Dell, Scott 1903-1989 . . . . DLB-52

Odets, Clifford 1906-1963 . . . . . . DLB-7, 26

Odhams Press Limited DLB-112

O'Donnell, Peter 1920- DLB-87

O'Donovan, Michael (see O'Connor, Frank)

Ōe, Kenzaburō 1935- DLB-182

O'Faolain, Julia 1932- DLB-14

O'Faolain, Sean 1900- DLB-15, 162

Off Broadway and Off-Off Broadway . . DLB-7

Off-Loop Theatres DLB-7

Offord, Carl Ruthven 1910- DLB-76

O'Flaherty, Liam
1896-1984 . . . . DLB-36, 162; Y-84

Ogilvie, J. S., and Company DLB-49

Ogot, Grace 1930- DLB-125

O'Grady, Desmond 1935- DLB-40

Ogunyemi, Wale 1939- DLB-157

O'Hagan, Howard 1902-1982 . . . . . DLB-68

O'Hara, Frank 1926-1966 . . . . . . DLB-5, 16

O'Hara, John 1905-1970 . . . . DLB-9, 86; DS-2

Okara, Gabriel 1921- DLB-125

O'Keeffe, John 1747-1833 . . . . DLB-89

Okes, Nicholas
[publishing house] DLB-170

Okigbo, Christopher 1930-1967 . . . . . DLB-125

Okot p'Bitek 1931-1982 . . . . DLB-125

Okpewho, Isidore 1941- DLB-157

Okri, Ben 1959- DLB-157

Olaudah Equiano and Unfinished Journeys:
The Slave-Narrative Tradition and
Twentieth-Century Continuities, by
Paul Edwards and Pauline T.
Wangman DLB-117

Old English Literature:
An Introduction DLB-146

Old English Riddles
eighth to tenth centuries DLB-146

Old Franklin Publishing House DLB-49

Old German Genesis and *Old German Exodus*
circa 1050-circa 1130 . . . . DLB-148

Old High German Charms and
Blessings DLB-148

The *Old High German Isidor*
circa 790-800 . . . . DLB-148

Older, Fremont 1856-1935 . . . . . . DLB-25

Oldham, John 1653-1683 . . . . DLB-131

Olds, Sharon 1942- DLB-120

Olearius, Adam 1599-1671 . . . . . . DLB-164

Oliphant, Laurence
1829?-1888 . . . . DLB-18, 166

Oliphant, Margaret 1828-1897 . . . . . DLB-18

Oliver, Chad 1928- DLB-8

Oliver, Mary 1935- DLB-5

Ollier, Claude 1922- DLB-83

Olsen, Tillie 1913?- DLB-28; Y-80

Olson, Charles 1910-1970 . . . . . . DLB-5, 16

Olson, Elder 1909- DLB-48, 63

Omotoso, Kole 1943- DLB-125

"On Art in Fiction" (1838),
by Edward Bulwer DLB-21

On Learning to Write Y-88

On Some of the Characteristics of Modern
  Poetry and On the Lyrical Poems of
  Alfred Tennyson (1831), by Arthur
  Henry Hallam DLB-32

"On Style in English Prose" (1898), by
  Frederic Harrison DLB-57

"On Style in Literature: Its Technical
  Elements" (1885), by Robert Louis
  Stevenson DLB-57

"On the Writing of Essays" (1862),
  by Alexander Smith DLB-57

Ondaatje, Michael 1943- DLB-60

O'Neill, Eugene 1888-1953 . . . . . . DLB-7

Onetti, Juan Carlos 1909-1994 . . . . DLB-113

Onions, George Oliver
  1872-1961 . . . . DLB-153

Onofri, Arturo 1885-1928 . . . . DLB-114

Opie, Amelia 1769-1853 . . . . . DLB-116, 159

Opitz, Martin 1597-1639 . . . . DLB-164

Oppen, George 1908-1984 . . . . . DLB-5, 165

Oppenheim, E. Phillips 1866-1946 . . . DLB-70

Oppenheim, James 1882-1932 . . . . . DLB-28

Oppenheimer, Joel 1930- DLB-5

Optic, Oliver (see Adams, William Taylor)

Orczy, Emma, Baroness
  1865-1947 . . . . DLB-70

Origo, Iris 1902-1988 . . . . DLB-155

Orlovitz, Gil 1918-1973 . . . . DLB-2, 5

Orlovsky, Peter 1933- DLB-16

Ormond, John 1923- DLB-27

Ornitz, Samuel 1890-1957 . . . . . DLB-28, 44

Ortese, Anna Maria 1914- DLB-177

Ortiz, Simon J. 1941- DLB-120, 175

Ortnit and Wolfdietrich
  circa 1225-1250 . . . . DLB-138

Orton, Joe 1933-1967 . . . . DLB-13

Orwell, George 1903-1950 . . . . . DLB-15, 98

The Orwell Year Y-84

Ory, Carlos Edmundo de 1923- . . . DLB-134

Osbey, Brenda Marie 1957- DLB-120

Osbon, B. S. 1827-1912 . . . . DLB-43

Osborne, John 1929-1994 . . . . DLB-13

Osgood, Herbert L. 1855-1918 . . . . . DLB-47

Osgood, James R., and
  Company DLB-49

Osgood, McIlvaine and
  Company DLB-112

O'Shaughnessy, Arthur
  1844-1881 . . . . DLB-35

O'Shea, Patrick
  [publishing house] DLB-49

Osipov, Nikolai Petrovich
  1751-1799 . . . . DLB-150

Oskison, John Milton 1879-1947 . . . DLB-175

Osofisan, Femi 1946- DLB-125

Ostenso, Martha 1900-1963 . . . . . . DLB-92

Ostriker, Alicia 1937- DLB-120

Osundare, Niyi 1947- DLB-157

Oswald, Eleazer 1755-1795 . . . . . . DLB-43

Oswald von Wolkenstein
  1376 or 1377-1445 . . . . DLB-179

Otero, Blas de 1916-1979 . . . . . . DLB-134

Otero, Miguel Antonio
  1859-1944 . . . . DLB-82

Otero Silva, Miguel 1908-1985 . . . . DLB-145

Otfried von Weißenburg
  circa 800-circa 875? DLB-148

Otis, James (see Kaler, James Otis)

Otis, James, Jr. 1725-1783 . . . . . . DLB-31

Otis, Broaders and Company DLB-49

Ottaway, James 1911- DLB-127

Ottendorfer, Oswald 1826-1900 . . . . DLB-23

Ottieri, Ottiero 1924- DLB-177

Otto-Peters, Louise 1819-1895 . . . . DLB-129

Otway, Thomas 1652-1685 . . . . . . DLB-80

Ouellette, Fernand 1930- DLB-60

Ouida 1839-1908 . . . . DLB-18, 156

Outing Publishing Company DLB-46

Outlaw Days, by Joyce Johnson DLB-16

Overbury, Sir Thomas
  circa 1581-1613 . . . . DLB-151

The Overlook Press DLB-46

Overview of U.S. Book Publishing,
  1910-1945 . . . . DLB-9

Owen, Guy 1925- DLB-5

Owen, John 1564-1622 . . . . DLB-121

Owen, John [publishing house] DLB-49

Owen, Robert 1771-1858 . . . . . DLB-107, 158

Owen, Wilfred 1893-1918 . . . . DLB-20

Owen, Peter, Limited DLB-112

The Owl and the Nightingale
  circa 1189-1199 . . . . DLB-146

Owsley, Frank L. 1890-1956 . . . . . . DLB-17

Oxford, Seventeenth Earl of, Edward de Vere
  1550-1604 . . . . DLB-172

Ozerov, Vladislav Aleksandrovich
  1769-1816 . . . . DLB-150

Ozick, Cynthia 1928- DLB-28, 152; Y-82

P

Pace, Richard 1482?-1536 . . . . DLB-167

Pacey, Desmond 1917-1975 . . . . . . DLB-88

Pack, Robert 1929- DLB-5

Packaging Papa: The Garden of Eden Y-86

Padell Publishing Company DLB-46

Padgett, Ron 1942- DLB-5

Padilla, Ernesto Chávez 1944- DLB-122

Page, L. C., and Company DLB-49

Page, P. K. 1916- DLB-68

Page, Thomas Nelson
  1853-1922 . . . . DLB-12, 78; DS-13

Page, Walter Hines 1855-1918 . . . . DLB-71, 91

Paget, Francis Edward
  1806-1882 . . . . DLB-163

Paget, Violet (see Lee, Vernon)

Pagliarani, Elio 1927- DLB-128

Pain, Barry 1864-1928 . . . . DLB-135

Pain, Philip ?-circa 1666 . . . . DLB-24

Paine, Robert Treat, Jr. 1773-1811 . . . DLB-37

Paine, Thomas
  1737-1809 . . . . DLB-31, 43, 73, 158

Painter, George D. 1914- DLB-155

Painter, William 1540?-1594 . . . . . DLB-136

Palazzeschi, Aldo 1885-1974 . . . . . DLB-114

Paley, Grace 1922- DLB-28

Palfrey, John Gorham
  1796-1881 . . . . DLB-1, 30

Palgrave, Francis Turner
  1824-1897 . . . . DLB-35

Palmer, Joe H. 1904-1952 . . . . . . DLB-171

Palmer, Michael 1943- DLB-169

Paltock, Robert 1697-1767 . . . . . . DLB-39

Pan Books Limited DLB-112

Panama, Norman 1914- and
  Frank, Melvin 1913-1988 . . . . . . DLB-26

Pancake, Breece D'J 1952-1979 . . . . DLB-130

Panero, Leopoldo 1909-1962 . . . . . DLB-108

Pangborn, Edgar 1909-1976 . . . . . . DLB-8

"Panic Among the Philistines": A Postscript,
  An Interview with Bryan Griffin Y-81

Panneton, Philippe (see Ringuet)

Panshin, Alexei 1940- DLB-8

Pansy (see Alden, Isabella)

Pantheon Books DLB-46

Paperback Library DLB-46

Paperback Science Fiction DLB-8

Paquet, Alfons 1881-1944 . . . . DLB-66

Paracelsus 1493-1541 . . . . DLB-179

Paradis, Suzanne 1936- DLB-53

Pareja Diezcanseco, Alfredo
  1908-1993 . . . . DLB-145

Pardoe, Julia 1804-1862 . . . . DLB-166

Parents' Magazine Press DLB-46

Parise, Goffredo 1929-1986 . . . . . . DLB-177

Parisian Theater, Fall 1984: Toward
  A New Baroque Y-85

Parizeau, Alice 1930- DLB-60

Parke, John 1754-1789 . . . . DLB-31

Parker, Dorothy 1893-1967 . . . . DLB-11, 45, 86

Parker, Gilbert 1860-1932 . . . . DLB-99

Parker, James 1714-1770 . . . . DLB-43

Parker, Theodore 1810-1860 . . . . DLB-1

Parker, William Riley 1906-1968 . . . . DLB-103

Parker, J. H. [publishing house] DLB-106

Parker, John [publishing house] DLB-106

Parkman, Francis, Jr. 1823-1893 . . . . DLB-1, 30, 183

Parks, Gordon 1912- DLB-33

Parks, William 1698-1750 . . . . DLB-43

Parks, William [publishing house] DLB-49

Parley, Peter (see Goodrich, Samuel Griswold)

Parmenides late sixth-fifth century B.C. DLB-176

Parnell, Thomas 1679-1718 . . . . DLB-95

Parr, Catherine 1513?-1548 . . . . DLB-136

Parrington, Vernon L. 1871-1929 . . . . DLB-17, 63

Parronchi, Alessandro 1914- DLB-128

Partridge, S. W., and Company DLB-106

Parton, James 1822-1891 . . . . DLB-30

Parton, Sara Payson Willis 1811-1872 . . . . DLB-43, 74

Parun, Vesna 1922- DLB-181

Pasinetti, Pier Maria 1913- DLB-177

Pasolini, Pier Paolo 1922- DLB-128, 177

Pastan, Linda 1932- DLB-5

Paston, George 1860-1936 . . . . DLB-149

The *Paston Letters* 1422-1509 . . . . . . DLB-146

Pastorius, Francis Daniel 1651-circa 1720 . . . . DLB-24

Patchen, Kenneth 1911-1972 . . . . . DLB-16, 48

Pater, Walter 1839-1894 . . . . . . DLB-57, 156

Paterson, Katherine 1932- DLB-52

Patmore, Coventry 1823-1896 . . . . DLB-35, 98

Paton, Joseph Noel 1821-1901 . . . . . DLB-35

Paton Walsh, Jill 1937- DLB-161

Patrick, Edwin Hill ("Ted") 1901-1964 . . . . DLB-137

Patrick, John 1906- DLB-7

Pattee, Fred Lewis 1863-1950 . . . . . DLB-71

Pattern and Paradigm: History as Design, by Judith Ryan DLB-75

Patterson, Alicia 1906-1963 . . . . . . DLB-127

Patterson, Eleanor Medill 1881-1948 . . . . DLB-29

Patterson, Eugene 1923- DLB-127

Patterson, Joseph Medill 1879-1946 . . . . DLB-29

Pattillo, Henry 1726-1801 . . . . DLB-37

Paul, Elliot 1891-1958 . . . . DLB-4

Paul, Jean (see Richter, Johann Paul Friedrich)

Paul, Kegan, Trench, Trubner and Company Limited DLB-106

Paul, Peter, Book Company DLB-49

Paul, Stanley, and Company Limited DLB-112

Paulding, James Kirke 1778-1860 . . . . DLB-3, 59, 74

Paulin, Tom 1949- DLB-40

Pauper, Peter, Press DLB-46

Pavese, Cesare 1908-1950 . . . . DLB-128, 177

Pavić, Milorad 1929- DLB-181

Pavlov, Konstantin 1933- DLB-181

Pavlović, Miodrag 1928- DLB-181

Paxton, John 1911-1985 . . . . DLB-44

Payn, James 1830-1898 . . . . DLB-18

Payne, John 1842-1916 . . . . DLB-35

Payne, John Howard 1791-1852 . . . . DLB-37

Payson and Clarke DLB-46

Peabody, Elizabeth Palmer 1804-1894 . . . . DLB-1

Peabody, Elizabeth Palmer [publishing house] DLB-49

Peabody, Oliver William Bourn 1799-1848 . . . . DLB-59

Peace, Roger 1899-1968 . . . . DLB-127

Peacham, Henry 1578-1644? DLB-151

Peacham, Henry, the Elder 1547-1634 . . . . DLB-172

Peachtree Publishers, Limited DLB-46

Peacock, Molly 1947- DLB-120

Peacock, Thomas Love 1785-1866 . . . . DLB-96, 116

Pead, Deuel ?-1727 . . . . DLB-24

Peake, Mervyn 1911-1968 . . . . DLB-15, 160

Peale, Rembrandt 1778-1860 . . . . . DLB-183

Pear Tree Press DLB-112

Pearce, Philippa 1920- DLB-161

Pearson, H. B. [publishing house] DLB-49

Pearson, Hesketh 1887-1964 . . . . . . DLB-149

Peck, George W. 1840-1916 . . . . DLB-23, 42

Peck, H. C., and Theo. Bliss [publishing house] DLB-49

Peck, Harry Thurston 1856-1914 . . . . DLB-71, 91

Peele, George 1556-1596 . . . . DLB-62, 167

Pegler, Westbrook 1894-1969 . . . . . DLB-171

Pekić, Borislav 1930-1992 . . . . . . DLB-181

Pelletier, Aimé (see Vac, Bertrand)

Pellegrini and Cudahy DLB-46

Pemberton, Sir Max 1863-1950 . . . . DLB-70

Penguin Books [U.S.] DLB-46

Penguin Books [U.K.] DLB-112

Penn Publishing Company DLB-49

Penn, William 1644-1718 . . . . DLB-24

Penna, Sandro 1906-1977 . . . . . . DLB-114

Penner, Jonathan 1940- Y-83

Pennington, Lee 1939- Y-82

Pepys, Samuel 1633-1703 . . . . . . DLB-101

Percy, Thomas 1729-1811 . . . . . . DLB-104

Percy, Walker 1916-1990 . . . . DLB-2; Y-80, 90

Percy, William 1575-1648 . . . . . . DLB-172

Perec, Georges 1936-1982 . . . . . . DLB-83

Perelman, S. J. 1904-1979 . . . . . DLB-11, 44

Perez, Raymundo "Tigre" 1946- DLB-122

Peri Rossi, Cristina 1941- DLB-145

Periodicals of the Beat Generation DLB-16

Perkins, Eugene 1932- DLB-41

Perkoff, Stuart Z. 1930-1974 . . . . . DLB-16

Perley, Moses Henry 1804-1862 . . . . . DLB-99

Permabooks DLB-46

Perrin, Alice 1867-1934 . . . . DLB-156

Perry, Bliss 1860-1954 . . . . DLB-71

Perry, Eleanor 1915-1981 . . . . DLB-44

Perry, Matthew 1794-1858 . . . . . . DLB-183

Perry, Sampson 1747-1823 . . . . . . DLB-158

"Personal Style" (1890), by John Addington Symonds DLB-57

Perutz, Leo 1882-1957 . . . . DLB-81

Pesetsky, Bette 1932- DLB-130

Pestalozzi, Johann Heinrich 1746-1827 . . . . DLB-94

Peter, Laurence J. 1919-1990 . . . . . DLB-53

Peter of Spain circa 1205-1277 . . . . . DLB-115

Peterkin, Julia 1880-1961 . . . . DLB-9

Peters, Lenrie 1932- DLB-117

Peters, Robert 1924- DLB-105

Peters, Robert, Foreword to Ludwig of Bavaria DLB-105

Petersham, Maud 1889-1971 and Petersham, Miska 1888-1960 . . . . . DLB-22

Peterson, Charles Jacobs 1819-1887 . . . . DLB-79

Peterson, Len 1917- DLB-88

Peterson, Louis 1922- DLB-76

Peterson, T. B., and Brothers DLB-49

Petitclair, Pierre 1813-1860 . . . . . . DLB-99

Petrov, Aleksandar 1938- DLB-181

Petrov, Gavriil 1730-1801 . . . . . . DLB-150

Petrov, Vasilii Petrovich 1736-1799 . . . . DLB-150

Petrov, Valeri 1920- DLB-181

Petrović, Rastko 1898-1949 . . . . . . DLB-147

Petruslied circa 854? DLB-148

Petry, Ann 1908- DLB-76

Pettie, George circa 1548-1589 . . . . . DLB-136

Peyton, K. M. 1929- DLB-161

Pfaffe Konrad
    flourished circa 1172 . . . . DLB-148

Pfaffe Lamprecht
    flourished circa 1150 . . . . DLB-148

Pforzheimer, Carl H. 1879-1957 . . . . DLB-140

Phaer, Thomas 1510?-1560 . . . . DLB-167

Phaidon Press Limited. DLB-112

Pharr, Robert Deane 1916-1992 . . . . . DLB-33

Phelps, Elizabeth Stuart
    1844-1911 . . . . DLB-74

Philander von der Linde
    (see Mencke, Johann Burckhard)

Philip, Marlene Nourbese
    1947- DLB-157

Philippe, Charles-Louis
    1874-1909 . . . . DLB-65

Philips, John 1676-1708 . . . . DLB-95

Philips, Katherine 1632-1664 . . . . . DLB-131

Phillips, Caryl 1958- DLB-157

Phillips, David Graham
    1867-1911 . . . . DLB-9, 12

Phillips, Jayne Anne 1952- Y-80

Phillips, Robert 1938- DLB-105

Phillips, Robert, Finding, Losing,
    Reclaiming: A Note on My
    Poems DLB-105

Phillips, Stephen 1864-1915 . . . . . . DLB-10

Phillips, Ulrich B. 1877-1934 . . . . . . DLB-17

Phillips, Willard 1784-1873 . . . . . . DLB-59

Phillips, William 1907- DLB-137

Phillips, Sampson and Company. DLB-49

Phillpotts, Eden
    1862-1960 . . . . . . DLB-10, 70, 135, 153

Philo circa 20-15 B.C.-circa A.D. 50
    . . . . DLB-176

Philosophical Library DLB-46

"The Philosophy of Style" (1852), by
    Herbert Spencer. DLB-57

Phinney, Elihu [publishing house] DLB-49

Phoenix, John (see Derby, George Horatio)

PHYLON (Fourth Quarter, 1950),
    The Negro in Literature:
    The Current Scene DLB-76

Physiologus
    circa 1070-circa 1150 . . . . DLB-148

Piccolo, Lucio 1903-1969 . . . . DLB-114

Pickard, Tom 1946- DLB-40

Pickering, William
    [publishing house] DLB-106

Pickthall, Marjorie 1883-1922 . . . . . . DLB-92

Pictorial Printing Company. DLB-49

Piel, Gerard 1915- DLB-137

Piercy, Marge 1936- DLB-120

Pierro, Albino 1916- DLB-128

Pignotti, Lamberto 1926- DLB-128

Pike, Albert 1809-1891 . . . . DLB-74

Pike, Zebulon Montgomery 1779-1813 . . DLB-183

Pilon, Jean-Guy 1930- DLB-60

Pinckney, Josephine 1895-1957 . . . . . DLB-6

Pindar circa 518 B.C.-circa 438 B.C.
    . . . . DLB-176

Pindar, Peter (see Wolcot, John)

Pinero, Arthur Wing 1855-1934 . . . . . DLB-10

Pinget, Robert 1919- DLB-83

Pinnacle Books DLB-46

Piñon, Nélida 1935- DLB-145

Pinsky, Robert 1940- Y-82

Pinter, Harold 1930- DLB-13

Piontek, Heinz 1925- DLB-75

Piozzi, Hester Lynch [Thrale]
    1741-1821. . . . . DLB-104, 142

Piper, H. Beam 1904-1964. . . . . . . DLB-8

Piper, Watty. DLB-22

Pirckheimer, Caritas 1467-1532 . . . . . DLB-179

Pirckheimer, Willibald
    1470-1530 . . . . DLB-179

Pisar, Samuel 1929- Y-83

Pitkin, Timothy 1766-1847 . . . . DLB-30

The Pitt Poetry Series: Poetry Publishing Today
    . . . . Y-85

Pitter, Ruth 1897- DLB-20

Pix, Mary 1666-1709 . . . . DLB-80

Plaatje, Sol T. 1876-1932 . . . . DLB-125

The Place of Realism in Fiction (1895), by
    George Gissing DLB-18

Plante, David 1940- Y-83

Platen, August von 1796-1835 . . . . . DLB-90

Plath, Sylvia 1932-1963 . . . . . DLB-5, 6, 152

Plato circa 428 B.C.-348-347 B.C.
    . . . . DLB-176

Platon 1737-1812. . . . . DLB-150

Platt and Munk Company DLB-46

Playboy Press DLB-46

Playford, John
    [publishing house] DLB-170

Plays, Playwrights, and Playgoers DLB-84

Playwrights and Professors, by
    Tom Stoppard DLB-13

Playwrights on the Theater DLB-80

Der Pleier flourished circa 1250 . . . . DLB-138

Plenzdorf, Ulrich 1934- DLB-75

Plessen, Elizabeth 1944- DLB-75

Plievier, Theodor 1892-1955 . . . . . . DLB-69

Plomer, William 1903-1973 . . . . DLB-20, 162

Plotinus 204-270 . . . . DLB-176

Plumly, Stanley 1939- DLB-5

Plumpp, Sterling D. 1940- DLB-41

Plunkett, James 1920- DLB-14

Plutarch circa 46-circa 120 . . . . . . DLB-176

Plymell, Charles 1935- DLB-16

Pocket Books DLB-46

Poe, Edgar Allan
    1809-1849 . . . . DLB-3, 59, 73, 74

Poe, James 1921-1980 . . . . DLB-44

The Poet Laureate of the United States
    Statements from Former Consultants
    in Poetry Y-86

Pohl, Frederik 1919- DLB-8

Poirier, Louis (see Gracq, Julien)

Polanyi, Michael 1891-1976 . . . . . . DLB-100

Pole, Reginald 1500-1558 . . . . DLB-132

Poliakoff, Stephen 1952- DLB-13

Polidori, John William
    1795-1821 . . . . DLB-116

Polite, Carlene Hatcher 1932- DLB-33

Pollard, Edward A. 1832-1872 . . . . . DLB-30

Pollard, Percival 1869-1911 . . . . . . DLB-71

Pollard and Moss DLB-49

Pollock, Sharon 1936- DLB-60

Polonsky, Abraham 1910- DLB-26

Polotsky, Simeon 1629-1680. . . . . . . DLB-150

Polybius circa 200 B.C.-118 B.C. DLB-176

Pomilio, Mario 1921-1990 . . . . DLB-177

Ponce, Mary Helen 1938- DLB-122

Ponce-Montoya, Juanita 1949- DLB-122

Ponet, John 1516?-1556 . . . . DLB-132

Poniatowski, Elena 1933- DLB-113

Ponsonby, William
    [publishing house] DLB-170

Pony Stories DLB-160

Poole, Ernest 1880-1950 . . . . DLB-9

Poole, Sophia 1804-1891. . . . . DLB-166

Poore, Benjamin Perley
    1820-1887 . . . . DLB-23

Popa, Vasko 1922-1991 . . . . DLB-181

Pope, Abbie Hanscom
    1858-1894 . . . . DLB-140

Pope, Alexander 1688-1744 . . . . . DLB-95, 101

Popov, Mikhail Ivanovich
    1742-circa 1790 . . . . DLB-150

Popović, Aleksandar 1929-1996 . . . . . DLB-181

Popular Library DLB-46

Porlock, Martin (see MacDonald, Philip)

Porpoise Press DLB-112

Porta, Antonio 1935-1989 . . . . DLB-128

Porter, Anna Maria
    1780-1832. . . . . DLB-116, 159

Porter, David 1780-1843. . . . . DLB-183

Porter, Eleanor H. 1868-1920 . . . . . . DLB-9

Porter, Gene Stratton (see Stratton-Porter, Gene)

Porter, Henry ?-? DLB-62

Porter, Jane 1776-1850 . . . . . . DLB-116, 159

Porter, Katherine Anne
    1890-1980 . . . . DLB-4, 9, 102; Y-80; DS-12

Porter, Peter 1929- DLB-40

Porter, William Sydney
    1862-1910 . . . . DLB-12, 78, 79

Porter, William T. 1809-1858 . . . . . DLB-3, 43

Porter and Coates DLB-49

Portis, Charles 1933- DLB-6

Posey, Alexander 1873-1908 . . . . . . DLB-175

Postans, Marianne
    circa 1810-1865 . . . . DLB-166

Postl, Carl (see Sealsfield, Carl)

Poston, Ted 1906-1974 . . . . DLB-51

Postscript to [the Third Edition of] *Clarissa*
    (1751), by Samuel Richardson DLB-39

Potok, Chaim 1929- . . . DLB-28, 152; Y-84

Potter, Beatrix 1866-1943 . . . . DLB-141

Potter, David M. 1910-1971 . . . . . . DLB-17

Potter, John E., and Company DLB-49

Pottle, Frederick A.
    1897-1987 . . . . DLB-103; Y-87

Poulin, Jacques 1937- DLB-60

Pound, Ezra 1885-1972 . . DLB-4, 45, 63; DS-15

Povich, Shirley 1905- DLB-171

Powell, Anthony 1905- DLB-15

Powers, J. F. 1917- DLB-130

Pownall, David 1938- DLB-14

Powys, John Cowper 1872-1963 . . . . DLB-15

Powys, Llewelyn 1884-1939 . . . . . . DLB-98

Powys, T. F. 1875-1953 . . . . . DLB-36, 162

Poynter, Nelson 1903-1978 . . . . . . DLB-127

The Practice of Biography: An Interview
    with Stanley Weintraub Y-82

The Practice of Biography II: An Interview
    with B. L. Reid Y-83

The Practice of Biography III: An Interview
    with Humphrey Carpenter Y-84

The Practice of Biography IV: An Interview with
    William Manchester Y-85

The Practice of Biography V: An Interview
    with Justin Kaplan Y-86

The Practice of Biography VI: An Interview with
    David Herbert Donald Y-87

The Practice of Biography VII: An Interview with
    John Caldwell Guilds Y-92

The Practice of Biography VIII: An Interview
    with Joan Mellen Y-94

The Practice of Biography IX: An Interview
    with Michael Reynolds Y-95

Prados, Emilio 1899-1962 . . . . DLB-134

Praed, Winthrop Mackworth
    1802-1839 . . . . DLB-96

Praeger Publishers DLB-46

Praetorius, Johannes 1630-1680 . . . . DLB-168

Pratolini, Vasco 1913—1991 . . . . . . DLB-177

Pratt, E. J. 1882-1964 . . . . DLB-92

Pratt, Samuel Jackson 1749-1814 . . . . DLB-39

Preface to *Alwyn* (1780), by
    Thomas Holcroft DLB-39

Preface to *Colonel Jack* (1722), by
    Daniel Defoe DLB-39

Preface to *Evelina* (1778), by
    Fanny Burney DLB-39

Preface to *Ferdinand Count Fathom* (1753), by
    Tobias Smollett DLB-39

Preface to *Incognita* (1692), by
    William Congreve DLB-39

Preface to *Joseph Andrews* (1742), by
    Henry Fielding DLB-39

Preface to *Moll Flanders* (1722), by
    Daniel Defoe DLB-39

Preface to *Poems* (1853), by
    Matthew Arnold DLB-32

Preface to *Robinson Crusoe* (1719), by
    Daniel Defoe DLB-39

Preface to *Roderick Random* (1748), by
    Tobias Smollett DLB-39

Preface to *Roxana* (1724), by
    Daniel Defoe DLB-39

Preface to *St. Leon* (1799), by
    William Godwin DLB-39

Preface to Sarah Fielding's *Familiar Letters*
    (1747), by Henry Fielding
    [excerpt] DLB-39

Preface to Sarah Fielding's *The Adventures of
    David Simple* (1744), by
    Henry Fielding DLB-39

Preface to *The Cry* (1754), by
    Sarah Fielding DLB-39

Preface to *The Delicate Distress* (1769), by
    Elizabeth Griffin DLB-39

Preface to *The Disguis'd Prince* (1733), by
    Eliza Haywood [excerpt] DLB-39

Preface to *The Farther Adventures of Robinson
    Crusoe* (1719), by Daniel Defoe . . . DLB-39

Preface to the First Edition of *Pamela* (1740), by
    Samuel Richardson DLB-39

Preface to the First Edition of *The Castle of
    Otranto* (1764), by
    Horace Walpole DLB-39

Preface to *The History of Romances* (1715), by
    Pierre Daniel Huet [excerpts] DLB-39

Preface to *The Life of Charlotta du Pont* (1723),
    by Penelope Aubin DLB-39

Preface to *The Old English Baron* (1778), by
    Clara Reeve DLB-39

Preface to the Second Edition of *The Castle of
    Otranto* (1765), by Horace
    Walpole DLB-39

Preface to *The Secret History, of Queen Zarah,
    and the Zarazians* (1705), by Delariviere
    Manley DLB-39

Preface to the Third Edition of *Clarissa* (1751),
    by Samuel Richardson
    [excerpt] DLB-39

Preface to *The Works of Mrs. Davys* (1725), by
    Mary Davys DLB-39

Preface to Volume 1 of *Clarissa* (1747), by
    Samuel Richardson DLB-39

Preface to Volume 3 of *Clarissa* (1748), by
    Samuel Richardson DLB-39

Préfontaine, Yves 1937- DLB-53

Prelutsky, Jack 1940- DLB-61

Premisses, by Michael Hamburger DLB-66

Prentice, George D. 1802-1870 . . . . . DLB-43

Prentice-Hall DLB-46

Prescott, Orville 1906-1996 . . . . Y-96

Prescott, William Hickling
    1796-1859 . . . . DLB-1, 30, 59

The Present State of the English Novel (1892),
    by George Saintsbury DLB-18

Prešeren, Francè 1800-1849 . . . . . . DLB-147

Preston, Thomas 1537-1598 . . . . . . DLB-62

Price, Reynolds 1933- DLB-2

Price, Richard 1723-1791 . . . . DLB-158

Price, Richard 1949- Y-81

Priest, Christopher 1943- DLB-14

Priestley, J. B. 1894-1984
    . . . . . . DLB-10, 34, 77, 100, 139; Y-84

Primary Bibliography: A
    Retrospective Y-95

Prime, Benjamin Young 1733-1791 . . . DLB-31

Primrose, Diana
    floruit circa 1630 . . . . DLB-126

Prince, F. T. 1912- DLB-20

Prince, Thomas 1687-1758 . . . . . DLB-24, 140

The Principles of Success in Literature (1865), by
    George Henry Lewes [excerpt] . . . DLB-57

Printz, Wolfgang Casper
    1641-1717 . . . . DLB-168

Prior, Matthew 1664-1721 . . . . DLB-95

Prisco, Michele 1920- DLB-177

Pritchard, William H. 1932- DLB-111

Pritchett, V. S. 1900- DLB-15, 139

Procter, Adelaide Anne 1825-1864 . . . . DLB-32

Procter, Bryan Waller
    1787-1874 . . . . DLB-96, 144

The Profession of Authorship:
    Scribblers for Bread Y-89

The Progress of Romance (1785), by Clara Reeve
    [excerpt] DLB-39

Prokopovich, Feofan 1681?-1736 . . . . DLB-150

Prokosch, Frederic 1906-1989 . . . . . DLB-48

The Proletarian Novel DLB-9

Propper, Dan 1937- DLB-16

The Prospect of Peace (1778), by
    Joel Barlow DLB-37

Protagoras circa 490 B.C.-420 B.C.
. . . . DLB-176

Proud, Robert 1728-1813 . . . . DLB-30

Proust, Marcel 1871-1922 . . . . DLB-65

Prynne, J. H. 1936- DLB-40

Przybyszewski, Stanislaw
1868-1927 . . . . DLB-66

Pseudo-Dionysius the Areopagite floruit
circa 500 . . . . DLB-115

The Public Lending Right in America
Statement by Sen. Charles McC.
Mathias, Jr. PLR and the Meaning
of Literary Property Statements on
PLR by American Writers Y-83

The Public Lending Right in the United Kingdom
Public Lending Right: The First Year in the
United Kingdom Y-83

The Publication of English
Renaissance Plays DLB-62

Publications and Social Movements
[Transcendentalism] DLB-1

Publishers and Agents: The Columbia
Connection Y-87

A Publisher's Archives: G. P. Putnam . . . Y-92

Publishing Fiction at LSU Press Y-87

Pückler-Muskau, Hermann von
1785-1871 . . . . DLB-133

Pufendorf, Samuel von
1632-1694 . . . . DLB-168

Pugh, Edwin William 1874-1930 . . . . DLB-135

Pugin, A. Welby 1812-1852 . . . . DLB-55

Puig, Manuel 1932-1990 . . . . DLB-113

Pulitzer, Joseph 1847-1911 . . . . DLB-23

Pulitzer, Joseph, Jr. 1885-1955 . . . . . DLB-29

Pulitzer Prizes for the Novel,
1917-1945 . . . . DLB-9

Pulliam, Eugene 1889-1975 . . . . . . DLB-127

Purchas, Samuel 1577?-1626 . . . . . DLB-151

Purdy, Al 1918- DLB-88

Purdy, James 1923- DLB-2

Purdy, Ken W. 1913-1972 . . . . . DLB-137

Pusey, Edward Bouverie
1800-1882 . . . . DLB-55

Putnam, George Palmer
1814-1872 . . . . DLB-3, 79

Putnam, Samuel 1892-1950 . . . . . . DLB-4

G. P. Putnam's Sons [U.S.] DLB-49

G. P. Putnam's Sons [U.K.] DLB-106

Puzo, Mario 1920- DLB-6

Pyle, Ernie 1900-1945 . . . . DLB-29

Pyle, Howard 1853-1911 . . . . . DLB-42; DS-13

Pym, Barbara 1913-1980 . . . . . DLB-14; Y-87

Pynchon, Thomas 1937- DLB-2, 173

Pyramid Books DLB-46

Pyrnelle, Louise-Clarke 1850-1907 . . . DLB-42

Pythagoras circa 570 B.C.-? DLB-176

Q

Quad, M. (see Lewis, Charles B.)

Quarles, Francis 1592-1644 . . . . . . DLB-126

The Quarterly Review
1809-1967 . . . . DLB-110

Quasimodo, Salvatore 1901-1968 . . . . DLB-114

Queen, Ellery (see Dannay, Frederic, and
Manfred B. Lee)

The Queen City Publishing House . . . DLB-49

Queneau, Raymond 1903-1976 . . . . . DLB-72

Quennell, Sir Peter 1905-1993 . . . . DLB-155

Quesnel, Joseph 1746-1809 . . . . . . DLB-99

The Question of American Copyright
in the Nineteenth Century
Headnote
Preface, by George Haven Putnam
The Evolution of Copyright, by Brander
Matthews
Summary of Copyright Legislation in
the United States, by R. R. Bowker
Analysis of the Provisions of the
Copyright Law of 1891, by
George Haven Putnam
The Contest for International Copyright,
by George Haven Putnam
Cheap Books and Good Books,
by Brander Matthews DLB-49

Quiller-Couch, Sir Arthur Thomas
1863-1944 . . . . DLB-135, 153

Quin, Ann 1936-1973 . . . . DLB-14

Quincy, Samuel, of Georgia ?-? DLB-31

Quincy, Samuel, of Massachusetts
1734-1789 . . . . DLB-31

Quinn, Anthony 1915- DLB-122

Quintana, Leroy V. 1944- DLB-82

Quintana, Miguel de 1671-1748
A Forerunner of Chicano
Literature DLB-122

Quist, Harlin, Books DLB-46

Quoirez, Françoise (see Sagan, Françoise)

R

Raabe, Wilhelm 1831-1910 . . . . . . DLB-129

Rabe, David 1940- DLB-7

Raboni, Giovanni 1932- DLB-128

Rachilde 1860-1953 . . . . DLB-123

Racin, Kočo 1908-1943 . . . . DLB-147

Rackham, Arthur 1867-1939 . . . . . DLB-141

Radcliffe, Ann 1764-1823 . . . . . DLB-39, 178

Raddall, Thomas 1903- DLB-68

Radichkov, Yordan 1929- DLB-181

Radiguet, Raymond 1903-1923 . . . . . DLB-65

Radishchev, Aleksandr Nikolaevich
1749-1802 . . . . DLB-150

Radványi, Netty Reiling (see Seghers, Anna)

Rahv, Philip 1908-1973 . . . . DLB-137

Raičković, Stevan 1928- DLB-181

Raimund, Ferdinand Jakob
1790-1836 . . . . DLB-90

Raine, Craig 1944- DLB-40

Raine, Kathleen 1908- DLB-20

Rainolde, Richard
circa 1530-1606 . . . . DLB-136

Rakić, Milan 1876-1938 . . . . DLB-147

Ralegh, Sir Walter 1554?-1618 . . . . DLB-172

Ralin, Radoy 1923- DLB-181

Ralph, Julian 1853-1903 . . . . DLB-23

Ralph Waldo Emerson in 1982 . . . . . Y-82

Ramat, Silvio 1939- DLB-128

Rambler, no. 4 (1750), by Samuel Johnson
[excerpt] DLB-39

Ramée, Marie Louise de la (see Ouida)

Ramírez, Sergío 1942- DLB-145

Ramke, Bin 1947- DLB-120

Ramler, Karl Wilhelm 1725-1798 . . . DLB-97

Ramon Ribeyro, Julio 1929- DLB-145

Ramous, Mario 1924- DLB-128

Rampersad, Arnold 1941- DLB-111

Ramsay, Allan 1684 or 1685-1758 . . . DLB-95

Ramsay, David 1749-1815 . . . . . . DLB-30

Ranck, Katherine Quintana
1942- DLB-122

Rand, Avery and Company DLB-49

Rand McNally and Company DLB-49

Randall, David Anton
1905-1975 . . . . DLB-140

Randall, Dudley 1914- DLB-41

Randall, Henry S. 1811-1876 . . . . . DLB-30

Randall, James G. 1881-1953 . . . . . DLB-17

The Randall Jarrell Symposium: A Small
Collection of Randall Jarrells
Excerpts From Papers Delivered at
the Randall Jarrell
Symposium Y-86

Randolph, A. Philip 1889-1979 . . . . . DLB-91

Randolph, Anson D. F.
[publishing house] DLB-49

Randolph, Thomas 1605-1635 . . . DLB-58, 126

Random House DLB-46

Ranlet, Henry [publishing house] . . . DLB-49

Ransom, John Crowe
1888-1974 . . . . DLB-45, 63

Ransome, Arthur 1884-1967 . . . . . DLB-160

Raphael, Frederic 1931- DLB-14

Raphaelson, Samson 1896-1983 . . . . DLB-44

Raskin, Ellen 1928-1984 . . . . DLB-52

Rastell, John 1475?-1536 . . . . . DLB-136, 170

Rattigan, Terence 1911-1977 . . . . . DLB-13

Rawlings, Marjorie Kinnan
  1896-1953 . . . . DLB-9, 22, 102

Raworth, Tom 1938- DLB-40

Ray, David 1932- DLB-5

Ray, Gordon Norton
  1915-1986 . . . . DLB-103, 140

Ray, Henrietta Cordelia
  1849-1916 . . . . DLB-50

Raymond, Henry J. 1820-1869 . . . DLB-43, 79

Raymond Chandler Centenary Tributes
  from Michael Avallone, James Elroy, Joe
  Gores,
  and William F. Nolan Y-88

Reach, Angus 1821-1856 . . . . DLB-70

Read, Herbert 1893-1968 . . . . . DLB-20, 149

Read, Herbert, "The Practice of Biography," in
  *The English Sense of Humour and Other
  Essays* DLB-149

Read, Opie 1852-1939 . . . . DLB-23

Read, Piers Paul 1941- DLB-14

Reade, Charles 1814-1884 . . . . DLB-21

Reader's Digest Condensed
  Books DLB-46

Reading, Peter 1946- DLB-40

Reading Series in New York City Y-96

Reaney, James 1926- DLB-68

Rebhun, Paul 1500?-1546 . . . . DLB-179

Rèbora, Clemente 1885-1957 . . . . . DLB-114

Rechy, John 1934- DLB-122; Y-82

The Recovery of Literature: Criticism in the
  1990s: A Symposium Y-91

Redding, J. Saunders
  1906-1988 . . . . DLB-63, 76

Redfield, J. S. [publishing house] DLB-49

Redgrove, Peter 1932- DLB-40

Redmon, Anne 1943- Y-86

Redmond, Eugene B. 1937- DLB-41

Redpath, James [publishing house] . . . DLB-49

Reed, Henry 1808-1854 . . . . DLB-59

Reed, Henry 1914- DLB-27

Reed, Ishmael
  1938- DLB-2, 5, 33, 169; DS-8

Reed, Sampson 1800-1880 . . . . DLB-1

Reed, Talbot Baines 1852-1893 . . . . DLB-141

Reedy, William Marion 1862-1920 . . . DLB-91

Reese, Lizette Woodworth
  1856-1935 . . . . DLB-54

Reese, Thomas 1742-1796 . . . . DLB-37

Reeve, Clara 1729-1807 . . . . DLB-39

Reeves, James 1909-1978 . . . . DLB-161

Reeves, John 1926- DLB-88

Regnery, Henry, Company DLB-46

Rehberg, Hans 1901-1963 . . . . DLB-124

Rehfisch, Hans José 1891-1960 . . . . DLB-124

Reid, Alastair 1926- DLB-27

Reid, B. L. 1918-1990 . . . . DLB-111

Reid, Christopher 1949- DLB-40

Reid, Forrest 1875-1947 . . . . DLB-153

Reid, Helen Rogers 1882-1970 . . . . . DLB-29

Reid, James ?-? DLB-31

Reid, Mayne 1818-1883 . . . . . DLB-21, 163

Reid, Thomas 1710-1796 . . . . DLB-31

Reid, V. S. (Vic) 1913-1987 . . . . . DLB-125

Reid, Whitelaw 1837-1912 . . . . DLB-23

Reilly and Lee Publishing
  Company DLB-46

Reimann, Brigitte 1933-1973 . . . . . . DLB-75

Reinmar der Alte
  circa 1165-circa 1205 . . . . DLB-138

Reinmar von Zweter
  circa 1200-circa 1250 . . . . DLB-138

Reisch, Walter 1903-1983 . . . . DLB-44

Remarque, Erich Maria 1898-1970 . . . DLB-56

"Re-meeting of Old Friends": The Jack
  Kerouac Conference Y-82

Remington, Frederic 1861-1909 . . . . . DLB-12

Renaud, Jacques 1943- DLB-60

Renault, Mary 1905-1983 . . . . Y-83

Rendell, Ruth 1930- DLB-87

Representative Men and Women: A Historical
  Perspective on the British Novel,
  1930-1960 . . . . DLB-15

(Re-)Publishing Orwell Y-86

Rettenbacher, Simon 1634-1706 . . . . DLB-168

Reuchlin, Johannes 1455-1522 . . . . . DLB-179

Reuter, Christian 1665-after 1712 . . . . DLB-168

Reuter, Fritz 1810-1874 . . . . DLB-129

Reuter, Gabriele 1859-1941 . . . . DLB-66

Revell, Fleming H., Company DLB-49

Reventlow, Franziska Gräfin zu
  1871-1918 . . . . DLB-66

Review of Reviews Office DLB-112

Review of [Samuel Richardson's] *Clarissa* (1748),
  by Henry Fielding DLB-39

The Revolt (1937), by Mary Colum
  [excerpts] DLB-36

Rexroth, Kenneth
  1905-1982 . . . . . DLB-16, 48, 165; Y-82

Rey, H. A. 1898-1977 . . . . DLB-22

Reynal and Hitchcock DLB-46

Reynolds, G. W. M. 1814-1879 . . . . . DLB-21

Reynolds, John Hamilton
  1794-1852 . . . . DLB-96

Reynolds, Mack 1917- DLB-8

Reynolds, Sir Joshua 1723-1792 . . . . DLB-104

Reznikoff, Charles 1894-1976 . . . . DLB-28, 45

"Rhetoric" (1828; revised, 1859), by
  Thomas de Quincey [excerpt] . . . DLB-57

Rhett, Robert Barnwell 1800-1876 . . . . DLB-43

Rhode, John 1884-1964 . . . . DLB-77

Rhodes, James Ford 1848-1927 . . . . . DLB-47

Rhys, Jean 1890-1979 . . . . DLB-36, 117, 162

Ricardo, David 1772-1823 . . . . DLB-107, 158

Ricardou, Jean 1932- DLB-83

Rice, Elmer 1892-1967 . . . . DLB-4, 7

Rice, Grantland 1880-1954 . . . . . DLB-29, 171

Rich, Adrienne 1929- DLB-5, 67

Richards, David Adams 1950- DLB-53

Richards, George circa 1760-1814 . . . . DLB-37

Richards, I. A. 1893-1979 . . . . DLB-27

Richards, Laura E. 1850-1943 . . . . . DLB-42

Richards, William Carey
  1818-1892 . . . . DLB-73

Richards, Grant
  [publishing house] DLB-112

Richardson, Charles F. 1851-1913 . . . DLB-71

Richardson, Dorothy M.
  1873-1957 . . . . DLB-36

Richardson, Jack 1935- DLB-7

Richardson, John 1796-1852 . . . . . . DLB-99

Richardson, Samuel
  1689-1761 . . . . DLB-39, 154

Richardson, Willis 1889-1977 . . . . . DLB-51

Riche, Barnabe 1542-1617 . . . . . . DLB-136

Richler, Mordecai 1931- DLB-53

Richter, Conrad 1890-1968 . . . . DLB-9

Richter, Hans Werner 1908- DLB-69

Richter, Johann Paul Friedrich
  1763-1825 . . . . DLB-94

Rickerby, Joseph
  [publishing house] DLB-106

Rickword, Edgell 1898-1982 . . . . . . DLB-20

Riddell, Charlotte 1832-1906 . . . . . DLB-156

Riddell, John (see Ford, Corey)

Ridge, John Rollin 1827-1867 . . . . . DLB-175

Ridge, Lola 1873-1941 . . . . DLB-54

Ridge, William Pett 1859-1930 . . . . DLB-135

Riding, Laura (see Jackson, Laura Riding)

Ridler, Anne 1912- DLB-27

Ridruego, Dionisio 1912-1975 . . . . . DLB-108

Riel, Louis 1844-1885 . . . . DLB-99

Riemer, Johannes 1648-1714 . . . . . DLB-168

Riffaterre, Michael 1924- DLB-67

Riggs, Lynn 1899-1954 . . . . DLB-175

Riis, Jacob 1849-1914 . . . . DLB-23

Riker, John C. [publishing house] . . . DLB-49

Riley, James 1777-1840 . . . . DLB-183

Riley, John 1938-1978 . . . . DLB-40

Rilke, Rainer Maria 1875-1926 . . . . . DLB-81

Rimanelli, Giose 1926- DLB-177

Rinehart and Company. DLB-46

Ringuet 1895-1960. . . . . DLB-68

Ringwood, Gwen Pharis
1910-1984 . . . . DLB-88

Rinser, Luise 1911- DLB-69

Ríos, Alberto 1952- DLB-122

Ríos, Isabella 1948- DLB-82

Ripley, Arthur 1895-1961. . . . . DLB-44

Ripley, George 1802-1880. . . . . DLB-1, 64, 73

The Rising Glory of America:
Three Poems DLB-37

The Rising Glory of America: Written in 1771
(1786), by Hugh Henry Brackenridge and
Philip Freneau. DLB-37

Riskin, Robert 1897-1955. . . . . . . DLB-26

Risse, Heinz 1898- DLB-69

Rist, Johann 1607-1667 . . . . DLB-164

Ritchie, Anna Mowatt 1819-1870 . . . . DLB-3

Ritchie, Anne Thackeray
1837-1919 . . . . DLB-18

Ritchie, Thomas 1778-1854. . . . . . . DLB-43

Rites of Passage
[on William Saroyan] Y-83

The Ritz Paris Hemingway Award Y-85

Rivard, Adjutor 1868-1945 . . . . DLB-92

Rive, Richard 1931-1989 . . . . DLB-125

Rivera, Marina 1942- DLB-122

Rivera, Tomás 1935-1984 . . . . DLB-82

Rivers, Conrad Kent 1933-1968 . . . . DLB-41

Riverside Press DLB-49

Rivington, James circa 1724-1802 . . . DLB-43

Rivington, Charles
[publishing house] DLB-154

Rivkin, Allen 1903-1990 . . . . DLB-26

Roa Bastos, Augusto 1917- DLB-113

Robbe-Grillet, Alain 1922- DLB-83

Robbins, Tom 1936- Y-80

Roberts, Charles G. D. 1860-1943. . . . DLB-92

Roberts, Dorothy 1906-1993 . . . . . . DLB-88

Roberts, Elizabeth Madox
1881-1941. . . . . DLB-9, 54, 102

Roberts, Kenneth 1885-1957. . . . . . DLB-9

Roberts, William 1767-1849. . . . . . DLB-142

Roberts Brothers DLB-49

Roberts, James [publishing house] . . . DLB-154

Robertson, A. M., and Company DLB-49

Robertson, William 1721-1793 . . . . . DLB-104

Robinson, Casey 1903-1979 . . . . . . DLB-44

Robinson, Edwin Arlington
1869-1935 . . . . DLB-54

Robinson, Henry Crabb
1775-1867 . . . . DLB-107

Robinson, James Harvey
1863-1936 . . . . DLB-47

Robinson, Lennox 1886-1958. . . . . . DLB-10

Robinson, Mabel Louise
1874-1962 . . . . DLB-22

Robinson, Mary 1758-1800 . . . . . . DLB-158

Robinson, Richard
circa 1545-1607 . . . . DLB-167

Robinson, Therese
1797-1870 . . . . DLB-59, 133

Robison, Mary 1949- DLB-130

Roblès, Emmanuel 1914- DLB-83

Roccatagliata Ceccardi, Ceccardo
1871-1919 . . . . DLB-114

Rochester, John Wilmot, Earl of
1647-1680 . . . . DLB-131

Rock, Howard 1911-1976 . . . . DLB-127

Rodgers, Carolyn M. 1945- DLB-41

Rodgers, W. R. 1909-1969 . . . . DLB-20

Rodríguez, Claudio 1934- DLB-134

Rodriguez, Richard 1944- DLB-82

Rodríguez Julia, Edgardo
1946- DLB-145

Roethke, Theodore 1908-1963. . . . . DLB-5

Rogers, Pattiann 1940- DLB-105

Rogers, Samuel 1763-1855 . . . . DLB-93

Rogers, Will 1879-1935. . . . . DLB-11

Rohmer, Sax 1883-1959 . . . . DLB-70

Roiphe, Anne 1935- Y-80

Rojas, Arnold R. 1896-1988 . . . . . . DLB-82

Rolfe, Frederick William
1860-1913 . . . . DLB-34, 156

Rolland, Romain 1866-1944 . . . . . . DLB-65

Rolle, Richard
circa 1290-1300 - 1340 . . . . . . DLB-146

Rölvaag, O. E. 1876-1931 . . . . DLB-9

Romains, Jules 1885-1972. . . . . . . DLB-65

Roman, A., and Company DLB-49

Romano, Lalla 1906- DLB-177

Romano, Octavio 1923- DLB-122

Romero, Leo 1950- DLB-122

Romero, Lin 1947- DLB-122

Romero, Orlando 1945- DLB-82

Rook, Clarence 1863-1915 . . . . DLB-135

Roosevelt, Theodore 1858-1919 . . . . DLB-47

Root, Waverley 1903-1982. . . . . . . DLB-4

Root, William Pitt 1941- DLB-120

Roquebrune, Robert de 1889-1978. . . . DLB-68

Rosa, João Guimarães
1908-1967 . . . . DLB-113

Rosales, Luis 1910-1992 . . . . DLB-134

Roscoe, William 1753-1831 . . . . . . DLB-163

Rose, Reginald 1920- DLB-26

Rose, Wendy 1948- DLB-175

Rosegger, Peter 1843-1918. . . . . . . DLB-129

Rosei, Peter 1946- DLB-85

Rosen, Norma 1925- DLB-28

Rosenbach, A. S. W. 1876-1952 . . . . DLB-140

Rosenberg, Isaac 1890-1918. . . . . . DLB-20

Rosenfeld, Isaac 1918-1956 . . . . . . DLB-28

Rosenthal, M. L. 1917- DLB-5

Ross, Alexander 1591-1654 . . . . . . DLB-151

Ross, Harold 1892-1951 . . . . DLB-137

Ross, Leonard Q. (see Rosten, Leo)

Ross, Martin 1862-1915 . . . . DLB-135

Ross, Sinclair 1908- DLB-88

Ross, W. W. E. 1894-1966 . . . . DLB-88

Rosselli, Amelia 1930- DLB-128

Rossen, Robert 1908-1966 . . . . . . DLB-26

Rossetti, Christina Georgina
1830-1894 . . . . DLB-35, 163

Rossetti, Dante Gabriel 1828-1882 . . . DLB-35

Rossner, Judith 1935- DLB-6

Rosten, Leo 1908- DLB-11

Rostenberg, Leona 1908- DLB-140

Rostovsky, Dimitrii 1651-1709 . . . . . DLB-150

Bertram Rota and His Bookshop Y-91

Roth, Gerhard 1942- DLB-85, 124

Roth, Henry 1906?- DLB-28

Roth, Joseph 1894-1939 . . . . DLB-85

Roth, Philip 1933- DLB-2, 28, 173; Y-82

Rothenberg, Jerome 1931- DLB-5

Rotimi, Ola 1938- DLB-125

Routhier, Adolphe-Basile
1839-1920 . . . . DLB-99

Routier, Simone 1901-1987 . . . . DLB-88

Routledge, George, and Sons DLB-106

Roversi, Roberto 1923- DLB-128

Rowe, Elizabeth Singer
1674-1737 . . . . DLB-39, 95

Rowe, Nicholas 1674-1718 . . . . DLB-84

Rowlands, Samuel
circa 1570-1630 . . . . DLB-121

Rowlandson, Mary
circa 1635-circa 1678 . . . . DLB-24

Rowley, William circa 1585-1626 . . . . DLB-58

Rowse, A. L. 1903- DLB-155

Rowson, Susanna Haswell
circa 1762-1824 . . . . DLB-37

Roy, Camille 1870-1943 . . . . DLB-92

Roy, Gabrielle 1909-1983 . . . . DLB-68

Roy, Jules 1907- DLB-83

The Royal Court Theatre and the English
Stage Company. DLB-13

The Royal Court Theatre and the New Drama
. . . . DLB-10

The Royal Shakespeare Company
at the Swan Y-88

Royall, Anne 1769-1854 . . . . DLB-43

The Roycroft Printing Shop DLB-49

Royster, Vermont 1914- DLB-127

Royston, Richard
[publishing house] DLB-170

Ruark, Gibbons 1941- DLB-120

Ruban, Vasilii Grigorevich
1742-1795 . . . . DLB-150

Rubens, Bernice 1928- DLB-14

Rudd and Carleton DLB-49

Rudkin, David 1936- DLB-13

Rudolf von Ems
circa 1200-circa 1254 . . . . DLB-138

Ruffin, Josephine St. Pierre
1842-1924 . . . . DLB-79

Ruganda, John 1941- DLB-157

Ruggles, Henry Joseph 1813-1906 . . . . DLB-64

Rukeyser, Muriel 1913-1980 . . . . . . DLB-48

Rule, Jane 1931- DLB-60

Rulfo, Juan 1918-1986 . . . . DLB-113

Rumaker, Michael 1932- DLB-16

Rumens, Carol 1944- DLB-40

Runyon, Damon 1880-1946 . . DLB-11, 86, 171

Ruodlieb circa 1050-1075 . . . . DLB-148

Rush, Benjamin 1746-1813 . . . . DLB-37

Rusk, Ralph L. 1888-1962 . . . . . . DLB-103

Ruskin, John 1819-1900 . . . . . . DLB-55, 163

Russ, Joanna 1937- DLB-8

Russell, B. B., and Company DLB-49

Russell, Benjamin 1761-1845 . . . . . DLB-43

Russell, Bertrand 1872-1970 . . . . . . DLB-100

Russell, Charles Edward
1860-1941 . . . . DLB-25

Russell, George William (see AE)

Russell, R. H., and Son DLB-49

Rutherford, Mark 1831-1913 . . . . . . DLB-18

Ryan, Michael 1946- Y-82

Ryan, Oscar 1904- DLB-68

Ryga, George 1932- DLB-60

Rymer, Thomas 1643?-1713 . . . . . DLB-101

Ryskind, Morrie 1895-1985 . . . . . . DLB-26

Rzhevsky, Aleksei Andreevich
1737-1804 . . . . DLB-150

S

The Saalfield Publishing
Company DLB-46

Saba, Umberto 1883-1957 . . . . . . DLB-114

Sábato, Ernesto 1911- DLB-145

Saberhagen, Fred 1930- DLB-8

Sacer, Gottfried Wilhelm
1635-1699 . . . . DLB-168

Sachs, Hans 1494-1576 . . . . DLB-179

Sackler, Howard 1929-1982 . . . . DLB-7

Sackville, Thomas 1536-1608 . . . . . DLB-132

Sackville, Thomas 1536-1608
and Norton, Thomas
1532-1584 . . . . DLB-62

Sackville-West, V. 1892-1962 . . . . . . DLB-34

Sadlier, D. and J., and Company DLB-49

Sadlier, Mary Anne 1820-1903 . . . . . DLB-99

Sadoff, Ira 1945- DLB-120

Saenz, Jaime 1921-1986 . . . . DLB-145

Saffin, John circa 1626-1710 . . . . . . DLB-24

Sagan, Françoise 1935- DLB-83

Sage, Robert 1899-1962 . . . . DLB-4

Sagel, Jim 1947- DLB-82

Sagendorph, Robb Hansell
1900-1970 . . . . DLB-137

Sahagún, Carlos 1938- DLB-108

Sahkomaapii, Piitai (see Highwater, Jamake)

Sahl, Hans 1902- DLB-69

Said, Edward W. 1935- DLB-67

Saiko, George 1892-1962 . . . . DLB-85

St. Dominic's Press DLB-112

Saint-Exupéry, Antoine de
1900-1944 . . . . DLB-72

St. Johns, Adela Rogers 1894-1988 . . . DLB-29

St. Martin's Press DLB-46

St. Omer, Garth 1931- DLB-117

Saint Pierre, Michel de 1916-1987 . . . . DLB-83

Saintsbury, George
1845-1933 . . . . DLB-57, 149

Saki (see Munro, H. H.)

Salaam, Kalamu ya 1947- DLB-38

Šalamun, Tomaž 1941- DLB-181

Salas, Floyd 1931- DLB-82

Sálaz-Marquez, Rubén 1935- DLB-122

Salemson, Harold J. 1910-1988 . . . . . DLB-4

Salinas, Luis Omar 1937- DLB-82

Salinas, Pedro 1891-1951 . . . . DLB-134

Salinger, J. D. 1919- DLB-2, 102, 173

Salkey, Andrew 1928- DLB-125

Salt, Waldo 1914- DLB-44

Salter, James 1925- DLB-130

Salter, Mary Jo 1954- DLB-120

Salustri, Carlo Alberto (see Trilussa)

Salverson, Laura Goodman
1890-1970 . . . . DLB-92

Sampson, Richard Henry (see Hull, Richard)

Samuels, Ernest 1903- DLB-111

Sanborn, Franklin Benjamin
1831-1917 . . . . DLB-1

Sánchez, Luis Rafael 1936- DLB-145

Sánchez, Philomeno "Phil"
1917- DLB-122

Sánchez, Ricardo 1941- DLB-82

Sanchez, Sonia 1934- DLB-41; DS-8

Sand, George 1804-1876 . . . . DLB-119

Sandburg, Carl 1878-1967 . . . . DLB-17, 54

Sanders, Ed 1939- DLB-16

Sandoz, Mari 1896-1966 . . . . DLB-9

Sandwell, B. K. 1876-1954 . . . . DLB-92

Sandy, Stephen 1934- DLB-165

Sandys, George 1578-1644 . . . DLB-24, 121

Sangster, Charles 1822-1893 . . . . . DLB-99

Sanguineti, Edoardo 1930- DLB-128

Sansom, William 1912-1976 . . . . . . DLB-139

Santayana, George
1863-1952 . . . . DLB-54, 71; DS-13

Santiago, Danny 1911-1988 . . . . . . DLB-122

Santmyer, Helen Hooven 1895-1986 . . . Y-84

Sapidus, Joannes 1490-1561 . . . . . . DLB-179

Sapir, Edward 1884-1939 . . . . DLB-92

Sapper (see McNeile, Herman Cyril)

Sappho circa 620 B.C.-circa 550 B.C.
. . . . DLB-176

Sarduy, Severo 1937- DLB-113

Sargent, Pamela 1948- DLB-8

Saro-Wiwa, Ken 1941- DLB-157

Saroyan, William
1908-1981 . . . . DLB-7, 9, 86; Y-81

Sarraute, Nathalie 1900- DLB-83

Sarrazin, Albertine 1937-1967 . . . . . DLB-83

Sarris, Greg 1952- DLB-175

Sarton, May 1912- DLB-48; Y-81

Sartre, Jean-Paul 1905-1980 . . . . . . DLB-72

Sassoon, Siegfried 1886-1967 . . . . . DLB-20

Sata, Ineko 1904- DLB-180

Saturday Review Press DLB-46

Saunders, James 1925- DLB-13

Saunders, John Monk 1897-1940 . . . . DLB-26

Saunders, Margaret Marshall
1861-1947 . . . . DLB-92

Saunders and Otley DLB-106

Savage, James 1784-1873 . . . . DLB-30

Savage, Marmion W. 1803?-1872 . . . . DLB-21

Savage, Richard 1697?-1743 . . . . . . DLB-95

Savard, Félix-Antoine 1896-1982 . . . . DLB-68

Saville, (Leonard) Malcolm
1901-1982 . . . . DLB-160

Sawyer, Ruth 1880-1970 . . . . DLB-22

Sayers, Dorothy L.
1893-1957 . . . . DLB-10, 36, 77, 100

Sayles, John Thomas 1950- DLB-44

Sbarbaro, Camillo 1888-1967 . . . . . DLB-114

Scannell, Vernon 1922- DLB-27

Scarry, Richard 1919-1994 . . . . DLB-61

Schaeffer, Albrecht 1885-1950 . . . . . DLB-66

Schaeffer, Susan Fromberg 1941- DLB-28

Schaff, Philip 1819-1893 . . . . DS-13

Schaper, Edzard 1908-1984 . . . . DLB-69

Scharf, J. Thomas 1843-1898 . . . . . . DLB-47

Schede, Paul Melissus 1539-1602 . . . . DLB-179

Scheffel, Joseph Viktor von
1826-1886 . . . . DLB-129

Scheffler, Johann 1624-1677 . . . . . . DLB-164

Schelling, Friedrich Wilhelm Joseph von
1775-1854 . . . . DLB-90

Scherer, Wilhelm 1841-1886 . . . . . . DLB-129

Schickele, René 1883-1940 . . . . DLB-66

Schiff, Dorothy 1903-1989 . . . . DLB-127

Schiller, Friedrich 1759-1805 . . . . . . DLB-94

Schirmer, David 1623-1687 . . . . . . DLB-164

Schlaf, Johannes 1862-1941 . . . . . . DLB-118

Schlegel, August Wilhelm
1767-1845 . . . . DLB-94

Schlegel, Dorothea 1763-1839 . . . . . DLB-90

Schlegel, Friedrich 1772-1829 . . . . . DLB-90

Schleiermacher, Friedrich
1768-1834 . . . . DLB-90

Schlesinger, Arthur M., Jr. 1917- . . . DLB-17

Schlumberger, Jean 1877-1968 . . . . . DLB-65

Schmid, Eduard Hermann Wilhelm (see Edschmid,
Kasimir)

Schmidt, Arno 1914-1979 . . . . DLB-69

Schmidt, Johann Kaspar (see Stirner, Max)

Schmidt, Michael 1947- DLB-40

Schmidtbonn, Wilhelm August
1876-1952 . . . . DLB-118

Schmitz, James H. 1911- DLB-8

Schnabel, Johann Gottfried
1692-1760 . . . . DLB-168

Schnackenberg, Gjertrud 1953- DLB-120

Schnitzler, Arthur 1862-1931 . . . . DLB-81, 118

Schnurre, Wolfdietrich 1920- DLB-69

Schocken Books DLB-46

Scholartis Press DLB-112

The Schomburg Center for Research
in Black Culture DLB-76

Schönbeck, Virgilio (see Giotti, Virgilio)

Schönherr, Karl 1867-1943 . . . . . . DLB-118

Schoolcraft, Jane Johnston
1800-1841 . . . . DLB-175

School Stories, 1914-1960 . . . . DLB-160

Schopenhauer, Arthur 1788-1860 . . . . DLB-90

Schopenhauer, Johanna 1766-1838 . . . . DLB-90

Schorer, Mark 1908-1977 . . . . DLB-103

Schottelius, Justus Georg
1612-1676 . . . . DLB-164

Schouler, James 1839-1920 . . . . DLB-47

Schrader, Paul 1946- DLB-44

Schreiner, Olive 1855-1920 . . . . DLB-18, 156

Schroeder, Andreas 1946- DLB-53

Schubart, Christian Friedrich Daniel
1739-1791 . . . . DLB-97

Schubert, Gotthilf Heinrich
1780-1860 . . . . DLB-90

Schücking, Levin 1814-1883 . . . . . . DLB-133

Schulberg, Budd
1914- DLB-6, 26, 28; Y-81

Schulte, F. J., and Company DLB-49

Schulze, Hans (see Praetorius, Johannes)

Schupp, Johann Balthasar
1610-1661 . . . . DLB-164

Schurz, Carl 1829-1906 . . . . DLB-23

Schuyler, George S. 1895-1977 . . . DLB-29, 51

Schuyler, James 1923-1991 . . . . DLB-5, 169

Schwartz, Delmore 1913-1966 . . . . DLB-28, 48

Schwartz, Jonathan 1938- Y-82

Schwarz, Sibylle 1621-1638 . . . . . . DLB-164

Schwerner, Armand 1927- DLB-165

Schwob, Marcel 1867-1905 . . . . . . DLB-123

Sciascia, Leonardo 1921-1989 . . . . . DLB-177

Science Fantasy DLB-8

Science-Fiction Fandom and
Conventions DLB-8

Science-Fiction Fanzines: The Time
Binders DLB-8

Science-Fiction Films DLB-8

Science Fiction Writers of America and the
Nebula Awards DLB-8

Scot, Reginald circa 1538-1599 . . . . DLB-136

Scotellaro, Rocco 1923-1953 . . . . . . DLB-128

Scott, Dennis 1939-1991 . . . . DLB-125

Scott, Dixon 1881-1915 . . . . DLB-98

Scott, Duncan Campbell
1862-1947 . . . . DLB-92

Scott, Evelyn 1893-1963 . . . . . . DLB-9, 48

Scott, F. R. 1899-1985 . . . . DLB-88

Scott, Frederick George
1861-1944 . . . . DLB-92

Scott, Geoffrey 1884-1929 . . . . . . DLB-149

Scott, Harvey W. 1838-1910 . . . . . . DLB-23

Scott, Paul 1920-1978 . . . . DLB-14

Scott, Sarah 1723-1795 . . . . DLB-39

Scott, Tom 1918- DLB-27

Scott, Sir Walter
1771-1832 . . . . DLB-93, 107, 116, 144, 159

Scott, William Bell 1811-1890 . . . . . DLB-32

Scott, Walter, Publishing
Company Limited DLB-112

Scott, William R.
[publishing house] DLB-46

Scott-Heron, Gil 1949- DLB-41

Scribner, Charles, Jr. 1921-1995 . . . . Y-95

Charles Scribner's Sons DLB-49; DS-13

Scripps, E. W. 1854-1926 . . . . DLB-25

Scudder, Horace Elisha
1838-1902 . . . . DLB-42, 71

Scudder, Vida Dutton 1861-1954 . . . . DLB-71

Scupham, Peter 1933- DLB-40

Seabrook, William 1886-1945 . . . . . . DLB-4

Seabury, Samuel 1729-1796 . . . . . . DLB-31

Seacole, Mary Jane Grant
1805-1881 . . . . DLB-166

The Seafarer circa 970 . . . . DLB-146

Sealsfield, Charles 1793-1864 . . . . . DLB-133

Sears, Edward I. 1819?-1876 . . . . . . DLB-79

Sears Publishing Company DLB-46

Seaton, George 1911-1979 . . . . DLB-44

Seaton, William Winston
1785-1866 . . . . DLB-43

Secker, Martin, and Warburg
Limited DLB-112

Secker, Martin [publishing house] DLB-112

Second-Generation Minor Poets of the
Seventeenth Century DLB-126

Sedgwick, Arthur George
1844-1915 . . . . DLB-64

Sedgwick, Catharine Maria
1789-1867 . . . . DLB-1, 74, 183

Sedgwick, Ellery 1872-1930 . . . . . . DLB-91

Sedley, Sir Charles 1639-1701 . . . . . DLB-131

Seeger, Alan 1888-1916 . . . . DLB-45

Seers, Eugene (see Dantin, Louis)

Segal, Erich 1937- Y-86

Šegedin, Petar 1909- DLB-181

Seghers, Anna 1900-1983 . . . . DLB-69

Seid, Ruth (see Sinclair, Jo)

Seidel, Frederick Lewis 1936- Y-84

Seidel, Ina 1885-1974 . . . . DLB-56

Seigenthaler, John 1927- DLB-127

Seizin Press DLB-112

Séjour, Victor 1817-1874 . . . . DLB-50

Séjour Marcou et Ferrand, Juan Victor (see Séjour,
Victor)

Selby, Hubert, Jr. 1928- DLB-2

Selden, George 1929-1989 . . . . DLB-52

Selected English-Language Little Magazines
and Newspapers [France,
1920-1939] DLB-4

Selected Humorous Magazines
(1820-1950) DLB-11

Selected Science-Fiction Magazines and
Anthologies DLB-8

Selenić, Slobodan 1933-1995 . . . . . . DLB-181

Self, Edwin F. 1920- DLB-137

Seligman, Edwin R. A. 1861-1939 . . . . DLB-47

Selimović, Meša 1910-1982 . . . . DLB-181

Selous, Frederick Courteney
   1851-1917 . . . . DLB-174

Seltzer, Chester E. (see Muro, Amado)

Seltzer, Thomas
   [publishing house] DLB-46

Selvon, Sam 1923-1994 . . . . DLB-125

Senancour, Etienne de 1770-1846 . . . . DLB-119

Sendak, Maurice 1928- DLB-61

Senécal, Eva 1905- DLB-92

Sengstacke, John 1912- DLB-127

Senior, Olive 1941- DLB-157

Šenoa, August 1838-1881 . . . . DLB-147

"Sensation Novels" (1863), by
   H. L. Manse DLB-21

Sepamla, Sipho 1932- DLB-157

Seredy, Kate 1899-1975 . . . . DLB-22

Sereni, Vittorio 1913-1983 . . . . DLB-128

Seres, William
   [publishing house] DLB-170

Serling, Rod 1924-1975 . . . . DLB-26

Serote, Mongane Wally 1944- DLB-125

Serraillier, Ian 1912-1994 . . . . DLB-161

Serrano, Nina 1934- DLB-122

Service, Robert 1874-1958 . . . . DLB-92

Seth, Vikram 1952- DLB-120

Seton, Ernest Thompson
   1860-1942 . . . . DLB-92; DS-13

Setouchi, Harumi 1922- DLB-182

Settle, Mary Lee 1918- DLB-6

Seume, Johann Gottfried
   1763-1810 . . . . DLB-94

Seuse, Heinrich 1295?-1366 . . . . . . DLB-179

Seuss, Dr. (see Geisel, Theodor Seuss)

The Seventy-fifth Anniversary of the Armistice:
   The Wilfred Owen Centenary and the Great
   War Exhibit at the University of
   Virginia Y-93

Sewall, Joseph 1688-1769 . . . . DLB-24

Sewall, Richard B. 1908- DLB-111

Sewell, Anna 1820-1878 . . . . DLB-163

Sewell, Samuel 1652-1730 . . . . DLB-24

Sex, Class, Politics, and Religion [in the
   British Novel, 1930-1959] DLB-15

Sexton, Anne 1928-1974 . . . . . . DLB-5, 169

Seymour-Smith, Martin 1928- DLB-155

Shaara, Michael 1929-1988 . . . . Y-83

Shadwell, Thomas 1641?-1692 . . . . . DLB-80

Shaffer, Anthony 1926- DLB-13

Shaffer, Peter 1926- DLB-13

Shaftesbury, Anthony Ashley Cooper,
   Third Earl of 1671-1713 . . . . . DLB-101

Shairp, Mordaunt 1887-1939 . . . . . . DLB-10

Shakespeare, William
   1564-1616 . . . . DLB-62, 172

The Shakespeare Globe Trust Y-93

Shakespeare Head Press DLB-112

Shakhovskoi, Aleksandr Aleksandrovich
   1777-1846 . . . . DLB-150

Shange, Ntozake 1948- DLB-38

Shapiro, Karl 1913- DLB-48

Sharon Publications DLB-46

Sharp, Margery 1905-1991 . . . . DLB-161

Sharp, William 1855-1905 . . . . DLB-156

Sharpe, Tom 1928- DLB-14

Shaw, Albert 1857-1947 . . . . DLB-91

Shaw, Bernard 1856-1950 . . . . . DLB-10, 57

Shaw, Henry Wheeler 1818-1885 . . . . DLB-11

Shaw, Joseph T. 1874-1952 . . . . DLB-137

Shaw, Irwin 1913-1984 . . . . DLB-6, 102; Y-84

Shaw, Robert 1927-1978 . . . . . . DLB-13, 14

Shaw, Robert B. 1947- DLB-120

Shawn, William 1907-1992 . . . . DLB-137

Shay, Frank [publishing house] DLB-46

Shea, John Gilmary 1824-1892 . . . . . DLB-30

Sheaffer, Louis 1912-1993 . . . . DLB-103

Shearing, Joseph 1886-1952 . . . . . . DLB-70

Shebbeare, John 1709-1788 . . . . DLB-39

Sheckley, Robert 1928- DLB-8

Shedd, William G. T. 1820-1894 . . . . DLB-64

Sheed, Wilfred 1930- DLB-6

Sheed and Ward [U.S.] DLB-46

Sheed and Ward Limited [U.K.] DLB-112

Sheldon, Alice B. (see Tiptree, James, Jr.)

Sheldon, Edward 1886-1946 . . . . DLB-7

Sheldon and Company DLB-49

Shelley, Mary Wollstonecraft
   1797-1851 . . . . . DLB-110, 116, 159, 178

Shelley, Percy Bysshe
   1792-1822 . . . . DLB-96, 110, 158

Shelnutt, Eve 1941- DLB-130

Shenstone, William 1714-1763 . . . . . DLB-95

Shepard, Ernest Howard
   1879-1976 . . . . DLB-160

Shepard, Sam 1943- DLB-7

Shepard, Thomas I,
   1604 or 1605-1649 . . . . DLB-24

Shepard, Thomas II, 1635-1677 . . . . . DLB-24

Shepard, Clark and Brown DLB-49

Shepherd, Luke
   flourished 1547-1554 . . . . DLB-136

Sherburne, Edward 1616-1702 . . . . . DLB-131

Sheridan, Frances 1724-1766 . . . . DLB-39, 84

Sheridan, Richard Brinsley
   1751-1816 . . . . DLB-89

Sherman, Francis 1871-1926 . . . . . . DLB-92

Sherriff, R. C. 1896-1975 . . . . DLB-10

Sherry, Norman 1935- DLB-155

Sherwood, Mary Martha
   1775-1851 . . . . DLB-163

Sherwood, Robert 1896-1955 . . . . DLB-7, 26

Shiel, M. P. 1865-1947 . . . . DLB-153

Shiels, George 1886-1949 . . . . DLB-10

Shiga, Naoya 1883-1971 . . . . DLB-180

Shiina, Rinzō 1911-1973 . . . . DLB-182

Shillaber, B.[enjamin] P.[enhallow]
   1814-1890 . . . . DLB-1, 11

Shimao, Toshio 1917-1986 . . . . DLB-182

Shimazaki, Tōson 1872-1943 . . . . . . DLB-180

Shine, Ted 1931- DLB-38

Ship, Reuben 1915-1975 . . . . DLB-88

Shirer, William L. 1904-1993 . . . . . . DLB-4

Shirinsky-Shikhmatov, Sergii Aleksandrovich
   1783-1837 . . . . DLB-150

Shirley, James 1596-1666 . . . . DLB-58

Shishkov, Aleksandr Semenovich
   1753-1841 . . . . DLB-150

Shockley, Ann Allen 1927- DLB-33

Shōno, Junzō 1921- DLB-182

Short, Peter
   [publishing house] DLB-170

Shorthouse, Joseph Henry
   1834-1903 . . . . DLB-18

Showalter, Elaine 1941- DLB-67

Shulevitz, Uri 1935- DLB-61

Shulman, Max 1919-1988 . . . . DLB-11

Shute, Henry A. 1856-1943 . . . . DLB-9

Shuttle, Penelope 1947- DLB-14, 40

Sibbes, Richard 1577-1635 . . . . DLB-151

Sidgwick and Jackson Limited DLB-112

Sidney, Margaret (see Lothrop, Harriet M.)

Sidney, Mary 1561-1621 . . . . DLB-167

Sidney, Sir Philip 1554-1586 . . . . . . DLB-167

Sidney's Press DLB-49

Siegfried Loraine Sassoon: A Centenary Essay
   Tributes from Vivien F. Clarke and
   Michael Thorpe Y-86

Sierra, Rubén 1946- DLB-122

Sierra Club Books DLB-49

Siger of Brabant
   circa 1240-circa 1284 . . . . DLB-115

Sigourney, Lydia Howard (Huntley)
   1791-1865 . . . . DLB-1, 42, 73, 183

Silkin, Jon 1930- DLB-27

Silko, Leslie Marmon
   1948- DLB-143, 175

Silliman, Benjamin 1779-1864 . . . . . DLB-183

Silliman, Ron 1946- DLB-169

Silliphant, Stirling 1918- DLB-26

Sillitoe, Alan 1928- DLB-14, 139

Silman, Roberta 1934- DLB-28

Silva, Beverly 1930- DLB-122

Silverberg, Robert 1935- DLB-8

Silverman, Kenneth 1936- DLB-111

Simak, Clifford D. 1904-1988 . . . . . . DLB-8

Simcoe, Elizabeth 1762-1850 . . . . . . DLB-99

Simcox, George Augustus
1841-1905 . . . . DLB-35

Sime, Jessie Georgina 1868-1958 . . . . DLB-92

Simenon, Georges
1903-1989. . . . . DLB-72; Y-89

Simic, Charles 1938- DLB-105

Simic, Charles,
Images and "Images" DLB-105

Simmel, Johannes Mario 1924- DLB-69

Simmes, Valentine
[publishing house] DLB-170

Simmons, Ernest J. 1903-1972 . . . . DLB-103

Simmons, Herbert Alfred 1930- DLB-33

Simmons, James 1933- DLB-40

Simms, William Gilmore
1806-1870 . . . . DLB-3, 30, 59, 73

Simms and M'Intyre. DLB-106

Simon, Claude 1913- DLB-83

Simon, Neil 1927- DLB-7

Simon and Schuster. DLB-46

Simons, Katherine Drayton Mayrant
1890-1969 . . . . Y-83

Simović, Ljubomir 1935- DLB-181

Simpkin and Marshall
[publishing house] DLB-154

Simpson, Helen 1897-1940 . . . . . . DLB-77

Simpson, Louis 1923- DLB-5

Simpson, N. F. 1919- DLB-13

Sims, George 1923- DLB-87

Sims, George Robert
1847-1922 . . . . DLB-35, 70, 135

Sinán, Rogelio 1904- DLB-145

Sinclair, Andrew 1935- DLB-14

Sinclair, Bertrand William
1881-1972 . . . . DLB-92

Sinclair, Catherine
1800-1864 . . . . DLB-163

Sinclair, Jo 1913- DLB-28

Sinclair Lewis Centennial
Conference Y-85

Sinclair, Lister 1921- DLB-88

Sinclair, May 1863-1946. . . . . . DLB-36, 135

Sinclair, Upton 1878-1968 . . . . DLB-9

Sinclair, Upton [publishing house] DLB-46

Singer, Isaac Bashevis
1904-1991 . . . . DLB-6, 28, 52; Y-91

Singmaster, Elsie 1879-1958 . . . . DLB-9

Sinisgalli, Leonardo 1908-1981 . . . . . DLB-114

Siodmak, Curt 1902- DLB-44

Sissman, L. E. 1928-1976 . . . . DLB-5

Sisson, C. H. 1914- DLB-27

Sitwell, Edith 1887-1964 . . . . DLB-20

Sitwell, Osbert 1892-1969 . . . . DLB-100

Skármeta, Antonio 1940- DLB-145

Skeffington, William
[publishing house] DLB-106

Skelton, John 1463-1529 . . . . DLB-136

Skelton, Robin 1925- DLB-27, 53

Skinner, Constance Lindsay
1877-1939 . . . . DLB-92

Skinner, John Stuart 1788-1851 . . . . DLB-73

Skipsey, Joseph 1832-1903 . . . . DLB-35

Slade, Bernard 1930- DLB-53

Slamnig, Ivan 1930- DLB-181

Slater, Patrick 1880-1951 . . . . DLB-68

Slaveykov, Pencho 1866-1912 . . . . . DLB-147

Slaviček, Milivoj 1929- DLB-181

Slavitt, David 1935- DLB-5, 6

Sleigh, Burrows Willcocks Arthur
1821-1869 . . . . DLB-99

A Slender Thread of Hope: The Kennedy
Center Black Theatre Project DLB-38

Slesinger, Tess 1905-1945 . . . . DLB-102

Slick, Sam (see Haliburton, Thomas Chandler)

Sloane, William, Associates DLB-46

Small, Maynard and Company DLB-49

Small Presses in Great Britain and Ireland,
1960-1985 . . . . DLB-40

Small Presses I: Jargon Society Y-84

Small Presses II: The Spirit That Moves
Us Press Y-85

Small Presses III: Pushcart Press Y-87

Smart, Christopher 1722-1771 . . . . . DLB-109

Smart, David A. 1892-1957 . . . . . . DLB-137

Smart, Elizabeth 1913-1986 . . . . . . DLB-88

Smellie, William
[publishing house] DLB-154

Smiles, Samuel 1812-1904 . . . . DLB-55

Smith, A. J. M. 1902-1980 . . . . . . DLB-88

Smith, Adam 1723-1790 . . . . DLB-104

Smith, Alexander 1829-1867 . . . . DLB-32, 55

Smith, Betty 1896-1972. . . . . Y-82

Smith, Carol Sturm 1938- Y-81

Smith, Charles Henry 1826-1903 . . . DLB-11

Smith, Charlotte 1749-1806 . . . . DLB-39, 109

Smith, Chet 1899-1973 . . . . DLB-171

Smith, Cordwainer 1913-1966 . . . . . . DLB-8

Smith, Dave 1942- DLB-5

Smith, Dodie 1896- DLB-10

Smith, Doris Buchanan 1934- DLB-52

Smith, E. E. 1890-1965 . . . . DLB-8

Smith, Elihu Hubbard 1771-1798 . . . . DLB-37

Smith, Elizabeth Oakes (Prince)
1806-1893. . . . . DLB-1

Smith, F. Hopkinson 1838-1915 . . . . . DS-13

Smith, George D. 1870-1920 . . . . . DLB-140

Smith, George O. 1911-1981 . . . . . . DLB-8

Smith, Goldwin 1823-1910 . . . . DLB-99

Smith, H. Allen 1907-1976. . . . . DLB-11, 29

Smith, Hazel Brannon 1914- DLB-127

Smith, Henry
circa 1560-circa 1591 . . . . DLB-136

Smith, Horatio (Horace)
1779-1849 . . . . DLB-116

Smith, Horatio (Horace) 1779-1849 and
James Smith 1775-1839 . . . . DLB-96

Smith, Iain Crichton
1928- DLB-40, 139

Smith, J. Allen 1860-1924. . . . . . . DLB-47

Smith, John 1580-1631 . . . . . . DLB-24, 30

Smith, Josiah 1704-1781. . . . . DLB-24

Smith, Ken 1938- DLB-40

Smith, Lee 1944- DLB-143; Y-83

Smith, Logan Pearsall 1865-1946. . . . DLB-98

Smith, Mark 1935- Y-82

Smith, Michael 1698-circa 1771 . . . . DLB-31

Smith, Red 1905-1982. . . . . . DLB-29, 171

Smith, Roswell 1829-1892 . . . . DLB-79

Smith, Samuel Harrison
1772-1845 . . . . DLB-43

Smith, Samuel Stanhope
1751-1819 . . . . DLB-37

Smith, Sarah (see Stretton, Hesba)

Smith, Seba 1792-1868. . . . . . . DLB-1, 11

Smith, Sir Thomas 1513-1577. . . . . DLB-132

Smith, Stevie 1902-1971. . . . . DLB-20

Smith, Sydney 1771-1845 . . . . DLB-107

Smith, Sydney Goodsir 1915-1975 . . . DLB-27

Smith, Wendell 1914-1972. . . . . . . DLB-171

Smith, William
flourished 1595-1597 . . . . DLB-136

Smith, William 1727-1803 . . . . . . DLB-31

Smith, William 1728-1793 . . . . . . DLB-30

Smith, William Gardner
1927-1974 . . . . DLB-76

Smith, William Henry
1808-1872 . . . . DLB-159

Smith, William Jay 1918- DLB-5

Smith, Elder and Company. DLB-154

Smith, Harrison, and Robert Haas
[publishing house] DLB-46

Smith, J. Stilman, and Company DLB-49

Smith, W. B., and Company DLB-49

Smith, W. H., and Son DLB-106

Smithers, Leonard
[publishing house] DLB-112

Smollett, Tobias 1721-1771 . . . . . DLB-39, 104

Snellings, Rolland (see Touré, Askia
Muhammad)

Snodgrass, W. D. 1926- DLB-5

Snow, C. P. 1905-1980 . . . . DLB-15, 77

Snyder, Gary 1930- DLB-5, 16, 165

Sobiloff, Hy 1912-1970 . . . . DLB-48

The Society for Textual Scholarship and
TEXT Y-87

The Society for the History of Authorship, Reading and Publishing Y-92

Soffici, Ardengo 1879-1964 . . . . . . DLB-114

Sofola, 'Zulu 1938- DLB-157

Solano, Solita 1888-1975 . . . . DLB-4

Soldati, Mario 1906- DLB-177

Šoljan, Antun 1932-1993 . . . . DLB-181

Sollers, Philippe 1936- DLB-83

Solmi, Sergio 1899-1981 . . . . DLB-114

Solomon, Carl 1928- DLB-16

Solway, David 1941- DLB-53

Solzhenitsyn and America Y-85

Somerville, Edith Œnone
1858-1949 . . . . DLB-135

Song, Cathy 1955- DLB-169

Sono, Ayako 1931- DLB-182

Sontag, Susan 1933- DLB-2, 67

Sophocles 497/496 B.C.-406/405 B.C.
. . . . DLB-176

Šopov, Aco 1923-1982 . . . . DLB-181

Sorge, Reinhard Johannes
1892-1916 . . . . DLB-118

Sorrentino, Gilbert
1929- DLB-5, 173; Y-80

Sotheby, William 1757-1833 . . . . . . DLB-93

Soto, Gary 1952- DLB-82

Sources for the Study of Tudor and Stuart Drama
DLB-62

Souster, Raymond 1921- DLB-88

The *South English Legendary*
circa thirteenth-fifteenth
centuries DLB-146

Southerland, Ellease 1943- DLB-33

Southern Illinois University Press Y-95

Southern, Terry 1924- DLB-2

Southern Writers Between the
Wars DLB-9

Southerne, Thomas 1659-1746 . . . . . DLB-80

Southey, Caroline Anne Bowles
1786-1854 . . . . DLB-116

Southey, Robert
1774-1843 . . . . DLB-93, 107, 142

Southwell, Robert 1561?-1595 . . . . . DLB-167

Sowande, Bode 1948- DLB-157

Sowle, Tace
[publishing house] DLB-170

Soyfer, Jura 1912-1939 . . . . DLB-124

Soyinka, Wole 1934- DLB-125; Y-86, 87

Spacks, Barry 1931- DLB-105

Spalding, Frances 1950- DLB-155

Spark, Muriel 1918- DLB-15, 139

Sparke, Michael
[publishing house] DLB-170

Sparks, Jared 1789-1866 . . . . DLB-1, 30

Sparshott, Francis 1926- DLB-60

Späth, Gerold 1939- DLB-75

Spatola, Adriano 1941-1988 . . . . . . DLB-128

Spaziani, Maria Luisa 1924- DLB-128

The Spectator 1828- DLB-110

Spedding, James 1808-1881 . . . . . . DLB-144

Spee von Langenfeld, Friedrich
1591-1635 . . . . DLB-164

Speght, Rachel 1597-after 1630 . . . . DLB-126

Speke, John Hanning 1827-1864 . . . . DLB-166

Spellman, A. B. 1935- DLB-41

Spence, Thomas 1750-1814 . . . . . . DLB-158

Spencer, Anne 1882-1975 . . . . . . DLB-51, 54

Spencer, Elizabeth 1921- DLB-6

Spencer, Herbert 1820-1903 . . . . . . DLB-57

Spencer, Scott 1945- Y-86

Spender, J. A. 1862-1942 . . . . DLB-98

Spender, Stephen 1909- DLB-20

Spener, Philipp Jakob 1635-1705 . . . . DLB-164

Spenser, Edmund circa 1552-1599 . . . DLB-167

Sperr, Martin 1944- DLB-124

Spicer, Jack 1925-1965 . . . . DLB-5, 16

Spielberg, Peter 1929- Y-81

Spielhagen, Friedrich 1829-1911 . . . . DLB-129

"*Spielmannsepen*"
(circa 1152-circa 1500) DLB-148

Spier, Peter 1927- DLB-61

Spinrad, Norman 1940- DLB-8

Spires, Elizabeth 1952- DLB-120

Spitteler, Carl 1845-1924 . . . . DLB-129

Spivak, Lawrence E. 1900- DLB-137

Spofford, Harriet Prescott
1835-1921 . . . . DLB-74

Squibob (see Derby, George Horatio)

The St. John's College Robert Graves Trust
. . . . Y-96

Stacpoole, H. de Vere
1863-1951 . . . . DLB-153

Staël, Germaine de 1766-1817 . . . . . DLB-119

Staël-Holstein, Anne-Louise Germaine de
(see Staël, Germaine de)

Stafford, Jean 1915-1979 . . . . . . DLB-2, 173

Stafford, William 1914- DLB-5

Stage Censorship: "The Rejected Statement"
(1911), by Bernard Shaw
[excerpts] DLB-10

Stallings, Laurence 1894-1968 . . . . . DLB-7, 44

Stallworthy, Jon 1935- DLB-40

Stampp, Kenneth M. 1912- DLB-17

Stanev, Emiliyan 1907-1979 . . . . . . DLB-181

Stanford, Ann 1916- DLB-5

Stanković, Borisav ("Bora")
1876-1927 . . . . DLB-147

Stanley, Henry M. 1841-1904 . . . . . . DS-13

Stanley, Thomas 1625-1678 . . . . . . DLB-131

Stannard, Martin 1947- DLB-155

Stansby, William
[publishing house] DLB-170

Stanton, Elizabeth Cady 1815-1902 . . . DLB-79

Stanton, Frank L. 1857-1927 . . . . . . DLB-25

Stanton, Maura 1946- DLB-120

Stapledon, Olaf 1886-1950 . . . . DLB-15

Star Spangled Banner Office DLB-49

Starkey, Thomas circa 1499-1538 . . . . DLB-132

Starkweather, David 1935- DLB-7

Statements on the Art of Poetry DLB-54

Stationers' Company of
London, The DLB-170

Stead, Robert J. C. 1880-1959 . . . . . DLB-92

Steadman, Mark 1930- DLB-6

The Stealthy School of Criticism (1871), by
Dante Gabriel Rossetti DLB-35

Stearns, Harold E. 1891-1943 . . . . . . DLB-4

Stedman, Edmund Clarence
1833-1908 . . . . DLB-64

Steegmuller, Francis 1906-1994 . . . . . DLB-111

Steel, Flora Annie
1847-1929 . . . . DLB-153, 156

Steele, Max 1922- Y-80

Steele, Richard 1672-1729 . . . . . DLB-84, 101

Steele, Timothy 1948- DLB-120

Steele, Wilbur Daniel 1886-1970 . . . . DLB-86

Steere, Richard circa 1643-1721 . . . . DLB-24

Stefanovski, Goran 1952- DLB-181

Stegner, Wallace 1909-1993 . . . . DLB-9; Y-93

Stehr, Hermann 1864-1940 . . . . DLB-66

Steig, William 1907- DLB-61

Stein, Gertrude 1874-1946 DLB-4, 54, 86; DS-15

Stein, Leo 1872-1947 . . . . DLB-4

Stein and Day Publishers DLB-46

Steinbeck, John 1902-1968 . . . . DLB-7, 9; DS-2

Steiner, George 1929- DLB-67

Steinhoewel, Heinrich
1411/1412-1479 . . . . DLB-179

Stendhal 1783-1842 . . . . DLB-119

Stephen Crane: A Revaluation Virginia
Tech Conference, 1989 . . . . Y-89

Stephen, Leslie 1832-1904. . . . . DLB-57, 144

Stephens, Alexander H. 1812-1883. . . . DLB-47

Stephens, Ann 1810-1886 . . . . . . DLB-3, 73

Stephens, Charles Asbury
1844?-1931 . . . . DLB-42

Stephens, James
1882?-1950. . . . . DLB-19, 153, 162

Stephens, John Lloyd 1805-1852 . . . . DLB-183

Sterling, George 1869-1926 . . . . DLB-54

Sterling, James 1701-1763. . . . . DLB-24

Sterling, John 1806-1844. . . . . DLB-116

Stern, Gerald 1925- DLB-105

Stern, Madeleine B. 1912- DLB-111, 140

Stern, Gerald, Living in Ruin. DLB-105

Stern, Richard 1928- Y-87

Stern, Stewart 1922- DLB-26

Sterne, Laurence 1713-1768. . . . . . . DLB-39

Sternheim, Carl 1878-1942 . . . . DLB-56, 118

Sternhold, Thomas ?-1549 and
John Hopkins ?-1570 . . . . DLB-132

Stevens, Henry 1819-1886. . . . . . . DLB-140

Stevens, Wallace 1879-1955. . . . . . . DLB-54

Stevenson, Anne 1933- DLB-40

Stevenson, Lionel 1902-1973 . . . . . DLB-155

Stevenson, Robert Louis 1850-1894
. . . . DLB-18, 57, 141, 156, 174; DS-13

Stewart, Donald Ogden
1894-1980 . . . . DLB-4, 11, 26

Stewart, Dugald 1753-1828 . . . . DLB-31

Stewart, George, Jr. 1848-1906 . . . . . DLB-99

Stewart, George R. 1895-1980 . . . . . . DLB-8

Stewart and Kidd Company DLB-46

Stewart, Randall 1896-1964 . . . . . . DLB-103

Stickney, Trumbull 1874-1904 . . . . . DLB-54

Stieler, Caspar 1632-1707 . . . . DLB-164

Stifter, Adalbert 1805-1868 . . . . . . DLB-133

Stiles, Ezra 1727-1795. . . . . DLB-31

Still, James 1906- DLB-9

Stirner, Max 1806-1856 . . . . DLB-129

Stith, William 1707-1755 . . . . DLB-31

Stock, Elliot [publishing house] DLB-106

Stockton, Frank R.
1834-1902. . . . . DLB-42, 74; DS-13

Stoddard, Ashbel
[publishing house]. DLB-49

Stoddard, Richard Henry
1825-1903 . . . . DLB-3, 64; DS-13

Stoddard, Solomon 1643-1729 . . . . . . DLB-24

Stoker, Bram 1847-1912 . . . . DLB-36, 70, 178

Stokes, Frederick A., Company DLB-49

Stokes, Thomas L. 1898-1958 . . . . . . DLB-29

Stokesbury, Leon 1945- DLB-120

Stolberg, Christian Graf zu
1748-1821 . . . . DLB-94

Stolberg, Friedrich Leopold Graf zu
1750-1819 . . . . DLB-94

Stone, Herbert S., and Company DLB-49

Stone, Lucy 1818-1893 . . . . DLB-79

Stone, Melville 1848-1929. . . . . DLB-25

Stone, Robert 1937- DLB-152

Stone, Ruth 1915- DLB-105

Stone, Samuel 1602-1663 . . . . DLB-24

Stone and Kimball DLB-49

Stoppard, Tom 1937- DLB-13; Y-85

Storey, Anthony 1928- DLB-14

Storey, David 1933- DLB-13, 14

Storm, Theodor 1817-1888 . . . . . . DLB-129

Story, Thomas circa 1670-1742 . . . . . DLB-31

Story, William Wetmore 1819-1895. . . . DLB-1

Storytelling: A Contemporary
Renaissance. Y-84

Stoughton, William 1631-1701 . . . . . DLB-24

Stow, John 1525-1605 . . . . DLB-132

Stowe, Harriet Beecher
1811-1896 . . . . DLB-1, 12, 42, 74

Stowe, Leland 1899- DLB-29

Stoyanov, Dimitŭr Ivanov (see Elin Pelin)

Strabo 64 or 63 B.C.-circa A.D. 25
. . . . DLB-176

Strachey, Lytton
1880-1932 . . . . DLB-149; DS-10

Strachey, Lytton, Preface to Eminent
Victorians DLB-149

Strahan and Company DLB-106

Strahan, William
[publishing house] DLB-154

Strand, Mark 1934- DLB-5

The Strasbourg Oaths 842 . . . . . . DLB-148

Stratemeyer, Edward 1862-1930 . . . . DLB-42

Strati, Saverio 1924- DLB-177

Stratton and Barnard DLB-49

Stratton-Porter, Gene 1863-1924 . . . . . DS-14

Straub, Peter 1943- Y-84

Strauß, Botho 1944- DLB-124

Strauß, David Friedrich
1808-1874 . . . . DLB-133

The Strawberry Hill Press DLB-154

Streatfeild, Noel 1895-1986 . . . . . . DLB-160

Street, Cecil John Charles (see Rhode, John)

Street, G. S. 1867-1936 . . . . DLB-135

Street and Smith DLB-49

Streeter, Edward 1891-1976. . . . . . . DLB-11

Streeter, Thomas Winthrop
1883-1965 . . . . DLB-140

Stretton, Hesba 1832-1911. . . . . . . DLB-163

Stribling, T. S. 1881-1965 . . . . DLB-9

Der Stricker circa 1190-circa 1250 . . . DLB-138

Strickland, Samuel 1804-1867. . . . . . DLB-99

Stringer and Townsend. DLB-49

Stringer, Arthur 1874-1950 . . . . DLB-92

Strittmatter, Erwin 1912- DLB-69

Strniša, Gregor 1930-1987 . . . . DLB-181

Strode, William 1630-1645 . . . . . . DLB-126

Strother, David Hunter 1816-1888 . . . . DLB-3

Strouse, Jean 1945- DLB-111

Stuart, Dabney 1937- DLB-105

Stuart, Dabney, Knots into Webs: Some Autobiographical Sources. DLB-105

Stuart, Jesse
1906-1984 . . . . . . DLB-9, 48, 102; Y-84

Stuart, Lyle [publishing house] DLB-46

Stubbs, Harry Clement (see Clement, Hal)

Stubenberg, Johann Wilhelm von
1619-1663 . . . . DLB-164

Studio. DLB-112

The Study of Poetry (1880), by
Matthew Arnold DLB-35

Sturgeon, Theodore
1918-1985 . . . . DLB-8; Y-85

Sturges, Preston 1898-1959 . . . . DLB-26

"Style" (1840; revised, 1859), by
Thomas de Quincey [excerpt] DLB-57

"Style" (1888), by Walter Pater DLB-57

Style (1897), by Walter Raleigh
[excerpt] DLB-57

"Style" (1877), by T. H. Wright
[excerpt] DLB-57

"Le Style c'est l'homme" (1892), by
W. H. Mallock. DLB-57

Styron, William 1925- DLB-2, 143; Y-80

Suárez, Mario 1925- DLB-82

Such, Peter 1939- DLB-60

Suckling, Sir John 1609-1641? . . . DLB-58, 126

Suckow, Ruth 1892-1960. . . . . . . DLB-9, 102

Sudermann, Hermann 1857-1928 . . . . DLB-118

Sue, Eugène 1804-1857 . . . . DLB-119

Sue, Marie-Joseph (see Sue, Eugène)

Suggs, Simon (see Hooper, Johnson Jones)

Sukenick, Ronald 1932- DLB-173; Y-81

Suknaski, Andrew 1942- DLB-53

Sullivan, Alan 1868-1947 . . . . DLB-92

Sullivan, C. Gardner 1886-1965 . . . . . DLB-26

Sullivan, Frank 1892-1976 . . . . DLB-11

Sulte, Benjamin 1841-1923 . . . . DLB-99

Sulzberger, Arthur Hays
1891-1968 . . . . DLB-127

Sulzberger, Arthur Ochs 1926- DLB-127

Sulzer, Johann Georg 1720-1779 . . . . . DLB-97

Sumarokov, Aleksandr Petrovich
1717-1777 . . . . DLB-150

Summers, Hollis 1916- DLB-6

Sumner, Henry A.
[publishing house] DLB-49

Surtees, Robert Smith 1803-1864 . . . . . DLB-21

Surveys: Japanese Literature,
1987-1995 . . . . DLB-182

A Survey of Poetry Anthologies,
1879-1960 . . . . DLB-54

Surveys of the Year's Biographies

A Transit of Poets and Others: American
Biography in 1982 . . . . Y-82

The Year in Literary Biography . . . Y-83–Y-96

Survey of the Year's Book Publishing

The Year in Book Publishing Y-86

Survey of the Year's Children's Books

The Year in Children's Books Y-92–Y-96

Surveys of the Year's Drama

The Year in Drama
. . . . Y-82–Y-85, Y-87–Y-96

The Year in London Theatre Y-92

Surveys of the Year's Fiction

The Year's Work in Fiction:
A Survey Y-82

The Year in Fiction: A Biased View Y-83

The Year in
Fiction Y-84–Y-86, Y-89, Y-94–Y-96

The Year in the
Novel Y-87, Y-88, Y-90–Y-93

The Year in Short Stories Y-87

The Year in the
Short Story Y-88, Y-90–Y-93

Survey of the Year's Literary Theory

The Year in Literary Theory Y-92–Y-93

Surveys of the Year's Poetry

The Year's Work in American
Poetry Y-82

The Year in Poetry Y-83–Y-92, Y-94–Y-96

Sutherland, Efua Theodora
1924- DLB-117

Sutherland, John 1919-1956 . . . . DLB-68

Sutro, Alfred 1863-1933 . . . . DLB-10

Swados, Harvey 1920-1972 . . . . DLB-2

Swain, Charles 1801-1874 . . . . DLB-32

Swallow Press DLB-46

Swan Sonnenschein Limited DLB-106

Swanberg, W. A. 1907- DLB-103

Swenson, May 1919-1989 . . . . DLB-5

Swerling, Jo 1897- DLB-44

Swift, Jonathan
1667-1745 . . . . DLB-39, 95, 101

Swinburne, A. C. 1837-1909 . . . . . DLB-35, 57

Swineshead, Richard floruit
circa 1350 . . . . DLB-115

Swinnerton, Frank 1884-1982 . . . . . . DLB-34

Swisshelm, Jane Grey 1815-1884 . . . . . DLB-43

Swope, Herbert Bayard 1882-1958 . . . . DLB-25

Swords, T. and J., and Company DLB-49

Swords, Thomas 1763-1843 and
Swords, James ?-1844 . . . . DLB-73

Sykes, Ella C. ?-1939 . . . . DLB-174

Sylvester, Josuah
1562 or 1563 - 1618 . . . . DLB-121

Symonds, Emily Morse (see Paston, George)

Symonds, John Addington
1840-1893 . . . . DLB-57, 144

Symons, A. J. A. 1900-1941 . . . . . . DLB-149

Sùmons, Arthur
1865-1945 . . . . DLB-19, 57, 149

Symons, Julian
1912-1994 . . . . DLB-87, 155; Y-92

Symons, Scott 1933- DLB-53

A Symposium on *The Columbia History of
the Novel* Y-92

Synge, John Millington
1871-1909 . . . . DLB-10, 19

Synge Summer School: J. M. Synge and the Irish
Theater, Rathdrum, County Wiclow, Ireland
. . . . Y-93

Syrett, Netta 1865-1943 . . . . DLB-135

Szymborska, Wisława 1923- Y-96

T

Taban lo Liyong 1939?- DLB-125

Taché, Joseph-Charles 1820-1894 . . . . . DLB-99

Tachihara, Masaaki 1926-1980 . . . . . DLB-182

Tadijanović, Dragutin 1905- DLB-181

Tafolla, Carmen 1951- DLB-82

Taggard, Genevieve 1894-1948 . . . . . . DLB-45

Tagger, Theodor (see Bruckner, Ferdinand)

Tait, J. Selwin, and Sons DLB-49

Tait's Edinburgh Magazine
1832-1861 . . . . DLB-110

The Takarazaka Revue Company Y-91

Talander (see Bohse, August)

Talev, Dimitŭr 1898-1966 . . . . DLB-181

Tallent, Elizabeth 1954- DLB-130

Talvj 1797-1870 . . . . DLB-59, 133

Tan, Amy 1952- DLB-173

Tanizaki, Jun'ichirō 1886-1965 . . . . . DLB-180

Tapahonso, Luci 1953- DLB-175

Taradash, Daniel 1913- DLB-44

Tarbell, Ida M. 1857-1944 . . . . DLB-47

Tardivel, Jules-Paul 1851-1905 . . . . . . DLB-99

Targan, Barry 1932- DLB-130

Tarkington, Booth 1869-1946 . . . . DLB-9, 102

Tashlin, Frank 1913-1972 . . . . DLB-44

Tate, Allen 1899-1979 . . . . . . DLB-4, 45, 63

Tate, James 1943- DLB-5, 169

Tate, Nahum circa 1652-1715 . . . . . . DLB-80

Tatian circa 830 . . . . DLB-148

Taufer, Veno 1933- DLB-181

Tauler, Johannes circa 1300-1361 . . . . DLB-179

Tavčar, Ivan 1851-1923 . . . . DLB-147

Taylor, Ann 1782-1866 . . . . DLB-163

Taylor, Bayard 1825-1878 . . . . DLB-3

Taylor, Bert Leston 1866-1921 . . . . . . DLB-25

Taylor, Charles H. 1846-1921 . . . . . . DLB-25

Taylor, Edward circa 1642-1729 . . . . . DLB-24

Taylor, Elizabeth 1912-1975 . . . . . . DLB-139

Taylor, Henry 1942- DLB-5

Taylor, Sir Henry 1800-1886 . . . . . . DLB-32

Taylor, Jane 1783-1824 . . . . DLB-163

Taylor, Jeremy circa 1613-1667 . . . . . DLB-151

Taylor, John 1577 or 1578 - 1653 . . . DLB-121

Taylor, Mildred D. ?- DLB-52

Taylor, Peter 1917-1994 . . . . Y-81, Y-94

Taylor, William, and Company DLB-49

Taylor-Made Shakespeare? Or Is
"Shall I Die?" the Long-Lost Text
of Bottom's Dream? Y-85

Teasdale, Sara 1884-1933 . . . . DLB-45

The Tea-Table (1725), by Eliza Haywood [excerpt]
DLB-39

Telles, Lygia Fagundes 1924- DLB-113

Temple, Sir William 1628-1699 . . . . . DLB-101

Tenn, William 1919- DLB-8

Tennant, Emma 1937- DLB-14

Tenney, Tabitha Gilman 1762-1837 . . . DLB-37

Tennyson, Alfred 1809-1892 . . . . . . DLB-32

Tennyson, Frederick 1807-1898 . . . . . DLB-32

Terhune, Albert Payson 1872-1942 . . . . DLB-9

Terhune, Mary Virginia 1830-1922 . . . . DS-13

Terry, Megan 1932- DLB-7

Terson, Peter 1932- DLB-13

Tesich, Steve 1943- Y-83

Tessa, Delio 1886-1939 . . . . DLB-114

Testori, Giovanni 1923-1993 . . . . DLB-128, 177

Tey, Josephine 1896?-1952 . . . . DLB-77

Thacher, James 1754-1844 . . . . DLB-37

Thackeray, William Makepeace
1811-1863 . . . . DLB-21, 55, 159, 163

Thames and Hudson Limited DLB-112

Thanet, Octave (see French, Alice)

The Theater in Shakespeare's Time . . . DLB-62

The Theatre Guild DLB-7

Thegan and the Astronomer
flourished circa 850 . . . . DLB-148

Thelwall, John 1764-1834 . . . . . DLB-93, 158

Theocritus circa 300 B.C.-260 B.C.
. . . . DLB-176

Theodulf circa 760-circa 821 . . . . DLB-148

Theophrastus circa 371 B.C.-287 B.C.
. . . . DLB-176

Theriault, Yves 1915-1983 . . . . DLB-88

Thério, Adrien 1925- DLB-53

Theroux, Paul 1941- DLB-2

They All Came to Paris DS-16

Thibaudeau, Colleen 1925- DLB-88

Thielen, Benedict 1903-1965 . . . . . . DLB-102

Thiong'o Ngugi wa (see Ngugi wa Thiong'o)

Third-Generation Minor Poets of the
Seventeenth Century DLB-131

This Quarter 1925-1927, 1929-1932 . . . . . DS-15

Thoma, Ludwig 1867-1921 . . . . DLB-66

Thoma, Richard 1902- DLB-4

Thomas, Audrey 1935- DLB-60

Thomas, D. M. 1935- DLB-40

Thomas, Dylan
1914-1953 . . . . DLB-13, 20, 139

Thomas, Edward
1878-1917 . . . . DLB-19, 98, 156

Thomas, Gwyn 1913-1981 . . . . DLB-15

Thomas, Isaiah 1750-1831 . . . . . DLB-43, 73

Thomas, Isaiah [publishing house] DLB-49

Thomas, Johann 1624-1679 . . . . . . DLB-168

Thomas, John 1900-1932 . . . . DLB-4

Thomas, Joyce Carol 1938- DLB-33

Thomas, Lorenzo 1944- DLB-41

Thomas, R. S. 1915- DLB-27

Thomasîn von Zerclære
circa 1186-circa 1259 . . . . DLB-138

Thomasius, Christian 1655-1728 . . . . DLB-168

Thompson, David 1770-1857 . . . . . . DLB-99

Thompson, Dorothy 1893-1961 . . . . . DLB-29

Thompson, Francis 1859-1907 . . . . . DLB-19

Thompson, George Selden (see Selden, George)

Thompson, John 1938-1976 . . . . . . DLB-60

Thompson, John R. 1823-1873 . . . . DLB-3, 73

Thompson, Lawrance 1906-1973 . . . . DLB-103

Thompson, Maurice
1844-1901 . . . . DLB-71, 74

Thompson, Ruth Plumly
1891-1976 . . . . DLB-22

Thompson, Thomas Phillips
1843-1933 . . . . DLB-99

Thompson, William 1775-1833 . . . . . DLB-158

Thompson, William Tappan
1812-1882 . . . . DLB-3, 11

Thomson, Edward William
1849-1924 . . . . DLB-92

Thomson, James 1700-1748 . . . . DLB-95

Thomson, James 1834-1882 . . . . DLB-35

Thomson, Joseph 1858-1895 . . . . . . DLB-174

Thomson, Mortimer 1831-1875 . . . . . DLB-11

Thoreau, Henry David
1817-1862 . . . . DLB-1, 183

Thorpe, Thomas Bangs
1815-1878 . . . . DLB-3, 11

Thoughts on Poetry and Its Varieties (1833),
by John Stuart Mill DLB-32

Thrale, Hester Lynch (see Piozzi, Hester
Lynch [Thrale])

Thucydides circa 455 B.C.-circa 395 B.C.
. . . . DLB-176

Thümmel, Moritz August von
1738-1817 . . . . DLB-97

Thurber, James
1894-1961 . . . . DLB-4, 11, 22, 102

Thurman, Wallace 1902-1934 . . . . . . DLB-51

Thwaite, Anthony 1930- DLB-40

Thwaites, Reuben Gold
1853-1913 . . . . DLB-47

Ticknor, George
1791-1871 . . . . DLB-1, 59, 140

Ticknor and Fields DLB-49

Ticknor and Fields (revived) DLB-46

Tieck, Ludwig 1773-1853 . . . . DLB-90

Tietjens, Eunice 1884-1944 . . . . DLB-54

Tilney, Edmund circa 1536-1610 . . . . DLB-136

Tilt, Charles [publishing house] DLB-106

Tilton, J. E., and Company DLB-49

Time and Western Man (1927), by Wyndham
Lewis [excerpts] DLB-36

Time-Life Books DLB-46

Times Books DLB-46

Timothy, Peter circa 1725-1782 . . . . DLB-43

Timrod, Henry 1828-1867 . . . . DLB-3

Tinker, Chauncey Brewster
1876-1963 . . . . DLB-140

Tinsley Brothers DLB-106

Tiptree, James, Jr. 1915-1987 . . . . . . DLB-8

Tišma, Aleksandar 1924- DLB-181

Titus, Edward William
1870-1952 . . . . DLB-4; DS-15

Tlali, Miriam 1933- DLB-157

Todd, Barbara Euphan
1890-1976 . . . . DLB-160

Tofte, Robert
1561 or 1562-1619 or 1620 . . . . DLB-172

Toklas, Alice B. 1877-1967 . . . . DLB-4

Tokuda, Shūsei 1872-1943 . . . . DLB-180

Tolkien, J. R. R. 1892-1973 . . . . DLB-15, 160

Toller, Ernst 1893-1939 . . . . DLB-124

Tollet, Elizabeth 1694-1754 . . . . DLB-95

Tolson, Melvin B. 1898-1966 . . . . DLB-48, 76

Tom Jones (1749), by Henry Fielding
[excerpt] DLB-39

Tomalin, Claire 1933- DLB-155

Tomasi di Lampedusa,
Giuseppe 1896-1957 . . . . DLB-177

Tomlinson, Charles 1927- DLB-40

Tomlinson, H. M. 1873-1958 . . . DLB-36, 100

Tompkins, Abel [publishing house] . . . DLB-49

Tompson, Benjamin 1642-1714 . . . . . DLB-24

Tonks, Rosemary 1932- DLB-14

Tonna, Charlotte Elizabeth
1790-1846 . . . . DLB-163

Tonson, Jacob the Elder
[publishing house] DLB-170

Toole, John Kennedy 1937-1969 . . . . . Y-81

Toomer, Jean 1894-1967 . . . . . . DLB-45, 51

Tor Books DLB-46

Torberg, Friedrich 1908-1979 . . . . . . DLB-85

Torrence, Ridgely 1874-1950 . . . . . . DLB-54

Torres-Metzger, Joseph V.
1933- DLB-122

Toth, Susan Allen 1940- Y-86

Tottell, Richard
[publishing house] DLB-170

Tough-Guy Literature DLB-9

Touré, Askia Muhammad 1938- DLB-41

Tourgée, Albion W. 1838-1905 . . . . . DLB-79

Tourneur, Cyril circa 1580-1626 . . . . . DLB-58

Tournier, Michel 1924- DLB-83

Tousey, Frank [publishing house] DLB-49

Tower Publications DLB-46

Towne, Benjamin circa 1740-1793 . . . . DLB-43

Towne, Robert 1936- DLB-44

The Townely Plays
fifteenth and sixteenth
centuries DLB-146

Townshend, Aurelian
by 1583 - circa 1651 . . . . DLB-121

Tracy, Honor 1913- DLB-15

Traherne, Thomas 1637?-1674 . . . . . DLB-131

Traill, Catharine Parr 1802-1899 . . . . DLB-99

Train, Arthur 1875-1945 . . . . DLB-86

The Transatlantic Publishing
Company DLB-49

The Transatlantic Review 1924-1925 . . . . . DS-15

Transcendentalists, American DS-5

transition 1927-1938 . . . . DS-15

Translators of the Twelfth Century:
Literary Issues Raised and Impact
Created. DLB-115

Travel Writing, 1837-1875 . . . . . . DLB-166

Travel Writing, 1876-1909 . . . . . . DLB-174

Traven, B.
1882? or 1890?-1969?. DLB-9, 56

Travers, Ben 1886-1980 . . . . DLB-10

Travers, P. L. (Pamela Lyndon)
1899- DLB-160

Trediakovsky, Vasilii Kirillovich
1703-1769 . . . . DLB-150

Treece, Henry 1911-1966 . . . . DLB-160

Trejo, Ernesto 1950- DLB-122

Trelawny, Edward John
1792-1881. . . . . DLB-110, 116, 144

Tremain, Rose 1943- DLB-14

Tremblay, Michel 1942- DLB-60

Trends in Twentieth-Century
Mass Market Publishing DLB-46

Trent, William P. 1862-1939. . . . . . DLB-47

Trescot, William Henry
1822-1898 . . . . DLB-30

Trevelyan, Sir George Otto
1838-1928 . . . . DLB-144

Trevisa, John
circa 1342-circa 1402 . . . . DLB-146

Trevor, William 1928- DLB-14, 139

Trierer Floyris circa 1170-1180 . . . . . DLB-138

Trilling, Lionel 1905-1975 . . . . . . DLB-28, 63

Trilussa 1871-1950 . . . . DLB-114

Trimmer, Sarah 1741-1810 . . . . . . DLB-158

Triolet, Elsa 1896-1970 . . . . DLB-72

Tripp, John 1927- DLB-40

Trocchi, Alexander 1925- DLB-15

Trollope, Anthony
1815-1882 . . . . DLB-21, 57, 159

Trollope, Frances 1779-1863 . . . DLB-21, 166

Troop, Elizabeth 1931- DLB-14

Trotter, Catharine 1679-1749 . . . . . DLB-84

Trotti, Lamar 1898-1952 . . . . DLB-44

Trottier, Pierre 1925- DLB-60

Troupe, Quincy Thomas, Jr.
1943- DLB-41

Trow, John F., and Company DLB-49

Truillier-Lacombe, Joseph-Patrice
1807-1863 . . . . DLB-99

Trumbo, Dalton 1905-1976. . . . . . . DLB-26

Trumbull, Benjamin 1735-1820. . . . . DLB-30

Trumbull, John 1750-1831 . . . . DLB-31

Trumbull, John 1756-1843 . . . . . . DLB-183

Tscherning, Andreas 1611-1659. . . . . DLB-164

T. S. Eliot Centennial Y-88

Tsubouchi, Shōyō 1859-1935 . . . . . DLB-180

Tucholsky, Kurt 1890-1935. . . . . . . DLB-56

Tucker, Charlotte Maria
1821-1893 . . . . DLB-163

Tucker, George 1775-1861 . . . . . DLB-3, 30

Tucker, Nathaniel Beverley
1784-1851. . . . . DLB-3

Tucker, St. George 1752-1827 . . . . . DLB-37

Tuckerman, Henry Theodore
1813-1871 . . . . DLB-64

Tunis, John R. 1889-1975 . . . . . DLB-22, 171

Tunstall, Cuthbert 1474-1559 . . . . . DLB-132

Tuohy, Frank 1925- DLB-14, 139

Tupper, Martin F. 1810-1889 . . . . . DLB-32

Turbyfill, Mark 1896- DLB-45

Turco, Lewis 1934- Y-84

Turnbull, Andrew 1921-1970 . . . . . DLB-103

Turnbull, Gael 1928- DLB-40

Turner, Arlin 1909-1980. . . . . DLB-103

Turner, Charles (Tennyson)
1808-1879 . . . . DLB-32

Turner, Frederick 1943- DLB-40

Turner, Frederick Jackson
1861-1932 . . . . DLB-17

Turner, Joseph Addison
1826-1868 . . . . DLB-79

Turpin, Waters Edward
1910-1968 . . . . DLB-51

Turrini, Peter 1944- DLB-124

Tutuola, Amos 1920- DLB-125

Twain, Mark (see Clemens,
Samuel Langhorne)

Tweedie, Ethel Brilliana
circa 1860-1940 . . . . DLB-174

The 'Twenties and Berlin, by
Alex Natan DLB-66

Tyler, Anne 1941- DLB-6, 143; Y-82

Tyler, Moses Coit 1835-1900 . . . DLB-47, 64

Tyler, Royall 1757-1826 . . . . DLB-37

Tylor, Edward Burnett 1832-1917 . . . . DLB-57

Tynan, Katharine 1861-1931 . . . . . . DLB-153

Tyndale, William
circa 1494-1536 . . . . DLB-132

U

Udall, Nicholas 1504-1556 . . . . DLB-62

Ugrěsić, Dubravka 1949- DLB-181

Uhland, Ludwig 1787-1862. . . . . . . DLB-90

Uhse, Bodo 1904-1963 . . . . DLB-69

Ujević, Augustin ("Tin")
1891-1955. . . . . DLB-147

Ulenhart, Niclas
flourished circa 1600 . . . . DLB-164

Ulibarrí, Sabine R. 1919- DLB-82

Ulica, Jorge 1870-1926 . . . . DLB-82

Ulizio, B. George 1889-1969 . . . . . DLB-140

Ulrich von Liechtenstein
circa 1200-circa 1275 . . . . DLB-138

Ulrich von Zatzikhoven
before 1194-after 1214 . . . . . . DLB-138

Unamuno, Miguel de 1864-1936 . . . . DLB-108

Under the Microscope (1872), by
A. C. Swinburne DLB-35

Unger, Friederike Helene
1741-1813 . . . . DLB-94

Ungaretti, Giuseppe 1888-1970 . . . . . DLB-114

United States Book Company DLB-49

Universal Publishing and Distributing
Corporation DLB-46

The University of Iowa Writers' Workshop
Golden Jubilee Y-86

The University of South Carolina
Press Y-94

University of Wales Press. DLB-112

"The Unknown Public" (1858), by
Wilkie Collins [excerpt] DLB-57

Uno, Chiyo 1897-1996 . . . . DLB-180

Unruh, Fritz von 1885-1970 . . . . DLB-56, 118

Unspeakable Practices II: The Festival of
Vanguard Narrative at Brown
University. Y-93

Unwin, T. Fisher
[publishing house] DLB-106

Upchurch, Boyd B. (see Boyd, John)

Updike, John
1932- DLB-2, 5, 143; Y-80, 82; DS-3

Upton, Bertha 1849-1912 . . . . DLB-141

Upton, Charles 1948- DLB-16

Upton, Florence K. 1873-1922 . . . . . DLB-141

Upward, Allen 1863-1926. . . . . DLB-36

Urista, Alberto Baltazar (see Alurista)

Urzidil, Johannes 1896-1976. . . . . . DLB-85

Urquhart, Fred 1912- DLB-139

The Uses of Facsimile Y-90

Usk, Thomas died 1388 . . . . DLB-146

Uslar Pietri, Arturo 1906- DLB-113

Ustinov, Peter 1921- DLB-13

Uttley, Alison 1884-1976 . . . . DLB-160

Uz, Johann Peter 1720-1796 . . . . . . DLB-97

V

Vac, Bertrand 1914- DLB-88

Vail, Laurence 1891-1968 . . . . DLB-4

Vailland, Roger 1907-1965 . . . . DLB-83

Vajda, Ernest 1887-1954 . . . . DLB-44

Valdés, Gina 1943- DLB-122

Valdez, Luis Miguel 1940- DLB-122

Valduga, Patrizia 1953- DLB-128

Valente, José Angel 1929- DLB-108

Valenzuela, Luisa 1938- DLB-113

Valeri, Diego 1887-1976 . . . . DLB-128

Valgardson, W. D. 1939- DLB-60

Valle, Víctor Manuel 1950- DLB-122

Valle-Inclán, Ramón del
1866-1936 . . . . DLB-134

Vallejo, Armando 1949- DLB-122

Vallès, Jules 1832-1885 . . . . DLB-123

Vallette, Marguerite Eymery (see Rachilde)

Valverde, José María 1926- DLB-108

Van Allsburg, Chris 1949- DLB-61

Van Anda, Carr 1864-1945 . . . . . . DLB-25

Van Doren, Mark 1894-1972 . . . . . DLB-45

van Druten, John 1901-1957 . . . . . . DLB-10

Van Duyn, Mona 1921- DLB-5

Van Dyke, Henry
1852-1933 . . . . DLB-71; DS-13

Van Dyke, Henry 1928- DLB-33

van Itallie, Jean-Claude 1936- DLB-7

Van Loan, Charles E. 1876-1919 . . . . DLB-171

Van Rensselaer, Mariana Griswold
1851-1934 . . . . DLB-47

Van Rensselaer, Mrs. Schuyler (see Van
Rensselaer, Mariana Griswold)

Van Vechten, Carl 1880-1964 . . . . . DLB-4, 9

van Vogt, A. E. 1912- DLB-8

Vanbrugh, Sir John 1664-1726 . . . . . DLB-80

Vance, Jack 1916?- DLB-8

Vane, Sutton 1888-1963 . . . . DLB-10

Vanguard Press DLB-46

Vann, Robert L. 1879-1940 . . . . . . DLB-29

Vargas, Llosa, Mario 1936- DLB-145

Varley, John 1947- Y-81

Varnhagen von Ense, Karl August
1785-1858 . . . . DLB-90

Varnhagen von Ense, Rahel
1771-1833 . . . . DLB-90

Vásquez Montalbán, Manuel
1939- DLB-134

Vassa, Gustavus (see Equiano, Olaudah)

Vassalli, Sebastiano 1941- DLB-128

Vaughan, Henry 1621-1695 . . . . . . DLB-131

Vaughan, Thomas 1621-1666 . . . . . . DLB-131

Vaux, Thomas, Lord 1509-1556 . . . . DLB-132

Vazov, Ivan 1850-1921 . . . . DLB-147

Vega, Janine Pommy 1942- DLB-16

Veiller, Anthony 1903-1965 . . . . DLB-44

Velásquez-Trevino, Gloria
1949- DLB-122

Veloz Maggiolo, Marcio 1936- DLB-145

Venegas, Daniel ?-? DLB-82

Vergil, Polydore circa 1470-1555 . . . . DLB-132

Veríssimo, Erico 1905-1975 . . . . . . DLB-145

Verne, Jules 1828-1905 . . . . DLB-123

Verplanck, Gulian C. 1786-1870 . . . . DLB-59

Very, Jones 1813-1880 . . . . DLB-1

Vian, Boris 1920-1959 . . . . DLB-72

Vickers, Roy 1888?-1965 . . . . DLB-77

Victoria 1819-1901 . . . . DLB-55

Victoria Press DLB-106

Vidal, Gore 1925- DLB-6, 152

Viebig, Clara 1860-1952 . . . . DLB-66

Viereck, George Sylvester
1884-1962 . . . . DLB-54

Viereck, Peter 1916- DLB-5

Viets, Roger 1738-1811 . . . . DLB-99

Viewpoint: Politics and Performance, by
David Edgar DLB-13

Vigil-Piñon, Evangelina 1949- DLB-122

Vigneault, Gilles 1928- DLB-60

Vigny, Alfred de 1797-1863 . . . . . . DLB-119

Vigolo, Giorgio 1894-1983 . . . . . . DLB-114

The Viking Press DLB-46

Villanueva, Alma Luz 1944- DLB-122

Villanueva, Tino 1941- DLB-82

Villard, Henry 1835-1900 . . . . DLB-23

Villard, Oswald Garrison
1872-1949 . . . . DLB-25, 91

Villarreal, José Antonio 1924- DLB-82

Villegas de Magnón, Leonor
1876-1955 . . . . DLB-122

Villemaire, Yolande 1949- DLB-60

Villena, Luis Antonio de 1951- DLB-134

Villiers de l'Isle-Adam, Jean-Marie
Mathias Philippe-Auguste, Comte de
1838-1889 . . . . DLB-123

Villiers, George, Second Duke
of Buckingham 1628-1687 . . . . . DLB-80

Vine Press DLB-112

Viorst, Judith ?- DLB-52

Vipont, Elfrida (Elfrida Vipont Foulds,
Charles Vipont) 1902-1992 . . . . . DLB-160

Viramontes, Helena María
1954- DLB-122

Vischer, Friedrich Theodor
1807-1887 . . . . DLB-133

Vivanco, Luis Felipe 1907-1975 . . . . DLB-108

Viviani, Cesare 1947- DLB-128

Vizenor, Gerald 1934- DLB-175

Vizetelly and Company DLB-106

Voaden, Herman 1903- DLB-88

Voigt, Ellen Bryant 1943- DLB-120

Vojnović, Ivo 1857-1929 . . . . DLB-147

Volkoff, Vladimir 1932- DLB-83

Volland, P. F., Company DLB-46

Volponi, Paolo 1924- DLB-177

von der Grün, Max 1926- DLB-75

Vonnegut, Kurt
1922- DLB-2, 8, 152; Y-80; DS-3

Voranc, Prežihov 1893-1950 . . . . . . DLB-147

Voß, Johann Heinrich 1751-1826 . . . . DLB-90

Vroman, Mary Elizabeth
circa 1924-1967 . . . . DLB-33

W

Wace, Robert ("Maistre")
circa 1100-circa 1175 . . . . DLB-146

Wackenroder, Wilhelm Heinrich
1773-1798 . . . . DLB-90

Wackernagel, Wilhelm
1806-1869 . . . . DLB-133

Waddington, Miriam 1917- DLB-68

Wade, Henry 1887-1969 . . . . DLB-77

Wagenknecht, Edward 1900- DLB-103

Wagner, Heinrich Leopold
1747-1779 . . . . DLB-94

Wagner, Henry R. 1862-1957 . . . . . DLB-140

Wagner, Richard 1813-1883 . . . . . . DLB-129

Wagoner, David 1926- DLB-5

Wah, Fred 1939- DLB-60

Waiblinger, Wilhelm 1804-1830 . . . . DLB-90

Wain, John
1925-1994 . . . . . . DLB-15, 27, 139, 155

Wainwright, Jeffrey 1944- DLB-40

Waite, Peirce and Company DLB-49

Wakoski, Diane 1937- DLB-5

Walahfrid Strabo circa 808-849 . . . . DLB-148

Walck, Henry Z. DLB-46

Walcott, Derek
1930- DLB-117; Y-81, 92

Waldegrave, Robert
[publishing house] DLB-170

Waldman, Anne 1945- DLB-16

Waldrop, Rosmarie 1935- DLB-169

Walker, Alice 1944- DLB-6, 33, 143

Walker, George F. 1947- DLB-60

Walker, Joseph A. 1935- DLB-38

Walker, Margaret 1915- DLB-76, 152

Walker, Ted 1934- DLB-40

Walker and Company DLB-49

Walker, Evans and Cogswell
Company DLB-49

Walker, John Brisben 1847-1931 . . . . DLB-79

Wallace, Dewitt 1889-1981 and
   Lila Acheson Wallace
   1889-1984 . . . . DLB-137

Wallace, Edgar 1875-1932 . . . . DLB-70

Wallace, Lila Acheson (see Wallace, Dewitt,
   and Lila Acheson Wallace)

Wallant, Edward Lewis
   1926-1962. . . . . DLB-2, 28, 143

Waller, Edmund 1606-1687 . . . . DLB-126

Walpole, Horace 1717-1797. . . . . DLB-39, 104

Walpole, Hugh 1884-1941 . . . . DLB-34

Walrond, Eric 1898-1966 . . . . DLB-51

Walser, Martin 1927- DLB-75, 124

Walser, Robert 1878-1956 . . . . DLB-66

Walsh, Ernest 1895-1926 . . . . . . DLB-4, 45

Walsh, Robert 1784-1859. . . . . DLB-59

Waltharius circa 825 . . . . DLB-148

Walters, Henry 1848-1931 . . . . . . DLB-140

Walther von der Vogelweide
   circa 1170-circa 1230 . . . . DLB-138

Walton, Izaak 1593-1683 . . . . DLB-151

Wambaugh, Joseph 1937- DLB-6; Y-83

Waniek, Marilyn Nelson 1946- DLB-120

Warburton, William 1698-1779 . . . . DLB-104

Ward, Aileen 1919- DLB-111

Ward, Artemus (see Browne, Charles Farrar)

Ward, Arthur Henry Sarsfield
   (see Rohmer, Sax)

Ward, Douglas Turner 1930- DLB-7, 38

Ward, Lynd 1905-1985. . . . . DLB-22

Ward, Lock and Company DLB-106

Ward, Mrs. Humphry 1851-1920 . . . . DLB-18

Ward, Nathaniel circa 1578-1652 . . . . DLB-24

Ward, Theodore 1902-1983 . . . . . . DLB-76

Wardle, Ralph 1909-1988 . . . . DLB-103

Ware, William 1797-1852 . . . . DLB-1

Warne, Frederick, and
   Company [U.S.]. DLB-49

Warne, Frederick, and
   Company [U.K.]. DLB-106

Warner, Charles Dudley
   1829-1900 . . . . DLB-64

Warner, Rex 1905- DLB-15

Warner, Susan Bogert
   1819-1885 . . . . DLB-3, 42

Warner, Sylvia Townsend
   1893-1978 . . . . DLB-34, 139

Warner, William 1558-1609 . . . . . . DLB-172

Warner Books. DLB-46

Warr, Bertram 1917-1943 . . . . DLB-88

Warren, John Byrne Leicester (see De Tabley,
   Lord)

Warren, Lella 1899-1982 . . . . Y-83

Warren, Mercy Otis 1728-1814 . . . . . DLB-31

Warren, Robert Penn
   1905-1989 . . . . . DLB-2, 48, 152; Y-80, 89

Die Wartburgkrieg
   circa 1230-circa 1280 . . . . DLB-138

Warton, Joseph 1722-1800. . . . . DLB-104, 109

Warton, Thomas 1728-1790. . . . DLB-104, 109

Washington, George 1732-1799 . . . . . DLB-31

Wassermann, Jakob 1873-1934 . . . . . . DLB-66

Wasson, David Atwood 1823-1887 . . . . DLB-1

Waterhouse, Keith 1929- DLB-13, 15

Waterman, Andrew 1940- DLB-40

Waters, Frank 1902- Y-86

Waters, Michael 1949- DLB-120

Watkins, Tobias 1780-1855. . . . . . . DLB-73

Watkins, Vernon 1906-1967 . . . . . . DLB-20

Watmough, David 1926- DLB-53

Watson, James Wreford (see Wreford, James)

Watson, John 1850-1907 . . . . DLB-156

Watson, Sheila 1909- DLB-60

Watson, Thomas 1545?-1592 . . . . . DLB-132

Watson, Wilfred 1911- DLB-60

Watt, W. J., and Company DLB-46

Watterson, Henry 1840-1921. . . . . . DLB-25

Watts, Alan 1915-1973 . . . . DLB-16

Watts, Franklin [publishing house]. . . . DLB-46

Watts, Isaac 1674-1748 . . . . DLB-95

Waugh, Auberon 1939- DLB-14

Waugh, Evelyn 1903-1966 . . . . . DLB-15, 162

Way and Williams DLB-49

Wayman, Tom 1945- DLB-53

Weatherly, Tom 1942- DLB-41

Weaver, Gordon 1937- DLB-130

Weaver, Robert 1921- DLB-88

Webb, Frank J. ?-? DLB-50

Webb, James Watson 1802-1884. . . . . DLB-43

Webb, Mary 1881-1927 . . . . DLB-34

Webb, Phyllis 1927- DLB-53

Webb, Walter Prescott 1888-1963 . . . . DLB-17

Webbe, William ?-1591 . . . . DLB-132

Webster, Augusta 1837-1894 . . . . . . DLB-35

Webster, Charles L.,
   and Company. DLB-49

Webster, John
   1579 or 1580-1634? DLB-58

Webster, Noah
   1758-1843 . . . . . . DLB-1, 37, 42, 43, 73

Weckherlin, Georg Rodolf
   1584-1653 . . . . DLB-164

Wedekind, Frank 1864-1918 . . . . . . DLB-118

Weeks, Edward Augustus, Jr.
   1898-1989 . . . . DLB-137

Weems, Mason Locke
   1759-1825. . . . . DLB-30, 37, 42

Weerth, Georg 1822-1856 . . . . DLB-129

Weidenfeld and Nicolson DLB-112

Weidman, Jerome 1913- DLB-28

Weigl, Bruce 1949- DLB-120

Weinbaum, Stanley Grauman
   1902-1935. . . . . DLB-8

Weintraub, Stanley 1929- DLB-111

Weise, Christian 1642-1708 . . . . . . DLB-168

Weisenborn, Gunther
   1902-1969 . . . . DLB-69, 124

Weiß, Ernst 1882-1940 . . . . DLB-81

Weiss, John 1818-1879. . . . . DLB-1

Weiss, Peter 1916-1982 . . . . . . DLB-69, 124

Weiss, Theodore 1916- DLB-5

Weisse, Christian Felix 1726-1804 . . . . DLB-97

Weitling, Wilhelm 1808-1871 . . . . . DLB-129

Welch, James 1940- DLB-175

Welch, Lew 1926-1971? DLB-16

Weldon, Fay 1931- DLB-14

Wellek, René 1903- DLB-63

Wells, Carolyn 1862-1942 . . . . DLB-11

Wells, Charles Jeremiah
   circa 1800-1879 . . . . DLB-32

Wells, Gabriel 1862-1946 . . . . DLB-140

Wells, H. G.
   1866-1946 . . . . . . DLB-34, 70, 156, 178

Wells, Robert 1947- DLB-40

Wells-Barnett, Ida B. 1862-1931 . . . . DLB-23

Welty, Eudora
   1909- DLB-2, 102, 143; Y-87; DS-12

Wendell, Barrett 1855-1921. . . . . . . DLB-71

Wentworth, Patricia 1878-1961 . . . . . DLB-77

Werder, Diederich von dem
   1584-1657 . . . . DLB-164

Werfel, Franz 1890-1945 . . . . . DLB-81, 124

The Werner Company DLB-49

Werner, Zacharias 1768-1823. . . . . . DLB-94

Wersba, Barbara 1932- DLB-52

Wescott, Glenway 1901- DLB-4, 9, 102

Wesker, Arnold 1932- DLB-13

Wesley, Charles 1707-1788 . . . . DLB-95

Wesley, John 1703-1791 . . . . DLB-104

Wesley, Richard 1945- DLB-38

Wessels, A., and Company DLB-46

Wessobrunner Gebet
   circa 787-815. . . . . DLB-148

West, Anthony 1914-1988 . . . . DLB-15

West, Dorothy 1907- DLB-76

West, Jessamyn 1902-1984 . . . . . DLB-6; Y-84

West, Mae 1892-1980. . . . . DLB-44

West, Nathanael 1903-1940 . . . DLB-4, 9, 28

West, Paul 1930- DLB-14

West, Rebecca 1892-1983 . . . . . DLB-36; Y-83

West and Johnson DLB-49

Western Publishing Company DLB-46

The Westminster Review 1824-1914 . . . . DLB-110

Weston, Elizabeth Jane
circa 1582-1612 . . . . DLB-172

Wetherald, Agnes Ethelwyn
1857-1940 . . . . DLB-99

Wetherell, Elizabeth
(see Warner, Susan Bogert)

Wetzel, Friedrich Gottlob
1779-1819 . . . . DLB-90

Weyman, Stanley J.
1855-1928. . . . . DLB-141, 156

Wezel, Johann Karl 1747-1819 . . . . . DLB-94

Whalen, Philip 1923- DLB-16

Whalley, George 1915-1983 . . . . DLB-88

Wharton, Edith
1862-1937 . . . . . DLB-4, 9, 12, 78; DS-13

Wharton, William 1920s?- Y-80

Whately, Mary Louisa
1824-1889 . . . . DLB-166

What's Really Wrong With Bestseller
Lists Y-84

Wheatley, Dennis Yates
1897-1977 . . . . DLB-77

Wheatley, Phillis
circa 1754-1784 . . . . DLB-31, 50

Wheeler, Anna Doyle
1785-1848? DLB-158

Wheeler, Charles Stearns
1816-1843 . . . . DLB-1

Wheeler, Monroe 1900-1988 . . . . DLB-4

Wheelock, John Hall 1886-1978 . . . . . DLB-45

Wheelwright, John
circa 1592-1679 . . . . DLB-24

Wheelwright, J. B. 1897-1940 . . . . . . DLB-45

Whetstone, Colonel Pete
(see Noland, C. F. M.)

Whetstone, George 1550-1587 . . . . . DLB-136

Whicher, Stephen E. 1915-1961 . . . . DLB-111

Whipple, Edwin Percy
1819-1886 . . . . DLB-1, 64

Whitaker, Alexander 1585-1617 . . . . DLB-24

Whitaker, Daniel K. 1801-1881 . . . . . DLB-73

Whitcher, Frances Miriam
1814-1852 . . . . DLB-11

White, Andrew 1579-1656 . . . . DLB-24

White, Andrew Dickson
1832-1918 . . . . DLB-47

White, E. B. 1899-1985 . . . . . . DLB-11, 22

White, Edgar B. 1947- DLB-38

White, Ethel Lina 1887-1944 . . . . . . DLB-77

White, Henry Kirke 1785-1806 . . . . DLB-96

White, Horace 1834-1916 . . . . DLB-23

White, Phyllis Dorothy James
(see James, P. D.)

White, Richard Grant 1821-1885 . . . . DLB-64

White, T. H. 1906-1964 . . . . DLB-160

White, Walter 1893-1955 . . . . DLB-51

White, William, and Company DLB-49

White, William Allen
1868-1944 . . . . DLB-9, 25

White, William Anthony Parker (see Boucher, Anthony)

White, William Hale (see Rutherford, Mark)

Whitechurch, Victor L.
1868-1933 . . . . DLB-70

Whitehead, Alfred North
1861-1947 . . . . DLB-100

Whitehead, James 1936- Y-81

Whitehead, William
1715-1785 . . . . DLB-84, 109

Whitfield, James Monroe
1822-1871 . . . . DLB-50

Whitgift, John circa 1533-1604 . . . . . DLB-132

Whiting, John 1917-1963 . . . . DLB-13

Whiting, Samuel 1597-1679 . . . . . . DLB-24

Whitlock, Brand 1869-1934 . . . . . . DLB-12

Whitman, Albert, and Company DLB-46

Whitman, Albery Allson
1851-1901 . . . . DLB-50

Whitman, Alden 1913-1990 . . . . Y-91

Whitman, Sarah Helen (Power)
1803-1878 . . . . DLB-1

Whitman, Walt 1819-1892 . . . . . DLB-3, 64

Whitman Publishing Company DLB-46

Whitney, Geoffrey
1548 or 1552?-1601 . . . . DLB-136

Whitney, Isabella
flourished 1566-1573 . . . . DLB-136

Whitney, John Hay 1904-1982 . . . . . DLB-127

Whittemore, Reed 1919- DLB-5

Whittier, John Greenleaf 1807-1892 . . . . DLB-1

Whittlesey House DLB-46

Who Runs American Literature? Y-94

Wideman, John Edgar 1941- DLB-33, 143

Widener, Harry Elkins 1885-1912 . . . . DLB-140

Wiebe, Rudy 1934- DLB-60

Wiechert, Ernst 1887-1950 . . . . DLB-56

Wied, Martina 1882-1957 . . . . DLB-85

Wiehe, Evelyn May Clowes (see Mordaunt, Elinor)

Wieland, Christoph Martin
1733-1813 . . . . DLB-97

Wienbarg, Ludolf 1802-1872 . . . . . . DLB-133

Wieners, John 1934- DLB-16

Wier, Ester 1910- DLB-52

Wiesel, Elie 1928- DLB-83; Y-87

Wiggin, Kate Douglas 1856-1923 . . . . DLB-42

Wigglesworth, Michael 1631-1705 . . . . DLB-24

Wilberforce, William 1759-1833 . . . . . DLB-158

Wilbrandt, Adolf 1837-1911 . . . . . . DLB-129

Wilbur, Richard 1921- DLB-5, 169

Wild, Peter 1940- DLB-5

Wilde, Oscar
1854-1900 . . . . DLB-10, 19, 34, 57, 141, 156

Wilde, Richard Henry
1789-1847 . . . . DLB-3, 59

Wilde, W. A., Company DLB-49

Wilder, Billy 1906- DLB-26

Wilder, Laura Ingalls 1867-1957 . . . . DLB-22

Wilder, Thornton 1897-1975 . . . . DLB-4, 7, 9

Wildgans, Anton 1881-1932 . . . . . . DLB-118

Wiley, Bell Irvin 1906-1980 . . . . . . DLB-17

Wiley, John, and Sons DLB-49

Wilhelm, Kate 1928- DLB-8

Wilkes, Charles 1798-1877 . . . . . . DLB-183

Wilkes, George 1817-1885 . . . . DLB-79

Wilkinson, Anne 1910-1961 . . . . . . DLB-88

Wilkinson, Sylvia 1940- Y-86

Wilkinson, William Cleaver
1833-1920 . . . . DLB-71

Willard, Barbara 1909-1994 . . . . . . DLB-161

Willard, L. [publishing house] DLB-49

Willard, Nancy 1936- DLB-5, 52

Willard, Samuel 1640-1707 . . . . . . DLB-24

William of Auvergne 1190-1249 . . . . DLB-115

William of Conches
circa 1090-circa 1154 . . . . DLB-115

William of Ockham
circa 1285-1347 . . . . DLB-115

William of Sherwood
1200/1205 - 1266/1271 . . . . DLB-115

The William Chavrat American Fiction
Collection at the Ohio State University Libraries Y-92

Williams, A., and Company DLB-49

Williams, Ben Ames 1889-1953 . . . . DLB-102

Williams, C. K. 1936- DLB-5

Williams, Chancellor 1905- DLB-76

Williams, Charles
1886-1945 . . . . DLB-100, 153

Williams, Denis 1923- DLB-117

Williams, Emlyn 1905- DLB-10, 77

Williams, Garth 1912- DLB-22

Williams, George Washington
1849-1891 . . . . DLB-47

Williams, Heathcote 1941- DLB-13

Williams, Helen Maria
1761-1827 . . . . DLB-158

Williams, Hugo 1942- DLB-40

Williams, Isaac 1802-1865 . . . . . . DLB-32

Williams, Joan 1928- DLB-6

Williams, John A. 1925- DLB-2, 33

Williams, John E. 1922-1994 . . . . . . DLB-6

Williams, Jonathan 1929- DLB-5

Williams, Miller 1930- DLB-105

Williams, Raymond 1921- DLB-14

Williams, Roger circa 1603-1683. . . . . DLB-24

Williams, Samm-Art 1946- DLB-38

Williams, Sherley Anne 1944- DLB-41

Williams, T. Harry 1909-1979 . . . . . DLB-17

Williams, Tennessee
1911-1983. . . . . DLB-7; Y-83; DS-4

Williams, Ursula Moray 1911- DLB-160

Williams, Valentine 1883-1946 . . . . . DLB-77

Williams, William Appleman
1921- DLB-17

Williams, William Carlos
1883-1963 . . . . DLB-4, 16, 54, 86

Williams, Wirt 1921- DLB-6

Williams Brothers DLB-49

Williamson, Jack 1908- DLB-8

Willingham, Calder Baynard, Jr.
1922- DLB-2, 44

Williram of Ebersberg
circa 1020-1085 . . . . DLB-148

Willis, Nathaniel Parker
1806-1867 . . . DLB-3, 59, 73, 74, 183; DS-13

Willkomm, Ernst 1810-1886. . . . . . DLB-133

Wilmer, Clive 1945- DLB-40

Wilson, A. N. 1950- DLB-14, 155

Wilson, Angus
1913-1991 . . . . DLB-15, 139, 155

Wilson, Arthur 1595-1652 . . . . . . DLB-58

Wilson, Augusta Jane Evans
1835-1909 . . . . DLB-42

Wilson, Colin 1931- DLB-14

Wilson, Edmund 1895-1972 . . . . . . DLB-63

Wilson, Ethel 1888-1980 . . . . DLB-68

Wilson, Harriet E. Adams
1828?-1863? DLB-50

Wilson, Harry Leon 1867-1939 . . . . . DLB-9

Wilson, John 1588-1667 . . . . DLB-24

Wilson, John 1785-1854 . . . . DLB-110

Wilson, Lanford 1937- DLB-7

Wilson, Margaret 1882-1973 . . . . . . DLB-9

Wilson, Michael 1914-1978. . . . . . . DLB-44

Wilson, Mona 1872-1954 . . . . DLB-149

Wilson, Thomas
1523 or 1524-1581 . . . . DLB-132

Wilson, Woodrow 1856-1924 . . . . . . DLB-47

Wilson, Effingham
[publishing house] DLB-154

Wimsatt, William K., Jr.
1907-1975 . . . . DLB-63

Winchell, Walter 1897-1972 . . . . . . DLB-29

Winchester, J. [publishing house]. . . . DLB-49

Winckelmann, Johann Joachim
1717-1768 . . . . DLB-97

Winckler, Paul 1630-1686 . . . . DLB-164

Wind, Herbert Warren 1916- DLB-171

Windet, John [publishing house] DLB-170

Windham, Donald 1920- DLB-6

Wingate, Allan [publishing house] . . . DLB-112

Winnemucca, Sarah 1844-1921 . . . . . DLB-175

Winnifrith, Tom 1938- DLB-155

Winsloe, Christa 1888-1944 . . . . . . DLB-124

Winsor, Justin 1831-1897 . . . . DLB-47

John C. Winston Company DLB-49

Winters, Yvor 1900-1968 . . . . DLB-48

Winthrop, John 1588-1649 . . . . . DLB-24, 30

Winthrop, John, Jr. 1606-1676 . . . . . DLB-24

Wirt, William 1772-1834 . . . . DLB-37

Wise, John 1652-1725. . . . . DLB-24

Wiseman, Adele 1928- DLB-88

Wishart and Company DLB-112

Wisner, George 1812-1849 . . . . DLB-43

Wister, Owen 1860-1938 . . . . . . DLB-9, 78

Wither, George 1588-1667 . . . . . . DLB-121

Witherspoon, John 1723-1794 . . . . . DLB-31

Withrow, William Henry 1839-1908. . . . DLB-99

Wittig, Monique 1935- DLB-83

Wodehouse, P. G.
1881-1975 . . . . DLB-34, 162

Wohmann, Gabriele 1932- DLB-75

Woiwode, Larry 1941- DLB-6

Wolcot, John 1738-1819 . . . . DLB-109

Wolcott, Roger 1679-1767 . . . . DLB-24

Wolf, Christa 1929- DLB-75

Wolf, Friedrich 1888-1953. . . . . . . DLB-124

Wolfe, Gene 1931- DLB-8

Wolfe, John [publishing house] DLB-170

Wolfe, Reyner (Reginald)
[publishing house] DLB-170

Wolfe, Thomas
1900-1938 . . . . . DLB-9, 102; Y-85; DS-2

Wolfe, Tom 1931- DLB-152

Wolff, Helen 1906-1994 . . . . Y-94

Wolff, Tobias 1945- DLB-130

Wolfram von Eschenbach
circa 1170-after 1220 . . . . DLB-138

Wolfram von Eschenbach's *Parzival:*
Prologue and Book 3 . . . . DLB-138

Wollstonecraft, Mary
1759-1797 . . . . DLB-39, 104, 158

Wondratschek, Wolf 1943- DLB-75

Wood, Benjamin 1820-1900 . . . . . . DLB-23

Wood, Charles 1932- DLB-13

Wood, Mrs. Henry 1814-1887 . . . . . DLB-18

Wood, Joanna E. 1867-1927 . . . . . . DLB-92

Wood, Samuel [publishing house] DLB-49

Wood, William ?-? DLB-24

Woodberry, George Edward
1855-1930 . . . . DLB-71, 103

Woodbridge, Benjamin 1622-1684 . . . . DLB-24

Woodcock, George 1912- DLB-88

Woodhull, Victoria C. 1838-1927 . . . . DLB-79

Woodmason, Charles circa 1720-?. . . . DLB-31

Woodress, Jr., James Leslie
1916- DLB-111

Woodson, Carter G. 1875-1950 . . . . . DLB-17

Woodward, C. Vann 1908- DLB-17

Woodward, Stanley 1895-1965 . . . . . DLB-171

Wooler, Thomas
1785 or 1786-1853 . . . . DLB-158

Woolf, David (see Maddow, Ben)

Woolf, Leonard 1880-1969 . . . . DLB-100; DS-10

Woolf, Virginia
1882-1941 . . . . DLB-36, 100, 162; DS-10

Woolf, Virginia, "The New Biography," *New York
Herald Tribune,* 30 October 1927
. . . . DLB-149

Woollcott, Alexander 1887-1943 . . . . DLB-29

Woolman, John 1720-1772 . . . . DLB-31

Woolner, Thomas 1825-1892. . . . . . DLB-35

Woolsey, Sarah Chauncy
1835-1905 . . . . DLB-42

Woolson, Constance Fenimore
1840-1894. . . . . DLB-12, 74

Worcester, Joseph Emerson
1784-1865. . . . . DLB-1

Worde, Wynkyn de
[publishing house] DLB-170

Wordsworth, Christopher
1807-1885 . . . . DLB-166

Wordsworth, Dorothy
1771-1855 . . . . DLB-107

Wordsworth, Elizabeth
1840-1932 . . . . DLB-98

Wordsworth, William
1770-1850 . . . . DLB-93, 107

The Works of the Rev. John Witherspoon
(1800-1801) [excerpts]. DLB-31

A World Chronology of Important Science
Fiction Works (1818-1979) DLB-8

World Publishing Company DLB-46

World War II Writers Symposium at the
University of South Carolina,
12–14 April 1995 . . . . Y-95

Worthington, R., and Company. DLB-49

Wotton, Sir Henry 1568-1639 . . . . . DLB-121

Wouk, Herman 1915- Y-82

Wreford, James 1915- DLB-88

Wren, Percival Christopher
1885-1941 . . . . DLB-153

Wrenn, John Henry 1841-1911 . . . . . DLB-140

Wright, C. D. 1949- DLB-120

Wright, Charles 1935- DLB-165; Y-82

Wright, Charles Stevenson 1932- DLB-33

Wright, Frances 1795-1852 . . . . DLB-73

Wright, Harold Bell 1872-1944 . . . . . . DLB-9

Wright, James 1927-1980 . . . . . . DLB-5, 169

Wright, Jay 1935- DLB-41

Wright, Louis B. 1899-1984 . . . . . . DLB-17

Wright, Richard 1908-1960 . . DLB-76, 102; DS-2

Wright, Richard B. 1937- DLB-53

Wright, Sarah Elizabeth 1928- DLB-33

Writers and Politics: 1871-1918,
by Ronald Gray DLB-66

Writers and their Copyright Holders:
the WATCH Project Y-94

Writers' Forum Y-85

Writing for the Theatre, by
Harold Pinter DLB-13

Wroth, Lady Mary 1587-1653 . . . . . DLB-121

Wurlitzer, Rudolph 1937- DLB-173

Wyatt, Sir Thomas
circa 1503-1542 . . . . DLB-132

Wycherley, William 1641-1715 . . . . . . DLB-80

Wyclif, John
circa 1335-31 December 1384 . . . DLB-146

Wylie, Elinor 1885-1928 . . . . DLB-9, 45

Wylie, Philip 1902-1971 . . . . DLB-9

Wyllie, John Cook 1908-1968 . . . . DLB-140

X

Xenophon circa 430 B.C.-circa 356 B.C.
. . . . DLB-176

Y

Yasuoka, Shōtarō 1920- DLB-182

Yates, Dornford 1885-1960 . . . . DLB-77, 153

Yates, J. Michael 1938- DLB-60

Yates, Richard 1926-1992 . . . . DLB-2; Y-81, 92

Yavorov, Peyo 1878-1914 . . . . DLB-147

Yearsley, Ann 1753-1806 . . . . DLB-109

Yeats, William Butler
1865-1939 . . . . DLB-10, 19, 98, 156

Yep, Laurence 1948- DLB-52

Yerby, Frank 1916-1991 . . . . DLB-76

Yezierska, Anzia 1885-1970 . . . . DLB-28

Yolen, Jane 1939- DLB-52

Yonge, Charlotte Mary
1823-1901 . . . . DLB-18, 163

The York Cycle
circa 1376-circa 1569 . . . . DLB-146

A Yorkshire Tragedy DLB-58

Yoseloff, Thomas
[publishing house] DLB-46

Young, Al 1939- DLB-33

Young, Arthur 1741-1820 . . . . DLB-158

Young, Dick 1917 or 1918 - 1987 . . . DLB-171

Young, Edward 1683-1765 . . . . DLB-95

Young, Stark 1881-1963 . . . . . . DLB-9, 102

Young, Waldeman 1880-1938 . . . . . DLB-26

Young, William [publishing house] DLB-49

Young Bear, Ray A. 1950- DLB-175

Yourcenar, Marguerite
1903-1987 . . . . DLB-72; Y-88

"You've Never Had It So Good," Gusted by
"Winds of Change": British Fiction in the
1950s, 1960s, and After DLB-14

Yovkov, Yordan 1880-1937 . . . . . . DLB-147

Z

Zachariä, Friedrich Wilhelm
1726-1777 . . . . DLB-97

Zajc, Dane 1929- DLB-181

Zamora, Bernice 1938- DLB-82

Zand, Herbert 1923-1970 . . . . DLB-85

Zangwill, Israel 1864-1926 . . . . DLB-10, 135

Zanzotto, Andrea 1921- DLB-128

Zapata Olivella, Manuel 1920- . . . DLB-113

Zebra Books DLB-46

Zebrowski, George 1945- DLB-8

Zech, Paul 1881-1946 . . . . DLB-56

Zepheria DLB-172

Zeidner, Lisa 1955- DLB-120

Zelazny, Roger 1937-1995 . . . . DLB-8

Zenger, John Peter 1697-1746 . . . . DLB-24, 43

Zesen, Philipp von 1619-1689 . . . . . DLB-164

Zieber, G. B., and Company DLB-49

Zieroth, Dale 1946- DLB-60

Zigler und Kliphausen, Heinrich Anshelm von
1663-1697 . . . . DLB-168

Zimmer, Paul 1934- DLB-5

Zingref, Julius Wilhelm
1591-1635 . . . . DLB-164

Zindel, Paul 1936- DLB-7, 52

Zinzendorf, Nikolaus Ludwig von
1700-1760 . . . . DLB-168

Zitkala-Ša 1876-1938 . . . . DLB-175

Zola, Emile 1840-1902 . . . . DLB-123

Zolotow, Charlotte 1915- DLB-52

Zschokke, Heinrich 1771-1848 . . . . . DLB-94

Zubly, John Joachim 1724-1781 . . . . . DLB-31

Zu-Bolton II, Ahmos 1936- DLB-41

Zuckmayer, Carl 1896-1977 . . . . DLB-56, 124

Zukofsky, Louis 1904-1978 . . . . . DLB-5, 165

Zupan, Vitomil 1914-1987 . . . . DLB-181

Župančič, Oton 1878-1949 . . . . . . DLB-147

zur Mühlen, Hermynia 1883-1951 . . . . DLB-56

Zweig, Arnold 1887-1968 . . . . DLB-66

Zweig, Stefan 1881-1942 . . . . . . DLB-81, 118

ISBN 0-7876-1072-0